Praise for *Climate Just Global and Regional Go*

MW00848911

Climate change is the defining issue of humankind, involving and invoking a complex pastiche of science, fear, resignation, governance and human will. The question is whether, and if so how, justice can be done in adapting to the Anthropocene. Climate Justice: Case Studies in Global and Regional Governance Challenges *elevates the climate change conversation above the stultifying echo-chamber of what to do into the realm of how international, national, regional and local legal regimes can help to level otherwise unbalanced outcomes. The book's 24 chapters are a globe-trotting account of how to advance environmental justice, intergenerational equity, and human dignity in the wake of planetary changes more often than not disproportionately afflicting the poor, urban, indigenous, disenfranchised and disempowered, from the Arctic to Kenya, from Kiribati to Amazonia, and from all of us to each of us. So hold your frequent flyer miles at bay, and enjoy this eye-popping account of what climate justice means to the intercontinental human condition that connects us all.*

—James R. May
Distinguished Professor of Law & Chief Sustainability Officer, Widener University

This book explores the extraordinary challenges climate change is posing to the planet's environment. It provides a rich snapshot of the innovative legal and policy responses climate change is spawning in every corner of the world. A diverse group of scholars explores why fairness to present and future generations should be the touchstone for crafting climate policy and avenues for pursuing this important goal.

—Robert V. Percival
Robert F. Stanton Professor of Law & Director, Environmental Law Program
University of Maryland Francis King Carey School of Law

True to form, Prof. Randall Abate has again managed to provide us with a highly topical and comprehensively researched text on a critical issue: climate justice. The unique strengths, theoretical and practical relevance, and original added value of the text lie in its being fashioned on a wide range of case studies that have been authored by a terrifically cosmopolitan collection of multi-disciplinary experts working in a wide range of professions and hailing from developed and developing country contexts. The book provides new insights to an exceptionally broad audience on the urgency of achieving climate justice across a wide range of sectors, ranging from international governance, regional governance, domestic scenarios, and very pertinently, the global judiciary. The book will no doubt become an important resource for, among others, students, scholars, practitioners, governments and non-governmental organisations in their efforts to achieve global climate justice.

—Louis J. Kotzé
Research Professor, North-West University, South Africa

While climate change is often framed as a problem of science, of economics, and of politics, climate justice reminds us that it is law that is called upon for solutions. Professor Abate's new edited volume on climate justice cuts new ground in centering justice as the core around which issues of finance, of governance, of participation, and of litigation strategy rotate (and sometimes flounder). Finally there is a resource which brings together perspectives, and detailed new case studies, from all corners of the globe to address an issue which respects few boundaries.
—Natasha Affolder
Associate Dean, Research and International, Peter A. Allard School of Law,
The University of British Columbia

Climate Justice: Case Studies in Global and Regional Governance Challenges *is essential reading for policy makers, activists, and citizens interested in moving beyond the polarizing rhetoric on climate change and toward real solutions to protect present and future generations. The text addresses a remarkably diverse set of topics that collectively demonstrate the increasing complexity of addressing climate change and its impacts on some of the most vulnerable communities of the world. Topics include the physical impacts of climate change, energy infrastructure and financing, human rights, environmental justice, global policy initiatives and other emerging issues. Each chapter provides a thorough, insightful, and engaging examination of a key issue impacting climate justice throughout the world. Through evidence-based case studies and thoughtful analysis of existing law and policy, the text provides a valuable roadmap for effectively responding to the many challenges of climate change.*
—Eric V. Hull
Professor of Law, Florida Coastal School of Law

The overarching message of the spectacular Climate Justice: Case Studies in Global and Regional Governance Challenges *is: the means are the ends in the making. That is to say, how we address the present and future, urgent threats of climate change will determine what our planet looks like and who will survive and thrive. Professor Abate's volume brings together a stellar array of scholars to address this most important ethical problem of our generation.*
—David Takacs
Professor, University of California Hastings College of Law

CLIMATE JUSTICE

Case Studies in Global and Regional Governance Challenges

Randall S. Abate, Editor

ENVIRONMENTAL LAW INSTITUTE
Washington, D.C.

Published December 2016.

Cover design by A.J.-Miles Media, Inc.
www.ajmilesmedia.com

Printed in the United States of America
ISBN 978-1-58576-181-4

For present and future generations throughout the world who are suffering from or live in fear of their vulnerability to climate change impacts.

Contents

Editor and Contributor Biographies

Editor

Randall S. Abate is the associate dean for academic affairs and a professor of law at Florida Agricultural and Mechanical University College of Law in Orlando, Florida. Professor Abate teaches climate change law and justice, international environmental law, climate change and indigenous peoples, climate change impacts on ocean and coastal law, constitutional law I and II, and animal law. Professor Abate joined the Florida A&M College of Law faculty in 2009 with 15 years of full-time law teaching experience at Vermont Law School, Widener Law School-Harrisburg, Rutgers School of Law-Camden, Florida Coastal School of Law, and Florida State College of Law. He has taught international and comparative environmental law courses in Argentina, Canada, the Cayman Islands, China, India, Kenya, Kyrgyzstan, Spain, Ukraine, and the United Kingdom. Professor Abate was awarded a Sustainability Institute faculty fellowship from Florida A&M University for the 2016/2017 academic year.

Professor Abate has published and presented widely on environmental law topics, with a recent emphasis on climate change law and justice. His articles on climate change law and justice have appeared in the *Stanford Environmental Law Journal, Cornell Journal of Law and Public Policy, Connecticut Law Review, Duke Environmental Law and Policy Forum, Washington Law Review, William and Mary Environmental Law and Policy Review, Tulane Journal of International and Comparative Law, Seattle Journal of Environmental Law, Ottawa Law Review, Tulane Environmental Law Journal, Fordham Environmental Law Review,* and *UCLA Journal of International Law and Foreign Affairs.* He is the editor of WHAT CAN ANIMAL LAW LEARN FROM ENVIRONMENTAL LAW? (ELI Press 2015) and CLIMATE CHANGE IMPACTS ON OCEAN AND COASTAL LAW: U.S. AND INTERNATIONAL PERSPECTIVES (Oxford University Press 2015) and co-editor of CLIMATE CHANGE AND INDIGENOUS PEOPLES: THE SEARCH FOR LEGAL REMEDIES (Edward Elgar 2013). Early in his career, Professor Abate handled environmental law matters at two law firms in Manhattan. He holds a B.A. from the University of

Rochester and a J.D. and M.S.E.L. (environmental law and policy) from Vermont Law School.

Contributing Authors

Nadia B. Ahmad is an assistant professor of law at Barry University Dwayne O. Andreas School of Law. Previously, she was the visiting assistant professor of environmental law at Pace Law School. Professor Ahmad's research explores the intersections of energy law and the environment and draws on international investment law, energy justice, corporate best practices, and corporate social responsibility. Alongside her scholarship on energy law and the environment, Professor Ahmad also writes about women's legal rights in South Asia and the Middle East. Prior to joining Pace Law School, Professor Ahmad worked for a multinational oil and gas company. Additionally, as a legal fellow with the Colorado-based nongovernmental organization Sustainable Development Strategies Group, Professor Ahmad analyzed foreign mining and natural resource development laws for compliance with sustainable development principles. Previously, Professor Ahmad was an attorney in private practice in Florida and handled civil litigation, real property, land use and zoning, corporate, and employment law matters. Professor Ahmad earned a B.A. in comparative literature with language emphases in Latin and English from the University of California at Berkeley with high honors, a J.D. from the University of Florida Levin College of Law, and an LL.M. in environmental and natural resources law from the University of Denver Sturm College of Law. She is a member of the state bars of Florida and Colorado. She has delivered presentations at Columbia Law School, Harvard Law School, Yale University, University of Georgia School of Law, University of Washington School of Law, Albany Law School, American University in Cairo, Texas A&M School of Law, and George Washington University Law School.

Naysa Ahuja is a senior associate at Enviro Legal Defence Firm, the first environmental law firm in India. She works as a consultant on the interface of natural resource management, forest and landscape governance, community access rights, gender justice, and environmental rule of law in India, the United States, and other Asian countries. She is interested in studying the implications of international climate change discussion on resilience-building actions and financing at the national and village levels. Ms. Ahuja has worked with environmental law firms, U.N. agencies, and international think tanks including the World Resources Institute (WRI) and World Wildlife Fund-India. At WRI, she helped develop an Environmental Democracy Index (launched in May 2015), which ranks 70 countries against the tenets of Principle 10 of the Rio Declaration. A strong advocate for participative legal and institutional reforms, Ms. Ahuja has conducted several field investigations and multi-stakeholder consultations to submit policy recommendations on strengthening forest and mountain governance to the Government of India. She holds an LL.M. in environmental law from The George Washington University Law School, where she was the Thomas Buergenthal scholar of 2013. She is also a recipient of an NFP fellowship at the Centre for Development Innovation, Wageningen University, to study landscape approach in Indonesia (2015). She received her LL.B. from the University of Delhi and practices in the Supreme Court of India and the National Green Tribunal. She has delivered guest lectures, presentations, and conducted training at universities, government agencies, and the United Nations on several occasions. Ms. Ahuja is currently a visiting attorney at the Environmental Law Institute in Washington, D.C., while developing her Ph.D. research questions around existing environmental dispute resolution mechanisms to address transboundary resource conflicts.

Dr. Sumudu Anopama Atapattu is the director of research centers and senior lecturer at the University of Wisconsin Law School. She teaches seminar classes on international environmental law and climate change, human rights, and the environment. She is affiliated with UW-Madison's Nelson Institute for Environmental Studies and the Center for South Asia and coordinates the campus-wide interdisciplinary Human Rights Program. She was a visiting professor at Doshisha University Law School, Japan, in summer 2014. Dr. Atapattu serves as the lead counsel for human rights at the Center for International Sustainable Development Law based in Montreal, Canada, and is on the advisory board of the *McGill International Journal of Sustainable Development Law and Policy*. She has participated in several consultations organized by the United Nations Independent Expert on Human Rights and the Environment, including a consultation on climate change and human rights with the United Nations Office of the High Commissioner for Human Rights. Dr. Atapattu has published widely in the fields of international environmental law, climate change, environmental rights, and sustainable development, and is the author of HUMAN RIGHTS APPROACHES TO CLIMATE CHANGE: CHALLENGES AND OPPORTUNITIES (Routledge 2016). She holds an LL.M. (public international law) and a Ph.D. (international environmental law) from the University of Cambridge, U.K., and is an attorney-at-law of the Supreme Court of Sri Lanka.

Ara Azad is managing partner at AzP Consulting, LLC, a regulatory consulting firm with a primary focus on the energy and utilities industry. Ms. Azad is a certified public accountant with a B.S. in molecular biosciences from the University of Kansas and an M.S. in accounting from the University of Missouri-Kansas City. Prior to her career in regulated utilities consulting, she worked at the international accounting firm PricewaterhouseCoopers as a financial statement auditor. During her career as a consultant, she has provided finance and accounting consulting services to regulators in their public interest reviews of utility mergers and acquisitions, property valuations, and operational and compliance audits. Ms. Azad has served as an expert in the statutory reviews of some of the largest proposed electric and natural gas utility mergers in the United States, having served as an expert witness addressing ratepayer protection issues including accounting and tax matters, merger costs, energy efficiency, impact on employment, community support, and cost allocation.

Ava Azad is an attorney-advisor in the Federal Facilities Enforcement Office of the U.S. Environmental Protection Agency headquarters in Washington, D.C. She holds a J.D. with an environmental and natural resources law certificate from the University of Kansas, where she received the Hershberger, Patterson, Jones & Roth Energy Law Award. She earned a B.A. in environmental studies and a B.A. in Spanish from the University of Kansas, where she graduated with honors. Ms. Azad has worked at the Conservation Law Foundation (CLF) in Boston in the Clean Energy and Climate Change Program and the Healthy Communities and Environmental Justice Program. At CLF, her projects included analysis and advocacy of clean transportation and environmental justice in the energy, transportation, and food industries in New England. Ms. Azad has also worked in the environmental division of Shook, Hardy & Bacon LLP and the Kansas Department of Health & Environment. She has published on international environmental justice implications of foreign oil exploration in the *Florida A&M University Law Review*, and has also been published in the *Kansas Law Review*.

Josephine M. Balzac is a visiting assistant professor at Rollins College in the Department of Business. She is also an adjunct law professor at Barry University School of Law teaching sustainability in business. She is admitted to practice in Florida and the U.S. District Court, Middle District of Florida. She serves her community on the board of directors for IDEAS For Us and the EarthWeb Foundation. Professor Balzac previously worked as an associate attorney at an AV-rated trial litigation firm and also worked for a food safety regulatory consulting group. She holds a J.D. from Florida A&M University College of Law, where she graduated as valedictorian of her class. While at Florida A&M, Ms. Balzac received several scholarships, including the prestigious Holland & Knight Scholarship. She also won the Third Best Oralist Award during the Stetson International Environmental Moot Court Competition, where her team reached the semifinals. She received her LL.M. in international environmental law at The George Washington University Law School. While attending GWU Law, she served as a Randolph C. Shaw research fellow for the associate dean of environmental studies and interned at the U.S. Environmental Protection Agency in the Office of Resource Conservation and Recovery in the International Transportation Branch. Ms. Balzac is actively involved in the environmental community, frequently educating and promoting awareness by being an avid speaker on environmental, food, conservation, and social justice issues. Professor Balzac has also published articles on sustainable development, international trade, human rights, and environmental justice in the *Florida A&M University Law Review* and the *Loyola University of Chicago International Law Review*.

Mushtaq ur Rasool Bilal is a Ph.D. candidate in postcolonial feminism at the National University of Modern Languages in Islamabad, Pakistan. His book-length collection of long-form interviews with Pakistani English fiction writers was published in 2016 by HarperCollins India. He is also working as an editor-at-large at *Kitaab*, which is both a literary magazine and a publishing house based in Singapore. His work has appeared in academic journals— *South Asia: Journal of South Asian Studies, Postcolonial Text, Contemporary South Asia, the Annual of Urdu Studies*—as well as in popular publications, including *The News on Sunday, Dawn-Books and Authors, The Missing Slate*, and *Himal Southasian*.

Dr. Keely Boom is an Australian Aboriginal woman who is executive officer of the Climate Justice Programme, a nonprofit organization that encourages, supports, and tracks the enforcement of law and legal initiatives to combat climate change. She holds a Ph.D. from the University of Wollongong in international climate change law. Dr. Boom is a research associate at the University of Technology, Sydney, and a research fellow at the University of Wollongong. She is author of the chapter *The Rising Tide of International Climate Litigation: An Illustrative Hypothetical of Tuvalu v. Australia*, in CLIMATE CHANGE AND INDIGENOUS PEOPLES: THE SEARCH FOR LEGAL REMEDIES (Randall S. Abate & Elizabeth Ann Kronk Warner eds., 2013). She lives in a rural area and holds a practicing certificate in the state of New South Wales. Dr. Boom is a mother and is passionate about protecting the climate for future generations.

Dr. Wil Burns is the founding co-director of the Forum for Climate Engineering Assessment, a scholarly initiative of American University. He is based in its western office in Berkeley, California. Dr. Burns previously served as the director of the Master of Science, Energy Policy & Climate Program at Johns Hopkins University in Washington, D.C. He also serves as the co-chair of the International Environmental Law Committee of the American Branch of the International Law Association. Dr. Burns is the former president of the Association for Environmental Studies & Sciences and former co-chair of the International Environmental Law Interest Group of the American Society of International Law and chair of the International Wildlife Law Interest Group of the Society. He has published more than 75 articles in law, science, and policy journals and has co-edited four books. Prior to becoming an academic, he served as assistant secretary of state for public affairs for the state of Wisconsin and worked in the nongovernmental sector for 20 years, including as executive director of the Pacific Center for International Studies, a think-tank that focused on implementation of international wildlife treaty regimes, including the Convention on Biological Diversity and International Convention for the Regulation of Whaling. His current areas of research focus are climate geoengineering; international climate change litigation; and adaptation strategies to address climate change, with a focus on the potential role of microinsurance. Dr. Burns holds a Ph.D. in international environmental law from the University of Wales-Cardiff School of Law.

Dr. Onita Das is a senior lecturer in law at the University of the West of England, Bristol. She received her LL.M. in international law at the University of Bristol and Ph.D. in international law at the University of the West of England. Dr. Das currently teaches environmental law at the undergraduate level and contributes to teaching on the international environmental law, natural resources law, and European environmental law and policy modules at the postgraduate level. Her principal research areas are sustainable development, environmental protection relevant to security and armed conflict, and land grabbing in the context of sustainable development and human rights. She is a core member of the Global Network on Human Rights and the Environment, and in 2015 was a visiting fellow at the Lauterpacht Centre for International Law in Cambridge. Dr. Das also serves as the head of the Environmental Law Research Unit at the University of the West of England.

Dr. Verónica de la Rosa Jaimes is a research fellow at the Canadian Institute of Resources Law and the Latin American Research Centre at the University of Calgary. She previously served as an Eyes High postdoctoral scholar in the Canadian Institute of Resources Law of the University of Calgary Faculty of Law, where she researched issues in energy development and climate change litigation. Dr. de la Rosa Jaimes holds a J.D., a master's in international law, and a Ph.D. (Hon.) from the National Autonomous University of Mexico (UNAM). She spent one year conducting research for her doctoral thesis at the University of Montpellier in France, where she was a visiting professor. She has been a lecturer at the University of Calgary, UNAM, and TEC de Monterrey. Dr. de la Rosa Jaimes is a certified attorney in Mexico, where she worked for several government agencies in managing regulatory and legal projects. She has published several books and articles in law journals in Mexico and the United States in the areas of international law, human rights law, and environmental law.

Dr. Patrícia G. Ferreira is a postdoctoral fellow with the Centre for International Governance Innovation's (CIGI's) International Law Research Program. Dr. Ferreira's research at CIGI focuses on how the intersection of international law institutions with domestic legal institutions may facilitate sustainable development outcomes, with an emphasis on international environmental law. Current research projects include a study on how emerging economies like China, India, Brazil, and South Africa have been shifting their positions in relation to key international law principles, norms, and institutions that may impact sustainable development outcomes. She holds an S.J.D. in law and development from the University of Toronto, which she earned concurrently with an interdisciplinary doctorate in the dynamics of global change from the Munk School of Global Affairs. She has an LL.B. from the Federal University of Bahia and an LL.M. from the University of Notre Dame. A Brazilian national, Dr. Ferreira is a research associate at the Institute for Studies on Labor and Society in Rio de Janeiro. In 2013, she was a visiting scholar and Joaquim Nabuco Chair in Brazilian studies at the Center for Latin American Studies at Stanford University and a visiting scholar at the Fundação Getúlio Vargas Law School in São Paulo. Before earning her doctoral degree, she worked for nearly 20 years in the fields of human rights and international development. Her professional experience ranges from litigating major Brazilian human rights cases before international bodies as a lawyer for the Center for Justice and International Law to grant writing with the Open Society Initiative for Southern Africa.

Steven Ferrey is a professor of law at Suffolk University Law School in Boston, and has served as visiting professor of law at Harvard Law School and Boston University Law School. He has testified as an expert witness before seven committees of the U.S. Congress on energy, and was appointed by the president of the United States to serve on three national energy boards. Since 1993, he has served as primary legal advisor to the World Bank and the United Nations on renewable energy and climate change projects in several developing countries in Asia, Africa, and elsewhere. He has served as vice-chair of two different American Bar Association Energy Committees. Professor Ferrey is the author of seven books and 100 articles on environmental and energy law and regulatory topics. His books include the three-volume Law of Independent Power (40th ed. 2016); Environmental Law: Examples and Explanations (7th ed. 2016); Renewable Power in Developing Countries (2006); and Unlocking the Global Warming Toolbox (2010). In addition to a J.D. degree from Boalt Hall at the University of California at Berkeley, he holds a B.A. in economics from Pomona College in California, a master's degree in urban and regional environmental/energy planning from U.C. Berkeley, and was a Fulbright fellow in London between his graduate degrees.

Dr. Teresa Giménez-Candela is a professor of law; director and founder of the postgraduate Animals, Law, and Society Program; and director of the master's in animal law and society at the Universitat Autònoma de Barcelona in Spain. She has the distinction of being the first law professor in Spain to teach a course on animal law. Dr. Giménez-Candela is the director of the research group Animales, Derecho y Sociedad, which was awarded official recognition by the autonomous government of Catalonia. She is the founder and editor of the web page www.derechoanimal.info, the first database on animal policy and case law in Spain. She is the founder and director of the collection *Animals and the Law*, printed by the Tirant lo Blanch publishing house in Valencia. She is also the founder of the European Group of Animal Law Studies. Dr. Giménez-Candela has more than 25 years of law teaching experience at universities on four continents, including Universidad de Navarra; Universidad de Valencia; Universitat de les Illes Balears; University of Köln; Fukuoka; UNAM of Mexico; Mayor de S. Simón; Università di Tor Vergata; Università Federico II di Napoli; and New York University. She has received multiple fellowships from the Alexander-von-Humboldt-Stiftung, which enabled her to conduct research at the German universities of München and Heidelberg, in addition to the University of Rome La Sapienza, in the manuscript section of the Vatican Library, and the Maruccelliana Library. She has worked in the *Thesaurus Linguae Latinae* in München, and in the Department of Papyrology of the Ashmolean Museum in Oxford. Dr. Giménez-Candela was trained in Roman law and Latin legal epigraphy and holds an LL.B. and Ph.D. in law with special prize for merit from the Universidad de Navarra in Pamplona.

Dr. Kamrul Hossain is an associate professor and director of the Northern Institute for Environmental and Minority Law at the Arctic Centre in the University of Lapland. He has previously served the Faculty of Law of the University of Lapland as acting professor of public international law. He is also an adjunct professor of international law at the University of Lapland. Dr. Hossain leads the research project, HuSArctic, funded by the Academy of Finland. He has been actively involved in a number of significant research projects funded by the European Union, Nordic Council of Ministers, and the Academy of Finland. Dr. Hossain has published scholarly articles in many highly regarded international journals. He served as the special editor for Volume 3 of the Yearbook of Polar Law, published in 2011. He regularly teaches at the University of Lapland, and periodically at other foreign universities. He completed visiting fellowships at a number of foreign universities, including the University of Toronto, Scott Polar Research Institute of the University of Cambridge, and the Muroran Institute of Technology in Japan. He has received a number of prestigious awards, including the SYLFF fellowship at the University of Helsinki. In 2012, Dr. Hossain was awarded a faculty research fellowship by the Canadian Department of Foreign Affairs and International Trade.

Jennifer Huang is an international fellow at the Center for Climate and Energy Solutions (C2ES). Ms. Huang tracks and researches international climate policy, focusing on key issues in the United Nations Framework Convention on Climate Change (UNFCCC) negotiations, including transparency, the global stocktake under the Paris Agreement, and adaptation.

She also helps facilitate dialogues among international policymakers and stakeholders. Prior to joining C2ES, she worked as a law clerk at the White House Council on Environmental Quality and as a legal intern in the Ad Hoc Working Group on the Durban Platform for Enhanced Action Implementation Strategy Unit at the UNFCCC secretariat in Bonn, Germany. Ms. Huang also has a background in international criminal law and international human rights, with a special interest in human rights and climate change. She co-authored the chapter *Governance of Climate Change Impacts on the Antarctic Marine Environment,* in CLIMATE CHANGE IMPACTS ON OCEAN AND COASTAL LAW: U.S. AND INTERNATIONAL PERSPECTIVES (Randall S. Abate ed., 2015). She has authored articles on transparency, renewable energy, and the U.S. military, and on Darfur genocide reparations before the International Criminal Court. She is also a member of the New York City Bar Association's International Environmental Law Committee. Ms. Huang holds an LL.M. degree in environmental law with a focus on climate change and a J.D. with certificates in international and environmental law from Pace Law School (now the Elisabeth Haub School of Law at Pace University). She holds an interdisciplinary B.A. in war and military studies from New York University.

Dr. Cameron S.G. Jefferies is an assistant professor and Borden Ladner Gervais energy law fellow at the Faculty of Law, University of Alberta. He holds a B.Sc. and LL.B. from the University of Alberta and an LL.M. and S.J.D. from the University of Virginia School of Law, where he studied as a Fulbright Scholar. Before entering academia, he practiced at Field LLP in Edmonton, Alberta, and worked as a research associate at the Health Law Institute at the University of Alberta. Dr. Jefferies currently researches and teaches in the areas of international law, environmental law, natural resources law, ocean law, and animal law, and is a member of the Intersections of Sustainability Collaborative Research Network on Water Governance, Climate Change, and the Futures of Communities at the University of Alberta. He is keenly interested in public interest law and advocacy and works to promote local environmental law reform. Most recently, his efforts have focused on a Canadian municipal environmental rights movement. He has published several book chapters and articles in U.S. and Canadian law journals, including the *Energy Law Journal* and the *Journal of Environmental Law and Practice,* and is the author of MARINE MAMMAL CONSERVATION AND THE LAW OF THE SEA (Oxford University Press 2016).

Dr. Robert Kibugi is a lecturer in law at the University of Nairobi's Centre for Advanced Studies in Environmental Law and School of Law. He previously taught at the Faculty of Law, University of Ottawa, in Canada. He holds an LL.B. and an LL.M. from the School of Law, University of Nairobi, and an LL.D. from the Faculty of Law, University of Ottawa. He is an advocate of the High Court of Kenya. His legal and policy research agenda focuses on public participation in natural resource governance; land use law for sustainable development; climate change, including the role of law and policy in the adaptation and mitigation of climate change; energy law; water resources management and rights; and water and sanitation. Since November 2013, Dr. Kibugi has been legal advisor and consultant to the government of Kenya on drafting climate change legislation and policy for the country. He has published various chapters and articles in peer-reviewed books and journals. His current research addresses enhancing community benefits in large-scale land acquisitions for investments, supported by the International Development Research Centre. Dr. Kibugi is a member of the governing board of the International Union for Conservation of Nature Academy of Environmental Law, elected in 2013 to represent the African continent. He is a member of the Climate Change Adaptation Specialist Group at the Asia Pacific Environmental Law Centre at the National University of Singapore, and chief legal counsel for climate change at the Centre for International Sustainable Development Law in Montreal, Canada.

Dr. Itzchak Kornfeld is the Giordano research fellow at the Faculty of Law of the Hebrew University of Jerusalem in Israel. He holds a Sc.B. (geology), M.A. (geochemistry), J.D. (Tulane), LL.M. (Georgetown), and LL.D./Ph.D. (Hebrew University). Dr. Kornfeld's main research interests are international environmental law, particularly how courts and tribunals adjudicate issues related to natural resources and water law. He also researches energy law issues, concentrating on the human right to energy. He has written widely on these subjects. Dr. Kornfeld is currently finishing two books. The first is titled ADJUDICATING INTERNATIONAL WATER DISPUTES IN NORTH AMERICA, and the second is DAM(N)ING NATURAL RESOURCES: DAMS AND THE DESTRUCTION OF PEOPLE AND THE ENVIRONMENT. He was a co-founder and managing articles editor of the *Tulane Environmental Law Journal*, and clerked for the Honorable David I. Gertler. Dr. Kornfeld worked as a petroleum geologist for 10 years. Early in his career, Dr. Kornfeld litigated numerous environmental and energy cases, including a landmark Comprehensive Environmental Response, Compensation, and Liability Act (CERCLA) case of first impression, where the district court held that the city of Philadelphia's sewer systems were not per se exempt from CERCLA's definition of "facilities," subject to liability for contribution costs (*United States v. Union Corp.*, 277 F. Supp. 2d 478 (E.D. Pa. 2003)). His environment and natural resources blog is available at itzchakkornfeld.com.

Clement Yow Mulalap, a native of the island of Yap in the Federated States of Micronesia, is the legal adviser for the Permanent Mission of the Federated States of Micronesia to the United Nations, where he primarily reviews international conventions, tracks international organizations, covers United Nations meetings, and negotiates United Nations resolutions on legal matters on behalf of the Federated States of Micronesia. He is the author of the chapter *Islands in the Stream: Addressing Climate Change From a Small Island Developing State Perspective*, in CLIMATE CHANGE AND INDIGENOUS PEOPLES: THE SEARCH FOR LEGAL REMEDIES (Randall S. Abate & Elizabeth Ann Kronk Warner eds., 2013). He holds a B.A. in economics (with minors in political science and English) from the University of Hawai'i at Mānoa, a J.D. (with a certificate in Asia-Pacific law) from the William S. Richardson School of Law, and an LL.M. in international legal studies from New York University School of Law.

Dr. Chilenye Nwapi is a research associate at the Canadian Institute of Resources Law, University of Calgary. He is also a senior fellow at the Institute for Oil, Gas, Energy, Environment, and Sustainable Development, Afe Babalola University, Nigeria. Dr. Nwapi's research interests cut across various aspects of extractive resource development, including issues of human and environmental rights abuses, extractive sector transparency, and environmental and social impact assessments. He has published extensively in these and other areas in various peer-reviewed journals and has presented his research at national and international conferences in several countries. Dr. Nwapi holds a Ph.D. in transnational litigation from the University of British Columbia (Canada), an LL.M. in energy and environmental law from the University of Calgary (Canada), and an LL.B. from Imo State University, Nigeria. He has been a visiting fellow at the Uppsala Forum for Democracy, Peace, and Justice at Uppsala Universitet in Sweden. He has taught at the University of British Columbia and the University of Calgary and is an associate editor of the *Journal of Sustainable Development Law and Policy*. In addition to the prestigious Banting Fellowship, he has been awarded numerous other fellowships and scholarships, including the Social Sciences and

Humanities Research Council Postdoctoral Fellowship, the Law Foundation of British Columbia Fellowship, and the Alberta Law Foundation Scholarship. He is a barrister and solicitor of the Supreme Court of Nigeria.

Dr. Damilola S. Olawuyi is an associate professor of petroleum, energy and environmental law at the HBKU Law School, Qatar, and chancellor's fellow at the Institute for Oil, Gas, Energy and Environment, Nigeria. A prolific and highly regarded scholar, Dr. Olawuyi has published more than 30 peer-reviewed articles, books, and reports on carbon finance, climate justice, extractive resource governance, and the intersections of human rights and the environment. His most recent publication is THE HUMAN RIGHTS-BASED APPROACH TO CARBON FINANCE (Cambridge University Press 2016). Dr. Olawuyi was formerly deputy director and head of international environmental law at the Centre for International Governance Innovation (CIGI), Canada. He also practiced as an international energy lawyer at Norton Rose Fulbright Canada LLP, Calgary, where he served on the firm's global committee on extractive resource investments in Africa. He has lectured on energy and environmental law in more than 20 countries, including Australia, Canada, China, Indonesia, Denmark, France, India, Kenya, Nigeria, Spain, the United Kingdom, and the United States. Dr. Olawuyi holds a doctoral degree in energy and environmental law from the University of Oxford, an LL.M. from Harvard Law School, another LL.M. from the University of Calgary, and a diploma in international environmental law from the United Nations Institute for Training and Research (Switzerland). He earned his LL.B. from Igbinedion University, Nigeria, graduating with first-class honors, and his B.L. from the Nigerian Law School, also graduating with first-class honors. He serves on the executive committees and boards of the American Society of International Law (co-chair, African Interest Group), the International Law Association (London), and the Environmental Law Centre (Alberta). He is vice president of the International Law Association (Nigerian branch), editor-in-chief of the *Journal of Sustainable Development Law and Policy*, associate fellow of the Centre for International Sustainable Development Law (Montreal), and, most recently, the David Sive scholar at the Sabin Center for Climate Change Law, Columbia Law School.

Karine Péloffy has been a lawyer since 2007 and is the executive director of the Quebec Center for Environmental Law (CQDE). As the CQDE director, she has been active on the Center's legal filings, such as two successful injunctions to protect species at risk in the past year, including against a proposed oil export terminal in a beluga whale nursery in the Saint Lawrence River. Ms. Péloffy formerly practiced commercial litigation at a top-tier Canadian law firm and served as a community rights lawyer for forest communities and civil society organizations in the Congo Basin countries of Africa. In 2013, she published the first comparative law article on climate litigation in Canada and the United States, which analyzed the case of *Kivalina v. Exxon-Mobil* in light of the jurisprudence of the Supreme Courts of both countries. She has presented the results of this article before government commissions and at university conferences. She also has campaigned with the Eradicating Ecocide Global Initiative in London and has lived, traveled, and volunteered with several initiatives dedicated to social and environmental justice in America, Africa, Europe, and Australasia. Ms. Péloffy was awarded the Lawyer of the Year/Tomorrow's Leader in the alternative career category by the Montreal Young Bar Association. She holds an M.Sc. in environmental change and management from the University of Oxford and a B.C.L./LL.B. from McGill University's unique transsystemic law program.

Noor Jahan Punam holds a master's degree in law from the University of Eastern Finland. She has previously completed a post graduate certificate in management of land acquisition, rehabilitation, and resettlement at Brac University, Bangladesh. In 2011, she completed a postgraduate diploma in bar professional training from Northumbria University, U.K., and she was called to the Bar of England and Wales in 2012. Ms. Punam holds an LL.B. degree from the University of London's international program. She has worked at the Bangladesh Institute of Law and International Affairs as a research assistant assisting the editorial process of the *Bangladesh Journal of Law*. She has also worked as an associate lawyer at Giambrone Law in Palermo, Italy. In addition, Ms. Punam worked for the law desk at the *Daily Star, Bangladesh* writing on contemporary legal issues in Bangladesh. Ms. Punam also has delivered lectures at various authorized institutions of the University of London in Bangladesh.

Keith W. Rizzardi joined the St. Thomas law faculty in 2011 after many years of government service to the U.S. Department of Justice and the South Florida Water Management District. An accomplished litigator, he appeared in water and wildlife cases before administrative, trial, or appellate courts from the Florida Everglades to the California Central Valley Project, and from Washington, D.C., to Hawaii. As a counselor and policy advisor, he chaired the Marine Fisheries Advisory Committee, assisted local governments with the challenges of compliance with public records laws, and volunteers as an ombudsman for the U.S. Department of Defense. A Florida Bar leader, he chaired the Government Lawyer Section, served on the state bar's ethics and professionalism committees, and earned recognition as a board certified specialist in state and federal administrative practice. Professor Rizzardi has authored nearly two dozen articles and book chapters, and his teaching and scholarship have focused on administrative law, civil procedure, environmental law, negotiation, professional responsibility, and regulatory compliance. He is a graduate of the University of Virginia (B.A. 1991), University of Florida (J.D. 1994), and Florida Atlantic University (M.P.A. 1998). Professor Rizzardi has shared his education, experience, and writings at dozens of conferences, and he taught internationally at the United Nations Educational, Scientific, and Cultural Organization Water Institute in the Netherlands and at the China University of Political Science and Law in Beijing.

David Roche is a staff attorney with the Environmental Law Institute (ELI), where he specializes in coastal community health and resilience in the Gulf of Mexico, Arctic, and Caribbean. In the past two years, his work has been published in *The Environmental Forum*, the *National Wetlands Newsletter* (cover article), the *Duke Environmental Law and Policy Forum*, and by Oxford University Press and ELI Press. In addition to published work, Mr. Roche writes a blog on ocean issues entitled "Ocean Talk" for ELI, writes many online-only articles on ocean and coastal issues, and develops interactive tools to assist coastal communities in engaging with environmental issues. He also has been a featured speaker at a number of conferences, including Restore America's Estuaries and State of Our Coast, and moderates ELI's Ocean Seminar Series. He graduated from Duke University School of Law magna cum laude, where he was editor-in-chief of the *Duke Environmental Law and Policy Forum*, and also received a master's degree in environmental science from Duke's Nicholas School. His undergraduate degree is in environmental science from Columbia University.

Carly Elizabeth Souther is a researcher for the International Center for Animal Law and Policy and an adjunct professor in the Master's of Animal Law and Society Program at Universitat Autónoma de Barcelona. She co-authored the chapter *Invasive Animal Species: International Impacts and Inadequate Interventions*, in WHAT CAN ANIMAL LAW LEARN FROM ENVIRONMENTAL LAW? (Randall S. Abate ed., 2015). She has published on a wide range of issues in both legal and medical journals, including the *Georgetown Journal* *on Poverty Law & Policy* and the *Care Management Journal*. Ms. Souther formerly served as assistant general counsel at Florida's Agency for Health Care Administration, a research fellow at the Center for Innovative Collaboration in Medicine and the Law of the Florida State University College of Medicine, and second-chair of the Juvenile Justice course at the Florida State University College of Law. Ms. Souther is co-founder, pro bono chair, and past president of Petagon International, Inc., and is a member of the Florida Bar. She holds a master's in animal law and society from the Universitat Autónoma de Barcelona, a J.D. from the Florida State University College of Law, and a B.A. in political science from Mercer University.

Maria Antonia Tigre is an attorney in the environment program at the Cyrus R. Vance Center for International Justice. She works with nongovernmental organizations across the globe on environmental law issues, especially on forests and the interface between climate change and human rights. Ms. Tigre has worked with environmental law firms, infrastructure companies, and international nongovernmental organizations, including the World Resources Institute (WRI). She began her career in Brazil, where she assisted infrastructure companies in environmental impact assessments, environmental permitting procedures, and due diligence requirements. At WRI, she developed a toolkit for urban governance in developing world cities through a comparative analysis of best practices. Ms. Tigre holds a double LL.M., magna cum laude, from Pace Law School (environmental law and comparative legal studies). She received her LL.B. from the Pontifícia Universidade Católica of Rio de Janeiro, Brazil. Ms. Tigre was a visiting scholar at Widener Law School and Maurice A. Dean Law School at Hofstra University. Her research focuses on comparative environmental law in Latin America. She is writing a book on cooperation between the countries that share the Amazon rainforest, which analyzes national, regional, and international forest law and the Amazon Cooperation Treaty Organization. She recently published an article, *Cooperation for Climate Mitigation in Amazonia: Brazil's Emerging Role as a Regional Leader*, in the Fall 2016 issue of the *Transnational Environmental Law* (TEL) journal published by Cambridge University Press. Ms. Tigre is fluent in Portuguese, English, and German, with basic understanding of French and Spanish.

Acknowledgments

This book addresses a daunting global challenge and it demanded a substantial and collaborative global effort in research and writing. The book would not have been possible without the outstanding chapters and indispensable insights and support from the 29 contributing authors from 16 countries in this volume. The chapters contain detailed and thoughtful analysis on cutting-edge issues from both established and rising scholars and practitioners who work in a wide range of settings including academia, private practice, government agencies, and nongovernmental organizations within and outside the legal profession. The editor is grateful to have had the privilege to work with such a remarkable team on this book project.

A small army of volunteer research assistants throughout the United States and abroad provided essential support in the book manuscript assembly and review process. Volunteer research assistants who provided outstanding assistance above and beyond the call of duty were attorney Mackenzie Landa and students Jomayra Belmonte, Chelsea Hernandez-Silk, and April Williams. Several other volunteer research assistants who provided valuable assistance were attorneys Jess Beaulieu, Jacqueline Bertelsen, Christine Castro, Claribel Gonzalez, Jerry Leakey, Vanessa McCarthy, Sabrina Persaud, Divya Pillai, Dan Schreiber, Teodora Siderova, and Karina Valencia, and students Miles Archabal, Oscar Burkholder, Tatiana Devia, Sacha Dixon, Sean Fann, Katheryn Goulfine, Kohinoor Mahi, Leara Morris-Stokes, Kaleigh Pappas, Justin Pon, Michael Scott, Latravia Smith, Kayleen Tinoco, Emily Wajert, Marlon White, and Demetrius Wilson.

This work was supported in part by Florida A&M University's Sustainability Institute. The editor is grateful to his wife, Nigara, for her love and support.

TABLE OF CASES

India

**Inter-American Commission on Human Rights &
Inter-American Court of Human Rights**

United States

Introduction

Climate change is one of the most complex political, social, and environmental issues of this century at all levels of governance. Climate change regulation rose to prominence in the 1990s with the United Nations Framework Convention on Climate Change (UNFCCC) and Kyoto Protocol mitigation mandates. It soon became clear, however, that an exclusive focus on greenhouse gas mitigation in climate change regulation would be insufficient to address the challenge of global climate change. Although climate change mitigation must continue to proceed as ambitiously as possible, severe climate change impacts have occurred and will continue to occur with increasing intensity.

Consequently, climate change adaptation has become an increasingly large focus of global efforts to address climate change. Although climate change adaptation measures are underway worldwide in many forms and in many sectors of society, the international community's attention regarding climate change adaptation has been on developing countries' needs. Consensus emerged that additional protection is necessary to ensure the health and safety of the most vulnerable communities of the world such as the urban and rural poor, low-lying island nations, indigenous peoples, and future generations in the face of climate change impacts. Early case studies that gained international attention regarding the need for effective adaptation include the Inuit indigenous community in the Arctic, and South Pacific island nations like Tuvalu and Kiribati, whose cultures and physical environments are on the brink of extermination from climate change impacts.

Climate justice evolved in response to this need for equity in the global response to these and other challenges associated with the disparate burdens of these impacts. Climate justice can be defined generally as addressing the disproportionate burden of climate change impacts on poor and marginalized communities and as seeking to promote more equitable allocation of the burdens of these impacts at the local, national, and global levels through proactive regulatory initiatives and reactive judicial remedies that draw on international human rights and domestic environmental justice theories. Efforts to define climate justice as a field of inquiry can be elusive and underinclusive, however, because the concept is so vast in scope.

This book provides an overview of the landscape of climate justice from a variety of legal and geographic perspectives in a case study format. It analyzes climate justice from an international law perspective and from the perspectives of legal responses to promote climate justice in several regions of the world, including Pacific island nations, South Asia, North America, and Africa and the Middle East. It addresses proposed solutions to a range of regulatory obstacles under international law, U.S. law, and foreign domestic law in seeking to promote climate justice on a global scale.

The book underscores how climate justice involves multiple legal parameters and regulatory strategies. First, there are procedural and substantive dimensions to promoting climate justice. Procedural dimensions involve efforts to enhance public participation, consultation with affected communities, and access to justice on these issues. Chapter 8 addresses procedural dimensions of climate justice for affected communities in the Gulf of Mexico in the wake of the *Deepwater Horizon* oil spill, whereas Chapter 9 addresses procedural-based climate justice protections for indigenous peoples in Alberta's oils sands region. Substantive dimensions of climate justice involve efforts to assert human rights-based protections as a response to climate change impacts. Chapters 1, 6, and 10 address various dimensions of the potential role of substantive human rights-based protections.

Second, climate justice involves both mitigation and adaptation dimensions. Climate justice can be achieved in part through mitigation policies and efforts at the international level. Examples include international climate regulation negotiations pursuant to the common but differentiated responsibility paradigm addressed in Chapter 2, exploring potential climate geoengineering strategies discussed in Chapter 6, and approving an amendment to the Montreal Protocol stratospheric ozone depletion regime to address hydrofluorocarbons as a potent greenhouse gas, as discussed in Chapter 12. To the extent that climate mitigation efforts are successful, climate justice for vulnerable communities is achieved to some degree. But the focus of climate justice is primarily in the adaptation domain. Legal responses such as the loss and damage mechanism in the Paris Agreement and climate justice litigation strategies focus on helping vulnerable communities adapt to the devastating climate impacts that they are experiencing. Adaptation measures range from financial and technological assistance from developed countries to developing countries, as addressed in Chapter 3, to preservation of cultural heritage and potential relocation of displaced communities and nations, as discussed in Chapters 11–13.

Third, climate justice also explores the role of climate change impacts as a "threat multiplier," which refers to how climate change impacts can exacerbate an existing context of social and environmental vulnerability. Chapters 14 and 15 address this concept in Africa and the Middle East. Chapter 14 discusses how climate change impacts such as drought act as a threat multiplier to an already compromised system of agricultural productivity in Kenya. Chapter 15 discusses how climate change impacts exacerbated an already volatile context for conflict in Syria and South Sudan.

Fourth, the quest for climate justice proceeds in proactive and reactive forms. Both types of responses are necessary. Proactive regulation of climate change adaptation and mitigation has occurred at the international, regional, national, subnational, and local levels of governance. Though well-intentioned, these efforts are incapable of offering complete or even minimally effective responses to promote climate justice. Therefore, much of the focus of recent climate justice has been in response to dissatisfaction with the adequacy of proactive responses or, in some instances, the failure to implement any form of proactive response. The book contains a unit on climate justice litigation to explore the range of reactive litigation strategies that have been employed, which includes the most famous of these efforts to date—the *Urgenda* case in the Netherlands (Chapter 21). Other climate justice litigation theories explored in the book include atmospheric justice litigation in the United States and abroad (Chapter 20), fossil fuel divestment litigation (Chapter 5), the World Heritage Convention (Chapter 22), and international and regional human rights protections, and domestic law protections, for indigenous peoples (Chapters 10, 23, and 24). These creative and unique litigation strategies share a common theme at their foundation in relying on the principle of intergenerational equity as the basis for their relief.

Within academic circles, climate change law has grown rapidly in the past three decades as a specialty area within environmental law and international law. Dozens of law schools in the United States and abroad offer courses and have developed specialty programs relating to climate change regulation. Climate justice has emerged as a subspecialty in this field and is drawing increased attention. In the international diplomacy context, the prelude to the much-anticipated 21st Conference of the Parties to the UNFCCC climate change negotiations in Paris in November 2015, and the unresolved human rights issues in its wake, have propelled climate justice to the forefront as a focus to help define future efforts to ensure a sustainable planet for future generations through effective climate change regulation.

International Governance Perspectives

Chapter I

Advancing Climate Justice in National Climate Actions: The Promise and Limitations of the United Nations Human Rights-Based Approach

Damilola S. Olawuyi

Introduction

One of the contemporary issues in climate justice debates is the need to anticipate, prevent, and address the potential infringement of fundamental human rights by projects undertaken to combat climate change.[1] Climate change mitigation measures, particularly Clean Development Mechanism (CDM) and Reducing Emissions From Deforestation and Forest Degradation in Developing Countries (REDD+) projects, have recently been linked with human rights violations, land grabs, forced displacements, marginalization, exclusions, and governmental repressions in developing countries.[2]

---

1. For detailed discussions of these debates, see Damilola Olawuyi, The Human Rights-Based Approach to Carbon Finance 1–15 (2016); *see also* Damilola Olawuyi, *Climate Justice and Corporate Responsibility: Taking Human Rights Seriously in Climate Actions and Projects*, 34 J. Energy & Nat. Resources L. 1 (2016).

2. Scientific studies show that deforestation and forest degradation, through agricultural expansion, conversion to pastureland, infrastructure development, destructive logging, and fires account for

The gaps and the high incidence of human rights violations resulting from CDM projects have increased the calls for a more transparent, accountable, and human rights-based approach to climate change mitigation.[3] Emerging debates on climate justice, therefore, recognize the growing indirect impacts that climate change mitigation and adaptation efforts have on human rights and examine how international law could provide legal frameworks to address these impacts.

This expansive view of climate justice is well captured by the 2014 Report of the International Bar Association (IBA), which defines climate justice as a process that seeks:

> To ensure communities, individuals and governments have substantive legal and procedural rights relating to the enjoyment of a safe, clean, healthy and sustainable environment and the means to take or cause measures to be taken within their national legislative and judicial systems and, where necessary, at regional and international levels, to mitigate sources of climate change and provide for adaptation to its effects *in a manner that respects human rights*.[4]

The IBA report emphasizes the ongoing search for legal and governance frameworks that will ensure that the global climate change conundrum is addressed in a manner that respects human rights.

The need to incorporate human rights considerations has also been addressed in international climate change negotiations under the United Nations Framework Convention on Climate Change (UNFCCC). For example, the 21st Conference of the Parties to the UNFCCC (COP21) in Paris recognized, in the Paris Agreement, that Parties should, "when taking action

---

nearly 20% of global greenhouse gas emissions, more than the entire global transportation sector and second only to the energy sector. The United Nations therefore recommends actions aimed at reducing emissions from deforestation and forest degradation, sustainable management of forests and conservation, and enhancement of forest carbon stocks (REDD+). The Bali Action Plan identified REDD+ as a prominent potential emission mitigation strategy. *See Report of the Conference of the Parties on Its Thirteenth Session, Held in Bali From 3 to 15 December 2017—Addendum, Part Two: Action Taken by the Conference of the Parties at Its Thirteenth Session, Decisions Adopted by the Conference of the Parties*, UNFCCC, 13th Sess., Decision 2/CP.13–Decision 4/CP.13, U.N. Doc. FCCC/CP/2010/7/ Add.1 (2010); *see also* ARILD ANGELSEN ET AL., REDUCING EMISSIONS FROM DEFORESTATION AND FOREST DEGRADATION: AN OPTIONS ASSESSMENT REPORT (2009), http://www.redd-oar.org/links/ REDD-OAR_en.pdf.

3. *See* Olawuyi, *Climate Justice and Corporate Responsibility, supra* note 1; *see also* UNITED NATIONS ENVIRONMENT PROGRAMME (UNEP), CLIMATE CHANGE AND HUMAN RIGHTS 9–10 (2015); Naomi Roht-Arriaza, *Human Rights in the Climate Change Regime*, 1 J. HUM. RTS. & ENV'T 211 (2010) (identifying areas where current climate change regimes may cause human rights violations in local communities, including projects under the CDM, large hydropower and biomass projects, use of biofuels, choices on energy and adaptation, and REDD+ projects).

4. INTERNATIONAL BAR ASSOCIATION, ACHIEVING JUSTICE AND HUMAN RIGHTS IN AN ERA OF CLIMATE DISRUPTION (2014) (emphasis added), http://www.ibanet.org/PresidentialTaskForceClimateChange-Justice2014Report.aspx.

to address climate change, respect, promote and consider their respective obligations on human rights."[5] This includes the right to health; the rights of indigenous peoples, local communities, migrants, children, persons with disabilities, and people in vulnerable situations; and the right to development, as well as gender equality, empowerment of women, and intergenerational equity.[6] Prior to the Paris Agreement, COP16 in Cancun, Mexico, emphasized that when undertaking REDD+ projects, countries must respect, protect, and promote the following safeguards:

> Respect for the knowledge and rights of indigenous peoples and members of local communities, by taking into account relevant international obligations, national circumstances and laws, and noting that the United Nations General Assembly has adopted the United Nations Declaration on the Rights of Indigenous Peoples; [and]

> The full and effective participation of relevant stakeholders, in particular, indigenous peoples and local communities, in actions referred to in paragraphs 70 and 72 of this decision.[7]

Despite these recognitions and declarations, however, the search for robust legal remedies and protection for traditional lands and rights in the implementation of climate actions remains a complex and contentious concern in several jurisdictions.[8] Recent scholarly writing on climate change and human rights has focused on approaches aimed at recognizing climate change as a human rights issue.[9] Different approaches have been suggested, ranging from

---

5.   *See Adoption of the Paris Agreement*, UNFCC Conference of the Parties, 21st Sess., U.N. Doc. FCCC/ CP/2015/10/Add.1 (Dec. 12, 2015), http://unfccc.int/files/home/application/pdf/paris_agreement. pdf.

6.   *See* Robert Chambers et al., *The Rise of Rights: Rights-based Approaches to International Development*, 17 IDS Policy Briefing (2003), http://www.ids.ac.uk/files/Pb17.pdf; Raymond C. Offenheiser & Susan H. Holcombe, *Challenges and Opportunities in Implementing a Rights-Based Approach to Development: An Oxfam America Perspective*, 32 Nonprofit & Voluntary Sector Q. 268, 300 (2003), http://nvs. sagepub.com/content/32/2/268.full.pdf+html.

7.   *See Outcome of the Work of the Ad Hoc Working Group on Long-Term Cooperative Action Under the Convention*, UNFCCC, unfccc.int/files/meetings/cop_16/application/pdf/cop16_lca.pdf.

8.   *See* Marcos Orellana, *A Human Rights-Based Approach to Climate Change, in* The Human Rights-Based Approach: A Field of Action for Human Rights Education 58 (J. Parra ed., 2012) (noting that "a large-scale hydroelectric project in a developing country under the CDM could force local communities to relocate from their traditional lands and livelihoods resulting in infringement of their rights to self-determination, property and life"); *see also* Damilola Olawuyi, *Aguan Biogas Project and the Government of the United Kingdom: Legal and International Human Rights Assessment*, 4 Queen Mary L.J. 37 (2013); Robin Bronen, *Climate-Induced Community Relocations: Creating an Adaptive Governance Framework Based in Human Rights Doctrine*, 35 N.Y.U. Rev. L. & Soc. Change 357 (2011).

9.   For recent and detailed analyses, see Olawuyi, The Human Rights-Based Approach to Carbon Finance, *supra* note 1, at 1–15; *see also* Sumudu Atapattu, The Human Rights Approaches to Climate Change: Challenges and Opportunities 1–20 (2015).

the introduction of a new substantive human right on climate change to the reinterpretation of existing human rights to provide for climate justice.[10]

Furthermore, since the United Nations human rights-based approach (HRBA) emerged in the early 2000s, it has gained rapid ascendancy and mention in the scholarly literature as a normative framework for mainstreaming human rights norms into the design, approval, finance, and implementation of climate change projects as a means to avoid human rights impacts.[11] The normative strengths of the HRBA as a strong process-based option for addressing the interaction of human rights and climate issues in the design, approval, finance, and implementation of climate change projects have been comprehensively unpacked elsewhere, and will not be discussed in this chapter.[12] By providing a template for implementing existing and recognized international human rights in a climate change context, the HRBA avoids redundancy, rights proliferation, and lack of political will concerns that have for many years stifled the development of substantive human rights to environmental protection.[13] Therefore, mainstreaming human rights into policymaking, through the HRBA, has been rightly described as the "wonder drug" for equal opportunities, justice, and human rights protection in development actions and projects.[14]

Despite the potential of the HRBA to advance climate justice at the global level, the HRBA faces several practical constraints at national levels. Due to its history, content, and structure, many of the elements of the HRBA experience varying levels of recognition, protection, and implementation in countries where climate injustices are most severe. Furthermore, local challenges such as inadequacy or absence of climate change laws, restrictive property regimes, inadequate capacity, and lack of resources impact the capacity of

---

10. *See* OLAWUYI, THE HUMAN RIGHTS-BASED APPROACH TO CARBON FINANCE, *supra* note 1, at 1–15; *see also* UNEP, CLIMATE CHANGE AND HUMAN RIGHTS, *supra* note 3, at 5–25.

11. *See* Lavanya Rajamani, *The Increasing Currency and Relevance of Rights-Based Perspectives in the International Negotiations on Climate Change*, 22 J. ENVTL. L. 391 (2010).

12. *See* Damilola Olawuyi, *Advancing Climate Justice in International Law: An Evaluation of the United Nations Human Rights-Based Approach*, 11 FLA. A&M L. REV. 1 (2016); Dinah Shelton, *Equitable Utilization of the Atmosphere: A Rights-Based Approach to Climate Change*, in HUMAN RIGHTS AND CLIMATE CHANGE 91–126 (Stephen Humphreys ed., 2010), http://scholarship.law.gwu.edu/cgi/viewcontent.cgi?article=1230&context=faculty_publications.

13. For a review of these debates, see Olawuyi, *Advancing Climate Justice in International Law, supra* note 12.

14. TAHNYA BARNETT DONAGHY, MAINSTREAMING: NORTHERN IRELAND'S PARTICIPATIVE-DEMOCRATIC APPROACH 1–2 (Hawkes Institute 2002); *see also* Navi Pillay, United Nations High Commissioner for Human Rights, Statement at the Launch of the United Nations Development Group Human Rights Mainstreaming Mechanism (UNDG-HRM) Multi-Donor Trust Fund (Nov. 27, 2011), https://undg.org/wp-content/uploads/2014/08/Statement-by-High-Commissioner-for-Human-Rights-Ms.-Navi-Pillay.pdf.

vulnerable groups to invoke human rights norms to seek redress when climate change projects threaten their ways of life.

This chapter examines practical and logistical barriers that stifle the promise and potential of the HRBA to deliver climate justice at national levels. Unless national regimes are revitalized and strengthened to provide requisite legal and governance infrastructure for climate justice programs, attempts to mainstream human rights norms into national climate regimes may not attain the desired level of coherence and effectiveness. Considering the roles of national institutions in approving climate strategies, actions, and projects, efforts to promote human rights norms in international climate instruments must also take root at national levels. The approval and implementation of climate projects by national authorities must be underpinned and guided by rights-based processes and safeguards.

Part I describes the guiding principles of the HRBA. Part II discusses practical and logistical questions that have stifled the overall efficacy of the HRBA in surveyed national regimes. It also includes legal and institutional proposals and recommendations on how national regimes on climate change can be revitalized and reformed to be more rights-based, transparent, and accountable, consistent with the core precepts of the HRBA.

I.   The United Nations Human Rights-Based Approach

The HRBA is a process-based governance framework that emphasizes the need to respect, protect, and fulfill human rights in development actions and projects. The aim of the HRBA is to ensure that projects or actions designed to advance development do not result in adverse human rights consequences.[15] A rights-based approach provides normative procedural frameworks for addressing systemic and structural injustices, social exclusions, and human rights repressions in the development of climate change solutions.[16]

The HRBA originated in 1997 when the United Nations secretary-general launched the United Nations Programme for Reform. This action plan called on all entities of the United Nations to mainstream human rights norms into their respective mandates and activities.[17] Since 1997, the idea

---

15.   See United Nations Practitioners' Portal on Human Rights Based Approaches to Programming (HRBA Portal), *The Human Rights-Based Approach to Development Cooperation: Towards a Common Understanding Among UN Agencies*, http://hrbaportal.org/the-human-rights-based-approach-to-development-cooperation-towards-a-common-understanding-among-un-agencies (last visited Aug. 20, 2016) [hereinafter HRBA Portal].

16.   *Id.*

17.   See *Renewing the United Nations: A Programme for Reform: Report of the Secretary-General*, U.N. GAOR, 51st Sess., Agenda Item 168, U.N. Doc. A/51/950 (1997). *See also* United Nations Children's

of integrating human rights principles into development efforts has gained significant recognition and popularity from United Nations agencies, the European Union, the World Bank, and national governments as a planning and programming framework.[18] From the early 2000s, human rights mainstreaming began to develop increasingly but somehow haphazardly by different international organizations leading to a lack of coordination or common understanding of its meaning, scope, and content. For example, the idea of mainstreaming has generated significant literature on the idea of gender mainstreaming. It has also been reflected in the work of gender equality agencies.[19] Since 1998, the United Nations Children's Emergency Fund (UNICEF) has developed a comprehensive program on mainstreaming human rights into its work.[20] The same is true for the United Nations Development Group (UNDG), which has delivered massive endorsements for the idea.[21] However, the difference in the scope of activities of these agencies generated confusion regarding the terminology on human rights mainstreaming.

To resolve this terminological conflict, United Nations agencies came together to establish a human rights-based approach framework. The *Common Understanding on HRBAs*, which spells out the meaning, nature, design, and essential attributes of an HRBA framework, was adopted in 2003.[22] It identifies the HRBA as a policy frame for mainstreaming human rights norms, standards, and principles into legislation, policies, and planning to ensure that citizens' interests are protected at all times. The *Common Understanding* spells out the basics of the HRBA and encourages agencies covered

---

Emergency Fund (UNICEF), *Guidelines for Human Rights-Based Programming Approach, Executive Directives* (CF/EXD/1998-004) (1998), http://www.unicefinemergencies.com/downloads/eresource/docs/Human%20Rights%20Based%20Approach/Executive%20Director%20Guidelines%20for%20HRB%20Programming.pdf (last visited Aug. 20, 2016).

18. *See* ANDRÉ FRANKOVITS, UNESCO STRATEGY ON HUMAN RIGHTS: THE HUMAN RIGHTS-BASED APPROACH AND THE UNITED NATIONS SYSTEM (UNESCO 2006), http://unesdoc.unesco.org/images/0014/001469/146999e.pdf; KARIN SVADLENAK-GOMEZ, HUMAN RIGHTS AND CONSERVATION: INTEGRATING HUMAN RIGHTS IN CONSERVATION PROGRAMMING 48 (2007); LISA VENEKLASEN ET AL., RIGHTS-BASED APPROACHES AND BEYOND: CHALLENGES OF LINKING RIGHTS AND PARTICIPATION 3–5 (2004), http://www.ids.ac.uk/ids/bookshop/wp/wp235.pdf; JOACHIM THEIS, PROMOTING RIGHTS-BASED APPROACHES: EXPERIENCES AND IDEAS FROM ASIA AND THE PACIFIC 10 (2004), http://www.redenderechos.org/webdav/publico/01_sc_experiencias_ap.pdf; Brigitte I. Hamm, *A Human Rights Approach to Development*, 23 HUM. RTS. Q. 1005, 1031 (2001).

19. *See* ANDRÉ FRANKOVITS, *supra* note 18.

20. *See* UNICEF, *Guidelines for Human Rights-Based Programming Approach, supra* note 17; *see also* OLAWUYI, THE HUMAN RIGHTS-BASED APPROACH TO CARBON FINANCE, *supra* note 1, at 20–40.

21. *See* UNDG, UNDG HUMAN RIGHTS MAINSTREAMING MECHANISM: OPERATIONAL PLAN 2011–2013 (2011), https://undg.org/wp-content/uploads/2015/04/UNDG-HRM-Operational-Plan-Nov-20-2011.pdf.

22. *See* HRBA Portal, *supra* note 15.

by United Nations operations to develop specialized standards tailored to cover their activities.[23]

The HRBA seeks to mainstream five interconnected human rights norms and principles into development planning and decisionmaking. These human rights norms are: (1) participation and inclusion; (2) access to information; (3) non-discrimination and equality; (4) empowerment and accountability; and (5) legality and access to justice (the "PANEL principles"). By implementing the PANEL principles in the design, approval, finance, and implementation of projects, policymakers are better positioned to anticipate and consider the impacts of a project on the public and then take steps to mitigate those impacts.

In practical terms, the HRBA seeks to reform the existing international climate change regime to establish project approval guidelines that include the PANEL principles.[24] It would provide a threshold that would require governments and project proponents to demonstrate that these elements have been complied with and are guaranteed to citizens in project planning and execution.[25] Any project that does not satisfy the elements would either be referred back or refused approval by supervisory bodies of climate change mitigation projects, for example, the CDM executive board (CDM EB) and designated operational entities (DOEs). It would also include establishing complaint mechanisms and procedures for stakeholders or private individuals whose human rights have been infringed to seek redress, to block approval of such projects, or to seek review of approved projects.[26] Mary Robinson has expertly summarized the crux of the HRBA:

> In each situation we confront, a rights-based approach requires us to ask: what is the content of the right? Who are the human rights claim-holders? Who are the corresponding duty-bearers? Are claim-holders and duty-bearers able to claim their rights and fulfill their responsibilities? If not, how can we help them to do so? This is the heart of a human rights based approach.[27]

---

23. The *Common Understanding* is based on three essential principles: that all development programs should further the realization of human rights articulated in the Universal Declaration of Human Rights and other international human rights instruments; that human rights standards and norms guide all development cooperation and programming in all sectors and in all phases of the programming process; and that programs contribute to the development of the capacities of duty-bearers to meet their obligations and of "rights-holders" to claim their rights. *Id.*

24. OLAWUYI, THE HUMAN RIGHTS-BASED APPROACH TO CARBON FINANCE, *supra* note 1, at 20–40.

25. *Id.*

26. *Id.*

27. Mary Robinson, Former United Nations High Commissioner for Human Rights, Comments at the Second Interagency Workshop on Implementing a Rights-Based Approach in the Context of United Nations Reform (May 2003), quoted in http://www.ihrnetwork.org/files/IHRN-AI%20HRBA%20Ireland%20Sept05%20FINAL.pdf.

The HRBA seeks to ensure that projects designed to combat climate change are conceived, planned, and implemented with the objective of protecting, respecting, and fulfilling human rights.[28] The HRBA integrates human rights safeguards into project plans and implementation.[29] This way, human rights principles are not only invoked when there is a protest or violation about a project but are integrated into design and approval processes to ensure that projects that violate human rights are not approved, registered, or implemented. The HRBA, therefore, represents a shift from a needs-based approach to an approach that requires governments and project proponents to consider the impact of a particular project on the enjoyment of existing human rights.[30]

Secondly, the HRBA is generally a less contentious approach for reinforcing legal intersections and linkages between human rights and the environment.[31] Attempts to codify substantive rights to the environment have generally recorded little progress in international law due to several debates on its theoretical basis and practical underpinnings.[32] The HRBA avoids these debates by drawing on several existing rights instruments, conventions, and internationally agreed norms and standards that have been recognized and ratified by many countries.[33] The core elements of the PANEL principles are procedural human rights that have been endorsed and recognized in core human rights treaties and conventions. The HRBA does not seek to create new rights or call for adoption of new principles. Rather, it outlines normative guidelines that would assist international regimes and national authorities to translate existing human rights goals and standards into practical and achievable results.[34]

---

28. *See* Shelton, *Equitable Utilization of the Atmosphere, supra* note 12, at 91–126.
29. Anita Cheria et al., A Human Rights Approach to Development: Resource Book 2–4 (2004).
30. *Id.*
31. *See* Dinah Shelton, *Whiplash and Backlash—Reflections on a Human Rights Approach to Environmental Protection*, 13 Santa Clara J. Int'l L. 11, 21, 29 (2015) (stating that a "rights-based approach" to environmental protection avoids many of the problems found in private litigation, as well as the limitations of environmental regulation and market-based incentives).
32. *See* Dinah Shelton, *Developing Substantive Environmental Rights*, 1 Geo. Wash. J. Hum. Rts. & Env't 89, 89–120 (2010); Stephen Turner, A Substantive Environmental Right: An Examination of the Legal Obligations of Decision-Makers Towards the Environment 2–15 (2009); Marc Pallemaerts, *The Human Right to the Healthy Environment as a Substantive Right, in* Human Rights and the Environment: Compendium of Instruments and Other International Texts on Individual and Collective Rights Relating to the Environment and the International and European Framework 11, 15 (Maguelonne Dejeant-Pons & Marc Pallemaerts eds., 2002).
33. *See* United Nations Population Fund, *Core Concepts of a Human Rights-Based Approach, in* A Human Rights-Based Approach to Programming: Practical Implementation Manual and Training Materials 10–117 (2010), http://www.unfpa.org/sites/default/files/resource-pdf/hrba_manual_in%20full.pdf.
34. Rajamani, *supra* note 11.

Thirdly, the HRBA provides a framework for addressing root causes of climate change injustices, human rights violations, and well-entrenched power imbalances that tend to exclude members of the public from playing active roles in climate change mitigation. The HRBA focuses on protecting, fulfilling, and realizing rights of excluded and marginalized populations, and those whose rights are at risk of being violated.[35] For example, the HRBA to climate change would place a focus on addressing project-planning approaches that target or concentrate large-scale mitigation and adaptation projects in vulnerable communities by ensuring that all people enjoy human rights irrespective of status or economic strengths. It would also provide opportunities for every segment of society to play active roles in regulatory approval processes leading to the implementation of climate change projects. Through the HRBA, human rights could be harmonized and integrated into international climate change regimes so as to give the public a legal basis to freely air their views about a project and to demand a review when such views are not taken into consideration in project design and implementation.[36]

Furthermore, the HRBA provides a normative framework for reducing the fragmentation of obligations in international law that has resulted in an overlap of climate change and human rights obligations.[37] Through the HRBA, several climate change and human rights obligations could be harmonized and protected in a holistic and coherent manner. The PANEL principles of the HRBA, for example, emphasize the need to integrate and harmonize all human rights norms and obligations into the processes of planning and executing mitigation projects. By harmonizing human rights and climate change obligations, attempts to combat climate change-related human rights violations would be less likely to occur.

Despite the potential and promise of the HRBA as a holistic policy framework for advancing climate justice, the implementation of the HRBA faces several practical constraints at national levels. Generally, many of the elements of the HRBA enjoy varying levels of recognition, protection, and implementation in countries where climate injustices are most severe. Furthermore, local challenges such as arbitrary land tenure systems, inadequacy or absence of climate change laws, exclusionary customary practices, and inadequate capacity impact vulnerable groups' ability to invoke human rights norms to

---

35. OFFICE OF THE UNITED NATIONS HIGH COMMISSIONER FOR HUMAN RIGHTS, FREQUENTLY ASKED QUESTIONS ON A HUMAN RIGHTS-BASED APPROACH TO DEVELOPMENT COOPERATION 37 (2006), http://www.ohchr.org/Documents/Publications/FAQen.pdf.
36. *See* HRBA Portal, *supra* note 15.
37. *See* Harro van Asselt et al., *Global Climate Change and the Fragmentation of International Law*, 30 L. & POL'Y 423 (2008); *see also* Sean Stephenson, *Jobs, Justice, Climate: Conflicting State Obligations in the International Human Rights and Climate Change Regimes*, 42 OTTAWA L. REV. 155, 180 (2010).

seek redress when climate change projects threaten their ways of life. These practical, on-the-ground challenges are discussed in the next section.

II.   Implementing the HRBA at National Levels: Practical Barriers and Limitations

A number of legal and institutional barriers and paradoxes stifle the utility and relevance of the HRBA at national levels. These practical concerns are discussed in this section under four key headings: absence or inadequacy of climate change laws; restrictive property regimes; limited implementation capacity; and limited resources.

A.   *Absence or Inadequacy of Climate Change Laws*

One of the key limitations to protecting and enshrining climate justice in many developing countries is the absence or inadequacy of domestic climate change laws. A comprehensive review of global climate change laws reveals that many of the countries in Africa and Latin America, such as in Nigeria, Panama, and Honduras, where CDM and REDD+ projects have been controversial, have no climate change laws.[38] In Nigeria, there is currently no direct legislation on climate change at the federal, state, or municipal levels. Ever since 2010 when the Nigerian National Climate Change Commission Bill was adopted by the Nigerian federal parliament, it has not received presidential assent.[39] The result is that there is currently no legislative framework that addresses direct and indirect impacts of climate change on local and vulnerable communities in Nigeria.[40]

The importance of domestic legislation and regulation in addressing local manifestations of climate injustice cannot be overemphasized.[41] For example, one key requirement in the approval of international climate projects,

---

38.   *See* Sabin Center for Climate Change, *Climate Change Laws of the World*, http://web.law.columbia. edu/climate-change/resources/climate-change-laws-world (last visited Aug. 20, 2016).

39.   For information on the status of climate legislation in Nigeria, see Federal Government of Nigeria, Climate Change Unit, http://environment.gov.ng/index.php/about-moe/initiative/86-special-units/137-special-climate-change.

40.   A new Climate Change and Global Greenhouse Emission Reduction Bill 2015 is currently under consideration in Nigeria's parliament. If passed, this bill will provide a comprehensive legal framework for combating climate change in Nigeria. *See* Henry Umoru & Joseph Erunke, *Nigeria: Climate Change Bill Scales Second Reading in Senate*, VANGUARD, May 4, 2016, http://allafrica.com/stories/201605040252. html.

41.   *See* UNEP, GUIDELINES FOR THE DEVELOPMENT OF NATIONAL LEGISLATION ON ACCESS TO INFOR-MATION, PUBLIC PARTICIPATION, AND ACCESS TO JUSTICE IN ENVIRONMENTAL MATTERS—ADOPTED BY THE GOVERNING COUNCIL OF THE UNITED NATIONS ENVIRONMENT PROGRAMME IN DECISION SS.XI/5, Part A of 26 Feb. 2010 (2011).

such as CDM and REDD+, is that such projects receive host country approval.[42] This requirement places great responsibilities on national authorities to approve climate actions and projects as meeting national sustainability criteria before their implementation nationally or under existing international climate project mechanisms.[43] Without a legal framework that defines a country's sustainability criteria or basis for implementing and approving climate projects, many of the key issues of exclusions, lack of participation, and discrimination in climate actions and responses discussed by the HRBA are either left unaddressed or unprotected under local laws.[44] Failure to establish legal frameworks on climate change in a systematic approach that reflects fundamental human rights norms often leaves victims of climate injustices without robust legal protection or remedy.

Establishing a legal framework on climate change will provide a basis for local communities to demand enforcement and action by national authorities for lack of action on climate change, or for the implementation of climate actions that increase local vulnerabilities or affect human rights. A national law on climate change will also define a country's vision and objectives for tackling climate change, while providing procedural and rights-based mechanisms to increase awareness, foster participation, build capacity, and initiate public information disclosure programs.

To speak of climate justice in countries without climate laws is paradoxical and contentious for two main reasons. The first paradox is whether countries that have, several years after the UNFCCC was adopted, been unwilling or unable to enact climate change laws will be able to generate the requisite political will to support climate change legislation. There are several causative factors for such lack of political will in emerging economies. One key reason is that in many developing countries, especially in Africa, climate change has not attracted the required level of legislative attention from government and

---

42. *See* United Nations Framework Convention on Climate Change, *CDM Project Activity Cycle*, https://cdm.unfccc.int/Projects/pac/index.html.

43. Para. 40(2) of the CDM modalities and procedures requires host countries to confirm that "project activity assists in achieving sustainable development." Furthermore, Parties are required to "publish the criteria they use in assessing the contribution of project activities to sustainable development." *See Report of the Conference of the Parties Serving as the Meeting of the Parties to the Kyoto Protocol on Its First Session, Held at Montreal From 28 November to 10 December 2005, Decisions Adopted by the Conference of the Parties Serving as the Meeting of the Parties to the Kyoto Protocol*, UNFCCC, 1st Sess., Decision 3/CMP.1, at 6, U.N. Doc. FCCC/KP/CMP/2005/8/Add.1 (2006), http://unfccc.int/resource/docs/2005/cmp1/eng/08a01.pdf; *see also Draft Decision CMP.5: Further Guidance Relating to the Clean Development Mechanism: Proposal by the President*, UNFCCC, Conference of the Parties Serving as the Meeting of the Parties to the Kyoto Protocol, 5th Sess., Agenda Item 6, at sec. VI, para. 46, U.N. Doc. FCCC/KP/CMP/2009/L.10 (2009), http://unfccc.int/resource/docs/2009/cmp5/eng/l10.pdf.

44. Decision 3/CMP.1, *supra* note 43.

policymakers.[45] The culture of approving energy projects, exploiting natural resources, and promoting foreign investments, irrespective of their environmental and human rights impacts on local communities, remains prevalent in many emerging economies.[46] Governments in many African countries are not even asking how climate change should be regulated; rather, the focus remains on attracting foreign investments and combating poverty.[47]

Furthermore, lopsided political culture, pre-existing ethnic tensions, and lack of bipartisan cooperation have stifled progress on environmental issues. In Nigeria, due to perennial political tensions between southern Nigeria, where much of Nigeria's vast oil resources are located, and northern Nigeria, a largely agriculture-based region, achieving legislative consensus on environmental issues has been nearly impossible.[48] This national North/South divide has been responsible for the non-domestication of several international treaties in Nigeria, including the Kyoto Protocol.[49] Political bifurcations and lack of political will have also been problematic in many other emerging democracies in Africa and Latin America, such as Tanzania, Zambia, Panama, and Honduras.[50] This lack of political consensus has made it impossible

---

45.   *See* ROBERT MBURIA, AFRICA CLIMATE POLICY: AN ADAPTATION AND DEVELOPMENT CHALLENGE IN A CHANGING WORLD 2–10 (2015) (stating that the challenges facing climate change regulation in African countries include sluggish political systems; weak institutional capacity and framework; poor coordination and implementation of existing legislation; absence of foresight in national development planning and climate resilience; international abandonment; and unfavorable global settings to enhance Africa's capacity to develop climate change adaptation and mitigation), http://www.fao.org/fsnforum/sites/default/files/discussions/contributions/AFRICA_CLIMATE_CHANGE_POLICY-CEI_3.pdf.

46.   *Id.*

47.   *Id.*

48.   As Sagay rightly notes:
      No bill can pass through the Nigerian National Assembly without the concurrence of the Northern States, but bills will sail smoothly through both Houses even if the whole of the Southern Representatives oppose them. That is permanent power vested in the North by a combination of the colonial masters, the Arewa political oligarchy and the military governments.
      Itse Sagay, Nigeria: Federalism, the Constitution, and Resource Control, Speech Delivered at the Fourth Sensitisation Programme Organized by the Ibori Vanguard (May 19, 2001), http://www.waado.org/NigerDelta/Essays/ResourceControl/Sagay.html (last visited Aug. 20, 2016).

49.   In many African countries, regional or international declarations and treaties will only be recognized at the national level after they have been domesticated and translated into local laws. For example, Nigeria is a Party to the Kyoto Protocol, having ratified the instrument on Dec. 10, 2004. However, the Kyoto Protocol remains unrecognized and undomesticated in Nigeria. As the Supreme Court of Nigeria held in the leading case of General Sani Abacha and 3 Others v. Chief Gani Fawehinmi, 77 Law Reports of Courts of Nigeria, 1254–1401 (2000), no international treaty can be said to come into effect in Nigeria unless the provisions of such treaty have been enacted into law by the Nigerian National Assembly. The Court explained: "when we have an international treaty of this nature, it only becomes binding when enacted into law by our National Assembly . . . it is such law that breathes life into it in Nigeria."

50.   For a detailed and excellent examination of how domestication requirements affect the implementation of international treaties across Africa, see MAGNUS KILLANDER ed., INTERNATIONAL LAW AND DOMESTIC HUMAN RIGHTS LITIGATION IN AFRICA 68–69 (2010).

to promote and execute short- and long-term programs on climate awareness, capacity development, and human rights protection.

A second paradox is whether countries lacking clear climate laws, or a framework for climate projects, will garner the political will to adopt a right-based process that could holistically empower the public to block mitigation and adaptation projects, demand accountability, request project information, and even challenge project decisions before international supervisory bodies. This is the question whether a justice-based proposal to integrate human rights norms into national action plans on climate change will not be resisted as an attempt to grant the public a cudgel with which to beat the State into submission, or to empower nongovernmental organizations (NGOs) to habitually oppose climate change projects. These concerns are reasonable, particularly the fear that NGOs and interest groups could capture and frustrate mitigation projects and plans through the proposed rights-based processes.[51]

These two paradoxes on the lack of political will to adopt climate change laws, or implement climate justice precepts in emerging democracies, are intricately intertwined and therefore call for holistic legal solutions. A starting point is to promote greater awareness of the meaning, basis, and value of climate justice. The HRBA does not necessarily introduce new obligations that many States do not already have under several international human rights treaties. The rights-based framework builds on existing human rights obligations under international law, which virtually all the Parties to the climate change regimes already agreed to protect, respect, and fulfill.[52] As such, the HRBA would not grant new or revolutionary rights that NGOs and the public do not already possess. It would only provide an opportunity for countries to comply with their treaty obligations under both the international climate and international human rights regimes.

B.   Restrictive Property Regimes

Many of the key contentions on the implementation of CDM and REDD+ projects relate to the arbitrary confiscation of traditional and tribal lands

---

51. *See* Maria Lee et al., *Public Participation and Climate Change Infrastructure*, 25 J. ENVTL. L. 33, 33 (2012) (discussing how untempered public participation might become a "simple bureaucratic hurdle, frustrating for all concerned"); *see also* Maria Lee & Carolyn Abbot, *The Usual Suspects? Public Participation Under the Aarhus Convention*, 66 MOD. L. REV. 80, 82–83 (2003).

52. There are 166 Parties to the International Covenant on Civil and Political Rights and 160 to the International Covenant on Economic, Social and Cultural Rights (ICESCR). The majority of these Parties have signed the UNFCCC and the Kyoto Protocol. *See* Rajamani, *supra* note 11, at 412.

by national authorities as sites for climate projects.[53] Concerns regarding the impacts of climate projects on indigenous lands and forests have been raised in several countries including Nigeria, Brazil, Peru, Panama, Honduras, and Indonesia.[54] The HRBA, as well as several United Nations declarations and resolutions, provide comprehensive guidelines on stakeholder engagement and consultation to avoid such human rights impacts on traditional lands.[55] However, local laws that fail to recognize or protect such traditional rights have stifled implementation of such international resolutions at national levels. In many of the above-listed countries, indigenous groups face significant legal hurdles and challenges to maintaining their rights vis-à-vis State policies, regulations, and development processes that fail to recognize or implement international instruments. In many of these countries, traditional lands and forests are either under government control with only occupancy rights for traditional groups, or the government retains arbitrary legal rights to confiscate traditional lands and forests for public reason, and in many cases without compensation.[56] For instance, a 2012 report from the International Fund for Agricultural Development (IFAD) points to the example of East Kalimantan in Indonesia where, due to the lack of legal recognition and protection of customary rights over land and natural resources, "the local government took lands and forests of indigenous peoples and allocated it for logging concessions, mining, and plantations without prior consultation with or adequate compensation to the affected communities."[57]

Similarly, in Nigeria, the government retains arbitrary statutory powers to confiscate forests and lands for public purpose. The anachronistic provisions of Nigeria's Land Use Act vests absolute ownership, management, and control of land in each state of the federation of Nigeria in the governor, leaving

---

53. See OLAWUYI, THE HUMAN RIGHTS-BASED APPROACH TO CARBON FINANCE, *supra* note 1, at 15–30.

54. For excellent and detailed analyses of the human rights impacts of REDD+ projects in Brazil and Peru, see Kristen Taylor, *Improving Substantive and Procedural Protections for Indigenous Rights in REDD+ Projects: Possible Lessons From Brazil*, 5 AFE BABALOLA U.J. SUSTAINABLE DEV. L. & POL'Y 32 (2015); Carlos Soria Dall'Orso, *Increased Relevance and Influence of Free Prior Informed Consent, REDD, and Green Economy Principles on Sustainable Commons Management in Peru*, 5 AFE BABALOLA U.J. SUSTAINABLE DEV. L. & POL'Y 4 (2015).

55. See OLAWUYI, THE HUMAN RIGHTS-BASED APPROACH TO CARBON FINANCE, *supra* note 1.

56. See, for example, the United Nations' first Universal Periodic Review—a report assessing the state of human rights in the United Nations' 193 Member countries over the course of four years, which noted "Indonesia treats its indigenous and tribal people . . . worse than any other country in the world." *See Report of the Working Group on the Universal Periodic Review: Indonesia*, U.N. Human Rights Council, 21st Sess., Agenda Item 6, U.N. Doc. A/HRC/217 (2012), http://www.redd-monitor.org/wp-content/uploads/2012/10/upr-indonesia-report.pdf.

57. ALIANSI MASYARAKAT ADAT NUSANTARA, REPUBLIC OF INDONESIA: COUNTRY TECHNICAL NOTES ON INDIGENOUS PEOPLES' ISSUES (2012), https://www.ifad.org/documents/10180/a1fe61f8-837b-4d94-b1b7-da17c3543d14.

individuals with "rights of occupancy."[58] Secondly, the Act fails to recognize any right of control or administration by community leaders or tribal chiefs. Furthermore, §28 of the Act provides that land may be appropriated for "overriding public interests." This includes "the requirement of the land for mining purposes or oil pipelines or for any purpose connected therewith."[59] Due to the arbitrary provisions of this Act, the Nigerian government has come under the microscope for failing to protect community lands from arbitrary expropriation for REDD+ and CDM projects.[60] For example, a REDD+ project financed by Shell Canada and Gazprom has been resisted by local communities in Nigeria's Cross River state as a scam and the "largest land grab of all time"[61] Due to inadequate legal protection for traditional forests and property land rights of communities, and lack of stakeholder accommodation in the process leading to the approval of REDD+ projects, it is anticipated that several tribal groups in Cross River state could be evicted from ancestral lands that have been annexed as sites for REDD+ projects.[62]

While REDD+ projects would contribute to climate change mitigation, confiscating a large proportion of land from indigenous communities without providing compensation or settlement options is a major human rights concern that requires legislative attention consistent with international human rights norms.[63] It is imperative for countries to reform local property laws to

58. Land Use Act, Laws of the Federation of Nigeria, CAP 202 L.F.N. 1990 ACT CAP L5 L.F.N. 2004.
59. *See* Abioye v. Yakub, (1991) 5 NWLR (pt. 190) 130, 223, paras. (d)–(g).
60. For an excellent and detailed criticism of this section and the Land Use Act in general, see Rhuks T. Ako, *Nigeria's Land Use Act: An Anti-Thesis to Environmental Justice*, 53 J. Afr. L. 289 (2009).
61. It has been described as "perverse incentives" to convert natural forests into monoculture tree plantations and to actually increase deforestation. According to Nigeria's environmental group: "Most of the forests of the world are found in Indigenous Peoples' land. REDD-type projects have already resulted in land grabs, violations of human rights, threats to cultural survival, militarization, scams and servitude." *See* Rita Osarogiagbon, REDD & Its Implication on Community People, Presentation Made at Cross River State Stakeholders Forum on Climate Change (Mar. 1, 2011), http://www.redd-monitor.org/wp-content/uploads/2011/04/Appendix-21.pdf (last visited Aug. 20, 2016); *see also* Chris Lang, *"Our Forest Is Not for Sale!" NGO Statement on REDD in Nigeria*, REDD Monitor, Sept. 1, 2010, http://www.redd-monitor.org/2010/09/01/our-forest-is-not-for-sale-ngo-statement-on-redd-in-nigeria.
62. As the official spokesperson of the indigenous community noted:
    Forests in Cross Rivers State—some of the few remaining tracks of mangrove and rainforest reserve in the world targeted for REDD—are in grave danger due to the scheme, hence the need for participants to uncover any cover-ups by government which is detrimental to community forests and the environment. To us, carbon trading/market mechanisms promoted by REDD are false solutions to climate change; REDD promotes deforestation, more plantation and corporate land grabs . . . Forest is not for sale! It is our life and source of livelihoods for millions of forest-dependent peoples in forest-bearing communities in Africa. World Bank, IMF, UNEP and other multilateral institutions should [keep their] hands off our forests.
    See Lang, *supra* note 61.
63. Land grabs due to REDD+ projects reduce access to the resources through which indigenous peoples could feed and sustain themselves, thereby threatening their subsistence. This is a violation of the international human right to enjoy the benefits of culture. Article 27 of the ICESCR provides that

provide more robust protection for property rights, especially the protection of traditional forests and tribal lands. Without developing national legal regimes that recognize and protect traditional land rights, efforts to implement global HRBA norms on stakeholder engagement, access to information, and access to justice will remain stifled and unrealized at national levels.

C.   Limited Implementation Capacity

The HRBA framework seeks to establish a legal partnership between the human rights and climate change regimes and incorporate human rights norms into climate change action plans and programs.[64] This includes the expansion of national climate strategies and project approval guidelines to include human rights requirements, and the expansion of mandates of environmental ministries, departments, and climate change-designated national authorities to incorporate human rights assessment and review of climate actions and projects. These are complex transitions that could expand the scope of activities of an environmental entity into uncharted areas such as interpreting human rights and making decisions on the human rights impacts of a project.

Concerns have been raised regarding whether environmental ministries, which in many countries consist of environmentalists, urban planners, scientists, and outsiders to human rights, have the requisite capacity to apply, interpret, and implement justice and human rights norms.[65] For example, placing the task of interpreting and applying human rights norms in the hands of administrative bodies consisting mainly of professional administrators and scientists who arguably know little or nothing about international human rights is dangerous.[66] The United Nations Development Programme (UNDP) defines capacity as the ability of individuals, institutions, and societies to perform functions, solve problems, and set and achieve objectives in a

---

persons belonging to minorities have the right to enjoy their own culture. Article 27 further provides that "persons belonging to minorities shall not be denied the right in community with other members of the group to enjoy their own cultures . . . ." International Covenant on Economic, Social, and Cultural Rights, 993 U.N.T.S. 3, 6 I.L.M. 360 (entered into force Jan. 3, 1976); International Covenant on Civil and Political Rights, 999 U.N.T.S. 171 (entered into force Mar. 23, 1976).

64.   *See* HRBA Portal, *supra* note 15.

65.   *See* J. Christopher McCrudden, *Mainstreaming Human Rights, in* HUMAN RIGHTS IN THE COMMUNITY: RIGHTS AS AGENTS FOR CHANGE (Colin Harvey ed., 2005).

66.   Koskoniemi takes these arguments further when he notes that entrusting human rights interpretation to outsiders would further blur the already thinning line between human rights experts and outsiders. *See* Martti Koskieniemi, *Human Rights Mainstreaming as a Strategy for Institutional Power*, 1 HUMAN. 47 (2010).

sustainable manner.[67] The need for environmental institutions to understand and develop an in-depth understanding of key philosophical principles and norms underpinning the HRBA to climate justice, and how they apply on the ground in local development contexts, is critical to the task of mainstreaming the HRBA at national levels.[68]

Many countries, especially those that have been the epicenter of climate justice protests relating to climate action, lack robust institutional capacity to coordinate and implement human rights and climate programs. In Nigeria, one of the key problems identified with the Nigerian Climate Change Unit (CCU), within the Ministry of Environment, is its composition. Largely comprised of environmentalists and planners, with little or no expertise on justice and human rights, the CCU has been unable to develop coherent rights-based policy responses to several human rights issues identified in CDM and REDD+ projects in Nigeria. Despite Nigeria's participation and attendance in recent COP meetings where countries have been encouraged to address human rights issues in climate action, the legal implications of climate change on human rights remain unaddressed by the CCU.

The HRBA to climate justice can be enhanced at national levels by a radical restructuring of human rights and climate institutions to foster coordination, coherence, and systemic integration.[69] The gap between climate and human rights institutions is fueled by the tendency of actors to remain within the formal confines of their areas of mandate, i.e., of human rights ministries or within climate change units.[70] This is due to the absence of a formal agenda or obligations to collaborate between actors; the lack of fluid programmatic activity between human rights ministries and environmental ministries and departments; the lack of a coherent agenda between human rights and environmental interest groups; and personal unwillingness by actors to collaborate across sectors and agendas spurred by the absence of

---

67. *See* Carlos Lopes & Thomas Theisohn, Ownership, Leadership, and Transformation: Can We Do Better for Capacity Development? (2003).

68. *See* Offenheiser & Holcombe, *supra* note 6.

69. For the Alston/Petersmann debate, see Ernst-Ulrich Petersmann, *Time for a United Nations "Global Compact" for Integrating Human Rights Into the Law of Worldwide Organizations: Lessons From European Integration*, 13 Eur. J. Int'l L. 621 (2002); Philip Alston, *Resisting the Merger and Acquisition of Human Rights by Trade Law: A Reply to Petersmann*, 13 Eur. J. Int'l L. 815 (2002); Ernst-Ulrich Petersmann, *Taking Human Dignity, Poverty, and Empowerment of Individuals More Seriously: Rejoinder to Alston*, 13 Eur. J. Int'l L. 845 (2002).

70. John H. Knox, Forging Stronger Cooperation Between Human Rights and Climate Change Communities: Assessing the Impacts of Climate Change on Human Rights, Address Before the United Nations Seminar to Address the Adverse Impacts of Climate Change on the Full Enjoyment of Human Rights (Feb. 24, 2012), http://www.ohchr.org/Documents/Issues/ClimateChange/Seminar2012/JohnKnox24Feb2012.pdf.

training and capacity to do so.[71] As such, human rights have no place, visibility, or political support in climate actions, while climate change is not a priority issue in the everyday affairs of human rights institutions.

Fostering institutional coordination and constructive engagement between human rights and climate change, such that programs and projects to address climate vulnerability are designed, financed, and implemented together by both communities, is a holistic way of improving capacity at national levels. Appointing human rights experts into environmental ministries, and vice versa, will ensure that human rights and human rights instruments are understood, internalized, implemented, and enforced in climate actions; and that climate actions do not violate human rights.[72]

It is also pertinent for countries to provide human rights education and training for climate change leaders and institutions. For example, the United Nations Declaration on Human Rights Education and Training emphasizes that human rights education and training is essential for the "promotion of universal respect for and observance of all human rights and fundamental freedoms for all."[73] Article 7(4) provides that States should ensure adequate training in human rights and, where appropriate, international humanitarian law and international criminal law, of State officials, civil servants, judges, law enforcement officials, and military personnel, as well as promote adequate training in human rights for teachers, trainers, and other educators and private personnel acting on behalf of the State. Article 11 also provides that human rights education and training should be provided for civilian personnel, and military and police personnel serving under their mandates.[74] A robust implementation of this declaration at national levels will educate security agents on how to prevent concerns of brutality and repression that have trailed several CDM and REDD+ projects. It will also guide environmental ministries on the key elements and scope of human rights and the HRBA as a normative governance approach.

D.   Limited Resources

Linked to the question of capacity and institutional coordination is the question of resources. Realizing and enforcing human rights come with consider-

---

71.   *Id.*
72.   *See* John Knox, *Linking Human Rights and Climate Change at the United Nations*, 33 HARV. ENVTL. L. REV. 477 (2009).
73.   United Nations Human Rights Council Res. 16/1, United Nations Declaration on Human Rights, Education, and Training, 16th Sess., U.N. Doc. A/HRC/RES/16/1 (2011).
74.   *Id.*

able costs.[75] The institutional harmonization and transformation under the HRBA to climate justice comes with significant financial implications, for example, the expansion of the current institutions, cost of staffing, training, field inspections, project review panels, and program funding.[76] Due to limited resources and competing budget priorities, the HRBA may run into implementation problems, especially in emerging economies.[77] While the international climate regime has promoted the need for human rights protection in climate actions, questions on how domestic initiatives on human rights mainstreaming and climate justice will be financed have not been exhaustively considered and addressed. Much of the existing literature, and many of the United Nations instruments, on climate finance focus on how climate change mitigation and adaptation projects can be financed. Lack of attention to how international and national regimes can support and finance the integration of human rights in climate change institutions is a key impediment to realizing climate justice.

There is a need to move beyond mere preambular or textual recognition of the need for countries to respect human rights in climate action. The international community must foster a focused discussion on how human rights training and climate justice awareness programs can be developed, financed, and delivered in developing countries. A needed step forward in implementing textual recognitions on climate justice and human rights in the Paris Agreement is for the international climate regime to establish a specialized fund for human rights capacity development in the context of climate change.

Considering the importance of fostering justice and human rights in national climate actions, countries must also devote greater attention, resources, and institutional accountability to climate justice programs. One of the key problems in many African countries is the lack of an independent and sustained budget for environmental programs. The abilities of environmental departments and ministries to launch and implement long-term environmental justice programs have been hampered by a lack of consistent funding by successive government and corrupt diversion of environmental restoration funds.[78] Due to differing priorities placed on environmental

---

75. SANDRA FREDMAN, HUMAN RIGHTS TRANSFORMED: POSITIVE RIGHTS AND POSITIVE DUTIES 1–25 (2008).
76. *See* THOMAS GREIBER ET AL., IUCN, CONSERVATION WITH JUSTICE: A RIGHTS-BASED APPROACH (2009), https://cmsdata.iucn.org/downloads/eplp_071.pdf.
77. McCrudden, *supra* note 65.
78. A significant portion of funds marked for environmental programs have been perennially looted by successive Nigerian governments. *See* Ronald Mutum, *Nigeria: ICPC Returns N1 Billion Looted Funds to Environment Ministry*, DAILY TRUST, Sept. 16, 2015, http://allafrica.com/stories/201509160545.

matters by successive governments, environmental justice policies and projects are inconsistently implemented, and largely depend on the visions and priorities of the government in power.[79] Lack of continuity and sustained funding for environmental justice in Nigeria often results in the mid-cycle abandonment or stagnation of lofty programs on environmental justice; the result is the lack of sustained progress in addressing the root causes of environmental injustice.

This concern emphasizes the need to establish specialized bodies on climate justice with continuing mandates and funding to tackle local impacts and concerns irrespective of the government in power. A good example is the Office of the Commissioner of the Environment and Sustainable Development, an independent and authoritative environmental unit, housed within the Office of the Auditor General of Canada to investigate and address root causes of environmental complaints from the public.[80] The continuity of the Office of the Commissioner ensures that its activities can continue irrespective of the government in power. To seriously deliver and maintain climate justice programs, similar institutions can be established with direct responsibility, independence, and funding to continually pursue climate justice mandates irrespective of the ruling or governing political party or government.

Linked to the question of continuity is the lack of institutional independence by environmental ministries and departments to pursue needed climate justice initiatives and programs. For example, since ministries of environment (MOEs) are typically supervised by cabinet ministers, they are accountable to the government, and arguably lack the required level of institutional independence required to hold policymakers accountable for their actions that threaten climate justice. MOEs arguably lack the status

---

html. *See Senate Promises to Intervene in Non-Payment of HYPREP Workers Salary*, CHANNELS TELE-VISION NEWS, Aug. 2, 2014 (stating how workers were owed more than 18 months in salaries and allowances), http://www.channelstv.com/2014/08/02/senate-promises-intervene-non-payment-hyprep-workers-salary/; *see also* Bassey Udo, *Recruitment Fraud Rocks Nigeria Anti-Pollution Agency Stalling Workers Pay for Years*, PREMIUM TIMES, Jan. 17, 2015, http://www.premiumtimesng.com/business/175104-recruitment-fraud-rocks-nigeria-anti-pollution-agency-stalling-workers-pay-years.html.

79. A good example is the Nigerian government's long delay in implementing the United Nations report calling for environmental restoration and cleanup in the Niger Delta. *See* UNEP, *Environmental Assessment of Ogoniland Report*, http://www.unep.org/disastersandconflicts/CountryOperations/Nigeria/EnvironmentalAssessmentofOgonilandreport/tabid/54419/Default.aspx (last visited Aug. 20, 2016).

80. The commissioner conducts performance audits, and is responsible for assessing whether federal government departments are meeting their sustainable development objectives, and overseeing the environmental petitions process. *See* Office of the Auditor General of Canada, *Commissioner of the Environment and Sustainable Development*, http://www.oag-bvg.gc.ca/internet/English/cesd_fs_e_921.html (last visited Aug. 20, 2016).

and independence needed to serve as "watchdogs" to monitor and report on the sustainability of government operations and policies. For example, the Canadian commissioner of the environment and sustainable development has legislative powers to conduct performance audits and to launch independent assessments as to whether federal government departments are meeting their sustainable development objectives and responding to environmental petitions from the public. Due to the fact that the commissioner is not a cabinet-level member, incumbents are able to pursue their mandates independently and report to the public without fear of reprimand. This is the level of institutional independence required to truly embed climate justice in governance. Ministries and departments, under the leadership of a cabinet member appointed, and terminable, by the executive arguably lack the institutional independence to fairly monitor, appraise, and launch independent investigations into the activities of government that stifle climate justice, accountability, and transparency. The need for accountability, independence, and transparency in implementing climate justice programs is even more apparent in countries, such as Nigeria, Panama, and Honduras, where governments have been perennially accused of colluding with international oil companies to stifle climate justice.

The above problems underscore the need for national governments to reassess and revitalize the architecture for delivering climate justice programs to avoid the perennial challenges of corruption, diversion of program funding, and lack of sustained funding to pursue environmental justice programs and initiatives. A way forward is to establish independent and focal institutions on climate justice with independent and continuing mandates to tackle environmental injustice irrespective of the government in power. Providing direct mandates and funding for climate justice programs can reduce problems of political patronage, nepotism, and corrupt diversion of program funds that have been prevalent in many of the surveyed countries.

Conclusion

Without a climate justice perspective, projects and actions designed to combat climate change may exacerbate social exclusions, land grabs, and human rights concerns in many countries. The HRBA provides a procedural framework through which countries can combat climate change in a manner that respects human rights. By integrating human rights norms into the design, approval, finance, and implementation of climate change projects, perennial justice and human rights concerns that have accompanied several climate mitigation and adaptation projects can be holistically addressed and prevented.

To ensure that the HRBA moves from theory to successful practical integration and adoption, national climate strategies and frameworks, and logistical concerns that stifle the utility and relevance of the HRBA at local levels, must be carefully reviewed and addressed. There is a need for a coherent understanding of the importance of respecting, protecting, and fulfilling rights in climate change measures to avoid overlap. The 2015 Paris climate agreement reflects renewed global consensus on the need for Parties to respect human rights in all climate actions. To advance this objective, there is a need to develop robust legal and institutional frameworks at national levels to ensure that climate actions and projects do not exacerbate poverty and societal exclusions in poor and vulnerable communities, i.e., combating climate change in a way that is fair and beneficial to all members of society. This is not only desirable, but imperative to ensure that human rights and climate change obligations are coherently and systemically integrated, to avoid duplication, overlap, inefficiency, and waste of resources.

Barriers to the implementation and adoption of the HRBA must be holistically addressed by invigorating national climate change policies and legislation with human rights safeguards; harmonizing climate change and human rights institutions and regimes; updating existing laws that stifle the realization of rights; and promoting human rights awareness at all levels of governance. Countries must develop a systemic integration of human rights norms into national actions and institutions on climate change to ensure that climate actions and projects that threaten human rights are not approved.

Chapter 2

From Justice to Participation: The Paris Agreement's Pragmatic Approach to Differentiation

Patrícia G. Ferreira

Introduction

Recent debates on climate justice have centered primarily on questions such as the inverse relationship between climate vulnerabilities and contributions to climate change, the need for a rights-based approach to climate action, inter-generational equity, and climate litigation.[1] This chapter focuses on another climate justice question, a question that has informed one of the earliest and most enduring debates in the area. The question is how to fairly allocate

---

1.   *See, e.g.*, INTERNATIONAL BAR ASSOCIATION, ACHIEVING JUSTICE AND HUMAN RIGHTS IN AN ERA OF CLIMATE DISRUPTION (2014), http://www.ibanet.org/PresidentialTaskForceClimateChangeJustice-2014Report.aspx; Edith Brown Weiss, *Climate Change, Intergenerational Equity, and International Law*, 9 VT. J. ENVTL. L. 615 (2008); WILLIAM C.G. BURNS & HARI OSOFSKY EDS., ADJUDICATING CLIMATE CHANGE: STATE, NATIONAL, AND INTERNATIONAL APPROACHES (2009); R. LORD ET AL. EDS., CLIMATE CHANGE LIABILITY: TRANSNATIONAL LAW AND PRACTICE (2012); JACQUELINE PEEL & HARI OSOFSKY, CLIMATE CHANGE LITIGATION: REGULATORY PATHWAYS TO CLEANER ENERGY (2015).

the burdens and costs of collective climate action among vastly asymmetric countries when it comes to contributions to climate change (historic and current greenhouse gas (GHG), absolute, and per capita emissions), capabilities to address the climate challenge, development needs, and vulnerabilities to the impacts of global warming.[2] Since its inception, this climate justice debate has been framed as a question of intragenerational equity between rich nations in the global North and poor nations in the global South.[3]

The literature places the principle of common but differentiated responsibilities and respective capabilities (CBDR) as the "focal point of the divide between Northern and Southern countries"[4] when it comes to the fair allocation of climate action under the 1992 United Nations Framework Convention on Climate Change (UNFCCC).[5] Accordingly, debates on the evolution of CBDR have often been framed as part of broader academic discussions on how contemporary international law, and more specifically international environmental law, has been profoundly shaped by tensions along a geopolitical North-South divide, one that has pitted developed countries against developing countries.[6] Since the mid-2000s, environmental justice debates related to differentiation in international law have focused on this North-South divide, while recognizing the growing constraints of this conceptual framework in a geopolitical world in flux.[7] For the global South, CBDR has been primarily a legal instrument to ensure a measure of intragenerational climate justice. For the global North, differentiation in international envi-

---

2. For a thorough justice-based analysis of the allocation of climate burdens and costs across countries, see HENRY SHUE, CLIMATE JUSTICE: VULNERABILITY AND PROTECTION (2014); *see also* ERIC A. POSNER & DAVID WEISBACH, CLIMATE CHANGE JUSTICE (2010); Michael Trebilcock, *Climate Change Policy: Managing More Heat in the World's Kitchens, in* DEALING WITH LOSERS: THE POLITICAL ECONOMY OF POLICY TRANSITIONS (2014); WARWICK J. MCKIBBIN & PETER J. WILCOXEN, THE ROLE OF ECONOMICS IN CLIMATE CHANGE POLICY (2002); Yoram Margalioth & Yinon Rudich, *Close Examination of the Principle of Global Per Capita: Allocation of the Earth's Ability to Absorb Greenhouse Gas*, 14 THEORETICAL INQUIRIES L. 191 (2013).

3. SHUE, *supra* note 2.

4. SUMUDU ATAPATTU, HUMAN RIGHTS APPROACHES TO CLIMATE CHANGE: CHALLENGES AND OPPORTUNITIES 29 (2015); *see also* Rowena Maguire & Xiaoyi Jiang, *Emerging Powerful Southern Voices: Role of BASIC Nations in Shaping Climate Change Mitigation Commitments, in* INTERNATIONAL ENVIRONMENTAL LAW AND THE GLOBAL SOUTH (Shawkat Alam, Sumudu Atapattu, Carmen G. Gonzalez & Jona Razzaque eds., 2015).

5. United Nations Framework Convention on Climate Change, May 9, 1992, 1771 U.N.T.S. 107, 31 I.L.M. 849 (entered into force Mar. 21, 1994) [hereinafter UNFCCC].

6. INTERNATIONAL ENVIRONMENTAL LAW AND THE GLOBAL SOUTH, *supra* note 4. ANDREW HURREL & BENEDICT KINGSBURY EDS., THE INTERNATIONAL POLITICS OF THE ENVIRONMENT (1992); MARIAN A.L. MILLER, THE THIRD WORLD IN GLOBAL ENVIRONMENTAL POLITICS (1995).

7. *See* ANITA M. HALVORSSEN, EQUALITY AMONG UNEQUALS IN INTERNATIONAL ENVIRONMENTAL LAW: DIFFERENTIAL TREATMENT FOR DEVELOPING COUNTRIES (1999); Karin Michelson, *South, North, International Environmental Law, and International Environmental Lawyers*, 11 Y.B. INT'L ENVTL. L. 52 (2000); RUCHI ANAND, INTERNATIONAL ENVIRONMENTAL JUSTICE, A NORTH-SOUTH DIMENSION (2004); SUMUDU ATAPATTU, EMERGING PRINCIPLES OF INTERNATIONAL ENVIRONMENTAL LAW (2006).

ronmental law, especially in the climate regime, has been primarily a question of enlisting the participation of developing countries in collective efforts to address global environmental problems.

In the past decade, scholars have increasingly emphasized that the differentiation formula enshrined in the UNFCCC and in the Kyoto Protocol did not take into account the growing responsibilities of emerging economies for the GHG emissions that are at the root of the climate change problem. Compounding the high emissions of developed countries, these rising emissions jeopardize the countries that are most vulnerable to climate change like the least developed countries (LDCs) and small island nations, and the most vulnerable communities within emerging economies and developed countries.[8] The marked economic and political rise of emerging economies like China, Brazil, India, and South Africa, known as the BASIC countries for the name of the coalition they formed at the climate negotiations, brings those countries to a space not yet among the developed world, but no longer among the broad majority of developing countries.[9] As the geopolitical North-South line becomes increasingly blurred, CBDR has produced cleavages not only along this line, but also along a South-South line.[10]

This chapter builds on and contributes to this ongoing debate. It looks into the evolution of CBDR from a justice perspective that goes beyond the North-South divide. It investigates whether the BASIC countries have maintained the same approach to CBDR as their responsibilities for GHG emissions and their financial and technological capabilities grew over time. Based on the model of CBDR adopted in the 2015 Paris Agreement, it concludes that the BASIC countries have significantly changed their approach to differentiation in the climate regime over time, and argues that this change has implications for the question of just allocation of climate burdens and costs. The BASIC countries are no longer relying on CBDR as the key legal instrument to promote intragenerational climate justice, but rather are looking into other legal and political instruments within and outside the climate regime as important tools to advance their climate justice agenda. Though retaining a measure of North-South justice considerations,

---

8.   *See* Andrew Hurrell & Sandeep Sengupta, *Emerging Powers, North-South Relations and Global Climate Politics*, 88 Int'l Aff. 463 (2012).

9.   Karl Hallding et al., Together Alone: Brazil, South Africa, India, China (BASIC) and the Climate Change Conundrum (2011), https://www.sei-international.org/mediamanager/documents/Publications/Climate/sei-basic-preview-jun2011.pdf.

10. *See* Carmen Gonzalez, *Bridging the North-South Divide: International Environmental Law in the Anthropocene*, 32 Pace Envtl. L. Rev. 407 (2015); Maguire & Jiang, *supra* note 4; Karin Mickelson, *Beyond a Politics of the Possible? South-North Relations and Climate Justice*, 10 Melb. J. Int'l L. 411 (2009); Ulrich Beyerlin, *Bridging the North-South Divide in International Environmental Law*, 66 ZaoRV 259, 279 (2006), http://www.zaoerv.de/66_2006/66_2006_2_a_259_296.pdf.

the Paris Agreement CBDR has become closer to the more pragmatic model of differentiation present in other multilateral environmental agreements (MEAs), which take into account special circumstances of developing countries to promote their effective participation in collective efforts to address global environmental problems.

Part I of this chapter addresses two realities that have made it impossible for the BASIC countries to remain in the same category as lower-income developing countries with respect to fair allocation of global climate burdens and costs: (1) their significant and growing responsibilities for the climate change problem; and (2) their sufficient financial and technological capabilities to act decisively to address climate change. Part II considers how the rise of a South-South divide complicates the already elusive search for a CBDR model that balances participation and justice in the climate regime. Part III argues that the Paris Agreement marks a shift in the the BASIC countries' position on CBDR in the global climate regime, from one primarily guided by justice considerations along a North-South divide, to a pragmatic approach to differentiation that emphasizes broad participation. The chapter concludes that a positive result of this shift in the position of the BASIC countries was the end of a protracted deadlock that had prevented the climate negotiations from moving forward. As CBDR has lost this robust link to intragenerational justice in the climate regime, the battle for just allocation of burdens and costs now depends on the strategic political use of other provisions in the Paris Agreement (such as the transparency framework and the stocktaking mechanisms) and mechanisms outside of the climate regime (including domestic and transnational political efforts to promote responses by all major emitters, including BASIC countries).

I.   The Distinguishable Responsibilities and Capabilities of the BASIC Countries

Much has been written on how enduring disputes and tensions over global environmental governance—such as disagreements over priority setting and the distribution of burdens and costs of environmental action—can be understood as a consequence of a geopolitical North-South divide.[11] The literature has also increasingly recognized the North against South framework as an oversimplification.[12] As the geopolitical context evolves, cleavages along

---

11.   *See supra* notes 6, 7, and 8; *see also* LAURIE SUSSKIND & CONNIE OZAWA, ENVIRONMENTAL DIPLOMACY: STRATEGIES FOR NEGOTIATING MORE EFFECTIVE INTERNATIONAL AGREEMENTS (1990).

12.   In the early 1990s, Henry Shue proposed that examinations of justice in climate negotiations should take into account a differentiation between "poor nations with the most leverage" in climate negotia-

North-North and South-South divides will need to be considered to fully understand the important aspects of the evolution of global environmental governance.[13] As a small group of developing countries such as China, India, Brazil, and South Africa disproportionately increase their economic might and their influence on the global stage when compared to most other developing countries, the possibility of a South-South rift over interests and priorities is amplified. Understanding the recent evolution of global climate governance requires taking into account a divide between the so-called emerging economies and other developing countries.

It has proved impossible to define which countries belong to the category of "emerging economies." The significant economic growth of a group of developing countries and their rising profile on the global stage is still fairly recent; it has neither happened in a linear fashion nor has it been homogenous. There are no agreed-upon criteria to define a country as an "emerging economy." Some authors include Mexico, Turkey, and South Korea, based on their higher per capita incomes. Others may refer to the BRICS group (Brazil, Russia, India, China, and South Africa), formed by countries with large populations and landmasses, regional leadership, and a significant share of global gross domestic product (GDP). This chapter does not address the difficult question of what constitutes an emerging economy. Instead, it focuses on the BASIC political group, formed by Brazil, China, India, and South Africa, developing countries that found common ground to negotiate a joint position in climate negotiations since 2009. When the chapter refers to the BASIC countries among an expanded set of high-middle income developing countries, as defined by the World Bank, it is based on the available data relevant to the discussion.

This section provides an overview of two characteristics commonly considered in climate justice debates on fair allocation of climate burdens to illustrate why a growing South-South divide among the BASIC countries and other developing countries is becoming increasingly significant to global climate governance. These characteristics are: (1) significant contribution to the climate change problem; and (2) enhanced capabilities to act on climate change. The section is not meant to provide a comprehensive comparative

---

tions (due to their potential rising share of global emissions linked to major population and expected economic growth), and "poor nations with the least leverage" (which pose no threats to the environment of developed countries). For Shue, no general solidarity across the developing world could be assumed because developing countries with large populations and significant landmass were expected to prioritize their interests if they clashed with the interests of smaller developing countries. SHUE, *supra* note 2, at 27–46; *see also* Gonzalez, *supra* note 10; Maguire & Jiang, *supra* note 4.

13.   *See* INTERNATIONAL ENVIRONMENTAL LAW AND THE GLOBAL SOUTH, *supra* note 4. Maguire & Jiang, *supra* note 4.

assessment of the evolution of these characteristics in the BASIC countries, other emerging economies, and the larger group of developing countries. This would require a detailed analysis with all the nuances that it deserves.[14] Rather, the objective is to provide anecdotal evidence of the changing profile of the BASIC countries and other emerging economies in the global climate regime, and to discuss the implications of these changes for climate justice debates.

A.   Significant and Growing Responsibilities for Climate Change

In the lead up to the 1992 UNFCCC and the 1997 Kyoto Protocol, emerging economies consistently invoked the polluter-pays principle—those who cause or who have caused a pollution problem should pay for the resulting damage—as one important equity indicator[15] to justify why developed countries should embrace a larger share of the burdens and costs of climate action.[16] At the time, the group of developed countries was responsible for a disproportionate share of total GHG emissions, per capita emissions, and cumulative historic emissions.[17] The contributions of developing countries as a group were expected to rise because their development needs justified priority to address poverty reduction and economic development concerns over climate mitigation.[18]

---

14.   Except for the extensive information contained in the Intergovernmental Panel on Climate Change (IPCC) reports, it is surprisingly difficult to find information on the evolution of GHG contributions and capabilities of BASIC countries and other emerging economies in comparison to other developing countries.

15.   For a list of criteria used to guide the equitable allocation of burdens and costs of collective international action among asymmetric countries, including contributions to a problem, capabilities, development needs, and entitlements, see Dinah Shelton, *Equity, in* The Oxford Handbook of International Environmental Law 639–62 (Daniel Bodansky, Jutta Brunnée & Ellen Hey eds., 2008); *see also* Eric Neumayer, *In Defence of Historical Accountability for Greenhouse Gas Emissions,* 33 Ecological Econ. 185 (2000).

16.   Simon Caney, *Climate Change and the Duties of the Advantaged,* 13 Critical Rev. Int'l & Pol. Phil. 203, 206 (2010); *see also Paper No. 1 Brazil: Proposed Elements of a Protocol to the United Nations Framework Convention on Climate Change, Presented by Brazil in Response to the Berlin Mandate,* UNFCCC, 7th Sess., Provisional Agenda Item 3, U.N. Doc. FCCC/AGBM/1997/MISC.1/Add.3 (1997) (describing the official position of Brazil in the UNFCCC negotiations preceding the Kyoto Protocol), http://unfccc.int/cop5/resource/docs/1997/agbm/misc01a3.htm.

17.   *Summary for Policymakers: The Economic and Social Dimensions of Climate Change, in* Climate Change 1995. Contribution of Working Group III to the Second Assessment Report of the Intergovernmental Panel on Climate Change 45 (James P. Bruce, Hoesung Lee & Erik F. Haites eds., 1995).

18.   The preamble to the UNFCCC provides, in pertinent part: "Noting that the largest share of historical and current global emissions of greenhouse gases has originated in developed countries, that per capita emissions in developing countries are still relatively low and that the share of global emissions originating in developing countries will grow to meet their social and development needs." UNFCCC, *supra* note 5, at pmbl.

The collective emissions from developing countries did rise, though it was concentrated in a few of these countries, especially the members of BASIC. Since 1992, the global distribution of GHG emissions has changed significantly.[19] A marked shift in industrial economic activities from developed countries towards a group of developing countries, notably China, and robust economic and population growth have deeply affected the emissions patterns of the BASIC countries. The BASIC countries experienced a significant rise in total GHG emissions in the past decade.[20] In 2005, the four BASIC countries collectively accounted for nearly 60% of the total annual GHG emissions from non-Annex 1 countries and almost 29% of total global emissions.[21]

Meanwhile, notwithstanding continuing economic growth from the early 1990s to 2010, the emissions trajectories of developed countries as a group have remained largely unchanged, if not slowed down.[22] This outcome is attributed to the adoption of policies to reduce GHG emissions in European Union (EU) countries, and to enhance energy efficiency and reliance on renewable energy technologies in other developed countries.[23] In 2010, China surpassed the United States as the largest emitter of GHGs, whereas India was just behind the EU in fourth place. Brazil rose to seventh place, while Mexico and Indonesia, two other developing countries often considered among the emerging economies, joined the group of top 10 emitters in 2010, the last year the Intergovernmental Panel on Climate Change (IPCC) has calculated global emissions.[24]

In 2010, per capita emissions were still significantly higher in developed countries, with Canada, the United States, Russia, Japan, and the EU in the top five places. Yet, per capita emissions in industrialized countries have remained stable over the past 10 years. Per capita emissions in lowest income countries have also remained flat.[25] The only group that experienced a steady increase in per capita emissions over the past decade was a group of emerging

---

19. CLIMATE CHANGE 2014: MITIGATION OF CLIMATE CHANGE, WORKING GROUP III CONTRIBUTION TO THE FIFTH ASSESSMENT REPORT OF THE INTERGOVERNMENTAL PANEL ON CLIMATE CHANGE (O. Edenhofer et al. eds., 2014).
20. Each emerging economy has its own emissions profile and national circumstances. Brazil, for example, has seen emissions growth primarily from deforestation and forest degradation; India has experienced sharp total emissions growth, but its per capita emissions remain significantly lower than other emerging economies; whereas South Africa has high emissions per capita, but low total emissions. For the most updated assessment of emissions trends, see CLIMATE CHANGE 2014, *supra* note 19.
21. *See* HALLDING ET AL., *supra* note 9.
22. *See* CLIMATE CHANGE 2014, *supra* note 19.
23. *Id.*
24. *Id.*
25. *Id.*

economies, including all the BASIC countries.[26] In 2010, China, Brazil, and India already appeared among the top 10 countries based on per capita emissions.[27] In 2010 (the last year calculated by IPCC), only 20 countries, both developed and emerging economies, accounted for 75% of the total GHG emissions in the world.[28] Only five countries accounted for half of the world's emissions, and two of these countries are among the emerging economies: China (21.9%), the United States (18.1%), India (6%), Japan (4.5%), and Russia (4.1%).

Given that climate change is caused by the stock of accumulated GHG emissions over time, many studies on shares of contributions to climate change measure cumulative emissions. There are two ways to consider cumulative emissions: starting from pre-industrial times since about 1750 to 2010 (due to the long atmospheric residence time—around 100 years— of GHGs like carbon dioxide), or starting from 1990 to 2010 (when scientific evidence of the potential effects of GHG emissions in the climate was first acknowledged by the international community). In both scenarios, the BASIC countries already appear within the top 10 emitters of cumulative GHG emissions, with China in second place, behind the United States.[29] Between 1990 and 2002, the share of cumulative emissions from the BASIC countries had already risen from 11.8% to 20.6%.[30]

Contributions should not be considered in isolation from other criteria usually taken into consideration in discussions on equitable allocation, such as development needs. The UNFCCC included specific language recognizing that emissions in developing countries were expected to rise to meet their development needs.[31] The BASIC countries and other emerging economies should be afforded some room to increase their emissions temporarily, while developed countries should be reducing their emissions significantly faster. Yet, when compared to other developing countries, which have development needs that are even higher in some cases than in the emerging economies, the BASIC countries already contribute significantly more to the climate problem, in all measures: total emissions, per capita emissions, and historic emissions. Therefore, although the BASIC countries cannot be compared

---

26. *Id.*
27. *Id.*
28. CLIMATE CHANGE 2014, *supra* note 19, at 131.
29. *Id.* For a perspective from India, see NAVROZ DUBASH ED., HANDBOOK OF CLIMATE CHANGE AND INDIA: DEVELOPMENT, POLITICS, AND GOVERNANCE (2012).
30. ANDREAS GOLDTHAU ED., THE HANDBOOK OF GLOBAL ENERGY POLICY (2013).
31. *See* ANIL AGARWAL & SUNITA NARAIN, GLOBAL WARMING IN AN UNEQUAL WORLD: A CASE FOR ENVIRONMENTAL COLONIALISM (1990) (offering a strong critique of the idea that developing countries, including China and India, should have the same responsibilities related to their emissions when compared to developed countries).

directly to developed countries in assessing their contributions, they cannot be classified in the same category as developing countries either.

B. Enhanced Capabilities

Another key factor considered in studies on the allocation of differentiated burdens and costs in the climate regime has been the capacity or capability of each country to act on climate, or "from each according to his or her ability."[32] Capabilities can be understood in terms of both financial resources and technological capacity to undertake effective climate action.[33] In both measures, the North-South divide persists, especially in per capita terms. Nevertheless, there has been a slow but significant convergence among the BASIC countries and developed countries over time, and a growing divide among the BASIC countries and the rest of the developing world.

From 1988 to 2013, Chinese GDP rose from $310 billion to $7,379 billion.[34] Increases in GDP of other BASIC countries were less striking but equally significant. In 1992, the gross national income (GNI) disparities between the developed countries[35] and the large group of developing countries were stark. In that year, the high-income countries had accumulated a total of $14.78 trillion in GNI,[36] while the group of the BASIC countries plus Mexico and Turkey accumulated a total of $1.39 trillion.[37] The total GNI of developed countries was more than 10 times the total GNI of the group of emerging economies. The contrast with the GNI of LDCs was much starker—the LDCs accumulated only $0.12 trillion of GNI.

In 2009, the year of the Copenhagen Accord, the GNI of the high income Organisation for Economic Co-operation and Development (OECD) countries as a group was $41.93 trillion,[38] five times the total GNI of the group of emerging economies at $8.32 trillion[39] (compared to having been 10 times greater in 1992). The GNI of the least developed countries as a group was $0.52 trillion in 2009. China's GNI alone that year was higher than the total GNI of all lower-middle-income countries combined. In 2014, the GNI of the group of high-income developed countries together rose to $47.40 tril-

---

32. Shelton, *supra* note 15, at 655.
33. Duncan French, *Developing States and International Environmental Law: The Importance of Differentiated Responsibilities*, 49 INT'L & COMP. L.Q. 35, 50 (2000).
34. KARIN BACKSTRAND & EVA LOVBRAND EDS., RESEARCH HANDBOOK ON CLIMATE GOVERNANCE 19 (2015).
35. *See* World Bank Database, *Indicators*, http://data.worldbank.org/indicator (last visited Aug. 28, 2016).
36. *Id.*
37. *Id.*
38. *Id.*
39. *Id.*

lion. The BASIC countries' GNI, combined, reached $15.2 trillion, whereas LDCs combined had a GNI of only $0.72 trillion. While the GNI of the United States continued to be far ahead of any other country in the world, at $17.66 trillion, China's GNI reached $10.72 trillion, in second place, double the GNI of the third place country, Japan, with $4.66 trillion.[40]

Even though the per capita incomes of the BASIC countries are still significantly lower when compared to developed countries, they already accumulated a critical mass of financial resources that dwarfs the resources available in lower-income countries. The BASIC countries are also all major regional powers. China, Brazil, and South Africa each account for more than 30% of the GDP in their respective regions.[41] India's GDP accounts for more than 80% of the share in South Asia.[42] The BASIC countries are significantly underdeveloped when compared to wealthy industrialized countries, yet they are significantly ahead of many of their developing country peers when it comes to financial resources. There is a pool of financial resources in the BASIC countries that could be invested in climate mitigation and other climate actions that could advance sustainable development goals.[43]

The development of technological capacity in the BASIC countries has also been remarkable. In 1992, developed countries concentrated most of the world's technological capacity. It was widely understood that without the strong financial and technological contributions of developed countries there could be no effective climate mitigation and climate adaptation actions.[44] In 2001, the RAND Corporation's Science and Technology Policy Institute created a global index of scientific and technological capacity for the World Bank to compare developing countries' potential to innovate and cooperate with more scientifically advanced nations.[45] Unsurprisingly, the United States, Japan, and Germany were in the scientifically advanced group, at the top of the ranking. Already in 2001, surprisingly, all four BASIC countries were ranked in the second group of scientifically proficient nations, with the rest of the developed countries.[46] In 2011, the study was replicated, and the results defied the common perception about the limitations of technological

---

40. *Id.*
41. Praful Bidwai, The Emerging Economies and Climate Change: A Case Study of the BASIC Grouping, TNI Working Papers 4 (2014).
42. *Id.*
43. Climate Change 2007: Impacts, Adaptation, and Vulnerability. Contribution of Working Group II to the Fourth Assessment Report of the Intergovernmental Panel on Climate Change (M.L. Parry et al. eds., 2007).
44. Shue, *supra* note 2, at 29.
45. *See* Gayle Allard, *Science and Technology Capacity in Africa: A New Index*, 7 J. Afr. Stud. & Dev. 137, 137 (2015).
46. *Id.* at 139.

capacity in developing countries: China had climbed from 38th place in the ranking to the third place; India from the 44th place to 12th; and Brazil from 39th to 16th.[47] South Africa showed the weakest improvement, only climbing from 43rd to 37th place within the technologically proficient group.[48]

The fact that the BASIC countries still have a significantly lower percentage of inhabitants with higher education compared to developed countries is indisputable. Yet the BASIC countries already have a critical mass of highly educated people, including scientists and engineers, which distinguishes them from lower-income developing countries.[49] The same is true regarding infrastructure to spur technological innovation. According to the 2014 IPCC Fifth Assessment Report, a shift occurred in the global landscape for innovation related to climate change in the past 20 years.[50] By 2014, all of the largest emerging economies in the global South had already established effective systems for innovation and for the deployment of new technologies, leading to increasing South-South technology transfer, including in the climate area.[51] Indeed, the BASIC countries are increasingly cooperating to develop climate-related technology. One example is the Sino-Brazil wind technology cooperation, which has existed since 2011, to foster joint research and development investments in wind technology in both countries.[52]

Developed countries still possess superior financial and technological capabilities that justify requiring them to shoulder a greater share of climate burdens and costs, and provide technological transfers to the global South as a whole. Nevertheless, the BASIC countries can no longer use capabili-

---

47. *Id.* at 140.
48. *Id.* at 145.
49. *See* Carl J. Dahlman, *Innovation Strategies in Brazil, India & China: From Imitation to Deepening Technological Capability in the South, in* THE RISE OF TECHNOLOGICAL POWER IN THE SOUTH (Xiaolan Fu & Luc Soete eds., 2010); CARL J. DAHLMAN, THE WORLD UNDER PRESSURE: HOW CHINA AND INDIA ARE INFLUENCING THE GLOBAL ECONOMY AND ENVIRONMENT (2011).
50. CLIMATE CHANGE 2014, *supra* note 19.
51. *Id.* at 118. Illustrative examples are the strong wind turbine industry in China, largely based on homegrown technology; India's well-established sectors of information technology and biotechnology; and Brazil's leading biofuel technology. *See* Gabriel Blanco et al., *Drivers, Trends and Mitigation, in* CLIMATE CHANGE 2014: MITIGATION OF CLIMATE CHANGE, WORKING GROUP III CONTRIBUTION TO THE FIFTH ASSESSMENT REPORT OF THE INTERGOVERNMENTAL PANEL ON CLIMATE CHANGE 393 (O. Edenhofer et al. eds., 2014); Daniel Cusick, *Chinese Wind Turbine Maker Is Now World's Largest,* SCI. AM., Feb. 23, 2016, http://www.scientificamerican.com/article/chinese-wind-turbine-maker-is-now-world-s-largest/; ANDRE D. MARQUEZ, THE BRAZILIAN ENERGY REVOLUTION: LESSONS FROM THE BIOFUEL INDUSTRY BOOM (2007).
52. *See* Hyosun Bae & Zoraida Velasco, *Brazil-China Wind Energy Technology Cooperation,* GSDR PROTOTYPE BRIEFS, 2014, https://sustainabledevelopment.un.org/content/documents/5565Brazil-China%20Wind%20Energy%20Technology%20Cooperation.pdf; DENNIS BEST & JOERG HUSAR, ENERGY INVESTMENTS AND TECHNOLOGY TRANSFER ACROSS EMERGING ECONOMIES: THE CASE OF BRAZIL AND CHINA (2013), https://www.iea.org/publications/freepublications/publication/PCS_ChinaBrazil_FINAL_WEB.pdf.

ties constraints as a valid excuse to evade assuming a proportionately greater share of climate burdens and costs when compared to lower-income developing countries that lack financial and technological capacity. This marked shift in the global position of the BASIC countries and other emerging economies regarding their responsibilities for GHG emissions and their capabilities to act on climate has provoked a change in the way these countries have approached the principle of differentiation in the climate regime. This transformation is addressed in the next two sections.

II.   The Elusive Balance Between Justice and Participation in Differentiation

The literature commonly advances two explanations as to why States have established differential treatment in multilateral environmental agreements. One (value-driven) explanation is based on moral principles of justice and solidarity among States, while a second (instrumental or pragmatic) explanation is based on broad participation and effectiveness considerations.[53] The value-driven explanation asserts that the international community's decision to establish differential treatment was rooted in the concept of justice and equality to international law. The value-driven or equity explanation is typically divided into two distinct propositions.[54] Differential international norms based on the idea of justice were created to avoid imposing equal burdens on countries that are unequal in relevant ways—like their development needs or their financial, institutional, and technological capabilities to implement treaty obligations. Equal treatment would inflict unfair or impracticable burdens on those least able to bear such burdens, thus exacerbating existing inequalities among States. In this case, differential treatment would represent an application of the principle of distributive justice in international law.[55]

A second proposition based on the idea of justice claims that when some States have disproportionately contributed to a collective problem, allocating burdens and costs equally among all States would be unfair to those

---

53.   For a discussion of the value-driven approach, see PHILIPPE SANDS & JACQUELINE PEEL, PRINCIPLES OF INTERNATIONAL ENVIRONMENTAL LAW (2012); PIETER PAUW ET AL., DIFFERENT PERSPECTIVES ON DIFFERENTIATED RESPONSIBILITIES IN INTERNATIONAL NEGOTIATIONS—A STATE-OF-THE-ART REVIEW OF THE NOTION OF COMMON BUT DIFFERENTIATED RESPONSIBILITIES IN INTERNATIONAL NEGOTIATIONS, DISCUSSION PAPER 6, GERMAN DEVELOPMENT INSTITUTE (2014); PHILIPPE CULLET, DIFFERENTIAL TREATMENT IN INTERNATIONAL ENVIRONMENTAL LAW 84 (2003); ATAPATTU, *supra* note 7; HALVORSSEN, *supra* note 7.

54.   *See* Dinah Shelton, *Describing the Elephant: International Justice and Environmental Law, in* ENVIRONMENTAL LAW AND JUSTICE IN CONTEXT (Jonas Ebbesson & Phoebe Okowa eds., 2009).

55.   *Id.*

less responsible. Consequently, those States responsible for a larger share of contribution to the collective problem should be allocated a larger share of the burdens and costs to address it. This idea is associated with the polluter-pays principle in environmental law, which establishes that those who have caused a problem shall pay to fix it proportionally.[56] In this case, differential treatment would be an application of the principle of corrective justice in international law.[57]

In both cases discussed above, seeking justice through differential treatment of unequal States Parties constitutes an end in itself.[58] An instrumental explanation, on the other hand, considers differentiation as a means to achieve the objective of a multilateral agreement. Scott Barrett argues that international agreements perceived as fair in their allocation of burdens and costs induce broader participation and favor treaty compliance.[59] By offering preferential treatment in trade agreements, for example, developed countries can enlist the participation and cooperation of developing countries in developed countries' preferred goal of global commerce liberalization. Broader participation in the global climate regime potentially improves effectiveness by covering a larger share of the global emissions, and by reducing leakage opportunities.[60]

States respond to both value-driven and interest-driven motivations when negotiating international agreements.[61] In each international treaty, the manifestation of differential treatment likely reflects the result of the political balancing of diverse and often conflicting value-driven and interest-driven goals within each State, and among various States. Nevertheless, it is possible to identify which type of motivation has prevailed in the position of a country, or a group of countries, by analyzing the political process involved in

---

56. Caney, *supra* note 16; LAVANYA RAJAMANI, DIFFERENTIAL TREATMENT IN INTERNATIONAL ENVIRON-MENTAL LAW 73 (2006).

57. *See* Shelton, *supra* note 54.

58. *Id*. Rajamani distinguishes between two ideological premises behind the differentiation in the climate agreement: the consideration/capacity premise (based on morality, humanity, and goodwill) and the culpability/entitlement premise (based on legal obligation and liability). RAJAMANI, *supra* note 56, at 86.

59. With no centralized top-down government in international law, and States free to join or not join international treaties that are essentially self-enforcing, there is a greater need for a perception of fairness as a source of legitimacy and incentive for broader participation and compliance. *See* SCOTT BARRETT, ENVIRONMENT AND STATECRAFT: THE STRATEGY OF ENVIRONMENTAL TREATY MAKING (2003); Scott Barrett & Robert Stavins, *Increasing Participation and Compliance in International Climate Change Agreements*, 3 INT'L ENVTL. AGREEMENTS: POL., L. & ECON. 349 (2003); *see also* CULLET, *supra* note 53.

60. CLIMATE CHANGE 2014, *supra* note 19, ch. 13.

61. *See* Kenneth W. Abbott & Duncan Snidal, *Values and Interests: International Legalization in the Fight Against Corruption*, 31 J. LEGAL STUD. 141 (2002); WALTER MATTLI & NGAIRE WOODS EDS., THE POLITICS OF GLOBAL REGULATION (2010).

each treaty, as well as the State practice and doctrine related to it. Identifying the prevailing motivations behind States' positions on differential treatments in international agreements is necessary to understand fully the dynamic evolution of the principle of CBDR in international law.

Can the climate CBDR function as an internal instrument that effectively promotes fair allocations of burdens and costs among countries with asymmetric contributions, capabilities, and development needs? Or should CBDR serve primarily as an instrument to promote the broadest possible participation in collective efforts, with the battle for just allocation of burdens and costs being primarily a political issue, using different instruments from within and outside the multilateral regime? The answer may lie in the prevailing motivations of key stakeholders shaping the climate regime, beyond the North-South divide. The next section investigates how the prevailing motivations of the BASIC countries when advancing their favored model of CBDR shifted from the inception of the climate regime in 1992 to the 2015 Paris Agreement. Therefore, the term "early CBDR" will be used to refer to the differentiation arrangement that was enshrined in the UNFCCC and the Kyoto Protocol, in contrast to the new approach to CBDR that began in 2009 in Copenhagen and was formally incorporated into the legal text of the 2015 Paris Agreement.

III.   The BASIC Countries and CBDR: From Justice to Pragmatic Considerations

Differential treatment in favor of developing countries became a common feature in the "new generation" of MEAs that followed the 1972 Stockholm Conference on the Human Environment.[62] The predominant view was that developed countries accepted to engage in equity-based considerations when negotiating global environmental obligations primarily to incentivize the participation of developing countries in collective efforts to address common environmental problems. Since developed countries were unable to solve these problems unilaterally, or by coordinating only among themselves, universal participation was deemed indispensable.[63]

Developing countries resisted participating in global efforts to address environmental problems for several reasons, including: (1) economic develop-

---

62.   See Lavanya Rajamani, *The Changing Fortunes of Differential Treatment in the Evolution of International Environmental Law*, 88 INT'L AFF. 605 (2012). For an account of forms of differentiation in international law since the 1919 International Labour Organization Treaty of Versailles, see Christopher D. Stone, *Common but Differentiated Responsibilities in International Law*, 92 AM. J. INT'L L. 276 (2004).

63.   See HALVORSSEN, *supra* note 7; RAJAMANI, *supra* note 56.

ment and poverty reduction were their overriding priorities; (2) they lacked sufficient financial and technological capabilities to comply with proposed global environmental standards; and (3) developed countries had been predominantly responsible for global environmental problems. A fair allocation of the burdens of costs of environmental action would need to take these asymmetries into consideration. In other words, developed countries agreed to insert differentiated provisions reflecting equity considerations into MEAs in exchange for the participation of developing countries. Developing countries only agreed to participate in MEAs that took into consideration their low contributions to the problems, weak capabilities to act, and their greater development needs.

The question of whether by embracing differentiation developed countries could be seen as accepting legal responsibility for their historic and current contributions to the problems (corrective justice), or only accepting responsibility based on their capabilities (distributive justice), has remained unsettled.[64] The attempts of developing countries to expressly link obligations to historic responsibilities of developed countries in operational clauses of MEAs have failed. They did succeed in placing such a reference into preambles of agreements, most notably in the preamble of the UNFCCC.[65] The United States has consistently emphasized that differentiation should not trigger liability for developed countries' past contributions.[66]

The agreed-upon differentiation provisions in international environmental law were most often vague enough to allow developed countries and developing countries to claim their preferred approach to differentiation. This uneasy balance between participation and justice considerations has worked well for most MEAs, with Parties agreeing to common substantive obligations, tempered by differentiated regimes to facilitate implementation by developing countries. Developing countries have been granted, in different measures and modalities: deferred base years to start implementation and delayed reporting schedules provisions; financial and technical assistance;[67] capacity-building; and technology transfers to support the implementation of treaty obligations.[68] In this way, developed countries achieved their goal to attract the participation of developing countries, while developing countries

---

64.   See Shelton, *supra* note 15.
65.   UNFCCC, *supra* note 5, at pmbl.
66.   See Rajamani, *supra* note 56.
67.   UNFCCC, *supra* note 5, at arts. 4.3., 4.4, 4.5.
68.   See Lavanya Rajamani, *The Nature, Promise, and Limits of Differential Treatment in the Climate Regime*, 16 Yb. Int'l Envtl. L. 81 (2005); Lavanya Rajamani, Differentiation in a 2015 Climate Agreement 2 (Center for Climate and Energy Solutions (C2ES) 2015), http://www.c2es.org/docUploads/differentiation-brief-06-2015.pdf; Cullet, *supra* note 53.

won concessions from developed countries that they were unable to get in other ways.[69]

A.   Early CBDR: North-South Justice Over Pragmatism

In contrast to differentiation in most MEAs, which remained largely uncontroversial, the early CBDR has been highly contested. The early CBDR diverged markedly from differentiation in other MEAs.[70] Most MEAs include provisions that differentiate between countries with respect to the implementation of the particular treaty. The Montreal Protocol, for example, provides a grace period (10 years) before developing countries are to meet their obligations (Article 5), and establishes that they will receive financial and technical assistance to meet these obligations.[71] Unlike other MEAs, the UNFCCC and Kyoto Protocol established a regime of differentiation between developed and developing countries with respect to central obligations like mitigation.[72] The UNFCCC establishes that developed countries listed in Annex I shall adopt national mitigation policies demonstrating that they are taking the lead in modifying long-term trends in climate change,[73] while non-Annex I countries (all developing countries) should voluntarily adopt national mitigation programs.[74] The Kyoto Protocol only established mitigation obligations for Annex I countries.[75] The UNFCCC was also the only MEA to expressly mention the historic responsibilities of developed countries in the preamble, followed by repeated provisions stating that "developed countries should take the lead" in meeting the objective of the Convention while exempting developing countries from most substantive obligations.[76]

In other words, under early CBDR, developing countries (including the BASIC countries) were not simply given flexibility and support towards the implementation of core obligations. Instead, they were completely exempt from binding obligations towards the central objective of the climate regime: to reduce the anthropogenic GHG emissions. The participation of the

---

69.   Shelton, *supra* note 15.
70.   Rajamani, *supra* note 68.
71.   Montreal Protocol on Substances That Deplete the Ozone Layer, Sept. 16, 1987, 1522 U.N.T.S. 29, 34 (entered into force Jan. 1, 1989).
72.   Rajamani, *supra* note 68.
73.   UNFCCC, *supra* note 5, at arts. 4.1, 4.2.
74.   *Id.* at art. 4. Rajamani emphasizes this unique feature of differentiation under the UNFCCC. Rajamani, *supra* note 68, at 89.
75.   Kyoto Protocol to the United Nations Framework Convention on Climate Change, Dec. 10, 1997, arts. 2, 3, 2303 U.N.T.S. 148, 37 I.L.M. 22 (entered into force Feb. 16, 2005).
76.   UNFCCC, *supra* note 5.

BASIC countries and other developing countries was, therefore, voluntary and conditioned on developed countries taking the lead in climate action and in financial and technological support. This stark model of North-South differentiation, resulting from the unique political bargaining process of climate negotiations, was the closest to the concept of corrective justice that developing countries could get in international law.[77] The BASIC countries were heavily invested in advancing this model of differentiation in the climate regime.[78]

Considered a political win for developing countries, the early CBDR sacrificed the original idea of universal participation for North-South justice. First, the BASIC countries, already expected to increase their emissions significantly over time, were entirely exempted from the obligations of the Kyoto Protocol. Their development needs could have been taken into account by granting long deferral periods for implementation, for example, coupled with strong financial support, capacity-building, and technology transfer. Expressly rejecting the idea of granting emerging economies exemptions from common climate mitigation obligations,[79] the United States refused to participate in the climate regime under the Kyoto Protocol terms.[80] Other developed countries including Canada, Japan, and Australia embraced the U.S. position, and over time rejected exempting emerging economies with significant emissions from fulfilling legal obligations under the climate regime.[81]

By 2008, the Kyoto Protocol covered only 15% of global emissions, with participation primarily from EU countries.[82] The fact that emerging economies were exempt from any obligation has also given developed countries excuse to delay necessary climate action, while accusing the BASIC countries

---

77. RAJAMANI, *supra* note 56.
78. Kathryn Hochstetler & Manjana Milkoreit, *Responsibilities in Transition: Emerging Powers in the Climate Change Negotiations*, 21 GLOBAL GOVERNANCE: REV. MULTILATERALISM & INT'L ORGS. 205 (2015).
79. *See* Kathryn Hochstetler, *Climate Rights and Obligations for Emerging States: The Cases of Brazil and South Africa*, 79 SOC. RES. 957 (2012).
80. *Id.*
81. On several occasions, developed countries expressed their view that the division between Annex I and non-Annex I countries for the effects of the climate regime did not reflect current realities as it related to GHG emissions, capabilities, and development needs. *See* Thomas Deleuil & Tuula Honkonen, *Vertical, Horizontal, Concentric: The Mechanisms of Differential Treatment in the Climate Regime*, 5 CLIMATE L. 82 (2015). For a detailed political science account of the changing negotiating group dynamics in climate negotiations, with an emphasis on emerging economies, see Hochstetler, *supra* note 79; Hochstetler & Milkoreit, *supra* note 78; Jutta Brunee & Charlotte Streck, *The UNFCCC as a Negotiation Forum: Towards Commom but More Differentiated Responsibilities*, 13 CLIMATE POL'Y 589 (2013).
82. *See* Hochstetler, *supra* note 79.

of being the "great irresponsibles" in the climate regime.[83] The conundrum was that by insisting on a justice-based regime, the BASIC countries ended up contributing to delay in climate action by developed countries. As developed countries failed to take the lead in climate action, the BASIC countries resisted assuming their own responsibilities.

B.   Paris Agreement: Pragmatism Over Justice

The Kyoto Protocol is an example of an environmental agreement that endorsed justice over participation. The BASIC countries were all strong supporters of the differentiation arrangement of the Kyoto Protocol. Yet, in covering only 15% of emissions, the Kyoto Protocol's approach was unsustainable. One option to restore the balance between justice and participation would be for the BASIC countries to accept obligations that did not match the obligations of developed countries, but that would be distinguishable from the obligations of low-income developing countries without significant levels of contribution or capabilities. Developed countries did not oppose the concept of taking the lead in climate action, based on their greater contributions and capabilities. Many developed countries insisted that the BASIC countries and other emerging economies accept some form of meaningful participation that was closer to developed country obligations, and not voluntary as under the Kyoto Protocol.[84] Many attempts to arrive at a formula of fair differentiation that included emerging economies have failed, primarily due to strong resistance from the BASIC countries to assume legal responsibility for their contributions and capabilities.[85] A new compromise seemed elusive, as developed countries and emerging economies could not agree on an allocation formula that reflected this balance.[86]

With the multilateral system in gridlock, the BASIC countries came under mounting political pressure in the run-up to the 15th Conference of the Parties (COP15) in Copenhagen in 2009.[87] The Major Economies Forum on Energy and Climate, created by the United States to facilitate political discussions on climate action among developed countries, invited the BASIC countries to their meetings.[88] The G8 proposed a G8 + 5 Cli-

---

83.   Hurrell & Segupta, *supra* note 8, at 467.
84.   *See* RAJAMANI, *supra* note 56.
85.   The literature on the attempts to arrive at a more "fair and equitable" form of differentiation in the climate regime is extensive. The IPCC Fifth Assessment Report offers a good review of this literature. *See* CLIMATE CHANGE 2014, *supra* note 19.
86.   *See* Brunee & Streck, *supra* note 81.
87.   *See* Karl Hallding et al., *Rising Powers: The Evolving Role of BASIC Countries*, 13 CLIMATE POL'Y 638 (2013).
88.   *Id.*

mate Dialogue that included the four BASIC countries plus Mexico, to discuss climate action among leading emitters. From the other side of the spectrum, the groups of LDCs and small island nations, the most vulnerable to climate change, began to press the BASIC countries to accept greater responsibility for climate action.[89] The BASIC countries, and especially China, were perceived as the enemies of climate progress. Karl Hallding et al. argue that this escalating political pressure and loss of legitimacy led the BASIC countries to fear that, without the UNFCCC shield of CBDR, they would be compelled to take climate actions similar to those expected from developed countries.[90]

Copenhagen was expected to be the testing ground for the negotiation of a new climate agreement that restored the balance between participation and justice. The BASIC countries would finally accept their measure of legal responsibility, commensurate to their contributions, capabilities, and development needs. Developed countries, including the United States, would finally take the lead by embracing climate obligations that were more stringent and faster than the BASIC countries and other developing countries. As is well known, Parties did not arrive at a binding agreement at Copenhagen, signing instead a nonbinding accord.

The dominant view in the aftermath of COP15 in Copenhagen was that the Conference illustrated the incapacity of multilateral negotiations to address climate change and that one of the main obstacles was the lingering tension regarding CBDR.[91] However, as countries engaged in negotiations towards a new agreement after Copenhagen, it became clear that the Conference had in fact firmly planted the seeds for a change in the paradigm of differentiation in the climate regime.[92] Copenhagen also came to be recognized as the Conference where the BASIC countries and the United States, followed by other developed countries, agreed on a new compromise that would significantly shape the 2015 Paris Agreement.[93] Copenhagen was the first COP to the UNFCCC where the BASIC countries formed a coalition to participate in the negotiations. For the first time, there were noticeable divergences in the positions of the BASIC countries and other developing

---

89. *Id.*
90. *Id.*
91. *See* Navroz K. Dubash, *Copenhagen: Climate of Mistrust*, ECON. & POL. WKLY., Dec. 26, 2009; Lavanya Rajamani, *Copenhagen Accord: Neither Fish Nor Fowl*, Centre for Policy Research Seminar Paper 606, at 26 (2010), http://www.india-seminar.com/2010/606/606_lavanya_rajamani.htm.
92. *See* Daniel Bodansky, *The Copenhagen Climate Change Conference: A Postmortem*, 104 AM. J. INT'L L. 230 (2010).
93. *See* Hallding et al., *supra* note 87.

countries in the climate regime on key areas such as the legal nature of the regime and the levels of ambition.[94]

In Copenhagen, developed countries and the BASIC countries began to develop a new paradigm for differentiation in the climate regime. Instead of a top-down differentiation establishing different levels of legal obligation for different countries, the new paradigm was based on a bottom-up system where countries self-defined their pledges, which were voluntary in nature. This bottom-up approach relies on pledges that are defined at the national level, based on the respective contributions, capabilities, and national circumstances of each country. In 2014, China and the United States announced their intention to cooperate bilaterally on climate change, presenting for the first time a proposal for a new concept for differentiation, one that read: "common but differentiated responsibilities and capabilities in the light of different national circumstances."[95] The expression "in light of different national circumstances" allows Parties to take into account criteria such as stages of development, geographic size, and natural resources endowments when proposing their pledges. With the addition of this expression, the earlier strong correlation between responsibilities for GHG emissions and capabilities and corresponding climate burdens and costs in CBDR has been attenuated, with a broadening of the parameters of differentiation.[96]

This new paradigm of differentiation was incorporated into the 2015 Paris Agreement.[97] There is broad recognition that the 2015 Paris Agreement represents a fundamental shift away from the categorical binary approach of the Kyoto Protocol toward more nuanced forms of differentiation.[98] The Paris Agreement still builds on the normative legacy of the UNFCCC, and

94. *Id.*

95. Press Release, The White House, U.S.-China Joint Announcement on Climate Change (Nov. 11, 2014), para. 2 (committing to reach an ambitious agreement in 2015 in COP21 in Paris that reflects the principle of common but differentiated responsibilities and respective capabilities, in light of different national circumstances), https://www.whitehouse.gov/the-press-office/2014/11/11/us-china-joint-announcement-climate-change; *see also* Daniel Bodansky, Building Flexibility and Ambition Into a 2015 Climate Agreement (Center for Climate and Energy Solutions (C2ES) 2014), http://www.c2es.org/docUploads/int-flexibility-06-14.pdf; Daniel Bodansky & Lavanya Rajamani, Key Legal Issues in the 2015 Climate Negotiations (Center for Climate and Energy Solutions (C2ES) 2015), http://papers.ssrn.com/sol3/papers.cfm?abstract_id=2652001.

96. Christina Voigt & Felipe Ferreira, *Dynamic Differentiation in the Paris Agreement: The Interplay of the Principles of Common but Differentiated Responsibilities and Respective Capabilities, Progression and Highest Possible Ambition*, 6 Climate L. 58, 66 (2016).

97. For analyses of the Paris Agreement, see a *Compendium of Commentary on the Paris Agreement/COP21*, organized by Wil Burns, http://teachingclimatelaw.org/compendium-of-commentary-on-the-paris-agreementcop21/ (last visited Aug. 20, 2016).

98. Meinhard Doelle, *The Paris Agreement: Historic Breakthrough or High Stakes Experiment?*, 6 Climate L. 1, 2 (2016); Daniel Bodansky, *The Paris Climate Agreement: A New Hope?*, 110 Am. J. Int'l L. 1, 4 (2016); Lavanya Rajamani, *Ambition and Differentiation in the 2015 Paris Agreement: Interpretive Possibilities and Underlying Politics*, 65 Int'l & Comp. L.Q. 493, 494 (2016).

therefore it maintains some elements of North-South differentiation.[99] For example, it calls for developed countries to continue taking the lead in climate action. It sets exclusive legal obligations for developed countries to provide financial resources for climate action in developing countries; however, for the first time in international environmental law, language was introduced to encourage those developing countries "able to do so" to also provide funding and assistance for less developed countries.[100] In this way, the differentiation in the climate regime still remains stronger than in other MEAs. On the other hand, the common nature of the responsibilities was strengthened, with all Parties in the Paris Agreement mandated to formulate, communicate, and update their nationally determined contributions (NDCs).[101] However, NDCs are not legally binding, in that their implementation is voluntary. Instead of different levels of binding obligations for all countries with significant emissions and sufficient capabilities, all commitments became voluntary.

Christina Voigt and Felipe Ferreira argue that while the Paris Agreement differentiation builds on the categories of "developed" and "developing," it has moved away from a bifurcated or binary approach and could eventually over time lead to common types of mitigation efforts.[102] This is true, but the BASIC countries will have no specific timeline to conclude this "graduation" under the Paris Agreement. There is now a common system of reporting and review, with flexibility mechanisms that do not follow the developed vs. developing divide, but rather that take into account various national capacities and circumstances.[103] BASIC countries remain legally allowed to claim the same flexibility of lower-income countries when it comes to reporting and review.

The Paris Agreement has introduced a hybrid system of differentiation,[104] which reflected a compromise between developed countries and the BASIC emerging economies to combine universal responsibility based on self-defined voluntary pledges while maintaining some elements of the North-South differentiation. There was no introduction of legal differentiation for the BASIC

---

99. *See* Voigt & Ferreira, *supra* note 96.

100. Pauwelyn argues that the long-term trend is away from differential treatment of developing countries as a broad group, towards more individualized differentiation according to specific criteria and tailored to each negotiation or regime. The Paris Agreement would thus be a first step in this direction. *See* Joost Pauwelyn, *The End of Differential Treatment for Developing Countries? Lessons From the Trade and Climate Change Regimes*, 22 Rev. Eur., Comp. & Int'l Envtl. L. 29 (2013).

101. Obligations of conduct when it comes to preparing and submitting nationally determined contributions are now universal, and do not follow a North-South divide.

102. Voigt & Ferreira, *supra* note 96, at 67.

103. *Id.* at 70, 71.

104. Bodansky, *supra* note 98, at 19.

countries, and developed countries' commitments also became voluntary. Parties to the Paris Agreement were able to ensure broad participation in the new agreement, with all major emitters, both developed and developing, signing the document. Yet to ensure this high uptake among countries, including all major emitters, the differentiation model in the Paris Agreement has departed from the strong focus on climate justice, which associated climate burdens and costs with responsibilities for contributions and capabilities to act on climate, a model that characterized the early CBDR.

For Voigt and Ferreira, rather than promoting a mere burden-sharing concept, "differentiation under the Paris Agreement has the potential to function as a catalyst for a race to the top on climate action."[105] Lavanya Rajamani also concludes that the Paris Agreement contains "aspirational goals, binding obligations of conduct in relation to mitigation, a rigorous system of oversight, and a nuanced form of differentiation between developed and developing countries" that is conducive to ambition.[106] To date, the sum of the mitigation pledges that Parties presented in their NDCs during the 2015 COP21 in Paris will not enable the international community to reach the goal of keeping temperature increases to well below 2°C. Only time will tell if the architecture of the Paris Agreement will effectively lead to sufficiently ambitious climate action to meet this goal. What is certain is that in the negotiations leading to the Paris Agreement, the BASIC countries gave up the concept of differentiation as the primary justice-based burden-sharing principle that had prevailed until Copenhagen.

Conclusion

This chapter has analyzed how the Paris Agreement CBDR reflects the BASIC countries' shift in position on climate differentiation, as their responsibilities for emissions and their capabilities to act on climate have significantly evolved over time. BASIC countries have abandoned their emphasis on a justice-based concept of rigid binary differentiation along a North-South divide, according to respective contributions and capabilities, to invest in a more nuanced differentiation that promotes broad participation of all large and smaller emitters. Therefore, BASIC countries have sacrificed the concept of justice-based differentiation that made the controversial climate CBDR stand out from differentiation in other MEAs. The implication is that whether the allocation of climate burdens and costs among countries

---

105. Voigt & Ferreira, *supra* note 96, at 74.
106. Rajamani, *supra* note 98, at 494.

will be more or less closely related to respective responsibilities and capabilities, instead of merely based on self-determined national circumstances, will depend on the political will of developed countries and BASIC countries implementing the agreement. The innovative legal instruments of the Paris Agreement, such as the transparency mechanism, the stocktaking system, and the progression principle, are expected to help in shaping this political will closer to the intragenerational justice ideal.

Only time will tell whether the softer approach to differentiation (without different levels of legally binding mitigation obligations), together with the innovative compliance mechanisms, will be enough to prevent those countries that contributed less to the climate problem and that are less able to respond to the climate challenge from shouldering an unfair share of burdens and costs. Climate justice related to the fair allocation of burdens and costs of climate action among countries according to their respective responsibilities and capabilities has left the realm of mere principles of international environmental law and has entered the realm of international environmental law implementation.

Chapter 3

The Green Climate Fund, International Governance, and Climate Justice in Developing Nations

Steven Ferrey

Introduction: The Largest Transfer of Wealth in History

Several developed countries have committed to the largest sustained international transfer of wealth in history: a commitment of an additional $100 billion per year of foreign aid continuing in perpetuity for the explicit purpose of dealing with global climate change.[1] Since the current warming trend is irreversible and will last over a period of 100 years or more,[2] this com-

---

1.   United Nations Secretary-General, Report of the Secretary-General's High-Level Advisory Group on Climate Change Financing 2 (2010), http://www.un.org/wcm/webdav/site/climatechange/shared/Documents/AGF_reports/AGF%20Report.pdf [hereinafter United Nations Secretary-General].

2.   Susan Solomon et al., *Irreversible Climate Change Due to Carbon Dioxide Emissions*, 106 Proc. Nat'l Acad. Sci. 1704, 1704 (2009).

mitment constitutes trillions of dollars of additional cross-national financial assistance from some wealthier developed nations to the bulk of countries. It is of unprecedented dimension, scale, and longevity.

New climate change financing will need to come from a wide variety of sources, public and private, bilateral and multilateral, including alternative sources of finance and the scaling up of existing sources and increased private flows. Commitments to domestic mitigation of warming and the introduction of new public instruments based on carbon pricing will be important for mobilizing adequate climate financing.[3] Developing nations want these funds to be administered through newer organizations set up with the dominant governing board control exercised by recipient nations, in which there would be fewer administrative requirements and less monitoring of recipients' decisions and accounting for use of the proceeds. The donor countries typically prefer administration by the traditional multilateral international organizations, in which there would be traditional monitoring of recipient fund use and accountability, and where the boards are constituted with a majority of donor countries. An international battle over the administration of trillions of dollars of discretionary funds is not merely a fight over funds. In a larger dimension, it maps the future of 21st century international law and regulation.

This scenario will represent a different form of wealth transfer compared to tradition. The entire world is dependent on scores of countries making significant and successful greenhouse gas (GHG) emissions reductions; the failure of any one country to follow through has irreversible impacts on all. The battle against global climate change can only be successful if developing countries make immediate fundamental changes in their electrified economies. The newly pledged massive financial transfers are the engine for developing country climate change mitigation. If they are misapplied, the entire world economy bears the climate warming burdens and consequences. Therefore, unlike most other kinds of foreign assistance, accountability and control of how this assistance is used is of unusual importance. A misstep by any nation equally impacts all nations with warming consequences. An effective solution cannot be centralized; it must be achieved in every country according to the nation's particular culture, regulatory system, and unique situation.

In December 2009, at the United Nations Climate Change Conference in Copenhagen, industrialized countries set a goal of mobilizing $100 billion per year by 2020 to support mitigation and adaptation activities in devel-

---

3.   UNITED NATIONS SECRETARY-GENERAL, *supra* note 1, at 5.

oping countries.[4] It will matter for climate justice how this unprecedented financial flow is or is not controlled. As a starting point for the detail that follows, only mitigation of emission of greenhouse gases by all nations will reduce climate warming. Since climate change is expected to most severely affect those countries with the least resources to adapt, mitigation activities with worldwide impacts can increase global equity.

Adaptation to the effects of warming does not itself reduce the amount of climate warming, but funds for this purpose can be expended in a manner that promotes climate justice. Whether adaptation funds promote climate justice depends on where these funds go and how they are spent. This is a function of the local governments through which climate mitigation and adaptation funds are funneled. It is also a function of accounting and control over disbursement of these funds, which is influenced by the international organizations that administer the flow and allocation of these funds. This chapter examines the different components and the moving parts in this choreography.

This $100 billion annual pledge is an unprecedented amount of wealth transfer. For context, the total annual 2016-2017 United Nations budget, including all of its remote worldwide posts, is $5.4 billion annually; added peacekeeping operations raise annual expenditures by $7.87 billion to $13.3 billion.[5] About half of this latter amount comes from mandatory United Nations assessments, and the other half from voluntary donations by Member nations. The assessments are based on gross national product (GNP); richer countries pay more than poorer countries.[6] The top 10 most-assessed countries by the United Nations are the most developed affluent counties, which contribute 76.44% of the regular United Nations budget, although representing only 5% of world nations.[7]

For multilateral agencies that finance infrastructure in developing countries, the annual operating budget of the World Bank (excluding loans and grants) is approximately $1.5 billion.[8] The annual budget of the International

---

4. UNITED NATIONS SECRETARY-GENERAL, *supra* note 1, at 2.
5. *See* United Nations, UN Budget for 2016/17 adopted by UN General Assembly, http://www.un.org/pga/70/2015/12/23/general-assembly-adopts-un-budget-for-2016-17/; United Nations, Financing Peacekeeping, http://www.un.org/en/peacekeeping/operations/financing.shtml (last visited Sept. 18, 2016).
6. *Id.* There are some exceptions, however. For example, Brazil pays more than Liechtenstein even though Brazil's per capita income is much lower, because as a larger country its total GNP is much higher.
7. Matt Rosenberg, *The Number of Countries in the World: By Most Accounts, There Are 196 Countries in the World*, ABOUT.COM, http://geography.about.com/cs/countries/a/numbercountries.htm (last visited Aug. 21, 2016). There are 193 Members of the United Nations, among 196 countries in the world. Taiwan, Puerto Rico, Bermuda, Greenland, and Palestine are not recognized as countries.
8. *See* World Bank, *World Bank Budget Increase*, http://web.worldbank.org/WBSITE/EXTERNAL/EXTABOUTUS/ORGANIZATION/EXTPRESIDENT2007/EXTPASTPRESIDENTS/PRESID

Monetary Fund (IMF) is about $1 billion annually for administration, in addition to its lending.[9] Both groups have 187 Member countries,[10] which includes most of the world's countries. By any measure, $100 billion of new annual financial assistance, on an ongoing indefinite basis, is a significant amount of additional money. There are now battles about this funding commitment along two dimensions. First, as for managerial control of carbon funds, which organizations will administer this huge carbon fund? Second, regarding distributional control, will donors or donee recipients control the expenditure and verification of funds and their use?

These funding management battles will have substantial impacts on climate justice. Adaptation funds could be flexibly directed at both the international and recipient national levels to promote climate justice for the most vulnerable populations. Or they could promote the opposite if not carefully directed and managed. Climate mitigation funds, effectively implemented, will most benefit the most vulnerable people in the most vulnerable nations, by reducing the impacts of a warmer world. If carefully managed at both the international and national levels, the impact of a pledged transfer of $100 billion each year can have an unprecedented impact on climate justice. This chapter examines how we got to where the world now is, and the options and alternatives going forward with this pending, massive international transfer.

Developing countries are on the cutting edge of the challenge to control climate change because they are expected to add around 80% of all new electric generation capacity and resulting GHG emissions worldwide during the critical next two decades. While often overlooked, to address climate change and its impact on world populations, the structure and accountability of international mechanisms are critical. Part I of this chapter addresses the evolution of the emission reduction commitments in the United Nations Framework Convention on Climate Change (UNFCCC) from Copenhagen to Paris and the corresponding funding mechanisms to support those goals. Part II examines the structural and operational differences between the more traditional international agencies and the newer institutional conduits though which these massive amounts of international climate funds may flow. The legal differences in executive council membership and pro-

---

ENTEXTERNAL/0,,contentMDK:20095591~menuPK:235080~pagePK:159837~piPK:159808~theSitePK:227585,00.html (last visited Aug. 21, 2016).

9.   *See* IMF, IMF Annual Report 2010: Supporting a Balanced Global Recovery, at 59, tbl. 5.1 (2010), http://www.imf.org/external/pubs/ft/ar/2010/eng/pdf/ar10_eng.pdf.

10.   *See* IMF, *Factsheet—The IMF at a Glance* 1, http://www.imf.org/external/np/exr/facts/glance.htm (last visited Aug. 21, 2016).

cedures for governance and decisionmaking of these various international climate funding mechanisms make a difference in how funds are directed and monitored, and the resulting cash flow for warming gas mitigation and climate justice. Part III examines in full perspective the critical distinctions in the international financial conduits through which this massive flow of climate funds may take and the importance of these choices for mitigation of warming. Correctly applied, mitigation funds will minimize future climate change, and adaptation funds can save populations and economies and promote greater climate justice.

I. Comparing International Commitments on Climate Change

A. The Commitments in Copenhagen and Cancun

As a starting point, it is critical to understand how international law responses to climate change have evolved and assess how effective the mechanisms deployed in the past decade have or have not been in promoting climate justice as the world addresses climate warming. This inquiry provides a baseline against which to compare commitments in terms of time and amount to be able to value reductions.

With 191 national Parties and the European Union, the UNFCCC has near universal membership of world countries.[11] The Convention is the parent treaty that generated the 1997 Kyoto Protocol, which has, to date, 192 Member Parties.[12] Under the Protocol, 42 States, consisting of industrialized countries and the European community, initially agreed to implement GHG emission limitation and reduction commitments, while the remaining 155 developing countries among the 192 signatories, including the largest GHG emitter among all nations, have non-binding generic undertakings to limit emissions.[13] Four of these 42 Annex I countries either did not ratify the Protocol (United States), withdrew after ratification (Canada), or announced that they would not take on additional obligations after 2011 (Japan and Russian Federation).

---

11. *See* UNFCCC, *Status of Ratification of the Kyoto Protocol*, http://unfccc.int/kyoto_protocol/status_of_ratification/items/2613.php (last visited Aug. 21, 2016).
12. *Id.*
13. *See* UNFCC, *Kyoto Protocol*, http://unfccc.int/kyoto_protocol/items/2830.php (last visited Aug. 21, 2016).

There were GHG reduction pledges made by developed countries at the 1997 Kyoto Protocol,[14] at the 2007 Bali Conference of the Parties (COP),[15] at the 2009 Copenhagen COP,[16] at the 2010 Cancun COP[17] (as well as a fast-start pledge),[18] and at the 2011 Durban COP. The Copenhagen Accord marked the beginning of a new approach to international climate agreements, breaking from past methods by allowing each country to choose its own base year and to express its commitment in terms other than absolute reductions in emissions. This flexibility promoted consensus on the regulatory concept and allowed an agreement to be reached. At the same time, however, with no common metric, it significantly complicates comparing the emissions reductions and economic efforts implicit in the commitments made by the participants.[19] Commitments expressed in different algorithms or over different time periods will affect climate justice in both the "how much" and "when" aspects of climate mitigation of warming impacts that will most affect the most vulnerable populations.

Here is why the numbers pledged by different countries do not align for easy comparison. Comparisons among countries are not straightforward because even among countries that pledge to reduce emissions from a self-chosen baseline year, those chosen baseline years vary significantly country by country. Normalizing these values is not straightforward. Also, countries differ in their metrics; for instance, China and India committed to reduce their emissions per unit of gross domestic product (GDP) relative to 2005 by 40% and 20%, respectively. Commitments of developed

14. *Id.*
15. COP is the Conference of the Parties to the Kyoto Protocol, an annual meeting to attempt to implement the goals of the Protocol. *See* Jessica Aldred, *Q&A: Bali Climate Change Conference*, THE GUARDIAN, Dec. 3, 2007, http://www.guardian.co.uk/environment/2007/nov/30/bali.climatechange; *Report of the Conference of the Parties on Its Thirteenth Session, Held in Bali From 3 to 15 December 2007—Addendum, Part Two: Action Taken by the Conference of the Parties at Its Thirteenth Session, Decisions Adopted by the Conference of the Parties*, UNFCCC, 13th Sess., Decision 1/CP.13, at 3, U.N. Doc. FCCC/CP/2007/6/Add.1 (2008), http://unfccc.int/resource/docs/2007/cop13/eng/06a01.pdf#page=3. *See also Deal Agreed in Bali Climate Talks*, THE GUARDIAN, Dec. 15, 2007, http://www.guardian.co.uk/environment/2007/dec/15/bali.climatechange4.
16. *See Report of the Conference of the Parties on Its Fifteenth Session, Held in Copenhagen From 7 to 9 December 2009—Addendum, Part Two: Action Taken by the Conference of the Parties at Its Fifteenth Session, Decisions Adopted by the Conference of the Parties*, UNFCCC, 15th Sess., Decision 2/CP.15, at 4, U.N. Doc. FCCC/CP/2009/11/Add.1 (2010), http://unfccc.int/resource/docs/2009/cop15/eng/11a01.pdf#page=4.
17. *See* UNFCCC, *The Cancun Agreements*, http://cancun.unfccc.int/mitigation/developed-country-emission-reduction-targets/ (last visited Aug. 21, 2016).
18. *See* KIRSTEN STASIO ET AL., SUMMARY OF DEVELOPED COUNTRY FAST-START CLIMATE FINANCE PLEDGES (World Resources Institute 2010), http://pdf.wri.org/climate_finance_pledges_2010-10-27.pdf.
19. WARWICK J. MCKIBBEN, ADELE MORRIS & PETER J. WILCOXEN, COMPARING CLIMATE COMMITMENTS: A MODEL-BASED ANALYSIS OF THE COPENHAGEN ACCORD 6 (2010), http://belfercenter.ksg.harvard.edu/files/McKibbin-DP-June2010-final.pdf [hereinafter MCKIBBEN].

countries[20] and developing countries[21] also vary. Table 1 sets forth the 2009 Copenhagen commitments voluntarily elected by countries and reported to the UNFCCC.[22] These differ from the commitments to the 1997 Kyoto Protocol, which capped total emissions over a five-year period ending in 2012.[23] The base year for reductions also varies by country: the United States and Canada promised reductions of 17% relative to their 2005 levels, while Australia used 2000 as its baseline, and the European Union, Russia, and Japan chose a base year of 1990.

Table 1. Commitments Under the Copenhagen Accord[24]

Country	Greenhouse Gas Emissions Targets for 2020	Base Year
USA	[Reduction of emissions] in the range of 17% in conformity with anticipated U.S. energy and climate legislation, recognizing that the final target will be reported to the secretariat in light of enacted legislation.	2005
Japan	25% reduction, which is premised on the establishment of a fair and effective international framework in which all major economies participate and agree on ambitious targets.	1990
Australia	5% unconditionally; up to 15% or 25% with international action. Australia will reduce its GHG emissions by 25% of 2000 levels by 2020 if the world agrees to an ambitious global deal capable of stabilizing levels of GHGs in the atmosphere at 450 parts per million carbon dioxide equivalent (ppm CO_2-eq) or lower. Australia will unconditionally reduce emissions by 5% below 2000 levels by 2020, and by up to 15% by 2020 if there is a global agreement that falls short of securing atmospheric stabilization at 450 ppm CO_2-eq and under which major developing economies commit to substantially restrain emissions and advanced economies take on commitments comparable to Australia's.	2000

---

20. Emissions commitments by Annex I countries appear in Appendix I of the Accord, formulated as economy-wide reductions in GHG emissions relative to a base year of each country's choosing. UNFCCC, *Appendix I—Quantified Economy-Wide Emissions Targets for 2020*, http://unfccc.int/home/items/5264.php (last visited Aug. 21, 2016).
21. Their commitments are more varied and include, for example, emissions reduction targets relative to business-as-usual projections, reductions in emissions per unit of GDP, expansions in forest cover, and investments in energy efficiency and biofuels. *See* UNFCCC, *Appendix II—Nationally Appropriate Mitigation Actions of Developing Country Parties*, http://unfccc.int/home/items/5265.php (last visited Aug. 21, 2016).
22. McKibben, *supra* note 19, at 6.
23. *See* UNFCCC, *Kyoto Protocol, supra* note 13.
24. *See* McKibben, *supra* note 19, at 6, tbl. 2.

Country	Greenhouse Gas Emissions Targets for 2020	Base Year
European Union	20%/30%; as part of a global and comprehensive agreement for the period beyond 2012, the European Union reiterates its conditional offer to move to a 30% reduction by 2020 compared to 1990 levels, provided that other developed countries commit themselves to comparable emission reductions and that developing countries contribute adequately according to their responsibilities and respective capabilities.	1990
Canada	17%; to be aligned with the final economy-wide emissions target of the United States in enacted legislation.	2005
Russia	15–25%; the range of the GHG emission reductions will depend on the following conditions: • Appropriate accounting of the potential of Russia's forestry sequestration contribution in meeting the obligations of the anthropogenic emissions reduction; • Undertaking by all major emitters the legally binding obligations to reduce anthropogenic GHG emissions.	1990
China	Increase forest coverage by 40 million ha and forest stock volume by 1.3 billion m3.	2005
India	Reduce the emissions intensity of its GDP by 20–25% by 2020 in comparison to the 2005 level.	2005

In context, China and India committed to reducing by 40% and 20%, respectively, their emissions per unit of national GDP.[25] There is no agreement even among developed countries as to how to measure the "how much" and "when" commitments to limit emissions of warming gases. The Brookings Institution work compares agreements reached by world nations in the Copenhagen Accord in December 2009.[26] The 42 original covered Annex I countries subject to Kyoto Protocol carbon emission reductions represent approximately 20% of world countries and less than 40% of world carbon sources.[27] Table 2 illustrates the Copenhagen Accord emissions commitments for 2020 transposed to common historical base years (1990, 2000, and 2005) and relative to emissions in the 2020 baseline scenario, or business-as-usual (BAU) emissions.[28]

---

25.   McKibben, *supra* note 19, at 7.

26.   *Id.* at 4.

27.   *See* UNFCCC, *GHG Data From UNFCCC*, http://unfccc.int/ghg_data/ghg_data_unfccc/items/4146. php (last visited Aug. 21, 2016).

28.   McKibben, *supra* note 19, at 17. For China and India, commitments are reported using the emissions levels in 2020 that produce the targeted reductions in emissions per unit real GDP. For the regions without Accord targets (Brazil, the least developed countries (LDCs), and the Organization of the Petroleum Exporting Countries (OPEC)), emissions in the policy scenario are measured against their historical emissions and BAU projections for 2020.

Table 2. Emissions in 2020 That Result From Copenhagen Accord[29]

Country	2020 Target as a Percent Change in Emissions in 2020 Relative to Emissions in the Indicated Year			BAU in 2020
	1990	2000	2005	
USA	-1	-15	-17	-33
Japan	-25	-37	-39	-48
Australia	30	-5	-18	-35
Europe	-20	-24	-27	-36
ROECD	10	-7	-17	-25
China	496	350	146	-22
India	346	159	120	0.4
EEFSU	-15	28	18	-1.3
Brazil	168	73	61	0.6
LDC	211	119	85	0.9
OPEC	180	105	60	1.3
World	90	70	43	-17.5

Note: Here and throughout, ROECD = the rest of the Organisation for Economic Co-operation and Development, EEFSU = Eastern Europe and the former Soviet Union, LDC = least developed countries, and OPEC = the Organization of Petroleum Exporting Countries.

Table 3 ranks each regions' commitments, normalized to equivalent baseline values, in order of the greatest percent emissions reductions.[30] The highlighted boxes in Table 3 also indicate which base year was chosen by the highlighted country(ies).

---

29. *Id.* at 18. The United States, Japan, Australia, China, India, and Brazil are each represented by a self-contained single-modeled country; the rest of the world is aggregated into western Europe; the rest of the OECD (ROECD), not including Mexico and Korea; eastern Europe and the former Soviet Union (EEFSU); OPEC oil-exporting economies; and all other developing countries (LDC).

30. *Id.* at 19. Highlighted cells in the table differentiate the commitment formulas chosen by each country for its Copenhagen Accord commitment.

Table 3. Ranking of Participants by
Reductions in Emissions Levels

Rank	Change Relative to 1990 Base Year Emissions	Change Relative to 2000 Base Year Emissions	Change Relative to 2005 Base Year Emissions	Change From 2020 BAU Emissions
1	Japan	Japan	Japan	Japan
2	Europe	Europe	Europe	Europe
3	EEFSU	USA	Australia	Australia
4	USA	ROECD	USA/ROECD	USA
5	ROECD	Australia		ROECD
6	Australia	EEFSU	EEFSU	China
7	India	India	India	EEFSU
8	China	China	China	India

These comparative tables indicate that the United States does relatively well on a comparative and absolute basis in its Copenhagen Accord commitment. The United States is in the top half of countries, regardless of what base year is used for comparison.

The United States committed to similar departures from BAU with projected emissions declines by 2020 of 36%, 35%, and 33%, respectively.[31] These are the last quantitative commitments by world nations, because the Paris COP21 commitments were not quantitative on a national basis. China and India are in last position in Table 3, along with the former eastern Soviet Union countries.[32] The different baselines and commitment levels illustrated in the tables above also illustrate the complexity of carbon regulations to implement GHG control.

Table 4 recasts Table 2 data in terms of emissions per unit of GDP, or emissions intensity. Column 4 of Table 4 shows that emissions intensity declines from 2005 to 2020 in all regions in the baseline, with the greatest decline of 37% in Brazil.[33]

---

31. *Id.* at 20, tbl. 3.
32. *Id.* at tbl. 4.
33. *Id.* at tbl. 5.

Table 4. Copenhagen Accord Emissions Commitments in Intensity Terms[34]

Region	Emissions Intensity in 2005 (MMtCO$_2$/ $2006GDP)	Baseline Emissions Intensity in 2020 (MMtCO$_2$/ $2006GDP)	Emissions Intensity in 2020 Under Accord	Percent Change in Intensity From 2005 to 2020 in Baseline	Percent Change in Intensity From 2005 to 2020 Under Copenhagen Accord	Percent Change in 2020 Emissions Intensity Relative to BAU
USA	0.47	0.38	0.26	-18	-44	-31
Japan	0.28	0.27	0.15	-3	-47	-46
Australia	0.56	0.45	0.31	-20	-44	-30
W. Europe	0.27	0.21	0.14	-20	-46	-33
ROECD	0.53	0.38	0.30	-28	-43	-20
China	2.35	1.73	1.41	-26	-40	-18
India	1.40	1.13	1.12	-20	-20	0
EEFSU	1.61	1.20	1.22	-26	-25	2
Brazil	0.40	0.25	0.25	-37	-37	1
LDC	0.76	0.49	0.50	-35	-34	1
OPEC	1.12	0.91	0.98	-18	-12	8
World	0.61	0.58	0.49	-5	-19	-15

Table 5 recasts Table 4 values as per capita values, to take account of the population of each region or country. Even under this measure, Japan, Western Europe, Australia, and the United States lead world nations in demanding the most per citizen for climate control from the BAU scenario. With the exception of China, the developing country commitments are modest or even exacerbate GHG emissions compared to BAU over the next decade.

---

34. *Id.* at 21. The second column in Table 4 is emissions intensity in 2020 in the baseline and the third column is the same measure under the policy scenario. The sixth column of Table 4 shows the percent change in intensities in the policy scenario relative to the 2020 baseline. Boldface numbers represent commitments as articulated in the Copenhagen Accord.

**Table 5. Copenhagen Accord Emissions
Commitments in Per Capita Terms**[35]

Region	Emissions per Capita in 2005	Emissions per Capita in 2020 in Baseline	Emissions per Capita in 2020 Under Accord	Change in 2020 per Capita Emissions Relative to BAU
USA	20	22	15	-33
Japan	10	12	6	-48
Australia	21	23	15	-35
W. Europe	12	14	9	-36
ROECD	18	18	14	-25
China	4	13	10	-22
India	1	2	2	0
EEFSU	11	14	14	-1
Brazil	2	3	3	1
LDC	2	2	2	1
OPEC	8	10	11	1
World	4	7	5	-17

These different relative comparisons under the Copenhagen Accord target levels, intensity, and per capita values are summarized in Table 6. The United States is within 10% of western Europe and Australia.[36] On all absolute and per capita measures, the developed countries are committing to undertake the largest carbon emission reductions among all world countries. Countries not covered by any concrete restriction pursuant to the Kyoto Protocol or the Paris Agreement, developing countries including India, China, and the former Soviet Union countries, are committing to the least reductions under all comparative measures. So this obligates the more affluent countries to greater commitments. However, greater commitments do not necessarily translate to lesser climate vulnerability of all populations. Many of the less developed countries are in more arid zones, on islands, or with populations more vulnerable to dislocations from climate warming. Similarly, the developed countries that are undertaking the largest GHG reductions also experience the largest declines in average annual growth rate, ranging from declines of 0.1 to 0.3 percentage points, with the largest reductions

---

35.   *Id.*
36.   *Id.* at tbl. 6.

in Japan and Western Europe.[37] The decline for the United States is 0.23 percentage points.[38] Therefore, climate justice exhibits many changing factors in a still-to-be-determined warming future.

Table 6. Normalized GHG Reduction Commitment Ranking of Participants

Rank	Change in 2010 Emissions Levels Relative to BAU	Change in 2020 Emissions Intensity Relative to BAU	Change in 2020 per Capita Emissions Relative to BAU
1	Japan	Japan	Japan
2	Europe	Europe	Europe
3	Australia	USA	Australia
4	USA	Australia	USA
5	ROECD	ROECD	ROECD
6	China	China	China
7	EEFSU	India	EEFSU
8	India	EEFSU	India

These commitments of various countries for climate warming mitigation are expressed in different metrics by the pledging nations, which require an independent mediator to translate these into a comparative form. In 2014, the Organisation for Economic Co-operation and Development's (OECD's) Development Assistance Committee (collaborating with multilateral development banks (MDBs) and other international organizations) introduced a cohesive accounting system for bilateral and multilateral public development finance; these reports followed a common reporting format for the first time.[39] To ensure a balanced assessment of climate justice and equity, it is important to account for the emission inputs of all countries to CO_2 concentrations in the atmosphere. It is very difficult for the typical observer to make sense of all the differently expressed commitments unless they are expressed in a common numeric manner. Going forward, these are the critical numbers as to what each nation commits to limiting its warming emissions. The latest agreement was in Paris.

---

37. *Id.* at 27.
38. *Id.*
39. *Id.* Previous reporting and the common tabular formats had no internationally agreed upon definitions and provided no methodology for basic financial reporting. *Id.* at 33. It also did not specify a meaning for the term "climate-specific finance." There has been and is substantial progress towards developing a more global "climate finance" definition.

B.   The 2015 Paris Agreement

Switching now to present tense: the Paris Agreement in December 2015. At a time when there is an imperative to radically and very quickly reduce their carbon emissions, a critical variable is which countries are decreasing their warming emissions and which are not. Developed and developing countries have disagreed as to whether all countries must contribute equally, or each according to its in-country means. To cause developing countries to contribute to emission mitigation to the degree that is necessary, there will need to be new financial mechanisms to redirect adequate capital.

A common way to assess what really happened in Paris regarding climate change is necessary. During the 2015 Paris COP21, the OECD/International Energy Agency Climate Change Expert Group (CCXG), the World Resources Institute (WRI), and the Children's Invest Fund Foundation (CIFF) assessed the COP21 agreements and addressed "the transparency, or measurement, reporting and verification (MRV) framework." The analysis included gaps in the current UNFCCC reporting framework regarding how to achieve a more transparent framework post-2020, how to address gaps in the "verification" of the MRV framework, and how to enhance capacity-building.[40]

The next decade will make or break the now generally recognized necessity to limit increases in average global temperature to no more than 2°C. Figure 1 depicts from which nations of the world CO_2 emissions are estimated to emanate over the next decade in the baseline scenario that expresses BAU under the current patterns of carbon utilization.[41] China is the largest source of projected world emissions, as well as contributing the largest growth of emissions. China is not covered by the Kyoto Protocol or any other international regulation of carbon emissions.[42] Other developing countries also contribute a growing share of increases, as shown in Figure 1. At the margin, these countries contribute substantially to pushing the world over the so-called "tipping point" of unsustainable global warming, from the already high levels of carbon emissions to which the developed countries have significantly contributed over the past century. This will have significant implications for climate justice affecting developing countries.

---

40.   OECD, *COP21 Session—Identifying Gaps in the UNFCCC Reporting Framework*, http://www.oecd.org/environment/cc/cop21session-identifyinggapsintheunfcccreportingframework.htm (last visited Aug. 21, 2016).
41.   *Id.* at 38.
42.   *See* UNFCCC, *Kyoto Protocol, supra* note 13.

Figure 1: Baseline Scenario Fossil CO₂ Emissions[43]

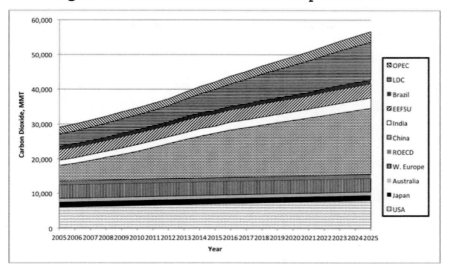

Either carbon regulation imposing enforceable country limits, or a carbon tax, could redirect this warming vector. Figure 2 shows fossil CO_2 emissions by country/region through imposition of a carbon price for emissions (assuming it started in 2012) by Copenhagen Accord participant countries.[44] This figure shows that world emissions would be almost 10,000 MMt CO_2 lower, more than 15%, in 2020 compared to the baseline BAU scenario in Figure 1.[45] Since this assumes that these prices would be imposed only in developed countries pursuant to the Accord, it is those countries where emissions are notably reduced. China and developing countries continue to increase emissions dramatically between the present and 2020 in this model. As noted below, this is a scenario in which the world warms dramatically and climate justice is not furthered. Infusion of capital sources is necessary, as it is critical for targeting and accounting of the use of these funds. This underscores the need for additional and perhaps new institutions and financing that address developing countries' needs and the necessity that they participate in reducing carbon emissions.

---

43.   McKibben, *supra* note 19, at 38.
44.   *Id.* at 41.
45.   *Id.*

Figure 2: Policy Scenario Fossil CO$_2$ Emissions[46]

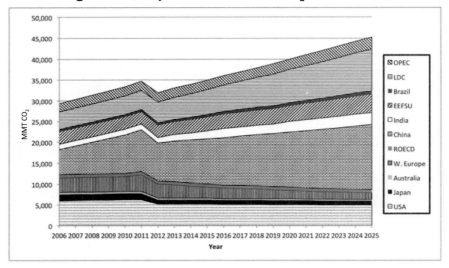

What is the significance going forward of these impacts and commitments in the Copenhagen Accord? The developed nations, under every source of measurement—in absolute terms, in per capita terms, in terms of impact on GDP, and in terms of comparison to BAU scenarios—were undertaking virtually all of the required world GHG reductions into the foreseeable future. This, alone, will not achieve acceptable GHG emission reductions as per international climate agreement requirements.[47] With the burgeoning increase in GHG emissions occurring and forecast in developing countries, they must be involved as part of any solution.[48] Toward this necessity, the Copenhagen Accord committed $30 billion in immediate funds leading to $100 billion per year in additional funding for developing countries' emissions mitigation and adaptation. The Paris Agreement took another step.

Which countries are obligated under the Paris Agreement? Article 2 of the 2015 Paris Agreement establishes a target: "holding the increase in global average temperature to well below 2°C above pre-industrial levels and to pursue efforts to limit temperature increase to 1.5°C." The Paris Agreement calls on all countries to strengthen their pledges to reduce GHG emissions, and to

---

46.   *Id.* at 41.
47.   *See generally* Steven Ferrey, *Cubing the Kyoto Protocol: Post-Copenhagen Regulatory Reforms to Reset the Global Thermostat*, 28 UCLA J. ENVTL. L. & POL'Y 343 (2011).
48.   *Id.*

monitor their progress and report it to the world: "All parties should strive to formulate and communicate long-term low greenhouse gas emission development strategies."[49]

Many countries committed publicly to submit plans of action they intend to take after 2020, called intended nationally determined contributions (INDCs).[50] By June 2016, INDCs from 161 nations had been submitted.[51] Here is the oddity in terms of law: under the Vienna Convention, while the COP21 2015 Paris Agreement is considered an international treaty and has some legal force[52] (even though the Obama Administration did not treat it as a treaty or submit it to the U.S. Senate for ratification), long-term goals and national reporting requirements are legally binding, but the INDC pledges are not.[53] "Under U.S. insistence, the 31-page agreement was explicitly crafted to exclude emissions reductions targets and finance from the legally binding parts of the deal."[54]

Other parts of the agreement, including its five-year review cycles, do carry legal force: "[t]he long term goals and the national reporting requirements are legally binding."[55] Nonetheless, there are no international enforcement mechanisms to penalize any country for noncompliance in its GHG emissions varying from its pledge.[56] However, many domestic laws are binding, and they will become a powerful tool to force early planning, or at least disclosures. Of note, the tables and figures above do not take account of the cost of funding a $100 billion annual contribution to developing countries, which is the other critical pledge.

49. *Adoption of the Paris Agreement*, UNFCC Conference of the Parties, 21st Sess., art. 4, para. 19, U.N. Doc. FCCC/CP/2015/10/Add.1 (Dec. 12, 2015), http://unfccc.int/files/home/application/pdf/paris_agreement.pdf [hereinafter *Paris Agreement*].
50. WRI, *What Is an INDC?*, http://www.wri.org/indc-definition (last visited Aug. 21, 2016).
51. UNFCC, *INDCs as Communicated by Parties*, http://www4.unfccc.int/submissions/indc/Submission%20Pages/submissions.aspx (last visited Aug. 21, 2016).
52. Thomas Day et al., *What the Paris Agreement Means for Global Climate Change Mitigation*, NEW CLIMATE INSTITUTE, Dec. 14, 2015, http://newclimate.org/2015/12/14/what-the-paris-agreement-means-for-global-climate-change-mitigation/.
53. *See id.*
54. *See* Suzanne Goldenberg, *How US Negotiators Ensured Landmark Paris Climate Deal Was Republican-Proof*, THE GUARDIAN, Dec. 13, 2015, http://www.theguardian.com/us-news/2015/dec/13/climate-change-paris-deal-cop21-obama-administration-congress-republicans-environment. The other exclusion zone was any clause in the agreement that would expose the United States to liability and compensation claims for causing climate change.
55. *Id.* On the other hand, national mitigation targets submitted for the post-2020 period as INDCs are not legally binding (the first is written that the countries "shall undertake" these contributions (Article 3); the latter is written as "are to undertake").
56. *Id.*

C.   Financial Demands of the Agreements

I.   The Sources of Finance for Developing Countries

Achieving the goal of the 2015 Paris climate agreement—to limit global warming to 2°C (3.6°F) above pre-industrial levels—would require investment of $12 trillion.[57] Clean energy investments hit a record $329 billion in 2015; investment in wind, solar, and other clean technologies is projected to reach about $7 trillion over the next 25 years.[58] Public and private financing for climate action will need to be scaled up significantly in the near-term years. Building on commitments from the Copenhagen Accord, in the 2015 Paris Agreement developed countries agreed to extend the $100 billion per year financing from 2020 to 2025 at which point a new goal of equal or greater amount will be agreed.[59] Reiterating the pledge made in Copenhagen in 2009, the Cancun Agreements of December 2010 formally commit developed countries to collectively provide resources.[60]

The financial mechanism for this cash flow was established in Paris to provide funds from Parties for developing countries, with more resources allocated to more vulnerable developing country Parties.[61] In the Adoption of the Paris Agreement, the COP decided that the Green Climate Fund (GCF) and the Global Environment Facility (GEF) are entrusted with operating the financial mechanism of the Convention.[62]

GCF is an international climate change fund that will offer loans, concessional loans, grants, and structural insurance to developing countries.[63] More than $10 billion had been pledged to the GCF as of early 2016, mostly from

---

57.   Andrea Vittorio, *Climate Deal Requires Trillions More in Investment*, 47 Env't Rep. (BNA) No. 308 (Jan. 27, 2016).
58.   *Id.*
59.   Han Chen, *Paris Climate Agreement Explained: Climate Finance*, NAT. RESOURCES DEF. COUNCIL, Dec. 12, 2015, http://switchboard.nrdc.org/blogs/hchen/climate_finance_newly_adopted_paris_agreement_cop21.html.
60.   *See* UNFCCC, *Cancun Agreements*, http://cancun.unfccc.int/. The Cancun Agreements mandate that fast-start funds have a "balanced allocation between adaptation and mitigation, are "new and additional, are prioritized for the most vulnerable developing countries, such as the least developed countries, small island developing States and Africa," and include "forestry and investments through international institutions."
61.   UNFCC, *Climate Finance*, http://unfccc.int/cooperation_and_support/financial_mechanism/items/2807.php (last visited Aug. 21, 2016).
62.   *Paris Agreement, supra* note 49, para. 59.
63.   Bill Hinchberger, *100 Billion Questions Remain for the Green Climate Fund*, DEVEX, Oct. 2, 2015, https://www.devex.com/news/100-billion-questions-remain-for-the-green-climate-fund-87039. GCF Executive Director Héla Cheikhrouhou noted that "GCF is the only international financing institution set up with the sole goal of supporting the UNFCCC's objective of keeping global warming below 2 degrees Celsius."

developed nations.[64] While as of October 2015, GCF had received pledges of $10.2 billion, only $5.83 billion had been formally agreed upon and only $852 million had actually been received.[65] The United States alone pledged $3 billion of that, and as of March 2016, the first $500,000 of the four-year, $3 billion dollar pledge was confirmed.

The U.S. pledge to the GCF is part of that broader $100 billion commitment from the group of industrialized nations.[66] The United States committed more than $4.5 billion in bilateral climate finance to its developing country partners and committed $921 million to multilateral climate change funds in the 2013 and 2014 fiscal years.[67] President Obama's fiscal year 2017 budget request also includes what is a down payment on a $30 million climate insurance pledge he made in Paris to convince small island nations to join the global climate deal reached in France.[68] Ten billion was supposed to be collected before the GCF began disbursing funding to mitigation and adaptation projects. The $100 billion annual figure promised by developed countries can come from private sources as well as public sources.[69]

---

64. Dean Scott, *Climate Aid Should Go to Pressing U.S. Needs, Chairman Says*, ENERGY & CLIMATE REP. (BNA), Feb. 13, 2016.

65. Sanjay Kumar, *Green Climate Fund Faces Slew of Criticism*, NATURE, Nov. 20, 2015, http://www.nature.com/news/green-climate-fund-faces-slew-of-criticism-1.18815.

66. Scott, *supra* note 64. Five hundred million of the $750 million in U.S. fast-start funding for FY 2017 as part of the $3 billion pledge to be dispersed through the GCF is requested through the U.S. State Department's FY 2017 budget, while the remaining $250 million is requested by the U.S. Treasury Department. Dean Scott, *Final Obama Budget Seeks $750 Million for Green Climate Fund*, ENERGY & CLIMATE REP. (BNA), Feb. 9, 2016.

67. *Supporting the Global Community: International Climate Finance and Other Activities*, *in* 2016 SECOND BIENNIAL REPORT OF THE UNITED STATES OF AMERICA UNDER THE UNITED NATIONS FRAMEWORK CONVENTION ON CLIMATE CHANGE 40–55 (U.S. Dept. of State 2016), http://unfccc.int/files/national_reports/biennial_reports_and_iar/submitted_biennial_reports/application/pdf/2016_second_biennial_report_of_the_united_states_.pdf.

68. Scott, *supra* note 64. The first-time budget request is $12.5 million, which would fund climate insurance initiatives in Central America and the Caribbean. The funding—included in the FY 2017 budget request for the U.S. State Department, the U.S. Agency for International Development, and other international agencies—would be administered by the World Bank's International Bank for Reconstruction and Development. The U.S. contribution "will support the availability of affordable insurance against natural disaster to as many as six Central American countries and the Dominican Republic, by expanding coverage," which is already being offered under the Caribbean Catastrophic Risk Insurance Facility, according to the U.S. State Department's FY 2017 budget request. One climate insurance approach—the use of parametric insurance, where payments are triggered by an event such as a certain amount of rainfall, as opposed to the economic damages sustained by landowners during severe storms—"can be a sustainable and cost-effective way to increase financial resilience in vulnerable countries," the budget request said.

69. Scott, *supra* note 64.

2.   Accessible Institutional Funds

Recent estimates of current public and private *financing* from developed to developing countries, specifically targeted to mitigation activities, is around $50 billion per year, which accounts for less than one-sixth of public and private financial flows to sectors where investment can lead to GHG emissions reduction.[70] Public *funding* flowing from developed to developing countries for climate change is estimated to be much lower—on the order of $12 billion per year.[71] Of this, funding for adaptation is only a fraction; annual financial flows for adaptation are estimated to be on the order of $100 to $200 million per year forthcoming.[72]

In 1992, public financial flows were greater than private financial flows; however, by 1996, private financial flows were more than five times larger.[73] To date, countries are electing to channel their funding through a mix of existing multilateral, bilateral, and public-private institutions, particularly Climate Investment Funds (CIFs) and GEF, as well as through export credit agencies and other public-private channels, in the form of grants, loans, equity, loan guarantees, and insurance.[74] Different channels and organizational involvement has caused friction to grow over climate change funding.

The OECD provides an up-to-date estimate of public and private climate finance mobilized by developed countries for climate action in developing countries towards their UNFCCC 2010 Cancun commitment. The study estimated public and private finance were at $62 billion in 2014, a step up from the $52 billion dollars in 2013, for an average of $57 billion annually over the 2013/2014 period.[75] Public finance, either bilateral or multilateral in derivation, accounted for more than 70% of these flows during 2013/2014, while mobilized private finance made up more than 25% and export credits constituted the remainder.[76] More than three-quarters of total estimated cli-

---

70.   OECD, Financing Climate Change Action and Boosting Technology Change (2011), http://www.oecd.org/dataoecd/34/44/46534686.pdf (last updated Mar. 10, 2011).

71.   Corfee-Morlot et al., Financing Climate Change Mitigation: Towards a Framework for Measurement, Reporting, and Verification (2009), http://www.oecd.org/environment/cc/44028376.pdf.

72.   *Id.*

73.   WRI, *Climate Finance*, http://www.wri.org/project/international-financial-flows (last visited Aug. 21, 2016).

74.   Clifford Polycarp et al., *Summary of Developed Country "Fast-Start" Climate Finance Pledges, World Resources Institute Working Paper*, http://www.wri.org/publication/summary-of-developed-country-fast-start-climate-finance-pledges (last visited Aug. 21, 2016).

75.   OECD, *Climate Finance in 2013–14 and the USD 100 Billion Goal*, http://www.oecd.org/environment/cc/OECD-CPI-Climate-Finance-Report.htm (last Aug. 21, 2016).

76.   *Id.* The estimates are based on the following sections of public and private finance:
    • Provisional estimates of bilateral public climate finance based on Parties' expected reporting to the UNFCCC;

mate finance was to support mitigation activities, with about one-sixth going to support adaptation and a small share targeting both purposes[77]:

- Bilateral public climate finances are allocated 68% to mitigation, 18% to adaptation, and 14% to both;

- The MDBs allocated 76% of funds to mitigation, 20% to adaptation, and 4% to both;

- Climate funds allotted 69% to mitigation, 29% to adaptation, and 2% to both;

- Export credit agencies gave 100% of funds to mitigation; and

- Private funds distributed 90% of funds to mitigation and 10% to adaptation.[78]

What this says about the flow of funds and climate equity and justice is interesting. To date, the great majority of climate income transfers to developing countries has been devoted to mitigation, and the distinct minority to adaptation purposes. In addition, the multilateral development banks, private nongovernment funds, and national export credit agencies favor to date channeling funds to mitigation activities instead of to adaptation. To some degree this is explained by the fact that export credit agencies support sale of in-country-produced goods and services, which are more likely to be low-carbon-emission technologies, rather than the more amorphous category of adaptation activities for local application. Adaptation activities are more likely to be comprised of domestic civil works, relocation, and alternative arrangements for populations and activities.

Emission mitigation activities contribute to world goals to limit warming. Adaptation does not limit global warming; it assists local populations to adapt to climate change. Both have climate justice implications. Because CO_2 stays in the atmosphere for a century or more, and it is accumulated carbon concentrations rather than current emissions that changes climate, emissions mitigation investment is an investment in the climate status for the next 100 years or more. It benefits all countries.

- Multilateral public climate finance from MDBs and key climate funds that can be attributed to developed countries;
- Climate-related officially supported export credits, predominately to renewable energy, together with supplementary Party reporting.

77. *Id.* Climate change mitigation objectives are reported as 77% of the climate finance amount estimates; adaptation is reported as 16%; activities that target both are given as 7%.

78. *Id.*

Investments in adaptation to assist individual recipient countries has significant appeal to developing countries. There is palpable tension between developed and developing countries in terms of which agencies administer this pledged largest transfer of funds in history, and required accountability for allowed use. These tensions over choice of funding conduits are examined in Part III of this chapter.

The private sector is investing in climate-related green funding. HSBC has predicted $55 billion to $80 billion of green bonds will be issued in 2016; Moody's Corp. said the market for green bonds may exceed $50 billion for the first time this year.[79]

Public finance also can be used as a catalyst to leverage private investments wherever possible. Experience with the GEF funds illustrates that public funds expended as part of climate change mitigation can draw in an additional devotion of seven times that amount of private sector financing, which is made more secure by public sector guarantees and financial risk mitigation.[80] Each of the three mechanisms described below creates multipliers in fostering increased gross carbon financing flows:

- the multilateral development banks[81];

- bilateral risk-mitigating instruments[82]; and

- carbon offsets.[83]

How these funds are moved, and through which international organizations they flow under different respective rules and procedures, is more than mere form when addressing climate change and climate justice. The various international organizations which could administer this largest transfer of wealth in history are substantively different in terms of donor country versus recipient country control and requirements for donee accountability for

---

79. Jessica Shankleman, *Apple's $1.5B Green Bond Seen Spurring Corporate Issuers*, ENERGY & CLIMATE REP. (BNA), Feb. 17, 2016. Despite a record $41 billion of green bonds issued globally in 2015, the rate of growth for corporate green bonds slowed last year to 7% and to 35% in 2014, according to data compiled by the Climate Bonds Initiative.

80. OECD, FINANCING CLIMATE CHANGE ACTION AND BOOSTING TECHNOLOGY CHANGE, *supra* note 70, at 6; JOY AEREE KIM ET AL., LINKING MITIGATION ACTIONS IN DEVELOPING COUNTRIES WITH MITIGATION SUPPORT: A CONCEPTUAL FRAMEWORK (2009), http://www.environmentportal.in/files/linking-mitigation.pdf.

81. *Id.* at 40. MDBs have the capacity to translate one dollar of public capital into up to four dollars of gross lending, and each dollar of lending is estimated to generate three dollars of private capital co-investment, of which approximately 50% is mobilized from international sources.

82. *Id.* Each public dollar invested in such risk mitigation instruments is estimated to generate three dollars of gross international resource flows.

83. *Id.* at 40. At an assumed $25/t carbon price, offset volumes would be approximately 2 billion tons, which generates up to $50 billion in gross flows, crowding in up to $75 billion in additional international private capital investment.

use of funds. Here, the intermediary administrative agencies have different operational elements and rules that can change how climate change funds flow and are allocated. Different choices can affect substantive, as well as mere procedural, impacts. These differences in international organizational procedures and protocols have created tensions between donor and donee countries. The next section examines these key differences and distinctions.

II. Institutions That Control Climate Capital Flow

Funds from developed countries to developing countries can flow through the approved GCF and GEF facilities, or through other institutions, at the donor country's discretion. There are palpable, apparent splits among world nations on how to structure, govern, and fund these major carbon financing agencies, centering around:

- voting control between developed and developing nations;
- funds from public or private sources;
- delivery through new or existing institutions;
- fiduciary obligations and duties imposed for financial management of billions of dollars of financial transfer;
- a single centralized institution or a decentralized approach to fund transfer;
- the role of the UNFCCC institutions; and
- control between donor and recipient countries.

A. Traditional Development Banks and Climate Funding

The decision to employ the MDBs as trustees for the CIFs and other funding mechanisms, as analyzed by the U.S. Congressional Research Service, identifies advantages to using the traditional MDBs as the funding mechanism for international climate change financing.[84] Developed countries tend to favor existing institutions that have in place systems to measure and manage their investments,[85] including commitment to private sector development, capac-

---

84. RICHARD K. LATTANZIO, INTERNATIONAL CLIMATE CHANGE FINANCING: THE CLIMATE INVESTMENT FUNDS (CIFs) (U.S. Congressional Research Service 2013), https://www.fas.org/sgp/crs/misc/R41302.pdf.
85. ATHENA BALLESTEROS ET AL., POWER, RESPONSIBILITY, AND ACCOUNTABILITY: RE-THINKING THE LEGITIMACY OF INSTITUTIONS FOR CLIMATE FINANCE, WORLD RESOURCES INSTITUTE WORKING PAPER 5 (2010), http://www.wri.org/publication/power-responsibility-accountability.

ity to leverage large co-financing arrangements, responsiveness to donor countries, and fiduciary standards and institutional expertise.[86]

The World Bank and other multilateral agencies provide one form of management structure in which donor countries maintain some control over management of activities and funds. The World Bank is administered by a board of governors comprised of 187 countries,[87] along with executive directors.[88] The board of governors[89] consists of one governor and one alternate governor appointed by each Member country. The office is usually held by the country's minister of finance, governor of its central bank, or a senior official of similar rank. The governors and alternates serve for terms of five years and can be reappointed.[90] The executive directors of the World Bank are the top five countries that contribute the most United Nations annual funding.[91] Collectively, these five nations contribute almost two-thirds of all United Nations funding, while only representing 3% of all Member nations.[92] Given that three of these five Members also are Members of the European Union, the nations of the European Union, along with the United States and Japan, contribute almost 80% of total World Bank funding, while these nations constitute only about 15% of total Member nations.[93] In terms of promotion of climate justice, investments by the World Bank require that the funded projects address direct poverty reduction, country fiscal stabilization, governance and private sector development, and environmental sustainability.

The Multilateral Investment Guarantee Agency (MIGA) seeks to foster foreign direct investment (FDI) in developing countries to advance economic growth, decrease poverty, and improve quality of life.[94] The agency's total membership is 174 countries.[95] MIGA provides political risk insurance for projects in developing Member countries, when such investment

---

86. *Id.*

87. World Bank, International Bank for Reconstruction and Development, International Finance Corporation, International Development Association, Governors and Alternates (2016), http://siteresources.worldbank.org/BODINT/Resources/278027-1215526322295/BankGovernors.pdf.

88. World Bank, Executive Directors and Alternates of The World Bank and Their Voting Power (2010), http://siteresources.worldbank.org/EXTANNREP2010/Resources/leadership2_eds-alts.pdf.

89. World Bank, Organization Chart of The World Bank (2013), http://siteresources.worldbank.org/EXTABOUTUS/Resources/bank.pdf.

90. *Id.*

91. *See* World Bank, *Boards of Directors*, http://www.worldbank.org/en/about/leadership/directors#Role_of_the_Executive_Directors (last visited Aug. 21, 2016).

92. *See* Table 1, *supra* (showing the top five country contributions).

93. *Id.* These five nations represent less than 3% of the 196 world nations. *See* Rosenberg, *supra* note 7.

94. MIGA, *Who We Are—Overview*, https://www.miga.org/who-we-are (last visited Aug. 31, 2016).

95. World Bank Group Multilateral Investment Guarantee Agency, 2009 Annual Report (2009), http://www.miga.org/documents/09ar_highlights.pdf.

is made by a Member in another Member's country, or in certain cases an investment made by a national of the host country if the funds originate from outside that country and the host government specifically approves the investment.[96]

The International Financing Corporation (IFC) is the private sector arm of the World Bank Group,[97] which provides assistance in the form of loans, grants, credit guarantees, equity, structured finance, trade finance, and risk management products.[98] IFC's 182 Member countries provide its authorized share of capital of $2.4 billion, collectively determine its policies, and approve investments.[99]

B.   New International Carbon Financing Structures

Critics highlight several criticisms and concerns regarding use of traditional institutions, including a lack of transparency, coordination, "polluter-pays" responsibilities, a potential for new lending conditions or requirements that investments be demonstrated to be "additional," and resulting increased debt burdens on developing countries.[100] A variety of recipient countries, nongovernmental organizations (NGOs), and civil society groups[101] have articulated arguments to not employ the traditional MDBs, or to adapt the CIFs that they currently administer.[102] Developed countries prefer traditional institutions; developing countries are skeptical of these institutions, which are

---

96.   MIGA, *Investment Guarantees—Overview*, https://www.miga.org/investment-guarantees (last visited Aug. 21, 2016).

97.   IFC, PHILANTHROPY AND IFC: PARTNERS IN PRIVATE SECTOR DEVELOPMENT BROCHURE, http://www.ifc.org/ifcext/about.nsf/AttachmentsByTitle/Philanthropy_brochure/$FILE/Philanthropy_brochure.pdf.

98.   IFC, *Financing FAQs*, http://www.ifc.org/wps/wcm/connect/CORP_EXT_Content/IFC_External_Corporate_Site/IFC+Projects+Database/Projects/AIP+Policy+in+Detail/ProjectFAQs (last visited Sept. 8, 2016).

99.   IFC, *Overview*, http://www.ifc.org/wps/wcm/connect/corp_ext_content/ifc_external_corporate_site/about+ifc_new (last visited Sept. 8, 2016).

100.   LATTANZIO, *supra* note 84, at 1.

101.   *Id.* at 13 (citing CELINE TAN, NO ADDITIONALITY, NEW CONDITIONALITY: A CRITIQUE OF THE WORLD BANK'S PROPOSED CLIMATE INVESTMENT FUNDS (Third World Network 2008), http://www.choike.org/documentos/wb_climate_change_celinetan.pdf; SMITA NAKHOODA, CATALYZING LOW-CARBON DEVELOPMENT? THE CLEAN TECHNOLOGY FUND, WRI WORKING PAPER (2009), http://pdf.wri.org/working_papers/development_clean_technology_fund.pdf; *Fuelling Contradictions: The World Bank's Energy Lending and Climate Change*, BRETTON WOODS PROJECT, Apr. 19, 2010, http://www.brettonwoodsproject.org/art-566198. "Additionality" requires screening an application for funding or carbon credits to demonstrate that the investment would not be made under BAU conditions absent the financial incentive provided as part of the program. *See* Steven Ferrey, *When 1 + 1 No Longer Equals 2: The New Math of Legal "Additionality" Controlling World and U.S. Global Warming*, 10 MINN. J.L. SCI. & TECH. 591 (2009); Steven Ferrey, *Post-Copenhagen: The "New" Math, Legal "Additionality," and Climate Warming*, 23 ELECTRICITY J. 6 (2010).

102.   LATTANZIO, *supra* note 84, at 13–15.

structured to reflect donor power. Developing countries prefer new institutions without donor control.[103]

There are various recent operating funding models that take individual country donor dollars and reallocate them to various climate change mitigation or adaptation projects in developing countries. Fund governance can be split between developed and developing countries, or in some instances, with majority control of the fund vested in developing countries. Each of these funds is much smaller in funding than the $100 billion in annual funding pledged in the Copenhagen Accord.[104] These various international funds, and their differences in donor/donee control and decisionmaking in how funds are allocated for climate mitigation and/or equitable climate adaptation and justice, are summarized below.

I. Administered Through Traditional Organizations

Created under the Kyoto Protocol, the Adaptation Fund[105] is funded by an automatic set-aside of 2% of certified emissions reductions (CERs) certified by the Kyoto Protocol Clean Development Mechanism (CDM). It is administered by an adaptation fund board (AFB) of 16 members, with the majority constituted by non-Annex I countries.[106] Therefore, recipient developing countries control the most positions on the AFB. The GEF secretariat serves as the interim secretariat for administrative support."[107]

Since its formation in 1994, the GEF, has served as the *de jure* interim financial mechanism of the UNFCCC, making it the longest serving operating entity of the UNFCCC financial mechanism. GEF is referenced in the Adoption to the Paris Agreement three times. The largest funder of projects to benefit the global environment, GEF has 182 participating countries and is structured as a trust fund that works with three implementing agencies: the United Nations Development Programme (UNDP), the United Nations Environment Programme (UNEP), and the World Bank.[108] It is administered by the assembly of representatives of Member countries and a council

103. BALLESTEROS ET AL., *supra* note 85.
104. UNITED NATIONS SECRETARY-GENERAL, *supra* note 1, at 2.
105. For information about the Adaptation Fund, see UNFCCC, *Adaptation Fund*, http://unfccc.int/cooperation_and_support/financial_mechanism/adaptation_fund/items/3659.php (last visited Aug. 21, 2016).
106. *Id.* Two from each of five United Nations Regional Groups, one from the small island developing States (SIDS), one from an LDC, two from Annex I Parties, and two from non-Annex I Parties.
107. Adaptation Fund, *About the Adaptation Fund*, http://www.adaptation-fund.org/About_(last visited Aug. 21, 2016).
108. The GEF Small Grants Programme, *About GEF*, http://sgp.undp.org/index.cfm?module=ActiveWeb&page=WebPage&s=AboutGEF (last visited Aug. 21, 2016).

with 32 members comprised of 16 from developing countries, 14 from developed countries, and 2 from economies in transition (EITs), acting by double majority vote if no consensus is attained.[109] Therefore, donee countries have half or more of the votes on council decisions.

GEF has total resources after its GEF-5 replenishment of $15.9 billion.[110] In 2010, the GEF funded $8.7 billion in projects through the Trust Fund, the Least Developed Country Fund (LDCF), and Special Climate Change Fund (SCCF), leveraging approximately $33 billion in co-financing.[111] It is funded by donations from 25 developed and 7 developing countries. Funding from the GEF is approximately $401 million, plus $407 million from other partners.[112] GEF administers several special subprograms that can fund climate change mitigation projects, including the Small Grant Program,[113] SCCF,[114] and LDCF.[115]

Backed by the World Bank and GEF, the Global Platform for Sustainable Cities (GPSC) launched a multimillion dollar project to promote sustainable urban development in more than 23 cities around the world. GEF is contributing $151.6 million to the pilot project, which is backed by a number of countries including Brazil, China, India, Mexico, Peru, South Africa, and Vietnam. An additional $1.15 billion is expected from co-financing investment over the next five years.[116] The GEF also has a Small Grants Program (GEF/SGP) the focus of which is on funding local community-based projects and developing grant requests of NGOs, community-based organizations, and academic research organizations.[117]

---

109. *Id.*
110. Smita Nakhooda, Getting to Work: A Review of the Operations of the Clean Technology Fund, WRI Working Paper 2 (2010).
111. *Id.*
112. The GEF Small Grants Programme, *SGP at a Glance*, http://sgp.undp.org/index.cfm?module=Activ eWeb&page=WebPage&s=AboutSGP (last visited Aug. 21, 2016). Grants are channeled directly to community-based organizations and NGOs.
113. *Id.*
114. *See* The GEF, *Special Climate Change Fund (SCCF)*, http://www.thegef.org/gef/SCCF (last visited Aug. 21, 2016).
115. *See* The GEF, *Least Developed Countries Fund (LDCF)*, http://www.thegef.org/gef/LDCF (last visited Aug. 21, 2016).
116. Madeleine Cuff, *World Bank and Global Environment Facility Launch $150m Green Cities Project*, BusinessGreen, Mar. 10, 2016. Municipal leaders with the support of the GPSC will develop urban sustainability indicators and an "evidence-based" approach to urban planning.
117. Kebalepile Phuthego, *Botswana: Environment Facility Uptake Slow*, Daily News, Mar. 8, 2016, http://allafrica.com/stories/201603090031.html.

2.   Administered Through Alternative Governance Structures

Operational in 2014, the GCF was designated as an operating entity of the financial mechanism of the UNFCCC.[118] The GCF is the largest public climate fund in history, with more than $10 billion pledged towards the GCF's initial capitalization by developed and developing countries in 2014.[119] "The GCF will seek to balance its funding between adaptation and mitigation over time, with 50% of the funds, on a grant equivalent basis, dedicated to adaptation, half of which will target developing countries most vulnerable to the adverse effects of climate change."[120]

The COP21 2015 Paris Agreement institutionalizes certain funding mechanisms. First, the GCF enjoys a special, if not absolutely preferred, place in the December 2015 Adoption to the Paris Agreement in which it is referenced three times as a financing source. It directs the GCF to expedite support for the least developed countries' adaptation efforts,[121] for predictable financial resources referencing the GCF only as an example and not as a required funding mechanism,[122] and designates the GCF as one of four financial institutions that will service the convention.[123] The GEF is also referenced in the Adoption to the Paris Agreement three times.

The GCF's board consists of 24 members from developed and developing countries, which were selected by the UNFCCC regional constituencies.[124] Each of the LDCs and small island developing States (SIDS) receive one dedicated seat. The board elects two co-chairs, one from a developing coun-

---

118. *Id.* Its intention is to encourage a change towards low emissions and climate resilient development by supporting developing countries to limit and reduce their GHG emissions and to adapt to climate changes and its impacts.

119. *Id.*

120. *Id.*

121. The Paris Agreement includes: "47. *Further requests* the Green Climate Fund to expedite support for the least developed countries and other developing country Parties for the formulation of national adaptation plans, consistent with decisions 1/CP.16 and 5/CP.17, and for the subsequent implementation of policies, projects and programmes identified by them." *Paris Agreement, supra* note 49, at 7.

122. The Paris Agreement includes:

        55. *Recognizes* the importance of adequate and predictable financial resources . . . while reaffirming the importance of non-carbon benefits associated with such approaches; encouraging the coordination of support from, inter alia, public and private, bilateral and multilateral sources, such as the Green Climate Fund, and alternative sources in accordance with relevant decisions by the Conference of the Parties.

        Paris Agreement, supra note 49, at 8.

123. The Paris Agreement includes: "59. *Decides* that the Green Climate Fund and the Global Environment Facility, the entities entrusted with the operation of the Financial Mechanism of the Convention, as well as the Least Developed Countries Fund and the Special Climate Change Fund, administered by the Global Environment Facility, shall serve the Agreement." *Paris Agreement, supra* note 49, at 8.

124. Green Climate Fund, *Behind The Fund*, http://www.greenclimate.fund/the-fund/behind-the-fund/#management (last visited Aug. 21, 2016).

try and one from a developed country, to each serve a one-year term.[125] Decisions by the board are taken by consensus.[126]

GCF's lack of financial expertise resulted in accrediting 33 entities to assist with financing, ranging from private sector financial institutions, NGOs, United Nations agencies, and national and regional development banks.[127] There are other alternative funding programs.

- **Forest Carbon Partnership Facility (FCPF).**[128] FCPF administers $115 million against a $200 million goal,[129] governed by a Participant Committee of 10 donor countries and 10 recipient country participants, with the World Bank serving as trustee.

- **Climate Investment Funds (CIFs).**[130] CIFs are investment programs administered by the World Bank Group composed of two trust funds:

  - The Clean Technology Fund (CTF)[131] administered by a Trust Fund Committee of eight donor and eight developing country governments[132] (including all eight of the governments contributing funds to the CTF—Australia, France, Germany, Japan, Spain, Sweden, United Kingdom, and United States). Representatives of the World Bank and each of the partnering regional development banks are also represented, but do not vote.[133] Decisions are exercised by con-

125. Climate Funds Update, *Green Climate Fund*, http://www.climatefundsupdate.org/listing/green-climate-fund (last visited Aug. 21, 2016).

126. Green Climate Fund, Rules of Procedure of the Board, www.greenclimate.fund/documents/20182/56440/Rules_of_Procedure.pdf/9d55fae7-f4df-45fe-a3f3-754bc0d98e67.

127. Patrick Goodenough, *Days After $500 Million US Contribution, U.N. Green Climate Fund Increases Staff by 150%*, CNSNews.com, Mar. 14, 2016, http://www.cnsnews.com/news/article/patrick-goodenough/days-after-500000-us-contribution-un-green-climate-fund-increases. There has been criticism that it is extremely difficult for small-scale local projects to receive funding.

128. Benoît Bosquet & Ken Andrasko, Introduction and Early Lessons—Briefing to Guyana Civil Society, Forest Carbon Partnership Facility Management Team (2010), http://www.forestcarbonpartnership.org/fcp/sites/forestcarbonpartnership.org/files/Documents/FCPF_Intro_Early_Lessons_Guyana_Final%20_04-21-10.pdf.

129. Nakhooda, *supra* note 111, at 9.

130. *See* Climate Investment Funds, *Homepage*, http://www-cif.climateinvestmentfunds.org/ (last visited Aug. 21, 2016).

131. Climate Investment Funds, Design Document for the Program of Scaling Up Renewable Energy in Low Income Countries (SREP), A Targeted Program Under the Strategic Climate Fund (2009), http://www.climateinvestmentfunds.org/cif/sites/climateinvestmentfunds.org/files/SREP_design_Document.pdf; Climate Investment Funds, Criteria for Selecting Country and Regional Pilots Under the Program for Scaling Up Renewable Energy in Low Income Countries (2010), http://www.climateinvestmentfunds.org/cif/sites/climateinvestmentfunds.org/files/March_criteria_for_selecting_pilots_SREP_031410.pdf.

132. Represented on the committee, but not participating in funding decisions are the World Bank, IFC, and the MDBs (MDBs include the Asian Development Bank, African Development Bank, European Bank for Reconstruction and Development, and Inter-American Development Bank).

133. Nakhooda, *supra* note 111, at 4.

sensus.[134] The CTF trustee is the World Bank—which holds in trust, as the legal owner and administrator, the funds, assets, and receipts that constitute the trust fund, pursuant to the terms entered into with the contributors. CTF earmarked $4.35 billion to support investment plans in 12 countries.[135]

- The Strategic Climate Fund (SCF),[136] overseen by a SCF Trust Fund Committee composed of eight representatives of contributor countries plus eight recipient countries, a representative of the World Bank, and one representative for the other MDBs. It is actually a suite of three separate funds:

  - The Pilot Program for Climate Resilience (PPCR),[137] which as of spring 2011 had pledges of $987 million, $615 million of which was grant contributions, with the remaining $372 million going toward capital contributions.[138] It is governed by six donor countries and an equal number of recipient countries selected on a regional basis.[139]

  - The Forest Investment Program (FIP),[140] with governance equally split between donors and recipients, with decisionmaking by consensus.[141] As of spring 2011, the pledging level to the FIP was $577 million, $404 million of which was provided in the form of grant contributions, with the remaining $173 million provided as capital contributions.[142]

---

134. *Id.* at 9.
135. *Id.*
136. *Id.*
137. Climate Investment Funds, *Strategic Climate Fund*, http://www.climateinvestmentfunds.org/cif/node/3 (last visited Aug. 21, 2016).
138. Climate Investment Funds, Semi-annual Report on PPCR Operations 3 (2011), http://www.climateinvestmentfunds.org/cif/sites/climateinvestmentfunds.org/files/PPCR%209%20Semi-Annual%20Operational%20Report.pdf.
139. Climate Investment Funds, *Pilot Program for Climate Resilience Sub-Committee*, http://www-cif.climateinvestmentfunds.org/about/committee-governance #ppcr (last visited Aug. 21, 2016).
140. Climate Investment Funds, Design Document for the Program of Scaling up Renewable Energy in Low Income Countries (SREP), A Targeted Program Under the Strategic Climate Fund, *supra* note 132; Climate Investment Funds, Criteria for Selecting Country and Regional Pilots Under the Program for Scaling Up Renewable Energy in Low Income Countries (2010), http://www.climateinvestmentfunds.org/cif/sites/climateinvestmentfunds.org/files/March_criteria_for_selecting_pilots_SREP_031410.pdf; Bosquet & Andrasko, *supra* note 129.
141. Climate Investment Funds, *Forest Investment Program Sub-Committee*, http://www-cif.climateinvestmentfunds.org/about/committee-governance#fip (last visited Aug. 21, 2016).
142. Climate Investment Funds, Semi-Annual Report on FIP Operations 3 (2011), http://www.climateinvestmentfunds.org/cif/sites/climateinvestmentfunds.org/files/FIP%203%20Semi-Annual%20Operational%20Report%2067.pdf.

- The Scaling Up Renewable Energy Program in Low Income Countries (SREP),[143] which as of fall 2011 had $352 million pledged for grants and concessional loans for deployment of proven "new" renewable energy technologies.[144] Governance is from up to six donor countries with an equal number of recipient countries.[145]

Each of the CIFs is governed by a Trust Fund Committee composed of 16 participants, with an equal number of representatives of donor governments and developing country governments. Decisions are taken by consensus. Donor countries had pledged $6.1 billion to the funds since September 2008 from 13 of the world's largest donors, administered through multilateral channels.[146]

The differences in membership and governance of these various international climate funding mechanisms make a difference in how funds are directed and monitored. There has occurred since the Copenhagen COP conference a visible split of opinions between donor and donee countries as to which mechanisms each wishes to employ. The Paris Agreement mentions GEF and GCF as identified funding mechanisms, but does not require all, or for that matter any, funds donated for climate mitigation, adaptation, or climate justice to flow through these particular channels. As yet, there is no agreed form for accounting and monitoring contributions to developing countries. Because the Kyoto Protocol, the Copenhagen Accord, and the Paris Agreement each operates without sanctions and are unenforceable, nations are free to count, direct, and monitor their donated funds in any manner, if and until more specifications are agreed by world nations.

There are many examples of this lack of a common modality and resultant friction in how the funds flow for climate mitigation, adaptation, and equity. China had pledged $3.1 billion in bilateral climate finance flowed through South-South Climate Finance (SSCF), the Asian Infrastructure Investment Bank (AIIB), and the New Development Bank (BRICS Bank).[147] Xie Zhenhua, vice chairman of China's National Development and Reform Commission, stated that China had no intention of putting

---

143. Climate Investment Funds, *Funds & Programs: SREP—Scaling Up Renewable Energy Program*, http://www-cif.climateinvestmentfunds.org/fund/scaling-renewable-energy-program (last visited Aug. 21, 2016).

144. Climate Funds Updates, *Scaling Up Renewable Energy Program for Low Income Countries*, http://www.climatefundsupdate.org/listing/scaling-up-renewable-energy-program (last visited Aug. 21, 2016).

145. Climate Investment Funds, *Scaling Up Renewable Energy Program Sub-Committee*, http://www-cif.climateinvestmentfunds.org/about/committee-governance#srep (last visited Aug. 21, 2016).

146. NAKHOODA, *supra* note 111, at 2. The U.S. pledge is $2 billion.

147. Sangjung Ha et al., *After Paris, It's "All Hands on Deck" for Climate Finance*, GLOBAL POL'Y, Feb. 12, 2016, http://www.globalpolicyjournal.com/blog/12/02/2016/after-paris-it%E2%80%99s-%E2%80%9Call-hands-deck%E2%80%9D-climate-finance.

money into the GCF because that fund is for developed countries to fund. Many developing countries have expressed concern with the World Bank's role in the GCF: Brazil prefers China's SSCF model, which will use the new AIIB and BRICS Bank institutions.[148] The Climate Policy Initiative (CPI) estimated that South-South cross-border climate finance reached $10 billion in 2013, which is as much as 30% of the climate finance mobilized from public and private sources in developed countries for developing countries in the same period ($34 billion), and 10% of total climate finance flows globally ($331 billion).[149]

III.   The Critical Nature of the International Financial Conduit

The current need for climate change international capital flows to support current climate needs is different in design and function than traditional foreign aid that is provided for multiple purposes. These past capital flows have sometimes been diverted, and there is particular concern about the same happening with climate change funding.[150] There are many reports of donor countries freezing tens and hundreds of billions of dollars in financial accounts associated with countries in political transitions.[151] When bilateral aid is diverted within a recipient country from one beneficiary to another, it may still achieve its general objective of helping development.

Climate change funding, because it serves an urgent international objective to physically arrest climate warming, cannot be subject to fund diversion among effective and ineffective projects. There is also the need to support climate justice in how these funds are allocated and used. More than just national development is involved with carbon financing. Limiting global warming to a no more than 2°C increase from pre-Industrial Revolution levels will require stabilizing CO_2 concentrations in the atmosphere to no more than 450 ppm.[152]

---

148. Lisa Friedman, *China Launches Separate International Climate Aid Fund and Sparks "Interesting" Politics*, EENEWS.NET, Dec. 9, 2014, http://www.eenews.net/stories/1060010175.

149. *See* Sangjung Ha et al., *Climate Finance in and Between Developing Countries: An Emerging Opportunity to Build On*, 7 GLOBAL POL'Y 102 (2016), http://onlinelibrary.wiley.com/doi/10.1111/1758-5899.12293/epdf.

150. *See* Transparency International, Climate Change, https://www.transparency.org/topic/detail/climate_chang (last visited Sept. 18, 2018).

151. Deborah Ball & Cassell Bryan-Low, *Swiss Banks Scrutinise Regimes' Assets*, WALL ST. J., Feb. 13, 2011, *reprinted in* FIN. TIMES, http://www.efinancialnews.com/story/2011-02-23/swiss-banks-freeze-assets; Helene Cooper, *U.S. Freezes a Record $30 Billion in Libyan Assets*, N.Y. TIMES, Feb. 28, 2011, http://www.nytimes.com/2011/03/01/world/africa/01assets.html.

152. *See* STEVEN FERREY, ENVIRONMENTAL LAW: EXAMPLES & EXPLANATIONS 235 (5th ed. 2010). At such modest levels, the degree of warming is not expected to result in radical loss of ice sheets, sea-level

Therefore, climate funding must ensure that donated expenditures yield absolute physical results, and that there is no deviation, displacement, or so-called "leakage" of carbon generation from one source or region to another.[153] An official with the Intergovernmental Panel on Climate Change (IPCC) concluded that developed nations will need to slash CO_2 emissions almost entirely by 80–90% by 2050 to hold GHGs to 450 ppm in the atmosphere.[154] Complicating this reality, CO_2 lingers in the atmosphere, thus causing concentrations to hold steady for decades,[155] perhaps even hundreds of years.[156] Within a century, if all nations of the world do not significantly limit their GHG emissions, "the average global temperature will climb anywhere from 1.4° to 5.8° Celsius" (or 2.5° to 10°F).[157] This will require a sharp reduction of emissions over the next generation, and to "near zero by 2100."[158]

Precise targeting and accountability of international fund use is important in climate change funding to a degree not experienced in many other kinds of traditional lending and grants. Unless used precisely for the intended projects and accounted for, not only will internal country welfare be affected, but world welfare may be irreversibly altered. The urgent and interdependent nature of the problem has implications for how international climate aid is managed and channeled. Developing countries are at the forefront of this challenge because they are expected to add around 80% of all new electric generation capacity and GHG emissions worldwide in the next two decades.[159] The correct institutions are necessary for distribution and

---

rise, and shift of agricultural areas.

153. Carbon "leakage" is the ability of carbon emitting activities to relocate from a country or region within a country in which they are regulated, taxed, or restricted, to another country or region in which their emissions are not regulated and where they can operate at lower cost. Thereafter, their product can be shipped to world markets. Leakage has been a concern in U.S. carbon markets in California and in the Regional Greenhouse Gas Initiative, as well as in Europe. *See* Steven Ferrey, *Carbon Outlasts the Law: States Walk the Constitutional Line*, 41 B.C. Envtl. Aff. L. Rev. 309 (2014); Rocío Hiraldo & Thomas Tanner, The Global Political Economy of REDD+: Engaging Social Dimensions in the Emerging Green Economy, U.N. Research Institute for Social Development (2011), http://www.unrisd.org/80256B3C005BCCF9/%28LookupAllDocumentsByUNID%29/B0B96C3 130210583C12579760057FA24?OpenDocument.

154. Steven Ferrey, *The Failure of International Global Warming Regulation to Promote Needed Renewable Energy*, 37 B.C. Envtl. Aff. L. Rev. 67, 72 (2010) (citing Rick Mitchell, *IPCC Official Says Industrialized Nations Must Cut Emissions Up to 95 Percent*, 39 Env't Rep. (BNA) No. 1917 (2008)).

155. National Academies of Science et al., Understanding and Responding to Climate Change 16 (2006).

156. *See* Solomon et al., *supra* note 2 (noting that CO_2 warming impacts could last 1,000 years or more).

157. Climate Change 2007: Impacts, Adaptation, and Vulnerability. Contribution of Working Group II to the Fourth Assessment Report of the Intergovernmental Panel on Climate Change 45, tbl. 3.1 (Martin Parry et al. eds. 2007).

158. Michael MacCracken, *Prospects for Future Climate Change and the Reasons for Early Action*, 58 J. Air & Waste Mgmt. Ass'n 735, 735 (2008).

159. Lutz Weischer et al., Grounding Green Power: Bottom-Up Perspectives on Smart Renewable Energy Policy in Developing Countries 1 (WRI 2011), http://www.wri.org/sites/default/

management of these funds to achieve the most long-term lifecycle efficient means to ensure that cost-effective projects are funded to limit additional carbon emissions.

International structure and accountability matter. To be successful in limiting severe climate change, every country needs to turn the energy generation base to more renewable sources of electric power and more sustainable solutions. Therefore, it matters that international capital flows designed to mitigate GHG emissions effectively find their targeted applications. This pledged climate change aid is of unprecedented amounts, scope, and duration: $100 billion in annual capital flow commitment is unprecedented in size. In duration, the problem of climate change shows every sign of being a long-term international issue for many decades to come, with warming gases, once emitted, lasting from 100 to several thousand years.[160]

The financial mechanism for the 2015 Paris COP Agreement does not cover the entire inflow and outflow of the $100 billion in annual funding, which can proceed, at donor discretion, through bilateral and multilateral channels. Different developed and BRIC donor nations seem to prefer different institutions to handle their contributions. Form matters. The devil is in the details.

Conclusion

Form matters. The flow of money between nations is and will remain a critical part of the carbon equation. For addressing climate change in real time, the amount of money pledged exceeds all other transfers of wealth in human history. However, there is not much time in which to accomplish a feasible, but nonetheless Herculean, task. Correctly applied, mitigation funds will minimize future climate change; adaptation funds can save populations and economies at risk, and promote greater climate justice.

But of almost equal importance to the commitment of unprecedented amounts of capital are the international institutions through which this money is channeled and dispersed. Unlike many types of traditional international financial aid, these funds must be immediately devoted effectively to specific aspects of warming mitigation, adaptation, and justice, to be part of an effective solution. If not carefully managed to do so, the repercussions are severe for all populations in the world.

---

files/grounding_green_power.pdf.
160. *See* Solomon et al., *supra* note 2.

A rift has emerged between developed donor countries of climate financing, and developing recipient countries of financing, through which mechanisms these funds will be transferred. These disagreements include control over the funding agency, monitoring, and requirements for accountability in the expenditure of funds. While the 2015 Paris Agreement identifies the GEF and GCF as authorized conduits for these funds, there is no requirement in the Paris Agreement or prior international climate agreements that donor countries utilize these mechanisms. Many aspects and requirements for financing are still under discussion in the wake of the Paris Agreement. These are critical decisions, which have become more political with each passing year approaching the 2020 threshold for this funding of $100 billion annually in transfers to developing countries to address climate change. Although not the issues about climate that are in current headlines, these are critical decisions that will determine the future of the earth's environment and climate justice on the earth.

Chapter 4

Energy Access, Climate Justice, and Financing Innovation

Ara Azad and Ava Azad[*]

* *The authors would like to thank Ryan Pfaff for his helpful review of this chapter. This chapter was prepared by the authors in their personal capacities. The opinions expressed in this chapter are solely those of the authors, and do not reflect the views of the U.S. Environmental Protection Agency or the U.S. government.*

Introduction

The field of climate justice provides a forum to evaluate the global inequalities resulting from historic contributions to and current and projected effects of climate change. It is widely recognized that some nations and private actors are more responsible for human-induced climate change than others.[1] Climate change equity discussions primarily focus on how to take these unequal contributions into account in determining who shall pay to mitigate the harms caused, and who, if anyone, will be subsidized in combating climate change impacts.

The concept of developed and developing nations' differing historical contributions and future responsibilities was a focus of the discussions at the December 2015 Paris Climate Conference—the 21st Conference of the Parties (COP21) of the United Nations Framework Convention on Climate Change (UNFCCC).[2] The UNFCCC recognized this idea of "common but differentiated" responsibilities and capabilities of developed versus developing countries as far back as 1992, five years before adoption of the Kyoto Protocol.[3]

As land dries, seas rise, and storms cause devastation, developing countries—historically poor and some only recently experiencing economic growth—face great economic challenges in restoring their communities in response to these acts of nature. Environmental concerns are especially daunting for these nations as they must simultaneously tend to the separate but related task of continuing to develop their economies, communities, and governments so that their citizens can enjoy privileges that citizens of developed nations have experienced for years.[4]

---

1. *See generally* Hans-Martin Füssel, *How Inequitable Is the Global Distribution of Responsibility, Capability, and Vulnerability to Climate Change: A Comprehensive Indicator-Based Assessment*, 20 GLOBAL ENVTL. CHANGE 597 (2010) (finding a "double inequity" between responsibility for climate change on the one hand and capability to combat climate change and vulnerabilities to food security, human health, and coastal populations on the other); John Crump, *Snow, Sand, Ice, and Sun: Climate Change and Equity in the Arctic and Small Island Developing States*, 8 SUSTAINABLE DEV. L. & POL'Y 8 (2008) (discussing the disproportionate impacts of climate change on the Arctic and small island developing States despite their limited contributions to anthropogenic climate change); FAIRNESS IN ADAPTATION TO CLIMATE CHANGE (W. Neil Adger et al. eds., 2006) (discussing global fairness considerations in addressing climate change).
2. European Commission, *Climate Action—Paris Agreement*, http://ec.europa.eu/clima/policies/international/negotiations/paris/index_en.htm (last visited Aug. 21, 2016).
3. UNITED NATIONS, UNITED NATIONS FRAMEWORK CONVENTION ON CLIMATE CHANGE (1992) (U.N. Doc. FCCC/INFORMAL/84), https://unfccc.int/resource/docs/convkp/conveng.pdf.
4. *See* Alefu Chinasho, *Challenges and Opportunities to the Adaptation and Mitigation of Climate Change in Developing Countries: Review*, 6 AM. J. SOC. & MGMT. SCI. 34 (2015), http://scihub.org/media/pdf/2016/02/AJSMS-6-2-34-39.pdf.

Access to energy is one of the most fundamental benefits that developed countries have made universal and that developing countries strive to make universal.[5] Not only does energy access provide for greater comfort and convenience by, for example, allowing people to control household temperatures and use time-saving appliances, it also equips those who have it with greater opportunities for professional and personal success. One significant example of this is students' ability to continue their studies after sunset with the availability of electricity.[6] The potential for success in education feeds one's potential for greater professional opportunities, achieving intellectual potential, increased feelings of satisfaction and self-worth, and adopting a lifestyle choice that translates to fewer births per family, which ultimately mitigates the dilemma of providing energy access to a growing human population.[7]

Anthropogenic climate change and the urgent need to address its consequences are all but accepted, as evidenced most recently by COP21, during which 195 countries adopted the first-ever[8] universal global climate deal.[9] The undeniable value of access to energy is also relatively uncontroversial.[10] Discrepancy and controversy arise where these two issues intersect.[11] While

5. *E.g.*, Gwénaëlle Legros et al., The Energy Access Situation in Developing Countries: A Review Focusing on the Least Developed Countries and Sub-Saharan Africa (World Health Organization & United Nations Development Programme 2009), http://www.undp.org/content/dam/undp/library/Environment%20and%20Energy/Sustainable%20Energy/energy-access-situation-in-developing-countries.pdf; World Bank, *Access to Electricity (% of Population)*, http://data.worldbank.org/indicator/EG.ELC.ACCS.ZS?end=2012%start=2012%view=bar (last visited Aug. 21, 2016); International Energy Agency, *Energy Access Database* (stating "95% of those living without electricity are in countries in sub-Saharan Africa and developing Asia"), http://www.worldenergyoutlook.org/resources/energydevelopment/energyaccessdatabase/ (last visited Aug. 21, 2016).

6. United Nations Department of Economic and Social Affairs, Electricity and Education: The Benefits, Barriers, and Recommendations for Achieving the Electrification of Primary and Secondary Schools 9 (2014), https://sustainabledevelopment.un.org/content/documents/1608Electricity%20and%20Education.pdf.

7. United Nations Educational, Scientific, and Cultural Organization, Fact Sheet: Girls' Education—The Facts (2013), http://en.unesco.org/gem-report/sites/gem-report/files/girls-factsheet-en.pdf.

8. While the 1997 Kyoto Protocol was the first international agreement to reduce greenhouse gas (GHG) emissions, developing countries were essentially exempt from its targets. UNFCCC, *Kyoto Protocol*, http://unfccc.int/kyoto_protocol/items/2830.php (last visited Aug. 21, 2016). While 37 industrialized countries and the European community committed to reducing GHG emissions in the first commitment period of Kyoto, the 195 countries that came together to adopt the Paris Agreement in 2015 included developing as well as developed nations, making this the first universal global climate deal.

9. *Adoption of the Paris Agreement*, UNFCC Conference of the Parties, 21st Sess., U.N. Doc. FCCC/CP/2015/L.9/ (2015), https://unfccc.int/resource/docs/2015/cop21/eng/l09.pdf.

10. *E.g.*, Adrian J. Bradbrook & Judith G. Gardam, *Placing Access to Energy Services Within a Human Rights Framework*, 28 Hum. Rts. Q. 389 (2006); Stephen Tully, *The Human Right to Access Electricity*, 19 Electricity J. 30 (2006).

11. *See* Amie Gaye, Access to Energy and Human Development, United Nations Development Programme 12–13 (2007) (arguing that, "While fossil fuel use, exploration, transportation, transformation and distribution have detrimental effects on the world's atmosphere, any strategies to deal

climate justice is often used to frame the fact that those least responsible for climate change will suffer the worst of its environmental consequences, another manifestation of climate injustice is the fact that those least responsible for climate change are now at risk of suffering the worst of its economic and political consequences. To ensure comprehensive climate justice, it is critical to avoid creating a socioeconomic justice problem for those same marginalized communities unable to deal with climate change environmentally by also preventing them from gaining access to energy.

Developing countries are those with the highest number of citizens without access to energy.[12] In working to provide energy to their citizens, many of these nations continue to rely heavily on fossil fuels.[13] At a time when the global community has agreed to reduce greenhouse gas (GHG) emissions, this means that these developing countries are actually on track to *increase* their GHG emissions.[14]

The continued reliance on fossil fuels is not only disconcerting because it perpetuates the cycle of global anthropogenic climate change, but also because of its heavy impact on local and national communities. Major sources of GHG emissions, such as coal-fired power plants, are also the sources of other air pollutants like particulate matter, which contribute to health problems.[15] Consequently, geographical areas with the highest GHG emission contributors are also the areas in which populations suffer most from the negative health consequences of poor air quality. According to the World Health Organization (WHO), in 2012, 3.7 million deaths worldwide were "attributable to ambient air pollution." Note also that 88% of these deaths occurred in low- and middle-income countries,[16] with 12 of the 25 cities with the worst air quality located in India.[17] An urban air pollution study released by the WHO in 2016 found that while 56% of cities in high-income

---

with climate change should not limit the developing countries' quest to meet their basic energy needs for development and poverty reduction."), http://citeseerx.ist.psu.edu/viewdoc/download?doi=10.1.1.422.3937&rep=rep1&type=pdf.

12. *See supra* note 5 and accompanying text.

13. GLOBAL CCS INSTITUTE, THE GLOBAL STATUS OF CCS 2015 SUMMARY REPORT 3 (2015), https://hub.globalccsinstitute.com/sites/default/files/publications/196843/global-status-ccs-2015-summary.pdf.

14. U.S. ENERGY INFORMATION ADMINISTRATION, INTERNATIONAL ENERGY OUTLOOK (2016) (emphasis added), http://www.eia.gov/forecasts/ieo/pdf/exec_summ.pdf.

15. WORLD HEALTH ORGANIZATION, FREQUENTLY ASKED QUESTIONS: AMBIENT AND HOUSEHOLD AIR POLLUTION AND HEALTH 1 (2014), http://www.who.int/phe/health_topics/outdoorair/databases/faqs_air_pollution.pdf?ua=1.

16. *Id.* at 1–2. The WHO acknowledges in the same document other factors that could contribute to outdoor air pollution deaths, including smoking, unhealthy diet, and lack of physical activity. *Id.* at 3.

17. WHO, *WHO Global Urban Ambient Air Pollution Database (Update 2016)*, http://www.who.int/phe/health_topics/outdoorair/databases/cities/en/ (last visited Aug. 21, 2016).

countries with 100,000 or more inhabitants did not meet the WHO's air quality guidelines, in cities of low- and middle-income countries, 98% did not meet those guidelines.[18] Not only are the poorest nations least capable of implementing climate change adaptation measures, the sources of their GHG emissions also compound the harm by threatening the health of their human and animal populations in addition to their environments.

The same problem exists in the opposite context where developing countries' residents are energy poor.[19] Such populations that do not have access to modern energy predominately rely on biomass for household fuel.[20] Burning biomass in the home leads to high levels of indoor air pollution and associated health concerns.[21] This results in a complex, nation-specific, yet global justice and climate change problem.[22]

The question then becomes how to guarantee reliable energy access to those who desire it while realistically promoting reduced reliance on fossil fuels and reduced GHG emissions. The answer is that developed countries must financially support the development of technologies that make energy production clean and affordable. This response reflects the historical inequities underpinning actual climate change contributions and couples it with the near universal consensus in favor of a more equitable distribution of burdens and responsibilities. Achieving this balance may come through innovations in renewable energy production, but more practically would be through innovations in "clean" fossil fuel use, given that the latter continues to be a more affordable option for developing nations.

The current dilemma is that the international community expects developed nations, which are independently moving away from fossil fuels and toward renewable energy, to continue to invest in fossil fuels for the sake of developing countries and the world at large.[23] Increasingly stringent envi-

---

18. Press Release, WHO, *Air Pollution Levels Rising in Many of the World's Poorest Cities* (May 12, 2016), http://www.who.int/mediacentre/news/releases/2016/air-pollution-rising/en/.

19. "Energy poverty" is defined as the "inability to cook with modern cooking fuels and the lack of a bare minimum of electric lighting to read or for other household and productive activities at sunset." GAYE, *supra* note 11, at 4.

20. *Id.*

21. *See* Duncan G. Fullerton et al., *Indoor Air Pollution From Biomass Fuel Smoke Is a Major Health Concern in the Developing World*, 102 TRANSACTIONS ROYAL SOC'Y TROPICAL MED. & HYGIENE 843 (2008); GAYE, *supra* note 11, at 6–7.

22. *See* FREQUENTLY ASKED QUESTIONS, *supra* note 15, at 3 ("Public health recognizes air pollution as an important determinant of health. Today this is especially the case in developing countries where exposure to air pollution is now higher than in developed countries, where mitigation measures led to reductions in exposure. There is significant inequality in the exposure to air pollution and related health risks: air pollution combines with other aspects of the social and physical environment to create a disproportional disease burden in less affluent parts of society.").

23. GLOBAL CCS INSTITUTE, *supra* note 13, at 3.

ronmental regulations and the environmental component of climate justice are pushing these nations in one direction, while ideals of equal access to energy and the economic component of climate justice push them in another. To add to the complications, wherever the investments are initiated—the government, energy companies, other private companies—those ultimately paying the price for technology development projects will be the citizens of developed countries—taxpayers, ratepayers, customers, and investors. Thus, as is the issue on a global scale, low-income and marginalized communities within developed countries will have to bear some of the burden of enabling climate justice globally.

Determining the most effective manner by which developed countries may fulfill their ethical and political obligations to fund clean energy development globally requires careful consideration of the legal, economic, and practical limitations embedded in this complex equation. This chapter presents these limitations and the corresponding issues of justice in the context of comparing developed nations and developing nations, their respective energy market histories, and their anticipated futures. Part I discusses developed nations with a focus on the United States, given its immense historical carbon footprint and robust environmental regulations. Part II addresses developing nations with a focus on India and China, in light of their key roles as fossil-fuel-reliant developing countries, and their commitments and efforts to reduce GHG emissions to date. Part III proposes that the most promising options for the future should involve a significant shift in energy subsidization in developed countries toward renewable energy, increasing research and development for cleaner fossil fuel energy, a stronger push toward private-public partnerships, and developed countries' fostering of an autonomous-yet-accountable application of clean energy funds by developing nations.

I. Developed Countries

A. High Historical Climate Change Contributions

Beginning with their industrialization in the 1800s, developed countries have contributed far more than an equitable share to total global carbon emissions.[24] National historical emissions data from 1750 to 2010 illustrate that until about the 1950s, the United States and European countries (and Japan to a lesser degree) were the sole significant contributors to global GHG emissions.[25] Other

---

24. FAIRNESS IN ADAPTATION TO CLIMATE CHANGE viii (W. Neil Adger et al. eds., 2006).
25. CARBON DIOXIDE INFORMATION ANALYSIS CENTER, NATIONAL CO_2 EMISSIONS FROM FOSSIL-FUEL BURNING, CEMENT MANUFACTURE, AND GAS FLARING: 1751–2013 (2016), http://cdiac.ornl.gov/

countries (with China contributing the most) have only begun to significantly contribute over the last three decades.[26] Emissions have increased drastically over the past 15 years as emerging economies have begun to grow.[27]

According to the PBL Netherlands Environmental Assessment Agency (NEAA), regional GHG emissions from the last two decades provide the most telling information about the varying contributions to climate change.[28] Taking a broader look, the NEAA shows that the United States and Europe rank first and second, respectively, in their contributions to climate change when compared to other contributors from 1850 and projected to 2030.[29] In accordance with their heightened responsibility for climate change, developed nations have also been the leaders in shifting laws and technologies away from energy production that results in high GHG emissions and toward cleaner energy sources.[30] The following section describes in detail the trajectory of this shift in the United States specifically.

B. Outlook on Political and Economic Shift Away From Traditional Fossil Fuel Reliance

In May 2016, the U.S. Energy Information Administration (EIA) reported that energy-related carbon dioxide (CO_2) emissions in the United States in 2015 were 12% below 2005 levels.[31] These emissions reductions are the result of a shifting electric power sector,[32] in which the use of coal is steadily declining while its competitors enjoy growing market shares. As the greatest source of CO_2 emissions in the electricity sector, the focus on coal as the major culprit of the group is a predictable policy reaction from climate change-concerned citizens and government actors.

According to an April 2016 report by the EIA, the consumption of coal to generate electricity fell 29% in the United States from its peak in 2007

ftp/ndp030/nation.1751_2013.ems.

26. *Id.*
27. *Id.*
28. *See* Michel G.J. den Elzen et al., *Countries' Contributions to Climate Change: Effect of Accounting for All Greenhouse Gases, Recent Trends, Basic Needs, and Technological Progress*, 121 CLIMATIC CHANGE 397 (2013), http://www.pbl.nl/en/publications/countries-contributions-to-climate-change.
29. *Id.*
30. *See infra* section I.B.
31. Perry Lindstrom (principal contributor), *U.S. Energy-Related Carbon Dioxide Emissions in 2015 Are 12% Below Their 2005 Levels*, U.S. ENERGY INFO. ADMIN., May 9, 2016, http://www.eia.gov/todayinenergy/detail.cfm?id=26152.
32. In 2015 in the United States, coal accounted for 71% of total CO_2 emissions from the national electric power sector. U.S. ENERGY INFORMATION ADMINISTRATION, *Frequently Asked Questions—How Much of U.S. Carbon Dioxide Emissions Are Associated With Electricity Generation?*, http://www.eia.gov/tools/faqs/faq.cfm?id=77&t=11 (last visited Aug. 21, 2016).

to 2015.[33] Considering that electricity generation accounts for 97% of the steam coal market, a 29% drop signifies nearly a one-third reduction in total coal consumption.[34] While six states accounted for nearly half the overall decline, coal consumption fell in every state except Nebraska and Alaska.[35] The EIA reported that the largest declines occurred in the Midwest and Southeast, followed by the Rocky Mountain region.[36] The report cites significant increases in electricity generation from natural gas, wind, and solar power as the catalysts for coal's decline, and specifically mentions federal tax credits and state-level mandates for wind and solar energy as key drivers of the success of those fuel sources.[37]

As the EIA report and legal realities in the United States demonstrate, the industry is guided, in no small part, by state and federal laws. Policy shifts in the legislative arena[38] translate into support for certain industry players by way of tax incentives, but can also give rise to restrictive regulations that seek to protect the public interest. In the United States, both sides of the regulatory coin have had a profound effect on the energy market.

A number of existing and proposed Clean Air Act (CAA) environmental regulations from the U.S. Environmental Protection Agency (EPA) have and will continue to shape the progression of the electric utility sector in the United States. One such initiative, EPA's now-infamous Clean Power Plan (CPP), aims to reduce CO_2 emissions from existing power plants in the utility power sector to 32% below 2005 levels by 2030.[39] Together with EPA, states are to establish plans to achieve CO_2 emissions performance rates for the power plants within that state, as established in the CPP, using the best system of emission reduction (BSER).[40] The CPP's

33. Brian Park (principal contributor), *Power Sector Coal Demand Has Fallen in Nearly Every State Since 2007*, U.S. ENERGY INFO. ADMIN., Apr. 28, 2016, https://www.eia.gov/todayinenergy/detail.cfm?id=26012.
34. *Id.*
35. *Id.*
36. *Id.*
37. *Id.* Though it sometimes goes unmentioned in such reports and, thus, in this chapter, hydropower is also a significant renewable energy source in the United States. For a recent review of the history and projected future of hydropower in the United States, see U.S. DEPT. OF ENERGY, HYDROPOWER VISION: A NEW CHAPTER FOR AMERICA'S 1ST RENEWABLE ELECTRICITY SOURCE (2016), http://energy.gov/eere/water/articles/hydropower-vision-new-chapter-america-s-1st-renewable-electricity-source.
38. For an example of executive branch policy with potential market implications, see Memorandum from Christina Goldfuss, Council on Envtl. Quality, to Heads of Federal Departments and Agencies (Aug. 1, 2016) (providing guidance to federal agencies on consideration of GHG emissions and the effects of climate change in National Environmental Policy Act reviews), https://www.whitehouse.gov/sites/whitehouse.gov/files/documents/nepa_final_ghg_guidance.pdf.
39. Carbon Pollution Emission Guidelines for Existing Stationary Sources: Electric Utility Generating Units, 80 Fed. Reg. 64661, 64665 (Oct. 23, 2015) (to be codified at 40 C.F.R. pt. 60).
40. *Id.* at 64663–64.

BSER standards are source-specific, with one performance rate for coal and oil steam plants and another for natural gas plants.[41] The performance rates were used to generate rate-based goals, measured in pounds per megawatt hour, and mass-based goals, measured in short tons of CO_2, to provide states with flexibility in creating their plans.[42] Unfortunately for purposes of inducing technological innovation, EPA relied on "actions, technologies and strategies already in widespread use by states and utilities that result in reduction of carbon pollution" to develop its BSER standards.[43] The CPP has received harsh criticism from its inception. It is currently embroiled in a heated legal battle initiated by industry and several states in an effort to overturn the rule.[44]

A number of other CAA environmental regulations limit the fossil fuel industry. The March 2013 Mercury and Air Toxics Standards (MATS) rule, aimed at reducing mercury and other air toxics emissions, places restrictions on emissions of those pollutants from new coal- and oil-fired electric generating units.[45] Power plants emit more mercury than any other anthropogenic source.[46] Yet, even before the most recent MATS rule, utility companies complained that EPA's regulation of mercury emissions put a strain on the

---

41. EPA, *FACT SHEET: Clean Power Plan Key Changes and Improvements*, https://www.epa.gov/clean-powerplan/fact-sheet-clean-power-plan-key-changes-and-improvements (last visited Aug. 21, 2016).

42. Carbon Pollution Emission Guidelines for Existing Stationary Sources: Electric Utility Generating Units, 80 Fed. Reg. 64661, 64664 (Oct. 23, 2015) (to be codified at 40 C.F.R. pt. 60); EPA, *FACT SHEET: Clean Power Plan Key Changes and Improvements, supra* note 41; EPA, *FACT SHEET: Overview of the Clean Power Plan*, https://www.epa.gov/cleanpowerplan/fact-sheet-overview-clean-power-plan (last visited Aug. 21, 2016).

43. EPA, *FACT SHEET: Clean Power Plan Key Changes and Improvements, supra* note 41; *see also* Carbon Pollution Emission Guidelines for Existing Stationary Sources: Electric Utility Generating Units, 80 Fed. Reg. 64661, 64666–67 (Oct. 23, 2015) (to be codified at 40 C.F.R. pt. 60).

44. *See* Oral Argument Part I, West Virginia v. EPA, No. 15-1363 (D.C. Cir. 2016), https://www.cadc.uscourts.gov/recordings/recordings2017.nsf/70BB3CF9D847F2288525803B007B8232/$file/15-1363.mp3; Oral Argument Part II, *West Virginia*, No. 15-1363, https://www.cadc.uscourts.gov/recordings/recordings2017.nsf/093F16FCFE643B358525803B007BC85E/$file/09272016partIIb.mp3; West Virginia v. EPA, No. 15A773 (U.S. Feb. 9, 2016) (staying CPP pending disposition of D.C. Circuit case and potential U.S. Supreme Court case if writ of certiorari is granted following D.C. Circuit decision); Environmental Defense Fund, *Clean Power Plan Case Resources* (containing links to CPP lawsuit case filings), https://www.edf.org/climate/clean-power-plan-case-resources (last visited Aug. 21, 2016).

45. Reconsideration of Certain New Source Issues: National Emission Standards for Hazardous Air Pollutants From Coal- and Oil-Fired Electric Utility Steam Generating Units and Standards of Performance for Fossil-Fuel-Fired Electric Utility, Industrial-Commercial-Institutional, and Small Industrial-Commercial-Institutional Steam Generating Units, 78 Fed. Reg. 24073 (Apr. 24, 2013) (to be codified at 40 C.F.R. pts. 60 & 63); EPA, Fact Sheet: Updates of the Limits for New Power Plants Under the Mercury and Air Toxics Standards (MATS) (2013), https://www.epa.gov/sites/production/files/2016-05/documents/20130328fs.pdf; EPA, *EPA Updates the Mercury and Air Toxics Standards for New Power Plants*, https://www.epa.gov/mats/epa-updates-mercury-and-air-toxics-standards-new-power-plants (last visited Aug. 21, 2016).

46. EIA, *What Is the Role of Coal in the United States?*, http://www.eia.gov/energy_in_brief/article/role_coal_us.cfm (last visited Aug. 21, 2016).

fossil fuel industry. In February 2012, FirstEnergy announced the closing of three of its oldest coal-fired power plants in West Virginia, claiming that the cost of compliance with environmental regulations made the operation of those plants too expensive.[47] Within the same period, FirstEnergy closed six other coal plants in Ohio, Pennsylvania, and Maryland.[48]

Another relevant CAA rule is the July 2011 Cross-State Air Pollution Rule (CSAPR), which regulates nitrogen oxide (NO_x) and sulfur dioxide (SO_2) emissions from power plants in 28 states.[49] The purpose of CSAPR is to improve air quality and enable states to achieve National Ambient Air Quality Standards (NAAQS) by reducing particulate matter and ground-level ozone in the atmosphere.[50] Regulations implementing the CAA's NAAQS,[51] air toxics provisions,[52] and new source performance standards[53] place further requirements on the fossil fuel industry.

Environmental regulation of the fossil fuel industry is not limited to that addressing air emissions, however. The Disposal of Coal Combustion Residuals from Electric Utilities rule, published in the *Federal Register* in April 2015, imposes requirements for the proper disposal of coal ash from coal-fired power plants.[54] The rule was authorized by subtitle D of the Resource Conservation and Recovery Act, the nation's cradle-to-grave statute for solid and hazardous waste regulation.[55] EPA also uses §316(b) of the Clean Water Act to regulate power plants' cooling water intake structures.[56] These regulations are intended to minimize the adverse effects of using water to cool power plants.[57]

47. *E.g.*, Christopher Flavelle, *What Happens After the Coal Plant Closes?*, Bloomberg, July 22, 2015, https://www.bloomberg.com/view/articles/2015-07-22/what-happens-after-the-coal-plant-closes-; *FirstEnergy to Snuff Albright, Rivesville, Willow Island Plants*, State J., Mar. 9, 2012, http://www.statejournal.com/story/16768718/firstenergy-to-snuff-albright-rivesville-willow-island-plants; Ken Ward Jr., *3 W.Va. Plants Latest to Close Under Utility Restructuring*, W. Va. Gazette Mail, Feb. 8, 2012, http://www.wvgazettemail.com/News/201202080125.

48. *E.g.*, *FirstEnergy to Snuff Albright, Rivesville, Willow Island Plants*, *supra* note 47; Bob Downing, *FirstEnergy Closing 6 Coal-Fired Power Plants*, Beacon J., Jan. 26, 2012, http://www.ohio.com/news/break-news/firstenergy-closing-6-coal-fired-power-plants-1.257090.

49. Federal Implementation Plans: Interstate Transport of Fine Particulate Matter and Ozone and Correction of SIP Approvals, 76 Fed. Reg. 48208 (Aug. 8, 2011) (to be codified at 40 C.F.R. pts. 51, 52, 72, 78, & 97); EPA, *Cross-State Air Pollution Rule (CSAPR)*, https://www3.epa.gov/crossstaterule/ (last visited Aug. 21, 2016).

50. Federal Implementation Plans: Interstate Transport of Fine Particulate Matter and Ozone and Correction of SIP Approvals, 76 Fed. Reg. 48208, 48208 (Aug. 8, 2011) (to be codified at 40 C.F.R. pts. 51, 52, 72, 78, & 97); *Cross-State Air Pollution Rule (CSAPR)*, *supra* note 49.

51. National Primary and Secondary Ambient Air Quality Standards, 40 C.F.R. §§ 50.1–.19.

52. 40 C.F.R. §§ 61.01–63.12099.

53. Standards of Performance for New Stationary Sources, 40 C.F.R. § 60.1–.5880.

54. Hazardous and Solid Waste Management System; Disposal of Coal Combustion Residuals From Electric Utilities, 80 Fed. Reg. 21302 (Apr. 17, 2015) (to be codified at 40 C.F.R. pts. 257 & 261).

55. *Id.* at 21302.

56. 40 C.F.R. §§ 122, 125.80–.99 & 125.130–139.

57. 40 C.F.R. § 125.80(a).

In addition to regulatory and administrative controls, the prevalence of citizen-initiated lawsuits presents a threat to U.S. companies that is far less common and often nonexistent in other nations.[58] In the United States, companies must adapt and respond not only to regulations of state and federal governments, but also to lawsuits from citizens groups, shareholders, and insurance companies.[59] The recent accusations of and investigations into ExxonMobil Corp. for its alleged concealment of climate change evidence[60] could be a precursor for climate change litigation encompassing a range of causes of action. The information discovered in these investigations may be used in a manner similar to that used by the federal government against tobacco companies in suits filed under the Racketeer Influenced and Corrupt Organizations Act (RICO).[61] Citizens may also use this new data to file suit under false advertising, misrepresentation, and state consumer protection laws.[62]

Attorneys on both sides of the potential litigation predict a litany of novel plaintiffs and arguments to enter the scene as new science becomes available and enables plaintiffs to attribute types and quantities of climate change-related harms to distinct companies and practices.[63] The future of climate litigation has even been compared to the federal Superfund program, where a party historically responsible for polluting a given site is responsible

---

58. *See* Oliver A. Houck, Taking Back Eden: Eight Environmental Cases That Changed the World (2012) (telling the story of the citizen suit phenomenon—with its beginnings in the 1960s in the United States—through eight landmark cases brought in the United States and in seven other countries that later adopted the concept).

59. *See, e.g.*, Connecticut v. American Elec. Power Co., 406 F. Supp. 2d 265 (S.D.N.Y. 2005) (dismissing on political question grounds plaintiffs' public nuisance claim against electric companies for contributions to global warming), *vacated*, 582 F.3d 309 (2d Cir. 2009), *aff'd in part by an equally divided court, rev'd in part*, 131 S. Ct. 2527 (2011); Comer v. Murphy Oil USA, 839 F. Supp. 2d 849 (S.D. Miss. 2012) (dismissing plaintiffs' claims against oil, gas, and chemical companies for damages suffered as a result of Hurricane Katrina, which plaintiffs alleged was intensified by defendants' contributions to global warming); Douglas A. Kysar, *What Climate Change Can Do About Tort Law*, 42 ELR 10739, 10740 n.1 (Aug. 2012) (citing various other climate change citizen suits brought on tort claim grounds); Amanda Reilly, *Exxon Case Launches "Novel and Creative" Era of Litigation*, Greenwire, May 6, 2016 (discussing predictions from various environmental attorneys on future climate litigation cases), http://www.eenews.net/greenwire/2016/05/06/stories/1060036846.

60. Press Release, Attorney General Eric T. Schneiderman, A.G. Schneiderman, Former Vice President Al Gore and a Coalition of Attorneys General From Across the Country Announce Historic State-based Effort to Combat Climate Change (Mar. 29, 2016), http://www.ag.ny.gov/press-release/ag-schneiderman-former-vice-president-al-gore-and-coalition-attorneys-general-across.

61. United States v. Philip Morris USA Inc., 449 F. Supp. 2d 1 (D.D.C. 2006), *aff'd in part & vacated in part*, 566 F.3d 1095 (D.C. Cir. 2009) (per curiam), *cert. denied*, 130 S. Ct. 3501 (2010); *see also* U.S. Department of Justice, *Litigation Against Tobacco Companies Home* (describing the progression of the United States' tobacco litigation and containing links to court documents, orders, and opinions), https://www.justice.gov/civil/case-4 (last visited Aug. 21, 2016).

62. Reilly, *supra* note 59 (citing statements from Center for International Environmental Law attorney Alyssa Johl).

63. *Id.*

for the cleanup.[64] In a similar way, companies historically responsible for GHG emissions may be held accountable for the resulting harm. Attempts to hold them accountable may even come from shareholder- and insurance company-plaintiffs.[65]

Holding GHG emitters financially liable for climate change contributions will not be without numerous political challenges and legal nuances, however. Increasing numbers of bankruptcy filings by coal-based companies provide one obstacle. The Chapter 11 bankruptcy filing of Peabody Energy Corp., the largest coal mining company in the United States, is an example of the challenge to ensure that companies have the financial solvency to pay for the damage they cause.[66] The environmental cleanup costs associated with Peabody's mining operations are in the hundreds of millions of dollars, causing great concern for environmental groups.[67] Though the issue in the Peabody case is land-directed mine site cleanup rather than atmosphere-directed climate change mitigation, the reality of such companies' lack of financial capacity to respond to environmental liability is a shared detriment.

While environmentally charged challenges tend to be the focus of law-based discussions on energy market drivers, financial incentives also play a significant role in dictating who the market players are, how they operate, and their likelihood of success. In March 2015, the EIA released a report examining tax expenditures, direct expenditures, and research and development (R&D) expenditures in energy.[68] Electricity-related subsidies and sup-

---

64. *Id.* (citing statements from David Doniger, director of the Climate and Clean Air Program at the Natural Resources Defense Council).

65. *Id. Accord* Original Class Action Complaint and Demand for Jury Trial, Illinois Farmers Ins. Co. v. County of McHenry, No. 1:14-cv-03282 (N.D. Ill. 2014).

66. In re Peabody Energy Corp. et al., No. 16-42529-399 (Bankr. E.D. Mo. 2016); Press Release, Peabody Energy Corp., Amid Prolonged Industry Downturn, Peabody Energy Takes Major Step to Strengthen Liquidity and Reduce Debt Through Chapter 11 Protection (Apr. 13, 2016), https://mscusppegrs01. blob.core.windows.net/mmfiles/sitemedia/ch11/announcement%20press%20release.pdf; John W. Miller & Matt Jarzemsky, *Peabody Energy Files for Chapter 11 Bankruptcy Protection*, WALL ST. J., Apr. 14, 2016, http://www.wsj.com/articles/peabody-energy-files-for-chapter-11-protection-from-creditors-1460533760; Tiffany Kary et al., *Coal Slump Sends Mining Giant Peabody Energy Into Bankruptcy*, BLOOMBERG, Apr. 13, 2016, http://www.bloomberg.com/news/articles/2016-04-13/peabody-majority-of-its-u-s-entities-file-for-chapter-11; Steven Mufson & Joby Warrick, *Can Coal Companies Afford to Clean Up Coal Country?*, WASH. POST, Apr. 2, 2016, https://www.washingtonpost.com/business/economy/can-coal-companies-afford-to-clean-up-coal-country/2016/04/01/c175570c-ec73-11e5-a6f3-21ccdbc5f74e_story.html?tid=a_inl.

67. *E.g.*, Susan Cosier, *Who Pays for Mine Cleanup After Big Coal Goes Bankrupt?*, onEarth, June 22, 2016, https://www.nrdc.org/onearth/who-pays-mine-cleanup-after-big-coal-goes-bankrupt; Video: Coal: ELPC's Learner Talks Self-Bonding Liabilities Following Peabody Bankruptcy, (E&ETV OnPoint 2016), http://www.eenews.net/tv/2016/04/28; Miller & Jarzemsky, *supra* note 66.

68. EIA, DIRECT FEDERAL FINANCIAL INTERVENTIONS AND SUBSIDIES IN ENERGY IN FISCAL YEAR 2013 (2015).

port in the United States grew from $11.7 billion in 2011 to $16.1 billion in fiscal year 2013—a 38% increase, the largest component of which was attributed to a $4.2 billion increase in support of solar energy, which comprised $5.3 billion of the $16.1 billion.[69] According to this report, renewable beneficiaries accounted for 72% of total electric-related U.S. government subsidies and support.[70] A significant consideration in determining the effect of these subsidies is that, despite renewables' receipt of a significant majority of government electricity subsidies, renewable energy accounted for only 13% of energy generation in calendar year 2013.[71] This serves as evidence that the funding of renewable energy projects through subsidies and tax incentives does not go far enough to remove the obstacles that prevent renewables from entering the market with greater force. Affordability and efficiency of those energy sources must be supported to a greater extent through R&D funding, which would bring renewables closer to the status of fossil fuels with regard to financial viability.

Though the EIA report reflects the federal government's preference for renewable energy sources in the electricity sector, federal subsidies for fossil fuels remain significant. In its 2014 Progress Report on Fossil Fuel Subsidies, presented to the G20,[72] the U.S. Department of the Treasury outlined preferences for fossil fuels codified as permanent provisions in the U.S. tax code.[73] The Treasury identified 11 federal fossil fuel production tax provisions, which in the aggregate result in $4.7 billion in annual revenue costs to the United States.[74] The five provisions with the greatest annual revenue costs address: the expensing of intangible drilling costs ($1.2 billion per year), the percentage depletion for oil and natural gas wells ($1.3 billion per year), domestic manufacturing deductions for fossil fuels ($1.3 billion per year), the two-year amortization period for geological and geographical expenditures ($305 million per year), and the percentage depletion for hard mineral fossil fuels ($205 million per year).[75] Despite the Obama Administration's proposal that the preferential treatment for fossil fuels be eliminated from

---

69.   *Id.* at viii.
70.   *Id.* at xviii–xix.
71.   *Id.* at xviii.
72.   The G20, started in 1999, consists of 19 countries and the European Union, and serves as a forum for participating countries to discuss international financial policy and development. G20, *About G20*, http://www.g20.org/English/aboutg20/AboutG20/201511/t20151127_1609.html (last visited Aug. 21, 2016).
73.   U.S. Treasury, United States—Progress Report on Fossil Fuel Subsidies (2014), https://www.treasury.gov/open/Documents/USA%20FFSR%20progress%20report%20to%20G20%202014%20Final.pdf.
74.   *Id.* at 1.
75.   *Id.* at 2–4.

the tax code, Congress has not amended the tax code to effectuate that proposal.[76] The progress report provides insight into the financial support that the U.S. fossil fuel industry receives and is anticipated to receive from the U.S. government. It further demonstrates the absence of sufficient financial incentives for R&D to induce clean energy technology. Not only is investment in R&D not among the five provisions with the greatest annual revenue costs—it is not at all represented in the tax code incentives.[77] If the government is to continue to financially support fossil fuels through tax incentives, it should do so in an energy-progressive manner to promote technological development for cleaner burning of fossil fuels.

Another important financial tool in energy policy that Congress has failed to facilitate is the continuation of the §1705 Loan Program for projects of technological innovation in reducing air pollutants and GHG emissions, a program that expired on September 30, 2011.[78] Section 1705 permitted the U.S. Department of Energy (DOE) to provide loans for energy production projects with a technological innovation component meeting the definition of that term in the statute.[79] The program served as a useful resource for researchers and industry actors to fund otherwise risky or uneconomical projects with the potential to advance clean energy. However, Congress did not renew the loan program beyond its September 2011 expiration.[80]

As the legal and economic shifts above indicate, the general culture in recent years in the United States appears to be moving strongly toward cleaner energy production. Nevertheless, the transition has not been without conflict. The shifting legal and economic climates in energy production have produced tension in many U.S. cities with a legacy of reliance on coal. Colstrip, Montana, is one such example. In a town of 2,300 residents, 770 of whom are employed at the power plant, the 2,094-MW Colstrip Generating Station is a powerful symbol of the town's economic stability.[81] The plant primarily provides

---

76.   *Id.* at 8.
77.   *See generally id.*
78.   Incentives for Innovative Technologies, Pub. L. No. 109-58, 119 Stat. 1117.
79.   *Id.*
80.   For more information about the program, see U.S. Department of Energy, *Section 1705 Loan Program*, http://energy.gov/lpo/services/section-1705-loan-program (last visited Aug. 21, 2016); Loan Guarantees for Projects That Employ Innovative Technologies, 74 Fed. Reg. 63544 (Dec. 4, 2009) (to be codified at 10 C.F.R. pt. 609).
81.   Elizabeth Harball, *Powder River Basin: Inside a Town That Won't Give Up on Coal*, CLIMATEWIRE, Apr. 12, 2016, http://www.eenews.net/climatewire/2016/04/12/stories/1060035404. Just two of the four coal-fired units at the plant produce $14.2 million in tax revenue for the state and local governments. *Id.* The city's website provides further evidence of pride in the coal-based economy. City of Colstrip, *About Colstrip*, http://www.cityofcolstrip.com/index.php?option=com_content&view=article&id=7 2&Itemid=1193 (last visited Aug. 21, 2016).

power to the Pacific Northwest, powering approximately 1.5 million homes.[82] According to data reported to EPA, it also emits nearly 15 million metric tons of CO_2 annually, and is among the top 15 most carbon-polluting plants in the nation.[83] Accordingly, viability of the Colstrip plant is threatened by environmental regulations from three jurisdictions: the federal government,[84] Oregon,[85] and Washington.[86] Though the residents of Colstrip fight to protect their coal-based economy, other sources of power that fall within current market trends are available, if not abundant, in Montana. One such source is the state's natural gas reserve.[87] More importantly, the American Wind Energy Association ranks Montana third in U.S. states in potential for land-based wind power generation.[88] Though certain infrastructure obstacles must be overcome to achieve this potential for wind energy production, the opportunity for a shift toward renewable energy is an entirely viable option for the state.[89]

Meanwhile, Iowa, along with other Midwestern states historically reliant on coal, is increasingly buying into the renewable energy market and shifting energy investments from coal to wind and natural gas.[90] In April 2016, Des Moines-based utility company MidAmerican Energy Co. announced a 2,000-MW wind project, which will be complete in 2019.[91] Once the project is complete, more than 40% of Iowa's electricity will be fueled by wind.[92] Unlike the financial hit feared by the residents of Colstrip, Iowa's transition to renewable energy has been a proven opportunity, providing economic benefits that include millions of dollars through tax payments, income for

---

82. Harball, *supra* note 81.
83. From 2014 data populated from EPA's FLIGHT database. EPA, *Facility Level Information on Greenhouse Gases Tool (FLIGHT)*, https://ghgdata.epa.gov/ghgp/main.do (last visited Aug. 21, 2016).
84. Proposed emissions standards for Montana under the CPP would put great pressure on the state to reduce the emissions from the Colstrip plant. Carbon Pollution Emission Guidelines for Existing Stationary Sources: Electric Utility Generating Units, 80 Fed. Reg. 64661, 64824–25, 64889, 64962–63 (Oct. 23, 2015) (to be codified at 40 C.F.R. pt. 60).
85. In March 2016, a new Oregon law increased the state's renewable portfolio standard to 50% by 2040, and would require the state to end its reliance on Colstrip power by 2030. S. 1547, 78th Leg., Reg. Sess. (Or. 2016); Press Release, Oregon Governor's Office, Governor Brown to Sign Bill Adding Renewable Energy and Eliminating Coal From Oregon's Energy Resources (Mar. 10, 2016), http://www.oregon.gov/newsroom/Pages/NewsDetail.aspx?newsid=1032.
86. In April 2016, a new Washington law enabled Puget Sound Energy, co-owner of two of the plant's older units, to decommission those units. S. 6248, 64th Leg., Reg. Sess. (Wa. 2016).
87. Amy Martin, *New EPA Rules Motivate Montana to Look Beyond Coal*, NPR, Sept. 10, 2015, http://www.npr.org/2015/09/10/439152956/new-epa-rules-motivate-montana-to-look-beyond-coal.
88. *Id.*
89. *Id.*
90. Jeffrey Tomich, *Iowa Wind Boom Highlights Transformation in Midwest*, ENERGYWIRE, May 9, 2016, http://www.eenews.net/energywire/2016/05/09/stories/1060036884.
91. *Id.*
92. *Id.*

turbine-hosting farmers, jobs for more than 7,000 people in parts manufacturing, and billions in investment by companies looking for affordable wind energy to fuel their businesses.[93]

Solar energy is also making large strides in the U.S. energy market, with a shift from individualized, limited-capacity solar installments to large-scale projects and advanced battery storage. One major player in the industry, SolarCity, announced in May 2016 its plans to expand its customer base to include electric utilities.[94] The leader of rooftop solar's announcement to enter the centralized power grid signifies a shift in solar energy production toward a scale that can compete with fossil fuel energy production.[95]

Despite ominous messages from environmentalists, regulators, and the market, the coal industry is reluctant to admit defeat. Instead, many in the coal business expect to aim their oversupply at overseas demand, optimistic that their decreasing role in the U.S. energy market will not mean the demise of the industry given the increasing demand for coal abroad.[96] Though coal plants are being closed throughout the United States,[97] 1,200 coal plants were being planned globally as recently as 2012, with 455 plants in China and 363 in India.[98] As home to approximately 26% of the world's total coal reserves and with declining national demand, the U.S. coal industry is ripe for expansion of exports.[99]

Currently, the destination for most of the United States' exported coal is Europe.[100] A number of factors, including Europe's high gas prices, oversupply of pollution permits, and Germany's phase-out of nuclear energy, have created the market for U.S. coal in Europe.[101] Given the EU's move toward more stringent pollution regulations, the viability of U.S. coal

---

93.   *Id.*

94.   David Ferris, *SolarCity, Duke of the Rooftop, Expands Into Solar Farms*, ENERGYWIRE, May 6, 2016, http://www.eenews.net/energywire/2016/05/06/stories/1060036818.

95.   *Id.*

96.   Dylan Brown, *Export Ambitions Down, But Not Out*, GREENWIRE, Apr. 26, 2016, http://www.eenews.net/greenwire/2016/04/26/stories/1060036277.

97.   *See, e.g.*, Robert Ferris, *What Shuttering Coal Plants Means for Energy Jobs*, CNBC, Apr. 13, 2016 (discussing coal plant closures and their effect on jobs), http://www.cnbc.com/2015/04/13/what-shuttering-coal-plants-means-for-energy-jobs.html.

98.   Jacopo Zenti, *The Future of the American Coal Industry*, NAT'L CENTER FOR POL'Y ANALYSIS, Jan. 30, 2015, http://www.ncpa.org/pub/ba806.

99.   *Id.; see also* EIA, *What Is the Role of Coal in the United States?* (describing the United States' recoverable coal reserves as estimated to be the world's largest), http://www.eia.gov/energy_in_brief/article/role_coal_us.cfm (last visited Aug. 21, 2016).

100. Kieran Cooke, *Is the U.S. Exporting Coal Pollution?*, SCI. AM., Mar. 23, 2013, http://www.scientificamerican.com/article/is-the-us-exporting-coal-pollution/; EIA, QUARTERLY COAL REPORT (ABBREVIATED), Oct.–Dec. 2015, tbl. 7: U.S. COAL EXPORTS, https://www.eia.gov/coal/production/quarterly/pdf/t7p01p1.pdf.

101. *Id.*

exports to Europe may be greatly reduced in the near future.[102] In that case, however, U.S. coal producers would turn to Asia for their primary customer base, likely a safe business move given the size of the Chinese and Indian coal markets.[103]

While coal export terminals on the United States' east coast are at full capacity, forward-looking coal producers are fighting for the construction and operation of export terminals in the Pacific Northwest to enable greater coal export capacity to Asia.[104] With a handful of export terminals in Washington and Oregon, coal companies could export as much as 150 million tons of coal per year.[105] Legal challenges to the construction of export terminals in the West result in the practical inability of some companies to export their coal to Asia, and currently present the biggest challenge to those companies seeking to export coal. The legal challenges are based on both local environmental concerns (i.e., the negative environmental effects of those terminals on the immediately surrounding environments) and concerns from local residents about the potential disruptions to their communities.[106] The environmental legal challenges also raise the issue of curbing GHG emissions, which anticipates the global environmental effects of permitting construction of export terminals.[107]

From an environmental perspective, if coal is to be extracted at all, it is likely better it be extracted in the United States, where mining activities are subject to numerous environmental statutes and regulations.[108] However, the emissions incurred to transport the coal overseas and the burning of that coal in countries with limited environmental regulations and technological advancements result in the same predicament those countries, and the world, must address in the face of developing countries' increased reliance on coal. Thus, even in cases of U.S.-led extraction, the United States' facilitation of coal burning abroad, without regard for enhanced technology to mitigate emissions, is a contributing factor to the global crisis of climate change and of the especially powerful impacts climate change will have on poorer nations

---

102. *Id.*
103. *Id.*
104. *Id.*
105. Bryan Walsh, *Drawing Battle Lines Over American Coal Exports to Asia*, Time, May 31, 2012, http://science.time.com/2012/05/31/drawing-battle-lines-over-american-coal-exports-to-asia/.
106. *Id.*
107. Press Release, Earthjustice, Coalition Challenges Permit Allowing Dirty Coal Export to Asia From WA Port (Dec. 13, 2010), http://earthjustice.org/news/press/2010/coalition-challenges-permit-allowing-dirty-coal-export-to-asia-from-wa-port#.
108. These include, but are not limited to: the Clean Water Act, the Clean Air Act, the Safe Drinking Water Act, the Resource Conservation and Recovery Act, and the Comprehensive Environmental Response, Compensation, and Liability Act.

unable to afford adaptation strategies. Legal and social precautions should continue to be taken to prevent increasing coal exports from the United States, and allow the focus of U.S.-facilitated energy production in developing countries to come in the form of shareable technology advancements in the United States and funding of clean energy initiatives and technology advancements outside the United States.

C.   Case Study: Kemper IGCC

As the discussion in the previous section reflects, the financing of and financial forecast for energy projects play significant roles in determining the extent to which those projects will succeed in the changing energy market. Pursuing the ideal of funding of technology innovation in the United States as a method for supporting the global shift away from emissions-heavy technologies requires consideration of such funding in practice. The case of a carbon capture initiative by a Mississippi utility presented in this section demonstrates some of the practical implications of developed countries taking on high-risk technology innovation projects. The Mississippi case study illustrates the critical need for government funding for technology R&D, financing of clean energy projects, and use of federal funds—as opposed to relying more heavily on ratepayers—to enable utilities to recover costs.

In the United States, utility cost-of-service ratemaking in the energy industry generally allows for local distribution companies to recover costs that have been deemed reasonably incurred[109] for the purpose of providing safe and reliable services to consumers,[110] and that have been approved by regulators (state public service commissions). These costs must pass a number of tests, including a demonstration by the utility that the utility assets were "used and useful"[111] for providing services to the ratepayers to whom costs will be passed down.

A number of factors, including jurisdiction, determine the treatment of the various costs under consideration in rate case proceedings. Costs associated with meeting clean air standards[112] and costs incurred for improvements to plant infrastructure for compliance with environmental regulations are generally deemed necessary for the provision of safe and reliable services,

---

109. KARL McDERMOTT, COST OF SERVICE REGULATION IN THE INVESTOR-OWNED ELECTRIC UTILITY INDUSTRY vii (Edison Electric Institute 2012), http://www.eei.org/issuesandpolicy/stateregulation/documents/cosr_history_final.pdf.
110. *Id.* at 9.
111. *Id.*
112. *Id.* at 32.

and are recovered from consumers.[113] Costs associated with construction of new facilities, however, are generally not recovered in rates until the facility is demonstrated to be providing services to the ratepayers; that is, until the facility becomes used and useful. In some instances, public utility commissions have greater latitude to assess the cost of construction work in progress for inclusion in rates. Improvements to existing facilities as well as planning for and construction of new generation facilities require substantial capital investment. The financial responsibilities of benefiting parties can vary widely depending on the regulations of the state in which a company operates.

The case from Kemper County, Mississippi, illustrates the financial implications of regulation of carbon capture and sequestration (CCS)[114] technologies in the fossil fuel industry in the United States. Mississippi's Baseload Act[115] provides for an alternative method of cost recovery for certain forms of base load generation.[116] Generally, prior to the Baseload Act, the cost of construction of new facilities would first be estimated by the company and approved by the Mississippi Public Service Commission (MPSC or the Commission). After construction, the utility would seek rate recovery of the construction costs, allowing the Commission to compare the actual costs of construction to those estimated, and assess their pru-

---

113. *Id.* at 35.
114. While natural gas energy production is more likely to meet the increasingly stringent standards for GHG emissions (for example, the BSER standards in the CPP), average emission rates from coal-fired plants make similar compliance at those plants much more difficult. Carbon Pollution Emission Guidelines for Existing Stationary Sources: Electric Utility Generating Units, 80 Fed. Reg. 64661 (Oct. 23, 2015) (to be codified at 40 C.F.R. pt. 60); Christopher Helman, *The War on Coal Goes Global: China Bans New Plants as Obama EPA Plans Killer Regs*, Forbes, Sept. 12, 2013, http:// www.forbes.com/sites/christopherhelman/2013/09/12/the-war-on-coal-goes-global-china-bans-new-plants-as-obama-epa-plans-killer-regs/print/. Some analysts project that trapping the CO_2 emissions and injecting them underground would double the capital costs of a coal power plant to nearly $112 per mWh of capacity. *Id.* While CCS technologies are not currently deemed a proven method by regulators, the abundance and affordability of coal make use of CCS a viable option for enabling the continued use of coal plants while ensuring compliance with GHG emission regulations. Carbon Pollution Emission Guidelines for Existing Stationary Sources: Electric Utility Generating Units, 80 Fed. Reg. 64661, 64728 (Oct. 23, 2015) (to be codified at 40 C.F.R. pt. 60). Accordingly, the U.S. government has dedicated resources to research in developing such "cleaner" fossil fuel sources of energy production. In 2011, the U.S. Department of Energy funded six projects with $14 million "aimed at developing technologies to lower the cost of producing electricity in integrated gasification combined cycle (IGCC) power plants using carbon capture." *Secretary Chu Announces $14 Million for Six New Projects to Advance IGCC Technology*, U.S. Department of Energy, Sept. 9, 2011, http:// www.energy.gov/fe/articles/secretary-chu-announces-14-million-six-new-projects-advance. EPA notes that the number of CCS patents have been sharply increasing since 2007, with 160 issued in 2014. EPA, Technical Support Document: Literature Survey of Carbon Capture Technology (2015), https://www.epa.gov/sites/production/files/2015-11/documents/tsd-cps-literature-survey-carbon-capture-technology.pdf.
115. Miss. Code Ann. §§ 77-3-101–77-3-109 (2009).
116. No. 2012-UR-01108-SCT Consolidated with No. 2013-UR-00477-SCT, at 40 (Miss. 2015) (reversing and remanding Mississippi Public Service Commission decision).

dence. By enacting the Baseload Act, the Mississippi legislature created a new section of the Mississippi Code that favors baseload generation and allows the Commission to approve alternate recovery of construction costs for baseload generating plants if the Commission finds such recovery consistent with the public interest.[117]

In 2010, Mississippi Power Company (MPC), a Mississippi electric generation, transmission, and distribution company, began construction of the Kemper County integrated gasification combined cycle (IGCC) power plant (Kemper IGCC).[118] The Kemper IGCC was designed by MPC parent company Southern Company, KBR, and DOE.[119] It was designed to use lignite, a soft coal abundant in the region, as its primary source of fuel.[120] The coal would then be converted into natural gas using transport integrated gasification (TRIG) technology. The natural gas would be used to power turbines to generate electricity. MPC believed that the plant's IGCC and carbon capture technologies would result in cleaner production of energy[121] by capturing 65% of the CO_2 produced by the plant, thereby reducing its carbon emissions to a level comparable to that emitted by a similar-sized natural gas plant.[122] The Kemper IGCC was the first of its kind and scale to be built in the United States,[123] with an initial anticipated construction cost of $2.2 billion.[124]

The project was funded in part by grants from DOE—$270 million under the Clean Coal Power Initiative[125]—and received nearly $280 million in tax credits from the Internal Revenue Service (IRS).[126] In 2010, the MPSC issued a Certificate of Public Convenience and Necessity, which authorized the acquisition, construction, and operation of the Kemper IGCC. In 2013, the Commission approved recovery of Kemper-related costs for construction

---

117. Final Order on Remand Granting a Certificate of Public Convenience and Necessity, Authorizing Application of Baseload Act, and Approving Prudent Pre-Construction Costs, Docket No. 2009-UA-014, at 40 (Miss. Pub. Serv. Comm'n 2012).

118. Massachusetts Institute of Technology, *Kemper County IGCC Fact Sheet: Carbon Dioxide Capture and Storage Project*, https://sequestration.mit.edu/tools/projects/kemper.html (last visited Aug. 21, 2016).

119. Mississippi Power Co., *21st-century Technology*, http://www.mississippipower.com/about-energy/plants/kemper-county-energy-facility/21st-century-technology (last visited Sept. 18, 2016).

120. *Id.*

121. *Id.*

122. *Id.*

123. Final Order on Remand Granting a Certificate of Public Convenience and Necessity, Authorizing Application of Baseload Act, and Approving Prudent Pre-Construction Costs, Docket No. 2009-UA-014, at 18 (Miss. Pub. Serv. Comm'n 2012).

124. *Kemper County IGCC Fact Sheet, supra* note 118.

125. Final Order on Remand Granting a Certificate of Public Convenience and Necessity, Authorizing Application of Baseload Act, and Approving Prudent Pre-Construction Costs, Docket No. 2009-UA-014, at 59 (Miss. Pub. Serv. Comm'n 2012).

126. *Id.* at 19, 59.

work in progress (CWIP) in utility rates recovered from customers in 2012, 2013, and 2014.[127] The Commission found construction costs up to $2.88 billion to be appropriate for recovery from ratepayers.[128]

The Kemper IGCC project experienced a number of challenges. Five years after starting construction, the estimated completion time and financial budget had far surpassed initial projections, in large part due to design flaws involving miscalculations of pipe thickness, length, quantity, and metallurgy, and the resulting changes necessary for the support structures.[129] As of April 2016, the estimated cost of the Kemper IGCC plant was $6.66 billion—more than three times that of the original $2.2 billion estimate, and its revised anticipated startup date, set in August 2016, was nearly three years behind schedule. As a result of missing the project's deadline, the company will have to repay $133 million to the federal government and return $234 million in investment tax credits to the IRS.[130] In addition, in 2010, the MPSC ordered the annual rate increases[131] that MPC had been collecting from utility ratepayers to be refunded to customers as a result of a Mississippi Supreme Court decision that found the collection of CWIP costs from ratepayers to be unlawful.[132]

The challenges associated with the Kemper IGCC illustrate a number of relevant points. First, proper planning and assessment of technological capabilities are necessary to effect significant changes in emissions from coal-fired electric power generators. Second, the financial assurances required to build state-of-the-art infrastructure, even when undertaken in a developed country with cutting-edge scientific and technological advances, presents copious challenges. Third, government involvement, subsidization, and alleviation of both technological and financial[133] burdens on stakeholders—that is, investors, ratepayers, taxpayers, and the environment—play substantial roles in determining financial viability of clean energy projects.

The first point supports the need for R&D in developed countries to establish a stronger foundation of knowledge in clean energy technologies,

127. *Id.* at 22.
128. This represented a 20% cap above MPC's approved project estimate of $2.4 billion. *Id.* at 106.
129. *Kemper Country IGCC Fact Sheet*, *supra* note 118.
130. *Id.*
131. No. 2012-UR-01108-SCT Consolidated with No. 2013-UR-00477-SCT, at 3 (Miss. 2015) (reversing and remanding Mississippi Public Service Commission decision).
132. This was a result of a Mississippi Supreme Court ruling that found the recovery unlawful and remanded the case back to the commission for remuneration to the ratepayers. Order on remand, Docket No. 2013-UN-14 (Miss. Pub. Serv. Comm'n 2015).
133. MPC estimates of government incentives included upfront capital costs of $296 million as well as reductions in operating costs of more than $1 billion. Final Order on Remand Granting a Certificate of Public Convenience and Necessity, Authorizing Application of Baseload Act, and Approving Prudent Pre-Construction Costs, Docket No. 2009-UA-014 87 (Miss. Pub. Serv. Comm'n 2012).

including technologies for systems that rely on fossil fuels. The second point emphasizes the need for government intervention in the process because, financially, the risks and challenges associated with such clean energy projects often function to discourage investment by investors and industry actors. Given that the company and its investors absorb expenses beyond the commission-approved recoverable cost cap,[134] additional incentives via policy-based government financing are necessary to promote risky clean energy projects.

The third point indicates how the government should use its cost recovery authority to pass on the costs of energy projects to the public. To the extent costs are recovered through government grants and tax credits on the one hand and through utility rates and surcharges on the other, they are funded by taxpayers and ratepayers, respectively. When the federal government— i.e., taxpayers—provides the funding, the cost is nationally distributed, with those of higher income contributing more dollars to the government funds used to provide grants, tax credits, and subsidies. When ratepayers pay, cost is recovered from the local/regional population that is subject to the services of the utility. Thus, greater cost recovery from ratepayers would create a greater burden for financially vulnerable communities, while federal government support would ensure a broader distribution of the costs of energy projects, which are likely to result in national and global benefits. Consequently, to ensure that efforts to advance clean energy technology to support global climate justice do not, in turn, cause domestic climate injustice, there should be a greater focus on government financing of projects rather than reliance on localized funding from ratepayers.

II.   Developing Countries

While developed countries enjoyed an earlier industrialization era and are now moving toward more climate-responsible energy practices, developing countries are working hard to catch up. Given that developing countries do not have the financial resources to continue to develop without relying on cheap fossil fuels, the global community must identify the most effective strategies for developing countries to provide their citizens with opportunities similar to their developed counterparts, while preventing further GHG emissions to the greatest extent possible.[135] This section provides background

---

134. However, a negative financial impact on the company, such as increase in cost of capital, would also result in an increase in rates recovered from customers.

135. For an informative report on the industrialization of developing countries, and associated economic and environmental implications, see generally UNITED NATIONS DEPARTMENT OF ECONOMIC AND

on the historical economic and environmental conditions of developing countries with regard to climate change, demonstrating their relatively limited historical contributions. The section then describes the energy future projected for these nations, which indicates a need to rely on fossil fuels in the near term until they are able to achieve greater affluence. The section concludes with a review of cases in which developing countries were provided with clean energy infrastructure, and concludes that the resulting challenges and successes in the different cases demonstrate the need to carefully evaluate divergent capabilities and provide for ongoing sources of funding if such clean energy projects are to be functional and sustainable.

A. Low Historical Climate Change Contributions

The relationship between and responsibilities of developed and developing countries and their respective access to energy and related impacts on their environments have been under consideration for decades. In a 1991 report, the U.S. Congress Office of Technology Assessment recognized the relatively historically limited—though quickly growing—energy consumption of developing nations,[136] the critical role of technology in access to energy by developing countries, and the related environmental impacts.[137] In particular, the report focused on the potentially determinative role of the United States in the availability of such technologies to underdeveloped nations.[138] The report explored the environmental impacts of various fuel sources, including coal, oil, gas, and nuclear energy, as well as hydroelectricity, biomass, solar, wind, and other renewable energy sources.[139] The report also recognized the catch-22 that exists with regard to rural communities—on the one hand, the critical role of access to energy in modernization of developing societies, and on the other, the impact of energy extraction and production on the rural environment.[140]

Given that developing countries have entered the energy market more recently than developed countries, they have a much shorter history of industrialized energy production and contribution to the global emissions problem from large-scale power production.[141] In many developing countries, tradi-

---

SOCIAL AFFAIRS, INDUSTRIAL DEVELOPMENT FOR THE 21ST CENTURY: SUSTAINABLE DEVELOPMENT PERSPECTIVES (2007), https://sustainabledevelopment.un.org/content/documents/full_report.pdf.

136. *See* U.S. CONGRESS OFFICE OF TECHNOLOGY ASSESSMENT, ENERGY IN DEVELOPING COUNTRIES 8–9 (1991) (OTA-E-486) (discussing the rapidly growing share of developing countries' global commercial energy consumption), http://ota.fas.org/reports/9118.pdf.

137. *Id.*

138. *Id.* at 3.

139. *Id.* at 15–18.

140. *Id.* at 128.

141. *See supra* note 136 and accompanying text.

tional uses of biomass have played a major role in producing energy and have been in the form of fuelwood, manure and crop residues, and charcoal.[142] While the development of the bioenergy systems that have traditionally served the energy needs of developing countries have many potential benefits, including climate change mitigation in some respects, they can also lead to deforestation, reduced biodiversity, and increased GHG emissions.[143]

On a positive note, innovative developments in sustainable fuels have been taking place among some developing countries for years. In Brazil, for example, a large-scale sugar cane ethanol program has been in place since the 1970s.[144] The program has been described as the "best example of a large growth in the use of renewables" in developing countries, citing Brazil's annual 16-billion-liter (4.2-billion-gallon) ethanol production as evidence.[145] Moreover, at the end of 2006, overall ethanol production subsidies of $30 billion over a 20-year period were heavily outweighed by the benefit of $50 billion in foregone petroleum imports over the same period.[146] By 2004, ethanol had become fully competitive with gasoline in the global market *without* government intervention—that is, Brazil achieved economies of scale in producing ethanol to a degree that no longer required government subsidy.[147] In addition to utilizing ethanol in automobile fuel, Brazil has been selling surplus ethanol to the electric power grid for use in high-pressure boilers that allow cogeneration of electricity.[148]

In 2004, the Food and Agriculture Organization of the United Nations (FAO) reported that the then-13% share of global renewable sources was not expected to change significantly over the decades to follow.[149] Countries in Africa and Central and South America, which include primarily developing economies, accounted for the only significant shares of renewable energy in total energy consumption by region.[150] Renewable energy generation represented approximately 49% of total energy generation in Africa and 29% of total energy generation in Central and South America.[151] In Central and South America, the large renewable energy sources

---

142. Ivan Tomaselli, Forests and Energy Working Paper 2: Forests and Energy in Developing Countries, Food and Agriculture Organization of the United Nations v (2007), ftp://ftp.fao.org/docrep/fao/010/k1140e/k1140e00.pdf.
143. *Id.* at 8.
144. José Goldemberg et al., *Ethanol for a Sustainable Energy Future*, 315 Sci. 808 (2007).
145. Donald Kennedy, Science Magazine's State of the Planet 2008–2009: With a Special Section on Energy and Sustainability 24 (2008).
146. *Id.* at 25.
147. *Id.* at 24–25.
148. Goldemberg et al., *supra* note 145.
149. *See* Tomaselli, *supra* note 143.
150. *Id.* at 6–7.
151. *Id.* at 7, fig. 4.

were driven primarily by Brazil, where 45% of all energy consumed was derived from hydroelectric, wood, and sugar cane ethanol.[152] As of 2007, Brazil consumed about 90 million tons of wood per year for energy generation.[153] As of 2004, about 75% of the world's renewable energy sources were consumed in developing countries with biomass accounting for the greatest portion.[154]

These examples illustrate the willingness and ability of developing countries to take initiative in mitigating climate change through reliance on renewable energy sources. This also demonstrates that given the opportunity and sufficient autonomy, developing countries have been able to deliver their citizens more sustainable energy and can do so to meet their future needs. However, to do so in place of fossil fuels will require additional support as discussed in the following section, which explores projected energy needs and the related climate justice challenges for developing countries, particularly India and China, where challenges of overcoming fossil-fuel-sourced energy are expected to be particularly significant in the coming years.

B.   Outlook on Curbing Emissions Through Political and Economic Shifts in Fossil Fuel Reliance

Though the long-term history of developing countries has seen relatively low energy consumption, the recent history of many developing nations shows dramatic increases in both energy needs and consumption. This section explains these growing needs, citing as examples the two top players among developing nations, China and India, and discusses these nations' commitments to decreasing emissions and potential limitations to satisfying those commitments.

Headquartered in Paris, France, the Organisation for Economic Co-operation and Development (OECD) was established in 1961 with a mission "to promote policies that will improve the economic and social well-being of people around the world."[155] As of 2016, the OECD is comprised of 34 Member countries, most of which classify as developed, with the exception of Chile, Israel, Korea, Mexico, and Turkey.[156] By the end of 2013, the

---

152. *Id.* at 6.
153. *Id.* at 7.
154. *Id.*
155. OECD, *About the OECD*, http://www.oecd.org/about (last visited Aug. 21, 2016).
156. Member countries list was obtained from the OECD website. OECD, *Members and Partners*, http://www.oecd.org/about/membersandpartners/#d.en.194378 (last visited Aug. 21, 2016). The classification of countries is based on the categorization by the United Nations. UNITED NATIONS, WORLD

EIA's International Energy Outlook 2013 (IEO 2013) predicted growth in global energy use through 2040 to be driven primarily by countries outside the OECD.[157] The EIA's projections forecasted steady energy consumption among OECD countries during the period 2010 through 2040, with energy use increasing at approximately the rate of population growth, at 0.5% per year, and remaining around 250 quadrillion British thermal units (Btu).[158] For non-OECD countries, however, the EIA projects that energy consumption from 2010 to 2040 will grow by 2.2% each year.[159] The non-OECD countries' proportion of total global energy use would increase as a result, from 54% in 2010 to 65% of total global energy use in 2040.[160] These projections predict the significant and disproportionate rate at which developing countries are expected to consume energy over the next three decades. Factors that have historically led to increased utilization of fossil fuels in developed countries can be expected to have the same effect in developing countries unless otherwise mitigated. For example, in 2007, the FAO projected that reduced availability of fuelwood, increased urbanization, and increased per capita incomes would be among the factors leading to reduced reliance on traditional biomass in developing countries over the coming decades, noting further that these factors have historically led to a replacement of traditional biomass by fossil fuels in developed countries.[161]

Energy use per capita is projected to remain relatively constant from 2010 to 2040 among OECD countries at about 193 million Btu (MMBtu), and expected to increase among non-OECD countries during the same period from 50 MMBtu to 73 MMBtu.[162] African countries are anticipated to experience the greatest population growth during these three decades, but the energy use per capita in these countries is anticipated to remain low.[163] India, by contrast, is projected to experience population growth at a rate twice that of the remaining non-OECD countries, and is also anticipated to see growth in its energy use per capita during this period.[164]

ECONOMIC SITUATION AND PROSPECTS 2014, http://www.un.org/en/development/desa/policy/wesp/wesp_current/2014wesp_country_classification.pdf.

157. David Peterson (principal contributor), *Today in Energy: Future World Energy Demand Driven by Trends in Developing Countries*, U.S. ENERGY INFO. ADMIN., Dec. 3, 2013, http://www.eia.gov/todayinenergy/detail.cfm?id=14011.

158. *Id.*

159. *Id.*

160. *Id.*

161. TOMASELLI, *supra* note 143, at 8.

162. Peterson, *supra* note 158.

163. *Id.*

164. *Id.*

The leader of developing countries in GHG emissions, China appears to be struggling more with the challenge of managing its grid than with technological or financial limitations.[165] This is important given China's key role in managing the challenges of climate change that proliferate in the energy industry. China's anticipated strategies, along with its successes and failures, account for a substantial contribution on the part of developing countries. In April 2015, the National Development and Reform Commission (NDRC) of China banned construction of new coal-fired thermal power plants in areas with an excess power supply.[166] From 2012 to 2016, China's solar energy capacity increased nearly seven times and wind energy capacity doubled, but sales from renewables have been limited due to lack of planning and congestion in the network.[167] The ban on new coal-fired plant construction is anticipated to curb GHG emissions both from coal-fired energy generation, and by allowing a greater proportion of the country's energy demand to be satisfied from renewable sources.[168] China's decrease in coal consumption two years in a row—2.9% in 2014 and 3.7% in 2015—provides hope that the country's commitment to reducing carbon emissions may come to fruition earlier than anticipated in its Paris pledge.[169]

India has also made promises of increased renewables and increased investment in R&D on an international platform, as part of its nationally determined contribution to the Paris Agreement. The country pledged to obtain between 30% and 40% of its power from non-fossil-fuel sources by 2030.[170] India also anticipates increasing its clean energy R&D funding from $72 million to $145 million by 2019.[171]

While India's involvement in the Paris talks was significant, and Prime Minister Narendra Modi has taken on climate change as an issue of spiritual responsibility, the national government's recent pledges may translate into limited implementation.[172] In India, authority to regulate the electric power sector falls within the powers of states.[173] Only nine of India's 29 states are under the leadership of Modi's Bharatiya Janata Party, making

165. *China Ban on New Coal Power Eases Clean Energy Waste, WRI Says*, BLOOMBERG, Apr. 29, 2016, http://www.bloomberg.com/news/articles/2016-04-29/china-ban-on-new-coal-power-eases-clean-energy-waste-wri-says.

166. Shiv Mehta, *China Bans New Coal-Fired Power Plants*, INVESTOPEDIA, Apr. 27, 2016, http://www.investopedia.com/articles/insights/042716/china-bans-new-coalfired-power-plants.asp#.

167. *China Ban on New Coal Power Eases Clean Energy Waste, supra* note 166.

168. *Id.*

169. Jean Chemnick, *Nations: China Coal Cuts Might Bring Emissions Peak Closer to Reality*, CLIMATEWIRE, Mar. 1, 2016, http://www.eenews.net/climatewire/2016/03/01/stories/1060033218.

170. *Id.*

171. *Id.*

172. *Id.*

173. *Id.*

nationwide realization of Modi's Paris promises a challenge.[174] However, the national government can use financial incentives for the states to encourage energy efficiency and growth in renewables, an action the government is currently taking.[175] That, coupled with states' support for renewables and Modi's support for a free market at a time when private party investment is a key resource for success, indicates that India appears to be on track for mitigating climate change consequences of energy production.[176] This effort will not, however, proceed without challenges, as illustrated in the case study that follows, which demonstrates the importance of a tailored approach for meeting the challenges of balancing climate change mitigation and access to energy. While the initiative and governmental support behind a shift to renewable energy are imperative for the necessary global shift toward renewables, practical limitations in developing countries may, in many cases, mean that a hasty transition to renewable energy in unprepared communities will be ineffective and unsustainable.

C.   Case Studies: Greenpeace in Dharnai and Contrasting Success Stories

Economic and political obstacles prevent communities around the world from gaining access to electricity. An economic injustice is created when climate policy prevents those who were historically non-players in climate change contributions from now having the opportunity to gain reliable access to energy. The issue is further complicated by the fact that many of these impoverished or rural communities are unable to access electricity due not only to policy, but also to economic constraints. This economic injustice issue means these groups are not only more vulnerable to the environmental harms of climate change, but are also without energy access at a time when energy production is more controversial than ever. These communities either await the doom of too much or too little water on their land or seek refuge during what some anticipate will be one of the world's worst refugee crises, all the while living without a luxury and comfort that many in developed nations take for granted.

The case that follows, of Greenpeace's solar power initiative in Dharnai, India, provides an example of this conflict, while the examples that follow it serve as models of similar, successful attempts to provide clean energy to low-income communities in developing nations. These cases demonstrate the

---

174. *Id.*
175. *Id.*
176. *Id.*

need for project-/location-specific analyses to determine the unique needs of each community when providing financial or technological support for establishing access to clean energy. Further, they demonstrate the need for ongoing funding, particularly for projects in areas where the communities are unable to sustain the project financially once it is in place.

Dharnai is a town of approximately 3,200 people in eastern India.[177] The community was without electricity for decades, until Greenpeace India implemented an initiative in July 2014 to bring solar-powered electricity to the rural community in the form of microgrids.[178] While settling to some extent for the electricity they could get from this initiative, Greenpeace's efforts were met with a demand from the residents to their government that they receive "real" electricity from the central grid, primarily powered by coal.[179] Dharnai is fraught with political struggle, caught geographically in the midst of the Naxalism guerilla communist movement.[180] It is one of many towns in rural Bihar and Uttar Pradesh that house the 400 million people in that region who do not have electric power.[181] While organizations like Greenpeace see this as an opportunity to power these communities through renewable energy, the realities of the limitations in such communities can be discouraging.[182]

The investment in Dharnai consisted of 70 kW of photovoltaic cells throughout the village, 224 batteries for energy storage and $407,050.[183] Though the power was free for the first six months, the subsequent monthly payments required of the families were more than many could afford.[184] For one family that needed to power one compact fluorescent light bulb and a wall outlet to charge a mobile phone, the cost was about $1 per month, while the average earnings per person in the town was about 30 cents per day.[185] The wealthier Dharnai residents already had rooftop solar panels, but many still took advantage of Greenpeace's offer, thought to provide a more reliable microgrid.[186] However, this resulted in wealthier residents draining the town's solar battery power with their appliances, while poorer families were

177. Gayathri Vaidyanathan, *Nations: Activists Say Solar Can Power India, but Politics and Economics of Coal Win Out*, CLIMATEWIRE, Oct. 19, 2015, http://www.eenews.net/special_reports/greater_expectations/stories/1060026477.
178. *Id.*
179. *Id.*
180. *Id.*
181. *Id.*
182. *Access to Electricity (% of Population)*, *supra* note 5.
183. *Id.*
184. *Id.*
185. *Id.*
186. *Id.*

left unable to power the single light bulb in their homes.[187] The residents of Dharnai took advantage of the publicity resulting from Greenpeace's solar initiative to draw attention to their desire to be placed on the central grid.[188] A few weeks after Greenpeace entered the scene, Dharnai received a 100-kW transformer and was connected to the central grid.[189] Residents below the poverty line now have free access to electricity, which, for the residents who pay for the service, costs one-third that of solar grid power.[190]

As this example demonstrates, the discrepancies in justice that are involved in closing the energy access gap while addressing CO_2 emissions can result in challenges that, at present, weigh more in favor of economic rather than environmental considerations. The case in Dharnai, however, is not the only one in which an attempt has been made to power a rural community through renewable energy. As the following examples demonstrate, other such cases have proven successful.

A project of the World Bank that is now in its second installation, the Rural Electrification and Renewable Energy Development Project (RERED) was originally approved in 2002 with the goal of powering rural communities in Bangladesh through solar power.[191] Approximately 60% of rural households in Bangladesh do not have access to grid electricity due to their remote location and because they are the first volunteered to lose power in the event of a shortage.[192] The RERED project aimed to provide a more reliable source of energy for these communities through reliance on renewables.[193]

The first RERED project established more than 650,000 new connections to the power grid and more than 1.2 million solar home systems in remote areas.[194] The second RERED project, which began in 2014, was the fastest growing solar home systems program in the world, resulting in the installation of 50,000 solar home systems every month.[195] Impact evaluation studies on solar home systems "confirmed increased study time for children, increased mobility and sense of security for women, and increased use of

187. *Id.*
188. *Id.*
189. *Id.*
190. *Id.*
191. World Bank, *Rural Electrification and Renewable Energy Development*, http://www.worldbank.org/projects/P071794/rural-electrification-renewable-energy-development?lang=en&tab=details (last visited Sept. 3, 2016).
192. *Id.*
193. Stephan Bachenheimer, *Lighting Up Rural Communities in Bangladesh*, WORLD BANK, Jan. 15, 2014, http://www.worldbank.org/en/news/feature/2014/01/15/lighting-up-rural-communities-in-bangladesh.
194. *Id.*
195. *Id.*

contraceptives and fall in recent fertility in [solar home system] households, thanks to awareness from watching TV."[196]

The apparent success of this project as compared to that in Dharnai is likely a result of the financial support behind RERED. With the backing of the World Bank, and monetary commitments from national and international nongovernmental organizations (NGOs) and from other nations (e.g., Germany), the RERED project has been sustained for nearly one and a half decades, while Greenpeace's financial contributions to Dharnai's solar power did not go far beyond initial installations and the first six months of the project.[197]

Another promising case emerged in China. In April 2016, China's State Council, the country's top decisionmaking body, announced an initiative to "help finance distributed and centralized solar photovoltaic projects in 3,500 villages in 16 provinces over the next five years."[198] The subsidies will allow families to finance up to 5 kW of solar power and will allow for centralized projects for up to 25 kW.[199]

Home to the greatest number of nations with the lowest levels of energy access, Africa is also a prime candidate for renewable energy. Some initiatives, such as Innovation: Africa, already exist to this end.[200] Similarly, in 2013, the Obama Administration pledged $7 billion for its Power Africa initiative with the goal of expanding energy access across the continent.[201] With two-thirds of sub-Saharan Africans—85% in rural areas—living without electricity, initiatives such as these are critical in addressing the problem of energy access justice.[202] Though not a requirement of the program, Power Africa uses GHG emissions reduction and climate change mitigation as key factors in its efforts.[203]

---

196. *Id.*
197. World Bank, *Rural Electrification and Renewable Energy Development II (RERED II) Project, Financing Plan at Board Presentation (US$ Millions)*, http://www.worldbank.org/projects/P131263/rural-electrification-renewable-energy-development-ii-rered-ii-project?lang=en&tab=financial (last visited Sept. 3, 2016).
198. Michael Standaert, *China to Subsidize Solar to Help Environment, Poor*, Bloomberg BNA, Apr. 5, 2016.
199. *Id.*
200. Ashoka, *Will Obama's Power Africa Initiative Reach the Rural Poor?*, Forbes, Aug. 20, 2013, http://www.forbes.com/sites/ashoka/2013/08/20/will-obamas-power-africa-initiative-reach-the-rural-poor/#19e0f9be1d0b.
201. *Id.*
202. *Id.*
203. Fact Sheet, The White House, Office of the Press Secretary, Power Africa (July 25, 2015), https://www.whitehouse.gov/the-press-office/2015/07/25/fact-sheet-power-africa. The International Institute for Environment and Development is yet another proponent of powering the poor through sustainable energy, and uses research, case studies, and collaboration with governments and NGOs to further that objective. *Improving People's Access to Sustainable Energy*, Int'l Inst. Env't & Dev., Oct. 26, 2012, http://www.iied.org/improving-people-s-access-sustainable-energy.

As the OECD recognized in a brief for policymakers, renewable energy has significant potential to bring energy access, revenue sources, jobs, community building, and more to rural communities and countries.[204] Additionally, access to communities that are accustomed to living without electricity provides the renewable energy industry with a unique opportunity for innovation and experimentation.[205] In fact, according to the OECD, "Some form of innovation related to renewable energy has been observed in all the case studies."[206] In this way, such projects serve as valuable economic investments for renewable energy companies, and as valuable economic and political investments for governments due to the technology-driving contributions with benefits beyond those to the rural communities. As evidenced by the cases presented in this section, the keys to success in these projects are an accurate analysis of each community's specific needs and capabilities in maintaining the energy system, and securing sources of ongoing funding, whether it be a community that can afford to continuously maintain the project, or a government or private grant that remains available for some time after installation of the infrastructure.

III. The Future of Global Energy and Climate Change: Financing Innovation Through Cooperative Partnerships and a Tailored Approach

In addition to financial support and incentives aimed at ameliorating the environmental impacts of energy consumption, efficacy of policy is a key determinant in achieving climate justice both environmentally and economically. This is particularly important as developed nations devote greater attention and resources to measures aimed at mitigating climate change. This section considers the implications of the challenges identified in this chapter, and concludes with recommendations for promoting climate justice. In addition to continued investment in clean energy, this section also presents the need to enhance private-public partnerships in both developed and developing countries to ensure both sides of the equation (financial viability, and environmental and public health) are represented and working in concert, to reassess domestic allocation of public funds (e.g., subsidies, grants, tax incentives) to ensure that renewable energy production and clean energy R&D

---

204. OECD, Linking Renewable Energy to Rural Development: Executive Summary Brief for Policy Makers 1 (n.d.), https://www.oecd.org/regional/regional-policy/Renewable-rural-energy-summary.pdf.
205. *Id.*
206. *Id.*

are the recipients of the funds, to carefully assess the capabilities of and best practices for communities receiving clean energy funds, and to allow for flexibility in developing countries' application of the financial support provided by developing countries.

As the basis for clean energy advancement, countries, especially those of higher economic status, should continue—if not greatly increase—to foster technological innovation to support clean energy production. The United States, with its marked investment trend toward clean energy and clean technologies, can in many ways serve as a model for this objective. The Clean Energy Trust is an example of this trend. The Clean Energy Trust Challenge is an annual, one-day clean technology funding competition for startups in the Midwest, with more than 80 companies funded to date.[207] Investments from such initiatives, along with R&D investments and incentives from government and industry, have encouraged rapid advancement in clean technologies in the United States. These national achievements are essential to paving the path forward for the United States, and when combined with international-scale initiatives, provide for truly meaningful strides toward cleaner energy technologies.

As a related consideration, both developed and developing nations must make conscious efforts to close the divide between industry goals and government/public interest goals. This goal can be achieved through public-private partnerships that allow for open communication and collaboration between the two, often conflicting, sides, and can serve to minimize economic and political tensions that exist in the energy and climate justice contexts. As efforts to further develop emissions-curbing technologies progress in the electric utility sector, agencies, businesses, and organizations invested in these efforts would be wise to emulate models in related sectors that have successfully addressed industries of global concern. For example, the transportation sector's recent efforts to curb CO_2 emissions from airplanes provides helpful examples of successful cooperative endeavors that may serve as a best practice in the energy sector.

Airplanes have been identified as contributing 2% of global CO_2 emissions for nearly two and a half decades.[208] The United States contributes 29%

---

207. Clean Energy Trust, *Clean Energy Trust Challenge 2016*, http://cleanenergytrust.org/challenge/ (last visited Aug. 21, 2016).
208. *See* Kristin Rypdal, Aircraft Emissions, Good Practice Guidance and Uncertainty Management in National Greenhouse Gas Inventories, Background Paper (2000) (citing 1990 numbers), http://www.ipcc-nggip.iges.or.jp/public/gp/bgp/2_5_Aircraft.pdf; Intergovernmental Panel on Climate Change, *Aviation and the Global Atmosphere* (citing 1992 numbers), http://www.ipcc.ch/ipccreports/sres/aviation/006.htm (last visited Aug. 21, 2006); International Civil Aviation Org. (ICAO), ICAO Environmental Report 2013: Aviation and Climate Change 11 (2013)

of all global aircraft GHG emissions,[209] the largest share of global contributions.[210] The United Nations' International Civil Aviation Organization discussions and negotiations for establishing international standards for GHG emissions from airplanes may become another significant forum for distinctions between developed and developing nations and what each side may be expected to contribute to global efforts, making this example in particular a useful parallel for the energy sector.[211]

In addressing aviation industry emissions, the United States has established private-public partnerships that strike a balance between industry needs and environmental needs. In 2010, the Federal Aviation Administration (FAA) created the Continuous Lower Energy, Emissions, and Noise (CLEEN) program to facilitate the development of technologies that, among other things, reduce emissions and fuel burn in the aviation sector.[212] More than half of the money invested in the CLEEN program, $250 million, came from contributions from the five aviation manufacturers—Boeing, General Electric, Honeywell, Pratt &Whitney, and Rolls-Royce—working in partnership with the FAA.[213] The FAA is not alone among U.S. agencies in driving aviation emissions-reducing technology. The National Aeronautics and Space Administration (NASA) and the U.S. Air Force are also spearheading technology-advancing initiatives.[214]

(stating that emissions are 2% of total anthropogenic CO_2 emissions globally), http://cfapp.icao.int/Environmental-Report-2013/files/assets/common/downloads/ICAO_2013_Environmental_Report.pdf; Air Transport Action Group, *Facts & Figures* (confirming 2% figure), http://www.atag.org/facts-and-figures.html (last visited Aug. 21, 2016).

209. Proposed Finding That Greenhouse Gas Emissions From Aircraft Cause or Contribute to Air Pollution That May Reasonably Be Anticipated to Endanger Public Health and Welfare and Advance Notice of Proposed Rulemaking, 80 Fed. Reg. 37758, 37788–89 (July 1, 2015).

210. *See, e.g.*, Jad Mouawad & Coral Davenport, *U.N. Agency Proposes Limits on Airlines' Carbon Emissions*, N.Y. TIMES, Feb. 8, 2016 (citing a Center for Biological Diversity report that attributes half of global CO_2 emissions from airplanes to the United States), http://www.nytimes.com/2016/02/09/business/energy-environment/un-agency-proposes-limits-on-airlines-carbon-emissions.html?_r=0; Christie Aschwanden, *Every Time You Fly, You Trash the Planet—And There's No Easy Fix*, FIVETHIRTYEIGHT, Jan. 2, 2015 (attributing one-third of global CO_2 emissions from airplanes to the United States), http://fivethirtyeight.com/features/every-time-you-fly-you-trash-the-planet-and-theres-no-easy-fix/.

211. Anthony Adragna, *"Key Moment" for Global Aircraft Emissions This Week*, BLOOMBERG BNA, May 10, 2016, http://www.bna.com/key-moment-global-n57982070918/?utm_source=feedburner&utm_medium=feed&utm_campaign=Feed%3A+WWF-InTheNews+%28World+Wildlife+Fund+In+the+News%29#!; *see also* ICAO, *Environmental Protection* (containing information on ICAO's environmental protection initiatives), http://www.icao.int/environmental-protection/Pages/default.aspx (last visited Aug. 21, 2006).

212. UNITED STATES AVIATION GREENHOUSE GAS EMISSIONS REDUCTION PLAN, SUBMITTED TO THE INTERNATIONAL CIVIL AVIATION ORGANIZATION 12 (2015), http://www.icao.int/environmental-protection/Lists/ActionPlan/Attachments/30/UnitedStates_Action_Plan-2015.pdf.

213. *Id.*

214. *Id.* at 13.

Europe has also developed airplane technologies for greater energy efficiency through private-public partnerships. The EU's Joint Technology Initiative CleanSky and the Advisory Council for Aeronautics Research in Europe's Vision 2020 are examples of such programs.[215] The private-public partnerships developed to address airline emissions, along with the national and continental efforts that parallel those in the energy sector, demonstrate how an industry's financing and collaboration with regulators puts both sides in the best position to make progress. Applying this success story to the energy sector, fossil fuel industry players may be more likely to succeed amidst inevitable actions to address climate change if those stakeholders join rather than reject regulators in conceiving plans to abate GHG emissions while ensuring the industry's economic needs are met. This approach of cooperation, as contrasted with the government-versus-industry struggle presented in Part I.B., is a fundamental catalyst of climate justice progress that also addresses the world's energy needs.

Cooperation and collaboration are necessary not only among industry and government, but also among the leaders of the world's nations and their communities.[216] The collaborative efforts observed in the recent international agreement developed in Paris set an important tone for the necessary efforts to come, and provide a model for controversial issues that must be addressed in present and future climate justice efforts. The Paris Agreement encourages Parties to implement measures that represent their most ambitious efforts in light of the circumstances unique to each nation, including the best available science, and based on the "provision of finance, technology and capacity-building to developing countries."[217] The key to ensuring that climate change actions are environmentally and economically just is to acknowledge the divergent needs and capabilities of different countries and regions within them, and to identify the most effective clean energy initiative to correspond with those needs and capabilities. For instance, an essential consideration of Greenpeace in its Dharnai efforts should have been the projected ability of the community to maintain the new solar energy system. Where the organization or government entity developing energy infrastructure in poor or rural

---

215. ICAO ENVIRONMENTAL REPORT 2013, *supra* note 209, at 101.

216. For an example of a case involving collaboration between nations, private-public partnership, and federal financing of clean energy R&D, see DOE, *Energy Department Announces $30 Million Expansion of U.S.-India Partnership to Advance Clean Energy Research* (describing a $30 million combined pledge by the United States and India to fund private-public clean energy research as part of the countries' Partnership to Advance Clean Energy Research (PACE-R)), http://energy.gov/articles/energy-department-announces-30-million-expansion-us-india-partnership-advance-clean-energy (last visited Sept. 18, 2016).

217. *Adoption of the Paris Agreement*, UNFCC Conference of the Parties, 21st Sess., at 2, U.N. Doc. FCCC/CP/2015/L.9/Rev.1 (2015), https://unfccc.int/resource/docs/2015/cop21/eng/l09.pdf.

areas will not itself be able to continuously fund the project, that entity must conduct an analysis to determine what form of energy production will provide the most long-term, efficient energy access to the community.[218] In some cases, the best form of energy production will be from renewable sources, an inherently better fuel source for the environment.[219] Situations where this is not the case can help to determine how clean energy efforts must be allocated to developing technologies that mitigate GHG emissions from fossil fuels.

In order to implement effective programs, there must be an understanding of the case-specific opportunities and limitations present, and the needs that must be satisfied to ensure a successful project. For example, as illustrated in the Kemper IGCC case study in Part I.C., to construct a facility that can emit CO_2 from coal use at a level comparable to that of natural gas requires significant technological advances and financial investments beyond those feasible in rural areas in the most underdeveloped regions of a developing country such as India. Thus, subsidies play a decisive role in the advancement of otherwise cost-prohibitive measures toward achieving cleaner energies. Subsidies, tax incentives, and other forms of financial support from the government must continue to be available for industry and researchers to justify financially high-risk technology innovation projects. The forms of government financial support that will be most relevant and necessary for achieving the latter are funds that support R&D. Thus, in order to effectively promote a clean energy and climate-just future, governments should provide such funding and incentives via support for renewable energy production and clean energy R&D, but not via support for fossil fuel production and use. As demonstrated in the Kemper IGCC case study, taxpayer funding as opposed to ratepayer funding provides for a more widely distributed, and thus more just, sharing of these costs by the public and is greater evidence of the need for federal financing.[220]

The use of tax subsidies for energy production has also been examined at the international level. According to a 2015 International Monetary Fund (IMF)

---

218. For an example of such an analysis, see Ram M. Shrestha et al., *Institutional Reforms and Electricity Access: Lessons From Bangladesh and Thailand*, 8 ENERGY SUSTAINABLE DEV. 41 (2004).

219. *See* M.R. Nouni, et al., *Providing Electricity Access to Remote Areas in India: Niche Areas for Decentralized Electricity Supply*, 34 RENEWABLE ENERGY 430 (2009).

220. DOE's August 2016 announcement of a $28 million investment in R&D projects to advance cleaner fossil fuel energy production is a notable example of such federal financing. DOE, *Energy Department Invests $28 Million to Advance Cleaner Fossil Fuel-Based Power Generation*, http://energy.gov/fe/articles/energy-department-invests-28-million-advance-cleaner-fossil-fuel-based-power-generation (last visited Sept. 18, 2016). Another example is DOE's funding of projects to develop technologies for use of CO_2 from coal-fired power plants. DOE, *DOE Seeks Projects to Advance Carbon Dioxide Utilization From Coal-Fired Power Plants*, http://energy.gov/fe/articles/doe-seeks-projects-advance-carbon-dioxide-utilization-coal-fired-power-plants (last visited Sept. 18, 2016).

report, global post-tax energy subsidies have significantly exceeded their projections. In 2011, 2013, and 2015, global post-tax subsidies totaled $4.2 trillion, $4.9 trillion, and $5.3 trillion, that is, 5.8%, 6.5%, and 6.5% of global gross domestic product, respectively.[221] Post-tax subsidies were eight times that of pre-tax subsidies in 2011 and 16 times that of pre-tax subsidies in 2015.[222] While international energy prices have experienced a sharp decline, post-tax subsidies have remained high.[223] The IMF cites high growth in energy consumption, namely coal, as the primary reason for this reality, in particular in countries with significant environmental damage from coal.[224] The IMF states, "This trend suggests that energy subsidy reform is as urgent as ever, in particular to tackle the un-priced externalities from energy consumption."[225] The IMF further suggests that current conditions present an opportunity to eliminate pre-tax subsidies and raise energy taxes, especially because the impact on and response from the public would be mitigated in part due to lower international energy prices.[226] These considerations, along with examples from other countries, should be evaluated in global efforts to develop the strongest public funding structures for clean energy.

Shifting considerations from domestic funding schemes to international ones, a climate-just future must involve the funding by developed countries of developing countries' energy and environmental security in a manner that protects developing countries' sovereignty and flexibility while still addressing their unique needs. Regarding funding, many programs already exist for developed countries to submit funds to or for developing countries' clean energy futures. One global initiative that is part of a combined effort to achieve climate justice is the Green Climate Fund (GCF). The GCF is a financial initiative in which developed countries support developing countries' future greening and adaptation to climate change.[227] The GCF was established to prevent the global temperature from rising beyond 2°C by way of developed countries contributing to a fund to be used by developing countries to keep emissions low as they continue to develop.[228] The Obama Administration has pledged $3 billion to the fund, $500 million of which

221. David Coady et al., How Large Are Global Energy Subsidies? 18 (International Monetary Fund 2015) (WP/15/105), https://www.imf.org/external/pubs/ft/wp/2015/wp15105.pdf.
222. Id.
223. Id.
224. Id.
225. Id. at 29.
226. Id.
227. See Chapter 3 of this volume, for a detailed analysis of the GCF.
228. Green Climate Fund, Homepage, http://www.greenclimate.fund/home (last visited Aug. 21, 2016).

the administration transmitted to the World Bank on March 7, 2016.[229] One outstanding question in applying the fund, and key to the issue of maintaining sovereignty and flexibility, is who will determine how the funds are allocated—i.e., whether the developed donors will have the authority to determine how the funds are utilized, or whether the developing countries will receive the funds as cash and decide how they will apply the funds in their respective countries.

This question presents an opportunity to reflect on the notion that, while developed countries are the ones funding global-scale clean energy initiatives, they should relinquish those funds with an appreciation for developing countries' expectation of and need for a reasonable level of autonomy and flexibility in progressing toward clean energy. While it is vital that developing countries be held accountable for using the funds in accordance with principles of advancing cleaner energy, micromanagement by developed countries is not appropriate given the unique challenges each developing country—even each city within that country—faces. Neglecting these challenges and exercising too much control over the business of other nations creates the risk of repeating unsuccessful efforts like those observed in Dharnai. Conversely, allowing developing nations to determine the application of funds they receive would enable them to invest in such technologies as carbon capture and sequestration that allow them to continue fossil fuel use while reducing atmospheric GHG emissions.

A British case study from the University of Oxford further emphasizes the importance of demand-side policy.[230] There, researchers found that an examination of the energy efficiency measures proposed by the Department of Energy and Climate Change through its "Green Deal" initiative revealed that it would be *less* effective than the policies already in place.[231] The researchers held that to ensure maximum positive impact, social factors—including the level of national acceptance of proposed strategies—are to be considered relative to their required scale to achieve the desired impact.[232]

Countries applying the considerations and strategies offered here will better ensure both environmental and economic climate justice in their efforts, domestically and internationally, to secure a clean energy future.

---

229. Dean Scott, *U.S. Makes $500 Million Green Climate Fund Payment*, BLOOMBERG BNA, Mar. 9, 2016, http://www.bna.com/us-makes-500-n57982068259/?elqTrackId=8fe69c1f19a8451f8c5683fd0b104 c8f&elq=917323b86ca44cbabf09a623eab89b0e&elqaid=4761&elqat=1&elqCampaignId=2830.

230. UNIVERSITY OF OXFORD, POLICY DESIGN TO PROMOTE ENERGY EFFICIENCY (2013), http://www. energy.ox.ac.uk/wordpress/wp-content/uploads/2013/09/CaseStudies_4.pdf.

231. *Id.*

232. *Id.*

Conclusion

While development of new policies and technologies are necessary to mitigate the harms of increased energy use, such initiatives must acknowledge the double-edged sword of climate justice. Meeting the demands of an ever-increasing human population should be approached with prudence to ensure that finance and technology sharing among parties and governments' support of clean energy initiatives incorporate considerations of the risks of all, rather than any one (i.e., environmental) detriment. In this way, countries can ensure that they are sensitive to the many negative impacts of climate change, and that an overemphasis in mitigating one risk does not result in the creation of another.

A global consensus exists that to make progress toward climate justice and achieve equitable access to energy throughout the world, information sharing and financial access to innovation and infrastructure are the cornerstones of the common but differentiated responsibility of the global community. This progress must be achieved through providing support for a cultural and economic shift toward cleaner energy in developing countries while maintaining a base of reliable traditional sources of energy to facilitate a smooth and realistic transition. The greater the citizens and policymakers in developed and developing countries are informed of the potentially divergent implications of climate justice, the better the position of all parties to build a system to address the world's energy demands in a manner that leads to a more just outcome for all.

Chapter 5

Corporate Responsibility: Promoting Climate Justice Through the Divestment of Fossil Fuels and Socially Responsible Investment

Josephine Balzac

Introduction

> People of conscience need to break their ties . . . it makes no sense
> to invest in companies that undermine our future.
>
> *—Desmond Tutu*

The perpetuation of business as usual in the climate change era endangers the future of human existence and, consequently, imperils the realization of human rights.[1] The recent signing and adoption of the Paris Agreement signifies a global consensus that climate change is an urgent threat and common concern of humankind that needs ambitious mitigation and adaptation efforts to solve the problem.[2] The Agreement requires holding the increase in global temperature to well below 2°C while pursuing efforts to limit the temperature increase to 1.5°C above pre-industrial levels.[3] The Paris Agreement is undergirded by principles of equity, common but differentiated responsibilities, sustainable development, and poverty eradication.[4]

Protecting the environment and eradicating poverty are an "indispensable requirement and integral part of achieving sustainable development."[5] Sustainable development incorporates three components: environmental protection, social development, and economic development. On January 1, 2016, the 17 Sustainable Development Goals of the 2030 Agenda for Sustainable Development officially became effective.[6] The goals include women's rights, eradicating poverty, climate action, food security, environmental protection, health, education, equality, and job opportunities.[7] The Sustainable Development Goals promote equitable economic growth, equitable social development, and integrated and sustainable management of natural resources and ecosystems.[8]

Sustainable development is rooted in equitably meeting the developmental and environmental needs of present and future generations.[9] This concept of intergenerational equity was first emphasized in the Stockholm Declaration preamble, stating that "[t]o defend and improve the human environment for present and future generations has become an imperative goal of humankind."[10] Furthermore, the United Nations Framework Convention

---

1.   Webinar: Business and Climate Justice: What Role Can Business Play in Tackling the Human Rights of Impacts of Climate Change? (U.N. Global Compact and Mary Robinson Foundation 2015), https://www.unglobalcompact.org/library/1231.

2.   *Adoption of the Paris Agreement*, UNFCCC Conference of the Parties, 21st Sess., U.N. Doc. FCCC/CP/2015/10/Add.1 (Dec. 12, 2015), http://unfccc.int/files/home/application/pdf/paris_agreement.pdf.

3.   *Id.*

4.   *Id.*

5.   *Rio Declaration on Environment and Development*, U.N. Conference on Environment and Development, Rio de Janeiro, Brazil, June 3–14, 1992, Annex 1, U.N. Doc. A/CONF.151/26 (Vol. I) (1992), http://www.un.org/documents/ga/conf151/aconf15126-1annex1.htm [hereinafter *Rio Declaration*].

6.   United Nations, *The Sustainable Development Agenda*, http://www.un.org/sustainabledevelopment/development-agenda/ (last visited Aug. 21, 2016).

7.   *Id.*

8.   *Id.*

9.   *Rio Declaration, supra* note 5, at Annex I, Princ. 3 (noting that the "right to development must be fulfilled so as to equitably meet developmental and environmental needs of present and future generations").

10.   *Declaration of the United Nations Conference on the Human Environment*, U.N. Conference on the Human Environment, Stockholm, Sweden, June 5–16, 1972, U.N. Doc. A/CONF.48/14 (1972),

on Climate Change (UNFCCC) requires countries to protect the climate system for the benefit of present and future generations of humankind on the basis of equity and in accordance with their common but differentiated responsibilities and respective capabilities.[11]

Viewing the scientific evidence and impacts of climate change through a human rights lens, climate change impacts endanger the effective enjoyment of a range of human rights. The connection between human rights and climate change has been recognized by the United Nations in a variety of documents by the Human Rights Council and the Office of the High Commissioner for Human Rights.[12] In 2000, at the UNFCCC Sixth Conference of the Parties (COP6), the summit's mission stated: "We affirm that climate change is a rights issue. It affects our livelihoods, our health, our children and our natural resources."

The Mary Robinson Foundation is a leading climate justice organization that seeks to put justice and equity at the heart of climate change responses and identifies the strong connection between human rights and climate change.[13] In its Principles of Climate Justice, the Foundation observed that "[c]limate justice links human rights and development to achieve a human-centered approach safeguarding the rights of the most vulnerable and sharing the burdens and benefits of climate change and its resolution equitably and fairly."[14] The climate "injustice" is that the people most vulnerable and marginalized are the ones that have had little to do with generating the greenhouse gas (GHG) emissions that cause climate change. Climate justice affirms the need to significantly reduce the emission of GHGs and associated local pollutants.[15] The Bali Principles identified the 27 principles of climate justice.[16]

The business community is now recognizing this connection between human rights and climate change.[17] Businesses play a role in addressing cli-

revised by U.N. Doc. A/CONF.48/14/Corr.1 (1972), _reprinted in_ 11 I.L.M. 1416 (1972); _see also_ David Hunter et al., International Environmental Law and Policy 492 (3d ed. 2007).

11. United Nations Framework Convention on Climate Change, May 9, 1992, 1771 U.N.T.S. 107 (entered into force Mar. 21, 1994).

12. Webinar, _supra_ note 1; _see also_ John H. Knox, U.N. Special Rapporteur, Mapping Report on Climate Change and Human Rights (2014), http://srenvironment.org/wp-content/uploads/2014/08/Climate-Change-mapping-report-15-August-final.docx; United Nations Human Rights Office of the High Commissioner, Key Messages on Human Rights and Climate Change 2 (2015), http://www.ohchr.org/Documents/Issues/ClimateChange/KeyMessages_on_HR_CC.pdf.

13. Mary Robinson Foundation-Climate Justice, _Mission and Vision_, http://www.mrfcj.org/about/mission-and-vision/ (last visited Aug. 21, 2016).

14. Mary Robinson Foundation-Climate Justice, Principles of Climate Justice (n.d.), http://www.mrfcj.org/pdf/Principles-of-Climate-Justice.pdf.

15. Bali Principles of Climate Justice (2002), http://www.ejnet.org/ej/bali.pdf.

16. _Id._

17. Webinar, _supra_ note 1.

mate change impacts on human rights.[18] Until recently, businesses addressed these two subjects independently of the other. Due to the growing awareness and recognition of the nexus between the two, however, businesses are now addressing climate change and human rights concerns holistically.[19] Recent actions in the business and investment sectors reflect a new focus on protecting human rights in the face of climate change impacts.

This heightened awareness of climate change has inspired various institutional investors to divest from fossil fuels.[20] Investors have embraced the same thinking by pushing for a new sustainable energy economy with socially and environmentally responsible investments.[21] This fossil fuel divestment and investment in sustainable and socially responsible businesses will become a powerful driver of change.[22] This transition will promote climate justice by taking a human-centered approach to climate change and safeguarding the rights of present and future generations in the investment decisionmaking process.

This chapter examines the ethical motivations behind the movement to divest from dirty energy in order to protect our planet and present and future generations. Part I of this chapter discusses the moral origins of the fossil fuel divestment movement, the litigation that has ensued, and the movement's reach beyond its college campus origins. Part II identifies the sustainable business model through a corporate social responsibility (CSR) framework and discusses how CSR voluntary initiatives undertaken by companies can help promote climate justice. It addresses how climate change impacts are driving responsible investments and prompting investors to consider environmental, social, and governance criteria in the investment decisionmaking process.

I.   The Fossil Fuel Divestment Movement

Movements seeking ecological equity for future generations and rights of nature have been gaining momentum in the 21st century.[23] Divestment is a social responsibility campaign in which owners can decide to withhold their capital by selling investments in reprehensible activity.[24] It is the process of

---

18.   *Id.*
19.   *Id.*
20.   Divestor.org, *Reinvest: Your Home*, https://divestor.org/YHreinvesting.html (last visited Aug. 21, 2016).
21.   *Id.*
22.   *Id.*
23.   Judith E. Koons, *At the Tipping Point: Defining an Earth Jurisprudence for Social and Ecological Justice*, 58 Loy. L. Rev. 349, 349 (2012).
24.   Atif Ansar et al., Stranded Assets and the Fossil Fuel Divestment Campaign: What Does Divestment Mean for the Valuation of Fossil Fuel Assets? (Smith School of Enterprise and

removing investments that are unethical or morally ambiguous.[25] Divesting is a form of social investing, defined as "the systematic incorporation of ethical values and objectives in the investment decision-making process."[26] The objective of divestment is to promote a certain behavior or policy.[27]

In the 20th century, reprehensible activity subject to divestment campaigns included tobacco, munitions, corporations in apartheid South Africa, adult services, and gaming.[28] These divestment campaigns have been successful, but the largest and most impactful was the South African apartheid context.[29] Divesting in multinationals doing business in South Africa helped break the back of the apartheid government and usher in a new era of democracy and equality.[30] The success of this campaign is the inspiration for the current fossil fuel divestment movement.[31]

The fossil fuel divestment movement has quickly become the fastest growing divestment corporate campaign in history, surpassing the South Africa apartheid divestment movement.[32] The spark began in August 2012 when *Rolling Stone Magazine* published an article by Bill McKibben, founder of the organization 350.org, which detailed the risk of increasing the global temperatures above 2°C.[33] A tour called Do the Math was launched by 350.org explaining the need to limit the release of fossil fuels and keep the fossil fuels in the ground.[34] The tour led to the 350.org Fossil Free Divesture Movement, "a network of independent campaigns petitioning institutions and investors to divest from fossil fuels."[35]

The first major victory was in May 2014 when Stanford University agreed to divest its $18.7 billion endowment from coal companies.[36] By

the Environment 2013), http://www.smithschool.ox.ac.uk/research-programmes/stranded-assets/SAP-divestment-report-final.pdf.

25. Fossil Free, *What Is Fossil Fuel Divestment?*, http://gofossilfree.org/what-is-fossil-fuel-divestment/ (last visited Aug. 21, 2016).

26. Surbhi Sarang, Note, *Combating Climate Change Through a Duty to Divest*, 49 COLUM. J.L. & SOC. PROBS. 295, 300 (2016).

27. *What Is Fossil Fuel Divestment?*, *supra* note 25.

28. ANSAR ET AL., *supra* note 24, at 9 (noting that the private wealth owners making the decision to divest typically are university endowments, public pension funds, or their appointed asset managers).

29. *What Is Fossil Fuel Divestment?*, *supra* note 25.

30. *Id.*

31. ANSAR ET AL., *supra* note 24.

32. Marc Gunther, *Why the Fossil Fuel Divestment Movement May Ultimately Win*, YALE ENV'T 360, July 26, 2015, http://e360.yale.edu/feature/why_the_fossil_fuel_divestment_movement_may_ultimately_win/2898; Desmond Tutu, *We Need an Apartheid-Style Boycott to Save the Planet*, THE GUARDIAN, Apr. 10, 2014, http://www.theguardian.com/commentisfree/2014/apr/10/divest-fossil-fuels-climate-change-keystone-xl.

33. Sarang, *supra* note 26, at 298.

34. *Id.*

35. *Id.* at 299.

36. *Id.*

December 2015, 500 institutions representing $3.4 trillion in assets committed to divesting.[37]

A.   Moral Dimensions of the Fossil Fuel Divestment Movement

The fossil fuel divestment campaign focuses on the moral dimensions of climate change by spotlighting the immoral actions and impacts of the polluting fossil fuel industry.[38] It is a climate justice initiative that seeks to stand in solidarity with vulnerable frontline communities and those already experiencing the impacts of climate change.[39] The students of the campaign make a further plea that their futures are at stake because they are inheriting the consequences of global warming beyond 2°C.[40] They emphasize the injustice in this reality because they did not create the crisis but have a responsibility to fix it.[41] This intergenerational equity focus of the campaign seeks to ensure that future generations are not worse off by our choices.[42] It requires utilizing resources sustainably to avoid irreversible damage to the environment.[43]

The movement focuses on "living up to our values, changing the business as usual mentality, and redefining our future."[44] Our values as humans are what determine how we will behave in certain situations.[45] In order to have integrity, there must be consistency in what we say we value and what our actions say we value.[46] Ethical decisions involve self-restraint: (1) not doing what you have the power to do and (2) not doing what you have the right to do.[47]

The goal of divesting from fossil fuels is to "diminish the influence and power of the fossil fuel industry in the market, our political system, and in the social conscience overall."[48] Fossil fuel divestment has three aims:

---

37. Fossil Free, *Divestment Commitments*, http://gofossilfree.org/commitments/ (last visited Aug. 21, 2016).

38. Brett Fleishman, *The Decarbonizer and the Moral Case for Divestment*, 350, Feb. 5, 2016, https://350.org/the-decarbonizer-and-the-moral-case-for-divestment/.

39. We Are Power Shift, *Fossil Fuel Divestment*, http://www.wearepowershift.org/campaigns/divest (last visited Aug. 21, 2016).

40. *Id.*

41. *Id.*

42. Hunter et al., *supra* note 10, at 491.

43. *Id.*

44. Fleishman, *supra* note 38.

45. Michael Josephson, Making Ethical Decisions 5–6 (Josephson Inst. of Ethics n.d.), http://www.sfjohnson.com/acad/ethics/making_ethical_decisions.pdf.

46. *Id.*

47. *Id.* (explaining that an act is not proper simply because it is permissible or you can get away with it. There is a big difference between what you have the right to do and what is right to do.).

48. *Fossil Fuel Divestment, supra* note 39.

(i) "force the hand" of the fossil fuel companies and pressure government to leave the fossil fuels "down there"; (ii) pressure fossil fuel companies to undergo "transformative change" that can cause a drastic reduction in carbon emissions; [and] (iii) pressure governments to enact legislation such as a ban on further drilling or a carbon tax.[49]

It demands institutions and investors to eradicate the environmental and social injustices created by "dirty energy" by adopting sustainable investment policies.[50]

The Bali Principles on Climate Justice intended to shift "the discursive framework of climate change from a scientific-technical debate to one about ethics focused on human rights and justice."[51] "Divesting is a form of social investing . . . incorporating ethical values and objectives in the investment decision making process."[52] The campaign is not just to fight climate change "but to fight the racism, classism, and imperialism that the fossil fuel industries perpetuate."[53] This future generation is shifting the way of thinking "business as usual" and propelling change. This shift is necessary to change these social and political realities and have a meaningful response to climate change impacts on the environment and human rights.[54]

B.   College Campus Future Generations Lead Divestment Campaigns

The Fossil Free Divestment Movement mobilized and trained thousands of students and young people to organize against the threats of climate change.[55] Social movements use confrontational strategies, including media protests, to emphasize the negative social and environmental practices of highly visible corporations.[56] With social media commanding the public's attention, these corporations realize they are not immune to "naming and shaming" strategies when their valuable brands and reputation are linked to objectionable

---

49.   ANSAR ET AL., *supra* note 24.
50.   *What Is Fossil Fuel Divestment?*, *supra* note 25.
51.   BALI PRINCIPLES OF CLIMATE JUSTICE, *supra* note 15; ROBERT COX, ENVIRONMENTAL COMMUNICA-
      TION AND THE PUBLIC SPHERE 121 (3d. ed. 2013) (citing J. Agyeman et al., *The Climate-Justice Link:
      Communicating Risk With Low-Income and Minority Audiences*, *in* COMMUNICATING A CLIMATE FOR
      CHANGE: COMMUNICATING CLIMATE CHANGE AND FACILITATING SOCIAL CHANGE (S.C. Moser & L.
      Dillings eds., 2007).
52.   Sarang, *supra* note 26, at 300–01.
53.   *Fossil Fuel Divestment*, *supra* note 39.
54.   Koons, *supra* note 23, at 351.
55.   Fossil Fuel Divestment Student Network, *Organizing Pledge Project*, http://www.studentsdivest.org/
      organizing_pledge (last visited Aug. 21, 2016).
56.   Carmen Bain & Tamera Dandachi, *Governing GMOs: The (Counter) Movement for Mandatory and
      Voluntary Non-GMO Labels*, 6 SUSTAINABILITY 9456, 9459 (2014).

and social practices.[57] Social movements have emerged as key forces in mobilizing political consumers to address their concerns through the market.[58]

The students are demanding full divestment of fossil fuels and are doing it in the name of "climate justice." Students and graduates are making campaign pledges such as: "[M]illennials, we must rise to our historic moment and lead the call for climate justice. This is truly the fight of our lives."; "[W]e will not stop until we confront, dismantle and ultimately transform oppressive structures that perpetuate climate injustice, gender violence, and economic equality"; and "[B]ecause I want a more just and sustainable world that protects humanity over profits, environment over exploitation."[59] The "fossil fuel divestment [movement] is a moral campaign at its core."[60] In an open publication, Divest Harvard students criticized the Harvard Management Company (HMC) for betraying its moral obligations to its students by investing new capital in oil and gas exploration and refusing to divest.[61]

Most of the divestments to which colleges, universities, or schools have committed are only partial, such as only divesting in coal or tar sands, and are mostly from smaller private colleges.[62] Students are being advocates by writing and signing petitions, scheduling meetings, and conducting protests, week-long blockades, and sit-ins.[63]

Recently, this type of social activism generated real change on a university campus. On May 25, 2016, the University of Massachusetts became the first major public university to fully divest its endowment from fossil fuels.[64] Divestment of coal at UMass first began last year in response to a petition from the Student Fossil Fuel Divestment Campaign at UMass.[65] In April 2016, in efforts to call for full divestment of fossil fuels, the Campaign staged a series

57. *Id.*
58. *Id.*
59. *Organizing Pledge Project, supra* note 55.
60. 350, *In the Space of Just 10 Weeks . . .* , https://350.org/in-the-space-of-just-10-weeks/ (last visited Aug. 21, 2016).
61. *Open Publication: Divest Harvard Requests Meeting With Stephen Blyth*, Divest Harv., Mar. 9, 2016 (stating that "[a]bsent strong action, those of us who are young will likely see some of the world's great cities begin to be submerged underwater and millions of people displaced or killed by droughts, floods and famines. In our view, this crisis calls for new intergenerational accountability entailing drastic reductions in fossil fuel investment, production, and use." In order to reach the goal of 2°C, Divest Harvard states that "at least half of current reserves must remain in the ground, and investments in fossil fuel production must decrease considerably"), http://divestharvard.com/updates/.
62. *Divestment Commitments, supra* note 37.
63. Mariel A. Klein, *Student Protesters Appeal Dismissal of Divestment Lawsuit*, Harv. Crimson, Oct. 13, 2015, http://www.thecrimson.com/article/2015/10/13/divestment-appeal-lawsuit-dismiss/.
64. Robert P. Connolly, *UMass Becomes First Major Public University to Divest From Direct Fossil Fuel Holdings*, UMass Amherst, May 25, 2016, http://www.umass.edu/newsoffice/article/umass-becomes-first-major-public.
65. *Id.*

of protests that led to student arrests at UMass Amherst.[66] This student activism resulted in a unanimous decision by the board of directors of the UMass Foundation to fully divest from fossil fuels.[67] The board of trustees chairman stated that he will endorse the Foundation's decision, "because members of the UMass community have urged us to consider divestment in moral terms . . . and we acknowledge the moral imperative."[68] The UMass Amherst chancellor stated in regards to the decision to divest, "[T]he Foundation's action today . . . speaks volumes about our students' passionate commitment to social justice and the environment. It is largely due to their advocacy that this important issue has received the attention that it deserves."[69]

Although the divestment movement started on university campuses, it has spread beyond campuses and reached diverse institutions and cities throughout the world.[70] Of the more than 500 institutions divesting, only 13% are universities, colleges, and schools.[71] Other institutions divesting include faith-based organizations (26%), foundations (24%), governmental agencies (14%), pension funds (13%), nongovernmental organizations (6%), and for-profit corporations (3%).[72]

More than 70 cities worldwide have divested from fossil fuels, including Oslo, Norway; Paris, France; Newcastle, Australia; Muenster, Germany; Copenhagen, Denmark; San Francisco, California; Boulder, Colorado; and Minneapolis, Minnesota.[73] In addition, Stockholm, Sweden, and Berlin, Germany, are reviewing their fossil fuel investments.[74] Copenhagen's mayor stated in his proposal to divest that it would be wrong to continue investing in fossil fuels when Copenhagen is leading the world in the transition to a green economy.[75] Similarly, in deciding to divest from fossil fuels, the UMass board of trustees chairman shared a similar vision in stating, "[D]ivestment from fossil fuel companies is in keeping with our status as a national leader in environmental sustainability with cutting-edge programs in alternative energy research, sustainable agriculture, and sustainable built environment."[76] The decisionmakers deciding to divest are recognizing that

---

66. *Id.*
67. *Id.*
68. *Id.*
69. *Id.*
70. *Fossil Fuel Divestment, supra* note 39.
71. *Divestment Commitments, supra* note 37.
72. *Id.*
73. *Fossil Fuel Divestment, supra* note 39.
74. Melanie Mattauch, *Mayor Wants to Rid Copenhagen of "Totally Wrong" Investments in Coal, Oil, and Gas,* Fossil Free, Feb. 3, 2016, http://gofossilfree.org/mayor-wants-to-rid-copenhagen-of-totally-wrong-investments-in-coal-oil-and-gas/; *In the Space of Just 10 Weeks, supra* note 60.
75. Mattauch, *supra* note 74.
76. Connolly, *supra* note 64 (quoting Kumble Subbaswamy, UMass Amherst chancellor).

their investments must align with their values to convey the proper message and uphold integrity in promoting their goals.

C.   Fossil Fuel Divestment Litigation

Social activism in the fossil fuel divestment movement has been taken to the courts, as students demand climate justice.[77] The litigation arose out of Harvard students' frustration with the university's refusal to divest from fossil fuels after demanding divestment from the university endowment through their campaigns and petitions.[78] The students decided to take their advocacy to another level.

On November 19, 2014, the Harvard Climate Justice Coalition filed a complaint against the Harvard president and fellows of Harvard College, the HMC, and the attorney general of Massachusetts.[79] The plaintiffs are a group of seven students, consisting of law, graduate, and undergraduate students.[80] The students are bringing this suit seeking climate justice on behalf of future generations.[81] The complaint names "individuals not yet born or too young to assert their rights but whose future health, safety, and welfare depend on slowing the pace of climate change."[82]

The innovative causes of action listed in the complaint are twofold: (1) mismanagement of charitable funds and (2) intentional investment in abnormally dangerous activity.[83] The statement of facts describes the vesting of responsibility in the "President and Fellows" by the charter of the Harvard Corporation to further the goals of "the advancement and education of youth."[84] They are suing the attorney general of Massachusetts by citing the duty of Massachusetts "'legislatures and magistrates' to ensure the charitable operation of schools . . . [by] acting in the public interest, furthering the education and welfare of the students, and refraining from actions known to cause harm to the public and students."[85]

---

77.   John Schwartz, *Harvard Students Move Fossil Fuel Stock Fight to Court*, N.Y. Times, Nov. 19, 2014, http://www.nytimes.com/2014/11/20/us/harvard-students-move-fossil-fuel-divestment-fight-to-court.html?ref=us&_r=1.

78.   *Id.*

79.   Harvard Complaint (Nov. 19, 2014), http://www.divestproject.org/wp-content/uploads/2014/10/Read-the-Complaint.pdf.

80.   Harvard Climate Justice Coalition v. President and Fellows of Harvard College, *About The Plaintiffs*, http://www.divestproject.org/about-the-plaintiffs/ (last visited Aug. 21, 2016).

81.   *See* Harvard Complaint, *supra* note 79.

82.   *Id.* para. 2.

83.   *See id.* paras. 41, 63.

84.   *Id.* para. 29.

85.   *Id.* paras. 29–31.

The lawsuit identified $79 million in direct holdings in publicly traded fossil fuel companies in Harvard's endowment.[86] The endowment also contains additional indirect holdings in fossil fuels, but the amount is not listed.[87] The plaintiffs connect investing in fossil fuels with creating environmental and social harms because the universities are helping finance the fossil fuel industry's business activities.[88] The complaint identifies the catastrophic consequences that endanger the health, safety, and welfare of present and future generations if businesses continue to burn fossil fuels and emit GHGs.[89] The complaint is supported by significant evidence labeled as exhibits, including reports from scientists (James Hansen) and international organizations (the Intergovernmental Panel on Climate Change), federal agencies (U.S. Environmental Protection Agency), Harvard's U.S. Securities and Exchange Commission (SEC) filing, Harvard's charter, the Massachusetts Constitution, news articles, and academic studies.[90]

The mismanagement of charitable funds cause of action stems from Harvard Corporation's breach of fiduciary and charitable duties as a public charity and nonprofit.[91] The complaint asserts that investing in fossil fuels damages Harvard's reputation, and the students' and graduates' reputations.[92] The students are unable to be free of the threats of climate change, and the future damage to the university's physical campus as a result of sea-level rise.[93] The second count—intentional investment in abnormally dangerous activities—identifies the fossil fuel industries' business activities as abnormally dangerous "because they inevitably contribute to climate change, causing serious harm to Plaintiff's Future Generations' persons and property."[94] The argument continues that there is no amount of reasonable care that can be taken by a fossil fuel company to substantially reduce the risk of harm.[95] The complaint alleges that Harvard has knowledge or should have known that fossil fuel companies contribute to climate change and cause harm, and that these harms are well understood among institutions of higher education.[96]

---

86. *Id.* para. 32.
87. *Id.*
88. *Id.* para. 33.
89. *Id.* paras. 21–28.
90. Harvard Climate Justice Coalition v. President and Fellows of Harvard College, *The Evidence*, http://www.divestproject.org/the-evidence/ (last visited Aug. 21 2016).
91. Harvard Complaint, *supra* note 79, para. 47.
92. *Id.*
93. *Id.*
94. *Id.* para. 66.
95. *Id.*
96. *Id.* para. 67.

The Harvard Climate Justice Coalition complaint requests "an injunction ordering Defendants to immediately withdraw Defendant Harvard Corporation's direct holdings in fossil fuel companies and an injunction for Defendants to take immediate steps to begin withdrawing indirect holdings and to complete withdrawal within a reasonable period of time."[97] The plaintiffs also request a declaration that Harvard breached its obligations contained in its charter.[98]

The plaintiffs acknowledged the difficulty of meeting the "special interest" requirement to have standing to sue.[99] The lawsuit was ultimately dismissed on the ground that the plaintiffs lacked standing because they claimed the threat was to "future generations."[100] The court reasoned that the plaintiffs' status as Harvard students did not give them personal rights enough to have standing to charge Harvard with the mismanagement of its charitable assets.[101]

The Harvard students appealed the dismissal of the divestment lawsuit.[102] The appellate brief was supported by amicus curiae briefs by Dr. James E. Hansen and the Animal Legal Defense Fund.[103] The brief from the Animal Legal Defense Fund supported the moral obligation for the protection of future generations, as a recognized principle in international and domestic law.[104] The city of Cambridge, Massachusetts, also supported the lawsuit.[105] Dr. Hansen's amicus brief also cites the moral obligation to protect future generations by phasing out fossil fuels.[106] The appeal focuses on the same arguments that Harvard mismanaged its endowment by investing in "abnormally dangerous activities."[107] On June 7, 2016 the Harvard Climate Justice Coalition appeared for oral arguments in the Massachusetts Appeals Court and the appeal is pending as of this writing.[108]

---

97. *Id.*
98. *Id.*
99. Schwartz, *supra* note 77.
100. Theodore R. Delwiche & Mariel A Klein, *Judge Dismisses Divestment Lawsuit*, HARV. CRIMSON, Mar. 24, 2015, http://www.thecrimson.com/article/2015/3/24/judge-dismisses-divestment-lawsuit/.
101. *Id.*
102. Klein, *supra* note 63; Brief for Petitioner-Appellant Harvard Climate Justice Coalition v. President & Fellows of Harvard Coll., No. 2015-P-0905 (Nov. 19 2014), http://www.divestproject.org/wp-content/uploads/2015/10/HCJC-Appellants-Brief.pdf.
103. Klein, *supra* note 63; Harvard Climate Justice Coalition v. President and Fellows of Harvard College, *Court Documents*, http://www.divestproject.org/documents-2/ (last visited Aug. 21, 2016).
104. Animal Legal Defense Fund Amicus Brief, 36-9, http://www.divestproject.org/wp-content/uploads/2015/10/ALDF-Amicus.pdf.
105. Klein, *supra* note 63.
106. Dr. James Hansen Amicus Brief, 2015-P-0905 (Oct. 23, 2015), http://www.divestproject.org/wp-content/uploads/2015/10/Hansen-Amicus.pdf.
107. Klein, *supra* note 63.
108. Appellant Harvard Climate Justice Coalition v. President & Fellows of Harvard Coll., No. 2015-p-0905, Appeals Court, Full Case Panel Court Docket http://www.ma-appellatecourts.org/search_number.php?dno=2015-P-0905&get=Search (last visited Sept. 20, 2016).

Even in the face of this social activism and litigation, the HMC still decided not to divest but instead became the first university endowment in the United States to join the Principles for Responsible Investment (PRI) and the Carbon Disclosure Project (CDP).[109] The HMC has dedicated a web page to their sustainable investments, reporting their focus on investments based on environmental, social, and governance (ESG) factors.[110] The HMC assesses and manages ESG risks, and documents and considers risk before making a decision on the investment.[111] The faculty members in support of divestment responded by saying that the PRI and CDP are "utterly ineffective."[112] These voluntary measures are not as effective in mitigating climate change as mandatory legal standards or full divestment; however, in lieu of full divestment, these initiatives can be seen as steps in the right direction toward a more sustainable future within businesses. If the intent behind the initiative is purely for public relations reasons, however, it would be deemed to be merely "greenwashing."[113] A sustainable business model "should not be a discretionary preference, to follow only if corporate leaders perceive an economic benefit."[114] What is necessary is the acceptance of an ethical responsibility to do what is right and act for environmental and social well-being, regardless of financial gain.[115]

II.   Corporate Social Responsibility and Responsible Investment

Divestment of fossil fuels is promoting climate justice by bringing awareness to the moral obligation of corporations, wealth owners, and investors, and to the duty to protect the interest of society, future generations, and the environment. The campaign creates stigma and advocates for more socially responsible investment practices. Divestment of fossil fuels is the "people

---

109. Press Release, Harvard, Harvard to Sign on to United Nations-Supported Principles for Responsible Investment (Apr. 7, 2014), http://news.harvard.edu/gazette/story/2014/04/harvard-to-sign-on-to-united-nations-supported-principles-for-responsible-investment/.

110. Harvard Management Co., *Investing for the Long-Term: Integrating ESG Factors*, http://www.hmc.harvard.edu/investment-management/sustainable_investment.html (last visited Aug. 21, 2016).

111. *Id.*

112. *The Divestment Debate*, HARV. MAG., July–Aug. 2014, http://harvardmagazine.com/2014/07/the-divestment-debate.

113. Thomas P. Lyon & John W. Maxwell, *Greenwash: Corporate Environmental Disclosure Under Threat of Audit*, 20 J. ECON. MGMT. STRATEGY 3, 4 (2011) (defining greenwashing as "the selective disclosure of positive information about a company's environmental or social performance, while withholding negative information on these dimensions").

114. BEATE SJAFJELL & BENJAMIN J. RICHARDSON, COMPANY LAW AND SUSTAINABILITY: LEGAL BARRIERS AND SUSTAINABILITY 2 (2015).

115. *Id.* at 2.

demanding institutions and corporations to adopt comprehensive sustainable investment policies that eliminate the environmental and social injustices that the fossil fuel industry is creating."[116] Climate justice will be achieved not just by divesting from fossil fuels, but also by businesses incorporating sustainable policies, practices, and standards into everyday business activities. Since divestment is the opposite of investment, sustainable and socially responsible investments are also needed to promote climate justice.

Achieving a sustainable future does not occur in a vacuum, however. Although often the primary source of environmental pollution, business must be part of the long-term solution.[117] Compared to government, business has greater capital, research, development capacity, and influence in the market to push towards sustainable development and climate justice.[118] The United Nations acknowledged the significant role of business in mitigating and adapting to climate change.[119] Caring for Climate is a joint initiative convened by the United Nations Global Compact, the United Nations Environment Programme (UNEP), and UNFCCC and recognizes that "only through a critical mass of engaged companies can the private sector be an effective part of the climate solution."[120] The initiative calls on all companies to commit to corporate responsibility policies on climate action.[121]

Since the Earth Summit in 1992, the field of CSR has evolved to become part of mainstream thinking in corporate compliance with environmental and human rights principles.[122] CSR is premised on the idea that businesses have a responsibility to society and all its stakeholders, not just to their shareholders or their bottom line profits.[123] The World Business Council for Sustainable Development defines CSR as "the continuing commitment by business to behave ethically and contribute to economic development while improving the quality of life of the workforce and their families as well as of the local community and society at large."[124] CSR encompasses the sustainability agenda by thinking in terms of the "triple bottom line," focusing on economic prosperity, environmental quality, and social justice.[125] John Elk-

---

116. *What Is Fossil Fuel Divestment?*, *supra* note 25; Fleishman, *supra* note 38.
117. SJAFJELL & RICHARDSON, *supra* note 114, at 35–36.
118. *Id.*
119. Caring for Climate, *Homepage*, http://caringforclimate.org/ (last visited Aug. 21, 2016).
120. *Id.*
121. Caring for Climate, *Responsible Corporate Engagement in Climate Policy*, http://caringforclimate.org/workstreams/climate-policy-engagement/ (last visited Aug. 21, 2016).
122. HUNTER ET AL., *supra* note 10, at 1489.
123. Donal Crilly et al., *The Grammar of Decoupling: A Cognitive-linguistic Perspective on Firms' Sustainability Claims and Stakeholders' Interpretation*, 59 ACAD. MGMT. J. 705 (2016).
124. SJAFJELL & RICHARDSON, *supra* note 114, at 3.
125. JOHN ELKINGTON, CANNIBALS WITH FORKS: THE TRIPLE BOTTOM LINE OF 21ST CENTURY BUSINESS 22 (1998).

ington wrote, "[t]o refuse the challenge implied by the triple bottom line is to risk extinction."[126] This shift in thinking for business priorities stems from a reshaping of society's expectations.[127]

The severe financial crisis and climate change risks have underscored the need for businesses to incorporate ESG factors into their financial statements, policies, and disclosures.[128] Businesses feel pressure from all stakeholders, customers, investors, financial institutions, and shareholders.[129] Lenders and investors, of course, want the best return on their investments with the least amount of risks.[130] Moreover, investors today understand that financial success and good corporate citizenship are connected.[131]

Therefore, investing in fossil fuels is a risky business not only because of the financial risks, but also because of the environmental and social risks. Al Gore made a comparison of the risks of investing in fossil fuels to the meltdown in the market for subprime mortgages: "The assumption that you can safely invest in assets that come from business models that assume carbon is free is an assumption that is about to go splat. Many companies have lots of assets in your portfolios that are chock full of 'subprime' carbon assets."[132]

ESG issues have a material impact on those risks and fulfill fiduciary duties.[133] These ESG practices and considerations are evident across the spectrum of business entities including financial institutions, institutional investors, individual investors, corporations engaging in CSR practices, and consumers. CSR and ESG performance, monitoring, and improvement provide the greater transparency that all sectors are demanding.[134] After the financial crisis and the looming threat of climate change, consumers, investors, stakeholders, and suppliers are demanding greater transparency.[135] This pressure caused an increase in CSR reporting to publicize companies' ESG data.[136]

---

126. *Id.*
127. *Id.*
128. Kevin Wilhelm, Return on Sustainability: How Business Can Increase Profitability and Address Climate Change in an Uncertain Economy 105 (2013).
129. *Id.*
130. *Id.*
131. *Id.*
132. *Id.*
133. US SIF: The Forum for Sustainable and Responsible Investment, *SRI Basics*, http://www.ussif.org/sribasics (last visited Aug. 21, 2016).
134. Wilhelm, *supra* note 128, at 166.
135. *Id.*
136. Hunter et al., *supra* note 10, at 1490.

A.   Corporate Social Responsibility Reporting and Disclosures

It is becoming the norm in corporate practice to submit sustainability reports or CSR reports using at least one voluntary initiative.[137] CSR disclosure focuses on the paradigm of sustainability reporting, with the information reported being relative to the triple bottom line of social, environmental, and economic impacts of a corporation's activities.[138] Executives are now considering the environmental issues, such as climate change, to be among the most important issues affecting business.[139] The Governance and Accountability Institute reported that in 2015, 75% of the Standard & Poor's 500 Index produced sustainability reports, an increase from 20% in 2011.[140]

There are many voluntary initiatives and providers of CSR reporting, but the major providers offering sustainability reporting include: the Global Reporting Initiative (GRI) (GRI's Sustainability Reporting Standards), the Organisation for Economic Co-operation and Development (OECD) (OECD Guidelines for Multinational Enterprises), the United Nations Global Compact (the Communication on Progress), the International Organization for Standardization (ISO) (ISO 26000, International Standard for social responsibility), and the Carbon Disclosure Project.[141] The GRI is the best example of the CSR reporting trends.[142] It was launched in 1997 by the Coalition for Environmentally Responsible Economies (CERES)[143] and it included the participation of organizations such as CEP, UNEP, and the World Business Council for Sustainable Development.[144] The GRI's mission

---

137. David W. Case, *Corporate Environmental Reporting as Informational Regulation: A Law and Economics Perspective*, 76 U. Colo. L. Rev. 379, 389 (2005).

138. *Id.*

139. Wilhelm, *supra* note 128, at 166.

140. Emily Chasan, *Investors Want More From Sustainability Reporting, Says Former SEC Head*, Wall St. J., Nov. 12, 2015 (citing Governance & Accountability Institute, *Flash Report—Seventy-Five Percent (75%) of the S&P 500 Index Published Corporate Sustainability Reports in 2014*, http://www.ga-institute.com/nc/issue-master-system/news-details/article/flash-report-seventy-five-percent-75-of-the-sp-index-published-corporate-sustainability-rep.html), http://blogs.wsj.com/cfo/2015/11/12/investors-want-more-from-sustainability-reporting-says-former-sec-head/.

141. Wilhelm, *supra* note 128, at 161; Carbon Disclosure Project, *Homepage*, https://www.cdp.net/en-US/Pages/HomePage.aspx (last visited Aug. 21, 2016).

142. Case, *supra* note 137, at 389; *see also* GRI, *Homepage*, https://www.globalreporting.org/Pages/default.aspx (last visited Aug. 21, 2016).

143. The organization describes itself as follows: "CERES is a non-profit organization advocating for sustainability leadership. We mobilize a powerful network of investors, companies and public interest groups to accelerate and expand the adoption of sustainable business practices and solutions to build a healthy global economy." http://www.ceres.org/ (last visited Aug. 31, 2016). CERES established a 10-point code of conduct that companies voluntarily commit to reporting on corporate environmental activities. *Id.*

144. Case, *supra* note 137, at 389; *see also* GRI, *supra* note 142.

is "to elevate the comparability and credibility of sustainability reporting practices worldwide."[145] Currently, 92% of the 250 largest corporations in the world report on their sustainability performance utilizing the GRI.[146] The GRI's goal is to make sustainability reporting as commonplace as financial reporting.[147]

True sustainability reporting allows for greater transparency into corporate practices that either achieve CSR or impede its achievement. Sustainability reporting is valuable because it ensures that the organizations reporting consider their impacts on environmental and social issues and allows them to be transparent about the risks and opportunities that they encounter.[148] A trusting relationship amongst stakeholders is necessary to receive good support.[149] Transparency builds and maintains trust and credibility[150] in businesses because it shows honesty, openness, and self-criticism.[151] CSR reporting on ESG issues promotes better decisionmaking because it informs the decisions of investors, consumers, local communities, and civil society.[152] Reporting in a transparent manner is an essential part of committing to sustainability.[153]

Businesses need to make sure that they report the good, the bad, and the ugly of their companies. Voluntary self-reporting can tempt companies to only reveal the greatest achievements and omit negative information.[154] This type of reporting is seen as greenwashing and is only concerned with image and not with accurate reporting.[155] This practice causes distrust in stakeholders because they fear a cover up and, therefore, are unable to be fully informed of the risks and benefits of the company.[156] To avoid creating suspicion, companies should report achievements and weaknesses and identify the steps to fix the problems.[157]

---

145. Hunter et al., *supra* note 10, at 1491; *see also* GRI, *Homepage,* https://www.globalreporting.org/Pages/default.aspx (last visited Aug. 21, 2016).
146. GRI, *Homepage, supra* note 145.
147. Hunter et al., *supra* note 10, at 1491.
148. GRI, *About Sustainability Reporting,* https://www.globalreporting.org/information/sustainability-reporting/Pages/default.aspx (last visited Aug. 21, 2016).
149. William R. Blackburn, The Sustainability Handbook: The Complete Management Guide to Achieving Social, Economic, and Environmental Responsibility 285 (2d ed. 2015).
150. *Id.*
151. *Id.; About Sustainability Reporting, supra* note 148.
152. United Nations Global Impact, *Participation,* https://www.unglobalcompact.org/participation/report (last visited Aug. 21, 2016).
153. *Id.*
154. Case, *supra* note 137, at 389.
155. *Id.*
156. Blackburn, *supra* note 149, at 285.
157. *Id.* at 285–86.

B.   International Voluntary ESG and CSR Initiatives

The growing public awareness of environmental performance is driving companies to adopt voluntary or self-imposed standards, guidelines, and codes.[158] Those supporting ESG and CSR considerations in any sector must rely on international voluntary corporate standards because transnational corporate activities are minimally governed by international law.[159] These voluntary standards or initiatives usually do not have any verification methods or enforcement measures.[160] The only enforcement mechanism available is to "name and shame" the companies that fail to meet these standards.[161] These standards also lack explicit performance benchmarks.[162] Some companies become signatories to these third-party initiatives committing to standards and codes of conducts to improve their public image.[163] Others view these initiatives as attempts to prevent more stringent regulations through preemptive measures by the market.[164] Others do it out of a commitment to true sustainability. Although there is no substitute for legally binding standards, these voluntary initiatives signify a change of consciousness, a change in values, a change in priorities, and a commitment across the globe to create a more sustainable and just future for our present and future generations in the face of climate change. The "business as usual" model is no longer mainstream, it is no longer popular, and the market has responded.

CSR voluntary corporate codes of conduct are becoming the norm as companies want to convey their core values and ethical business practices to all stakeholders. This shift in thinking to employ CSR has caused an increase in the majority of corporations dedicated to addressing larger social problems.[165] The United Nations Global Compact is the world's largest voluntary corporate sustainability initiative.[166] More than 8,000 companies and 4,000 non-businesses have become signatories to the compact.[167] The mission of the compact is for businesses to be responsible by aligning their strategies and operations with principles on human rights, labor, environment, and

---

158. HUNTER ET AL., *supra* note 10, at 1488.
159. *Id.* at 1493.
160. *Id.* at 1501.
161. *Id.* at 1488.
162. SJAFJELL & RICHARDSON, *supra* note 114, at 4.
163. HUNTER ET AL., *supra* note 10, at 1501.
164. SJAFJELL & RICHARDSON, *supra* note 114, at 18.
165. Crilly et al., *supra* note 123.
166. United Nations Global Impact, *What Is U.N. Global Impact?*, https://www.unglobalcompact.org/what-is-gc (last visited Aug. 21, 2016).
167. *Id.*

anti-corruption.[168] The United Nations Global Compact's General Assembly mandate is to "promote responsible business practices and UN values among the global business community and the UN System."[169]

The 10 principles of the United Nations Global Compact are derived from the Universal Declaration of Human Rights, the International Labour Organization's Declaration on Fundamental Principles and Rights at Work, the Rio Declaration on Environment and Development, and the United Nations Convention Against Corruption.[170] The Compact principles have been endorsed by the Human Rights Council, which has confirmed the interconnectedness between climate change and human rights.[171] The Global Compact institutes these principles as the core values to be shared among businesses, trade unions, and civil society.[172] The United Nations Guiding Principles on Human Rights have been incorporated into the Compact commitments for the past four years.[173] The Compact requires businesses to make a policy commitment to respect human rights and take proactive steps to prevent violations and remediate any adverse human rights impacts.[174]

Commitments to the Compact also include taking action to advance societal goals, such as the United Nations Sustainable Development Goals 2030.[175] Through the Global Compact, businesses have played an important role in the process of shaping the Sustainable Development Goals and helping companies implement them.[176] The efforts through partnerships created by the Compact include the Post-2015 Business Engagement Architecture, Rio+20 Corporate Sustainability Forum, Global Compact Local Networks, SDG Industry Matrix, Caring for Climate, and Global Compact LEAD.[177]

---

168. United Nations Global Impact, *Our Mission*, https://www.unglobalcompact.org/what-is-gc/mission (last visited Aug. 21, 2016).

169. United Nations Global Impact, *Our Governance*, https://www.unglobalcompact.org/about/governance (last visited Aug. 21, 2016); G.A. Res. 70/224, U.N. GAOR, 70th Sess., at 2, U.N. Doc. A/RES/70/224 (2016).

170. United Nations Global Impact, *The Ten Principles of the UN Global Compact*, https://www.unglobalcompact.org/what-is-gc/mission/principles (last visited Aug. 21, 2016).

171. *See* E. Cameron et al., Business in a Climate-Constrained World: Catalyzing a Climate-Resilient Future Through the Power of the Private Sector 6 (2014), http://www.bsr.org/reports/BSR_Business_in_a_Climate_Constrained_World_Report.pdf.

172. United Nations Global Impact, *Global Compact +15: General Assembly Session*, https://www.unglobalcompact.org/library/3861 (last visited Aug. 21, 2016); Video: GC + 15: General Assembly Session (U.N. Global Compact 2016), https://www.youtube.com/watch?v=DFMaTKadtfs.

173. *Id.*

174. *Id.*

175. United Nations Global Impact, *Our Mission*, *supra* note 168.

176. United Nations Global Impact, *UN Global Compact and the Sustainable Development Goals*, https://www.unglobalcompact.org/what-is-gc/our-work/sustainable-development/background (last visited Aug. 21, 2016).

177. *Id.*

C.   Opportunities for Responsible Investment

While CSR reporting has been on the rise within corporations, investors have been able to use this information to determine in which sectors of the stock market they want to invest. Socially responsible investing (SRI) is "an investment discipline that considers environmental, social, and governance (ESG) criteria to generate long-term competitive financial returns and positive societal impact."[178] The motivations for SRI investing include personal goals, institutional missions, and the demands of clients and stakeholders.[179] Investors also are seeking strong financial performance in their investments to contribute to advancement in ESG practices.[180] SRI allows investors to match financial investments with ethical and moral values.[181] These SRI investments focus on considering ESG criteria.[182] SRI investments were more than $6.57 trillion in 2014, a 76% increase compared to 2012 figures.[183]

The SRI practice used to focus on weeding out companies from specific industries that investors did not want to support, such as natural resource extraction and nuclear energy.[184] This approach is a negative screen; positive screens focus on promoting positive change and rewarding good behavior by investing in companies that promote positive social and environmental impacts.[185] This section discusses three important SRI opportunities to promote climate justice.

I.   United Nations Principles for Responsible Investment

The United Nations Principles for Responsible Investment (PRI) is a voluntary set of guidelines for investors that seek to combine financial return with a moral and ethical obligation by giving consideration to the ESG issues of companies in which parties choose to invest.[186] Ethical values are

---

178. US SIF, *supra* note 133.
179. *Id.*
180. *Id.*
181. WILHELM, *supra* note 128, at 166.
182. US SIF, *supra* note 133.
183. *Id.*
184. *Id.*
185. WILHELM, *supra* note 128, at 115.
186. Principles for Responsible Investment, *About the PRI*, https://www.unpri.org/about (last visited Aug. 21, 2016); WILHELM, *supra* note 128, at 161 (The six principles are: (1) Incorporate ESG issues into investment analysis and decisionmaking process; (2) Incorporate ESG issues into ownership policies and practices; (3) Seek appropriate disclosure on ESG issues by the entities invested; (4) Promote acceptance and implementation of the Principles within the investment industry; (5) Work together to enhance effectiveness in implementing the Principles; and (6) Report on activities and progress toward implementing the Principles).

the essence of climate justice and instilling these principles into investment decisions allows for greater protection of the rights of vulnerable communities. The goal was to incorporate "ESG issues into mainstream investment decision-making and ownership practices."[187] This momentum is driven by recognizing that ESG factors play a material role in determining risk and return within the financial community.[188] Investors understand that part of their fiduciary duty is incorporating ESG factors and that beneficiaries are demanding more transparency.[189] Responsible investment is also grounded in the fact that companies could face serious reputational risk by destroying value on environmental (climate change and pollution), social (employee diversity and working conditions), and economic issues (aggressive tax strategies).[190] The PRI has nearly 1,500 signatories that represent $60 trillion from more than 50 countries.[191]

2. Shareholder Resolutions

An important aspect of SRI is shareholder advocacy. Through shareholder resolutions, investors are given the opportunity to file resolutions to raise ESG issues.[192] These resolutions involve human rights, working conditions, and climate change issues.[193] In 2007, only 43 climate shareholder resolutions were filed with U.S. companies.[194] That number increased in 2009, with 68 shareholder proposals on climate change.[195] In the 2015 proxy season, a record-breaking 433 social and environmental shareholder resolutions were filed with climate change as one of the leading drivers of the uptick in activity.[196] By filing shareholder resolutions, active shareholders are able to bring important issues to the attention of company management.[197] Filing these resolutions gains media attention and educates the public.[198] The mere

---

187. WILHELM, *supra* note 128, at 107.
188. Principles for Responsible Investment, *What Is Responsible Investment?*, https://www.unpri.org/about/what-is-responsible-investment (last visited Aug. 21, 2016).
189. *Id.*
190. *Id.*
191. Principles for Responsible Investment, *About the PRI, supra* note 186.
192. US SIF, *supra* note 133.
193. *Id.*
194. WILHELM, *supra* note 128, at 116.
195. LAWRENCE P. SCHANPF, ENVIRONMENTAL ISSUES IN BUSINESS TRANSACTIONS 461 (2014).
196. Caitlin Kauffman, *Proxy Preview 2015 Examines Record-Breaking Number of Sustainability-Related Shareholder Resolutions*, SUSTAINABLE BRANDS, Mar. 11, 2015, http://www.sustainablebrands.com/news_and_views/marketing_comms/caitlin_kauffman/proxy_preview_2015_examines_record-breaking_number_s.
197. US SIF: The Forum for Sustainable and Responsible Investment, *SRI Basics*, http://www.ussif.org/sribasics (last visited Aug. 21, 2016).
198. *Id.*

process of filing resolutions prompts productive discussions and agreements, and the receipt of the shareholders' majority vote further pressures action by the corporation's management.[199]

Recently, an Exxon climate justice shareholder resolution, "Acknowledge Moral Imperative to Limit Global Warming to 2° Celsius," was filed.[200] It stated that the poor and most vulnerable are the first to suffer, while future generations, holding no responsibility, will live with greater impacts of global warming.[201] Shareholders called on the board of directors to act by adopting a policy acknowledging the imperative to limit global average temperature increases to 2°C above pre-industrial levels.[202] Exxon challenged the proposal as "vague" to exclude the climate justice proposal from this year's proxy ballot so that the shareholders would not be allowed to vote, fearing a majority in favor of the resolution.[203] The SEC reviewed the resolution and denied Exxon's challenge.[204] This outcome is a significant victory, as shareholders will have the opportunity to vote on Exxon's moral responsibilities regarding climate change.[205] These moral and ESG considerations are continuing to take center stage in the investment decisionmaking process in seeking to promote climate justice.

3.   Equator Principles ESG Guidelines for Financial Institutions

This framework sets out minimum standards for institutions to implement to ensure due diligence in determining, assessing, and managing environmental and social risks when determining whether to finance projects.[206] Financing of the project is conditioned on complying with the Equator Principles (EP). If companies will not or are unable to comply with the EP, then no project finance or project-related corporate loans will be provided.[207] Borrowers must categorize and fully disclose environmental and social risks and

---

199. *Id.*
200. Acknowledge Moral Imperative to Limit Global Warming to 2°C, 2016—Exxon Mobil Corporation (Feb. 1, 2016), http://www.iccr.org/sites/default/files/resources_attachments/exxonreso.pdf.
201. *Id.*
202. *Id.*
203. *Id.*
204. Press Release, Interfaith Center on Corporate Responsibility, ExxonMobil Seeks to Deny Shareholders a Vote on Climate Justice Proposal (Feb. 1, 2015), http://www.iccr.org/sites/default/files/blog_attachments/pr_exxon_-_moral_reso_1-31-15_final_3.pdf.
205. *See* Press Release, Interfaith Center on Corporate Responsibility, ExxonMobil Fails to Block Climate Justice Proposal at the SEC (Mar. 24, 2016), http://www.iccr.org/sites/default/files/blog_attachments/exxon_pr_sec-moral_reso_3-24-16final.pdf.
206. WILHELM, *supra* note 128, at 106.
207. The Equator Principles Association, *About the Equator Principles*, http://www.equator-principles.com/index.php/about-ep (last visited Aug. 21, 2016).

provide a mitigation plan to manage the risks to obtain loans from these Equator Principles Financial Institutions (EPFIs).[208]

Currently, 83 EPFIs[209] in 36 countries have adopted the EP.[210] This number of institutions covers more than 70% of international project finance debt in emerging markets.[211] The EPs incorporate principles of climate justice by including comprehensive standards for indigenous peoples and consultation with locally affected communities within the project.[212] Borrowers must also disclose to affected communities "a mechanism for addressing grievances, and third-party verified review, monitoring, and annual public reporting."[213] Studies show that after the financial crisis of 2008, only four of the largest financial institutions—Bank of America, Wells Fargo, JP Morgan Chase, and Citibank—survived and they were all signatories to the EPs.[214] This outcome is further proof that incorporating ESG principles into lending practices helps manage and identify risks and opportunities.

Conclusion

The impacts of climate change are the biggest threat of our time, imperiling both natural resources and human rights. This connection between climate change and human rights has significantly impacted decisionmaking in financial markets from divesting to investing. Companies, consumers, and investors are prioritizing ESG considerations and responsible business practices. The detrimental impacts of climate change have prompted the recognition that there is an ethical and moral obligation to invest responsibly by choosing to divest from morally reprehensible activities such as fossil fuel extraction.

These actions promote climate justice via the financial investment markets. Investors are recognizing not only the financial incentives of considering ESG factors, but most importantly the ethical need to invest in sustainable and socially responsible companies to protect the needs of present and future generations. Investors now understand and recognize climate change risks and social injustices and do not want to invest in or support companies that

---

208. WILHELM, *supra* note 128, at 106.
209. The Equator Principles Association, *Equator Principles Association Members & Reporting*, http://www.equator-principles.com/index.php/members-reporting (last visited Aug. 21, 2016).
210. The Equator Principles Association, *Homepage*, http://www.equator-principles.com/ (last visited Aug. 21, 2016).
211. *Id.*
212. The Equator Principles Association, *About the Equator Principles*, *supra* note 207.
213. WILHELM, *supra* 128, at 106.
214. *Id.*

are not concerned with their moral duty to be good citizens of the world. The businesses that survive are the ones that have a genuine interest in caring about the people and the planet while also making a profit.

Divesting from fossil fuels and SRI reduces GHG emissions, helps eradicate poverty, promotes sustainability, and protects future generations. Although the actions undertaken are voluntary in nature, they represent an important shift in thinking necessary for a sustainable future. Therefore, these actions promote the goal of climate justice for the most vulnerable communities of the world.

Chapter 6

Human Rights Dimensions of Bioenergy With Carbon Capture and Storage: A Framework for Climate Justice in the Realm of Climate Geoengineering

*William C.G. Burns**

* Co-executive director, Forum for Climate Engineering Assessment, School of International Service, American University, Washington, D.C. I wish to extend my heartfelt appreciation for the research assistance of Sharon Moraes of the University of Chicago Law School and Marlon White of Florida A&M College of Law. The author also wishes to thank the Centre for International Governance Innovation for financial support in the preparation of this chapter.

Introduction

One of the most striking aspects of the new Paris Agreement[1] to the United Nations Framework Convention on Climate Change (UNFCCC)[2] is the incorporation of human rights language in its preamble. While the human rights community in recent years has sought to highlight the nexus between climate change and human rights,[3] the climate change community has historically been far more reluctant to do so.[4] In 2010, however, the Parties to the UNFCCC adopted a resolution providing that the Parties "should, in all *climate change related actions*, fully respect human rights."[5] After contentious debate,[6] the Paris Agreement became the first climate change instrument, and one of the first environmental

---

1. *Adoption of the Paris Agreement*, UNFCC Conference of the Parties, 21st Sess., U.N. Doc. FCCC/CP/2015/10/Add.1 (Dec. 12, 2015), http://unfccc.int/files/home/application/pdf/paris_agreement.pdf [hereinafter *Paris Agreement*].

2. United Nations Framework Convention on Climate Change, May 9, 1992, 31 I.L.M. 849.

3. *See, e.g.*, United Nations Human Rights Council Res. 29/15, Human Rights and Climate Change (2015) ("Affirming that human rights obligations, standards and principles have the potential to inform and strengthen international, regional and national policymaking in the area of climate change"), http://ap.ohchr.org/documents/dpage_e.aspx?si=A/HRC/29/L.21; United Nations Human Rights Council Res. 26/27, Human Rights and Climate Change, 26th Sess., U.N. Doc. A/HRC/RES/26/27 (2014) ("Emphasizing that the adverse effects of climate change have a range of implications, both direct and indirect, for the effective enjoyment of human rights"), http://ap.ohchr.org/documents/dpage_e.aspx?si=A/HRC/26/L.33/Rev.1; United Nations Human Rights Council Res. 10/4, Human Rights and Climate Change, 10th Sess., U.N. Doc. A/HRC/10/L.11 (2009) ("Climate change-related impacts have a range of implications, both direct and indirect, for the effective enjoyment of human rights"), http://ap.ohchr.org/documents/E/HRC/resolutions/A_HRC_RES_10_4.pdf; *Report of the Office of the United Nations High Commissioner for Human Rights on the Relationship Between Climate Change and Human Rights*, U.N. Human Rights Council, 10th Sess., Provisional Agenda Item 2, at para. 75, U.N. Doc. A/HRC/10/61 (2009).

4. Sheila R. Foster & Paolo Galizzi, *Human Rights and Climate Change: Building Synergies for a Common Future, in* CLIMATE CHANGE LAW 43, 44 (Daniel A. Farber & Marjan Peeters eds., 2016); Megan H. Herzog, *Coastal Climate Change Adaptation and International Human Rights, in* CLIMATE CHANGE IMPACTS ON OCEAN AND COASTAL LAW 593, 605 (Randall S. Abate ed., 2015).

5. *Report of the Conference of the Parties on Its Sixteenth Session, Held in Cancun From 29 November to 10 December 2010—Addendum, Part Two: Action Taken by the Conference of the Parties at Its Sixteenth Session, Decisions Adopted by the Conference of the Parties*, UNFCCC, 16th Sess., Decision 1/CP.16, at 4, para. 8, U.N. Doc. FCCC/CP/2010/7/Add.1 (2010) (emphasis added), http://unfccc.int/resource/docs/2010/cop16/eng/07a01.pdf. While not explicitly referring to human rights impacts, the Kyoto Protocol to the UNFCCC includes consistent language, providing that industrialized countries should strive to "minimize adverse social, environmental and economic impacts on developing country Parties" in terms of mitigation response measures. *Decisions Adopted by the Conference of the Parties*, UNFCCC, Decision 1/CP.3, U.N. Doc. FCCC/CP/1997/L.7/Add.1 (1997), *reprinted in* 37 I.L.M. 22 (1997), at art. 3(14).

6. *Human Rights in Climate Pact Under Fire: Norway, Saudis, US Blocking Strong Position*, HUM. RTS. WATCH, Dec. 7, 2015, https://www.hrw.org/news/2015/12/07/human-rights-climate-pact-under-fire; Marc Limon, *Why Human Rights Must Be at Heart of Climate Change Decisions*, WORLD ECON. F., Sept. 14, 2015, https://www.weforum.org/agenda/2015/09/why-human-rights-must-be-at-the-heart-of-climate-change-decisions/.

agreements, to explicitly recognize the relevance of human rights in the context of climate change policymaking.[7]

In pertinent part, the Agreement provides:

> Parties should, when taking action to address climate change, respect, promote and consider their respective obligations on human rights, the right to health, the rights of indigenous peoples, local communities, migrants, children, persons with disabilities and people in vulnerable situations and the right to development, as well as gender equality, empowerment of women and intergenerational equity.[8]

While the Paris Agreement's recognition of the potential human rights impacts of responses to climate change is a positive step forward, there is a compelling need to translate this provision, as Basil Ugochukwu observed in 2015, "in ways that integrate human rights into practical actions in specific climate change policies."[9]

This chapter proposes a framework for operationalizing the Paris Agreement's human rights language in the context of an emerging potential response to climate change, bioenergy with carbon capture and storage (BECCS). BECCS seeks to reduce concentrations of carbon dioxide (CO_2) in the atmosphere in a process by which biomass is converted to heat, electricity, or liquid or gas fuels, coupled with CO_2 capture and sequestration (CCS), whereby CO_2 is stored terrestrially or in the ocean.[10] BECCS is denominated a "negative emissions technology" because it can effectuate a permanent net removal of CO_2, as opposed to processes that merely reduce emissions to the atmosphere.[11] BECCS facilitates this by absorption of carbon dioxide by the burning of biomass feedstocks, and subsequent storage for indefinite periods of time in geological formations.[12] More broadly,

---

7.   *Report of the Special Rapporteur on the Issue of Human Rights Obligations Relating to the Enjoyment of a Safe, Clean, Healthy, and Sustainable Environment*, U.N. Human Rights Council, 31st Sess., Agenda Item 36, at 6, U.N. Doc. A/HRC/31/52 (2006), http://www.ohchr.org/EN/HRBodies/HRC/RegularSessions/Session31/Documents/A%20HRC%2031%2052_E.docx.

8.   *Paris Agreement, supra* note 1, at pmbl.

9.   Basil Ugochukwu, CIGI Papers, No. 82—Climate Change and Human Rights: How? Where? When? 9 (2015). *See also* International Human Rights Law Clinic et al., Protecting People and the Planet: A Proposal to Address the Human Rights Impacts of Climate Change Policy 7 (2009), https://repositories.lib.utexas.edu/bitstream/handle/2152/7464/Protecting_People_and_the_Planet-Berkeley.pdf?sequence=2&isAllowed=y.

10.   European Biofuels Technology Platform, Biomass With CO_2 Capture and Storage (Bio-CCS) 5 (2012), http://biofuelstp.eu/downloads/bioccsjtf/EBTP-ZEP-Report-Bio-CCS-The-Way-Forward.pdf.

11.   International Energy Agency, Combining Bioenergy With CCS: Reporting and Accounting for Negative Emissions Under UNFCCC and the Kyoto Protocol 6 (2011), https://www.iea.org/publications/freepublications/publication/bioenergy_ccs.pdf.

12.   C. Gough & N.E. Vaughan, Synthesizing Existing Knowledge on the Feasibility of BECCS 5 (Feb. 2015), http://avoid-net-uk.cc.ic.ac.uk/wp-content/uploads/delightful-downloads/2015/07/

BECCS is a technological option that falls under the broader rubric of "climate geoengineering," defined by the U.K.'s Royal Society as "the deliberate large-scale manipulation of the planetary environment to counteract anthropogenic climate change."[13]

Part I of the chapter provides an overview of climate geoengineering options, with a focus on BECCS, and considers why these options are being actively discussed in the climate policymaking community. Part II discusses the potential human rights implications of BECCS, including within the context of the Paris Agreement. Part III proposes a human rights-based approach to operationalizing the human rights provisions of the Paris Agreement in the context of BECCS. It suggests that a human rights-based approach is an important safeguard to address intrinsic issues of equity and justice that would arise if the international community opts to implement this climate geoengineering strategy.[14]

I.   The Growing Impetus for Climate Geoengineering and BECCS

In recent years, there has been mounting evidence that temperature increases of 1.5–2°C above pre-industrial levels could have extremely serious impacts on global ecosystems and human institutions, especially in vulnerable developing countries.[15] There has also been growing concern that feckless climate policy responses may ensure that the globe exceeds critical climatic thresholds during this century, or that we could pass critical "tipping points" that precipitate abrupt, and nonlinear, climatic change on the earth.[16] As a consequence,

Synthesising-existing-knowledge-on-the-feasibility-of-BECCS-AVOID-2_WPD1a_v1.pdf.

13. The Royal Society, Geoengineering the Climate: Science, Governance, and Uncertainty 11 (2009), https://royalsociety.org/~/media/Royal_Society_Content/policy/publications/2009/8693.pdf.

14. Michael Burger & Jessica Wentz, Climate Change and Human Rights 10 (United Nations Environment Programme 2015), http://apps.unep.org/publications/index.php?option=com_pub&task=download&file=011917.

15. Carl-Friedrich Schleussner et al., *Differential Climate Impacts for Policy-Relevant Limits to Global Warming: The Case of 1.5 C and 2 C*, 7 Earth Sys. Dynamics 327–51 (2016); Hannah Osborne, *Paris COP21 Climate Talks: What Is the 2C Limit and What Happens if Global Warming Exceeds It?*, Int'l Bus. Times, Nov. 28, 2015, http://www.ibtimes.co.uk/paris-cop21-climate-talks-what-2c-limit-what-happens-if-global-warming-exceeds-it-1530851; World Bank Group, Turn Down the Heat 5–29 (2014), https://openknowledge.worldbank.org/handle/10986/20595; V. Ramanathan & Y. Feng, *On Avoiding Dangerous Anthropogenic Interference With the Climate System: Formidable Challenges Ahead*, 105 Proc. Nat'l Acad. Sci. 14245, 14245 (2008).

16. U.S. Government Accountability Office (GAO), Report to the Chairman, Committee on Science and Technology, House of Representatives, Climate Change: A Coordinated Strategy Could Focus Federal Geoengineering Research and Inform Governance Efforts 6 (2010) (GAO-10-903), http://www.gao.gov/assets/320/310105.pdf. Mason Inman, *Planning for Plan B*, 4 Nature Climate Change 7, 7 (2010).

climate geoengineering options, considered largely outside the mainstream of climate policymaking until a decade ago,[17] have emerged from the shadows, leading to legislative hearings,[18] calls for government-sponsored research programs,[19] limited scientific research,[20] and extensive assessment by the Intergovernmental Panel on Climate Change (IPCC).[21] Many members of the climate community were extremely hopeful that the Paris Agreement would prove to be a transformative moment in terms of climate policymaking. However, while the Agreement aims to hold temperatures to within this range,[22] the emissions reduction pledges made by the Parties to the UNFCCC to date put

---

17. Nils Markusson et al., *"In Case of Emergency Press Here": Framing Geoengineering as a Response to Dangerous Climate Change*, 5 WIREs CLIMATE CHANGE 281, 281 (2014); GAO, *supra* note 16; *see* Wil Burns & Simon Nicholson, *Governing Climate Geoengineering, in* NEW EARTH POLITICS 345–50 (Simon Nicholson & Sikina Jinnah eds., 2016).

18. CHAIRMAN BART GORDON, U.S. HOUSE COMMITTEE ON SCIENCE AND TECHNOLOGY, ENGINEERING THE CLIMATE: RESEARCH NEEDS AND STRATEGIES FOR INTERNATIONAL COORDINATION ii (2010), http://democrats.science.house.gov/sites/democrats.science.house.gov/files/10-29%20Chairman%20 Gordon%20Climate%20Engineering%20report%20-%20FINAL.pdf; U.K. HOUSE OF COMMONS SCIENCE AND TECHNOLOGY COMMITTEE, THE REGULATION OF GEOENGINEERING—FIFTH REPORT OF SESSION 2009–10, at 27–43 (2010), http://www.publications.parliament.uk/pa/cm200910/cmselect/ cmsctech/221/221.pdf.

19. THE ROYAL SOCIETY, *supra* note 13, at ix; NATIONAL RESEARCH COUNCIL OF THE NATIONAL ACADEMIES, CLIMATE INTERVENTION: REFLECTING SUNLIGHT TO COOL EARTH 6 (2015), http://www.nap.edu/ catalog/18988/climate-intervention-reflecting-sunlight-to-cool-earth; NATIONAL RESEARCH COUNCIL OF THE NATIONAL ACADEMIES, CLIMATE INTERVENTION: CARBON DIOXIDE REMOVAL AND RELIABLE SEQUESTRATION 107 (2015), http://www.nap.edu/catalog/18805/climate-intervention-carbon-dioxide-removal-and-reliable-sequestration. Most recently, a bill, S. 2084, was introduced into the U.S. Senate calling for the U.S. Department of Energy to study one category of climate geoengineering, which it terms "albedo modification," also known as solar radiation management (*see infra* notes 24–35 and accompanying text); Energy and Water Development Appropriations Bill, S. REP. NO. 114-236, 114th Cong. (2015/2016).

20. Institute for Advanced Sustainability Studies, *Managing the Climate? The Risks and Uncertainties of Climate Engineering*, http://www.iass-potsdam.de/en/research/emerging-technologies/climate-engineering (last visited Aug. 22, 2016); Eli Kintisch, *Bill Gates Funding Geoengineering Research*, SCI., Jan. 26, 2010, http://www.sciencemag.org/news/2010/01/bill-gates-funding-geoengineering-research; Cao Long et al., *Geoengineering: Basic Science and Ongoing Research Efforts in China*, 6 ADVANCES IN CLIMATE CHANGE RES. 188–96 (2015).

21. IPCC, CLIMATE CHANGE 2013: THE PHYSICAL SCIENCE BASIS. CONTRIBUTION OF WORKING GROUP I TO THE FIFTH ASSESSMENT REPORT OF THE INTERGOVERNMENTAL PANEL ON CLIMATE CHANGE 29 (2013), http://www.climatechange2013.org/images/report/WG1AR5_ALL_FINAL.pdf [hereinafter CLIMATE CHANGE 2013]; IPCC, CLIMATE CHANGE 2014: IMPACTS, ADAPTATION AND VULNERABILITY. PART A: GLOBAL AND SECTORAL ASPECTS. CONTRIBUTION OF WORKING GROUP II TO THE FIFTH ASSESSMENT REPORT OF THE INTERGOVERNMENTAL PANEL ON CLIMATE CHANGE 92 (2014), https://www.ipcc.ch/ pdf/assessment-report/ar5/wg2/WGIIAR5-PartA_FINAL.pdf; OTTMAR EDENHOFER ET AL., CLIMATE CHANGE 2014: MITIGATION OF CLIMATE CHANGE, WORKING GROUP III CONTRIBUTION TO THE FIFTH ASSESSMENT REPORT OF THE INTERGOVERNMENTAL PANEL ON CLIMATE CHANGE 256 (2014), https:// www.ipcc.ch/pdf/assessment-report/ar5/wg3/ipcc_wg3_ar5_full.pdf. Moreover, the chair of the IPCC, Hoesung Lee, has advocated research on potential large-scale deployment of climate geoengineering, including governance considerations. Suzanne Goldenberg, *UN Climate Science Chief: It's Not Too Late to Avoid Dangerous Temperature Rise*, THE GUARDIAN, May 11, 2016, https://www.theguardian. com/environment/2016/may/11/un-climate-change-hoesung-lee-global-warming-interview.

22. *Paris Agreement, supra* note 1, at art. 2(1)(a).

the globe on track for temperature increases of between 2.6–3.7°C by 2100,[23] with even higher temperatures in centuries to come.[24]

Climate geoengineering options are generally divided into two broad categories: solar radiation management (SRM) and CO_2 removal (CDR).[25] SRM geoengineering approaches focus on reducing the amount of solar radiation absorbed by the earth (estimated at approximately 235 $W \cdot m^{-2}$ currently) by an amount sufficient to offset some, or all, of the increased trapping of infrared radiation by rising levels of greenhouse gases (GHGs).[26] There are three leading SRM options. The first is sulfur aerosol injection (SAI), which would seek to enhance planetary albedo (surface reflectivity of sun's radiation) through the injection of a gas, such as sulfur dioxide, into the stratosphere, potentially exerting a potent cooling effect.[27] The sec-

23. Joeri Rogelj et al., *Paris Agreement Climate Proposals Need a Boost to Keep Warming Well Below 2°C*, 534 NATURE 631, 634 (2016); *Paris Agreement: Stage Set to Ramp Up Climate Action*, CLIMATE ACTION TRACKER, Dec. 12, 2015, http://climateactiontracker.org/news/257/Paris-Agreement-stage-set-to-ramp-up-climate-action.html; Kelly Levin & Taryn Fransen, *INSIDER: Why Are INDC Studies Reaching Different Temperature Estimates?*, WORLD RESOURCES INST., Nov. 9, 2015, http://www.wri.org/blog/2015/11/insider-why-are-indc-studies-reaching-different-temperature-estimates. The Paris Agreement provides for a "global stocktake" every five years "to assess the collective progress towards achieving the purpose of this Agreement and its long-term goals," with an eye to enhancing domestic and international commitments to meet the Agreement's overarching objectives, if necessary. *Paris Agreement*, supra note 1, at art. 14. While this provision could help the Parties avoid passing the 2°C threshold, this would require strengthened commitments prior to the Agreement entering into force, and more ambitious long-term commitments. WOLFGANG OBERGASSEL ET AL., PHOENIX FROM THE ASHES—AN ANALYSIS OF THE PARIS AGREEMENT TO THE UNITED NATIONS FRAMEWORK CONVENTION ON CLIMATE CHANGE 45 (Wuppertal Institute for Climate, Environment, and Energy 2016), http://wupperinst.org/uploads/tx_wupperinst/Paris_Results.pdf. Economic models project that the 2°C target could be "lost" in terms of economic feasibility by 2027, and the 2.5°C target after 2040. GUIDO VISCONTI, FUNDAMENTALS OF PHYSICS AND CHEMISTRY 765, 771 (2016). Moreover, the world's remaining "carbon budget" to avert passing the 2°C threshold may also be far lower than many current estimates given uncertainties about many critical parameters. Glen P. Peters, *The "Best Available Science" to Inform 1.5°C Policy Choices*, 6 NATURE CLIMATE CHANGE 1 (2016), http://www.nature.com/nclimate/journal/vaop/ncurrent/pdf/nclimate3000.pdf.

24. Peter U. Clark et al., *Consequences of Twenty-First Century Policy for Multi-Millennial Climate and Sea-Level Change*, 6 NATURE CLIMATE CHANGE 360, 361 (2016); Gregory Trencher, *Climate Change: What Happens After 2100?*, OUR WORLD, Nov. 16, 2011, http://ourworld.unu.edu/en/climate-change-what-happens-after-2100.

25. William C.G. Burns, *Geoengineering the Climate: An Overview of Solar Radiation Management Options*, 46 TULSA L. REV. 283, 286 (2012). Alternatively, some commentators divide climate geoengineering options into "shortwave" and "longwave" approaches; *see* T.M. Lenton & N.E. Vaughan, *The Radiative Forcing Potential of Different Climate Geoengineering Options*, 9 ATMOSPHERIC CHEMISTRY & PHYSICS 5539, 5540 (2009), whereas the U.S. National Academy of Sciences uses the term "albedo modification" instead of "solar radiation management." CLIMATE INTERVENTION: REFLECTING SUNLIGHT TO COOL EARTH, supra note 19, at 6.

26. MICHAEL C. MACCRACKEN, BEYOND MITIGATION: POTENTIAL OPTIONS FOR COUNTER-BALANCING THE CLIMATIC AND ENVIRONMENTAL CONSEQUENCES OF THE RISING CONCENTRATIONS OF GREENHOUSE GASES, POLICY RESEARCH WORKING PAPER 4938, WORLD BANK, DEVELOPMENT ECONOMICS 15 (2009), https://openknowledge.worldbank.org/bitstream/handle/10986/4132/WPS4938.pdf;sequence=1.

27. Peter J. Irvine et al., *An Overview of the Earth System Science of Solar Geoengineering*, WIREs CLIMATE CHANGE, July 14, 2016, http://onlinelibrary.wiley.com/doi/10.1002/wcc.423/full; A.V. Eliseev, I.I. Mokhov & A.A. Karpenko, *Global Warming Mitigation by Means of Controlled Aerosol Emissions Into*

ond is marine cloud brightening schemes, which contemplate dispersal of seawater droplets approximately 1 μm in size into marine stratiform clouds to increase their albedo.[28] The third option is space-based systems, which involve positioning sun-shields in space to reflect or deflect solar radiation back to space.[29]

By contrast, CO_2 removal approaches seek to remove and sequester CO_2 from the atmosphere, either by enhancing natural sinks for carbon, or deploying chemical engineering to remove CO_2 from the atmosphere.[30] Examples of CDR approaches include: ocean iron fertilization, whereby certain ocean regions would be seeded with iron or other substances to stimulate phytoplankton production to sequester carbon[31]; terrestrial enhanced weathering, which seeks to increase natural chemical silicate rock weathering to capture atmospheric carbon dioxide[32]; direct air capture, which seeks to extract CO_2 from ambient air in a closed-loop industrial process[33]; and BECCS.

There has been some guarded support for research into SRM options in recent years.[34] Advocates have usually emphasized the potential to use such technologies to avoid passing critical climatic thresholds,[35] or to reverse potential catastrophic climatic changes, such as rapid melting of the Greenland ice sheets.[36] However, there has also been substantial resistance to SRM

the Stratosphere: Global and Regional Peculiarities of Temperature Response as Estimated in IAP RAS CM Simulations, 22 ATMOSPHERIC & OCEANIC OPTICS 388, 390 (2009).

28. Blaž Gasparini & Ulrike Lohmann, *Why Cirrus Cloud Seeding Cannot Substantially Cool the Planet*, 121 J. GEOPHYSICAL RES. ATMOSPHERES 4877, 4878 (2016); Keith Bower et al., *Computational Assessment of a Proposed Technique for Global Warming Mitigation Via Albedo-Enhancement of Marine Stratocumulus Clouds*, 82 ATMOSPHERIC RES. 328, 329 (2006).

29. Takanobu Kosugi, *Role of Sunshades in Space as a Climate Control Option*, 67 ACTA ASTRONAUTICA 241, 242 (2010); Roger Angel, *Feasibility of Cooling the Earth With a Cloud of Small Spacecraft Near the Inner Lagrange Point (L1)*, 103 PROC. NAT'L ACAD. SCI. 17184, 17184 (2006).

30. Timothy Lenton, *The Global Potential for Carbon Dioxide Removal*, in GEOENGINEERING OF THE CLIMATE SYSTEM 53 (Roy Harrison & Ron Hester eds., 2014); CLIMATE CHANGE 2013, *supra* note 21, at Annex III, Glossary, at 1449 (2013).

31. Matthew Hubbard, *Barometer Rising: The Cartagena Protocol on Biosafety as a Model for Holistic International Regulation of Ocean Fertilization Projects and Other Forms of Geoengineering*, 40 WM. & MARY ENVTL. L. & POL'Y REV. 591, 598 (2016).

32. Nils Moosdorf et al., *Carbon Dioxide Efficiency of Terrestrial Enhanced Weathering*, 48 ENVTL. SCI & TECH. 4809, 4890 (2014).

33. K.S. Lackner, *Capture of Carbon Dioxide From Ambient Air*, 176 EUR. PHYSICAL J. SPECIAL TOPICS 93–106 (2009).

34. M. Granger Morgan et al., *Needed: Research Guidelines for Solar Radiation Management*, 29 ISSUES SCI. & TECH. (2013), http://issues.org/29-3/morgan-3/; CLIMATE INTERVENTION: REFLECTING SUNLIGHT TO COOL EARTH, *supra* note 19, at 177–92.

35. THE ROYAL SOCIETY, *supra* note 13, at 50; Clive Hamilton, Ethical Anxieties About Geoengineering: Moral Hazard, Slippery Slope, and Playing God, Paper Presented to a Conference of the Australian Academy of Science, Canberra (Sept. 27, 2011), at 1–2, http://www.homepages.ed.ac.uk/shs/Climatechange/Geo-politics/ethical_anxieties_about_geoengineering.pdf.

36. Hamilton, *supra* note 35, at 2.

research or deployment, with opponents citing large potential risks, including potentially radical changes in precipitation patterns, which could, inter alia, radically alter monsoon patterns in some regions, including South Asia; deplete the ozone layer; and cause huge pulses of warming if the use of such technologies were terminated.[37]

Should society ultimately choose to deploy climate geoengineering strategies, policymakers will most likely embrace the CO_2 removal approach of BECCS. This is true for two reasons. First, whether wholly justified or not,[38] BECCS is increasingly being portrayed as a "benign"[39] or "safe solution,"[40] perhaps primarily in comparison to the risks associated with SRM approaches.[41] Additionally, large-scale deployment of BECCS has been identified in many climate integrated assessment models as "central to the feasibility of not exceeding 2°C."[42] For example, of the 204 scenarios in the IPCC's Fifth Assessment Report, which project temperature increases below 2°C by 2100, 184 contemplate large-scale deployment of BECCS.[43] However, as outlined in the next section, while BECCS provides great promise in helping the world address climate change, it presents great perils, some with substantial implications for human rights.

---

37.   William C.G. Burns, *Climate Geoengineering: Solar Radiation Management and Its Implications for Intergenerational Equity*, 4 STAN. J.L. SCI. & POL'Y 38–55 (2011).

38.   *See infra* Part II.

39.   Peter Read & Jonathan Lermit, *Bio-Energy With Carbon Storage (BECS): A Sequential Decision Approach to the Threat of Abrupt Climate Change*, 30 ENERGY 2654, 2666 (2005).

40.   Bobo Zheng & Jiuping Xu, *Carbon Capture and Storage Development Trends From a Techno-Paradigm Perspective*, 7 ENERGIES 5221, 5240 (2014).

41.   CLIMATE INTERVENTION: CARBON DIOXIDE REMOVAL AND RELIABLE SEQUESTRATION, *supra* note 19, ch. 2, at 5, http://www.nap.edu/read/18805/chapter/2.

42.   Gough & Vaughan, *supra* note 12, at 7. *See also* José Roberto Moreira et al., *BECCS Potential in Brazil: Achieving Negative Emissions in Ethanol and Electricity Production Based on Sugar Cane Bagasse and Other Residues*, 179 APPLIED ENERGY 55, 56 (2016) (noting that BECCS "will play a vital role in reaching the required level of emission reductions in the future").

43.   GOUGH & VAUGHAN, *supra* note 12, at 5. *See also* Pete Smith et al., *Agriculture, Forestry, and Other Land Use (AFOLU), in* CLIMATE CHANGE 2014: MITIGATION OF CLIMATE CHANGE. CONTRIBUTION OF WORKING GROUP IIII TO THE FIFTH ASSESSMENT REPORT OF THE INTERGOVERNMENTAL PANEL ON CLIMATE CHANGE 870 (2015), http://www.ipcc.ch/pdf/assessment-report/ar5/wg3/ipcc_wg3_ar5_chapter11.pdf; Olivier Boucher et al., *In the Wake of the Paris Agreement, Scientists Must Embrace New Directions for Climate Change Research*, 113 PROC. NAT'L ACAD. SCI. 7287, 7288 (2016); Sabine Fuss, *Optimal Mitigation Strategies With Negative Emission Technologies and Carbon Sinks Under Uncertainty*, 118 CLIMATIC CHANGE 73, 74 (2013). One recent study projected potential sequestration of 1.5 Gt CO_2/yr by 2050 and 5–16 Gt CO_2/yr by 2100. BEN CALDECOTT ET AL., STRANDED CARBON ASSETS AND NEGATIVE EMISSIONS TECHNOLOGIES, WORKING PAPER 19, 22 (Smith School of Enterprise and the Environment, University of Oxford 2015), http://www.smithschool.ox.ac.uk/research-programmes/stranded-assets/Stranded%20Carbon%20Assets%20and%20NETs%20-%2006.02.15.pdf. By comparison, 2015 global CO_2 emissions were projected to be 35.7 Gt CO_2. Robert B. Jackson, *Reaching Peak Emissions*, 6 NATURE CLIMATE CHANGE 7, 7 (2016).

II.   BECCS and Its Potential Ramifications for Human Rights

Human rights are universal standards supported by legal guarantees that seek to protect both individuals and groups from contravention of what are recognized as fundamental freedoms premised on protection of values such as freedom, dignity, and fairness.[44] As such, they establish minimum standards for individuals and groups that cannot be contravened in the pursuit of aggregate societal benefits.[45] Most fundamentally, human rights protections seek to ensure that laws and political and social structures are grounded in moral reasons and moral discourse, and are justifiable within a framework of appropriate legal and political structures.[46] Therefore, human rights provide a critical link between protection of a vital interest and imposition of a duty on others to protect and promote the interest.[47] Large-scale deployment of BECCS could threaten a number of human rights interests.

A.   BECCS and the Human Right to Food

The right to adequate food is established by a number of human rights instruments at the international and regional levels,[48] including the International Covenant on Economic, Social, and Cultural Rights (ICESCR), which seeks to protect "the fundamental right of everyone to be free from

44.   Office of the U.N. High Commissioner for Human Rights, Frequently Asked Questions on a Human Rights-Based Approach to Development Cooperation 1 (2006), http://www.ohchr.org/Documents/Publications/FAQen.pdf. *See also* Henry Shue, *Changing Images of Climate Change: Human Rights and Future Generations*, 5 J. Hum. Rts. & Env't 50, 58 (2014).

45.   Simon Caney, *Climate Change, Human Rights, and Moral Thresholds, in* Climate Ethics 73–90 (Stephen Gardiner et al. eds., 2010); Frédéric Mégret, *Nature of Obligations, in* International Human Rights Law 129 (Daniel Moeckli, Sangeeta Shah & Sandesh Sivakumaran eds., 2010).

46.   Rainer Frost, *The Justification of Human Rights and the Basic Right to Justification: A Reflexive Approach*, 120 Ethics 711, 734 (2010).

47.   Charles Jones, *The Human Rights to Subsistence*, 30 J. Applied Phil. 57, 58 (2013).

48.   *See, e.g.*, Universal Declaration of Human Rights art. 25, G.A. Res. 217A, U.N. GAOR, 3d Sess., 67th plen. mtg., U.N. Doc. A/810 (1948) (providing part of the right to an adequate standard of living), http://www.un.org/en/universal-declaration-human-rights/; Convention on the Rights of the Child (CRC), G.A. Res. 44/25, U.N. GAOR, 44th Sess., Annex, Supp. No. 49, at 167, U.N. Doc. A/44/49 (1989), at art. 24(2)(c) & (e), http://www1.umn.edu/humanrts/instree/k2crc.htm; Convention on the Rights of Persons With Disabilities, G.A. Res. 61/106, U.N. Doc. A/RES/61/106 (2006), at art. 25(f), http://www.un.org/disabilities/documents/convention/convoptprot-e.pdf; Convention on the Elimination of All Forms of Discrimination Against Women, G.A. Res. 34/180, U.N. GAOR, 34th Sess., Supp. No. 46, at 193, U.N. Doc. A/34/46 (1979), at art. 12, http://www.un.org/womenwatch/daw/cedaw/cedaw.htm; African Charter on Human and Peoples' Rights, OAU/CAB/LEG/67/3/Rev.5 (Org. of African Unity) (1996), *reprinted in* Human Rights Law in Africa (Christof Heyns ed., 1996) (implicit in Articles 4, 16, and 22), http://www.achpr.org/files/instruments/achpr/banjul_charter.pdf.

hunger."[49] A report of the Office of the High Commissioner on Human Rights (OHCHR) indicated that States must take necessary actions to ensure freedom from hunger and access to adequate food, "even in times of natural or other disasters."[50] The ICESCR Committee General Comment No. 12 states that "accessibility encompasses both economic and physical accessibility."[51] Therefore, the Comment continues, vulnerable groups such as displaced peoples and indigenous populations "may need attention through special [programs]."[52]

Deployment of BECCS could raise food prices, and/or displace agricultural production, in ways that could also imperil food security and violate the right to food. One striking feature of BECCS is the potential amount of land that may need to be diverted from other uses, including food production and livelihood-related activities, to provide bioenergy feedstocks. Delivery of a relatively modest 3 Gt of CO_2 equivalent (CO2-eq) negative emissions annually would require a land area of approximately 380–700 million ha 2100, translating into 7–25% of agricultural land and 25–46% of arable and permanent crop area.[53] The range of land demands would be 2–4 times larger than land areas that have been classified as abandoned or marginal.[54] This level of emissions removal would be equivalent to a startling 21% of total current human appropriate net primary productivity.[55] While it might be possible to reduce these impacts by more of an emphasis on the use of agricultural residue and waste feedstocks, this option could prove to be extremely limited.[56]

Demands on land of this magnitude could substantially raise food prices on basic commodities.[57] This could imperil food security for many of the world's most vulnerable, with many families in developing countries already

49. International Covenant on Economic, Social, and Cultural Rights, 993 U.N.T.S. 3, *reprinted in* 6 I.L.M. 360 (1967), at art. 11(2), http://www.ohchr.org/EN/ProfessionalInterest/Pages/CESCR.aspx.
50. *Report of the Office of the United Nations High Commissioner for Human Rights on the Relationship Between Climate Change and Human Rights, supra* note 3, at 9.
51. *CESCR General Comment No. 12: The Right to Adequate Food (Art. 11),* U.N. ESCOR Comm. on Economic, Social, and Cultural Rights, at para. 13, U.N. Doc. E/C.12/1999/5 (1999).
52. *Id.*
53. Pete Smith et al., *Biophysical and Economic Limits to Negative CO_2 Emissions,* 6 Nature Climate Change 42, 46 (2016). *See also* Phil Williamson, *Scrutinize CO_2 Removal Methods,* 530 Nature 153, 154 (2016).
54. Smith et al., *supra* note 53, at 46.
55. *Id.*
56. Caldecott, Lomax & Workman, *supra* note 43, at 16; David Sommerstein, *Is Burning Trees Still Green? Some Experts Now Question Biomass,* NPR, July 12, 2016, http://www.npr.org/2016/07/12/482937940/is-burning-trees-still-green-some-experts-now-question-biomass.
57. Scott Barrett, *Solar Geoengineering's Brave New World: Thoughts on the Governance of an Unprecedented Technology,* 8 Rev. Envtl. Econ. 249, 254 (2014).

expending 70–80% of their income on food.[58] There is empirical evidence to support this proposition in the context of efforts in the past decade to increase biofuel expansion. Biofuel expansion, in many cases at the expense of food production, was one of the major factors precipitating substantial spikes in food prices in 2007/2008 and 2012.[59] Food price increases and reduction of food production imperiled the food security of many in Africa and in other parts of the developing world.[60] Increases in food prices in 2007 led to food riots in a number of countries and elevated the number of people living in hunger to a historical high of over one billion.[61] According to a 2008 report by Oxfam, the "scramble to supply" biofuels like palm oil, which was partly driven by EU biofuel targets, exacerbated the food price crises, brought "30 million people into poverty," and put 60 million indigenous people at risk.[62] While it is difficult to estimate the impact of large-scale deployment of BECCS on food prices, even the far more modest goal of scaling up biofuels production could result in price increases of 15–40%.[63]

Efforts to develop feedstock for bioenergy can also result in displacement of the poor from land, which can undermine food security, as well as livelihoods, political power, and social identity.[64] A recent report listed more than

58. United Nations Office of the High Commissioner, Mandate of the Special Rapporteur on the Right to Food, Note on the Impacts of the EU Biofuels Policy on the Right to Food (2013), http://www.srfood.org/images/stories/pdf/otherdocuments/20130423_biofuelsstatement_en.pdf; Ottmar Edenhofer et al., *Addressing Transformation Pathways, in* Climate Change 2014: Mitigation of Climate Change, Working Group III Contribution to the Fifth Assessment Report of the Intergovernmental Panel on Climate Change 91 (2014), https://www.ipcc.ch/pdf/assessment-report/ar5/wg3/ipcc_wg3_ar5_full.pdf; GAO, Center for Science, Technology, and Engineering, Climate Engineering: Technical Status, Future Directions, and Potential Responses 25 (2011), http://www.gao.gov/assets/330/322208.pdf.

59. ActionAid, Caught in the Net: How "Net-Zero Emissions" Will Delay Real Climate Action and Drive Land Grabs 7 (2015), http://www.actionaid.org/sites/files/actionaid/caught_in_the_net_actionaid.pdf. Some studies have attributed 30% of grain price increases from 2000–2007 to demand for biofuels. Mark W. Rosegrant, Biofuels and Grain Prices: Impacts and Policy Responses 2 (International Food Policy Research Institute 2008), http://www.ifpri.org/publication/biofuels-and-grain-prices.

60. Bamikole Amigun et al., *Biofuels and Sustainability in Africa*, 15 Renewable & Sustainable Energy Rev. 1360, 1362 (2011).

61. International Bar Association, Climate Change Justice and Human Rights Task Force Report, Achieving Justice and Human Rights in an Era of Climate Disruption 183 (2014), http://www.ibanet.org/PresidentialTaskForceClimateChangeJustice2014Report.aspx.

62. Oxfam, Climate Wrongs and Human Rights: Putting People at the Heart of Climate-Change Policy 15–16 (2008). *See also* Center for Human Rights and Global Justice, New York University School of Law, Foreign Land Deals and Human Rights: Case Studies on Agricultural and Biofuel Investment (2010).

63. Hans Morten Haugen, *International Obligations and the Right to Food: Clarifying the Potentials and Limitations in Applying a Human Rights Approach When Facing Biofuels Expansion*, 11 J. Hum. Rts. 405, 406 (2012).

64. Lorenzo Cotula et al., Fuelling Exclusion? The Biofuels Boom and Poor People's Access to Land 14 (International Institute for the Environment and Development and Food and Agriculture Organization 2008), http://pubs.iied.org/pdfs/12551IIED.pdf.

293 reported "land grabs" for the purposes of biofuel plantation expansion, encompassing more than 17 million ha of land.[65] Moreover, there is ample historic evidence of land seizures from vulnerable populations for other economic enterprises, including mineral extraction and industrial projects.[66] While supporters of BECCS contend that bioenergy expansion can be effectuated primarily through "marginal," "degraded," or "abandoned" land,[67] primarily found in developing countries, the reality is that hundreds of millions may rely on these lands for income and sustenance.[68] For example, substantial portions of grazing lands are barren during the dry season in developing countries, and thus classified as "degraded." Yet these lands are often productive during the rainy season and relied on for food and income by poor families.[69] Moreover, there is likely to be substantial pressure to dedicate additional land to agricultural production in the future given projected increases in population and affluence.[70]

Finally, incentives for feedstock production may result in farmers converting substantial swaths of land from food crop production, reducing food supplies for local populations.[71] For example, in one region of Brazil, conversion of land from cassava and rice production to oil seed for biofuel production undermined food security.[72] A 2011 study indicated that more than half of the world's bioenergy potential is centered in two regions with very large poor and vulnerable populations: (1) sub-Saharan Africa and (2) Latin America and the Caribbean.[73]

---

65. ActionAid, *supra* note 59, at 7. *See also* Evadné Grant & Onita Das, *Land Grabbing, Sustainable Development, and Human Rights*, 4 Transnat'l Envtl. L. 289 (2015); Lili Fuhr & Niclas Hällström, *The Myth of Net-Zero Emissions*, Heinrich Böll Found., Dec. 10, 2014, https://www.boell.de/en/2014/12/10/myth-net-zero-emissions.

66. Prakash Kashwan, *The Politics of Rights-Based Approach in Conservation*, 31 Land Use Pol'y 613, 622 (2013).

67. Raphael Slade et al., *Global Bioenergy Resources*, 4 Nature Climate Change 99, 100 (2014); Secretariat of the Convention on Biological Diversity, CBD Technical Series No. 65: Biofuels and Biodiversity 32 (2012), https://www.cbd.int/doc/publications/cbd-ts-65-en.pdf.

68. Rachel Smolker & Almuth Ernsting, BECCS (Bioenergy With Carbon Capture and Storage): Climate Saviour or Dangerous Hype?, 8 (Biofuelwatch 2012), http://www.biofuelwatch.org.uk/2012/beccs_report/; Secretariat of the Convention on Biological Diversity, *supra* note 67, at 32.

69. Slade et al., *supra* note 67, at 103.

70. Stefan Bringezu et al., *Beyond Biofuels: Assessing Global Land Use for Domestic Consumption of Biomass: A Conceptual and Empirical Contribution to Sustainable Management of Global Resources*, 29 Land Use Pol'y 224, 228 (2012).

71. Cotula et al., *supra* note 64, at 14.

72. Marcus Vinicius Alves Finco & Werner Doppler, *Bioenergy and Sustainable Development: The Dilemma of Food Security and Climate Change in the Brazilian Savannah*, 14 Energy Sustainable Dev. 194, 198 (2010).

73. Helmut Haberl et al., *Global Bioenergy Potentials From Agricultural Land in 2050: Sensitivity to Climate Change, Diets, and Yields*, 35 Biomass & Bioenergy 4753, 4762 (2011).

B. BECCS and the Human Right to Water

Several human rights instruments recognize the human right to water.[74] The Committee on Economic, Social, and Cultural Rights (CESCR) in Comment 14 provides that the States' duty to respect the right to water requires refraining from interfering with the enjoyment of that right, and to protect the right by adopting measures to restrain third parties from interfering with the right.[75]

In 2010, the United Nations General Assembly also officially recognized the "right to water and sanitation."[76] The United Nations Human Rights Council subsequently adopted HRC Resolution 15/9, which "affirms that the rights to water and sanitation are part of existing international law and confirms that these rights are legally binding" on States Parties to the ICESCR.[77] A number of regional courts have found that the right to safe drinking water and sanitation derives from other human rights, such as the rights to life, health, and adequate housing,[78] even though the right is not explicitly mentioned in regional human rights instruments.[79]

BECCS could imperil the right to water in some regions of the world given its "very large water footprint" when implemented at a scale of between 1.1 and 3.3 Gt of CO_2-eq per year.[80] By 2100, BECCS feedstock production at scale could require approximately 10% of the cur-

---

74. *See, e.g.*, Convention on the Elimination of All Forms of Discrimination Against Women, *supra* note 48, at art. 14(2); CRC, *supra* note 48, at arts. 24, & 27(3); International Labour Organization Convention No. 161 Concerning Occupational Health Services, June 25, 1985, 71st I.L.C. Sess., at art. 5, http://www.ilo.org/dyn/normlex/en/f?p=NORMLEXPUB:12100:0::NO::P12100_INSTRUMENT_ID:312306; Additional Protocol to the American Convention on Human Rights, Inter-Am. C.H.R. Basic Documents Pertaining to Human Rights in the Inter-American System, OAS/ser.L/V/II.82, Doc. 6 rev. 1 (1992), at art. 11(1), http://www.oas.org/juridico/english/treaties/a-52.html; Arab Charter on Human Rights, May 22, 2004, *reprinted in* 12 Int'l Hum. Rts. Rep. 893 (2005) (entered into force Mar. 15, 2008), at art. 39, https://www1.umn.edu/humanrts/instree/loas2005.html.

75. *Substantive Issues Arising in the Implementation of the International Covenant on Economic, Social, and Cultural Rights, General Comment No. 15: The Right to Water (Arts. 11 and 12 of the Covenant)*, U.N. ESCOR Comm. on Economic, Social, and Cultural Rights, 29th Sess., at paras. 21, 23, U.N. Doc. E/C.12/2002/11 (2003).

76. The Human Right to Water, G.A. Res. 64/292, U.N. GAOR, 64th Sess., U.N. Doc. A/RES/64/292 (2010), http://www.un.org/es/comun/docs/?symbol=A/RES/64/292&lang=E.

77. United Nations Human Rights Council Res. 15/9, Human Rights and Access to Safe Drinking Water and Sanitation, 15th Sess., U.N. Doc. A/HRC/RES/15/9 (2010).

78. United Nations et al., Fact Sheet No. 35: The Right to Water 6 (2010), http://www.ohchr.org/Documents/Publications/FactSheet35en.pdf.

79. *See, e.g.*, European Social Charter, 529 U.N.T.S. 89, http://www1.umn.edu/humanrts/euro/z31escch.html; American Convention on Human Rights, OASTS No. 6, at 1, OEA/ser.K/XVI/1.1, Doc. 65 rev. 1 corr. 2 (1970), *reprinted in* 9 I.L.M. 673 (1970), http://www.oas.org/dil/treaties_B-32_American_Convention_on_Human_Rights.pdf, and the African Charter on Human and Peoples' Rights.

80. Pete Smith, *Soil Carbon Sequestration and Biochar as Negative Emission Technologies*, 22 Global Change Biology 1315, 1321 (2016).

rent evapotranspiration from all global cropland areas,[81] or of the same magnitude as *all current total agricultural water withdrawals.*[82] Moreover, water consumption for energy generation and carbon capture could have "intensive localized effects."[83] In a world of growing food demand, this could have serious implications, as maximum crop yields are only possible under conditions where water supplies are not restricted.[84] There is also concern that BECCS operations might contaminate underground sources of drinking water.[85]

C.   BECCS and Potential Contravention of Other Human Rights

The right to health is included in a large number of human rights treaties and soft law instruments.[86] It is most comprehensively established in the ICESCR as "the right of everyone to the enjoyment of the highest attainable standard of physical and mental health."[87]

The ICESCR Committee interprets the right to health in General Comment No. 14 to include "a wide range of socio-economic factors that promote conditions in which people can lead a healthy life, and extends to the underlying determinants of health, such as . . . a healthy environment."[88] General Comment 14 further states that the right to health includes "a right to the enjoyment of a variety of facilities, goods, services and conditions necessary

---

81.   Smith et al., *supra* note 53, at 47.

82.   Markus Bonsch et al., *Trade-offs Between Land and Water Requirements for Large-Scale Bioenergy Production*, 8 GCB BIOENERGY 11, 12 (2014). *See also* Vaibhav Chaturvedi et al., *Climate Mitigation Policy Implications for Global Irrigation Water Demand*, 20 MITIGATION ADAPTATION STRATEGIES FOR GLOBAL CHANGE 389, 396 (2015).

83.   Lydia J. Smith & Margaret S. Torn, *Ecological Limits to Terrestrial Biological Carbon Dioxide Removal*, 118 CLIMATIC CHANGE 89, 92 (2013).

84.   B.J. LEGG, YIELDS OF FARMED SPECIES: CONSTRAINTS AND OPPORTUNITIES IN THE 21ST CENTURY 31–50 (R. Sylvester-Bradley & Julian Wiseman eds., 2005).

85.   KELSI BRACMORT & RICHARD K. LATTANZIO, GEOENGINEERING: GOVERNANCE AND TECHNOLOGY POLICY 12 (Congressional Research Service 2013), https://www.fas.org/sgp/crs/misc/R41371.pdf.

86.   Universal Declaration of Human Rights, *supra* note 48, at art. 25; International Convention on the Elimination of All Forms of Racial Discrimination, Dec. 21, 1965, 660 U.N.T.S. 195, http://www.refworld.org/docid/3ae6b3940.html; CRC, *supra* note 48, at art. 24; Convention on the Elimination of All Forms of Discrimination Against Women, *supra* note 48, at arts. 11(1)(5), 12, 14(2)(b); International Convention on the Protection of the Rights of All Migrant Workers and Members of Their Families, G.A. Res. 45/158, U.N. GAOR, 45th Sess., Supp. No. 49A, Annex, arts. 28, 43(e), and 45(c), at 262, U.N. Doc. A/45/49 (1990), https://www1.umn.edu/humanrts/instree/n8icprmw.htm; African Charter on Human and Peoples' Rights, *supra* note 48, at art. 16; Additional Protocol to the American Convention on Human Rights, *supra* note 74, at art. 10; Constitution of the World Health Organization July 22, 1946, pmbl., 14 U.N.T.S. 185.

87.   International Covenant on Economic, Social and Cultural Rights, *supra* note 49, at art. 12.

88.   *CESCR General Comment No. 14: The Right to the Highest Attainable Standard of Health (Art. 12)*, U.N. ESCOR Comm. on Economic, Social, and Cultural Rights, U.N. Doc. HR1.GEN/1/REV.9 (Vol. I) (1984), http://www.ohchr.org/Documents/Issues/Women/WRGS/Health/GC14.pdf.

for the realization of the highest attainable standard of health."[89] To the extent that food production might be adversely impacted by deployment of BECCS, as outlined above, it would undermine one of the "underlying determinants of health."[90]

BECCS could "vastly accelerate the loss of primary forest and natural grassland."[91] This could result in habitat loss for many species and, ultimately, "massive" changes in species richness and abundance.[92] Indeed, Phil Williamson concluded that large-scale deployment of BECCS could result in a greater diminution of terrestrial species than temperature increases of 2.8°C above pre-industrial levels.[93]

Loss of biological diversity could undermine the right to health by leading to an increase in the transmission of infectious disease, such as hantavirus, Lyme disease, and schistosomiasis.[94] Moreover, products and services derived from biodiversity are a critical economic resource for many of the world's poor, including indigenous peoples.[95] Diminution of biodiversity through deployment of geoengineering options could undermine the right to livelihood,[96] which in turn is intimately linked to the human right to life and an adequate standard of living for health and well-being of individuals and families.[97] Loss of biodiversity could also undermine the right of indigenous peoples to access to such resources.[98]

---

89. *Id.*
90. *Id.* at para. 11.
91. Williamson, *supra* note 53, at 154.
92. ANDREW WILTSHIRE & T. DAVIES-BARNARD, PLANETARY LIMITS TO BECCS NEGATIVE EMISSIONS 15 (Mar. 2015), http://avoid-net-uk.cc.ic.ac.uk/wp-content/uploads/delightful-downloads/2015/07/Planetary-limits-to-BECCS-negative-emissions-AVOID-2_WPD2a_v1.1.pdf. *See also* GOUGH & VAUGHAN, *supra* note 12, at 15; SECRETARIAT OF THE CONVENTION ON BIOLOGICAL DIVERSITY, *supra* note 67, at 38.
93. Williamson, *supra* note 53, at 154.
94. *Report of the Special Rapporteur on the Issue of Human Rights Obligations Relating to the Enjoyment of a Safe, Clean, Healthy, and Sustainable Environment*, *supra* note 7, at 9.
95. ROUBINA BASSOUS/GHATTAS, BIODIVERSITY AND HUMAN RIGHTS FROM A PALESTINIAN PERSPECTIVE (The Applied Research Institute–Jerusalem/Society n.d.), http://www.arij.org/files/arijadmin/biodiversity.pdf; Tim Hayward, *Biodiversity, Human Rights, and Sustainability*, BOTANIC GARDENS CONSERVATION INT'L, July 2001, http://www.bgci.org/education/article/0423.
96. Universal Declaration of Human Rights, *supra* note 48, at art. 25(1).
97. Ryan Hartzell & C. Balisacan, *Harmonizing Biodiversity Conservation and the Human Right to Livelihood: Towards a Viable Model for Sustainable Community-based Ecotourism Using Lessons From the Donsol Whale Shark Project*, 57 ATENEO L.J. 423, 438 (2012).
98. Convention Concerning Indigenous and Tribal Peoples in Independent Countries, June 27, 1989, art. 15(1), 28 I.L.M. 1382, http://www.ilo.org/dyn/normlex/en/f?p=NORMLEXPUB:12100:0::N O::P12100_ILO_CODE:C169; United Nations Declaration on the Rights of Indigenous Peoples, U.N. ESCOR, Comm. on Hum. Rts., 11th Sess., Annex I, U.N. Doc. E/CN.4/Sub.2 (1993), at art. 8(2)(b), http://www.un.org/esa/socdev/unpfii/documents/DRIPS_en.pdf.

III.   Operationalizing Human Rights Protections Under the Paris Agreement in the Context of BECCS/ Climate Geoengineering

The Paris Agreement calls on its Parties to take human rights into account "when taking action to address climate change . . . ."[99] This section will suggest how the Parties might give effect to this language in the context of climate geoengineering.

A.   *The Contours of a Human Rights-Based Approach*

The suggested framework is known as a "human rights-based approach" (HRBA). The hallmark of the HRBA is a focus "on the relationship between the rights-holder and the duty-bearer and revealing gaps in legislation, institutions, policy and the possibility of the most vulnerable to influence decisions that have impact on their lives."[100] An HRBA establishes a normative framework "for addressing systematic and structural injustices, social exclusions and human rights repressions . . . ."[101] The HRBA has been embraced by international, national, and subnational governmental, and nongovernmental organizations in a wide array of contexts, including, health, development, and environmental protection.[102]

Drawing on guidelines developed by human rights and development institutions,[103] applying the HRBA to the consideration of BECCS as a climate geoengineering option should include the elements discussed below.

---

99.   *Paris Agreement, supra* note 1.
100. Alessandra Lundström Sarelin, *Human Rights-Based Approaches to Development Cooperation, HIV/ AIDS, and Food Security*, 29 Hum. Rts. L.Q. 460, 479 (2007), http://courses.arch.vt.edu/courses/ wdunaway/gia5434/sarelin07.pdf.
101. Damilola S. Olawuyi, *Advancing Climate Justice in International Law: An Evaluation of the United Nations Human Rights-Based Approach*, 11 Fla. A&M U. L. Rev. 1, 9 (2016).
102. Aled Dilwyn Fisher, A Human-Rights Based Approach to the Environment and Climate Change, GI-ESCR Practitioner's Guide (2014), http://globalinitiative-escr.org/wp-content/ uploads/2014/03/GI-ESCR-Practitioners-Guide-Human-Rights-Environment-and-Climate-Change.pdf; Leslie London, *What Is a Human-Rights Based Approach to Health and Does It Matter?*, 10 Health & Hum. Rts. 65–80 (2008), https://www.researchgate.net/profile/Leslie_London/ publication/46287024_What_is_a_human-rights_based_approach_to_health_and_does_it_matter/ links/54de290d0cf23bf2043af813.pdf; Andrea Cornwall & Celestine Nyamu-Musembi, *Putting the "Rights-Based Approach" to Development Into Perspective*, 25 Third World Q. 1415–37 (2004), http:// courses.arch.vt.edu/courses/wdunaway/gia5434/cornwall.pdf. For a detailed discussion of the HRBA in the climate justice context, see Chapter 1 of this volume.
103. International Human Rights Law Clinic et al., *supra* note 9, at 15; United Nations High Commissioner for Refugees, Climate Change, Natural Disasters, and Human Displacement: A UNHCR Perspective 11 (2009).

I.   Human Rights Impact Assessments

The HRBA would facilitate a process to identify the specific potential impacts of BECCS and associated potential human rights considerations, as well as the specific groups likely to be impacted. A reliable method to effectuate this goal would be to mandate the preparation of a human rights impact assessment (HRIA) for individual BECCS programs, and on a programmatic basis.

HRIAs are assessment protocols that assess the consistency of policies, legislation, projects, and programs with human rights.[104] It is a particularly appropriate instrument in the context of emerging high-risk technologies such as geoengineering in that its focus is not on past violations, but rather on developing tools to avoid violations of rights in the future.[105]

An HRIA process in the context of BECCS should include the following elements:

- *A scoping process that would identify rights-holders and duty-bearers, and develop relevant indicators to use in the process to help assess potential impacts and their relevance to the human rights interests of rights-holders*

  In identifying rights-holders, the HRBA focuses on protection of the rights of excluded and marginalized populations, including those whose rights are most likely to be threatened.[106] Indicators should be designed to assess State intent to comply with human rights mandates, measure State implementation of human rights obligations, and measure State human rights performance.

- *An evidence gathering process to help assess the potential impacts of deployment of BECCS*

  One critical requirement of the HRBA process would be greatly enhanced scientific understanding of the impacts of large-scale deployment of BECCS, including regional impacts that might adversely impact specific potential rights-holders.

---

104. World Bank & Nordic Trust Fund, Human Rights Impact Assessment: A Review of the Literature, Differences With Other Forms of Assessments and Relevance for Development 1 (2013), http://siteresources.worldbank.org/PROJECTS/Resources/40940-1331068268558/HRIA_Web.pdf.

105. *Id.*

106. Office of the U.N. High Commissioner for Human Rights, Frequently Asked Questions, *supra* note 44, at 16.

- *An ex ante deliberative process between rights-holders and duty-bearers that would help identify specific concerns of rights-holders and duty-bearers*

  An essential component of any potential governance architecture for climate geoengineering is engagement of populations in regions where impacts are likely to be most extreme, especially in developing countries.[107] This participatory component of the HRIA process could help promote this objective by operationalizing procedurally oriented human rights provisions, including the right to information and the right to public participation.

  In developing this component of the HRIA, efforts should be made to go beyond merely soliciting public opinion on geoengineering issues, usually characterized as public communication or public consultation,[108] to the establishment of large-scale public deliberative processes. Public deliberative processes seek to afford citizens, or a representative subset thereof, the opportunity to discuss, exchange arguments, and deliberate on critical issues,[109] as well as to seek to persuade one another of the judiciousness of their solutions.[110]

2.   Analysis and Recommendations

This element of the HRIA process should include assessment of the human rights impacts of BECCS proposals, and an assessment of State responsibilities to respect, protect, and fulfill human rights in this context. This step should also include the critical element of developing recommendations to avoid or ameliorate potential impacts on human rights, or alternative means to achieve climate mitigation goals that would avoid human rights violations. This obligation discussing mitigation and alternative options is also

---

107. Nick Pidgeon, *Deliberating Stratospheric Aerosols for Climate Geoengineering and the SPICE Project*, 3 NATURE CLIMATE CHANGE 451, 454 (2013).

108. For example:

    In public communication, information is conveyed from the sponsors of the initiative to the public . . . In public consultation, information is conveyed from members of the public to the sponsors of the initiative, following a process initiated by the sponsor. Significantly, no formal dialogue exists between individual members of the public and sponsors. The information elicited from the public is believed to represent currently held opinions on the topic in question.

    Gene Rowe & Lynn J. Frewer, *A Typology of Public Engagement Mechanisms*, 30 SCI. TECH. & HUM. VALUES 251, 254–55 (2005), http://www.academia.edu/214234/A_typology_of_public_engagement_mechanisms.

109. Paul Anderson, *Which Direction for International Environmental Law?*, 6 J. HUM. RTS. & ENV'T 98, 121 (2015).

110. J. Dryzek, *Ecology and Discursive Democracy*, in IS CAPITALISM SUSTAINABLE?: POLITICAL ECONOMY AND THE POLITICS OF ECOLOGY 176 (M. O'Connor ed., 1994); Anderson, *supra* note 109, at 121.

an important component of environmental impact assessments at both the international and national levels.[111]

- *Assessment of the capacity of rights-holders to exercise their rights and duty-bearers to fulfill their respective obligations, as well as strategies to bolster capacities*

  Capacity, broadly defined, is a critical consideration in determining the ability of duty-bearers to meet their obligations and rights-holders to claim their rights.[112] In the context of a human rights assessment of BECCS, this should include an assessment of human and economic capacity of duty-bearers to protect human rights interests. It should also involve an assessment of rights-holders' capacities, including access to pertinent information, especially for marginalized or traditionally excluded groups, and ability to obtain redress.[113]

- *Establishment of a program to monitor and evaluate both outcomes and processes, guided by human rights standards and principles*

  Implementation of a human rights monitoring program in the context of BECCS should include the use of role and capacity analysis to assess the obligations of institutions at the international and national levels to monitor the impacts of geoengineering, as well as their capacity and analysis of existing information systems and networks to assess critical

---

111. The Pew Charitable Trusts, High Seas Environmental Assessments: The Importance of Evaluation in Areas Beyond National Jurisdiction (2016), http://www.pewtrusts.org/en/research-and-analysis/issue-briefs/2016/03/high-seas-environmental-impact-assessments; Neil Craik, The International Law of Environmental Impact Assessment 67 (2008); Convention on Environmental Impact Assessment in a Transboundary Context, Feb. 25, 1991, art. 5(a), 1989 U.N.T.S. 310 (1997), 30 I.L.M. 800 (1991) (entered into force Sept. 10, 1997), http://www.unece.org/fileadmin/DAM/env/eia/documents/legaltexts/Espoo_Convention_authentic_ENG.pdf; National Environmental Policy Act, 42 U.S.C. §§4321–4347, at §4332, http://elr.info/sites/default/files/docs/statutes/full/nepa.pdf; National Wildlife Fed'n v. National Marine Fisheries Serv., 2016 WL 2353647, at *59 (D. Or. 2016); Directive 2014/52/EU of the European Parliament and Council of Apr. 16, 2014, amending Directive 2011/92/EU on the assessment of the effects of certain public and private projects on the environment, 2014 O.J. L124/1, at art. 5(1)(d), Annex IV.4.

112. Food and Agriculture Organization of the United Nations, Methods to Monitor the Human Right to Adequate Food Volume II 38 (2008), http://www.fao.org/3/a-i0351e.pdf; Urban Jonsson, Human Rights Approach to Development Programming 15 (UNICEF 2003), http://www.unicef.org/rightsresults/files/HRBDP_Urban_Jonsson_April_2003.pdf.

113. United Nations Development Programme Capacity Development Group, Applying a Human Rights-Based Approach to Development Cooperation and Programming: A UNDP Capacity Development Resource 8 (2006), http://waterwiki.net/images/e/ee/Applying_HRBA_To_Development_Programming.pdf.

information gaps to be effectively monitored by decisionmakers, rights-holders, and rights-bearers.[114]

Monitoring could be particularly effective in terms of deployment of BECCS. Projections of potentially sustainable levels of bioenergy deployment are "systematically optimistic" and not based on empirical observations or practical experience.[115] Raphael Slade et al. suggest fostering "learning by doing" by close monitoring of incremental efforts to expand the role of biomass in energy production.[116] Close monitoring of the first few exajoules[117] of energy crops would help realistically assess purported benefits of integrated crop and energy production, and the sustainability of energy crop extension into allegedly marginalized, degraded, and deforested lands.

• *Ensure that programs are informed by recommendations from international human rights bodies and mechanisms*

The UNFCCC would benefit from collaboration with human rights bodies, including United Nations bodies, such as the Office of the United Nations High Commissioner for Human Rights; the United Nations Human Rights Council; human rights treaty bodies, such as the Human Rights Committee and the Committee on the Rights of the Child; regional bodies, such as the Inter-American Commission on Human Rights and the African Commission on Human and People's Rights; and nongovernmental organizations, such as Human Rights Watch and the International Red Cross. Collaboration should also be explored with other organizations that may help inform the process, such as the Global Bioenergy Partnership (GBEP), comprised of both State and non-State actors. The GBEP has developed a set of sustainability indicators intended to inform

---

114. Maarten Immink & Margaret Vidar, *Monitoring the Human Right to Adequate Food at Country Level*, *in* International Human Rights Monitoring Mechanisms 322 (Gudmundur Alfredsson et al. eds., 2d. ed. 2009).

115. Raphael Slade et al., *Global Bioenergy Resources*, 4 Nature Climate Change 99, 103 (2014).

116. *Id.*

117. An exajoule (EJ) is a metric unit of energy that is often used in the context of global energy production. It is equivalent to 947.817 trillion British Thermal Units (BTUs). A BTU, in turn, is defined as the amount of heat required to raise the temperature of 1 lb of water by 1°F. Russ Rowlett & the University of North Carolina at Chapel Hill, *How Many? A Dictionary of Units of Measurement*, https://www.unc.edu/~rowlett/units/dictE.html (last visited Aug. 22, 2016). Projections for energy production from BECCS range from 30–600 EJ annually in the period of 2050–2100, dependent on the assumptions made in terms of factors such dietary trends, crop yields, population growth, and land use, Guy Lomax et al., *Investing in Negative Emissions*, 5 Nature Climate Change 498, 498 (2015); Raphael Slade et al., *Global Bioenergy Resources*, 4 Nature Climate Change 99–105 (2014).

decisionmaking and foster sustainability, including in the context of socioeconomic considerations.[118]

B. Implementing the HRBA for Climate Geoengineering Within the Paris Agreement

The optimal method to facilitate the HRBA process under the Paris Agreement would be to establish a human rights subsidiary body comprised of human rights and development experts. This body could be tasked, inter alia, with developing HRBA architecture, advising the Conference of the Parties (COP) on relevant human rights standards, and reporting on best national practices.[119]

Alternatively, the most appropriate existing institutions for operationalizing the HRBA process under the Paris Agreement would be its Subsidiary Body for Implementation (SBI) and Subsidiary Body for Scientific and Technological Advice (SBSTA). At the 17th COP, the Parties to the UNFCCC established a "forum on the impact of the implementation of response measures," which was mandated to meet twice annually under the rubric of the SBI and SBSTA.[120] The forum, whose mandate was subsequently extended, is tasked, inter alia, with assessment of the impacts of climate response measures, and engendering cooperation on response strategies.[121] It provides a platform to facilitate assessment of the potential impacts of implementation responses, and seeks to recommend specific plans of action.[122]

The forum would thus be an appropriate mechanism to implement the HRBA on behalf of the Parties to the Paris Agreement, or the Kyoto Protocol. It could establish an ad hoc technical expert group with expertise on both technological aspects of geoengineering, as well as experts in the field

---

118. GBEP, THE GLOBAL BIOENERGY PARTNERSHIP SUSTAINABILITY INDICATORS FOR BIOENERGY (1st ed. 2011), http://www.globalbioenergy.org/fileadmin/user_upload/gbep/docs/Indicators/The_GBEP_ Sustainability_Indicators_for_Bioenergy_FINAL.pdf. *See also* Yoshiko Naiki, *Trade and Bioenergy: Explaining and Assessing the Regime Complex for Sustainable Bioenergy*, 27 EUR. J. INT'L L. 129, 142–44 (2016).

119. Naomi Roht-Arriaza, *Human Rights in the Climate Change Regime*, 1 J. HUM. RTS. & ENV'T 211, 232 (2010).

120. UNFCCC, *Forum on the Impact of the Implementation of Response Measures*, http://unfccc.int/cooperation_support/response_measures/items/7418.php (last visited Aug. 2 2016).

121. *Id.*

122. *Report of the Conference of the Parties on Its Twenty-First Session, Held in Paris From 30 November to 13 December 2015—Addendum, Part Two: Action Taken by the Conference of the Parties at Its Twenty-First Session, Decisions Adopted by the Conference of the Parties*, UNFCCC, 21st Sess., Decision 11/CP.21, at 25, U.N. Doc. FCCC/CP/2015/10/Add.1 (2016), http://unfccc.int/resource/docs/2015/cop21/eng/10a02.pdf.

of human rights law.[123] Under the terms of reference for the forum, it could develop guidance to the Parties and the subsidiary bodies for development of HRBAs, as well as facilitating ongoing sharing of information.[124]

This framework may also prove helpful in assessing the human rights implications of mitigation and adaptation options. To date, consideration of the human rights implications of adaptation responses has been "peripheral."[125] Similar concerns have been raised in the context of mitigation responses, including the Clean Development Mechanism of the Kyoto Protocol[126] and efforts to reduce deforestation (REDD+).[127]

Conclusion

The Paris Agreement provides a framework for taking human rights into account in responding to climate change. This chapter has proposed a framework for operationalizing this broad mandate in the context of one climate geoengineering option.

The Paris Agreement may ultimately be viewed as a major breakthrough in the field of climate policymaking, as well as a powerful force for defending the human rights of the most vulnerable in our society from environmental change. The emerging field of climate geoengineering affords an opportunity to develop a framework to make human rights more than merely an aspiration in the context of climate policymaking.

---

123. CENTER FOR INTERNATIONAL ENVIRONMENTAL LAW, HUMAN RIGHTS AND CLIMATE CHANGE: PRACTICAL STEPS FOR IMPLEMENTATION 29 (2009), http://www.ciel.org/Publications/CCandHRE_Feb09.pdf.

124. *Report of the Conference of the Parties on Its Twenty-First Session, supra* note 122, at 25–26.

125. HUMAN RIGHTS AND EQUAL OPPORTUNITY COMMISSION, HUMAN RIGHTS AND CLIMATE CHANGE 14 (2008), https://www.humanrights.gov.au/papers-human-rights-and-climate-change-background-paper.

126. INTERNATIONAL BAR ASSOCIATION, *supra* note 61, at 50; Roht-Arriaza, *supra* note 119, at 215–16; MISEREOR, CIDSE & CARBON MARKET WATCH, HUMAN RIGHTS IMPLICATIONS OF CLIMATE MITIGATION ACTIONS 17–18 (2d ed. 2016), http://carbonmarketwatch.org/wp-content/uploads/2016/05/NC-HUMAN-RIGHTS-IMPLICATIONS-OF-CLIMATE-CHANGE-MITIGATION-ACTIONS-VERSION-02-MAY-2016-OK-WEB-spread-page-.pdf.

127. Kirsty Gover, *REDD+, Tenure, and Indigenous Property: The Promise and Peril of a "Human Rights-based Approach," in* RESEARCH HANDBOOK ON REDD+ AND INTERNATIONAL LAW 249–83 (2016); Annalisa Savaresi, *The Role of REDD in the Harmonisation of Overlapping International Obligations, in* CLIMATE CHANGE AND THE LAW 391, 414 (E.J. Hollo ed., 2013).

North American Perspectives

Chapter 7

Flee the Rising Sea?
South Florida's Choice of
Leadership or Litigation

Keith W. Rizzardi

Introduction: A Slow-Motion Crisis, Speeding Up

For coastal cities—and for south Florida in particular—rising seas represent a potential existential crisis. While uncertainty exists as to when and how much our physical communities and ecosystems will change, policymakers must make hard decisions about the risks ahead. Communities will choose between action and adaptation, or inaction and litigation.

To some extent, humanity is making progress in the effort to confront a frightening future. At the international level, nations have achieved new, common understandings. Implementing the United Nations Framework Convention on Climate Change (UNFCCC),[1] a 2015 Conference of the Parties in Paris set objectives to minimize and mitigate the harms of climate change.[2] Due to melting land-based ice and thermal expansion of the ocean,

---

* *The author extends special thanks to Stephanie Schellhorn-Masonbrink (J.D. 2016, St. Thomas University) for her research and editorial assistance.*

1. UNFCCC, *First Steps to a Safer Future: Introducing the United Nations Framework Convention on Climate Change*, http://unfccc.int/essential_background/convention/items/6036.php (last visited Aug. 22, 2016).

2. *Report of the Conference of the Parties on Its Twenty-First Session, Held in Paris From 30 November to 13 December 2015—Addendum, Part Two: Action Taken by the Conference of the Parties at its Twenty-First Session, Decisions Adopted by the Conference of the Parties*, UNFCCC, 21st Sess., U.N. Doc. FCCC/CP/2015/10/Add.1 (2016), http://unfccc.int/resource/docs/2015/cop21/eng/10a01.pdf.

rising seas are among the harmful and recognized consequences of climate change.[3] At the federal level, the U.S. Global Change Research Program (USGCRP) continues to provide dramatic assessments of the issues.[4]

Simultaneously, the news is frightening for the next generation, especially in Florida, where the risks created by sea-level rise are acute. According to a regional vulnerability analysis, with a mere one foot of sea-level rise, four hospitals, 65% of the schools and 71% of the emergency shelters in the Florida Keys are vulnerable; power plant properties in Miami-Dade and Broward are exposed; and more than 81 mi of roadway from Miami-Dade County to Palm Beach County are at elevations below sea level.[5] The upper estimate of taxable property values vulnerable across the region is greater than $4 billion at just one foot of sea-level rise, with values rising to more than $31 billion at the 3-ft scenario.[6] The fact that these analyses occurred at all is a tribute to local leadership, and the South Florida Climate Change Compact has successfully united the local leaders of four Florida coastal counties to engage in planning and dialogue.[7] Still, awareness and aspiration are not enough. In fact, Florida has likely underestimated the coming catastrophe. Recent scientific studies concluded that the rate of sea-level rise is increasing faster than expected, and the melting of ice in Antarctica means that the estimates should be doubled.[8] The slow-motion crisis is speeding up.

Climate justice necessitates climate action. The real question is, action by whom—the engineers or the lawyers? This chapter explores the next steps in a dialogue about rising seas, with a focus on south Florida. Part I considers the magnitude of the risks ahead, offering insights into the many ways

---

3.   UNFCCC, *Climate Change Information Sheet 11: Sea Levels, Oceans, and Coastal Areas*, http://unfccc. int/essential_background/background_publications_htmlpdf/climate_change_information_kit/ items/290.php (last visited Aug. 22, 2016).

4.   Jerry M. Melillo et al., Climate Change Impacts in the United States: The Third National Climate Assessment. (U.S. Global Change Research Program 2014), http://s3.amazonaws.com/ nca2014/high/NCA3_Climate_Change_Impacts_in_the_United%20States_HighRes.pdf [hereinafter USGCRP].

5.   Southeast Florida Regional Climate Change Compact Inundation Mapping and Vulnerability Assessment Work Group, Analysis of the Vulnerability of Southeast Florida to Sea Level Rise 6–11 (2012), http://www.southeastfloridaclimatecompact.org//wp-content/uploads/2014/09/ vulnerability-assessment.pdf.

6.   *Id.* at 6, 9.

7.   *See, e.g.*, Southeast Florida Regional Climate Change Compact, *Homepage*, http://www.southeast-floridaclimatecompact.org/ (last visited Aug. 22, 2016).

8.   Camille von Kaenel, *Antarctica Meltdown Could Double Sea Level Rise*, Sci. Am., Mar. 31, 2016 (citing Robert M. DeConto & David Pollard, *Contribution of Antarctica to Past and Future Sea Level Rise*, 531 Nature 591 (2016)), http://www.scientificamerican.com/article/antarctica-meltdown-could-double-sea-level-rise/. *See also* Doyle Rice, *Sea Levels Rising Faster Now Than in Past 3,000 Years*, USA Today, Feb. 22, 2016.

that sea-level rise will impact south Florida's coastal communities. Part II considers the status quo, revealing patterns of denial and delay, while also highlighting the current planning efforts. Applying the lessons of history, and seeking to predict our destiny, Part III explores the most likely paths: either coastal leadership emerges to implement projects and laws that confront, mitigate, and otherwise disclose the risks, or the people harmed by the do-nothing option will pursue litigation as a way to blame others and recover their losses. The chapter concludes with a call for an immediate sense of urgency to address this crisis.

I.   The Risks Tomorrow: Diminishing Flood Control and Retreat

Sea-level rise presents a substantial threat to society, acknowledged by every branch of the U.S. government. Thirty years ago, Congress acknowledged the risks of rising seas in §1102 of the Global Climate Protection Act of 1987, which stated that an increase in earth temperature could "cause thermal expansion of the oceans and partial melting of the polar ice caps and glaciers, resulting in rising sea levels."[9] President Obama has explained that the oceans and coasts are subject to significant environmental challenges,[10] and has issued numerous Executive Orders on the subject.[11] The U.S. Supreme Court acknowledged that sea-level rise, as predicted, had begun, harmed, and would continue to harm Massachusetts, noting that "[t]he risk of catastrophic harm, though remote, is nevertheless real."[12]

In *Laudato Si'*, also known as the Papal Encyclical on Climate Change, the leader of the Catholic Church warned that rising seas have consequences for all humankind:

> If present trends continue, this century may well witness extraordinary climate change and an unprecedented destruction of ecosystems, with serious consequences for all of us. A rise in the sea level, for example, can create extremely serious situations, if we consider that a quarter of the world's popu-

---

9. Global Climate Protection Act, Pub. L. No. 100-204, §1102, 101 Stat. 1407, 1408 (1987).

10. THE WHITE HOUSE COUNCIL ON ENVIRONMENTAL JUSTICE, FINAL RECOMMENDATIONS OF THE INTERAGENCY OCEAN POLICY TASK FORCE (2010), https://www.whitehouse.gov/files/documents/OPTF_FinalRecs.pdf.

11. *See generally* Federal Leadership in Environmental, Energy, and Economic Performance, Exec. Order No. 13514, 74 Fed. Reg. 52117 (Oct. 5, 2009); Preparing the United States for the Impacts of Climate Change, Exec. Order No. 13653, 78 Fed. Reg. 66819 (Nov. 1, 2013); Planning for Federal Sustainability in the Next Decade, Exec. Order No. 13693, 80 Fed. Reg. 15871 (Mar. 19, 2015).

12. Massachusetts v. EPA, 549 U.S. 497, 526 (2007).

lation lives on the coast or nearby, and that the majority of our megacities are situated in coastal areas.[13]

Rising seas are neither politics nor religion.[14] While expressed as a range, with upper and lower boundaries, there is a scientific consensus that rising seas present a significant coastal risk. The Fifth Assessment Report (AR5) prepared by the Intergovernmental Panel on Climate Change (IPCC), consisting of 830 authors from 80 countries nominated by both government and observer organizations, includes a report of more than 50 chapters responding to more than 142,000 comments.[15] In a summary for policymakers on the subject of sea-level rise, the IPCC declared with "high confidence" that "the rate of sea level rise since the mid-19th century has been larger than the mean rate during the previous two millennia"[16] and that "[b]y the end of the 21st century, it is very likely that sea level will rise in more than about 95% of the ocean area."[17] In fact, "[i]t is virtually certain that global mean sea level rise will continue for many centuries beyond 2100, with the amount of rise dependent on future emissions."[18] Updated computer models projected between .5 and 1 m of sea-level rise by 2100.[19]

---

13. POPE FRANCIS, ENCYCLICAL LETTER, LAUDATO SI', para. 12 (2015), http://w2.vatican.va/content/dam/francesco/pdf/encyclicals/documents/papa-francesco_20150524_enciclica-laudato-si_en.pdf [hereinafter LAUDATO SI'].

14. Some readers may be surprised by this reference to an overtly religious document in a legal text. The Pope responds to that comment as well:
    I would add that "religious classics can prove meaningful in every age; they have an enduring power to open new horizons . . . Is it reasonable and enlightened to dismiss certain writings simply because they arose in the context of religious belief?" It would be quite simplistic to think that ethical principles present themselves purely in the abstract, detached from any context.
    Id. at para. 199. *See also* John Copeland Nagle, *Pope Francis, Environmental Anthropologist*, 28 REGENT U. L. REV. 7 (2015).

15. *See* IPCC, *Activities*, http://www.ipcc.ch/activities/activities.shtml (last visited Aug. 22, 2016).

16. Christopher B. Field et al., *Summary for Policymakers, in* CLIMATE CHANGE 2014: IMPACTS, ADAPTATIONS, AND VULNERABILITY 13 (IPCC 2014), http://ipcc-wg2.gov/AR5/images/uploads/WG2AR5_SPM_FINAL.pdf.

17. *Id.* at 14. In addition, "coastal systems and low-lying areas are at risk from sea level rise, which will continue for centuries even if the global mean temperature is stabilized (high confidence)." *Id.* at 13, 15.

18. *Id.* at 16. Though cautious in addressing the potential for melting the Greenland Ice Cap, the IPCC explained that a 7 m rise in sea levels was not unrealistic:
    The threshold for the loss of the Greenland ice sheet over a millennium or more, and an associated sea level rise of up to 7 m, is greater than about 1°C (low confidence) but less than about 4°C (medium confidence) of global warming with respect to pre-industrial temperatures. Abrupt and irreversible ice loss from the Antarctic ice sheet is possible, but current evidence and understanding is insufficient to make a quantitative assessment.
    Id.

19. *Id.* at 11.

Some American leaders have been reluctant to accept the IPCC report.[20] Senate Majority Leader Mitchell McConnell (R-Ky.) sent top aides to warn representatives of foreign nations of the U.S. resistance to any dealmaking on climate change.[21] The opposition exists despite the extraordinary efforts of the USGCRP, which gathered more than 300 experts, over a three-year period, to evaluate the information related to climate change and its potential effects.[22]

Through the USGCRP, the facts and risks of sea-level rise, and its consequences, have been made abundantly and unquestionably clear, using a remarkably transparent and comprehensive process that engaged domestic scientists. Agency participants in the USGCRP effort included the U.S. Departments of Agriculture, Commerce, Defense, Health and Human Services, Interior, State, and Transportation, and independent agencies such as the National Aeronautics and Space Administration (NASA), the National Oceanic and Atmospheric Administration (NOAA), and the U.S. Environmental Protection Agency (EPA).[23] More than two dozen academic and university experts were engaged as editors,[24] and the draft report was subjected to a transparent peer review by outside experts from the National Research Council of the National Academy of Sciences.[25] Organized into three major parts discussing economic sectors, geographic regions, and response strategies, the "key messages" in each chapter leave no question about the substantial risks to freshwater supplies,[26] energy systems,[27] and transportation systems.[28] Regional risks are also addressed. In the Southeast and Caribbean,

---

20. *See, e.g.*, U.S. SENATOR JAMES INHOFE, THE GREATEST HOAX: HOW THE GLOBAL WARMING CONSPIRACY THREATENS YOUR FUTURE (2012).

21. Andrew Restuccia, *GOP to Attack Climate Pact at Home and Abroad*, POLITICO, Sept. 7, 2015, http://www.politico.com/story/2015/09/gop-congress-climate-pact-paris-213382#ixzz45LKdHHK7.

22. USGCRP, *supra* note 4, at iii.

23. *Id.* at vii–viii.

24. *Id.* at vi–vii (naming editors from Arizona State University, Brown University, Colorado State University, Columbia University, George Mason University, Indiana University, Lehigh University, Massachusetts Institute of Technology, Michigan State University, New Mexico State University, Pennsylvania State University, Purdue University, Rutgers University, Stanford University, Syracuse University, University of Arizona, University of British Columbia, University of Calgary, University of Colorado, University of Maine, University of Maryland, University of Michigan, University of Minnesota, University of New Mexico, University of North Carolina, University of Washington, University of Wyoming, Washington State University, Woods Hole Oceanographic Institution, and Yale University).

25. *Id.* at iii.

26. USGCRP, *supra* note 4, at 108 ("Sea level rise, storms and storm surges, and changes in surface and groundwater use patterns are expected to compromise the sustainability of coastal freshwater aquifers and wetlands.").

27. *Id.* at 114 ("In the longer term, sea level rise, extreme storm surge events, and high tides will affect coastal facilities and infrastructure on which many energy systems, markets, and consumers depend."); *see also id.* at 119.

28. *Id.* at 131 ("Sea level rise, coupled with storm surge, will continue to increase the risk of major coastal impacts on transportation infrastructure, including both temporary and permanent flooding

in particular, rising seas pose widespread and continuing threats to natural environments, built environments, and the economy.[29]

Applying these risks of sea-level rise on a local scale, the four counties of south Florida created the Unified Sea Level Rise Projection for Southeast Florida.[30] According to the document, which relies on the projections developed by NASA, NOAA, the U.S. Army Corps of Engineers, and the IPCC, sea-level rise is projected to be 6 to 10 in by 2030, 14 to 26 in by 2060, and 31 to 61 in by 2100.[31] For critical infrastructure projects with design lives in excess of 50 years, the compact counties recommend planning values of 34 in (nearly 3 ft of sea-level rise) by 2060 and 81 in—*nearly 7 ft of sea-level rise*—by 2100.[32]

These projections may prove difficult for people to accept. Yet, the compact counties have noted that the changes related to rising seas are already underway. Based on an analysis of nuisance flooding during the period from 1998 to 2013, flooding due to heavy rain events had increased by 33%, and flooding after the fall equinox tides, regardless of rain events, had increased by 400%.[33] Believe it or not, the world is changing, before our eyes.

In south Florida, a regional governmental entity, the South Florida Water Management District (SFWMD), possesses authority to manage floods, wetlands, and water supplies.[34] For decades, the Corps, along with SFWMD and its predecessor, the Central and South Florida Flood Control District, have operated pumps, canals, and structures that drained surface waters from the lands, converting a patchwork of wetlands and marshes into uplands available to people for agricultural and economic development.[35]

---

of airports, ports and harbors, roads, rail lines, tunnels, and bridges."). *See also id.* at 134, 146.

29. *Id.* at 397. *See also id.* at 379 ("Infrastructure of the Northeast will be stressed and increasingly compromised by climate-related hazards, including sea level rise, coastal flooding, and intense precipitation events."); *id.* at 469 ("Flooding and erosion in coastal areas are already occurring even at existing sea levels and damaging some California coastal areas during storms and extreme high tides. Sea level rise is projected to increase as Earth continues to warm, resulting in major damage as wind-driven waves ride upon higher seas and reach farther inland."); *id.* at 492 ("In the Pacific Northwest, sea level rise threatens infrastructure and habitat."); *id.* at 538 ("In Hawaii, saltwater intrusion associated with sea level rise will reduce the quantity and quality of freshwater in coastal aquifers.").

30. SOUTHEAST FLORIDA REGIONAL CLIMATE CHANGE COMPACT, SEA LEVEL RISE WORK GROUP (COMPACT), UNIFIED SEA LEVEL RISE PROJECTION: SOUTHEAST FLORIDA (2015), http://www.southeastfloridaclimatecompact.org/wp-content/uploads/2015/10/2015-Compact-Unified-Sea-Level-Rise-Projection.pdf.

31. *Id.* at 1.

32. *Id.*

33. *Id.* at 9.

34. *See generally* FLA. STAT. §373.036 (2014).

35. In 1949, the Central and Southern Florida Flood Control District was created to act as local sponsors for the federal project built to drain Florida's Everglades. Flood Control Act of 1948, Pub. L. No. 80-858, 62 Stat. 1171 (1948). In 1972, pursuant to the Florida Water Resources Act, the state created five water management districts, with expanded responsibilities for regional water resource

The flood control system helps protect people from storms, hurricanes, and floods. However, as SFWMD has recognized, sea-level rise undermines the effectiveness of that flood control system, because water in coastal canals is typically higher on the land side, so higher levels in the ocean will limit the ability to open flood gates and move excess waters.[36] According to the agency, 28 coastal water control structures on Florida's east coast, and 6 more on the west coast, are vulnerable to sea-level rise.[37] In addition, the rising seas will affect coastal freshwater supplies, due to the intrusion of salty ocean water into the groundwater systems. Coastal ecosystems will be at risk due to permanent inundation of coastal habitats, changing salinity zones, the spread of invasive species, and altered cycles of flood and drought.[38]

Rising seas will have compounding economic impacts, too.[39] As the counties of south Florida have noted, critical at-risk coastal facilities include 2 nuclear power plants, 3 state prisons, 68 hospitals, 74 airports, 115 solid waste disposal sites, 140 water treatment facilities, 334 public schools, and 341 hazardous material cleanup sites, including 5 Superfund sites.[40] Residential and commercial buildings may be harmed, too, as well as community ecosystems. Property values would inevitably decline.[41] Additional indirect impacts will occur if and when beaches erode, tourism declines, health quality declines, and communities shrink.[42] In other words, as seas rise, communities incur increasing costs to protect themselves, but lost tourism and abandoned homes

---

management and environmental protection. FLA. STAT. §373.036. *See also* John J. Fumero & Keith W. Rizzardi, *The Everglades Ecosystem: From Engineering to Litigation to Consensus-Based Restoration*, 13 ST. THOMAS L. REV. 667 (2000).

36.   SOUTH FLORIDA WATER MANAGEMENT DISTRICT, WATER MANAGEMENT CONCERNS OF RISING SEAS (n.d), http://www.sfwmd.gov/portal/page/portal/xrepository/sfwmd_repository_pdf/display_sea_level_rise. pdf.

37.   *Id.*

38.   *Id.*

39.   *See, e.g.*, DAVID W. YOSKOWITZ, PH.D. ET AL., THE SOCIO-ECONOMIC IMPACT OF SEA LEVEL RISE IN THE GALVESTON BAY REGION (Environmental Defense Fund 2009), https://www.edf.org/sites/default/ files/9901_EDF_Sea_Level_Rise_Report.pdf.

40.   SOUTHEAST FLORIDA REGIONAL CLIMATE CHANGE COMPACT, *supra* note 5, at 2. *See also* Giselle Peruyera, *A Future Submerged: Implications of Sea Level Rise for South Florida*, 8 FLA. A&M L. REV. 297 (2013).

41.   Jason P. Oppenheim, *The Waters Are Rising! Why Isn't My Tax Basis Sinking? Why Coastal Land Should Be a Depreciable Asset in Light of Global Warming and the Rise in Sea Level*, 8 U. MASS. L. REV. 228, 230–31 (2013) (noting that "in light of the rising sea level, coastal properties that are at risk of becoming completely inundated, which meet all other requirements for depreciation other than being land, should now be depreciable because they have a finite useful life").

42.   *See, e.g.*, Press Release, San Francisco State University, Study Predicts Sea-level Rise May Take Economic Toll on California Coast (Sept. 13, 2011), http://www.sfsu.edu/news/prsrelea/fy12/005.htm; *see also* NEW YORK STATE SEA LEVEL RISE TASK FORCE, REPORT TO THE LEGISLATURE (2010), http:// www.dec.ny.gov/docs/administration_pdf/slrtffinalrep.pdf.

results in diminishing tax revenues to pay for the needed adaptations.[43] The slow-motion disaster of sea-level rise has many dimensions, and it threatens to fundamentally transform the economy and society.[44]

The effects of sea-level rise may have the most severe effects on the poorest people, who are reduced to collateral damage by the political discourse and dissonance.[45] Eventually, in some coastal communities, rising seas will displace people and create mass migrations.[46] Worse yet, as Pope Francis recognized: "rises in the sea level mainly affect impoverished coastal populations who have nowhere else to go within the lowest lying elevations of coastal communities."[47] Continuing his environmental justice perspective, geography is destiny. When the decisions are made on which places will be protected, and which ones are forced to retreat, communities will try to save their tax-generating regions, while the politically powerless are "confined to national environmental sacrifice areas."[48]

In a 2010 report, the Florida Department of Environmental Protection (Florida DEP) acknowledged that "[s]ea-level rise is not a science fiction scenario but a reality."[49] Florida has approximately 1,350 mi of generalized coastline, more than any state in the continental United States.[50] High tide is coming to Main Street, and Miami has the largest amount of exposed assets and the fourth-largest population vulnerable to sea-level rise in the world.[51]

---

43. Valerie Seidel et al., *Evaluating Coastal Real Estate Value vs. Risk in the Wake of Sea Level Rise*, 38 REAL ESTATE ISSUES 3, 16 (2013) ("In some communities, future revenues from tourist spending and property tax revenue are projected to fall by more than 30 percent by 2050 because of shifting shoreline patterns and loss of beach area.") [hereinafter Seidel et al.].

44. Ryan McNeill et al., *As the Seas Rise, a Slow-Motion Disaster Gnaws at America's Shores*, REUTERS, Sept. 4, 2014, http://www.reuters.com/investigates/special-report/waters-edge-the-crisis-of-rising-sea-levels/.

45. LAUDATO SI', *supra* note 13, at para. 49.

46. *See generally* Julia Toscano, *Climate Change Displacement and Forced Migration: An International Crisis*, 6 ARIZ. J. ENVTL. L. & POL'Y 457 (2015); Mostafa Mahmud Naser, *Climate Change, Environmental Degradation, and Migration: A Complex Nexus*, 36 WM. & MARY ENVTL. L. & POL'Y REV. 713 (2012).

47. LAUDATO SI', *supra* note 13, at para. 48.

48. Maxine Burkett, *Just Solutions to Climate Change: A Climate Justice Proposal for a Domestic Clean Development Mechanism*, 56 BUFF. L. REV. 169, 189 (2008) (quoting David Naguib Pellow & Robert J. Brulle, *Power, Justice, and the Environment: Toward Critical Environmental Justice Studies, in* POWER, JUSTICE, AND THE ENVIRONMENT: A CRITICAL APPRAISAL OF THE ENVIRONMENTAL JUSTICE MOVEMENT 2 (2005)).

49. FLORIDA OCEANS AND COASTAL COUNCIL, CLIMATE CHANGE AND SEA-LEVEL RISE IN FLORIDA: AN UPDATE OF THE EFFECTS OF CLIMATE CHANGE ON FLORIDA'S OCEAN AND COASTAL RESOURCES 1 (2010), http://www.dep.state.fl.us/oceanscouncil/reports/climate_change_and_sea_level_rise.pdf.

50. Florida Department of Environmental Protection, *Geographical Summary* (At a finer, detailed scale, Florida's coast has more than 8,000 mi to be protected from rising seas.), http://www.dep.state.fl.us/secretary/stats/geographical.htm (last visited Aug. 22, 2016).

51. JOHN ENGLANDER, HIGH TIDE ON MAIN STREET: RISING SEA LEVEL AND THE COMING COASTAL CRISIS 118 (2d ed. 2012) ("Miami is used as the 'poster child' of potential sea level rise impact, for good reason.") (discussing PETER WARD, THE FLOODED EARTH: OUR FUTURE IN A WORLD WITHOUT ICE CAPS (2010)); FORBES TOMPKINS & CHRISTINA DECONCINI, SEA-LEVEL RISE AND ITS IMPACT

Much of Broward County, to the north of Miami, lies at just 2 to 6 ft above sea level.[52] As the Florida DEP noted:

> With a 1-meter (about 40-inch) rise in sea level by 2100, there will be impacts on 9% of Florida's land area, which includes more than 4,700 square miles and 1/10 of the state's population. Without successful steps to build up or otherwise protect this land area, which will be expensive and in some areas is likely to be impossible, the land will be submerged at normal high tide.[53]

In other words, the people of south Florida are vulnerable, and need help.

II.   The Reality Today: Deny, Ignore, Delay, or Plan

Science, at times, lacks certainty. Explanations of the risks of rising seas, using projections with high end (worst-case) and low end (best-case) estimates, have left room for a "debate," but climate science has been irresponsibly rejected or dismissed by political and business leaders who decline the opportunity to lead.[54] Given the substantial scientific efforts and consensus, the explicit warnings, and the specific statements by south Florida's leaders, the debate, and refusal to respond to the risks, is astonishing. There is certainly room for disagreement over how much to do, how much to spend, and when to spend it. But honest discussion, and disclosure of the risks to the people living in these communities, is essential.

As of this writing, and despite President Obama's many Executive Orders on climate change,[55] federal leadership has significant limitations. Congress resists and limits the funding.[56] A federal lawmaker publicly boycotted the Pope's address to Congress.[57] Political leaders claim that the President's various actions lack congressional authorization, threaten American jobs, create more bureaucracy, and impose new litigation costs and regulatory uncer-

---

ON MIAMI-DADE COUNTY, WORLD RESOURCES INSTITUTE FACT SHEET (2014), http://www.wri.org/sites/default/files/sealevelrise_miami_florida_factsheet_final.pdf.

52.   David Fleshler, *Rising Seas: Inching Toward Disaster*, SUN SENTINEL, Apr. 6, 2014 (citing U.S. Geological Survey as the source for the chart), http://interactive.sun-sentinel.com/rising-seas/north.html.

53.   FLORIDA OCEANS AND COASTAL COUNCIL, *supra* note 49.

54.   Michael E. Mann, *The Assault on Climate Science*, N.Y. TIMES, Dec. 8, 2015, at A31.

55.   *See supra* note 11 (listing recent Executive Orders on climate change).

56.   Devin Henry, *House Panel Approves $30.17B Bill Cutting EPA Funds, Blocking Rules*, THE HILL, June 16, 2015 (discussing the House Appropriations Committee's decision to cut EPA funding by 9% in an effort to block EPA policies and rules), http://thehill.com/policy/energy-environment/245137-house-panel-approves-3017b-bill-to-cut-epa-funds-block-climate.

57.   Timothy Cama, *GOP Rep Has No Regrets About Skipping Pope's Speech*, THE HILL, Sept. 24, 2015, http://thehill.com/policy/energy-environment/254836-gop-rep-has-no-regrets-about-skipping-popes-speech.

tainties.[58] Presidential aspirants evade hard facts. Despite their Florida ties, Jeb Bush and Marco Rubio claimed that climate change is a distant threat.[59] Donald Trump—despite owning a historic oceanfront property, the Mar Lago home in Palm Beach—also says he "is not a believer"[60] and declared, on Twitter, that the concept of global warming "was created by and for the Chinese in order to make U.S. manufacturing non-competitive."[61] Of special note, when EPA adopted regulations and a Clean Power Plan,[62] industries opposed the effort, litigated the issue, and the Supreme Court issued an unprecedented stay.[63]

State leaders also resist the need to take action on climate change or sea-level rise. Twenty-four states, including Florida, oppose the EPA rules and the Clean Power Plan, which attempted to reduce carbon emissions in the energy industry.[64] But Florida's inaction and climate denial—reversing prior statements in 2010—is especially troubling. The *Miami Herald* described how the governor of Florida, Rick Scott, ordered state employees not to use

---

58. The "top 10" talking points used to critique the National Ocean Policy have been used to critique the Clean Power Plan and its attempts to address climate change. *Compare Top 10 Things to Know About President Obama's Plan to Zone the Oceans*, HOUSE COMMITTEE ON NAT. RESOURCES, Sept. 30, 2011, http://naturalresources.house.gov/newsroom/documentsingle.aspx?DocumentID=262435, *with* LEAGUE OF CONSERVATION VOTERS, IN THEIR OWN WORDS: 2016 PRESIDENTIAL CANDIDATES ON THE CLEAN POWER PLAN (2015), http://www.lcv.org/media/11_13-pres-candidates-cpp.pdf.

59. Patricia Mazzei, *They Live at Ground Zero, but Jeb Bush and Marco Rubio Say Climate Change Is a Distant Threat*, MIAMI HERALD, Jan. 15, 2016, http://www.miamiherald.com/news/politics-government/elections-2016/article54945660.html. Similarly, New Jersey Governor Chris Christie, despite previously acknowledging that "climate change is occurring" and a need to "defer to the experts," later insisted that the climate is always changing and then said climate change is not a crisis. Dick Polman, *Crisis? What Crisis? Welcome to the Chris Christie School of Science*, NEWSWORKS, Dec. 2, 2015, http://www.newsworks.org/index.php/local/national-interest/88727-crisis-what-crisis-welcome-to-the-chris-christie-school-of-science.

60. Trump stated:
    So I am not a believer, and I will, unless somebody can prove something to me, I believe there's weather. I believe there's change, and I believe it goes up and it goes down, and it goes up again. And it changes depending on years and centuries, but I am not a believer, and we have much bigger problems.
    Hugh Hewitt, *Donald Trump Returns*, HUGH HEWITT SHOW, Sept. 21, 2015, http://www.hughhewitt.com/donald-trump-returns/.

61. Donald Trump (realdonaldtrump) (Nov. 6, 2012) [Twitter post], https://twitter.com/realdonaldtrump/status/265895292191248385?lang=en.

62. Eric Anthony DeBellis, *EPA Unveils Final Clean Power Plan: So What's All the Fuss About?*, ENVTL. L. REV. SYNDICATE, Dec. 7, 2015 (noting that EPA had regulated air pollutants through emission permits, but now takes a broader approach through the Clean Power Plan than was enacted under the Clean Air Act), http://georgetown1372.rssing.com/browser.php?indx=58543913&item=5.

63. West Virginia v. EPA, 2016 WL 502947, at *1 (U.S. 2016) (granting application for a stay pending review in the U.S. Court of Appeals for the D.C. Circuit).

64. Kristen Clark, *Florida Among 24 States Suing Over EPA Carbon Emissions Rule*, TAMPA BAY TIMES, Oct. 23, 2015, http://www.tampabay.com/news/environment/airquality/florida-among-24-states-suing-over-epa-carbon-emissions-rule/2251030. *See also* Petition for Extraordinary Writ, In re West Virginia, No. 15-1277 (D.C. Cir. Aug. 15, 2015), http://www.eenews.net/assets/2015/08/14/document_ew_04.pdf.

the term "climate change."[65] Demonstrating disinterest in mitigation of the risks ahead, Florida also passed the Florida Climate Protection Act, a law that repealed the state's effort to address greenhouse gas (GHG) emissions.[66] Instead, Florida's state leaders (and North Carolina's leaders, too) have left the consequences of climate change to local governments, allowing them to define an "[a]daptation action area" to identify "one or more areas that experience coastal flooding due to extreme high tides and storm surge and that are vulnerable to the related impacts of rising sea levels for the purpose of prioritizing funding for infrastructure needs and adaptation planning."[67]

Meanwhile, the south Florida real estate industry continues to construct new buildings along the vulnerable coastline, and housing prices are on the rise again in one of the least affordable real estate markets in the nation.[68] As an article in *Bloomberg Businessweek* cynically explained, the governor's denials, and the continued building boom, might be rational—but only in the short term.[69] South Florida relies on real estate taxes to fund public infrastructure, so communities need to maintain the value of real estate if they are to have any hope in the future of implementing measures to adapt to sea-level rise risks.[70]

Informed by the science, and in stark contrast to Florida, other state governments have taken action. California is planning for sea-level rise and using a state-run database to coordinate efforts.[71] Connecticut has also established a state policy of planning for rising seas,[72] collecting and assembling its

---

65. Tristram Korten, *In Florida, Officials Ban Term "Climate Change,"* MIAMI HERALD, Mar. 8, 2015, www.miamiherald.com/news/state/florida/article12983720.html; Tristram Korten, *Gov. Rick Scott's Ban on Climate Change Term Extended to Other State Agencies,* MIAMI HERALD, Mar. 11, 2015, http://www.miamiherald.com/news/state/florida/article13576691.html.

66. *See* H.R. 4001, 2012 Leg., Reg. Sess. (Fla. 2012) (repealing Florida's efforts to implement climate change protections through a Department of Environmental Protection regulatory program).

67. FLA. STAT. §163.3164(1) (2015). The North Carolina Legislature took a similar approach, declaring that the General Assembly would not mandate the development of a sea-level rise policy, but leaving the issue open to local governments. N.C. GEN. STAT. §113A-107.1 (2012) ("Nothing in this section shall be construed to prohibit a county, municipality, or other local government entity from defining rates of sea-level change for regulatory purposes.").

68. Nicholas Nehamas, *Home Prices Up but Slowdown Looms for South Florida Real Estate,* MIAMI HERALD, June 23, 2015, http://www.miamiherald.com/news/business/real-estate-news/article25357552.html.

69. Robert Meyer, *How Climate Change Is Fueling the Miami Real Estate Boom,* BLOOMBERG BUSINESSWEEK, Oct. 20, 2014 ("South Florida's best shot at coping with the long-term environmental threat may be a strategy that no doubt seems perverse to environmentalists: aggressively foster a collective belief that sea level rise is not something we urgently need to worry about."), http://www.businessweek.com/articles/2014-10-20/how-climate-change-is-fueling-the-miami-real-estate-boom#p2.

70. *Id.*

71. CAL. PUB. RES. CODE §§30963–30964 (2015). *See* Sara C. Aminzadeh, *California Coastal Climate Adaptation, in* CLIMATE CHANGE IMPACTS ON OCEAN AND COASTAL LAW: U.S. AND INTERNATIONAL PERSPECTIVES 553–56 (Randall S. Abate ed., 2015).

72. CONN. GEN. STAT. §22a-92 (2013).

climate change data,[73] and developing a best practices guide for coastal structures permitting.[74] New York requires state agencies to adopt future projections of sea-level rise, and to consider its consequences in decisionmaking.[75]
New York City, taking a step beyond planning and regulation and learning
hard lessons from Superstorm Sandy, has pilot projects and project designs
for the modification and upgrading of soft and hard infrastructure.[76]

Lacking similar leadership in the Sunshine State, local governments and
public-private partnerships serve as the leading voices in south Florida.
Through the Southeast Florida Regional Climate Change Compact, the
counties have prepared numerous documents addressing the risks of sea-level
rise and a climate-changed future. Going beyond a mere identification of
risk, the Compact created an ambitious regional climate action plan.[77]

In that plan, the Southeast Florida Regional Climate Change Compact
Counties addressed a variety of issues: transportation planning, water supply,
management and infrastructure, natural systems, agriculture, energy and
fuel, risk reduction and emergency management, and outreach and public
policy.[78] But despite the document title, the counties remain a long way from
action. Discussing the need for risk reduction and emergency management,
the plan identifies a goal of providing "a more resilient natural and built
physical environment in light of climate change."[79] In 2013 and thereafter, local mayors signed the Mayors' Climate Action Pledge, which "agrees
to consider integrating the Regional Climate Action Plan framework," but
only "where and when appropriate and financially feasible."[80] Revealing just
how much more work remains to be done, the Climate Compact's Implementation Guide identifies more than 110 tasks and subtasks, nearly all of
them requiring funding sources, legislation, or additional resources.[81] The

---

73. CONN. S. No. 1013 (2015), 2013 Conn. Spec. Acts. No. 13-9.
74. 2013 Conn. Pub. Acts. No. 13-179.
75. Community Risk and Resiliency Act, Chapter 355 of the Laws of 2014.
76. *See, e.g.*, NYC SPECIAL INITIATIVE FOR REBUILDING AND RESILIENCY, CHAPTER 15: INITIATIVES FOR
    INCREASING RESILIENCY IN EAST AND SOUTH SHORES OF STATEN ISLAND (n.d.), http://www.nyc.gov/
    html/sirr/downloads/pdf/final_report/Ch15_Staten_Island_FINAL_singles.pdf; Lauren Coleman,
    *Making Soft Infrastructures a Reality in New York City: Incorporating Unconventional Storm Defense
    Systems as Sea Levels Rise*, 36 WM. & MARY ENVTL. L. & POL'Y REV. 529, 536–41 (2012) (discussing
    current climate change programs in New York City).
77. SOUTHEAST FLORIDA REGIONAL CLIMATE CHANGE COMPACT COUNTIES, A REGION RESPONDS TO A
    CHANGING CLIMATE: REGIONAL CLIMATE ACTION PLAN (2012), http://www.southeastfloridaclimate-
    compact.org/wp-content/uploads/2014/09/regional-climate-action-plan-final-ada-compliant.pdf.
78. *Id.* at 11 (referencing Table of Contents).
79. *Id.* at 37.
80. Mayors' Climate Action Pledge (2013), http://www.southeastfloridaclimatecompact.org/wp-content/
    uploads/2015/12/MAYORS-CLIMATE-PLEDGE-municipalities-general.pdf.
81. SOUTHEAST FLORIDA REGIONAL CLIMATE CHANGE COMPACT, REGIONAL CLIMATE ACTION FRAME-
    WORK: IMPLEMENTATION GUIDE (n.d.), http://www.southeastfloridaclimatecompact.org//wp-content/

next step of actually starting (and completing) the physical upgrades to the regional flood control and stormwater management infrastructure—which requires a project manager, engineering design, and substantial funding—is still a paper concept.[82]

Paralleling the efforts of the climate compact counties, a public-private partnership including dozens of organizations from the seven counties of southeast Florida developed the Seven50 plan to offer a vision for the next 50 years.[83] Addressing regional priorities, the document recognized the impact of climate change and sea-level rise on private and public investment, and expressly acknowledged the potential for rising insurance rates and the costs of new resilient infrastructure.[84] The Seven50 plan further called for leadership,[85] and discussed potential sea-level rise adaptations, including mangrove restoration, beach nourishment, and water control structures including pumps and backflow preventers, levees, seawalls, rip rap walls, raising land elevations, reinforcing bridges, and—really—a subterranean ice wall.[86]

Still, these local and partnership efforts produced only ideas. In 2014, a Miami task force praised these efforts as "laying the foundation for action," but its first recommendation was to accelerate the process, select the engineers, and develop a robust capital plan to begin the needed changes.[87] As the introductory letter by the task force chairman explained:

> This report is an urgent, though optimistic, call to begin the step by step process needed to design and build a re-engineered urban infrastructure that over time will withstand a worst case scenario . . . Make no mistake, it will be costly, but its costs are dwarfed by the potential human, physical and economic values at stake.[88]

III.   The Responsibility to Act: From History to Destiny

Fueled by the denials, empowered by the ignorance, and contrary to the well-intentioned plans, the risks of rising seas remain. The Department of

---

uploads/2014/09/implementation-guide.pdf.

82. *Id.* at WS-6.
83. Seven50, SE Florida Prosperity Plan: Better Region, Better Life (2014), http://seven50report. org/.
84. *Id.* at 10, 12, 18, 41.
85. *Id.* at 292–99.
86. *Id.* at 278–85.
87. Miami-Dade Sea Level Rise Task Force Report and Recommendations 4, 14 (2014), http://www.miamidade.gov/planning/library/reports/sea-level-rise-report-recommendations.pdf.
88. *Id.* at 2.

Defense, in a report to Congress, considered sea-level rise to be a matter of national security.[89] Yet, the responsibility to decide whether, when, and how to act falls on the shoulders of local governments, businesses, and individual homeowners. South Florida has reached a critical fork in the road. Which way will it go?

Local leaders must relearn the lessons we learned long ago, and international experience offers important lessons.[90] In 1972, at the United Nations Conference on the Human Environment, the signatories to the Stockholm Accord recognized the growing class of environmental problems, the need for applied science, and the burden on local and national governments to engage in actions within their jurisdictions.[91] In 1987, the Montreal Protocol on Substances that Deplete the Ozone Layer and subsequent Clean Air Act amendments helped reduce the planetary risk of harm to the stratospheric ozone layer.[92] And just before the historic Paris Agreement, the Parties to the Montreal Protocol agreed to pursue additional amendments in 2016 that would regulate additional types of climate-change-inducing hydrofluorocarbons in the same way that the planet united to regulate chlorofluorocarbons.[93]

At the heart of these policies is the precautionary principle, an approach to policymaking that makes protection of people a priority. Though certainly not a mandate,[94] Principle 15 of the Rio Declaration on Environment and Development, adopted in 1992, spoke directly to the types of problems Florida now faces, and the proper responses:

> In order to protect the environment, the precautionary approach shall be widely applied by States according to their capabilities. Where there are threats of serious or irreversible damage, lack of full scientific certainty shall

89. U.S. Department of Defense, National Security Implications of Climate-Related Risks and a Changing Climate (2015) ("Sea level rise and temperature changes lead to greater chance of flooding in coastal communities and increase adverse impacts to navigation safety, damages to port facilities and cooperative security locations, and displaced populations."), http://archive.defense.gov/pubs/150724-congressional-report-on-national-implications-of-climate-change.pdf.

90. *See* Andronico O. Adede, *The Treaty System From Stockholm (1972) to Rio de Janeiro (1992)*, 13 Pace Envtl. L. Rev. 33 (1995).

91. *Declaration of the United Nations Conference on the Human Environment*, U.N. Conference on the Human Environment, Stockholm, Sweden, June 5–16, 1972, U.N. Doc. A/CONF.48/14 (1972).

92. *See* Louis P. Oliva, *The International Struggle to Save the Ozone Layer*, 7 Pace Envtl. L. Rev. 213 (1989).

93. *Montreal Protocol Parties Devise Way Forward to Protect Climate Ahead of Paris COP21*, UNEP News Centre, Nov. 6, 2015, http://www.unep.org/newscentre/Default.aspx?DocumentID=26854&ArticleID=35543.

94. U.S. Department of State, *U.S. Interpretive Statement on World Summit on Sustainable Development Declaration* ("The United States does not accept any interpretation of principle 7 that would imply a recognition or acceptance by the United States of any international obligations or liabilities, or any diminution of the responsibilities of developing countries under international law."), http://www.state.gov/s/l/38717.htm (last visited Aug. 22, 2016).

not be used as a reason for postponing cost-effective measures to prevent environmental degradation.[95]

Stated succinctly, scientific uncertainty never justifies an irresponsible failure to act.

The history of environmental policy in the United States shows that our federal government is capable of implementing the precautionary principle, too. The lessons of history can also be found at the national scale. Responding to mass protests on Earth Day, Rachel Carson's *Silent Spring*, a growing environmental awareness, and images of a river burning in Ohio, Congress passed numerous environmental laws in the 1970s.[96] The National Environmental Policy Act, for example, states that it is the continuing responsibility of the federal government to use all practicable means to "attain the widest range of beneficial uses of the environment without degradation, risk to health or safety, or other undesirable and unintended consequences."[97] In 1977, even before the Montreal Protocol was adopted unanimously by the United Nations, the United States cut chlorofluorocarbon-propelled aerosols by 90%, and banned all non-essential uses.[98] As amended, the Marine Mammal Protection Act of 1972[99] and the Endangered Species Act of 1973[100] both regulate the death, harm, and harassment of wildlife, and also reflect precautionary efforts to protect wildlife from threats and extinction. Even the Oil Pollution Act of 1990, although passed in response to the tragic Exxon Valdez oil spill in Alaska, created a forward-looking framework that holds actors accountable and provides funding for the prompt recovery of habitat and cleanup of future oil spills.[101] In every instance, science revealed

---

95. *Rio Declaration on Environment and Development*, U.N. Conference on Environment and Development, Rio de Janeiro, Brazil, June 3–14, 1992, U.N. Doc. A/CONF.151/26 (Vol. I) (1992), http://www.un.org/documents/ga/conf151/aconf15126-1annex1.htm.

96. Jennifer Latson, *The Burning River That Sparked a Revolution*, Time, June 22, 2015 (noting that on June 22, 1969, the Cuyahoga River burst into flames when sparks from a passing train set fire to an oil slick that was floating on the water's surface), http://time.com/3921976/cuyahoga-fire/; Jamie Henn, *When Earth Day Changed the World*, Msnbc, Apr. 19, 2015 (describing how an estimated 20 million people took to the streets in 1970 and helped turn environmentalism into a mass social movement and made an immediate political impact), http://www.msnbc.com/msnbc/what-the-original-earth-day-can-teach-us.

97. 42 U.S.C. §4331(b)(3).

98. Oliva, *supra* note 92, at 224.

99. 16 U.S.C. §§1361–1423(h); H.R. Rep. No. 92-707, at 15 (1971) ("It seems elementary common sense to the Committee that legislation should be adopted to require that we act conservatively—that no steps should be taken regarding these animals that might prove to be adverse or even irreversible in their effects until more is known.").

100. Endangered Species Act of 1973, Pub. L. No. 93-205, 87 Stat. 884 (codified at 16 U.S.C. §§1531–1544). *See also* Defenders of Wildlife v. Babbitt, 958 F. Supp. 670, 680 (D.D.C. 1997), quoting Conner v. Burford, 848 F.2d 1441, 1454 (9th Cir. 1988) (stating that the principle of institutionalized caution at the heart of the Endangered Species Act means giving "benefit of the doubt" to species).

101. Elizabeth R. Millard, *Anatomy of an Oil Spill: The Exxon Valdez and the Oil Pollution Act of 1990*, 18 Seton Hall Legis. J. 331, 360 (1993) (explaining that the Exxon Valdez oil spill caused Alaska

the need to act, and the United States has ample experience with rational and localized application of environmental science, despite uncertainties. In fact, the U.S. Supreme Court, as a basic principle of administrative law, has held that it is not sufficient for an agency to merely recite the terms "substantial uncertainty" as justification for its actions.[102] An administrative agency must explain the evidence that is available, and must offer a "rational connection between the facts found and the choice made."[103] Somehow, when it comes to sea level rise, facts and policy have been disconnected.

The precautionary principle and the lessons of international and national policy must now be downscaled to south Florida. The environmental movement has long promoted thinking globally and acting locally.[104] Grassroots activism also invokes the phrase "not in my backyard"—a particularly appropriate perspective when it comes to keeping floodwaters away.[105] In Miami-Dade County, a group of environmental activists, wearing bright orange life jackets, stood at the podium to protest the proposed budget and convinced the county commissioners to increase funds for sea-level rise adaptation.[106] In Miami Beach, a successful mayoral candidate ran a campaign advertisement showing him kayaking through traffic on the flooded streets.[107] After all, Miami Beach has $30 billion in assets at risk, and now, through the Rising Above initiative, the city is engaging the community and adapting to sea-level rise.[108]

significant environmental and economic tragedy that provided the necessary catalyst to create the Oil Pollution Liability and Compensation Act of 1989).

102. Motor Vehicles Mfrs. Ass'n v. State Farm, 463 U.S. 29, 43 (1983).

103. *Id.*

104. The attribution of this phrase is disputed. *See, e.g.*, Fred Shapiro, *Quotes Uncovered: The Real McCoy and Acting Locally*, FREAKONOMICS BLOG, Mar. 11, 2010 (attributing phrase to Rene Dubois), http://freakonomics.com/2010/03/11/quotes-uncovered-the-real-mccoy-and-acting-locally/; RALPH KEYES, THE QUOTE VERIFIER: WHO SAID WHAT, WHERE, WHEN (2006) (attributing phrase to French theologian Jacques Ellul); Stuart R. Grauer, Think Globally, Act Locally: A Delphi Study of Educational Leadership Through the Development of International Resources in the Local Community (1989) (D. Educ. thesis, University of San Diego) (attributing phrase to Harlan Cleveland).

105. Nicholas Freudenberg & Carol Steinsapir, *Not in Our Backyards: The Grassroots Environmental Movement, Special Issue: Two Decades of American Environmentalism: The U.S. Environmental Movement*, 4 SOC'Y & NAT. RESOURCES: AN INT'L J. 3 (1991).

106. Douglas Hanks & Michael Vasquez, *Climate Change Gets Last-Minute Nod in New Miami-Dade Budget*, MIAMI HERALD, Sept. 17, 2015, http://www.miamiherald.com/news/local/community/miami-dade/article35657733.html#storylink=cpy.

107. David Kamp, *Can Miami Beach Survive Global Warming?*, VANITY FAIR, Dec. 2015, http://www.vanityfair.com/news/2015/11/miami-beach-global-warming.

108. City of South Miami, Res. No. 167-15-14506 (2015), http://miamibeachfl.gov/WorkArea/DownloadAsset.aspx?id=85505. *See also* City of Miami Beach, *Rising Above*, http://miamibeachfl.gov/risingabove/ (last visited Aug. 22, 2016); Joey Flechas & Jenny Staletovich, *Miami Beach's Battle to Stem Rising Tides*, MIAMI HERALD, Oct. 23, 2015, http://www.miamiherald.com/news/local/community/miami-dade/miami-beach/article41141856.html.

Local politics, however, must eventually produce local policies. Communities are in the process of developing new codes to upgrade the physical environment and infrastructure.[109] In the near future, a host of new requirements are possible for Miami Beach, including increases in base flood elevation by measuring heights from the finished floor, stormwater retention basins, elevated seawalls, lot grading, and green spaces to absorb flood events.[110] Georgetown University's Climate Center, in fact, has prepared a model zoning ordinance.[111] Forward-looking property owners can even obtain private consulting services to assist them with the assessment of coastal risk and the potential for seasonal or permanent inundation.[112] In Fort Lauderdale, a few neighborhoods have even taken action, upgrading their local storm drainage systems.[113]

But no single individual, nor single local government, can spare south Florida the anguish of dramatically rising seas. Indeed, if any coastal community fails to act, the neighbors will still suffer when water encroaches in unwelcome places. True water management will require the coordinated construction and operation of an integrated regional system.

A.   What Can We Do? Coastal Defense Inspired by the Everglades

To protect itself from floods, Florida has taken large-scale measures in the past. Historically, the Corps and state flood control organizations, usually the SFWMD or its predecessor districts, have provided regional approaches to improve flood control and to better manage the tensions between lands and waters.[114] After a series of hurricanes in the 1920s, more than 67 mi of dikes were built around Lake Okeechobee to protect various communities from flooding.[115] In the 1940s and 1950s, the Central and South Florida Flood Control Project was built to provide enhanced flood control for thou-

---

109. City of Miami, *Beach, Storm Water Management Master Plan*, http://miamibeachfl.gov/publicworks/scroll.aspx?id=27280 (last visited Aug. 22, 2016). *See also* CITY OF ANNAPOLIS, REGULATORY RESPONSE TO SEA LEVEL RISE AND STORM SURGE INUNDATION (2011), http://dnr2.maryland.gov/ccs/Publication/Annapolis_RRSLRnSSI.pdf.

110. *Id.*

111. Georgetown Climate Center, *Zoning for Sea Level Rise*, http://www.georgetownclimate.org/zoning-for-sea-level-rise (last visited Aug. 22, 2016).

112. *See, e.g.*, Coastal Risk Consulting LLC, *Homepage*, http://coastalriskconsulting.com/ (last visited Aug. 22, 2016); *see also* Jess Swanson, *Ten South Florida ZIP Codes Most Vulnerable to Sea-Level Rise*, NEW TIMES, Mar. 14, 2016, http://www.browardpalmbeach.com/news/ten-south-florida-zip-codes-most-vulnerable-to-sea-level-rise-7642106.

113. Mary Hladky, *Against the Tide*, FORT LAUDERDALE MAG., Apr. 17, 2015, http://flmag.com/features/against-tide.

114. *See generally* MATTHEW C. GODFREY, RIVER OF INTERESTS: WATER MANAGEMENT IN SOUTH FLORIDA AND THE EVERGLADES, 1948–2000 (2006).

115. *Id.* at 11–14.

sands of square miles in south Florida.[116] In the 1970s, additional measures were added to benefit Everglades National Park and the southwestern Miami-Dade County region.[117] Today, the SFWMD operates that system, including 2,100 mi of canals, another 2,000 mi of levees and berms, 71 pump stations, more than 600 water control structures, and 625 project culverts.[118] Increasingly, these systems will require upgrades to meet flood control needs, as demonstrated by recent efforts to upgrade nearly 60 mi of the East Coast Protective Levee that separates the developed areas of Palm Beach and Broward County from the water conservation areas and Everglades ecosystem.[119]

Projects like these take many years—many decades—to plan, design, construct, and refine. Taking an optimistic view, the planning process has begun.[120] In recent years, the state's accomplishments include the creation of the regional climate change compact discussed above, and the passage of state legislation authorizing an optional planning tool for local governments to designate "adaptation action areas."[121] Another legislative change provided that local governments' coastal management plans should address sea-level rise "when opportunities arise," and "reduce the flood risk in coastal areas which results from high-tide events, storm surge, flash floods, stormwater runoff, and the related impacts of sea-level rise."[122] This combination of voluntary measures and uncertain terminology simply marks the beginning of a long process, because the lawyers, and the accompanying cycles of legislation, litigation, and modification, have not yet been fully engaged.[123] As Floridians consider how and when to respond to sea-level rise, they should recall the struggles in the Everglades, and recognize why a sense of urgency is needed.

---

116. *Id.* at 27–69.
117. *Id.* at 80–91.
118. South Florida Water Management District, *Canal and Structure Operations*, http://www.sfwmd.gov/portal/page/portal/xweb%20drought%20%20and%20%20flood/canal%20and%20structure%20operations (last visited Aug. 22, 2016).
119. Press Release, South Florida Water Management District, SFWMD Completes Upgrade of the Levee Protecting East Coast Population: Reinforcement Work Meets Federal Flood Insurance Standards (Dec. 10, 2015), http://www.sfwmd.gov/portal/page/portal/xrepository/sfwmd_repository_pdf/nr_2015_1212_ecpl_update.pdf.
120. *See generally* David L. Markell, *Emerging Legal and Institutional Responses to Sea-level Rise in Florida and Beyond*, 42 Colum. J. Envtl. L. (forthcoming 2016), http://papers.ssrn.com/sol3/papers.cfm?abstract_id=2765569.
121. Fla. Stat. §163.3177(6)(g)(10) (2015). *See supra* Part I. For an overview of Florida's efforts prior to the 2011 legislation, see Erin Deady & Thomas Ruppert, *The Link Between Future Flood Risk and Comprehensive Planning*, 2 ELULS Rep. 7–8 (2015).
122. Fla. Stat. §163.3178(f)(1) (2015).
123. Markell, *supra* note 120, at 23 ("There is considerable uncertainty in the legal landscape that will shape such efforts. It is far too early to know how this mandate will be implemented, and how much flood risk will be reduced."). *See also* Fumero & Rizzardi, *supra* note 35.

The Everglades Construction Project (ECP) involved the construction, over the course of decades, of nearly 70,000 acres of stormwater treatment areas, large retention areas that cleansed runoff from the sugar cane fields of the Everglades Agricultural Area before it flowed into the Everglades ecosystems.[124] Agency planning efforts began in the 1980s, and a 1988 lawsuit eventually led to a 1991 settlement agreement and passage of the Everglades Forever Act in 1994.[125] Decades later, the "A-1" flow equalization basin added another 15,000 acres of water management storage to the system.[126] Still, after more than three decades of effort, compliance with water quality standards—the fundamental goal of the project—was not fully achieved.[127]

Building a new "Florida Coastal Defense Construction Project" to protect people from the rising seas will require a long-term vision akin to—and likely much bigger than—the ECP. Funding mechanisms must be created and land must be acquired.[128] Engineers must design and build coastal levees, water storage basins, and upgraded pumping stations. When designing these coastal defense projects, some especially low-lying private communities, too difficult to protect, may be sacrificed and turned into retention areas to hold flood waters. Even if limited solely to the four counties at the

---

124. Lawrence Gerry, *Appendix 5B-4: Implementation of the Long-Term Plan for Achieving Water Quality Goals in the Everglades Protection Area*, in SOUTH FLORIDA ENVIRONMENTAL REPORT App. 5B-4-1 (2014), http://my.sfwmd.gov/portal/page/portal/pg_grp_sfwmd_sfer/portlet_prevreport/2014_sfer/v1/appendices/v1_app5b-4.pdf.

125. Lance H. Gunderson et al., *Escaping a Rigidity Trap: Governance and Adaptive Capacity to Climate Change in the Everglades Social Ecological System*, 51 IDAHO L. REV. 127, 134, 136 (2014) [hereinafter Gunderson et al.]; FLA. STAT. §373.4592 (2015).

126. SOUTH FLORIDA WATER MANAGEMENT DISTRICT, EVERGLADES CONSTRUCTION PROJECT: DESIGN AND CONSTRUCTION (n.d.), http://www.sfwmd.gov/portal/page/portal/pg_grp_sfwmd_watershed/subtabs_stamanagement_home/tab1834093/egladpro.pdf; *see also* SOUTH FLORIDA WATER MANAGEMENT DISTRICT, A-1 FLOW EQUALIZATION BASIN (FEB) (2016), http://www.sfwmd.gov/portal/page/portal/xrepository/sfwmd_repository_pdf/jtf_a1_feb.pdf.

127. SOUTH FLORIDA WATER MANAGEMENT DISTRICT, 2015 SOUTH FLORIDA ENVIRONMENTAL REPORT (2015) ("With more than 140 active stations and in excess of 2,500 sampling events, the majority of analytical results indicate general compliance with state water quality standards."), http://my.sfwmd.gov/portal/page/portal/xrepository/sfwmd_repository_pdf/2015_sfer_at_a_glance.pdf. In fact, in a further dose of irony, the ECP was designed, in part, to ensure compliance with a federal consent decree to protect Everglades National Park, a region that will be fundamentally transformed as rising seas push ocean saltwater into the freshwater marshes. Amartya K. Saha et al., *Sea Level Rise and South Florida Coastal Forests*, CLIMATIC CHANGE 2001, http://www2.fiu.edu/~pricer/Saha_Climatic%20change%20coastal%20forests.pdf.

128. The Everglades Construction Project was funded by a dedicated tax and the Everglades Forever Act expressly empowered the District to exercise eminent domain authority. FLA. STAT. §373.4592(4)(a) ("The district shall not levy ad valorem taxes in excess of 0.1 mill within the Okeechobee Basin for the purposes of the design, construction, and acquisition of the Everglades Construction Project."), FLA. STAT. §373.4592(5)(b) ("The Legislature further declares that certain lands may be needed for the treatment or storage of water prior to its release into the Everglades Protection Area. The acquisition of real property for this objective constitutes a public purpose for which public funds may be expended.").

southern tip of Florida—Broward, Collier, Miami-Dade, and Monroe coun-ties—the projects must protect hundreds of miles of coastline and thousands of square miles of lands that are just a few feet above sea level. Hard decisions will need to be made about what to build, and where and when to build it. As the Corps acknowledges in its important policy document, Sea Level Rise Guidance, "the conundrum of the planning process, and any decision support process, is in doing sufficient work to support a decision while avoid-ing decision paralysis or, worse, making decisions that ignore important uncertainties."[129] Once a decision is finally made, periodic revisions will be needed to adapt to changing conditions.[130]

It can be done, and the Netherlands, where lands are often below sea level, offers an example of how policy solutions can be implemented and funded over time. In 1953, a historic flood killed more than 1,800 peo-ple and inundated more than 9% of the nation's farmlands, leading to the "Delta Works."[131] Implementing the 1958 Delta Act, the Dutch con-structed a massive chain of dams, levees, and structures, including more than 10,000 mi of dikes, to provide national flood protection.[132] Forty years later, the Dutch government estimated that the modified water man-agement infrastructure had reduced the risk of flooding to survive the 1-in-4,000 year event.[133] But in 2008, the Dutch recognized that the existing Delta Works were not enough. Adapting to rising seas became a matter of national urgency.[134] Through the Delta Programme and the Water Act of 2009, a Delta Fund now provides an additional €1 billion annually for implementation of projects to protect the Netherlands from the surging North Sea.[135]

The lessons from the Dutch will not fully translate to Florida, where unique challenges exist due to the massive scale of the Florida coastline and

129. Technical Letter from U.S. Army Corps of Engineers, Procedures to Evaluate Sea Level Change: Im-pacts, Responses, and Adaptation, at 3-1 (June 30, 2014) (No. 1100-2-1), http://www.publications. usace.army.mil/Portals/76/Publications/EngineerTechnicalLetters/ETL_1100-2-1.pdf.
130. *Id.*
131. KEES D'ANGREMOND, FROM DISASTER TO DELTA PROJECT: THE STORM FLOOD OF 1953, https://www. iadc-dredging.com/ul/cms/terraetaqua/document/1/2/4/124/124/1/terra-et-aqua-nr90-01.pdf.
132. Deltawerken Online, *The Delta Works*, http://www.deltawerken.com/Deltaworks/23.html (last visited Aug. 22, 2016).
133. Water-Technology.net, *Delta Works Flood Protection, Rhine-Meuse-Scheldt Delta, Netherlands*, http:// www.water-technology.net/projects/delta-works-flood-netherlands/ (last visited Aug. 22, 2016).
134. DELTA COMMISSIE, WORKING TOGETHER WITH WATER: A LIVING LAND BUILDS FOR ITS FUTURE (2008), http://www.deltacommissie.com/doc/deltareport_full.pdf. *See generally* HUNT JANIN & SCOTT A. MANDIA, RISING SEA LEVELS: AN INTRODUCTION TO CAUSE AND IMPACT (2012), http://ncse.com/ files/pub/evolution/excerpt--rising.pdf.
135. Jonathan Verschuuren, *Country Report: Netherlands, Climate Change and Coasts*, 2012 IUCN ACAD. ENVTL. L. E-J. 146 (2012).

population, coupled with a porous limestone bedrock.[136] In all likelihood, the region will require an all-of-the-above approach to problem solving, with widespread participation from federal, state, and local governments, and support from the private sector. Engineers will implement public works projects, while financial professionals issue bonds to pay for them. Regulators will adopt and enforce new standards. New lands will be purchased to make room for water retention areas and other coastal defense projects. Grant dollars and tax policies will create new incentives and disincentives. Private companies and individuals will undertake additional voluntary measures. Some areas may no longer be productive and nature must be allowed to take over.

Remarkably, every one of these approaches is found in the Everglades Forever Act, the law that created the blueprint for the Everglades Construction Project.[137] In other words, the past efforts to restore the Florida Everglades required state and federal partners to develop and fund a massive project that included the construction of new levees and pump stations, and the conversion of some agricultural lands into large scale constructed wetlands. The future effort of adapting to sea-level rise will require those same partners to construct new levees and pump stations and convert urbanized lands in low-lying areas into flood control and storm surge basins. Learning from the Dutch, and its own recent state history, Florida must once again fulfill its duty to protect the public, and draw new blueprints for the Florida Coastal Defense Construction Project.[138]

Florida's early history is also relevant. When much of Florida was swamplands, state and federal laws incentivized private efforts to drain and protect lands from floods.[139] Lawyers, developers, and real estate professionals helped their clients navigate through creative property transactions. Most notably, in 1881, Hamilton Disston's historic purchase of 4,000,000 acres

---

136. United States Senate Committee on Energy and Natural Resources, Impacts of Sea Level Rise on Florida's Domestic Energy and Water Infrastructure, Dr. Leonard Berry's Testimony, Apr. 19, 2012, http://www.energy.senate.gov/public/index.cfm/files/serve?File_id=e0f5e6f1-34f1-4bd9-8243-8b3c77e1d27d (visited Sept. 19, 2016).

137. FLA. STAT. §373.4592 (2015). The subsections of the Everglades Forever Act included design, construction, and funding requirements for the Everglades Construction Project, which included the conversion of agricultural lands into natural stormwater marshes, FLA. STAT. §373.4592(4)(a) (2015); regulatory requirements related to private sector best management practices, FLA. STAT. §373.4592(4)(f) (2015); authority and procedures for land acquisition, FLA. STAT. §373.4592(5) (2015); and taxation and special assessment authority, FLA. STAT. §373.4592(6), (7), and (8) (2015).

138. Alfred R. Light, *The Intergovernmental Relations of Water Policy and Management: Florida-Holland Parallels*, 23 TUL. ENVTL. L.J. 1 (2010) (noting that Holland and Florida have an "overwhelming imperative in both jurisdictions to defend the public safety").

139. F.T. IZUNO, A BRIEF HISTORY OF WATER MANAGEMENT IN THE EVERGLADES AGRICULTURAL AREA (IFAS Circular 815 n.d.), http://share.disl.org/stanton/Shared%20Documents/Everglades/Izuno_Water%20management%20in%20the%20EAA.pdf.

of Florida swampland, and agreement to drain vast lands, saved Florida's trustees of the Internal Improvement Trust Fund from the embarrassment of bankruptcy.[140] South Florida may go back to the future, with state property law becoming creative once more. Public purchases of lands, and private investments in flood defense, could involve land swaps, transfers of development rights, and rights to redevelop sites with increased density.[141]

The implementation of these measures adapting Florida to sea-level rise will take decades. Even the initial step of developing an environmental impact statement for sea-level rise adaptation may prove to be difficult.[142] The overlay of our current legal system, with its occasionally inflexible regulatory requirements, could delay or prevent the implementation of necessary projects.[143] A wide range of laws—not just property law—must be passed or rewritten as a result of climate change and sea-level rise.[144] The costs of adaptation, however, seem trivial when compared to the worst-case scenarios that inaction creates.[145]

B.   Who Can I Sue? The Litigation Conundrum

A refusal to adapt to the risks of rising seas leaves people to suffer the consequences on their own. Retreat will be the solution by default. One United Nations report suggested that the risk of vulnerability of coastal

---

140. Junius E. Dovell, *A History of the Everglades of Florida* (1947), http://sofia.usgs.gov/memorials/ dovell#thesis; *see also* R.E. Rose, *The Swamp and Overflow Lands of Florida: The Disston Drainage Company and the Disston Purchase, A Reminiscence* (1916), http://ufdc.ufl.edu/FS00000077/00001/1j.

141. Seidel et al., *supra* note 43, at 21–23.

142. Even the planning and project selection will require the development of a large-scale environmental impact statement. *See* Jessica Wentz, *Assessing the Impacts of Climate Change on the Built Environment: A Framework for Environmental Reviews*, 45 ELR 11015 (Nov. 2015), http://web.law.columbia.edu/ sites/default/files/microsites/climate-change/wentz_-_assessing_impacts_of_cc_on_the_built_envt_- _a_framework_for_envtl_reviews.pdf.

143. *See, e.g.*, Keith W. Rizzardi, *Regulating Restoration: Why the Perfect Permit Is the Enemy of the Good Project*, 27 Nova L. Rev. 51 (2002).

144. Richard J. Lazarus, *Super Wicked Problems and Climate Change: Restraining the Present to Liberate the Future*, 40 ELR 10749, 10749 (Aug. 2010) ("For climate change legislation to be successful, the new legal framework must simultaneously be flexible in certain respects and steadfast in others."), http:// www.law.harvard.edu/faculty/rlazarus/docs/articles/Lazarus_WickedELRArticle.pdf.

145. Robert J. Nicholls et al., *Sea-level Rise and Its Possible Impacts Given a "Beyond 4°C World" in the Twenty-First Century*, 369 Phil. Transaction Royal Soc'y A 1–21 (2012), ftp://soest.hawaii.edu/ coastal/Climate%20Articles/Sea%20Level%20Nicholls%20et%20al%202010%20Phil%20Trans. pdf (explaining that pessimists assume that protection is unaffordable, while optimists assume that protection will be widespread and largely succeed, concluding that long-term strategic adaptation plans for the full range of possible sea-level rise (and other changes) need to be widely developed. The analysis further praised schemes like the United Kingdoms' Thames Estuary 2100 project and the Netherlands' Delta Commission, which "establish a flexible approach to management where there is some upgrading of defences and a logical sequence of additional measures to reduce risk and diversion of investment into new and upgraded coastal defences and other forms of adaptation.").

people, the uncertain magnitude and pace of sea-level rise, and the likely migration and resettlement that follows "might be the biggest challenge for humanity in the 21st century."[146] If the consequences manifest as predicted, without the construction of coastal defense projects, then the communities of south Florida will face a relentless cycle of flood, retreat, and economic decline. Some of the displaced victims, having lost their property investments, will seek justice. As they did in the Everglades, lawyers will shape the future of Florida.

Some lawsuits will focus on the government. For example, people might sue the government, demanding that it must change its regulations to adapt to sea-level rise.[147] Others might frame the same debate in budgetary terms, arguing that the government should place moratoria or setbacks on coastal development to avoid future government obligations and financial exposures.[148] Challenges to government decisions related to coastal zone construction, however, have often fared poorly, because courts often give great deference to the agencies.[149]

Alternatively, if and when the government fails to act, other landowners might demand government compensation for the taking of lands due to an alleged failure to provide flood control and the resulting loss of property.[150] These cases will raise complex questions about the extent to which sovereign immunity applies.[151] However, in 2015, the U.S. Court of Federal Claims held a federal agency accountable for the acts and omissions associated with the management of the Mississippi River Gulf Outlet, and the catastrophic storm surge it created when Hurricane Katrina hit New Orleans. Sovereign immunity failed to save the Corps from liability for its contribution to a temporary taking by flooding:

---

146. Anthony Oliver-Smith, Sea Level Rise and the Vulnerability of Coastal Peoples: Responding to the Local Challenges of Global Climate Change in the 21st Century i (2009), http://www.munichre-foundation.org/dms/MRS/Documents/InterSection2009_OliverSmit_Sealevelrise.pdf.

147. See generally Jacqueline Peel & Hari M. Osofsky, Sue to Adapt?, 99 Minn. L. Rev. 2177 (2015).

148. Thomas Ruppert & Carly Grimm, Drowning in Place: Local Government Costs and Liabilities for Flooding Due to Sea-Level Rise, 87 Fla. B.J. 29 (2013), http://www.floridabar.org/DIVCOM/JN/JNJournal01.nsf/d59e2cf27607c0cf85256ad1005ba53f/d1cd8a7e6519800885257c1200482c39!OpenDocument.

149. See, e.g., Island Harbor Beach Club v. Department of Natural Res., 495 So. 2d 209 (Fla. App. 1986).

150. Christopher Serkin, Passive Takings: The State's Affirmative Duty to Protect Property, 113 Mich. L. Rev. 345, 346 (2014) ("Takings liability for regulatory inaction—what this Article calls passive takings—means that property owners could be constitutionally entitled either to governmental intervention on their behalf or to compensation if the government fails to act."). See also Ruppert & Grimm, supra note 148.

151. See generally Theresa K. Bowley, A Blanket of Immunity Will Not Keep Florida Dry: Proposed Adjustments to Florida's Drainage Regulations and Sovereign Immunity Laws to Account for Climate Change Impacts, 10 Fla. A&M L. Rev. 387 (2015).

Weighing all the evidence in this case, the court has determined that Plaintiffs established that the Army Corps' construction, expansions, operation, and failure to maintain the MR-GO caused subsequent storm surge that was exacerbated by a "funnel effect" during Hurricane Katrina and subsequent hurricanes and severe storms, causing flooding on Plaintiffs' properties that effected a temporary taking under the Fifth Amendment to the United States Constitution . . . . Certainly by 2004, the Army Corps no longer had any choice but to recognize that a hurricane inevitably would provide the meteorological conditions to trigger the ticking time bomb created by a substantially expanded and eroded, [Mississippi River-Gulf Outlet navigational channel] and the resulting destruction of wetlands that had shielded the St. Bernard Polder for centuries . . . .[152]

With damages still to be determined, the Corps pursued an interlocutory appeal of that order.[153] Nevertheless, the willingness of a court to assign liability to the Corps may offer a sneak preview of the future of climate change litigation, and the expanding potential for government liability.[154]

The government will not be the only defendant. Another category of litigation will involve the insurance industry, and debates over whether a particular event is covered by an insurance policy.[155] In another line of cases related to Hurricane Katrina, insurance companies successfully defended themselves from liability by invoking the policy exclusion clauses.[156] Property insurance may be the most obvious underwriting risk, but many other areas of insurance—liability insurance, life and health insurance, and workers' compensation, for example—could all be affected by climate change.[157]

---

152. St. Bernard Parish Gov't v. United States, Memorandum Opinion and Order on Liability re: Temporary Taking by Flooding, 45 ELR 20084, No. 05-1119 (Ct. Fed. Cl. 2015).

153. Juan Carlos Rodriguez, *Army Corps Asks Judge for Appeal of Katrina Liability Finding*, Law360, Dec. 1, 2015, http://www.law360.com/articles/732641/army-corps-asks-judge-for-appeal-of-katrina-liability-finding.

154. Jennifer Klein, *Government Found Liable for Hurricane Katrina Flooding*, Columbia Law School Climate Law Blog, May 11, 2015 ("Notably, *Saint Bernard Parish*, if it survives appeal, expands government liability from situations in which the government deliberately causes flooding, for example by releasing water from a dam, to include situations in which inaction by the government exacerbates flooding from severe weather. This developing area of law will also have broad implications for local and state governments seeking to prepare for—or deliberately deciding not to prepare for—climate change impacts."), http://blogs.law.columbia.edu/climatechange/2015/05/11/government-found-liable-for-hurricane-katrina-flooding/#sthash.JmDWco0T.dpuf.

155. *See, e.g.*, Joseph MacDougald & Peter Kochenburger, *Insurance and Climate Change*, 47 J. Marshall L. Rev. 719, 726–30 (2013).

156. A federal appellate court also concluded that the flood exclusions in property insurance policies precluded coverage for flood damage in these circumstances. *See* In re Katrina Canal Breaches Litig., 495 F.3d 191 (5th Cir. 2007).

157. *Id.* at 731 (citing Christina M. Carroll et al., Climate Change and Insurance 135–37 (2012)).

At times, the insurance industry might even become a plaintiff. In April 2013, Farmers Insurance Company sued Chicago-area governmental entities alleging that their negligent failures to act on climate change resulted in financial harms.[158] It later withdrew the lawsuit, stating that its lawsuit had "brought important issues to the attention of the respective cities and counties."[159]

Yet, the federal government is part of the insurance equation, too. Federal law authorizes the regional director of the Federal Emergency Management Agency (FEMA) to "approve funding for and require restoration of a destroyed facility at a new location" when a facility will be subject to repetitive heavy damage and the project is cost efficient and not otherwise prohibited by law.[160] Indeed, on rare occasions in U.S. history, entire communities—Love Canal in New York,[161] Centralia in Pennsylvania, and Valmeyer, Illinois[162]—have been forced to relocate, receiving millions of dollars in federal disaster relief assistance. FEMA's fact sheet on permanent relocation offers examples of this type of funding, suggesting amounts given to individual landowners from $100,000 to $400,000.[163] But the National Flood Insurance Program now caps coverage at $250,000 for the structure and $100,000 for the contents.[164] In the worst cases, such as New Orleans after Hurricane Katrina, FEMA can reimburse eligible applicants for relocation expenses[165] but the Individuals and Households Program (IHP) capped financial assistance for individuals who left New Orleans at $26,200.[166]

158. Akiko Shimizu, *Farmers Insurance Withdraws Class Action Alleging Failure to Adapt to Climate Change*, Columbia Law School Climate Law Blog, June 16, 2014 (containing links to cases), http://blogs. law.columbia.edu/climatechange/2014/06/16/farmers-insurance-withdraws-class-action-alleging-failure-to-adapt-to-climate-change/#sthash.SSKpkabb.dpuf.

159. Robert McCoppin, *Insurance Company Drops Suits Over Chicago-Area Flooding*, Chicago Trib., June 3, 2014, http://www.chicagotribune.com/news/local/breaking/chi-chicago-flooding-insurance-lawsuit-20140603-story.html.

160. 44 C.F.R. §206.226(g) (2015).

161. New York State Department of Health, *Love Canal: A Special Report to the Governor & Legislature: April 1981*, https://www.health.ny.gov/environmental/investigations/love_canal/lcreport.htm#relocation (last visited Aug. 22, 2016).

162. Dennis M. Knobloch, *Moving a Community in the Aftermath of the Great 1993 Midwest Flood*, 130 J. Contemp. Water Res. & Educ. 45–46 (2005), http://opensiuc.lib.siu.edu/cgi/viewcontent. cgi?article=1070&context=jcwre.

163. FEMA Recovery Division, Fact Sheet 9580.102: Permanent Relocation (n.d.), https://www. fema.gov/pdf/government/grant/pa/policy_archive/9580_102.pdf.

164. National Flood Insurance Program, *Policy Rates*, https://www.floodsmart.gov/floodsmart/pages/ residential_coverage/policy_rates.jsp (last visited Aug. 22, 2016).

165. FEMA, *FEMA Funds Relocation of Displaced Katrina/Rita Households, Release Number: HQ-07-203*, https://www.fema.gov/news-release/2007/10/15/fema-funds-relocation-displaced-katrina/rita-households (last visited Aug. 22, 2016).

166. FEMA, Disaster Specific Guidance: Disaster Assistance Directorate (2007), https://www. fema.gov/media-library-data/20130726-1818-25045-3610/hurricane_katrina_and_rita_relocation_assistance.pdf.

Although undeniably tragic and expensive, the circumstances in New Orleans affected a much smaller community[167] than the one at risk in south Florida, where 2.4 million people, and $2 trillion dollars of coastal property, exist at less than four feet above the high-tide line.[168] Optimists might note that with sound, visionary planning, the necessary abandonment of the lowest-lying areas could be conducted gradually and in an orderly fashion.[169] The pessimist, however, has plenty to discuss. FEMA's cost-benefit analysis expects the states to consider sea-level rise in its planning efforts, but Florida's lack of leadership and mitigation efforts could reduce the funding available for some communities.[170] Moreover, FEMA and the National Flood Insurance Program may lack the financial capacity to solve the problems at this scale.[171] Coastal property owners in Florida demonstrate remarkably little understanding of these risks and realities.[172]

Based on their ethical codes, certified and licensed professionals involved in the real estate and coastal development industries have a duty to know better.[173] Florida law already requires sellers of certain coastal property, partially or totally seaward of the coastal construction control line, to inform buyers when lands are subject to "frequent and severe fluctuations" or "significant erosion conditions."[174] Competent private sector professionals, unlike their unsophisticated clients, must recognize that sea-level rise—especially in south Florida—will affect inland communities, too,

---

167. The population of Orleans Parish in 2005 was 454,863, but after Hurricane Katrina, as of Jan. 1, 2006, the city's population fell to 158,000. NARAYAN SASTRY, WORKING PAPER: TRACING THE EFFECTS OF HURRICANE KATRINA ON THE POPULATION OF NEW ORLEANS: THE DISPLACED NEW ORLEANS RESIDENTS PILOT STUDY (2007), http://www.rand.org/pubs/working_papers/WR483.html.

168. Laura Parker, *Treading Water*, NAT'L GEOGRAPHIC, Feb. 2015, at 107, http://ngm.nationalgeographic.com/2015/02/climate-change-economics/parker-text.

169. *See, e.g.*, James Titus, *Planning for Sea Level Rise Before and After a Coastal Disaster*, *in* GREENHOUSE EFFECT AND SEA LEVEL RISE: A CHALLENGE FOR THIS GENERATION (Michael C. Barth & James G. Titus eds., 1984) (remarkably, this visionary chapter dates to 1984).

170. Dave Boyer, *FEMA Targets Climate Change Skeptic Governors, Could Withhold Funding*, WASH. TIMES, Mar. 23, 2015, http://www.washingtontimes.com/news/2015/mar/23/fema-targets-climate-change-denier-governors-could/.

171. *See generally* Ernest B. Abbott, *Flood Insurance and Climate Change: Rising Sea Levels Challenge the NFIP*, 26 FORDHAM ENVTL. L. REV. 10 (2015). FEMA's flood insurance policies are also capped, with limits of $250,000 for building property and $100,000 for personal property. FEMA, NATIONAL FLOOD INSURANCE PROGRAM: SUMMARY OF COVERAGE (2012) (FEMA F-679), http://www.fema.gov/media-library-data/20130726-1620-20490-4648/f_679_summaryofcoverage_11_2012.pdf.

172. KEVIN WOZNIAK, GARIN DAVIDSON & TOM ANKERSEN, FLORIDA'S COASTAL HAZARDS DISCLOSURE LAW: PROPERTY OWNER PERCEPTIONS OF THE PHYSICAL AND REGULATORY ENVIRONMENT (2012) (According to survey data, when asked whether sea-level rise will ever threaten their coastal property during their lifetime, only 3.7% of the respondents answered yes, and barely 25% knew that sea levels were rising in Florida.), http://nsgl.gso.uri.edu/flsgp/flsgps12001.pdf.

173. *See generally* Keith W. Rizzardi, *Rising Seas, Receding Ethics: Why Real Estate Professionals Should Seek the Moral High Ground*, 6 WASH. & LEE J. ENERGY, CLIMATE & ENV'T 402 (2015).

174. FLA. STAT. §161.57 (2006).

and dramatically reduce regional flood control. Professionals who knew (or should have known) and who failed to properly advise and protect their clients should be held accountable. Architects speaking in their professional capacity must avoid fraud and shall not knowingly make false statements of material fact.[175] Civil engineers should "hold paramount the safety, health and welfare of the public and shall strive to comply with the principles of sustainable development in the performance of their professional duties."[176] Lawyers cannot make false statements of material fact to third persons, nor fail to disclose material facts when disclosure is necessary to avoid assisting a fraud.[177] Planners "shall not deliberately or with reckless indifference fail to provide adequate, timely, clear and accurate information on planning issues."[178] Realtors "shall avoid exaggeration, misrepresentation, or concealment of pertinent facts relating to the property or the transaction."[179] Failure to adhere to these standards and many other standards could result in tort claims and allegations of fraud, misconduct, or malpractice. The professionals' own ethical standards will be held up as the evidence of the necessary standard of care, and its breach.

Absent the construction of a coastal defense system, or some other type of planned retreat that allows for communities to transition as the seas rise, the existing systems created by government and insurers could fail. The lawsuits will follow. Admittedly, thus far, tort law has not been an effective tool for stopping carbon emissions. Cases based on public nuisance law have fared poorly,[180] and the U.S. Supreme Court has held that the Clean Air Act displaced any federal common law right to seek abatement of carbon dioxide emissions from fossil-fuel fired power plants.[181] Still, creative litigators will find a way to bring sea-level rise into the courtroom. Prof. Michael Gerrard and his colleagues at the Sabin Center for Climate Change at Columbia Law School continue to explore the vast potential for the use of tort law to

---

175. *See* American Institute of Architects, Code of Ethics and Professional Conduct, at Rules 2.104, 2.106, and 4.103 (2012), http://www.aia.org/aiaucmp/groups/aia/documents/pdf/aiap074122.pdf.

176. *See* American Society of Civil Engineers, *Code of Ethics*, at Canon 1 (2006), http://www.asce.org/code_of_ethics/ (last visited Aug. 31, 2016).

177. *See* Rules Regulating the Florida Bar, Rules of Professional Conduct, at Rule 4-4.1 (2014); *see also* Keith W. Rizzardi, *Sea Level Lies: The Duty to Confront the Deniers*, 44 STETSON L. REV. 75 (2014).

178. *See* American Planning Association, *AICP Code of Ethics and Professional Conduct*, at §B.1 (2009), https://www.planning.org/ethics/ethicscode.htm (last visited Aug. 31, 2016).

179. *See* National Association of Realtors, *Code of Ethics*, at art. 1 (2012) (recognizing a duty for realtors to "treat all parties honestly"), http://www.realtor.org/mempolweb.nsf/pages/code (last visited Aug. 31, 2016).

180. *See, e.g.*, Native Village of Kivalina v. ExxonMobil Corp., 696 F.3d 849 (9th Cir. 2012); Comer v. Murphy Oil USA., 607 F.3d 1049 (5th Cir. 2010); California v. General Motors Corp., No. C06-05755, 2007 WL 272681 (N.D. Cal. Sept. 17, 2007).

181. American Elec. Power Co. v. Connecticut, 564 U.S. 410 (2011).

require compensation and deter irresponsible actions.[182] Some law firms have warned their clients to obtain directors and officers liability insurance to protect against the risks of climate change litigation.[183]

If a breach of duty can be established, the next point of dispute will be the causation of damages. Importantly, sea-level rise, unlike atmospheric GHGs, is not invisible. Damages may be easy to demonstrate because individual landowners will experience property damage, or in some cases, complete loss of inundated lands. The photos of flooded structures will often speak for themselves. So, in the future malpractice cases against these professionals, causation is likely to become the trickiest argument.

In another line of federal cases involving Hurricane Katrina and the Federal Tort Claims Act, the court openly discussed the difficulty of proving a causal link between the storm and the defendant's GHG emissions.[184] In a decision viewed by some scholars as further evidence of environmental injustice,[185] the Corps escaped liability because the Flood Control Act of 1928 granted the agency "virtually absolute immunity, no matter how negligent it might have been in designing and overseeing the construction of the levees" that provided regional flood protection.[186] Private companies and professionals who profit from the coastal real estate marketplace, however, lack the Corps' immunity and could be held accountable. Increasingly, science is able to demonstrate that climate change or sea-level rise was a defining

---

182. *See, e.g.*, Global Climate Change and U.S. Law (Michael B. Gerrard ed., 2007); Michael B. Gerrard, *What the Law and Lawyers Can and Cannot Do About Global Warming*, 16 South-eastern Envtl. L.J. 1, 53 (2007); Michael B. Gerrard, *What Litigation of a Climate Nuisance Suit Might Look Like*, Yale L.J. Online, Sept. 13, 2011, http://www.yalelawjournal.org/forum/what-litigation-of-a-climate-nuisance-suit-might-look-like.

183. *See, e.g.*, Collin J. Hite & Sung B. Yhim, Global Warming Litigation and D&O Insurance Coverage Issues (McGuire Woods n.d.), https://www.mcguirewoods.com/news-resources/publications/global%20warming%20and%20insurance%20coverage.pdf.

184. Comer v. Nationwide Mut. Ins. Co., No. 05 CV 436, 2006 WL 1066645 (S.D. Miss. Feb. 23, 2006) (now referenced as Comer v. Murphy Oil USA).

185. *See, e.g.*, Reilly Morse, Environmental Justice Through the Eye of Hurricane Katrina (2008), http://inequality.stanford.edu/_media/pdf/key_issues/Environment_policy.pdf; Christopher R. Dyess, *Off With His Head: The King Can Do No Wrong, Hurricane Katrina, and the Mississippi River Gulf Outlet*, 9 Nw. J. L. & Soc. Pol'y 302 (2014).

186. In re Katrina Canal Breaches Consol. Litig., 2013 U.S. Dist. LEXIS 53802, at **139–42, 2013 WL 1562765 (E.D. La. Apr. 12, 2013) (ending with a remarkable word of caution from the Judge: "I feel obligated to note that the bureaucratic behemoth that is the Army Corps of Engineers is virtually unaccountable to the citizens it protects despite the Federal Tort Claims Act. The public fisc will very possibly be more jeopardized by a lack of accountability than a rare judgment granting relief. The untold billions of dollars of damage incurred by the Greater New Orleans area as a result of the LPV levee failures during Katrina speak eloquently to that point. I take note that the Corps of Engineers has many excellent and dedicated engineers, supervisors, and staff. I also note that if individuals, corporations, and bureaucracies are never brought to task for substantial negligence, each will be much less assiduous in discharging their respective duties."); *see also* Kent C. Hofman, *An Enduring Anachronism: Arguments for the Repeal of the §702(c) Immunity Provision of the Flood Control Act of 1928*, 79 Tex. L. Rev. 791, 793 (2001).

or contributing factor to a specific weather event.[187] Competent professionals know, right now, that sea-level rise will cause more flood events and higher storm surges during extreme weather events.[188] Someday, customers will be suing professionals who committed malpractice by failing to account for these entirely foreseeable circumstances.[189]

Rising seas may seem a long way off, but the litigation may come soon. As a practical matter, there is an incentive not to wait. In the real estate arena, a victorious plaintiff in a negligence case will have difficulty recovering from a real estate development company that sold all its properties and no longer exists. Sophisticated south Florida tort lawyers are probably preparing now, planning their class action cases, to be filed the moment the next storm surge event occurs. Ironically, while politicians debate the "existence" of climate change, the judges will decide whether to bar claims related to sea-level rise based upon the statute of limitations. Although claimants are not necessarily required to sue when it is still uncertain whether the gradual process will result in a permanent taking,[190] the obligation to sue may arise once the permanent nature of the action is evident, regardless of whether damages are complete and fully calculable.[191] For example, when litigants in South Florida argued that the Army Corps flood control system was severely polluting the rivers and local estuary and causing algae blooms, the courts held that the takings claims had gone stale, because evidence of the environmental harms had been apparent many years earlier.[192]

---

187. *Is It Global Warming or Just the Weather?*, THE ECONOMIST, May 9, 2015, http://www.economist.com/news/international/21650552-scientists-are-getting-more-confident-about-attributing-heatwaves-and-droughts-human.

188. Evan Lehmann & Peter Behr, *Rising Seas Pose Growing Flood Threat*, SCI. AM., Oct. 27, 2015, http://www.scientificamerican.com/article/rising-seas-pose-growing-flood-threat/. *See also* RACHEL CLEE-TUS, OVERWHELMING RISK: RETHINKING FLOOD INSURANCE IN A WORLD OF RISING SEAS (Union of Concerned Scientists 2013), http://www.ucsusa.org/sites/default/files/legacy/assets/documents/global_warming/Overwhelming-Risk-Full-Report.pdf.

189. Maxine Burkett, *Litigating Climate Change Adaptation: Theory, Practice, and Corrective (Climate) Justice*, 42 ELR 11144, 11145 (Dec. 2012) ("A plaintiff, for example, would only need to prove the unreasonableness of defendant's actions in light of the well-established science of climate change—still a formidable task, though far less so than proving the causal link between a given climate impact and a distant entity's emissions. Further, even if establishing the causal link between a flooding event and climate change remains necessary to prove legal cause, advances in the ability to attribute a given impact to global warming is improving—at least enough to threaten more widespread civil liability.").

190. Columbia Basin Orchard v. United States, 88 F. Supp. 738, 739 (Ct. Cl. 1950).

191. Goodrich v. United States, 434 F.3d 1329, 1336 (Fed. Cir. 2006).

192. Mildenberger v. United States, 643 F.3d 938, 944 (Fed. Cir. 2011), citing Mildenberger v. United States, 91 Fed. Cl. 217, 235 (2010)("plaintiffs should have been aware of the permanence of defendant's discharges into the St. Lucie River long before November 13, 2000.").

Although the merits and timing of courtroom claims remains uncertain, the lawyers are coming. These types of arguments are already being made at the international level. The Republic of the Marshall Islands has even argued that the actions of the rest of the planet have put their nation in harm's way. Rising seas, they explain, threaten their life, property, culture, food, housing, health and water—all of which are elementary principles codified in the Universal Declaration of Human Rights (UDHR).[193] Human rights litigation is unavailable for Floridians.[194] Nevertheless, a future shaped by litigation in the state and federal courts will fit a familiar Florida pattern, and the Everglades, again, offers an insight.

In 1988, the federal government sued the state of Florida over water quality concerns in the Everglades. Since then, the many stakeholders have spent countless hours and fortunes arguing and litigating over water quality, wildlife, and other aspects of the ecosystem restoration. Yet, as one study of the Everglades socio-ecological system explained, despite more than 80 cases, the litigation process created no winners:

> Any one case can alter decades of planning, and every case—even the meritless ones—can bring publicity that still succeeds in undermining public confidence in the overall policy objectives. But in the future, as the forces of climate change re-shape the Everglades, countless decisions will be subjected to stakeholder and judicial second-guessing . . . .[195]

The crisis of rising seas, and the complete failure of our legal and governance systems, might finally motivate the reform needed to build a more adaptive system capable of confronting our changing future.[196] But for the property owners who lose their homes and investments to the ocean, those changes may come too late.

---

193. The Republic of the Marshall Islands, a former U.S. territory located in the Pacific Ocean, fears the potential loss of its national lands as a result of sea-level rise, and even submitted a communication to the United Nations decrying the potential violations of the Universal Declaration of Human Rights, the International Covenant on Economic, Social, and Political Rights, and the International Covenant on Civil and Political Rights. *See* Phillip H. Muller, *National Communication Regarding the Relationship Between Human Rights & the Impacts of Climate Change—UN Human Rights Council Res. 7/23* (Dec. 31, 2008); *see also* INTERNATIONAL COUNCIL ON HUMAN RIGHTS POLICY, CLIMATE CHANGE AND HUMAN RIGHTS: A ROUGH GUIDE (2009), http://www.ohchr.org/Documents/Issues/ ClimateChange/Submissions/136_report.pdf.

194. UNITED STATES SUBMISSION TO THE OFFICE OF U.N. HIGH COMMISSIONER FOR HUMAN RIGHTS, OBSERVATIONS BY THE UNITED STATES OF AMERICA ON THE RELATIONSHIP BETWEEN CLIMATE CHANGE AND HUMAN RIGHTS (2008) ("The U.S. Department of State has made its position clear that it did not recognize a "right to a safe environment" and concluded that a human rights approach to addressing climate change was unlikely to be effective."), http://www.ohchr.org/Documents/Issues/ ClimateChange/Submissions/USA.pdf.

195. Gunderson et al., *supra* note 125, at 154.

196. *Id.* at 156.

Conclusion: Urgency, Now

Despite a series of extraordinary events—shocking images of glacial melting over time,[197] open expanses of ocean in the Arctic during
wintertime,[198] and increasingly common flooding events in Miami[199]—
Florida's response to the risks of rising seas remains tepid.[200] How much
more evidence could policymakers possibly need before they take greater
precautions to protect the public? Pope Francis has even scolded society's
leaders for this complacency:

> Superficially, apart from a few obvious signs of pollution and deterioration,
> things do not look that serious, and the planet could continue as it is for some
> time. Such evasiveness serves as a license to carrying on with our present
> lifestyles and models of production and consumption. This is the way human
> beings contrive to feed their self-destructive vices: trying not to see them, try-
> ing not to acknowledge them, delaying the important decisions and pretend-
> ing that nothing will happen.[201]

Sea-level rise comes with uncertainties,[202] but south Florida cannot whis-
tle past the flooded graveyard. As the Everglades experience has proven, the
transition from ideas to investment to implementation can be achieved, but it
will take decades. Floridians can still choose the option of coastal leadership.
Inaction, however, is injustice by default, and nothing more than a decision
to let the lawyers sort out the consequences.

197. U.S. Geological Survey, *Repeat Photography Project*, https://www.usgs.gov/centers/norock/science/
    repeat-photography-project?qt-science_center_objects=0#qt-science_center_objects (last visited Aug.
    31, 2016).
198. Thomas Homer-Dixon, *Disaster at the Top of the World*, N.Y. TIMES, Aug. 22, 2010 (stating that the
    Arctic is warming twice as fast as the rest of the planet, and with the sun heating newly open water it
    will take longer to refreeze during winter), http://www.nytimes.com/2010/08/23/opinion/23homer-
    dixon.html.
199. Coral Davenport, *Miami Finds Itself Ankle-Deep in Climate Change Debate*, N.Y. TIMES, May 7, 2014,
    http://www.nytimes.com/2014/05/08/us/florida-finds-itself-in-the-eye-of-the-storm-on-climate-
    change.html.
200. Robin McKie, *Miami, the Great World City, Is Drowning While the Powers That Be Look Away*, THE
    GUARDIAN, July 11, 2014, https://www.theguardian.com/world/2014/jul/11/miami-drowning-
    climate-change-deniers-sea-levels-rising.
201. LAUDATO SI', *supra* note 13, at para 59.
202. J.T. Reager et al., *A Decade of Sea Level Rise Slowed by Climate-Driven Hydrology*, 351 SCI. 699–703
    (2016). *Compare* Press Release, NASA, University Study Shows Rising Seas Slowed by Increasing
    Water on Land (Feb. 11, 2016) (explaining that this "University Study Shows Rising Seas Slowed
    by Increasing Water on Land"), http://www.nasa.gov/press-release/nasa-university-study-shows-
    rising-seas-slowed-by-increasing-water-on-land, *with* Marc Morano, *NASA Study Concludes "Global
    Warming" Is Actually Slowing Sea Level Rise*, CLIMATE DEPOT, Feb. 12, 2016 ("Settled Science: Global
    warming causes sea levels to rise—oops—fall, er slowdown? Whatever!"), http://www.climatedepot.
    com/2016/02/12/flashback-1987-global-warming-causes-sea-levels-to-fall-2016-global-warming-
    causes-slowdown-in-sea-level-rise/#ixzz40GODwHFD.

Chapter 8

The Seas Are Rising and So Are Community Voices: Coastal Resilience and Climate Justice Through Public Participation After the *Deepwater Horizon* Oil Spill

David Roche

Introduction: Climate, Communities, and the Spill

Climate change and sea-level rise are reshaping the coastline along the Gulf of Mexico.[1] Land is being lost at an alarming rate, especially in Louisiana, where subsidence is compounding the effects of sea-level rise.[2] Across the Gulf Coast, communities are increasingly vulnerable as the seas rise, land subsides, saltwater intrudes, and marshes retreat.[3] In the face of such monumental change, it is essential for communities to plan and adapt.

Another major challenge for the Gulf of Mexico region is how to achieve restoration in the wake of the *Deepwater Horizon* oil spill.[4] Billions of dollars will support projects and programs stemming from the spill and these funds should be spent in ways that appropriately consider climate projections— something that may not be occurring in the early phases of restoration.[5] Following the oil spill, multiple processes were established to address restoration and recovery from environmental disaster.[6] Through three of these processes—the Natural Resource Damage Assessment (NRDA), the National Fish and Wildlife Fund's (NFWF's) grant programs, and the Resources and Ecosystem Sustainability, Tourist Opportunities, and Revived Economies of the Gulf Coast States Act (RESTORE Act) —$16.7 billion will be available to fund restoration projects.[7] As of this writing, just over $1 billion worth

---

1. Cindy A. Thatcher et al., *Economic Vulnerability to Sea-Level Rise Along the Northern U.S. Gulf Coast*, 63. J. Coastal Res. 234, 234 (2013).
2. *See id.* at 235.
3. *Id.* at 241–44.
4. The oil spill began on April 20, 2010, after 11 men lost their lives in a blowout on the *Deepwater Horizon* oil rig. National Commission on the BP Deepwater Horizon Oil Spill and Offshore Drilling, Report to the President, Deep Water: The Gulf Oil Disaster and the Future of Offshore Drilling vi (2011), https://www.gpo.gov/fdsys/pkg/GPO-OILCOMMISSION/pdf/GPO-OILCOMMISSION.pdf. For the next 87 days, oil gushed into the Gulf of Mexico, releasing millions of barrels total. *Id.* As the oil flowed, underwater cameras broadcast the environmental disaster in real-time to an increasingly horrified, angry, and helpless audience. *See id.* When the well was finally capped in July, the spill was being called the worst environmental disaster in U.S. history. Press Release, The White House, Remarks by the President to the Nation on the BP Oil Spill (June 15, 2010), https://www.whitehouse.gov/the-press-office/remarks-president-nation-bp-oil-spill. Environmental impacts were both immediate and persistent, and they are only beginning to be understood. Drew Griffin et al., *5 Years After the Gulf Oil Spill: What We Do (and Don't) Know*, CNN.com, Apr. 20, 2015, http://www.cnn.com/2015/04/14/us/gulf-oil-spill-unknowns. Monumental impacts were felt by species, ecosystems, and human communities of the Gulf region. *Id.*
5. *See* Webinar: Climate Change, Community Resilience, and Restoration in the Gulf of Mexico (ELI Ocean Seminar Series 2015), http://eli-ocean.org/gulf/climatechangewebinar. During the webinar, panelists and attendees expressed concern that restoration was not adequately considering climate and community resilience.
6. *See generally* Environmental Law Institute, *Introduction to Gulf Recovery*, http://eli-ocean.org/gulf/intro-gulf-recovery/ (last visited Aug. 22, 2016).
7. *See id.*

of projects have been approved.[8] The billions remaining will be spent in the coming decades based on local, state, and regional plans to support restoration of the Gulf Coast.

From the challenges of climate change and restoration planning emerges an opportunity: incorporating climate justice into the future of the Gulf region. Here, climate justice is achieved by policies that "address the issues and concerns that arise from the intersection of climate change with race, poverty, and preexisting environmental risks,"[9] confronting inequity by considering civil, social, and human rights in decisionmaking.

The five Gulf states all rank near the bottom nationally for economic inequality,[10] a microcosm of the disenfranchisement that is felt by many communities in the region. The restoration processes were designed in a way that could support community-driven restoration, and in the process support justice for the people of the Gulf region. However, to accomplish community-driven restoration, it is essential to understand the applicable laws and policies to ensure that coastal communities have a meaningful voice in the process.

Part I of the chapter examines the ecological problems facing the Gulf region—rising seas, catastrophic storms, and resource extraction from marine and coastal ecosystems. Part II describes the legal parameters of restoration in the wake of the *Deepwater Horizon* oil spill, focusing on how the processes incorporate public engagement and planning. Part III reviews success stories for climate justice in Gulf restoration. The chapter concludes by recommending actions that can be taken from within and outside the restoration processes to support climate justice in coastal planning decisions.

Climate justice in this context does not necessarily require a specific outcome for coastal communities. But it does require that those communities are given a meaningful voice.[11] Gulf restoration could provide a compelling case study in how to secure climate justice from a procedural rights perspective. And in the process, it could provide a template for giving coastal communities across the United States a louder voice in decisions that affect them.

---

8. Environmental Law Institute, *Restoration Projects Map*, http://eli-ocean.org/gulf/map (last visited Aug. 22, 2015).

9. Maxine Burkett, *Just Solutions to Climate Change: A Climate Justice Proposal for a Domestic Clean Development Mechanism*, 56 Buff. L. Rev. 169, 170 (2008).

10. *See* U.S. Census Bureau, Household Income Inequality Within U.S. Counties: 2006–2010, at 2 (2012), https://www.census.gov/prod/2012pubs/acsbr10-18.pdf.

11. *See* R. Gregory Roberts, *Environmental Justice and Community Empowerment: Learning From the Civil Rights Movement*, 48 Am. U. L. Rev. 229, 233 (1998) (describing "powerlessness" as root of environmental injustice).

I.   Coastal Resilience in the Gulf of Mexico

Given sea-level rise, increased prevalence of extreme events, and vulnerability to a number of coastal threats, it is essential for planning decisions to support coastal resilience—or "reduce the ecological and socioeconomic risks of coastal hazards."[12] Coastal resilience has become one of those popular terms that is mentioned so often that it has lost some of its meaning. At its core, it is a simple idea that is complex to implement. It consists of three interconnected prongs: preventing risk when possible, mitigating unavoidable risk, and adapting to risk moving forward.

The importance of decisionmaking based on coastal resilience principles is especially evident in the Gulf of Mexico region. Along the Gulf Coast, catastrophic storms, vulnerable coastlines, and economic disparity interact to create the potential for horrific human and environmental disasters. Two disasters in particular stand out: Hurricane Katrina in 2005 and the *Deepwater Horizon* oil spill in 2010.

A.   Hurricane Katrina in 2005

In 2005, Hurricane Katrina devastated much of the Gulf Coast, demonstrating the extent of the damage that extreme storm events can have on both the ecology and economy of the region.[13] Hurricane Rita shortly thereafter provided further evidence of the risks facing the Gulf Coast.[14] Both storms caused devastation beyond measure, exacting an economic toll of well over $100 billion,[15] but the human toll was incalculable. The most straightforward explanation of the disaster was the ferocity of the storms. And they certainly were fierce—sustained winds of 175 mph for both storms.[16] There is some evidence that such violent storms may become more common with climate change.[17] Regardless of whether the intensification projections come

---

12.   National Oceanic and Atmospheric Administration (NOAA), *Coastal Resilience Mapping Portal* (defining coastal resilience), http://coast.noaa.gov/digitalcoast/tools/coastalresilience (last visited Aug. 22, 2016).

13.   *See generally* Harold A. McDougall, *Hurricane Katrina: A Story of Race, Poverty, and Environmental Injustice*, 51 How. L.J. 533 (2008).

14.   *See id.* at 547.

15.   *See* Congressional Budget Office, The Macroeconomic and Budgetary Effects of Hurricanes Katrina and Rita: An Update (2005), https://www.cbo.gov/sites/default/files/109th-congress-2005-2006/reports/09-29-effectsofhurricanes.pdf.

16.   NOAA, Hurricane Katrina (2005), http://www.ncdc.noaa.gov/extremeevents/specialreports/Hurricane-Katrina.pdf; NOAA, Hurricane Rita, (2005), http://www.ncdc.noaa.gov/extremeevents/specialreports/Hurricane-Rita2005.pdf.

17.   *See* Greg Holland & Cindy L. Bruyère, *Recent Intense Hurricane Response to Global Climate Change*, 42 Climate Dynamics 617 (2014).

to fruition, there will be future storms, and the storms will tell familiar stories of despair for coastal communities if more is not done to enhance coastal resilience.

Perhaps even more unique to the Gulf region than intense hurricanes is a particularly vulnerable coastline. Much of the coastal zone is low lying and at risk of damage from storm surge, which can be dangerously exacerbated by sea-level rise.[18] In addition, subsidence is causing land to plummet beneath the waves at alarming rates along parts of the coast. One projection indicates that nearly 250 km^2 will be lost per year by 2050 in the Lower Mississippi River Basin.[19] In other locations, land is eroding from wave action. In essence, the sea is rising everywhere, and already low-lying land is falling or eroding in some locations. It is the old cliché turned on its head—an unstoppable force meeting a movable (and actively moving) object. Hurricane Katrina exploited the vulnerable coast, devastating hundreds of miles of shoreline along the Gulf of Mexico.

Hurricane Katrina was strong, and parts of the coast were somewhat weak. But what made Katrina an immense catastrophe was economic disparity. The storm had disproportionately negative impacts for low-income communities.[20] These communities had been subject to environmental injustice for many years prior to the storm, including injustices built into the legal system in the form of structural protections that favored certain communities over others and nonstructural protections that were inadequate.[21] Thus, when the surge came, in many instances the individuals in the communities had nowhere to go and nothing to protect them.[22] Coastal development had stripped the coastal zone of many of its natural protections, and the man-made protections were concentrated in areas of relative affluence.

Altogether, the result was a tragedy that embodied the failure of all prongs of coastal resilience. Risk prevention, mitigation, and adaptation were inadequate for many of the coastal communities of the Gulf region. When the 2005 storms were over, thousands of lives would be lost and many more lives changed forever due to a lack of coastal resilience and climate justice.

---

18. *See* Thatcher et al., *supra* note 1.
19. Lei Zou et al., *Evaluating Land Subsidence Rates and Their Implications for Land Loss in the Lower Mississippi River Basin*, 8 WATER 10, 15–18 (2016).
20. *See* McDougall, *supra* note 13.
21. *See id.*
22. *See id. See also* CARMEN GONZALEZ ET AL., CENTER FOR PROGRESSIVE REFORM, CLIMATE CHANGE, RESILIENCE, AND FAIRNESS (2016) (discussing structural and non-structural protection, among other things), http://progressivereform.org/articles/Climate_Change_Resilience_Gulf_Coast_1603.pdf.

B.   Deepwater Horizon *Oil Spill in 2010*

The need for coastal resilience is not limited to natural environmental tragedy; it also extends to man-made environmental disasters. On April 20, 2010, the *Deepwater Horizon* drilling rig exploded off of the coast of Louisiana, triggering one of the nation's worst oil spills. The public stood transfixed as millions of barrels of oil spilled into the Gulf of Mexico over 87 days.[23] More than six years later, the economic and environmental impacts of the spill are only beginning to be understood.

Like Hurricanes Katrina and Rita, low-income communities bore the brunt of the disaster, with fishing and tourism industries suffering significant impacts.[24] Perhaps most telling in relation to the Gulf region's coastal resilience history is not the economic impact, but the emotional one.[25] Speaking with community members along the Gulf Coast often reveals a lingering fatigue about facing these massive issues. Some feel that their voice is being drowned out by other influences, with the *Deepwater Horizon* spill being yet another instance of injustice. Resource extraction in particular can be a sore subject. There is a perception that billions of dollars come out of the ground, but very little of that money makes it back to the communities that have to cope with the impacts of extraction, like oil spills.

C.   *Oil Spill Restoration and Climate Justice*

With the 2010 spill, though, came a chance to fight back against that injustice and put coastal resilience principles into practice. Several restoration and recovery processes have been initiated to address impacts from *Deepwater Horizon*. Under these processes, $16.7 billion has been allocated to coastal projects and programs in all five Gulf states, with payments spread out over the next two decades. The money is important, but what it stands for is even more integral to the future of the Gulf Coast—it represents a chance to use planning processes rooted in law to influence the trajectory of environmental justice in the entire region.

The imperative to do something is only getting stronger. National Oceanic and Atmospheric Administration (NOAA) projections show the progressively greater effects that will be felt throughout the region from climate

---

23.   *See, e.g., Disaster Unfolds Slowly in the Gulf of Mexico,* Boston.com, May 12, 2010, http://www. boston.com/bigpicture/2010/05/disaster_unfolds_slowly_in_the.html.

24.   *See* Hari M. Osofsky et al., *Environmental Justice and the BP Deepwater Horizon Oil Spill,* 20 N.Y.U. Envtl. L.J. 99 (2012).

25.   J. Glenn Morris Jr. et al., *Psychological Responses and Resilience of People and Communities Impacted by the Deepwater Horizon Oil Spill,* 124 Transactions Clinical & Climatological Ass'n 191 (2013).

change, sea-level rise, and subsidence in the coming years and decades.[26] Much of the U.S. coast is at risk for climate impacts; however, the simultaneous threats facing the Gulf Coast make it an ideal laboratory for long-term coastal resilience planning.

In the wake of Hurricanes Katrina and Rita, the *Deepwater Horizon* oil spill, and decades of research, all of the elements for actualizing coastal resilience are present. The need is clear and the money is available. However, there must be a nexus between the need and the funding, so that available monies go to projects and programs that give coastal communities a voice and facilitate coastal resilience objectives.

II.   Gulf Restoration Overview

As soon as the extent of the spill became evident in summer 2010, dialogue began about how to make things right. The images of oil spewing into the ocean for months led to visceral reactions throughout the nation. BP would pay to restore the Gulf.

Now, more than six years later, the red-hot reactions have mostly simmered and cooled for much of the country. However, there are pockets of passionate advocates centered in the Gulf Coast but present around the country who have been fighting for the region and its people in the wake of the spill. These advocates are essential because while the visceral reactions may have worn off for the most part, restoration is only just beginning.

In April 2016, the BP Consent Decree was entered by the U.S. District Court for the Eastern District of Louisiana.[27] The case had meandered through the court for years, and the consent decree represented the culmination of countless legal arguments in that time.[28] With the consent decree, the public now knows how much money is going to the Gulf, and for what types of activities.

Six years after the spill, the money is finally on the table. And the stack of chips is towering—$16.7 billion total for restoration through the three main processes. For the most part, those chips are yet to be divvied out to restoration activities. On one side of the table, there is ecological

---

26.   *See, e.g.*, NOAA, *Sea Level Rise Viewer* (showing that even one foot of sea-level rise will have massive impacts on the geography of the Gulf Coast), http://coast.noaa.gov/digitalcoast/tools/slr (last visited Aug. 22, 2016).

27.   Consent Decree Among Defendant BP Exploration & Production Inc. ("BPXP"), the United States of America, and the States of Alabama, Florida, Louisiana, Mississippi, and Texas, In re: Oil Spill by the Oil Rig "Deepwater Horizon" in the Gulf of Mexico, on April 20, 2010, MDL No. 2179, https://www.justice.gov/enrd/file/838066/download [hereinafter Consent Decree].

28.   *See id.* para. A-T.

restoration. On the other side is economic restoration. No matter where the chips fall, it is essential that coastal communities have a voice in how they are cashed in. Given the history of injustice in the Gulf region, climate justice can only be achieved through a democratic approach to Gulf restoration. Community-driven restoration is possible for every stack of chips available.[29]

Restoration of the Gulf region after the *Deepwater Horizon* oil spill is primarily being carried out through three processes: the NRDA, the NFWF's Gulf Environmental Benefit Fund, and the RESTORE Act. Through the consent decree, previous agreements, and several rulings, $16.7 billion will flow through these three processes spread out over approximately the next 20 years, with just over $1 billion currently dedicated to projects.

To access the funds, each process has varying planning requirements, involving local governments, state governments, regional entities, and federal agencies. All plans have baseline requirements involving transparency, accountability, and public participation, and these avenues of engagement have already had massive impacts on the types of projects that get funded. Coastal communities have had their voice heard, and there is evidence that it has caused billions more dollars to go to coastal resilience objectives (like shoreline strengthening and marsh rebuilding), rather than more politically expedient goals (like stadiums and convention centers).[30]

Through planning and engagement requirements, the funding thus presents a massive opportunity to institutionalize climate justice considerations into coastal planning and restoration. The public participation, project planning, and climate justice requirements are described briefly below.

A.   Natural Resource Damage Assessment (NRDA)

The Oil Pollution Act of 1990[31] requires that the government undertake an NRDA following an oil release to help resources harmed by the spill.[32] The goal is to return natural resources to the condition they would have been in, had the oil spill not occurred (called "baseline").[33] NRDA trustees assess injuries to natural resources and then draft restoration plans to address these injuries.[34] The Deepwater Horizon Oil Spill Trustee Council was established

---

29.   *See infra* Part III.
30.   *Id.*
31.   Oil Pollution Act of 1990, Pub. L. No. 101-380, 104 Stat. 507 (codified at 33 U.S.C. §§2701–2719).
32.   33 U.S.C. §2706.
33.   15 C.F.R. §990.30 (2016).
34.   *Id.* at §990.12.

in 2010 by a memorandum of understanding.[35] The trustees include federal agencies and state agencies from all five Gulf states.[36]

After the NRDA process began in 2010, it became clear that the assessment was unprecedented in scope and would take several years. In the face of this drawn-out assessment process, on the one-year anniversary of the spill, the trustees and BP announced an early restoration agreement that would provide $1 billion for restoration projects as the assessment was being completed (to be credited against BP's total liability).[37] Then, in October 2015, the consent decree with BP was announced along with the Programmatic Damage Assessment and Restoration Plan (PDARP)[38] that would together determine how much money would be available through NRDA. In total, $8.8 billion is slated to flow through the NRDA process in the Gulf of Mexico.[39] Thus far, through early restoration, $870 million worth of projects have been funded,[40] leaving approximately $8 billion for future restoration activities under NRDA.

NRDA funds are allocated to projects through restoration plans, which are drafted periodically by trustees at the state and regional levels.[41] Restoration plans include environmental analysis under the National Environmental Policy Act (NEPA),[42] the Endangered Species Act,[43] and other laws when applicable. Prior to restoration plans being released, the trustees hold periodic public meetings, and they have submission portals for projects online.[44] After plans are drafted, they are open for public review and comment.[45]

In addition to engagement opportunities, climate change and environmental justice are important considerations in plan design, content, and

---

35. Memorandum of Understanding Relating to the Natural Resource Damage Assessment and Restoration Resulting From the *Deepwater Horizon* Mobile Offshore Drilling Unit and the Subsea Macondo Well (Nov. 17, 2010), https://www.doi.gov/sites/doi.gov/files/migrated/deepwaterhorizon/adminrecord/upload/DWH-NRDAR-Trustee-MOU-signed-version-but-2.pdf.
36. *Id.*
37. Framework for Early Restoration Addressing Injuries Resulting From the Deepwater Horizon Oil Spill (May 2011), http://www.gulfspillrestoration.noaa.gov/wp-content/uploads/2011/05/framework-for-early-restoration-04212011.pdf.
38. Gulf Spill Restoration, *Final Programmatic Damage Assessment and Restoration Plan (PDARP) and Final Programmatic Environmental Impact Statement (PEIS)*, http://www.gulfspillrestoration.noaa.gov/restoration-planning/gulf-plan (last visited Aug. 22, 2016) [hereinafter *PDARP*].
39. Consent Decree, *supra* note 27, para. 15.
40. *See* Environmental Law Institute, *Gulf of Mexico Restoration Projects Database*, eli-ocean.org/gulf/restoration-projects-database (last visited Aug. 22, 2016) [hereinafter *Restoration Projects Database*].
41. 15 C.F.R. §990.50 (2016).
42. 42 U.S.C. §§4321–4347.
43. 16 U.S.C. §§1531–1544.
44. *See* Gulf Spill Restoration, *Restoration*, http://www.gulfspillrestoration.noaa.gov/restoration/ (last visited Aug. 22, 2016).
45. 15 C.F.R. §990.23 (2016).

implementation. Regarding climate change, a 2015 restoration plan (for phase IV of early restoration) states that, "Consideration of factors such as sea-level rise, changes to shorelines, and altered hydrology at the project design stage has allowed, and will allow, for the anticipation of a range of environmental changes and the development of Early Restoration projects that would be more resilient over time."[46] In addition, the plan aims to incorporate Executive Order 13653, which directs agencies to develop projects and programs that consider climate impacts.[47] A preliminary search shows that several NRDA projects include climate considerations.[48] However, it is unclear how much weight climate change impacts were given in the decisionmaking process. In addition, there is little discussion of why some projects were selected instead of others, even though many project footprints include areas projected to be directly affected by sea-level rise in the coming decades.

Environmental justice and socioeconomic impacts are reviewed under NEPA for each project, including impacts to minority and low-income communities.[49] In addition, projects are reviewed under Executive Order 12898, which directs agencies to consider environmental justice in decisionmaking.[50] However, environmental justice has not been used to justify projects outright. Rather, environmental justice review primarily examines whether there will be adverse impacts to affected communities.

Read together, the focus on public participation, climate change, and environmental justice necessitates that community priorities and perspectives be considered in the NRDA process. The NRDA trustees have already made shifts in the type of projects they approve, possibly in response to community concerns.[51] While climate justice is moving in a positive direction in the NRDA process, only 9.9% of the $8.8 billion has been allocated to projects. Thus, the remaining portion of funds presents an even greater opportunity to incorporate climate justice into decisionmaking.

---

46. DEEPWATER HORIZON TRUSTEES, DEEPWATER HORIZON OIL SPILL FINAL PHASE IV ENVIRONMENTAL RESTORATION PLAN AND ENVIRONMENTAL ASSESSMENTS 4–17 (2015), http://www.gulfspillrestoration. noaa.gov/wp-content/uploads/Final-Phase-IV-ERP-EA.pdf.
47. Exec. Order No. 13653, 78 Fed. Reg. 66819 (Nov. 1, 2013) ("Preparing the United States for the Impacts of Climate Change").
48. See, e.g., PHASE IV ENVIRONMENTAL RESTORATION PLAN, supra note 46, §12 (describing climate change impacts at Gulf Islands National Seashore).
49. See Council on Environmental Quality, Environmental Justice and NEPA, https://ceq.doe.gov/ nepa_information/justice.html (last visited Aug. 22, 2016).
50. Exec. Order No. 12898, 3 C.F.R. §859 (1995), reprinted as amended in 42 U.S.C. §4321 (1994 & Supp. I 1995).
51. See infra Part III.

B.   National Fish & Wildlife Foundation (NFWF)

NFWF is a private, nonprofit organization created by Congress in 1984 to protect and restore fish and wildlife and their habitats.[52] The organization funds a wide variety of conservation projects across the country, leveraging public funds with private investment dollars. NFWF is governed by a board of directors, which consists of 30 members who are approved by the U.S. Secretary of the Interior.[53]

As part of the criminal settlements that BP and Transocean (another company responsible for the spill) reached with the federal government, NFWF will receive a total of $2.544 billion "[t]o remedy harm and eliminate or reduce the risk of future harm" to natural resources in the Gulf.[54] The funds are held in the Gulf Environmental Benefit Fund. Approximately $500 million worth of projects have been approved to date.[55]

In Alabama, Florida, Mississippi, and Texas, the money funds natural resource projects.[56] In Louisiana, the money funds barrier island or river diversion projects.[57] In practice, NFWF works closely with the states to determine which projects will be funded. Each state has a portal where the public can submit project ideas for consideration under NFWF.

Because it is not a government agency, NFWF does not have statutory or regulatory planning requirements, including under NEPA. However, an April 2015 webinar on climate change and Gulf restoration included a presentation from NFWF's senior manager for coastal habitat restoration, who explained that the program requires the integration of climate change and environmental justice impacts into restoration projects.[58] Proposals must discuss linkages to adjacent existing and planned projects and major project risks, such as sea-level rise.[59] In addition, under the terms of the agreements,

---

52. NFWF, *About National Fish and Wildlife Foundation*, http://www.nfwf.org/whoweare/Pages/home. aspx (last visited Aug. 22, 2016).
53. *Id.*
54. *See* Guilty Plea Agreement para. 35, United States v. BP (Jan. 21, 2013), http://www.nfwf.org/gulf/ Documents/us-v-bp-plea-agreement.pdf; Cooperation Guilty Plea Agreement at Exhibit B1, United States v. Transocean Deepwater Inc. (Jan. 3, 2013), http://www.nfwf.org/gulf/Documents/transocean-plea-agreement%20p2.pdf.
55. *See Restoration Projects Database, supra* note 40.
56. *Guilty Plea Agreement* para. 37.
57. *Id.*
58. Environmental Law Institute, Webinar Summary: Climate Change, Community Resilience, and Restoration in the Gulf of Mexico 4 (2015), http://eli-ocean.org/wp-content/blogs.dir/2/ files/Climate-Restoration-Webinar-Summary.pdf.
59. *Id.*

NFWF must consult with the Gulf states to, "maximize the environmental benefits of such projects."[60]

Therefore, states, federal agencies, and NFWF itself must incorporate climate planning into NFWF proposals and NFWF must determine how much weight to give the various aspects of each proposal. However, climate change and environmental justice considerations are rarely included in public project descriptions and it is unclear what role they play in project design and selection.

Through other funded projects outside of the Gulf region, NFWF has prioritized environmental justice and climate resilience.[61] In the absence of legal requirements, NFWF must take the initiative to consider public input about project priorities to ensure that climate justice is a part of oil spill restoration as well.

C.   RESTORE Act

The RESTORE Act[62] was enacted to direct 80% of the Clean Water Act (CWA) civil penalties from the *Deepwater Horizon* disaster to Gulf restoration.[63] The funds will support a variety of projects aimed at helping the Gulf recover from environmental and economic injuries experienced as a result of decades of oil and gas development in the region, including the effects of the *Deepwater Horizon*. The Act does not include the terms "climate" or "justice" anywhere in the text. In total, $5.328 billion will be available through the RESTORE Act.[64]

Under the RESTORE Act, there are three primary "pots" of funding determining where 95% of all monies go, each with different planning requirements, eligible activities, and engagement opportunities. Thus, each pot has different avenues for incorporating climate justice into restoration.

Pot one is the direct component, which directs 35% of funds to the five Gulf states in equal shares[65] ($1.9 billion total; a small portion of which is

---

60. *Guilty Plea Agreement* para. 37.
61. *See* NFWF, *Five Star & Urban Waters Restoration Program 2015 Request for Proposals* (requiring the applicant to identify "demographic characteristics of underserved or environmental justice communities benefiting from the project"), http://www.nfwf.org/fivestar/Pages/2015rfp.aspx (last visited Aug. 22, 2016).
62. Resources and Ecosystems Sustainability, Tourist Opportunities, and Revived Economies of the Gulf Coast States Act of 2012 (RESTORE Act), Pub. L. No. 112-141, 126 Stat. 588, https://www.treasury.gov/services/restore-act/Documents/Final-Restore-Act.pdf.
63. Environmental Law Institute, *RESTORE Act*, http://eli-ocean.org/gulf/clean-water-act-restore/ (last visited Aug. 22, 2016).
64. *See* Consent Decree, *supra* note 27.
65. RESTORE Act, Pub. L. No. 112-141, §1603.

currently allocated to projects). To receive the funds, each of the Gulf states (in addition to coastal parishes in Louisiana and coastal counties in Florida) must draft a multi-year implementation plan.[66] Under pot one, eligible activities include ecological and economic restoration.[67]

There are two main avenues for public engagement in pot one. First, states and local governments often solicit comments on approaches in public meetings and online. Second, each plan is required to be open for comment prior to being finalized.[68] While these opportunities exist, they often are announced in local print newspapers or in the nooks and crannies of government websites. Thus, it can be difficult to engage effectively in many instances.[69]

Climate justice could be an integral component of project planning requirements. Guidance issued by the U.S. Treasury Department includes one reference to climate change.[70] Within dozens of questions to help applicants determine whether they complied with all applicable environmental laws, the guidance states that to comply with Executive Order 13653, the applicant should consider the following question: "Will the proposed activity incorporate elements that promote climate resilience (e.g., to rising sea levels)?"[71] If yes, the state (or local) government should include a brief description of the climate-resilient elements in the grant application.[72] As of this writing, 11 plans developed under pot one have been accepted by the U.S. Treasury Department, and none of the narratives addresses climate impacts in detail.[73] In addition, it is unclear how state and local governments are considering climate change during project selection.

---

66. *Id.*
67. *Id.*
68. *Id.*
69. *See generally* LeRoy Paddock, *Environmental Accountability and Public Involvement*, 21 Pace Envtl. L. Rev. 243 (2004) (discussing link between public participation opportunities, accountability, and environmental justice); Scott Kuhn, *Expanding Public Participation Is Essential to Environmental Justice and the Democratic Decisionmaking Process*, 25 Ecology L.Q. 647, 648 (1999) ("True public participation and environmental justice cannot be realized until the communities that are impacted by environmental regulations have a voice in the process . . ."); Robert D. Bullard & Glenn S. Johnson, *Environmental Justice: Grassroots Activism and Its Impact on Public Policy Decision Making*, 56 J. Soc. Issues 555 (2000) (detailing the effectiveness of nongovernmental organizations and other activists in promoting environmental justice).
70. U.S. Department of the Treasury, RESTORE Act Direct Component Guidance and Application to Receive Federal Financial Assistance 36 (2014), http://www.treasury.gov/services/restore-act/Documents/Direct%20Component%20Guidance_August%202014.pdf.
71. *Id.*
72. *Id.*
73. *See* U.S. Department of the Treasury, *RESTORE Act: Direct Component* (providing links to accepted plans), https://www.treasury.gov/services/restore-act/Pages/Direct%20Component/Direct-Component.aspx (last visited Aug. 22, 2016).

Another question within the guidance addresses environmental justice. To comply with Executive Order 12898, the applicant should consider the following question: "Will the proposed activity have disproportionately high and adverse human health or environmental effects on minority or low-income populations?"[74] If yes, the applicant should refer to further guidance on environmental justice from the Council on Environmental Quality. Current plans have not addressed environmental justice in detail. In addition, given that the state and local governments are carrying out the projects, the U.S. Treasury Department has indicated that NEPA review is not required unless there is another triggering mechanism.[75] Altogether, pot one has distinct opportunities to consider public input and incorporate climate justice, but it is unclear whether those opportunities have meaningfully influenced restoration thus far.

Pot two is the Gulf Coast Ecosystem Restoration Council component, which directs 30% of funding to a new federal agency (the Gulf Coast Ecosystem Restoration Council, or "Council") with representatives from the five Gulf states and relevant federal agencies[76] ($1.6 billion is available, but less than $200 million is allocated to projects). The Council selects from projects submitted by these members.[77] Projects are focused on ecological restoration.[78]

The RESTORE Act requires the Council to incorporate a Gulf Coast Ecosystem Restoration Task Force strategy into project planning and selection; develop a comprehensive plan for restoring the Gulf Coast; and develop a funded priorities list (FPL) of projects and programs selected for funding, which is updated as more funding becomes available.[79] Each component includes general climate and environmental justice considerations.[80] Additionally, NEPA review is required for Council projects, which incorporates environmental justice analysis.[81] In December 2015, the initial FPL described the first $140 million of projects proposed for funding.[82]

---

74. RESTORE ACT DIRECT COMPONENT GUIDANCE, *supra* note 70.

75. *See* ENVIRONMENTAL LAW INSTITUTE, THE RESTORE ACT & NEPA (2014), http://eli-ocean.org/wp-content/blogs.dir/6/files/RESTORE-and-NEPA.pdf.

76. RESTORE Act, Pub. L. No. 112-141, §1603.

77. *Id.*

78. *Id.*

79. *Id.*

80. *See, e.g.,* GULF COAST ECOSYSTEM RESTORATION COUNCIL, INITIAL COMPREHENSIVE PLAN: RESTORING THE GULF COAST'S ECOSYSTEM AND ECONOMY 11 (2013) ("It also includes protecting and conserving ecosystems so they can continue to reduce impacts from tropical storms and other disasters, support robust economies, and assist in mitigating and adapting to the impacts of climate change.").

81. RESTORE Act & NEPA, *supra* note 75.

82. RESTORE COUNCIL, RESOURCES AND ECOSYSTEMS SUSTAINABILITY, TOURIST OPPORTUNITIES, AND REVISED ECONOMIES OF THE GULF COAST STATES ACT (RESTORE ACT) INITIAL FUNDED PRIORITIES

The Council has taken a proactive approach in soliciting engagement from the public and incorporating climate justice concerns into projects. Prior to FPL drafting, the Council hosted meetings to get ideas about restoration. After the draft FPL was released, the Council incorporated comments into its approach to restoration.[83] Before the next FPL is drafted, the Council has pledged to host sessions that review lessons learned and chart a path forward based on public input. Moreover, each project description includes the life of the activity, with many describing environmental justice considerations over time, sea-level rise, and extreme weather event impacts.[84]

Though climate justice appears to be at the forefront of the Council's considerations, the weight given to climate change and environmental justice in project selection is unclear. Additionally, the criteria that Council members (including Gulf states) employ to select projects for submission varies.

Pot three is the spill impact component, which directs 30% of funds to the five Gulf states based on impacts from the oil spill[85] ($1.6 billion available). Like pot one, projects can be ecological or economic in nature.[86] Under pot three, the states have substantial discretion in choosing funded projects to include in their expenditure plans, and it is unclear how each plan will consider climate justice. Most likely, project selection and engagement will closely mirror pot one, with engagement opportunities before and after plan drafting.

Pots four and five are research-oriented,[87] directing $266 million combined to research efforts. While the funding can play a role in designing tools for planning, mitigation, and adaptation, most of the projects are science-focused and unlikely to address climate justice directly.[88]

III. Climate Justice in Gulf Restoration

Like many important governance principles, climate justice is an easy value to talk about generally, but a hard concept to implement in specific manage-

---

LIST (2015), https://www.restorethegulf.gov/sites/default/files/FPL_forDec9Vote_Errata_04-07-2016.pdf [hereinafter INITIAL FPL].

83. *See id.* at 7.
84. *See id.* at 64.
85. RESTORE Act, Pub. L. No. 112-141, §1603.
86. *Id.*
87. *Id.* at §§1604, 1605.
88. In addition to the restoration processes, there are numerous existing programs at the local, state, and federal levels. *See* Environmental Law Institute, *Building Bridges* (summarizing plans and programs at the federal, state, and local level), http://eli-ocean.org/gulf/building-bridges/ (last visited Aug. 22, 2016). Many of these programs have separate avenues for incorporating climate justice into Gulf restoration, but they are beyond the scope of this analysis.

ment decisions. Gulf restoration provides an opportunity to pursue the hard actions that actualize the easy ideals.

The Gulf region has a history of injustice with a legacy that reverberates to present inequality.[89] That inequality and injustice was felt in the aftermath of Hurricane Katrina,[90] and it was felt again after the *Deepwater Horizon* oil spill.[91] Now, though, there is an unprecedented chance to reverse course and instill climate justice values into environmental decisionmaking in the Gulf region. Because it is unprecedented, Gulf restoration does not have a preexisting structure with its own status quo. Thus, there is less inertia to overcome in moving toward climate justice.

As a threshold requirement, climate justice in the Gulf necessitates that coastal communities have a meaningful voice in the decisions that affect them.[92] For that voice to be meaningful, the restoration processes must be transparent and accountable, with decisionmaking based on public participation, rather than simply checking the box of the legal requirements described in the previous section. By integrating the law on the books with how the restoration processes work in practice, it is possible to encourage a climate justice-based framework for engagement that empowers communities, rather than a framework that silences them.

Of the $16.7 billion allocated to Gulf restoration through the three main processes discussed above, just over $1 billion has been obligated to projects. The current trickle of funds has some success stories that can illustrate how climate justice can reinforce coastal resilience in the Gulf region by integrating the voices of coastal communities. By examining those success stories, lessons can be institutionalized when that trickle becomes a deluge over the next decade.

A.   NRDA Success Stories

Funds were allocated to Gulf restoration relatively soon after the spill. Several of the early restoration efforts serve as examples of climate justice in action. When the first restoration plans were announced (there have now been five plans),[93] the NRDA trustees were taking a step into the unknown. Early restoration had no precedent. Now, many years later with only 10% of NRDA

---

89.   *See* McDougall, *supra* note 13.
90.   *Id.*
91.   Osofsky et al., *supra* note 24.
92.   Roberts, *supra* note 11.
93.   *See* Gulf Spill Restoration, Early *Restoration*, http://www.gulfspillrestoration.noaa.gov/restoration/early-restoration/ (last visited Aug. 22, 2016).

funds spent, early restoration set some of its own precedent. Those experiences help show how climate justice can be driven by public participation.

A pending lawsuit demonstrates the conflict inherent in NRDA that drives the need for climate justice approaches to restoration.[94] Under NRDA, funds can be used to restore resources harmed by the spill or to compensate for the loss of use of resources due to the spill.[95] That first prong leads to many of the projects associated with coastal resilience, like barrier island restoration or living shorelines. The second prong, also called "lost recreational use" projects, can be used for a variety of economic purposes, like boat ramps or park facilities. In 2014, the NRDA trustees proposed an $85 million lost recreational use project to construct a convention center in Gulf State Park in Gulf Shores, Alabama.[96] Outrage ensued.

At the heart of the outrage was a concern that the convention center stretched the intent of the Oil Pollution Act's "loss of use" provision. The Gulf Restoration Network (a nonprofit based in Louisiana) filed a lawsuit contending that the project violated both the Oil Pollution Act and NEPA.[97] In 2016, the court ruled that the project could not proceed without further environmental review, effectively scrapping the project for now.[98]

While the convention center is just one battle about the use of less than 1% of total NRDA funds, it could play a monumental role in Gulf restoration. The NRDA trustees received countless comments deriding the use of funds for a convention center.[99] In public meetings, the outcry was even more pronounced. A cacophony of voices spoke out about the use of funds (and the interpretation of NRDA it embodied). The NRDA trustees seem to have heard those voices.

Prior to the convention center lawsuit and outrage, 33.7% of early restoration funds went to lost recreational use projects.[100] Afterward, just 5.6% of early restoration funds were used for the same purpose.[101] And most signifi-

---

94. Complaint for Declaratory and Injunctive Relief, Gulf Restoration Network v. Jewell et al. (Oct. 23, 2014), http://www.healthygulf.org/sites/healthygulf.org/files/1_grn_complaint_10-23-2014.pdf.

95. 33 U.S.C. §2702(b).

96. NRDA Trustees, Final Programmatic and Phase III Early Restoration Plan and Early Restoration Programmatic Environmental Impact Statement 11–55 (2014), http://www.gulfspillrestoration.noaa.gov/wp-content/uploads/ERP-PEIS-Part-3-Chapter-10-through-Chapter-11.pdf.

97. Opinion and Order at 2–3, Gulf Restoration Network v. Jewell et al. (Feb. 15, 2016), https://www.scribd.com/doc/299485884/Judge-blocks-BP-funds-for-Gulf-State-Park-Lodge.

98. Id. at 14–20.

99. NRDA Trustees, Final Programmatic and Phase III Early Restoration Plan and Early Restoration Programmatic Environmental Impact Statement 13–66 (2014), http://www.gulfspillrestoration.noaa.gov/wp-content/uploads/ERP-PEIS-Part-6-Chapter-13.pdf.

100. See Restoration Projects Database, supra note 40.

101. Id.

cantly, for the remaining $7.9 billion to flow through the NRDA process, less than 2% will go to such projects.[102]

While it is impossible to trace a line from public engagement to substantive change in most instances, it is safe to say that the voices of the public were heard. In the courtroom and in meetings, voices spoke for climate resilience for the Gulf Coast, instead of more of the same for the region. The NRDA trustees were listening, and Gulf restoration will likely include billions more dollars dedicated to coastal resilience because of it.

B.   NFWF Success Stories

NFWF has fewer opportunities for engagement built directly into the process. Nevertheless, NFWF has been proactive about seeking public input, and has overcome the process hurdles by creating projects that take planning to the people.

Thus far, there are two strategic planning projects—one in Mississippi[103] and one in Florida.[104] Both are designed to spark community conversations about how to use restoration funds to achieve the goals of coastal communities. From those conversations, similar themes have emerged: use the funds for coastal resilience, support community development and adaptation, and focus on coordinated restoration across geographic areas.[105]

In those two states, the projects are designed to give a voice to the people, supporting climate justice in future projects. In Alabama, Louisiana, and Texas, however, there are no analogous projects to open up a somewhat closed process. However, in each state, NFWF seems to be listening to the concerns of coastal communities. In general, project announcements are met with approval from the public, rather than push-back. Moving forward, though, more can be done to ensure that NFWF funds are spent in a way that is transparent and accountable, based on public input.

C.   RESTORE Act Success Stories

At its best, the RESTORE Act can feel like a maze with a difficult but rewarding solution. At its worst, it can feel like a set of M.C. Escher stairs,

102. Consent Decree, *supra* note 27, app. 2; *PDARP*, *supra* note 38, ch. 5.
103. NFWF, Mississippi Coastal Restoration Plan (2014), http://www.nfwf.org/gulf/Documents/ms-coastal-restoration-plan.pdf.
104. NFWF, Florida Gulf Environmental Benefit Fund Restoration Strategy (2015), http://www.nfwf.org/gulf/Documents/fl-restoration%20planning-15oc.pdf.
105. *See* Mississippi Department of Environmental Quality, Mississippi Coastal Restoration Plan (2015), http://msrestoreteam.com/NFWFPlan2015/.

forever winding around and impossible to understand. The problem many people see with RESTORE is that it is essentially five processes—one for each funding pot described above. Each process has different entry points and goals. Thus, each process requires a new set of strategies for engagement, which can stress the capacity and patience of people who are not involved with oil spill restoration on a day-to-day basis.

While there is a risk that complexity presents a barrier to climate justice, there have been success stories that demonstrate the opportunity that exists if the processes can be simplified to encourage engagement. A positive example of front-end participation (rather than reacting to an announcement, as in the NRDA example above) is the initial list of projects proposed by the RESTORE Council under pot two.[106] The list selected $140 million worth of projects for the first tranche of funding.[107] The project ideas came from Council members, which included the Gulf states.[108] However, going upstream from the approved projects to the lists submitted by the states (the headwaters), then from the state lists to the genesis of the idea in the state project portals,[109] reveals the source. Often, many project elements were suggested by community members expressing concern about coastal resilience in the place they call home.[110] Participation led to projects that support the community voice, buttressing restoration that is based on climate justice principles.

The RESTORE Council provides other apt examples as well. For example, in the initial list of projects, special emphasis was given to workforce development for local communities.[111] Adapting to climate change—like Gulf restoration generally—requires skilled laborers, and the RESTORE Council listened to suggestions to build employment opportunities into restoration design. The RESTORE Council recognized that achieving climate justice will require efforts that combat economic disparity while also strengthening coastal resilience.

On the flip side of the engagement coin are some of the multiyear implementation plans under pot one of the RESTORE Act. Of the 11 plans approved so far, five did not receive any public comments, even though such

---

106. *See* INITIAL FPL, *supra* note 82.
107. *Id.*
108. *See* Gulf Coast Ecosystem Restoration Council, *Council-selected Restoration Component Proposals and Context Reports*, https://www.restorethegulf.gov/release/2015/03/12/council-selected-restoration-component-proposals-and-context-reports (last visited Aug. 22, 2016).
109. *See, e.g.*, RESTORE Mississippi, *Review Submitted Project Ideas*, http://www.restore.ms/review-submitted-project-ideas-2/ (last visited Aug. 22, 2015).
110. *See id.*
111. *See, e.g.*, INITIAL FPL, *supra* note 82, at 254 (describing the Conservation Corps Partnerships, which "will establish a regional workforce-training program to benefit local communities and support long-term Gulf coast restoration implementation").

comments can influence where tens of millions of dollars will go.[112] While these projects could support coastal resilience, there is a concern that lack of engagement will diminish transparency and accountability, which could reinforce the status quo in environmental decisionmaking. And if the general history of Gulf environmental management is any indication, the status quo may not support climate justice principles.

IV.   Integrating Climate Justice Into Gulf Restoration

Climate justice in the Gulf requires advocates that can break the status quo of environmental management in the region. Those advocates can come from within governance institutions and funding entities (i.e., the Council or NFWF) or from outside (i.e., communities, nongovernmental organizations, other engaged citizens). The strategies that have been effective thus far depend on the category at issue.

A.   Governance Institutions and Funding Entities

It is essential not to paint Gulf restoration as an adversarial process. In fact, most of the people working in the Gulf have the same goals—long-term, sustainable restoration that benefits the region's ecosystems and communities. Within governance institutions and funding entities, many of the successes of integrating climate justice thus far have come from those shared goals. Failings, meanwhile, usually come from inadequate legal or institutional structure rather than personal animus toward climate justice principles.

1.   Climate Justice Through NRDA Trustees

For example, the NRDA process was shrouded by the threat of litigation until October 2015, when the BP Consent Decree was announced. As a result, much of what was happening was subject to confidentiality requirements, and the public could not engage. However, despite that obstacle, the NRDA trustees seemed eager to engage when possible, with a staffer dedicated to public outreach and many public meetings. In addition, the trustees set up advanced mapping tools to show the public where projects were taking place, what stage they were in, and what their goals were.[113]

---

112. U.S. Department of the Treasury, *RESTORE Act: Direct Component, supra* note 73 (providing links to accepted plans).

113. Gulf Spill Restoration, *Early Restoration Project Atlas,* http://www.gulfspillrestoration.noaa.gov/restoration/early-restoration/early-restoration-projects-atlas/ (last visited Aug. 22, 2016).

Although efforts were made, as discussed above in relation to the convention center lawsuit,[114] most of the discord thus far has resulted from
what some perceive as an insular and deceptive process for approving some
of the early restoration projects. Projects were announced and subject to
public comment, but rarely altered in any way based on public input.[115]
Notably, the process for early restoration (which is now complete) was different from the process used for the remainder of the funds.[116] In early
restoration, BP and the trustees had to unanimously agree to fund each
project,[117] which likely introduced a dynamic of compromise in order to
move forward.

With the rest of the funds, BP is not involved, and unanimity among all
of the trustees is not required. Instead, projects will be determined by Trustee
Implementation Groups, which usually consist of representatives from the
state where the project is taking place and federal agencies.[118] Moreover, the
funds are allocated in the PDARP to specific project types.[119] Therefore, the
next phase of NRDA will likely center on how goals are reached (i.e., how
to restore bird populations), rather than what goals to pursue (i.e., recreation
versus habitat).

Although the general funding structure is decided, it is essential that the
remainder of the NRDA process is transparent and accountable. Agencies
in the Trustee Implementation Groups should make their activities open,
and projects should be subject to more than the legally obligated comment
period. Simultaneously, NRDA trustees' admirable efforts to display project
locations and outcomes should continue. Climate justice should be a consideration in all project types when it is applicable.

2.   Climate Justice Through NFWF

Unlike NRDA and the RESTORE Act, NFWF is not subject to NEPA
because it is not a federal actor. Therefore, one of the primary avenues for
engagement built into the legal system is not available for NFWF projects.
In lieu of public participation requirements, it is essential that NFWF proac-
tively engage with the public.

---

114. *See supra* note 97 and accompanying text.
115. *See* NRDA TRUSTEES, FINAL PROGRAMMATIC AND PHASE III EARLY RESTORATION PLAN, *supra* note
    99, ch. 13 (describing no substantive changes based on public comments).
116. *See supra* note 37 and accompanying text.
117. Framework for Early Restoration Addressing Injuries Resulting From the Deepwater Horizon Oil
    Spill, *supra* note 37.
118. *PDARP, supra* note 38, ch. 8.
119. *Id.* ch. 5.

Thus far, that engagement has occurred through consultations with state agencies that help to determine projects, along with informal outreach by NFWF staff in the form of webinars and meetings. In addition, NFWF is partnering with both state agencies and nongovernmental organizations like the Nature Conservancy to implement projects,[120] which provides an indirect link to public input. As mentioned above, NFWF is also funding projects that go directly to coastal communities to help determine project priorities.

Moving forward, NFWF should implement the priorities described by communities in Florida and Mississippi. In addition, it should consider other similar projects in Alabama, Louisiana, and Texas. Absent those sorts of projects, it should continue to try to solicit public input through informal means. After project approval, NFWF should consider setting up an apparatus to solicit feedback, even if it is not required by law.

3.   Climate Justice Through the RESTORE Act

The RESTORE Act's integration of climate justice depends on the funding pot at issue. For pots one and three, funds are going directly to the states (and local governments in Florida and Louisiana).[121] The legal requirement is for a comment window after project plans are decided.[122] Some of these project plans already have fallen through the cracks, and received no comments at all.

Some states and local governments are actively soliciting proposals and public input through RESTORE Act meetings.[123] These meetings provide an avenue for coastal communities to have their voices heard. However, the extent to which comments are considered and public input has a meaningful impact is primarily dependent on the capacity of decisionmakers within each state and local government entity. Some, like Jim Muller (the RESTORE Act coordinator for Bay County, Florida), are doing a particularly admirable job. Muller provides constant updates on Bay County's website, in addition to linking with other Florida counties to keep coastal residents apprised of Gulf restoration on both the local and statewide scales.[124]

---

120. *See, e.g.*, NFWF, Galveston Bay Sustainable Oyster Reef Restoration (2015) (including partners The Nature Conservancy, the Galveston Bay Foundation, and the Texas Parks & Wildlife Department), http://www.nfwf.org/gulf/Documents/tx-galveston%20oyster-15.pdf.
121. RESTORE Act, Pub. L. No. 112-141, §1603.
122. *Id.*
123. *See* Bay County, Florida, *The RESTORE Act and Bay County, Florida* (listing engagement opportunities), http://www.co.bay.fl.us/restore/index.php (last visited Aug. 22, 2016).
124. *See id.* Mr. Muller has maintained a status report that he emails to all Gulf Coast counties in Florida.

In the coming years, it is essential that participation requirements in pots one and three are not viewed as a box-check, but as a meaningful part of project design, selection, and implementation. Much of that will be based on the capacity and discretion of politicians and government personnel in the Gulf states. In addition, opportunities should be publicized openly, and not buried in hidden niches of government websites. A cross-jurisdiction portal could provide an option to consolidate participation opportunities.

For pot two, the RESTORE Council has gone beyond statutory requirements to support climate justice in Gulf restoration. In addition to the examples above, Council staff have readily engaged with the public in a way that is open, transparent, and inclusive. Most recently, the Council launched a 360-degree review process that aims to find out how operations can be improved moving forward.[125] The review is based on informal discussions over meetings and webinars, designed to provide a meaningful voice to citizens and groups.[126] In addition, the Council is funding monitoring projects that will help display the progress of restoration over time, increasing transparency and accountability.[127] And perhaps most significantly, the Council is leveraging funds by partnering with local groups to bring projects into the coastal communities with additional resources than would be available from the RESTORE Act alone.[128]

Given the time and effort that it takes to listen to the voices of coastal communities, it is important that the positive efforts of the Council are supported. The Council is a federal agency, and political winds could shift. Precedent that is started now should be built upon in the coming years and decades.

B.   Nongovernmental Organizations and the Public

In the immediate aftermath of the spill, outrage flowed from all corners of the world just as the oil spewed from the well. Over time, the outrage became less pronounced generally, but specific pockets of advocates continued the fight. Often, the advocates built upon existing coalitions that began in response to environmental injustice in the wake of Hurricane Katrina.[129] These networks of groups and citizens that are fighting for Gulf restoration

---

125. Email From RESTORE Council Staff to Many Recipients (Mar. 16, 2016) (on file with author).
126. *Id.*
127. RESTORE COUNCIL, GULF-WIDE FOUNDATIONAL INVESTMENT: COUNCIL MONITORING AND ASSESSMENT PROGRAM DEVELOPMENT (2015), https://www.restorethegulf.gov/sites/default/files/FPL_FS_K1_GW%20Monitoring%20and%20Assessment%20v11.15.15.pdf.
128. INITIAL FPL, *supra* note 82, at 19 (describing leveraging greater than $1 billion).
129. *See* Gulf Future Coalition, *Homepage*, http://www.gulffuture.org/ (last visited Aug. 22, 2016).

based on climate justice principles have three primary modes of action: litigation, policy advocacy, and supporting transparency and accountability.

1.   Litigation

Nongovernmental organizations like the Gulf Restoration Network, Ocean Conservancy, the Environmental Defense Fund, and Earthjustice have been at the forefront of using litigation as part of a broader strategy to integrate climate justice into restoration. As described above, the Gulf Restoration Network and Earthjustice led a successful lawsuit to contest an $85 million convention center under NRDA.[130] That lawsuit could have played a role in the increased proportion of funds for coastal resilience projects later in the process. Outside of NRDA, NFWF, and the RESTORE Act, legal actions have addressed marine wildlife issues related to oil and gas drilling in the Gulf of Mexico[131] and economic damages from the oil spill,[132] among many other issues.

The threat of litigation also could play a role. These engaged organizations and others could file suit related to decisions that do not support climate justice, which helps determine how legal mandates are implemented under the restoration processes.

2.   Policy Advocacy

Climate justice in Gulf restoration has numerous policy advocates, from nongovernmental organizations to foundations that support advocacy to private citizens. One particular policy advocate fighting for climate justice in the Gulf is Colette Pichon Battle, executive director of the Gulf Coast Center for Law & Policy.[133] Battle argues that supporting climate justice is the way to fight economic inequality and environmental degradation.[134] She works to

---

130. Dennis Pillion, *Court Blocks Use of BP Restoration Funds for Gulf State Park Convention Center*, AL.COM, Feb. 16, 2016, http://www.al.com/news/index.ssf/2016/02/court_blocks_use_of_bp_restora.html.

131. *See, e.g.*, Letter from Michael Jasny, Senior Policy Analyst, Natural Resources Defense Council, to Ken Salazar et al., Re: Notice of Intent to Pursue Legal Action for Violations of the Endangered Species Act and the Marine Mammal Protection Act in Connection With Unauthorized Take of Marine Mammals Related to Offshore Oil and Gas Activities in the Gulf of Mexico (Feb. 9, 2011), http://www.biologicaldiversity.org/campaigns/ocean_noise/pdfs/NOI_letter_re_GOM_activities_Feb11.pdf.

132. *See, e.g.*, Order and Judgment Granting Final Approval of Economic and Property Damages Settlement and Confirming Certification of the Economic and Property Damages Settlement Class, *In re* Oil Spill by the Oil Rig "Deepwater Horizon" in the Gulf of Mexico, on April 20, 2010 (Dec. 21, 2012), http://www.lieffcabraser.com/pdf/Order-and-Judgment-Granting-Final-Approval-of-the-Economic-and-Property-Damages-Settlement-Agreement.pdf.

133. Gulf Coast Center for Law & Policy, *Homepage*, http://gcclp.org/ (last visited Aug. 22, 2016).

134. Webinar summary, *supra* note 5.

ensure that restoration not only considers vulnerable communities, but emanates from these communities as well.[135] The organization is multifaceted, working with decisionmakers and community members in everything from public comments to planning. Battle also organized the Gulf South Rising coalition, with the motto, "The Seas Are Rising and So Are We."[136] Gulf South Rising "demands a just transition away from extractive industries, discriminatory policies, and unjust practices that hinder equitable disaster recovery and impede the development of sustainable communities."[137] It achieves those goals through community organization, convening, and movement-building, among other things.

Battle's work is a tour de force, encompassing numerous advocacy strategies. Other individuals and organizations utilize similarly diverse strategies. A non-exhaustive list of strategies are: submitting project proposals through the restoration processes, commenting through formal opportunities, engaging with decisionmakers at the local, state, and federal levels, convening people and organizations, campaigning for political candidates, and educating communities and decisionmakers. One advocacy option that was discussed but has not been used in Gulf restoration is developing citizen advisory groups within the processes. After the Exxon Valdez oil spill, these groups played a role in coastal restoration,[138] and they could be a part of the Gulf's future as well.

Other significant pieces of the advocacy puzzle are foundations and funding organizations that support climate justice. Over the coming decades, similar investments of time, energy, and money are needed to support the voices of coastal communities in Gulf restoration.

3. Transparency and Accountability

Gulf restoration's complexity and expansiveness introduce a risk that climate justice will get steamrolled by the momentum of so many moving parts. Groups like the Gulf of Mexico Alliance, Sea Grant Colleges, and the Trust for Public Land are focused on tracking opportunities for engagement, summarizing what is happening, and monitoring implementation.

Transparency and accountability are important at every stage of restoration. Before restoration begins, it is essential to know when and where there

---

135. *Id.*
136. Gulf South Rising, *Homepage*, http://www.gulfsouthrising.org/ (last visited Aug. 22, 2016).
137. *Id.*
138. *See* Christina Marshall Santarpio, *From Lapdog to Watchdog: Giving Citizens a Voice in Monitoring the Oil Industry Through RCACs*, 40 B.C. L. Rev. 297, 299 (2013).

are opportunities to get involved. Effective actions so far have been bulletin boards of participation opportunities[139] and handbooks on how to engage.[140] During restoration, it is important that decisions are not made in a vacuum, but in the open air. Groups are tracking what is happening and when decisions are being made,[141] allowing the public to decide whether restoration is being carried out in an effective manner. After restoration, monitoring and maintenance rely on a comprehensive understanding of where restoration is happening and what its effects are for the people and places of the Gulf. Maps, research projects, and reports will be especially important as hundreds more projects are approved in the coming years.[142]

Together, groups and individuals are working to influence Gulf restoration from outside the restoration processes. Achieving climate justice requires everyone—from decisionmakers to nongovernmental organizations to engaged citizens—to stay engaged and support restoration based on resilience principles.

Conclusion: Fast-Tracking Climate Justice

This chapter reviewed the landscape of coastal resilience in the Gulf Coast region and the potential for climate justice through restoration processes stemming from the *Deepwater Horizon* oil spill. Climate justice is not explicitly written into restoration laws, regulations, and policies. Reactive efforts to establish substantive climate justice rights through legislation or lawsuits could possibly be effective, but it is essential to recognize the existing procedural opportunities. Proactive procedural protections may be more effective at promoting climate justice in the long term because they utilize the legal framework and institutional capacity that is already in place. Litigation, policy advocacy, and public participation could help instill climate justice values into environmental decisionmaking for the Gulf Coast. In the process, these procedural protections could help shift the narrative for the region away from a legacy of environmental injustice.

The *Deepwater Horizon* oil spill occurred more than six years ago. Six years is a long time—long enough that most people not engaged with the Gulf

---

139. *See* Environmental Law Institute, *Public Participation Bulletin Board*, http://eli-ocean.org/gulf/the-bulletin-board/ (last visited Aug. 22, 2016).
140. *See* Environmental Law Institute, *Gulf Restoration Educational Materials*, http://eli-ocean.org/gulf/educational-resources/ (last visited Aug. 22, 2016).
141. *See* Environmental Law Institute, *Where Are We Now?*, http://eli-ocean.org/gulf/updates/ (last visited Aug. 22, 2016).
142. *See* Deepwater Horizon Project Tracker, *Homepage*, http://www.dwhprojecttracker.org/ (last visited Aug. 22, 2016).

would probably think restoration was nearly complete. In fact, restoration is just beginning. The legal processes to determine funding moved slowly and the scientific analysis to determine damages moved slowly. But now that the BP Consent Decree is final and all of the money is on the table, restoration is going to move fast. By understanding the law and policy of Gulf restoration, it is possible that climate justice also gets put on the fast track for the entire region. And if the opportunity is not seized, there is a chance that climate justice gets left in the dust.

Chapter 9

Justice in an Unconventional World: First Nations' Treaty Rights and Procedural Climate Justice in Alberta's Oil Sands Region

Cameron S.G. Jefferies *

Introduction

Canada is at a crucial juncture for both environmental law and First Nations[1] relations. With respect to environmental law, Canada's retreat from science-

* *The author gratefully acknowledges Heather Parker for her able and enthusiastic research assistance. Ms. Parker graduated from the Willamette University College of Law in May 2016.*

1.   Section 35 of the Constitution Act, 1982, *being* Schedule B to the Canada Act, 1982, ch. 11 (U.K.) (Constitution Act) defines "aboriginal peoples of Canada" as "Indian, Inuit and Métis." This definition is controversial as it incorporates language from the long-standing and intensely colonial Indian Act, which has been used by the federal government for the registration of status-Indians, for benefit determination, and also individual and community marginalization and disenfranchisement. In this chapter, the term "First Nation" will be used, recognizing that Aboriginal and indigenous are also frequently used. The Inuit (Canada's northern Aboriginal peoples) and Métis (individuals of both Aboriginal and European heritage) are not the focus of this chapter.

based precautionary decisionmaking and ecosystem-based management under Prime Minister Stephen Harper's federal Conservative government (2006–2015) has been well described and critiqued.[2] In addition to sweeping amendments to long-standing federal statutes, deep budget cuts to environmental agencies and research funds, and the abolition of the national environmental advisory board, the Conservative government's regression and stagnation was particularly pronounced in the area of climate change law and policy. Internationally, Canada became the first nation to withdraw its ratification of the Kyoto Protocol,[3] further cementing its reputation as a climate laggard.[4] Domestically, and despite broad federal regulatory powers afforded by virtue of greenhouse gases (GHGs) being listed as "toxic substances" under the Canadian Environmental Protection Act, 1999,[5] Canadian emissions continued to rise through 2014, driven largely by oil and gas sector emissions, which were exempted from Canada's sectoral response.

Turning to Aboriginal relations, Canada continues to atone for many colonial and post-colonial wrongs, and this chapter's climate justice discussion must be understood within this broader context. Particularly noteworthy injustices include: (1) the custodial state-sponsored religious residential school program that ran from 1880 until the mid-1990s. Driven by a Eurocentric worldview of culture and civilization, the residential school program forcibly separated Aboriginal children from their families and communities to "kill the Indian in the child."[6] The abuses suffered by many of the 150,000 children who attended the residential school system produced intergenerational trauma, precipitated the largest class action settlement in Canadian history in 2007,[7] elicited a formal apology from then-Prime Minister Harper in 2008,[8] and spurred the creation of a Truth and Reconciliation Commission to initiate and pursue the healing process[9]; (2) the

---

2.   See Robert B. Gibson, *In Full Retreat: The Canadian Government's New Environmental Assessment Law Undoes Decades of Progress*, 30 Impact Assessment & Project Appraisal 179 (2012); Nigel Kinney, *Burning Down the House: Environmental Policy Dismantling by the Harper Government*, in The Harper Record: 2008–2015, at 337–47 (Teresa Healy & Stuart Trew eds., 2015); Chris Turner, The War on Science: Muzzled Scientists and Wilful Blindness in Stephen Harper's Canada (Nancy Flight et al. eds., 2013).

3.   Kyoto Protocol to the United Nations Framework Convention on Climate Change, Dec. 10, 1997, 37 I.L.M. 22.

4.   See Cameron Jefferies, *Filling the Gaps in Canada's Climate Change Strategy: "All Litigation, All the Time. . ."?*, 38 Fordham Int'l L.J. 1372 (2015).

5.   Canadian Environmental Protection Act, 1999, S.C. 1999, ch. 33, §64.

6.   Truth and Reconciliation Commission of Canada, *About the Commission*, http://www.trc.ca/websites/trcinstitution/index.php?p=39 (last visited Aug. 22 2016.

7.   *Id.*

8.   *Id.*

9.   The Truth and Reconciliation Commission produced a final report in 2015. Titled Honouring the Truth, Reconciling for the Future (2015), this report provides an extensive history of these

disproportionate rate at which Aboriginal women and girls are murdered or disappear, as brought to light by Amnesty International's 2004 report, "Stolen Sisters: A Human Rights Response to Violence and Discrimination against Indigenous Women in Canada"[10]; (3) the heightened rate of suicide attempts and deaths amongst First Nations youth, as most recently exemplified at the Attawapiskat First Nation in northern Ontario where a state of emergency was declared for the community of 2,000 people after 28 suicide attempts occurred in March 2016, followed by 11 more on one day the following month[11]; and (4) the ongoing investigation into third world living conditions on many reserves, as exemplified by a clean drinking water crisis,[12] which the United Nations Committee on Economic, Social, and Cultural Rights (CESCR) called on Canada to rectify as recently as March 2016.[13] According to James Anaya, former special rapporteur on the rights of indigenous peoples, "Canada faces a continuing crisis when it comes to the situation of indigenous peoples of the country."[14] Moving forward, the *raison d'être* of enhanced Aboriginal relations and crisis resolution (and ideally prevention) must be the meaningful reconciliation of First Nations and non-First Nations peoples in our shared country.[15]

Two significant Canadian elections in 2015 have shifted official policy and rhetoric and promise meaningful reform of climate change law and First Nations relations. First, on May 5, 2015, the province of Alberta—home to the oil sands—voted out a Progressive Conservative government that had been in power for 44 consecutive years in favor of the social-democratic New Democratic Party (NDP) led by Premier Rachel Notley. Then, on October 20, 2015, the federal election replaced the Conservative government with a Liberal government, led by Prime Minister Justin Trudeau. Though it is

---

events and then offers a number of calls to action in the context of future reconciliation.

10. Stop Violence Against Women, Amnesty International, Stolen Sisters: A Human Rights Response to Violence and Discrimination Against Indigenous Women in Canada (2014).

11. *Attawapiskat: Four Things to Help Understand the Suicide Crisis*, The Globe & Mail, July 8, 2016, http://www.theglobeandmail.com/news/national/attawapiskat-four-things-to-help-understand-the-suicidecrisis/article29583059/.

12. Maya Basdeo & Lalita Bharadwaj, *Beyond Physical: Social Dimensions of the Water Crisis on Canada's First Nations and Considerations for Governance*, 23 Indigenous Pol'y J. 1 (2013); Lalita Bharadwaj, *Vulnerability of First Nations Communities in Canada to Environmental Degradation*, in Impact of Climate Change on Water and Health (Velma I. Grover ed., 2012); Joanne Levasseur & Jacques Marcoux, *Bad Water: "Third World" Conditions on First Nations in Canada*, CBC, Oct. 15, 2015, http://www.cbc.ca/news/canada/manitoba/bad-water-third-world-conditions-on-first-nations-in-canada-1.3269500.

13. *Concluding Observations on the Sixth Periodic Report of Canada*, U.N. Committee on Economic, Social, and Cultural Rights, U.N. Doc. E/C.12/CAN/CO/6 (2016).

14. *The Situation of Indigenous Peoples in Canada: Report of the Special Rapporteur on the Rights of Indigenous Peoples*, James Anaya, U.N. Human Rights Council, 27th Sess., Agenda Item 3, U.N. Doc. A/HRC/27/52/Add.2 (2014).

15. Tsilhqot'in Nation v. British Columbia, [2014] 2 S.C.R. 257, para. 82.

still early in the regime change, certain developments indicate that meaningful change is imminent. Federally, Prime Minister Trudeau's post-election mandate letter to the minister of indigenous and northern affairs declared: "No relationship is more important to me and to Canada than the one with Indigenous peoples."[16] Then, on May 9, 2016, Canada revoked its objector status to the United Nations Declaration on the Rights of Indigenous Peoples (UNDRIP)[17] and committed to implement its principles and enhance First Nations' participation in decisionmaking.[18] Alberta has also committed to utilizing UNDRIP to revamp and rebuild the federal government's relations with First Nations.[19]

In terms of repairing its international reputation and reforming its regulatory approach to climate law, Canada actively participated in the final push to the Paris Agreement and on April 22, 2016, signed the Agreement, reiterating its commitment to reducing, at a minimum, GHG emissions by 30% by 2030 as compared to 2005 levels.[20] The federal government has committed to creating a pan-Canadian climate change framework to coordinate federal, territorial, and provincial action.[21] Alberta has also revised its climate change strategy, largely in response to the recommendations contained in a commissioned climate leadership report.[22] Importantly, this report acknowledges that First Nations communities are the most directly affected by climate change and recommends the creation of "a defined process in which the government works directly with Aboriginal communities and traditional knowledge systems to ensure Treaty and other Aboriginal rights are understood and

16.   Letter from Justin Trudeau, Prime Minister of Canada, to Dr. Carolyn Bennett, Minister of Indigenous and Northern Affairs (undated mandate letter), http://pm.gc.ca/eng/minister-indigenous-and-northern-affairs-mandate-letter.

17.   United Nations Declaration on the Rights of Indigenous Peoples, G.A. Res. 61/295, U.N. GAOR, 61st Sess., U.N. Doc. A/RES/61/295 (2007), 46 I.L.M. 1013 (2007) [hereinafter UNDRIP].

18.   Brian Hill, *Canada Endorses United Nations Declaration on the Rights of Indigenous Peoples*, GLOBAL NEWS, May 11, 2016, http://globalnews.ca/news/2689538/canada-endorses-united-nations-declaration-on-the-rights-of-indigenous-peoples/.

19.   Letter from Rachel Notley, Premier of Alberta, to Government of Alberta Cabinet Ministers (July 7, 2015), http://indigenous.alberta.ca/documents/Premier-Notley-Letter-Cabinet-Ministers.pdf.

20.   *Adoption of the Paris Agreement*, UNFCC Conference of the Parties, 21st Sess., U.N. Doc. FCCC/CP/2015/10/Add.1 (Dec. 12, 2015), http://unfccc.int/files/home/application/pdf/paris_agreement. pdf (noting that the Paris Agreement has yet to be ratified by the requisite 55 States that account for approximately 55% of global emissions as is required to enter into force). There are legitimate concerns that this target does not meaningfully deviate from the previous Conservative government's voluntary reduction targets and that it does not accord with Prime Minister Trudeau's support for limiting global warming to 1.5°C. Further, a recent study suggests that Canada's emissions trajectory, even accounting for Alberta's new measures, will overshoot the 2030 target by 91 Mt. *See* DAVE SAWYER & CHRIS BATAILLE, STILL MINDING THE GAP: AN ASSESSMENT OF CANADA'S GREENHOUSE GAS REDUCTION OBLIGATIONS (2016).

21.   Government of Canada, *Canada's Way Forward on Climate Change*, http://www.climatechange.gc.ca/default.asp?lang=En&n=72F16A84-1 (last visited Aug. 22, 2016).

22.   ANDREW LEACH ET AL., CLIMATE LEADERSHIP: REPORT TO MINISTER (2015).

addressed as policies for climate solutions are refined and implemented."[23] To date, the NDP's strategy has committed to phasing out coal-fired electrical generation by 2030, introduced a consumer carbon levy on heating and transport fuels, capped allowable annual oil sands emissions at 100 Mt, and implemented measures to capture fugitive methane emissions.[24]

It is against this contextual and highly dynamic backdrop that this chapter analyzes one aspect of Canada's emergent climate justice discourse and proposes practical solutions that ought to figure prominently in Canada's new approach. This chapter introduces Canada's emergent climate justice movement by focusing on Alberta's First Nations communities that are geographically proximate to the oil sands deposits and, accordingly, most significantly and disproportionately impacted by their development and by Alberta's changing climate. This chapter focuses on the procedural dimension of climate justice in the context of the constitutional duty to consult First Nations communities when their rights may be impacted by government decisionmaking and industrial development and also as a dimension of the environmental assessment (EA) processes. Specifically, the chapter concludes that climate change law and policy reform coupled with bolstered commitments for further reconciliation with First Nations peoples should manifest as, or at a minimum promote, a just construction of constitutionally protected treaty rights held by those First Nations communities living in Alberta's oil sands region. This, in turn, lends itself to procedurally just and more robust climate decisionmaking that allows for meaningful participation by Canada's original inhabitants.

Part I of this chapter introduces Canada's emerging climate justice movement. Part II situates climate justice concerns within the context of oil sands development in northern Alberta. Part III critiques the constitutional duty to consult First Nations peoples and environmental assessment as two exist-

---

23. *Id.* at 87. Note that this recommendation comes at a time when the province is involved in ongoing litigation and policy reform.

24. Government of Alberta, *Climate Leadership Plan*, http://www.alberta.ca/climate-leadership-plan.cfm (last visited Aug. 22, 2016). *See also* Government of Alberta, *Oil Sands Advisory Group*, http://www.alberta.ca/oilsands-advisory-group.cfm (last visited Aug. 22, 2016). The government of Alberta recently appointed the Oil Sands Advisory Group (OSAG) to help guide implementation of its GHG reduction strategy. The group is "composed of members from industry, environmental organizations and Indigenous and non-Indigenous communities to advise government on the oil sands aspects of the Climate Leadership Plan and ensure that its initiatives are effective and widely supported." OSAG has three co-chairs. The industry co-chair is Dave Collyer, former president and chief executive officer of the Canadian Association of Petroleum Producers; the environmental nongovernmental organization co-chair is prominent environmental campaigner Tzepbora Berman; and the co-chair representing communities is Melody Lepine, a member of the Mikisew Cree First Nation. OSAG has their work cut out for them in reaching consensus on its recommended reduction strategies, but they are united by a common mandate so there is considerable optimism that this approach will yield positive results.

ing participatory avenues that can be enhanced through implementation of UNDRIP's core principle of "free, prior and informed consent."[25] Part IV concludes with recommendations to promote climate justice for First Nations in Canada.

I.   Canada's Emergent Climate Justice Movement

Climate justice exists at the nexus of climate science, human rights, sustainability and the right to develop, and intergenerational equity. Substantively, it acknowledges, describes, and responds to concerns that marginalized or disadvantaged peoples are disproportionately impacted by the consequences of a changing climate to which they have minimally or negligibly contributed.[26] Procedurally, climate justice considers whether the decisionmaking processes that inform climate negotiations and/or the promulgation of law and policy meaningfully engage and respond to the concerns of those same disproportionately impacted peoples.[27] The normative objective of climate justice is the redistribution of the costs and benefits of climate change, which demands both "fair treatment" and "meaningful involvement"[28] that recognizes different perspectives. Climate justice concerns are operative at all governance levels: international, national, and subnational. Climate justice has the potential to act as a strong driver of change; however, it is only now rooting itself in Canadian discourse.

In the United States, the Environmental Protection Agency is mandated to consider the "fair treatment and meaningful involvement of all people regardless of race, color, national origin, or income" throughout "the development, implementation, and enforcement of environmental laws, regulations, and policies."[29] In contrast, "Canada has no laws that address the concept of environmental justice—the fair and consistent distribution of environmental benefits and burden, without discrimination on the basis of socio-economic status, race, ethnic origin, or residence on an Aboriginal reserve."[30] In 2008,

25. UNDRIP, *supra* note 17. "Free, prior, and informed consent" is a requirement that recurs in numerous articles.
26. *See* Nathalie J. Chalifour, *Environmental Justice and the Charter: Do Environmental Injustices Infringe Sections 7 and 15 of the* Charter?, 28 J. ENVTL. L. & PRAC. 89, 95–98 (2015) (describing the different normative dimensions of the environmental justice movement).
27. Margaux J. Hall, *Advancing Climate Justice and the Right to Health Through Procedural Rights*, 16 HEALTH & HUM. RTS. 8, 9–10 (2014).
28. Dayna Nadine Scott, *The Networked Infrastructure of Fossil Fuel Capitalism: Implications of the New Pipeline Debates for Environmental Justice in Canada*, 43 REVUE GÉNÉRALE DE DROIT 11, 17–18 (2013).
29. U.S. Environmental Protection Agency, *Environmental Justice*, https://www.epa.gov/environmental-justice (last visited Aug. 22, 2016).
30. *See* Margot Venton & Kaitlyn Mitchell (EcoJustice), *A Dark Day for Environmental Justice in Canada*, HUFFINGTON POST, Jan. 29, 2015, http://www.huffingtonpost.ca/ecojustice/environmental-justice-

Prof. Michael Buzzelli suggested that Canada is at a "nascent stage of EJ discourse."[31] Fast-forward to 2016 and a staff lawyer at EcoJustice (Canada's only national environmental law charity) proffered that "[w]e are only now beginning an important discussion in Canada which recognizes that socio-economic status, race, and environmental health are interrelated concepts."[32] The relatively recent emergence of a Canadian discourse on environmental justice and climate justice and the absence of explicit recognition in existing laws must not be misconstrued as an absence of concern about these issues.

First Nations often bear a disproportionate share of environmental burdens. Aboriginal peoples in Canada suffer from the environmental contamination, decreased availability, and lower safety of traditional food due to the impact of climate change on ecosystems.[33] Communities in the Arctic have already begun to experience the health implications of climate change effects, such as the increased probability and severity of extreme weather events, and sea-level rise and associated coastal erosion.[34] The adverse environmental impacts of industrial activity on Aboriginal communities has also been observed. Numerous Aboriginal communities, including Aamjiwaang First Nation and Grassy Narrows First Nation in Ontario, Fort Chipewyan in Alberta, and Mi'kmaw communities in Nova Scotia, have expressed concerns with regard to contamination of their air, water, and soil, and have reported high rates of cancer and other illnesses in their communities.[35]

First Nations have also been at the forefront of grassroots efforts on climate justice. For example, the national Idle No More movement is "one of

---

canada_b_6547682.html.

31. MICHAEL BUZZELLI, ENVIRONMENTAL JUSTICE IN CANADA—IT MATTERS WHERE YOU LIVE 11 (2008).

32. Kaitlyn Mitchell & Zachary D'Onofrio, *Environmental Injustice and Racism in Canada: The First Step Is Admitting We Have a Problem*, 29 J. ENVTL. L. & PRAC. 305, 307 (2016).

33. *See generally* Nathalie J. Chalifour, *Bringing Justice to Environmental Assessment: An Examination of Kearl Oil Sands Joint Review Panel and the Health Concerns of the Community of Fort Chipewyan*, 21 J. ENVTL. L. & PRAC. 31 (2010) [hereinafter Chalifour, *Environmental Assessment*]; *see also* Mitchell & D'Onofrio, *supra* note 32, at 322 (citing Elaine M. Power, *Conceptualizing Food Security for Aboriginal People in Canada*, 99 CANADIAN J. PUB. HEALTH 95 (2008); SPEAKING FOR OURSELVES: ENVIRONMENTAL JUSTICE IN CANADA (Julian Agyeman et al. eds., 2009).

34. *See generally* James D. Ford et al., *Vulnerability to Climate Change in the Arctic: A Case Study From Arctic Bay, Canada*, 16 GLOBAL ENVTL. CHANGE 145 (2006); *see also* James D. Ford et al., *Climate Change Policy Responses for Canada's Inuit Population: The Importance of and Opportunities for Adaptation*, 20 GLOBAL ENVTL. CHANGE 177 (2010).

35. James D. Ford et al., *Vulnerability of Aboriginal Health Systems in Canada to Climate Change*, 20 GLOBAL ENVTL. CHANGE 668 (2010); Danya Scott, *Situating Sarnia: "Unimagined Communities" in the New National Energy Debate*, 25 J. ENVTL. L. & PRAC. 81 (2013); Isaac Luginaah & Kevin Smith, *Surrounded by Chemical Valley and "Living in a Bubble": The Case of the Aamjiwnaang First Nation, Ontario*, 53 J. ENVTL. PLAN. MGMT. 353 (2010); Deborah Jackson, *Scents of Place: The Dysplacement of a First Nation Community in Canada*, 113 AM. ANTHROPOLOGY 606 (2011); Ingrid R.G. Waldron, *Findings From the Series of Workshops in Whose Backyard? Exploring Toxic Legacies in Mi'kmaw and African Nova Scotian Communities*, 8 ENVTL. JUST. 1 (2015); PATRICIA SELLERS, HUMAN AND ECOLOGICAL HEALTH IN ASUBPEESCHOSEEWAGONG NETUM ANISHINABEK (2014).

the largest Indigenous mass movements in Canadian history" and began in late 2012 in protest to federal environmental law reforms that threatened "Indigenous sovereignty and environmental protections . . . . [and] the social and political landscape of Canada."[36] Idle No More has recently partnered with like-minded environmental groups and other First Nations organizations to propose the justice-based People's Climate Plan that, among other goals, advances First Nations sovereignty and reconciliation.[37] First Nations communities have also demonstrated a willingness to take the government to court over industrial development on traditional lands, proposed pipeline infrastructure, and the government's interpretation of constitutionally protected Aboriginal rights.[38] If the goal is to secure climate justice for Canada's First Nations communities, impacted First Nations both deserve and are prepared to occupy a more central role in the *ex ante* decisionmaking that will guide Canada's next iteration of climate change law and policy. The focus of the remainder of this chapter is how appreciable movement in this regard can be achieved in Alberta's oil sands region.

II.   Oil Sands, Treaty 8, and Climate Change

A.   The Oil Sands and Greenhouse Gas Emissions

Alberta's oil sands are the world's third largest proven oil reserve[39] and are found in three separate accumulations under northern Alberta's boreal forest: (1) the Peace River deposit, (2) the Athabasca deposit, and (3) the Cold Lake deposit. Together, the oil sands underlie some 54,000 mi^2 of land.[40] Bitumen (the technical term for the oily sand) is a high viscosity unconventional crude. It is recovered using open pit mining (for shallow deposits) or in situ steam-assisted gravity drainage (for deep deposits). Extracted bitumen requires some initial upgrading to reduce viscosity prior to being transported for further upgrading or international export. Prior to the oil and gas market sag of 2015/2016, oil sands production from some 120 active oil sands projects peaked at 2.3 million barrels per day in mid-2014.[41] The Canadian

---

36.   Idle No More, *The Story*, http://www.idlenomore.ca/story (last visited Aug. 22, 2016).
37.   People's Climate Plan, *Background*, http://peoplesclimate.ca/#principles (last visited Aug. 22, 2016).
38.   *See* Gitxaala Nation v. Canada, [2016] F.C.A. 187, where the Federal Court of Appeal quashed an Order in Council (federal Cabinet decision) to approve the controversial Northern Gateway pipeline connecting Alberta's oil sands to a Kitimat port terminal in British Columbia on the basis that the federal government failed to meaningfully consult First Nations.
39.   Alberta Energy, *About Oil Sands: Facts and Statistics*, http://www.energy.alberta.ca/oilsands/791. asp#Geography (last visited Aug. 22, 2016).
40.   *Id.*
41.   *Id.*

Association of Petroleum Producers forecasts a steady increase in oil sands production over the next 15 years with production reaching 4 million barrels per day in 2030.[42] This rate of development has significant implications for Canada's national carbon budget.

The government of Canada's most recent national GHG inventory was produced in accordance with the United Nations Framework Convention on Climate Change's (UNFCCC's) updated reporting guidelines and it tracks and estimates national emissions between 1990 and 2014. As of the end of 2014, Canada's total emissions were estimated at 732 Mt of carbon dioxide equivalent (CO^2-eq).[43] Canada's energy sector (including stationary combustion sources, transportation, and fugitive emissions) accounted for 594 Mt (81%) of these emissions.[44] To understand Alberta's contribution, consider that in 2014 only 4.15 of Canada's 35 million citizens (11.9%) lived in Alberta, but the province accounted for 37.4% (273.8 Mt) of Canada's total emissions.[45] Canada's recent commitment to reduce GHGs by 30% by 2030 compared to the 2005 baseline translates to a 524 Mt budget in 2030, which is a 208 Mt reduction.[46] This is an ambitious target that will require considerable regulatory and market-based innovation and it is appropriate to assume that achieving it demands overall reductions across the economy. Contrarily, the oil sands represent Canada's fastest growing emissions source. Environment Canada projects that "oil sands-related emissions" may increase from 64 Mt (2010) to 115 Mt in 2030, even in the face of significant gains in reducing emissions intensity.[47] The NDP's 100 Mt cap on oil sands emissions will likely prevent oil sands exploitation from reaching 115 Mt; however, even this cap facilitates considerable expansion.

Much of the political debate surrounding the short- and long-term future of oil sands development pertains to the construction of new pipeline infrastructure to get bitumen to west coast and/or east coast tidewater for export to China or India. Two pipeline projects—Enbridge's Northern Gateway pipeline and Kinder Morgan's Trans Mountain expansion—have received conditional approval by Canada's National Energy Board (NEB) and some political support, but political and legal obstacles remain. TransCanada's Energy East pipeline that would connect the oil sands to eastern Canadian

42. CANADIAN ASSOCIATION OF PETROLEUM PRODUCERS, THE FACTS ON: OIL SANDS 11 (2014/2015).
43. ENVIRONMENT AND CLIMATE CHANGE CANADA, NATIONAL INVENTORY REPORT 1990–2014: GREEN-HOUSE GAS SOURCES AND SINKS IN CANADA 3–11 (2016).
44. Id.
45. Id.
46. Government of Canada, Key Issues—Climate Change, https://www.canada.ca/en/environment-climate-change/briefing/key-issues-climate-change.html (last visited Aug. 22, 2016).
47. Id.

refineries and a port terminal in New Brunswick is even less along in the approval process as it is currently before the NEB. While much could be said about the substantive and procedural climate justice implications of these pipeline projects from the First Nations' perspective,[48] this analysis focuses on those First Nations communities within the Treaty 8 boundary in Alberta that are geographically proximate to oil sands development.

B.   *Treaty 8 and Climate Change*

From Canada's earliest colonial days, Great Britain and France signed treaties with First Nations peoples to facilitate European settlement, expand fur trading, develop strategic military partnerships, and memorialize different versions of "peace and friendship."[49] Post-Canadian Confederation in 1867 and the Crown's acquisition of the large swath of western and northern land previously held by the Hudson's Bay Company (and obviously occupied and utilized by Aboriginal peoples well before that time), European settlers continued to push west, new provinces were contemplated, and the Crown's treaty-making efforts focused on securing land surrender[50] from Aboriginal peoples in the prairies and the north. To this end, 11 numbered treaties were executed between the Crown and Aboriginal groups between 1871 and 1921.

Treaty 8 was signed in 1899 between Her Majesty the Queen and a number of Cree and Dene communities and is the largest of the land surrender treaties, covering some 325,000 mi^2 (which, for context, is approximately 50,000 mi^2 larger than Texas).[51] As the land surrender characterization suggests, Treaty 8 declares that "said Indians do hereby cede, release, surrender and yield up to the Government of the Dominion of Canada . . . . All their rights, titles and privileges whatsoever" held in the land.[52] In return, Her Majesty the Queen provided a number of financial incentives and material goods, land "reserves for such bands as desire reserves," and the guarantee that

> said Indians shall have the right to pursue their usual vocations of hunting, trapping and fishing *throughout the tract surrendered* as heretofore described,

---

48. *See* Kristen Mikadze, *Pipelines and the Changing Face of Public Participation*, 29 J. ENVTL. L. & PRAC. 83 (2016).
49. *See generally* INDIAN AND NORTHERN AFFAIRS CANADA, A HISTORY OF TREATY-MAKING IN CANADA (2010). Early Atlantic Canada treaties were referred to as "Peace and Friendship Agreements" as they were designed to reduce hostilities between colonizing powers and original inhabitants.
50. The extent of actual land "surrender" is contested as this calls into question the extent to which First Nations as original occupants construed land ownership in a similar manner to the Crown or settlers.
51. Mikisew Cree First Nation v. Canada (Minister of Canadian Heritage), [2005] 3 S.C.R. 388, para. 2.
52. Treaty No. 8 Made June 21, 1899 and Adhesions, Reports, Etc. (1966 reprint of 1899 original) [hereinafter Treaty 8].

subject to such regulations as may from time to time be made by the Government of Canada of the country . . . . and saving and excepting such tracts of land as may be required or taken up from time to time for settlement, mining, lumbering, trading or other purposes.[53]

By guaranteeing the right to hunt, fish, and trap throughout treaty lands, Treaty 8 affirms and protects a traditional way of life that is intimately connected to the land, nature, and the local environment. In 1982, the federal government constitutionalized and entrenched the reconciliation process and Aboriginal rights in §35 of the Constitution Act, 1982, which declares: "The existing aboriginal and treaty rights of the aboriginal peoples of Canada are hereby recognized and affirmed."[54]

The land area covered by Treaty 8 encompasses present-day northern Alberta, northeast British Columbia, northwest Saskatchewan, and limited southern portions of the Northwest Territories. There are 39 First Nations communities within Treaty 8, 23 of which are in Alberta. Each First Nation community has its own chief, council, and associated administrative structures. Treaty 8, as a whole, is represented by the Treaty 8 Tribal Association, which has a grand chief and its own administrative bodies. The Peace River and Athabasca oil sands deposits occur wholly within the traditional lands encompassed by Treaty 8 and many First Nations communities have been vocal in expressing their opposition to the rate and scale of development.[55] For example, prominent members from the Athabasca Chipewyan First Nation, Mikisew Cree First Nation, Fort McMurray First Nation, and Fort McKay First Nation have organized and opposed further oil sands development and its localized impacts.[56] Still, it must be acknowledged that the oil and gas industry employs nearly 2,000 Aboriginal people and that the money that has flowed to Aboriginal communities as a result of tribal oil ownership or venture partnership is in the billions of dollars.[57] This difficult

---

53. *Id.* (emphasis added).
54. Constitution Act, 1982, *being* Schedule B to the Canada Act, 1982, ch. 11 (U.K.). "Existing" refers to and affirms the fact that Aboriginal rights that were extinguished by the Crown through its declaration of sovereignty or statutory action prior to the provision of constitutional protection remain unavailable to the peoples that once exercised such rights.
55. The Cold Lake deposit occurs within Treaty 6 territory where the Beaver Lake Cree similarly contest future development. For a summary of Beaver Lake's ongoing litigation over the cumulative impacts of oil sands development in their traditional territory, see RAVEN, *Tar Sands Trial: Beaver Lake Cree vs Alberta and Canada*, http://raventrust.com/tar-sands-trial/ (last visited Aug. 22, 2016).
56. Shawn McCarthy, *Where Oil and Water Mix*, THE GLOBE & MAIL, Nov. 6, 2015, http://www.theglobeandmail.com/news/alberta/where-oil-and-water-mix-oil-sands-development-leaves-fort-mckays-indigenous-communitytorn/article27151333/; Indigenous Environmental Network, *Tar Sands*, http://www.ienearth.org/what-we-do/tar-sands/ (last visited Aug. 22, 2016).
57. Government of Canada, *Oil Sands: A Strategic Resource for Canada, North America and the Global Market*, http://publications.gc.ca/collections/collection_2011/rncan-nrcan/M164-4-5-1-2011-eng.

balancing of economic, environmental, and cultural considerations within Treaty 8's territory and framework underscores the difficulty in generalizing experiences across First Nation communities in this region. Despite being unified by shared constitutionally protected treaty rights, each community has its own political and ideological preferences as well as its own unique history of interaction with industry and government.

A second commonality affecting all of Treaty 8's First Nations communities is the region's changing climate, which has warmed by 1.4°C over the last century.[58] While the impacts of Canada's changing climate are not as well documented in Treaty 8 territory as they are in Canada's far north where changes to permafrost underlying northern boreal forest and the distribution and extent of sea ice are quite pronounced, scientific evidence is clear that demonstrable changes are occurring within boreal forest ecosystems. Moreover, spatiotemporal temperature changes to this region have been confirmed through historical and current tree-ring and pollen-based measurements,[59] while 20th century monitoring data coupled with general circulation models predict "an average warming of at least 2.0°C (relative to ca. 2000) seems very probable across the Canadian boreal zone by 2050: these temperatures would match the warmest 100-year periods estimate for the paleo reconstructions of the Holocene."[60] While some of the predicted changes associated with this temperature are potentially positive (i.e., boosted forest productivity resulting from increased precipitation and atmospheric CO_2), "many of the anticipated changes will be substantially negative for Canada's boreal ecosystems."[61] These impacts include: (1) a dramatic range expansion of pest insect species; (2) an increased risk of tree diseases; (3) an increased frequency and severity of both forest fires and storm weather; and (4) drought conditions in the southern boreal range (which includes Alberta).[62] Other studies report similar predictions, suggesting that the boreal forest region that covers

pdf (last visited Sept. 17, 2016). *See also* KEN COATES, FIRST NATIONS ENGAGEMENT IN THE ENERGY SECTOR IN WESTERN CANADA (2016). In this report prepared for the Indian Resource Council, Coates makes the case for more extensive First Nations' participation in the energy sector moving forward and describes the "thousands of Aboriginal people working in the industry, First Nations' equity investments in oil and gas fields, hundreds of Indigenous-owned service and supply companies, and long but typically successful negotiations of impact and benefit agreements with Indigenous companies."*Id.* at 4.

58.   RICHARD R. SCHNEIDER, ALBERTA'S NATURAL SUBREGIONS UNDER A CHANGING CLIMATE: PAST, PRESENT, AND FUTURE 28 (2013).

59.   David T. Price et al., *Anticipating the Consequences of Climate Change for Canada's Boreal Forest Ecosystems*, 21 ENVTL. REV. 322, 323–25 (2013).

60.   *Id.* at 328 (noting that this estimate accounts for recognized uncertainties such as positive and negative feedback responses).

61.   *Id.* at 354.

62.   *Id.*

Treaty 8 can also expect a decrease in river flow as a result of diminishing glaciers and snowpack in the Rocky Mountains,[63] and biodiversity in the boreal region is expected to decline as ecosystems shift (largely northward) and some species find themselves unable to respond.[64]

There is no doubt that ongoing and projected climatic changes within the boundaries of Treaty 8 will impact the ability of First Nations communities to practice their constitutionally protected treaty rights. The right to fish, hunt, trap, and gather on the land are only meaningful if the animals and their habitat are present. The threat that climate change poses to the long-term viability of Treaty 8 rights is exacerbated by the cumulative effects associated with the significant land, air, and water disruption that has resulted from human settlement, forestry, and oil sands operations. If Treaty 8's guarantees are truly going to survive "as long as the sun shines, grass grows and river flows," as Federal Treaty Commissioner James Morrison once promised, then efforts must be taken to secure climate justice for these First Nations communities whose very way of life is seriously threatened.[65] Ideally, existing procedural mechanisms can be engaged and enhanced to prevent substantive injustices from occurring, to the maximum extent practicable.

III. Existing Procedural Mechanisms and Corresponding Limitations

Enhanced procedural climate justice for First Nations communities in Alberta's oil sands region does not require the invention of novel participatory mechanisms. Rather, what is needed is a reconsideration of existing procedures and meaningful reforms that respect and engage affected communities. Alberta's First Nations have used all of the tools at their disposal to voice their discontent over perceived inadequacies in existing environmental and energy decisionmaking processes. Communities and individuals have organized and opposed development at the grassroots level to exert political

---

63. D.W. Schindler & W.F. Donahue, *An Impending Water Crisis in Canada's Western Prairie Provinces*, 103 Proc. Nat'l Acad. Sci. 7210, 7211-14 (2006). This reduction will likely be exacerbated by consumptive water practices that occur in the oil sands region along one of the main waterways in Treaty 8, the Athabasca River. *See* David J. Sauchyn et al., *Long-Term Reliability of the Athabasca River (Alberta, Canada) as the Water Source for Oil Sands Mining*, 112 Proc. Nat'l Acad. Sci. 12621 (2015); Doris Leong & Simon Donner, *Climate Change Impacts on Streamflow Availability for the Athabasca Oil Sands*, 133 Climate Change 651 (2015).

64. *See* Richard Schneider, Conserving Alberta's Biodiversity Under a Changing Climate: A Review and Analysis of Adaptation Measures (2014); *see also* Christopher C. Shank & Amy Nixon, Climate Change Vulnerability of Alberta's Terrestrial Biodiversity: A Preliminary Assessment (2014).

65. Jamie Wilson, *In Canada We Are All "Treaty People,"* Winnipeg Free Press, May 31, 2012, http://www.winnipegfreepress.com/opinion/analysis/in-canada-we-are-all-treaty-people-155890525.html.

pressure, they have worked cooperatively (and uncooperatively) with government and industry, and they have taken government and industry to court asserting procedural shortcomings and violations of various rights.[66] The two existing mechanisms that hold the most potential to advance climate justice in the oil sands region are the constitutional duty to consult and accommodate First Nations communities and the EA process.

A.   The Constitutional Duty to Consult and Accommodate

Constitutionalizing Aboriginal and treaty rights in 1982 offered First Nations peoples a new point of access to the courts to challenge government action or inaction and substantive rights infringements. That said, the Supreme Court of Canada confirmed that Aboriginal rights (including treaty rights, like those enumerated in Treaty 8) are not absolute and that the Crown can justify a violation through the two-step test articulated in *R v. Sparrow*: (1) does the action further a "compelling and substantial" purpose; and (2) does the action account for the Aboriginal interest, which holds "priority."[67] Essentially this test demands that the court balance and reconcile Aboriginal rights with broader societal concerns that drive government action. While it is conceivable that government inaction in addressing climate change could ground an infringement action, this is quite speculative and would again leave the affected community seeking *ex post facto* redress rather than anticipatory or preventative justice.

The procedural aspect of §35 of the Constitution Act, 1982 that offers hope for *ex ante* climate justice and the long-term integrity of many First Nations' rights is the Crown's duty to consult and accommodate First

---

66.   The Canadian Charter of Rights and Freedoms, Part I of the Constitution Act, 1982, *being* Schedule B to the Canada Act, 1982, ch. 11 (U.K.) protects, amongst other fundamental human rights, the right to life, liberty, and security of the person (§7) and the right to equality (§15). In *Environmental Justice and the Charter: Do Environmental Injustices Infringe Sections 7 and 15 of the Charter?*, Professor Chalifour reviews existing Charter jurisprudence and presents a compelling argument that there is "ample scope" within §15 and especially §7 to "capture many different types of environmental justice claims." Chalifour, *supra* note 26, at 93. One potential shortcoming of Charter protection is that its application is limited to provincial, territorial, or federal government action. *See* §32. Chalifour concludes that this means "the Charter is not helpful to environmental justice claimants seeking redress directly from the private sector. However, much of the environmental harm created by private entities is subject to government regulation, and that regulation *is* subject to the Charter's protections." Chalifour, *supra* note 26, at 110. She suggests that Alberta's First Nations communities proximate to the oil sands regions "could point to the provincial regulatory scheme within which industrial activity adjacent to their communities is authorized" as the public angle needed to initiate a legal challenge. *Id.* at 110–11. *See also* Andrew Stobo Sniderman & Adam Shedletzky, *Aboriginal Peoples and Legal Challenges to Canadian Climate Change Policy*, 4 W. J. Legal Stud. 1 (2014).

67.   R v. Sparrow, [1990] 1 S.C.R. 1075, at 1113–19 (most recently affirmed in *Tsilhqot'in Nation v. British Columbia*, [2014] 2 S.C.R. 257).

Nations peoples. Since at least 1984, the judiciary's assessment of historical interactions between the Crown and Canada's original inhabitants has led courts to characterize the relationship between the Crown and Aboriginal peoples as fiduciary.[68] Similar concerns have grounded the court's development of the Crown's duty to consult and accommodate.

First contemplated by the Canadian courts in *R v. Sparrow* in 1990, the transformative moment for the duty to consult and accommodate occurred in 2004 when its content and scope of the Crown's obligation was articulated by the Supreme Court of Canada in *Haida Nation v. British Columbia (Minister of Forests)*[69] and *Taku River Tingit First Nation v. British Columbia (Project Assessment Director).*[70] In brief, owing to the Crown's assertion of sovereignty over previously occupied lands, the Crown's subsequent dealings with First Nations must be guided by good faith. If the Crown has real or constructive knowledge of a substantive Aboriginal right (proven or not) and is considering an action that might impact such right,[71] the consultation duty is triggered and, depending on the outcome of the consultation, accommodation may be required.

The content of the consultation duty varies based on the strength of the right in question and the potential impact of the proposed activity. On the low end of the spectrum, the government may be able to discharge its obligation simply by giving notice or disclosing information; however, when the proposed activity involves possibly taking up land for mining, settlement, or forestry (as the numbered treaties allow) or a more significant adverse impact, then consultation will engage more significant negotiations that are undertaken with an eye to addressing the Aboriginal community's con-

---

68. R v. Guerin, [1984] 2 S.C.R. 335. There is also a growing body of jurisprudence from the Inter-American Court of Human Rights that addresses free, prior, and informed consent. *See generally* Tara Ward, *The Right to Free, Prior, and Informed Consent: Indigenous Peoples' Participation Rights Within International Law*, 10 Nw. J. Int'l Hum. Rts. 54 (2011). While Canada has been a member of the Organization of American States since 1990, it has not ratified any of its major treaties and, accordingly, is not subject to the Inter-American Court of Human Rights' jurisdiction. For a detailed assessment of Canada's participation in the Inter-American human rights regime, see Bernard Dunham, *Canada and the Inter-American Human Rights System*, 67 Int'l L.J. 639 (2012).

69. Haida Nation v. British Columbia (Minister of Forests), [2004] 3 S.C.R. 511.

70. Taku River Tingit First Nation v. British Columbia (Project Assessment Dir.), [2004] 3 S.C.R. 550. *See also* Rio Tinto Alcan Inc. v. Carrier Sekani Tribal Council, [2010] 2 S.C.R. 650, para. 51 (opining on the test for establishing the duty to consult, observing: "As we have seen, the duty to consult arises when: (1) the Crown has knowledge, actual or constructive, of potential aboriginal claims or rights; (2) the Crown proposes conduct or a decision; and (3) that conduct or decision may have an adverse impact on the Aboriginal claims or rights. This requires demonstration of a causal connection between the proposed Crown conduct and a potential adverse impact on an Aboriginal claim or right.").

71. It is not necessary for an Aboriginal community to prove actual harm at this stage. The Supreme Court of Canada confirmed at *Haida Nation*, 3 S.C.R. 511, para. 35, that the "potential existence" of harm is sufficient to trigger the duty.

cerns.[72] At the opposite end of the spectrum, the Supreme Court of Canada acknowledges "some cases may even require the full consent of an aboriginal nation, particularly when provinces enact hunting and fishing regulations in relation to aboriginal lands."[73] Leading duty of consultation expert Prof. Dwight Newman has identified "notice and appropriate timelines for response, appropriate disclosure of relevant information, discussion appropriate to the circumstances, responding to concerns raised in discussions, and potentially accommodating concerns in appropriate circumstances" as the "fundamental components of meaningful consultation."[74]

The appropriateness of the Crown's consultation is judicially reviewable on a reasonableness standard (i.e., reviewed for intelligibility and justifiability).[75] Both the federal and provincial governments maintain policies and laws to formalize their consultation processes but these are often contested by Aboriginal communities who hold different expectations and approach such negotiations as nation-to-nation rather than something that is simply *pro forma*. These contextually variable duties are to be interpreted purposively rather than technically and the federal court has concluded that they even extend to legislative action.[76]

Despite appearing as a potentially potent leverage point, the shortcomings of the duty of consultation and accommodation are evident in two recent federal court cases. The first limitation relates to the range of remedies that the courts are willing to award in the face of the breach.[77] Courts appear to have broad discretion in crafting an appropriate remedy if an Aboriginal community proves that the Crown has breached its duty. The Supreme Court of Canada affirmed the breadth of possible remedies in the 2014 Tsilhqot'in decision: "If the Crown fails to discharge its duty to consult, various remedies are available including injunctive relief, damages, or an order that consultation or accommodation be carried out."[78] Determining the appropriate remedy turns on "what stage matters have reached."[79] Has the proposed development already commenced or is it still in the planning stage? Were any efforts taken to negotiate or consult or has

---

72. *Haida Nation*, 3 S.C.R. 511, paras. 43–45; Grassy Narrows First Nation v. Ontario (Natural Res.), [2014] 2 S.C.R. 447, paras. 50–52.
73. Delgamuukw v. British Columbia, [1997] 3 S.C.R. 1010, para. 168.
74. Dwight G. Newman, Revisiting the Duty to Consult Aboriginal Peoples 103 (2014).
75. Adam v. Canada, [2014] F.C. 1185, para. 65.
76. Courtoreille v. Canada, [2014] F.C. 1244.
77. Professor Newman asserts that "[t]he duty to consult doctrine has developed precisely as a means to avoid extra litigation and as a means of fostering better relationships and negotiated agreements." Newman, *supra* note 74, at 79.
78. Tsilhqot'in Nation v. British Columbia, [2014] 2 S.C.R. 257 paras. 89–90.
79. Newman, *supra* note 74, at 78.

the affected community been totally excluded from the process? The most concerning scenario is that in which a development or action has already been initiated—or worse yet completed—without Aboriginal consultation. Here, a court might be willing to issue some form of injunctive relief or perhaps only damages.[80]

A breach of the duty to consult may not result in a meaningful remedy for affected First Nations. For example, in response to the sweeping reforms to Canadian federal environmental laws conducted by Canada's previous Conservative administration, the Mikisew Cree First Nation of Treaty 8 challenged the amendment process, which utilized expansive omnibus bills that dealt mostly with financial matters but also shoehorned in "significant changes to Canada's environmental laws,"[81] including the Fisheries Act,[82] Species at Risk Act,[83] Navigable Waters Protection Act,[84] and the Canadian Environmental Assessment Act, 2012 (CEAA, 2012).[85] The federal court agreed that the "effect of the amendments to those *Acts* is arguably to reduce the number of bodies of water within Canada which are required to be monitored by federal officials thereby affecting fishing, trapping and navigation."[86] These legislative changes occurred without any consultation during the amendment process and the court was satisfied that this violated the duty to consult because the potentially affected First Nation should have, minimally, been given notice and the opportunity to make submissions in response.[87]

In crafting its remedy for the breach and declining to award the injunctive relief sought by the First Nation, the court referenced the principle of separation of powers that maintains Canadian constitutional order and the deference that should be afforded to the legislative branch in its law making responsibility. Ultimately, the court simply offered a "declaration to the effect that the Crown ought to have given the Mikisew notice when each of the Bills were introduced into Parliament together with a reasonable opportunity to make submissions."[88] In many ways the very fact that the federal court was willing to issue *any* remedy that pertained to the law making process is a significant development; however, the outcome highlights how

---

80. *Id.*
81. *Courtoreille*, F.C. 1244, para. 2.
82. R.S.C. 1985, ch. F-14.
83. S.C. 2002, ch. 29.
84. R.S.C. 1985, ch. N-22.
85. S.C. 2012, ch. 19 (replacing the Canadian Environmental Assessment Act, 1992, S.C. 1992, ch. 37).
86. *Courtoreille*, F.C. 1244, para. 4.
87. *Id.* paras. 103–104.
88. *Id.* para. 109.

the remedy following from a breach of the duty to consult may be perceived as nothing more than a slap on the wrist by the Aboriginal community that has been neglected.

The second limitation pertains to the limited circumstances in which actual consent from a First Nations community is required as part of the consultation process. Despite the Supreme Court's recognition in 1997 that "some cases may . . . require the full consent,"[89] only one case to date expressly contemplates a consent requirement. The Supreme Court of Canada's decision in *Tsilhquot'in* in 2014 is widely regarded as a watershed development in Canadian Aboriginal law since it was the first time that a court awarded a First Nation community a unique Aboriginal right called Aboriginal title. Many First Nations communities in British Columbia never concluded land surrender agreements like Treaty 8 and as such they have outstanding land claims. Aboriginal title is a "unique product of the historic relationship between the Crown and the Aboriginal group in question"[90] that "burdens the Crown's underlying title" as an "independent legal interest" and affords the Aboriginal title holders with "the right to the benefits associated with the land—to use it, enjoy it and profit from its economic development."[91] Aboriginal titleholders are not limited to using title land in a manner that it has been used for in the past, but are limited by the fact that title land cannot be used in a manner that severs or destroys the group's original connection to the land. The test to establish Aboriginal title is quite onerous and turns on both historic and continuous occupation of the land in question.[92] After finding that the Tsilhquot'in Nation satisfied this test for some 1,180 mi^2, the court commented on the incidents of title and opined:

> The right to control the land conferred by Aboriginal title means that governments and others seeking to use the land must obtain the consent of the Aboriginal title holders. If the Aboriginal group does not consent to the use, the government's only recourse is to establish that the proposed incursion on the land is justified under s. 35 of the Constitution Act, 1982 [i.e., has a compelling and substantial objective and otherwise passes the *Sparrow* test].[93]

---

89. Delgamuukw v. British Columbia, [1997] 3 S.C.R. 1010.
90. Tsilhqot'in Nation v. British Columbia, [2014] 2 S.C.R. 257, para. 72.
91. *Id.* paras 69–70.
92. The test for title was set out in *Delgamuukw v. British Columbia*, [1997] 3 S.C.R. 1010, para. 143: [T]he [A]boriginal group asserting title must satisfy the following criteria: (i) the land must have been occupied prior to sovereignty; (ii) if present occupation is relied on as proof of occupation pre-sovereignty, there must be a continuity between present and pre-sovereignty occupation, and (iii) at sovereignty, that occupation must have been exclusive.
93. Tsilhqot'in Nation v. British Columbia, [2014] 2 S.C.R. 257, para. 76.

The extension of a consent requirement to the Aboriginal title situation is quite logical owing to the broad level of control over land use decisions that it vests in the titleholders. This finding is also potentially important for the future of the duty to consult, more generally. Specifically, *Tsilhquot'in* opens the door for courts to recognize other scenarios where the Crown's consultation obligation requires full consent from the rights holder before a development proceeds or an action can be taken. While the prospect of a successful Aboriginal title claim within the boundaries of Treaty 8[94] is quite low owing to the preexisting land surrender agreement, it is possible that significant strategic decisions related to land use or perhaps even climate change mitigation or adaptation efforts that compromise recognized treaty rights could require full participation and consent from First Nations communities. Consider, for example, a scenario in which a new provincial energy policy demands a large-scale shift to hydroelectric power generation in a manner that compromises rivers and lakes that are important traditional fishing grounds. Or, alternatively, consider the possibility that changing climatic conditions and associated ecosystem alterations threaten the continued survival of some game species that are important to certain First Nations and the federal government responds with regulatory action that prohibits any further hunting or trapping totally or at least within areas designated as critical habitat. These sorts of decisions should fully engage impacted First Nations and the government, at least arguably, ought to strive to secure consent.

The ongoing interpretation of treaty rights and the associated procedural duty to consult remain contentious exercises as First Nations communities and governments hold different opinions on what is required to preserve and protect substantive rights and also what qualifies as appropriate consultation or accommodation. As the Supreme Court of Canada observed in *Mikisew Cree First Nation v. Canada (Minister of Canadian Heritage)*, in the context of 21st century land use changes, "consultation is key to achievement of the overall objective of the modern law of treaty and aboriginal rights, namely reconciliation."[95] Despite its limitations, there can be no doubt that consultation will feature prominently in the future of Canada's provincial and federal climate change response.

---

94. One caveat to this statement might be the Lubicon Lake Cree. This community's traditional lands are located within the boundaries of Treaty 8 but were missed by the Federal Treaty Commissioner in 1899 during the signing of Treaty 8. As such, the Lubicon have a long-standing and contentious land claim that awaits formal resolution through a modern treaty or potentially even through the assertion of Aboriginal title. *See A History of Struggle: A Chronology of the Lubicon Cree Land Rights Struggle*, BRIARPATCH MAG., Feb. 28, 2012, http://briarpatchmagazine.com/articles/view/a-history-of-struggle.

95. Mikisew Cree First Nation v. Canada (Minister of Canadian Heritage), [2005] 3 S.C.R. 388, para. 63.

B.   Environmental Assessment

The second procedural mechanism is the Canadian EA process. Similar to EA processes in other jurisdictions, Canada's EA laws represent, at least in theory, "an attempt to avoid, or at least minimize, environmental damage by changing the nature of project planning, design, and implementation."[96] The potential for EAs to advance preventative, precautionary, and integrated decisionmaking within the sustainable development paradigm are well documented in the literature and need not be recited here.[97] Canada's EA process is admittedly related to the duty to consult since an EA often constitutes a significant dimension of the consultation process.[98]

Canadian EAs are largely proponent (industry) driven, but their substance and form are dictated by the regulatory parameters established by provincial and federal law and policy.[99] Canada's federal EA process was substantially overhauled as part of the Conservative government's reformation of environmental law, which resulted in CEAA, 2012. Alberta's provincial EA process is set down in the Environmental Protection and Enhancement Act (EPEA).[100] In the context of oil sands development, owing to the scope and significant negative environmental impacts associated with extraction, most projects engage a joint provincial-federal review, coordinated and conducted through agreement. Turning to the climate justice context, EAs have the potential to ensure that First Nations communities "do not bear a disproportionate burden of harm from development projects and that their account of risk is given due consideration."[101] Unfortunately, experience to date indicates that EAs have not yet lived up to their potential in this regard.

A first order concern is the extent to which climate justice concerns are required to be considered by EA legislation. Starting with CEAA, 2012, §4 ("Purposes") declares that one purpose is "to promote communication and cooperation with aboriginal peoples with respect to environmental assess-

---

96. PAUL MULDOON ET AL., AN INTRODUCTION TO ENVIRONMENTAL LAW AND POLICY IN CANADA 225 (2d ed. 2015).
97. *See* B.F. NOBLE, INTRODUCTION TO ENVIRONMENTAL IMPACT ASSESSMENT: A GUIDE TO PRINCIPLES AND PRACTICE 16–17 (2010) (explaining how EAs can reduce project costs, integrate environmental concerns into planning and implementation, offer a forum for public debate and public participation, and enhance transparency, accountability, and public acceptance of potentially controversial projects).
98. *See* Taku River Tingit First Nation v. British Columbia (Project Assessment Dir.), [2004] 3 S.C.R. 550, para. 40, where the Supreme Court of Canada articulated that in certain circumstances an EA can completely satisfy the procedural duty to consult.
99. The environment is an area of shared jurisdiction between federal and provincial governments owing to the fact that it is not an area of legislative competence that was expressly assigned by Canada's constitutional instruments.
100. R.S.A. 2000, ch. E-12.
101. Chalifour, *Environmental Assessment, supra* note 33, at 56.

ments." Another purpose of CEAA, 2012 is to "to ensure that opportunities are provided for meaningful public participation during an environmental assessment." In order to qualify for participation in an EA, CEAA, 2012 requires that the "interested party" be "directly affected" or have "relevant information or expertise."[102] CEAA, 2012 then articulates the "environmental effects" that are to be considered during assessment in §5. Here, environmental effect "with respect to aboriginal peoples" is defined as

> an effect occurring in Canada of any change that may be caused to the environment on . . . health and socio-economic conditions, physical and cultural heritage, the current use of lands and resources for traditional purposes, or any structure, site or thing that is of historical, archaeological, paleontological or architectural significance.

CEAA, 2012 directs that "[t]he environmental assessment of a designated project *may* take into account community knowledge and Aboriginal traditional knowledge"[103] and requires the responsible agency "to engage in consultation with Aboriginal peoples on policy issues related to this Act."[104] Alberta's EPEA lacks analogous guidance with respect to considering unique impacts of projects on Aboriginal peoples.

As promising as these provisions in CEAA, 2012 seem, the overarching objective of the reform to the EA process was to streamline the process to accommodate industry's concerns that EAs were delaying business and development.[105] The government's response was dramatic, as CEAA, 2012 "eliminated between 4,000 to 6,000 environmental assessments per year, limited the effects that get considered in an assessment, restricted the public's rights to participate in the EA process, offloaded the responsibility of EA to provincial governments without clear national guidelines, and set arbitrary

102. CEAA, S.C. 2012, ch. 19, §2 (replacing the Canadian Environmental Assessment Act, 1992, S.C. 1992, ch. 37). While this can be quite a difficult threshold for many interested parties to meet, senior civil litigator Timothy Leadem, Q.C. correctly observes that:

> it is difficult to conceive of a situation where an Aboriginal band or group that could show a connection with its constitutionally protected rights and the proposal brought forward by a designated project would not be considered to be an interested party with full rights of standing at any review that may emanate from a decision to hold an environmental assessment.

ENVIRONMENTAL ASSESSMENT IN CANADA AND ABORIGINAL LAW: SOME PRACTICAL CONSIDERATIONS FOR NAVIGATING THROUGH A CHANGING LANDSCAPE, at 1.2.3 (Aboriginal Law Conference 2013), https://www.cle.bc.ca/PracticePoints/ENV/13-EnvironmentalAssessmentinCanadaandAboriginalLaw.pdf.

103. CEAA, S.C. 2012, ch. 19, §19(3) (replacing the Canadian Environmental Assessment Act, 1992, S.C. 1992, ch. 37) (emphasis added).

104. *Id.* at §105(g).

105. Anna Johnston & Monisha Sebastian, *Working Towards a Next-Generation Environmental Assessment Law for Canada*, W. COAST ENVTL. L., May 20, 2016, http://wcel.org/resources/environmental-law-alert/working-towards-next-generation-environmental-assessment-law-canad.

timelines for environmental reviews."[106] In assessing the consequences of this streamlining on the ability for First Nations communities to participate in EAs, Denis Kirchhoff, Holly L. Gardner, and Leonard J.S. Tsuji posit that reduction in the overall number of assessments and the short statutory time-lines make it considerably more difficult for First Nations communities to fully participate—a problem that is exacerbated for more remote communities.[107] They assert that fulsome Aboriginal participation was further eroded by significant funding cuts to "both Aboriginal Representative Organizations and Tribal Councils."[108]

Another shortcoming in CEAA, 2012 is its narrow focus on simply mitigating the negative effects of development. A more robust assessment process should go one step further and require that the proponent demonstrate how the proposed project "make[s] a positive contribution to sustainability."[109] Demanding this longer-term thinking would be particularly useful in the oil sands context as it would force a review panel to consider sustainability-related issues that may otherwise be disregarded, including whether or how the proposed oil sands project fits within national and international climate targets, whether the local Aboriginal community is uniquely positioned to benefit economically or socially from the proposed development, or even whether the scope and projected life-span for the project aligns with the provincial/federal shift towards renewable energy development, and how the proposed project may "help promote justice for . . . marginalized communities and avoid further entrenching existing inequalities."[110]

Despite CEAA, 2012's specific mention of the need to account for cumulative effects during an EA, the reality is that EAs continue on a project-by-project basis that largely excludes the holistic thinking required to achieve preventative and precautionary decisionmaking in the climate change context. The sort of coordinated decisionmaking that is necessary to position oil sands development within the broader climate justice and regulatory climate change approach demands EA-style review of "government policies, plans, programs, and other broad-scale initiatives."[111] This sort of higher-order review, known as a strategic-level assessment, is particularly suitable for the oil sands region where decisions about the preferred intensity of development and its corresponding GHG emission budget ultimately have intergenera-

---

106. *Id.*
107. Denis Kirchhoff et al., *The Canadian Environmental Assessment Act, 2012 and Associated Policy: Implications for Aboriginal Peoples*, 4 INT'L INDIGENOUS POL'Y J. 1, 5–6 (2013).
108. *Id.* at 9.
109. Chalifour, *Environmental Assessment, supra* note 33, at 61.
110. *Id.*
111. MULDOON ET AL., *supra* note 96, at 235.

tional consequences for the permanent First Nations residents who are intimately connected to the land and a traditional way of life. It is imperative
that their world experience is both respected and accommodated as the world
gradually shifts away from fossil fuels in favor of renewable energy options.

A final concern with the EA process comes back to the thorny issues
of consent, the Crown's constitutional duty to consult First Nations, and
the government's broad discretion to approve projects even in the face of
staunch opposition. It is common for the duty to consult and accommodate
to form part of the EA process; indeed, EAs quite often constitute one piece
of the large consultation and accommodation puzzle. In the case of *Adam
v. Canada (Environment)*, the Athabasca Chipewyan First Nation (ACFN)
from Treaty 8 sought judicial review of the Government of Canada's decision that the "significant adverse environmental effects" of the Shell Canada
Energy Jackpine Mine were "justified in the circumstances."[112] The ACFN
had opposed the proposed expansion since 2007, and their concerns were
bolstered when the joint provincial-federal environmental review panel operating under CEAA, 2012 concluded that:

> the Project offered significant economic benefits and should not be delayed.
> In addition, the Project was likely to cause significant adverse environmen-
> tal effects—some of them irreversible and inadequately mitigated—for the
> landscape, flora, fauna, and Indigenous peoples of the lands in question. The
> cumulative effects of this and other projects in the region, however, would
> likely result in significant harm to Aboriginal rights and the environment.[113]

The government ultimately determined that the expansion should proceed and imposed a number of binding conditions on Shell, based largely on
the joint panel's recommendations. The court substantially agreed with the
review panel's findings, reaffirming that the development would "adversely
affect the ACFN's rights, notably its Treaty 8 rights to hunting, fishing, and
the harvesting of animals and plants . . . [and] would interfere with the maintenance of the ACFN's culture and way of life."[114]

The ACFN asserted that the government's discretionary decision to
approve the mine's expansion violated the constitutional duty to consult
and accommodate. They argued that the consultation was rushed, secretive,
failed to adequately consider cumulative effects,[115] and that accommoda-

---

112. Adam v. Canada (Env't), [2014] F.C. 1185, para. 1.
113. *Id.* para. 11.
114. *Id.* para. 6.
115. *Id.* paras. 26–30.

tion minimally addressed their concerns.[116] The court determined that the Crown's duty to consult fell on the "more involved" end of the consultation spectrum since the proposed expansion "would destroy a large part of the ACFN's traditional lands and might also impinge upon the maintenance of their culture and way of life."[117] Nevertheless, the court was satisfied that the consultation had been quite involved over a number of years, including full participation in the review panel aspect of the EA, and ultimately dismissed ACFN's application. Through the course of its decision, the court went out of its way to articulate that the duty to consult does not afford an Aboriginal people with a "veto" or a "guarantee" to "everything that they wish to obtain."[118]

It is highly questionable as to whether the ACFN received procedural justice in this scenario. The court appeared to be satisfied that so long as government and industry check off their base consultative obligations then the government's discretionary decision somehow becomes infallible. Worse still, the court noted that the "Crown did consult the ACFN on the cumulative adverse effects on Treaty 8 rights, the flora and fauna, and the maintenance of the ACFN's culture and way of life" and that "[m]uch of the work of the Panel addressed these very issues."[119] While it is fair that one particular proponent should not have to bear full responsibility for the cumulative effects of regional development, at some point the manifestation of that aspect must be weighed against the fairness of allowing further development in a region that is already disproportionately impacted where its original inhabitants have decided that enough is enough. Surely there must come a point when a First Nations community is entitled to simply say no, this development may not proceed. The remainder of this chapter considers this scenario in the Canadian context.

IV.   Practical Solutions

Despite their limitations, the constitutional duty to consult and accommodate and Canada's EA processes are well-developed and entrenched aspects of First Nations' relations and environmental decisionmaking. In the search for practical and feasible procedural climate justice solutions for Aboriginal people in the Treaty 8 region, targeted reforms to these existing mechanisms is a logical starting point. Here, such reform is guided by the goal that Can-

---

116. *Id.* paras. 41–42.
117. *Id.* para. 71.
118. *Id.* paras. 66, 104.
119. *Id.* para. 85.

ada's First Nations be granted a true seat at the table where Canada's critical resource extraction and climate law decisions are being made.

This solutions section begins with three initial observations. The first observation is extra-legal in nature but nevertheless critically instrumental to the regulatory process. It is imperative that Canada's First Nations communities become meaningfully engaged in future studies that assess and measure the impact of both the oil sands development and Alberta's changing climate. This must be prioritized. As a 2015 opinion piece from the journal *Nature Climate Change* observes: "assessment and monitoring programmes for sociocultural and livelihood impacts in the oil sands [upon First Nations communities] remain inadequate."[120] If decisions are going to fully account for the unique First Nations' perspective, then it is essential that environmental baselines are established and that traditional ecological knowledge is garnered. The government, scientists, and academics should seek to establish cooperative relationships that empower First Nations communities as active participants in the process of monitoring and reporting on their environment and how its changes impact their way of life. This should strive to further reconcile the scientific way of knowing with the traditional ecological knowledge transmitted through First Nations communities.

The second observation is that time is of the essence. Not only is time short in the ecological sense in that we only have so long to get GHG emissions under control to avoid the catastrophic consequences of climate change, time is also limited—or at the very least highly uncertain—in the political sense so it is incredibly important that First Nations communities secure pragmatic and meaningful procedural reforms that help address climate justice concerns while Canada's political landscape is more open and receptive to such initiatives and fully committed to furthering the reconciliation process.

A final observation is that Canada should look to UNDRIP to guide these reforms. As a declaration from the General Assembly of the United Nations, UNDRIP exists as international soft law. This means, in essence, that those States that fully endorse UNDRIP may be expected to conduct themselves in accordance with its tenets, but it cannot be enforced against a State in the event of a breach. As introduced earlier, Canada initially voted against UNDRIP in 2007, largely because of its perceived implications for resource development and the recurring use of the phrase "free, prior and informed consent" (FPIC), and then in 2010 the Conservative government indicated that it supported UNDIRIP in principle but maintained its reser-

---

120. C.S. Mantyka-Pringle et al., *Honouring Indigenous Treaty Rights for Climate Justice*, 5 Nature Climate Change 798, 799 (2015).

vations about FPIC on the basis that it could be interpreted as a veto. This changed in May 2016, when Canada withdrew its permanent objector status and promised to fully implement UNDRIP.

Canada has work to do in giving full effect to many of UNDRIP's principles. The following articles seem to present the greatest opportunities to secure procedural climate justice:

Article 18

Indigenous peoples have the *right to participate in decision-making in matters which would affect their rights*, through representatives chosen by themselves in accordance with their own procedures, as well as to maintain and develop their own indigenous decision-making institutions.

Article 19

States shall consult and cooperate in good faith with the indigenous peoples concerned through their own representative institutions *in order to obtain their free, prior and informed consent before adopting and implementing legislative or administrative measures that may affect them.*

Article 32

1. Indigenous peoples have the right to determine and develop priorities and strategies for the development or use of their lands or territories and other resources.

2. States shall *consult and cooperate in good faith with the indigenous peoples concerned through their own representative institutions in order to obtain their free and informed consent prior to the approval of any project affecting their lands or territories and other resources, particularly in connection with the development, utilization or exploitation of mineral, water or other resources.*

3. States shall provide effective mechanisms for just and fair redress for any such activities, and appropriate measures shall be taken to mitigate adverse environmental, economic, social, cultural or spiritual impact.[121]

The participatory right guaranteed by Article 18 of UNDRIP is largely met by the constitutional duty to consult and accommodate in its current form. The added requirement of consultation for the purposes of obtaining FPIC before "adopting and implementing legislative or administrative measures that may affect them" (Article 19) and "prior to the approval of any project affecting their lands or territories and other resources, particularly

---

121. UNDRIP, *supra* note 17 (emphasis added).

in connection with the development, utilization or exploitation of mineral, water or other resources" (Article 32) is arguably where Canada's process falls short. The remainder of this section considers how these principles may inform practical reform to the duty to consult and the EA process.

A.   Revisiting the Duty to Consult

The duty to consult and accommodate requires consent from First Nations communities in very limited situations such as the development on land covered by Aboriginal title. And, even when consent is required, the government is still able to override the "Aboriginal title-holding group's wishes on the basis of the broader public good."[122] The consent requirement definitely does not yet extend to legislative or administrative decisionmaking or to development in the oil sands. The question is whether Canada's commitment to implement UNDRIP can help enhance the duty to consult's efficacy as a procedural mechanism that promotes climate justice.

A sharp divergence of opinion already exists on the meaning of UNDIRP's FPIC requirement and its potential impact in the Canadian context. On one end of the spectrum is the position taken by Perry Bellegarde, the national chief of the Assembly of First Nations, who views FPIC as "the right to say yes, and the right to say no [to development on traditional lands and territories]. It is much more than a process of consultation."[123] To Chief Bellegarde, implementation requires that this be enshrined in law. True implementation would require a review of every existing law to ensure it accords and perhaps even constitutional entrenchment. On the other end of the spectrum is the position held by some lawyers and politicians that FPIC simply cannot be construed as a veto power, which would run counter to existing Canadian law and State sovereignty.[124] This perspective endorses informal implementation that eschews broad legal reform and can point to some practical problems with true implementation.

Consider, for example, the feasibility of trying to secure FPIC from every First Nations community across Canada for federal legislative action or even trying to secure FPIC from each of Alberta's Treaty 8 Aboriginal communities that might be impacted by the cumulative effects of additional oil sands

---

122. Tsilhqot'in Nation v. British Columbia, [2014] 2 S.C.R. 257, para. 77.

123. Shawn McCarthy, *Liberals Must Give Indigenous People "Right to Say No," AFN Chief Says*, THE GLOBE & MAIL, May 12, 2016, http://www.theglobeandmail.com/news/politics/liberals-must-give-indigenous-people-right-to-say-no-afn-chief-says/article30006459/.

124. Mackenzie Scrimshaw, *Unpacking UNDRIP: How Trudeau Could Take Crown/First Nations Law Into Uncharted Waters*, IPOLITICS, Jan. 12, 2016, http://ipolitics.ca/2016/01/12/unpacking-undrip-how-trudeau-could-take-crownfirst-nations-law-into-uncharted-waters/.

development.[125] Each Aboriginal community has its own goals, priorities, and perspectives on industry and government, a reality that likely negates the possibility of ever securing unanimous consent.

Professor Newman's review of interpretive evidence suggests a sensible and pragmatic middle ground: the wording contained in the articles in UNDRIP that addresses FPIC "does not create a veto power, in this it does not create an obligation to engage in a good faith process with the genuine objective of obtaining consent" even if such efforts fall short, and that the intention is to "create a spectrum of obligations, depending on the seriousness of impact on the Indigenous community affected by particular actions."[126] Building on this approach, Canada's implementation efforts can work to improve procedural climate justice for First Nations communities by reconsidering the scenarios in which the Crown's consultation duty requires consent. For example, while it has always made practical sense for governments to engage in a meaningful consultative process with First Nations communities prior to the development of climate change policy, implementing Article 19 of UNDRIP should require governments to seek and secure consent from First Nations communities prior to enacting and implementing climate change laws that affect First Nations peoples. Setting this down in policy—or preferably law—would offer a guarantee to First Nations that their worldviews and existing disparities would be fully considered. This approach could even remedy some of the federal court's concerns in *Courtoreille*[127] where it struggled to determine an appropriate remedy for the government's failure to consult prior to enacting laws that impacted First Nations' rights that were protected by §35. A court would not have the same reservations about injecting itself into the legislative process and even invalidating legislation if that remedial action is statutorily authorized.

Second, the government should work with First Nations communities in Treaty 8 to identify those core tracts of land that are currently essential for communities to conduct the activities protected by their treaty rights and/ or to list certain development activities that presumptively have a significant impact on treaty rights and require consent. This could reverse the burden, thereby requiring a proponent to refute the presumption before any development activity takes place. Assuming that such a mapping/listing exercise is

---

125. *See* Dwight Newman, *Why the Duty to Consult May Be Harming Aboriginal Communities*, THE GLOBE & MAIL, May 6, 2014 (surveying some of the practical problems with conducting very broad-scale formal consultations), http://www.theglobeandmail.com/opinion/why-the-duty-to-consult-may-be-harming-aboriginal-communities/article18482956 [hereinafter Newman, *Duty to Consult*].

126. NEWMAN, *supra* note 74, at 148–49.

127. Courtoreille v. Canada, [2014] F.C. 1244.

possible, the government could then establish additional zones within the boundaries of Treaty 8 where any future oil sands development or expansion would have to secure FPIC before proceeding, in accordance with the purpose of UNDRIP's Article 32. This proposed course of action would help move the consultation spectrum and rationally integrate the intentions of FPIC in the Canadian context. For such a plan to succeed, First Nations communities would also have to turn their attention to determining which "representative institutions"[128] should participate in these consultations and governments would have to consider the sorts of situations in which they would be justified in deviating from FPIC in the name of the public good. Still, given the rapid pace at which the duty to consult has taken hold and developed through jurisprudence, these hurdles should not be insurmountable.

B.   Revamping Environmental Assessment

No fewer than five federal government ministers have been tasked with reviewing the current EA process under CEAA, 2012.[129] Major changes to this process are coming; the question is not *whether* reform will occur but rather *what form* it will take. For concerned First Nations communities, such reform may hold the key to securing enhanced procedural climate justice.

A revamped EA law should formally incorporate both a sustainability-based assessment approach and a strategic environmental assessment (SEA). With regard to the former, this would mandate that a proponent and the responsible government agency

> ask whether the project makes a positive contribution to sustainability writ large, but also include consideration of whether a given community [such as a proximate First Nations community] would be unfairly burdened by a project . . . [and] require investigation whether the project perpetuates systemic inequalities or contributes towards addressing them.[130]

These requirements could be built directly into the EA's terms of reference. Prof. Nathalie J. Chalifour posits that advancing this perspective of justice in the EA process could be aided by the mandatory inclusion of at least one person on each review panel who is from the marginalized community or

---

128. *See* Newman, *Duty to Consult, supra* note 125, where Professor Newman suggests that "[t]here needs to be an orderly means of consulting with national representative organizations that can represent the interests of grassroots First Nations." I would add to this by noting that it is important to consider ways in which groups such as the freshly minted "Indigenous civil society vehicle" called "Indigenous Climate Action" can formally engage in climate change discourse.

129. Johnston & Sebastian, *supra* note 105.

130. Chalifour, *Environmental Assessment, supra* note 33, at 50.

who has "adequate training in systemic inequality."[131] Alternatively, or perhaps complimentarily, the panel's work could be supplemented by a "friend of the panel" who is "responsible for bringing forward a justice perspective" throughout the review.[132] Procedural justice can also be enhanced by reviewing existing funding mechanisms with an eye to ensuring that communities are able to meaningfully and fully contribute throughout in a timely fashion.[133] Finally, this sustainability-based approach should engage "mechanisms for Aboriginal review processes that run parallel to or in tandem with Crown processes" to help ensure that the Aboriginal worldview and perspective is accounted for in a manner that is not simply "imposed by the Crown."[134] It should be mandatory for a review panel to consider traditional ecological knowledge.

With respect to SEAs, a revamped EA process should expand beyond project-based review and seek to integrate environmental considerations into the assessment of higher-order government plans, policies, and programs, to review

> whether there are adequate ecological, social, and administrative capacities to deal with the cumulative effects of multiple undertakings in an area, and whether we should permit initial or further development along a questionable path when attractive alternative strategies may exist (e.g., promoting energy efficiencies and renewable energy sources rather than facilitating more extraction and use of hydrocarbons).[135]

Engaging in this sort of review in the climate change context, provincially or federally, necessitates a preemptive public review of the sort of decisions that often seem shrouded in secrecy or buried in government bureaucracy and affords participants an opportunity to debate the extent to which economic development ought to be restricted to account for environmental and social concerns. Any SEA process should also have an express mandate of including First Nations communities and other disproportionately impacted communities.

To help address concerns over the broad level of discretion that government has retained through CEAA, 2012, the EA process is also a logical place to implement UNDRIP's goal of FPIC. Aboriginal law expert Tom

---

131. *Id.* at 62.
132. *Id.*
133. *Id.* at 62–64.
134. RACHEL S. FORBES ET AL., ENVIRONMENTAL ASSESSMENT LAW FOR A HEALTHY, SECURE, AND SUSTAINABLE CANADA: A CHECKLIST FOR STRONG ENVIRONMENTAL LAWS 7 (2012).
135. MULDOON ET AL., *supra* note 96, at 241–42.

Isaac views revamped EA policy as the "appropriate starting place" for the government to articulate that its "preference is going to be to approve projects where aboriginal consent is evident."[136] West Coast Environmental Law, a pro bono legal group in British Columbia that is "engaged directly in law reform, legal education and test case litigation,"[137] takes Isaac's suggestion one step further by asserting that UNDRIP's FPIC should be expressly "reflected in Canada's EA legislation" rather than as a simple policy preference.[138] In other words, rework the notion of Aboriginal participation to work in a consent requirement. The EA process is an appropriate place to implement the list of recognized core traditional lands and presumptively disruptive activities that ought to be recognized as engaging the FPIC principle. This is a logical starting point that ensures that consent and the broader duty to consult occupy a meaningful position within Canada's EA process to move forward with nation-to-nation reconciliation.

Conclusion

Eriel Deranger, an indigenous rights advocate and member of the Treaty 8 Athabasca Chipewyan First Nation, is one of many prominent First Nations women in Alberta who are leading the charge for procedural and substantive climate justice for their communities. As exemplified by the following statement, Deranger views procedural climate justice as a core element of environmental protection and the ongoing process of reconciliation:

> If our communities are not active participants in creating pathways for a just future we will continue to participate on the fringes of society, continually playing a marginalized role. It's time for Canada, [Prime Minister] Trudeau, and provincial leaders to step up and live up to the promises of Treaty and the foundation of UNDRIP and allow our people to take back our roles as true leaders and stewards of our land and peoples.[139]

It was during the early days of negotiating and completing the numbered treaties between the Crown and prairie and northern First Nations communities that Federal Treaty Commissioner Alexander Morris exclaimed that

---

136. Scrimshaw, *supra* note 124.
137. West Coast Environmental Law, *West Coast—Participating in the Creation of All Significant Environmental Legislation in BC Since 1974*, http://wcel.org/about-us/west-coast-%E2%80%93-participating-creation-all-significant-environmental-legislation-bc-1974 (last visited Aug. 22, 2016).
138. FORBES ET AL., *supra* note 134.
139. Eriel Deranger, *First Nations Target Trudeau's Climate Plan With Indigenous Climate Action*, NAT'L OBSERVER, Apr. 27, 2016, http://www.nationalobserver.com/2016/04/27/opinion/first-nations-target-trudeaus-climate-plan-indigenous-climate-action.

these numbered treaties would last "as long as the sun shines, grass grows and river flows."[140] Some 150 years later, treaty implementation remains a contentious process; however, the treaties remain. The integrity and longevity of core treaty rights is now threatened by the equally complex problem of climate change.

Numerous injustices continue to ravage Canada's First Nations communities. As Canada continues down the path of atonement and reconciliation, it is prudent to approach law and policy reform in the area of climate change, environmental law, and First Nations relations as a unique opportunity to embrace the tenets of Canada's emergent climate justice movement and to act to avoid or at least significantly soften climate change's impact on some of Canada's most disproportionately burdened communities. This chapter has explored the content of the constitutional duty to consult and EAs as two logical procedural mechanisms that are ripe for targeted and pragmatic reforms. Reconciliation will not occur overnight, but all Canadians owe it to our future generations to help make it right and respond to this legacy of injustice.

---

140. *See* Jefferies, *supra* note 4.

Chapter 10

The Impact of Climate Change on American and Canadian Indigenous Peoples and Their Water Resources: A Climate Justice Perspective

Itzchak Kornfeld

Introduction

Across the world, indigenous communities face threats to their access to water as a consequence of climate change. Indeed, water management is one of the most fundamental climate change-related issues in North America and internationally. It involves issues of equity, and is related to significant political, social, and ecological struggles that indigenous peoples face. These characteristics are defined as both cause and symptom of the precarious life on reservations, other tribal territories, and urban areas and their relation to climate change.

To date, national, state/provincial, and local governments have done little, if anything, to address the problems of access to water and the impacts of climate change on that access. Courts have also been unreceptive to these issues. These inequities have caused conflict between indigenous peoples and governmental authorities.

Two responses to these conflicts and inequities include (1) mediation, and (2) a program for the long-term sustainable development of water resources in the face of climate change. Such efforts require the participation of the very public whose human rights have been abused. However, those people that are most affected by the scarcity of water in the areas in which they live are also those least likely to participate in policy and governance organizations. Their ability to participate is limited by the time demands of fetching water, and making a living, and because they do not trust "the system."

This chapter addresses the indigenous peoples of Canada and the United States. It reviews international and national laws, relevant case law, and commission reports. The international laws addressed are the 1966 International Covenant on Economic, Social, and Cultural Rights (ICESCR), the Convention on the Elimination of All Forms of Discrimination Against Women (CEDAW), the United Nations Convention on the Rights of the Child (CRC), the ILO Convention Concerning Indigenous and Tribal Peoples in Independent Countries (ILO No. 169), the International Convention on the Elimination of All Forms of Racial Discrimination (CAFRD), and the Inter-American Declaration of Human Rights (IADHR).

The United States is not a Party to the ICESCR, the CEDAW, the CRC, or ILO No. 169. Canada, however, is a Party to all of these conventions. Canada and the United States are both Parties to the CAFRD and the Inter-American Convention on Human Rights (IACHR), except that the United States does not recognize the jurisdiction of the Inter-American Court. Indigenous peoples face several challenges in seeking protection under these international law instruments to address climate change impacts on their lands and cultures. One significant hurdle is causation, i.e., the difficulty a litigant faces in proving that climate change impacted his or her access to water. On the national level, Canada and the United States each has treaties with their indigenous peoples—the American Indians/Alaska Natives in the United States and the First Nations in Canada—and there are applicable municipal laws and court rulings.

Numerous indigenous communities lack access to fresh and potable water and sanitation, and climate change will impact these peoples' continued access to this resource. For example, the recent drought in California impacted the Bishop Paiute, California Valley Miwok, and the Fort Mojave Indians more than other Californians because these indigenous communities do not have the modern conveniences or resources that most other state residents enjoy.

Part I of this chapter introduces how climate change is impacting select U.S. and Canadian indigenous communities' natural resources and cultures. Part II addresses international law instruments that are potentially applicable to these indigenous peoples' efforts to adapt to climate change impacts. Part III examines the right to water for American and Canadian indigenous peoples. Part IV concludes the chapter by offering recommendations to help secure justice for these peoples.

I.   Climate Change Impacts on Indigenous Communities in the United States and Canada

There are approximately 570 federally recognized American Indian tribes and Alaska Native (AI/AN) villages in the United States.[1] They vary significantly in terms of their culture, economic status, land base, language, location, and population size. Despite these distinguishing features, many of these tribal communities share several characteristics. Specifically, the majority are situated in isolated and often environmentally challenging areas,[2] such as deserts, extra-rural areas, or regions far from any major population centers. The U.S. Census Bureau has identified some 25% of AI/AN that live below the national poverty line, contrasted with about 9% for non-Hispanic whites.[3] Indeed, the U.S. Environmental Protection Agency (EPA) has also noted that throughout Indian country and in Alaska Native villages a disproportionate percentage of tribal homes lack access to safe drinking water and safe wastewater disposal. According to 2007 data from the Indian Health

---

1.   U.S. Environmental Protection Agency et al., Infrastructure Task Force Access Subgroup, Meeting the Access Goal: Strategies for Increasing Access to Safe Drinking Water and Wastewater Treatment to American Indian and Alaska Native Homes 6 (2008), https://www.epa.gov/sites/production/files/2015-07/documents/meeting-the-access-goal-strategies-for-increasing-access-to-safe-drinking-water-and-wastewater-treatment-american-indian-alaska-native-villages.pdf.
2.   Id.
3.   Id.

Service (IHS), approximately 13% of AI/AN homes do not have safe water or wastewater disposal facilities. This is an extremely high percentage compared with the 0.6% of non-native homes in the United States that lack such infrastructure as measured in 2005 by the U.S. Census. The lack of access to these basic services in Indian country continues to threaten the public health of tribal communities.[4]

Climate change is a daunting global regulatory challenge. Climate change impacts will be variable; harsher in some areas, and less harsh in others. A recent study[5] recalled that less than 2°C of global warming for the earth was the target agreed by leaders at the 21st Conference of the Parties climate conference in Paris in November 2015.[6] However, such targets may fail to communicate the urgency of reducing carbon dioxide emissions. Regional hot spots cited are the Mediterranean countries, Brazil, and the United States, where 2°C of global warming could translate into local temperature increases of more than 3°C. But the region expected to suffer most is the Arctic, where nighttime temperatures are predicted to soar by 6°C.[7]

In 2015, the U.S. National Oceanic and Atmospheric Administration (NOAA) issued a report card on the state of the Arctic.[8] It disclosed that the annual average air temperature was 1.3°C above the long-term average.[9] This increase is a peak since the keeping of modern records in 1900.[10] Moreover, temperatures topped 3°C above the average, from 1981 to 2010.[11] The record heat has been attended by shrinking levels of ice. In 2015, "[t]he Arctic Ocean reached its peak ice cover on 25 February—a full 15 days earlier than the long-term average and the lowest extent recorded since satellite records began in 1979. The minimum ice cover, which occurred on 11 September, was the fourth smallest in area on record."[12]

Climate change poses multiple threats to indigenous communities' natural resources and cultures. These communities' close ties to the land make them especially vulnerable to climate change impacts. Lack of precipitation,

---

4.   *Id.* at 4.
5.   Sonia I. Senerviratne et al., *Allowable CO₂ Emissions Based on Regional and Impact-related Climate Targets*, 529 NATURE 477, 477 (2016).
6.   *Id.* at 477–78.
7.   Kate Ravilious, *Global Warming: Uneven Changes Across Planet*, THE GUARDIAN, Feb. 10, 2016, http://www.theguardian.com/news/2016/feb/10/weatherwatch-ravilious-global-warming-limit-climate-change-uneven-arctic-europe-us.
8.   Oliver Milman, *Record High Arctic Temperatures in 2015 Having "Profound Effects" on Region*, THE GUARDIAN, Dec. 15, 2015, http://www.theguardian.com/world/2015/dec/15/arctic-noaa-report-record-high-temperatures-diminishing-sea-ice.
9.   *Id.*
10.   *Id.*
11.   *Id.*
12.   *Id.*

attributed to climate change, has proven to be disastrous to indigenous peoples' subsistence cultures in the United States' North Country.[13] For example, in 2012, for only the second time in the past decade, the Ojibwe Bad River Reservation in northern Wisconsin and the Fond du Lac Band of Lake Superior Chippewa near Duluth, Minnesota, had to cancel their manoomin (wild rice) harvests.[14]

Over the past few years, the contiguous United States has witnessed record heat and the most severe drought since the 1950s.[15] Moreover, January 2013 was warmer and wetter than the average for the 20th century.[16] This has had a profound impact on Indian country.[17] For example, the wildfires that have swept the western United States beginning in 2011 and continuing through 2015 have seen some of the worst seasons in recorded history.[18] "In Indian country that translated into damage or outright devastation on several reservations, including the Northern Cheyenne Indian Reservation, where the 2,000-population town of Lame Deer, the tribal hub, was briefly evacuated in August 2012 after a fire in southeastern Montana made its way onto the reservation."[19] Fires in New Mexico threatened both the Fort Apache and the San Carlos Apache reservations, which have seen hundreds of thousands of acres burned to the ground, impacting farming and other interests.[20]

The tribes discussed below were selected for this discussion because they are among the poorest and will be some of the most impacted by climate change. Additionally, poverty on a reservation increasingly means that members of the tribes addressed do not have indoor plumbing, and that they will have to rely solely on other sources of water such as streams and water holes. As these sources dry due to droughts and high temperatures associated with climate change, access to water will become more problematic.

A.   The Pine Ridge Indian Reservation

Located in South Dakota, the Pine Ridge is the eighth-largest reservation in the United States and one of the poorest. The reservation is home to the Oglala Lakota Sioux Nation. Established in 1889, the Pine Ridge Reserva-

---

13.   Indian Country Today Media Network Staff, *The 7 Most Alarming Effects of Climate Change on North America, 2013 Edition*, INDIAN COUNTRY, Feb. 22, 2013, http://indiancountrytodaymedianetwork.com/2013/02/22/seven-most-alarming-effects-climate-change-north-america-2013-edition-147835.
14.   *Id.*
15.   *Id.*
16.   *Id.*
17.   *Id.*
18.   *Id.*
19.   *Id.*
20.   *Id.*

tion today is 3,469 mi^2 (8,984 km^2) in size.[21] The Lakota population of the Pine Ridge Reservation suffers from major health conditions, which include high mortality rates, alcoholism,[22] and malnutrition. For example, the reservation's average life expectancy is approximately 47 years for men and 52 for women,[23] as compared to approximately 79 years of age for the average American.[24] These are the lowest life expectancy figures in the Western Hemisphere outside of Haiti.[25]

Ninety-seven percent of the reservation's population lives below the federal government's poverty level of $24,250,[26] with the median income of $2,600 to $3,500;[27] the unemployment rate hovers in excess of 85%;[28] at least 60% of homes lack running water, connection to electricity, or sewage systems;[29] and the infant mortality (age 1-4 years) is the highest in North America, and is 300% higher than the U.S. national average.[30] Health care access is also limited and inadequate as compared to that in urban areas and "many reservation homes lack stoves, refrigerators, beds and/or basic furniture."[31]

The federal government, which is the trustee for the American Indians, has to date not expended a great deal of money to improve these native peoples' lives and it does not appear that it will.[32] This lack of caring continues

21. Re-Member, *Pine Ridge Indian Reservation*, http://www.re-member.org/pine-ridge-reservation.aspx (last visited Aug. 24, 2016).

22. *Id.* ("Alcoholism rate estimated as high as 80%; 1 in 4 infants born with fetal alcohol syndrome or effects").

23. American Indian Humanitarian Foundation, *Pine Ridge Statistics, Pine Ridge Reservation Humanitarian Rescue, Statistical Data*, http://www.4aihf.org/id40.html (last visited Aug. 24, 2016).

24. S.C. Kulkarni et al., *Falling Behind: Life Expectancy in U.S. Counties From 2000 to 2007 in an International Context*, 9 POPULATION HEALTH METRICS 16, 18 (2011). A 1998 study estimated life expectancy in Oglala Lakota County to be the lowest of any county in the United States; men—56.5 years, women—66 years. C.J.L. MURRAY ET AL., U.S. PATTERNS OF MORTALITY BY COUNTY AND RACE: 1965–1994: THE U.S. BURDEN OF DISEASE AND INJURY MONOGRAPH SERIES (Harvard Center for Population and Development Studies 1998). The Harvard School of Public Health has reported estimates of longevity for men at 48 years and women at 52 years. *See* A Pine Ridge Story, *Pine Ridge Today*, http://www.pineridgesioux.com (last visited Aug. 24, 2016).

25. American Indian Humanitarian Foundation, *supra* note 23.

26. Obamacare Facts, *Federal Poverty Level*, http://obamacarefacts.com/federal-poverty-level (last visited Aug. 24, 2016).

27. American Indian Humanitarian Foundation, *supra* note 23.

28. *Id.*

29. *Id.*

30. *Id.*

31. *Id.*; Re-Member, *supra* note 21.

32. *See, e.g.*, The American Presidency Project, *Special Message From President Richard Nixon to the Congress on Indian Affairs* (July 8, 1970) ("The first Americans—the Indians—are the most deprived and most isolated minority group in our nation. On virtually every scale of measurement—employment, income, education, health—the condition of the Indian people ranks at the bottom."), http://www.presidency.ucsb.edu/ws/?pid=2573; U.S. COMMISSION ON CIVIL RIGHTS, A QUIET CRISIS: FEDERAL FUNDING AND UNMET NEEDS IN INDIAN COUNTRY iii (2003) ("This study reveals that federal funding directed to Native Americans through programs at these agencies has not been sufficient to address the basic and very urgent needs of indigenous peoples. Among the myriad unmet needs are: health

to demonstrate the United States' disregard for human rights[33] and second and third generation rights.[34]

The Oglala Lakota will have difficulty adapting to the impacts of climate change on temperature and water wells.[35] Their cattle ranching and farming operations will surely be impacted.[36] Moreover, scientists do not yet know what effect the melting permafrost in Alaska and northern Canada and the concomitant melting of the Arctic ice sheet will have on this region of South Dakota.[37]

---

care, education, public safety, housing, and rural development."), http://www.usccr.gov/pubs/na0703/na0204.pdf.

33. *Special Message From President Richard Nixon, supra* note 32 ("This condition is the heritage of centuries of injustice. From the time of their first contact with European settlers, the American Indians have been oppressed and brutalized, deprived of their ancestral lands and denied the opportunity to control their own destiny."); Native American Rights Fund, *Promote Native American Human Rights* ("American Indian and Alaska Native individuals, like all people, are entitled to inalienable, fundamental human rights. In addition, tribes have fundamental collective human rights."), http://www.narf.org/our-work/promotion-human-rights (last visited Aug. 24, 2016).

34. First generation rights are defined as follows:

   civil and political rights such as free speech and conscience and freedom from torture and arbitrary detention . . . . Second generation rights are social, economic and cultural and include the rights to reasonable levels of education, healthcare, and housing and minority language rights . . . . Most recently third generation rights have shifted focus from the individual person (first generation rights) and the communities in which they live (social, economic and cultural rights) to the natural world, such as the right to a clean and healthy environment, and the right to species biodiversity.

   Helen Stacy, Second and Third Generation Rights in Africa, (Stanford Center on Democracy, Development, and the Rule of Law 2011), http://fsi.stanford.edu/research/second_and_third_generation_rights_in_africa.

35. *See, e.g.,* Daniel Cordalis & Dean B. Suagee, *The Effects of Climate Change on American Indian and Alaska Native Tribes,* 22 Nat. Resources & Env't 45, 45 (2008) ("Climate change will affect American Indian tribes differently than the larger American society. Tribal cultures are integrated into the ecosystems of North America, and many tribal economies are heavily dependent on the use of fish, wildlife, and native plants. Even where tribal economies are integrated into the national economy, tribal cultural identities continue to be deeply rooted in the natural world. As global warming disrupts biological communities, the survival of some tribes as distinct cultures may be at risk. The loss of traditional cultural practices because important plants and animals are no longer available may prove to be too much for some tribal cultures to withstand on top of the external pressures they have faced during recent generations.") *See also* Press Release, The White House, Fact Sheet: What Climate Change Means for South Dakota and the Great Plains (May 6, 2014) ("The Great Plains is a diverse region where climate is woven into the fabric of life. Daily, monthly, and yearly variations in the weather can be dramatic and challenging. The region experiences multiple climate and weather hazards, including floods, droughts, severe storms, tornadoes, hurricanes, and winter storms. In much of the Great Plains, too little precipitation falls to replace that needed by humans, plants, and animals. These variable conditions already stress communities and cause billions of dollars in damage. *Climate change will add to both stress and costs.*") (emphasis added), https://www.whitehouse.gov/sites/default/files/docs/state-reports/SOUTHDAKOTA_NCA_2014.pdf.

36. Press Release, The White House, *supra* note 35 ("Changes to crop growth cycles due to warming winters and alterations in the timing and magnitude of rainfall events have already been observed; as these trends continue, they will require new agriculture and livestock management practices.").

37. *See generally* Justin Gillis, *As Permafrost Melts, Scientists Study the Risks,* N.Y. Times, Dec. 16, 2011, http://www.nytimes.com/2011/12/17/science/earth/warming-arctic-permafrost-fuels-climate-change-worries.html.

Nevertheless, the Oglala Lakota community has not stood still in the face of climate change impacts. Indeed, it has taken steps to fight these potential effects, as well as the impacts of other environmental changes.[38] Since a large percentage of the reservation is suitable for grazing, and some farming, that effort has been successful, but for the lack of water.[39] Moreover, despite its natural beauty, Pine Ridge is geographically isolated and has limited water resources, which have made it quite difficult for the Lakota to launch themselves economically. The droughts that have impacted the western United States have had harsh impacts on the Lakota reservation, and have made a bad situation worse.[40] Over time, climate change will increase its toll on the reservation.[41] That is why the federal government's Bureau of Indian Affairs has to increase its footprint in Indian country.

The burdening of vulnerable and marginalized communities is not limited to Indian country. Similarly, as was observed in March 2016 with regards to the Flint, Michigan, contamination of water by lead (Pb), "Congress, which has refused to invest sufficiently in the nation's public works and has been antagonistic to environmental protection, must also learn from the crisis. For years, poor and minority communities have suffered disproportionately from environmental degradation."[42]

In the case of Flint, residents alleged racial discrimination over the change in drinking water from Lake Huron to the Flint River and high incidences of Pb in the water. The change in water source was initiated by Michigan's Republican governor, Rick Snyder.[43] In an effort to save money, the city manager, apparently in consultation with the governor's office and the Michigan Department of Environmental Quality, unhooked the city's potable

---

38. *See generally* Cordalis & Suagee, *supra* note 35; Tom Weis, *Why a Climate Activist Fasted Nine Days for Immigrant Families*, THE HUFFINGTON POST, Dec. 13, 2013 ("The moment you step into the fasting tent, you know you have entered a different dimension. It's not something I've experienced often with people I don't know (the last time, I felt it was in ceremony *with my brothers and sisters of the Great Sioux Nation*). In the tent, mutual respect reigns and egos melt away. Here, everyone is equal. Here, everyone has a voice. In the tent, you're family.") (emphasis added), http://www.huffingtonpost.com/ tom-weis/why-a-climate-justice-act_b_4409357.html.

39. Press Release, The White House, *supra* note 35 ("Rising temperatures are leading to increased demand for water and energy. In parts of the region, this will constrain development, stress natural resources, and increase competition for water among communities, agriculture, energy production, and ecological needs.").

40. *Id.*

41. *Id.*

42. Editorial Board, *The Racism at the Heart of Flint's Crisis*, N.Y. TIMES, Mar. 25, 2016, http://www. nytimes.com/2016/03/25/opinion/the-racism-at-the-heart-of-flints-crisis.html?action=click&pgtyp e=Homepage&clickSource=story-heading&module=opinion-c-col-left-region&region=opinion-c- col-left-region&WT.nav=opinion-c-col-left-region&_r=0.

43. Michael Moore, *10 Things They Won't Tell You About the Flint Water Tragedy. But I Will.*, http://mich- aelmoore.com/10FactsOnFlint/ (last visited Aug. 24, 2016).

water source and hooked up the water works to the toxic Flint River. The city undertook these actions even though it was warned by EPA that doing so would be dangerous for the residents. According to Michael Moore, a former resident of Flint, "[w]hen the governor's office discovered just how toxic the water was, they decided to keep quiet about it and covered up the extent of the damage being done to Flint's residents, most notably the lead affecting the children, causing irreversible and permanent brain damage. Citizen activists uncovered these actions."[44]

B.   Alaska Natives

In indigenous communities in Alaska, the impacts of climate change have been evident for almost a decade. For example, in 2007, the Fourth Assessment Report of the United Nations Intergovernmental Panel on Climate Change's (IPCC's) Working Group II[45] recognized that "American indigenous communities are among the most sensitive to climate change in North America."[46] Moreover, "indigenous communities in northern Canada and Alaska are already experiencing constraints on lifestyles and economic activity from less reliable sea and lake ice (for travelling, hunting, fishing, and whaling), loss of forest resources from insect damage, stress on caribou, and more exposed coastal infrastructure from diminishing sea ice."[47]

Indeed, Alaska, because of its melting permafrost, is likely to experience the effects of global warming more than any other location on earth.[48] Furthermore, due to their northern location, Alaska Native tribes are among the first American populations to feel the impacts of global climate change.[49] Eighty-six percent of Alaska Native villages have suffered some degree of flooding and erosion, with the greatest impacts of this destruction having been felt along the Alaskan coast.[50]

Increased variability in temperature, ice formation, wind speed, and ocean currents in the Bering and Chukchi Seas has occurred along the barrier island

---

44. *Id.*

45. CLIMATE CHANGE 2007: IMPACTS, ADAPTATION, AND VULNERABILITY. CONTRIBUTION OF WORKING GROUP II TO THE FOURTH ASSESSMENT REPORT OF THE INTERGOVERNMENTAL PANEL ON CLIMATE CHANGE (M.L. Parry et al. eds., 2007), www.ipcc.ch/ipccreports/ar4-wg2.htm [hereinafter IPCC FOURTH ASSESSMENT REPORT].

46. Cordalis & Suagee, *supra* note 35, at 45.

47. *Id.* (citing IPCC, FOURTH ASSESSMENT REPORT, *supra* note 45).

48. *See, e.g.*, Randall S. Abate & Elizabeth Ann Kronk, *Commonality Among Unique Indigenous Communities: An Introduction to Climate Change and Its Impacts on Indigenous Peoples*, 26 TUL. ENVTL. L.J. 179, 183 (2013).

49. *See id.*

50. GENERAL ACCOUNTING OFFICE, ALASKA NATIVE VILLAGES: MOST ARE AFFECTED BY FLOODING AND EROSION, BUT FEW QUALIFY FOR FEDERAL ASSISTANCE (2003) (GAO-04-142 2-3).

chain over the past few decades, changing the climate patterns to which the native villagers had been accustomed.[51] Sea ice formation is occurring later in the fall due to warmer temperatures and high winds.[52] The ice that builds up is often thinner, making it dangerous to cross and more susceptible to early breakup in the spring.[53]

Precipitation patterns have changed, with little snowfall in the autumn and early winter, but heavy amounts in late winter and spring.[54] The lack of snow makes it difficult for polar bears and ringed seals to make dens for giving birth or, in the case of male polar bears, to seek protection from the weather.[55] These environmental stresses will cause polar bears who go hungry to seek other sources of food, including in villages.

In response to the predictions of these impacts, speaking at the National Museum of the American Indian in Washington, D.C., Cheyenne elder Henrietta Mann, "issued an American Indian 'Call to Consciousness' on global climate change that calls 'upon all the peoples of the world to awaken and respond to our collective human responsibility to the seventh generation.'"[56]

---

51.   *See* Peter A. Bieniek et al., *Climate Drivers Linked to Changing Seasonality of Alaska Coastal Tundra Vegetation Productivity*, 19 EARTH INTERACTIONS 1, 2 (2015) ("The [Alaskan] tundra region generally has warmed over the summer but intraseasonal analysis shows a decline in midsummer land surface temperatures. The midsummer cooling is consistent with recent large-scale circulation changes characterized by lower sea level pressures, which favor increased cloud cover."), http://journals.ametsoc.org/doi/pdf/10.1175/EI-D-15-0013.1; *see also* NOAA, *Arctic Change, Human and Economic Indicators—Shishmaref* ("Sarichef Island (on which Shishmaref is located) is part of a dynamic, 100km-long barrier island chain that records human and environmental history spanning the past 2000 years . . . Erosion is occurring along the entire island chain, but it is exacerbated at Sarichef Island in part *because of the hydrographic impacts* of hard armoring of a sandy shoreface and permafrost degradation that is accelerated by infrastructure. Residents are experiencing the effects of coastal retreat on residential and commercial properties and there is a need to develop solutions, potentially including the difficult choice to abandon the island."), http://www.arctic.noaa.gov/detect/human-shishmaref.shtml (last visited Aug. 24, 2016).

52.   Bieniek et al., *supra* note 51, at 2 ("Many climatic changes have been documented in the Arctic summer over the satellite record and at longer time scales, most notably increasing surface air temperatures and a decline in sea ice.").

53.   *Id.* ("The decline in sea ice has had far-reaching terrestrial consequences not only for the climate but also for vegetation and other biota in the Arctic.").

54.   KEVIN GALLOWAY ET AL., ALASKA CLIMATE DISPATCH: A STATE-WIDE SEASONAL SUMMARY AND OUTLOOK (2014) ("Winter 2013–14 was memorable across Alaska not just for the records but for the significant impacts over many regions of the state. The National Climatic Data Center ranked this as the 8th warmest and 27th wettest mid-winter (December through February) statewide since 1915, and the impacts were from both individual weather events and the cumulative effects of the mild winter."), https://accap.uaf.edu/sites/default/files/AK_climate_dispatch_mar14_final.pdf.

55.   *See generally* Cordalis & Suagee, *supra* note 35, at 47; Mark Nuttall, *Chapter 12: Hunting, Herding, Fishing, and Gathering: Indigenous Peoples and Renewable Resource Use in the Arctic, in* ARCTIC CLIMATE IMPACT ASSESSMENT—SCIENTIFIC REPORT 660 (2005).

56.   Cordalis & Suagee, *supra* note 35, at 45 (citing Jose Barreiro, *A Call to Consciousness on the Fate of Mother Earth*, 8 NAT'L MUSEUM OF THE AM. INDIAN MAG. 34, 36 (2007)).

Furthermore, a 2010 report[57] explored the links between energy and water insecurity in rural Iñupiaq Eskimo villages in Alaska's Northwest Arctic Borough.[58] Required fuel-based transportation, such as snowmobiles, and high energy costs are two of the significant factors in domestic water access for the Iñupiaq community.[59] Dramatic increases in the costs of energy have led to decreased domestic water access, with adverse effects on household hygiene practices. The author of the report considers energy to be "a public health issue."[60] Indeed, she traces the manner in which high energy costs regulate "water consumption from production to household acquisition and use."[61] Thus, the author posits that in order to improve sanitation and access to potable water necessitates bearing in mind the water-energy nexus[62]: the amount and cost of energy required to treat and distribute water as well as manage waste.

Finally, with respect to water production, resource extraction, subsistence uses, and protection of instream flows,[63] it is essential that the federal government consider the disproportionate impacts of climate change,[64] water diversions, and water development on Alaska Native villages, as well as the possible management by Alaskan tribal governments.

---

57. Laura Palen Eichelberger, *Living in Utility Scarcity: Energy and Water Insecurity in Northwest Alaska*, 100 Am. J. Pub. Health 1010 (2010) ("I seek to demonstrate that sanitation, domestic water access, and hygiene practices in the Alaskan Arctic depend on the availability and cost of energy.").

58. Northwest Arctic Borough, *About* (indicating that the population is 7,523 based on the July 2010 U.S. Census), http://www.nwabor.org/about (last visited Aug. 24, 2016).

59. Eichelberger, *supra* note 57, at 1010.
     Lena: "Before, there was no payments."
     Ruth: "There were no bills."
     Lena: "The lights, the toilet . . . it spoiled us. But we can't go back and unravel it."
     Ruth: "If there's no fuel, there will be no electricity, there will be nothing. It will be hard time. We'll go back to cutting wood and hauling water."
         —Two elderly Iñupiaq women
     Id.

60. *Id.* at 1011.

61. *Id.* at 1010.

62. *Id.*

63. Instream flow is defined as "the water flowing in a stream channel . . . This simple concept belies the difficulty of determining what that flow should be among competing uses of water, such as irrigation, public supply, recreation, hydropower, and aquatic habitat." National Research Council (U.S.), The Science of Instream Flows: A Review of the Texas Instream Flow Program 32 (2005), http://www.nap.edu/read/11197/chapter/5.

64. Harold Shepherd, Water Justice in Alaskan Native Communities: A White Paper for Review by the Obama Administration and the Current Congress 1 (The Center for Water Advocacy n.d.), http://www.trunity.net/files/61501_61600/61508/cwa_wp_water-justice-in-alaska.pdf.

C.   The Piikani[65] First Nation Peoples of Alberta

In 1991, the Supreme Court of Canada heard a case that involved Alberta's construction of the Oldman Dam, on the Oldman River.[66] Until that time, very few people outside of Alberta were aware of the Northern Blackfeet Piikani (Scabby Robe) First Nation people, even though this band has been in Alberta since time immemorial.[67] Their plight became publicized when the government of Alberta sought to build a dam that would flood portions of their reserved lands, and the Piikani (then-Peigan), sued the Canadian government to require an environmental impact assessment.

When the Piikani entered into a treaty with the government, they requested that the Oldman River, the Porcupine Hills, and Crow Creeks be designated as their home base, because these were their preferred buffalo hunting wintering grounds.[68] Following the slaughter of the buffalo by the white man, the Piikani were persuaded to learn agriculture and to move to their newly designated reserve.[69] However, climatic conditions made farming untenable, and they turned their energies towards ranching, an economic activity that they are still engaged in today.

Nevertheless, like all First Nations across Canada, the Piikani face challenging and unique economic conditions, specifically a consistently low standard of living.[70] Indeed, in Canada, which is rated by the United Nations as one of the top four economically advanced nations in the world, "First Nation people experience employment rates of approximately 50% (on reserve) and 61% (off-reserve)."[71] As a consequence of these poor economic conditions, there is commonly an inability to cope with large-scale economic, social, and environmental changes in First Nation communities.[72] One of the reasons for this inability to deal with these changes is that the First Nations' econo-

---

65.   The Piikani were formally known as the Peigan.

66.   Friends of the Oldman River Soc'y v. Canada (Minister of Transport), [1992] 1 S.C.R. 3.

67.   *See generally* Alberta Government, Aboriginal Peoples of Alberta: Yesterday, Today, and Tomorrow 19 (2013), http://indigenous.alberta.ca/documents/aboriginalpeoples.pdf.

68.   *See* Jay Hansford C. Vest, *The Oldman River and the Sacred: A Meditation Upon Aputosi Pii'kani Tradition and Environmental Ethics*, 2 Can. J. Native Stud. 571 (2005), http://www3.brandonu.ca/cjns/25.2/cjnsv25no2_pg571-607.pdf.

69.   *See id.*

70.   Centre for Indigenous Environmental Resources, Report 3: Impacts of Climate Change on First Nation Economies 1 (2006), http://www.afn.ca/uploads/files/env/report_3_-_climate_change_and_fn_economies_final_draft_001.pdf. For the level of disparity among indigenous and non-Aboriginal populations gathered by Statistics Canada, *see id.* fig. 2-1.

71.   *Id.* at 8.

72.   *See generally id.*

mies are generally based on subsistence income-generating activities, such as forestry and tourism.[73]

These subsistence activities are vulnerable to changes in the climate.[74] Similarly, hunting and gathering of wild fruits and vegetables are also impacted by climatic conditions. Although the Piikani have benefited from alternative energy projects in which their band is involved, e.g., hydroelectricity and wind,[75] they still remain vulnerable to the vagaries of the climate.

As the subsistence economy gives way as a result of climate change, there are no "short-term or medium-term prospects that the subsistence sector can be replaced by the wage sector and industrial economy"[76] because there are simply no jobs to be had or created on and off the reserves for indigenous peoples.[77] Moreover, current research demonstrates that "climate change is presently having an impact on many northern communities [north of the 60° parallel] and on their ability to continue subsistence activities."[78] For instance, numerous First Nation peoples have reported retreating and thinning ice, drying tundra, reduced summer rain, warmer winters, and increased storms, among others.[79] Although the 60th parallel lies just north of the Piikani peoples reserve, there is no question that as the climate changes in the decades ahead, this band's lifestyle will be impacted, perhaps severely, if temperatures warm to the predicted 3–5°C.

Each of these changes or effects will require adaptation and mitigation by the Piikani and other First Nation communities.[80] Indeed, such efforts will also require resources for capacity-building, e.g., changes in hunting and fishing will demand new types of gear.[81] Given the lack of economic resources in these communities, it will be difficult to make the necessary transition without government aid. Provincial governments and the federal government have not provided the required financial assistance to First Nations.

II.   Applicable International Law

This section describes international human rights instruments that may be employed by indigenous Canadians and Americans in pursuing protection

---

73. *Id.* at 1.
74. *Id.*
75. *Id.* at 36, app. 1.
76. *Id.* at 10.
77. *Id.*
78. *Id.*
79. *Id.*
80. *Id.*
81. *Id.*

and justice in light of the impacts of climate changes. Efforts to employ these instruments will likely not be fruitful, especially in the near future.

A.   The United Nations Charter[82]

Every State that is a Member of the United Nations is a Party to the Charter.[83] The Charter was signed on June 26, 1945, and entered into force on October 24, 1945.[84] Articles 55[85] and 56[86] of the United Nations Charter provide in pertinent part:

> Article 55. With a view to the creation of conditions of stability and well-being which are necessary for peaceful and friendly relations among nations based on respect for the principle of equal rights and self-determination of peoples, the United Nations shall promote: a. higher standards of living, full employment, and conditions of economic and social progress and development; b. solutions of international economic, social, health, and related problems; and international cultural and educational cooperation; and c. universal respect for, and observance of, human rights and fundamental freedoms for all without distinction as to race, sex, language, or religion.

> Article 56. All Members pledge themselves to take joint and separate action in cooperation with the Organization for the achievement of the purposes set forth in Article 55.

Thus, the right of self-determination and the conditions of stability and well-being are paramount ends for each State Party. Charter rights are applicable to both Canadians and Americans. All United Nations Members are bound by Articles 55 and 56, by virtue of their status as Parties to the Charter and the United Nations' Universal Declaration of Human Rights, with which every Member, including the United States, must comply.

B.   The Universal Declaration of Human Rights

The Universal Declaration of Human Rights[87] provides in relevant part that human dignity is the hallmark of all human activity. It states

---

82. U.N. Charter, Oct. 24, 1945, 1 U.N.T.S. XVI, http://www.refworld.org/docid/3ae6b3930.html.
83. Article 102 of the Charter makes it binding on all Parties that are Members of the United Nations.
84. United Nations, *The UN Charter: The 70th Anniversary*, http://www.un.org/en/charter-united-nations (last visited Aug. 24, 2016).
85. U.N. Charter art. 55.
86. *Id.* at art. 56.
87. Universal Declaration of Human Rights, G.A. Res. 217A (III), U.N. GAOR, 3d Sess., 1st plen. mtg., U.N. Doc. A/810 (1948).

unequivocally that "[a]ll human beings are born free and equal in dignity and rights. They are endowed with reason and conscience and should act towards one another in a spirit of brotherhood."[88] Furthermore, Article 2 states that:

> Everyone is entitled to all the rights and freedoms set forth in this Declaration, without distinction of any kind, such as race, colour, sex, language, religion, political or other opinion, national or social origin, property, birth or other status. Furthermore, no distinction shall be made on the basis of the political, jurisdictional or international status of the country or territory to which a person belongs, whether it be independent, trust, non-self-governing or under any other limitation of sovereignty.[89]

Article 3 further provides that "[e]veryone has the right to life, liberty and security of person."[90] Similarly, Articles 6[91] and 7[92] of the Declaration provide that every person must be recognized as a person before the law, and that all people are equal before the law. The underlying theme of the Declaration is the importance of human self-esteem and respect. Indeed, it establishes common standards of treatment for all peoples and all Member States. It set out, for the first time, basic human rights to be universally protected. These fundamental rights were subsequently incorporated in other international instruments, including the European Declaration of Human Rights.[93]

C.   The 1966 International Covenant on Economic, Social, and Cultural Rights[94]

Economic, social, and cultural rights, known as second generation rights, encompass the rights to (1) adequate food, (2) health, (3) adequate housing, (4) education, (5) work, (6) social security, (7) participate in cultural life, (8)

---

88.   *Id.* at art. 1.
89.   *Id.* at art. 2.
90.   *Id.* at art. 3.
91.   *Id.* at art. 6. ("Everyone has the right to recognition everywhere as a person before the law.").
92.   *Id.* at art. 7. ("All are equal before the law and are entitled without any discrimination to equal protection of the law. All are entitled to equal protection against any discrimination in violation of this Declaration and against any incitement to such discrimination.").
93.   *See, e.g.*, Protocol No. 13 to the Convention for the Protection of Human Rights and Fundamental Freedoms, May 3, 2002, E.T.S. 187, which states:
> The Member States of the Council of Europe, signatory hereto, Convinced that everyone's right to life is a basic value in a democratic society and that the abolition of the death penalty is essential for the protection of this right and for the full recognition of the inherent dignity of all human beings . . . .
94.   International Covenant on Economic, Social, and Cultural Rights, Dec. 19, 1966, 993 U.N.T.S. 3.

water, and (9) sanitation. The hallmark of the ICESCR is self-determination, as reflected in the following language:

> 1. All peoples have the right of self-determination. By virtue of that right they freely determine their political status and freely pursue their economic, social and cultural development.

> 2. All peoples may, for their own ends, freely dispose of their natural wealth and resources without prejudice to any obligations arising out of international economic co-operation, based upon the principle of mutual benefit, and international law. In no case may a people be deprived of its own means of subsistence.[95]

The States Parties' obligations under the Covenant, specifically pursuant to Article 2, include a showing that they are making every effort to take concrete steps to implement the treaty.[96] One of these obligations is the duty to undertake administrative actions that will mitigate the effects of climate change. Such adaptation measures require providing indigenous populations with the opportunity for self-determination. Self-determination has been defined as the process by which indigenous peoples demonstrate that they have "particular ties to the territory whose fate is in question, ties which legitimize their participation in the vote."[97]

One area where self-determination and climate change intersect is health and health effects. A 2010 study found that

> [t]he existing burden of ill-health increases the sensitivity of Indigenous peoples to the adverse impacts of climate change, which combined with a proportionally higher dependence of many Indigenous livelihoods on the environment, spiritual and cultural ties to the land, demographic trends, and experience of marginalization, makes Indigenous peoples particularly vulnerable.[98]

Accordingly, the study's authors recommend that public health interventions concentrated on indigenous peoples in North America are required in order to prepare for, avert, and manage climate change perils, such as adaptation.[99] Indeed, the authors note that "Canada has been a leader in vulnerability assessment in public health."[100]

---

95. *Id.* at art. 1.
96. *Id.* at art. 14.
97. Marie-Hélène Gillot et al. v. France, U.N. Hum. Rts. Comm., 75th Sess., para. 8.14, U.N. Doc. CCPR/C/75/D/932/2000 (2002).
98. James D. Ford et al., *Vulnerability of Aboriginal Health Systems in Canada to Climate Change*, 20 GLOBAL ENVTL. CHANGE 668, 670 (2010).
99. *Id.*
100. *Id.*

D. The International Convention on the Elimination of All Forms of Racial Discrimination[101]

The International Convention on the Elimination of All Forms of Racial Discrimination (CAFRD) provides that segregation, as an outgrowth of colonialism and doctrines of superiority—including the white man's burden, Social Darwinism, and racial discrimination—must be eliminated. Moreover, the Parties to the Convention undertook to stop engaging, as governments, in acts or practices that support or encourage discrimination. Below are some of the provisions from the Convention that are relevant to the protection of indigenous peoples.

> Considering that the United Nations has condemned colonialism and all practices of segregation and discrimination associated therewith, in whatever form and wherever they exist . . .
>
> Article 1
> 1. In this Convention, the term "racial discrimination" shall mean any distinction, exclusion, restriction or preference based on race, colour, descent, or national or ethnic origin which has the purpose or effect of nullifying or impairing the recognition, enjoyment or exercise, on an equal footing, of human rights and fundamental freedoms in the political, economic, social, cultural or any other field of public life.
>
> Article 2
> 1. State Parties condemn racial discrimination and undertake to pursue by all appropriate means and without delay a policy of eliminating racial discrimination in all its forms and promoting understanding among all races . . .[102]

A committee was established as part of the Convention. Referred to as the Committee on the Elimination of Racial Discrimination, it held its 85th session in August 2014, where the Committee considered reports, comments, and information that the United States and Canada submitted under Article 9 of the Convention.[103] The United States noted that with regards to dis-

---

101. The International Convention on the Elimination of All Forms of Racial Discrimination, *opened for signature* Dec. 21, 1965, 660 U.N.T.S. 195 (entered into force Jan. 4, 1969) (Canada signed on Aug. 24, 1966, and ratified Oct. 14, 1970; United States signed on Sept. 28, 1966, and ratified Oct. 21, 1994), http://www.ohchr.org/EN/ProfessionalInterest/Pages/CERD.aspx.

102. *Id.*

103. United Nations Human Rights Office of the High Commissioner, *Committee on the Elimination of Racial Discrimination: Membership*, http://ohchr.org/EN/HRBodies/CERD/Pages/Membership.aspx (last visited Aug. 24, 2016).

crimination against indigenous peoples, the United States asserted that there remain

(a) Obstacles to the recognition of tribes . . .

(d) Progress made to improve the situation of indigenous peoples, including poverty, unemployment, health-care gaps, violent crime, including violence against women, low levels of academic achievement and the lack of access to safe drinking water and basic sanitation.[104]

In Canada's submission, the country reported that its indigenous First Nation citizens still suffer from continuing racial discrimination as follows:

3. Situation of Aboriginal people:

(b) Discriminatory effects of the Indian Act on the rights of Aboriginal women and children to marry, own property and inherit on reserve lands . . .;

(c) Overrepresentation of Aboriginal people in correctional facilities and their reintegration into the society: results of initiatives undertaken, in particular by British Colombia province . . .;

(d) Enjoyment of economic, social and cultural rights by Aboriginal people: access to public and private labour market, conditions of work, qualification recognition, job security and education . . .;

(f) Land issues, negotiation of treaties and land claims with Aboriginal people, including the Lubicon Lake case . . . .[105]

Given the discriminatory effects of the Indian Act on the rights of Aboriginal women and children, specifically with regards to the rights of marriage, ownership of property, and inheritance on reserve lands, as well as the continued lack of access to public and private labor markets, including conditions of work, job security, and education, and violations of treaties and land claims, it appears that these peoples will not fare well in efforts to prepare

---

104. *International Convention on the Elimination of All Forms Racial Discrimination—List of Themes in Relation to the Combined Seventh to Ninth Periodic Reports of United States of America (CERD/C/USA/7–9)*, U.N. Comm. on the Elimination of Racial Discrimination, 85th Sess., Provisional Agenda Item 4, U.N. Doc. CERD/C/USA/Q/7-9 (2014), http://docstore.ohchr.org/SelfServices/FilesHandler. ashx?enc=6QkG1d%2FPPRiCAqhKb7yhspzOl9YwTXeABruAM8pBAK2Wyp226L00wco36MQ ybB2d%2BztJSjxeRwa%2BJOQnvi2adxwohXw8hfhAG3Y3KRe0EU4M6Aq7je1UwoxEwATkFS vr.

105. *International Convention on the Elimination of All Forms of Racial Discrimination—List of Themes to Be Taken up in Connection With the Consideration of the Nineteenth and Twentieth Periodic Reports of Canada (CERD/C/CAN/19–20)*, U.N. Comm. on the Elimination of Racial Discrimination, 80th Sess., U.N. Doc. CERD/C/CAN/Q/19-20 (2012), http://tbinternet.ohchr.org/_layouts/treatybodyexternal/ Download.aspx?symbolno=CERD%2fC%2fCAN%2fQ%2f19-20&Lang=en.

for the impact of climate change. Furthermore, Canada has had decades to correct its colonialist ways in equalizing the treatment between its European and Aboriginal populations since it entered into the Convention, and yet it continues to fail to do so.

E.   The Convention on the Elimination of All Forms of Discrimination Against Women

Canada signed the Convention on the Elimination of All Forms of Discrimination Against Women (CEDAW) on July 17, 1980, and ratified it on December 10, 1981.[106] The United States has not ratified the Convention; however, its government signed the instrument on July 17, 1980.[107]

The Convention defines discrimination against women as

any distinction, exclusion or restriction made on the basis of sex which has the effect or purpose of impairing or nullifying the recognition, enjoyment or exercise by women, irrespective of their marital status, on a basis of equality of men and women, of human rights and fundamental freedoms in the political, economic, social, cultural, civil or any other field.[108]

In assenting to the Convention, States Parties obligate themselves to assume certain procedures to put an end to bias against women in all forms, including:

- to incorporate the principle of equality of men and women in their legal system, abolish all discriminatory laws and adopt appropriate ones prohibiting discrimination against women;

- to establish tribunals and other public institutions to ensure the effective protection of women against discrimination; and

- to ensure elimination of all acts of discrimination against women by persons, organizations or enterprises.[109]

On March 6, 2015, the CEDAW Committee found that Canada committed "grave violations" of the rights of Aboriginal women by failing to quickly

---

106. *See* The Convention on the Elimination of All Forms of Discrimination Against Women, *opened for signature* Mar. 1, 1980, 1249 U.N.T.S. 13 (entered into force Sept. 3, 1981), http://www.un.org/womenwatch/daw/cedaw/cedaw.htm.
107. *Id.*
108. *Id.* at art. 1.
109. *Id.* at art. 2.

and systematically scrutinize the high incidences of brutality and cruelty that they suffer, including murder and disappearances.[110]

F. The American Convention on Human Rights[111] and the American Declaration of the Rights and Duties of Man[112]

The American Convention on Human Rights and the American Declaration of the Rights and Duties of Man cover the countries of the Americas— North, Central, and South—and both Canada and the United States are Parties. With regards to human rights, Article 21 of the Convention, entitled the Right to Property, provides the following:

1. Everyone has the right to the use and enjoyment of his property. The law may subordinate such use and enjoyment to the interest of society.

2. No one shall be deprived of his property except upon payment of just compensation, for reasons of public utility or social interest, and in the cases and according to the forms established by law.[113]

The lands (property) in Canadian reserves, American reservations, and Inuit and Alaska Native territories are degraded, primarily based on their location, but also because these lands are not served by sewage or water treatment services.[114] This lack of basic services is a deprivation of property rights since other citizens, particularly those in urban centers, are provided these services. Moreover, the First Nations and the Inuit are not being justly compensated for the deficiency or denial of these services.

Article II of the Declaration provides that a fundamental rule of law is that "[a]ll persons are equal before the law and have the rights and duties established in this Declaration, without distinction as to race, sex, language, creed or

---

110. *See* Press Report, United Nations Human Rights Office of the High Commissioner, Canada's Failure to Effectively Address Murder and Disappearance of Aboriginal Women "Grave Rights Violation"—UN Experts (Mar. 6, 2015), http://www.ohchr.org/en/NewsEvents/Pages/DisplayNews.aspx?NewsID=15656&LangID=E. Although this chapter deals specifically with water security and climate change, the violence perpetrated against women by native and non-native men demonstrates the breadth of the issues that First Nations women must deal with on a daily basis.

111. American Convention on Human Rights, "Pact of San Jose, Costa Rica," Nov. 22, 1969, O.A.S. Treaty Series No. 36, 1144 U.N.T.S. 123, http://www.refworld.org/docid/3ae6b36510.html.

112. American Declaration of the Rights and Duties of Man, May 2, 1948, O.A.S. Res. XXX, http://www.oas.org/en/iachr/mandate/Basics/declaration.asp.

113. American Convention on Human Rights, *supra* note 111, at art. 21.

114. *See, e.g.*, David R. Boyd, No Taps, No Toilets: First Nations and the Constitutional Right to Water in Canada—Executive Summary (n.d.) ("As of 2010, 49 First Nations communities have high-risk drinking water systems and more than 100 First Nations face ongoing boil water advisories (out of roughly 600 First Nations in Canada . . . Many of these deplorable situations have been dragging on for years and in some cases decades."), http://www.onwa.ca/upload/documents/first-nations-right-to-water-in-canada.pdf.

any other factor."[115] In turn, Article VI further provides that "[e]very person has the right to establish a family, the basic element of society, and to receive protection therefore."[116]

The question that arises is how can one establish a family when one has no basic services, such as drinking water and sanitation? That endeavor is very hampered if not impossible. Moreover, it is commonly known that the family is "the basic element of society." Nevertheless, the very society that an Aboriginal (First Nations or Inuit) is part of routinely deprives these indigenous persons of the basic necessities to raise a family. Indeed, the State is depriving indigenous citizens of basic services. Article II appears to foreclose such actions; however, this is what is occurring on the ground.

Similarly, Article XI of the Declaration states that "[e]very person has the right to the preservation of his health through sanitary and social measures, relating to food [which should include water], clothing, housing and medical care, to the extent permitted by public and community resources."[117] In turn, Article XIII provides in pertinent part that "[e]very person has the right to take part in the cultural life of the community . . . ."[118] Native peoples in North America have a rich and varied culture, which includes the ability to feed and clothe themselves, and sustain their own languages and cultural traditions. For the most part, that culture is now destroyed. The lack of water and sanitation is an insult to the original injury of being pushed into reserves that are much less productive than their original lands.

Furthermore, culture includes a way of life. The native peoples of the Americas have an ethos that includes reverence for the land and water. When modern governments, such as the governments of Canada and the United States, maintain the underfunding of potable water and sewage systems on the reserves or reservations, they are depriving these peoples of their culture.

Similarly, Article XXIII states that "[e]very person has a right to own such private property as meets the essential needs of decent living and helps to maintain the dignity of the individual and of the home."[119] Native peoples' original or now reserved property cannot meet their essential needs or maintain their dignity if they do not have potable water and sanitation.

The right to property was tested in an Inter-American Commission on Human Rights case, *Mary and Carrie Dann v. United States*.[120] There, the

---

115. American Declaration of the Rights and Duties of Man, *supra* note 112, at art. II.
116. *Id.* at art. VI.
117. *Id.* at art. XI.
118. *Id.* at art. XIII.
119. *Id.* at art. XXIII.
120. Case 11.140, Inter-Am. C.H.R., Report No. 75/02, OEA/ser.L/V/II.117, doc. 5 rev., para. 140 (2002).

Danns, members of the Western Shoshone people, had their property condemned under the laws of the state of Nevada, under the normal due process rules of the state. The sisters sued to stop the condemnation but lost at all levels of the United States court system. They then brought their case before the Inter-American Commission, which held that both the American Declaration of the Rights and Duties of Man and the American Convention on Human Rights require that indigenous and tribal peoples' property rights over their territories are equivalent to those of non-indigenous private property rights, because of the duty of non-discrimination.

The Commission also cited Article XIII, the Right to Property, and found that it was violated since the Danns belonged to the Western Shoshone people, and that the tribe had experienced historical forced expropriation from their lands, in violation of the Treaty of Ruby Valley. Moreover, the Commission found that the tribe was moved, without profiting from any of the guarantees provided by the U.S. Constitution that protect persons from arbitrary takings of property: a violation of Article XXIII.

Given the *Dann* precedent, the First Nations and Inuit of Canada, who were also moved without just compensation, can be seen as suffering violations of their property rights and their rights to legal process under Article II. Similarly, given that the Dann sisters' facts are similar to those of their Canadian counterparts, a deprivation of property rights is sure to be found were a case filed before the Inter-American Commission. Indeed, the Commission would likely also find that these peoples' cultural rights were also violated.

The United States generally hides behind its Constitution and uses that instrument as a shield against second and third generation human rights. Nevertheless, as was noted in the case of Mary and Carrie Dann, there are other avenues for enforcing basic human rights in forums outside the United States. The same provision of the American Declaration of the Rights and Duties of Man and the Convention on Human Rights that apply to Canada are applicable with equal force against the United States.

Indian tribes are separate nations or entities that have some degree of sovereignty.[121] This fact has long been recognized by the U.S. Supreme Court. Tribal law and tribal courts govern Indian activity. Federal and state courts govern Indians where treaties, the Constitution, and federal statutes provide for jurisdiction.[122]

---

121. Colliflower v. Garland, Sheriff of County of Blaine, 342 F.2d 369, 374 (9th Cir. 1965).
122. Talton v. Mayes, 163 U.S. 376, 380–82 (1896). *See* Cherokee Nation v. Southern Kansas Ry. Co., 135 U.S. 641 (1890).

The leading decision is *Worcester v. Georgia*.[123] That case upheld, against the pretensions of the state of Georgia, the treaty rights of the Cherokee Nation. In so doing, Chief Justice Marshall stated: "The Indian nations had always been considered as distinct, independent, political communities, retaining their original natural rights, as the undisputed possessors of the soil, from time immemorial."[124]

Federal courts thus have jurisdiction to hear most, if not all, cases that involve Indian issues.[125] They therefore can utilize as indirect precedents the cases cited above, with regards to discrimination in the provision of drinking water.[126] In the same vein, Sioux (and other tribes) may sue for rights of sanitation. The basis of most of these suits is the U.S. Constitution's Fifth or Fourteenth Amendments, which require equal protection, before the law, for all citizens. Thus, if urban centers are provided with sanitary systems, tribal communities should likewise receive these services.

Treaty rights are also a basis for recovery. Thus, in *Tlingit & Haida Indians v. United States*,[127] the tribal entities were successful in their suit, which alleged that under certain federal laws, the United States impaired their title rights to certain land and water purchased from the United States and Russia.[128]

A challenge to a regulatory scheme was the issue in *Akiachak Native Community v. Salazar*.[129] There, four Alaska Native tribes and one native person, brought suit to challenge the Secretary of the Interior's decision to leave in place a regulation regarding trust lands that treated Alaska Natives differently from other native peoples. The challenged regulation governed the taking of land into trust under §5 of the Indian Reorganization Act.[130] It also

---

123. Worcester v. Georgia, 31 U.S. 515 (1832).
124. *Id.* at 519.
125. *See Colliflower*, 342 F.2d 369.
126. Although the General Assembly of the United Nations voted 50-1 for the right to water, the United States cast the dissenting vote. *See* G.A. Res. 64/292, U.N. GAOR, 64th Sess., U.N. Doc. A/RES/64/292 (2010). Therefore, as in other areas of human rights, that provision will likely have no effect on the behavior of the government of the United States. Few, if any, American federal courts would adopt a right to water. For further discussion of the right to water, see generally Itzchak E. Kornfeld, *Constitutions, Courts, Subsidiarity, Legitimacy, and the Right to Potable Water*, 21 WIDENER L. REV. 257 (2015); *see also* CENTRE ON HOUSING RIGHTS AND EVICTIONS, RIGHT TO WATER AND SANITATION PROGRAM, LEGAL RESOURCES FOR THE RIGHT TO WATER AND SANITATION: INTERNATIONAL AND NATIONAL STANDARDS (2d ed. 2008), http://www.worldwatercouncil.org/fileadmin/wwc/Programs/Right_to_Water/Pdf_doct/RWP-Legal_Res_1st_Draft_web.pdf.
127. Tlingit & Haida Indians v. United States, 147 Ct. Cl. 315 (1959).
128. *Id.* at 342.
129. Akiachak Native Cmty. v. Salazar, 935 F. Supp. 2d 195 (D. D.C. 2013).
130. 25 U.S.C. §465.

provided that, with one exception, the regulatory procedures "do not cover the acquisition of land in trust status in the State of Alaska."[131]

Plaintiffs argued that this exclusion of Alaska Natives—*and only Alaska Natives*—accordingly nullifies the regulation, as it discriminates among the various Indian tribes. The state of Alaska intervened to argue that the disparity in treatment is required by the Alaska Native Claims Settlement Act, which (upon the state's account) deprived the secretary of the statutory authority to take most Alaska land into trust. The secretary disagreed. The court concluded that the secretary retained his statutory authority to take land into trust on behalf of all Alaska Natives, and that his decision to maintain the exclusion of most Natives from the land-into-trust regulation violates 25 U.S.C. §476(g), which provides that contrary regulations "shall have no force or effect."[132] The court therefore granted summary judgment to the plaintiffs, and ordered additional briefing on the question of the proper remedy. Here again, discrimination by a government entity was not tolerated or sanctioned by the courts.

Canada and the United States were the defendants in another case in which the primary cause of action was destruction of hunting grounds due to climate change.[133] The plaintiff's petition sought relief from violations of the human rights of the Inuit community, caused by global warming resulting from greenhouse gas (GHG) emissions from the United States.[134] Moreover, it documented existing and projected destruction of the Arctic environment and the Inuit's cultural and hunting-based economy, which the petitioners asserted was caused by global warming.[135]

Indeed, the Inuit claimed that the specific rights they were seeking to protect were "the benefits of culture, to property, to the preservation of health, life, physical integrity, security, and a means of subsistence, and to residence, movement, and inviolability of the home."[136] Furthermore, they argued that the government of the United States ought to be held answer-

131. *Akiachak Native Cmty.*, 935 F. Supp. 2d at 197.
132. *Id.*
133. The 163-page petition was filed on December 7, 2005, with the Inter-American Commission on Human Rights, and supported by testimony from 63 named Inuit from northern Canada and Alaska. Press Release, Inuit Circumpolar Council Canada, Inuit Petition Inter-American Commission on Human Rights to Oppose Climate Change Caused by the United States of America (Dec. 7, 2005), www.inuitcircumpolar.com/inuit-petition-inter-american-commission-on-human-rights-to-oppose-climate-change-caused-by-the-united-states-of-america.html.
134. *Id.*
135. *Id.*
136. Inuit Circumpolar Conference v. Bush Administration: Petition to the Inter-American Commission on Human Rights Seeking Relief From Violations Resulting From Global Warming Caused by Acts and Omissions of the United States, at 5 (Dec. 7, 2005), http://www.ciel.org/Publications/ICC_Petition_7Dec05.pdf.

able for these violations so far as they resulted from two of its actions (or omissions): contributing disproportionately to GHG emissions and failing to take consequential steps to reduce GHG emissions and to counter climate change.[137]

The Inuit petitioners faced a number of obstacles, not the least of which was the fact that the United States has not accepted the jurisdiction of the Inter-American Court of Human Rights. Thus, the petition could only be brought before the Commission, which only issues recommendations and not binding judgments.[138] However, a bigger hurdle for the Inuit was proving a causal nexus between the harm caused by climate change and the actions and omissions of the U.S. government.[139] Notwithstanding the Inuit's efforts, on November 16, 2006, the Commission dismissed their petition without prejudice.[140]

III. The Status of American and Canadian Indigenous Peoples' Right to Water

In 1992, Prof. Stephen McCaffrey proposed a human right to water.[141] Thereafter, the United Nations Committee on Economic, Social, and Cultural Rights found a human right to water,[142] and issued its General Comment No. 15: The Right to Water, pursuant to the Convention's Articles 11 and 12.[143] Although not binding, the General Comment has been adopted by a number of national courts, including the Israel Supreme Court.[144] On July 28, 2010, the United Nations General Assembly unequivocally established a

---

137. *Id.* at 103–08.
138. Megan Chapman, *Climate Change and the Regional Human Rights Systems*, 10 Sustainable Dev. L. & Pol'y 37–38 (2010), http://digitalcommons.wcl.american.edu/cgi/viewcontent.cgi?article=1031&context=sdlp.
139. *Id.*
140. *Id.*
141. Stephen C. McCaffrey, *A Human Right to Water: Domestic and International Implications*, 5 Geo. Int'l Envtl. L. Rev. 1, 12 (1992).
142. *Substantive Issues Arising in the Implementation of the International Covenant on Economic, Social, and Cultural Rights, General Comment No. 15: The Right to Water (Arts. 11 and 12 of the Covenant)*, U.N. ESCOR Comm. on Economic, Social, and Cultural Rights, 29th Sess., U.N. Doc. E/C.12/2002/11 (2003), http://www2.ohchr.org/english/issues/water/docs/CESCR_GC_15.pdf.
143. *Id.; see also* Comm.155/96, Social & Econ. Rights Action Ctr. v. Nigeria, AHRLR 60 (ACHPR 2001); Aoife Nolan, *Addressing Economic and Social Rights Violations by Non-state Actors Through the Role of the State: A Comparison of Regional Approaches to the "Obligation to Protect,"* 9 Hum. Rts. L. Rev. 225 (2009).
144. *See, e.g.*, C.A. 9535/06 Abdallah Abu Masad v. Water Comm'r (2011) (Israel). The opinion was authored in Hebrew; however, an English translation is available, http://adalah.org/upfiles/2012/Supreme%20Court%20Ruling,%20Civil%20Appeal%20No.%209535.06%20-%20Abu%20Masad,%20Right%20to%20Water%20-%20English.pdf.

human right to water and sanitation[145] "and acknowledged that clean drinking water and sanitation are essential to the realisation of all human rights."[146]

Canada has yet to adopt either of these two instruments into its national law. Furthermore, since the United States is not a Party to the Convention on Economic, Social, and Cultural Rights, it is not bound by the Committee on Economic, Social, and Cultural Rights', General Comment 15, The Right to Water.[147] Thus, there is no right to or for water for any Canadian or U.S. citizen, regardless of whether indigenous or not.

As a Party to the Covenant on Economic, Social, and Cultural Rights, Canada must submit reports regarding its government's violations of human rights. Indeed, Canada has acknowledged that it has violated the human rights of indigenous peoples. That government has also acknowledged that it has violated the human right to water. These revelations were recently reported by the government's Department of Indian and Northern Affairs Canada. The agency issued a National Assessment of First Nations Water and Wastewater Systems—National Roll-up Report in 2011.[148] Similarly, in 2012, the nongovernmental organization Council of Canadians issued a report as part of its Blue Planet Project.[149] The latter report noted that in the two-year span between 2009 and 2011, Canada's federal government—as opposed to a provincial one—undertook an analysis of the First Nations communities' water and wastewater systems across Canada.[150]

That assessment encompassed 571 First Nations communities, which represent 97% of First Nations communities in the country.[151] The Council's report revealed that more than a third of these communities' systems were considered high risk for poor health, i.e., in 171 communities the water qual-

---

145. *Resolution Adopted by the General Assembly on 28 July 2010, 64/292. The Human Right to Water and Sanitation*, U.N. GAOR, 65th Sess., U.N. Doc. A/RES/64/292 (2010), http://www.un.org/es/comun/docs/?symbol=A/RES/64/292&lang=E.

146. United Nations Department of Economic and Social Affairs, *International Decade for Action "Water for Life" 2005–2015*, http://www.un.org/waterforlifedecade/human_right_to_water.shtml (last visited Aug. 24, 2014).

147. *Substantive Issues Arising in the Implementation of the International Covenant on Economic, Social, and Cultural Rights, General Comment No. 15: The Right to Water (Arts. 11 and 12 of the Covenant), supra* note 142.

148. *See* Neegan Burnside Ltd., National Assessment of First Nations Water and Wastewater Systems: National Roll-up Report—Final (Department of Indian Affairs and Northern Development 2011), http://www.aadnc-aandc.gc.ca/DAM/DAM-INTER-HQ/STAGING/texte-text/enr_wtr_nawws_rurnat_rurnat_1313761126676_eng.pdf.

149. *See* Meera Karunananthan & Johanna Willows, Canada's Violations of the Human Right to Water—Council of Canadians' Blue Planet Project (2012), http://lib.ohchr.org/HRBodies/UPR/Documents/Session16/CA/CC_UPR_CAN_S16_2013_CouncilofCanadiansBluePlanetProject_E.pdf.

150. *Id.* at 3.

151. *Id.*

ity was so deficient that it was detrimental to these citizens' health and safety.[152] Furthermore, some water systems were so run down that they would likely lead to substantial harm to health for members of the communities. Indeed, 143 communities, or 25% of the First Nations population across the country, were found to be served by high risk water systems.[153] A total of 312 systems were unable to meet Canadian health standards for drinking water.[154]

Furthermore,

[a]ccording to Health Canada, as of April 31, 2012, 119 First Nations communities across Canada are under drinking water advisories. Some of these advisories have been in place for over a decade . . . Incidence of waterborne diseases in First Nations communities is 26 times higher than in the general Canadian population . . . ."[155]

The Council of Canadians has particularly focused on three First Nation tribal communities: the Ontario-based Attawapiskat First Nation, the Pikangikum First Nation, and the northern Manitoba-based Manitoba Keewatinowi Okimakanak. For example, in 2011, significant media attention was focused on the Attawapiskat. Living conditions were found to be so significantly decayed that the Canadian Red Cross was forced to provide the community humanitarian aid.[156]

The situation for the entire First Nation community is even worse. A recent report observed that:

As of 2010, 49 First Nations communities have high-risk drinking water systems and more than 100 First Nations face ongoing boil water advisories (out of roughly 600 First Nations in Canada) . . . Many of these deplorable situations have been dragging on for years and in some cases decades . . . The federal government estimates that there are approximately 5,000 homes in First Nations communities (representing an estimated 20,000+ residents) that lack basic water and sewage services . . . Compared to other Canadians, First Nations' homes are 90 times more likely to be without running water . . . .[157]

---

152. *Id.*
153. *Id.*
154. *Id.*
155. *Id.*
156. *Id.* at 4.
157. BOYD, *supra* note 114 (citing *Implementation of the International Covenant on Economic, Social, and Cultural Rights: Addendum to the Fourth Periodic Reports Submitted by State Parties, Canada*, U.N. ESCOR, 19th Sess., U.N. Doc. E/C.12/4/Add.15 (2004)).

However, there is some collaboration between two Canadian government agencies: the Indigenous and Northern Affairs Department and Health Canada.[158] The latter assists portions of the First Nations community in assuring safe drinking water in their homes. Health Canada also provides environmental public health services to First Nations communities via its Environmental Public Health Program. As part of this program, Health Canada screens potable water quality and offers advice on potable water quality to First Nations communities and Indigenous and Northern Affairs Canada. Health Canada also provides wastewater programming such as public health inspections and public education in First Nations communities.

From a financial perspective, recent government outlays have also been positive. For example, before 2001, Health Canada was investing $5 million annually in its Drinking Water Safety Program for First Nation communities and one of the few reports discussing data from April 2001 to March 2003 demonstrated that Health Canada invested an additional $5 million to protect and enhance drinking water quality on reserves.[159]

Furthermore, "[i]n the 2003 budget, $600 million over five years was announced to support the implementation of the First Nations Water Management Strategy developed by Indigenous and Northern Affairs Canada and Health Canada to promote the safety of water supplies in First Nation communities from 2003–2008. Of the $600 million, $116 million was allocated to Health Canada to":

- provide resources to monitor drinking water quality in distribution systems with five or more connections as per the latest edition of the *Guidelines for Canadian Drinking Water Quality*;

- provide resources to monitor drinking water quality in distribution systems with five or more connections as per the latest edition of the *Guidelines for Canadian Drinking Water Quality*;

- increase resources allocated to communities with water treatment plants identified as being at high and medium risk;

- build First Nations' capacity;

- increase quality assurance/quality control of drinking water quality test results;

---

158. *See, e.g.*, Health Canada, *First Nations and Inuit Health, Drinking Water and Wastewater*, http://www.hc-sc.gc.ca/fniah-spnia/promotion/public-publique/water-eau-eng.php (last visited Aug. 24, 2016).
159. *Id.*

- increase accountability for implementation and delivery of the Drinking Water Safety Program;

- increase ability to make timely and informed decisions; and

- increase ability to detect potential drinking water quality problems."[160]

As for the United States, it has no federal constitutional guarantee for the right to water. However it has two statutory provisions that seek to enhance certain features of the right.[161] The two main statutes, the Safe Drinking Water Act[162] and the Clean Water Act,[163] merely address water quality. With regards to the individual states, in 2012 California passed a law that acknowledges the human right to water.[164] Moreover, Massachusetts' and Pennsylvania's constitutions recognize the right to water.[165]

Indeed, in the United States, current governmental processes deprive groups who in the past have endured discrimination, of equal access to basic levels of safe and affordable drinking water.[166] In her review of conditions in the United States, following her country visit, the United Nations special rapporteur on the human right to safe drinking water and sanitation noted in 2011[167] that those "who are facing obstacles in the enjoyment of the rights to water and sanitation are disproportionately Black, Latino, American Indian, homeless, or otherwise disadvantaged."[168] These communities lack access to water as a result of one or both of the following problems: they cannot afford a basic level of drinking water, or available drinking water is not safe for human consumption. Women and children face additional risks as a result of this situation.

---

160. *Id.*
161. See, *e.g., Report of the Special Rapporteur on the Human Right to Safe Drinking Water and Sanitation, Catarina de Albuquerque, Mission to the United States of America*, U.N. Human Rights Council, 18th Sess., paras. 7–13, U.N. Doc. A/HRC/18/33/Add.4 (2011), http://www2.ohchr.org/english/bodies/hrcouncil/docs/18session/A-HRC-18-33-Add4_en.pdf.
162. 42 U.S.C. §§300f–300k.
163. 33 U.S.C. §§1251–1387.
164. A.B. 685, 2011–2012 Leg., Reg. Sess. (Cal. 2012) (codified at Cal. Water Code §106.3 (West 2012)).
165. See Mass. Const. art. XCVII; Pa. Const. art. 1, §27.
166. *See generally* International Human Rights Law Clinic, Berkeley Law, United States Government Consultation on Environmental Issues Relating to the United Nations Universal Periodic Review: A Summary 8 (2014), https://www.law.berkeley.edu/files/UPR_Enviro_Consultation_Outcome_Doc_141208.pdf; International Human Rights Law Clinic at Santa Clara University School of Law, The Human Right to Water in the United States (2015), http://law.scu.edu/wp-content/uploads/150915_IACHR-Water-Rts-Questionnaire_United-States_Santa-Clara.pdf.
167. *Report of the Special Rapporteur on the Human Right to Safe Drinking Water and Sanitation, Catarina de Albuquerque, Mission to the United States of America, supra* note 161.
168. *Id.* at 3. *See also* International Human Rights Law Clinic at Santa Clara University School of Law, *supra* note 166, at 4.

IV.   Climate Justice Recommendations for Reform

For generations, Canada and the United States have ignored the human rights of its indigenous peoples. The law has withered in the face of these injustices. One would be foolish to believe that these nations will suddenly address such inequalities and wrongs in the face of climate change, particularly in the United States, where a large part of the populace and the government believes it is a hoax or a natural process that does not require regulation. Lawyers and advocates must therefore urge governments to address the universal human right to a healthy, clean, safe, and sustainable environment.

One response that is worth pursuing is the continued efforts to wean these countries off of fossil fuels, which will reduce climate change impacts on marginalized communities. As a result of these efforts, Alaska Natives and indigenous communities in the Arctic region of Canada would face less of a crisis in the potential loss of land, and loss of the ice required by polar bears and seals. Another proposal is to green investment treaties, particularly bilateral ones, which would include commitments to reduce GHGs and eliminate trade measures that conflict with climate change rules.

Other actions include the imposition of responsibilities on corporations to not only recognize, but to meet certain standards to reduce their carbon footprint and diminish their impact on human rights. Moreover, the United Nations' universal periodic review[169] process could be engaged to bring climate justice concerns to the broader population. Relocation is another issue that will have to be confronted. How and where to relocate Alaska Natives will be important adaptation responses by the United States. Similarly, planning will need to be undertaken to adapt to the flooding caused by climate change, such as the creation of flood insurance programs. Numerous other suggestions regarding the protection of human rights as a consequence of climate change have been made by the International Bar Association.[170]

---

169. The United Nations Human Rights Office of the High Commissioner explains the process as follows: The Universal Periodic Review (UPR) is a unique process which involves a review of the human rights records of all UN Member States. The UPR is a State-driven process, under the auspices of the Human Rights Council, which provides the opportunity for each State to declare what actions they have taken to improve the human rights situations in their countries and to fulfil their human rights obligations. As one of the main features of the Council, the UPR is designed to ensure equal treatment for every country when their human rights situations are assessed.
United Nations Human Rights Office of the High Commissioner, *Universal Periodic Review*, http://www.ohchr.org/EN/HRBodies/UPR/Pages/UPRMain.aspx (last visited Aug. 24, 2016).

170. *See generally Climate Laws Inadequate to Protect Human Rights—New Legal Frameworks Needed, States New IBA Report*, INT'L BAR ASS'N, Sept. 22, 2014, http://www.ibanet.org/Article/Detail.aspx?ArticleUid=96b93592-3761-4418-8a52-54a81b02c5f1.

Finally, native peoples in the United States can rely on environmental justice precedent to seek justice in Indian country. For example, in *Kennedy v. City of Zanesville*,[171] jury verdicts totaling approximately $11 million were issued for the illegal denial, to a purely African-American community, of a water supply system for 50 years, while ensuring connections to all of the surrounding white neighborhoods. The verdicts were issued against the city of Zanesville, Ohio; Muskingum County, Ohio; and the East Muskingum Water Authority. The jury found that the defendants violated fair housing and constitutional protections afforded to the plaintiffs under U.S. federal law. Similarly, in *Dowdell v. City of Apopka*,[172] the court concluded that the city engaged in prohibited discrimination by failing to provide access to water infrastructure in marginalized African-American neighborhoods. The court ordered that the marginalized community be provided water in an expedited fashion and that the remedy should be implemented before provision to any predominantly white neighborhoods was undertaken. These two cases can offer a foundation for environmental justice-based relief to support indigenous communities' right to access drinking water in the face of climate change impacts. Failing to ensure indigenous communities' access to water and use of natural resources may constitute a violation of treaty-based and federal trust protections.

Conclusion

This chapter first discussed the status of American and Canadian indigenous communities and focused on specific tribes in North America. Following a brief introduction of Canadian and American indigenous peoples, this chapter addressed the threats faced by these communities as a consequence of climate change. The chapter then discussed case law and international law instruments that these indigenous peoples may employ in pursuing legal avenues to vindicate their rights, specifically the right to water, in light of global warming and the loss of their lands and way of life. It also highlights the fact that indigenous peoples in Canada and the United States, who live in extra-rural reservations and in remote and climate-vulnerable locations, will suffer much more than the non-indigenous populations in cities and the suburbs.

Finally, the chapter provided recommendations for mitigation and adaptation measures for these indigenous communities. These proposals for reform

---

171. Kennedy v. City of Zanesville, Case No. 2:03-cv-1047 (S.D. Ohio July 10, 2008).
172. Dowdell v. City of Apopka, 698 F.2d 1181 (11th Cir. 1983).

include decreasing fossil fuel consumption through government action, imposing responsibility on corporations to reduce their carbon footprint and impact on human rights, and utilizing environmental justice case law precedent.

Island Nation
Perspectives

Chapter 11

Justice for Small Island Nations: Intersections of Equity, Human Rights, and Environmental Justice

*Sumudu Anopama Atapattu**

Introduction

> *We live in constant fear of the adverse impacts of climate change. For a coral atoll nation, sea level rise and more severe weather events loom as a growing threat to our entire population. The threat is real and serious, and is of no difference to a slow and insidious form of terrorism against us.*
>
> — Prime Minister of Tuvalu, Saufatu Sapo'aga[1]

After the euphoria at the adoption of the Paris Agreement has died down and its formal signing on Earth Day completed, the above quote from the prime minister of Tuvalu at the 21st meeting of the Conference of the Parties

---

* *The author gratefully acknowledges the research assistance of Dan Schreiber, Esq.*

1. Harsha Walia, *Why Migration Should Be Central to Paris COP21 Climate Talks*, TELESURTV.NET, Nov 30, 2015 (quoting statement of prime minister of Tuvalu at the United Nations), http://www.telesurtv.net/english/opinion/Why-Migration-Should-Be-Central-to-Paris-COP21-Climate-Talks-20151125-0011.html.

(COP21) offers a dose of reality. Likewise, a May 2016 news story that five of the Solomon Islands have disappeared into the Pacific Ocean and six more have experienced a dramatic reduction in their shorelines[2] should send alarm bells to even the most ardent climate skeptic. These adverse consequences, certainly the disappearance of islands, were expected to take place in the distant future, not during our lifetime. Thus, addressing the plight of small island States has become an urgent issue.

Nevertheless, the international community has dragged its feet and not taken meaningful action to reduce greenhouse gas (GHG) emissions, despite the adoption of the Paris Agreement. The significant gap between what States have pledged under their nationally determined contributions (NDCs) in the run up to the Paris Agreement and what is required to avert tipping points is disconcerting.[3] Small island States are understandably very worried. Even more disconcerting are the climate skeptics who, in the face of overwhelming scientific evidence, continue to dispute its existence.[4] "Wet feet marching"[5] could become a reality sooner than anticipated.

Climate change poses unprecedented challenges to the global community. Nowhere are these challenges more pronounced and dire than in relation to small island States.[6] With sea-level rise associated with increased temperatures and melting of glaciers, these small island States are facing a bleak future. They are already experiencing increased severe weather events, which are causing extensive hardship to this vulnerable group of States.[7] These nations and their people stand to lose everything they have, including statehood, which is crucial to exist as a legal entity under international law.[8]

---

2. Angela Dewan, *Five Solomon Islands Swallowed by the Sea*, CNN.COM, May 10, 2016, http://edition. cnn.com/2016/05/10/world/pacific-solomon-islands-disappear/.

3. U.N. ENVIRONMENT PROGRAMME (UNEP), THE EMISSIONS GAP REPORT 2015: A UNEP SYNTHESIS REPORT (2015), http://uneplive.unep.org/media/docs/theme/13/EGR_2015_301115_lores.pdf.

4. *See* NAOMI KLEIN, THIS CHANGES EVERYTHING: CAPITALISM VS. THE CLIMATE (2014); ROB NIXON, SLOW VIOLENCE AND THE ENVIRONMENTALISM OF THE POOR (2011).

5. "Wet feet marching" has become the slogan to refer to climate refugees, especially from small island States, after the impassioned speech of Atiq Rahaman of Bangladesh before the COP in Berlin in 1995: "If climate change makes our countries uninhabitable. . . . we will march with our wet feet into your living rooms." *See* Marissa Knodel, *Wet Feet Marching: Climate Justice and Sustainable Development for Climate Displaced Nations in the South Pacific*, 14 VT. J. ENVTL. L. 127 (2012).

6. The emphasis on small island States should not be taken as an indication that the impact on other countries is not important. Areas such as sub-Saharan Africa and low-lying countries such as Bangladesh are also extremely vulnerable.

7. Leonard A. Nurse et al., *Small Islands*, *in* CLIMATE CHANGE 2014: IMPACTS, ADAPTATION, AND VULNERABILITY. PART B: REGIONAL ASPECTS. CONTRIBUTION OF WORKING GROUP II TO THE FIFTH ASSESSMENT REPORT OF THE INTERGOVERNMENTAL PANEL ON CLIMATE CHANGE 1613 (V.R. Barros et al. eds., 2014), http://www.ipcc.ch/pdf/assessment-report/ar5/wg2/WGIIAR5-Chap29_FINAL. pdf.

8. Whether a State ceases to become a State once it loses its territory, which is one of the criteria of statehood, (or as some contend, its population) is a hotly debated issue. *See* SUMUDU ATAPATTU, HUMAN

Because these nations are disproportionately affected by a phenomenon to which they hardly contributed, climate change raises serious justice issues for this group of States. As the United Nations Human Rights Council recognized, "the effects of climate change will be felt most acutely by those segments of the population who are already in vulnerable situations owing to factors such as geography, poverty, gender, age, indigenous or minority status and disability."[9]

This chapter discusses environmental justice and climate justice frameworks to examine their applicability to small island States and their people. It reviews literature on environmental justice and climate justice and evaluates its relevance for small island States. Part I of the chapter addresses climate change impacts on small island States. Part II discusses environmental justice, including its various definitions and the four-fold definition proposed by Robert Kuehn and the tripartite framework proposed by Hari M. Osofsky. Part III examines climate justice and small island States and evaluates what climate justice means for the people of small island States and for the island nations themselves. It reviews the Warsaw International Mechanism for Loss and Damage under the United Nations Framework Convention on Climate Change (UNFCCC) and evaluates the degree to which it can provide relief to this vulnerable group of States and their people. Part IV discusses the Paris Agreement and its reference to climate justice and concludes with some recommendations for both small island States and their inhabitants on how the climate justice framework can provide relief for their plight.[10]

I.   Climate Change and Small Island States

The United Nations Office of the High Representative for the Least Developed Countries, Landlocked Developing Countries, and Small Island Devel-

---

RIGHTS APPROACHES TO CLIMATE CHANGE: CHALLENGES AND OPPORTUNITIES ch. 11 (2015). Under the Montevideo Convention on the Rights and Duties of States, an entity must satisfy four criteria in order to be considered a State: territory, population, government, and the capacity to enter into international relations. *See generally* JAMES CRAWFORD, CREATION OF STATES IN INTERNATIONAL LAW (2d ed. 2006).

9.   United Nations Human Rights Council Res. 10/4, Human Rights and Climate Change, 10th Sess., U.N. Doc. A/HRC/10/L.11 (2009), http://ap.ohchr.org/documents/E/HRC/resolutions/A_HRC_RES_10_4.pdf.

10. Although these small island States are at risk of becoming completely submerged from sea-level rise, this chapter will not discuss the legal issues arising from the disappearance of States or those relating to displacement of the inhabitants of small island States in depth. For a discussion of the legal issues relating to disappearance of States, see ATAPATTU, *supra* note 8, at ch. 9. For a discussion of climate change displacement issues, see ROBERT A. MCLERMAN, CLIMATE AND HUMAN MIGRATION: PAST EXPERIENCES, FUTURE CHALLENGES (2013); JANE MCADAM, CLIMATE CHANGE, FORCED MIGRATION, AND INTERNATIONAL LAW (2012); ATAPATTU, *supra* note 8, at ch. 6.

oping States (UN-OHRLLS) identifies small island developing States (SIDS) as "a distinct group of developing countries facing specific social, economic and environmental vulnerabilities."[11] There are 52 countries in this group.

Similarly, the Intergovernmental Panel on Climate Change (IPCC) confirms that small island States are especially vulnerable to climate change.[12] The IPCC noted that sea-level rise "poses one of the most widely recognized climate change threats to low-lying coastal areas."[13] The report pointed out that this is significant because the majority of communities and infrastructure is located in coastal zones and on-land relocation opportunities are limited.[14] Despite the enormous impact of climate change on these small islands, climate change is not the only factor that is contributing to the negative impacts experienced by these islands.[15] As with many other issues, human activities, including beach mining, population pressures, and expanding settlements, have contributed to coastal erosion and other environmental problems facing these States.

These small island States are not homogenous, even though they are often treated as such. While there are some obvious similarities, their culture, populations, ecosystems and, therefore, their vulnerability vary. As the IPCC report noted: "Vulnerabilities and adaptation needs are as diverse as the variety of islands between regions and even within nation states."[16] The IPCC report also highlights that there are gaps in research with regard to the impact of climate change on these islands that need to be addressed. It further noted that while sea-level rise poses one of the most widely recognized threats to low-lying coastal areas on islands, the long-term impacts depend on the type of island and the adaptation strategy adopted. Small island States have 16% of their land area in low elevation coastal areas, yet there is limited evidence as to which regions will experience the largest sea-level rise and which island will experience the worst climate impacts.[17] In this regard, the IPCC report concluded:

> More research is needed to produce *robust agreement* on the impact of SLR [sea-level rise] on small islands, and on the range of adaptation strategies that

---

11. UN-OHRLLS, Small Island Developing States: Small Islands Big(ger) States (2011), http://unohrlls.org/custom-content/uploads/2013/08/SIDS-Small-Islands-Bigger-Stakes.pdf.
12. Climate Change 2014: Impacts, Adaptation and Vulnerability. Part A: Global and Sectoral Aspects. Contribution of Working Group II to the Fifth Assessment Report of the Intergovernmental Panel on Climate Change (2014), http://www.ipcc.ch/report/ar5/wg2/ [hereinafter IPCC, Climate Change 2014].
13. *Id.* at 1619.
14. *Id.*
15. *Id.* at 1620.
16. *Id.* at 1635.
17. *Id.* at 1639.

could be appropriate for different island types under those scenarios. Research into the possible un-inhabitability of islands has to be undertaken sensitively to avoid short-term risk (i.e., to avoid depopulation and ultimately island abandonment) associated with a loss of confidence in an island's future.[18]

Many States and communities are now engaged in preparing adaptation plans and many least developed countries, including some small island States, have prepared national adaptation programs of action (NAPAs).[19] Small island States face particular challenges as their adaptation options are limited by their physical characteristics. The IPCC identifies some of these challenges as:

[i]nadequate access to financial, technological, and human resources; issues related to cultural and social acceptability of measures; constraints imposed by the existing political and legal framework; the emphasis on island development as opposed to sustainability; a tendency to focus on addressing short-term climate variability rather than long-term climate change; and community preference for "hard" adaptation measures such as seawalls instead of "soft" measures such as beach nourishment.[20]

The IPCC report was very careful not to refer to total inundation of these islands and what it would mean for the States and their people. The UN-OHRLLS report on SIDS, by contrast, acknowledges that the very survival of some low-lying SIDS will be threatened by climate change.[21] Unless States reduce their GHG emissions drastically such that global temperature increase is limited to 1.5°C from pre-industrial levels, this seems to be the fate awaiting the small island States. The potential impacts of climate change on SIDS are considered extreme. In addition to the adverse impacts that are common to all States, "SIDS will also suffer a series of problems which will be uniquely detrimental to them."[22]

II.   Environmental Justice as a Framework

Given the grossly disproportionate impact of climate change on small island States in relation to their overall GHG emissions, environmental justice pro-

---

18. *Id.*
19. For a list of countries that have prepared NAPAs, see UNFCCC, *NAPAs Received by the Secretariat*, http://unfccc.int/adaptation/workstreams/national_adaptation_programmes_of_action/items/4585. php (last visited Aug. 22, 2016).
20. *See* IPCC, CLIMATE CHANGE 2014, *supra* note 12, at 1640.
21. *Id.*
22. Alexander Gillespie, *Small Island States in the Face of Climate Change: The End of the Line in International Environmental Responsibility*, 22 UCLA J. ENVTL. L. & POL'Y 107, 115 (2003).

vides a useful lens to examine the consequences of climate change on small island States and their people. While many equate justice with *access* to justice, and international human rights law requires States to provide access to judicial bodies and tribunals,[23] access to justice is only one dimension of environmental justice.

Scholars use various definitions of environmental justice and it seems to mean "many things to many people."[24] It also depends on whether one is referring to local communities, regulated entities, or governmental officials, and whether the issue is occurring at the international, national, or local level.[25] Similarly, Dinah Shelton equates environmental justice to "Aesop's elephant," where in the fable of Aesop, several blind men who touch an elephant describe it in different ways depending on where they touch.[26] This aptly describes the various interpretations of environmental justice adopted by scholars, activists, and victims. While some argue that it signifies the moral underpinning from which law emerges, others contend that it is the ultimate objective to be achieved by legal norms.[27] Whatever definition one adopts, law and justice are clearly related, yet not synonymous, and notions of fairness and equity are inherent in the concept of justice.[28] It also recognizes the disproportionate impact of adverse consequences of environmental pollution and degradation on certain communities due to historic marginalization, subordination, and underlying power asymmetry often dating back to the colonial era.[29] Rather than attempt to define environmental justice, this chapter will use the four-part categorization of environmental justice proposed by Kuehn—distributive justice, procedural justice, corrective justice, and social justice[30]—supplemented, to the extent relevant, by the tripartite definition proposed by Osofsky—geographic scope, severity, and duration.[31]

---

23. *See* International Covenant on Civil and Political Rights, Dec. 16, 1966, art. 2, 999 U.N.T.S. 171, http://www.ohchr.org/en/professionalinterest/pages/ccpr.aspx.
24. *See* Robert Kuehn, *A Taxonomy of Environmental Justice*, 30 ELR 10681 (2000).
25. *Id.*
26. *See* Dinah Shelton, *Describing the Elephant: International Justice and Environmental Law*, *in* ENVIRONMENTAL LAW AND JUSTICE IN CONTEXT 55 (Jonas Ebbesson & Phoebe Okowa eds., 2009).
27. *Id.*
28. *See* Lea Brilmayer, *International Justice and International Law*, 98 W. VA. L. REV. 611 (1996).
29. For a comprehensive discussion of how the North-South divisions have shaped international environmental law, see SHAWKAT ALAM, SUMUDU ATAPATTU, CARMEN GONZALEZ & JONA RAZZAQUE EDS., INTERNATIONAL ENVIRONMENTAL LAW AND THE GLOBAL SOUTH (2015).
30. *See* Kuehn, *supra* note 24; Carmen Gonzalez, *Environmental Justice and International Environmental Law*, *in* ROUTLEDGE HANDBOOK OF INTERNATIONAL ENVIRONMENTAL LAW 79–80 (Shawkat Alam et al. eds., 2013).
31. *See* Hari M. Osofsky, *Learning From Environmental Justice: A New Model for International Environmental Rights*, 24 STAN. ENVTL. L. J. 71 (2005).

While human rights law is related to environmental justice and could be a useful tool to achieve justice, some contend that the human rights framework is *itself* the problem and has resulted in further marginalizing certain groups and communities.[32] Others claim that the reach of human rights is overstated. Some commentators claim that the language of human rights has become the dominant mode of moral discourse in the past 50 years, edging out moral tropes such as distributive justice, the common good, and solidarity. Such claims to dominance and universality seem to be overstated.[33]

Despite these criticisms, the human rights framework has provided relief to many victims and communities, particularly at the regional level, and has provided a powerful tool to victims who have suffered at the hands of their own State to seek redress. Human rights law is constrained by the limits of international law itself and displays those drawbacks, but it has given a voice to marginalized communities and a powerful tool to activists to seek justice on behalf of those marginalized communities. Moreover, it has constrained State behavior vis-à-vis its own citizens and given direct standing to individual victims before these international and regional fora, which no other framework has done. In the context of climate change with its disproportionate impacts on vulnerable States and communities, justice and human rights provide useful frameworks to address issues facing small island States, their people, those who are forced to migrate as a result of climate change, current victims in least developed countries, and future generations[34] who will face the brunt of the problem.

Adopting a justice and rights framework is the best approach for the victims of climate change, especially for inhabitants of small island States. Its significance has not been more apparent than in relation to climate change. While those who contributed most to the problem will hide behind adaptation fortifications, those who contributed the least will become even more impoverished, and in the worst case, be forced to migrate, leaving behind ancestral lands and cultural practices, and losing the protection of their State. They will be at the mercy of the very States that created the problem. In anticipation of this plight, developing countries lobbied hard to get the loss and damage mechanism included in climate agreements. After years of negotiations, they succeeded at COP19 in Warsaw, and the Paris Agreement included this mechanism as the fourth pillar of climate action, despite

---

32. *See* Gonzalez, *supra* note 30.
33. *See* William Twining, *Law, Justice, and Rights: Some Implications of a Global Perspective, in* Ebbesson & Okowa, *supra* note 26, at 88.
34. *See* Peter Lawrence, Justice for Future Generations (2014).

intense opposition from developed countries.[35] The United Nations Global Conference for Sustainable Development of Small Island Developing States emphasized the need for a justice framework.

The environmental justice movement originated in the United States to address the growing practice of siting polluting and hazardous activities in poor and minority neighborhoods.[36] It was one of the early manifestations of the environmental protection field converging with the human (civil) rights movement. It led to an Executive Order on environmental justice issued by President Clinton in 1994.[37] The U.S. Environmental Protection Agency (EPA) has moved from its initial definition of "environmental equity" to mean equal distribution of environmental risks across population groups to encompass fair treatment of people of all races, cultures, incomes, and educational levels.[38] It then moved beyond that definition to the following version:

> Environmental justice is based on the premise that: 1) it is a basic right of all Americans to live and work in "safe, healthful, productive, and aesthetically and culturally pleasing surroundings"; 2) it is not only an environmental issue but a public health issue; 3) it is forward-looking and goal-oriented; and 4) it is also inclusive since it is based on the concept of fundamental fairness, which includes the concept of economic prejudices as well as racial prejudices.[39]

Some refer to the desired end results,[40] while yet others identify principles inherent in the environmental justice framework: (1) protect all persons from environmental degradation; (2) adopt a public health prevention of harm approach; (3) place the burden of proof on the polluter; (4) remove the requirement to prove intent to discriminate; and (5) redress existing inequities.[41] In other words, ask the question, "who gets what, why and how much."[42] The next section outlines Kuehn's four-fold framework for environmental justice.

---

35. *See* CLIMATE FOCUS, LOSS AND DAMAGE IN THE PARIS AGREEMENT: CLIMATE FOCUS CLIENT BRIEF ON THE PARIS AGREEMENT IV (2015), http://www.climatefocus.com/sites/default/files/20160214%20 Loss%20and%20Damage%20Paris_FIN.pdf.

36. *See* Kuehn, *supra* note 24; Carmen Gonzalez, *Environmental Justice, Human Rights, and the Global South*, 13 SANTA CLARA J. INT'L L. 151, 155 (2015).

37. Federal Actions to Address Environmental Justice in Minority Populations and Low-income Populations, Exec. Order No. 12898, 59 Fed. Reg. 7629 (Feb. 16, 1994), http://www.ejnet.org/ej/execorder. html.

38. Kuehn, *supra* note 24, at 10682.

39. *Id.* at 10683.

40. *Id.* (citing the 1991 First People of Color Environmental Leadership Summit and Its Principles of Environmental Justice).

41. Kuehn, *supra* note 24, at 10683 (quoting Dr. Robert Bullard).

42. *Id.*

A. Distributive Justice

Distributive justice is closely related to equal treatment—i.e., the right to the same distribution of goods and opportunities as anyone else.[43] In the environmental context, this does not mean distributing pollution or risk equally. Instead, environmental justice advocates have called for equal protection for all and the need to eliminate environmental hazards: "In other words, distributive justice is achieved through a *lowering* of risks, not a shifting or equalizing of existing risks."[44] Distributive justice also refers to the equal distribution of benefits, including access to parks, safe drinking water and sanitation, and public transportation.[45]

While distributive justice requires equal treatment, sometimes it becomes necessary to favor a particular group to redress past imbalances or inequities and level the playing field. Law has developed tools to promote this objective: affirmative action under national law[46] and the common but differentiated responsibility (CBDR) principle at the international level.[47] While a detailed analysis of these topics is beyond the scope of this chapter, both tools are based on the notion of justice and fairness and seek to redress past injustices. In fact, the CBDR principle underlies the legal regime governing climate change and forms one of its core principles.[48] It requires developed countries (Annex I countries) to help developing countries with both mitigation and adaptation measures, including technology transfer and the establishment of funds. Not surprisingly, it has also been the subject of intense controversy, and action on climate change has often stalled as a result of it. Nonetheless, its adoption breaks new ground in international law, a system based essentially on the principle of sovereign equality.[49]

The Paris Agreement adopted an ingenious way to circumvent application of distributive justice principles by avoiding any differentiation of States according to their level of development. Instead, it encapsulated voluntary commitments made by States within a legally binding framework, thereby

---

43. *Id.*
44. *Id.* at 10684 (emphasis added).
45. *Id.*
46. *See, e.g.,* Executive Order No. 11246, 20 Fed. Reg. 12319 (Sept. 28, 1965) (addressing affirmative action), https://www.eeoc.gov/eeoc/history/35th/thelaw/eo-11246.html.
47. For a detailed discussion of the CBDR principle, see Lavanya Rajamani, Differential Treatment in International Law (2006).
48. United Nations Framework Convention on Climate Change, May 9, 1992, art. 3, 1771 U.N.T.S. 107, 31 I.L.M. 849.
49. *See* U.N. Charter art. 2(1), which provides: "The Organization is based on the principle of the sovereign equality of all its Members."

ensuring that all States participated in the legal regime.[50] In light of this approach, while CBDR continues to form part of the climate legal regime, its significance has diminished somewhat. However, it remains relevant to other issues such as adaptation, climate financing, and the loss and damage mechanism.[51]

B.　Procedural Justice

Procedural justice is probably the best known and most developed of the four components of environmental justice. Decisions are often made without the participation of the relevant stakeholders, information is not available or not provided, and access to justice is not available. The three related rights—access to information, participation in the decisionmaking process, and access to justice—are often referred to as environmental democracy and overlap significantly with international human rights law.[52] These rights were included in an international environmental law instrument, albeit nonbinding, for the first time in the Rio Declaration on Environment and Development.[53] They have been codified in the Aarhus Convention,[54] form the procedural components of sustainable development,[55] and comprise what are now part of environmental rights.[56] These procedural rights have become most relevant in the context of environmental impact assessments, although they are not confined to that context.

In addition to requiring the facilitation of participation in the decisionmaking process, procedural justice also questions whether the process

---

50.　*See* Wolfgang Obergassel et al., Phoenix from the Ashes—An Analysis of the Paris Agreement to the United Nations Framework Convention on Climate Change, Wuppertal Institute for Climate, Environment, and Energy 10 (2016) (calling this a "climate diplomacy masterpiece"). The paper discusses whether the Paris Agreement is a binding document. Since it is an agreement adopted with the UNFCCC it is essentially a protocol and hence binding. However, for the United States, which sought to avoid at all costs referring it to the Senate for ratification, this may be "an international agreement other than a treaty." *Id.* at 13.

51.　*See infra* Part IV for discussion of the loss and damage mechanism.

52.　*See* Olivier De Schutter, International Human Rights Law (2d ed. 2010).

53.　*Rio Declaration on Environment and Development*, U.N. Conference on Environment and Development, Rio de Janeiro, Brazil, June 3–14, 1992, Princ. 10, U.N. Doc. A/CONF.151/26 (1992), http://www.unep.org/documents.multilingual/default.asp?documentid=78&articleid=1163.

54.　Convention on Access to Information, Public Participation in making, and Access to Justice in Environmental Matters, June 25, 1998, signed at Aarhus, Denmark, http://www.unece.org/fileadmin/DAM/env/pp/documents/cep43e.pdf.

55.　*See* Sumudu Atapattu, Emerging Principles of International Environmental Law ch. 2 (2006).

56.　*See* Svetlana Kravchenko, *Procedural Rights as a Crucial Tool to Combat Climate Change*, 28 Ga. J. Int'l & Comp. L. 613 (2010); Svetlana Kravchenko & John Bonine eds., Human Rights and the Environment: Cases, Law, and Policy (2008); Dinah Shelton, *Whiplash and Backlash—Reflections on a Human Rights Approach to Environmental Protection*, 13 Santa Clara J. Int'l L. 11 (2015).

has been designed in a way to lead to a fair outcome.[57] Moreover, in some instances, the mere provision of information is not sufficient, as the relevant stakeholders may lack the ability to grasp the significance of the proposed activity. In such instances, there may be an obligation on public authorities to actually educate the stakeholders of the proposed activity and its potential impact. Furthermore, people living in poverty or those who are marginalized may not participate in the decisionmaking process as they have other pressing issues to worry about[58] so there may be an additional obligation on officials to provide disadvantaged groups with legal and technical resources to ensure greater access to decisionmaking.[59] In addition, due process and the implementation of the process in a just manner is also important. With regard to some communities, these procedural protections may be even more stringent. Thus, for indigenous communities, international law requires the application of the free, prior, and informed consent principle in some instances, particularly in the event that activities are likely to displace these populations from their ancestral land.[60]

C.   Corrective Justice

Corrective justice involves fairness in punishment and remedying harm inflicted on individuals and communities. It encompasses aspects of retributive justice and restorative justice.[61] In the environmental context, this means that polluters are punished and not allowed to reap the benefits of disregarding the law, as well as remedying the injuries caused by the wrongful act. Many cases in the environmental field involve a combination of procedural and corrective justice.

Controlling the activities of private actors and punishing the wrongdoers has been a constant challenge in the environmental field. Many of the serious environmental and human rights abuses are carried out by multinational companies operating in developing countries. These companies have

---

57.   Kuehn, *supra* note 24, at 10688.
58.   *See* Svitlana Kravchenko, *The Myth of Public Participation in a World of Poverty*, 23 Tul. Envtl. L.J. 33 (2009).
59.   Kuehn, *supra* note 24, at 10689.
60.   *See* United Nations Declaration on the Rights of Indigenous Peoples, G.A. Res. 61/295, U.N. GAOR, 61st Sess., U.N. Doc. A/RES/61/295 (2007), 46 I.L.M. 1013 (2007), http://www.un.org/esa/socdev/ unpfii/documents/DRIPS_en.pdf. *See also* Parshuram Tamang, An Overview of the Principle of Free, Prior, and Informed Consent and Indigenous Peoples in International and Domestic Law and Practices, Presented at the United Nations Workshop on Free, Prior, and Informed Consent and Indigenous Peoples (Jan. 19, 2005); Alex Page, *Indigenous Peoples' Free Prior and Informed Consent in the Inter-American Human Rights System*, 4 Sustainable Dev. L. & Pol'y 17 (2004).
61.   Kuehn, *supra* note 24, at 10689.

escaped liability for several reasons including lax environmental regulations in the host country, investment treaties that favor the investor,[62] and project finance structures that shield these companies.[63] In addition, the power asymmetry between the investor and the host country complicates matters.

D.   Social Justice

This pillar is the least developed and possibly the most nebulous aspect of environmental justice.[64] It remains under-theorized but is closely related to the social pillar of sustainable development.[65] It coincides with the goal of achieving a more just society and some have described environmental justice as a "marriage of the movement for social justice with environmentalism" integrating environmental concerns into a broader agenda that emphasizes social, racial, and economic justice.[66] This pillar shows that environmental justice cannot be separated from struggles for other forms of justice that often underlie the reasons for environmental problems. As Sheila Foster points out, focusing on distributive justice alone neglects the social structures and agents that are causing environmental problems.[67] The link with the social pillar contributes to a vicious cycle of racial, economic, and political factors leading to environmental degradation and injustice, which, in turn, exacerbates living conditions of people and contributes to further marginalization and social and economic degradation.[68] Thus, adopting a holistic approach to environmental justice that encompasses social justice helps to break this vicious cycle and identify underlying causes of injustice. On the other hand, while these struggles and injustices are intertwined and cannot be separated from each other, the wider focus can also seem overwhelming. Moreover, it

---

62. *See* Shyami Puvimanasinghe, *From a Divided Heritage to a Common Future? International Investment Law, Human Rights, and Sustainable Development*, *in* INTERNATIONAL ENVIRONMENTAL LAW AND THE GLOBAL SOUTH, *supra* note 29, at 317.

63. *See* Shalanda Baker, *Project Finance and Sustainable Development in the Global South*, *in* INTERNATIONAL ENVIRONMENTAL LAW AND THE GLOBAL SOUTH, *supra* note 29, at 338.

64. Kuehn, *supra* note 24, at 10699.

65. Sustainable development consists of three pillars—environmental, social, and economic. *See* UNITED NATIONS, REPORT OF THE WORLD SUMMIT ON SUSTAINABLE DEVELOPMENT, JOHANNESBURG, SOUTH AFRICA, 26 AUGUST–4 SEPTEMBER 2002, U.N. Doc. A/CONF. 199/20 (2002), http://www.unmillenniumproject.org/documents/131302_wssd_report_reissued.pdf. The Brundtland definition had only two pillars—economic and environmental. *See Our Common Future*, World Commission on Environment and Development, Annex, U.N. Doc. A/42/427 (1987). The social pillar was added later at the Johannesburg Conference on Sustainable Development in 2002.

66. Kuehn, *supra* note 24, at 10699.

67. *See* Sheila Foster, *Justice From the Ground Up: Distributive Inequities, Grassroots Resistance, and the Transformative Politics of the Environmental Justice Movement*, 86 CAL. L. REV. 775 (1998).

68. Kuehn, *supra* note 24, at 10699.

could overlook other factors such as the role played by the market, which contributes to these inequities.[69]

In addition to the four-fold approach discussed above, the tripartite approach to environmental justice proposed by Osofsky is also useful, especially in relation to environmental problems like climate change that have a severe and often long-lasting impact on victims. Drawing on environmental, tort, and civil rights laws, Osofsky proposes the following test:

> Domestic environmental law provides a lens for examining the harm as a violation of universally applicable environmental standards. The tort law perspective, with its emphases on harm, duty of care, and causation, provides a mechanism for examining the complex relationships that underlie international problems. Finally, civil rights law challenges the unfairness inherent in the current distribution of environmental harm; the problem may not be simply that environmental harm occurred, but rather that it disproportionately affects a particular individual or group or constitutes a part of a broader pattern of discrimination.[70]

Osofsky notes that three factors may be instructive in evaluating whether environmental damage also constitutes a human rights violation: geographic scope, severity, and duration.[71] The adverse effects of climate change meet all three criteria. The next section applies these frameworks to small island States and their people.

III.   Climate Justice and Small Island States

In addition to environmental justice, climate justice[72] has received considerable attention from both scholars and activists in recent years. The Mary Robinson Foundation-Climate Justice, for example, believes that "climate justice links human rights and development to achieve a human-centred approach, safeguarding the rights of the most vulnerable and sharing the burdens and benefits of climate change and its resolution equitably and fairly."[73] It identifies the following core principles that inform climate justice: (a) respect and protect human rights; (b) support the right to development; (c) share benefits and burdens equitably; (d) ensure that decisions on climate change are

---

69.   *Id.*
70.   *See* Osofsky, *supra* note 31.
71.   *Id. See also* ATAPATTU, *supra* note 8, at 66.
72.   This section draws from the author's book HUMAN RIGHTS APPROACHES TO CLIMATE CHANGE: CHALLENGES AND OPPORTUNITIES, *supra* note 8, at ch. 3 (with permission from the publisher).
73.   MARY ROBINSON FOUNDATION-CLIMATE JUSTICE, PRINCIPLES OF CLIMATE JUSTICE, http://www.mrfcj.org/pdf/Principles-of-Climate-Justice.pdf.

participatory, transparent, and accountable; (e) ensure gender equality and equity; (f) harness the transformative power of education for climate stewardship; and (g) use effective partnerships to secure climate justice.[74] These principles share elements common with the environmental justice framework discussed in the previous section. Thus, participation of relevant stakeholders—including women as a vital component of society and other vulnerable groups—falls within participatory justice while sharing benefits and burdens equitably falls within distributive justice. Right to development also displays characteristics of distributive justice and overlaps with the intragenerational equity component of sustainable development:

> The vast disparity in resources between rich and poor, evident in the gaps between countries in the North and South and also within many countries (both North and South), is the deepest injustice of our age. This failure of resource-fairness makes it impossible for billions of humans to lead decent lives. Climate change both highlights and exacerbates this gulf in equality.[75]

Some scholars base climate justice—the elephant in the room—on four interrelated arguments: (1) the disjuncture between responsibility for climate change and its impacts; (2) the capacity (or lack thereof) to take adaptation measures; (3) the need for economic development for poorer nations; and (4) insufficient atmospheric space to allow developing countries to emit GHGs to the same level as developed countries.[76] The International Bar Association (IBA) Task Force on Climate Justice, on the other hand, adopts a more rights-based definition of climate justice:

> To ensure that communities, individuals and governments have substantive legal and procedural rights to the enjoyment of a safe, clean, healthy and sustainable environment and the means to take or cause measures to be taken within their national legislative and judicial systems and, where necessary, at regional and international levels, to mitigate sources of climate change and provide for adaptation to its effects in a manner that respects human rights.[77]

As the above definitions indicate, and in contrast to environmental justice, climate justice is being applied in relation to both vulnerable communities within States and vulnerable States themselves. The IBA definition does not

---

74. *Id.*
75. *Id.*
76. *See* Jeremy Baskin, *The Impossible Necessity of Climate Justice?*, 10 MELB. J. INT'L L. 424 (2009).
77. *See* DAVID ESTRIN & BARONESS HELENA KENNEDY QC, ACHIEVING JUSTICE AND HUMAN RIGHTS IN AN ERA OF CLIMATE DISRUPTION: INTERNATIONAL BAR ASSOCIATION CLIMATE CHANGE JUSTICE AND HUMAN RIGHTS TASK FORCE REPORT 35 (2014), http://www.ibanet.org/Article/Detail.aspx?ArticleUid=96b93592-3761-4418-8a52-54a81b02c5f1 [hereinafter IBA REPORT].

specifically refer to distributive, procedural, or corrective justice, but adopts a human rights approach by applying a substantive right to a healthy environment in the context of both mitigation and adaptation. It contains elements of procedural justice, hence its reference to procedural rights.

Climate justice and human rights are not interchangeable concepts, however. Working together, they form a good framework to address the plight of small island States. The limitations of the human rights framework in relation to climate change were highlighted by participants of the initial consultations held by the Human Rights Council and the Office of the United Nations High Commissioner for Human Rights (OHCHR) on climate change and human rights:

> Bangladesh noted that in dealing with the global problem of climate change, too much emphasis was put on national responsibility. The least developed countries and small island States would be the worst affected by climate change, although they had contributed least to global greenhouse gas emissions. It was not only unfair, but also unjustified, to hold these countries responsible fully for protecting their populations. While human rights based efforts to [promote] adaptation and mitigation were useful, such an approach should not only focus on the obligations of national authorities as duty bearers for protecting individuals' human rights.[78]

While there are elements of human rights within the justice framework and human rights would be a useful tool to seek justice, climate justice is wider because it takes the disparities in the global community into account and seeks to remedy the imbalance. Hence, distributive, procedural, and corrective justice would be useful in addressing these disparities especially in the context of climate change, whereas social justice would be more appropriate for vulnerable communities within States and across generations.[79] The present generation is feeling the impact of decisions taken by our forefathers, while our children and grandchildren will suffer the consequences of our actions today, making it an intergenerational justice issue.[80]

While developed nations have the resources and the technology to adapt to the adverse impacts of climate change, such as building seawalls and storing food stocks against droughts, poor nations and communities do not enjoy

---

78. OHCHR, *Human Rights Council Panel Discussion on Human Rights and Climate Change*, http://www. ohchr.org/EN/Issues/HRAndClimateChange/Pages/Panel.aspx (last visited Aug. 22, 2016).

79. *See* IBA Report, *supra* note 77, at 45.

80. *Id.* at 45. Intergenerational equity is another principle that forms part of the climate change legal regime. *See* United Nations Framework Convention on Climate Change, May 9, 1992, art. 3, 1771 U.N.T.S. 107, 31 I.L.M. 849.

such luxuries.[81] Although the international community recognized the vulnerability of small island States and least developed nations with the adoption of the Warsaw loss and damage mechanism,[82] the general consensus is that this response and the existing legal regime overall do not go far enough. Thus, a justice-centered approach that introduces ethics into policymaking and fosters a human rights-based perspective to climate change is necessary. Furthermore, a climate justice agenda must embrace the implications of climate change on development imbalances, including the fact that the distribution of climate change impacts is inherently unjust:

> [C]limate justice seeks to combine the climate change discussion with human rights in a way that is equitable for the most climate-vulnerable groups. Practically speaking, this means not just thinking of the political and moral issues inherent in tackling climate change as questions of distributive justice, but rather as a matter of avoiding (i) worsening climate change by continuing to emit enormous quantities of GHGs and (ii) hindering development for poorer nations in the methods we find to reduce those emissions.[83]

Intergenerational equity[84] and gender equity[85] are essential elements of climate justice. Both intergenerational equity and intragenerational equity principles are inherent in the notion of sustainable development, all of which are included as principles in the UNFCCC.[86] A notable omission in Article 3 of the UNFCCC was a reference to gender equality as a principle. Although the Paris Agreement rectified this omission, it failed, yet again, to identify women as a *vulnerable group*.[87]

---

81. *Id. See also* Zackary L. Stillings, *Human Rights and the New Reality of Climate Change: Adaptation's Limitations in Achieving Climate Justice*, 35 Mich. J. Int'l L. 637, 643 (2014) (applying an environmental justice framework to States because States are harmed by damage suffered by individuals).

82. Although the Paris Agreement included a separate provision on loss and damage, the decision adopted there made it clear that this provision did not confer any liability or compensation. This seems like giving with one hand and taking away with the other. *See* Obergassel et al., *supra* note 50.

83. *Id.* at 46.

84. Edith Brown Weiss was the first scholar to advance a theory of intergenerational justice. *See* Edith Brown Weiss, In Fairness to Future Generations: International Law, Common Patrimony, and Intergenerational Equity (1989); Edith Brown Weiss, *Climate Change, Intergenerational Equity, and International Law*, 9 Vt. J. Envtl. L. 618 (2008).

85. Gender equity was included in the Cancun Adaptation Framework and the Paris Agreement. *See* Bernadette P. Resurreccion, *Persistent Women and Environment Linkages in Climate Change and Sustainable Development Agendas*, 40 Women's Stud. Int'l F. 37 (2013).

86. United Nations Framework Convention on Climate Change, May 9, 1992, art. 3, 1771 U.N.T.S. 107, 31 I.L.M. 849. *See also* Mary Robinson Foundation-Climate Justice, Climate Justice: An Intergenerational Approach (2013), http://www.mrfcj.org/media/pdf/Intergenerational-Equity-Position-Paper-2013-11-16.pdf.

87. *See Adoption of the Paris Agreement*, UNFCCC Conference of the Parties, 21st Sess., pmbl., U.N. Doc. FCCC/CP/2015/10/Add.1 (Dec. 12, 2015), http://unfccc.int/files/home/application/pdf/paris_agreement.pdf (emphasis added) [hereinafter *Paris Agreement*]. The section of the preamble that

Not all scholars are enamored by the notion of climate justice, however. Eric A. Posner and David Weisbach contend:

> Our argument is unusual. We strongly favor a climate change agreement, especially because it would help poor people in poor nations, and we also favor redistribution from the rich to the poor. At the same time, we reject the claim that certain intuitive ideas about justice should play a major role in the design of a climate agreement.[88]

They provide several central themes to their argument including looking forward, not backward, and relying less on moral arguments that may not make sense for States.[89] They categorically reject the calls for the inclusion of principles of corrective and distributive justice in the climate change regime because, they argue, its proponents "treat climate negotiations as an opportunity to solve some of the world's most serious problems—the admittedly unfair distribution of wealth across northern and southern countries, the lingering harms of the legacy of colonialism, and so forth."[90] This argument ignores the very reason for the current disparity between the global North and the global South and turns a blind eye to the suffering of the majority of the global population: the current capitalist economy that favors only an elite minority[91] with roots in imperialism and colonialism.[92] It disregards the communities that are already suffering the adverse consequences of climate change. To ignore the roots of injustice and the current manifestation of the North-South divide is to continue to ignore the elephant in the room and pretend that there is nothing wrong with the current system.[93] Climate change is a prime example of the current development paradigm with its roots in capitalism gone wrong—without addressing the root causes of climate change, it is impossible to design an effective legal regime.[94] This is precisely why the climate negotiations to date have failed. The global North is essentially engaged in window dressing while the global South is demanding real action and real answers.[95] As eloquently articulated by Carmen Gonzalez: "environmental injustice cannot be separated from

---

refers to human rights is an odd assortment of principles, a list of vulnerable groups, and aspirations, included to appease the human rights community and other interest groups.

88.   Eric A. Posner & David Weisbach, Climate Change Justice 5 (2010).
89.   Id.
90.   Id.
91.   Klein, supra note 4, at 18.
92.   See International Environmental Law and the Global South, supra note 29, at ch. 1.
93.   Klein, supra note 4, at 18. Klein asks the question, "What is wrong with us?"
94.   Id.
95.   For an in-depth analysis of the North-South divide in relation to international environmental law, see International Environmental Law and the Global South, supra note 29.

economic inequality, race and gender subordination, and the colonial and post-colonial domination of the global South."[96]

In a critique of the position taken by Posner and Weisbach, Daniel Farber urges that ethical considerations should inform climate policy:

> This Review suggests that ethical considerations should play an even greater role than Posner and Weisbach suggest. The injustice of causing harm to the poorest countries and future generations provides powerful arguments for stringent limitations on emissions or, where feasible, strenuous efforts to limit the human toll of climate impacts—and cash compensation for possible catastrophic harm may not be adequate even if feasible. To the extent that harmful climate change cannot be avoided, the rich countries that have contributed so much to emissions should provide funding for adaptation and mitigation efforts to reduce harm in the poorest countries.[97]

In stark contrast to the position taken by Posner and Weisbach, a joint paper issued by the World Resources Institute and the Mary Robinson Foundation argues that equity and justice *should* inform a new climate agreement.[98] Premised on the notion that climate change is an issue of injustice and a human tragedy in the making, the report posits:

> Climate change is far more than an environmental challenge. It is profoundly a human issue with immediate and far-reaching implications for jobs, homes, health, food and lives . . . . It is also increasingly seen as a justice issue as climate change undermines the realization of a host of internationally recognized human rights, has asymmetrical impacts on the poor and vulnerable, and increasingly requires disproportionate action from developing countries.[99]

The paper argues for "an effective and equitable agreement that places people at the center, protects the most vulnerable and equitably shares the burdens and benefits of our response to climate change."[100] In order to apply equity within the new climate agreement, the paper proposes the application of principles of climate justice: (1) giving a voice to the most vulnerable; (2) ensuring transparency in decisionmaking and accountability for decisions;

---

96. *See* Carmen Gonzalez, *Environmental Justice and International Environmental Law*, *in* ROUTLEDGE HANDBOOK OF INTERNATIONAL ENVIRONMENTAL LAW 79 (Shawkat Alam et al. eds., 2013).

97. *See* Daniel Farber, *Climate Justice*, 110 MICH. L. REV. 985 (2012).

98. *See* EDWARD CAMERON, TARA SHINE & WENDI BEVINS, CLIMATE JUSTICE: EQUITY AND JUSTICE INFORMING A NEW CLIMATE AGREEMENT, CLIMATE JUSTICE WORKING PAPER (World Resources Institute & Mary Robinson Foundation 2013), http://www.wri.org/sites/default/files/climate_justice_equity_and_justice_informing_a_new_climate_agreement.pdf.

99. *Id.* at 3.

100. *Id.* at 16.

(3) applying human rights in informing how equity is applied; (4) ensuring the application of both inter- and intragenerational equity principles; (5) ensuring the protection of human rights; and (6) transitioning to a new type of economic growth.[101]

Can the above four-fold justice framework, complemented by the tripartite framework and the human rights framework, help small island States and their people? Or is climate justice as articulated by the Mary Robinson Foundation a better fit? These definitions overlap with one another—the basic features can be identified as: sharing burdens and benefits equally, participation and transparency, gender equality, intergenerational equity, protecting human rights, and ensuring the right to development.

For small island States, a justice framework is very much needed. But what would a justice framework look like for them? First, acknowledging that their present plight is due to the unabated emission of GHGs by developed countries would be a good start. Second, offering some form of compensation for their loss would ensure some relief for the victims. The loss and damage mechanism seems to address this situation, but despite its adoption at Warsaw and inclusion in the Paris Agreement, the decision adopted at COP21 made it clear that it does not involve liability or compensation.[102] Third, helping them with adaptation would be necessary. Fourth—and it gets more difficult as the list progresses—all States, especially the major emitters, will have to start reducing emissions in earnest if limiting the temperature rise to not more than 1.5°C will be possible. Fifth, the international community will need to seriously look into the issue of relocating the inhabitants of the small island States.

Finally, deciding the fate of the islands themselves as legal entities would be necessary. The question here is whether these islands would lose statehood if they lose territory or, as some contend will happen first, their population.[103] If they lose statehood and with it their sovereignty, do their populations become stateless? Currently, international law addresses situations where people have been made stateless as a result of the operation of law, not due to the collective action of States that resulted in climate change. Furthermore, international law has never dealt with the phenomenon of States physically disappearing. This unprecedented situation needs attention by the international community. It will be necessary to adopt another legal fiction similar

---

101. *Id.* at 17.
102. *Adoption of the Paris Agreement*, UNFCCC Conference of the Parties, 21st Sess., U.N. Doc. FCCC/CP/2015/10/Add.1 (Dec. 12, 2015), http://unfccc.int/files/home/application/pdf/paris_agreement.pdf.
103. *See* MCADAM, *supra* note 10.

to "States" and "statehood" to cover the entities that lose some attributes of statehood.[104] In addition, the international community needs to address the legal vacuum that currently exists in relation to "climate refugees." While not proposing the adoption of a stand-alone treaty for climate refugees or the expansion of the existing legal framework, this chapter nonetheless suggests that this category of people must be afforded some legal protection.[105] Although the IPCC recognized in its first assessment report that the greatest single impact of climate change could be on human migration,[106] the international community is still grappling with terminology while policymakers are busy trying to sweep the issue under the carpet possibly hoping that it will go away. The next section discusses the implications of including climate justice in the Paris Agreement for small island States.

IV.   Climate Justice and the Paris Agreement

In addition to including a provision on human rights, the Paris Agreement took the unusual step of including a provision on climate justice as well. While the wording is very soft and the reference is limited to the preamble, its inclusion was unexpected. The preamble states as follows:

> Noting the importance of ensuring the integrity of all ecosystems, including oceans, and the protection of biodiversity, recognized by some cultures as Mother Earth, and noting the importance *for some* of the concept of "climate justice," when taking action to address climate change.[107]

This is a curious provision indeed. Climate justice, which usually applies in relation to vulnerable communities and groups, is lumped together with the need to protect all ecosystems and biodiversity and Mother Earth. The reference to "importance for some" conveys the idea that not everybody agrees on its relevance or importance. This rather half-hearted way of including concepts sometimes can do more harm than good.

---

104. Several legal fictions have been proposed by scholars, including deterritorialized States, nations ex situ, and States in exile. *See* Maxine Burkette, *The Nation Ex-situ: On Climate Change, Deterritorialized Nationhood, and the Post-climate Era*, 2 CLIMATE L. 345 (2011).

105. "Climate refugees" is not a legal term. It merely describes those who will be forced to move as a result of climate change. Several terms have been proposed to address the plight of those who will be forced to migrate as a result of climate change. *See* Jane McAdam, *Swimming Against the Tide: Why a Climate Change Displacement Treaty Is Not the Answer*, 23 INT'L J. REFUGEE L. 2 (2011) (asserting that a universal treaty may be inappropriate, local or regional responses would be better, and that local and regional responses provide an opportunity to plan relocation measures). While she is correct for the most part, no relocation planning has taken place.

106. IPCC, CLIMATE CHANGE: THE IPCC SCIENTIFIC ASSESSMENT, *Policymakers Summary* (1990), at https://www.ipcc.ch/ipccreports/far/wg_I/ipcc_far_wg_I_spm.pdf.

107. *Paris Agreement, supra* note 87, at pmbl. (emphasis added).

However, for small island States and their people, in addition to the human rights hook, climate justice provides another valuable hook. If major emitters do not take measures to reduce their GHG emissions significantly and limit the temperature rise to 1.5°C, there is no real hope for small island States. As they have consistently reminded the international community, a 2°C increase is like a death sentence for them.[108]

Tired of waiting for the international community to act, the Maldives decided to construct an artificial island to meet the future housing and industrial development needs of the country. Hulhumale Island was constructed at a cost of $63 million.[109] While the construction of artificial islands would certainly solve the problem relating to sovereignty, it is unlikely that the small island States can afford such a high price tag. If this indeed is a viable option, coupled with the justice framework and the CBDR principle that forms part of the climate legal regime, the high emitters can be asked to contribute to a fund to construct these islands to resettle the small island States and their people. As artificial islands are not entitled to maritime zones under the United Nations Convention on the Law of the Sea, this issue will have to be resolved before embarking on a project of this massive scale. However, this should be considered as a last resort—cutting down emissions should be the first step. Helping small island States with their immediate adaptation needs should be addressed simultaneously. One of the most perplexing and controversial issues is whether major emitters should compensate the victim States for the adverse consequences, which relates to the corrective justice component discussed above. The loss and damage mechanism seems to address this concern to some degree, but without any admission of liability.

The international mechanism for loss and damage was adopted at COP19 in Warsaw "to address loss and damage associated with impacts of climate change, including extreme events and slow onset events, in developing countries that are particularly vulnerable to the adverse effects of climate change."[110] Extreme events and slow onset events are included; however, loss

108. At the OHCHR consultation on climate change and human rights, the Maldives, speaking on behalf of 14 small island States, noted that entire populations of low-lying States might in the future have no choice but to leave their own country as a result of climate change. *See Human Rights Council Panel Discussion on the Relationship Between Climate Change and Human Rights—Summary of Discussions* (2009), http://www.ohchr.org/EN/Issues/HRAndClimateChange/Pages/Panel.aspx.

109. *See Hulhumalé and the Last Stand of the Maldives,* THE BASEMENT GEOGRAPHER, Apr. 14, 2011, http://basementgeographer.com/hulhumale-and-the-last-stand-of-the-maldives/. Kiribati also pursued this option. *See Kiribati Looks to Artificial Islands to Save Nation From Rising Sea Levels,* ABC.NET, Feb. 16, 2016, http://www.abc.net.au/news/2016-02-17/artificial-islands-perhaps-the-only-option-to-save-kiribati/7175688.

110. UNFCCC, *Warsaw International Mechanism for Loss and Damage Associated with Climate Change Impacts,* http://unfccc.int/adaptation/workstreams/loss_and_damage/items/8134.php (last visited Aug. 22, 2016).

and damage itself it not defined.[111] The UNFCCC web page elaborates on these impacts as including both extreme events such as hurricanes and heat waves, and slow-onset events such as desertification, sea-level rise, and ocean acidification.[112] The loss and damage mechanism seeks to approach this topic in essentially three ways: (1) enhancing knowledge and understanding of comprehensive risk management approaches; (2) strengthening dialogue and coordination among relevant stakeholders; and (3) enhancing action and support, including finance, technology, and capacity-building.[113]

The loss and damage mechanism further provides that action to address gaps in the understanding of various topics includes the risk of slow-onset events, noneconomic loss and damage, and how impacts of climate change are affecting patterns of migration, displacement, and human mobility. The loss and damage mechanism was incorporated into Article 8 of the Paris Agreement. It provides: "Parties recognize the importance of averting, mini-mizing and addressing loss and damage associated with the adverse effects of climate change, including extreme weather events and slow onset events, and the role of sustainable development in reducing the risk of loss and damage."[114]

At COP21, the Warsaw International Mechanism was brought under the guidance and authority of the COP. According to the decisions adopted at Paris, the areas of cooperation include: early warning systems; emergency preparedness; slow-onset events; events that may involve irreversible and permanent loss and damage; risk insurance; noneconomic losses; and resil-ience of communities, livelihoods, and ecosystems.[115] Climate displace-ment, included in the negotiating draft, unfortunately did not find a place in the Paris Agreement itself. However, according to the decisions adopted at COP21, the executive committee has been requested to establish a task force "to develop recommendations for integrated approaches to avert, minimize and address displacement related to the adverse impacts of climate change."[116]

This decision is welcome and long overdue. The executive committee was requested to operationalize the provisions referred to under paragraphs 48

---

111. See CLIMATE FOCUS CLIENT BRIEF, *supra* note 35 (noting that "conceptually, loss and damage arises when the adverse effects are not avoided through mitigation and adaptation (i.e. the impacts exceed adaptive capacities)").

112. *Id.*

113. *Id.*

114. *Paris Agreement, supra* note 87, at art. 8.

115. *Report of the Conference of the Parties on Its Twenty-first Session, Held in Paris From 30 November to 13 December 2015—Addendum, Part Two: Action Taken by the Conference of the Parties at Its Twenty-first Session, Decisions Adopted by the Conference of the Parties*, UNFCCC, 21st Sess., U.N. Doc. FCCC/CP/2015/10/Add.1 (2016).

116. *Id.* para. 49.

and 49 (on loss and damage) and to report on the progress in its annual report. While the Parties stressed that Article 8 does not provide a basis for any liability or compensation, they nonetheless agreed to set a new collective quantified goal of $100 billion per year, taking into account the needs and priorities of developing countries,[117] which was another welcome development. It remains to be seen how this goal will be reached—one option would be to divert some funds from the security budget of countries, but given the recent heightened risks and concerns surrounding terrorism, this is unlikely to happen. The inclusion of the loss and damage mechanism in the Paris Agreement was a huge victory for developing countries, particularly for small island States and least developed countries who pushed hard for its inclusion as a separate pillar of climate action.[118] Now the international community must ensure that it will not get bogged down in bureaucracy and politics similar to the fate of many other issues.

The loss and damage mechanism appears to come closest to what is sought to be achieved under climate justice. Given how contentious its adoption has been,[119] and the express exclusion of liability and compensation under the Paris decision, it is unlikely to be considered akin to corrective justice, but it seems to be the next best thing.[120]

Conclusion

This chapter discussed the notion of environmental justice as well as climate justice in the context of small island States and their inhabitants. Climate change is a very complex issue and solutions to it are equally complex. The longer the international community delays in implementing effective responses for small island nations, however, the options available to respond effectively will diminish, with respect to both mitigation and adaptation.

---

117. *Id.* para 53.
118. *See* CLIMATE FOCUS CLIENT BRIEF, *supra* note 35 (noting that loss and damage constituted one of the most debated topics at COP21 and "its inclusion in the final text remained controversial until the very last hours of negotiations").
119. *Id.* The brief points out that ever since the Alliance of Small Island States proposed in 1991 that developed countries should make mandatory payments to compensate losses suffered by vulnerable countries, this has been a contentious issue.
120. *Cf.* Stephen Humphreys, *In the Shadow of Paris: Theories of Justice and Principles of Harm*, 7 J. HUM. RTS. & ENV'T 3 (2016) (noting that the Warsaw Mechanism presents "an invidious Catch-22 for SIDS" because it is based on insurance rather than on compensation. Insurance depends on risk reduction through adaptation measures and SIDS lack the resources to take such measures); *see also* Sam Adelman, *Climate Justice, Loss and Damage, and Compensation for Small Island Developing States*, 7 J. HUM. RTS. & ENV'T 32 (2016) (arguing for the establishment of an international fund to compensate SIDS: "An international compensation fund offers a relatively simple and ethically satisfactory way of acknowledging the physical loss and psychological damage resulting from climate change and from the extensive violation of islanders' human rights.").

The crucial question with regard to small island States and their people is whether the international community will allow 52 sovereign nations to get washed away into the sea. While it may be too late to stop the forces that have been set in motion with global climate change, it is not too late to address the plight of the small island nations and their people. Indeed, notions of justice and equity demand it. The very foundations of international law may need to be reconsidered and a legal regime designed to accommodate this new category of States—those without land territory—and their deterritorialized people may need to be adopted. The Paris Agreement was a hopeful step in the right direction. But it is only a start. What is needed now is action—drastic, serious action.

At the Human Rights Council consultation on climate change and human rights, the Maldives highlighted the difficulty facing small island States. Speaking on behalf of 14 small island States, the Maldives underscored the increasing difficulty for SIDS acting alone to protect human rights affected by climate change. It considered international cooperation to be a vital legal obligation under international human rights treaties. In particular, States had an obligation to refrain from acting in ways that knowingly undermined human rights in other countries, as well as an obligation to take steps through international assistance and cooperation to facilitate the fulfillment of human rights in other countries.[121]

As highlighted here, international cooperation is vital. Moreover, the recognition that the international community created this problem for the small island States and for humanity as a whole should be sobering. Despite what the skeptics say, future generations deserve decisive action now. The urgent plea from Minister Tony de Brum of the Marshall Islands is relevant in this regard: "My country will be destroyed by climate change. It will be removed from the map by rising seas. Because it is happening inch by inch does not make the situation any less desperate, or any less urgent. This is an emergency."[122]

It would be naïve to think that climate justice and human rights will solve the issues facing small island States if States continue to put their self-interest first and let politics dictate the agenda. As Upendra Baxi points out: "existing justice principles cannot yet achieve the political urgency that global climate change summons."[123]

---

121. OHCHR, *supra* note 78.
122. Minister Tony de Brum, Speech at the United Nations Security Council (Feb. 15, 2013) (copy on file with author).
123. Upendra Baxi, *Towards a Climate Change Justice Theory*, 7 J. Hum. Rts. & Env't 7, 12 (2016) (raising the question, "How does one even begin to conduct conversation about justice in this epoch of climate change?").

Chapter 12

"To Preserve the Heritage of the Past, and to Protect the Promise of the Future": Intergenerational Equity Challenges from Climate Change in the Federated States of Micronesia

Clement Yow Mulalap

Introduction

Every four years, delegations from Pacific islands convene in a location in Oceania and engage in a two-week celebration of traditional Pacific arts. Officially called the Festival of Pacific Arts and colloquially described as the Pacific Olympics of Arts, the event features traditional dances, chants, handicraft, and other forms of cultural exchange and exhibits. In 2016, the island of Guam hosted the festival from May 22 to June 4.[1] At dawn on the opening day, several canoes sailed into Tumon Bay to launch the festival. The canoes were from the island groups of Yap and Chuuk in the Federated States of Micronesia (FSM), a sovereign nation comprised of approximately 600 low-lying islands and atolls in the North Pacific. The canoes were fash-

---

1. For more information on the 2016 festival, see https://festpac.visitguam.com/ (last visited Aug. 23, 2016).

ioned from local, natural materials, in accordance with ancient Yapese and Chuukese practice. To the delight of the festival-goers, the canoes had sailed from the various islands of Yap and Chuuk to Guam—a voyage of hundreds of miles over the open Pacific Ocean—without using any modern navigational instruments. Instead, the crews on the canoes employed traditional navigational skills that rely on the positions and movements of stars and other celestial bodies, the swells and directions of ocean currents, and the behavior of seabirds and marine life in the high seas.[2]

The arrival of the canoes was a profound testament to the genius of ancient Pacific mariners and the deep links they forged with their natural environments, including the skyscape, as they sought and settled the far-flung islands of the Pacific millennia ago, long before Europeans "discovered" those islands. It was also a celebration of the commitment of past and current generations of islanders from Yap and Chuuk to learn the challenging skill of noninstrumental traditional wayfinding and transmit the knowledge of that skill to future generations, even as indigenous populations elsewhere in the Pacific lost their own knowledge of wayfinding.[3]

Amidst the celebration, however, one of the traditional navigators from an outer island of Yap sounded a note of caution. Larry Raigetal, the founder of Waa'gey, a nongovernmental organization from Yap that uses traditional skills to address the social, economic, and environmental challenges faced by the people of Yap, warned that climate change was already having adverse effects on the traditional navigation practiced in Yap and Chuuk.[4] Raigetal cited ancient knowledge about how the positions of stars in the nightscape are supposed to augur prohibitive sailing weather, but nowadays do not cor-

2.   For news reports about the arrival of the canoes and the official opening of the festival, see Jerick Sablan, *Traditional Seafarers Arrive in Guam*, Pac. Daily News, May 17, 2016, http://www.guampdn. com/story/news/2016/05/16/traditional-seafarers-arrive-guam/84432448/; *see also* Jojo Santo Thomas, *FestPac Welcomed With Full Day of Celebration*, Pac. Daily News, May 23, 2016, http://www.guampdn. com/story/news/2016/05/22/canoe-arrivals-mark-beginning-festpac/84734934/.

3.   In contrast to other indigenous Pacific populations, the Native Hawaiians managed to rectify their loss of wayfinding, but only with the magnanimous assistance of Pius "Mau" Piailug, a master navigator from the island of Satawal in the Federated States of Micronesia who taught a small group of Native Hawaiians in the 1970s how to navigate like their ancestors did, with the stars and currents and other natural elements as guides. That gesture by Piailug triggered a strong Hawaiian cultural renaissance that continues today. *See generally* Sam Low, Hawaiki Rising: Hokule'a, Nainoa Thompson, and the Hawaiian Renaissance (2013); *see also* Cynthia Franklin, *Introduction*, *in* Navigating Islands and Continents: Conversation and Contestations in and Around the Pacific: Selected Essays xxiv (Cynthia Franklin ed., 2000).

4.   Raigetal gave his comments at a conference held in connection with the 2016 festival. *See* Louella Losinio, *Traditional Navigation and Climate Change*, Guam Daily Post, May 15, 2016, http://www. postguam.com/news/local/traditional-navigation-and-climate-change/article_89f5a9c2-19d6-11e6-8ea6-93d7a1b7b168.html. For additional commentary by Raigetal on the impacts of climate change on traditional navigation, see Video: Climate Change vs. Traditional Navigation, https://vimeo.com/157791925.

respond with actual storm events in a reliable manner. Raigetal also discussed how climate change—particularly the sea-level rise and drought conditions that climate change enables—drives people from the low-lying atolls and outer islands of Yap to the main island in search of stable food sources and land for resettlement. Such climate-induced migration threatens to disrupt the careful sociopolitical relationship between the main island of Yap and its outer islands, a relationship that ascribes specific cultural spheres for particular groups of Yapese. These cultural spheres will inevitably come into conflict with each other as more outer islanders settle in the main island, jostle for equitable access to the limited food resources of the main island, and interact with main islanders to a greater extent than traditionally allowed.

Most profoundly, Raigetal warned that as climate change forces people from the outer islands to migrate to the main island of Yap and beyond, the passing of ancient traditional knowledge from generation to generation will be disrupted, perhaps irreversibly. This transmission of culture is best performed in situ, i.e., in the waters and shores and community houses and inland areas of the islands where such cultural practices have occurred for millennia. As the people of the islands depart their ancestral homes, they also leave behind their best opportunities to learn what makes them unique in this world: ancient skills, knowledge, practices, legends, and other elements of cultural identity. In abandoning that cultural heritage, the islanders lose some of the best tools available to fight climate change and reverse their exodus from their island homes.[5]

Raigetal voiced his warnings about a year after Supertyphoon Maysak pummeled the outer islands and atolls of Chuuk and Yap in April 2015. Maysak wrought $8.5 million in damage to public infrastructure, destroyed 80–90% of food crops and freshwater systems, caused five fatalities, and affected the lives of approximately 30,000 people (about a third of the FSM's population), making Maysak one of the worst storm events ever recorded in the FSM.[6] On the outer island of Ulithi in the Yap island group, traditional

---

5. For more information about the threats posed by climate change to traditional Pacific wayfinding and other examples of traditional environmental knowledge, see AKATSUKI TAKAHASHI & BOYOUNG CHA, TRADITIONAL KNOWLEDGE FOR ADAPTING TO CLIMATE CHANGE: SAFEGUARDING INTANGIBLE CULTURAL HERITAGE IN THE PACIFIC 8 (2013), http://unesdoc.unesco.org/images/0022/002253/225313E.pdf; see generally D.J. NAKASHIMA, K. GALLOWAY MCLEAN, H.D. THULSTRUP, A. RAMOS CASTILLO & J.T. RUBIS, WEATHERING UNCERTAINTY: TRADITIONAL KNOWLEDGE FOR CLIMATE CHANGE ASSESSMENT AND ADAPTATION (2012); Maxine Burkett, *Indigenous Environmental Knowledge and Climate Change Adaptation, in* CLIMATE CHANGE AND INDIGENOUS PEOPLES: THE SEARCH FOR LEGAL REMEDIES 96 (Randall S. Abate & Elizabeth Ann Kronk Warner eds., 2013).

6. See UNITED STATES OF AMERICA INTERNATIONAL DEVELOPMENT, MICRONESIA—TYPHOON MAYSAK, FACT SHEET #3, FISCAL YEAR (FY) 2015 (2015), http://reliefweb.int/sites/reliefweb.int/files/resources/04.22.15%20-%20USAID-DCHA%20Typhoon%20Maysak%20Fact%20Sheet%20%233.pdf. Maysak also had the dubious honor of being the most powerful pre-April typhoon ever recorded. *See*

meeting houses collapsed, taro patches and other staple croplands drowned from saltwater inundation, and freshwater supplies dwindled in the wake of Maysak.[7] The images of this destruction remain searing and haunting.[8] A year after Maysak's landfall, many of the traditional meeting houses where cultural learning occurs in the outer islands of Yap and Chuuk are still unreconstructed, and the transmission of cultural knowledge is endangered—including knowledge about traditional navigation.

As its experience with Maysak attests, and as Raigetal's discourse indicates, the FSM is already suffering from many of the adverse effects of climate change and is poised for even more disruptive conditions in the not-too-distant future. Such disruptions will undermine the ability of present and future generations of the FSM's indigenous population to practice their ancient customs and traditions in harmony with their natural environments, just as their ancestors did for millennia; as well as to enjoy the bounty of the FSM's natural environment for sustainable development purposes and for its own sake. The preamble of the Constitution of the FSM expresses a core commitment of the founders of the federation: in crafting the FSM Constitution and establishing a new nation, the "People of Micronesia . . . affirm our common wish to live together in peace and harmony, to preserve the heritage of the past, and to protect the promise of the future."[9] The present generation of people in the FSM has a solemn, constitutional obligation to bequeath to future generations of the FSM populace the social, environmental, economic, political, and cultural "heritage" handed to the current generation by previous generations. Confronted with climate change, however, the discharge of that obligation is highly uncertain.

This chapter examines the concept of intergenerational equity in the face of climate change from the perspective of the FSM. Part I identifies various ways in which climate change is undermining the ability of present and future generations of the FSM people to enjoy their natural environment, develop their economies in a sustainable manner, preserve their territorial integrity, and practice their ancient customs and traditions as their ancestors did for millennia. Part II situates this struggle in the context of intergenera-

---

Jeff Masters, *Category 5 Super Typhoon Maysak Pounding Micronesia*, WEATHER UNDERGROUND, Mar. 31, 2015, https://www.wunderground.com/blog/JeffMasters/comment.html?entrynum=2946.

7.   Zain Haidar, *Typhoon Maysak Flattens Ulithi Atoll, Devastates Flood Supply*, WEATHER CHANNEL, Apr. 3, 2015, https://weather.com/storms/typhoon/news/typhoon-maysak-impacts-ulithi-yap-federated-states-micronesia-philippines.

8.   Bethany Keats, *Typhoon Maysak: Photographer Brad Holland Captures the Recovery on Islands of Yap in Micronesia*, AUSTRALIA BROADCASTING CORP., Apr. 8, 2015, http://www.abc.net.au/news/2015-04-08/pictures-show-devastation-typhoon-maysak-micronesia/6378904.

9.   FSM CONST. pmbl. para. 2.

tional equity as a legal obligation. Specifically, Part II defines intergenerational equity as an obligation under international law that must be respected, protected, and enforced by the international community for the protection of future generations, particularly with regard to those activities that will be adversely affected by climate change. Building on the legal analysis of intergenerational equity and the examination of the intergenerational impacts of climate change in the FSM, Part III discusses ways in which the FSM can use international law—including in bilateral settings—to achieve the FSM's obligations to future generations of the FSM people, with an emphasis on securing commitments from the international community to aid the FSM in discharging those obligations. Part III also proposes that the FSM, as a minimal contributor to climate change, is entitled to demand action from the international community for the sake of future generations of the FSM people, especially action addressing climate change taken by developed countries with historical responsibilities for climate change. Climate justice demands this approach.

I.   Climate Change Impacts in the FSM

The FSM is a sovereign Pacific nation of more than 600 low-lying islands and atolls that are politically grouped into four states: Yap, Chuuk, Pohnpei, and Kosrae. The FSM commands more than one million square miles of ocean space by virtue of the exclusive economic zone generated by the FSM's islands and atolls. The population of the FSM is predominantly native; however, this population does not qualify as "indigenous" under normal international legal and political discourse. Although international law has not provided a strict and universal definition for an indigenous population, it is commonly understood that an indigenous population is a discrete and nondominant community within a nation-state or some other broader governing entity that operates in some manner to subjugate the interests of the indigenous population to those of the governing entity, despite the longstanding historical and cultural connections of that community to the space they inhabit in the governing entity.[10] In the FSM, however, almost all of its inhabitants

---

10.   Perhaps the most widely cited working definition of indigenous peoples is from the 1986 Martinez Cobo Study, which was commissioned by the United Nations Sub-commission on the Prevention of Discrimination and the Protection of Minorities to examine discrimination against indigenous populations and recommend international and domestic measures to address that discrimination. The study laid the foundation for the eventual adoption of the United Nations Declaration on the Rights of Indigenous Peoples. According to the study:
       Indigenous communities, peoples and nations are those which, having a historical continuity with pre-invasion and pre-colonial societies that developed on their territories, consider

belong to at least one of four ethnolinguistic groups—Chuukese, Kosraeans, Pohnpeians, and Yapese—that comprise approximately 90% of the national population.[11] Those inhabitants enjoy all the rights and privileges accorded by the laws of the FSM to its citizens. Additionally, those inhabitants enjoy special cultural protections under the national and state constitutions of the FSM, wherein any conflicts between Western-inspired jurisprudence and cultural practices should be decided—even in a Western-style court of law— in favor of indigenous traditions.[12] The legal and political institutions of the FSM thus accord tremendous respect to the traditions and cultural practices of its native population. This further underscores the compelling nature of the intergenerational equity obligations of the present generation of the peo- ple of the FSM. The people of the FSM cannot claim disenfranchisement or other obstacles typically faced by indigenous peoples; the people of the FSM are responsible for their own fates, as well as the fates of their descendants.

The discharge of that responsibility is challenged by the adverse effects of climate change in the FSM, which are extensive and stark. Sea-level rise poses the gravest long-term threat. The mean sea level in the FSM is pro- jected to rise as much as 18 cm by 2030 and up to 90 cm by 2090.[13] Put

---

themselves distinct from other sectors of the societies now prevailing on those territories, or parts of them. They form at present non-dominant sectors of society and are determined to preserve, develop and transmit to future generations their ancestral territories, and their ethnic identity, as the basis of their continued existence as peoples, in accordance with their own cultural patterns, social institutions and legal system.

Study of Discrimination Against Indigenous Populations, U.N. Economic & Social Council, Subcom- mision on Prevention of Discrimination & Protection of Minorities, para. 379, U.N. Doc. E/CN.4/ Sub.2/1986/7/Add.4 (1987) (*prepared by* Jose Martinez Cobo).

11. FSM DIVISION OF STATISTICS, THE FSM 2000 CENSUS OF POPULATION AND HOUSING, http:// www.pacificdisaster.net/pdnadmin/data/original/FSM_DEA_2000_Ppltn_hsng_cnsus.pdf; *see also* Secretariat of the Pacific Community Applied Geoscience and Technology Division, *Federated States of Micronesia Country Statistics*, http://www.sopac.org/index.php/member-countries/federated-states- of-micronesia (last visited Aug. 23, 2016) [hereinafter SPC].

12. The FSM Constitution protects the "role or function of a traditional leader as recognized by custom and tradition," FSM CONST. art. V, §1, and deems that the "protection of Micronesian tradition shall be considered a compelling social purpose warranting . . . governmental action" to protect indigenous traditions even at the expense of other constitutionally guaranteed rights. FSM CONST. art. V, §2; *see also* YAP CONST. art. III, §3 ("Due recognition shall be given to customs and traditions in provid- ing a system of law, and nothing in this Constitution shall be construed to limit or invalidate any recognized tradition or custom."); POHNPEI CONST. art. V, §1 ("This Constitution upholds, respects, and protects the customs and traditions of the traditional kingdoms of Pohnpei."); CHUUK CONST. art. IV, §4 ("Traditional rights over all reefs, tidelands, and other submerged lands, including their water columns, and successor rights thereto, are recognized."); KOSRAE CONST. art. II, §2 ("The State Government shall protect the State's traditions as may be required by the public interest.").

13. AUSTRALIAN BUREAU OF METEOROLOGY AND COMMONWEALTH SCIENTIFIC AND INDUSTRIAL RESEARCH ORGANIZATION, CLIMATE VARIABILITY, EXTREMES AND CHANGES IN THE WESTERN TROPICAL PACIFIC: NEW SCIENCE AND UPDATED COUNTRY REPORTS, PACIFIC-AUSTRALIA CLIMATE CHANGE SCIENCE AND ADAPTATION PLANNING PROGRAM TECHNICAL REPORT 85 (2014), http://www.pacificclimatechang- escience.org/wp-content/uploads/2014/07/PACCSAP_CountryReports2014_WEB_140710.pdf [hereinafter PACSSAP].

into context, the low-lying atolls and islands of the FSM have average eleva-tions of four to five feet above sea level.[14] Many homes and commercial properties are located on and near the shorelines of the islands in the FSM. Coastal erosion and coastal flooding are commonplace in the FSM, affect-ing not just the households and businesses on the coasts but also nearshore croplands (e.g., taro patches), freshwater wells, mangrove ecosystems that anchor landmasses, and burial plots established long before the sea began rising.[15] A series of tidal surges swept across many of the islands in the FSM in December 2008, necessitating unprecedented evacuations of households and businesses.[16]

The sea is not just rising in the FSM—it is also acidifying and warming. The increase in atmospheric concentrations of carbon dioxide (CO_2) causes ocean water to acidify as that water absorbs more CO_2 than normal. The most immediate consequence of ocean acidification is the stunting of the growth rate of coral reefs in the affected ocean space, as represented by the decreased aragonite saturation in that space. In the FSM, the aragonite saturation will decrease by nearly 25% compared to pre-industrial levels toward the end of the 21st century, at which point coral reefs will not be able to grow.[17] This stunting undermines a major natural defense in low-lying islands and atolls against tidal surges and other destructive tidal events.

In addition to acidifying, the ocean in the FSM will continue warming in response to increased atmospheric concentrations of CO_2 and other green-house gases (GHGs). A warming ocean results in, among other things, the phenomenon of coral bleaching, wherein coral reefs expel microalgae that live in them and turn white. Coral bleaching events in the FSM are pro-jected to occur more frequently and last longer as the 21st century progresses, imperiling the long-term viability of the FSM's coral reef ecosystems.[18] The expulsion of algae from coral reefs due to ocean warming deprives reef fish and other marine life of nutrients they normally derive from the coral reefs, thus imperiling the maritime food chain and the human communities that depend on that food chain.

---

14. For a representative sample of elevations in the FSM, see Charles H. Fletcher and Bruce Rich-mond, Climate Change in the Federated States of Micronesia: Food and Water Security, Climate Risk Management, and Adaptive Strategies 94–100 (2009) (working paper).

15. See Charles H. Fletcher & Bruce Richmond, Climate Change in the Federated States of Micronesia: Food and Water Security, Climate Risk Management, and Adaptive Strategies 5 (2010).

16. Bill Jaynes, Tidal Swell Washes Over Pacific Islands, The Kaselehlie Press, Dec. 24, 2008; see also M. Shigetani, Preliminary Damage Assessment, Federated States of Micronesia: High Tide Event, December 7–12, 2008 (2009).

17. PACSSAP, supra note 13, at 82–83.

18. Id. at 85.

The physical toll of climate change is visible and quantifiable, but climate change impacts life in the FSM in less salient ways that are still devastating and profound. Climate change is having an insidious effect on sociocultural conditions in the FSM. Residents of the outer islands of Yap, Chuuk, and Pohnpei are fleeing rising sea levels and migrating to the relatively "high" main islands in the FSM,[19] which in turn strains limited food and water resources on the main islands, threatens to undermine delicate power hierarchies that have existed in the islands for millennia,[20] and disrupts transmissions of cultural knowledge and practices. Climate change is also altering wave patterns in the FSM's ocean space, particularly wave height and periodicity in the western region of the FSM.[21] This has profound implications for traditional instrument-free canoe navigation by seafarers in the FSM, who use wave patterns as elemental guides for their voyages on the open ocean. All those seafarers are from Yap and Chuuk in the western half of the FSM.

As climate change endangers the cultural identity of the people of the FSM, it also threatens the FSM's sovereign rights, territorial integrity, and development aspirations. Under the 1982 United Nations Convention on the Law of the Sea (UNCLOS), each coastal State is entitled to establish a maritime area called an exclusive economic zone (EEZ) up to 200 nautical miles measured from the State's coastal baselines.[22] Baselines in outlying islands of a coastal State can generate an EEZ for that State, underscoring the value of having widely dispersed outer islands like those in the FSM.[23] Under UNCLOS, the coastal State has sovereign rights to exploit the resources in its EEZ.[24] However, with sea-level rise in the FSM, the baselines of the low-lying islands and atolls that help generate the FSM's EEZ (not to mention the baselines from the coastal areas of the "high"

---

19. For an analysis of the latest FSM Census figures on internal migration, see FSM DIVISION OF STATISTICS, NATIONAL CENSUS REPORT: THE FSM 2000 CENSUS OF POPULATION AND HOUSING 47 (2002); see also SPC, supra note 11.

20. For an example of land-centric leadership and power hierarchies in Micronesia, see SHERWOOD LINGENFELTER, YAP: POLITICAL LEADERSHIP AND CULTURAL CHANGE IN AN ISLAND SOCIETY 77 (1975). In the Yap island group, inhabitants of the outer islands are barred by Yapese customs and traditions from owning land on Yap's main island, in part to preserve the traditional power balance on the main island that is based primarily on land ownership. Emigration from the outer islands to the main island threatens to upend that balance. See also GLENN PETERSEN, TRADITIONAL MICRONESIAN SOCIETIES: ADAPTATION, INTEGRATION, AND POLITICAL ORGANIZATION 85 (2009).

21. PACSSAP, supra note 13, at 86. On the connection between increases in anthropogenic GHGs and a weakening of the Pacific Ocean's Walker Circulation (which regulates the trade winds and current behavior of the Pacific Ocean), see generally Gabriel A. Vecchi et al., Weakening of Tropical Pacific Atmospheric Circulation Due to Anthropogenic Forcing, NATURE, May 4, 2006, at 73.

22. United Nations Convention on the Law of the Sea, Dec. 10, 1982, art. 57, 1833 U.N.T.S. 3.

23. Id. at art. 121.

24. Id. at art. 56.

islands in the FSM) will recede, which will potentially retract the extent of the FSM's EEZ. Additionally, the loss of any of the FSM's low-lying atolls and islands will jeopardize the FSM's territorial integrity and potentially weaken the FSM's claims to sovereign statehood.[25] The loss of EEZ space will hamper the FSM's sustainable development aspirations, particularly the FSM's ability to benefit from the sustainable harvesting of the fish stocks in its EEZ.[26]

Faced with such harsh and extensive climate change impacts, the FSM must contend with the growing probability that future generations of its population will not enjoy the FSM's natural environment, development opportunities, political stability, and cultural practices to the same extent as the current FSM population. In order to minimize that probability, the FSM must sound a clarion call about the injustice that the present-day international community is perpetuating against future generations, particularly through the international community's contributions to climate change. To sound that clarion call, the FSM must establish the legal and moral imperative of intergenerational equity as an obligation that must be enforced by the current generation of humankind for the benefit of future generations, especially through actions to combat climate change. The next part of this chapter surveys the state of international law regarding intergenerational equity and its applicability as a tool to address climate change.

---

25. This issue was addressed at a three-day conference on "Legal Implications of Rising Seas and a Changing Climate" held at Columbia Law School from May 23–25, 2011, *see* Columbia Law School, *Conference Materials*, http://www.law.columbia.edu/centers/climatechange/resources/threatened-island-nations/ Conference_Materials (last visited Aug. 23, 2016). *See also Report of the United Nations Secretary General on Climate Change and Its Possible Security Implications*, U.N. Doc. A/64/350 (2009) (recognizing that adverse effects of climate change, particularly sea-level rise, jeopardize the continued existence of low-lying States). According to an oft-cited international convention, one of the main requirements for statehood is a defined territory. Montevideo Convention on the Rights and Duties of States, Dec. 26, 1933, art. 1(b), 165 L.N.T.S. 1915.

26. *See generally* VULNERABILITY OF TROPICAL PACIFIC FISHERIES AND AQUACULTURE TO CLIMATE CHANGE (Johann D. Bell, Johanna E. Johnson & Alistair J. Hobday eds., 2011). The pelagic fish stocks that spawn and range through the FSM's EEZ—e.g., skipjack tuna and bigeye tuna—may alter their spawning and migratory preferences because of warming ocean temperatures, particularly in El Niño events, and because of changes in ocean currents associated with climate change. *See id.* at 433. This will have major ramifications for the FSM, which realized nearly $50 million in revenues from the sale of fishing access licenses in 2014, or more than a third of the FSM's total government revenues that year; and which is currently aiming to generate up to $85 million in annual fisheries access revenues in the near future, or more than half of projected annual government revenues. *See* Press Release, FSM National Ocean Resource Management Authority, FSM Policy Revamp for Fisheries Aims to Double "Blue Gold" Millions (May 24, 2016), http://myfsm.blogspot.com/2016/05/fsm-policy-revamp-for-fisheries-aims-to.html.

II.   Intergenerational Equity, the Natural Environment, and Human Rights

Breaking down the concept of intergenerational equity into its two main components is instructive as a prelude to defining the concept as a whole. Intergenerationality is fairly self-explanatory. It is the notion that there are links between the present generation and the future generations of human-kind, with the "present generation" encompassing all generations currently living. Equity, in contrast to intergenerationality, has a complex pedigree in international law, with somewhat nebulous permutations. Equity in international law is usually defined in terms of fairness or justice, with procedural and substantive elements that aim to ensure that individuals and entities are able to access international legal processes and receive judgments on the merits that are fair and reasonable.[27] In the context of sustainable development, equity is treated as the basis for the fair allocation and sharing of limited resources, as well as for the fair distribution of the burdens for caring for those resources and the natural environments from which they are derived.[28]

Despite the foregoing, international law has not explicitly defined intergenerational equity. However, the concept is discussed in various classic sources of international law—including influential soft law instruments—as well as in the writings of respected international law jurists and scholars, particularly in the context of sustainable development, cultural preservation, and the natural environment.

For sustainable development, there is a tradition of soft international instruments referring to the needs and interests of future generations when implementing development agendas in the present. The Stockholm Declaration adopted by the 1972 United Nations Conference on the Human Environment provides that the "natural resources of the earth, including the air, water, land, flora and fauna and especially representative samples of natural ecosystems, must be safeguarded for the benefit of present and future generations through careful planning or management."[29] The World Commission on Environment and Development, in its 1987 report "Our Common Future," builds on the Principles of the Stockholm Declaration by defining sustainable development as "meeting the needs of the present without

---

27.   *See, e.g.,* Thomas Franck, Fairness in International Law and Institutions 7–9 (1995).
28.   *See generally* Edith Brown Weiss, *In Fairness to Future Generations and Sustainable Development,* 8 Am. U. Int'l L. Rev. 19 (1992).
29.   *Declaration of the United Nations Conference on the Human Environment,* U.N. Conference on the Human Environment, Stockholm, Sweden, June 5–16, 1972, Princ. 2, U.N. Doc. A/CONF.48/14/ Rev.1 (1972) [hereinafter Stockholm Declaration]; *see also id.* at Princ. 1.

compromising the ability of future generations to meet their own needs."[30] The 1992 Rio Declaration on Environment and Development, echoing Our Common Future and revisiting the 1972 Stockholm Declaration, confirms that the "right to development must be fulfilled so as to equitably meet developmental and environmental needs of present and future generations."[31] Finally, in "The Future We Want," the outcome document of the 2012 United Nations Conference on Sustainable Development, States "renew [their] commitment to sustainable development and to ensuring the promotion of an economically, socially and environmentally sustainable future for our planet and for present and future generations."[32] In the same outcome document, States further acknowledge that "some countries recognize the rights of nature in the context of the promotion of sustainable development" and proclaim their conviction that "in order to achieve a just balance among the economic, social and environmental needs of present and future generations, it is necessary to promote harmony with nature."[33] And, in the context of cultural resources and preservation, perhaps the most stirring statement in an international instrument about intergenerational equity comes from the 2007 United Nations Declaration on the Rights of Indigenous Peoples, which proclaims the right of indigenous peoples "to maintain, protect and develop the present and future manifestations of their cultures";[34] as well as "to maintain and strengthen their distinctive spiritual relationships with their traditionally owned or otherwise occupied and used lands, territories, waters and coastal seas and other resources and to uphold their responsibilities to future generations in this regard."[35]

The concept of intergenerational equity has also long enjoyed substantive representation in a number of "hard" international environmental law instruments. The 1972 Convention Concerning the Protection of the World Cultural and Natural Heritage—which, among other things, is responsible for populating a World Heritage List with sites of cultural significance,

---

30. *Our Common Future*, World Commission on Environment and Development, Annex, para. 8, U.N. Doc. A/42/427 (1987).

31. *Rio Declaration on Environment and Development*, U.N. Conference on Environment and Development, Rio de Janeiro, Brazil, June 3–14, 1992, Princ. 3, U.N. Doc. A/CONF.151/26 (1992) [hereinafter Rio Declaration].

32. *The Future We Want—Outcome of the Conference*, Rio+20 United Nations Conference on Sustainable Development, Rio de Janeiro, Brazil, June 3–14, 1992, para. 1, U.N. Doc. A/CONF.216/L.1 (2012).

33. *Id.* para. 39; *see also id.* para. 86 ("promoting intergenerational solidarity for the achievement of sustainable development") and para. 158 (committing to "protect, and restore, the health, productivity and resilience of oceans and marine ecosystems, to maintain their biodiversity, enabling their conservation and sustainable use for present and future generations").

34. United Nations Declaration on the Rights of Indigenous Peoples art. 11(1), G.A. Res. 61/295, U.N. GAOR, 61st Sess., U.N. Doc. A/RES/61/295 (2007), 46 I.L.M. 1013 (2007).

35. *Id.* at art. 25.

including environmental locations—confers upon States Parties the "duty of ensuring the identification, protection, conservation, presentation, and transmission to future generations of the cultural and natural heritage" inscribed in the World Heritage List.[36] The 1973 Convention on International Trade in Endangered Species of Wild Fauna and Flora recognizes that "wild fauna and flora in their many beautiful and varied forms are an irreplaceable part of the natural systems of the earth which must be protected for this and the generations to come."[37] The 1992 Convention on Biological Diversity expresses the determination of its contracting Parties to "conserve and sustainably use biological diversity for the benefit of present and future generations,"[38] with "sustainabl[e] use" defined as the use of components of biodiversity "at a rate that does not lead to the long-term decline of biological diversity, thereby maintaining its potential to meet the needs and aspirations of present and future generations."[39] The 1996 Protocol to the 1972 London Convention on the Prevention of Marine Pollution by Dumping of Wastes and Other Matter expresses the conviction of its States Parties that international action to protect and preserve the marine environment by preventing, reducing, and possibly eliminating maritime pollution is crucial to "meet the needs of present and future generations."[40] Lastly, the 1992 United Nations Framework Convention on Climate Change (UNFCCC) commits its States Parties "to protect the climate system for the benefit of present and future generations of humankind."[41]

International and regional adjudicatory regimes have addressed intergenerational equity on a number of occasions. The International Court of Justice (ICJ), in its advisory opinion on the legality of the threat or use of nuclear weapons, explicitly asserted that "it is imperative for the Court to take account of the unique characteristics of nuclear weapons, and in

---

36. Convention Concerning the Protection of the World and Cultural Heritage, Nov. 23, 1972, art. 4, 1037 U.N.T.S. 151 [hereinafter World Heritage Convention].
37. Convention on International Trade in Endangered Species of Wild Fauna and Flora, Mar. 3, 1973, pmbl. para. 1, 27 U.S.T. 1087, 993 U.N.T.S. 243.
38. Convention on Biological Diversity, June 5, 1992, pmbl. para. 23, 1760 U.N.T.S. 79 [hereinafter CBD].
39. *Id.* at art. 2.
40. 1996 Protocol to the Convention on the Prevention of Marine Pollution by Dumping of Wastes and Other Matter, Nov. 11, 1996, pmbl. para. 8, 36 I.L.M. 1 ("BEING CONVINCED that further international action to prevent, reduce and where practicable eliminate pollution of the sea caused by dumping can and must be taken without delay to protect and preserve the marine environment and to manage human activities in such a manner that the marine ecosystem will continue to sustain the legitimate uses of the sea and will continue to meet the needs of present and future generations").
41. United Nations Framework Convention on Climate Change, May 9, 1992, art. 3.1, 1771 U.N.T.S. 107 [hereinafter UNFCCC].

particular their ability to cause damage to generations to come."[42] The ICJ also stressed the great significance it attached to respect for the environment, noting that "the environment is not an abstraction but represents the living space, the quality of life and the very health of human beings, including generations unborn."[43] In a separate opinion in the 1993 *Denmark v. Norway* case regarding maritime delimitation, Judge Weeramantry surveyed the notions of reasonableness and fairness in the customary law of traditional societies around the world and identified various examples "of equit[able principles] broad-based upon global jurisprudence" that emerge from those societies, including "the sacrosanct nature of earth resources, harmony of human activity with the environment, respect for the rights of future generations, and the custody of earth resources with the standard of due diligence expected of a trustee."[44] At a regional level, the Inter-American Court of Human Rights discussed intergenerational equity in *Mayagna (Sumo) Awas Tingni Community v. Nicaragua*, wherein the main decision recognized the relationship of the indigenous community of the Awas Tingni to their ancestral land as critical to "preserve their cultural legacy and transmit it to future generations."[45]

Perhaps the most influential consideration of the concept of intergenerational equity can be found in the work of Edith Brown Weiss. In her seminal 1989 work, IN FAIRNESS TO FUTURE GENERATIONS: INTERNATIONAL LAW, COMMON PATRIMONY, AND INTERGENERATIONAL EQUITY, Brown Weiss argues that intergenerational equity is achieved when the present generation:

- ensures a conservation of options, i.e., "conserve[s] the diversity of the natural and cultural base, so that it does not unduly restrict the options available to future generations in solving their problems and satisfying their own values"[46] and acknowledges that future generations are "entitled to diversity [of natural and cultural resources] comparable to that enjoyed by previous generations";[47]

---

42. Legality of the Threat or Use of Nuclear Weapons, Advisory Opinion, 1996 I.C.J. 226, 244 (July 8).
43. *Id.* at 241–42. *See also* Gabcikovo-Nagymaros Project (Hun. v. Slovak.), 1997 I.C.J. 7, 53 (Sept. 25) ("The Court recalls that it has recently had occasion to stress, in the following terms, the great significance that it attaches to respect for the environment, not only for States but also for the whole of mankind . . . 'including generations unborn'") [hereinafter *Nagymaros*].
44. Maritime Delimitation in the Area Between Greenland and Jan Mayen (Den. v. Nor.), 1993 I.C.J. 211, 276 (June 14) (separate opinion of Judge Weeramantry).
45. Mayagna (Sumo) Awas Tingni Community v. Nicaragua, Inter-Am. C.H.R. (ser. C) No. 68, at 149 (2000).
46. EDITH BROWN WEISS, IN FAIRNESS TO FUTURE GENERATIONS: INTERNATIONAL LAW, COMMON PATRIMONY, AND INTERGENERATIONAL EQUITY 38 (1989).
47. *Id.*

- ensures a conservation of quality, i.e., "maintain[s] the quality of the earth so that it is passed on in no worse condition than [the present generation] received it";[48] and

- ensures a conservation of access, i.e., "provide[s] its members with equitable rights of access to the legacy from past generations and . . . conserve[s] this access for future generations."[49]

Brown Weiss's examination of intergenerational equity as the conservation of options, quality, and access for future generations, particularly with regard to natural and cultural resources, has profound implications for action to combat climate change, which should be seen as part of an overall obligation of the present generation to protect the interests of future generations in relation to the natural environment. As Judge Weeramantry of the ICJ has noted, Brown Weiss's work is an important citation

> for the recognition by diverse cultures that each generation is a trustee or steward of the natural environment for the benefit of generations yet unborn, and for the fact that intergenerational fairness can be addressed under principles of equity in accordance with a long tradition in international law of using equitable principles to achieve a just result.[50]

The work also resonates with traditional societies like that of the FSM, where the safeguarding of environmental and cultural endowments for future generations has always been a profound obligation of each generation.

However, while the present generation acts as a "trustee" of the natural environment for future generations, does that mean that future generations have a right to that natural environment whose protection and preservation are stewarded by the present generation? Is it possible for an unborn person (let alone an entire unborn generation) to have a right to anything? Or, does intergenerational equity impose obligations on the present generation without necessarily creating concomitant rights for future generations? In his dissenting opinion for the ICJ's advisory opinion on the legality of the threat or use of nuclear weapons, Judge Weeramantry used especially strong language on intergenerational equity, insisting that the ICJ, "as the principal judicial organ of the United Nations, empowered to state and apply international law with an authority matched by no other tribunal, must, in

---

48. *Id.*
49. *Id.*
50. C.G. WEERAMANTRY, UNIVERSALISING INTERNATIONAL LAW 307 (2004).

its jurisprudence, pay due recognition to the *rights* of future generations."[51] By contrast, the 1997 United Nations Educational, Scientific, and Cultural Organization (UNESCO) Declaration on the Responsibilities of the Present Generations Towards Future Generations asserts that the present generation must ensure that "the needs and interests of present and future generations are fully safeguarded,"[52] without characterizing those needs and interests as rights.

The question of whether future generations have rights—including in relation to environmental resources—does not need to be answered. The primary issue is whether the *present* generation has an obligation to preserve, protect, and use the natural environment in a sustainable manner for the sake of future generations, so that those future generations can enjoy that natural environment to at least the same degree as the present generation. The foregoing discussion has identified numerous references to such a legal obligation in various international instruments, case law, and credible writings of respected jurists and scholars. The obligation exists, and it must be discharged, regardless of whether the future generations have rights to the subject of the obligation.

Nevertheless, the language of "rights" can be instructive for this discussion. The present generation of humankind cannot be proper trustees of the environment for the benefit of future generations if that environment is not entitled to protection and preservation in the present day. That entitlement is best expressed in the human right to a healthy environment, particularly an environment that is protected from the ravages of climate change. International law has not explicitly established a human right to a healthy environment. However, a person who is unable to enjoy a healthy environment will also be unable to enjoy a panoply of rights contained in a large number of international and regional human rights instruments, including the rights to life,[53] to ade-

---

51. Legality of the Threat or Use of Nuclear Weapons, Advisory Opinion, 1996 I.C.J. 226, 455 (July 8) (dissenting opinion of Judge Weeramantry) (emphasis added).

52. *Declaration on the Responsibilities of Present Generations Towards Future Generations*, General Conference of the United Nations Educational, Scientific, and Cultural Organization, Oct. 21 to Nov. 12, 1997, art. 1 (1997).

53. *See, e.g.*, Universal Declaration of Human Rights art. 3, G.A. Res. 217A, U.N. GAOR, 3d Sess., 1st plen. mtg., at 71, U.N. Doc. A/810 (1948); International Covenant on Civil and Political Rights, Dec. 16, 1966, art. 6, 999 U.N.T.S. 171 [hereinafter ICCPR]; Convention on the Rights of the Child, Nov. 20, 1989, art. 6, 1577 U.N.T.S. 3 [hereinafter CRC]; American Convention on Human Rights, Nov. 21 1969, art. 4, 1144 U.N.T.S. 143 [hereinafter ACHR]; European Convention for the Protection of Human Rights and Fundamental Freedoms, Nov. 4 1950, art. 3, 213 U.N.T.S. 221; African Charter on Human and Peoples' Rights, June 27 1981, art. 4, 1520 U.N.T.S. 217. A devastated natural environment poses mortal dangers to human populations, thus threatening their right to life.

quate food,[54] to water,[55] to health,[56] to an adequate standard of living (including adequate housing),[57] to the productive use and enjoyment of property,[58] to cultural practices and traditions,[59] and to self-determination.[60] International and human rights courts have arguably stepped into the gap in international conventions and identified the right to a healthy environment, or at least to the resources therein, pursuant to sustainable development that respects the rights of indigenous peoples.[61] Additionally, a number of nonbinding instruments have recognized at least an entitlement (if not an explicit right) to a healthy environment.[62]

---

54. *See, e.g.*, International Covenant on Economic, Social, and Cultural Rights, Dec. 11 1966, art. 11, 993 U.N.T.S. 3 [hereinafter ICESCR]; CRC, *supra* note 53, at art. 24(c); International Convention on the Protection and Promotion of the Rights and Dignity of Persons With Disabilities arts. 25(f) and 28(1), G.A. Res. 61/106, U.N. GAOR, 61st Sess., Supp. No. 49, Annex I, at 65, U.N. Doc. A/61/49 (2006) [hereinafter CRPD]; Convention on the Elimination of All Forms of Discrimination Against Women, Dec. 18 1979, art. 14(2)(h), 1249 U.N.T.S. 13 [hereinafter CEDAW]; International Convention on the Elimination of All Forms of Racial Discrimination, Mar. 7, 1966, art. 5(e), 660 U.N.T.S. 195 [hereinafter ICERD]. Rising global temperatures undermine agricultural production at lower latitudes and raise the potential for widespread food shortages, especially for poorer regions of the world.

55. *See, e.g.*, CEDAW, supra note 54; CRPD, *supra* note 54, at art. 2(2)(a); CRC, *supra* note 53, at art. 24(2)(c). Climate change exacerbates droughts, floods, and the intrusion of saltwater into coastal water wells in low-lying islands, thereby undermining the right to water.

56. *See, e.g.*, ICESCR, *supra* note 54, at art. 12; CEDAW, *supra* note 54, at art. 12; ICERD, *supra* note 54, at art. 5(e)(iv); CRC, *supra* note 53, at art. 24; CRPD, *supra* note 54, at art. 16(4); European Social Charter, Oct. 18, 1961, art. 11, 529 U.N.T.S. 89. Droughts—including those worsened by climate change—imperil water security, access to food, and the containment of diseases such as malaria, thereby diminishing health standards for those affected.

57. *See, e.g.*, ICESCR, *supra* note 54, at art. 11; ICERD, *supra* note 54, at art. 5(e)(iii); CEDAW, *supra* note 54, at art. 14(2); CRC, *supra* note 53, at art. 27(3). Sea-level rise threatens coastal settlements, particularly in low-lying islands and atolls where populations have little choice but to establish households on the coasts.

58. *See, e.g.*, Protocol to the Convention for the Protection of Human Rights and Fundamental Freedoms, Mar. 20, 1952, art. 1, E.T.S. 9; ACHR, *supra* note 53, at art. 21. In indigenous populations, natural environments are the source of property holdings as well as resources for fashioning new properties (e.g., houses and the items therein), so the destruction of those environments will hinder the enjoyment of those properties.

59. *See, e.g.*, ICCPR, *supra* note 53, at art. 27. Cultural and traditional practices that are connected to land and sea are undermined by climate change and other harmful impacts on the natural environments.

60. *See, e.g.*, U.N. Charter art. 1(2); ICESCR, *supra* note 54, at art. 1; ICCPR, *supra* note 53, at art. 1. The right to self-determination is undermined if sea-level rise diminishes territories and causes emigration of populations that wish to exercise self-determination.

61. *See, e.g.*, *Nagymaros*, *supra* note 43, at 88 (separate opinion of Judge Weeramantry) ("The protection of the environment is . . . a vital part of contemporary human rights doctrine, for it is a sine qua non for numerous human rights such as the right to health and the right to life itself"); Mayagna (Sumo) Awas Tingni Community v. Nicaragua, Inter-Am. C.H.R. (ser. C) No. 68 (2000) (affirming the collective rights of the Awas Tingni indigenous peoples to enjoy and utilize their environment and its resources); Port Hope Environmental Group v. Canada, Decision of the Human Rights Committee Under the Optional Protocol to the International Covenant on Civil and Political Rights, U.N. Communication CCPR/C/17/D/67/1980 (recognizing environmental harms as potentially violating the right to life, as established in the ICCPR).

62. *See, e.g.*, Stockholm Declaration, *supra* note 29, at Princ. 1 ("Man has the fundamental right to freedom, equality and adequate conditions of life, in an environment of a quality that permits a life of

Perhaps most significantly, the United Nations Human Rights Council (UNHRC) has explicitly stated that "environmental damage can have negative implications, both indirect and direct, for the effective enjoyment of human rights."[63] In a landmark set of 14 mapping reports, John H. Knox, the independent expert (later special rapporteur) on the issue of human rights obligations relating to the enjoyment of a safe, clean, healthy, and sustainable environment, analyzed the United Nations human rights bodies and mechanisms, international human rights treaties, regional human rights systems, and international environmental instruments to fully assess the connections between human rights and a healthy environment. Knox's reports established "overwhelming support" for the abovementioned statement of the UNHRC, noting that "[v]irtually every source reviewed identifies rights whose enjoyment is infringed or threatened by environmental harm."[64] Knox's reports also underscored "strong evidence of converging trends towards greater uniformity and certainty in the human rights obligations [of States] relating to the environment."[65]

This survey of rights underscores a critical point. States have an obligation to take steps to address environmental harms that threaten their citizens' enjoyment of a panoply of core human rights. Climate change is perhaps the most potent source of environmental harms, at least in the long run, so States logically have an obligation to address climate change in order to, among other things, protect natural environments and safeguard the human rights of their citizens. At the same time, the present generation of humankind has an obligation to transmit its natural environment and cultural resources to future generations in as whole a manner as possible. The necessary synergy is clear: addressing climate change is a prerequisite to discharging the intergenerational equity obligations of the present generation of humankind to future generations. It is extremely difficult for the present generation to (in the language of Brown Weiss) ensure the conservation of options, quality, and access for future generations with regard to environmental and cultural resources when climate change has devastated those resources in the present day.

The FSM has historically been a minimal contributor to climate change, but the FSM is burdened with discharging core obligations to provide a

---

dignity and well-being"); Rio Declaration, *supra* note 31, at Princ. 1 ("Human beings are . . . entitled to a healthy and productive life in harmony with nature").

63.   United Nations Human Rights Council Res. 16/11, pmbl. para. 14, U.N. Doc. A/HRC/RES/16/11 (2011).

64.   *Report of the Independent Expert on the Issue of Human Rights Obligations Relating to the Enjoyment of a Safe, Clean, Healthy, and Sustainable Environment,* U.N. Human Rights Council, 25th Sess., Agenda Item 3, para. 17U.N. Doc. A/HRC/25/53/Add.1 (2014).

65.   *Id.* para. 27.

healthy environment for its present generation as well as its future generations. It is a grave miscarriage of justice to saddle the FSM with such obligations absent actions and other contributions by the international community,
particularly major GHG emitters that bear proportionately larger responsibility for climate change based on their past and current emissions.

III. Triggering International Action to Combat Climate Change for the Protection of Future Generations

This part considers the options that the FSM can pursue to trigger action by
the international community on climate change by relying on existing international legal instruments and institutions and bilateral bases for protection.
Such action must be taken pursuant to the overall objective of discharging
the obligation of the present generation of the FSM people to transmit the
FSM's environmental and cultural resources to the future generations of the
FSM people with the same care and sanctity as the ancestors of the FSM
people transmitted these resources to the present generation.

As a small island developing State (SIDS), the FSM faces daunting obstacles in not just dealing with the adverse effects of climate change, but also
compelling the international community to do its part to prevent or otherwise address those adverse effects. Nevertheless, international law provides the FSM with a number of ways to hold the international community
accountable for its contributions to climate change and aid the FSM in discharging its obligations to future generations of the FSM people. Indeed, the
FSM's status as a SIDS arguably enhances the FSM's ability to secure such
accountability and assistance. Developed countries bear historical responsibilities for their emissions, whereas SIDS like the FSM are recognized as having special circumstances and particular vulnerabilities in the fight against
climate change that developed countries must respect and accommodate.
Additionally, SIDS like the FSM tend to attach special significance to the
environmental and cultural endowments they inherit from their past generations and place great importance on transmitting those endowments as
completely as possible to their future generations.[66] Getting the international
community to honor its commitments to tackle climate change will in turn
aid the FSM in discharging its own obligations to the future generations of
its people.

---

66. For further discussion on the impact of climate change on the economic and sociocultural resources
    of SIDS, see UNFCCC CLIMATE CHANGE SECRETARIAT, CLIMATE CHANGE AND SMALL ISLAND
    DEVELOPING STATES 16 (2005), http://unfccc.int/resource/docs/publications/cc_sids.pdf.

The FSM can utilize language in a number of major international environmental treaties to push for broader and deeper accountability from certain States for the adverse effects of climate change, particularly for the benefit of the FSM and other SIDS. The primary international instrument addressing climate change is the 1992 UNFCCC. The UNFCCC does not impose binding emissions targets or limits on its Parties. However, the UNFCCC does establish the principle of common but differentiated responsibilities (CBDR), which is the recognition that while all States should do their part to address climate change, certain States have historically been high emitters of GHGs and should therefore take the lead in addressing climate change.[67] The UNFCCC also recognizes the particular vulnerability of "small island countries" to the adverse effects of climate changes[68] and prioritizes the "specific needs and concerns" of small island countries in the implementation of commitments under the UNFCCC.[69]

On December 12, 2015, the 21st Conference of the Parties (COP21) to the UNFCCC adopted a decision containing the Paris Agreement (Agreement), the first universally applicable agreement to reduce GHGs.[70] The Agreement adopts long-term temperature goals of holding the increase in the global average temperature to "well below 2 [degrees] Celsius above pre-industrial levels and pursuing efforts to limit the temperature increase to 1.5 [degrees] Celsius above pre-industrial levels, recognizing that this would significantly reduce the risks and impacts of climate change."[71] Like the UNFCCC, the Agreement does not establish emissions targets for its Parties. However, unlike the UNFCCC, the Agreement does obligate its Parties to adopt nationally determined contributions (NDCs) aimed at mitigating their GHG emissions and taking other actions to address climate change and meet the Agreement's ambitious long-term temperature goals.[72] The Agreement also obligates its Parties to submit new and progressively ambitious NDCs at set intervals in the future.[73] It further requires its Parties to pursue domestic measures to implement and achieve their NDCs.[74] In sum, Parties are free to formulate their own NDCs as they see fit, but they must achieve those NDCs, and they must produce successive NDCs that are more ambi-

---

67.   UNFCCC, *supra* note 41, at art. 3.1.
68.   *Id.* at pmbl. para. 19.
69.   *Id.* at art. 4.8.
70.   For the full text of the Agreement, see *Adoption of the Paris Agreement*, UNFCCC Conference of the Parties, 21st Sess., U.N. Doc. FCCC/CP/2015/10/Add.1 (Dec. 12, 2015), http://unfccc.int/files/home/application/pdf/paris_agreement.pdf [hereinafter *Paris Agreement*].
71.   *Id.* at art. 2.1(a).
72.   *See id.* at art. 4.2.
73.   *Id.* at art. 4.3.
74.   *Id.* at art. 4.2.

tious than previous NDCs. Additionally, although all Parties are expected to take action to tackle climate change, the concept of CBDR continues to apply under the Agreement, and major historical emitters are expected to do their part in proportion to their emissions histories, including adopting progressively ambitious new NDCs in the years to come.

Getting the language on 1.5°C into the Paris Agreement was a major objective of the Alliance of Small Island States (AOSIS), of which the FSM is a member. Another primary objective for AOSIS was to include language on loss and damage as a stand-alone article of the Agreement, separate from other articles, particularly the article on adaptation. Loss and damage is a concept that refers to harms that cannot be prevented by mitigation or addressed by adaptation, such as the loss of an atoll due to sea-level rise; as well as harms that, while reparable, are not fully avoidable through mitigation or adaptation, such as severe infrastructural damage by strong storms.[75] The concept encompasses, among other things, noneconomic losses, including cultural harms,[76] as well as slow-onset events and irreversible harms.[77] The concept's links to intergenerational equity are clear: loss and damage represents unavoidable and perhaps even permanent harm, and it affects the cultural and environmental endowments of not just the present generation, but also of future generations.

AOSIS succeeded in getting a stand-alone article on loss and damage into the Agreement,[78] but at a serious cost: language in the COP21 Decision that excludes compensation and liability being considered in connection with that stand-alone article.[79] Compensation and liability for loss and damage was deemed a strict negotiating "redline" by many developed country Parties in the negotiations for the Agreement, citing concerns that they would be on the hook legally and financially above and beyond the obligations they would have under the Agreement and perhaps in perpetuity, given the nature of slow-onset climate change impacts like ocean acidification and other examples of loss and damage.

Despite the foregoing language in the COP21 Decision, the FSM and other members of AOSIS are arguably not barred from pursuing compensation and liability for loss and damage, even under the Agreement. The exclu-

---

75. KASHMALA KAKAKHEL, LOSS AND DAMAGE—FROM DEFINING TO UNDERSTANDING TO ACTION (2012).

76. See generally Non-economic Losses in the Context of the Work Programme on Loss and Damage: UNFCCC Secretariat, U.N. Doc. FCCC/TP/2013/2 (2013); see also OLIVIA SERDECZNY, ELEANOR WATERS & SANDER CHAN, NON-ECONOMIC LOSS AND DAMAGE IN THE CONTEXT OF CLIMATE CHANGE: UNDERSTANDING THE CHALLENGES (2016), https://www.die-gdi.de/uploads/media/DP_3.2016.pdf.

77. See generally Slow Onset Events: UNFCCC Secretariat, U.N. Doc. FCCC/TP/2012/7 (2012).

78. See Paris Agreement, supra note 70, at art. 8.

79. Paris Agreement, supra note 70, para. 51.

sionary language in the COP21 Decision deals only with Article 8 on loss and damage. There are other articles in the Agreement that can be utilized to seek at least compensation for loss and damage, including the article on climate finance[80] and the article on capacity-building.[81] Additionally, Parties are not barred from pursuing claims for compensation and liability for loss and damage outside the institutions of the Agreement, even if they cite provisions of the Agreement (other than Article 8) to support their claims. In light of those opportunities, the FSM and several other members of AOSIS (i.e., the Cook Islands, Nauru, the Republic of the Marshall Islands, Solomon Islands, Tuvalu, and the Republic of Vanuatu) attached interpretative declarations to their instruments of ratification for the Agreement that express their retention of all rights under international law to pursue claims for compensation and liability in relation to loss and damage, notwithstanding the provisions of the Agreement and the COP21 Decision.[82] The FSM's declaration underscores the FSM's continued ability to pursue redress for the unavoidable and permanent cultural and environmental harms encompassed by the notion of loss and damage—harms which will be felt by future generations of the FSM people.

In addition to the UNFCCC and the Paris Agreement, the Montreal Protocol on Substances that Deplete the Ozone Layer can provide a relatively effective method for addressing climate change in a substantial manner in the near future. A protocol to the Vienna Convention for the Protection of the Ozone Layer, the Montreal Protocol aims to repair and protect the

---

80. *Paris Agreement, supra* note 70, at art. 9. Article 9 deals with financial resources primarily for mitigation and adaptation, whereas AOSIS prefers that loss and damage be treated separately from adaptation. AOSIS might wish to moderate that preference and allow loss and damage to remain paired with adaptation (as it is under the UNFCCC process, despite the separate articles in the Agreement) if it wishes to secure loss and damage compensation under the finance article of the Agreement.

81. *Id.* at art. 11. Article 11 calls on developed country Parties to "enhance the capacity and ability of developing country Parties, in particular countries with the least capacity, such as the least developed countries, and those that are particularly vulnerable to the adverse effects of climate change, such as small island developing States, to take effective climate change action." Such action is not limited to mitigation and adaptation, so it is possible for SIDS to secure financial and technical assistance (if not "compensation") to aid their responses to loss and damage, including slow-onset events and noneconomic losses like cultural degradation.

82. For example, the relevant declaration by the FSM reads:
    The Government of the Federated States of Micronesia declares its understanding that its ratification of the Paris Agreement does not constitute a renunciation of any rights of the Government of the Federated States of Micronesia under international law concerning State responsibility for the adverse effects of climate change, and that no provision in the Paris Agreement can be interpreted as derogating from principles of general international law or any claims or rights concerning compensation and liability due to the adverse effects of climate change[.]
    For the texts of all the declarations, see https://treaties.un.org/doc/Publication/MTDSG/Volume%20II/Chapter%20XXVII/XXVII-7-d.en.pdf.

stratospheric ozone layer by phasing out the production and consumption of certain ozone-depleting substances. The Montreal Protocol has enjoyed great success in that mission, with successful reductions of a number of harmful substances.[83] The Parties to the Montreal Protocol—including the FSM—are now poised to adopt an amendment that will phase down the production and consumption of hydrofluorocarbons (HFCs). HFCs are substances that are used in refrigerators and air conditioners. They are also GHGs with global warming potential that is thousands of times more potent than that of CO_2.[84] Phasing down their production and consumption will likely avert up to a .5°C global average temperature increase, and some scientists insist that this is necessary if the international community is to have a chance at meeting the 1.5°C long-term temperature goal of the Paris Agreement.[85]

The FSM was the first Party to the Montreal Protocol to propose an amendment to phase down the production and consumption of HFCs.[86] Since the FSM's proposal, a number of similar amendments have been proposed by a wide range of Parties, including the United States, China, India, and various African States.[87] The major stumbling block to approving an amendment has been the insistence of certain developing countries—particularly India—that they should not have to be burdened with phasing down their use of HFCs unless they receive sufficient financial and technical assistance for their transition to a post-HFC world and are allowed to make that transition on a different timetable than developed countries.[88] As of this writing, parties are close to achieving a deal that will unlock financial and technical assistance and allow for the transition to proceed worldwide in an equitable manner. The FSM should continue to urge Parties to adopt a much-needed HFC amendment as soon as possible.

---

83. For a history of the phase downs pursuant to the Montreal Protocol, *see* DAVID HUNTER, JAMES SALZMAN & DURWOOD ZAELKE, INTERNATIONAL ENVIRONMENTAL LAW AND POLICY 544–99 (4th ed. 2011).

84. For additional information on HFCs and their global warming potential, see generally DURWOOD ZAELKE, NATHAN BORGFORD-PARNELL & STEPHEN O. ANDERSEN, PRIMER ON HFCS: FAST ACTION UNDER THE MONTREAL PROTOCOL CAN LIMIT GROWTH OF HYDROFLUOROCARBONS (HFCS), PREVENT 100 TO 200 BILLION TONNES OF CO_2-EQ BY 2050, AND AVOID UP TO 0.5°C OF WARMING BY 2100 (2015) (working paper).

85. *Id.* at 6.

86. *See Proposed Amendment to the Montreal Protocol*, Open-ended Working Group of the Parties to the Montreal Protocol on Substances that Deplete the Ozone Layer, Geneva, Switzerland, June 15–18, 2010, 30th mtg., U.N. Doc. UNEP/OzL.Pro.WG.1/30/4 (2010).

87. For more on the FSM's leadership in phasing down HFCs and the positive response of the international community, see Peter M. Christian, *Scoring a Goal*, OUR PLANET, May 2016, at 10, http://apps.unep.org/publications/index.php?option=com_pub&task=download&file=012101_en.

88. *See* Amitabh Sinha, *India Embraces HFC Phase-out Under Montreal Protocol*, THE INDIAN EXPRESS, Apr. 18, 2015, http://indianexpress.com/article/india/india-others/india-embraces-hfc-phase-out-under-montreal-protocol/.

Another treaty with ties to climate change and intergenerational equity that the FSM can utilize to get the international community to address climate change is the World Heritage Convention (WHC).[89] The WHC creates a World Heritage Committee which, among other things, designates sites around the world as having strong cultural and natural heritage and deserving of preservation for future generations. Specifically, the WHC obligates each State Party to "do all it can to [preserve its cultural and natural heritage for future generations], to the utmost of its own resources,"[90] to assist other States Parties in the preservation of their cultural and natural heritage,[91] and "not to take any deliberate measures which might damage directly or indirectly the cultural and natural heritage situated on the territory of other States Parties."[92]

In order for a site to be subject to the WHC's protective provisions, the site must first be listed by the WHC's World Heritage Committee as a World Heritage site, and then be listed in a separate List of World Heritage in Danger. The FSM, as a State Party to the WHC, recently succeeded in securing the inclusion of the majestic Nan Madol ruins in both lists.[93] The ruins are a coastal complex of massive stone fortresses and waterways that was home to a powerful Micronesian dynasty and whose construction continues to defy explanation.[94] With rising sea levels, the Nan Madol site—much of which is situated on a marshy coastline—is in danger of crumbling, if not sinking outright. The FSM can now petition the World Heritage Committee to require States Parties to develop comprehensive strategies to reduce their GHG emissions and curb the adverse effects that climate change has on heritage sites like Nan Madol. This approach has particular resonance for the people of the FSM, whose stewardship of the FSM's natural and cultural resources for the sake of future generations may be thoroughly upended by climate forces beyond their control.

As the FSM works through the UNFCCC, the Montreal Protocol, and the WHC, the FSM is poised to utilize other treaties to press for action on climate change by the international community. Specifically, the FSM can

---

89. For a fuller discussion of this approach, see generally Erica J. Thorson, *The World Heritage Convention and Climate Change: The Case for a Climate-change Mitigation Strategy Beyond the Kyoto Protocol, in* Adjudicating Climate Change: State, National, and International Approaches 255 (William C.G. Burns & Hari Osofsky eds., 2009).

90. World Heritage Convention, *supra* note 36, at art. 4.

91. *Id.* at art. 6(2).

92. *Id.* at art. 6(3).

93. UNESCO, *Nan Madol: First World Heritage Site in Micronesia,* http://www.unesco.org/new/en/apia/about-this-office/single-view/news/nan_madol_first_world_heritage_site_in_micronesia (last visited Sept. 17, 2016).

94. *Id.*

use procedures under a number of core international human rights treaties as well as special processes in the United Nations to highlight the obligations of States to acknowledge and enforce a number of basic human rights that their citizens enjoy in connection with the environment. Although international human rights law does not explicitly define a right to a healthy environment, it does enshrine a number of core rights whose enjoyment by rights holders is violated when the natural environments of those rights holders are harmed. The United Nations recognizes nine core human rights treaties, and each treaty has a committee or some other formal body that regularly receives reports from States Parties about their fulfillment of their obligations under the relevant treaty and engages in a review and dialogue process with those States Parties about their records.[95] The treaty body can also receive communications from individuals about human rights abuses committed by particular States Parties, although the States Parties might have to first ratify an optional protocol for the relevant treaty.[96] The treaty body also can receive "shadow reports" from civil society, which can be done in conjunction with States Parties or independently. The FSM can encourage civil society and individuals in developed country States Parties that assent to individual communications to produce shadow reports and lodge individual communications asserting that those States Parties must do more to combat climate change—including mitigating their GHG emissions—to avoid infringing on core human rights, including the right to life, the right to health, and the right to food.

In addition to the core human rights treaties, the UNHRC conducts a process called the Universal Periodic Review (UPR), wherein every Member State of the United Nations undergoes a thorough evaluation of its entire human rights record.[97] Civil society can produce shadow reports in the UPR process. Additionally, all other Member States can participate in the review of a Member State in the UPR process, primarily by submitting questions about the human rights record of the Member State under review. As with the processes involving the human rights treaties, the FSM can encourage civil society to raise linkages between the protection of core human rights

---

95.   For a full listing of the instruments, see United Nations Human Rights Office of the High Commissioner, *The Core International Human Rights Instruments and Their Monitoring Bodies*, http://www.ohchr.org/EN/ProfessionalInterest/Pages/CoreInstruments.aspx (last visited Aug. 23, 2016).

96.   Five of the nine core human rights treaties have optional protocols that allow for individual communications. Most of the remaining treaties provide for individual communications, assuming State Party assent. *Id.*

97.   For an overview of the UPR process, see United Nations Human Rights Office of the High Commissioner, *Basic Facts About the UPR*, http://www.ohchr.org/EN/HRBodies/UPR/Pages/BasicFacts.aspx (last visited Aug. 23, 2016).

and the fight against climate change. The FSM can also participate in the UPR process for developed country Member States and pose questions to them highlighting those linkages.

As the FSM works through various international treaties to advance the fight against climate change, it is also making contributions to the work of the International Law Commission (ILC)[98] on a highly relevant topic: the protection of the atmosphere. The ILC began its consideration of the topic in 2013, when it appointed Shinya Murase as the special rapporteur for the topic. Mindful of the then-ongoing negotiations for what would eventually become the Paris Agreement, the ILC agreed to include the topic on its program of work only with the understanding that the ILC's work on the topic would not interfere with ongoing negotiations on climate change and ozone depletion; would not deal with questions of State liability, the polluter-pays principle, the transfer of funds and technology to developing countries, and the precautionary principle; and would not deal with specific substances such as black carbon that are the subject of ongoing international political negotiations. The ILC also decided that the outcome of its work will be draft guidelines that do not impose on existing treaty regimes legal rules or principles that those regimes do not currently contain.[99]

Despite the restrictions placed on the ILC's work, Murase has produced three reports to date that feature robust legal analyses of the topic of the protection of the atmosphere. His reports are engrossing explorations of international law's consideration of the obligations of States to protect the atmosphere. His reports also highlight a major point of contention among ILC Members that strikes at the heart of the topic: whether the protection of the atmosphere is a "common concern of humankind" or (more softly) a "pressing concern for the international community as a whole." Murase favors the former formulation, in large part because it signals that the protection of the atmosphere creates obligations *erga omnes*, but many ILC Members resist that formulation, opting for the softer formulation to avoid acknowledging obligations *erga omnes*.[100]

Obligations *erga omnes*, as defined by the ICJ in the *Barcelona Traction* case, are the "obligations of a State towards the international community as a

---

98. The ILC's core mission is "the promotion of the progressive development of international law and its codification," and its work is carried out by members "of recognized competence in international law." G.A. Res. 174 (II), U.N. Doc. A/504 (1947).
99. For the full text of the restrictions that the ILC placed on the topic's consideration, see *First Report on the Protection of the Atmosphere: Special Rapporteur*, para. 5, U.N. Doc. A/CN.4/667 (2014).
100. For the special rapporteur's analysis of the debate, see *Second Report on the Protection of the Atmosphere: Special Rapporteur*, Part IV, U.N. Doc. A/CN.4/681 (2015).

whole" and which "by their very nature . . . are the concern of all States."[101] The ICJ further noted in *Barcelona Traction* that obligations *erga omnes* create corresponding rights in the States that are Members of the international community, and in that regard, "[i]n view of the importance of the rights involved, all States can be held to have a legal interest in their protection; they are obligations *erga omnes*."[102] In other words, there are certain matters that are of such tremendous importance to the international community that all States are obligated to address those matters in a way that benefits the international community. Although the ICJ's discussion of this concept of obligations *erga omnes* was dicta, it has been reinforced on numerous occasions in the jurisprudence of the ICJ since *Barcelona Traction*[103] and the writings of eminent international law scholars.[104] The ILC embraced the concept in its landmark 2001 articles on the responsibility of States for internationally wrongful acts, whose draft Article 48(1) notes that:

> Any State other than an injured State is entitled to invoke the responsibility of another State . . . if: (a) the obligation breached is owed to a group of States including that State, and is established for the protection of a collective interest of the group; or (b) the obligation breached is owed to the international community as a whole.[105]

The concept of "common concern of humankind" has significant implications for intergenerational equity in the context of climate change, especially if one accepts that this principle has a temporal element that creates obligations *erga omnes* for the present generation of humankind to protect the atmosphere for the sake of future generations. There is strong support for the concept of the common concern of humankind in international law.

---

101. Barcelona Traction, Light, and Power Company, Limited (Belg. v. Sp.), Second Phase, 1970 I.C.J. 3, 32 (Feb. 5).
102. *Id.*
103. For instance, the ICJ deemed that respect for self-determination is a right and obligation *erga omnes* in East Timor (Port. v. Austl.), 1995 I.C.J. 90, 105 (June 30), and Legal Consequences of the Construction of a Wall in the Occupied Palestinian Territory, Advisory Opinion, 2004 I.C.J. 136, 172, 199 (July 9). *See also* Application of the Convention on the Prevention and Punishment of the Crime of Genocide (Bosnia and Herzegovina v. Yugo.), Preliminary Objections, 1996 I.C.J. 595, 616 (July 11), and Application of the Convention on the Prevention and Punishment of the Crime of Genocide (Croat. v. Serb.), 2015 I.C.J. paras. 87–88 (Feb. 3).
104. *See, e.g.*, RESOLUTION ON OBLIGATIONS *ERGA OMNES* IN INTERNATIONAL LAW ART. 1(a), FIFTH COMMISSION, INSTITUTE OF INTERNATIONAL LAW (2005) (defining obligations *erga omnes* as "an obligation under general international law that a State owes in any given case to the international community, in view of its common values and its concern for compliance, so that a breach of that obligation enables all States to take action"), http://www.justitiaetpace.org/idiE/resolutionsE/2005_kra_01_en.pdf.
105. Draft articles on Responsibility of States for Internationally Wrongful Acts art. 48(1), *in Report of the International Law Commission on the Work of its Fifty-third Session*, U.N. GAOR, 56th Sess., Supp. No. 10, at 43, U.N. Doc. A/56/10 (2001).

The preamble of the UNFCCC announces that "change in the Earth's climate and its adverse effects are a common concern of humankind."[106] Other major environmental treaties employ the same or similar language in connection with the environmental protection they espouse, including the Convention on Biological Diversity,[107] the United Nations Convention to Combat Desertification in Those Countries Experiencing Serious Drought and/or Desertification, Particularly in Africa,[108] the Stockholm Convention on Persistent Organic Pollutants,[109] the Vienna Convention for the Protection of the Ozone Layer,[110] and the Minamata Convention on Mercury.[111] The FSM is a Party to all those cited treaties except for the Minamata Convention.

In response to the resistance of some ILC Members to the concept of the common concern of humankind in connection with the protection of the atmosphere, the FSM delivered a statement in the United Nations Sixth Committee strongly supporting the retention of the concept and chiding the ILC for not acknowledging the global nature of the challenge posed by the degradation of the atmosphere.[112] The Sixth Committee has an important role to play in the ILC's work, with statements delivered in the Sixth Committee routinely affecting the conclusions adopted by the ILC. The FSM and other SIDS can continue calling in the Sixth Committee for the ILC to acknowledge that the protection of the atmosphere is a common concern of

---

106. UNFCCC, *supra* note 41, at pmbl. para. 1.

107. CBD, *supra* note 38, at pmbl paras. 2–3 (Contracting Parties are "[c]onscious . . . of the importance of biological diversity for evolution and for maintaining life sustaining systems of the biosphere" and affirm that "the conservation of biological diversity is a common concern of humankind"). The CBD arguably applies to the atmosphere because its Article 2.1 defines "biological diversity" as "the variability among living organisms from all sources including, inter alia, terrestrial, marine and other aquatic ecosystems and the ecological complexes of which they are part;" and its Article 4 provides that the CBD is applicable to paragraph (b) "In case of processes and activities, *regardless of where their effects occur,* carried out under its jurisdiction or control within the area of its national jurisdiction or *beyond the limits of national jurisdiction*") (emphases added).

108. Convention to Combat Desertification in Those Countries Experiencing Serious Drought and/or Desertification, Particularly in Africa, Oct. 14, 1994, pmbl., 1954 U.N.T.S. 3 (employs a number of phrases similar to common concern, including "centre of concerns" and "urgent concern of the international community").

109. Stockholm Convention on Persistent Organic Pollutants, May 22, 2001, pmbl. para. 1, 2256 U.N.T.S. 119 ("persistent organic pollutants . . . are transported, through air, water and migratory species, across international boundaries and deposited far from their place of release, where they accumulate in terrestrial and aquatic ecosystems").

110. Vienna Convention for the Protection of the Ozone Layer, Mar. 22, 1985, pmbl. para. 6, 1513 U.N.T.S. 323 ("measures to protect the ozone layer . . . require international cooperation and action").

111. Minamata Convention on Mercury, Oct. 13, 2013, pmbl. para. 1 (treating mercury as "a chemical of global concern owing to its long-range atmospheric transport"), https://treaties.un.org/doc/Treaties/2013/10/20131010%2011-16%20AM/CTC-XXVII-17.pdf.

112. Delegation of the Federated States of Micronesia, Statement on Agenda Item 83: Report of the International Law Commission on the Work of its Sixty-seventh Session, Delivered to the Sixth Committee (2015), http://statements.unmeetings.org/media2/7654512/micronesia.pdf.

humankind that triggers obligations *erga omnes*. Even if such a concept is not well-settled in international law, it is certainly pervasive enough for the ILC to justify adopting it as part of the ILC's mission of the "promotion of the progressive development of international law."

The link between climate change, the "common concern of humankind," and obligations *erga omnes* is relevant when considering climate change litigation. The United States has a federal law on the books—the Alien Tort Statute (ATS)—that the FSM can wield to hold certain entities accountable for their contributions to climate change. Enacted in the late 18th century, the ATS states the following: "The district courts [of the United States] shall have original jurisdiction of any civil action by an alien for a tort only, committed in violation of the law of nations or a treaty of the United States."[113] The U.S. Supreme Court has ruled that the ATS applies only to claims that "rest on a norm of international character accepted by the civilized world and defined with a specificity comparable to the features of the 18th-century paradigms" recognized by the Court as being in existence when the ATS was enacted.[114] Federal courts in the United States have identified a number of international law violations that are comparable to those 18th-century paradigms, including war crimes, genocide, torture, crimes against humanity, and prolonged arbitrary detention.[115]

In April 2013, the U.S. Supreme Court held in *Kiobel v. Royal Dutch Petroleum Co.* that the presumption against the extraterritorial application of the laws of the United States applies to ATS cases, but the Court left open the possibility of bringing an ATS case against a defendant—including a corporate defendant—whose actions are connected to the United States with "sufficient force to displace the presumption against extraterritorial application."[116] In *Kiobel*, the Court held that the corporate defendant allegedly committed its torts outside the United States and did not have sufficient contacts with the United States—a low bar to clear for post-*Kiobel* ATS if

---

113. 28 U.S.C. §1350.
114. Sosa v. Alvarez-Machain, 542 U.S. 692, 721–22 (2004).
115. *See, e.g.*, Abebe-Jira v. Negewo, 72 F.3d 844, 847–48 (11th Cir. 1996) (holding that the ATS allows for a private right of action for aliens alleging torture, as defined in the Torture Victim Protection Act of 1991); Kadic v. Karadzic, 70 F.3d 232, 242–44 (2d Cir. 1995) (holding that the ATS allows for a private right of action for aliens alleging torture and genocide); Doe v. Islamic Salvation Front, 993 F. Supp. 3, 5–6 (D.D.C. 1998) (holding that the ATS allows for a private right of action for aliens alleging torture, summary execution, and other crimes against humanity); Xuncax v. Gramajo, 886 F. Supp. 162, 183–84 (D. Mass. 1995) (holding that the ATS allows for a private right of action for aliens alleging acts drawing "universal condemnation and opprobrium," including torture, summary execution, disappearance, and prolonged arbitrary detention); Forti v. Suarez-Mason, 672 F. Supp. 1531, 1535, 1552 (N.D. Cal. 1987) (holding that the ATS allows for a private right of action for aliens alleging torture, summary execution, and prolonged arbitrary detention).
116. Kiobel v. Royal Dutch Petroleum Co., 133 S. Ct. 1659 (2013).

most (or all) of the alleged tortious activities occur in the United States. Thus, post-*Kiobel*, an ATS plaintiff must establish that she is an alien to the United States and the defendant allegedly committed a tort in the United States (or in a manner sufficiently connected to the United States) that violates an international law of widespread acceptance.[117]

The aforementioned international law violations identified by federal courts in the United States as actionable under the ATS arguably impose obligations *erga omnes*, demanding that all States have the obligation to prevent their occurrence and prosecute those who engage in them if they do occur.[118] In this regard, the FSM can argue that the protection of the natural environment from the adverse effects of climate change is a "common concern of humankind" that triggers obligations *erga omnes* similar to international law violations that have already been deemed by courts in the United States to be covered by the ATS. Specifically, a citizen of the FSM who is an alien in the United States can use the ATS to sue a fossil fuel corporation in the United States (e.g., Exxon) for continuing to engage in the drilling for and supplying of fossil fuels despite knowing about the hard science on the links between fossil fuel use and climate change, thereby committing an egregious affront to the "common concern of humankind" about the adverse effects of climate change. The FSM citizen can meet the *Kiobel* requirement of sufficient contacts by establishing that the corporate defendant carried out its tortious conduct in the United States, including in its laboratories, boardrooms, and extraction sites located in the United States.[119] The FSM citizen, being from a SIDS that is already experiencing many of the adverse effects of climate change, should be able to establish standing.[120]

---

117. See Jaclyn Lopez, *The New Normal: Climate Change Victims in Post-*Kiobel *United States Federal Courts*, 8 Charleston L. Rev. 113, 146 (2013).

118. For a discussion of the obligations *erga omnes* triggered by these major international crimes, see generally M. Cherif Bassiouni, *International Crimes:* Jus Cogens *and* Obligatio Erga Omnes, 59 L. & Contemp. Probs. 63 (1996).

119. Inside Climate News, an independent, nonpartisan, and nonprofit news organization, recently published a series of articles exposing how Exxon conducted groundbreaking climate change research in the United States decades ago, realized the reality of the adverse effects of climate change, and engaged in a systematic campaign of climate change denial. For the series, see *Exxon: The Road Not Taken*, http://insideclimatenews.org/content/Exxon-The-Road-Not-Taken (last visited Aug. 23, 2016). The series was named as a finalist for the 2016 Pulitzer Prize for Public Service and helped launch a formal investigation by more than a dozen states attorneys general in the United States. *See, e.g.*, Justin Gillis & Clifford Krauss, *Exxon Mobil Investigated for Possible Climate Change Lies by New York Attorney General*, N.Y. Times, Nov. 5, 2015, http://www.nytimes.com/2015/11/06/science/exxon-mobil-under-investigation-in-new-york-over-climate-statements.html; *ExxonMobil Climate Change Cover-up Probe to Expand as 17 AGs Join NY to Tackle Fossil Fuel Firms*, RT, Mar. 30, 2016, https://www.rt.com/usa/337698-exxonmobil-lawsuit-climate-change/.

120. In addition to pursuing litigation on its own, the FSM can also encourage climate change litigation by other Parties in other States. The recent success of a group of litigants in the Netherlands in securing a court judgment requiring the Dutch government to take stronger actions to mitigate climate change is a

As the FSM considers and pursues various avenues in international treaties and fora to compel the international community to address the adverse
effects of climate change, the FSM can also utilize perhaps its most important bilateral treaty relationship: the Compact of Free Association between
the FSM and the United States (Compact). The FSM and the United States
entered into the Compact in 1986.[121] According to the terms of the Compact, the United States provides tens of millions of dollars in annual grants
to the FSM national government to be disbursed to the four FSM states and
the national government according to a certain formula;[122] grants the FSM
national government, the four FSM state governments, and FSM citizens
access to a number of federal programs in the United States;[123] provides for
the military defense of the FSM;[124] and allows FSM citizens to travel to, and
reside in, the United States without a visa.[125] In return, the United States has
exclusive military operating rights in the FSM, as well as the right to deny
military access to the FSM by any other country.[126]

More pertinent to this chapter, the United States is obligated under the
Compact "to promote efforts to prevent or eliminate damage to the environment and biosphere and to enrich understanding of the natural resources of
the Federated States of Micronesia."[127] The Compact empowers the FSM
national government to "bring an action for judicial review of any adminis-

---

model for holding individual governments accountable for their obligations to tackle climate change—
obligations that they formally assume under international treaties, as well as obligations *erga omnes* that
all States arguably have in connection with countering the adverse effects of climate change. *See* Arthur
Neslen, *Dutch Government Ordered to Cut Carbon Emissions in Landmark Ruling*, THE GUARDIAN, June
24, 2015, https://www.theguardian.com/environment/2015/jun/24/dutch-government-ordered-cut-
carbon-emissions-landmark-ruling. The same is true for a lawsuit in Oregon filed on behalf of 21 teenagers
and children that a federal magistrate judge allowed to proceed despite strong opposition from the Obama
Administration and fossil fuel companies. *See* James Conca, *Federal Court Rules on Climate Change in
Favor of Today's Children*, FORBES, Apr. 10, 2016, http://www.forbes.com/sites/jamesconca/2016/04/10/
federal-court-rules-on-climate-change-in-favor-of-todays-children/#4b7a00856219.

121. For a fuller description of the history behind the founding of the FSM, the negotiations for the Com-
      pact, and the enduring relationship between the FSM and the United States, see generally FRANCIS
      X. HEZEL, STRANGERS IN THEIR OWN LAND: A CENTURY OF COLONIAL RULE IN THE CAROLINE AND
      MARSHALL ISLANDS (2003); *see also* Clement Yow Mulalap, *Islands in the Stream: Addressing Climate
      Change From a Small Island Developing State Perspective, in* CLIMATE CHANGE AND INDIGENOUS
      PEOPLES: THE SEARCH FOR LEGAL REMEDIES 377, 394–97 (Randall S. Abate & Elizabeth Ann Kronk
      Warner eds., 2013).
122. Compact of Free Association, June 25, 2004, U.S.-F.S.M., §211, 117 Stat. 2721. The original Compact
      was adopted in 1986. All the provisions of the original Compact last indefinitely (barring the Parties
      deciding to terminate them) except for its economic provisions. Those provisions (among others)
      were renegotiated beginning in 2001 and adopted in 2003 to incorporate a number of amendments.
      All citations to the Compact in this chapter are to the 2003 Amended Compact.
123. *Id.* §221(a).
124. *Id.* §311(a)–(b).
125. *Id.* §141(a).
126. *Id.* at tit. three.
127. *Id.* §161.

trative agency action or any activity of the Government of the United States pursuant to [§161] or for enforcement of the obligations of the Government of the United States arising thereunder."[128] Thus, the FSM can bring an action against the U.S. Environmental Protection Agency alleging that the Agency's failure to impose national GHG emissions limits on U.S. industrial sectors beyond what the Agency is currently imposing contributes to climate change in a manner that ultimately damages the FSM's "environment and biosphere" and violates the United States' Compact obligations.[129]

Conclusion

The people of the FSM are proud guardians of their cultural and environmental heritage, cognizant of the hardships that their ancestors endured in preserving that heritage while navigating the Pacific Ocean without modern instruments, settling hundreds of remote islands, developing complex societies over millennia, surviving centuries of outside contact and colonial domination, and forging an independent and sovereign State. In order to transmit that heritage to future generations, the people of the FSM must contend with present-day threats. The most insidious of those threats is climate change, with its potential to irreversibly mar the natural environments of the FSM and undermine the cultural practices that stem from and depend on those environments. Being a minimal contributor to climate change, the FSM cannot be expected to address climate change on its own. To insist otherwise is a grave miscarriage of climate justice. Instead, the international community—particularly major contributors to climate change—must do its part to address climate change. Fortunately, the FSM has a raft of options it can pursue under international law to push the international community to address climate change in a robust manner—and, in turn, to aid the FSM in meeting its intergenerational equity obligations to future generations of the FSM people.

---

128. *Id.* §162.
129. The U.S. District Court for the District of Hawaii and the U.S. District Court for the District of Columbia have jurisdiction over such an action, with their decisions subject to review in the U.S. Court of Appeals for the Ninth Circuit and the U.S. Court of Appeals for the District of Columbia, respectively, as well as potentially in the U.S. Supreme Court. *Id.*

Chapter 13

Climate Justice for Human *and* Nonhuman Islanders: Domestic Duties, Regional Responsibilities, and International Interventions

Carly Elizabeth Souther* and
Teresa Giménez-Candela**

* We dedicate this chapter to the memory of Danny Markel, a brilliant criminal legal theorist and an irreplaceable member of the Florida State community. This chapter benefitted from years of conversation with the brilliant Teresa Giménez-Candela. I thank my mentor, editor, and friend Randy Abate for his insightful edits and invaluable guidance. Many thanks to the editors of the Environmental Law Institute for their excellent editorial support. Exceptional research from Katheryn Goulfine is gratefully acknowledged. Thanks are also in order for my parents, Greg and Patti Souther, for their unwavering love and support of my profesional and academic pursuits. Finally, I owe a debt of gratitude to my Doberman, Bama, who patiently waits for walks while I write. May his lazy dog days never end!

** I would like to thank our colleague, Prof. Randall Abate for his assistance at every phase of this project. Without the keen eye and profesional standard of Carly Souther, no portion of this text would have seen the light of day. She transformed our collaboration into an exciting academic experience for which I am truly grateful. I would also like to thank Katheryn Goulfine for her helpful research.

Introduction

The delegates of the 21st Conference of the Parties (COP21) adopted a historic climate action agreement in Paris, France, in December 2015.[1] The Paris Agreement reflected the consensus of climate scientists that the risks of global warming are dire and imminent.[2] The increased carbon emissions of nations, cities, corporations, and individuals in the industrialized world have placed the climate system under dangerous anthropogenic pressure. The varied impacts of human-induced climate change disproportionately affect impoverished nations and deepen existing inequalities.[3] Although "those likely to suffer the most from the impacts of climate change are those who have contributed least to the problem," the big emitters remain largely unaccountable for, and seemingly nonplussed by, this pervasive injustice.[4]

The Intergovernmental Panel on Climate Change's (IPCC's) Fifth Assessment Report identifies eight key risks of human-accelerated climate change.[5] The first climate-related risk recognizes that the lives and livelihoods of people in small island developing States (SIDS) are particularly vulnerable

---

1.   *Adoption of the Paris Agreement*, UNFCC Conference of the Parties, 21st Sess., U.N. Doc. FCCC/
     CP/2015/10/Add.1 (Dec. 12, 2015), http://unfccc.int/files/home/application/pdf/paris_agreement.
     pdf [hereinafter *Paris Agreement*]. COP21 is also known as the 2015 Paris Climate Conference. *See*
     Climate Action, *Find Out More About COP21*, http://www.cop21paris.org/about/cop21 (last visited
     Aug. 23, 2016).
2.   *See* National Aeronautics and Space Administration (NASA) Global Climate Change, *Facts—Scientific
     Consensus: Earth's Climate Is Warming*, http://climate.nasa.gov/scientific-consensus/ (last visited Aug.
     23, 2016).
3.   *See* WORLD BANK, WORLD DEVELOPMENT REPORT 2010: DEVELOPMENT IN A CHANGING CLI-
     MATE—CONCEPT NOTE (2008), http://siteresources.worldbank.org/INTWDR2010/Resourc-
     es/5287678-1226014527953/5555566-1226014549177/WDR2010_CN_oct14v3.pdf.
4.   Siobhán McInerney-Lankford, *Climate Change and Human Rights: An Introduction to Legal Issues*, 33
     HARV. ENVTL. L. REV. 431, 431 (2009).
5.   Christopher B. Field et al., *Summary for Policymakers*, *in* CLIMATE CHANGE 2014: IMPACTS, ADAPTA-
     TIONS, AND VULNERABILITY 13 (IPCC 2014), http://www.ipcc.ch/pdf/assessment-report/ar5/wg2/
     WGIIAR5-IntegrationBrochure_FINAL.pdf.

to climate change.[6] The other risks—inland flooding, infrastructural issues, extreme heat, severe weather-related events, insufficient access to freshwater reserves, coral ecosystem change, or the risks to inland water systems—have only exacerbated the vulnerability of island inhabitants in the face of climate change.[7] These island nations are not culturally, politically, or socially homogenous, nor are they necessarily similar in terms of topography or economic development. Despite the tendency to overgeneralize about the impact of climate change on small islands, these States possess certain characteristics that distinguish them from non-island developing countries. SIDS are not only afflicted by the same difficulties and inequities as these unindustrialized countries (such as poverty, inequality, and conflict), but "their small size, remoteness, narrow resource and export base, and exposure to global environmental challenges and external economic shocks, including to a large range of impacts from climate change and potentially more frequent and intense natural disasters," renders them particularly vulnerable to an additional, unique layer of economic, social, and environmental problems.[8]

This chapter considers serious implications of climate change for the 39 small island Member States of the Barbados Programme of Action (BPOA) as well as the 14 SIDS that are not members of the United Nations,[9] with an emphasis on seven of the most vulnerable low-lying island nations (the SIDS-Seven) located within the tropics of the Pacific Ocean[10] and the Indian Ocean.[11] A substantial number of commentators have examined the profound climate impacts on SIDS and surveyed a range of remedies available to small island nationals.[12]

---

6. This chapter concentrates on "islands" created by water barriers that are relatively small in size. For example, Great Britain (including the territories of England, Scotland, and Wales) is an island created by water barriers, yet with landmass totaling more than 80,000 mi^2, it can hardly be described as "small."

7. This chapter does not consider the various other risks except as they relate to island communities. It is the consequences of climate change for SIDS, rather than climate-related risks in general, that are central to this analysis.

8. United Nations Department of Economic and Social Affairs Division for Sustainable Development, *Small Island Developing States*, https://sustainabledevelopment.un.org/topics/sids (last visited Aug. 23, 2016).

9. *See* United Nations Office of the High Representative for the Least Developed Countries, Landlocked Developing Countries, and Small Island Developing States (UN-OHRLLS) Small Island Developing States: Small Islands Big(ger) Stakes, http://unohrlls.org/custom-content/uploads/2013/08/SIDS-Small-Islands-Bigger-Stakes.pdf (last visited Sept. 21, 2016).

10. The Cook Islands and Tonga are located in the southern Pacific Ocean. The Federated States of Micronesia and the Marshall Islands are located in the western Pacific Ocean. Kiribati and Tuvalu are located in the central Pacific Ocean.

11. The Maldives is located in the central Indian Ocean. *See* Table 1.

12. *See, e.g.,* Maxine Burkett, *A Justice Paradox: On Climate Change, Small Island Developing States, and the Quest for Effective Legal Remedy*, 35 U. Haw. L. Rev. 633 (2013); Marc Limon, *Human Rights and Climate Change: Constructing a Case for Political Action*, 33 Harv. Envtl. L. Rev. 439 (2009);

This discourse has suffered from lack of consideration for island animal protection and climate change, with a number of acute consequences underpinning this specific link. At present, the critical challenge in connecting human rights and nonhuman animal protection is the pervasive perception that it is disrespectful to seek enhanced protection for animals when a significant number of humans neither have nor expect certain rights and freedoms to which they are entitled under the international human rights framework.[13]

Through several island animal examples, this chapter highlights the unchecked, unethical treatment of nonhuman animals to enhance the understanding of island communities and culture. It seeks to illustrate how, absent international interventions and protective efforts, climate-related changes in SIDS can drive island animal populations to extinction. The chapter describes how climate change exacerbates the vulnerability of an already-vulnerable population of animal islanders and calls for urgent international action to address climate change impacts in all relevant forums. It also proposes that global animal law duties are emerging to help support this effort.[14]

In surveying potential strategies to minimize climate change impacts on nonhuman animals, the chapter proposes a new framework for accommodating the consequences of climate change in SIDS with a climate-justice agenda.[15] It redirects existing global climate change initiatives toward "species-centered climate-justice reform"—the right of human *and* nonhuman animals to enjoy a secure and sustainable environment through national, regional, and international efforts to mitigate climate change and adapt to its effects.

John H. Knox, *Linking Human Rights and Climate Change in the United Nations*, 33 Harv. Envtl. L. Rev. 477 (2009); Xing-Yin Ni, *A Nation Going Under: Legal Protection for "Climate Change Refugees,"* 38 B.C. Int'l & Comp. L. Rev. 329 (2015).

13. In Kiribati, for example, human rights problems include violence and discrimination against women, child abuse, and threats to freedoms of speech and press. *See* U.S. Department of State, *Country Reports on Human Rights Practices for 2014—Kiribati*, http://www.state.gov/j/drl/rls/hrrpt/humanrightsreport/index.htm?year=2014&dlid=236446 (last visited Aug. 23, 2016).

14. Global governance centers on the creation of binding, universal laws that regulate how each country treats its citizens. This concept, especially if extended to nonhuman animals, could become a critical tool for advocates to influence the treatment of island animals. *See* Carly Elizabeth Souther, *The Cruel Culture of Conservation Country: Non-native Animals and the Consequences of Predator-free New Zealand*, 26 Transnat'l L. & Contemp. Probs. (forthcoming spring 2017).

15. Climate justice "recognises climate change will disproportionately affect people who have less ability to prevent, adapt or otherwise respond to increasingly extreme weather events, rising sea levels and new resource constraints. A climate-justice agenda embraces a conscious recognition of the development imbalances brought into relief by climate change." David Estrin & Baroness Helena Kennedy QC, Achieving Justice and Human Rights in an Era of Climate Disruption: International Bar Association Climate Change Justice and Human Rights Task Force Report 2–3 (2014), http://www.ibanet.org/Article/Detail.aspx?ArticleUid=96b93592-3761-4418-8a52-54a81b02c5f1.

Climate justice for human islanders is inextricably connected to the humane treatment and management of nonhuman animal islanders. Because the inherent value of any unthreatened species of island animal—with, perhaps, the notable exception of the dog—is unlikely to persuade developed countries to provide the financial resources necessary to integrate protective animal policies into adaptation plans, the chapter seeks to transform protection for animal islanders into animal-related measures that reduce human islanders' vulnerability to climate change. Under the "new" conception of international law,[16] the principle of absolute State sovereignty has gradually eroded in matters of universal interest such as human rights and environmental protection.[17] It therefore follows that if animal protection initiatives are repackaged as a means to advance accepted international objectives such as the protection of public health or the preservation of public morals—rather than as measures for advancing the interests of animals—they will be perceived as credible obligations instead of unjustifiable impositions. By emphasizing the economic, environmental, and public health values of animal-related adaptation actions, principles of animal protection are integrated into legal arguments regarding climate justice for humans.

The interplay between wildlife conservation, the emerging field of global animal law, and established principles of international law such as human rights and State sovereignty is assessed in this chapter to determine the duties and rights of both large emitters and small island inhabitants. It promotes species-centered reform to awaken the international community to the moral and ethical consequences of climate change on animal life in small islands. Part I of this chapter addresses climate change and the geography of atoll islands,[18] and discusses both recognized and unrecognized risks of climate change impacts on SIDS. Part II considers how species-centered reform in SIDS can be used to achieve climate justice for animal islanders. Part III identifies six animal-related adaptation proposals for SIDS to strengthen animal islanders' resilience and reduce their vulnerability to climate change. Each recommendation supports an animal control and sterilization-driven adaptation plan, which helps fill the gap between climate justice and island land animal protection.[19]

---

16. Julian Ku & John Yoo, *Globalization and Sovereignty*, 31 Berkeley J. Int'l L. 210, 213 (2013). "New international law," also referred to as "cosmopolitan law," "purports to create universal binding obligations regulating a nation-state's treatment of its own citizens." *Id.*

17. *Id. See also* David J. Bederman, Globalization and International Law 3–54 (2008).

18. An atoll is "a coral island consisting of a reef surrounding a lagoon." Merriam-Webster Dictionary, http://www.merriam-webster.com/dictionary/atoll. *Cf. to* an island, which is "a tract of land surrounded by water and smaller than a continent." Merriam-Webster Dictionary, http://www.merriam-webster.com/dictionary/island.

19. Detailed implementation of this strategy, or any facet thereof, is a matter for future scholarship.

I.   Animals: The Unacknowledged Climate-vulnerable Group

The implications of climate change for island animals have been unintentionally documented in the context of resource use and the societal and financial costs associated with island animals. For example, there is evidence that higher temperatures will lead to an increased island invasion of non-native flora and fauna.[20] Leaders from the IPCC to the Pacific Islands Forum recognized that agricultural and livestock production relies on stable precipitation patterns, and is vulnerable to cyclones and other extreme weather events.[21] This indirect consideration of nonhuman island inhabitants demonstrates the particular vulnerability of island animals (not simply farm animals), which are heavily dependent on seasonal rainfall for fresh drinking water. A sudden-onset natural disaster threatens the viability of all indigenous and non-native inhabitants. Another subsistence concern is that the livelihoods of many islanders depend on access to and favorable conditions for marine animals.[22] Unfortunately for the nonhuman islanders, SIDS governments do not have plans in place to assist these vulnerable animals.

At the global level, conservation efforts surrounding climate-related impacts on animals, such as the North Atlantic right whale and Indonesia's orangutans, highlight the connection between species survival and human-induced climate change.[23] As extensively documented elsewhere, marine ecosystems are undergoing rapid "regime shifts" that continue to reduce biodiversity and disrupt the behaviors and abundance of marine mammals.[24] Likewise, *National Geographic* confirmed that the recent extinction of two

---

20.   *See* Field et al., *Summary for Policymakers*, *supra* note 5, at 12.
21.   *See* LESLEY RUSSELL, POVERTY, CLIMATE CHANGE, AND HEALTH IN PACIFIC ISLAND COUNTRIES: ISSUES TO CONSIDER IN DISCUSSION, DEBATE, AND POLICY DEVELOPMENT 13 (2011), http://ses.library.usyd.edu.au//bitstream/2123/9202/1/lrpacificislands2011.pdf.
22.   *See* Field et al., *Summary for Policymakers*, *supra* note 5, at 122.
23.   *See* World Wide Fund for Nature, *Impact of Climate Change on Species: A Growing Need for Species to Adapt to a Changing World*, http://wwf.panda.org/about_our_earth/species/problems/climate_change/ (last visited Sep. 22, 2016).
24.   *See* Field et al., *Summary for Policymakers*, *supra* note 5, at 116–27. Warming does not uniformly impact coexisting marine species, as certain species are affected by larger thermal windows, which therefore causes differential changes in growth, reproductive success, larval output, early juvenile survival, and recruitment, implying shifts in the relative performance of animal species and, thus, their competitiveness. Such effects may underlie abundance losses or local extinctions, "regime shifts" between coexisting species, or critical mismatches between predator and prey organisms, resulting in changes in local and regional species richness, abundance, community composition, productivity, energy flows, and invasion resistance.
    Id. at 127. *See generally* Eric V. Hull, *Using Climate Change Impacts as Leverage to Protect the Polar Bear: The Value of Habitat Protection in Promoting Animal Welfare, in* WHAT CAN ANIMAL LAW LEARN FROM ENVIRONMENTAL LAW? 147–65 (Randall S. Abate ed., 2015) (charging climate-related changes with the loss of polar bear habitat).

amphibian species "has been attributed with medium confidence to climate change."[25]

Scientists have also noticed that many terrestrial "animal species have shifted their geographic ranges and seasonal activities and altered their abundance in response to observed climate change over recent decades."[26] Displaced animal populations are highly susceptible to disease in a new habitat because they are likely to encounter foreign bacteria and other disease organisms.[27] Additionally, heat waves may trigger mass mortality of livestock, and there is high confidence that heat stress reduces animal feeding, reproductive and growth rates, and overall strength.[28]

However, while there has been extensive media coverage of, and scholarship on, the fate of polar bears and SIDS,[29] the plight of island animals and migratory birds has been largely overlooked.[30] Nonhuman animals were not considered in the SIDS-Seven's intended nationally determined contribution plans (INDC), required pursuant to Decision 1/CP.21 of the Paris Agreement, nor in their respective national adaptation program of action (NAPA) plans, if applicable. Likewise, while the Paris Agreement

---

25. Christine Dell'Amore, *7 Species Hit Hard by Climate Change—Including One That's Already Extinct*, NAT'L GEOGRAPHIC, Apr. 2, 2014, http://news.nationalgeographic.com/news/2014/03/140331-global-warming-climate-change-ipcc-animals-science-environment/.

26. Field et al., *Summary for Policymakers*, *supra* note 5, at 44. The distribution of animals due to climate change has also been noted in Europe. *Id.* at 120 (noting that temperature change "increases the spatial distribution and seasonality of pests and diseases").

27. *Id.* at 120.

28. *Id.* at 112.

29. There have also been meaningful measures to strengthen the ability of small islands to adapt to climate change and manage future risks at the international level. In 2012, the United Nations Framework Convention on Climate Change (UNFCCC) Parties agreed that they "should, in all climate change-related actions, fully respect human rights." *See* ESTRIN & KENNEDY, *supra* note 15.

30. *But see* Leonard A. Nurse & Roger F. McLean et al., *Small Islands, in* CLIMATE CHANGE 2014: IMPACTS, ADAPTATIONS, AND VULNERABILITY 1622 (IPCC 2014) (noting that climate change can affect terrestrial species, by decreasing or altering their range or increasing the number of non-native species; however, protective measures for nonhuman animals are neither discussed nor proposed), http://ipcc-wg2.gov/AR5/images/uploads/WGIIAR5-Chap29_FINAL.pdf [hereinafter *Small Islands*]. *See also* Field et al., *Summary for Policymakers*, *supra* note 5, at 119. The International Union for the Conservation of Nature (IUCN) was the only organization the authors found that explicitly noted the adverse impacts of climate change on island animal species. *See* IUCN, FEDERATED STATES OF MICRONESIA (FSM): SUMMARY OF SPECIES ON THE 2008 IUCN RED LIST (n.d.) (noting that endemic plant and animal species in FSM are "vulnerable to extinction from climate change"), http://cmsdata.iucn.org/downloads/federated_states_of_micronesia.pdf [hereinafter FSM: SUMMARY OF SPECIES]. *Cf.* CENTER FOR BIOLOGICAL DIVERSITY, DEADLY WATERS: HOW RISING SEAS THREATEN 233 ENDANGERED SPECIES 1–2 (2013) (listing five of the most threatened species: Key deer, loggerhead sea turtle, Delmarva Peninsula fox squirrel, western snowy plover, and the Hawaiian monk seal), http://www.biologicaldiversity.org/campaigns/sea-level_rise/pdfs/Sea_Level_Rise_Report_2013_web.pdf [hereinafter DEADLY WATERS]. The Center for Biological Diversity has emphasized that rising sea levels pose a risk to 44 endangered or threatened mammals, reptiles, and birds in 23 coastal U.S. states. *See* Center for Biological Diversity, *Appendix*, http://www.biologicaldiversity.org/campaigns/sea-level_rise/appendix.html (last visited Aug. 23, 2016).

encourages State Parties, "when taking action to address climate change," to "respect, promote, and consider their respective obligations on human rights, the right to health, the rights of indigenous peoples, local communities, migrants, children, persons with disabilities, and people in vulnerable situations,"[31] responsibilities for the significant number of nonhuman islanders have been omitted. It follows that the well-being of nonhuman island inhabitants is neither protected nor necessarily desirable. For example, despite the fact that possessing, killing, and consuming sea turtle meat and eggs are prohibited acts,[32] i-Kiribati routinely dig up nests of sea turtle eggs from the beach, and fishermen often catch endangered sea turtles for the purposes of consumption.[33]

The following subparts assess the impacts of climate change on two species of animal islanders. By evaluating the key climate and ocean drivers of change, as well as the lethal and sublethal impacts that such changes will have on island animals, the need for climate justice for nonhuman islanders—and the nexus between this objective and the health, safety, and economic security of human islanders—becomes apparent. Subpart A examines the threat that climate change poses to the survival of the black noddy, a terrestrial island bird species, and explores the economic, agricultural, ecological, and public health impacts that such risks pose in SIDS. Subpart B considers the adverse impacts of climate change on canine islanders and discusses the threat of zoonosis, in addition to traditional Western concerns for protection of dogs, which can have serious fiscal ramifications for island economies that rely on revenue from tourism.

A.   A Nod to the Black Noddy

With respect to island animals, birds are the most common native terrestrial vertebrates, and "avian endemism increases with the isolation and topographic diversity of the islands, with most endemic species being found in the larger and higher islands."[34] Many endemic bird species have been clas-

---

31. *Paris Agreement, supra* note 1.
32. *See* Western Pacific Regional Fishery Council, Hawaii: A Center for Pacific Sea Turtle Research & Conservation 8 (2006), http://www.wpcouncil.org/wp-content/uploads/2013/03/Turtle-Excellence_FINAL.pdf.
33. The i-Kiribati (the demonym for native islanders) are not the only people to seize turtles and their eggs for consumption. According to the Western Pacific Regional Fishery Council, "[t]hroughout the world, people consume sea turtle eggs and harvest turtles for their meat, oil, leather and shell." *Id.* at 7.
34. Mark McGinley, *Biological Diversity in Polynesia-Micronesia*, Encyclopedia of the Earth (Dec. 1, 2011) (on file with author) [hereinafter *Biological Diversity*].

sified as threatened species.[35] But not all birds are endemic or at-risk species.[36] The black noddy (*Anous minutus*), a terrestrial bird species with an estimated global population of 1.5 million, lives in each of the SIDS-Seven except the Maldives.[37] Distinguished by their brightly colored mouths and tongues,[38] as well as by white markings on their eyelids, black noddies have sooty black plumage, a white cap, black bill, gray body, and reddish feet.[39] The only nesting marine tern, monogamous black noddy pairs build large nests—constructed with mangroves and coastal shrubs and held in place with guano[40]—in trees, sea caves, or on cliff edges.[41] One black noddy egg is laid during each breeding season, and both parents are actively involved in rearing their hatchling.

For black noddies, the key climate and ocean drivers of change include variations in wind strength and direction, increasing air and sea temperatures, extreme weather events such as cyclones and drought, sea-level rise, and coastal squeeze.[42] Stronger winds may cause eggs to fall from nests, which could lead to a reduction in the numbers of black noddy populations because only one egg is laid per breeding season. Temperature rise can accelerate the growth of bacteria and influence the distribution of mosquitoes and other disease vectors, which may be conducive to the transmission of new illnesses to black noddies. The increasing atmospheric concentration of carbon

35. For example, the Yap islands group of the Federated States of Micronesia has three endemic bird species, as well as four restricted-range bird species. The endemic *Zosterops oleaginous* bird species is threatened, and the two other endemic species are near-threatened. *See* World Wildlife Fund, *Yap Islands State, Federated States of Micronesia*, http://www.worldwildlife.org/ecoregions/oc0204 (last visited Aug. 23, 2016) [hereinafter *Yap Islands*]. Two other vulnerable birds are endemic to the Cook Islands: the Atiu swiftlet (*Collocalia sawtelli*) and the Mangaia kingfisher (*Todiramphus ruficollis*). *Id.* The vulnerable Rarotonga monarch of the Cook Islands is another example of a threatened endemic bird species. *See* IUCN Red List of Threatened Species, *Pomarea dimidiata*, http://www.iucnredlist.org/details/22707172/0 (last visited Aug. 23, 2016).

36. *But see* Gary J. Patronek, *Cats and Islands—Outline of a Presentation*, in Proceedings of the Conference: Challenges of Animal Protection on Island Nations—With Special Emphasis on Cats and Dogs 11 (Humane Society International 2002) (estimating that 20% "of all birds are on islands. More than 90% of the bird species that have become extinct in historical times were island species. Islands constitute less than 7% of the earth's surface, yet 53% of endangered bird species are on islands."), http://www.hsi.org/assets/pdfs/eng_challenges_island_nations.pdf.

37. *See* Tanya Dewey, *Anous Minutus—Black Noddy*, Animal Diversity Web, 2009, http://animaldiversity. org/accounts/Anous_minutus/ (last visited Aug. 23, 2016). *See also* IUCN Red List of Threatened Species, *Anous Minutus*, http://www.iucnredlist.org/details/22694799/0 (last visited Aug. 23, 2016).

38. The color of the mouth lining and tongue differs by region. Black noddies in the Hawaiian Islands and around the Atlantic have an orange-yellow mouth and tongue, while Australian noddies have a pink mouth lining and yellow tongue. *See* Dewey, *supra* note 37.

39. *Id.*

40. Guano is another word for bird droppings.

41. Dewey, *supra* note 37.

42. Coastal squeeze is the process by which physical infrastructure and rapid human population growth in a coastal area prevents nonhuman animal species from retreating landward as an adaptation response to coastal erosion.

dioxide and thermal stress affects the viability of living coral reef systems and leads to a decrease in fish abundance. The loss of coastal fish has detrimental implications for black noddies because they rely on fish for sustenance. Extreme weather events like storm surges, cyclones, and king tides can be expected to have both short-term effects on black noddy health, including drowning, injuries, nest destruction, and starvation, and long-term effects associated with an increase in human hunting due to food insecurity or inadequate nutritional resources. Sea-level rise "is reported as the most significant climate change threat to the survival of mangroves," which is a key material used in the construction of black noddy nests.[43]

From an economic perspective, black noddies have a positive impact on agricultural processes because of their enriched guano deposits. Black noddies forage in large flocks, flying close to the surface of ocean, lagoon, or brackish coastal waters, where they seize small fish, crustaceans, mollusks, and squid. The terns rely on "predatory fish, such as tuna, to drive its prey towards the water surface where it can reach it without diving."[44] By foraging in nearby productive waters and depositing guano inland, black noddies and other terrestrial seabirds "act as a primary vector for transferring nutrients to terrestrial systems. The size of these nutrient inputs cannot be underestimated."[45] Guano influences island vegetation and serves as an invaluable fertilizer for crop production. Also significant from an economic standpoint is the fact that black noddies have no adverse impacts on humans.[46]

Yet, people have had a negative impact on black noddies, and the projected impacts of human-induced climate change will only exacerbate these adverse effects. As vertebrate zoologist expert Dr. Tanya Dewey points out, "[h]umans and introduced mammalian predators have driven some populations to extinction. Human degradation of habitats is a serious threat to nesting and roosting colonies . . . Many black noddy nesting islands are protected and human hunting is illegal in most areas."[47] But for laws to be effective, they must be enforced—and the enforcement of black noddy hunting bans varies considerably across the species' expansive range. Given SIDS' limited resources,[48] it is unsurprising that many islanders continue to feast

---

43.   *Small Islands*, *supra* note 30, at 1621.

44.   Wildscreen Arkive, *Black Noddy (Anous Minutus)*, http://www.arkive.org/black-noddy/anous-minutus/image-G91664.html (last visited Aug. 23, 2015).

45.   HOLOCENE EXTINCTIONS 163 (Samuel T. Turvey ed., 2009).

46.   *See* Dewey, *supra* note 37.

47.   *Id.* The black noddy's habitat is often cleared for the purposes of "cultivation, livestock grazing and developments." Wildscreen Arkive, *supra* note 44 (noting that "[o]n many South Pacific Islands, vegetation is often cleared for coconut palm plantations").

48.   Limited resources include both depleted governmental coffers and protein scarcity.

on the black noddy tern.[49] Despite the agricultural, ecological, economical, and public health consequences of decreasing black noddy populations, the adverse impacts will only intensify as sea levels rise and human-produced greenhouse gases incubate the planet.

B.   Dog Days Are Over

While very few island mammals are native species,[50] non-native mammals such as dogs and pigs—which accompanied the first human settlers—have been established in SIDS for hundreds of years. The consideration and treatment of island animals varies among nations; however, distinctions can be drawn based on whether the species is deemed as a wild/feral, stray, companion,[51] or livestock animal. Nearly every household in Micronesia raises pigs for consumption during ceremonial, cultural, and celebratory occasions.[52] Under these circumstances, islanders are likely to treat pigs and other livestock as "assets" in a (relatively) humane manner, and supply livestock with adequate food and water and refrain from egregious acts of cruelty. Although inapplicable to the Maldives—a nation with a long-standing prohibition on both pigs and dogs[53]—the SIDS-Seven generally

---

49. *See, e.g.*, Wildscreen Arkive, *supra* note 44 (explaining that "the black noddy is still heavily harvested in the North Marshall Islands"); M.J. Szabo, *Black Noddy*, NEW ZEALAND BIRDS ONLINE, 2013 (noting that black noddies "are harvested as food in Micronesia"), http://nzbirdsonline.org.nz/species/black-noddy; FOOD AND NUTRITION IN FIJI: FOOD PRODUCTION, COMPOSITION, AND INTAKE 63 (A.A.J. Jansen et al. eds., 1990) (describing the black noddy as a "feasting food" in Fiji); *Tuvalu*, SPEAKZEASY, Dec. 16, 2014 (stating that the black noddy is a "traditional food source" in Tuvalu), https://speakzeasy.wordpress.com/2014/12/16/tuvalu/.

50. Native island mammals are primarily limited to different species of bats and, in certain locations, rats. *See Biological Diversity*, *supra* note 34 (explaining that 15 species of bats—11 of which are endemic—are the only native land mammals to the region of Polynesia-Micronesia). In Yap, the endemic flying-fox is classified as "[e]ndangered due to hunting and typhoons." *Yap Islands*, *supra* note 35.

51. Companion animals, in the Western conception of the category, are very uncommon. *See* Mandy Pederson, *Dogs in Tonga—Meet Franseen*, BENEATH A BALCONY OF STARS, Oct. 12, 2012 (calling pet dogs "a rarity. I have never seen or heard of an indoor dog in Tonga."), http://beneathabalconyofstars.blogspot.com.es/2012/10/dogs-in-tonga-meet-franseen.html.

52. *See* Federated States of Micronesia Visitors Board, *Traditional Culture*, http://www.visit-micronesia.fm/culture/index.html (last visited Aug. 23, 2016); EROAROME MARTIN AREGHEORE, FEDERATED STATES OF MICRONESIA (Food and Agriculture Organization of the United Nations 2009) (explaining that families "raise their animals in pens, backyards and often on free range or tethered. Under this sector, animals are raised for family consumption and for festive occasions such as weddings, traditional celebrations, source of immediate income, etc."), http://www.fao.org/ag/agp/agpc/doc/counprof/PDF%20files/Micronesia.pdf. According to one commentator in Micronesia, the more pigs a family owns, "and the fatter they were, the more assets" the family possesses. Rob Verger, *The Dogs of Pohnpei*, WORLD HUM, Jan. 3, 2008, http://www.worldhum.com/features/travel-stories/the_dogs_of_pohnpei_20080103/.

53. *See* MALDIVES CUSTOMS SERVICE, GOING THROUGH CUSTOMS (n.d.) (completely banning the importation of live pigs, as well as pork and its byproducts, without a permit from the Ministry of Economic Development), http://www.customs.gov.mv/Documents/251.

care for and consider the interests of farm animals because it is economically advantageous and necessary for the well-being and survival of most islanders.

To evaluate the key climate and ocean drivers of change for island dogs one need only examine those threatening people, with the notable distinction that in the unfortunate case of the canine, the adverse effects are intensified. In the long-term, what will become of island dogs when sea levels rise 1 m, thus "render[ing] some island countries uninhabitable?"[54] They surely cannot doggy paddle all the way to the mainland. Nonhuman land animals do not have the same opportunity as human land animals to flee threatened island nations. Sea-level rise also poses a contamination threat to freshwater resources causing potential threats of dehydration and death. These same risks are associated with warmer El Niño years, which have resulted in limited access to drinking water and droughts.

Coral bleaching could also affect island dogs in the long term. As food security and the economic well-being of island communities is threatened by the decline of coral reefs, human islanders may increasingly consume dogs for subsistence. A decrease in food supplies for humans could lead to canine starvation and cannibalism, as reduced quantities of human scraps means dogs have less to scavenge, which could lead them to prey on old, sick, and young dogs. The increase in air temperature also poses a risk to the lives of rarely vaccinated island dogs. If high temperatures stimulate the growth of disease organisms, island dogs could be infected more frequently and the transmission rate of disease could also increase. Likewise, a change in the distribution of disease vectors such as mosquitoes could expose dogs to an entirely new portfolio of diseases. The short-term effects of extreme weather events such as storm surges and cyclones on dog health include drowning and injuries, as well as limited freshwater reserves.

Unlike pigs and other livestock, wild or stray island dogs are viewed as a nuisance first and food source second.[55] There are two noteworthy features of roaming dog packs that raise serious concerns for animal protectionists. First, canines are openly killed and cooked (in a traditional outdoor oven) because

---

54. *Small Islands, supra* note 30, at 1618 (quoting TEGART ET AL., CLIMATE CHANGE: THE IPCC IMPACTS ASSESSMENT 4 (1990)).

55. Unfortunately, with the exception of the Maldives (which prohibits the possession of dogs in addition to pigs), dogs in developing island States are generally mistreated and unprotected. Consider, for example, the thousands of dogs of Pohnpei, Micronesia, which have been described as "mangy, filthy, flea-ridden, skinny [animals] . . . [that] prowled together in packs, fighting and yelping"; they are "treated like rats—taught to fend for themselves," and "killed, cooked, and eaten." Verger, *supra* note 52.

dog meat is considered a delicacy, not because food is scarce.[56] Consider, for example, that the Marshall Islands government has allowed "untagged street dogs . . . [to be] clubbed to death and fed to local prisoners."[57] This policy represents a substantial departure from the Western view that dogs are household pets to whom a moral duty of protection is owed. The second hallmark of canine islanders is that their treatment, when compared to farm animals like pigs, is markedly different. While both animals often suffer inhumane deaths,[58] the pig's economic status—and the corresponding degree of protection associated with such status—does not extend to dogs.[59] While it is advantageous for pig owners to provide adequate water, food, and shelter to their valuable livestock, dogs are not provided the same necessities and are subject to unsanitary and inhumane conditions for the duration of their lives.[60] Accordingly, many island dogs are infected with distemper,

---

56. *See id.* (noting that many people found dog meat delicious and "ate dog not out of a sense of need but instead, pleasure.").

57. Danielle Wolffe, *An Ex-pat's Adventures Helping Dogs on a Remote South Pacific Island*, THE HUFFINGTON POST, Apr. 15, 2015 (recognizing "small black dogs" as the type Marshallese considered to be the most delicious), http://www.huffingtonpost.com/danielle-wolffe/an-ex-pats-adventures-helping-dogs_b_7055676.html.

58. Dogs are often beaten to death with a baseball bat. *See* Lawrence Millman, *Wild Dogs I Have Eaten*, Apr. 20, 2012 (explaining that "[i]f you see a teenage kid walking around with a baseball bat on Pohnpei, he's not going to Little League practise. Rather, he's looking for the island's favorite feast food"—dog), http://lawrencemillman.com/wild-dogs-i-have-eaten/. One commentator on a Micronesia forum on animal welfare stated, "It is one thing to eat a dog, but quite another to starve it, run it over with a car, and beat it with a stick or baseball bat (all of which I have witnessed in Micronesia)." Bobson, *Animal Welfare in Micronesia*, MICRONESIA FORUM, Jan. 2012, http://www.micronesiaforum.org/index.php?p=/discussion/9650/animal-welfare-in-micronesia. Pigs, whose shrill cries islanders are coldly familiar with and unmoved by, are commonly bled to death. *See* Christy Brinkworth, *Taxi's, Sashimi, Prison, and Pig Slaughter: Just a Day in the Life*, THE ADVENTURE I CALL MY LIFE, June 24, 2012 (describing the cry of a pig being bled as "the most gut-wrenching sound of what I thought was a child being beaten"), http://christypeacecorps.blogspot.com.es/2012/06/taxis-sashimi-prison-and-pig-slaughter.html. *See also* Gabrielle Gill, *A Few Things Pohnpei Has Taught Me*, A JOURNEY ON THE EDGE OF THE WORLD, Oct. 31, 2011 (recognizing that humans can be conditioned to "watch a pig be killed and ripped apart and not even flinch."), http://kosraeanadventures.blogspot.com.es/2011/10/few-things-pohnpei-has-taught-me.html.

59. Animal welfare laws have not been enacted; therefore, when abuse is inflicted on an animal, the act is ignored.

60. Research indicates that the Cook Islands may be the only nation of the SIDS-Seven that has an established veterinarian clinic, which was founded in 1994. *See* The Esther Honey Foundation, *Who We Are*, http://estherhoney.org/who-we-are/ (last visited Aug. 23, 2016). Temporary veterinarian clinics have been established periodically. For example, in 2013, the Pacific Partnership Humanitarian Visit, a visiting veterinarian clinic, treated approximately 500 dogs for ailments ranging from the preventable such as worms and infections to sterilization and other surgeries. HUMANE SOCIETY INTERNATIONAL PROJECT, PROCEEDINGS OF THE CONFERENCE—CHALLENGES OF ANIMAL PROTECTION ON ISLAND NATIONS: WITH SPECIAL EMPHASIS ON DOGS AND CATS 7 (2012), http://www.hsi.org/assets/pdfs/eng_challenges_island_nations.pdf [hereinafter PROCEEDINGS OF THE CONFERENCE]. Because there is no permanent veterinarian or medical equipment in the Marshall Islands, volunteers send Skype messages to Hawaiian practitioners for advice on treating injured island animals. A local farmer, lacking formal veterinary training, has been recruited by volunteers to neuter dogs.

hepatitis, and canine parvovirus,[61] and very few are vaccinated to prevent the spread of such diseases and internal parasites.[62]

Yet, it is in fact advantageous for human islanders to provide for canine welfare because healthy and vaccinated dogs promote the goal of protecting human health. For example, human echinococcosis is a zoonosis caused by the "ingestion of parasite eggs in contaminated food, water or soil, or through direct contact with animal hosts."[63] The disease, which leads to the development of life-threatening hydatids (large, fluid-filled cysts), is preventable because the tapeworms rely on domestic animal hosts such as dogs and sheep.[64] The annual costs associated with the disease are $3 billion.[65] The World Health Organization believes one form of echinococcosis can be eliminated in humans in less than a decade if a simple program of deworming dogs, vaccinating lambs, and culling older sheep is implemented.[66] It therefore follows that in SIDS where deworming dogs is unlikely, islanders should refrain from eating dog meat, as canines are ideal hosts for the parasite.

Likewise, it is fiscally advantageous for SIDS to provide for canine health care because it protects the islands' tourist economies. On a domestic level, the economic argument is most likely to influence island governments to include animal protection provisions in adaptation and mitigation plans. Because tourism is vital for many island economies, and because "the largest number of complaints from tourists each year relates to concerns for the health and welfare of the dogs and cats on the streets, with some tourists stating that they will never return to the island(s)," this information could persuade SIDS to take actions to humanely manage island cats and dogs.[67]

---

61. *See* Yap Animal Protection Society, *White Chocolate* (recognizing that many dogs come into contact with contagious diseases), http://yapanimalprotectionsociety.tumblr.com/post/14520399515/white-chocolate/ (last visited Aug. 23, 2016). Furthermore, a permanent veterinarian is not located in any of the Federated States of Micronesia, so ill animals are left to suffer without proper medical treatment. Yap has neither a veterinarian nor medical supplies to treat sick animals. *Id.*

62. The threats of diseases and parasites for canines vary by geographical location. However, the following list highlights the wide range of vaccines and anthelmintics that each dog offered for sale in the state of Florida must receive and illuminates the diverse health risks such diseases and internal parasites pose to unvaccinated dogs: (1) canine distemper; (2) leptospirosis; (3) bordetella; (4) parainfluenza; (5) hepatitis; (6) canine parvo; (7) rabies; (8) roundworms; and (9) hookworms. *See* FLA. STAT. §828.29(1)(b) (2015).

63. World Health Organization, *Echinococcosis*, http://www.who.int/mediacentre/factsheets/fs377/en/ (last visited Aug. 23, 2016). Approximately 1 million people are infected with echinococcosis at any given time. *Id.*

64. *Id.*

65. *Id.*

66. *Id.*

67. *See* PROCEEDINGS OF THE CONFERENCE, *supra* note 60.

Table 1. Quick Facts—The SIDS-Seven

The following island nations have been recognized for their acute vulnerability to the adverse impacts of climate change. This chart provides information on island animal species. However, none of the SIDS-Seven has compiled a comprehensive list of animal islanders at the date of publication, so this chart is more than likely incomplete.

Country	No. of Islands	Human Population[a]	Animal[b] Species	It is Culturally Acceptable to Eat:
The Cook Islands[c]	• 9 coral atolls • 6 islands of volcanic origin	15,000	• 17 mammals (including pigs, goats, chickens, cattle, ducks, and the Pacific flying fox[d]) (2 species threatened) • 22 terrestrial birds[e] (6 endemic species: 4 species of which are vulnerable, and 1 species that is endangered) • 13 migratory birds • 40 seabirds[f] • 13 reptiles[g]	dogs
The Federated States of Micronesia[h]	607 islands in total (65 inhabited)	103,000	• 108 free-range birds • 28 terrestrial birds (9 endemic species & 9 threatened species) • 2 extinct birds • 25 mammals (6 threatened species) • 18 reptiles (3 threatened species; and invasive brown tree snake) • 2 sea turtles	• dogs • black noddy birds

Country	No. of Islands	Human Population[a]	Animal[b] Species	It is Culturally Acceptable to Eat:
Kiribati[i]	• 32 coral atolls (21 inhabited) • 1 island	105,700	• 75 birds (the Kiritimati reed-warbler is listed as Least Concern on International Union for Conservation of Nature (IUCN) Red List) • 21 mammals (rats, feral cats, dogs, pigs) • 4 reptiles (1 reptile is listed as threatened) • 1 amphibian (frog) • marine animals, including sea turtles, dolphins, sharks	• dogs • sea turtles • sea turtle eggs
Maldives[j]	25 coral atolls—1,190 islands (197 of which are inhabited)	393,200	• ·122 birds[k] (including endemic species such as the Maldivian pond heron, white tern, and lesser frigate) • 2 geckos • 2 agamid lizards • 2 fruit bats • 2 flying fox species (threatened) • 5 sea turtles (1 endangered) • 1 skink • 2 snakes • 1 frog • 1 toad • 3 non-native mammals (cats, rats, mice)	• eating pig is prohibited • sea turtles • sea turtle eggs

Country	No. of Islands	Human Population[a]	Animal[b] Species	It is Culturally Acceptable to Eat:
Marshall Islands[l]	29 coral atolls—1,156 individual islands	72,200	• 77 birds[m] • 22 mammals (including dogs, chickens, pigs) • 6 reptiles (1 of which is threatened)	• dogs • black noddy birds
Tonga[n]	4 coral atolls—176 islands extending across an archipelago located within the Ring of Fire	103,200	• mammals (Pacific flying fox,[o] a species of bat,[p] rats, pigs, dogs, horse, donkeys, mules, goats, sheep—1 threatened species) • 3 reptiles (including voracious dtella, a species of lizard;[q] banded sea snake)[r] • 5 freshwater birds[s] • 13 seabirds • 25 terrestrial birds	• dogs
Tuvalu[t]	6 atoll islands, 3 reef islands	10,900	• 19 birds[u] • 22 mammals • 5 reptiles (1 species is listed as threatened)	• dogs • black noddy birds

a.   This figure is based on the most recent State census or other official estimations.

b.   "Animal" species refers to terrestrial wild animals, companion animals, native or endemic terrestrial birds, seabirds, migratory birds, and marine creatures such as species of sea turtles and sea snakes that nest on land.

c.   *See generally* UNEP, *Cook Islands*, http://islands.unep.ch/CKK.htm (last visited Aug. 23, 2016). *See* World Wildlife Fund, *Pacific Ocean: Cook Islands*, http://www.worldwildlife.org/ecoregions/oc0103 (last visited Aug. 23, 2016) [hereinafter *Pacific Ocean: Cook Islands*]. *See* COOK ISLANDS COUNTRY REPORT ON ANIMAL GENETICS 3, ftp://ftp.fao.org/docrep/fao/010/a1250e/annexes/CountryReports/CookIslands.pdf. *See also* UNEP, PREVENTION, CONTROL, AND MANAGEMENT OF INVASIVE ALIEN SPECIES IN THE PACIFIC ISLANDS 18 (2015), https://www.sprep.org/attachments/gef-pas/ias/IAS_prodoc.pdf [hereinafter PACIFIC ISLANDS].

d.   The Pacific flying fox (*Pteropus tonganus*) is found in both the Cook Islands and Tonga. *See Pacific Ocean: Cook Islands, supra* note 70.

e.   Until recently the Rarotonga monarch was an endangered species; it is now considered vulnerable. *See* IUCN Red List of Endangered Species, *Pomarea dimidiata*, http://www.iucnredlist.org/details/22707172/0 (last visited Aug. 23, 2016). The Reed-warbler is listed as near threatened. *See* IUCN Red List of Endangered Species, *Acrocephalus Kerearako*, http://www.iucnredlist.org/details/22714821/0 (last visited Aug. 23, 2016). *See also* PACIFIC ISLANDS, *supra* note 70.

f.   One of these seabirds, the black noddy, can also be found in the Marshall Islands, Tonga, and Tuvalu. *See* Dewey, *supra* note 37.

g.   GERALD MCCORMACK, COOK ISLANDS BIODIVERSITY: STRATEGY AND ACTION PLAN 54 (Cook Islands Government 2002), https://www.cbd.int/doc/world/ck/ck-nbsap-01-en.pdf.

h. *See generally* PACIFIC ISLANDS,*supra* note 70. *See also* Federated States of Micronesia Office of Statistics, Budget, and Economic Management, *Summary of Census Results*, http://www.sboc.fm/index.php?id1= Vm0xMFUxSXhWWGhWYms1UIlrVndVbFpyVWtKUFVUMDk (last visited Aug. 23, 2016); FSM: SUMMARY OF SPECIES, *supra* note 30, at 2; Donald W. Buden, *The Reptiles of Pohnpei, Federated States of Micronesia* 32 MICRONESIA 155(2000),https://www.researchgate.net/publication/254945552_The_Reptiles_of_Pohnpei_Federated_States_of_Micronesia. *See also* PACIFIC ISLANDS, *supra* note 70.

i. The name of the nation is pronounced "Keer-ree-bahs." *See* Central Intelligence Agency (CIA), *The World Fact Book, Australia-Oceania—Kiribati*, https://www.cia.gov/library/publications/the-world-factbook/geos/kr.html (last visited Aug. 23, 2016). *See also* IUCN, KIRIBATI: SUMMARY OF SPECIES ON THE 2008 IUCN RED LIST (n.d.), http://cmsdata.iucn.org/downloads/kiribati.pdf [hereinafter KIRIBATI: SUMMARY OF SPECIES]; FRANK R. THOMAS, KIRIBATI: "SOME ASPECTS OF HUMAN ECOLOGY," FORTY YEARS LATER 22 (2003), http://www.sil.si.edu/DigitalCollections/AtollResearchBulletin/issues/00501.pdf; TERERE ABETE-REEMA & KAUTOA TONGANIBEIA ET AL., ENVIRONMENT AND CONSERVATION DIVISION, KIRIBATI STATE OF THE ENVIRONMENT REPORT, 2000–2002 (on file with authors). On average, Kiribati land is elevated 2 m above sea level. *Id. See also* PACIFIC ISLANDS, *supra* note 70.

j. *See* LUBNA MOOSA ET AL., NATIONAL ADAPTATION PROGRAM OF ACTION: REPUBLIC OF MALDIVES, MINISTRY OF ENVIRONMENT, ENERGY & WATER (2006), http://unfccc.int/resource/docs/napa/mdv01.pdf. Eighty percent of total land area in the Maldives is less than 1 m above water, distinguishing the island as the world's lowest-lying nation. *Id. See also* CIA, *The World Fact Book, South Asia—Maldives*, https:// www.cia.gov/library/publications/the-world-factbook/geos/mv.html (last visited Aug. 23, 2016).

k. *See* World Heritage Encyclopedia, *List of Birds of the Maldives* (citing Martin Collinson, *Splitting Headaches? Recent Taxonomic Changes Affecting the British and Western Palaearctic Lists*, 99 BRIT. BIRDS, 306–26 (June 2006), http://kindle.worldlibrary.net/articles/List_of_birds_of_the_Maldives (last visited Aug. 23, 2016).

l. *See generally* REPUBLIC OF THE MARSHALL ISLANDS, INTENDED NATIONALLY DETERMINED CONTRIBUTION (2015), http://www4.unfccc.int/submissions/INDC/Published%20Documents/Marshall%20 Islands/1/150721%20RMI%20INDC%20JULY%202015%20FINAL%20SUBMITTED.pdf. On average, land in the Marshall Islands is elevated 2 m above sea level. *Id. See also* CIA, *The World Fact Book, Australia-Oceania—Marshall Islands*, https://www.cia.gov/library/publications/the-world-factbook/ geos/rm.html (last visited Aug. 23, 2015).

m. *See* Dewey, *supra* note 37.

n. *See* TONGA MINISTRY OF FINANCE & NATIONAL PLANNING, TONGA STRATEGIC DEVELOPMENT FRAMEWORK 2015–2025 (2015),http://www.adb.org/sites/default/files/linked-documents/cobp-ton-2016-2018- ld-05.pdf; CIA, *The World Fact Book, Australia-Oceania—Tonga*, https://www.cia.gov/library/publications/the-world-factbook/geos/tn.html (last visited Aug. 23, 2016). *See also* PACIFIC ISLANDS, *supra* note 70.

o. The Pacific flying fox (*Pteropus tonganus*) is found in both the Cook Islands and Tonga. *See Pacific Ocean: Cook Islands*, *supra* note 70.

p. Leslie Avalos, *Pteropus tonganus—Pacific Flying Fox*, ANIMAL DIVERSITY WEB, 2003, http://animal-diversity.org/accounts/Pteropus_tonganus/ (last visited Aug. 23, 2016).

q. Elizabeth Holmes, *Gehyra vorax—Voracious Dtella*, ANIMAL DIVERSITY WEB, 2000, http://animal-diversity.org/accounts/Gehyra_vorax/ (last visited Aug. 23, 2016).

r. Eric Wright, *Laticauda colubrina—Colubrine or Yellow-lipped Sea Krait*, ANIMAL DIVERSITY WEB, 2011, http://animaldiversity.org/accounts/Laticauda_colubrina/ (last visited Aug. 23, 2016).

s. *See* Dewey, *supra* note 37.

t. *See, e.g.*, MINISTRY OF NATURAL RESOURCES, ENVIRONMENT, AGRICULTURE & LANDS, TUVALU'S NATIONAL ADAPTATION PROGRAMME OF ACTION (2007),http://www.sids2014.org/content/documents/162NAPA. pdf; GOVERNMENT OF TUVALU, INTENDED NATIONALLY DETERMINED CONTRIBUTIONS (2015), http:// www4.unfccc.int/submissions/INDC/Published%20Documents/Tuvalu/1/TUVALU%20INDC.pdf. In Tuvalu, land is rarely elevated higher than 3 m above sea level, and no area exceeds 5 m above the water. *Id. See also* CIA, *The World Fact Book, Australia-Oceania—Tuvalu*, https://www.cia.gov/ library/publications/the-world-factbook/geos/tv.html (last visited Aug. 23, 2016); IUCN, TUVALU: SUMMARY OF SPECIES ON THE 2008 IUCN RED LIST, http://cmsdata.iucn.org/downloads/tuvalu.pdf [hereinafter TUVALU: SUMMARY OF SPECIES].

u. *See* Dewey, *supra* note 37.

II. Climate Justice for Human and Nonhuman Island Inhabitants

In pursuing an analysis of the nexus between human rights, global animal protection,[68] and climate change, it is necessary to disaggregate the issues because each issue has a unique evolutionary path, built on separate foundations and distinct yet not dissimilar principles, analytical approaches, and struggles for legitimacy. However, growing awareness of the complex mental capacities of animals has led to increased legal protection of creatures that were historically reduced to "machines of flesh—living robots."[69]

The field of animal law has gained traction and momentum in only the past 50 years, and as a result, many disciplinary areas have yet to be discussed or discovered. The field has historically been focused on issues of domestic animal policy, rather than concerns of comparative or international animal law.[70] Yet, in the past decade, as people in developed countries have expressed a growing opposition to animal cruelty regardless of where the mistreatment occurred, animal law has likewise begun to shift toward an international orientation.[71] The International Court of Justice (ICJ) recently rejected established precedent that the only whales entitled to legal protection were those who are members of a vulnerable or endangered species; rather, the ICJ implicitly found that all individual whales—regardless of species vulnerability—have a right to protection as a principle of international law.[72] One scholar has suggested that this biocentric approach to valuing whales reflects

---

68. The authors prefer the term "animal protection," as opposed to the currently polarizing concepts of "animal welfare" and "animal rights," to help unify factions of the global animal protection movement and redefine the focus toward developing new theories of protection under the law (regardless of whether those protections are rights- or welfare-based).

69. *Animals Think, Therefore . . .*, THE ECONOMIST, Dec. 19, 2015, at 63 (paraphrasing RENÉ DESCARTES, DISCOURSE ON THE METHOD OF RIGHTLY CONDUCTING THE REASON, AND SEEKING THE TRUTH IN THE SCIENCES—PART V (1st ed. 1637), https://ebooks.adelaide.edu.au/d/descartes/rene/d44dm/part5.html).

70. *See* MICHAEL BOWMAN ET AL. EDS., INTERNATIONAL WILDLIFE LAW 90–91 (2d ed. 2010) (highlighting the "need for greater attention to be paid to the wellbeing of individual creatures, a matter which international law has as yet addressed in only a desultory fashion.").

71. *See, e.g.*, Whaling in the Antarctic (Austl. v. Japan: N.Z. intervening), 2014 I.C.J. 226 (Mar. 31, http://www.icj-cij.org/docket/files/148/18136.pdf [hereinafter Whaling in the Antarctic]; World Trade Organization, Report of the Appellate Body, *European Communities—Measures Prohibiting the Importation and Marketing of Seal Products*, WT/DS400/AB/R & WT/DS401/AB/R (May 22, 2014) (notably the first case to recognize animal welfare as a component of public morals under GATT art. XX(a)). This mounting opposition to animal cruelty can be largely attributed to the effects of globalization. For example, 20 years ago, footage of cruel animal treatment may remain largely unseen, but today, the video can "go viral" and be seen by millions of people around the world in a matter of minutes or hours. *See* Nick Bryant, *Australia Bans All Live Cattle Exports to Indonesia*, BBC, June 8, 2011, http://www.bbc.com/news/world-asia-pacific-13692211.

72. *See* Whaling in the Antarctic, *supra* note 92 (both parties agree that international opinion strongly supports whale protection). *See generally* Katie Sykes, *The Appeal to Science and the Formation of*

"evolving international discourse about whale protection"; this analysis relied on the ICJ's evaluation of "deeper questions of values and ethics that have for so long surrounded lethal taking of whales."[73] While disagreement exists as to whether a State practice or custom toward humane animal treatment has developed or is merely developing, the growing concern for nonhuman animals indicates that an international animal-protective "norm" will soon be established as a principle of international law.

In considering how emerging global principles of animal protection can be used to set the international climate justice agenda and secure recognition of new norms, animal advocates should recognize two broad objectives. First, animal protectionists must be aware of evolving cultural, political, and institutional landscapes to ensure the animal-related climate justice agenda is aligned with developing international standards. How the principles are conveyed should not ostracize or antagonize citizens in developing island nations who may lack civil liberties or basic necessities like food security and clean freshwater reserves.[74] If animal-related climate financing obligations were imposed on SIDS for the explicit purpose of protecting island animals, this measure would likely increase both resentment of developed countries and resistance to future animal protection efforts.

Second, the animal-related climate justice agenda should concentrate less on the principles' values in protecting small island animals, and focus more on promoting the economic, environmental, and public health values of mobilizing climate finance for animal-related adaptation actions.[75] Despite the fact that animal protectionists believe each animal islander has intrinsic value independent of that individual's perceived usefulness to humans, this argument is unlikely to persuade developing countries that animal-related adaptation practices should be prioritized. For the animal-related climate justice agenda to be effective, developing countries must perceive it as a tool to facilitate the protection of the economy, the environment, and human health and welfare.[76] This also means animal protectionists should avoid becoming entangled in ideological battles that have ensnared previous advocacy efforts,

---

Global Animal Law, Eur. J. Int'l L. (forthcoming 2016), http://papers.ssrn.com/sol3/papers.cfm?abstract_id=2632812.

73. Sykes, *supra* note 93, at 31.

74. *See* U.S. Department of State, *Country Reports on Human Rights Practices for 2014—Kiribati, supra* note 13.

75. *See supra* Part I.B. for an example of echinococcosis, a zoonosis that human islanders can contract from eating infected canines.

76. *See supra* Part I.B. for an argument related to tourism and the protection of the economy.

as such squabbles undermine the ultimate objective of advancing the interests of all nonhuman animals.[77]

Scholars have suggested a range of novel legal theories and justice mechanisms to address the consequences of climate change for SIDS. One of the most obvious, yet impractical, "solutions" is to relocate and reestablish island land animals to areas of the world less threatened by rising sea levels. Relocation is not a viable strategy for several economic and ecological reasons, two of which will be briefly addressed.[78] First, reestablishing any species can cost millions of dollars; the total relocation expenses depend on numerous factors, including the total number of animals being relocated; the species-acquisition process; the transportation distance; and other costs associated with shipping.[79] Not only are most of these animals already unwanted on their current islands of residence, it is hard to justify relocating non-endemic, or at the very least unthreatened, species as a public expenditure.[80]

Second, introducing a non-native species—even if close relatives peacefully inhabit the new habitat—could create even costlier economic and environmental consequences if the animal thrives in his or her new surroundings without predatory check.[81] Likewise, several animal islanders in need of protection are already considered "invasive" species in their current habitats; crafting a convincing argument to relocate destructive non-native species to the mainland would be quite challenging.[82] Because relocation could contribute to a potential invasive species problem in the selected destination, this "solution" is undesirable. It obfuscates the objective of achieving the animal-related climate justice agenda through accepted channels of international law, such as protection initiatives promoted in the interest of public health rather than on behalf of animal welfare.

---

77. For example, among other negative effects, bickering over the merits of the animal welfare versus animal rights approach to animal protection creates division when unity is desperately needed to validate the movement's credibility at the global level.

78. Potential exceptions include dogs, endangered or endemic animal species, or those otherwise legally protected under international law.

79. For example, relocating 60 tuatara, a rare reptile endemic to New Zealand, from Lady Alice Island to Motuihe—a distance of less than 6 mi—costs 33,000 NZD. *See* John R. Platt, *60 Rare Tuatara Reptiles Moved to Predator-free New Zealand Island*, Sci. Am., Apr. 14, 2012, http://blogs.scientificamerican.com/extinction-countdown/tuatara-reptiles-moved-predator-free-new-zealand-island/.

80. To be sure, this entire hypothetical rests on the unlikely, underlying assumption that a developed country would agree to accept the island animals into its territory.

81. *See* Dr. Teresa Giménez-Candela & Carly Elizabeth Souther, *Invasive Animal Species: International Impacts and Inadequate Interventions, in* What Can Animal Law Learn From Environmental Law? 334–40 (Randall S. Abate ed., 2015).

82. For example, the non-native brown tree snake is "one of the biggest threats to the economies and the environments of the Micronesian Islands." Pacific Islands, *supra* note 70, at 60.

Regarding island animals' eligibility to be protected from the adverse impacts of climate change, such protection will likely be granted to the species that humans perceive as "most valuable." Speciesism may be unfortunate, but it is an unsurprising reality.[83] The industrialized world "has a long history of exploiting animals for human advancement and comfort in much the same way that natural resources have been exploited since the industrial revolution."[84] While livestock animals will receive preferential treatment by islanders, endemic or threatened species will be prioritized at the regional level, and, finally, the international community will be largely supportive of measures that benefit companion animals.

Although the impacts of climate change on terrestrial and migratory animals are indiscriminate, the effects are disproportionately hostile to species on low-lying island States. In short, all the catastrophic climatic change impacts that threaten the livelihood and lives of SIDS' nationals also touch their animal populations, with one important distinction. The international community has not acknowledged the need to assist these vulnerable animal islanders.

III.   Global Call to Action: Ethics and Justice in International Law

It is nonhuman animal islanders—not human islanders—who are most likely to suffer from climate change and yet they have contributed the least to this global crisis.[85] Animal protection duties of developed States can usefully inform the design and implementation of climate justice policy for SIDS animals. Each Party to the United Nations Framework Convention on Climate Change (UNFCCC) should embrace common but differentiated responsibilities—dependent on national circumstances—to protect animals in small island nations.

While several international laws and non-binding general declarations address important aspects of animal protection, they are not particularly

---

83.   Peter Singer defined "speciesism" in his revolutionary 1975 book, *Animal Liberation*, as "a prejudice or bias in favour of the interests of members of one's own species and against those of members of other species." BBC, *Ethics Guide, The Ethics of Speciesism* (quoting PETER SINGER, ANIMAL LIBERATION (1975)), http://www.bbc.co.uk/ethics/animals/rights/speciesism.shtml (last visited Aug. 23, 2016). This term has naturally evolved, and now includes a secondary definition: a prejudice or bias in favor of the members of nonhuman animals that humans perceive to be valuable and against those of members of nonhuman animals that humans do not perceive to be valuable.

84.   Randall S. Abate, *Introduction, in* WHAT CAN ANIMAL LAW LEARN FROM ENVIRONMENTAL LAW? xxix, xxix (Randall S. Abate ed., 2015).

85.   *See* McInerney-Lankford, *supra* note 4.

useful in the context of the animal-related climate justice agenda.[86] However, the language of the Paris Agreement is broad enough to support the integration of animal-related policies into national mitigation and adaptation plans.[87] Capacity-building animal-related activities can be financed by the Green Climate Fund, which is expected to allocate $100 billion per year to assist SIDS and other developing nations in the battle against climate change.[88]

An animal control and sterilization-driven adaptation plan is a viable solution because it relies on a universally supported measure of animal control and does not call into play philosophical issues regarding human rights, nonhuman animal rights, or other hotly contested concerns. At the domestic level, the islands have a vested interest in sterilizing and inoculating packs of roaming dogs, who are an immediate threat to human health.[89] Controlling the island dog population also contributes to continued development of human rights in SIDS, a principle that is recognized throughout the Paris Agreement as an important objective. The obligations of States for island animal contraception and castration control will range in form from the integration of island animal birth control strategies into SIDS' national policy;[90] to campaigning for qualified veterinarians, as well as ample quantities of canine and cat vaccines, at the regional level;[91] to allocating funding for sterilization research at the international level.[92]

---

86. *But see* Part III.C.1, which proposes that island animals are a vulnerable group entitled to protection under the Paris Agreement.

87. For instance, the importance of protecting biodiversity is noted in the preamble. *Paris Agreement, supra* note 1.

88. *See* Coral Davenport, *The Marshall Islands Are Disappearing*, N.Y. Times, Dec 2. 2015, http://www.nytimes.com/interactive/2015/12/02/world/The-Marshall-Islands-Are-Disappearing.html?.

89. Large numbers of unvaccinated dogs are a threat to human health in many ways. They contaminate fresh drinking water reserves. They serve as a vector for disease and can spread certain illnesses to other animal species, including humans. Dog bites often become infected and, depending on the severity of the bite, can cause permanent disfiguration.

90. For example, the Chicago Transit Authority is testing new bait technology that would make rats infertile: "After the rats eat the bait multiple times, they typically make fewer babies within four weeks . . . Full sterility usually occurs within eight to 12 weeks . . . [T]he bait doesn't kill the rats or poison them, and it doesn't harm humans or the environment." Tracy Swartz, *CTA to Put Rats on Birth Control*, Chicago Trib., Dec. 22, 2014, http://www.chicagotribune.com/news/redeye-cta-to-put-rats-on-birth-control-20141222-story.html.

91. Although permanent veterinary clinics are desirable, temporary clinics, such as the one opened by U.S. Ambassador Larry Dinger in Pohnpei in 2002, could be established to spay and neuter island mammals. *See* Press Release, Federal States of Micronesia, U.S. Ambassador Dinger Opens Successful Animal Clinic in Pohnpei (Apr. 9, 2002) (in five days, four veterinarians "treated a total of 124 dogs and cats, of which 88 were sterilized, and visited over 30 piggeries."), http://www.fsmgov.org/press/nw040902.htm.

92. Since at least the 1990s, many scientists and researchers have concluded that "[b]iological control, especially immunocontraception targeting female fertility, is potentially an inexpensive, efficient, and humane option for addressing the possum problem." The development of new sterilization methods of non-native animal control is not only appropriate for possums but also for most, if not

This section offers six recommendations for integrated approaches to avert, minimize, and address nonhuman island animal displacement related to the adverse impacts of climate change.[93] Each recommendation supports a sterilization-driven adaptation plan, which, in many ways, begins to fill the gap between climate justice and island land animal protection.

A.   Domestic Duties: Database and Deliverables

The case of island animals illustrates the difficulty of identifying and responding to all groups marginalized by climate change. The IUCN has noted, "For a region known for its biodiversity hotspots, data is lacking and there are few links to regional and national policies."[94] Similar to how SIDS are heterogeneous territories that share preexisting vulnerabilities, the composition of animal species is geographically disparate across island nations, yet all island animals are acutely vulnerable to climatic changes. More broadly, island animal protection is not a feasible option for most climate change-impacted SIDS at this time. Not only are sterilization, relocation, and other animal adaptation strategies prohibitively costly, they require island nations to take the preliminary step of identifying and documenting their respective animal species in a consistent and comprehensive manner.

1.   Strategy 1. Animal Appendix

To promote climate justice for island animals, the current number and status of every species of terrestrial vertebrate and migratory bird must be accounted for by each island nation. Comprehensive species lists regarding the mammal, bird, reptile, and amphibian fauna of most developing island nations are lacking. International cooperation is necessary to promote the establishment of domestic institutions designed to systematically review and catalogue an annotated list of island animals.

---

all, vertebrate species. Weihong Ji, *A Review of the Potential of Fertility Control to Manage Brushtail Possums in New Zealand*, 3 Hum.-Wildlife Conflicts 20, 24 (2009), http://digitalcommons.unl.edu/cgi/viewcontent.cgi?article=1037&context=hwi. *See also* N.D. Barlow, *The Ecological Challenge of Immunocontraception: Editor's Introduction*, 37 J. Applied Ecology 897 (2000).

93.   This area of scholarship is extensive. To underscore the interest in SIDS climate-justice research, consider that three chapters in this volume are devoted to identifying meaningful remedies for SIDS.

94.   FSM: Summary of Species, *supra* note 30; IUCN, Marshall Islands: Summary of Species on the 2008 IUCN Red List (n.d.), http://cmsdata.iucn.org/downloads/marshall_islands.pdf; IUCN, Tonga: Summary of Species on the 2008 IUCN Red List (n.d.), http://cmsdata.iucn.org/downloads/tonga.pdf; Tuvalu: Summary of Species, *supra* note 87; Kiribati: Summary of Species, *supra* note 76.

To expedite the development of small island species lists, developed countries should assist SIDS in appropriate planning measures and in implementing good practices for systematic observation of animal species. For example, the Center for Biological Diversity, which has identified 44 endangered or threatened mammals, reptiles, and birds in 23 coastal U.S. states who are currently under increased threat due to rising sea levels,[95] could advise developing island nations on experiences and lessons learned and provide technical support and guidance on the process to develop and implement an animal appendix database. Once an assessment of island animals is completed and a database is established, the first obstacle to island animal protection will be overcome, as advocates will then be aware of the specific species in need.

2. Strategy 2. Ban Live Animal Imports

To complement the use of birth control methods for island animal management, developing island nations could follow the lead of the Maldives and enact a law to prohibit the importation of all living animals. Initially, this strategy is unlikely to be popular with developing island nations, as they may perceive it as a measure that exacerbates their inequitable access to sustainable development. However, this initiative does not undermine "the fundamental priority of safeguarding food" for several reasons.[96] First, most islanders subsist on a coastal diet based on fish consumption. Second, existing livestock need not be depleted in numbers, and breeding could continue, at least for the immediate future. Third, this effort could actually safeguard food production systems because islanders could focus on building the resilience of agricultural systems in a manner consistent with averting the adverse impacts of climate change.[97]

For example, the Cook Islands could ban the importation of livestock and companion animals as a voluntary mitigation action to enhance the effectiveness of a sterilization-driven adaptation plan. According to the Agricultural Census of 2011, 68% of Cook Islanders own livestock, with pigs being the most popular farm animal.[98] Yet, each year an average of $5.5 million is

---

95. *See* DEADLY WATERS, *supra* note 30.
96. *Paris Agreement, supra* note 1, at pmbl.
97. The Food and Agriculture Organization of the United Nations says that "[a] priority activity, common to all SIDS [is] to reduce vulnerability and increase resilience… through diversification of agriculture. Diversification through integrated farming systems remains a key action." FOOD & AGRICULTURE ORGANIZATION OF THE UNITED NATIONS, NATURAL RESOURCES MANAGEMENT AND THE ENVIRONMENT IN SMALL ISLAND DEVELOPING STATES (SIDS) 7 (2014), http://www.fao.org/3/a-i3928e.pdf.
98. *See* MINISTRY OF AGRICULTURE, COOK ISLANDS 2011 CENSUS OF AGRICULTURE & FISHERIES, at 17, http://www.fao.org/fileadmin/templates/ess/ess_test_folder/World_Census_Agriculture/Country_info_2010/Reports/Reports_5/COK_EN_REP_2011.pdf (last visited Sep. 22, 2016) (reporting

spent on importing beef, mutton, frozen chickens, and pork into the Cook Islands.[99] The most desirable solution, in the case of aligning the principles of animal protection and public health, is for islanders to begin controlling animal populations and gradually decrease reliance on imported sources of protein.

B.   Regional Responsibilities: Rallies and Relocation

At the regional level, intergovernmental organizations have developed instruments to adequately address human-driven climate change in the Pacific.[100] For instance, the Pacific Islands Framework for Action on Climate Change (PIFACC) was endorsed in 2005 by leaders of the Pacific Islands Forum,[101] an intergovernmental organization established in 1971 by 16 nations to enhance cooperation among the nations in the region.[102] The primary goal of the PIFACC is to enhance the resilience of SIDS in the Pacific by educating the public about the impacts of climate change and providing guidance on developing and implementing effective mitigation and adaptation measures.[103] The SAMOA Pathway is another regional initiative designed to increase international awareness of climate-related threats to SIDS' biodiversity and to promote partnerships in support of these conservation efforts.

These regional intergovernmental organizations have effectively championed the international community on behalf of human islanders and successfully shed light on the plight of SIDS in the face of climate change. These regional organizations should be tasked with coordinating sterilization-driven adaptation plans and animal birth control programs of member-nations' island animals. To avoid duplication of effort, one entity in each region should be designated as the agency directly responsible for island animal contraception and castration control.

---

that "[o]f the 2,334 households interviewed, 1,595 households were recorded as keeping livestock or poultry.").

99. *Id.*

100. *See, e.g.*, Secretariat of the Pacific Regional Environment Programme, Pacific Islands Framework for Action on Climate Change 2006–2015, at 3–4 (2d ed. 2011*)*, http://www.sprep.org/attachments/Publications/PIFACC-ref.pdf [hereinafter PIFACC]; Pacific Islands Forum, The NIUE Declaration on Climate Change, Annex B 24, http://www.sprep.org/att/irc/ecopies/pacific_region/463.pdf.

101. The Pacific Islands Forum endorsed the Niue Declaration on Climate Change—the first declaration on climate change in the Pacific—in 2008. *See* Tangata Vainerere, *Pacific Island Forum Leaders Endorse the Niue Declaration on Climate Change*, Secretariat of the Pac. Community, Aug. 26, 2008, http://www.spc.int/ppapd/index.php?option=com_content&task=view&id=131&Itemid=1. The goal of the Niue Declaration was to bridge the various climate change initiatives in the Pacific.

102. *See* PIFACC, *supra* note 100, at 5.

103. *See id.* at 3–4.

1. Strategy 1. Vocalize Vulnerabilities: Championing Climate Justice for Island Animals

Regional island organizations are primarily responsible for the increased international awareness of climate change threats to SIDS. These island nations have captured the attention of developed countries, if only momentarily. The animal-related climate justice agenda should take advantage of this spotlight by encouraging these regional networks to vocalize the need for integration of animal protection measures into adaptation plans. For example, a coalition of regional island organizations could launch a global education campaign to increase awareness of the public health and economic risks associated with island animals and climate change.

Regional institutions should also ensure that education and training related to interaction with and treatment of island animals is provided in SIDS. For instance, regional organizations can foster dialogue about the health concerns and risks of eating dog meat. The success of such strategies will depend on the magnitude of the campaigns and whether enough information is disseminated to influence citizens and policymakers in both developed and developing countries.

2. Strategy 2. Export the Endemic and Endangered

One potential consequence of island nations becoming uninhabitable is the irreversible and permanent loss of endemic species. The IUCN Red List reports that four of the SIDS-Seven have threatened endemic species: the Cook Islands has seven endemic birds, five of which are threatened; there are two endemic bird species in Kiribati (one is threatened); in Micronesia, there are two threatened endemic mammals, and 19 endemic birds, five of which are threatened; and, lastly, Tonga has three endemic birds (one is threatened).[104] Because the IUCN Red List relies on the voluntary submission of a Red List assessment, it is possible that unreported threatened endemic species are living in the SIDS-Seven. The assessment of annotated animal appendixes will help the appropriate agency formulate regionally determined prioritized actions, taking into account the species most at risk.

Preservation efforts of endemic species should focus on conservation translocation, which means humans will facilitate the transportation of endangered endemic island animals to new habitats. If these animals are not relocated, they will be at increased risk for extinction, which is a global

---

104. *See* IUCN Red List, IUCN Red List Version 2011.2: Table (2011) (on file with authors).

concern associated with climate change impacts. Regional economic integration organizations shall identify the environments in which each endemic species is likely to flourish without becoming invasive.[105] Although reversing defaunation is expensive, the costs may be justified, as several examples prove that endangered species restoration measures can succeed.[106] The international community has recognized the importance of protecting biodiversity, so support for intentionally moving endemic island animals to new habitats is likely to exist, in theory, at the global level. More importantly, the political will from developed countries must exist to fund these efforts through an international mechanism such as the Green Climate Fund under the UNFCCC. The success of this strategy will depend on whether relocating island animal populations outside their indigenous habitat is worth the risk of an invasive species problem.

C.   *International Implications: Investments and Interventions*

The limited international approach to animal protection is spread across many species-oriented or habitat-based treaties and agreements.[107] Although these international laws and non-binding general declarations touch on elements of animal protection, they do not directly advance the animal-related climate justice agenda.[108]

I.   Strategy I. COP21: Coordination and Collaboration for Island Animals

Although the Paris Agreement only provides indirect consideration for animals,[109] language regarding the development of mitigation and adap-

---

105. Although the Paris Agreement does not define "regional economic integration organization," the term is defined in the U.S. Code as "an organization that is constituted by, and composed of, foreign states, and on which such foreign states have conferred sovereign authority to make decisions that are binding on such foreign states, and that are directly applicable to and binding on persons within such foreign states . . . ." 15 U.S.C. §6211(9).

106. For example, "New Zealand has managed to bring back from the very edge of oblivion several fantastic birds, including the kakapo, the South Island saddleback, the Campbell Island teal, and the black robin." Elizabeth Kolbert, *The Big Kill*, New Yorker, Dec. 22, 2014, http://www.newyorker.com/magazine/2014/12/22/big-kill.

107. For a comprehensive examination of international agreements that offer some degree of protection for animals, see generally Sabine Brels, *The Evolution of International Animal Law: From Wildlife Conservation to Animal Welfare*, in What Can Animal Law Learn From Environmental Law? 365–83 (Randall S. Abate ed., 2015).

108. *But see* Part III.C.1., which proposes that island animals are a vulnerable group entitled to protection under the Paris Agreement.

109. For instance, the importance of protecting biodiversity is noted in the preamble. *Paris Agreement*, *supra* note 1.

tation measures is broad enough to facilitate the mobilization of support for integrating animal-related policies into national adaptation plans. For example, the argument that Paris Committees should develop recommendations for integrated measures to avert and mitigate climate change impacts on island animals is viable for the numerous economic, environmental, and public health concerns noted in this chapter.[110]

Likewise, the Paris Committee on Capacity-building (PCCB) should identify animal-related gaps and fulfill its objective of enhancing SIDS' resilience to climate change.[111] The PCCB is responsible for managing a work plan with nine objectives, including recommending solutions to capacity gaps, "[p]romoting the development and dissemination of tools and methodologies for the implementation of capacity-building . . . and collecting good practices, challenges, experiences, and lessons learned from work on capacity-building."[112] Taking into account these objectives, the PCCB can identify animal control as a capacity gap, and among other measures, take action to spay and neuter appropriate island animals; promote the development of immunocontraception for wild mammals such as rats and the flying fox; and research innovative sterilization tools for non-mammals. The PCCB can also foster coordination among domestic, regional, and international Parties to establish veterinary clinics and provide medical services for island animals.

At the 25th session of the Conference of the Parties in November 2019, the PCCB must take action with a view toward making animal-related recommendations to enhance "institutional arrangements for capacity-building."[113] The Green Climate Fund, which is expected to mobilize $100 billion per year to assist developing countries cope with the effects of climate change, can finance these capacity-building animal-related activities.[114] While this section briefly identified one potential strategy to protect island animals, incorporating sterilization programs and related policies into national adaptation plans could be a catalyst to facilitate attaining the goal of increasing international acceptance of animal protection generally.

---

110. Specifically, the Adaptation Committee, the Least Developed Countries Expert Group, the Standing Committee on Finance, and other relevant institutions should spearhead these integrated measures, which should build on the sterilization-driven strategies proposed in this chapter. *Id.* at I/CP.21, para. 46.
111. *Id.* at I/CP.21, para. 72.
112. *Id.* at I/CP.21, para. 74(c)–(b).
113. *Id.* at I/CP.21, para. 82.
114. *See* Davenport, *supra* note 109.

2.   **Strategy 2. Capitalize on Canine Culture: Conscientious Concern for Consumption, Control, Caretakers, and Costs**

One strategy to regulate SIDS' management of island animals to help promote the climate-justice animal protection agenda at the international level is to capture the attention and checkbooks of canine-protective Westerners. Because of North American and European canine adoration and attachment, this strategy, if implemented, could assist in advancing the humane treatment of island dogs. Moreover, this approach will not only raise awareness of the global plight of non-native animal species, but will also contribute to the growing body of evidence that animal protection is an issue of international concern.

As opposed to almost every other species—with the potential exception of cats—island dogs are well-positioned to appeal to the Western ethos, and with proper publicity, potentially redesign their destiny. North American and European societies pamper pooches, taking dogs to pet therapy (i.e., therapy to assist the animal's mental and emotional development), pet bakeries, for personalized pet massages, and to dogya (pronounced dough-guh, this word is a hybrid of "dog" and "yoga," and the activity is exactly that: yoga for dogs). Despite differing opinions on the treatment of farm animals, wild animals, and those in captivity, a strong consensus exists that companion animals are "part of the family."[115]

This sense of familial canine loyalty is so pronounced in the Western world that a mere whisper of the word "Yulin" is loud enough to cause transcontinental pandemonium from San Diego, California, to San Sebastián, Spain.[116] The so-called annual "dog-eating" festival has been protested

---

115. Ninety percent of U.S. pet owners consider their pets to be "part of the family." Rachel Hartigan Shea, *Q&A: Pets Are Becoming People, Legally Speaking*, Nat'l Geographic, Apr. 7, 2014, http://news.nationalgeographic.com/news/2014/04/140406-pets-cats-dogs-animal-rights-citizen-canine/.

116. Prior to the 2015 Yulin dog meat festival, everyone from comedians to academics to world leaders spoke out against the festival. *See* Lauren O'Neil, *Dog Meat Festival in China Takes Place Despite Massive Online Protest*, CBC News, Jun. 22, 2015, http://www.cbc.ca/news/trending/dog-meat-festival-in-china-takes-place-despite-massive-online-protest-1.3123266. British comedian Ricky Gervais tweeted, "Whether you're an atheist or believer, vegan or hunter, you must agree that torturing a dog then skinning it alive is wrong. #StopYuLin2015." Ricky Gervais, (rickygervais), (Jun. 20, 2015) [Twitter post], https://twitter.com/rickygervais. On April 6, 2016, Gervais once again protested Yulin via Twitter: "The dogs are tortured to 'make meat tastier'. They are also skinned and boiled alive. It's not a food festival. It's hell. #StopYulin." *Id.* at (Apr. 6, 2016). Almost 4.5 million people have signed an online petition against Yulin, and pledged to "be part of a compassionate world where we all come together to stand up and speak out for all innocent life, not just the life of humanity." Raise UR Paw, *Stop the Yulin Dog Meat Eating Festival*, Change.org, 2014, https://www.change.org/p/stop-the-yulin-dog-meat-eating-festival?source_location=search_index&algorithm=curated_trending (last visited Aug. 23, 2016). A second anti-Yulin dog meat eating online petition has more than 1.6 million signatures. *See* Duo Duo Animal Welfare Project, *Shut Down the Yulin Dog Meat Festival!*,

worldwide since its 2009 inception, but Yulin is not unique for this adverse reaction. Rather, Westerners have established the strict rule that they will vocally disavow any and all (known) instances in which other societies feast on Fido—and, importantly, the islands would not be the exception; it is simply a matter of raising awareness about canine consumption.[117] Because of Westerners' staunch commitment to canines, it is essential for animal protectionists to publicize the fact that islanders have extended Yulin's one-week annual festival by 358 days.

The emotional attachment of Westerners to dogs can be used to set the animal-related climate justice agenda and secure recognition of new international animal-protective norms. With this objective in mind, this section recommends one possibility that nongovernmental organizations (NGOs) could pursue independent of the Conference of the Parties to safeguard the healthcare of island animals. A two-part strategy could include the establishment of (1) full scholarships for nationals from SIDS who wish to pursue a doctor of veterinary medicine degree (DVM) in a developed country;[118] and (2) fully supplied veterinary clinics in SIDS, wherein scholarship recipients would practice upon graduation.[119] For example, an advocacy group could partner with an institution such as the University of Georgia College of Veterinary Medicine to reserve at least one incoming student position for a Tuvaluan national. This contractual relationship could be drafted to guarantee a position for an islander in each incoming class for a fixed number of years, depending on the needs of the specific nation; however, this term should never be less than two years (which would render two qualified veterinarians for the island in five years). During the students' four-year enrollment, the clinic could be constructed and stocked with appropriate medicines, vaccines, technology, and other products.

CHANGE.ORG, 2014, https://www.change.org/p/mr-chen-wu-yulin-governor-please-shut-down-the-yulin-dog-meat-festival-in-guangxi-china (last visited Aug. 23, 2016).

117. Western society not only protests eating dogs, but also the act of killing them. For example, North America and Europe were outraged when 2,000 stray dogs were ordered to be killed before the 2014 Winter Olympics in Sochi, Russia. For a discussion of reactions from animal rights groups to this practice, see Carla Hall, *Sochi Officials, Killing Stray Dogs Is No Way to Host the Olympics*, L.A. TIMES, Feb, 6, 2014, http://articles.latimes.com/2014/feb/06/news/la-ol-sochi-olympics-kill-stray-dogs-20140206; Ivan Watson, *Russians Say Authorities Rounding Up, Poisoning Stray Dogs Before Olympics*, CNN.COM, Feb. 5, 2014, http://www.cnn.com/2014/02/05/world/europe/russia-sochi-stray-dogs/.

118. Other developed countries offer the equivalent of the U.S. DVM degree; however, these veterinary degrees are referred to as "DVM" for simplicity and brevity.

119. As opposed to veterinarians visiting islands for temporary clinics, the scholarship-clinic program would promote small island self-sufficiency, which is also one component of the PCCB work plan. *See Paris Agreement, supra* note 1, at I/CP.21, para. 74(f) (directing the Committee to explore "how developing country Parties can take ownership of building and maintaining capacity over time and space.").

This option permits NGOs to target developed countries whose citizens feel strongly about dog abuse or inhumane animal practices to mobilize funding for full DVM scholarships, clinic establishments, medical supplies, and supplementing the salaries of island veterinarians (as all services should be provided without charge to SIDS). Because the recognition of canine protection is a Western value, the citizen fundraising strategy could be a helpful tool in encouraging islanders to seek treatment for ill animals, as well as to incentivize people to vaccinate and spay or neuter their pets.

Conclusion

Despite the momentum surrounding the SIDS-climate change discourse, protection of nonhuman island inhabitants has been largely overlooked. Failure to recognize and fight for the protection of small island animals contradicts and undermines a touchstone of animal advocacy. The animal protection movement has a duty to protect the health and welfare of *all* animals, including those on island nations imperiled by sea-level rise.

Conceptual questions persist regarding how to link the *separate but equal* issues of human rights and nonhuman animal protection. At this level, the obstacle remains how to connect the fully institutionalized field of human rights law, with its enhanced legitimacy in foreign domestic and international law fields, to the marginalized constructs of global animal law and the principles of climate justice.

Although the link between the consequences of climate change and impacts to island animals is evident, explicit measures of protection for these animals are unlikely to succeed on the domestic level because of prohibitive costs and cultural attitudes toward animals. However, if animal protection is repackaged as a mechanism for preserving the environment, economy, public health, or morals, then such initiatives could gain traction on the domestic and regional levels. Notably, at the international level, efforts to save human's best friend, the dog, will draw significant worldwide attention, and advocacy on behalf of island dogs could shine a spotlight on the current gap of animal protection in SIDS' climate change policies. Such efforts could increase understanding of climate-related risks to island animals, and help develop protective policies on their behalf.

African and Middle Eastern Perspectives

Chapter 14

Land Use and Climate Change: Using Planning Tools to Enhance Climate Adaptation in Kenya

Robert Kibugi

Introduction

This chapter examines how the adverse impacts of climate change affect socioeconomic and environmental activities in Kenya, and reviews how implementation of sustainable physical planning and development control tools can enhance adaptation options. The enactment of new climate change legislation in May 2016 reflects Kenya's commitment to implement responsive and coherent regulatory measures. Equally important is the codification of mainstreaming as the legal tool to guide internalization of climate change responses, such as adaptation, into various sectors of public policy.

389

Critical to these efforts is revisiting the concepts and principles that inform planning, including the emergence of stronger local governments through devolution of functions in Kenya within the past two years. Mainstreaming is crucial where governmental mandates on climate change are devolved to subnational levels, such as county governments in Kenya.

Adaptation to climate change is imperative to build resilience and enhance adaptive capacity. In this context, planned adaptation provides a valuable opportunity to set out interventions predictably, and to mainstream these efforts into other sectors. A key public policy sector is land use planning, particularly the application of physical and spatial planning tools to balance socioeconomic and environmental considerations. In the current legal landscape, the Climate Change Act of 2016 establishes a new legal tool to guide mainstreaming, the National Climate Change Action Plan (NCCAP). This action plan is to be implemented by mainstreaming into sectoral areas, such as physical planning, and to be further mainstreamed by county governments into their planning processes through County Integrated Development Plans (CIDP).

The detailed intersection of these tools is discussed further throughout this chapter, principally highlighting an important opportunity for Kenya. This includes taking steps to put in place national physical planning standards that counties can adopt as guidance to implement national physical planning standards, therefore providing a clear linkage between the physical planning system (under the national physical planning legislation) and the local government level CIDP and spatial planning structure set out by the County Governments Act. These adjustments will benefit and enhance adaptation planning and mainstreaming because clarity in the CIDP provides a better chance of mainstreaming the NCCAP through the CIDP, as required by the new climate change legislation.

Part I of this chapter describes climate change impacts in Kenya, while Part II discusses the regulatory approaches for climate change interventions in Kenya. Part III addresses the integration of adaptation planning and spatial planning through climate change mainstreaming, and evaluates opportunities for mainstreaming adaptation planning through physical planning legal tools in Kenya.

I.   Climate Change Impacts in Kenya

There is now no doubt regarding the adverse impacts of climate change. Globally, both the 2012 Rio Conference outcome document and the Sustainable Development Goals (SDGs) have raised climate change awareness, applying similar language that "climate change is one of the greatest challenges of our time . . . ."[1] The adoption of the Paris Agreement on climate change in December 2015 was a firm indication of the international community's willingness to both address climate change and avoid the emissions reduction challenges involved with implementing the 1997 Kyoto Protocol. Thus, the global consensus is that the adverse impacts of climate change undermine the ability of all countries to achieve sustainable development.[2] This is especially true for developing countries like Kenya, which are vulnerable to these adverse (and intensifying) impacts of climate change. Such impacts include persistent drought and extreme weather events, which further threaten food security and efforts to eradicate poverty and achieve sustainable development.[3]

Agriculture is a good example of vulnerability in Kenya, as farming is primarily small-scale, with about 75% of the total agricultural output produced on rainfed farmlands averaging 0.3 to 3 ha in size,[4] operated by about three million families.[5] This means that extreme weather events, such as droughts, can adversely affect the livelihoods of many households, thus enhancing vulnerability to climate change. When combined with the vulnerability of agriculture, drought can result in disasters like famine and potential economic ruin. In Kenya, droughts have been occurring more regularly, sometimes on an annual cycle.[6]

The national agriculture policy direction recognizes this vulnerability risk such that the national Agriculture Sector Development Strategy for the 2010–2020 period aims to "strategically position the agricultural sector as a key driver for delivering the 10 percent annual economic growth

---

1. *Transforming Our World: The 2030 Agenda for Sustainable Development*, G.A. Res. 70(1), U.N. GAOR, 70th Sess., U.N. Doc. A/RES/70/1, 5, para. 14, https://sustainabledevelopment.un.org/post2015/transformingourworld [hereinafter *Transforming Our World*]. *See also The Future We Want—Outcome of the Conference*, Rio+20 United Nations Conference on Sustainable Development, U.N. Doc. A/CONF.216/L.1, at 36, para. 190, https://sustainabledevelopment.un.org/rio20/futurewewant [hereinafter *Future We Want*].

2. *Transforming Our World, supra* note 1, para. 14.

3. *Future We Want, supra* note 1, para. 190.

4. Joab Osumba & Janie Rioux, Scoping Study on Climate-smart Agriculture in Kenya: Smallholder Integrated Crop-livestock Farming Systems 2 (2015), http://www.fao.org/3/a-i4367e.pdf.

5. Gordon O. Ojwang, Jaspat Agatsiva & Charles Situma, Analysis of Climate Change and Variability Risks in the Smallholder Sector: Case Studies of the Laikipia and Narok Districts Representing Major Agro-ecological Zones in Kenya 9 (2010), http://www.fao.org/docrep/013/i1785e/i1785e00.pdf.

6. Government of Kenya, National Climate Response Strategy 34 (2010), http://cdkn.org/wp-content/uploads/2012/04/National-Climate-Change-Response-Strategy_April-2010.pdf.

rate envisaged under the economic pillar of Vision 2030."[7] In addressing the agriculture sector, Vision 2030, which is Kenya's national development plan, aims for the development of an innovative, commercially oriented, and modern agriculture sector,[8] particularly through "transforming land use to ensure better utilization of high and medium potential lands."[9] To achieve this goal, it will be necessary to transform land use. There should be an aim, for instance, to increase productivity in medium-potential areas beyond 31% of land currently under crop production, and to enhance agriculture production in arid and semi-arid lands (ASALs) for livestock production, or crop farming through irrigation, to levels higher than the current 50% of the 24 million ha carrying capacity.[10] In the case of livestock farming, greater frequency of droughts in the ASALs increases livestock morbidity and mortality because of reduced availability of forage, increased disease incidences, and a breakdown of marketing infrastructure.[11] These impacts, together with enhanced irrigation for increased crop productivity in ASALs, require the implementation of adaptation measures to provide reliable water.

Physical infrastructure, such as transport and public works sectors, is an important and necessary enabler of socioeconomic development. This includes the road and rail network, water and sanitation services, and the development of small-scale but critical infrastructure such as footbridges in rural areas.[12] Climate change threatens vital infrastructure such as road and rail networks, as well as water and energy systems.[13] Sea-level rise, storms, rain and flooding, and higher temperatures pose a number of risks and impacts for infrastructure. In Kenya, the destruction of infrastructure including roads and bridges during storms is becoming increasingly common during extreme weather events.[14] Therefore, as an adaptation measure, it is necessary to "climate proof" infrastructure in a manner that anticipates the risks arising from climate change and internalizes the investments required to bypass

---

7.   GOVERNMENT OF KENYA, AGRICULTURAL SECTOR DEVELOPMENT STRATEGY 2010–2020 xiii (2010), http://faolex.fao.org/docs/pdf/ken140935.pdf.
8.   OFFICE OF THE PRIME MINISTER, KENYA, SESSIONAL PAPER NO. 10 OF 2012 ON KENYA VISION 2030, at 52, http://www.foresightfordevelopment.org/sobipro/55/1263-sessional-paper-no-10-of-2012-on-kenya-vision-2030.
9.   *Id.*
10.   *Id.* at 51.
11.   DAVID B. ADEGU, NATIONAL CLIMATE CHANGE SECRETARIAT OF KENYA, DRAFT NATIONAL CLIMATE CHANGE FRAMEWORK POLICY AND BILL 11 (2014), http://www.thecvf.org/wp-content/uploads/2015/07/Kenya.pdf [hereinafter KENYA, DRAFT NATIONAL CLIMATE CHANGE FRAMEWORK POLICY].
12.   KENYA, NATIONAL CLIMATE CHANGE ACTION PLAN ADAPTATION TECHNICAL ANALYSIS REPORT 14 (2012).
13.   *Id.*
14.   *Id.*

these risks.[15] Such an approach requires the integration of climate change resilience through planned adaptation measures in infrastructure (including in the spatial planning process) and internalization of climate proofing costs in the budgets for such infrastructure.

II. Regulatory Approaches for Policy-level Climate Change Interventions in Kenya

Against this background, Vision 2030 identifies climate change as a primary challenge to the sustainable development of Kenya, and calls for implementation of "measures to integrate climate change into development planning."[16] The Second Medium Term Plan (MTP) for Implementation of Vision 2030 for the period 2013–2017 further recognizes that "Kenya is susceptible to natural disasters such as drought and flooding which are likely to increase as a result of climate change."[17] This view is echoed in the 2014 Draft Climate Change Policy,[18] which notes that sustainable development in Kenya significantly depends on the design and implementation of mechanisms that trigger and enhance climate change resilience and adaptive capacity.[19]

A. Building Climate Resilience and Enhancing Adaptive Capacity

Enhancing climate change resilience and building adaptive capacity are two essential policy priorities that will enable Kenya to address its vulnerability to adverse impacts on agriculture and infrastructure. Adaptive capacity is defined by the Intergovernmental Panel on Climate Change (IPCC) as the "ability or potential of a system to respond successfully to climate variability and change, and includes adjustments in both behaviour and in resources and technologies."[20] The IPCC further states that adaptive capacity is a necessary condition for the design and implementation of effective adaptation strategies necessary to reduce vulnerability to the adverse impacts of climate

---

15. *Id.*
16. Office of the Prime Minister, Kenya, Sessional Paper No. 10, *supra* note 8, at 128.
17. Kenya, Vision 2030—Second Medium Term Plan (2013–2017), Transforming Kenya: Pathway to Devolution, Socioeconomic Development, Equity, and National Unity 41 (n.d.), http://www.sida.se/contentassets/855677b831b74ea0b226ce2db4eb93a3/kenya_second_medium_term_plan_2013_-_2017.pdf.
18. Kenya, Draft National Climate Change Framework Policy, *supra* note 11, at 20.
19. *Id.* at 5.
20. W.N. Adger et al., *Assessment of Adaptation Practices, Options, Constraints, and Capacity, in* Climate Change 2007: Impacts, Adaptation, and Vulnerability. Contribution of Working Group II to the Fourth Assessment Report of the Intergovernmental Panel on Climate Change 717, 727 (M.L. Parry et al. eds., 2007).

change.[21] A principal argument for planned adaptation is that application of adaptive capacity is a necessary condition to reduce the likelihood and the magnitude of harmful outcomes resulting from climate change.[22]

The Kenyan legal and policy framework is consistent with this approach, and the 2014 Draft Climate Change Policy highlights the priority to "enhance adaptive capacity and build resilience to climate variability and change." Furthermore, the draft policy stresses that adaptive capacity is key to improving socioeconomic characteristics of communities, households, and industry as it includes adjustments in both behavior and in resources and technologies. This adaptive capacity is closely linked to building climate resilience, which requires Kenyan systems of governance, ecosystems, and society to maintain competent functioning in the face of climate change,[23] where this competence is a critical ingredient for success in building adaptive capacity.

The 2016 Climate Change Act, which took effect on May 27, 2016, introduces a mandatory focus on all economic sectors in Kenya to promote resilience and adaptive capacity to the impacts of climate change.[24] It also requires the formulation of programs and plans to enhance the resilience and adaptive capacity of human and ecological systems to combat the impacts of climate change.[25] The role of a new legal tool, the NCCAP, in identifying priorities for adaptation (and mitigation) and in framing implementation through mainstreaming of climate change actions into the legal, policy, planning, budgeting, and implementation priorities of various economic sectors, is crucial in this effort. The NCCAP is discussed in detail in Subpart B of Part III below.

B.   Mainstreaming Climate Change Actions Into Planning and Implementation of Sectoral Mandates

In policy prioritization, Kenya has pursued a "low carbon climate resilient development" pathway,[26] which combines mitigation and adaptation, prioritizing the latter. The Climate Change Act of 2016 embraces this prioritization, noting that it "shall be applied for the development, management, implementation and regulation of mechanisms to enhance climate change resilience and low carbon development for the sustainable development of

---

21.   *Id.* at 727.
22.   *Id.*
23.   KENYA, DRAFT NATIONAL CLIMATE CHANGE FRAMEWORK POLICY, *supra* note 11, at 5.
24.   Climate Change Act, 2016, §3(2)(b), http://kenyalaw.org/kl/fileadmin/pdfdownloads/Acts/Climate ChangeActNo11of2016.pdf.
25.   *Id.* §3(2)(c).
26.   KENYA, DRAFT NATIONAL CLIMATE CHANGE FRAMEWORK POLICY, *supra* note 11, at 5.

Kenya."[27] An essential feature of climate-resilient development is the adoption of a mainstreaming approach for climate change actions, from development planning to budgeting and implementation, in conjunction with a focus on adaptation planning. Through mainstreaming, climate change risks are not addressed through separate initiatives but inform ongoing development policymaking, planning, and activities across all sectors.[28] This approach is important because climate-resilient development enables Kenya to adopt adaptation planning to slow the pace of an adaptation deficit. According to the United Nations Environment Programme (UNEP), an adaptation deficit is characterized by a country's failure to adapt adequately to existing climate risks.[29]

An example of an adaptation deficit in Kenya involves the continuing escalation of extreme weather events, such as droughts, into annually occurring disasters. While Kenya may not be able to do much to prevent droughts from occurring annually or biennially, adaptation planning can help minimize the impacts of such disasters. This can be achieved through minimizing the combination of the hazard (e.g., extreme weather events or drought) with vulnerability,[30] such as that arising from heavy national reliance on rainfed agriculture. In this scenario, the adoption of large- or small-holder irrigation, implemented together with watershed management to protect water sources, could reduce the vulnerability of agriculture and livelihoods to naturally occurring droughts, and possibly prevent famine. Such integrated adaptation planning, combining irrigation, agriculture, livelihoods, and watershed management, is consistent with the Sendai Framework for Disaster Risk Reduction (2015–2030).[31] This framework notes that it is critical to anticipate, plan for, and reduce disaster risk to more effectively protect persons, communities, their livelihoods, health, cultural heritage, socioeconomic assets, and ecosystems, and thus strengthen their resilience.[32] The mainstreaming approach is a facilitative tool for enhancing the interaction between planning and adaptation (as well as mitigation) actions identified as a priority for Kenya.

---

27. Climate Change Act, *supra* note 24, §3(1).
28. NAOMI OATES, DECLAN CONWAY & ROGER CALOW, THE "MAINSTREAMING" APPROACH TO CLIMATE CHANGE ADAPTATION: INSIGHTS FROM ETHIOPIA'S WATER SECTOR (2011), https://www.odi.org/sites/odi.org.uk/files/odi-assets/publications-opinion-files/7056.pdf.
29. United Nations Development Programme-UNEP, MAINSTREAMING CLIMATE CHANGE ADAPTATION INTO DEVELOPMENT PLANNING: A GUIDE FOR PRACTITIONERS 6 (2011), http://www.unep.org/pdf/mainstreaming-cc-adaptation-web.pdf.
30. For a definition of a disaster, see United Nations International Strategy for Disaster Reduction (UNISDR), *Terminology*, https://www.unisdr.org/we/inform/terminology (last visited Aug. 22, 2016).
31. UNISDR, SENDAI FRAMEWORK FOR DISASTER RISK REDUCTION 2015–2030, at 10 (2015), http://www.unisdr.org/files/43291_sendaiframeworkfordrren.pdf.
32. *Id.*

According to the Stockholm Environment Institute, mainstreaming is critical to secure the link between adaptation and development. The Food and Agriculture Organization of the United Nations (FAO) defines mainstreaming as the "incorporation of climate change considerations into established or on-going development programs, policies or management strategies, rather than developing adaptation and mitigation actions or priorities separately."[33] This process of mainstreaming planned adaptation mechanisms should, ideally, be iterative through application of a "climate lens" to sectoral plans and policies to identify key adaptation needs of those plans and policies,[34] and appropriate actions framed to be embedded in those sectoral plans and policies, including through budgetary allocations. Land use activities, which define the Kenyan socioeconomic context— including agriculture, forestry, infrastructure, and water resources—are some of the priority areas for adaptation, through which mainstreaming of climate change adaptation can be undertaken. As land use activities, these areas are subject to spatial planning processes that predetermine the holistic and integrated use of space, as well as the processes of planning, including the role of the public, budget allocation, and regulatory processes like development control.

The goals of the Kenyan national law on climate change are indicative of the priorities, and the linkages between mainstreaming and planning for adaptation. The law identifies some of its objectives as seeking to "mainstream climate change responses into development planning, decision making and implementation," and to "mainstream and reinforce climate change disaster risk reduction into strategies and actions of public and private entities."[35] Adaptation planning involves implementing regulatory measures to address the inevitable impacts of climate change and, in practice, the response can be proactive (anticipatory) or reactive. Mainstreaming of climate change actions into sectoral planning seeks to achieve proactive adaptation planning, with the application of a climate lens to potential impacts and the adjustment of budgets and other resource allocations. In addition, mainstreaming assists in preparing for unforeseeable impacts through internalization of disaster

---

33.   FAO POLICY LEARNING PROGRAMME, HOW TO MAINSTREAM CLIMATE CHANGE ADAPTATION AND MITIGATION INTO AGRICULTURE POLICIES 7 (2009), http://www.fao.org/docs/up/easypol/778/mainstream_clim_change_adaptation_agric_policies_slides_077en.pdf.
34.   STOCKHOLM ENVIRONMENTAL INSTITUTE, MAINSTREAMING ADAPTATION INTO DEVELOPMENT PLANS: LESSONS FROM THE REGIONAL CLIMATE CHANGE ADAPTATION KNOWLEDGE PLATFORM FOR ASIA, POLICY BRIEF (2013), https://www.sei-international.org/mediamanager/documents/Publications/Climate/SEI-AKP-PB-2013-Mainstreaming-adaptation.pdf.
35.   Climate Change Act, *supra* note 24, §3(2).

risk reduction elements into sectoral mandates as part of climate change integration.

In this approach of adaptation planning through mainstreaming, the concept of land use planning, and the practice of spatial or physical planning, can play an instrumental role. The foundation of national land use planning is established in the Constitution of Kenya, through Article 66, which empowers the State to "regulate the use of any land, or any interest in or right over any land, in the interest of defense, public safety, public order, public morality, public health, or land use planning."[36] This authority is part of the police power of the State and is, in practice, implemented through spatial and physical planning laws or by development control. Spatial planning is defined as the development of future-oriented, holistic policies that integrate and balance demands and requirements of society and various governmental policies into a desired future physical organization of space.[37]

According to the 1997 European Compendium of Spatial Planning, the object of spatial planning is to create a more rational territorial organization of land uses and to balance demands for development with the need to protect the environment and to achieve social and economic development objectives.[38] In this sense, spatial planning seeks to coordinate the spatial impacts of other sectoral policies to achieve an even distribution of physical activities, thereby striving to contend equitably with the social, economic, and environmental challenges that face a society. Spatial planning is concerned with land use and land development activities, which are correlated with vulnerability to climate change. As a consequence, spatial planning is essential to the implementation of adaptation priorities. Through mainstreaming, a regulatory system of spatial planning can be designed to integrate decisions on adaptation to climate change in the early stages of spatial planning to ensure a more comprehensive mix of tools to adapt to climate change in all spatial planning stages,[39] up to development control.

---

36. CONST. OF KENYA art. 66.
37. Bart Jan Davidse, Meike Othengrafen & Sonja Deppisch, *Spatial Planning Practices of Adapting to Climate Change*, 57 EUR. J. SPATIAL DEV. 1, 2 (2015), http://www.nordregio.se/Global/EJSD/Refereed%20articles/refereed57.pdf.
38. EUROPEAN COMMISSION, THE EU COMPENDIUM OF SPATIAL PLANNING SYSTEMS AND POLICIES 37–38 (1997), http://commin.org/upload/Glossaries/European_Glossary/EU_compendium_No_28_of_1997.pdf.
39. Davidse et al., *supra* note 37, at 2.

III. Physical Planning in Kenya: Mainstreaming Adaptation Planning

Land policy in Kenya[40] recognizes that land use planning is essential to the efficient and sustainable utilization and management of land and land-based resources. However, there are regulatory dysfunctions between planning and implementation of physical planning.[41] Therefore, with climate change impacts, the existing challenges of urban sprawl, land use conflicts, and environmental degradation continue to worsen.[42] Kenya has not had in place a national land use planning policy framework to guide national and local physical planning. Nor has the country had any guiding principles to support mainstreaming of physical planning objectives to guide integrated utilization of space. In May 2016, the government published the Draft National Land Use Policy, which recognizes the value of planned and integrated utilization of land resources, including the need to protect the social, economic, and environmental dimensions of sustainability.[43] Thus, for instance, climate change is identified as having resulted in declining agricultural productivity, requiring a need to implement adaptation measures. In addition, the draft policy identifies a need to respond to climate change through disaster response programs that "sensitize the communities on best land use practices that incorporate disaster mitigation . . . [and] adaptation and preparedness."[44]

The Draft Land Use Policy addresses the crucial policy questions of climate resilience and adaptive capacity, and the role of spatial planning in policymaking. The draft policy's call for adaptation measures in agriculture and disaster response raises the question of mainstreaming adaptation planning into physical planning. The Constitution of Kenya supports the linkage between physical planning and the pursuit of sustainability in land use decisionmaking. For example, Article 10 sets out binding values and principles of governance, and provides that public policy decisions, as well as legal frameworks, should integrate sustainable development.[45]

Although not defined in the Constitution, sustainable development concerns the balancing of social, economic, and environmental considerations,

---

40. Ministry of Lands Kenya, Sessional Paper No. 3 of 2009 on National Land Policy 52, http://www1.uneca.org/Portals/lpi/CrossArticle/1/Land%20Policy%20Documents/Sessional-paper-on-Kenya-National-Land-Policy.pdf.
41. *Id.*
42. *Id.*
43. Ministry of Lands and Physical Planning Kenya, Draft National Land Use Policy 10 (2016), http://www.ardhi.go.ke/wp-content/uploads/2016/06/Draft-National-Land-Use-Policy-May-2016.pdf.
44. *Id.* at 39.
45. Const. of Kenya art. 10.

which is also an objective of spatial planning, when making choices on the utilization of land resources. The IPCC has addressed the nexus between climate change and sustainable development, noting that society's priorities on sustainable development influence both the greenhouse gas (GHG) emissions that cause climate change and vulnerability. Thus, climate policy responses and socioeconomic development will affect the State's ability to achieve sustainable development goals, while the pursuit of those goals will in turn affect the success of those climate policies.[46] This suggests a need to pursue integration and mainstreaming of sustainability considerations into physical planning to ensure consistency with adaptation planning (and thus resilience and adaptive capacity). Such an approach is consistent with Sustainable Development Goal No. 13, which promotes the need to "integrate climate change measures into national policies, strategies and planning."[47]

A.   National Physical Planning Framework: Conceptual Linkage With Sustainability?

Currently, physical planning in Kenya is governed by the 1996 Physical Planning Act,[48] which predated the progressive 2010 Constitution of Kenya that makes sustainable development a binding principle of governance. Physical planning is the legal term used in Kenya to refer to land use planning through spatial and development planning. As framed in the physical planning legislation, physical planning extends to include the system of development control, which is administered by devolved county governments, as required by the Constitution.[49] On the basis of the current 1996 physical planning legislation, the existing system does not authorize national physical planning to provide guidance to other levels of spatial planning.

Instead, two categories of physical planning have been implemented, which are undertaken at the local (county) government level, but designed and approved through national government structures.[50] The first category

---

46.   IPCC, Climate Change 2007: Working Group III: Mitigation of Climate Change: The Dual Relationship Between Climate Change and Sustainable Development, https://www.ipcc.ch/publications_and_data/ar4/wg3/en/ch2s2-1-3.html.

47.   United Nations, *Sustainable Development Goals: 17 Goals to Transform Our World, Goal 13: Take Urgent Action to Combat Climate Change and Its Impacts*, http://www.un.org/sustainabledevelopment/climate-change-2/ (last visited Aug. 22, 2016).

48.   Physical Planning Act, 1996 (Cap. 286), http://www.ecolex.org/details/legislation/physical-planning-act-1996-cap-286-lex-faoc101236/.

49.   Const. of Kenya pt. II, fourth sched., §8.

50.   Physical Planning Act, *supra* note 48, §§16 & 24.

is through regional physical development plans[51] for areas considered rural, for purposes of

> improving the land and providing for the proper physical development of such land, and securing suitable provision for transportation, public purposes, utilities and services, commercial, industrial, residential and recreational areas, including parks, open spaces and reserves and also the making of suitable provision for the use of land for building or other purposes.[52]

Notably, the regional physical development plan may provide for planning, replanning, or reconstructing the "whole or part of the area" and "for controlling the order, nature and direction of development in that area."[53] The second category is through local physical development plans, which are designed and approved in urban areas to provide for the general purpose of "guiding and coordinating development of infrastructural facilities and services," including "the specific control of the use and development of land," such as through renewal or redevelopment."[54]

Even in the absence of a national spatial planning framework, the foregoing provisions reveal an appreciation for the subsidiarity principle of spatial planning,[55] whereby the planning process is focused on local requirements. However, some confusion arises because of provisions in two principal statutes governing devolved government authority. The 2012 County Governments Act provides for county planning, ostensibly implementing provisions of the 2010 Constitution of Kenya. This law requires county governments to develop and implement spatial plans for a period of 10 years, subject to review every five years.[56]

The county spatial plan is part of the mandatory County Integrated Development Plan,[57] and is required to provide a spatial depiction of the social and economic development program of the county as articulated in the integrated county development plan. The county spatial plan is required to indicate desired patterns of land use in the county; address the spatial construction or reconstruction of the county; provide strategic guidance regarding the location and nature of development within the county; and establish

51. *Id.* §16(1).
52. *Id.*
53. *Id.* §16(2).
54. *Id.* §24.
55. *Spatial Planning: Key Instrument for Development and Effective Governance With Special Reference to Countries in Transition,* U.N. Economic Commission for Europe, at 11, U.N. Doc. ECE/HBP/146 (2008), http://www.unece.org/fileadmin/DAM/hlm/documents/Publications/spatial_planning.e.pdf.
56. County Governments Act, 2012, §110, http://faolex.fao.org/cgi-bin/faolex.exe?database=faolex&search_type=link&table=result&lang=eng&format_name=@ERALL&rec_id=115452.
57. *Id.* §108.

basic guidelines for a land use management system in the county.[58] This law embraces the application of the spatial planning principle of integration[59] by requiring that the county spatial plan be aligned with the spatial planning frameworks of neighboring counties, and demonstrates how the county spatial plan is linked to the regional, national, and other county plans. This suggests that in addition to ensuring a holistic and integrated approach to planning, some link to the regional and local physical development plans is anticipated, although the law does not demonstrate how. Nonetheless, there is a requirement for the county spatial plans to demonstrate "the anticipated sustainable development outcomes."[60]

Notwithstanding the complexity of the spatial planning legal regime in Kenya, systems in the physical planning and county governments' legislation can be linked together for constructive integration with climate change legislation to facilitate the mainstreaming required for spatial planning to support planned adaptation. The regional and physical development plans are useful because although silent on the specific inputs, the laws are clear in their objective, which is to allow for short- to long-term predictable planning, including redevelopments, such as could be required for adaptation, to build resilience or enhance adaptive capacity. The spatial plans are more specific, and as long-term strategies, are well suited for adaptation planning. The law does not, however, address how spatial plans are to be enforced, or provide linkage to the process and practice of development control. In both cases, for implementation and enforcement to be clear, it will be necessary to implement administrative mechanisms for regulation and enforcement, including clear subsidiary legislation to provide for the process of developing these steps, and the manner in which they are to be enforced and implemented.

B.   Contribution of Spatial Planning to Adaptive Capacity

The physical planning system in Kenya is likely to change significantly should Parliament approve the 2015 Physical Planning Bill, which has been approved by the National Assembly.[61] As of this writing, the bill is under consideration in the Senate.[62] Several fundamental changes are proposed in the

---

58.   *Id.* §110.
59.   *Spatial Planning: Key Instrument for Development and Effective Governance With Special Reference to Countries in Transition, supra* note 55, at 12.
60.   County Governments Act, *supra* note 56, §110(xx).
61.   The Physical Planning Bill, 2015, was published in the Kenya Gazette Supplement No. 130 of 2015 and passed by the National Assembly, with amendments, on December 16, 2015, http://kenyalaw. org/kl/fileadmin/pdfdownloads/bills/2015/PhysicalPlanningBill2015.pdf.
62.   Bill No. 46 of 2015, https://www.google.com/url?sa=t&rct=j&q=&esrc=s&source=web&cd=1&ved= 0ahUKEwjE8dL-kanOAhWCuxQKHfjpAcUQFggeMAA&url=http%3A%2F%2Fwww.parliament.

draft law, which, if approved, will provide useful linkage between physical planning, climate change adaptation, and development control in a manner that is supportive of sustainable development. In its guiding principles, the Physical Planning Bill requires that physical planning should be guided by the principles of land policy under Article 60 of the Constitution of Kenya. These principles include the sustainable and productive management of land resources and the sound conservation and protection of ecologically sensitive areas. When read together with provisions of Article 10, which require mandatory application of the principle of sustainable development in implementing laws and making public policy, the guiding direction to balance socioeconomic and environmental considerations in the physical planning process is firmly established.

The draft physical planning law, together with provisions of the County Governments Act reviewed in Subpart A of this part and the 2016 Climate Change Act, can collectively provide a framework that links adaptation to physical planning and sustainability. This can be achieved through concrete implementation of a number of mechanisms in these different laws. First, a key objective of the Climate Change Act is for its application by the national and county governments to mainstream climate change responses into development planning, decisionmaking, and implementation. As such, the concept of mainstreaming obtains legal status in Kenyan law as the principal methodology of implementing climate change interventions. It is defined in the statute to mean "the integration of climate change actions into decision making and implementation of functions by sector ministries, state corporations and county governments."[63] In addition, to assist in this process of mainstreaming climate change responses, the national guiding policy is set as the attainment of low carbon, climate resilient development, which is a combination of both adaptation and mitigation.[64]

To help in this process, the new climate change law provides for the development of an NCCAP, which will "guide the country towards the achievement of low carbon climate resilient sustainable development,"[65] and develop "actions for mainstreaming climate change responses into sector functions."[66] The law further requires the NCCAP to mainstream other areas of policy considered strategic to attaining low carbon, climate-resilient

---

go.ke%2Fthe-senate%2Fhouse-business%2Fbills-from-national-assembly%2Fitem%2Fdownload%2F2047_8b7413ee7923642aeae8cde1c4ebcc54&usg=AFQjCNGWC-Ci1u45yDJNNmPpBlLMzF6Igg&sig2=ZqYUEVU1haa3FSh12pz9Pw.
63. Climate Change Act, *supra* note 24, §2.
64. *Id.*
65. *Id.* §13(3)(a).
66. *Id.* §13(3)(b).

development into sector functions. These policy areas include disaster risk reduction actions incorporated into development programs, or strategic areas of national infrastructure requiring climate proofing.[67] To advance both the strategic and legal importance of the NCCAP as a legal tool for Kenya to address vulnerability to climate change, and the importance of mainstreaming, the climate law requires the NCCAP "to address all sectors of the economy, and provide mechanisms for mainstreaming," into those sectors.[68]

I. Mainstreaming Climate Change Tools Into National Spatial Planning

In both the 2016 Climate Change Act and the draft 2015 Physical Planning Bill, there are two national legal tools that provide a clear intersection between physical planning and climate change actions. This is helpful to promote mainstreaming climate change actions into the physical planning system. It is also beneficial because to date there has not been a nationally focused physical planning system. Thus, the utility of the National Physical Development Plan and the NCCAP is crucial.

The purpose of the proposed National Physical Development Plan is to "define strategic policies for the determination of the general direction and trends of physical development and sectoral development in Kenya and provide a framework for the use and development of land."[69] When completed, this plan then becomes the basis for, among other priorities, promoting environmental conservation, socioeconomic development, and balanced national development; optimizing use of land resources; guiding local physical planning; coordinating sectoral planning and development; managing human settlements; and providing a framework for guiding the location and development of strategic national investments and infrastructural development.[70] In its development, the National Physical Development Plan should take into account the baseline analysis of physical development in Kenya, as well as necessary steps to optimize opportunities and potentials, and resolve challenges relating to physical development planning in Kenya. This approach can link national physical planning to adaptation planning, especially the dimension of enhancing adaptive capacity, if the baseline analysis of physical development in Kenya includes a vulnerability assessment. This approach is valuable because, according to the IPCC, much of the understanding

---

67. *Id.* §13(3)(f) & (h).
68. *Id.* §13(4).
69. Physical Planning Bill, *supra* note 61, §18.
70. *Id.* §18(2).

of adaptive capacity comes from vulnerability assessments, which provide important insights into the factors, processes, and structures that promote or constrain adaptive capacity.[71]

One major setback is the absence of a clear requirement for the National Physical Development Plan to undergo a strategic environmental assessment (SEA) prior to adoption because, at §20, the 2016 climate change law requires the integration of climate risk and vulnerability into all forms of environmental assessment. This, however, may not have a limiting effect as mandatory and binding requirements for undertaking an SEA are set out through §57A of the Environmental Management and Coordination Act (EMCA),[72] which requires that "*all* policies, plans and programmes for implementation shall be subject to strategic environmental assessment."[73] The EMCA clarifies the legal scope of a plan, policy, or program relative to the mandatory requirement of an SEA by noting that these (plans, policies, or programs) are those that are subject to "preparation or adoption by an authority at local, county, regional or national level," "prepared subsequent to a legislative procedure," and determined "likely to have significant effects on the environment."[74] In this context, the National Physical Development Plan, as well as the CIDPs, NCCAP, and other similar plans, must undergo a mandatory SEA.

In terms of the utility for mainstreaming, the proposed National Physical Development Plan will become a facilitative legal tool for integrating the adaptation priorities set out by the NCCAP into physical planning and development control. One illustration arises through addressing the challenge of land degradation in Kenya, which according to the Draft Land Reclamation Policy threatens food security and employment in agriculture-based industries.[75] Degradation is worsened by the significant and serious forms of soil erosion occurring in many parts of the country, as the removal of the top layer of fertile soil eventually leads to the formation of hard pans, rills, and gullies.[76] Therefore, addressing land degradation is important to eliminate vulnerability caused by land degradation to farming and other crucial land uses, the environment, and economic security.

---

71. IPCC, CLIMATE CHANGE 2007: WORKING GROUP II: IMPACTS, ADAPTATION, AND VULNERABILITY: ASSESSMENT OF ADAPTATION CAPACITY, OPTIONS AND CONSTRAINTS, https://www.ipcc.ch/publications_and_data/ar4/wg2/en/ch17s17-3.html.
72. Enacted in 1999 and revised through EMCA (Amendment) Act of 2015 (Kenya Gazette Supplement No. 74 of 2015).
73. *Id.* §57A (emphasis added).
74. *Id.* §2.
75. KENYA MINISTRY OF WATER AND IRRIGATION, FINAL DRAFT NATIONAL LAND RECLAMATION POLICY 5 (2013), http://www.environment.go.ke/wp-content/uploads/2015/06/LRP-Final-Draft-Policy.pdf.
76. *Id.*

According to the United Nations Convention to Combat Desertification (UNCCD) Secretariat, degradation arises when there is any loss or reduction in the biological or economic productive capacity of the land resource base.[77] This land degradation is caused by human activities, exacerbated by natural processes, and often magnified by and closely intertwined with climate change and biodiversity loss.[78] The challenge becomes complex because land degradation and climate change can, according to the UNCCD Secretariat, form a "positive feedback loop" whereby food production increases emissions while the loss of soil and vegetation significantly reduce potential carbon sinks, with more GHGs in the atmosphere feeding an energetic cycle of land degradation, biodiversity loss, and climate change.

The challenge of land degradation was highlighted by the Rio+20 outcome document, which called for urgent action to reverse land degradation, through efforts to achieve land-degradation neutrality in the context of sustainable development.[79] According to Alan Grainger, this requires strategies for managing land more sustainably to reduce the rate of degradation and subsequently increase the rate of restoration of degraded land, so that the outcome is a zero net rate of land degradation.[80] To achieve this goal, the scope of degraded lands should decrease or at least remain stable, and the rate of land degradation should not exceed that of land restoration.[81] Pamela Chasek argues that the challenge lies in making zero net land degradation operational because of the actions required, including: (1) scoping through determination of the spatial scale and geographical preference for attaining neutrality; (2) mapping lands based on current uses; and (3) prescribing management practices relevant for identifying lands for either reducing degradation or restoring productivity, or increasing resilience.[82]

Based on the foregoing analysis, the utility of physical planning tools in working to achieve zero net land degradation is key because the baseline analysis of physical developments can become a valuable tool for scoping the spatial scale and for mapping current uses. In its focus on low carbon,

77. UNCCD, Land Degradation Neutrality: Resilience at Local, National, and Regional Levels 4 (2014), http://www.unccd.int/Lists/SiteDocumentLibrary/Publications/Land_Degrad_Neutrality_E_Web.pdf.

78. Id.

79. Future We Want, supra note 1, para. 206.

80. Alan Grainger, Is Land Degradation Neutrality Feasible in Dry Areas?, 112 J. Arid Env'ts 14, 19 (2015), http://www.sciencedirect.com/science/article/pii/S0140196314001293.

81. Ilan Stavi & Rattan Lal, Achieving Zero Net Land Degradation: Challenges and Opportunities, 112 J. Arid Env'ts 44, 47 (2015), http://www.sciencedirect.com/science/article/pii/S0140196314000275.

82. See Pamela Chasek et al., Operationalizing Zero Net Land Degradation: The Next Stage in International Efforts to Combat Desertification?, 112 J. Arid Env'ts 5 (2015), http://www.sciencedirect.com/science/article/pii/S0140196314001359.

climate-resilient development, and the need to mainstream adaptation interventions into sectoral areas, the NCCAP represents an opportunity to utilize physical planning tools to guide analysis of technical inputs needed for zero net land degradation. Moreover, it also facilitates selection of land management practices necessary to reduce degradation, restore productivity, or increase resilience in the various sector functions, such as agriculture and forestry.

2.   Mainstreaming Climate Change Tools Into Local Spatial Planning

The role of local government authorities, such as the county governments in Kenya, in sustainability has widely been acknowledged, with Agenda 21 declaring that local authorities are globally indispensable in promoting sustainable development.[83] While the role and form of local government differs with legal context, Anel du Plessis argues that the broad functions of local authorities are central to integrating a wide range of national policy concerns on climate change,[84] particularly through the various sectoral executive and administrative functions they possess.[85] In the Kenyan context, the NCCAP as a legal tool for mainstreaming climate change is linked to county governments and their mandates including spatial planning. This connection is established through a provision in the Climate Change Act that requires county governments, when developing and approving CIDPs, to mainstream the implementation of the NCCAP, taking into account national and county priorities.[86]

The CIDP as a development planning tool involves a detailed consideration of all the relevant executive functions of a county government, which is a useful starting point for mainstreaming. The CIDP also includes a county spatial plan.[87] This spatial plan is developed for a long-term period, and when developed as part of the CIDP, this means that mainstreaming of the NCCAP priorities can be linked to the spatial planning process. Furthermore, the County Governments Act, under the authority of which the CIDP spatial plans are developed, requires that the spatial plan must not only dem-

---

83.   Anel du Plessis, *Climate Governance in South African Municipalities, in* LOCAL CLIMATE CHANGE LAW: ENVIRONMENTAL REGULATIONS IN CITIES AND OTHER LOCALITIES 354 (Benjamin J. Richardson ed., 2012). This argument references the provisions of article 28(1) of the United Nations' Agenda 21 (1992).
84.   *Id.*
85.   *Id.* at 358.
86.   Climate Change Act, *supra* note 24, §19(2).
87.   County Governments Act, *supra* note 56, §110.

onstrate the anticipated sustainable development outcomes,[88] but also must undergo a strategic environmental assessment of its impacts and be aligned with the spatial priorities of the neighboring counties.[89] Demonstration of anticipated sustainable development outcomes will require the county spatial plan to take a holistic approach in seeking to balance socioeconomic and environmental priorities, which is important when addressing vulnerabilities caused by climate change impacts through resilience and adaptive capacity measures. When the spatial plan is subjected to a strategic environmental assessment, and required by law to demonstrate anticipated sustainable development outcomes, a link arises through the need to mainstream measures needed for attaining low carbon, climate-resilient sustainable development. One of the changes introduced by the 2016 climate change law in Kenya is a mandatory requirement that the regulations on strategic and project-based environmental assessments must "integrate climate risk and vulnerability assessment into all forms of assessment."[90]

The mainstreaming of disaster risk reduction is a helpful example to demonstrate this linkage. Climate change adaptation and disaster risk reduction share a common element in that they both must be mainstreamed into other sectors (e.g., agriculture, water resources, roads, land use, and health) for effective internalization.[91] Disasters often arise where an existing sectoral vulnerability (such as that caused by climate change impacts) intersects with a natural hazard (such as extreme weather events). Disaster risk reduction involves preventing circumstances that result in a combination of the vulnerability and the hazard. In this case, linking the spatial planning process to the climate change mainstreaming process is critical, first because the law requires mainstreaming of disaster risk reduction into development priorities.[92] In addition, this is necessary because spatial planning is the precursor to development controls, the process through which approvals are given or denied for undertaking development activities within the scope defined in the spatial plan. Thus, identifying the disaster risk elements to the various components considered during spatial planning is important because adaptation tools to manage vulnerability of society, the economy, or the environment through building resilience, and enhancing adaptive capacity, can

---

88. *Id.* §110(1)(c).
89. *Id.* §110(2)(c)(vii).
90. Climate Change Act, *supra* note 24, §19.
91. Abdul Haseeb Ansari, *Legal and Policy Framework for Ecosystem-based Adaptation to Climate Change in Malaysia: A Reform-oriented Study, in* ADAPTATION TO CLIMATE CHANGE: ASEAN AND COMPARATIVE EXPERIENCES 110 (Koh Kheng Lian, Ilan Kelman, Robert Kibugi & Rose-Lia Eisma Osorio eds., 2015).
92. Climate Change Act, *supra* note 24, §3(2)(d).

be applied. Moreover, a strategic environmental assessment is required for each sectoral plan, and with modifications introduced by the 2016 climate law, climate risk and vulnerability assessment will become part of the strategic assessment, and the subsequent project-based environmental impact assessments.

Vulnerabilities, which could exacerbate the occurrence of disasters, can be reduced or managed through the strategic assessment process in which a more holistic view of development activities is taken. This implies that less risk would be under consideration at the development control stage, when only a project-based environmental assessment is legally necessary.[93] Disaster risk reduction is very closely affiliated with the concept of anticipatory or planned adaptation, as it involves proactive measures intended to reduce the adaptation deficit caused by persistent vulnerability in society, the economy, or the environment, which interacts with hazards to result in disasters.

Thus, the approach discussed here suggests that a supportive mechanism can be built into the local government planning process to mainstream climate change adaptation mechanisms into spatial planning. A significant challenge to this approach, however, is that the law does not provide a clear linkage between this spatial planning developed under the CIDP and the regional or local physical development plans developed under the physical planning legislation. This lack of clarity continues to exist in provisions of the draft physical planning law currently before Parliament, which makes extensive provisions for regional physical development plans (linking the spatial priorities of the various counties), as well as county-level physical development plans, that are further cascaded to local physical development plans. In planning practice, there are spatial elements required for the physical plans and, possibly, the elements of the spatial plan developed under the CIDP that can be integrated into the physical development plans.

In order to ensure efficacy in the application of the law, and to promote rule of law through compliance and enforcement, additional clarity needs to be provided through administrative mechanisms to foster linkage between the NCCAP and CIDP spatial plans, and the regional, county, and local physical development plans. These connections can be developed by utilizing the legislative authority of county assemblies[94] by establishing a model county physical planning law that counties can adopt to guide implementation of national physical planning standards, and therefore provide clear linkage between the national physical planning system under the CIDP and the spatial planning

---

93. Physical Planning Act, *supra* note 48, §36.
94. CONST. OF KENYA art. 177.

system under the County Governments Act. These adjustments will benefit and enhance adaptation planning and mainstreaming because clarity in the CIDP provides a better chance of mainstreaming the NCCAP through the CIDP, as required by §19 of the 2016 Climate Change Act.

Conclusion

Kenya's vulnerability to climate change impacts has been identified as a major threat to the country's goal to attain sustainable development. The recent enactment of a national law to guide the response to climate change with the objective of low carbon, climate-resilient development reflects the country's awareness of this threat. In addition, the choice of mainstreaming, as the legal concept through which priority climate change actions are integrated and internalized into sectoral functions at the national and county government levels, underscores Kenya's awareness of the need to build resilience and enhance adaptive capacity. Land use priorities are at the core of this process, particularly the linkage between climate change actions for adaptation and mitigation, and the development approval process.

Development control is at the bottom end of the land use planning process, which commences with the physical planning or spatial planning system, through which coherence of prioritization by competing sectors should be established. On the basis of this coherence, and the temporal scope of the use of geographical space, development proposals can be examined for approval or rejection. Similarly, the legal requirement for strategic environmental assessment for physical or spatial plans is crucial because the new climate law has added a requirement for climate risk vulnerability as part of the SEA and the project-based environmental impact assessment. Although the climate legal regime is quite new, and the physical planning system is expected to undertake major reforms upon enactment of the draft bill, an opportunity is available to utilize the mainstreaming approach and to capitalize on the centrality of physical planning's connection to other socioeconomic and environmental activities as a principal entry point for integrating climate change actions, particularly through adaptation planning.

Chapter 15

Climate Change and Armed Conflict: Challenges and Opportunities for Maintaining International Peace and Security Through Climate Justice

*Onita Das**

---

* I would like to thank Christine Castro, Esq. and Divya Pillai, Esq. for their invaluable
research assistance. Special thanks also goes to Dr. Ben Pontin and Elena Blanco for their
review and comments and to Prof. Randall Abate for his excellent comments and edits on
this chapter.

Introduction

> *Climate change is real; it is accelerating in a dangerous manner; and it not only exacerbates threats to international peace and security, it is a threat to international peace and security.*
>
> — United Nations Secretary General Ban Ki Moon[1]

Climate change is a global phenomenon. As the United Nations Intergovernmental Panel on Climate Change (IPCC) stated almost a decade ago, "warming of the climate system is unequivocal, as is now evident from observations of increases in global average air and ocean temperatures, wide-spread melting of snow and ice and rising global average sea level."[2] In addition, scientists have determined that such anthropogenic climate change can directly cause changes to the environment, which, in turn, may then indirectly affect human beings in the long term.[3]

This chapter argues that under certain circumstances, particularly where human adaptation to the changing climate is ineffective, climate change impacts can spark armed conflicts[4] that, in turn, negatively affect the environment and the population, thereby leading to a new cycle of destruction that engages the issues of climate justice. In these circumstances, the affected population has to adapt to the situation, or in some cases leave for a more habitable environment. Such migration or direct negative effects of climate change on the environment could trigger conflict within and with other communities as people compete for dwindling resources. For example, the United Nations Environment Programme (UNEP) highlighted the causal link between climate change and armed conflict in its 2007 report, "Sudan: Post-conflict Environmental Assessment."[5] More recently, the issue of climate change contributing to conflict has been raised in relation to the conflict in Syria.[6]

---

1. United Nations Secretary General Ban Ki Moon, Remarks to the Security Council on the Impact of Climate Change on International Peace and Security (July 20, 2011), http://www.un.org/sg/STATEMENTS/index.asp?nid=5424.

2. S. SOLOMON ET AL., CLIMATE CHANGE 2007: IMPACTS, ADAPTATION, AND VULNERABILITY. CONTRIBUTION OF WORKING GROUP I TO THE FOURTH ASSESSMENT REPORT OF THE INTERGOVERNMENTAL PANEL ON CLIMATE CHANGE (2007), https://www.ipcc.ch/publications_and_data/ar4/wg1/en/spmsspm-direct-observations.html.

3. *See generally* CLIMATE CHANGE 2014: IMPACTS, ADAPTATIONS, AND VULNERABILITY, PART A: GLOBAL AND SECTORAL ASPECTS (IPCC 2014); David Cohen, *Climate Change Could Kill 500,000 a Year by 2030*, NEW SCIENTIST, May 29, 2009, http://www.newscientist.com/article/dn17218-climate-change-could-kill-500000-a-year-by-2030.html.

4. The terms "armed conflict" and "conflict" will be used interchangeably throughout the chapter.

5. UNEP, SUDAN: POST-CONFLICT ENVIRONMENTAL ASSESSMENT 8 (2007).

6. Colin P. Kelley et al., *Climate Change in the Fertile Crescent and Implications of the Recent Syrian Drought*, 112 PROC. NAT'L ACAD. SCI. 3241 (2015).

While climate change regulation exists under mechanisms such as the United Nations Framework Convention on Climate Change (UNFCCC), such regulation primarily focuses on mitigating global greenhouse gases (GHGs). Though mitigating and combating emissions are important, such regulation may not be able to effectively address wider, more pervasive challenges resulting from climate change. Beyond regulating the primary sources of climate change, climate change adaptation is equally important and, as such, a climate justice approach to meeting adaptation issues is key. Climate justice—a concept built on the platform of equitable development, human rights, and environmental justice—focuses on the unequal burden of climate change impacts on the most vulnerable and seeks to safeguard their rights, particularly by promoting more equitable and fair allocation of such burdens at the local, national, and international levels.

Using the examples of the conflicts in Darfur and Syria, this chapter explores applying the concept of climate justice together with the existing climate change legal framework to more effectively meet the challenges created by climate change-related armed conflict issues. Part I of this chapter examines the nexus between climate change and armed conflict. Part II considers the challenges of climate change-related armed conflict and the limitations of existing climate change regulation. Part III proposes approaching climate change-related armed conflict through a climate justice lens.

I.   Climate Change and Armed Conflict

A 2014 IPCC report confirms that climate change threatens to disrupt weather patterns and ecosystems.[7] This includes "very likely" predictions of extreme hot and cold weather (e.g., heat waves, droughts, floods, cyclones, and wildfires),[8] unpredictable weather, and global rising sea levels.[9] Observed evidence of the impact of such climate changes globally extend from alteration of hydrological systems, which impacts water resources; ocean acidification, which threatens global marine life; increasing desertification, which reduces arable and habitable land; and disruption of global crop cycles.[10] As a

---

7.   CLIMATE CHANGE 2014: IMPACTS, ADAPTATIONS, AND VULNERABILITY, PART A: GLOBAL AND SECTORAL ASPECTS, *supra* note 3, at 10.

8.   *Id.* at 8.

9.   Owen Alterman, *Climate Change and Security: An Israeli Perspective*, 18 STRATEGIC ASSESSMENT 117, 118 (2015) (citing CLIMATE CHANGE 2014: IMPACTS, ADAPTATIONS, AND VULNERABILITY, PART A: GLOBAL AND SECTORAL ASPECTS, *supra* note 3, at 10).

10. CLIMATE CHANGE 2014: IMPACTS, ADAPTATIONS, AND VULNERABILITY, PART A: GLOBAL AND SECTORAL ASPECTS, *supra* note 3, at 6. *See also* UNITED NATIONS CONVENTION TO COMBAT DESERTIFICATION, CLIMATE CHANGE AND DESERTIFICATION, THEMATIC FACT SHEET SERIES No. 1 (2007), http://www.unccd.int/Lists/SiteDocumentLibrary/Publications/Desertificationandclimatechange.pdf.

result, climate change is also projected to threaten food security.[11] Thus, this chapter focuses on whether and to what degree climate change is a threat to international peace and security.

A.   The Nexus Between Climate Change and Armed Conflict

Climate change can be linked to armed conflict in a variety of ways. Not only will climate change threaten resource allocation, food and water security, and coastal societies, such threats will have significant implications on global stability—particularly for poor or fragile nations that lack good governance in institutions, resources, and the resilience required to adapt and respond to climate change impacts.[12] Moreover, as these adverse consequences accelerate, these stresses could in turn increase forced human migrations, raise tensions, and trigger or exacerbate conflict.[13] A causal link between climate change and armed conflict (in the context of Sudan) is explained by the 2007 UNEP report as follows: "complex but clear linkages exist between environmental problems and the ongoing conflict. Indeed, climate change, land degradation and the resulting competition over scarce natural resources are among the root causes as well as the consequences of the violence and grave humanitarian situation in the region."[14] However, in reality the link between climate change, environmental degradation, and armed conflict is more complicated.

Many factors condition the likelihood of violent conflict ensuing from change in climatic conditions. The extent to which factors like migration; inadequate responses to climate change pressures; and social, economic, and political instability increase the possibility of violent conflict "depends crucially on country-specific and contextual figures."[15] As Halvard Buhaug and

---

11.   CLIMATE CHANGE 2014: IMPACTS, ADAPTATIONS, AND VULNERABILITY, PART A: GLOBAL AND SECTORAL ASPECTS, *supra* note 3, at 13.

12.   *See, e.g.*, Oli Brown, Anne Hammill & Robert McLeman, *Climate Change as the "New" Security Threat: Implications for Africa*, INT'L AFF. 83, 1141 (2007); Michael Werz & Laura Conley, *Climate Change, Migration, and Conflict: Addressing Complex Crises Scenarios in the 21st Century*, CENTER FOR AM. PROGRESS 1 (2012), https://cdn.americanprogress.org/wpcontent/uploads/issues/2012/01/pdf/climate_migration.pdf; Solomon M. Hsiang et al., *Quantifying the Influence of Climate on Human Conflict*, SCI. 341 (2013); ASHOK SWAIN, UNDERSTANDING EMERGING SECURITY CHALLENGES: THREATS AND OPPORTUNITIES 28 (2013).

13.   Brown et al., *supra* note 12, at 1141. *See also* Werz & Conley, *supra* note 12, at 20; Hsiang et al., *supra* note 12.

14.   UNEP, *supra* note 5, at 22.

15.   HALVARD BUHAUG, NILS PETTER GLEDITSCH & OLE MAGNUS THEISEN, SOCIAL DIMENSIONS OF CLIMATE CHANGE: IMPLICATIONS OF CLIMATE CHANGE FOR ARMED CONFLICT, WORLD BANK SOCIAL DEVELOPMENT DEPARTMENT 2 (2008). *But cf.* Halvard Buhaug et al., *One Effect to Rule Them All? A Comment on Climate and Conflict*, 127 CLIMATE CHANGE 396 (2014) (acknowledging that this commentary on climate change-conflict research "should not be taken to imply that climate has no

Ida Rudolfsen note, "[c]ountries characterized by chronic political instability, large and heterogeneous populations, widespread poverty and inequality, and high dependence on rain-fed agriculture are much more likely to elicit any of the adverse social effects" that may exacerbate conflict.[16] The adverse consequences of climate change will not cause conflict in all situations, nor will it be the sole cause of armed conflict. It is the adverse impacts of climate change coalescing with existing divisions within society—whether political, economic, or social in nature—that could lead to or exacerbate violent conflict.

Research on the causal link between climate change and armed conflict to date is controversial and contradictory. For example, Nils Petter Gleditsch finds that at present there is not much evidence that climate change is an important driver of conflict.[17] Buhaug and Rudolfsen argue that while climate change is unlikely to have a uniform and universal effect on the risk of armed conflict, climate change may indirectly impact conflict through human migration, economic shocks, or food insecurity.[18] They also note that "many of the factors that drive armed conflict today also determines societies' vulnerability to climate change . . . ."[19] In contrast, Solomon M. Hsiang et al. conclude, having carried out a comprehensive review of climate-human conflict literature (60 previous studies), "that there is more agreement across studies regarding influence of climate on human conflict than has been recognized previously."[20] Hsiang et al. argue that a warming of global temperature from 2–4°C could amplify human conflict, but conclude that climate variability is not the sole or primary driver of conflict.[21] Therefore, climate change pressures are one of many variable factors that may trigger or

influence on armed conflict" but rather that "research to date has failed to converge on a specific and direct association between climate and violent conflict").

16.   HALVARD BUHAUG & IDA RUDOLFSEN, A CLIMATE OF CONFLICTS? CONFLICT TRENDS 05 OF THE PEACE RESEARCH INSTITUTE OF OSLO (2015), http://file.prio.no/publication_files/prio/Buhaug,%20 Rudolfsen%20-%20A%20Climate%20of%20Conflicts,%20Conflict%20Trends%2005-2015.pdf.

17.   Nils Petter Gleditsch, *Whither the Weather? Climate Change and Conflict*, 49 J. PEACE RES. 3, 5 (2012). *See also* Dan Smith & Janani Vivekananda, *Climate Change, Conflict, and Fragility: Getting the Institutions Right, in* CLIMATE CHANGE, HUMAN SECURITY, AND VIOLENT CONFLICT: CHALLENGES FOR SOCIETAL STABILITY 78 (Jürgen Scheffran et al. eds., 2012) (arguing that the climate change-conflict link is unsubstantiated by empirical evidence, but that "this lack of empirical evidence to date does not mean that there is no link between climate change and security").

18.   BUHAUG & RUDOLFSEN, *supra* note 16.

19.   *Id.*

20.   Hsiang et al., *supra* note 12. This research has been criticized by the scientific community for not being comprehensive enough. *See* WORLD BANK, 4° TURN DOWN THE HEAT: CONFRONTING THE NEW CLIMATE NORMAL 145 (2014), http://www-wds.worldbank.org/external/default/WDSContentServer/ WDSP/IB/2014/11/20/000406484_20141120090713/Rendered/PDF/927040v20WP00O0ull0R eport000English.pdf.

21.   Hsiang et al., *supra* note 12, at 1, 12.

exacerbate a potential conflict situation because such pressures will not cause elevated conflict risk in all societies.[22]

Numerous scholars and analysts agree that while climate change will not be a direct driver of conflict, it is considered a "threat multiplier," i.e., it is one factor that reinforces or exacerbates existing environmental, political, or socioeconomic tensions or vulnerabilities that present challenges to peace and security.[23] The negative effects of climate change will thus have serious implications for international peace and security, as not all nation States will be able to adapt to the unpredictable and changing climate conditions. Although many see climate change as a potential future threat with respect to armed conflict, some argue that in reality it has already had an impact.[24] The climate change-conflict link is explored in the following case studies.

B.   The Climate Change and Armed Conflict Nexus in Darfur and Syria

The climate change-conflict nexus is better understood by reviewing conflicts in practice. The case studies not only extend a descriptive view of the subject area, but also offer a reflection on human experience in such situations, thereby providing an important basis for ascertaining the appropriate action required. This section examines the link between climate change impacts and armed conflict by first exploring the 2003 Darfurian conflict and subsequently the most recent conflict in Syria.

The conflict in Darfur was caused by various factors. Despite its status as the largest region in the west of Sudan, Darfur is geographically isolated, which has caused it to be virtually ignored by the central Sudanese government in Khartoum.[25] Amidst a background of political marginalization and rising demographic pressure, the Darfur conflict was initiated by natural ecological adversity, which was exacerbated by serious government misman-

---

22. *See also* ONITA DAS, ENVIRONMENTAL PROTECTION, SECURITY, AND ARMED CONFLICT: A SUSTAINABLE DEVELOPMENT PERSPECTIVE 71 (2013) (arguing that climate change could add to the scarcity of natural resources, which could cause conflict in some situations).

23. *See, e.g.*, Stephen Marr, *Contextualizing Conflict: Trends and Challenges in the Syrian Civil War*, *in* INTERNATIONAL ORGANIZATIONS AND THE IMPLEMENTATION OF THE RESPONSIBILITY TO PROTECT: THE HUMANITARIAN CRISIS IN SYRIA 49 (Daniel Silander & Don Wallace eds., 2015); SWAIN, *supra* note 12, at 28; Christina Voigt, *Security in a "Warming World": Competences of the UN Security Council for Preventing Dangerous Climate Change*, *in* SECURITY: A MULTIDISCIPLINARY NORMATIVE APPROACH 294 (Cecilia M. Bailliet ed., 2009).

24. *See, e.g.*, Hsiang et al., *supra* note 12; Shirley V. Scott, *Climate Change and Peak Oil as Threats to International Peace and Security: Is it Time for the Security Council to Legislate?*, 9 MELB. J. INT'L L. 495, 504 (2008).

25. Leilani F. Battiste, *The Case for Intervention in the Humanitarian Crisis in Sudan*, 11 ANN. SURV. INT'L & COMP. L. 49, 51 (2005).

agement of natural resources such as land and water.[26] In northern Darfur, rain has decreased by a third over the past 80 years[27] and it has been suggested that the declining rainfall is attributed to some degree to global warming.[28] As the United Nations Secretary-General, Ban Ki-Moon, comments:

> Almost invariably, we discuss Darfur in a convenient military and political shorthand—an ethnic conflict pitting Arab militias against black rebels and farmers. Look to its roots, though, and you discover a more complex dynamic. Amid the diverse social and political causes, the Darfur conflict began as an ecological crisis, arising at least in part from climate change.[29]

Violence in Darfur erupted during the drought as a result of a combination of these factors. Once the rain stopped, there was no longer enough food and water for the population. Thus, fighting and conflict broke out when local groups rebelled, triggering counter attacks by the Khartoum-controlled Sudanese central army and government-backed Arab militia, the Janjaweed. By 2003, this spiraled into the tragedy that is evident today, in which nearly four years of armed conflict killed approximately 300,000 people and displaced more than five million.[30]

The 2007 UNEP report suggests that climate change and environmental degradation had a part to play in the conflict in Darfur.[31] The report claimed a strong causal link between climate-induced land degradation, desertification, and violent conflict in Darfur.[32] In contrast, many studies have disputed that the Darfurian conflict was primarily caused by climate change and conclude that the violence was driven by multiple factors (e.g., legacy of violence, ethnic fragmentation, ineffective governance, limited public services, and economic development), which are difficult to isolate as being the most influential.[33] Although violence erupted during the drought primarily as a result of diverse political and social problems with a combination of food

---

26. UNEP, From Conflict to Peacebuilding: The Role of Natural Resources and the Environment 9 (2009) [hereinafter From Conflict to Peacebuilding].
27. UNEP, *supra* note 5, at 60.
28. Ban Ki Moon, *A Climate Culprit in Darfur*, Wash. Post, June 16, 2007, at A15, http://www.washingtonpost.com/wp-dyn/content/article/2007/06/15/AR2007061501857_pf.html; From Conflict to Peacebuilding, *supra* note 26, at 9.
29. *Id.*
30. From Conflict to Peacebuilding, *supra* note 26, at 9.
31. UNEP, *supra* note 5, at 22.
32. *Id.*
33. W. Neil Adger et al., *Human Security*, *in* Climate Change 2014: Impacts, Adaptation and Vulnerability. Part A: Global and Sectoral Aspects. Contribution of Working Group II to the Fifth Assessment Report of the Intergovernmental Panel on Climate Change 773 (C.B. Field et al. eds., 2011) (citing Lyal S. Sunga, *Does Climate Change Kill People in Darfur?*, 1 J. Hum. Rts. & Env't 64, 85 (2011); H. Verhoeven, *Climate Change, Conflict and Development in Sudan: Global Neo-Malthusian Narratives and Local Power Struggles*, 42 Dev. & Change 679 (2011)).

and water insecurity and a lack of arable land, tensions in Darfur were simmering just below the surface, years before the drought, over water, land, and grazing rights between the mostly nomadic Arabs and farmers from local African tribal communities.

Such divisions within society provided fertile ground for tensions and violence, as conflicts do not occur simply due to desertification and drought caused by climate variability.[34] Though this is true, there is no doubt that in this situation, ecological factors compounded by climate change, in this case, lack of arable land and drought, contributed to the aggravation of tensions and conflict.[35] The Darfur example illustrates a complex situation in which existing socioeconomic and political problems in a vulnerable society are exacerbated into a security and armed conflict situation by climate change impacts, which can occur in less adaptive communities. UNEP has observed that as climate change may lead to further water and land stresses in Darfur and the Sahel region, there is a "need to place adaptation at the centre of their development and conflict prevention plan."[36]

Almost a decade later, in another region, climate change once again is believed to have contributed to conflict. In March 2011, in a rural Syrian town, a peaceful protest against President al-Assad's regime escalated into violent conflict. In August 2015, the United Nations confirmed that the death toll was more than 250,000 since the start of the conflict and that 12 million residents had been displaced.[37] Scholars, politicians, and environmental activists have argued that climate change caused the conflict in Syria.[38] However, as noted in the climate change-conflict link discussion above, environmental reasons—or in this case climate change impacts—are never the sole cause of an outbreak of

---

34. FROM CONFLICT TO PEACEBUILDING, *supra* note 26, at 9.

35. Linda Mbone Ndongo & Frank Maes, *Climate Change, Human Rights, and the Darfur Crisis, in* BIODIVERSITY AND CLIMATE CHANGE: LINKAGES AT INTERNATIONAL, NATIONAL, AND LOCAL LEVELS 140 (Frank Maes et al. eds., 2013).

36. FROM CONFLICT TO PEACEBUILDING, *supra* note 26, at 9.

37. *Alarmed by Continuing Syria Crisis, Security Council Affirms Its Support for Special Envoy's Approach in Moving Political Solution Forward*, U.N. Security Council, 7504th mtg. (2015), http://www.un.org/press/en/2015/sc12008.doc.htm.

38. *See, e.g.*, LUCAS RÜTTINGER ET AL., A NEW CLIMATE FOR PEACE: TAKING ACTION ON CLIMATE AND FRAGILITY RISKS, WOODROW WILSON INTERNATIONAL CENTER FOR SCHOLARS 31, 32 (European Union Inst. for Security Stud. 2015); David King et al., CLIMATE CHANGE: A RISK ASSESSMENT 10 (Centre for Sci. & Pol'y 2015); President Obama, Remarks by the President at the United States Coast Guard Academy Commencement (May 20, 2015), https://www.whitehouse.gov/the-press-office/2015/05/20/remarks-president-united-states-coast-guard-academy-commencement); George Monbiot, *How Fossil Fuel Burning Nearly Wiped out Life on Earth—250M Years Ago*, THE GUARDIAN, May 27, 2015, https://www.theguardian.com/commentisfree/2015/may/27/threat-islamic-state-fossil-fuel-burning. *But cf.* Jan Selby & Mike Hulme, *Is Climate Change Really to Blame for Syria's Civil War?*, THE GUARDIAN, Nov. 29, 2015 (criticizing claims of climate change causing conflict in Syria), https://www.theguardian.com/commentisfree/2015/nov/29/climate-change-syria-civil-war-prince-charles.

conflict. The Syrian uprising was triggered by a series of socioeconomic, political, and environmental factors, including increasing poverty (caused in part by cancelled state subsidies and rapid economic liberalization), rising unemployment, lack of political freedom, corruption, a widening rural/urban divide, long-term mismanagement of natural resources, severe drought, and climate change impacts on crop production and water.[39]

Syria experiences a semi-arid climate common to the region, where bouts of droughts are not unexpected.[40] However, prior to the unrest, around winter 2006/2007, Syria and the greater Fertile Crescent experienced one of the worst three-year droughts recorded.[41] This drought spell was consistent with human-induced climate change.[42] The drought caused widespread crop failure, reduction of water availability per capita, and mass migration of agricultural-based families.[43] As Colin P. Kelley et al. argue, "[D]rought can lead to devastating consequences when coupled with preexisting acute vulnerability, caused by poor policies and unsustainable land use practices in Syria's case and perpetuated by the slow and ineffective response to the Assad regime."[44] As such, Kelley et al. conclude that "[t]here is evidence that the 2007–2010 drought contributed to the conflict in Syria."[45]

On the other hand, Francesca de Châtel cautions against an "exaggerated focus on climate change" as the trigger of Syria's humanitarian crisis, arguing that doing so shifts the burden of responsibility away from the long-term government mismanagement that devastated Syria's natural resources.[46] This view is consistent with the argument that climate change is never the sole cause but contributes to the toxic mix of existing socioeconomic and environmental vulnerabilities that can lead to a humanitarian crisis. Shahrzad Mohtadi concedes that while the drought that may be attributable to climate change did not independently cause the civil war, the combined adverse effects of climate change, from drought, resource depletion, mass migration, and the Assad regime's failure to address and mitigate the consequences, propelled the country into civil conflict.[47]

---

39. *See, e.g.*, Rüttinger et al., *supra* note 38, at 52; Francesca de Châtel, *The Role of Drought and Climate Change in the Syrian Uprising: Untangling the Triggers of the Revolution*, 4 Middle E. Stud. 521 (2014).
40. de Châtel, *supra* note 39, at 522, 523.
41. Kelley et al., *supra* note 6, at 3241.
42. *Id.*
43. *See, e.g.*, Caitlin E. Werrell et al., *Did We See It Coming?: State Fragility, Climate Vulnerability, and the Uprisings in Syria and Egypt*, 35 SAIS Rev. Int'l Aff. 44 (2015); Kelley et al., *supra* note 6, at 3242.
44. Kelley et al., *supra* note 6, at 3242 (internal citations omitted).
45. *Id.* at 3241.
46. de Châtel, *supra* note 39, at 524.
47. Shahrzad Mohtadi, Climate Change and the Syrian Uprising, Bull. Atomic Scientists (2012). *See also* Peter H. Gleick, *Water, Drought, Climate Change, and Conflict in Syria*, 6 Weather, Climate & Soc'y 338 (2015).

While there is some recognition that climate change had a part to play in the Syrian uprising, Syria's vulnerability to climate change in the period leading up to the conflict may have been underestimated. As such, further research on "how climate vulnerability interacts with state fragility" may be necessary, as a better understanding of such interaction may prove "critical for ensuring that governments and publics are better prepared for and able to mitigate destabilizing trends."[48]

In the context of both Darfur and Syria, while climate change was not the "straw that broke the camel's back" in terms of causing conflict, there is evidence that the unusual human-induced climatic changes, which increase climate vulnerability in some fragile societies, can contribute to conflict. Therefore, these examples demonstrate the requirement for a more holistic climate justice-oriented adaptation approach to prevent situations in which simmering tensions can overflow into conflict. In situations where a humanitarian crisis has already occurred, these case studies showcase the need for holistic mitigation and adaptation policies looking toward climate justice principles to mitigate further reoccurring threats to international peace and security.

II.   Climate Change-related Armed Conflict and the Limitations of Existing Climate Change Regulation

The Darfur and Syria case studies have demonstrated that in some circumstances, climate change can be considered a threat to international peace and security. Given that some nation States will not be able to adapt to the adverse consequences of unpredictable and changing climate conditions, climate change is a growing security concern for nation states worldwide.[49] Climate change as a threat multiplier requires effective adaptation. Part A of this section describes the adaptation challenges of climate change-related armed conflict and Part B reviews the adequacy of existing climate change regulation in addressing these challenges.

A.   Challenges of Climate Change-related Armed Conflict

The challenges of climate change related-conflict should be considered from two perspectives: first, the prevention of climate change-related conflict, which requires adaptation of vulnerable societies to the adverse consequences

---

48.   Werrell et al., *supra* note 43, at 44.
49.   Alterman, *supra* note 9, at 117.

of climate change; and second, in the event of climate change-related conflict, adaptation to further climate change impacts by the war-torn society to prevent a relapse into future climate change-related conflict.

Due to the absence of generally supported theories and evidence about the causal nexus between climate change and conflict, it is not possible to make concrete statements about the effects of climate change on armed conflict.[50] Nevertheless, according to Ashok Swain, "[w]hile the exact impact of climate change is not known, it is clear that it will not only affect access to shared but also overall availability of resources."[51] Therefore, climate change-related conflict could include conflicts over resources (as seen in Darfur) or environmental conditions that could be affected by extreme weather, such as flooding or drought, diminishing water and food security, increasing desertification, and reducing arable land.[52] As mentioned above, such conflicts may occur in weak or failing States that lack the capacity to adapt to such climatic changes. As Linda Mbone Ndongo and Frank Maes note in the context of Darfur, "[t]he consequences of climate change in these regions are worse because there is a lack of capacity to adapt."[53]

In the event of a climate change-related conflict, it is difficult to determine the exact impact of climate change on armed conflict. It is most likely that the challenges of climate change-related armed conflict would include all adverse effects of traditional armed conflict with the added layer of the complexity of climate change. The impact of armed conflict generally includes the death and injury of the human population; destruction of infrastructure and institutions; disruption of markets, education, and development of human capital; and environmental damage.[54] Such disruption as a result of armed conflict also further limits livelihoods and creates and increases poverty, which in turn gives rise to vulnerability to climate change impacts.[55] Population displacement or forced human migration is another resulting impact—migration due to the conflict as well as the inability to adapt to climate change, i.e., environmentally induced migration.[56] Such migration could also lead to future conflict. According to the UN Refugee Agency (UNHCR), "[s]uch moves, or the adverse effects that climate change may have on natural resources, may spark conflict with

---

50. Adger et al., *supra* note 33, at 773.
51. SWAIN, *supra* note 12, at 28.
52. *See, e.g.*, Voigt, *supra* note 23, at 293.
53. Ndongo & Maes, *supra* note 35, at 133.
54. Adger et al., *supra* note 33, at 774 (internal citations omitted).
55. *Id.*
56. United Nations, *Refugees—Next Steps: New Dynamics of Displacement*, http://www.un.org/en/globalis-sues/briefingpapers/refugees/nextsteps.html (last visited Aug. 22, 2016).

other communities, as an increasing number of people compete for a decreasing amount of resources."[57]

The problem today is that while a particular conflict may end, the issues caused by climate change may not. Therefore, rebuilding the society or State post-conflict includes being able to adapt to the challenges of climate change, and for a war-torn fragile society or State, this would be difficult to achieve. This is corroborated by W. Neil Adger et al., observing that "where violent conflict emerges and persists the capacity to adapt to climate change is reduced for affected populations."[58]

Thus, in meeting the challenges of climate change, adaptation is key. According to Oli Brown et al., "[i]n the context of climate change, adaptation takes place through adjustments to reduce vulnerability or enhance resilience to observed or expected changes in climate, and involves changes in processes, perceptions, practices and function.'[59] However, as the discussion above shows, the complexities and variable factors involved in a climate change-related conflict situation means that adaptation to such climate change-conflict challenges has to be dynamic—differing across regions, nations, and communities, taking into consideration the existing socioeconomic, political, cultural, and environmental vulnerabilities of each situation. The case studies above set out the possible situations in which climate change-related conflict may occur and underscore the complexity of the adaptation policies required. The question that arises next is whether existing climate change regulation is adequate in setting out a framework to meet such adaptation needs.

B.   Existing Climate Change Regulation

The primary international legislation for climate change is the 1992 UNFCCC, which has the ultimate objective of preventing "dangerous" anthropogenic interference with the climate system.[60] There is now a political commitment in the international community, as reflected in the 2015 Paris Agreement, that GHGs should be limited to ensure that global temperatures do not increase beyond 2°C.[61] In 2010, Parties to the UNFCCC recognized

---

57. United Nations High Commissioner for Refugees, *Climate Change and Disasters*, http://www.unhcr. org/pages/49e4a5096.html (last visited Aug. 22, 2016).

58. Adger et al., *supra* note 33, at 774.

59. Brown et al., *supra* note 12, at 1149.

60. UNFCCC, *First Steps to a Safer Future: Introducing the United Nations Framework Convention on Climate Change*, http://unfccc.int/essential_background/convention/items/6036.php (last visited Aug. 22, 2016).

61. *Adoption of the Paris Agreement*, UNFCCC Conference of the Parties, 21st Sess., U.N. Doc. FCCC/ CP/2015/10/Add.1 (Dec. 12, 2015), http://unfccc.int/files/home/application/pdf/paris_agreement.

that adaptation to human-induced climate change must be addressed with the same level of priority as mitigation and adopted the Cancun Adaptation Framework (CAF) as part of the Cancun Agreements at the 2010 Climate Change Conference in Cancun, Mexico (16th Conference of the Parties (COP16)/Sixth Conference of the Parties serving as the meeting of the Parties (CMP6)).[62] The objective of CAF is to enhance action on adaptation, including through international cooperation.[63] Implementation of CAF was furthered in the 2011 Durban Climate Change Conference with the Parties agreeing on the Adaptation Committee, work program on loss and damage, and national adaptation plans of action (NAPA). Adaptation implementation plans continued in the 2012 Doha Climate Change Conference.[64] This focus on adaptation comes with the recognition that developing countries require international support (which includes technology transfer, capacity-building, and funding[65]) to meet adaptation challenges.[66]

While the UNFCCC's efforts to address adaptation are laudable and necessary,[67] the existing framework may not be equipped to rise to this complex dimension of adaptation challenge. While scholars note that the UNFCCC has been an invaluable resource in assisting "countries to prepare vulnerability assessments and climate change adaptation plans, as well as providing funding for the implementation of these funds," they also argue that it is challenging for already vulnerable and fragile nations to engage fully with UNFCCC-related activities.[68] It is further observed that climate vulnerability assessments "still lack significant discussion of the political or social impacts of climate change; in addition, most do not address drivers of fragility or other transboundary issues."[69] This limita-

pdf [hereinafter *Paris Agreement*]. Questions have been raised as to whether such commitments reflect obligations under international law. *See* Phillipe Sands, Public Lecture at King's College London: Climate Change and the Rule of Law: Adjudicating the Future in International Law 16 (Sept. 17, 2015), http://www.kcl.ac.uk/law/newsevents/climate-courts/assets/CLIMATE-CHANGE-INT-COURTS-17-Sept.pdf

62. For more information on the Cancun Adaptation Framework, see http://unfccc.int/adaptation/items/5852.php (last visited Aug. 22, 2016).

63. *See id.*

64. *See* UNFCCC, *Adaptation Overview*, http://unfccc.int/adaptation/items/7623.php (last visited Aug. 22, 2016).

65. Funding is provided through the financial mechanism of the UNFCCC. There are four funds set up by the Parties: Green Climate Fund, Special Climate Change Fund, Least Developed Countries Fund, and Adaptation Fund. For more information on funding opportunities, see UNFCCC, *Climate Finance*, http://unfccc.int/cooperation_and_support/financial_mechanism/items/2807.php (last visited Aug. 22, 2016).

66. *See* arts. 4.4, 4.8, and 4.9, UNFCCC; *see also* UNFCCC, *Adaptation Overview*, *supra* note 64.

67. For more information on the UNFCCC's work on adaptation, see UNFCCC, *Adaptation Overview*, *supra* note 64.

68. Rüttinger et al., *supra* note 38, at x.

69. *Id.* at xi.

tion is troublesome. As the case studies above show, climate change-related conflict will not occur in all situations, with particularly fragile nations being more at risk to the adverse consequences of climate change. Therefore, such climate vulnerability assessments may not capture the possibility of the risk of conflict in some situations, rendering adaptation efforts ineffective.

A more comprehensive notion of resilience is increasingly reflected in climate change adaptation plans.[70] This is evidenced by eight of the g7+ nations[71] having included climate-conflict risks in their NAPAs.[72] In addition, although the UNFCCC in 2014 published promising best practice examples for adaptation planning that showcased approaches to tackling human settlements, ecosystems, health, food, and water insecurity,[73] there are some gaps in guidance. For example, there is limited guidance on addressing transboundary issues of climate change consequences (e.g., shared river basins) or on how to develop NAPAs in fragile situations.[74] Transboundary dimensions of climate change that could contribute to transboundary climate fragility risks, in particular, could benefit from a more regional approach to tackling such issues. However, because of the traditional State-oriented nature of the UNFCCC, there is a distinct lack of regional focus in NAPAs.[75]

Climate change-related migration is suggested to be one of the factors that could contribute to conflict. However, scholars argue that despite the UNFCCC's focus on adaptation, the framework has limitations in terms of its structure and institutions in being able to address the issue of climate change refugees.[76] The UNFCCC program "was not designed for, and to date has not adequately dealt with, the problem of climate change refugees."[77] Nevertheless, in its ongoing UNFCCC negotiations, the UNFCCC, in its CAF Decision 14(f), included the need for Parties to take into account cli-

---

70. *Id.*
71. g7+ is a voluntary association of conflict-affected countries that are in the transition to the next stages of development and are part of the New Deal for Engagement in Fragile States. For more information, see g7+, *Who We Are*, http://www.g7plus.org/en/who-we-are (last visited Aug. 22, 2016).
72. Rüttinger et al., *supra* note 38, at xi.
73. See *Good Practices in and Lessons Learned From National Adaptation Planning, Submissions From Parties and Nairobi Work Programme Partner Organizations*, UNFCCC, Subsidiary Body for Scientific and Technological Advice, 41st Sess., Agenda Item 3, U.N. Doc. FCCC/SBSTA/2014/MISC.8 (2014).
74. Rüttinger et al., *supra* note 38, at xi and 83.
75. Dennis Tänzler et al., *Climate Change Adaptation and Peace*, 1 WILEY INTERDISC. REV. CLIMATE CHANGE 746, 747 (2010).
76. See, e.g., SUMUDU ATAPATTU, HUMAN RIGHTS APPROACHES TO CLIMATE CHANGE: CHALLENGES AND OPPORTUNITIES 158 (2016); David Hodgkinson et al., *Copenhagen, Climate Change "Refugees" and the Need for a Global Agreement*, 4 PUB. POL'Y 159 (2009).
77. Bonnie Docherty & Tyler Giannini, *Confronting a Rising Tide: A Proposal for a Convention on Climate Change Refugees*, 33 HARV. ENVTL. L. REV. 349, 358 (2009).

mate change-induced displacement and migration.[78] While such inclusion is significant as argued by Christine Gibb and James Ford, thereby placing the UNFCCC as an appropriate forum for the climate migration discourse, "it neither obliges signatories to take action nor specifies how implementation should occur . . . ."[79] According to Dennis Tänzler et al., although completed NAPAs to date have mentioned increasing migration as a possibility, "it is hardly addressed in a systematic way,"[80] which leaves another gap in the guidance for adaptation.

The funding mechanisms of the UNFCCC have been criticized by many for being fiscally and technically ineffective.[81] As the International Institute for Environment and Development (IIED) comments, UNFCCC funding streams "are not adequate to meet the adaptation needs in developing countries."[82] For example, States facing fragility risk situations "receive proportionately less climate financing than other developing countries."[83] In addition, access to climate finance by more fragile developing countries has been problematic. This could be due to the limitations of the internal capacity of those countries to access such funds as well as some financing mechanisms (e.g., Least Developed Countries Fund) being less complex and easier to access than others (e.g., Adaptation Fund).[84]

Criticism is also leveled at the implementation of climate change adaptation efforts. The complexity of climate change-conflict situations in which any adaptation efforts will impact "people's lives, livelihoods, asset base and power dynamics" requires adaptation approaches that apply the "do no harm" principle, which requires efforts to "distribute benefits and resources in a conflict-sensitive way that does not aggravate tensions between

---

78. *Report of the Conference of the Parties on Its Sixteenth Session, Held in Cancun From 29 November to 10 December 2010—Addendum, Part Two: Action Taken by the Conference of the Parties at Its Sixteenth Session, Decisions Adopted by the Conference of the Parties*, UNFCCC, 16th Sess., at 5, U.N. Doc. FCCC/CP/2010/7/Add.1 (2011).

79. Christine Gibb & James Ford, *Should the United Nations Framework Convention on Climate Change Recognize Climate Migrants?*, 7 ENVTL. RES. LETTERS 045601 (2012), http://iopscience.iop.org/article/10.1088/1748-9326/7/4/045601/pdf.

80. Tänzler et al., *supra* note 75, at 747.

81. *See, e.g.*, MARK GRASSO, JUSTICE IN FUNDING ADAPTATION UNDER THE INTERNATIONAL CLIMATE CHANGE REGIME 74 (2010); Ilona Miller et al., *Making Good the Loss: An Assessment of the Loss and Damage Mechanism Under the UNFCCC Process, in* THREATENED ISLAND NATIONS: LEGAL IMPLICATIONS OF RISING SEAS AND A CHANGING CLIMATE 464 (Michael B. Gerrard & Gregory E. Wannier eds., 2013).

82. *Supporting Adaptation to Climate Change: What Role for Official Development Assistance?*, INT'L INST. ENV'T & DEV., Nov. 14, 2008, http://www.iied.org/supporting-adaptation-climate-change-what-role-for-official-development-assistance.

83. Rüttinger et al., *supra* note 38, at 85. *See also* SMITA NAKHOODA, ET AL., CLIMATE FINANCE: IS IT MAKING A DIFFERENCE?, OVERSEAS DEVELOPMENT INSTITUTE REPORT 11 (2014).

84. Rüttinger et al., *supra* note 38, at xi, 85.

communities."[85] Unfortunately, in this regard, "there is limited guidance on how to 'conflict-proof' climate adaptation programmes."[86] There is, however, some evidence of progress in relation to NAPAs, with 45 NAPAs submitted to the UNFCCC by the end of 2010 (21 plans from States with a high risk of destabilization and 19 from States with increased risk of destabilization).[87] Nevertheless, Tänzler et al. caution that integration of adaptation measures can be superficial.[88] In order to ensure a more comprehensive "conflict-proof" climate adaptation approach, "[a] more systematic, integrated approach is needed to meaningfully incorporate existing conflict dynamics—as well as overarching socio-political and economic conditions—into the design of adaptation measures."[89]

As the impacts of climate change could constitute threats to international peace and security, and given the deficiencies in the UNFCCC's adaptation programs, the UNFCCC may not be the best forum to address climate adaptation related to security and armed conflict. Some scholars have argued that environmental protection can be derived from a broader interpretation of the United Nations Charter provisions—including climate change-related threats to peace and security.[90] The United Nations Security Council (UNSC), which has the primary responsibility for international peace and security,[91] appears reluctant to take a direct role in this matter at present. As Shirley V. Scott notes, "[t]here is as yet no consensus on whether the Security Council could or should be proactive in respect of climate change or, if so, of what its contribution to the global efforts might best consist."[92] In fact, both the UNSC and the United Nations General Assembly (UNGA) continue to reaffirm the UNFCCC as the "key instrument for addressing climate change."[93]

The UNFCCC continues to move forward and evolve as evidenced by the historic Paris Agreement adopted by States in December 2015.[94] The

---

85. *Id.* at xii.
86. *Id.*
87. Tänzler et al., *supra* note 75, at 9.
88. *Id.*
89. *Id.*
90. *See* Voigt, *supra* note 23, at 298; Shirley V. Scott, *Implications of Climate Change for the UN Security Council: Mapping the Range of Potential Policy Responses*, 91 INT'L AFF. 1317, 1333 (2015).
91. U.N. Charter ch. VII.
92. Scott, *supra* note 90, at 1333.
93. *See, e.g., Security Council, in Statement, Says "Contextual Information" on Possible Security Implications of Climate Change Important When Climate Impacts Drive Conflict*, U.N. Security Council, 6587th mtg., U.N. Doc. SC/10332 (2011); G.A. Res. 63/281, U.N. GAOR, 63rd Sess., U.N. Doc. A/RES/63/281 (2009).
94. *Paris Agreement, supra* note 61.

key outcomes from the Agreement and accompanying COP21's[95] decision include limiting global temperature rise to well below 2°C, binding commitments by States to make "nationally determined contributions" (NDCs) with regular reports on their progress, reaffirming the binding obligations of developed nations under the UNFCCC to support the efforts of developing countries, extending the current goal of mobilizing $100 billion per year, and incorporating a mechanism to address "loss and damage" resulting from climate change (though explicitly precluding liability and compensation).[96] In addition, the Paris Agreement places just as much importance on adaptation as it does mitigation,[97] establishing "a global goal to significantly strengthen adaptation to climate change through support and international cooperation."[98] However, it makes no specific mention of adaptation to climate change in relation to security and conflict. The Agreement is now open for signature[99] and how these commitments are turned into tangible action remains to be seen.

Even though the UNFCCC has taken a step in the right direction by focusing on adaptation issues as equally important to address as mitigation, there are gaps in the UNFCCC's present adaptation policies, particularly in relation to the vicious cycle of climate change, vulnerability, and conflict, i.e., a lack of more specific guidance on conflict-proof climate adaptation.

III. Climate Change-related Armed Conflict Through a Climate Justice Lens

Having discussed the limitations of the existing climate change regulatory framework, this section explores approaching climate change-related threats to international peace and security through a climate justice approach. Climate justice, with its multifaceted dimensions of equitable development, human rights, and environmental justice, and its overarching aim to promote more equitable and fair allocation of climate change impact burdens on society, provides a more holistic approach in seeking to meet the challenges of climate change-related conflict. Part A of this section, therefore,

---

95. *Report of the Conference of the Parties, Adoption of the Paris Agreement*, UNFCCC Conference of the Parties, 21st Sess., U.N. Doc. FCCC/CP/2015/10/Add.1 (2016), http://unfccc.int/resource/docs/2015/cop21/eng/10a01.pdf.

96. United Nations Climate Change Newsroom, *Historic Paris Agreement on Climate Change: 195 Nations Set Path to Keep Temperature Rise Well Below 2 Degrees Celsius*, http://newsroom.unfccc.int/unfccc-newsroom/finale-cop21/ (last visited Aug. 22, 2016).

97. *See Paris Agreement, supra* note 61, at art. 7.

98. United Nations Climate Change Newsroom, *supra* note 96. *See also Paris Agreement, supra* note 94.

99. UNFCCC, *Opening for Signature and High-level Signature Ceremony Convened by the UN Secretary-General*, http://unfccc.int/paris_agreement/items/9511.php (last visited Aug. 22, 2016).

provides a brief overview of the concept of climate justice and Part B explores the applicability of climate justice considerations to climate change-related armed conflict.

A. Climate Justice: A Brief Overview

The complexities of climate change-related conflict show that merely attempting to reduce GHG emissions, while crucial, is not enough. Although the UNFCCC framework has in recent years given equal priority to climate adaptation, the complexity of climate change-related conflict in countries with situations of fragility showcase the gaps in this area. The challenges associated with climate change-related conflict illustrate the need for a more holistic approach to tackling adaptation to climate change impacts. Therefore, climate justice[100] considerations may have a role to play in fashioning solutions to these challenges.

The Mary Robinson Foundation has formulated the Principles of Climate Justice, which include principles such as respect and protect human rights; support the right to development; share benefits and burdens equitably; ensure that decisions on climate change are participatory, transparent, and accountable; highlight gender equality and equity; harness the transformative power of education for climate stewardship; and use effective partnerships to secure climate justice.[101] These are principles that could assist societies or nations vulnerable to the adverse impacts of climate change to adapt.

As Jamieson aptly notes, "[c]limate justice is not a single dimension of justice."[102] This is to be expected as the unequal costs and burdens of anthropogenic climate change cannot be answered one dimensionally. Climate justice is thus an integration of principles focusing on the unequal burden of climate change impacts on the most vulnerable and seeks to safeguard their rights, particularly by promoting more equitable and fair allocation of such burdens at the local, national, and international levels. As Ayelet Banai states, "[c]limate justice connotes the normative, social scientific, and policy debates concerned with equitable distribution of these burdens and costs."[103]

---

100. For more detailed analysis on climate justice, see, e.g., Jouni Paavola & W. Neil Adger, Justice and Adaptation to Climate Change, Working Paper 23, at 1 (Tyndall Centre for Climate Change Research 2002); Chukwemerije Okereke, *Climate Justice and the International Regime*, 1 WIREs Climate Change 462 (2010).

101. Mary Robinson Foundation-Climate Justice, *Principles of Climate Justice*, http://www.mrfcj.org/principles-of-climate-justice/ (last visited Aug. 22, 2016).

102. Dale Jamieson, *Two Cheers for Climate Justice*, 82 Soc. Res. 791, 793 (2015).

103. Ayelet Banai, *Sovereignty Over Natural Resources and Its Implications for Climate Justice*, 7 WIREs Climate Change 238 (2016) (internal citations omitted).

In essence, climate justice is used to refer to distributive considerations associated with climate change consequences and response measures to it.

According to James Goodman, "climate justice responds to the intensifying crises generated by global warming, but also poses, in a double-sided way, the possibilities that the crisis generates."[104] This encapsulates the issues thrown up by climate change-conflict and provides a guiding framework through which to respond to the consequences of climate change. Jouni Paavola and W. Neil Adger argue that the discourse within the UNFCCC ignores many justice concerns, including questions such as "how do adaptive responses impact differentially on individuals and social groups? Do adaptation strategies alleviate or reinforce uneven distributions of power between and within social groups?"[105] Chukwemerije Okereke argues that "[i]n the climate debate, justice concern is rooted in the immense differences in countries' historical and projected contributions to global greenhouse gas emissions, their vulnerability to climate change, and their ability to bear the costs of mitigating or adapting to climate change."[106] What applies in the context of climate change-conflict discussed here would be justice in terms of climate adaptation, such as conflict-proof climate adaptation and bearing the costs of such adaptation.

B.   Applying Climate Justice Principles to Climate Change and Armed Conflict

While the UNFCCC taking on adaptation is admirable and necessary,[107] it cannot in its entirety appropriately address the complex adaptation challenges that climate change-related armed conflict presents. A holistic climate justice approach may be a more suitable solution in addressing such challenges. This subsection, therefore, argues that climate justice considerations could contribute to filling the gaps found in the UNFCCC's adaptation policies.

For example, climate vulnerability assessments under the UNFCCC adaptation activities may not appreciate the full account of a fragile State's position.[108] At present, climate vulnerability assessments within the UNFCCC framework lack significant discussion on crucial climate change-associated social and political consequences, drivers of fragility, or transboundary

---

104. James Goodman, *From Global Justice to Climate Justice? Justice Ecologism in an Era of Global Warming,* 31 NEW POL. SCI. 499, 500 (2009).

105. PAAVOLA & ADGER, *supra* note 100, at 2.

106. Okereke, *supra* note 100, at 464.

107. For more information on the UNFCCC's work on adaptation, see UNFCCC, *Adaptation Overview, supra* note 64.

108. Rüttinger et al., *supra* note 38, at 81.

issues.[109] Both case studies above have demonstrated the complexity of such underlying variable factors in contributing to climate change-related conflict. Climate justice concerns—from recognizing the variation of adaptive responses necessary for different social groups, nations, and regions as well as differences in the impact of such adaptive responses, to ensuring that assessments are participatory, transparent, and accountable—could be included to address the various issues that face developing, more vulnerable countries and produce more focused climate vulnerability assessments. More robust assessments, which include the identification of existing or potential climate change hotspots, could contribute to better early warning policies for preventing or mitigating climate change-conflict scenarios.

Climate change-related conflict in certain circumstances not only crosses State boundaries but also highlights the absence of climate justice. In many cases, it is the unequal burden of climate change impacts among the most vulnerable within society that can contribute towards conflict. Recognizing that these issues can in some circumstances intensify the fragility of a societal group, nation, or region, gaps in UNFCCC guidance for adaptation planning must be improved. At present, the UNFCCC's limited guidance on addressing climate migration and transboundary issues, including taking a regional approach to adaptation issues and the development of NAPAs in fragile situations,[110] makes it difficult for States or regions to develop appropriate climate change-conflict resilience. Plans and policies for adapting to the effects of climate change have to respond to the complex realities of climate-conflict situations. This includes incorporating the requirement for regional cooperation in the matter. Therefore, having some form of effective guidance, taking into consideration climate justice concerns, on how to develop and plan for conflict-proof climate adaptation within the UNFCCC framework is preferable.

The ability to bear the costs of climate change adaptation is another root of the climate justice concept. There are differences in the ability of countries to bear the costs of adapting to climate change impacts. While there are funding streams for adaptation under the UNFCCC framework, the discussion above highlights their inadequacies—including being insufficient to meet the needs of developing countries, States most vulnerable to fragility risk situations (including conflict) receiving much less climate financing, and difficulty in accessing some of the climate funds. Taking into account climate

---

109. *Id.*
110. *See, e.g.*, Gibb & Ford, *supra* note 79, at 1; Rüttinger et al., *supra* note 38, at xi; Tänzler et al., *supra* note 75, at 747.

justice concerns, the international community should endeavor to improve this existing reality because, without access to such funding required to implement the necessary climate change impact adaptation policies and programs, developing countries most vulnerable to climate change impacts will be unable to make their adaptation efforts climate-conflict proof.

More effective guidance should also be provided for implementation of NAPAs in practice, particularly in relation to implementing "conflict-proof" climate adaptation programs.[111] The equitable distribution of burdens and costs element of climate justice is particularly relevant at the implementation stage. This is because conflict-sensitive adaptation requires the distribution of "resources and benefits in ways that do not aggravate tensions between communities."[112] This means taking into account existing conflict or vulnerable dynamics, whether social, political, economic, or environmental, at all levels—within a community, State, or region. Guidance on implementation should also strongly encourage cooperation at all levels (local to regional), without which the actual implementation of NAPAs may face unnecessary obstacles. A failure to take all these factors into consideration could mean unsustainable development, exacerbation of existing fragility, and a lack of climate change resilience in vulnerable countries, contributing to potential hotspots for climate change-related conflict.

Conclusion

The impact of climate change transcends boundaries. It is a global issue. While scholarship on the climate change-conflict nexus remains divided, the difficulty of establishing the link between or the impact of climate change-related conflict does not mean there is no need to take action. The case studies have illustrated situations in which climate change impacts exacerbated fragile situations and contributed to conflict. Therefore, it is important not to sideline climate change as a contributing factor to current and future conflicts.

While the UNFCCC, as the primary international legal framework on climate change regulation at present, has taken a step in the right direction by enhancing its focus on adaptation issues, the gaps in its adaptation activities, particularly in relation to the vicious cycle of climate change, vulnerability, and conflict, need improvement. More conflict-sensitive climate vulnerability assessments, specific guidance on conflict-proof climate adaptation, conflict-

---

111. Rüttinger et al., *supra* note 38, at xii.
112. Rüttinger et al., *supra* note 38, at 87. *See also* Tänzler et al., *supra* note 75, at 741.

sensitive implementation of climate adaptation activities, and adequate funding to allow nations to harness the benefits of UNFCCC adaptation activities are needed. This includes the State-centric UNFCCC moving towards encouraging and strengthening regional cooperation to meet the challenges of climate change adaptation. In light of achieving climate justice, the international community must increase its commitment to climate change adaptation to ensure that vulnerable nations facing socioeconomic and political injustices are not pushed into conflict as a result of climate change impacts. In moving forward with the Paris Agreement, the international community should embrace climate-conflict sensitive factors relevant to adaptation.

South Asian Perspectives

Chapter 16

Taking Climate Justice to the Himalayan Heights: A Proposed Adaptive Mountain Governance Framework to Address Climate Change Impacts in the Indian Himalayan Region

Naysa Ahuja

Introduction

Mountain ecosystems cover one quarter of the earth's surface, representing irreplaceable sources of biological and cultural diversity.[1] These areas are havens for natural resource trade and tourism, contributing substantially to a country's gross domestic product (GDP). The ecosystem services of the mountains as carbon sinks and water towers further attach immeasurable value to these landscapes. Yet mountain communities suffer from high vulnerability factors such as poverty, isolation, and hunger, while the fragile ecosystem struggles with environmental degradation, especially from climate change impacts. This situation is exacerbated in developing countries where, due to limited resources and lack of political will, the environmental law discourse failed to address mountain contexts in their long-term governance models. However, mountain-specific governance is slowly becoming an emerging legal trend since the global importance of mountains and mountain communities was first recognized at the Earth Summit in 1992.[2]

Mountain regions throughout the world typically have peculiar environmental, climatic, economic, and social characteristics. These features primarily include geographic isolation, harsh climate, high natural resource dependency, and fragile ecosystems, coupled with political marginalization, weak infrastructure, and limited market access and means of communication. These characteristics have a considerable influence on the way the mountain laws and institutions are shaped to protect the environment and communities. This legal framework further establishes criteria for development and sets environmental priorities in the mountain context, given its political, geographical, and systemic concerns.[3]

Despite the rich biodiversity, high quality of agricultural produce, and valuable traditional knowledge (TK), most of the mountain regions are poor. Mountain people from developing countries form about 13% of the global population.[4] Yet, their limited access to climate-smart technology makes the mountain population extremely vulnerable to climate change impacts. Moreover, policy incoherence and institutional incapacity to adequately address

---

1. ANNIE VILLENEUVE ET AL., MOUNTAINS AND THE LAW: EMERGING TRENDS iii (2002).
2. United Nations Environment Programme (UNEP), *Managing Fragile Ecosystems: Sustainable Mountain Development*, http://www.unep.org/Documents.Multilingual/Default.asp?DocumentID=52&Article ID=61(last visited Aug. 23, 2016).
3. CAPRI, Publications: CIFOR's new series of legal studies (Apr. 11, 2016), http://capri.cgiar. org/2016/04/11/publications-cifors-new-series-of-legal-studies/?utm_source=feedburner&utm_ medium=email&utm_campaign=Feed%3A+ifpri-info+%28IFPRI.INFO%29.
4. Aruna Dutt, *Fund Launched to Help Mountain People Face Climate Change Threat*, INTER PRESS SERVICE, May 11, 2016, http://www.ipsnews.net/2016/05/fund-launched-to-help-mountain-people-face-climate-change-threat/.

mountain governance issues in the climate change era is a major source of climate injustice that mountain communities encounter. Mountain region legislation seeks to address these mountain-specific concerns, and countries have adopted a similar governance approach to these areas. However, it is only now that the climate-mountain nexus is being acknowledged at the policy level. With the immediacy of climate change threats and different levels of adaptive capacities, mountain States have taken different approaches to introduce effective adaptation and mitigation strategies.

To ensure sustainable development of mountains, the legal principles and policy measures are devised to enable mountain dwellers to live respectfully with their cultural identity intact and to find livelihood opportunities in their native place, without compromising their standard of living compared to other regions.[5] However, this governance framework in developing mountain countries often becomes a "tangled web of norms and rules" within which the institutions struggle to fulfill their respective roles, including governance of a unique ecosystem.[6] This is partly because most countries have conveniently extended the scope of national environmental laws and policies to the mountain regions without conducting any scientific and socioeconomic place-based needs assessment. This practice has failed to address the existing inequalities regarding opportunities and access between mountain-dwelling and lowland communities. It has further failed to appreciate the economic interdependence between mountains and lowland, to the detriment of mountain ecology and culture.[7] Therefore, an environmental governance mechanism sensitive to climate change impacts in the mountains can bring coherence between development and conservation goals only if the social, economic, and environmental policies are customized according to the needs and conditions of the region in an integrated manner. In response to climate change impacts, it is equally crucial for the mountain regions to have an adaptation governance framework that is flexible, responsive, and informed by both science and local traditions.

The ecological and economic relevance of the Indian Himalayan Region (IHR) with its geographical range of 5.37 lakh km^2 (0.537 million km^2) is incontestable.[8] The Himalayas are the youngest and highest mountain range

---

5. *Explanatory Memorandum—CG(10)9—Part II—The European Charter for Mountains*, Cong. of Local & Regional Auth., 10th Sess. (2003), https://wcd.coe.int/ViewDoc.jsp?p=&id=893235&Site=DC&direct=true.
6. *Id.*
7. Villeneuve et al., *supra* note 1, at 22.
8. Government of India, National Mission for Sustaining the Himalayan Ecosystem (NMSHE) 5 (2016), http://knowledgeportal-nmshe.in/Pdf/NMSHE%20brochure.pdf.

in the world.[9] Nine of the 10 highest peaks on the planet are in the Himalayas.[10] Apart from its vastness, it is the life source of major river systems and houses rich biodiversity including about 1,740 medicinal plants that support a large population of countries like India, Nepal, Bangladesh, China, Bhutan, and Pakistan.[11] A large portion of hydropower is generated in the IHR and supplied to downstream states. Sprawling over several international borders, the Himalayas are the watchtowers of the Indian subcontinent where strategic military bases are established and maintained through a strong network of road infrastructure.

Due to the unprecedented growth of development projects such as large-scale construction along with irresponsible tourism practices, the IHR has suffered a loss in biodiversity and has endured severe climate change impacts. A recent example is the flash floods in the state of Uttarakhand, which were a result of irrational exploitation of mountain resources, unabated tourism, and unexpected rainfall patterns.[12] In a region as vast as the IHR, there is a need for an integrated law and policy framework on adaptive environmental governance to address such threats from increasing anthropogenic pressures, climate change, and related environmental disasters.

To date, sustainable mountain development (SMD)[13] has received limited international and national attention in the larger environmental protection discourse. Very few attempts have been made to promote consensus building among the mountain countries to collectively protect the mountain ranges and to tackle environmental concerns that go beyond the national boundaries, such as climate change. A global agreement does not yet exist for the protection of mountain ecosystems and communities. Consequently, mountain countries—especially the developing ones—find themselves in a weaker position in the international climate negotiations. This governance gap has implications for political priorities of India because there is no holistic national-level environmental policy on the Himalayas in India. The gov-

9.   *Id.*
10. *Id.*
11. *Id.*
12. Shishir Prashant, *Combination of Many Factors Led to Uttarakhand floods*, Bus. Standard, Nov. 12, 2013, http://www.business-standard.com/article/current-affairs/combination-of-many-factors-led-to-uttarakhand-floods-113111201285_1.html.
13. "Sustainable mountain development" is a term that was coined in 1997 during the third session of the Commission on Sustainable Development and the 19th special session of the United Nations General Assembly. The term was the key subject of Chapter 13 of Agenda 21, which highlights the importance of mountains as an essential part of the global ecosystem and how mountain ecosystems are undergoing environmental degradation, threatening the dependence of the world population on its resources. It is reflected in Paragraph 33, Goal 15 of the 2030 Agenda on Sustainable Development. *See* United Nations Department of Economic and Social Affairs, *Mountains*, https://sustainabledevelopment.un.org/topics/mountains(last visited Aug. 23, 2016).

ernment of India had been more focused on industrial and economic growth after independence in 1947, which has created a perception of the mountain areas as resources to be exploited, and not as an essential part of the ecosystem necessary to ensure balance in nature. In the absence of this core understanding, weak interagency relationships, and lack of financial resources to deal with cross-cutting issues like climate change, implementing programs in an integrated manner is a daunting challenge.[14]

This chapter addresses the application of climate change adaptation strategies to key sectors of the IHR, including agriculture, water, forest, tourism, infrastructure, and energy. In the IHR context, the cultural and ecological interface cannot be ignored by policymakers in the sustainability discourse.[15] The Himalayan culture and its TK based on the available resources and the climatic conditions must be taken into account to support environmental stewardship and local adaptation efforts by mountain communities in a cross-cutting governance framework.[16] Efforts to develop IHR-specific governance, including mountain-specific policy, institutions, and financial resources, have recently become more of a focus in India and will be discussed in the chapter.

This chapter argues that mountain vulnerabilities have not been addressed holistically on the international legal map, and that has impacted the way national environmental and climate policy on the IHR is evolving. Part I discusses the significance and status of the IHR as a mountain ecosystem, highlighting how its unique features from a climate science standpoint make it a crucial region to address climate-related inequalities. Part II describes the key components of mountain governance and scrutinizes the climate change readiness of the IHR in the larger sustainable mountain governance discourse. Part III illustrates examples of good mountain governance practices for climate adaptation from Hindu Kush Himalayan (HKH) countries, IHR states, and community practices to emphasize the importance of regional knowledge sharing platforms. Part IV identifies policy gaps that contribute to climate injustices in the governance of the IHR. It further proposes policy recommendations for developing a dynamic and integrated environmental policy framework on IHR that empowers communities to have legal pro-

14. GOVERNMENT OF NEPAL NATIONAL PLANNING COMMISSION, CLIMATE CHANGE BUDGET CODE: APPLICATION REVIEW (2013), https://www.unpei.org/sites/default/files/e_library_documents/Nepal_Climate_Change_Budget_Code_Application_Review_2013.pdf.
15. INDIAN INSTITUTE OF ADVANCED STUDY, ENVIRONMENTAL GOVERNANCE IN THE CONTEXT OF SUSTAINABLE DEVELOPMENT IN INDIA: THE CASE OF MOUNTAIN ECOSYSTEMS 3 (2012), http://www.kas.de/wf/doc/kas_31785-1522-1-30.pdf?121030081537.
16. *Id.* at 4.

tection and adaptive capacities for bearing the disproportionate burden of climate change impacts.

I.   The Himalayan Context and Climate Change Adaptation

The IHR covers 16.2% of India's total geographical area, most of which is dotted with snow-clad peaks, towering glaciers, dense forests, and meandering perennial rivers.[17] Approximately 4% of the Indian population (46,961,740 as per Census 2011) lives in the 10 mountain states and the IHR experienced 17.3% decadal growth in population from 2001–2011, which is continuing to grow as development reaches these remote mountain regions.[18]Nevertheless, the population density in the IHR is thin and sparsely distributed, with the exception of the key hill towns.[19]

The unparalleled and unsustainable development in the IHR and increased anthropogenic pressures (especially tourism) due to better road connections has led to haphazard construction, encroachment over forestland, loss of biodiversity, and other climate-related risks such as the drying up of mountain streams. The recent examples of flash floods in Ladakh,[20] Uttarakhand,[21] and Jammu and Kashmir[22] reveal how unprepared this region is to withstand unsustainable human pressure and climate change impacts. The consequences of such pressure are evident in water resources,forest ecosystems, and the agricultural sector. There is a pressing need for effective environmental governance in the IHR, which would seek to develop climate adaptation measures for the Himalayan ecosystems and build adaptive capacities of the mountain dwellers to tackle distinct climate change impacts. Adaptation involves how communities adjust to the changing climate and reduce their vulnerabilities and, therefore, the involvement of local communities is essential.[23] To date, the need for an integrated regulatory framework for the IHR

17.   ENVIS Centre on Himalayan Ecology, *The Himalaya (Abode of Snow): The Highest Mountain Region in the World*, http://gbpihedenvis.nic.in/indian_him_reg.htm (last visited Aug. 23, 2016).

18.   ENVIS Centre on Himalayan Ecology, *FAQ Indian Himalayan Region*, http://gbpihedenvis.nic.in/PDFs/FAQ/Indian_Himalayan.pdf (last visited Aug. 23, 2016).

19.   *Id.* (181 per/km² as per Census 2011).

20.   *Was the Leh Disaster Man-made?*, Ndtv.com, Aug. 20, 2010, http://www.ndtv.com/india-news/was-the-leh-disaster-man-made-428069.

21.   *India Floods: More Than 50,700 People "Presumed Dead,"* BBC, July 15, 2013, http://www.bbc.com/news/world-asia-india-23282347.

22.   *Jammu and Kashmir Floods Killed 44 People, Injured 25 Others, Say State Govt*, Firstpost, Apr. 9, 2015, http://www.firstpost.com/india/jammu-kashmir-floods-killed-44-people-injured-25-others-says-state-govt-2189975.html.

23.   Neil Bird et al., The Climate Public Expenditure and Institutional Review (CPEIR): A Methodology to Review Climate Policy, Institutions and Expenditure (2012), https://www.

has been discussed, but the government has yet to formulate such a framework. The states coming under the IHR have their own legislation for the protection of the Himalayan region from climate change impacts; however, these laws are failing to comply with their objectives and the key principles of good governance.

The IHR has a rich cultural heritage that is defined by its environment. Its natural resources are the primary source of livelihood for the local communities. These communities not only extract and use the resources, but also give back to the environment through their environmentally sensitive indigenous practices. Despite the differences in resource management methods, the IHR states and their communities, along with the private sector, share a common region and climate change threats of varying intensity. Therefore, any legal and policy framework must take this commonality into consideration. To ensure effective governance of these common resources, the process must recognize and engage all of the stakeholders and institutions that influence the environment, locally as well as globally.[24] Also, the adaptive capacities of each of the IHR stakeholders must be assessed within the regional landscape. This landscape governance[25] approach is recommended to meet the goal of inclusive, just, and sustainable mountain development.

The entire Himalayan range witnesses natural disasters such as landslides, flash floods, and earthquakes. According to the climate change projections by the Intergovernmental Panel on Climate Change (IPCC), these natural disasters will only increase in intensity and frequency. The aim of resilient and adaptive Himalayan governance is to better equip the local bodies and communities to tackle or reduce the disastrous consequences over time.[26] Thus, continued climate change adaptation is an intrinsic objective of sustainable Himalayan development.

An important objective of an environmental governance framework is to ensure climate justice by capacity-building (especially adaptive capacity) and training of the communities on the science of climate change. Furthermore, outreach to communities and local agencies to sustain adaptation efforts beyond projects is also critical. "Barefoot science" needs to be introduced in

---

cbd.int/financial/climatechange/g-cpeirmethodology-undp.pdf[hereinafter Nepal CPEIR Report].

24. *See* UNEP, Environmental Governance (n.d.), http://unep.org/pdf/brochures/Environmental-Governance.pdf.

25. Landscape governance in a multifunctional ecosystem intricately maps and ties together the key institutional arrangements, procedures, and policy instruments along with local value system to meet the interests of multiple actors with respect to food, livelihood, and conservation. Raffaela Kozar et al., Toward Viable Landscape Governance Systems: What Works? (2014), http://www.cifor.org/publications/pdf_files/Papers/PSunderland1401.pdf.

26. G.B. Pant Institute of Himalayan Environment and Development, Action Plan for Himalaya 21 (1992), http://gbpihed.gov.in/PDF/Publication/Action%20Plan%20for%20Himalaya.pdf.

a systematic manner in which communities are trained to conduct scientific research, such as water quality testing. Before developing adaptive capacities of the institutions and communities, a pre-piloting assessment may be conducted. Finally, communication of all the complex climate science and information about its repercussions on the day-to-day lives of the mountain dwellers needs to be contextualized for the general public. It is essential to earn community acceptance for the new adaptation technology along with their traditional practices to ensure the information and policies are actualized on the ground. Overall, any possible solution should consider general principles of sustainable development, the precautionary principle, integrated management, decentralized governance, gender and equity, and respect for traditional or customary practices.[27]

There are several issues blocking implementation of holistic and robust environmental governance in the IHR. For proper implementation of an integrated climate change legal and policy framework, problems regarding "policy fragmentation" and "institutional barriers" should be addressed as a first step. Socioeconomic and environmental conditions are rapidly changing in the IHR and within the State as a whole; therefore, policy directed to Himalayan development must be mindful of these changes and be regularly assessed. Strengthening the institutional coordination and cumulative assessment of integrated projects from a climate adaptation perspective is required.

Data collection is one of the most challenging and vital tasks of environmental governance in a region where oral culture has been prevalent. It is difficult to develop a common policy in a region with culture, climatic conditions, land, and flora and fauna so diverse that all the relevant data must be mapped and analyzed for identifying common concerns and replicable measures. With the looming climate risks, only a proper vulnerability assessment (VA) report along with gap analysis activity from the data gathered (including scientific evidence) would feed directly into informed policymaking.

It is especially challenging to establish a one-size-fits-all environmental governance policy for such a vast region, particularly since the ecosystem, landscape, and community practices in the northwest and northeast Himalayas are dissimilar. Even if such an integrated climate policy framework is prepared, translating it into specific state laws would be difficult. In fact, the

---

27.   Ms. Ahuja has been an active contributor and rule of law advisor at the national and regional consultations of the Himalayan Sustainable Development Forum (HSDF) organized by the Swiss Agency for Development and Cooperation (SDC), and the Himalayan Climate Change Adaptation Programme (HICAP). She has been working with Himalayan communities on climate change issues since 2010. Much of the background information described in this chapter is based on her field observations from this experience.

existing pilot or model approaches on climate change adaptation introduced in one IHR state may not always be replicable in others. Perhaps a guidance framework, offering place-based adaptation approaches for western and eastern Himalayan regions, but with an integrated focus, would be appropriate.

The shortcomings of a project-based approach also support the arguments in favor of integrated IHR climate policy. The controlled pilot models do not sustain themselves beyond the period of the project. This is due to lack of coordination and capacity-building among the various departments responsible for implementing development and conservation objectives. Disregard for traditional practices and nonrecognition of community efforts in environmental protection is another concern that contributes to climate-induced socioeconomic inequalities.

Himalayan communities are dependent on agriculture, fruit growing, and animal husbandry. Agri-food industries from the IHR are the backbone of economic development in the region and are particularly vulnerable to climate change.[28] However, a reliable financial security net for small farmers, such as protection against climatic vagaries and financial support to agricultural adaptation measures, is missing in the economic policies in IHR. Even disaster management policy does not have a special focus to protect slope or terraced farmlands from permanent damage. Improper understanding of climate change and its impacts on the mountain resources and local livelihoods due to inadequate awareness amongst decisionmakers is a major reason for this unfortunate reality.

Other issues to be considered in IHR governance include ecosystem-based land use planning, cost-effective adaptation research, awareness and capacity-building, access to alternative resources or adaptation technologies, payment for ecosystem services, regular policy response assessment, and defined institutional support at different levels. There is a need to redefine IHR development goals and develop effective implementation mechanisms for attracting climate finance to support local adaptation efforts.

II. Indian Himalayan Region Environmental Governance

For proper management of natural resources from climate change impacts, well-directed policies and procedures must be in place to guide the communities, institutions, and other nongovernmental entities that are involved. Good

---

28. *Agriculture and Adapting to Climate Change in Himalayan Mountains of India*, CLIMATE HIMALAYA, July 6, 2012 (noting a 30–50% reduction in agricultural productivity in the mountains), http://chimalaya. org/2012/07/06/agriculture-and-adapting-to-climate-change-in-himalayan-mountains-of-india/.

environmental governance must ensure cooperation among key stakeholders, including government, local communities, businesses, and nongovernmental organizations (NGOs) to achieve two core outcomes: socioeconomic development and natural resource conservation. Governance mechanisms must also promote the rule of law by ensuring access to information, public participation, and justice.[29] However, in the mountain context, the unique social, geographical, and cultural realities also need to be addressed. Many existing IHR state laws were not enacted with a holistic understanding of climate change impacts on the lives of mountain people. Therefore, the current IHR policy gaps must be addressed by revisiting legal texts from a climate science perspective (top-down) and a mountain community perspective (bottom-up). Adaptation is by its nature a locally driven and conceptualized activity. The IHR policy can implement principles to empower local actors in mountain governance initiatives.

With respect to the general framework of mountain environmental governance, soft law instruments have been crucial in building consensus through a norm-creating process and have demonstrated potential to translate into hard law at the national level.[30] The most significant instrument that concerns mountain ecosystem and people is Chapter 13, Agenda 21 (Managing Fragile Ecosystems: Sustainable Mountain Development), which is a policy tool rather than a global agreement.[31] This instrument was followed by the Commission on Sustainable Development report in 2001 in which the economic status of mountain regions was recognized as "unacceptably low."[32] The World Summit on Sustainable Development in 2002 launched the International Partnership for Sustainable Development in Mountain Regions (Mountain Partnership), a multi-stakeholder platform on intersectoral concerns on SMD. The importance of mountains as sensitive indicators of climate change was first globally recognized in 2010.[33] A United Nations resolution explicitly declared that SMD is a key component of meeting Millennium Development Goals (MDGs) in many countries and, thus, should be part of intergovernmental and interministerial discussions on the United Nations Framework Convention on Climate Change (UNFCCC).[34]

29.   UNEP, *Rio Declaration on Environment and Development,* http://www.unep.org/documents.multilingual/default.asp?documentid=78&articleid=1163(last visited Aug. 23, 2016).
30.   VILLENEUVE ET AL., *supra* note 1, at 8.
31.   United Nations Earth Summit: *United Nations Conference on Environment & Development, Rio de Janerio, Brazil, 3 to 4 June 1992,* U.N. Sustainable Development, Agenda 21, Ch. 13 (1992).
32.   VILLENEUVE ET AL., *supra* note 1, at 9.
33.   *Sustainable Mountain Development,* G.A. Res. 205, U.N GAOR, 64th Sess., Agenda Item 53(h), para. 3, U.N. Doc. A/RES/64/205 (2010).
34.   *Id.* para. 4.

Thereafter, "The Future We Want" (outcome of the Rio+20 Summit) also highlighted the benefits that are derived from the mountains.[35] The Paris Agreement of 2015, however, did not even mention mountain ecosystems in its text. Apart from these global interventions on mountain ecosystems, some regional agreements such as the Alpine Convention (1991) and Carpathian Convention (2003) also contributed to the literature of SMD.

Mountains cross national borders quite often. It is therefore important to develop international understanding and cooperation in a formal legal manner.[36] However, in reality, mountain measures on conservation and development take place at a local level "within the state borders through national legislation."[37] Therefore, the IHR calls for a unique regulatory process to protect and sustainably manage its environment in perpetuity. The Food and Agriculture Organization of the United Nations (FAO) has identified four essential pillars to design a unique mountain governance framework. These need to be traced in the IHR context to identify potential gaps and opportunities to promote climate justice in Himalayan communities. These include: (a) mountain delimitation, (b) mountain legal framework, (c) mountain institutional framework, and (d) mountain financial mechanism, in addition to mountain socioeconomic development.[38]

A.   Mountain Delimitation

For effective implementation of any law, it is necessary to define the scope of its applicability.[39] Defining "mountain" is an important exercise for legislators at the national level to demarcate the coverage and reach of the laws.[40] However, it is also important to avoid over-defining the term.[41] With such range of mountain diversity within IHR, it is virtually impossible to have a fully inclusive definition of mountain. In practice, legislators consider various factors to determine what is "mountain" for the purpose of governance.[42] The geophysical elements include altitude (hypsometric criterion), topography, climate, and vegetation. Other factors are more anthropogenic in nature

35. *The Future We Want*, G.A. Res. 288, U.N GAOR, 66th Sess., U.N. Doc. A/RES/66/288 (2012), https://sustainabledevelopment.un.org/futurewewant.html.
36. VILLENEUVE ET AL., *supra* note 1, at 11.
37. *Id.*
38. *Id.* at 12.
39. *Id.* at 13.
40. *Id.*
41. *Id.*
42. *Id.*

such as food security, land use practices, culture, migration trends, and high-land-lowland interactions.[43]

The Himalayan range is not defined in any legal instrument of India. This is the case primarily because there are disagreements regarding the definition of what constitutes Himalayas due to internal diversity, a siloed regulatory approach, and political clashes on the Himalayan border.[44] IHR is divided into three regulatory zones: Sivaliks (lower Himalaya), trans-Himalaya, and higher Himalaya, covering about 95 districts in 10 states and hill regions of two states.[45] The Indian part of the Himalayas extends between latitudes 26°20' and 35°40'N, and between longitudes 74°50' and 95°40'E.[46] The ecological and cultural diversity in the IHR changes at every altitude, which shapes the local resource management mechanisms and cultural interaction with the changing climate in the region. Therefore, it has been difficult to extend the scope of mountain law to the entire Himalayan range within the country. To date, the administrative definition of IHR has been used. Policymakers have suggested that the administrative criteria (states/districts/blocks) may be replaced by functional criteria, where ecological units such as watershed-based integrated natural resource planning and implementation can prove more effective to address climate inequalities within the IHR state.[47] This is because the impact of climate change varies within a district itself while each watershed area as a functional ecological unit has unique interaction with climate change and surrounding communities. Thus, it can potentially offer requisite information to design place-based climate change adaptation measures in the overall environmental governance.

B.   Mountain Legal Framework

As long as the mountain laws are drafted to meet the particular needs of the mountain people and keep in mind the environmental conditions of the mountain area they cover, they will be effective governance tools.[48] What needs to be understood is that these mountains and the communities living in them are interdependent. Moreover, the communities living in the Himalayas are very poor and would not be able to afford even their basic needs if

---

43.   *Id.*
44.   *See* Indian Institute of Advanced Study, Environmental Governance in the Context of Sustainable Development in India: The Case of Mountain Ecosystems, *supra* note 15.
45.   ENVIS Centre on Himalayan Ecology, *FAQ Indian Himalayan Region*, *supra* note 18.
46.   *Id.*
47.   G.B. Pant Institute of Himalayan Environment and Development, Action Plan for Himalaya, *supra* note 26, at 26.
48.   Villeneuve et al., *supra* note 1, at 13.

IHR biodiversity is lost. Thus, a uniform set of rules and policies needs to be formulated, which not only checks the ongoing harm to the environment, but also encourages the interaction between the local communities and the governments of the concerned states. In addition, there is a need to develop laws that govern the industries and developmental projects in the Himalayan region.

The distinct Himalayan ecosystem demands a regulatory process and associated mechanisms and institutions that allow socioeconomic development of the Himalayan communities, continued security from climatic and border threats, and availability of ecosystem services. Despite this knowledge, there is no formal national-level law or policy in India that governs sustainable Himalayan development, unlike the coastal zone management laws and policies.[49] Initially, it was lack of knowledge on mountain ecosystems and later it was the lack of political will or integrity among the Himalayan states that no unified national policy statement was drafted on Himalayan ecosystem management. The interventions so far have been instructional, including guidelines and action plans that have no legally binding effect.

India has ample constitutional guarantees to ensure protection of its ecological systems. However, the Ministry of Environment, Forests, and Climate Change (MoEF&CC) had a more sectoral rather than regional or topographical focus for formulating national policies on management of natural resources such as forests, water, wildlife, and biological diversity. Each of the 12 IHR states' sectoral laws and policies are designed to cater to their unique topography and culture. Unfortunately, those laws are doing little to address climate change concerns. Consequently, the MoEF&CC and the respective state governments have issued various guidelines, policies, and action plans for better governance of IHR. Policies on climate change and ecosystem services are the latest additions to the IHR state policy framework, with some states incorporating climate justice considerations of the upstream and downstream populations into these policies.

In the wake of the Earth Summit in 1992,[50] MoEF&CC released its National Conservation Strategy and Policy Statement on Environment and Development (1992), which recognized the need for an Institute for Himalayan Environment and Development to enhance efforts to protect mountain

---

49. Integrated Coastal Zone Management Project, *Coastal Zone Management Laws and Policies, Coastal Regulation Management Notifications 2008 and 2011*, http://www.iczmpwb.org/main/czm_laws.php (last visited Aug. 23, 2016); *see also* R.R. Krishnamurthy et al., *Managing the Indian Coast in the Face of Disasters & Climate Change: A Review and Analysis of India's Coastal Zone Management Policies*, 18 J. Coastal Conservation 657 (2014), http://link.springer.com/article/10.1007/s11852-014-0339-7.
50. UNEP, *Managing Fragile Ecosystems: Sustainable Mountain Development*, *supra* note 2.

ecosystems from ecological degradation.[51] Thereafter, the G.B. Pant Institute of Himalayan Environment and Development (GBPIHED) prepared India's first Action Plan for the Himalayas in 1992. This document marked a shift from theory to concrete actions to promote sustainable Himalayan development.[52] Its forward-looking approach recognized the Himalayas as a priority area in India for the first time, and systematically recorded the gaps and constraints in its earlier development planning. It juxtaposed the desirable actions with feasible actions in 10 key sectors of the IHR.[53] However, the instrument did not delve into climate change impacts and the need for building adaptive capacities. By the very geographical and sociological nature of the Himalayas, or any mountain range for that matter, a decentralized form of governance is best suited to effectively manage the environmental concerns at the local level. At the outset, the 1992 Action Plan clarifies the role of government as "catalyst" and that of local communities as "fuel" in mountain management.[54]

India also attempted to develop its first National Policy on Integrated Development of the Himalayas in 1992 through an expert group formulated by the Planning Commission.[55] The report and recommendation of this expert group emphasized creation of special administrative mechanisms to meet the conservation and development goals of the IHR and a policy framework on development of IHR. A national-level apex body, the Himalayan Development Authority (HAD), and the National Himalayan Environment and Development Fund (NHEDF) also were recommended.[56] However, the recommendations were brushed aside until international political pressure on climate change was acutely felt. The National Action Plan on Climate Change (NAPCC), released in June 2008, discusses the existing and future policies as well as programs for effective climate change mitigation and adaptation. Of the eight national missions introduced under NAPCC, one focuses on sustainable Himalayan ecosystems.[57]

---

51. GOVERNMENT OF INDIA, NATIONAL CONSERVATION STRATEGY AND POLICY STATEMENT ON ENVIRONMENT AND DEVELOPMENT 5 (1992).
52. G.B. PANT INSTITUTE OF HIMALAYAN ENVIRONMENT AND DEVELOPMENT, ACTION PLAN FOR HIMALAYA, *supra* note 26, at 4.
53. *Id.* at 7.
54. *Id.* at 10.
55. Planning Commission, Government of India, *Mid-term Appraisal (1997–2002)*, http://planningcommission.nic.in/plans/mta/index.php?state=ap9702cont.htm (last visited Aug. 23, 2016).
56. M.L. DEWAN & PIYOOSH RAUTELA, PEOPLE'S MOVEMENT FOR HIMALAYAN REJUVENATION 242–43 (2d ed. 2001).
57. National missions under NAPCC are the key focus areas that have been identified as critically important themes to ensure the successful implementation and realization of the National Action Plan on Climate Change.

The National Mission for Sustaining the Himalayan Ecosystem (NMSHE) was launched in June 2010, but the action plan did not receive formal approval from the union government (central government) until 2014.[58] The NMSHE focuses on understanding the synergy between the Himalayan ecosystem and climate factors, and on ensuring sustainable development of the IHR. It aims to gather scientific data and develop sustainability measures based on the degree of vulnerability of the region and its population to climate change. The objective is to maintain the ecological and social sanctity of the region and ensure continuity of the Himalayan ecosystem services. For this, it focuses on building ecological resilience and national- and state-level capacities to assess, plan, and implement time-bound action plans for safeguarding Himalayan ecosystem services.[59] The focus on local community involvement and use of traditional resources and local material is the highlight of the NMSHE. NMSHE is the only mission under NAPCC that has a geographic rather than thematic focus.[60] The implementation of other national missions such as sustainable agriculture, promotion of solar energy, protection of watersheds and Himalayan rivers and glaciers, and traditional and indigenous knowledge management is also critically important to this mission.

The NMSHE is an integrated cross-sector mission with a multipronged approach covering the vast geographical region with all its diversity, from a rural and urban development standpoint.[61] Since its launch, six thematic task forces have been developed addressing natural and geological wealth, water, ice, snow (including glaciers), forest resources and plant diversity, microflora and fauna and wildlife, TK systems, and Himalayan agriculture.[62] Each of the task forces has been assigned a nodal coordinating institute and a set of collaborating institutes to fulfil their research objectives. These include academic research institutions, technical and management universities, and state training and research centers. The climate adaptation component is explored in each of the thematic research areas for appropriate policy formulation and action to meet the development needs.[63]

58. Vivek Venkataramani, National Mission for Sustaining the Himalayan Ecosystem ii (2015), http://www.ifmrlead.org/wp-content/uploads/2015/10/NAPCC/5_NMSHE%20Brief_CDF_IFM-RLEAD.pdf.

59. Himalayas Climate Change Portal, *NMSHE: National Mission for Sustaining the Himalayan Ecosystem*, http://knowledgeportal-nmshe.in/NMSHE.aspx (last visited Aug. 31, 2016).

60. Ministry of Science and Technology, Government of India, National Mission for Sustaining the Himalayan Ecosystem (NMSHE) (2016), http://knowledgeportal-nmshe.in/Pdf/NMSHE%20brochure.pdf.

61. Himalayas Climate Change Portal, *supra* note 59.

62. *Id.* at 7.

63. *Id.* at 11.

One of the primary objectives of the NMSHE is capacity-building. At one level, it facilitates capacity development of sector specialists and human resources.[64] At the state level, it facilitates capacity-building of institutions to develop coherent adaptation action plans and to implement the tasks effectively.[65] A pilot multilevel training program for improving adaptation planning and implementation capacities has also been developed for the state of Himachal Pradesh under NMSHE facilitation.[66] The modules of the training program range from basic understanding of climate change issues, interpreting of climate data, using climate tools to assess impacts and vulnerabilities, identifying adaptation options to reduce climate risks, developing a monitoring and evaluation framework, integrating adaptation measures into existing schemes and programs, and supporting the design of adaptation actions at the local levels where projects are implemented.[67]

Even though the action plans are being planned and implemented in a time-bound manner, the governance component of the NMSHE is essential to create a conducive policy environment. This forms the basis for achieving climate-resilient sustainable development.[68] Governance for Sustaining Himalayan Ecosystems (G-SHE) is a working document that for the first time gathered key findings from the scattered literature and practices on IHR to provide a set of guidelines and recommended practices to manage the increasing stress on Himalayan ecosystems.[69] These guidelines were formulated to fulfil the objectives in the NMSHE, NAPCC, and the National Environment Policy of 2006, with a focus on the IHR.

C.   Mountain Institutional Framework

The structural mechanism through which the mountain laws are implemented is a crucial aspect of environmental governance in any mountain country. The factors that influence the institutional structure with respect to mountain law are country-specific, such as the nature of the administrative system and the financial and socioeconomic conditions.[70] Gover-

---

64.   *Id.* at 14.
65.   *Id.*
66.   *Id.*
67.   *Id.* at 14–15. Other activities undertaken by the NMSHE include strengthening State Climate Change Cells in IHR; international and regional collaborations; and setting up the Himalayan Sustainable Development Forum (HSDF).
68.   *Id.* at 16.
69.   Press Release, Ministry of Environment and Forests, Government of India, India Releases Guidelines for Sustaining the Himalayan Ecosystem (Sept. 29, 2009), http://envfor.nic.in/sites/default/files/G-SHE_press_0.pdf.
70.   VILLENEUVE ET AL., *supra* note 1, at 14.

nance is more complicated at the international borders where political will and the power relationship between the border-sharing countries defines the final institutional arrangement for a mountain range. Based on these factors, the national mountain institutions are either developed as ad hoc bodies to meet specific requirements or the existing institutions can be stretched to govern certain overlapping sectors in the mountains.[71] The specialized mountain institutions can be seen as the primary government body to understand specific features and to meet specific demands such as researching, advising, and managing mountain-related governance tasks for the ministry.[72]

MoEF&CC is the national ministry that deals with environmental governance of the entire territory of India, whereas the Department of Science and Technology (DST), Ministry of Science and Technology, deals with climate science-related matters. DST has established the Himalayas Climate Change Portal, an initiative under the NMSHE that aims to enhance the scientific understanding of climate change, its impacts, and potential adaptation measures needed to protect the IHR. The Ministry works in coordination with Indian Himalayan states, the Planning Commission, and MoEF&CC.

Established in 1988, GBPIHED is an autonomous nodal agency of MoEF&CC that seeks "to advance scientific knowledge, evolve integrated management strategies, demonstrate their efficacy for conservation of natural resources, and ensure environmentally sound development in the entire IHR."[73] It is also responsible for creating linkages among different institutions working on varied aspects of mountain development and protection. Its major thematic areas of work are environmental governance and policy, socioeconomic development, climate change, capacity-building, and ecosystem services. GBPIHED is also secretariat of the Himalayan Sustainable Development Forum (HSDF), a platform for multi-stakeholder dialogue and knowledge exchange.[74] However, the institute does not have any authority to make policy decisions on IHR. It follows a multidisciplinary and landscape approach in its research and development programs including training, education, and awareness building.[75] The institute has a decentralized manner of operating through its five regional units in Himachal Pradesh and Uttara-

---

71. *Id.* at 15.
72. *Id.*
73. G.B. Plant National Institute of Himalayan Environment & Sustainable Development, Institute Profile (2009), http://gbpihed.gov.in/PDF/Publication/Institute%20Profile.pdf.
74. *Id.*
75. *Id.*

khand in the northwest Himalayas, two in Arunachal Pradesh and Sikkim in the Northeast, and one unit in MoEF&CC.[76]

Apart from mountain-specific government bodies, the role of specialized NGOs is increasingly becoming important to an inclusive lawmaking process or formulation of national strategy or implementation of actions and plans as it understands the local needs.[77] Many NGOs in India work on Himalayan issues ranging from waste management to endangered species protection to developing organic and resilient agricultural practices. Ideally, NGOs in the IHR should focus on eliminating reasons that lead to out-migration of mountain dwellers, especially threatened livelihoods of farmers and forest-dependent communities.[78] The gender transformative approach (GTA)[79] to livelihood generation can be another effective means to mitigate climate-induced gender inequalities by creating alternative livelihoods training that improves the socioeconomic status of women.

The existing sectoral departments in each of the IHR states are responsible for meeting the mountain-specific mandate within their state boundaries. Accordingly, the district-level committees carry out their duties to address the sociocultural and ecological needs of the immediate region. The village-level sectoral committees such as Biodiversity Management Committees, Joint Forest Management Committees, and Watershed Management Committees play important regulatory roles. Some of these local bodies are statutory, whereas others are traditional village bodies that play a fundamental role in contributing to natural resource management and implementation of adaptation programs in the IHR. Furthermore, Climate Change Cells have been established in each state of India, including IHR states, to specifically implement mitigation and adaptation programs. The Prime Minister's Council on Climate Change, an 18-member climate advisory team with the prime minister as its chairperson, was also established on June 5, 2007, but it was inactive for an extended period. Recently reconstituted, the Council aims to provide a coordinated response through interministerial consultations as well as oversee the formulation of national-level action plans related to climate

---

76.   *Id.* (four regional units are established in the IHR States with one in MoEF&CC, New Delhi, as the Mountain Division).

77.   *Id.* at 15.

78.   VILLENEUVE ET AL., *supra* note 1, at 15.

79.   "Gender transformative approaches (GTA) are programs and interventions that create opportunities for individuals to actively challenge gender norms, promote positions of social and political influence for women in communities, and address power inequities between persons of different genders." HEALTH COMMUNICATION CAPACITY COLLABORATIVE, GENDER TRANSFORMATIVE APPROACHES: AN HC3 RESEARCH PRIMER (n.d.), http://www.healthcommcapacity.org/wp-content/uploads/2014/08/Gender-Transformative-Approaches-An-HC3-Research-Primer.pdf.

change assessment, mitigation, and adaptation.[80] There is no special agenda for IHR within the Council. Moreover, the minister of rural development and minister of tribal affairs are not part of the Council. This omission can be seen as neglect of rural mountain dwellers of IHR in formulating national action plans.

The strong institutional presence of the International Centre for Integrated Mountain Development (ICIMOD) is also relevant. This regional cooperation framework for knowledge sharing among the eight regional Member countries of the HKH aims to prepare the communities and local bodies to respond to climate change impacts.[81] One of the objectives of the NMSHE is to partner with ICIMOD through DST in helping local governments and communities build climate change awareness and adapt accordingly while addressing social and ecological relations.[82]

D.   Mountain Financial Mechanism

Economic development is crucial for any country, but it holds special relevance to mountainous regions because of the unique development challenges that they face.[83] Economic growth in these areas is particularly tricky in the context of climate change adaptation, which needs investment to develop resilience and adaptive capacities of the people. Low investment per unit of area in the IHR is an oft-repeated factor responsible for the existing gaps in development planning.[84] Other factors include investment without assessing the needs and priorities of the Himalayan people based on their distinct culture and ecology, and isolated development efforts in one sector without appreciating its interconnectedness with others.[85] This limitation of financial and manpower resources requires national, regional, and international financial support for the Himalayan countries to support their mitigation and adaptation efforts.

There are two ways to design a national financial mechanism for IHR: one is to establish a special mountain fund,[86] such as NHEDF, as was suggested

80.   *See* Meena Menon, *PM's Climate Change Council Recast*, THE HINDU, Nov. 6, 2014, http://www.thehindu.com/sci-tech/energy-and-environment/govt-reconstitutes-pms-council-on-climate-change/article6567187.ece.

81.   ICIMOD, *About ICIMOD*, http://www.icimod.org/?q=abt (last visited Aug. 23, 2016).

82.   NMSHE, *Himalayas Climate Change Portal, Partnership With ICIMOD on Regional Cooperation in Himalayan Ecosystem*, http://knowledgeportal-nmshe.in/programme_details.aspx?C=0D16CF1B-4333-4C12-BD01-1E9F9EF79574 (last visited Aug. 23, 2016).

83.   VILLENEUVE ET AL., *supra* note 1, at 18.

84.   ACTION PLAN FOR HIMALAYA 1992, HIMAVIKAS OCCASIONAL PUBLICATION No. 2, at 27 (1992).

85.   *Id.*

86.   VILLENEUVE ET AL., *supra* note 1, at 18.

by the Planning Commission's expert group for accelerating the implementation of national Himalayan policy; the second is to create incentives for economic practices, including sustainable forest management, organic farming, and ecotourism.[87] The domestic mountain fund can receive resources in the form of revenues from exploitation of local resources and channel it towards local adaptation activities. Moreover, the Green Climate Fund is a source of multilateral funding from developed countries to support climate adaptation efforts in the IHR.[88] The newly launched Mountain Facility by the FAO is another exemplary funding mechanism that focuses on building local economic and adaptive capacities of the mountain people to manage their natural resources for food security.[89]

India currently spends more than 2.6% of its GDP on climate change adaptation in the agriculture, water, forests, and public health sectors, among others.[90] Funding is a priority for achieving emission reduction targets and for implementation of climate adaptation measures in India. Therefore, the Climate Change Financial Unit has been established within the Department of Economic Affairs, Ministry of Finance, as an institutional response to climate finance.[91] Unlike the coastal zone infrastructure or solar energy contexts, the climate finance discussion does not find a fertile policy environment for investment in building climate resilience in the IHR. This is due to an absence of a well-defined and integrated Himalayan policy at the national level, which, if complemented by national climate policy, can successfully receive funds from domestic and international sources. Climate finance strategies need to be developed to ensure equitable allocation of climate finance for protecting fragile Himalayan ecosystems.[92] The current fragmented climate finance scenario needs systematic mapping of stakeholders (national, subnational, public, and private), socio-ecological vulnerabilities, and adaptation financing opportunities, along with coordination efforts. Financial attention is also critically needed for evaluation of existing climate change adaptation responses in the region based on sector-specific vulnerability assessments.

87. *Id.*
88. *India Sets Up Pivotal Climate Change Financing Unit*, CLIMATE HIMALAYA, Aug. 9, 2012 (estimating that additional investment will be approximately $200–210 billion by 2030 for climate change adaptation), http://chimalaya.org/2012/08/09/india-sets-up-pivotal-climate-change-financing-unit/.
89. Dutt, *supra* note 4.
90. CLIMATE HIMALAYA, *supra* note 88.
91. *Id.*
92. VYOMA JHA, THE COORDINATION OF CLIMATE FINANCE IN INDIA 2 (Centre for Policy Research 2014), https://www.odi.org/sites/odi.org.uk/files/odi-assets/publications-opinion-files/9329.pdf.

An ideal investment in the IHR should focus on developing livelihood-based and gender-transformative adaptation strategies; strengthening disaster preparedness and risk reduction, knowledge exchange, and management; and promoting cross-border collaboration.[93] Financial aid must strengthen the local-level institutions to exercise the local wisdom and capacity to influence decisions.[94] This support can lead to increased income and better risk management capacity for both men and women in the IHR, and ultimately result in a more informed State Action Plan on climate change.

III.   Good Models of Himalayan Management for Effective Climate Adaptation

The IHR is part of the vast HKH region that crosses many international borders, covering countries from Afghanistan (west) to Myanmar (east).[95] It consists of eight countries connected by two mountain ranges—the Hindu Kush and the Himalayas. By virtue of geophysical linkage, these countries share common socioeconomic and ecological features that face similar climate change threats to varying degrees. Some of the major climate-related threats to HKH countries include drying watersheds and springs, melting glaciers, glacial lake outburst floods (GLOF), flash floods, forest fires, soil erosion, landslides, and unpredictable monsoons. Similar threats are managed within each IHR state by the concerned state and local governments based on their available resources, traditional practices, and socioeconomic priorities. Considering these shared concerns, there is an opportunity for exchange of conservation and climate adaptation practices in the region.

A.   International Practices

Much remains to be learned about the Himalayas at a scientific level; therefore, international and regional cooperation comparable to that involved in the Alpine Convention or Carpathian Convention would be useful. Though the general features of mountain ecosystems are similar in each of the HKH countries, there has been no attempt to develop a regional Himalayan agreement. In fact, Nepal and Bhutan fall within the scope of the IHR, yet the regional mountain governance on the borders has not been formalized. One

---

93.   Raising the Voice of the Mountains at UNFCCC COP20, ICIMOD, Dec. 11, 2014, http://www.icimod.org/?q=16034.
94.   INDIAN INSTITUTE OF ADVANCED STUDY, ENVIRONMENTAL GOVERNANCE IN THE CONTEXT OF SUSTAINABLE DEVELOPMENT IN INDIA: THE CASE OF MOUNTAIN ECOSYSTEMS, *supra* note 15, at 7.
95.   ICIMOD, *Hindu Kush Himalayan Region*, http://www.icimod.org/?q=1137 (last visited Aug. 23, 2016).

reason is the lack of political will among the developing countries. India seeks to bridge this knowledge gap on the Himalayas by nurturing international collaboration through the Indo-Swiss bilateral cooperation program called Indian Himalayas Climate Adaptation Programme (IHCAP).[96] The program seeks to promote understanding of the science of climate change and the Himalayas, particularly on glaciology, and facilitate need-based adaptation responses.[97]

ICIMOD's contribution to strengthening regional cooperation and building cross-border collaboration for the HKH countries is laudable. The Kailash Sacred Landscape Conservation and Development Initiative (KSLCDI) is an exemplary institutional attempt of ICIMOD to develop transboundary collaboration between India, Nepal, and China to protect the multicultural, ecologically significant, and fragile Himalayan landscape through participatory processes.[98] The highlight of the program is to develop long-term conservation strategies and action plans for the ecosystem while promoting livelihood-based resilience for communities without harming the sociocultural network of local people with the habitat.[99]

Most of the countries in the Himalayan belt are developing economies or economies in transition. It is necessary for these countries to continue on their path to development; however, their climate vulnerabilities make them choose a low-carbon economy path, focusing on building climate resilient government and communities. As a result of international support, each HKH country has been taking measures—legal, institutional, and financial—to promote climate adaptation in their respective development agendas. Some of these measures are discussed below to identify best practices for the IHR to replicate.

I.   Nepal's Climate Change Budget Code and Local Adaptation Plan

Climate change is an emerging policy theme in Nepal; however, meeting the diverse interests of each sector is a difficult task at the national level.[100] In order to map and address climate impacts and opportunities, Nepal has designed a National Adaptation Programme of Action (NAPA) based on a low-carbon

96. MINISTRY OF SCIENCE AND TECHNOLOGY, GOVERNMENT OF INDIA, NATIONAL MISSION FOR SUSTAINING THE HIMALAYAN ECOSYSTEM (NMSHE), *supra* note 60 (describing the partnership for capacity-building and knowledge sharing between India's Department of Science and Technology and the SDC).

97. *Id.*

98. ICIMOD, *Kailash Sacred Landscape Initiative*, http://www.icimod.org/?q=9457 (last visited Aug. 23, 2016).

99. *Id.*

100. NEPAL CPEIR REPORT, *supra* note 23, at 6.

climate-resilient development pathway.[101] The program seeks to identify and address the immediate multi-sectoral adaptation needs of the country at the multi-governance level.[102] Nepal also has established a Climate Change Knowledge Centre under NAPA,[103] in addition to a national-level Climate Change Policy and Climate Change Budget Code. Since translating climate policies into action requires adequate financing and robust institutional arrangements, Nepal underwent a comprehensive climate public expenditure and institutional review (CPEIR).[104] The analysis helped determine whether the national budget is sufficient to build capacities for institutions and whether it dovetails with broader proposed reforms within the public sector.[105]

Nepal's Climate Change Budget Code assists in prioritizing climate-related objectives and tracks public expenditure on relevant ministries and sectors to build a green economy.[106] It covers a multi-governance approach with a special focus on local-level bodies.[107] The Climate Budget Code, introduced in the annual budget of Fiscal Year 2012/2013, has been officially endorsed and has become an integral part of the national budget of Fiscal Year 2013/2014.[108] The Code compelled the ministries to identify the need for climate activities in their programs. Eleven ministries of Nepal now share one climate budget under the national budget announced by the Ministry of Finance using the climate budget codes developed for all climate activities under the public sector in a transparent manner.[109]

Apart from the above, the National Framework for Local Adaptation Plan of Action (LAPA) gives considerable importance to the decentralized approach to strengthen local-level adaptation systems, such as community forest management.[110] LAPA earmarks 80% of the funds to local adaptation programs and practices. This program is backed by the Climate Change

---

101. United Nations Capital Development Fund (UNCDF), Nepal LoCAL, http://www.local-uncdf.org/nepal.html.
102. GOVERNMENT OF NEPAL NATIONAL PLANNING COMMISSION, CLIMATE CHANGE BUDGET CODE: DOCUMENTING THE NATIONAL PROCESS OF ARRIVING AT MULTI-SECTORAL CONSENSUS, CRITERIA, AND METHOD (2012), http://www.npc.gov.np/images/download/Climate-change-budget-code.pdf.
103. UNCDF, Nepal LoCAL, *supra* note 101. This policy also appears under article 7 of Nepal's Climate Change Policy, 2011, https://ldcclimate.files.wordpress.com/2012/05/climate-change-policy-eng-nep.pdf.
104. NEPAL CPEIR REPORT, *supra* note 23, at 6.
105. *Id.*
106. GOVERNMENT OF NEPAL NATIONAL PLANNING COMMISSION, CLIMATE CHANGE BUDGET CODE, *supra* note 102.
107. *Id.*
108. *Id.* at 20 (noting that the total climate change budget allocated for FY 2013/2014 is 53,482,516,000, which is 10.3% of the total budget and 3.1% of the total GDP).
109. *Id.* at 21 (noting that the Ministry of Urban Development occupies the highest share, at 21.52% of the total climate budget, followed by the Ministry of Agriculture with 20.85%).
110. UNCDF, Nepal LoCAL, *supra* note 101 (Capital Development Fund).

Policy of 2011, which envisions access to financial resources and utilization for community-level program implementation.[111] In fact, LAPA was initiated with the help of district-level and village-level development committees. These local adaptation plans are developed with greater participation of the communities whose adaptive capacities need to be strengthened against climate change. Such initiatives of adaptive governance systems from Nepal have successfully qualified for United Nations Capital Development Fund (UNCDF) Local Climate Adaptive Living Facility (LoCAL).[112] Going forward, Nepal plans to establish a Climate Change Fund as envisioned in its climate change policy and to build the capacities of the local agencies to ensure effective climate financial management.

2.   Bhutan's Project-specific Adaptation Targets

Bhutan's commitment to natural resource conservation is evident in the Constitution of the Kingdom of Bhutan, which entrusts the protection of the natural environment and biodiversity from "all forms of ecological degradation" to every citizen.[113] The Constitution mandates the government to ensure that a minimum of 60% of Bhutan's land remain under forest cover "for all time."[114] This goal is also reflected in its climate adaptation program.

Bhutan was one of the first countries to prepare and submit its NAPA to the UNFCCC in 2006 and it implemented the program in 2007.[115] Bhutanese management work on Thorthormi Lake is a highly regarded adaptation model across the world.[116] Interesting aspects of Bhutan's NAPA is that it is a living document that is periodically revised and updated in a transparent manner by the National Environment Commission based on new scientific findings and the VAs conducted.[117] NAPA has a unique approach to ensure adaptation implementation based on urgent and immediate priorities, rather than applying a sectoral approach.[118] Some of the NAPA priority projects in 2006 were: artificial lowering of Thorthormi Lake, weather forecasting system to serve farmers and agriculture, flood protection of downstream indus-

---

111. Nepal Climate Change Policy, 2011, art. 11.3.
112. UNCDF, Nepal LoCAL, *supra* note 101 (describing LoCAL as a United Nations initiative that strengthens the role of local government bodies in building resilience of the local communities through easy access to climate finance for local adaptation planning and budgeting processes).
113. KINGDOM OF BHUTAN CONST. art. 5(1).
114. *Id.* at art. 5(3).
115. ROYAL GOVERNMENT OF BHUTAN, NATIONAL ENVIRONMENT COMMISSION, NAPA: UPDATES OF PROJECTS AND PROFILES 6 (2012) .
116. *Id.*
117. *Id.* at 7.
118. *Id.* at 13.

trial and agricultural areas, GLOF hazard zoning, and community-based forest fire management and prevention.[119]

As a result of this project-specific approach, adaptive management of resources has improved. This successful project has gathered additional partners from government and the private sector (hydropower industry) to co-finance upgrading of the GLOF early warning system.[120] A government notice for GLOF-resilient land use planning, based on the GLOF hazard zoning, has been issued and disseminated to the local authorities.[121] Moreover, lessons learned from the project are being captured and disseminated through the Adaptive Learning Mechanism (ALM) and knowledge sharing with other GLOF-prone areas.[122]

3.　Bangladesh's Climate Adaptation Action Plan and Food Security

Bangladesh is a developing country that is extremely vulnerable to climate change impacts. The fragile coastal and mountain regions of Bangladesh are frequently affected by extreme storm events and natural disasters. The Climate Change Strategy and Action Plan, 2009 is a "10-year program aimed at building the capacity and resilience of the country to meet the challenge of climate change."[123] The Action Plan is a comprehensive document focused on: (1) food security, public health, and livelihood protection of the poorest and most vulnerable; (2) disaster management and risk reduction from floods and cyclones by building climate-resilient communities; (3) improvement of urban infrastructure to adapt to increased extreme events; and (4) capacity-building and institutional strengthening.[124] The government of Bangladesh also established the Climate Change Trust in 2010 to finance projects for implementation of the Climate Change Strategy and Action Plan.[125]

The NAPA on Climate Change in 2005 provides a list of climate change adaptation measures that should be implemented.[126] Some measures call

---

119. *Id.* at 13.
120. *Id.* at 15.
121. *Id.* at 14.
122. *Id.* at 15.
123. Ministry of Environment & Forests, Government of the People's Republic of Bangladesh, Bangladesh Climate Change Strategy and Action Plan 2009 (2009), http://www.climatechangecell.org.bd/Documents/climate_change_strategy2009.pdf.
124. *Id.*
125. Bangladesh Climate Change Trust, *Homepage*, http://www.bcct.gov.bd/index.php/83-home/147-home-2 (last visited Aug. 23, 2016).
126. Ministry of Environment & Forests, Government of the People's Republic of Bangladesh, National Adaptation Programme of Action (NAPA) 22 (2005), http://unfccc.int/resource/docs/napa/ban01.pdf.

for intervention, such as adaptation to agriculture systems in areas prone to flash flooding and enhancing resilience of remote rural communities that face chronic under nutrition.[127] In 2013, FAO implemented an integrated household farming project for building resilience of traditional farming communities in Chittagong Hill Tract (CHT) to tackle food and livelihood insecurity.[128] These communities are highly vulnerable to natural shocks, including pest attacks, flash floods, and landslides.[129] The project provided livelihood diversification for women through horticulture and poultry interventions. With the support of ECHO and the Ministry of Chittagong Hill Tract Affairs, FAO enhanced the capacity of 200 local farmers as community seed providers and conducted a series of training and awareness camps on upland farming practices, fruit and vegetable production, and nutritional awareness to increase income and local resilience of 6,200 men and women.[130]

B. State Practices in the IHR

The IHR is spread across 10 Indian mountain states—Jammu and Kashmir, Himachal Pradesh, Uttarakhand, Arunachal Pradesh, Sikkim, Meghalaya, Mizoram, Nagaland, Manipur, and Tripura—and the hill regions of Assam and West Bengal.[131] With the topographical and cultural diversity within each state, the IHR creates a platform to innovate climate adaptation practices that are unique to a village community, region, or the state itself. Therefore, the environmental governance framework of the IHR must meet the national development agenda on one hand, while maintaining the sovereignty of the Indian Himalayan states to protect and manage their natural resources as per its sociocultural milieu on the other. Each of the 12 IHR states has developed its own State Action Plan on Climate Change (SAPCC) under the mandate of NAPCC. The approved SAPCC of each state designs its own plans, actions, and strategies for key sectors affected by climate change, unique to its socioeconomic, topographical, climatic, and cultural requirement. Some of the SAPCCs are discussed below under a few sectors that are critical to the livelihoods of the Himalayan communities and that need immediate adaptation measures.

---

127. *Id.*
128. FAO, *Achieving Food and Nutrition Security in Remote Areas of Chittagong Hill Tracts*, http://www.fao.org/in-action/achieving-food-and-nutrition-security-in-remote-areas-of-the-chittagong-hill-tracts/en/ (last visited Aug. 23, 2016).
129. *Id.*
130. *Id.*
131. Ministry of Science and Technology, Government of India, National Mission for Sustaining the Himalayan Ecosystem (NMSHE), *supra* note 60, at 17.

I. Forest and Biodiversity Management

The SAPCCs of the IHR states give great significance to the forests and biodiversity in the region. The Himachal Pradesh Climate Change Action Plan in 2012,[132] for instance, focuses on the efforts of the state to reduce the impacts of tourism and changing climate on the forest ecosystem such as deforestation, landslides, land degradation, and desertification. Other noteworthy strategies proposed within the plans include: mapping of available forest resources; conducting REDD+ feasibility studies for carbon sequestration; enhancing groundwater recharge in forest areas; enhancing forest quality using approaches outlined in the National Mission for a Green India; utilizing the National Afforestation Programme and the Compensatory Afforestation Fund Management and Planning Authority; linking protected areas to enable free movement of wildlife; enhancing fire prevention and fire management; preventing human-wildlife conflict; promoting use of renewable energy in fringe villages to decrease dependence on fuelwood from forests; reducing fragmentation of forests; promoting community forestry and participatory forest management; promoting agroforestry with multiple native species in farms and homestead gardens; and restructuring land use policy for *jhum* cultivation and climate proofing of existing forest program in the IHR states using the above-mentioned strategies.

Measures relating to increased livelihood opportunities include using Mahatma Gandhi Rural Employment Guarantee Schemes in afforestation and other forest development activities; developing microenterprises based on non-timber forest products (NTFPs), especially medicinal and aromatic plants and ecotourism ventures protecting traditional ecological knowledge of the local people and recording the same in People's Biodiversity Registers (PBRs); establishing scientific and sustainable harvesting methods for NTFPs; establishing gene banks and seed orchards and developing appropriate techniques for propagation and variety improvement including use of biotechnology; developing and providing good planting material that can be grown commercially by local communities; and developing effective market linkages for promotion of processed/unprocessed NTFPs.

---

132. *See* DEPARTMENT OF ENVIRONMENT, SCIENCE & TECHNOLOGY, GOVERNMENT OF HIMACHAL PRADESH, STATE STRATEGY & ACTION PLAN ON CLIMATE CHANGE (2012), http://www.moef.nic.in/sites/default/files/sapcc/Himachal-Pradesh.pdf [hereinafter HIMACHAL PRADESH SAPCC].

2.   Hill Town Planning and Urbanization

Urbanization and town planning have been recognized as an emerging sector that needs to be emphasized. However, a review of the specific strategies reveals a mixed response. West Bengal has no strategy for town planning. Nagaland, on the other hand, stresses that the guidelines for urban infrastructure underscore the need to develop sustainable urban infrastructure and identifies certain key priorities that need to be addressed.[133] In fact, Nagaland is one of the few states that has gone beyond formulating the strategy and has taken active steps to implement the strategy.[134]

Tripura talks about developing climate-responsible master plans for select cities under the City Development Plan (CDP) and formulating building guidelines with a provision for promoting traditional houses according to different agro-climatic zones, floodplains, and the seismic vulnerability of the state.[135] Though it sounds like a well-devised strategy, the Urban Development Plan of Tripura of 2013/2014 does not address any of the strategies mentioned in the SAPCC.

Sikkim's detailed SAPCC and its implementation plans have proposed collecting, separating, and converting waste to organic fertilizer in the short term, and the possibility of waste-to-energy generation in the long term.[136] Energy-efficient street lighting, stormwater management, and pedestrian-friendly paths are envisioned for the city of Gangtok.

3.   Agriculture and Food Security

Agricultural adaptation needs to receive better policy support from the IHR state governments to disseminate information and to address common local concerns that hamper agricultural productivity such as changes in crop patterns, water stress, natural disasters, and extreme rainfall. Innovative cultural events such as "local seeds exchange festivals" among the local communities

---

133. See GOVERNMENT OF NAGALAND, NAGALAND STATE ACTION PLAN ON CLIMATE CHANGE: ACHIEVING A LOW CARBON DEVELOPMENT TRAJECTORY (2012), http://www.moef.nic.in/sites/default/files/sapcc/Nagaland.pdf.
134. In a notification issued on March 19, 2015, the Urban Development Department stated that in accordance with the decision of the State Executive Committee of the Nagaland State Disaster Management Authority meeting on December 17, 2014, a special task force has been constituted to review the Nagaland Building Bylaws and recommend specific amendments.
135. GOVERNMENT OF TRIPURA, STATE ACTION PLAN ON CLIMATE CHANGE, http://www.moef.nic.in/sites/default/files/sapcc/TRIPURA.pdf [hereinafter TRIPURA SAPCC].
136. GOVERNMENT OF SIKKIM, SIKKIM ACTION PLAN ON CLIMATE CHANGE (2012–2030) (2011), http://www.nicra-icar.in/nicrarevised/images/State%20Action%20Plan/Sikkim-SAPCC.pdf [hereinafter SIKKIM SAPCC].

have been successful in the states of Himachal Pradesh and Uttarakhand.[137] Agricultural adaptation practices such as growing pulses for nitrogen fixation have been accepted by communities to increase the rice production from their fields in Tripura.[138]

Sikkim SAPCC addresses adapting agricultural practices to the changing climate by focusing agricultural research on identifying new climate-resilient crops that benefit from high temperatures and carbon concentrations, and that are not water reliant.[139] It encourages crop diversification to ensure conservation of indigenous plants with new resilient crops.[140] It has defined proactive strategies to study and develop infrastructural support to introduce adaptation strategies in the agriculture and food security sector.

These strategies have been complemented by the Sikkim Organic Farming Policy of 2003 (launched in 2010). The policy introduced the concept of a "bio village" to promote conversion to organic manure and biofertilizers, and to incentivize villages to shift to completely organic farming practices.[141] Furthermore, the principles and practices of the Sikkim Organic Mission of 2010 coincide with those of SAPCC; namely, pest management, nutrient management, disease management, and moisture management. However, there is no mention of climate-resilient technologies or adaptation of agriculture to the changing climate in the policy.

One concern in SAPCCs is the lack of joint climate adaptation and mitigation arrangements at the governance level on the borders of the states. Climate justice in the Himalayas must be ensured through interstate and transboundary consensus building and cooperative action. The NMSHE explicitly admits that state cooperation is valuable to successfully address the policy and institutional gaps in tackling climate change in the IHR.[142] In the spirit of "cooperative federalism," the mission interacts and engages with all IHR states to ensure climate change readiness through strengthening adaptive capacities, robust planning and adaptation action, conducting VAs, and awareness building on climate change.[143] Under the mission, states receive funds and technical assistance for adaptation planning and implementation.[144]

137. Himachal Pradesh SAPCC, *supra* note 132.
138. Tripura SAPCC, *supra* note 135.
139. Sikkim SAPCC, *supra* note 136.
140. *Id.*
141. Sikkim Organic Mission, State Policy on Organic Farming—Government of Sikkim, http://www.rvskvv.net/TaskForce/Organic_farming_policy_sikkim.pdf.
142. Government of India, National Mission for Sustaining the Himalayan Ecosystem 2 (2010), http://www.dst.gov.in/sites/default/files/NMSHE_June_2010.pdf.
143. Ministry of Science and Technology, Government of India, National Mission for Sustaining the Himalayan Ecosystem (NMSHE), *supra* note 60, at 17.
144. *Id.*

C.   Community Practices and Adaptation Mechanisms

The Himalayan region has geophysical features that largely influence the lives and livelihood of mountain communities. These unique features in the Himalayas have shaped traditional "human adaptation mechanisms" for sustainable use of available resources.[145] The five primordial elements (earth, fire, water, air, and sky) are, in fact, complementary to the local people's rituals, cognitive system, religious beliefs, and sacrificial practices in the IHR.[146] Based on their TK and wisdom, many communities have developed rituals and practices to protect their valuable resources through traditional mechanisms. It is therefore pertinent to recognize and validate such community efforts through legal measures. Furthermore, there is a need to integrate the various departmental programs, strategies, and action plans in key Himalayan sectors with community practices.

Some community practices of adapting to the changing climate or developing resilience against climate hazards from the IHR states must be recognized and documented. Some of these practices ensure availability of energy to remote communities while others promise continuous supply of water through artificial glaciers[147] and food security through integrated farming techniques.[148]

In Nagaland, communities are investing in small pico-hydro projects of up to 5 kW to generate power. Such smaller projects are more economical and do not harm the ecosystem. These hydro generators are mostly made of locally available material such as bamboo.[149] The unique aspect of these pico-hydro projects is that they create a sense of ownership of the energy pro-

145. INDIAN INSTITUTE OF ADVANCED STUDY, ENVIRONMENTAL GOVERNANCE IN THE CONTEXT OF SUSTAINABLE DEVELOPMENT IN INDIA: THE CASE OF MOUNTAIN ECOSYSTEMS, *supra* note 15, at 3.
146. *See* B.L. MALLA, WATER RESOURCES AND THEIR MANAGEMENT IN KASHMIR (Indira Gandhi Nat'l Center for the Arts 1998), http://ignca.nic.in/cd_07008.htm.
147. The Ice Stupa, or artificial glacier, is an extraordinary conical structure made from fresh snow and ice or sprinkling of surplus water in the winters near villages. The shape resembles that of a *stupa* (traditional mud structures near monasteries). An average Ice Stupa with a height of 40 m and a radius of 20 m can store about 16 million litres of water to be used during summers. *See* Sonam Wangchuk, *Ice Stupa Artificial Glaciers of Ladakh*, INDIEGOGO, https://www.indiegogo.com/projects/ice-stupa-artificial-glaciers-of-ladakh#/.
148. The traditional agrodiversity system of Sikkim is a common adaptation practice of the native farmers. It is a form of traditional integrated farming techniques in which a combination of crop, plant, and farm animals are placed on one piece of land, creating a mutually symbiotic ecosystem on the farmlands. This practice not only ensures food security and economic returns from high-value medicinal plants and large cardamom plantations, but also offers a range of supporting, provisioning, regulating, and cultural services.
149. JAYANTA KUMAR SARMA, SMALL IS BEAUTIFUL: "HYDROGER" A MEANS OF ENERGY AND SUSTAINABLE DEVELOPMENT 2 (n.d.), http://www.indiawaterportal.org/sites/indiawaterportal.org/files/small_is_beautiful.pdf.

duction process and an incentive among community members to collectively maintain the flow of water and protect its source for uninterrupted power supply.[150] The government of Nagaland has established Nagaland Empowerment of People through Energy Development (NEPeD) and village-level Hydroger Management Committees to institutionalize this sustainable practice and to provide technical assistance on the operation and management of the units.[151]

In Himachal Pradesh, the scarcity of water and rise in temperature due to climate change has led to a reduction in apple production in certain areas. For equitable and mindful use of water resources, a mechanism of payments for "ecosystem services" and a "riparian rights system" have been introduced at the community level. Under this arrangement, communities located on a lower altitude pay those at a higher altitude for not hindering their water supply and to protect the critical watershed areas in their vicinity. This model has been replicated in the city of Palampur in Himachal between a local *panchayat* (village governance body) and an urban civic body as the Palampur Water Governance Initiative.[152]

Flooding of the Brahmaputra River in the eastern Himalayas is a common occurrence during the rainy season, often disrupting the town of Dibrugarh in Assam. However, this flooding at one time was not perceived to be detrimental to people's lives. Traditional wisdom was used to predict the occurrence of these floods, such as the movement of ants or the behavior of the *gagini* locust. Local plantain and bamboo rafts called *bhoor* were rapidly built to escape the floodwaters while loose bamboo matting was used to form a barrier to trap fish in the flood waters.

Himalayan communities hold valuable TK attached to their ecology that has passed orally from one generation to the next. Such time-tested community knowledge needs to be conserved. Traditional practices of local communities, including local architecture, farming techniques, livestock and forest management, and medicinal treatments, must be given due regard in the governance of natural resources since it evolved from the deeper local understanding of their regional ecosystem. In the Vth and VIth Schedule areas under the Indian Constitution,[153] customary and traditional practices have been recognized and such recognition must be leveraged by incorporating traditional environmentally friendly practices into sector-specific laws.

---

150. *Id.* at 1.
151. *Id.*
152. *See Palampur Takes Lead in Water Governance in Himachal*, HimVani.com, Apr. 1, 2011, http://www. himvani.com/news/2011/04/01/palampur-takes-lead-in-water-governance-in-himachal/.
153. India Const. art. 244(1), fifth sched., and arts. 244(2) and 275(1), sixth sched. (1950).

TK on the existence of various natural resources such as NTFPs and their uses is a highly valued asset in these communities. IHR policy must have the requisite safeguards to protect, record, and validate such TK with science in a culturally sensitive manner. In this context, the role of a welfare official with an in-depth understanding of social and traditional sensibilities is pertinent to build community support for better management of their immediate landscape.

IV.   Proposals to Promote Climate Justice in the IHR With Increased Planning, Funding, and Coordination

Environmental governance involves a series of interventions that collectively aim to transform knowledge, decisions, and behaviors of people and institutions related to the environment.[154] Based on the foregoing detailed discussion of the environmental governance of the IHR, this part of the chapter addresses some of the key changes necessary for climate change adaptation governance in the IHR at the regional, state, and local levels.

There is a need to link climate change adaptation to good governance by making it an indicator of good governance. There are policy prescriptions at the government of India and state government levels that suggest that ecosystem-based planning and management should be integrated into Himalayan policies, beginning with the 7th Five Year Plan (1985–1990).[155] However, existing policies, mainly at the state government and municipality or panchayat levels, are not in alignment with these objectives. There are also significant implementation gaps in developing ecosystem resilience even when policies are aligned since the key sectors and government departments do not have tools to make climate-related decisions in an integrated manner.

Integrated policy for the IHR should have a mix of a sectoral approach with cross-cutting themes on governance, finance, and science, and a clustered approach where interdependent sectors and the immediate landscape can be studied together, with regional livelihoods and conservation priorities at its core. The IHR environmental governance policy also must be translated into state laws to ensure that climate change adaptation becomes part of the legislative, executive, and judicial fiber. One implementation pathway could be to enact a specific set of guidelines pertaining to the adaptive environmental governance of IHR, ranging from sector-specific guidelines to the consti-

---

154. INDIAN INSTITUTE OF ADVANCED STUDY, ENVIRONMENTAL GOVERNANCE IN THE CONTEXT OF SUSTAINABLE DEVELOPMENT IN INDIA: THE CASE OF MOUNTAIN ECOSYSTEMS, *supra* note 15, at 1.
155. G.B. PANT INSTITUTE OF HIMALAYAN ENVIRONMENT AND DEVELOPMENT, ACTION PLAN FOR HIMALAYA, *supra* note 26, at 26.

tutional status of different regions, including the Schedule V and VI unique governance context.[156] This could be a touchstone document for all the IHR states to review their environmental laws and policies. Given its statutory backing, unlike G-SHE, the incorporation of its principles could be ascertained through judicial action. Another way of ensuring climate justice in the IHR states is to incorporate the respective SAPCCs in the sector-specific policies to provide statutory backing, and thereafter monitor the implementation of these "action-based policies" in a time-bound manner.

Climate impact assessments should become part of the environmental impact assessment process, particularly in the IHR states, under the Environment Protection Act, given the area's high vulnerability to large development projects. Since all of the IHR states are part of one big transboundary Himalayan ecosystem, site-specific climate impact assessments should include input from the entire IHR prior to approval of any project. This process could contribute to consensus building among the IHR states as one national unit, and empower them to voice the IHR climate change concerns at the international level. Moreover, the procedure for clearance of a project in the IHR should be reviewed to identify potential climate adaptation practices or measures that can be introduced in the implementation of the project. Strengthening the institutional coordination and cumulative assessment of integrated projects from a climate adaptation perspective is essential in the IHR to reduce differential impacts of climate change on the poor mountain population within the Himalayan landscape. Therefore, special focus should be given to strengthening decentralized governance systems and local leadership to ensure holistic resilience building within the entire institutional framework.

For effective governance of the IHR in the climate change adaptation context, it will be important to shift "the environment" from its present "residuary" list status under the Constitution of India to a "concurrent"[157] subject list. This suggestion has also been mentioned in the Twelfth Five Year Plan document's Chapter 7, covering environment, forestry, and wildlife.[158] The main rationale behind this constitutional amendment is to enable the state governments and local authorities to enact and notify the public of their own enforcement laws and rules. The present residual status of the environment has arguably prevented the states from effectively

---

156. Under the Constitution of India, scheduled areas or states have different natural resources governance frameworks in which the community is the key decisionmaker on sustainable use and management of resources.

157. The subject matter of governance upon which both the central and the state governments can legislate.

158. Twelfth Five Year Plan (2012–2017), ch. 7 (particularly paras. 7.1, 7.2, 7.4, 7.5, and 7.6, at 202–03).

enforcing the various environmental laws and from implementing the State Action Plans.

Climate justice principles should be built into the psyche of the various line departments and other implementing agencies. Lack of coordination and depletion of funds among the various departments has often been cited as a recurrent problem in the implementation of development and conservation objectives in India. It is particularly true for the IHR due to difficult terrain and less connectivity during the winter season. Establishing a Climate Change Cell as a statewide, interdepartmental authority for climate change adaptation and mitigation with representation from the departments dealing with land, agriculture, forests, water, energy, meteorology, and finance would improve coordinated action plans. The proposed authority should have a scientific panel and a steering committee including representatives of business, civil society, and academia.

More emphasis should be placed on the use of TK in climate change adaptation planning, including community perceptions of the adaptation strategies. It would also be useful to document climate change-based TK and observations of mountain communities using the PBRs established under the Biological Diversity Act and rules.[159] Therefore, it would be crucial to enact and implement biodiversity rules in all of the IHR states as soon as possible. Lastly, the TK Digital Library at the central level must be linked to the PBRs from the IHR to recognize, evaluate, and track the conservation practices in the IHR.

Implementation of the policy measures will require significant financial and human resources. The central government should develop a long-term investment program for the IHR, commensurate with the contribution of this geographical region to the national GDP, to attract finance from various development schemes at the national and international levels. This can be done through public sector participation and need-based international funding, in addition to the regular budgetary allocation. The central government should also promote self-generating mechanisms on mobilization of resources such as value additions to forest products, market linkages, and tourism. Therefore, the environmental governance policy for the IHR must lay a foundation for generating finance for continuing Himalayan climate research, establishing sustainable mountain-based businesses, and strengthening the environmental governance framework in the region. A stronger financial security net should be provided to small farmers to protect them against climate vagaries. In this regard, expanding the use of weather or

---

159. Rule 22(6), BD Rules.

climate insurance products, such as subsidized rates under the crop insurance schemes, would be a valuable adjustment. Making such schemes and insurance available for the agricultural, energy generation, and other urban infrastructural adaptation programs will ensure involvement of IHR communities in adaptation efforts. The convergence of schemes from various departments at the state and regional levels can be a positive step in sustaining programs in the region. Adequate funding should also be made available to communities to explore climate adaptive strategies and practices at the local level through central- and state-level schemes such as the Mahatma Gandhi National Rural Employment Guarantee Act and through funds available under the Compensatory Afforestation Fund Management and Planning Authority.

The purpose of a climate budget code is underestimated at this stage. There are three reasons why a climate budget code would prove helpful in IHR climate governance: (1) to help prioritize the sectors and consequently the institutions that need additional funding; (2) to establish a procedure to track the finances allocated to the specified ministries; and (3) to allocate a fixed percentage of the overall climate finance at various levels, especially at the microlevel, for implementing pilots. A legal system such as the Nepal Climate Budget Code can be explored to ensure effective use of climate finance and to introduce long-term investment in building community-government-private sector consensus on climate adaptation efforts. Alternatively, the Climate Adaptation Fund may be considered to finance new scientific evidence-based research on different adaptation technologies and to investigate how such technologies improve the livelihoods of various IHR communities.

A joint ecological mechanism of India, China, Nepal, and Bhutan needs to be created. This joint platform is most important to prevent floods and reduce damage. This will lead to the development of joint policy and security mechanisms. There is also a need for an early warning system within the HKH region to prevent loss of life and property. Work to reduce the destructive power of rain needs to be taken up at a larger scale through gaining extensive knowledge about glaciers, lakes, and forests, as well as their sensitivity levels. The safe carrying capacity of hill towns must also be assessed.

Conclusion

After more than two decades of implementation of Chapter 13 of Agenda 21, mountain law and policy at both the international and national levels is in its infancy. There are, however, four lessons from the collective analysis of international, national, and state practices on mountain governance that enrich the IHR climate justice discourse. The first is the realization that the mountain communities are facing disproportionate burdens of climate change impacts on their lives and livelihoods that will gradually affect the lives of those from lowlands. There is also growing awareness that mountain policy, law, and institutions must be cognizant of such disparity to formulate conscious climate-resilient policy measures. The second is the need for a global treaty or regional convention on the Himalayas to negotiate and establish global guidelines for sustainable mountain development through collaboration of governments and other organizations in the absence of any mention of mountain environments in the Paris Agreement. Third, climate change adaptation should become a crucial consideration of IHR governance at the national, state, and local levels. The adaptation policies should be adopted and updated in relation to the ecological realities of time and place. Thus, clearer linkage between science, policy, and practice needs to be established. The fourth is to give climate adaptation policies the force of law to ensure that climate justice is delivered to mountain-dwelling communities.

With intensifying climate-related resource stress, the SAPCCs and state laws should ensure that place-based and locally driven adaptation measures are adopted with meaningful public participation in a time-bound manner. The existing siloed approach of separate policies governing each sector should be replaced by an adaptive, integrated, and cross-sectoral intervention for effective environmental governance, known as the landscape approach. Gender balancing in IHR environmental governance should also be given more attention. Finally, the transformative role of livelihood-based adaptation measures such as ecotourism, organic agriculture, and mountain labels for local products, among others, needs to be emphasized to check poverty, food crises, and out-migration. Given that climate adaptation is a more local practice, identification of sector-related, area-specific vulnerabilities is an imperative policy tool for IHR environmental management. Climate change vulnerability, sensitivity, and adaptive capacities as the pathway to meet climate justice goals should be studied through local interventions supported by climate scenarios. In this way, the resource utilization strategy would be mindful of mountain-specific vulnerabilities and needs as the climate changes.

Chapter 17

Monsoons, Hydropower, and Climate Justice in Pakistan's River Communities

Nadia B. Ahmad and Mushtaq ur Rasool Bilal*

Introduction

Floods from torrential monsoon rains have become a regular phenomenon in Pakistan. During the past 10 years, the country witnessed massive flooding, with the 2010 floods being the most devastating.[1] In order to comprehend the extent of losses caused by the 2010 floods, consider that the 20 million people affected by these floods were more than the entire populations hit by the Indian Ocean tsunami (2004), the Kashmir earthquake (2005), Cyclone Nargis (2008), and the Haiti earthquake (2010) combined based on figures from the United Nations. At the time of the flood, United Nations Secretary-General Ban Ki-moon said, "Make no mistake: this is a global disaster, a global challenge. It is one of the greatest tests of global solidarity in our times."[2]

---

* This chapter has benefited from the feedback of the presenters and participants of the Yale Department of Geology & Geophysics' Tropical Extremes Workshop on High-impact Weather Events in Monsoon Regions, which was jointly sponsored by the Yale Climate & Energy Institute and the Edward J. and Dorothy Clark Kempf Fund at the Yale MacMillan Center. Special thanks to Randall Abate for the invitation to contribute to this volume and to Tatiana Devia, Sacha Dixon, and Dillon Andreassi for their excellent research assistance. Reprint permission granted by Dawn and The News.

1.   *Monsoon 2011: Backlash of the Floods?—History of Pakistan Floods in Detail*, PAKISTAN WEATHER PORTAL, June 13, 2011, http://pakistanweatherportal.com/2011/06/13/monsoon-2011-backlash-of-the-floods-history-of-pakistan-floods-in-detail/.
2.   Press Release, United Nations General Assembly, General Assembly Calls for Strengthened Emergency Relief to Meet Pakistan's Urgent Needs After Massive Destruction Caused by Unprecedented, Devas-

The monsoon flooding has put Pakistan at the front lines of climate change. The country's river communities, coastal areas, and mountainous regions are subject to the dramatic effects of climate change, including droughts, heat waves, sea-level rise, erosion, and flooding. Infrastructure stability, agricultural yield, water and energy supplies, air quality, forestry, ecosystem balance, and public health are at risk because of the deleterious impacts of climate change. These negative consequences of climate change will strike Pakistan first and hardest. Existing conditions of poverty, drought, energy crisis, conflict, and political instability will aggravate the ongoing and future perils of climate change.

Climate change activists throughout the world applauded the outcome in the 2015 *Leghari* case in Pakistan.[3] In this landmark climate change lawsuit, Ashgar Leghari, a farmer in the Rahim Yar Khan District, in Pakistan's South Punjab region, sued the national government for failure to adhere to the actions stated in the 2012 National Climate Policy and Framework.[4] The Lahore High Court ruling, citing both the right to life and the right to human dignity, stated:

> Climate Change is a defining challenge of our time and has led to dramatic alterations in our planet's climate system. For Pakistan, these climatic variations have primarily resulted in heavy floods and droughts, raising serious concerns regarding water and food security. On a legal and constitutional plane this is a clarion call for the protection of fundamental rights of the citizens of Pakistan, in particular, the vulnerable and weak segments of the society who are unable to approach this Court.[5]

More than half of Pakistanis (53%) feel that life has become worse in the past five years, and nearly half of people in Pakistan (44%) feel that changes in the climate and environment are having an impact on their lives now.[6] These climate impacts include "the interrelated effects of increased temperatures, erratic rainfall, increased extreme weather events, and increased pests and mosquitoes."[7] Drawing on the recurring monsoon flooding, the increas-

---

tating Floods, U.N. Doc. GA/10969 (Aug. 19, 2010), http://www.un.org/press/en/2010/ga10969.doc.htm.

3.   Leghari v. Federation of Pakistan, W.P. No. 25501/2015 (Lahore High Court Sept. 14, 2015), http://edigest.elaw.org/sites/default/files/pk.leghari.091415.pdf.

4.   Jessica Wentz, *Lahore High Court Orders Pakistan to Act on Climate Change*, COLUMBIA LAW SCHOOL CLIMATE LAW BLOG, Sept. 26 2015, http://blogs.law.columbia.edu/climatechange/2015/09/26/lahore-high-court-orders-pakistan-to-act-on-climate-change/#sthash.LiJ8Tb4a.dpuf 20.

5.   *Leghari*, W.P. No. 25501/2015.

6.   KHADIJA ZAHEER & ANNA COLOM, PAKISTAN: HOW THE PEOPLE OF PAKISTAN LIVE WITH CLIMATE CHANGE AND WHAT COMMUNICATION CAN DO 4 (2013).

7.   *Id.*

ing threat of climate change, and the *Leghari* case, this chapter assesses the water-energy nexus in Pakistan and examines the climate justice ramifications of land use and urban planning in river communities. The notion of climate justice is used and defined in alternate landscapes, but is mainly deployed to contest the unequal impacts of climate change socially and geographically.[8] Climate justice principles include leaving fossil fuels in the ground, reasserting community control over energy development, relocalizing food production, reducing over-consumption with an emphasis on the global North, respecting indigenous and forest peoples' rights, and recognizing the ecological and climate debt owed to the global South by the societies of the global North necessitating the making of reparations.[9]

With respect to leaving fossil fuels in the ground and asserting community control over energy development, hydroelectricity has been a much sought after option in Pakistan. Hydroelectricity remains the most effective, and in some cases the only, energy source for various remote mountainous areas, rural farmland, and communities located along river banks in Pakistan. In the coming years, strengthening international relations through investment and innovation will be crucial to help improve infrastructure and develop a regional energy corridor of nascent renewable energy technologies, including small-scale hydroelectric power and hydrokinetic energy.

Pakistan is in an extremely precarious position as the country inches closer and closer to the choke point of its twin crises: energy and water. The situation in northern Pakistan is especially uncertain as a result of the heavy monsoon flooding that drenched its Himalayan foothills, valleys, and surrounding terrain on September 3, 2014.[10] According to the World Bank, Pakistan is one of the most water-stressed countries in the world, but at times there is too much water due to intense flooding. The idea of water scarcity itself is critical because it informs the views of policymakers on the urgency with which to address the water crisis. Floods in September 2014 affected 1.9 million people and resulted in more than 400 deaths in Pakistan.[11] The losses to various sectors of the economy undoubtedly ran into billions of dollars.

The dilemma of being a water-stressed country prone to the extreme effects of climate change, such as ongoing flooding, presents tremendous

---

8. Paul Chatterton, David Featherstone & Paul Routledge, *Articulating Climate Justice in Copenhagen: Antagonism, the Commons, and Solidarity*, 45 ANTIPODE 602, 603–06 (2013).

9. *Id.*

10. Munir Ahmed & Nirmala George, *Pakistani Military Diverts Swollen Rivers to Save Cities From Floods That Have Killed Hundreds*, U.S. NEWS & WORLD REP., Sept. 13, 2014, http://www.usnews.com/news/world/articles/2014/09/13/pakistan-diverts-rivers-to-save-cities-from-floods.

11. *See the Flooding in India and Pakistan, From Space*, TIME, Sept. 12, 2014, http://time.com/3341129/satellite-images-show-jammu-kashmir-submerged-underwater-after-floods/.

challenges for land use planning, climate change adaptation, environmental management, and natural resource conservation. According to the Falkenmark Water Stress Indicator, a country or region is "water stressed" if annual water supplies per person per year drop below 1,700 m^3.[12] A 2005 study of Pakistan indicates an available supply of water of little more than 1,000 m^3 per person, which places Pakistan in the high stress category. The overall water availability has decreased from 1,299 m^3 per capita in 1996/1997 to 1,101 m^3 per capita in 2004/2005.[13] This water-stress and flood proneness paradox can be explained with the help of two terms: (1) physical or absolute water scarcity, a condition where available water reserves fall short of meeting human requirements, and (2) economic water scarcity, a situation where a lack of investment in water infrastructure creates water scarcity.[14] While Pakistan has abundant "physical water" as is evident by the floods of the last decade, it is the "economic water" that is becoming increasingly scarce. This is a result of poor water management by successive Pakistani governments combined with such factors as interprovincial discord, lack of awareness toward efficient use of water, maladministration, and the gradual degradation of the existing water infrastructure.

The quest for increased capacity for energy resources and effective water management does not have a single solution. The International Hydropower Association recognizes the problem of hydropower as a clean energy solution, noting that energy and water for sustainable development rely not only on supply choices, but also on the implementation of those choices.[15] Sustainable water management needs to include all stakeholders in a participatory decisionmaking process.[16]

This chapter explores the conflicts between the construction of large dams and climate adaptation, and examines risks such as population displacement, increasing intensity of monsoons, energy access, and energy security. It addresses how environmental planning can help alleviate the social and environmental costs of large dams by considering climate justice concerns. Part I of this chapter discusses the ongoing water-energy crisis in Pakistan and how climate change disrupts existing and future hydroelectricity plans. Part II describes the benefits and drawbacks of a Sino-Pakistan collaboration

---

12. Malin Falkenmark, Jan Lundqvist & Carl Widstrand, *Macro-scale Water Scarcity Requires Micro-scale Approaches: Aspects of Vulnerability in Semi-arid Development*, 13 NAT. RESOURCES F. 258, 267 (1989).

13. GOVERNMENT OF PAKISTAN, OVERALL WATER AVAILABILITY, PAKISTAN STATISTICAL YEAR BOOK (Ministry of Economic Affairs and Statistics, Statistics Division, 2007).

14. Bilal Ibne Rasheed, *Are Big Dams the Solution?*, THE NEWS, Sept. 23, 2012, at 3.

15. INTERNATIONAL HYDROPOWER ASSOCIATION (IHA), THE ROLE OF HYDROPOWER IN SUSTAINABLE DEVELOPMENT, IHA WHITE PAPER 10 (2003).

16. *Id.*

to address energy needs and climate justice considerations. Part III offers recommendations for the climate justice movement to learn from this case study of Pakistan's river communities and the dam-building enterprise.

I. Ongoing Water-Energy Crisis and Trouble With Large Dams

The water-energy crisis that has plagued Pakistan's economy and society at large during the past decade is a corollary of the economic water scarcity in the country. In the absence of viable and sustainable alternative energy sources, Pakistan remains dependent on hydroelectricity to meet its energy requirements. Hydroelectricity is used to meet more than 25% of the total energy requirements of Pakistan (20,000 MW).[17] Since there is no shortage of physical water, the amount of hydroelectricity generated can be increased significantly by building large dams.

The complex interaction between nature and society forms a unique relationship, and dam construction is a strange instance of this complicated and multifarious interaction where social development seeks to overpower natural barriers.[18] But in doing so, dams lead to substantial ecological and climate disruption, negatively impact biodiversity, affect pastoral lands and forests along the stream, disturb communities dependent on these ecosystems, and result in the forced displacement of hundreds of thousands of people, causing irreparable social and cultural losses.[19] Financial corruption, violation of human rights, and deliberate nonadherence to international declarations and agreements concerning the planning and implementation of large dams further compound the situation.[20] However, in underdeveloped nations like Pakistan, large dams remain an unavoidable and necessary, if flawed, development option to deal with the escalating water and energy demands of a rapidly expanding population.[21]

Like Brazil,[22] Pakistan suffers from an overreliance on hydropower as a major single source for electricity generation, which results in greater energy

---

17. Saleem Shaikh & Sughra Tunio, *Pakistan Surges Into Coal-fired Power Plants to Meet Energy Demand*, Thomson Reuters, June 11, 2014, http://news.trust.org//item/20140611093028-fa051/.

18. Kevin Wehr, America's Fight Over Water: The Environmental and Political Effects of Large-scale Water Systems 27 (2004).

19. Ann Danaiya Usher, *Introduction, in* Dams as Aid: A Political Anatomy of Nordic Development Thinking 4 (Ann Danaiya Usher ed., 1997).

20. Thayer Scudder, The Future of Large Dams: Dealing With Social, Environmental, Institutional, and Political Costs 2 (2005).

21. *Id.*

22. World Bank, *Electricity Production From Hydroelectric Sources (% of Total)*, http://data.worldbank.org/indicator/EG.ELC.HYRO.ZS (last visited Aug. 22, 2016). Hydropower refers to electricity that is

insecurity and has climate justice implications.[23] The International Energy Agency explains that "[e]nergy insecurity stems from the welfare impact of either the physical unavailability of energy, or prices that are not competitive or overly volatile."[24] A Greenpeace report notes, "The predominance of hydroelectric power is susceptible to seasonal droughts, which are becoming more frequent and severe due to climate change."[25] The concern for energy security impacts the understanding and interpretation of Article 2 of the United Nations Framework Convention on Climate Change (UNFCCC), which points toward the "stabilization of greenhouse gas concentrations in the atmosphere at a level that would prevent dangerous anthropogenic interference with the climate system."[26] The time frame for climate adaptation measures should allow enough time for "ecosystems to adapt naturally to climate change, to ensure that food production is not threatened and to enable economic development to proceed in a sustainable manner."[27]

Michael Oppenheimer and Annie Petsonk recognize that nonquantitative and nonutilitarian frameworks have been suggested to explore "distributional questions in a way that emphasizes justice, equity, and rights."[28] They see the need for questioning tradeoffs and viewpoint consideration in that analysis.[29] To the extent which large dams can provide greater energy access, limit greenhouse gas (GHG) emissions, and serve the dual purpose of flood control and electrical generation devices requires serious consideration. Environmental planning and water management techniques working in concert as climate adaptation measures can reduce the negative social and environmental risks of large dam construction and use. Even the most sophisticated planning cannot eliminate the climate risks of large dams. The steps outlined in this chapter work only to mitigate the climate risks and work toward greater transparency and accountability to promote climate justice.

---

produced by hydroelectric power plants. *Id.* For the period 2006–2010, Brazil relied on hydropower for 68.6% of its electrical generation, whereas Pakistan relied on hydropower for 31.9% of its electrical generation needs countrywide.

23. Greenpeace, Large Scale Hydro Dams: A False Solution to the Climate Crisis (2014) (on file with authors).

24. International Energy Agency, Energy Security and Climate Policy: Accessing Interactions 12–13 (2007), https://www.iea.org/publications/freepublications/publication/energy_security_climate_policy.pdf.

25. Greenpeace, *supra* note 23.

26. United Nations Framework Convention on Climate Change, May 9, 1992, art. 2, 1771 U.N.T.S. 107, 31 I.L.M. 849, https://unfccc.int/resource/docs/convkp/conveng.pdf.

27. *Id.*

28. Michael Oppenheimer & Annie Petsonk, Article 2 of the UNFCC: Historical Origins, Recent Interpretations 35 (2004), http://citeseerx.ist.psu.edu/viewdoc/download?doi=10.1.1.462.8077&rep=rep1&type=pdf.

29. *Id.*

Civilization requires both water and energy for development. Integrated water resources management (IWRM) is an emerging approach to managing water resources that "promotes the coordinated development and management of water, land and related resources, in order to maximize the resultant economic and social welfare in an equitable manner without compromising the sustainability of vital eco-systems."[30] Energy issues are a critical component of the IWRM approach. An example of the link between water and energy is the increased use of small electric pumps in India and Pakistan for groundwater irrigation.[31] Due to political and economic concerns, farmers received extremely low-priced electricity and have limited incentive to conserve water, which results in the overexploitation of groundwater, long-term environmental degradation, and unsustainable food production.[32] An integrated approach to water and energy management is crucial for sustainability.[33] The IWRM approach is particularly critical in the context of large dams and climate justice.

In late-industrializing countries such as Pakistan, large dams have remained one of the most viable options to retain, store, and conserve available water resources in spite of virtually unanimous opposition to the construction of these projects.[34] In 1984, the World Bank proposed that Pakistan build a dam on the Indus River at Kalabagh, near Mianwali, to meet its future energy requirements.[35] The dam was supposed to be completed by 1989. However, the project was never undertaken because of interprovincial distrust and political manipulation by successive governments. After the 2010 floods, which resulted in huge losses to the country's economy—$49 million in communication infrastructure, $2.5 billion in the water and energy sector, a loss of over 5 million jobs, and 20 million internally displaced people—the then-Prime Minister Yousaf Raza Gilani conceded that the damage could have been averted if there had been a Kalabagh Dam.[36]

The Kalabagh Dam's development has been impeded by a number of factors, including project finance, regional tensions, and center-province disputes. In addition, ethnoregional politics has hurt communication and

---

30. Global Water Partnership, Towards Water Security: A Framework for Action 15 (2000).
31. IHA, *supra* note 15, at 36.
32. *Id.*
33. *Id.*
34. World Bank, The Agricultural Impact of the Kalabagh Dam (as Simulated by the Indus Basin Model Revised) (1987), http://documents.worldbank.org/curated/en/1987/06/15202470/agricultural-impact-kalabagh-dam-simulated-indus-basin-model-revised-vol-1-2-main-report.
35. *Id.*
36. Irfan Ghauri, *Kalabagh Dam: A Lingering Controversy*, Express Trib., Apr. 3, 2011, http://blogs.tribune.com.pk/story/4790/kalabagh-dam-a-lingering-controversy/.

diminished trust among stakeholders in hydropower development projects.[37] Usman Muhammad argues for a need to reactivate the Council of Common Interests (CCI) and improve the functioning of the Indus River System Authority (IRSA) to manage the hydropower conflict in the country.[38] Regarding settlement of disputes over water resources, Pakistan's provincial governments share authority for water resource management with the federal government in their bid for political autonomy. Center-province and interprovincial disputes involving water resources can be resolved through the CCI and through the IRSA.[39] Following the severe drought in southern Pakistan in the latter half of the 1990s, development proponents have been eyeing the construction of the Kalabagh Dam as "a surrogate for a litany of Sindhi grievances against the Punjabi-dominated political, military, and bureaucratic system in Pakistan."[40] The work to heighten water withdrawals and more fully regulate the Indus River system overcorrected the problem, which led to the massive flooding in 2010. The drought in the 1990s followed by the extreme flooding underscore the need to reevaluate the push for more dams for a more comprehensive water management system.[41]

These calls for large dams in Pakistan overlooked the GHG emissions associated with hydroelectricity. A blind insistence on large dams ignores greater climate change risks and the harm to marginalized communities and fragile ecosystems. In terms of direct GHG emissions, Greenpeace reported, "[F]orest areas flooded by reservoirs emit methane in the anaerobic decomposition of trees, vegetation and biomass submerged by the dam during its operation."[42] In other words, "emissions can be as high as in fossil thermal plants—in some cases, matching those of coal plants, as in the Balbina Hydro dam in the Brazilian Amazon."[43] The status quo of constructing and maintaining large dams to satisfy increasing energy demands has a negative impact on GHG emissions. "Although the number greatly varies according to the location and size of the dam, it is clear that tropical and subtropical areas tend to release much more carbon given its characteristics in terms of water temperature, hydrological cycles and biomass stock."[44] Poor and rural

---

37. Usman Muhammad, Hydro Politics and Interprovincial Relations in Pakistan: A Case Study of the Kalabagh Dam Controversy 28–29 (2012) (unpublished master's thesis, Uppsala on Rural Development and Natural Resources Management) (on file with author).
38. Id.
39. Id.
40. Daanish Mustafa, United States Institute for Peace Special Report: Hydropolitics in Pakistan's Indus Basin 2 (2010).
41. Id.
42. Greenpeace, supra note 23.
43. Id.
44. Id.

areas, as well as vulnerable and marginalized communities, are disproportionately affected by large dams and their climate change impacts.

These concerns about the environment and climate change management
impact choices that investors and international financing institutions make
regarding hydroelectricity projects.[45] The Report of the World Commission
on Dams (WCD) altered the perspective of the effect of large dams on the
relationship between human development, environmental protection, and
human rights.[46] The report highlights how large dams disrupt ecological
equilibrium, harm biodiversity irreversibly, and force riparian communities
to relocate permanently.[47] Moreover, the construction of large dams is a process that often involves large-scale financial corruption (of which the Kalabagh Dam project remains a quintessential example), violations of human
rights, and huge cultural losses. However, it would be wrong to assume that
the WCD report opposes large dams per se. The WCD report recognizes
that "governments face very real dilemmas in trying simultaneously to satisfy
urgent needs and advance the realisation of fundamental rights, even if the
goal of fulfilling all people's needs and entitlements is not questioned."[48] The
commission points out that "fulfilling development needs requires respect
for fundamental rights, and not a trade-off between them" and "that an equitable and sustainable approach to development requires that a decision to
build a dam or any other options must not, at the outset, sacrifice the rights
of any citizen or group of affected people."[49]

The construction of large dams to alleviate flooding is counterintuitive
based on the findings of the WCD report. Nonetheless, the government of
Pakistan's solution to flooding woes has been to plan to construct more dams,
but it has lacked the political consensus and financial resources to implement those plans. One of the motivations for dam construction is to control
water for agricultural irrigation. According to the WCD, "[t]he scale and
significance of large dams for irrigation varies significantly from country to
country in terms of the percentage of agricultural land irrigated, and the proportion of the irrigation water supplied from large dams."[50] Pakistan, China,
India, and the United States "account for more than 50% of the world's total

---

45. Ausilio Bauen, *Future Energy Sources and Systems—Acting on Climate Change and Energy Security*, 157 J. POWER SOURCES 893 (2006).
46. WORLD COMMISSION ON DAMS, DAMS AND DEVELOPMENT: A NEW FRAMEWORK FOR DECISION-MAKING, 106–08 (2000).
47. *Id.*
48. *Id.* at 204.
49. *Id.*
50. *Id.* at 13.

irrigated area."[51] In light of agricultural concerns, the farmers' organization, Kisan Board Pakistan (KBP), has urged the government to build new dams to store rainwater because flooding had damaged standing crops in Punjab, Khyber Pakhtunkhwa, Kashmir, and Balochistan.[52] KBP is concerned with the welfare of Pakistan's farming community and looks to introduce new production technologies to increase crop yields, organize forums for farmers at the village level, and represent the group's demands to the government. A KBP official indicated that "heavy rains and winds had affected the sugarcane crop" and would reduce productivity by 33% in 2014.[53] Other officials have pressed leaders within the Pakistan Tehreek-e-Insaf (PTI) (The Pakistan Justice Movement) and Pakistan Awami Tehreek to include the construction of large dams in their agenda with demands addressing water shortages and the acute energy crisis.[54] These officials continued to insist that large dams were the "only solution" to the water-energy crisis.[55] This narrative cannot be applied to the complex case of Pakistan.

With continued delays in dam-building projects (such as the Kalabagh Dam), the construction of illegal dikes by powerful landowners and political elites, the poor administration of provincial irrigation departments, and the absence of an integrated flood management system, devastating floods will continue to occur in the foreseeable future, as evidenced by the 2014 monsoon flooding in Pakistan mentioned earlier. The flooding will be worsened by ongoing and intensified climate change. In essence, the potential social, cultural, and economic impacts of flooding (exacerbated by climate change) must be considered more prominently and thoroughly in water and energy policy decisions. Accessing the social, cultural, and economic costs as well as climate change impacts of the permanent relocation of populations resulting from the construction of large dams, the consequences can be negotiated and brought under positive control if the guidelines enunciated in the WCD report are adhered to. The cost of floods is astronomically high when millions of people are displaced for an indefinite period of time. The construction of large dams, on the other hand, has caused the displacement of approximately 40 to 80 million people worldwide.[56] This problematic situation exemplifies

---

51.   *Id.*
52.   *KBP Urges Govt to Build New Dams*, Pakistan Today, Sept. 7, 2014, http://www.pakistantoday.com. pk/2014/09/07/business/kbp-urges-govt-to-build-new-dams/.
53.   *Id.*
54.   *PTI, PAT Asked to Include Construction of Mega Dams in Their Agenda*, The Nation, Aug. 18, 2014, http://nation.com.pk/business/18-Aug-2014/pti-pat-asked-to-include-construction-of-mega-dams-in-their-agenda.
55.   *Id.*
56.   WCD, *supra* note 46, at 16.

climate change mitigation measures that are required in the short term to address high-impact monsoon flooding. The tension between planning for the future and monsoon preparedness for the present creates unparalleled land use, infrastructure, and energy challenges.

Upendra Baxi argues that the WCD report provides for a range of readings: "[T]he Report is animated by the belief that large dams are, and remain, a necessary evil, and that the task is to lessen that evil through the pragmatic politics of the possible."[57] Baxi argues for a closer reading to more effectively protect the human rights impacted by these projects:

> The Report deserves close reading not only by both policy makers and activists, but also by all those concerned with the theory and practice of human rights. It holds diverse and constructive messages. The activists will find a wealth of facts and features to further legitimize their struggle. Policy makers, too, may find the facts sobering, and, in the end, enthusiasm for large dams will be seen as inhumane. Both constituencies have been provided with high stakes in evolving a new policy framework. Human rights theorists will no doubt remain engaged in the complexity of rights at risk and negotiating rights concerns. Human rights communities, in particular the NGO sector, will find the Report an embarrassment of riches in terms of improvising a whole range of new rights, tactics, and strategies.[58]

One of the major concerns for opponents of large dams is the involuntary displacement of people whose livelihoods are directly dependent on the free flow of a river. Climate change and resulting variations in the pattern of the South Asian monsoons are difficult to predict and even harder to plan for in advance. State-of-the-art general circulation models have difficulty simulating the regional distribution of monsoon rainfall, which in turn makes it challenging to determine how the monsoons will change because of climate change.[59] New climate science research has begun to examine more about processes driving the monsoon, its seasonal cycle, and modes of variability, which could improve climate change prediction models and thereby reduce the uncertainty in projections of future monsoon rainfall.[60] Having such simulation modeling for monsoons will provide a means to adjust human development impacts and plan the construction and maintenance projects for

---

57. Upendra Baxi, *What Happens Next Is Up To You: Human Rights at Risk in Dams and Development*, 16 AM. U. INT'L L. REV. 1507, 1509 (2001).

58. *Id.*

59. Andrew G. Turner & H. Annamalai, *Climate Change and the South Asian Summer Monsoon*, 2 NATURE CLIMATE CHANGE 587 (2012).

60. *Id.*

large dams. Avoiding infrastructure development in areas of high intensity and relocating those in the path of monsoons will work toward addressing the disproportionate impact of climate change on both poor and vulnerable populations and delicate ecosystems.

Typically, the most affected by large dams are peasants, tribal communities, landless people, and other marginalized groups. Large dams transfer a river's flow into electrical energy that is used to feed urban and industrial centers, and help concentrate the political power of already powerful individuals and groups, thereby further disempowering the marginalized and the poor.[61] Construction of large dams along with commercial logging and corporate agricultural farming "threaten tribal and indigenous peoples with loss of their rights over natural resources and thus with ultimate extinction."[62]

A study by the Minority Rights Group International examined the impact of dam construction on a riverine indigenous group, the Kihals, in the upper Indus River region, and revealed "the weakening of their already fragile identity and displacement from their livelihoods."[63] The impacts on indigenous boat peoples have largely been ignored:

> The government did not consider the adverse social, environmental and livelihood impacts on indigenous boat peoples, including Kihals, Jhabils, Mors and Mohanas, during the water resource development planning and implementation process. International financial institutions (IFIs) have also until very recently ignored the impacts of these processes on the identity and livelihoods of these indigenous groups. Currently, there are plans to construct a series of upstream storage and irrigation projects under Pakistan Water Vision 2025, which is an integral part of the Interim-Poverty Reduction Strategy Paper (I-PRSP). This document is blind to the adverse impacts on indigenous boat peoples, and lacks any measures to mitigate them. The recently prepared Pakistan Water Sector Strategy and the draft National Water Policy also pay little attention to the rights of indigenous and tribal groups. The only exception is the draft National Resettlement Policy that mentions and, to some extent, recognizes the rights of indigenous peoples. However, it lacks specific provisions with regard to the mega-water development projects and subsequent impacts on indigenous peoples. Indigenous groups and civil society

---

61. Ann Danaiya Usher ed., Dams as Aid: A Political Anatomy of Nordic Development Thinking (1997).

62. Mushtaq Gadi, Naeem Iqbal & Wasim Wagha, Unheard Indigenous Voices: The Kihals in Pakistan, Minority Rights Group International Microstudy (n.d.), http://minorityrights.org/wp-content/uploads/old-site-downloads/download-95-Unheard-Indigenous-Voices-The-Kihals-in-Pakistan.pdf.

63. Id.

organizations must mobilize to demand a comprehensive national policy on indigenous peoples.[64]

The benefits of flood control and the prospects of hydroelectricity provide a counterweight to the environmental and human rights impacts of large dams.[65] Dams are built not only to provide water as needed, but also for flood control by storing excess water.[66] Studies indicate 75% of the monsoon water drains into the sea following large-scale flooding events because of the lack of storage capacity.[67] While the reservoir of a dam stores water and is located where it can receive rainfall, the canals transport water to distant places that do not face any water scarcity.[68] The right to water and access to water for food production impact how large dams are considered. The viability and sustainability of dams includes assessment of "the engineering, environmental, social, economic and financial aspects within the context of an informed and participatory decision-making process." An integrated approach involves addressing "the entire basin when planning, developing and managing water resources, recognizing upstream and downstream interlinkages and being aware of particular stakeholder interests and areas of potential conflict."[69]

The United Nations Environment Programme (UNEP) has suggested that "the environmental, social and decision-making aspects of dams are usually less well understood and addressed than their engineering and financial aspects."[70] The UNEP recommendation is to recognize that "sustainability of large water resource infrastructure projects focuses on developing a comprehensive understanding of these issues and their incorporation into local normative frameworks and actual practices.[71] Formulating strategies for efficient water governance and sustainable conservation of water resources poses a daunting task for Pakistani hydro-strategists because the country has, unlike

---

64. *Id.*

65. *Id.*

66. Donald K. Anton & Dinah Shelton, *Problems in Human Rights and Large Dams, in* ENVIRONMENTAL PROTECTION AND HUMAN RIGHTS 12 (2011).

> According to a study conducted by the Central Water Commission in 1998, surface water resources were estimated at 1869 cu km and rechargeable groundwater resources at 432 cu km. It is believed that only 690 cu km of surface water resources (out of 1869 cu km) can be utilised by storage. At present the storage capacity of all dams in India is 174 cu km, which is incidentally less than the capacity of Kariba Dam in Zambia/Zimbabwe (180.6 cu km) and only 12 cu km more than Aswan High Dam of Egypt.

> *Id.*

67. *Id.*

68. *Id.*

69. UNITED NATIONS ENVIRONMENT PROGRAMME, DAMS AND DEVELOPMENT: RELEVANT PRACTICES FOR IMPROVED DECISION MAKING 1–2 (2007).

70. *Id.*

71. *Id.* at 12.

its neighbors India and China, only one major river system—the Indus River system—and no additional water can be injected into the system from outside. This lack of an alternative river system is further compounded by a variety of factors including lack of political will, rampant corruption, population explosion, interprovincial disharmony, indifference of citizens toward effective and economic utilization of available water resources, negligence toward repair and maintenance of water infrastructure, climate change, and inadequate production of knowledge.

Asserting the 1960 Indus Waters Treaty dispute resolution provision, Pakistan has sought international adjudication in recent years on account of two of India's hydroelectric projects that sought to alleviate electricity shortages in Kashmir.[72] Article IX of the Indus Water Treaty states: "Any question which arises between the Parties concerning the interpretation or application of this Treaty or the existence of any fact which, if established, might constitute a breach of this Treaty shall first be examined by the Commission, which will endeavor to resolve the question by agreement."[73] If the internal dispute resolution mechanism fails, the Treaty indicates, "A court of Arbitration shall be established to resolve the dispute."[74]

Pakistani officials objected to India's diversion of the Chenab River from construction of hydropower projects, including the 690-MW Ratli Dam, 1,000-MW Pikkal Dam, 1,190-MW Karthai Dam, and 600-MW Kero Dam, arguing that construction of these projects constituted a violation of the Indus River Treaty.[75] Brahma Chellaney noted:

> While railing against modestly sized run-of-the-river Indian dams, Pakistan has stirred local grassroots protests at home by embarking on much larger, storage-type dams such as the 4,500-megawatt Basha Dam . . . and the 7,000-megawatt Bunji Dam. While storage-type hydropower plants impound large volumes of water, run-of-the-river projects are located so as to use a river's natural flow energy and elevation drop to generate electricity without the aid of a large reservoir and dam.[76]

Chellaney underscores the smaller size of India's dam projects, but what is more significant is that most of the Himalayan rivers have been rela-

---

72. Indus Water Treaty, Sep. 19, 1960, India-Pakistan, art. IX, 419 U.N.T.S. 125, http://wrmin.nic.in/forms/list.aspx?lid=1202.
73. Id.
74. Id.
75. India Accused of Violating Indus Water Treaty, Dawn, Aug. 25, 2014, http://www.dawn.com/news/1127556.
76. Brahma Chellaney, Water, Power, and Competition in Asia, Asian Survey, July 2014, at 633.

tively untouched by dams near their sources.[77] A recent study points out that these "water grab" dams would be an environmental disaster.[78] The future dam projects create the highest dams in the world and generate energy capacity of more than 4,000 MW, the equivalent of the Hoover Dam.[79] "The result, over the next twenty years, 'could be that the Himalayas become the most dammed region in the world,'" according to scientist Ed Grumbine.[80]

An important aspect of climate justice is to recognize the ecological and climate debt that the global North owes to the peoples in the global South. Instead of transmitting ecologically sustainable small-scale hydroelectricity projects, the global South has inherited a callous disregard for the environment from the global North in the name of development. The need for energy access has translated into the production of mega dams. The beneficiaries of the dam construction projects are the people who benefit from reliable electricity, but also the development banks and private lending institutions and construction firms that handle and provide the finance and construction of the dams. The global South is subordinated by the technological advancements of the global North, which increases its detrimental reliance on the global North.

In addition, water is a finite resource to be shared by all the world's population. The damming of water limits access to the resource and also takes away the ability of the local population to control the water. Henry Shue argued:

> When human population and agricultural activity were sufficiently small, there was, for all practical purposes, an unlimited supply of water . . . . Even after it became necessary to move large quantities of water for the satisfaction of human demand, via dams and pipelines, plenty was available if human ingenuity could deliver it to the right place. But no more: some of the most vicious political battles . . . today are over water . . . . Relative to human

---

77. *Id.*
78. John Vidal, *China and India "Water Grab" Dams Put Ecology of Himalayas in Danger*, THE GUARDIAN, Aug. 10, 2013, http://www.theguardian.com/global-development/2013/aug/10/china-india-water-grab-dams-himalayas-danger.
79. *Id.*
80. Ed Grumbine explained:
    India aims to construct 292 dams . . . doubling current hydropower capacity and contributing 6% to projected national energy needs. If all dams are constructed as proposed, in 28 of 32 major river valleys, the Indian Himalayas would have one of the highest average dam densities in the world, with one dam for every 32km of river channel. Every neighbour of India with undeveloped hydropower sites is building or planning to build multiple dams, totalling at minimum 129 projects.
    Id.

demands for water, the supply of water is limited; the total natural supply cannot be changed by human action.[81]

The local communities' interests are secondary to those of the dam, which would provide access to electricity to those in far and away places. In other words, the needs of the local people to use water for irrigation, food production, and basic needs is limited by the use of water for hydroelectricity in the urban population centers. The vulnerability of people who rely on the dam for electricity is twofold. First, the overreliance on large dams leads to greater energy insecurity. Second, the use of water for large-scale hydroelectricity limits the availability of the water for other essential purposes and disrupts delicate ecosystems. Humans are unable to replace water once it has been consumed and polluted. The unequal access and use of water contributes to disproportionate climate impacts.

II.   Sino-Pakistan Collaboration

While large dams remain inevitable for meeting the water and energy requirements of Pakistan, the planning and implementation of these hydro projects must be well-regulated, the social ramifications deeply understood, and the "business as usual" approach with traditional and outdated thought processes and practices dramatically overhauled. In this regard, the expertise and experiences of one of Pakistan's neighboring countries and closest allies, China, can be extremely useful. With more than half of the world's large dams in China, the Chinese expertise in the planning, construction, maintenance, and implementation of large dams remains the most comprehensive.

The China-Pakistan Economic Corridor (CPEC) plan, which is a $46 billion investment package, includes a mix of transportation and energy projects.[82] The deal includes a number of energy projects, amounting to $34 billion, "including pipelines to transport oil and gas to Kashgar; the completion of the Iran-Pakistan gas pipeline; and a number of coal, wind, solar, and hydro energy plants that would add some 10,000 megawatts to energy-starved Pakistan by 2018."[83] This type of energy project would be more beneficial to Pakistan's long-term economic and social goals instead of previous aid projects contingent on military aid. At the same time, Pakistani officials

---

81.   HENRY SHUE, CLIMATE JUSTICE: VULNERABILITY AND PROTECTION 78 (2014).
82.   Claude Rakisits, *A Path to the Sea: China's Pakistan Plan*, WORLD AFFAIRS, Fall 2015, http://www.worldaffairsjournal.org/article/path-sea-china%E2%80%99s-pakistan-plan.
83.   *Id.*

should balance energy demands with sustainability of the projects and their impacts on climate change adaptation measures.

Despite a poor human rights record, China has been transitioning toward renewables faster than any other country. In 2014, Chinese leaders committed to seeing carbon emissions peak around 2030, which would require adding 1,000 GW of capacity from low-carbon emitting energy sources, equivalent to the total amount of electricity produced in the United States currently.[84] China was the largest renewables market in the world with 433 GW of generating capacity at the end of 2014, which was more than double the United States' 182 GW.[85] Pakistan can serve as an incubator for new renewable technologies for Chinese energy entrepreneurs. China could in turn serve as an ally to Pakistan in improving existing dam infrastructure and transitioning Pakistan to other renewables including, wind, solar, and small scale hydroelectricity, which have lower GHG emissions and environmental and social costs.

The WCD report states, "In the past, dam construction has caused environmental damage due to poor assessments, vested interests, lack of knowledge, lack of enforcement of mitigation measures, lack of sufficient resources, lack of ongoing monitoring or ignorance of ecosystem functions."[86] The WCD report indicates that "[r]esearch will continue to improve knowledge and understanding of ecosystem complexity."[87] However, "it is difficult to mitigate all ecosystem impacts and ecosystem responses are rarely fully predictable."[88] By collaborating with China, Pakistan would be able to draw on the unmatched Chinese knowledge and experience to construct large dams that are as efficient, equitable, and sustainable as possible. The WCD has noted that "a multi-layered approach is needed that prioritises avoidance, especially in sensitive areas, and has in-built checks that adapt and respond to observed ecosystem changes"; implementing this approach would be a significant step in the right direction.[89]

Moreover, to combat the immediate water crisis, dams for flood control would provide a solution. For these flood control dams, which could also simultaneously harness hydroelectric power through dams or hydrokinetic turbines, the Chinese can lend assistance. "Chinese dam developers have

---

84. Bloomberg News, *By the Numbers: China's Clean Energy Investments Show Big Strides*, BLOOMBERG, Nov. 2, 2015, http://www.bloomberg.com/news/articles/2015-11-02/by-the-numbers-china-s-clean-energy-investments-show-big-strides.

85. *Id.*

86. WCD, *supra* note 46, at 235.

87. *Id.*

88. *Id.*

89. *Id.*

been exporting hydropower expertise to Southeast Asia. While such involvement is limited to technical analyses and feasibility studies, it is likely that Chinese loans, construction expertise, and equipment will come into play."[90]

Because of China's growth, "the implications of its breakneck development for environmental sustainability and social stability" are garnering attention.[91] While the media has focused on the construction of large dams on southwestern China's transboundary rivers and the resulting environmental damage, the extent of China's engineering expertise in dam construction itself is also significant. China's hydroelectric powersheds are important because "large-scale hydropower is almost universally considered renewable and sustainable in China."[92] The ongoing focus on sustainability, scientific know-how, and renewable energy targets in the future will "more than double the existing installed hydropower generating capacity by 2020."[93] This rapid rise of hydroelectric projects would benefit from "robust analyses of the degree of sustainability of these projects, operationalized through the metrics of vulnerability and resilience."[94]

Dam-racing, the phenomenon of the rapid development of large dams, is distinctly Asian.[95] Much of the scale up leading toward large dam projects results from economic factors because of accelerated economic growth in the region and the resulting increase in energy demand. China is on the verge of becoming a water-stressed country with northern China already a water-scarce region. In order for China to overcome its worsening water situation and climate change risks, extensive research is underway to develop strategies to improve water governance, strengthen water rights administration, improve efficiency and equity in water supply pricing, control water pollution, and improve emergency response.[96] China has realized that it will have to reform and strengthen its water resource management framework and, therefore, the country is in the process of transitioning from a traditional system, with the government as the decisionmaking authority, towards a modern approach that incorporates sound legal framework, effective institutional arrangements, transparent decisionmaking, information disclosure, and active public participation.

---

90. Amy McNally et al., *Hydropower and Sustainability: Resilience and Vulnerability in China's Powersheds*, 90 J. ENVTL. MGMT. 1, 7 (2009).

91. *Id. See also* THAYER SCUDDER, THE FUTURE OF LARGE DAMS: DEALING WITH SOCIAL, ENVIRONMENTAL, INSTITUTIONAL, AND POLITICAL COSTS (2005); JIAN XIE ET AL., ADDRESSING CHINA'S WATER SCARCITY: RECOMMENDATIONS FOR SELECTED WATER RESOURCE MANAGEMENT ISSUES (2009).

92. McNally, *supra* note 90.

93. *Id.*

94. *Id.*

95. *See generally* BRAHMA CHELLANEY, FROM ARMS RACING TO "DAM RACING" IN ASIA (2012).

96. XIE ET AL., *supra* note 89.

China has been reluctant to embrace calls for statist approaches to climate justice, but it can be more open to assist in international efforts to tackle intranational equity concerns that "move beyond the simplistic developed-developing country dichotomy and . . . reassess justice among states in the context of the practical realities of climate change."[97] Even though it is difficult to calculate the total GHG emissions from affluent activities versus subsistence activities, there is a greater capacity for reduction of GHG emissions for nonessential and luxury purposes.[98] The billions of people who live in extreme poverty and who are most susceptible to climate change are the least able to contribute to mitigation efforts.[99] "A non-statist approach makes it possible to reconcile these simple facts by highlighting the role of individuals rather than focusing on the role of states."[100] This juncture of interpreting climate justice through a non-statist approach is where China can be most effective by supporting its own efforts at environmental and social equalities and that of its neighbor, Pakistan.

III.   Lessons for the Climate Justice Movement

The Pakistanis and the Chinese have been strategic allies for a number of years. Greater cooperation and stronger ties between the two countries are perceived to be mutually beneficial. Continued cooperation requires that the improvements in water management techniques be included in the national conversation and made a social responsibility priority.[101] Prime Minister Nawaz Sharif's political future teeters on whether he can find a solution to—literally—take the country out of darkness.[102] During Pakistan's last general election season in 2013, every candidate promised to revamp domestic industries and revitalize the country's faltering economy through mega-projects. Yet with power outages slicing upwards of 7% of the country's gross domestic product, the inability to turn on and keep on the lights is Pakistan's most pressing problem.[103] Pakistan's energy woes are epic, but they are surmount-

---

97. Paul G. Harris, Alice S.Y. Chow & Rasmus Karlsson, *China and Climate Justice: Moving Beyond Statism*, 13 Int'l Envtl. Agreements 291, 301 (2013).
98. *Id.*
99. *Id.*
100. *Id.*
101. Muhammad Amir Fahim, Impact of Water Scarcity on Food Security at Micro Level in Pakistan, MPRA Paper No. 35760, PMAS-Arid Agriculture University, Rawalpindi (Dec. 2011), http://mpra.ub.uni-muenchen.de/35760/. *See also* Tim Ambler & Morgen Witzel, Doing Business in China (2000).
102. Nadia Ahmad, *Shoring Up Power in Pakistan*, Dawn, June 19, 2013, http://www.dawn.com/news/1019094.
103. Nadeem Ul Haque, *On Power Sector Reform*, Dev. 2.0, June 19, 2016, http://development20.blogspot.com/2013/06/on-power-sector-reform.html.

able. Other less developed nations, including Sri Lanka[104] and Ghana,[105] have been able to utilize renewable energy, which begs the question as to why Pakistan cannot do so also.

Pakistan's energy crisis presents investment opportunity for potential jobs in the renewable energy sector, which is why Sharif has been galvanizing support for renewable projects. Solar, wind, and small-scale hydroelectric projects are more suitable for energy needs and climate change adaptation measures, but various political and financial interests will continue to put forward the option of large dams. The impact of climate change will vary from country to country and region to region. As such, infrastructure for hydroelectric energy designs should incorporate climate change adaptation measures, including variable flow turbine design, incremental power genera-tion, and flood attenuation designs.[106] The synergies between clean power production and the climate change modeling from hydroelectric projects must be configured.[107]

Large dams are not the ideal source of hydroelectric generation. Paki-stan generates more than 30% of its electricity from hydropower. The use of small-scale hydropower, including hydrokinetic energy, which harnesses power from the movements of waves and tides through underwater turbines, would be one of many potential energy sources to exploit because of the financial constraints of large dams. Small-scale hydropower technology can be used as a standalone energy system for rural power supply.[108] "[H]ydro-power can significantly contribute towards increased national energy access and security, mitigation of climate change and reduction of harmful air pol-lutants, creation of economic opportunities, and, thus, effectively leading to sustainable development."[109] Innovation in the energy sector, while thriving in neighboring China and India, has been stagnant in Pakistan. Prospects for coal in the Thar region and Iranian oil and gas imports, however, are not long-term solutions because an over-reliance on imported fossil fuels is unsustainable.

---

104. Bikash Pandey, *Clean Energy Options for Rural Pakistan: Lessons From South Asia, in* FUELING THE FUTURE: MEETING PAKISTAN'S ENERGY NEEDS IN THE 21ST CENTURY 167, 167–68 (Robert M. Ha-thaway et al. eds., Woodrow Wilson International Center for Scholars: Asia Program 2007), http://www.wilsoncenter.org/sites/default/files/Asia_FuelingtheFuture_rptmain.pdf.

105. *See* Veronica B. Miller et al., *Hydrokinetic Power for Energy Access in Rural Ghana*, 36 RENEWABLE ENERGY 673 (2011), http://mhk.pnnl.gov/wiki/images/0/06/Hydrokinetic_power_for_energy_ac-cess_in_rural_Ghanapdf.pdf.

106. Chiyembekezo S. Kaunda, Cuthbert Z. Kimambo & Torbjorn K. Nielsen, *Hydropower in the Context of Sustainable Energy Supply: A Review of Technologies and Challenges*, 2012 ISRN RENEWABLE ENERGY 1–15 (2012).

107. *Id.*

108. *Id.*

109. *Id.*

Large dams have served Pakistan for a number of years, but should be eliminated as a long-term energy access and security solution because of environmental degradation and aging and costly hydropower infrastructure. The United States has pledged more than $30 billion in aid to Pakistan since 1948, but has overlooked the feasibility of nascent energy technologies to relieve the country's acute energy crisis.[110] Half of that amount has been allocated for military assistance, and more than two-thirds of that amount was appropriated following 2001.[111] The U.S. Department of State and the U.S. Agency for International Development recognized the need to alleviate energy poverty and create sustainable energy options in Pakistan as part of the civilian assistance program to Pakistan.[112] Until now, hydrokinetic energy has been ignored as a possible solution for Pakistan's acute energy crisis. A part of the solution for Pakistan's power outages is hydrokinetic or tidal energy. The hydrokinetic energy option particularly presents an opportunity for Imran Khan and his party, PTI, because the Khyber Paktunawala region has steep mountainous rivers that can harness these energy resources in the monsoon and rainy seasons. Additionally, coastal areas in Karachi can develop offshore hydrokinetic energy projects. The country's unique topography is ideal for this type of tidal and wave energy.

Businesses in both urban centers of Karachi, Lahore, Islamabad, and Peshawar, and in rural areas, have managed to function with a dilapidated energy grid, but consider the possibilities if there were a sustainable energy solution. Previous projects, funded by the World Bank, Asian Development Bank, and the International Monetary Fund, have turned to small-scale dam proposals; however, they have not developed the possibility of hydrokinetic energy. Since Pakistan already derives 30% of its energy from hydroelectricity in the form of large dam projects,[113] hydrokinetic energy would be able to provide a low-cost energy solution using the existing energy grid. Scientists note that hydrokinetic energy is more reliable than solar and wind energy because it is not intermittent.[114] The power of the waves is the power for the future.

---

110. Susan B. Epstein & K. Alan Kronstadt, Congressional Research Service R41856, Pakistan: U.S. Foreign Assistance 2 (2012), http://www.fas.org/sgp/crs/row/R41856.pdf.

111. Id.

112. U.S. Department of State, Congressional Budget Justification, Volume i: Department of State Operations, Fiscal Year 2013, at 141 (2013), http://www.state.gov/documents/organization/181061.pdf.

113. Sumita Kumar, Pakistan's Energy Security: Challenges and Options, 34 Strategic Analysis 912–24 (2010). Figures provided in the Energy Yearbook by the Ministry of Petroleum and Natural Resources in Islamabad shows Pakistan's energy outlook.

114. Riaz Haq, Solar Energy for Pakistan, Haq's Musings, Feb. 27, 2009, http://www.riazhaq.com/2009/02/solar-energy-for-sunny-pakistan.html.

Conclusion

An enhanced water planning regime could work to combat the negative externalities associated with water scarcity.[115] These realizations and planning mechanisms should pave the way for infrastructure improvement for existing and planned dam projects in response to intranational attempts to address climate justice. The country's irrigation system requires urgent reform and stronger institutional arrangements. The rate at which underground water is being tapped is unsustainable, the coverage and quality of the urban water supply system is inadequate and unreliable, and there is no urban wastewater treatment system. Chinese collaboration in helping Pakistan reform its water policy and institutional framework, build greater capacity at the government level to efficiently manage available water resources, and ensure better coordination among the provinces will result in sustainable economic growth of the country. A further benefit of improved energy infrastructure would be the consideration of the water and energy needs of poor and marginalized populations, which is essential for climate justice on a nationwide level.

---

115. Fahim, *supra* note 99. *See also* WATER SCARCITY DRAFTING GROUP, WATER SCARCITY MANAGEMENT IN THE CONTEXT OF WFD, WATER DIRECTORS OF THE EUROPEAN UNION (2006), http://ec.europa.eu/environment/water/quantity/pdf/comm_droughts/8a_1.pdf.

Chapter 18

Climate Change Impacts and Human Rights of Rural Women in Bangladesh

Kamrul Hossain and Noor Jahan Punam

Introduction

Climate change and human rights are interconnected. The United Nations Human Rights Council declared in 2008 that climate change "poses an immediate and far-reaching threat" for the "full enjoyment of human rights."[1] This connection between climate change and human rights was subsequently affirmed by the Office of the United Nations High Commissioner for Human Rights (OHCHR) in a comprehensive report published in 2009.[2] Since that time, an extensive body of scholarly writing has analyzed the interrelationship between climate change and human rights as well as the adverse impacts of climate change on the enjoyment of basic human rights.[3]

---

1. United Nations Human Rights Council Res. 7/23, Human Rights and Climate Change, 7th Sess. (2008), http://www2.ohchr.org/english/issues/climatechange/docs/Resolution_7_23.pdf. *See also* United Nations Human Rights Council Res. 10/4, 10th Sess., U.N. Doc. A/HRC/10/L.11 (2009), https://www.un.org/ruleoflaw/files/edited_versionL.11Revised.pdf.

2. *Report of the Office of the United Nations High Commissioner for Human Rights on the Relationship Between Climate Change and Human Rights*, U.N. Human Rights Council, 10th Sess., Provisional Agenda Item 2, U.N. Doc. A/HRC/10/61 (2009).

3. *See, e.g.*, Timo Koivurova et al., *Climate Change and Human Rights, in* 21 Ius Gentium: Comparative Perspectives on Law and Justice, 287–325 (Erkki J. Hollo & Kati Kulovesi eds., 2013); Marc Limon, *Human Rights and Climate Change: Constructing a Case for Political Action*, 33 Harv. Envtl.

This growing awareness of the consequences of climate change can be traced to the scientific community, especially the Intergovernmental Panel on Climate Change's (IPCC's) Fifth Assessment Report.[4] The IPCC Fifth Assessment Report notes an escalation of the level of probability of the impacts, such as the worsening of the severity of drought, the acceleration of land degradation and desertification, the intensification of floods and tropical cyclones, and an increase in many infectious diseases in vulnerable and fragile key areas of the earth. Scientists argue that the risks of climate change are closely linked to social instability.[5] The risks disproportionately impact the most vulnerable people and communities who in most cases suffer from lack of societal infrastructure to adapt to the change, or are unable to adapt because of both the variation in the change as well as sociocultural norms and practices.

The impacts of climate change have made Bangladesh one of the most vulnerable countries along with several low-lying small island nations.[6] The country is regarded as one of the biggest deltas at the confluence of a number of large rivers including the Padma, Jamuna, and Meghna.[7] The densely populated country has a 147,610 km^2 area[8] inhabited by approximately 160 million people[9]—the third most populated country in Southeast Asia after India and Pakistan.[10] Around 10,000 km^2 of its land territory are covered with water[11] by virtue of the presence of various inland water bodies, and approximately 700 small and big rivers flowing to the south to the Bay of

---

L. Rev. 439 (2009); John H. Knox, *Linking Human Rights and Climate Change at the UN*, 33 Harv. Envtl. L. Rev. 477 (2009).

4. IPCC, Climate Change 2013: The Physical Science Basis. Contribution of Working Group I to the Fifth Assessment Report of the Intergovernmental Panel on Climate Change (2013)), http://www.climatechange2013.org/images/report/WG1AR5_ALL_FINAL.pdf.

5. Alex Kirby, *Climate Change "Makes Violence Likelier,"* Climate News Network, Mar. 31, 2014, http://climatenewsnetwork.net/climate-change-makes-violence-likelier/. *See also* Solomon M. Hsiang & Marshall Burke, *Climate, Conflict, and Social Stability: What Does the Evidence Say?*, 123 Climatic Change 39 (2014).

6. For further discussion of the issue, see Office of the High Representative for the Least Developed Countries, Landlocked Developing Countries, and Small Island Developing States, The Impact of Climate Change on the Development Prospects of the Least Developed Countries and Small Islands Developing States (2009), http://unohrlls.org/custom-content/uploads/2013/11/The-Impact-of-Climate-Change-on-The-Development-Prospects-of-the-Least-Developed-Countries-and-Small-Island-Developing-States1.pdf.

7. S.M. Imamul Huq & Jalal Uddin Md. Shoaib, The Soils of Bangladesh 15 (2013).

8. Bangladesh Ministry of Education, *Bangladesh Country Profile*, http://www.moedu.gov.bd/old/bangladesh.htm (last visited Aug. 23, 2016).

9. U.S. Central Intelligence Agency, The World Factbook (2015).

10. John R. Weeks, Population: An Introduction to Concepts and issues 50 (12th ed. 2016).

11. U.S. Library of Congress, *Geography of Bangladesh*, http://countrystudies.us/bangladesh/23.htm (last visited Aug. 23, 2016).

Bengal.[12] Most of the country lies less than 10 m above sea level.[13] While its soil is highly fertile, the country is vulnerable to regular flooding[14] primarily due to tropical monsoons causing heavy rainfall. At the same time, the dry season triggers an increase in temperature leading to drought in many parts of the country. These duel dilemmas make it an extremely disaster-prone country. According to the World Risk Index 2011, Bangladesh ranked sixth among countries that are most vulnerable to natural disasters, and second among Asian countries.[15]

While natural disasters are a common phenomenon in Bangladesh, climate change has caused the frequency of such disasters in Bangladesh to increase and they occur in an unpredictable manner. The duel pressures, caused by both seasonal stressors as well as impacts of climate change, exacerbate long-standing problems in the country such as poverty, hunger, food shortage, and homelessness. Thus, in addition to loss of life, infrastructural damage and adverse effects on livelihoods,[16] many parts of Bangladesh face large-scale population displacement.[17] A study revealed that 20 million people will be environmental refugees as 58,000 ha of agricultural land will be flooded.[18] For example, in 1995, half of Bhola Island in Bangladesh was submerged, leaving 500,000 people homeless.[19] Moreover, environmental degradation causing water pollution and groundwater contamination as a result of naturally occurring arsenic, soil degradation and erosion, and the proliferation of waterborne diseases are common features in most rural areas in Bangladesh.

Since human rights risks are a common component of the discourse on climate change regardless of the region, the problem of non-integrating human rights risks is more acute in the least developed or developing countries, such as Bangladesh. The absence of good governance in these

---

12. U.S. Library of Congress, *River Systems of Bangladesh*, http://countrystudies.us/bangladesh/25.htm (last visited Aug. 23, 2016).

13. S.A.I. Mahmood, *Impact of Climate Change in Bangladesh: The Role of Public Administration and Government's Integrity*, 4 J. Ecology & Nat. Env't 223, 225 (2012).

14. 1 IBP USA, Bangladesh Country Study Guide Strategic Information and Developments 44 (2012).

15. Mahmood, *supra* note 13, at 225.

16. Government of the People's Republic of Bangladesh, Ministry of Environment and Forests, Bangladesh Climate Change Strategy and Action Plan 2008, at 4 (2008).

17. Lilian Yamamoto & Miguel Esteban, Atoll Island States and International Law, Climate Change Displacement and Sovereignty 35 (2014).

18. Md. Shamsuddoha & Rezaul Karim Chowdhury, Climate Change Impact and Disaster Vulnerabilities in the Coastal Areas of Bangladesh (2007), http://www.unisdr.org/files/4032_DisasterBD.pdf.

19. *See* Aprna Kadian, Puja Kumari & Arpita Sharma, *Navigating Climate Change: Extenuating Strategies to Combat Climate Migration Threats*, 6 OIDA Int'l J. Sustainable Dev. 58 (2013).

countries poses an obstacle to the enjoyment of basic human rights in these countries. However, the consequences of climate change present serious implications for the enjoyment of most fundamental human rights such as the rights to life, adequate food, water, health, and adequate housing. While these climate change impacts affect the human rights of all people in Bangladesh, studies suggest that the most at risk due to climate change are the already vulnerable people, such as women, the elderly, indigenous peoples, and persons with disabilities, who generally suffer from severe inequality.[20] This chapter focuses exclusively on climate change impacts on the human rights of women in the rural areas in Bangladesh. Climate change impacts undermine the ability of women in these rural areas to live in dignity because of their exposure to poverty, fragile societal infrastructure, sexual harassment, and physical incapacity.[21]

This chapter addresses whether existing human rights mechanisms offer adequate protection to rural women in Bangladesh. Part I discusses the impacts of climate change on women in rural areas in Bangladesh. Part II examines international human rights standards applicable to women's rights in Bangladesh, in particular the rights to be addressed in the context of climate change-related consequences. Part III explores the challenges facing rural women in Bangladesh and their relationship to human rights norms. Part IV concludes the chapter by highlighting the mismatch between human rights norms and societal behaviors, which requires law reform to adequately address women's rights stemming from the threats of climate change in rural Bangladesh.

I.   Climate Change Impacts on Women in Bangladesh

As the world's biggest delta, Bangladesh is an acute example of climate change impacts. According to a study conducted by ActionAid,[22] Bangladesh is the fifth most vulnerable country to climate change.[23] The country is projected to become more exposed to climate change impacts in the future as polar melting will result in sea-level rise driving a significant part of the

---

20.   *See* Valerie Nelson, Gender, Generations, Social Protection & Climate Change: A Thematic Review (2011).

21.   Climate Change Cell et al., Climate Change Adaptation Research: Climate Change, Gender, and Vulnerable Groups in Bangladesh (2009), http://lib.icimod.org/record/13786/files/4600. PDF.

22.   ActionAid, On the Brink: Who's Best Prepared for a Climate and Hunger Crisis? 23 (n.d.), http://www.actionaidusa.org/sites/files/actionaid/scorecard_without_embargoe.pdf.

23.   Aminul Islam et al., *Bangladesh Climate Change Strategy and Action Plans, in* Climate Change Adaptation Actions in Bangladesh 109 (Rajiib Shaw, Fuad Mallick & Aminul Islam eds., 2013).

landmass of the countries like Bangladesh under water.[24] Scientific data projects that 15–17% of the country's land area (approximately 22,135–26,562 km²) will be under water by 2080.[25] Due to its unique geographical location and the hydrological influence of extreme rainfall in the monsoon season and patterns of regional water flow, the country cannot avoid the variant impacts of climate change. Between 1991 and 2009, more than 259 extreme natural disasters occurred in Bangladesh.[26] Approximately 140,000 people died in 1991 alone, 90% of whom were women.[27] Statistics also provide evidence of approximately 39 million people being displaced by floods and cyclones from 1970 to 2009.[28] Experts warn that approximately 6–8 million people from Bangladesh will be displaced by 2050 due to increasing global temperature and sea-level rise.[29]

The effect of climate change in Bangladesh will also bring other negative environmental implications, such as the loss of mangrove forests important for ensuring effective functioning of ecosystem services such as drawing down of groundwater, increased salinization of groundwater, and increased exposure to arsenic and iron in groundwater. The deterioration of these forests will result in serious impacts on human health generally and impose particularly adverse consequences on women.[30]

The adverse effects of climate change will subject vulnerable groups of the population, including rural women, to serious risks.[31] Climate change-induced internal displacement places women in Bangladesh at risk of a wide range of adverse impacts. The following subsections describe the status of women in rural Bangladesh and their vulnerability to these impacts.

---

24. Mahmood, *supra* note 13, at 227.
25. James S. Pender, What Is Climate Change? And How It Will Effect Bangladesh 54 (2008), https://www.kirkensnodhjelp.no/contentassets/c1403acd5da84d39a120090004899173/2008/final-draft-what-is-climate-change-and-how-it-may-affect-bangladesh.pdf.
26. Mahmood, *supra* note 13, at 227.
27. *See* Keiko Ikeda, *Gender Differences in Human Loss and Vulnerability in Natural Disasters: A Case Study From Bangladesh*, 2 Indian J. Gender Stud. 171 (1995).
28. *See* Tahera Akter, Climate Change and Flow of Environmental Displacement in Bangladesh (2009), http://bdresearch.org.bd/home/climate_knowledge/cd1/pdf/Bangladesh%20and%20climate%20change/Climate%20change%20impacts%20,vulnerability,%20risk/Climate_Change_and_Flow_of_Environmental_displacement.pdf.
29. *Dhaka to Stress Climate Compensation for LDCs*, Daily Star, Nov. 13, 2011, http://www.thedailystar.net/news-detail-209899.
30. *See* Shamsuddoha & Chowdhury, *supra* note 18; *see also* Farzana Nasrin, *Women, Environment, and Environmental Advocacy: Challenges for Bangladesh*, 1 Asian J. Soc. Sci. & Human. 149 (2012).
31. IPCC, Summary for Policymakers, Climate Change 2014: Synthesis Report, Contribution of Working Groups I, II, and III, Fifth Assessment Report of the Intergovernmental Panel on Climate Change 4 (2014), http://www.ipcc.ch/pdf/assessment-report/ar5/syr/AR5_SYR_FINAL_SPM.pdf.

A.   Status of Women in Rural Bangladesh

While climate change causes adverse impacts to both men and women,[32] the latter, particularly those residing in the rural areas in Bangladesh, are especially vulnerable to climate change.[33] Women's vulnerabilities are tied to prescribed gendered roles, prevailing societal norms, and socioeconomic and cultural factors. Within Bangladeshi society, violence against women is widespread and stems from the cultural attitudes regarding women as inferior to men.[34] Climate change and its impacts compound the suffering of these women.[35]

In Bangladesh, women are traditionally responsible for household tasks pertaining to securing food and water.[36] In most rural communities, these tasks also include basic household farming and agricultural activities. These tasks are climatically sensitive for women and impact their health.[37] However, as women are the major actors for these kinds of tasks, they are equipped with knowledge and expertise on various aspects of these tasks. Nevertheless, this traditional local knowledge is not properly incorporated into climate adaptation strategy because these women are not considered legitimate agents.[38] There are sociocultural factors that keep women outside of any formal role regarding policymaking or even policy shaping.[39] For example, social positioning of women is weaker as their work is not generally attached to tangible wealth. In most cases, therefore, women in Bangladesh lack decisionmaking power, which offers them little or no capacity to overcome environmental hazards caused by climate change. However, the importance of women's involvement is highly relevant in any responses to climate change as women are not only the victims but also the agents. They can help shape the solutions to adapt to climate change, as once expressed by former Finnish President Tarja Halonen:[40] "Women are powerful agents whose knowledge, skills and innovative ideas support the efforts to combat climate change."[41]

---

32. Mayesha Alam et al., Women and Climate Change: Impact and Agency in Human Rights, Security, and Economic Development, Georgetown Institute for Women, Peace, and Security 9 (2015).
33. Tabitha Black-Lock, Climate Change, Adaptation, and Gender in Bangladesh (2015), http://students.capi.uvic.ca/sites/default/files/climate_change_blog5.pdf.
34. Nasrin, *supra* note 30, at 149.
35. *Id.*
36. *Id.*
37. *Id.*
38. *Id.* at 153 (fig. 1).
39. Bangladesh Ministry of Environment and Forests, Climate Change and Gender in Bangladesh: Information Brief (n.d.), http://cmsdata.iucn.org/downloads/gender.pdf.
40. Tarja Halonen served as president of Finland from 2000–2012.
41. Equal Climate, *President of Finland, Tarja Halonen: Gender Equality Must Be Incorporated Into All Matters Connected to Climate Change*, http://www.equalclimate.org/en/background/President+of+Fi

Women are recognized as victims of climate impacts in Bangladesh, yet as agents they are not effectively acknowledged and integrated into decisionmaking roles. One of the reasons for this reality is lack of access to formal education. In 2008, a study found that girls in primary and secondary schools outnumbered boys.[42] However, the net attendance of girls in secondary schools is only at 53%, which is very low.[43] In tertiary education, the ratio of girls to boys is 6:10, which is significantly below the target of complete gender equality expressed in Millennium Development Goal 3.[44] However, compared to the education of older women, the education levels of girls in the new generation have improved. Older women typically received less education than men of their age.[45] Despite this improvement, concerns have been raised regarding dropout rates among young girls in most rural areas.[46] In addition to sexual abuse, harassment at schools, and harassment in transit to and from school, the structural and social barriers to quality education, such as deficiency of physical infrastructure, insufficient facilities for girls in schools, and adverse effects of early marriages, caused high dropout rates from schools among girls in the rural areas of Bangladesh.[47]

Education is a factor that influences the financial status of people to a certain extent. Any direct or indirect barrier to access to education for women limits the options for women to gain solid financial status as their opportunities to enter the work force become restricted. Today, women are nonetheless gradually becoming more engaged in gainful employment contributing to labor markets specifically due to the increasing development of garment industries and the nongovernmental organization (NGO) facilitated microcredit programs,[48] which offer work facilities in farming and other related economic sectors.[49] Because of lower educational qualifications, women gen-

nland,+Tarja+Halonen%3A+Gender+equality+must+be+incorporated+into+all+matters+connected
.9UFRrYYk.ips (last visited Aug. 23, 2016).

42. Press Release, Government of Bangladesh, Millennium Development Goals, Bangladesh Progress Report (2008).

43. United Nations International Children's' Emergency Fund (UNICEF) and Bangladesh Bureau of Statistics (BBS), Multiple Indicator Cluster Survey (MICS) 2009, Bangladesh (2010).

44. Id.

45. BBS, Report on Sample Vital Registration System (2008).

46. Concluding Observations of the Committee on the Elimination of Discrimination Against Women, U.N. Convention on the Elimination of All Forms of Discrimination Against Women, 48th Sess., U.N. Doc. CEDAW/C/BGD/CO/7 (2011), http://www2.ohchr.org/english/bodies/cedaw/docs/co/CEDAW-C-BGD-CO-7.pdf.

47. Id.

48. UNICEF, Women and Girls in Bangladesh (2010), http://www.unicef.org/bangladesh/Women_and_girls_in_Bangladesh.pdf.

49. Sohara Mehroze Shachi, Environment: Gender and Climate Change Adaptation, Dhaka Trib., July 23, 2015, http://www.dhakatribune.com/weekend/2015/jul/23/environment-gender-and-climate-

erally do not enjoy higher positions in the work force. Even where the educational status of a woman is well grounded, when it comes to employment women do not have options to switch from one employment to another, in particular if it is concerning change of location, simply because of her various other responsibilities attached to family.[50] Overall, the level of employment and ownership of financial resources of women is poorly managed. Moreover, decisions regarding the use of money earned by women are made by someone else.[51]

Women's status in Bangladesh is also determined by religious norms. Given that Bangladesh is a country with a Muslim majority,[52] the practice of purdah[53] or hijab works as a restraint on women's participation in the public sphere such as education, employment, and social engagement. The degree of restrictiveness varies depending on the individual families. However, in most cases, women are subject to seeking permission from husbands, fathers, or brothers prior to engaging in outside activities.[54] These religious aspects also have significance in terms of wealth inheritance, making women less wealthy than their male counterparts. For example, personal issues such as inheritance property are regulated by religious laws, which leave women with weaker rights than men in terms of ownership and leave women in a vulnerable economic condition. In some instances, women are even deprived of their entitlement to property inherited from their parents.[55]

B.   Examples of Vulnerability to Climate Change in Bangladeshi Women

The coastal area of Bangladesh consists of places located in the south, namely the districts of Satkhira, Khulna, Bagerhat, Cox's Bazar, and Patuakhali.[56] These areas are vulnerable to tropical cyclones, storm surges, flooding, salin-

---

change-adaptation#sthash.u2l9e6Rs.dpuf.

50.   Md. Sadequr Rahman, *Climate Change, Disaster, and Gender Vulnerability: A Study on Two Divisions of Bangladesh*, 2 Am. J. Hum. Ecology 72, 77 (2013).

51.   National Institute of Population Research and Training et al., Bangladesh Demographic and Health Survey (2007), http://dhsprogram.com/pubs/pdf/FR207/FR207%5BApril-10-2009%5D. pdf.

52.   David Lewis, Bangladesh: Politics, Economy, and Civil Society 5 (2011).

53.   For a discussion of Purdah, see *infra* Part IV.

54.   Organisation for Economic Co-operation and Development, Atlas of Gender and Development: How Social Norms Affect Gender Equality in Non-OECD Countries 181 (2010).

55.   *See* Farah D. Chowdhury, *Muslim Family Law in Bangladesh: Resistance to Secularisation, in* Managing Family Justice in Diverse Societies (Mavis Maclean & John Eekelaar eds., 2013).

56.   Norwegian Embassy et al., Assessment of Women's Livelihood Needs in Three Eco-zones of Bangladesh 34 (2014), http://www.uncclearn.org/sites/default/files/inventory/unwoman30112015_2. pdf [hereinafter Assessment of Women's Livelihood].

ity intrusion, droughts, cold waves, water logging, and bank erosion risks. Most vulnerable are those living in the Chars (new islands built of silt). Since the delta's rivers change their courses often, these Char lands are swept away during a disaster. These areas are susceptible to tidal surges and cyclones.

The drought-prone areas consist of places located in the northern part of Bangladesh. The districts of Chapainawabganj and Natore are particularly vulnerable.[57] Since the birth of Bangladesh in 1971, the country has faced severe droughts frequently. In 1973, 1978, 1979, 1981, 1982, 1992, 1994, 1995, 2000, and 2006, this northern part of the country suffered from serious drought. The drought in 1973 was one of the worst and caused famine in 1974 in the northern parts of Bangladesh,[58] which received worldwide attention. Droughts result in societal challenges, including the scarcity of clean water and sufficient food.

Apart from flood-prone and drought-prone areas, areas subject to regular flooding occupy 80% of Bangladesh.[59] The Active Ganges Floodplain on the River Padma, which falls within the district of Shariatpur, and Brahmaputra Jamuna Floodplain on the River Jamuna within the district of Sirajganj, are two notable examples. According to the Ministry of Environment and Forests, "[t]wo-thirds of the country is less than 5 meters above sea level and is susceptible to river and rainwater flooding and, in lower-lying coastal areas, to tidal flooding during storms."[60]

In all of these regions, the impacts of natural disasters, such as cyclones in the coastal areas, problems associated with drought, and flooding, contribute to significant adverse effects on women's livelihoods. Women require more time than men to recover from the adverse impacts of disasters and suffer the most due to the environmental degradation from climate change.[61] Women are particularly at risk because of their roles in the family, which include caring for children, the sick, and the elderly.[62] Due to their restricted mobility, they are unable to adapt to many of the challenges from climate change impacts.

Clear indicators of the vulnerability of women are evident in the disproportionate mortality rate of women due to their restricted mobility.[63] For

---

57. *Id.*
58. TASK FORCE REPORT, REPORT OF THE TASK FORCES ON BANGLADESH DEVELOPMENT STRATEGIES FOR THE 1990s (1991).
59. *See* ASSESSMENT OF WOMEN'S LIVELIHOOD, *supra* note 56.
60. MINISTRY OF ENVIRONMENT AND FORESTS GOVERNMENT OF THE PEOPLE'S REPUBLIC OF BANGLADESH, BANGLADESH CLIMATE CHANGE STRATEGY AND ACTION PLAN (2009).
61. *See* Momtaz Jahan, *The Impact of Environmental Degradation on Women in Bangladesh: An Overview*, 30 ASIAN AFF. J. 5 (2008).
62. Rahman, *supra* note 50, at 75.
63. ASIAN DEVELOPMENT BANK, COUNTRY GENDER ASSESSMENT: BANGLADESH (2010), http://www.adb.org/sites/default/files/institutional-document/31338/cga-women-bangladesh.pdf.

example, in coastal zones as well as in flood-prone areas where knowing how to swim is one of the major adaptation skills,[64] many women do not know how to swim. Furthermore, even those women with swimming skills are at risk because the traditional clothing that they generally wear—sari[65]— restricts their mobility in water. Women are not only vulnerable with regard to death and injury caused by natural disasters themselves, such as cyclones, but they are also vulnerable to post-disaster impacts, which can be as harsh as the impacts of the disasters.[66] For example, the mortality rate of women from waterborne diseases is high. Whereas sometimes social norms prevalent in the rural areas prohibit women from engaging in outside-of-home activities, such as in coastal zones, paradoxically in drought-prone areas, the search for clean water, food, and fuel are tasks typically undertaken by women, which make women's lives challenging and increases their vulnerability to post-disaster impacts. Studies suggest that during a disaster, 72.5% of women in rural areas are responsible for gathering drinking water.[67] Depending on how severe the drought is, women's regular household livelihood activities become limited in scope as they look for sources of food and clean water elsewhere.

Given their responsibility for most of the household work and as the principal caregiver as part of their traditional gender-oriented role, women opt to make sacrifices for the sake of the family's well-being. For example, in disaster scenarios, the general customary norm in rural Bangladesh is that women opt to eat less food than men,[68] and they eat after feeding the men and children, which leaves the least amount of food for them and makes them weaker. In contrast, the workload of women during disasters increases significantly. In disaster situations, "women's poorer nutritional status is a key aspect of their reduced capacity to cope with the effects of a hazard."[69] Insufficient food consumption, lack of nutritious food, and the extra workload of women in disaster situations make women become less healthy.[70] As the women become weaker, their immune systems falter, thus making them more prone to waterborne and other diseases.[71] In flood-prone areas, for example, more widespread health problems arise from unclean water. At the same time, inadequate medical facilities and

---

64. ASSESSMENT OF WOMEN'S LIVELIHOOD, *supra* note 56, at 44.
65. Sari is defined by Merriam-Webster Dictionary as "a garment of southern Asian women that consists of several yards of lightweight cloth draped so that one end forms a skirt and the other a head or shoulder covering."
66. *See* ASSESSMENT OF WOMEN'S LIVELIHOOD, *supra* note 56.
67. Rahman, *supra* note 50, at 77.
68. *See* ASSESSMENT OF WOMEN'S LIVELIHOOD, *supra* note 56.
69. *See* Terry Cannon, *Gender and Climate Hazards in Bangladesh*, 10 GENDER & DEV. 45 (2002).
70. *Id.*
71. *Id.* at 48.

lack of female healthcare professionals produce severe problems causing additional mental stress.[72] Other issues exclusive to female health during floods include lactation for nursing mothers and amplified perineal rashes and urinary tract infections in teenage girls as they cannot clean their menstrual rags properly.[73]

The vulnerabilities of women in any of the natural disasters extend also to the sociocultural, economic, religious, and personal spheres in the form of compromised safety and violence.[74] In drought-prone areas, both distance and safety issues involved in obtaining basic needs put women and girls at risk of violence, harassment, and sexual assault.[75] In the coastal zone during natural disasters women are subject to harassment, for example, in cyclone shelters.[76] The Guidebook on Gender and Social Inclusion in Disaster Risk Reduction by the Bangladesh government reported that women are often subjected to sexual harassment in pre- and post-disaster situations.[77] There have been many accounts of harassment in shelters,[78] specifically where there are no segregated spaces for women for use of toilets and showers, and to sleep.

Migration to seek employment in the post-disaster context also impacts rural women. It is generally the male head of the family who migrates. This often leads to break-up of families in the form of desertion, divorce, and polygamy resulting in an increase in women's economic vulnerability.[79] Consequently, these households that become female-headed see an increase in their level of poverty. Moreover, early marriage can be triggered as a related consequence resulting from the interconnected threats of natural disasters exacerbated by climate change and extreme poverty.[80] A report[81] by Plan International documented interviews with girls in Bangladesh and suggests that early marriages increased in the aftermath of Cyclone Sidr in 2007. Climate change-induced disasters aggravate child marriage and

---

72. *Id.*
73. Rahman, *supra* note 50, at 72–82.
74. *See* Assessment of Women's Livelihood, *supra* note 56.
75. *Id.*
76. *Id.*
77. A.K.M. Mamunur Rashid & Hasan Al Shafie, Facilitators Guidebook: Practicing Gender & Social Inclusion in Disaster Risk Reduction 18 (Government of Bangladesh 2009), https://www.gdnonline.org/resources/GSI%20Guide%20Book%20English_CDMP.pdf.
78. Assessment of Women's Livelihood, *supra* note 56, at 23.
79. *See* Farhana Sultana, *Living in Hazardous Waterscapes: Gendered Vulnerabilities and Experiences of Floods and Disasters*, 9 Envtl. Hazards 43 (2010).
80. Human Rights Watch, Marry Before Your House Is Swept Away: Child Marriage in Bangladesh (2015), https://www.hrw.org/sites/default/files/report_pdf/bangladesh0615_web.pdf.
81. Anita Swarup et al., Weathering the Storm: Adolescent Girls and Climate Change (UK Aid 2011), http://www.ungei.org/files/weatherTheStorm.pdf.

this tactic has been used as a survival strategy at times when floods and droughts hit.[82]

One of the other significant adverse consequences of climate change is population displacement. Displacement happens both internally and externally, and is defined as a condition where preferences are restricted and movement of people is forced by loss of land caused by, for example, sea-level rise or extreme drought. Loss of housing arrangements due to climate change leads to both temporary displacement and permanent migration. The displaced people, regardless of temporary or permanent displacement, are subjected to social exclusion, giving rise to other problems in relation to women's vulnerability. Climate change-related displacement has triggered increased trafficking of women and girls from disaster sites to the capital and across borders,[83] and an increase in forced child marriages.[84]

II.   Human Rights Norms Applicable to Climate Change Impacts on Women

For all of the reasons discussed in Part I of this chapter, women are a highly vulnerable and marginalized group that suffers from severe violations of a number of fundamental human rights as a result of climate change impacts. The rights to life, health, food, water, housing, property, social inclusion, and personal dignity are the most relevant ones requiring attention in this discussion. Many of these rights are interconnected, in particular concerning women's suffering in a climate change-related context. Therefore, infringement of one of the rights can jeopardize the other rights, where women in Bangladesh, either directly or indirectly, are affected.

According to the 2014 United Nations Human Development Report,[85] 200 million people were affected by disasters induced by climate change, particularly floods and droughts, between 2000 and 2012, most of which occurred in developing countries. The OHCHR relied on the United Nations

---

82.   Gayle Tzemach Lemmon, *Fragile States, Fragile Lives: Child Marriage Amid Disaster and Conflict*, GIRLS NOT BRIDES, July 30, 2014, http://www.girlsnotbrides.org/fragile-states-fragile-lives-child-marriage-amid-disaster-conflict/.

83.   *See* MARGARET ALSTON, WOMEN AND CLIMATE CHANGE IN BANGLADESH (2013); Sam Eaton, *After the Floods Come the Human Traffickers, but These Girls Are Fighting Back*, PRI's THE WORLD, Sept. 15, 2015, http://www.pri.org/stories/2015-09-15/after-floods-come-human-traffickers-these-girls-are-fighting-back.

84.   According to UNICEF, Bangladesh has the fourth highest rate of child marriage—after Niger, Central African Republic, and Chad—in the world.

85.   UNITED NATIONS DEVELOPMENT PROGRAMME (UNDP), HUMAN DEVELOPMENT REPORT—SUSTAINING HUMAN PROGRESS: REDUCING VULNERABILITIES AND BUILDING RESILIENCE (2014), http://hdr.undp.org/sites/default/files/hdr14-report-en-1.pdf.

Human Development Report 2007/2008[86] in its January 2009 report on climate change and human rights, which stated that the projected effects of climate change pose both direct and indirect threats to human lives.[87] While harm to lives is more immediate in some regions and countries than others, a report[88] by the Centre for Naval Analyses based in the United States concluded that climate change works as a "threat multiplier" in regions that are already vulnerable by accelerating the worsening of their conditions. Another report, by the Climate Vulnerable Forum[89] and DARA International,[90] in 2012 projected that climate change causes approximately 400,000 deaths every year, and this figure is estimated to increase to 700,000 by 2030.[91] Concerning human health, the IPCC Fourth Assessment Report[92] determined that climate change will impact the health of millions by way of malnutrition, diarrhea, respiratory illnesses, and increased health hazards caused by, for example, dengue fever—a disease common in Bangladesh that has claimed many lives in recent decades. Consequently, the threat to the right to life accelerates when risks to human health, which disproportionately affect women, increase. Moreover, the right to health is also affected due to lack of proper healthcare facilities; lack of adequate sanitation, safe water, and sufficient supply of food; and poor housing and access to health-related information.

As a result of climate change impacts, food production decreases significantly with the increase in temperatures speeding grain sterility; shifting patterns of rainfall inducing land infertility, increasing erosion, and desertification; and decreasing crop and livestock yields. Additionally, sea-level rise makes coastal lands unusable and causes fish species to migrate

---

86. *Id.*
87. United Nations Human Rights Office of the High Commissioner, 2009 Report: Activities and Results (2009), http://www.ohchr.org/Documents/Publications/I_OHCHR_Rep_2009_complete_final.pdf.
88. Center for Naval Analyses Corp., National Security and the Threat of Climate Change (2007), https://www.cna.org/CNA_files/pdf/National%20Security%20and%20the%20Threat%20of%20Climate%20Change.pdf.
89. The Climate Vulnerable Forum (CVF) is an "international partnership of countries highly vulnerable to a warming planet. The Forum serves as a South-South cooperation platform for participating governments to act together to deal with global climate change." CVF, About the Climate Vulnerable Forum, http://www.thecvf.org/web/climate-vulnerable-forum/(last visited Aug. 23, 2016).
90. DARA International is an "independent non-profit organisation committed to improving the quality and effectiveness of humanitarian action for vulnerable populations affected by armed conflicts and natural disasters." DARA Impact Matters, *Improving the Effectiveness of Humanitarian Aid: About Us,* http://daraint.org/about-us/ (last visited Aug. 23, 2016).
91. DARA and the Climate Vulnerable Forum, Climate Vulnerability Monitor: A Guide to the Cold Calculus of a Hot Planet 17 (2d ed. 2012).
92. Lenny Bernstein et al., Climate Change 2007 Synthesis Report, A Report of the Intergovernmental Panel on Climate Change (2007), https://www.ipcc.ch/pdf/assessment-report/ar4/syr/ar4_syr_full_report.pdf.

away. As the frequency of extreme weather conditions increase, agricultural activities are impacted. The IPCC report has indicated that climate change disrupts food security,[93] thereby threatening the realization of the right to food. According to a World Bank estimate,[94] a 2°C increase in the average global temperature will put 100 to 400 million more people at risk of hunger and could cause deaths in approximately 3 million additional people due to malnutrition every year. Climate change is also expected to intensify the risk of scarcity of water.[95] According to the IPCC report, climate change is expected to cause a decline in renewable surface water as well as groundwater resources in dry subtropical regions, making the competition for water even more intense.[96] A 2010 World Bank report concluded that a 2°C average global increase in temperature might lead to 1 to 2 billion people failing to have access to adequate water to meet their needs.[97] The decreased access to water will have disproportionate impacts on vulnerable groups of people.

Extreme storm events can also destroy homes and displace a significant number of people. Drought, erosion, and flooding can cause localities to be unfit for habitation, thus causing displacement and migration.[98] Sea-level rise poses challenges to land where housing is located, which is estimated to continue to severely impact the right to adequate housing.[99] All of these considerations are particularly relevant in the context of Bangladesh.

Rural women in Bangladesh are the most vulnerable potential victims of these impacts. They are the ones who face the most violations of human rights, including the rights to life, health, housing, water, and food. The mortality rate of women during disaster and post-disaster situations in Bangladesh is higher for the reasons described in Part I. In addition, lack of formal education and social and religious constraints restricting them to traditional roles in the family can result in non-recognition of their other rights, such as rights to education, inheritance, personal safety, freedom from displacement against one's will, and dignity of person.

---

93. *Id.* at 13.
94. World Bank, World Development Report 2010: Development and Climate Change 4–5 (2010), http://siteresources.worldbank.org/INTWDR2010/Resources/5287678-1226014527953/ WDR10-Full-Text.pdf.
95. Bernstein et al., *supra* note 92, at 15–16.
96. *Id.* at 13.
97. World Bank, *supra* note 94, at 5.
98. Md. Shamsuddoha et al., Displacement and Migration From Climate Hot-spots in Bangladesh: Causes and Consequences (ActionAid 2012), http://www.actionaidusa.org/sites/files/ actionaid/displacement_and_migration....pdf.
99. *Id.*

III. Human Rights Standards Applicable to Women in Bangladesh

The international human rights framework offers standards that are universally applicable to safeguard the aforementioned rights applicable to women. For example, the preamble and the articles of the Charter of the United Nations impose a general obligation on States "to reaffirm faith in fundamental human rights, in dignity and worth of the human person, in the equal rights of men and women"[100] and to support "promoting and encouraging respect for human rights and for fundamental freedoms for all without distinction as to race, sex, language, or religion . . . ."[101] In addition, Articles 55 and 56, respectively, demand promotion of universal respect for, and observance of, human rights and fundamental freedom, as well as joint and separate actions in cooperation with relevant organizations to achieve the goal of promoting human rights.[102]

Several international law instruments have been developed to provide a foundation for the protection of human rights. The most comprehensive is the international bill of rights consisting of three significant instruments—the Universal Declaration of Human Rights (UDHR), adopted in 1948; the International Covenant on Civil and Political Rights (ICCPR), adopted in 1966; and the International Covenant on Economic, Social, and Cultural Rights (ICESCR), adopted in 1966. In addition, there are several other instruments that recognize universal norms pertaining to human rights. Particularly relevant in the context of women's rights is the Convention on the Elimination of All Forms of Discrimination against Women (CEDAW), adopted in 1979.

Bangladesh has accepted the legal commitments within the framework of these instruments as it is a Party to all of these instruments. Bangladesh acceded to the ICCPR in 2000 and to the ICESCR in 1998. It also acceded to CEDAW in 1984, subject to reservations to Article 2 and Article 16(1)(c) to the extent these provisions conflict with the country's religious-based personal law issues. Article 2 of CEDAW obliges countries to eliminate discriminatory laws, policies, and practices within the domestic legal framework and Article 16 stipulates that women have equal rights to that of men with respect to marriage and family relations. These articles have been regarded by the OHCHR as integral to the due implementation of all other articles of the Convention.[103]

---

100. U.N. Charter pmbl.
101. *Id.* at art. 1.2.
102. *Id.* at arts. 55 and 56.
103. *Concluding Observations of the Committee on the Elimination of Discrimination Against Women, supra* note 46.

However, the Constitution of Bangladesh has embraced the essence of these internationally acknowledged norms in regard to the protection of fundamental human rights without any discrimination. With regards to women's rights stipulated in the aforementioned treaties, the following provisions of the Constitution of Bangladesh are deemed to comply with them. Article 10 provides for women's complete participation in national life and Article 19 makes the State responsible for ensuring equal opportunities for all citizens and to eliminate social and economic inequality between men and women and also assure equitable distribution of wealth and opportunities among citizens. Article 27 states that all citizens are equal and entitled to equal protection of law. Article 28 provides for the principles of non-discrimination, including that women are entitled to equal rights with men in all spheres of the State and public life. Article 31 addresses the right to be protected and treated in accordance with the law.

The right to life, the most basic of all human rights found in Article 3 of the UDHR and Article 6 of the ICCPR, appears in Article 32 of the Bangladesh Constitution. It is an inherent right and imposes both negative and positive obligations on States as confirmed by the United Nations Human Rights Committee,[104] which is the treaty monitoring body within the framework of the ICCPR. While articulated in many of the aforementioned instruments, the right to health is most comprehensively mentioned in Article 12 of the ICESCR, which entitles everyone to the right to health based on the "highest standard of physical and mental health"[105] In General Comment No. 12, the ICESCR notes that climate change challenges the right to health by distorting the environment, because one of the key factors in determining human health is a healthy environment. The ICESCR has interpreted this right to be inclusive of timely and proper healthcare, adequate sanitation and safe water, sufficient supply of food, housing, and access to health-related information. Although the Constitution of Bangladesh does not provide the right to protection of health, Article 32 is inclusive of the right to health[106] under the wider umbrella of the right to life.

In addition, the other rights affected by climate change can also be found guaranteed within the framework of human rights. For example, the right to food and the right to an adequate standard of living, including adequate

---

104. *General Comment No. 6: Article 6 (Right to Life)*, United Nations Human Rights Office of the High Commissioner, 16th Sess. (1982), http://tbinternet.ohchr.org/_layouts/treatybodyexternal/Download.aspx?symbolno=INT%2fCCPR%2fGEC%2f6630&Lang=en.
105. International Covenant on Economic, Social, and Cultural Rights, Jan. 3, 1976, http://www.ohchr.org/Documents/ProfessionalInterest/cescr.pdf.
106. Mehta v. India, (1998) 9 S.C.C. 589 (India).

housing, are guaranteed under Article 11 of the ICESCR. Rights to property (inheritance), inclusion, proper empowerment, and the right not to be arbitrarily displaced can be found in Article 17 of UDHR. A guarantee of these rights is either directly or indirectly reflected in the Constitution of Bangladesh.

The administrative bodies within the framework of the applicable treaties further interpret the scope of these rights. For example, in the Committee on Economic, Social, and Cultural Rights under the ICESCR, General Comment No. 12 obliges States Parties to assure freedom from hunger and to act positively to eradicate hunger even during natural or other disasters. While express recognition within the ICESCR framework does not yet exist, the right to water has been implied through General Comment No. 15 of the Committee on Economic, Social, and Cultural Rights, which provides that: "The human right to water entitles everyone to sufficient, safe, acceptable, physically accessible and affordable water for personal and domestic uses."[107] Other legal instruments, including Article 14 of CEDAW, recognize this right. Similarly, General Comment No. 4 of the Committee on Economic, Social, and Cultural Rights elaborated on the right to housing by emphasizing that this right is of core importance for the complete enjoyment of all other economic, social, and cultural rights.

IV. Challenges to Safeguarding Women's Rights in Bangladesh

Bangladesh is a country ruled by democratic governance, the Constitution of which ensures rule of law accommodating universally accepted norms. Subject to specific reservations, all internationally acknowledged human rights norms and standards, as shown in the previous section, are applicable to Bangladesh. Given its endorsement of international human rights instruments, Bangladesh not only has a duty to comply with the norms of human rights, but also bears the responsibility to prevent violation of, and to protect and promote, human rights. Even though the Constitution of Bangladesh adheres to most of the international obligations in terms of guaranteeing women's rights, the presence of law in itself does not guarantee the protection of human rights. It is also necessary to create an atmosphere promoting awareness inclusive of economic, sociocultural, and religious norms that offers clear roles for women as subjects, not objects, to ensure that they are

---

107. *General Comment No. 15: The Right to Water (arts. 11 and 12)*, United Nations Committee on Economic, Social, and Cultural Rights, 29th Sess., U.N. Doc. E/C.12/2002/11 (2003).

integrated as actors in all spheres of societal structure to promote their human rights. It requires measures to ensure equality, fairness, participation, access to justice, avoidance of arbitrariness, and transparency.[108]

The issue that gives rise to inconsistencies between legal rules and practical application of those rules is the traditional social structure. It assumes prescribed gendered roles, stereotypical images of women as childbearer or homemaker, religious misinterpretation of women's role, and strict practice of purdah.[109] Apart from sociocultural taboos, discussed elsewhere in this chapter, contributing to women's vulnerabilities, there are specific religious and social practices that restrict women from having a proper position despite constitutional guarantees. Social exclusion of women presents major challenges, which also accelerates their human insecurity. Therefore, while this chapter endorses the importance of the rule of law, it also highlights the need to promote social awareness, sustained economic growth, eradication of poverty, and access to education and an increase in the literacy rate so that overall quality of life is improved. The promotion of favorable social conditions greatly contributes to the promotion of human rights of women in response to the challenges identified in this chapter. Nevertheless, there is also inconsistency and ambiguity within the framework of law enshrined in the Constitution that result in discrimination against women.

Concerning rights enshrined in the Constitution, the Constitution of Bangladesh has been amended 15 times since its inception in 1972. Regarding fundamental principles, "secularism" is placed as one of the four,[110] the others being nationalism, democracy, and socialism. However, the recent version of the Constitution, as of 2011, is ambiguous with respect to the declaration of Islam as an official state religion in Article 2A. The upholding of the application of religious-based personal law is often regarded as the point of ambiguity and contradiction regarding gender equality. However, according to Tahrat Naushaba Shahid, reconciliation of these two aspects is generally interpreted pursuant to the discretion of the judicial system,[111] which does not necessarily preclude sexual equality as there are "jurisprudential avenues within *fiqh* or Islamic jurisprudence to offer women greater equality."[112]

---

108. *The Rule of Law and Transitional Justice in Conflict and Post-conflict Societies: Report of the Secretary-General*, U.N. SCOR, at 4, para. 6, U.N. Doc. S/2004/616 (2004).

109. *See* Abul Kalam, *Social Norms and Impediments of Women Development in Bangladesh*, 2 Int'l J. Soc. Sci. Stud. 100 (2014).

110. Const. of Bangladesh art. 8.

111. Tahrat Naushaba Shahid, Islam and Women in the Constitution of Bangladesh: The Impact on Family Laws for Muslim Women 2 (The Foundation for Law, Justice, and Society n.d.), http://www.fljs.org/files/publications/Tahrat.pdf.

112. *Id.* at 4.

Declaring Islam as the state religion has very little significance in terms of determining the role of religion in the context of legal practice. Article 28(2) of the Constitution ensures the equality of men and women both in the public and private spheres. An opposing view contends that the Constitution's primary reference to women's equality in reality lies in the public sphere only, such as in terms of enhancing women's presence in labor forces and in Parliament.[113] Yet the constitutional endorsement of equality of women held through Articles 27–29[114] does not clarify whether and how these provisions will take precedence in the event of a clash with classical Islamic jurisprudence. For example, the High Court of Bangladesh banned the issuance of fatwa in 2001.[115] The fatwa in question was directed at a young woman. Fatwa is a verdict issued by religious scholars or clerics in Islam. Clerics appealed against this decision in 2011 and the ban was lifted stating that no fatwa can be issued in defiance of existing laws of the country, and enforcement of such verdicts is forbidden.[116] Thus, there is a lack of clarity regarding the status of fatwa.

Women's constitutional rights in Bangladesh, in particular in the economic and political spheres, are heavily determined by political economy. Religion, particularly Islam, places some restrictions in the legal sphere,[117] which results in gender inequality in property rights. An example of this reality is evident in the reservation provided by the government of Bangladesh in 1984 concerning its legal obligation under CEDAW that the country "does not consider as binding upon itself the provisions of article 2, [. . . and . . .] 16 (1) (c) as they conflict with *Sharia* law based on Holy Quran and Sunna."[118] As such, within the framework of religious personal law, an unequal share of wealth arguably made women less empowered than men. For example, under Islamic law, the husband receives one-fourth of his wife's property on her death whereas the wife receives only one-eighth of her deceased husband's property provided that he left children[119] behind. In the Hindu religion, even where a Hindu woman inherits land, her rights in the land are restricted to

---

113. *Id.* at 6.

114. Article 29 of the Constitution ensures equality of opportunity in public employment.

115. *See* Fauzia Erfan Ahmed, *Ijtihad and Lower-middle-class Women: Secularism in Rural Bangladesh*, 31 Comp. Stud. S. Asia, Afr. & Middle E. 124 (2011).

116. *Bangladesh lifts fatwa ban but forbids enforcement*, BBC.com News, May 12, 2011, http://www.bbc.com/news/world-south-asia-13379016.

117. E.H. Chowdhury, *"Transnationalism Reversed": Engaging Religion, Development, and Women's Organizing in Bangladesh*, 32 Women's Stud. Int'l F. 414, 416 (2009).

118. Rule of Law in Armed Conflicts Projects, *Bangladesh: International Treaties Adherence*, http://www.geneva-academy.ch/RULAC/international_treaties.php?id_state=22 (last visited Aug. 23, 2016).

119. Shah I. Mobin Jinnah, Land and Property Rights of Rural Women in Bangladesh, Community Development Association (2013), http://www.ohchr.org/Documents/HRBodies/CEDAW/RuralWomen/CDABangladesh.pdf.

life interest. Accordingly, when she dies, the property will revert back to the person from whom she inherited the land. Hindu inheritance provisions govern the Buddhist community in Bangladesh.[120]

While the so-called personal law provides some concerns about women's rights in Bangladesh, women are generally well protected within the legal framework, as there are a number of widely used regulations available to protect women's rights; for example in case of violence against women, the regulations available are the Domestic Violence (Prevention and Protection) Act 2010 and Prevention of Women and Child Repression Act 2000. However, the protection and promotion of women's rights need to be integrated into strategies and action plans at various levels. Since restraints on the rights of women are imposed by the fact that women are subjected to sociocultural and religious stigma, a greater awareness will offer room for available legal provisions to be popularized.

There are several nongovernmental organizations (NGOs) working in the country to promote awareness of the challenges facing women in Bangladesh. For instance, NGOs like Proshika and BRAC are involved with microeconomic empowerment of women,[121] whereas NGOs like Ain o Salish Kendra works with the promotion of legal rights of women.[122] The adverse consequences of climate change impacts on women are increasingly becoming part of these NGOs' agendas. In addition, both government and NGOs often cooperate to promote the agenda for greater human development. For instance, in the health sector, the collaboration between government and NGOs has been prevalent specifically in controlling tuberculosis, maternal and child health, and family planning. Among many successful collaborations between the government and NGOs, CARE-Bangladesh's reproductive health project and BRAC's health and development programs had outstanding outcomes.[123] Initiatives such as these are capable of promoting the quality of life as they contribute to economic growth, efficiency in resource usages, sustainable development, social justice, and fairness in invocation of legal rules.

Apart from the presence of law, human development can stimulate the protection and promotion of human rights. The human development

---

120. *Id.*
121. *See* Mohammad A. Islam et al., *Micro-credit Programmes of Different NGOs/MFIs: A Comparative Study*, 10 J. BANGLADESH AGRIC. U. 297 (2012).
122. Ain o Salish Kendra's work is explained by Banglapedia. Banglapedia National Encyclopaedia of Bangladesh, Sayeed Ahmad, *Ain o Salish Kendra*, http://en.banglapedia.org/index.php?title=Ain_o_Salish_Kendra (last visited Aug. 23, 2016).
123. *See* HENRY B. PERRY, HEALTH FOR ALL IN BANGLADESH: LESSONS IN PRIMARY HEALTH CARE FOR THE TWENTY-FIRST CENTURY (2000); A.N. Zafar Ullah et al., *Government-NGO Collaboration: The Case of Tuberculosis Control in Bangladesh*, 21 HEALTH POL'Y PLAN. 143 (2006).

approach is involved in expanding the richness of human life instead of focusing solely on the richness of the economy where human beings live.[124] It focuses on people and their opportunities and choices. This approach was developed by the United Nations from Amartya Sen's work on "development as freedom."[125] The approach seeks to provide people with more freedom to lead their lives in ways that they value. This, in effect, touches on the capabilities of people in developing countries and provides them with the ability to utilize them. For instance, if a girl were provided with an education to strengthen her skills, it would not be of any use if she cannot access jobs or have the capabilities specifically required by the labor market of the locality. The foundations of the human development approach address three requirements: to live a long, healthy, and creative life; to be knowledgeable; and to have access to resources required for a decent standard of living.[126] Other factors that are deemed important are those that assist in creating the right conditions for human development, which can be achieved via ensuring participation in community life, environmental sustainability, human security and rights, and gender equality. Once these basic protections are achieved, they open up opportunities in all aspects of life.

Presence of law in itself cannot guarantee the protection of human rights. The protection of human rights must be found within a societal sphere having at least minimum standards for ensuring quality of life, and being free from unjust and unfair sociocultural and customary practices. Providing the society with a foundation for human development balances up the gender inequality and thereby assists in the eradication of issues highlighted above stemming from the adverse impacts of climate change.

Conclusion

This chapter addressed how impacts of climate change drastically affect the enjoyment of some of the most basic human rights of women in Bangladesh. It examined how climate change-related challenges cause women in Bangladesh, especially in its vast rural areas including the coastal zones, to face serious risks resulting not only in threats to life, but also in threats to overall sociocultural entitlements required for maintaining quality of life.

---

124. For further information, see UNDP, *Human Development Reports—About Human Development: What Is Human Development?*, http://hdr.undp.org/en/humandev(last visited Aug. 23, 2016).
125. *See* AMARTYA SEN, DEVELOPMENT AS FREEDOM (1999).
126. The Human Development Index considers these three attributes. UNDP, *Human Development Reports—Human Development Index (HDI)*, http://hdr.undp.org/en/content/human-development-index-hdi (last visited Aug. 23, 2016).

While these challenges have clear links to the established norms of human rights to which Bangladesh is fully committed as part of its constitutional and international obligations, adherence to the norm of human rights does not exist in a vacuum. Unless sociocultural elements and religious or related customary practices that substantially exclude women within the societal context are removed, legal guarantees will not by themselves be able to protect women from human rights violations. As a result, the promotion of social and political awareness concerning the challenges affecting these human rights in rural women is critical in conjunction with promoting overall human development to enhance quality of life for all, including women. Only this type of societal environment could better protect and promote women's rights in Bangladesh that are threatened by climate change impacts.

Climate Justice
in the Courts

Chapter 19

From Responsibility to Cost-Effectiveness to Litigation: The Evolution of Climate Change Regulation and the Emergence of Climate Justice Litigation

*Chilenye Nwapi**

* *The author gratefully acknowledges the research assistance of Leara Morris-Stokes and Demetrius Wilson, students at Florida A&M University College of Law.*

Introduction

The deleterious effects of climate change are well documented,[1] as is the link between human activities and climate change.[2] An article that appeared in *Scientific American* in 2006 declared that "[t]he debate on global warming is over. Present levels of carbon dioxide—nearing 400 ppm in the earth's atmosphere—are higher than they have been at any time in the past 650,000 years."[3] After examining 928 article abstracts published in scientific journals between 1993 and 2003 and listed in the Institute of Scientific Information database, Naomi Oreskes concluded that "the scientific consensus [about global warming] is clearly expressed" in the Intergovernmental Panel on Climate Change (IPCC) reports.[4] She described the study as follows:

> The 928 papers were divided into six categories: explicit endorsement of the consensus position, evaluation of impacts, mitigation proposals, methods, paleoclimate analysis, and rejection of the consensus position. Of all the papers, 75% fell into the first three categories, either explicitly or implicitly accepting the consensus view; 25% dealt with methods or paleoclimate, taking no position on current anthropogenic climate change. Remarkably, none of the papers disagreed with the consensus position.[5]

Despite this compelling data, States and other policymakers have struggled for more than 25 years to reach a consensus on the appropriate mechanisms to reduce greenhouse gas (GHG) emissions that contribute to global warming.[6]

---

1. The most authoritative sources are the various assessment reports of the Intergovernmental Panel on Climate Change (IPCC). To date, there have been five assessment reports, published in 1990, 1995, 2001, 2007, and 2014, plus a supplementary report published in 1992, http://www.ipcc.ch/publications_and_data/publications_and_data_reports.shtml.

2. *See* IPCC, CLIMATE CHANGE 2014: SYNTHESIS REPORT 2 (2015) (emphasizing that "[h]uman influence on the climate system is clear, and recent anthropogenic emissions of greenhouse gases are the highest in history"), http://www.ipcc.ch/pdf/assessment-report/ar5/syr/SYR_AR5_FINAL_full_wcover.pdf. The synthesis report distills the findings of the Working Groups to the Fifth Assessment Report.

3. Gary Stix, *A Climate Repair Manual*, 295 SCI. AM. 46, 46 (2006).

4. Naomi Oreskes, *Beyond the Ivory Tower: The Scientific Consensus on Climate Change*, 306 SCI. 1686, 1686 (2004), http://science.sciencemag.org/content/sci/306/5702/1686.full.pdf.

5. *Id.*

6. *See, e.g.*, Simon Chin-Yee, Briefing: *Africa and the Paris Climate Change Agreement*, AFR. AFF. 1, 3 (2016) (highlighting the "tensions and fears in the build-up to" the Paris Agreement); Raymond Clémencon, *The Two Sides of the Paris Climate Agreement: Dismal Failure or Historic Breakthrough*, 25 J. ENV'T & DEV. 3, 18, 20 (2016) (arguing that the Paris Agreement was a product of unprecedented global momentum for action on climate change, but concluding that it may represent "another missed opportunity where international leaders made promises they were in no position or unwilling to fulfil"); James W. Coleman, *Unilateral Climate Regulation*, 38 HARV. ENVTL. L. REV. 87, 89, 92 (2014) (observing that "the quest for a binding global treaty has proven to be a non-starter" and that "an international treaty remains unlikely"); DALE JAMIESON, REASON IN A DARK TIME: WHY THE

A central aspect of the struggle is the idea of climate justice. How should the costs of reducing GHG emissions be distributed among the multiple contributors to the emissions? Should any States be responsible for a greater share of that cost than other States and, if so, which states should bear such responsibility? How should the victims of climate change impacts be compensated and who should bear the burden of compensation? Controversy over these questions remains and has played out most prominently within the binary frame of developed and developing countries. Other dimensions to it involve indigenous peoples, women, youth, and environmental nongovernmental organizations (ENGOs) squaring off in litigation against fossil fuel companies and national and subnational governments entrusted with responsibility for protecting the environment.

Various mechanisms that reflect the influence of justice and equity considerations have been proposed to address climate change regulation, a review of which reveals three historical trends: (1) the age of responsibility, (2) the age of cost-effectiveness, and (3) the age of litigation. The age of responsibility refers to the "common but differentiated responsibility" (CBDR) principle characterized by political declarations affirming the recognition that climate change was a global problem. The age of cost-effectiveness produced ideas like emissions trading, the Clean Development Mechanism (CDM), and joint implementation (JI). The age of litigation is characterized by lawsuits in both domestic and regional fora seeking either judicial review of administrative decisions concerning climate change, mandatory action on climate change, or compensatory relief against contributors to climate change. But none of these approaches has gained extensive support, largely due to uncertainties over the costs of climate change and opposition from businesses.[7]

The age of responsibility has virtually been abandoned through its fundamental transformation under the Paris Agreement[8] from a strict differentiation between developed and developing States under the United Nations Framework Convention on Climate Change (UNFCCC)[9] and the accom-

---

STRUGGLE AGAINST CLIMATE CHANGE FAILED—AND WHAT IT MEANS FOR OUR FUTURE 2 (2014) (arguing that the climate change issue has "become too wrapped up in political slogans and partisan bickering" and that "[t]here is too much talk that purports to be about the science or policy but is really about posturing and positioning").

7. Eduardo M. Peñalver, *Acts of God or Toxic Torts? Applying Tort Principles to the Problem of Climate Change*, 38 NAT. RESOURCES J. 563, 564 (1998).

8. *Adoption of the Paris Agreement*, UNFCCC Conference of the Parties, 21st Sess., U.N. Doc. FCCC/CP/2015/10/Add.1 (Dec. 12, 2015), http://unfccc.int/files/home/application/pdf/paris_agreement.pdf.

9. United Nations Framework Convention on Climate Change (UNFCCC), May 9, 1992, 31 I.L.M. 849.

panying Kyoto Protocol[10] to a common, even if more nuanced, framework that commits all States to take action to combat global warming, albeit with developed States taking the lead. The age of cost-effectiveness is experiencing diminished acceptance despite the continuing presence of cost-effectiveness provisions in important legal instruments (including the Paris Agreement) that address climate change. In the wake of these developments, the age of litigation has been ushered in and is here to stay at least for the foreseeable future, despite the challenging issues of causation and proof that climate change litigation involves.

This chapter reviews these three trends, highlights the factors that necessitated their emergence, and takes stock of their gains and shortcomings. It highlights the significance of the Paris Agreement as the impetus for the phasing out of the responsibility and cost-effectiveness principles. It does not endorse one approach over another, but instead acknowledges that each approach has played an important role in the quest for climate justice. However, the chapter highlights the role that climate change litigation has played in the quest for climate justice, a role that reflects the frustration faced by certain segments of actors, such as indigenous communities and ENGOs, due to the international community's failure to take a proactive approach to support its avowed recognition of the urgent action that is needed to reduce GHG emissions.

Part I of the chapter considers the CBDR principle. It explains its meaning, its underlying rationale, and its status under the Paris Agreement. Part II addresses the cost-effectiveness principle and considers three mechanisms that have been adopted to implement it: emissions trading, the CDM, and JI. It also considers the current status of the principle and the role of these implementation mechanisms under the Paris Agreement. Part III discusses the idea of climate justice litigation. It identifies the factors that led to its emergence, considers some of the most significant cases that have been litigated, and evaluates the impact of litigation on climate change regulation and the search for climate justice.

I.   The CBDR Principle

The CBDR principle addresses the obligations of States to participate in international measures to combat global warming. The principle is rooted in the notion of the environment as part of the common heritage of man-

---

10.   Kyoto Protocol to the United Nations Framework Convention on Climate Change, Dec. 11, 1997, 37 I.L.M. 22.

kind.[11] The CBDR principle recognizes: (1) the varying levels of contribution of States to global environmental problems, (2) differences in States' respective capabilities to undertake measures to address the problems, and (3) the reality that the greatest impacts of global warming are felt by the poorer, developing States while the greatest per capita GHG emissions that cause global warming emanate from the wealthier, developed States.[12] While the principle requires States to cooperate to reduce the mutual risks involved in the destruction of the environment, it recognizes that developed States, which produce the most significant share of GHG emissions, have greater capacity to reduce their emissions than developing States. The principle therefore charges developed States to carry a greater share of the burden than developing States.

The CBDR principle is enshrined in several international instruments, including Principle 7 of the Rio Declaration.[13] Principle 7 provides that:

> In view of the different contributions to global environmental degradation, States have common but differentiated responsibilities. The developed countries acknowledge the responsibility that they bear in the international pursuit of sustainable development in view of the pressures their societies place on the global environment and of the technologies and financial resources they command.[14]

But the principle's most direct adoption, especially in the field of environmental protection, is in Article 3(1) of the UNFCCC, which commits States Parties to "protect the climate system . . . on the basis of equity and in accordance with their common but differentiated responsibilities and respective capabilities,"[15] with specific targets set in the Kyoto Protocol to the Convention. An important aspect of the principle is international assistance, including financial assistance and technology transfer, from developed to developing States.

The underlying rationale for the adoption of the CBDR principle in the UNFCCC and the Kyoto Protocol was that imposition of GHG reduction obligations on developing States would undermine developing States' economic development, which would in turn undermine global efforts to

---

11. Philippe Sands, Principles of International Environmental Law 217 (2d ed. 2003).
12. *See* Christopher D. Stone, *Common but Differentiated Responsibilities in International Law*, 98 Am. J. Int'l L. 276 (2004).
13. *Rio Declaration on Environment and Development*, U.N. Conference on Environment and Development, Rio de Janeiro, Brazil, June 3–14, 1992, princ. 7, U.N. Doc. A/CONF.151/26 (Vol. I) (1992), http://www.jus.uio.no/lm/environmental.development.rio.declaration.1992/portrait.a4.pdf.
14. *Id.*
15. UNFCCC, art. 3(1).

eradicate poverty.[16] It was believed that economic development had a direct correlation with fossil fuel use. To ask developing countries to reduce or avoid GHG emissions by reducing their fossil fuel use would place their economic development at risk.

The distinction between developed and developing States proved to be difficult to ascertain, however. For example, many States in transition (newly industrializing), such as China, India, Brazil, Mexico, and South Africa, are currently contributing more GHG emissions than they were before they began their transition or before the UNFCCC was drafted. Many scholars have argued that the rules of differentiation should be revised with a view to increasing the responsibilities of these States vis-à-vis other developing States.[17]

From the perspective of developed countries, the CBDR principle is an impediment to international efforts to combat climate change. This is because the principle was the basis upon which developing States refused to accept any obligations to reduce their emissions, a stance that resulted in a gridlock in future climate change negotiations when developed States insisted that a workable approach was one that imposed emissions reduction/avoidance obligations on all States, particularly on the newly industrializing States.[18] In fact, during the negotiations of the Kyoto Protocol, the United States vehemently asserted that it "will not assume binding obligations until developing countries make adequate commitments in terms of their own obligations."[19]

The differentiation element in the CBDR principle was a critical issue in the negotiation of the Paris Agreement, which lasted nearly a decade. The Agreement adopted a CBDR principle that departed from the conventional understanding of it towards what appears to be a more nuanced type of differentiation. While it explicitly adopts the principle under Article 2, with references to developed and developing States in several provisions, it abandons the establishment of separate and different categories of emissions reductions for developed and developing States and simply encourages developed States to take the lead. However, the Agreement adopts, albeit implicitly, what may be regarded as the principle of "self-differentiation." It does so by

---

16. Albert Mumma & David Hodas, *Designing a Global Post-Kyoto Climate Change Protocol That Advances Human Development*, 20 Geo. Int'l Envtl. L. Rev. 619, 625 (2007).
17. *See, e.g., id.* at 627; *see also* Tracy Bach & Rebecca Davidson, *Turning the Corner in Lima: The Language of Differentiation and the "Democratization" of Climate Change Negotiations*, 18 Ethics, Pol'y & Env't 169, 170 (2015) (arguing that fairness requires revisiting the CBDR rule). For a full discussion of the climate justice implications of CBDR, *see supra* Chapter 2 in this volume.
18. Mumma & Hodas, *supra* note 16, at 619–20.
19. *Id.* at 628 (internal citations omitted).

enlisting States to individually determine their own contributions towards climate goals in Article 4. Furthermore, the principle of "self-differentiation" is coupled with the principle of "self-identification." Under the Agreement, the terms "developed" and "developing" are not defined, implicitly allowing States to gauge where they fit within the spectrum. The potential implications of these two principles for poorer States, which bear the brunt of climate change impacts but lack the capacity to implement mitigation measures, remains to be seen and is beyond the scope of this chapter. While some have argued that the Agreement is "firmly anchored" in the CBDR principle,[20] from a developing State's perspective, the Agreement adopts a weakened form of the principle—though one that reflected a compromise without which the Agreement would very likely not have been adopted—thus indirectly enjoining developing States to do more than they are willing to do to combat climate change.

II.   The Principle of Cost Differentiation

Economists believe that conventional command-and-control methods do not achieve environmental objectives in the least costly manner. On the contrary, effectively designed market-based instruments would provide dynamic incentives for regulated entities to work more assiduously towards reducing their environmental imprints and at the least possible cost. Yielding to this economic theory during the negotiations leading up to the UNFCCC, the Ad Hoc Group on the Berlin Mandate—the negotiation group established by the first Conference of the Parties (COP) in 1995—submitted a series of proposals intended to enable industrialized States to implement measures that would enable them to achieve their emissions reduction targets.[21] The proposals resulted in the adoption of three flexible, market-based mechanisms that would allow industrialized States to pursue their emissions reduction targets by investing in or supporting emissions reduction projects in other States, primarily developing States.[22] The mechanisms are: (1) emissions trading, (2) the CDM, and (3) JI.

An important feature of these mechanisms was cost-effectiveness. The argument was that climate change commitments should be distributed in a

---

20.   Lavanya Rajamani, *Ambition and Differentiation in the 2015 Paris Agreement: International Possibilities and Underlying Politics*, 65 INT'L & COMP. L.Q. 493, 505 (2016).

21.   *Report of the Ad Hoc Group on the Berlin Mandate on the Work of Its Seventh Session, Bonn, 31 July–7 August 1997*, UNFCCC, 7th Sess., at 6, U.N. Doc. FCCC/AGBM/1997/5 (1997), http://unfccc.int/cop5/resource/docs/1997/agbm/05.pdf.

22.   Damilola S. Olawuyi, *Achieving Sustainable Development in Africa Through the Clean Development Mechanism: Legal and Institutional Issues Considered*, 17 AFR. J. INT'L & COMP. L. 270, 271–72 (2009).

manner that levels marginal costs of abatement across States.[23] The scope of the global effort needed to realize the objectives of the UNFCCC is enormous; however, the global resources are limited and the marginal cost of response strategies varies substantially by country. There is, therefore, a need for strategies that channel global investments to their most cost-effective uses.[24] Under the Paris Agreement, there is no mention of any of these cost-effectiveness principles. While this omission does not necessarily amount to an abandonment of the instruments because the Agreement is to be fleshed out through the COP, the lack of reference to these instruments may signal decreased enthusiasm for the instruments in the international community.

A.   Emissions Trading

Although emissions trading (or cap-and-trade) schemes were developed in the 1960s,[25] it was first utilized in the 1980s to address acid rain problems in North America and Europe.[26] They were introduced into climate change discussions during the negotiation of the Kyoto Protocol as a tool that would enable countries to meet their emissions reduction commitments.[27] Soon after its adoption in Kyoto, emissions trading became the "touchstone for both climate policy and controversy over the global response to climate change."[28] There are active emissions trading schemes in several jurisdictions, the largest being the European Union Emissions Trading Scheme (EU ETS). There are also emissions trading schemes in North America and the Asia-Pacific region. The United States' repudiation of the Kyoto Protocol affected the development of emissions trading in the United States. China—the world's largest GHG emitter—has implemented emissions trading schemes in several cities and provinces and has been considering a national scheme.[29]

Emissions trading is the commodification of GHG emissions. Its basic premise is that one State is allowed to pay another State to obtain permission

---

23.   Lasse Ringius, Asbjørn Torvanger & Arild Underdal, *Burden Sharing and Fairness Principles in International Climate Policy*, 2 INT'L ENVTL. AGREEMENTS: POL., L. & ECON. 1, 14 (2002).

24.   ONIO KUIK, PAUL PETERS & NICO SCHRIJVER EDS., JOINT IMPLEMENTATION TO CURB CLIMATE CHANGE: LEGAL AND ECONOMIC ASPECTS xii (1994).

25.   *See* Richard Lane, *The Promiscuous History of Market Efficiency: The Development of Early Emissions Trading Systems*, 21 ENVTL. POL. 585 (2012).

26.   *Id.*

27.   Michele Betsill & Matthew J. Hoffmann, *The Contours of "Cap and Trade": The Evolution of Emissions Trading Systems for Greenhouse Gases*, 28 REV. POL'Y RES. 83, 84 (2011).

28.   *Id.* at 83.

29.   Frank Jotzo & Andreas Löschel, *Emissions Trading in China: Emerging Experiences and International Lessons*, 75 ENERGY POL'Y 3, 3 (2014).

to emit GHGs. The buyer-State can use the purchased emission credits to emit GHGs instead of taking direct action to reduce its emissions. However, the government places a cap on GHG emissions from a specific group of sources. The cap may apply to the entire economy or to specific sectors of the economy. The government agency responsible for the trade allocates or sells a limited number of emissions permits to polluters to discharge stipulated quantities of pollutants within a given time period. Every polluter is required to hold a permit in an amount equal to its emissions and polluters that want to increase their emissions are required to buy permits from other polluters willing to sell their permits. Those polluters that can reduce their emissions more cost effectively are allowed to sell their excess allowances (if they have any) to other polluters unable to reduce their emissions in a similarly cost-effective manner. Polluters must either buy permits to emit or reduce their emissions in each stipulated time period.[30] Because emissions allowances are tradable, the actual distribution of emissions reduction efforts is determined by market forces and not by the government regulator.[31] In 2013, global emissions trading volume reached $54.9 billion.[32]

Emissions trading has several advantages. It is regarded by some as "the best way to reduce carbon emissions," especially when compared to carbon tax and command-and-control measures.[33] While carbon taxes provide greater certainty for compliance costs, their goals are more susceptible to compromise than emissions trading and, once legislated, carbon taxes do not provide the flexibility that emissions trading carries.[34] Emissions trading allows for flexibility in the timing of investments because the system affords emitters the discretion to determine when to purchase and install their emissions reduction facilities, unlike command-and-control measures that require emitters to install facilities within a specified time.[35]

But emissions trading has also faced several criticisms. In the EU, although emissions trading has been "up and running" for at least two decades, many observers believe that the system is not functioning as it should and that it has faced severe implementation problems. At least one commentator has

---

30. Alice H. Chang, *The Politics and Future of Carbon Cap-and-trade: Lessons From the European Union*, Claremont-UC Undergraduate Research Conference on the European Union, vol. 2014, art. 7, at 77 (2015), http://scholarship.claremont.edu/cgi/viewcontent.cgi?article=1092&context=urceu.

31. Robert N. Stavins, A U.S. Cap-and-trade System to Address Global Climate Change, Hamilton Project Discussion Paper 2007-13, at 8 (The Brookings Institution 2007), https://www.brookings.edu/research/a-u-s-cap-and-trade-system-to-address-global-climate-change/.

32. Ying Zhang, Kuang Jian Chao & Wang Chung, *Status Quo Analysis of Chinese and Foreign Carbon Trading Market*, 3 Foreign Energy Sources 1, 2 (2014).

33. *Id.*

34. Chang, *supra* note 30, at 77.

35. T.H. Tietenberg, Emissions Trading: Principles and Practice 5–6 (2d ed. 2006).

called for the system to be abandoned,[36] while another asserted that the system "has long been a mess" as it has resulted in "massive overcapacity in the carbon market" due in part to the granting of "too many allowances."[37] The EU system has also faced corruption and fraud charges,[38] as well as difficulties in achieving the appropriate cap during a financial crisis.[39]

In the United States, the prospects of a federal emissions trading scheme were scuttled by the death of the Kerry-Lieberman bill.[40] The Western Climate Initiative, originally launched in February 2007 by five western U.S. states (Arizona, California, New Mexico, Oregon, and Washington) and later joined by two other states (Utah and Montana) and four Canadian provinces (British Columbia, Manitoba, Ontario, and Quebec) with the goal of developing a multisector, market-based program to reduce GHG emissions, suffered serious setbacks with the withdrawal of Arizona and Utah from the emissions trading aspects of the initiative.[41] In Australia, lack of legislative approval delayed the development of the emissions trading system.[42] In China, the development or success of emissions trading is hampered by excessive state control of the energy sector.[43] For such a market-based instrument as emissions trading to work effectively, comprehensive deregulation of the energy sector must be undertaken.

B.   The Clean Development Mechanism

The CDM is provided for in Article 12 of the Kyoto Protocol. According to Article 12(2), the purpose of the CDM is to enable developed States to achieve their emissions reduction targets by investing in emissions-reducing projects in developing States and to assist developing States to achieve sustainable development and contribute to the overall objective of the UNFCCC. Studies show that it is much cheaper to reduce GHG emissions in developing

---

36.   Chris Lang, *The EU Emissions Trading Scheme Has Failed: "Time to Scrap the ETS,"* REDD MONITOR, Apr. 16, 2013, http://www.redd-monitor.org/2013/04/16/the-eu-emissions-trading-scheme-has-failed-time-to-scrap-the-ets/.

37.   *ETS, RIP?*, THE ECONOMIST, Apr. 18, 2013, http://www.economist.com/news/finance-and-economics/21576388-failure-reform-europes-carbon-market-will-reverberate-round-world-ets. *See also* Reuven S. Avi-Yonah & David M. Uhlmann, *Combating Global Climate Change: Why a Carbon Tax Is a Better Response to Global Warming Than Cap and Trade*, 28 STAN. ENVTL. L.J. 3, 49–50 (2009) (arguing that some of the claimed advantages of emissions trading are "largely illusory").

38.   Frédéric Branger, Oskar Lecuyer & Philippe Quirion, *The European Union Emissions Trading Scheme: Should We Throw the Flagship out With the Bathwater?*, 6 WILEY INTERDISCIPLINARY REV.: CLIMATE CHANGE 9–16 (2015).

39.   Betsill & Hoffmann, *supra* note 27, at 83.

40.   *Id.*

41.   *Id.*

42.   *Id.*

43.   Jotzo & Löschel, *supra* note 29, at 6.

States than in developed States[44] and that the costs can be up to three times cheaper.[45] The reason is that in developed States, in order to build natural gas facilities with cleaner technologies, for instance, it would be necessary to dismantle often decades-old existing coal-fired plants. This process can be very costly as it would involve expending significant capital, whereas in developing States where such coal-fired plants are often nonexistent, such wastage would likely not exist.[46]

The benefit is a two-way street. While CDM projects enable developed States to meet their emissions reduction commitments, developing States hosting such projects achieve a cleaner environment. The mechanism is also expected to stimulate international investments in developing States and provide an avenue for technology transfer from the developed to the developing States.[47] These investments and technology transfers would in turn enable developing States to address some of their socioeconomic problems through the infrastructure development and job creation that are associated with such projects. The ultimate benefit to developing States is more fast-tracked economic development.[48]

Participation in CDM projects is, however, voluntary and participants must have ratified the Kyoto Protocol. Since participation is voluntary, any developing State wishing to benefit from the mechanism must make itself attractive to developed States for CDM projects. Three attractiveness indicators have been identified: (1) mitigation potential—emissions reduction achievable in the State, (2) general investment climate—a safe business environment, predictable and reliable trade policy, availability of infrastructure facilities that enhance production and movement of goods and services, and (3) the legal and institutional capacity of a State for CDM projects—the existence of laws and institutions that enhance CDM implementation and the protection of property rights.[49]

According to the UNFCCC, as of April 30, 2016, a total of 7,710 CDM projects had been registered.[50] Studies show, however, that the placement

---

44. JEFFREY A. FRANKEL, GREENHOUSE GAS EMISSIONS, BROOKINGS POLICY BRIEF SERIES #50 (1999), http://www.brookings.edu/research/papers/1999/06/energy-frankel.

45. See Olawuyi, *Achieving Sustainable Development in Africa, supra* note 22, at 276.

46. See FRANKEL, *supra* note 44.

47. See Gary Cox, *The Clean Development Mechanism as a Vehicle for Technology Transfer and Sustainable Development—Myth or Reality?*, 6 L. ENV'T & DEV. J. 179 (2010).

48. See Christiana Figueres & Mary Gowan, *The Operation of the CDM, in* ESTABLISHING NATIONAL AUTHORITIES FOR THE CDM: A GUIDE FOR DEVELOPING COUNTRIES 21 (Christiana Figueres ed., 2002).

49. MARTINA JUNG, HOST COUNTRY ATTRACTIVENESS FOR CDM NON-SINK PROJECTS 6 (2005), http://ageconsearch.umn.edu/bitstream/26328/1/dp050312.pdf.

50. UNFCCC, *Project Activities—CDM*, http://cdm.unfccc.int/Statistics/Public/CDMinsights/index.html#reg (last visited Aug. 23, 2016).

of these projects has been predominantly located in a few States. Reviewing the destination of CDM projects, Damilola S. Olawuyi determined
that about 67% of developing States have been unable to attract CDM
projects and that African and Latin American States have been on the low
end of the spectrum.[51] Olawuyi divides the destinations into "very attractive," "attractive," "attractive to a limited extent," and "very unattractive."
Only eight States were considered "very attractive" for CDM projects.
These States include: Argentina, Brazil, China, India, Indonesia, Mexico,
South Africa, and Thailand. Fourteen States were considered "attractive,"
with Mauritius as the only African State.[52] Twenty-seven States had limited
attractiveness, out of which 8 were African, while 41 States were considered
very unattractive, 27 of which were African.[53] Since only eight States are
considered very attractive, it is not surprising that about 80% of CDM
projects have been concentrated in a few States, particularly China, India,
Brazil, and Mexico.[54] The uneven distribution of CDM projects is caused
by the profit-oriented attitude of developed States and their investors and
the inability of most developing States to meet the attractiveness criteria
outlined above. Since the attractiveness criteria are not such that a State
can meet them overnight, it will take time before many developing States
can begin to tap into the benefits of CDM.

In sum, CDM is a useful tool for climate change regulation in that it represents a win-win approach for developed and developing States. However, its
voluntary nature and the fact that its implementation is strongly influenced
by the profit motives of developed State investors render the mechanism a
weak tool for climate change regulation.

C.   Joint Implementation

JI is authorized under Articles 3, 4, and 6 of the Kyoto Protocol, which
allow Annex 1 (developed) States to implement jointly certain policies and
measures that would enable them to meet their emissions reduction commitments. JI allows one Annex 1 State to claim credits for reductions achieved
through projects jointly carried out with another Annex 1 State in that other

---

51.   *See* Damilola S. Olawuyi, *From Kyoto to Copenhagen: Rethinking the Place of Flexible Mechanisms in
      the Kyoto Protocol's Post 2012 Commitment Period*, 6 L. ENV'T & DEV. J. 31 (2010).
52.   The other countries are Antigua and Barbuda, Azerbaijan, Belize, Chile, Costa Rica, El Salvador,
      Jordan, Mongolia, Maldives, Malaysia, Panama, Trinidad and Tobago, and Uruguay.
53.   Olawuyi, *Achieving Sustainable Development in Africa, supra* note 22, at 283.
54.   Green Clean Guide, *CDM Projects Statistics*, http://greencleanguide.com/cdm-projects-statistics/ (last
      visited Aug. 23, 2016).

State.[55] Its main rationale is cost-effectiveness. Cost-effectiveness is achieved when the marginal cost of GHG reduction abroad through a JI project is lower than the marginal cost that can be achieved domestically.[56] If emissions reduction abroad can be used to offset international commitments, countries may be induced to invest in emissions reduction projects abroad where such efforts are cheaper than investments at home.

JI is similar to CDM in that it enables a State to invest in emissions reduction projects in another State where such efforts are considered more cost effective. The major difference between JI and CDM, however, is that CDM was designed to enable Annex 1 and non-Annex 1 States to work together for the purpose of identifying relevant projects in non-Annex 1 States, whereas JI was designed to enable one Annex 1 State to undertake emissions reduction projects in another Annex 1 State as an alternative to reducing emissions domestically. A State that undertakes a JI project in another State can claim credit (called emission reduction units) towards its compliance with its own Kyoto commitments. Another important difference between JI and CDM is that the JI projects take place in a State that has a commitment to reduce its emissions under the Kyoto Protocol, whereas for CDM projects, the project host State, being a non-Annex 1 State, is one without a Kyoto commitment. Like CDM, JI offers participating Parties a flexible and cost-effective means of fulfilling a part of their Kyoto commitments, while the host Party benefits from improved environmental measures, foreign investment, and technology transfer. Like CDM, JI is voluntary.

While the cost-effectiveness arguments of JI seem compelling, opponents of JI have noted that JI would discourage domestic action by developed States to take the lead in stemming global warming. Other criticisms include that JI would

> compromise the sovereignty and national interests of the "host" nations, decrease the incentive for technological innovation in the "donor" nations, impair the ability of "host" nations to harness indigenous resources and develop their own markets, [and] increase the transaction costs as well as the monitoring and verification costs associated with combating climate change.[57]

---

55. *See* A.S. Dagoumas, G.K. Papagiannis & P.S. Dokopoulos, *An Economic Assessment of the Kyoto Protocol Application*, 34 ENERGY POL'Y 26 (2006).

56. Axel Michaelowa, *Joint Implementation—The Baseline Issue: Economic and Political Aspects*, 8 GLOBAL ENVTL. CHANGE 81, 81 (1998).

57. Tim Jackson, *Joint Implementation and Cost-Effectiveness Under the Framework Convention on Climate Change*, 23 ENERGY POL'Y 117, 118 (1995).

States also expressed concerns that JI might lead to fraudulent and spurious emissions reductions claims.[58] The success of JI would therefore depend on the extent to which it can lead to actual emissions reductions, which requires establishing mechanisms for measuring reductions.

The rules and modalities relating to JI are provided for by the 2001 Marrakech Accords developed at the UNFCCC's COP7.[59] First, the Accords exclude from JI emissions reductions generated from nuclear facilities and urge economies in transition that are under Annex II to participate in JI projects. Second, they stipulate that a State can qualify to host a JI project through either of two tracks, depending on that State's ability to meet certain eligibility criteria. Under track I, a State is required to establish an assigned amount and create a national registry for tracking the transfer of any assigned amounts. Such a State must also establish a national system for estimating emissions reductions, submit an annual inventory to estimate emissions, and have accurate accounting of their assigned amount and submissions of information. To qualify for track II JI, a host State must only fulfil three of the eligibility requirements: they must be a Party to the Kyoto Protocol, establish an assigned amount, and have a national registry in place. Host State requirements under track I are stricter, but the State is subject to less international oversight.[60]

It has been suggested that central and eastern European States are the most likely destinations for JI projects.[61] This is because of lack of available project finance and a great potential for emissions reduction at low marginal costs in the region. Several JI projects have been implemented in this region. According to the UNFCCC, between 2006 and 2015, more than 871 million emission reduction units had been issued for emission reductions from more than 500 JI projects.[62] A 2012 study examining the implementation of JI in different States found that within the EU, although the development of JI was limited, its implications were "far-reaching: JI provided an opportunity for testing new clean technologies, estimating abatement costs, improving national GHG inventories and setting the benchmarks for emission

---

58. Michaelowa, *supra* note 56, at 81.
59. UNFCCC, THE MARRAKECH ACCORDS AND THE MARRAKECH DECLARATION, http://unfccc.int/cop7/documents/accords_draft.pdf.
60. KATIA KAROUSAKIS, JOINT IMPLEMENTATION: CURRENT ISSUES AND EMERGING CHALLENGES, ORGANIZATION FOR ECONOMIC COOPERATION AND DEVELOPMENT/INTERNATIONAL ENERGY AGENCY 6–7 (2006), https://www.oecd.org/env/cc/37672335.pdf.
61. FARHANA YAMIN, CLIMATE CHANGE AND CARBON MARKETS: A HANDBOOK OF EMISSION REDUCTION MECHANISMS 201 (2005).
62. UNFCCC, *CMP 11 Adopted Decision on JI*, http://ji.unfccc.int/JI_News/issues/issues/I_AFBF04P-G72BG7D5MMXZE26AEOFKKR0/viewnewsitem.html (last visited Aug. 23, 2016).

reductions."[63] There is, however, a risk of noncompliance with the requirements of the Kyoto Protocol scuttling ongoing projects.[64] Lack of political
support and efficient frameworks in some States, such as Russia, have also
limited the growth of JI.[65]

III. Climate Justice Litigation

This section considers the role of litigation in climate change regulation. It
identifies what necessitated the emergence of litigation as a regulatory tool
and reviews some of the most significant cases that have been litigated to
date. The section concludes with a consideration of the impact of litigation
on climate change regulation and the search for climate justice.

A. Climate Change Litigation as a Regulatory Tool to Stem Global Warming

Despite the hard facts substantiating global warming, States and other policymakers have failed to reach a consensus on the appropriate mechanism
to stem GHG emissions.[66] None of the mechanisms considered above has
gained widespread support due to uncertainties regarding the costs of climate
change as well as opposition from businesses. Especially since the adoption
of the Kyoto Protocol, further international action has been disappointingly
feeble due to the failure of States to agree on an acceptable mechanism to
tackle the challenge of climate change regulation, despite broad recognition
that urgent action is needed to reduce GHG emissions. There is a significant
gap between pledged emissions reductions and actual reductions.[67] Moreover, even the pledged reductions lag far behind what the scientific community has stated is needed to save the earth.[68]

---

63. Igor Shishlov, Valentin Bellassen & Benoit Leguet, Joint Implementation: A Frontier
Mechanism Within the Borders of an Emissions Cap 29 (2012), https://hal.archives-ouvertes.
fr/hal-01168452/document.
64. Yamin, *supra* note 61, at 214.
65. Shishlov, Bellassen & Leguet, *supra* note 63, at 1.
66. See, e.g., Joyeeta Gupta, *Climate Change Governance: History, Future, and Triple-loop Learning*, 7 Wires
Climate Change 192, 193 (2016); A.M. McCright, R.E. Dunlop & C. Xiao, *Perceived Scientific
Agreement and Support for Government Action on Climate Change in the USA*, 119 Climate Change
511, 512 (2013); Eric A. Posner, Climate Change and International Human Rights Litigation: A Critical Appraisal, John M. Olin Law and Economics Working Paper No. 329, at 2
(2007), http://www1.umn.edu/humanrts/links/CCIHRLitigation.pdf.
67. Jacqueline Peel & Hari M. Osofsky, Climate Change Litigation: Regulatory Pathways to
Cleaner Energy 11 (2015).
68. *Id.* at 12.

The Paris Agreement is a step forward in international efforts to stem global warming. However, as Jacqueline Peel and Hari M. Osofsky have argued, since climate change is a problem that cuts across different levels of governance—international, regional, national, state, and local—and involves different types of actors—both public and private—even if an effective treaty regime is implemented, it would still be difficult for such a regime to capture all the ways in which the different levels and types of actors interact.[69] In other words, something more is necessary to complement the treaty regimes.

Frustrated by the lack of international consensus to address climate change, environmental activists began exploring the possibility of using litigation as a legal tool to combat the climate change crisis. In fact, the Working Group III report of the Fourth Assessment Report of the IPCC noted that "litigation is likely to be used increasingly as countries and citizens become dissatisfied with the pace of international and national decision-making on climate change."[70] Perhaps the most distinguishing feature of climate change litigation from the mechanisms considered above is that while those mechanisms focus on what action should be taken to stem global warming, climate change litigation focuses frontally on the question of who is responsible for climate change and seeks to either compel action from those responsible or obtain damages awards from them.

Although climate change litigation is a fairly recent phenomenon, considerable work is already underway in the area in many States. In the United States, from 1989–2012, more than 450 climate change-related lawsuits were filed.[71] Other States with significant climate change litigation include Canada,[72] Australia,[73] and the EU.[74] In 2015, climate change cases had been brought in 18 countries across six continents and in international fora, totaling close to 700 claims.[75] The judicial fora have included national courts and regional bodies such as the Inter-American Commission on Human Rights and the European Court of Justice. Peel and Osofsky have divided ongoing

---

69. *Id.* at 13.
70. *See* S. Gupta et al., *Policies, Instruments, and Co-operative Arrangements, in* CLIMATE CHANGE 2007: MITIGATION: CONTRIBUTION OF WORKING GROUP III TO THE FOURTH ASSESSMENT REPORT OF THE INTERGOVERNMENTAL PANEL ON CLIMATE CHANGE 793 (B. Metz et al. eds., 2007).
71. MORGAN MCDONALD & KRISTEN BREWER, CLIMATE CHANGE LITIGATION: POTENTIAL REASONS CANADA LAGS BEHIND THE UNITED STATES 2 (2012), http://works.bepress.com/cgi/viewcontent.cg i?article=1000&context=mmcdonald.
72. *Id.*
73. *See* Hari M. Osofsky & Jacqueline Peel, *Litigation's Regulatory Pathways and the Administrative State: Lessons from U.S. and Australian Climate Change Governance,* 25 GEO. INT'L ENVTL. L. REV. 207 (2013).
74. *See* JOSEPHINE A.W. VAN ZEBEN, THE EUROPEAN EMISSIONS TRADING SCHEME CASE LAW, AMSTERDAM CENTRE FOR LAW AND ECONOMICS WORKING PAPER NO. 2009-12 (2009).
75. PEEL & OSOFSKY, *supra* note 67, at xi and 1.

climate change litigation into four classifications: (1) lawsuits that were not framed in climate change, but with implications for climate change regulation, e.g., those seeking to stop hydraulic fracturing, or fracking, (2) lawsuits that were motivated in part by climate change, but which did not specifically raise any climate change issues, e.g., lawsuits against coal-fired plants brought on environmental grounds, (3) lawsuits in which climate change was a "peripheral issue," and (4) lawsuits in which climate change was the principal issue.[76] The plaintiffs range from private citizens, environmental interest groups, indigenous peoples, subnational governments, States themselves (especially under the EU ETS), and even treaty bodies, such as the European Commission.[77] Although no major damages awards have resulted from any of the litigation due mostly to significant barriers to proving causation,[78] the cases "do reveal there is a decided interest in pursuing the legal route as the means to pushing for action on climate change."[79]

B.   Significant Climate Change Cases

While several climate change-related lawsuits have been brought in several jurisdictions around the world, some are particularly noteworthy. Four of these cases will be summarized: *Massachusetts v. EPA*,[80] *California v. General Motors Corp.*,[81] the Inuit Petition,[82] and *Kain v. Massachusetts Department of Environmental Protection*.[83]

1.   Massachusetts v. EPA

In 1999, the International Center for Technology Assessment and other parties petitioned the U.S. Environmental Protection Agency (EPA) to set standards for certain pollutants emitted by new motor vehicles. The petitioners asserted that motor vehicles emitting GHGs cause or contribute to

---

76.   *Id.* at 8.
77.   In *Commission v. Italy* and *Commission v. Finland*, for instance, the European Commission brought cases to the European Court of Justice against Italy and Finland for their failure to implement Directive 2003/87/EC establishing the EU ETS. *See* van Zeben, *supra* note 74, at 6–7.
78.   *See* Shi-Ling Hsu, *A Realistic Evaluation of Climate Change Litigation Through the Lens of a Hypothetical Lawsuit*, 79 U. Colo. L.J. 101, 103 (2008).
79.   Gupta et al., *supra* note 70, at 794.
80.   Massachusetts v. EPA, 549 U.S. 497 (2007).
81.   California v. General Motors Corp., No. C06-05755 MJJ (N.D. Cal. Sept. 17, 2007).
82.   Petition to the Inter-American Commission on Human Rights Seeking Relief From Violations Resulting From Global Warming Caused by Acts and Omissions of the United States (Dec. 7, 2005).
83.   Kain v. Massachusetts Dep't of Envtl. Prot., No. SUCV2014-02551, (Mass. Super. Ct. Mar. 23, 2015), http://masslegalresources.com/kain-et-al-v-department-of-environmental-protection-lawyers-weekly-no-10-066-16.

air pollution that potentially endangers public health within the meaning of the Clean Air Act (CAA). EPA denied the petition on several grounds, including that the CAA does not authorize climate change regulation and that it would not be appropriate or efficient for EPA to prescribe GHG standards for motor vehicles.[84] EPA held that GHGs were not "air pollutants" within the meaning of the CAA. A request for review by the District of Columbia Circuit Court of Appeals resulted in a split decision in favor of EPA. The Supreme Court held, in a 5-4 decision, that GHGs were "air pollutants" within the meaning of the CAA and that EPA had authority to regulate GHGs under the CAA. The Court did not, however, order EPA to regulate GHGs, but simply left EPA free to decide not to regulate, provided it offered adequate justification for not regulating, based on whether GHGs endanger public health.[85]

One of the most significant aspects of this decision was the Court's explicit recognition of the link between GHGs and global warming: "[W]hen carbon dioxide is released into the atmosphere, it acts like the ceiling of a greenhouse, trapping solar energy and retarding the escape of reflected heat. It is therefore a species—the most important species—of a 'greenhouse gas.'"[86] The court thus aligned with scientific consensus that global warming causes serious harm to the environment.

From a legal perspective, the decision is significant for its impact on two doctrinal issues: the standing of states in environmental matters and the standard of review applied to denials of petitions for rulemaking. On standing, the decision makes it clear that states have standing in climate change litigation based on "special solicitude," the power of states to bring claims on behalf of their citizens to protect the public.[87] On standard of review, the decision shrinks EPA's options with regard to regulating GHG emissions. As Prof. Lisa Heinzerling noted:

> Even if the agency found the science of climate change uncertain, the Court stated that the agency could not refuse to regulate greenhouse gases unless the science was so profoundly uncertain that the agency could not even form a judgment as to whether greenhouse gases were endangering public health or welfare.[88]

---

84. *See* Lisa Heinzerling, *Massachusetts v. EPA*, 22 J. ENVTL. L. & LITIG. 301, 302–03 (2007).
85. *Id.* at 305.
86. Massachusetts v. EPA, 549 U.S. 497, 505 (2007).
87. *See* Randall S. Abate, *Massachusetts v. EPA and the Future of Environmental Standing in Climate Change Litigation and Beyond*, 33 WM. & MARY ENVTL. L. & POL'Y REV. 121, 146 (2008).
88. Heinzerling, *supra* note 84, at 308.

It is significant that EPA acknowledged the link between climate change and GHGs as well as the threats posed by climate change. Given this recognition, it would be inconceivable that EPA would hold the science of climate change so uncertain that it would be unable to find that GHGs endanger public health and welfare. The far-reaching implications of the Supreme Court decision for the future of climate change litigation and environmental litigation generally has been extensively discussed in the literature.[89]

2.   *California v. General Motors Corp.*

The state of California sought damages against various automakers for creating and contributing to global warming. California asserted that it had expended millions of dollars studying, planning for, monitoring, and responding to the impacts of global warming on its environment. Those impacts included an increase in the winter average temperatures in the Sierra Nevada region; a reduction in the snow pack, which provides 35% of the state's water; an increased risk of flooding within the state due to melting temperatures, rising sea levels, and the risk of erosion along the state's coastline; and increases in the risk and intensity of wildfires.[90] California sought to hold each defendant automaker jointly and severally liable for creating, contributing to, and maintaining a public nuisance called global warming, based on the federal common law of public nuisance and, alternatively, California's state public nuisance law. It sought monetary damages, attorneys' fees, and a declaratory judgment for future monetary expenses and damages incurred by the state of California in connection with global warming.[91]

The defendants sought dismissal, arguing that the plaintiff was "attempting to create a new global warming tort that had no origins in federal or state law" and that the claims were nonjusticiable based on the political question doctrine.[92] The court granted the defendants' motion on political question doctrine grounds. Furthermore, it expressed concerns regarding the determination of causation in climate change litigation. Judge Jenkins denied the existence of any known method of discerning the entities causing or contributing to climate change, or any guidance to determine what amounts to an "unreasonable contribution" to climate change, as well as the bases to deter-

---

89.   *See, e.g.*, Heinzerling, *supra* note 84; Abate, *supra* note 87.
90.   PEEL & OSOFSKY, *supra* note 67, at 2.
91.   *Id.* at 3.
92.   *Id.*

mine the persons who should bear the costs associated with global climate change in the face of multiple contributors.[93]

In another case, however—*Comer v. Nationwide Mutual Insurance Co.*—rather than deny the existence of methods for determining causation, the court emphasized the

> daunting evidentiary problems for anyone who undertakes to prove, by a *preponderance of the evidence*, the degree to which global warming is caused by the emission of greenhouse gasses; the degree to which the actions of any individual oil company, and individual chemical company, or the collective action of these corporations contribute, through the emission of greenhouse gasses, to global warming.[94]

This judicial acceptance is significant for the future of climate change litigation even though it does not offer much to a plaintiff who must provide credible evidence to prove specific causation. However, a number of theories have already been developed that would facilitate the proof of causation in climate change litigation.[95]

3.   The Inuit Petition

In 2005, the Inuit Circumpolar Conference (ICC), a group representing the Inuit of the Arctic regions of Canada, Greenland, Russia, and the United States, brought a petition before the Inter-American Commission on Human Rights (IACHR) against the United States alleging that the negative impacts of climate change caused by U.S. GHG emitters violated their fundamental

---

93.   *Id.* at 21–22.
94.   Comer et al. v. Nationwide Mut. Ins. Co., No 1:05-CV-436 LTD RHW, 2006 WL 1066645, at *4 (S.D. Miss. Feb. 23, 2006).
95.   Four of these theories are the material contribution test, market share causation theory, the comingled product theory, and probabilistic analysis. *See* Clements v. Clements, 2012 S.C.C. 32 (Supreme Court of Canada) (adopting the material contribution test); British Columbia v. Imperial Tobacco Canada Ltd., 2005 2 S.C.R. 473 (Supreme Court of Canada) (where the "claim is made on an aggregate basis, [the plaintiff] may use statistical, epidemiological and sociological evidence to prove its case"); In re Methyl Tertiary Butyl Ether Prods. Liab. Litig., 379 F. Supp. 2d 348, 375 (S.D.N.Y. 2005) (recognizing the comingled product theory); Harrington v. Dow Corning Corp., 2000 11 W.W.R. 201 (Supreme Court of Canada) ("When a plaintiff produces epidemiological studies that treat products of all defendants as generic, it behooves any defendant who is of a contrary view to produce evidence supporting its view"); Sindell v. Abbott Labs., 26 Cal. 3d 588 (1980) (recognizing the market share theory). *See also* Emily H. Damron, *Reviving the Market for Liability Theories: The "Commingled Product" Theory of Market Share Liability Enters the Judicial Lexicon*, 111 Penn. St. L. Rev. 505 (2007); Samantha Lawson, *The Conundrum of Climate Change Causation: Using Market Share Liability to Satisfy the Identification Requirement in Native Village of Kivalina v. ExxonMobil Co.*, 22 Fordham Envtl. L. Rev. 433 (2011); David M. Schultz, *Market Share Liability in DES Cases: The Unwarranted Erosion of Causation in Fact*, 40 DePaul L. Rev. 771 (1991).

human rights.[96] The negative impacts included melting ice, rising sea levels, receding glaciers, increased coastal erosion, and warmer temperatures. The rights violated included the right to enjoy cultural benefits, the right to property, the right to health, the right to life, physical integrity and security, and the right to their own means of subsistence. They argued that the negative impacts of global warming hampered their full realization of these rights.

In 2006, however, the IACHR dismissed the petition through a brief letter to the ICC on the grounds that the information provided in the petition did not establish "whether the alleged facts would tend to characterize a violation of rights protected by the American Declaration."[97] It has been argued that even though the petition was dismissed, the petition exemplifies the way in which indigenous communities might proceed with a legal argument anchored in the extraordinary link between indigenous communities and their environment.[98] From an environmental justice perspective, leveraging the Inter-American human rights system in the quest for climate justice "constitutes an interesting legal development as the petition takes what is an environmental justice problem and explores it from a human rights perspective."[99]

4. *Kain v. Massachusetts Department of Environmental Protection*

This case is one of the most recent climate change decisions in the United States as of this writing. Four young children, together with two environmental interest groups, brought suit against the Massachusetts Department of Environmental Protection (DEP) asking the court to determine whether DEP had fulfilled its statutory obligations under the state's Global Warming Solutions Act (GWSA)—a legislative scheme designed to address the effects of climate change in Massachusetts by promoting "green" economic initiatives and reducing GHG emissions. Section 3(d) of the Act required DEP to "promulgate regulations establishing a desired level of declining annual aggregate emission limits for sources or categories of sources that

---

96. Petition to the Inter-American Commission on Human Rights Seeking Relief From Violations Resulting From Global Warming Caused by Acts and Omissions of the United States (Dec. 7, 2005), http://www.inuitcircumpolar.com/uploads/3/0/5/4/30542564/finalpetitionicc.pdf.

97. Letter from Ariel E. Dulitzky, Assistant Executive Secretary, IACHR, to Paul Crowley, Legal Representative, Re: Sheila Watt-Cloutier et al. (Nov. 16, 2006), http://graphics8.nytimes.com/packages/pdf/science/16commissionletter.pdf.

98. Elizabeth Ann Kronk & Randall S. Abate, *International and Domestic Law Dimensions of Climate Justice for Arctic Indigenous Peoples*, 43 Ottawa L. Rev. 113, 119 (2013). For a discussion of climate change litigation in the Inter-American human rights system, see Verónica de la Rosa Jaimes, *Climate Change and Human Rights Litigation in Europe and the Americas*, 5 Seattle J. Envtl. L. 165 (2015).

99. Kronk & Abate, *supra* note 98, at 138.

emit greenhouse gas emissions." Under the Act, the regulations were to be issued by January 1, 2012, to take effect on January 1, 2013, and to expire on December 31, 2020. DEP did not take any action by the 2012 statutory deadline.

In August 2014, the plaintiffs sued DEP seeking declaratory relief, or in the alternative, a writ of mandamus, on the grounds that DEP had failed to fulfil its statutory mandate under the GWSA. DEP argued that it had taken regulatory initiatives that included prescribed limits on sulfur hexafluoride leaks, a regional cap-and-trade market to manage carbon dioxide emissions, and a low emission vehicle program aimed at reducing automobile emissions and that these initiatives, singly and together, fulfilled its obligations under the Act. The Massachusetts Superior Court agreed with DEP.

On appeal, however, the Massachusetts Supreme Court reversed:

> [T]he unambiguous language of §3(d) requires the department to promulgate regulations that establish volumetric limits on multiple greenhouse gas emissions sources, expressed in carbon dioxide equivalents, and that such limits must decline on an annual basis. We further conclude that the sulfur hexafluoride, [the regional cap and trade initiative], and [the low emission vehicles] regulations fall short of complying with the requirements of §3(d), because they fail to ensure the type of mass-based reductions in greenhouse gases across the sources or categories of sources regulated under each of the programs, as intended by the Legislature.[100]

The court noted that while the initiatives designed by DEP were important in reducing GHG emissions, they did not meet the requirements of the GWSA, whose purpose is to attain actual, measurable, and permanent emissions reductions. The court vacated the superior court's judgment and remanded the matter for entry of a judgment declaring that the GWSA required DEP to enact regulation in accordance with §3(d).[101] The decision in this case not only requires governments to fulfil their obligations to stem global warming, but also exemplifies the role of children in prompting action on climate change on an intergenerational equity basis, which is a principle that forms part of the foundation of climate justice litigation.

---

100. Kain v. Massachusetts Dep't of Envtl. Prot., 45 ELR 20058, No. SUCV2014-02551, slip op. (Mass. Super. Ct. Mar. 23, 2015).
101. *Id.*

C. The Impact of Climate Justice Litigation on Climate Change Regulation

Although still in the early stages, some impact from climate change litigation is evident. The first impact is the mobilizing power of litigation towards sociopolitical change. To use the words of John Morrison, sociopolitical change means

> a fundamental alteration in the way an aspect of society is structured, in the way that people relate to one another or in the way that an issue is perceived and acted upon . . . . Law can tinker with the housekeeping of the legal system, it can codify, improve and refine doctrines, but if the final point of impact of such change is [only] within the legal system itself this does not count. Social change through law refers to change, originating from either outside the legal system or, more rarely, from within it, which moves through the legal system to make an impact outside it.[102]

Drawing on Pierre Bourdieu's "theory of the field" and what Bourdieu called "symbolic capital," transnational human rights litigation can provide marginalized groups the capital that would enable them to alter the operating standards in their system and to increase their bargaining power.[103] The capital improvement comes not necessarily through judicial victories and damages awards, but mostly through the damage that the existence or even the mere filing of a lawsuit can bring to corporate defendants. This idea of the indirect role of litigation in achieving sociopolitical change has been confirmed in the context of climate change litigation by several scholars.[104]

But climate change litigation has been shown to have a direct impact on climate change regulation. This was "in a particularly dramatic way," Osofsky points out, during the George W. Bush Administration when advocates for and against climate change used the courts to convey their views following the Bush Administration's rejection of the Kyoto Protocol.[105] The *Massachusetts v. EPA* decision provided the impetus for executive action under the Obama Administration in the face of congressional inaction.[106] *Mas-*

---

102. John Morrison, *How to Change Things With Rules*, in Law, Society, and Change 7 (Stephen Livingston & John Morrison eds., 1990).

103. Chilenye Nwapi, *Adjudicating Transnational Corporate Crimes in Foreign Courts: Imperialism or Assertion of Functional Jurisdiction?*, 19 Afr. Yb. Int'l L. 144, 183–84 (2012).

104. *See, e.g.*, Hari Osofsky, The Continuing Importance of Climate Change Litigation, Washington & Lee Public Legal Studies Research Paper Series No. 2010-3, at 6 (2009), http://papers.ssrn.com/sol3/papers.cfm?abstract_id=1529669.

105. *Id.* at 8.

106. *Id.*

sachusetts v. EPA and its associated jurisprudence have played a significant role in the development of federal climate change regulation under major U.S. environmental laws, such as the CAA.[107] In Australia, climate change litigation has been used in a strategic way to respond to inadequate legislative action with a view to spurring wider policy change.[108] Within the EU, emissions trading litigation before the European Court of Justice (ECJ) has helped to refine regulatory action by the EU. Josephine A.W. van Zeben has, for instance, noted that the ECJ jurisprudence has helped to provide some legal certainty for Member States regarding their obligations under the EU emissions trading directive with far-reaching consequences for the EU emissions trading market.[109] While litigation is not the only instrument for mobilizing public action on climate change, it occupies an extraordinary position in utilizing State apparatus to realize regulatory change.[110]

Lastly, the ongoing process of legal actions regarding climate change may well reenact what happened in the tobacco industry, which ultimately resulted in billions of dollars in settlement fees—plus a major shift in public attitude towards the product, with a resultant loss in tobacco sales and profits. Similar to what happened in the tobacco industry, some U.S. states are teaming up to bring legal action against fossil fuel companies for fraudulent denial of global warming.[111] ExxonMobil has been specifically singled out, following a newly discovered e-mail from one of its scientists, to have known about global warming as early as 1981 while spending millions of dollars for the next 27 years promoting climate change denial.[112]

Andrew Gage and Michael Byers observe that while there appears to be no imminent climate damages award in any jurisdiction, it is "premature" to assume that climate change litigation is unlikely to have a major impact on GHG producing companies, especially given what happened in the tobacco industry.[113] Soon after tobacco companies boasted that they had never lost or settled a case and did not expect the situation to change in the future, large-

107. PEEL & OSOFSKY, *supra* note 67, at 311–12.
108. *See* Jacqueline Peel, *The Role of Climate Change Litigation in Australia's Response to Global Warming*, 24 ENVTL. PLAN. L.J. 90 (2007).
109. VAN ZEBEN, *supra* note 74, at 12–14.
110. PEEL & OSOFSKY, *supra* note 67, at 31.
111. Mychaylo Prystupa, *US States Team Up to Nail Big Oil for Climate "Fraud,"* THE TYEE, Mar. 30, 2016, http://thetyee.ca/News/2016/03/30/US-AGs-Investigate-Climate-Fraud/.
112. Suzanne Goldenberg, *Exxon Knew of Climate Change in 1981, Email Says—But It Funded Deniers for 27 More Years*, THE GUARDIAN, July 8, 2015, https://www.theguardian.com/environment/2015/jul/08/exxon-climate-change-1981-climate-denier-funding.
113. ANDREW GAGE & MICHAEL BYERS, PAYBACK TIME? WHAT THE INTERNATIONALIZATION OF CLIMATE LITIGATION COULD MEAN FOR CANADIAN OIL AND GAS COMPANIES 13 (2014), http://wcel.org/sites/default/files/publications/Payback%20Time.pdf.

scale suits against them began to succeed with major damages awards against tobacco companies.[114] Gage and Byers add that

> the sheer number and diversity of venues, and means through which such litigation might be successful, suggest that civil liability is likely, particularly as the costs associated with climate change rise. Major greenhouse gas producers and their investors can manage this risk only by reducing their emissions, which may require moving away from fossil fuels, and by supporting efforts to conclude new international agreements that address climate liability, compensation demands, and emissions reductions in comprehensive and meaningful ways.[115]

There is no indication that the lawsuits will stop in the foreseeable future. Even though there has as yet been no major damages award, a June 2015 decision of the Dutch District Court in *Urgenda Foundation v. Government of the Netherlands (Ministry of Infrastructure and the Environment)* affirming the existence of a duty of care on the part of the government of the Netherlands to take action on climate change is remarkable.[116] It brings climate justice plaintiffs one step closer to finding corporate emitters of GHGs liable for climate change, which may occur in the near future. It is therefore important that investors in the energy industry, including large institutional investors such as pension funds, are fully aware of the nature, degree, and scope of climate justice litigation risk.

Conclusion

Regulatory action on climate change has witnessed various trends. These trends are not mutually exclusive, but are simultaneously operative within the same legal, political, and economic system. Each trend has its benefits and shortcomings and the global community can benefit by maximizing the benefits of each trend, while also finding ways to minimize their shortcomings. The nonexplicit mention of emissions trading, the CDM, and JI in the Paris Agreement may be reflective of the international community's diminished enthusiasm for these mechanisms. Of the three trends of regulatory action on climate change considered here, none is arguably more appreciative of the fact that anthropogenic factors are substantially responsible for climate

---

114. *Id.*
115. *Id.* at 10.
116. For a full discussion of this case and its implications, see Chapter 21 of this volume; *see also* Josephine van Zeben, *Establishing a Government Duty of Care for Climate Change Mitigation: Will Urgenda Turn the Tide?*, 4 TRANSNAT'L ENVT'L L. 339 (2016).

change than climate change litigation. And if the seeming diminished enthusiasm for emissions trading, CDM, and JI is real, it raises questions regarding the future of climate change regulation outside climate justice litigation.

While the other trends focus mostly on what can be done to curtail climate change, climate justice litigation is centered most directly on the question of who is responsible for climate change and providing relief for affected communities and States. Though the effects of climate change are beyond dispute, litigation would not be conceivable if the causes of climate change were purely natural without the contribution of man-made factors.[117] It is in fact the contribution of man-made factors that makes the injury suffered as a result of climate change a legally recognizable injury. Therefore, regardless of the obstacles that climate justice litigation may face, it is fair to say that climate justice litigation is here to stay. While it will take some time for its impacts to fully manifest, it is a potentially viable tool to vindicate human rights violations associated with climate change, either through international and regional human rights fora or through domestic courts drawing on intergenerational equity principles.

---

117. Alvaro Hasani, *Forecasting the End of Climate Change Litigation: Why Expert Testimony Based on Climate Models Should Not Be Admissible*, Law School Student Scholarship, Paper 108, at 6 (2012), http://scholarship.shu.edu/cgi/viewcontent.cgi?article=1108&context=student_scholarship.

Chapter 20

Atmospheric Trust Litigation in the United States: Pipe Dream or Pipeline to Justice for Future Generations?

Randall S. Abate [*]

Introduction

Climate justice litigation in the United States is in transition. It traces its origins to the environmental justice movement that began in the late 1980s.[1] The environmental justice movement was grounded in a growing awareness of the linkage between environmental and human rights problems and the need for law and policy responses to address the disproportionate impacts of envi-

---

[*] *The author gratefully acknowledges valuable research assistance from Mackenzie Landa, Esq.*

1. Elizabeth Ann Kronk Warner & Randall S. Abate, *International and Domestic Law Dimensions of Climate Justice for Arctic Indigenous Peoples*, 43 Ottawa L. J. 113, 121 (2013). For a helpful discussion of the legal and historical foundations of the environmental justice movement in the United States, see generally Michael B. Gerrard & Sheila R. Foster eds., The Law of Environmental Justice: Theories and Procedures to Address Disproportionate Risks (2d ed. 2009); Robert D. Bullard, Dumping in Dixie: Race, Class, and Environmental Quality (3d ed. 2000); Luke W. Cole & Sheila R. Foster, From the Ground Up: Environmental Racism and the Rise of the Environmental Justice Movement (2000).

ronmental problems on minority and low-income communities throughout the United States.[2] The implementation of environmental justice measures at the federal[3] and state[4] levels since the 1990s helped provide a foundation for climate justice litigation in the United States. Climate justice litigation in the United States also has drawn some of its inspiration from developments at the international level, where the connection between climate change and human rights became galvanized in response to the Inuit petition before the Inter-American Commission on Human Rights in 2005.[5] Climate justice litigation seeks to provide remedies to marginalized communities that are facing climate change impacts and that lack financial and technological resources to effectively adapt to these changes.[6]

The U.S. climate justice movement began with public nuisance lawsuits that sought injunctive relief or damages for climate change impacts.[7] Paralleling the evolution of the public nuisance line of climate justice lawsuits was the landmark case of *Massachusetts v. EPA*.[8] Massachusetts and several other states sued to compel the U.S. Environmental Protection Agency (EPA) to fulfill its duty to regulate carbon dioxide (CO_2) as a pollutant under the Clean Air Act. The U.S. Supreme Court concluded that the states had standing to bring the suit and that EPA had authority to regulate CO_2 as a pol-

---

2.   The environmental justice movement initially focused on "environmental racism" as manifested by the disproportionate siting of environmentally undesirable land uses in African American communities. The movement subsequently broadened its focus from environmental racism to "environmental justice," which expanded the movement's reach to include other disadvantaged communities, including low-income communities and Native American communities. *See* David H. Getches & David N. Pellow, *Beyond "Traditional" Environmental Justice, in* JUSTICE AND RESOURCES: CONCEPTS, STRATEGIES, AND APPLICATIONS 5–6, 24–25 (Katherine M. Mutz, Gary C. Bryner & Douglas S. Kenney eds., 2002).

3.   *See, e.g.,* OFFICE OF ENVIRONMENTAL JUSTICE, U.S. ENVIRONMENTAL PROTECTION AGENCY, PLAN EJ 2014 (2011), http://nepis.epa.gov/Exe/ZyPDF.cgi/P100DFCQ.PDF?Dockey=P100DFCQ.PDF (providing a roadmap for the U.S. Environmental Protection Agency (EPA) to integrate environmental justice considerations into all of its programs); Federal Actions to Address Environmental Justice in Minority Populations and Low-income Populations, Exec. Order No. 12898, 59 Fed. Reg. 7629 (Feb. 16, 1994) (directing federal agencies to incorporate environmental justice considerations into their decisionmaking processes).

4.   *See generally* UNIVERSITY OF CALIFORNIA HASTINGS COLLEGE OF THE LAW PUBLIC LAW RESEARCH INSTITUTE, ENVIRONMENTAL JUSTICE FOR ALL: A FIFTY STATE SURVEY OF LEGISLATION, POLICIES, AND CASES (4th ed. 2010), http://gov.uchastings.edu/public-law/docs/ejreport-fourthedition.pdf.

5.   *See generally* Hari M. Osofsky, *Complexities of Addressing the Impacts of Climate Change on Indigenous Peoples through International Law Petitions: A Case Study of the Inuit Petition to the Inter-American Commission on Human Rights, in* CLIMATE CHANGE AND INDIGENOUS PEOPLES: THE SEARCH FOR LEGAL REMEDIES (Randall S. Abate & Elizabeth Ann Kronk Warner eds., 2013).

6.   For a valuable and comprehensive discussion of the foundations and evolution of climate justice litigation, see generally INTERNATIONAL BAR ASSOCIATION, ACHIEVING JUSTICE AND HUMAN RIGHTS IN AN ERA OF CLIMATE DISRUPTION (2014), http://www.ibanet.org/PresidentialTaskForceClimate ChangeJustice2014Report.aspx.

7.   *See infra* Part I.

8.   Massachusetts v. EPA, 549 U.S. 497 (2007).

lutant under the Act.[9] This successful effort helped launch climate justice as a field in the United States because the case was not merely a citizen suit enforcement action under the Clean Air Act; it was a creative use of the courts to seek injunctive relief for climate change impacts in Massachusetts and elsewhere in response to Congress' and the executive branch's failure to regulate climate change.

Now in its "third wave" in the form of atmospheric trust litigation (ATL), climate justice litigation seeks to merge aspects of the public nuisance line of cases and the *Massachusetts v. Environmental Protection Agency* litigation theories. First, like *Massachusetts v. EPA*, ATL targets the most appropriate defendant—governmental entities—rather than singling out entities in the private sector as in the public nuisance line of cases. Second, like the public nuisance cases, ATL embraces a common law doctrine with a track record of success in environmental litigation—in this instance, the public trust doctrine. The public trust doctrine is even better suited than public nuisance for climate justice litigation because it has already evolved and broadened the focus of its applicability to issues beyond the initial tethering of the theory to the "traditional triad" of public trust uses (i.e., navigation, commerce, and fishing).[10] The extension of the public trust doctrine's applicability to atmospheric resources is a logical next step to include within the government's environmental stewardship responsibilities under the doctrine.

This chapter addresses the evolution of ATL from its public trust doctrine roots and the value of ATL as a tool to promote climate justice. Part I of this chapter examines the climate justice movement in the United States and describes the evolution of the public nuisance line of cases that launched this field. Part II describes the evolution of the public trust doctrine and how it serves as the conceptual foundation for ATL. Part III discusses how the ultimate goal of ATL—to apply this state law theory at the federal level[11]—faced a serious roadblock in *Alec L. v. McCarthy*.[12] Although this decision may have dimmed hopes for the applicability of ATL at the federal level, the success of recent ATL cases at the federal and state levels, and in foreign domestic courts, underscores how ATL will be a valuable tool to promote climate justice in the United States and abroad in the years ahead.

---

9.   *Id.* at 516–26.
10.   *See infra* note 31 and accompanying text.
11.   For a valuable discussion of the parameters of ATL from the scholar who conceived this theory, and its ultimate goal of applicability to the federal government, see generally Mary Christina Wood, *Atmospheric Trust Litigation*, in ADJUDICATING CLIMATE CHANGE: STATE, NATIONAL, AND INTERNATIONAL APPROACHES (William C.G. Burns & Hari M. Osofsky eds., 2009).
12.   Alec L. v. McCarthy, 561 Fed. App'x 7 (D.C. Cir. 2014).

I.   The Climate Justice Movement in the United States

Climate justice litigation in the United States would not have evolved as quickly as it did without building on the foundation from the environmental justice movement. Environmental regulation in the 1970s and 1980s was extremely effective in managing pollution of environmental resources such as air, water, land, and endangered species. Despite the success of federal environmental statutes enacted to protect these resources, and litigation to enforce the mandates of these statutes, a growing awareness emerged in the 1980s and 1990s that this environmental management scheme was missing an important component of the ecosystem: humans. The impacts of environmental problems are not limited to the impairment of the environmental resources—there are also serious human dimensions to environmental problems.

The environmental justice movement in the United States evolved to draw attention to the human dimensions of environmental problems by underscoring how minority and low-income communities are disproportionately burdened by these environmental problems. Environmental justice regulation consists largely of procedural mechanisms at the federal and state levels designed to consider and seek to mitigate the adverse environmental impacts of agency decisionmaking on affected communities.[13] This new area of law represented an important shift in thinking that helped climate justice litigation follow as a logical next step in the effort to provide protection to communities that are marginalized by environmental problems.

Building on the foundation of the environmental justice movement, climate justice litigation developed primarily as a response to the failure of the U.S. government to regulate greenhouse gas (GHG) emissions in a comprehensive manner at the federal level. The United States was not a Party to the Kyoto Protocol and did not implement Kyoto-like legislation to regulate climate change in the past two decades. The ultimate goal of climate justice litigation, therefore, was to apply pressure to the federal government to implement a regulatory framework to address this problem and to impose liability on significant emitters of GHGs in the private sector for their contributions to the climate change problem. Climate justice litigation against

---

13.   *See, e.g., supra* notes 3, 4. Federal courts have rejected litigants' efforts to establish a substantive remedy for disparate impacts of environmental problems on minority and low-income communities. *See, e.g.*, Alexander v. Sandoval, 532 U.S. 275 (2001) (holding that Title VI of the Civil Rights Act of 1964 does not authorize a private right of action in lawsuits alleging evidence of disparate impact); South Camden Citizens in Action v. New Jersey Dep't of Envtl. Prot., 274 F.3d 771 (3d Cir. 2001) (holding that Title VI does not authorize a private right of action under EPA's disparate impact regulations in the absence of evidence of intentional discrimination).

private sector entities seeking remedies for certain communities that were disproportionately burdened by the impacts of climate change followed shortly thereafter.

Public nuisance suits served as the foundation for climate justice litigation. These cases build on the foundation of the "federal common law of interstate pollution," which is a narrow doctrine established in air[14] and water[15] pollution cases. Climate change impacts are a form of interstate pollution, which triggered the potential applicability of this doctrine.

The first in this line of public nuisance cases was *American Electric Power (AEP) v. Connecticut*,[16] in which Connecticut and other states sought to integrate a public nuisance action and the federal common law of interstate pollution to obtain injunctive relief against several power plants for their significant collective contribution to climate change. The plaintiff sought injunctive relief against the power companies in requesting that the court issue an order to the companies to reduce their GHG emissions by a certain percentage. The U.S. Supreme Court in *AEP* ultimately concluded that this suit was barred on federal displacement grounds.[17]

The second step in this line of cases involved a shift in litigation strategy. Seeking injunctive relief for climate change issues raised concerns under the political question doctrine as to whether the courts were the proper forum to seek relief for climate change issues because such issues arguably need to be addressed first by either the executive or legislative branches. Therefore, in *California v. General Motors Corp.*,[18] the state of California sued major automakers for these companies' alleged contribution to the public nuisance of global warming and sought damages for the impacts from the current and future harms from global warming. The state voluntarily withdrew its claim, but the case laid an important foundation for future climate justice cases that sought damages under the public nuisance theory.

The litigation theory then adjusted slightly again in the next phase of the evolution of this theory, which involved public nuisance cases that affected

---

14. *See* Georgia v. Tennessee Copper Co., 206 U.S. 230 (1907) (holding that a state that is affected by air pollution from a neighboring state can seek injunctive relief from an emissions source in the neighboring state that caused the pollution problem).

15. *See* Illinois v. City of Milwaukee, 406 U.S. 91 (1972) (holding that federal district courts have jurisdiction over interstate water pollution disputes that create a public nuisance, even though the federal Clean Water Act was already in place to regulate water pollution issues, and that application of federal common law was consistent with the federal Clean Water Act).

16. American Elec. Power v. Connecticut, 131 S. Ct. 2527 (2011).

17. Federal displacement means that these public nuisance claims based on the federal common law of interstate pollution are nonjusticiable because such federal common law claims are barred when a federal statute—in this case, the Clean Air Act—addresses the subject matter at issue.

18. California v. General Motors Corp., No. C06-05755, 2007 WL 272681 (N.D. Cal. Sept. 17, 2007).

communities (rather than states) filed against private sector entities, including oil, gas, and chemical companies. The key lawsuits in this phase of the evolution were *Comer v. Murphy Oil USA*[19] and *Native Village of Kivalina v. ExxonMobil Corp.*[20] Seeking damages in these cases represented the essence of climate justice litigation under the public nuisance doctrine—affected communities that alleged that they had been disproportionately burdened by climate change impacts and that sought relief from private sector entities that contributed a significant percentage of GHG emissions to the global climate change problem. Unfortunately, the Ninth Circuit embraced the federal displacement reasoning from the *AEP* case in dismissing the Native Village of Kivalina's claim.[21] The U.S. Supreme Court declined review of the *Comer* and *Kivalina* cases, thereby severely limiting the future of public nuisance cases for climate change impacts based on federal common law. Such cases may still be filed if based on a state's common law doctrine of public nuisance, however.[22]

II.   The Evolution From the Public Trust Doctrine to Atmospheric Trust Litigation (ATL)

The public trust doctrine refers to the government's obligation to protect and maintain certain natural resources for the benefit of its citizens.[23] The principle originated in ancient Rome and was codified in the *Institutes of Justinian* in the sixth century A.D.[24] The ancient Romans acknowledged "public rights in water and the seashore which were unrestricted and common to all . . . ."[25]

---

19.   Comer v. Murphy Oil USA, 585 F.3d 855 (5th Cir. 2009) (plaintiffs were victims of Hurricane Katrina who alleged that climate change contributed to the increased intensity of the storm that caused them to be displaced from their homes in New Orleans, Louisiana).

20.   Native Village of Kivalina v. ExxonMobil Corp., 696 F.3d 849 (9th Cir. 2012), *cert. denied*, 133 S. Ct. 2390 (2013) (plaintiffs were a village of approximately 400 Native Alaskans who alleged that climate change caused coastal erosion that made their community uninhabitable and would require relocation to avoid losing their community due to sea-level rise).

21.   *Kivalina*, 696 F.3d at 897. For a discussion of the evolution of public nuisance suits seeking relief for climate change impacts, see generally Randall S. Abate, *Public Nuisance Suits for the Climate Justice Movement: The Right Thing and the Right Time*, 85 WASH. L. REV. 197 (2010).

22.   Tracy D. Hester, *A New Front Blowing in: State Law and the Future of Climate Change Public Nuisance Litigation*, 31 STAN. ENVTL. L.J. 49, 52 (2012) (citing American Elec. Power v. Connecticut, 131 S. Ct. 2527 (2011)).

23.   Gerald Torres & Nathan Bellinger, *The Public Trust: The Law's DNA*, 4 WAKE FOREST J.L. & POL'Y 281, 283 (2014).

24.   Melissa Kwaterski Scanlan, *The Evolution of the Public Trust Doctrine and the Degradation of Trust Resources: Courts, Trustees, and Political Power in Wisconsin*, 27 ECOLOGY L.Q. 135, 140 n.4 (2004).

25.   *Id.* at 140 n.4. *See also* HELEN ALTHAUS, PUBLIC TRUST RIGHTS 23 (1978) ("By the law of nature these things are common to mankind—the air, running water, the sea, and consequently the shores of the sea. No one, therefore, is forbidden to approach the seashore, provided that he respects habitations, monuments, and buildings . . .").

Under English common law, the concept developed into the idea of a public trust, pursuant to which title to navigable waters and "the bed or soil beneath tidal waters" was vested in the British Crown so that the Crown may "control the highways of commerce and navigation for the advantage of the public . . . ."[26] Thus, the British Crown acts as trustee to the citizens of Great Britain over the tidal waters and the submerged grounds beneath.[27] These natural resources are "not held in fee simple, but rather . . . in trust for the people and only for purposes that benefit the public interest."[28]

Following the American Revolution, the properties held in trust by the British Crown within the American colonies shifted to the now-former colonies as newly sovereign states.[29] Thus, the United States' doctrine initially recognized that the tidelands, and the lands beneath tidal and navigable waterways, should be held in trust by the states for the public to promote the interests of the public.[30] According to early public trust judicial opinions, those public interests were to promote navigation, commerce, and fishing.[31] The doctrine itself is a function of sovereignty that "imposes duties on government[,] instills certain inalienable rights in the people[,] and . . . constitutes the sovereign legal obligation that facilitates the reproduction and survival of our society . . . ."[32]

Legal scholars have identified language in the U.S. Constitution to illustrate the vital importance of the public trust concept in American law.[33] For example, the Equal Protection and Due Process Clauses reflect the framers' intentions to protect and reserve certain ideals and rights for future generations.[34] According to Prof. Gerald Torres, the public trust is the slate upon

---

26. *Id.* at 140.
27. *Id.*
28. Torres & Bellinger, *supra* note 23, at 287.
29. Scanlan, *supra* note 24, at 140. *See also* Martin v. Lessee of Waddell, 41 U.S. 367, 410 (1842) (recognizing that "[w]hen the Revolution took place the people of each State became themselves sovereign, and in that character hold the absolute right to all their navigable waters, and the soils under them, for their own common use, subject only to the rights since surrendered by the Constitution to the general government.").
30. Barton H. Thompson Jr., *The Public Trust Doctrine: A Conservative Reconstruction & Defense*, 15 SOUTHEASTERN ENVTL. L.J. 47, 67–68 (2006).
31. *Id.* at 68. These three uses came to be known as the "traditional triad" of public trust uses.
32. *Id.* at 289.
33. Torres & Bellinger, *supra* note 23, at 293–94.
34. Torres & Bellinger state:
    The Equal Protection Clause is designed to ensure that all persons are treated equally before the law. Temporal inequality requires a judicial mechanism to ensure the protection of future generations. The Due Process Clause of the Fifth Amendment incorporates unenumerated rights against the federal government. Whether a particular unenumerated right or limitation qualifies depends on "whether the right . . . is fundamental to our scheme of ordered liberty . . . or . . . whether this right is 'deeply rooted in this nation's history and tradition.'"
    Id. (internal citation omitted).

which "all constitutions and laws are written."[35] Prof. Mary Christina Wood characterizes the public trust as having a constitutional force based on "the inherent and inalienable rights of citizens as reserved through their social contract with government . . . ."[36] Notwithstanding these compelling theories from leading scholars, the U.S. Supreme Court has held that the public trust doctrine is a state law doctrine.[37] While many state constitutions incorporate elements of the public trust doctrine, most state courts find justification for the doctrine in the common law,[38] whereas some have found it to be a hybrid "of customary law but essentially constitutional in character."[39]

Early American jurisprudence only recognized navigable waterways, the lands beneath navigable waterways, and the seashore between high and low tides as public trust assets.[40] *Carson v. Blazer*, decided in 1810, was the first significant case to raise the public trust issue in the United States.[41] In an attempt to create a private fishery along the Susquehanna River, a riparian landowner claimed that his properties extended through the center of the river.[42] The Pennsylvania court held that "a riparian owner enjoys 'no exclusive right to fish in the river immediately in front of his lands . . . the right to fisheries in that river is vested in the state, and open to all . . . .'"[43] Subsequently, in 1821, the New Jersey Supreme Court ruled that lands below a beach's low water mark belong to the public and, therefore, the shellfish beds below the low mark could not be privately owned.[44] The most famous U.S. public trust case, *Illinois Central R.R. Co. v. Illinois*, was decided in 1892.[45] The U.S. Supreme Court held that the Illinois legislature's allocation of more than 1,000 acres of submerged lands in Lake Michigan, and along the Chicago waterfront, to a private railroad company was beyond the scope of the

---

35. Mary Christina Wood, Nature's Trust: Environmental Law for a New Ecological Age 129 (2013) (quoting Gerald Torres, Public Trust: The Law's DNA, Keynote Address at the University of Oregon School of Law (Feb. 23, 2012)).

36. Mary Christina Wood, *The Planet on the Docket: Atmospheric Trust Litigation to Protect Earth's Climate System and Habitability*, 9 Fla. A&M L. Rev. 259, 261 (2014).

37. Thompson, *supra* note 30, at 57. *See, e.g.*, Phillips Petroleum Co. v. Mississippi, 484 U.S. 469, 482 (1988) (relying on Mississippi law to determine the extent of public trust lands); Appleby v. City of New York, 271 U.S. 364, 395 (1926) (relying on New York common law to determine whether a private owner could restrain the city of New York from dredging the land and using the water).

38. S.C. Const. art. XIV, §4 ("All navigable waters shall forever remain public highways free to the citizens of the State."). *See also* Pa. Const. art. IX, §27; Tex. Const. art. XVI, §59; Haw. Const. art. I, §2 & art. XI, §1.

39. *See* Arnold v. Mundy, 6 N.J.L. 1, 16–17 (N.J. 1821); Glass v. Goeckel, 703 N.W.2d 58, 64 (Mich. 2005); In re Water Use Permit Applications, 9 P.3d 409, 425 (Haw. 2000).

40. Torres & Bellinger, *supra* note 23, at 286.

41. Carson v. Blazer, 2 Binn. 475 (Pa. 1810).

42. *Id.* at 486.

43. *Id.* at 495.

44. *Arnold*, 6 N.J.L. at 52.

45. Illinois Cent. R.R. v. Illinois, 146 U.S. 387 (1892).

legislature's authority because the property was held in trust for the public by the state.[46]

As society's perceptions of public resources have evolved, so too has the scope of resources protected by the public trust doctrine.[47] For example, though the commercial importance of waterways and the reliance on private fishing as a food source have declined, tidal areas and navigable waterways are still valuable public resources.[48] Coastal populations have increased, as have the recreational values of coastlines to those populations.[49] As a result, many state courts now safeguard natural resources for "general recreation, environmental protection, and aesthetics."[50] For example, in *Gould v. Greylock Reservation Commission* in 1966, citizens sued as public trust beneficiaries to prevent enforcement of a statute privatizing a large portion of a nature reserve for a ski resort.[51] The Supreme Court of Massachusetts held that the statute was invalid and enjoined the state from granting public lands for a private use.[52] In 1984, the New Jersey Supreme Court expanded the public trust doctrine to dry sand areas of the beach when it ruled that the public had a right to "cross and make reasonable use" of a privately owned, dry sand area of the beach when it "is essential or reasonably necessary for enjoyment of the ocean."[53]

In addition, scientific advances have raised climate change and environmental concerns that have augmented the ecological significance that society places on coastal areas, shorelines, and water resources.[54] As a result, some states now recognize non-navigable tributaries, wetlands, and groundwater as protected assets.[55] In 1971, the California Supreme Court recognized that the public trust is a flexible doctrine capable of adapting to changing public needs.[56] In *Marks v. Whitney*, the court prevented a property owner from developing tidelands because preservation of those

---

46. *Id.* at 456.
47. Thompson, *supra* note 30, at 67.
48. *Id.* at 67–68.
49. *Id.* at 68.
50. *Id.* at 70 n.12. Opinion of the Justices (Public Use of Coastal Beaches), 649 A.2d 604, 609 (N.H. 1994) (recognizing recreation as one of the purposes of the public trust doctrine); Borough of Neptune City v. Borough of Avon-by-the-Sea, 294 A.2d 47, 54 (N.J. 1972) (finding that public rights extend to "recreational uses, including bathing, swimming and other shore activities"). Not all courts, however, have been willing to expand the public trust purposes. *See, e.g.*, Bell v. Town of Wells, 557 A.2d 168, 173 (Me. 1989) (limiting trust rights to fishing, fowling, and navigation); Opinion of the Justices, 313 N.E.2d 561 (Mass. 1974) (limiting trust rights to fishing and navigation).
51. Gould v. Greylock Reservation Comm'n, 215 N.E.2d 114 (Mass. 1966).
52. *Id.* at 126.
53. Matthews v. Bay Head Improvement Ass'n, 471 A.2d 355, 365–66 (N.J. 1984).
54. Thompson, *supra* note 30, at 53.
55. Torres & Bellinger, *supra* note 23, at 297.
56. Thompson, *supra* note 30, at 52.

tidelands "in their natural state, so that they may serve as ecological units for scientific study, as open space, and as environments which provide food and habitat for birds and marine life, and which favorably affect the scenery and climate of the area" is an important objective for the public trust doctrine.[57]

The above cases underscore the public trust doctrine's role as "a legal framework that citizens can use to compel government to fulfill its fiduciary duties to protect natural resources."[58] In response to global climate change, a movement to extend the public trust doctrine to include the earth's atmosphere has led to ATL.[59] ATL proponents perceive the earth's atmosphere "as a single public trust asset in its entirety" over which all sovereigns are co-trustees with mutual responsibilities.[60] ATL attempts to impose a legal duty on governments to protect the atmosphere, and seeks to require governments to execute that duty based on scientific data and implement a policy of shared responsibility with regard to reducing CO_2 emissions.[61]

ATL pioneer and scholar, Professor Wood, sees ATL as a logical extension of the *Illinois Central* opinion. The *Illinois Central* Court announced that "the state can no more abdicate its trust over property in which the whole people are interested . . . than it can abdicate its police powers in the administration of government . . . ."[62] Nevertheless, courts have been reluctant to extend the public trust doctrine to include the atmosphere. ATL has had limited success at the state level to date; however, some recent developments appear promising.[63] An ATL case has not yet succeeded at the federal level. The *Alec L. v. McCarthy* case discussed in Part III presented the opportunity that ATL needed to apply the theory at the federal level, but the case was dismissed.

---

57. Marks v. Whitney, 491 P.2d 374, 380 (Cal. 1971) (concluding that the "public uses to which tidelands are subject are sufficiently flexible to encompass changing public needs," including environmental preservation).

58. Torres & Bellinger, *supra* note 23, at 316–17. *But see* Patrick Redmond, *The Public Trust in Wildlife: Two Steps Forward, Two Steps Back*, 49 Nat. Resources J. 249 (2009) (arguing that the public trust doctrine has expanded in an inconsistent and controversial manner that does not support application to wildlife protection efforts).

59. *See generally* Wood, *supra* note 36 (discussing the need for and viability of atmospheric trust litigation); *see also* Robin Kundis Craig, *Adapting to Climate Change: The Potential Role of State Common Law Public Trust Doctrines*, 34 Vt. L. Rev. 781 (2010) (arguing that the public trust doctrine can provide a legal mechanism for states to implement management-based climate change adaptation regimes).

60. Wood, *supra* note 36, at 270.

61. *Id.* at 271.

62. *Id.* at 261 (quoting Illinois Cent. R.R. v. Illinois, 146 U.S. 387, 453 (1892)).

63. *See infra* Part III.B. for a discussion of ATL state cases.

III. Moving Forward With ATL in the Wake of *Alec L. v. McCarthy*

After reviewing the D.C. Circuit's opinion in *Alec L. v. McCarthy*, and the subsequent pending federal ATL case in *Juliana*, Part III discusses how ATL and ATL-related cases at the state level in the United States and in foreign countries offer some hope for the continued viability of the ATL theory as a tool to secure climate justice in the courts.

A. The Federal Avenue for ATL

In *Alec L. v. Jackson*,[64] the plaintiffs—five youths[65] and two nongovernmental organizations (NGOs)[66]—filed suit in the U.S. District Court for the District of Columbia against Lisa Jackson, then-administrator of EPA, and other federal officials. The complaint alleged that each of the defendants, as agencies and officers of the federal government, "have wasted and failed to preserve and protect the atmosphere Public Trust asset."[67]

The district court held that the plaintiffs lacked standing to sue in federal court. The court determined that the key question is "whether Plaintiffs' public trust claim is a creature of state or federal common law."[68] The plaintiffs argued that the public trust doctrine presents a federal question because it "is not in any way exclusively a state law doctrine."[69] The court rejected this argument, relying on a 2012 Supreme Court decision[70] that stated that "the public trust doctrine remains a matter of state law" and its "contours . . . do not depend upon the Constitution."[71]

The parties disagreed as to whether the Supreme Court's declaration regarding the public trust doctrine is part of the holding or merely dicta.[72] The court determined that this concern is a non-issue because even carefully considered language in dicta generally must be regarded as authoritative.[73] The district court noted that even if the Supreme Court's

---

64. Alec L. v. Jackson, 863 F. Supp. 2d 11 (D.D.C. 2012).
65. The five youth plaintiffs were Alec L., Madeleine W., Garret & Grant S., and Zoe J.
66. The two NGO plaintiffs were Kids vs. Global Warming and WildEarth Guardians. According to Our Children's Trust (OCT), these plaintiffs partnered with OCT to file the lawsuit.
67. *Alec L. v. Jackson*, 863 F. Supp. 2d at 12.
68. *Id.* at 15.
69. *Id.*
70. PPL Montana v. Montana, 132 S. Ct. 1215 (2012). For a discussion of this case, see *infra* notes 116–22 and accompanying text.
71. *Alec L. v. Jackson,* 863 F. Supp. 2d at 15.
72. *Id.*
73. *Id.*

declaration were not binding, the court would at least regard the declaration as persuasive.[74]

The court also considered the argument of a federal common law public trust doctrine. Relying on the Supreme Court's decision in *AEP*, the court concluded that even if the public trust doctrine had been a federal common law claim at one time, it has subsequently been displaced by federal regulation, specifically the Clean Air Act.[75] In holding that the federal common law cause of action was displaced by the Clean Air Act, the court concluded that federal judges may not set limits on GHG emissions "in the face of a law empowering EPA to set the same limits, subject to judicial review only to ensure against action arbitrary, capricious, . . . or otherwise not in accordance with the law."[76]

The plaintiffs appealed the decision to the D.C. Circuit in *Alec L. v. McCarthy*.[77] In affirming the dismissal of the plaintiffs' complaint, the D.C. Circuit concluded in a two-page opinion that: (1) the plaintiffs failed to rely on any cases that indicate that violations of the public trust doctrine may apply as a federal question, and (2) the Supreme Court had recently reaffirmed that "the public trust doctrine remains a matter of state law."[78]

B.   ATL State Law Actions Remain Viable and Important

Despite the setback in the D.C. Circuit's decision in *Alec L. v. McCarthy*, several ATL cases are pending as of this writing in state courts throughout the United States.[79] Some type of climate change-related case has been filed in all 50 states, most of which have been administrative petitions that have realized limited success to date.[80] Several actions have received favorable rulings. For example, in *Bonser-Lain v. Texas*,[81] the Texas Environmental Law Center sued the Texas Commission on Environmental Quality (TCEQ), seeking judicial review of TCEQ's denial of a petition for rulemaking. While the court ultimately determined that the decision was a "reasonable exercise"

74.   *Id.*
75.   *Id.* at 16.
76.   *Id.* at 17.
77.   Alec L. v. McCarthy, 561 Fed. App'x 7 (2014).
78.   *Id.* at 8.
79.   *See* OCT, *State Legal Actions* (listing pending and past claims), http://ourchildrenstrust.org/Legal (last visited Aug. 24, 2016). OCT is an NGO based in Eugene, Oregon, that has undertaken impressive and inspiring work in advancing ATL in the United States and abroad.
80.   *Id.* (reporting that the 39 petitions for rulemaking that have been submitted to administrative agencies have been denied).
81.   Bonser-Lain v. Texas Comm'n on Envtl. Quality, No. D-1-GN-11-002194 (Tex. Dist. Ct. Aug. 2, 2012), http://www.law.uh.edu/faculty/thester/courses/Climate-Change-2012/BonserLain%20v%20 TCEQ.pdf.

of the agency's discretion, the court's opinion was supportive of the use of the public trust doctrine for protection of air and atmosphere.[82] The Texas district court invalidated the TCEQ's determination that the public trust doctrine applied only to water, stating "the public trust doctrine includes all natural resources of the State including the air and atmosphere."[83] The court further held that the federal Clean Air Act is a "floor, not a ceiling, for the protection of air quality," effectively rejecting the defendant's argument that the issue was preempted by the Clean Air Act.[84] This reasoning provides an important distinction from the U.S. Supreme Court decision in *AEP* in which the Court held that the plaintiffs' public nuisance claim was displaced by the Clean Air Act.

Five days after the Texas court decision in July 2012, a district court in New Mexico denied the state's motion to dismiss an ATL lawsuit. In *Sanders-Reed v. Martinez*,[85] the New Mexico governor's office was sued for failure to protect the atmospheric trust from the effects of climate change.[86] The district court denied the state's motion to dismiss and allowed the case to proceed to the merits.[87] Although the court granted the state's motion for summary judgment, this case is important because it is the first ATL case to proceed to the merits. The New Mexico Court of Appeals affirmed the district court's decision on procedural grounds; however, the court noted that the New Mexico Constitution supports the conclusion that the state's public trust encompasses the atmosphere.[88]

Progress on ATL at the state level suffered a setback in 2015 in Oregon. In *Chernaik v. Brown*, the plaintiffs alleged that their personal and economic well-being are "dependent upon the health of the state's natural resources held in trust for the benefit of its citizens, including water resources, sub-

---

82. *Id.* at 2.
83. *Id.* at 1.
84. *Id.*
85. Sanders-Reed v. Martinez, 42 ELR 20159, No. D-101-CV-2011-01514 (N.M. Dist. Ct. July 14, 2012).
86. *See* OCT, *New Mexico*, http://www.ourchildrenstrust.org/new-mexico (last visited Aug. 24, 2016).
87. Sanders-Reed v. Martinez, 42 ELR 20159, No. D-101-CV-2011-01514 (N.M. Dist. Ct. July 14, 2012), *order issued* (N.M. Dist. Ct. July 14, 2012).
88. *See* Sanders-Reed v. Martinez, 350 P.3d 1221 (N.M. Ct. App. 2015). Additional support for ATL can be found in the concurring opinion in an Iowa Court of Appeals case, *Filippone ex rel. Filippone v. Iowa Dep't of Natural Resources*, 829 N.W.2d 589 (Iowa Ct. App. 2013). In this case, the plaintiff petitioned the Iowa Department of Natural Resources to adopt new rules regarding the emission of GHGs. Although the court declined to expand the public trust doctrine to include the atmosphere, Judge Doyle's concurring opinion noted that "there is a sound public policy basis" to extend the public trust doctrine to include the atmosphere. Later in 2013, the Iowa Supreme Court upheld the dismissal of the case. *See* Press Release, Our Children's Trust et al., Iowa Supreme Court Declines to Review Climate Case, (May 10, 2013), http://ourchildrenstrust.org/sites/default/files/13.05.09-IowaSC-Decision_0.pdf.

merged and submersible lands, coastal lands, forests, and wildlife," all of which are threatened by climate change.[89] The plaintiffs contended that they will be "adversely and irreparable injured" by defendants' failure to limit GHG emissions.[90] The plaintiffs sought: (1) a declaration that the atmosphere, waters, shores, coastal areas, and wildlife are declared trust resources, that Oregon has an obligation to protect them, and that Oregon has failed in this obligation; (2) an order that Oregon develop an accurate accounting of its current GHG emissions and a plan to reduce those emissions that will protect public trust assets; and (3) a declaration that requires "carbon dioxide emissions to peak in 2012 and to be reduced by six percent each year until at least 2050."[91]

In 2007, Oregon's legislature enacted House Bill 3543, which found that climate change is a threat to Oregon's economy, public health, natural resources, and environment; adopted GHG reduction goals; and created the Oregon Global Warming Commission, whose responsibility is to create goals and methods for local and state governments, businesses, residents, and nonprofit organizations to decrease GHG emissions. Plaintiffs allege that the GHG emissions goals established in House Bill 3545 are inadequate and, even if they are adequate, Oregon has failed to meet these goals. The state filed a motion to dismiss for lack of subject matter jurisdiction and the court granted the motion. The court of appeals reversed and remanded and instructed the lower court to determine whether the natural resources identified by plaintiffs are trust resources and whether "'the State of Oregon, as trustee, has a fiduciary obligation to protect . . . from the impacts of climate change.'"[92]

In discussing the public trust doctrine, the court stated that "the States retain residual power to determine the scope of the public trust over navigable waters. . . . Therefore, the public trust doctrine is a matter of state law, subject to the federal power to regulate navigation under the Commerce Clause and the admiralty power."[93]

The court agreed with the state's position that the public trust doctrine includes only submerged and submersible lands. Regarding whether the atmosphere is encompassed by the public trust doctrine, the "Court first questions whether the atmosphere is a 'natural resource' at all, much less one to which the public trust doctrine applies."[94] The court ultimately decided

---

89.   Chernaik v. Brown, No. 16-11-09273, slip op. at 2 (Or. Cir. Ct. May 11, 2015).
90.   Id.
91.   Id. at 2–3.
92.   Id. at 5.
93.   Id. at 8.
94.   Id. at 10–11.

that the atmosphere does not legally fall under Oregon's public trust doctrine. It explained that the state does not hold title to the atmosphere. "[T]he public trust doctrine originated when title to the lands beneath navigable waters transferred to the State. Unlike submerged and submersible lands . . . the State has not been granted title to the atmosphere."[95] To further support its decision, the court stated the atmosphere is not "exhaustible and irreplaceable" and that, although it can be polluted, it is not a "resource that 'can only be spent once.'"[96]

The court further held that the state has no fiduciary obligation to protect resources encompassed in the public trust doctrine. The court reasoned that the state's obligation toward resources protected by the public trust doctrine is to prevent the state from alienating these resources, but that there is no affirmative fiduciary obligation to protect them. The court also held that the relief that the plaintiffs seek violates the separation of powers because asking the court to order defendants to develop a carbon reduction plan is to ask the "Court to substitute its judgment for that of the legislature."[97] The court reasoned that if it were to grant plaintiffs' request, it would strike down current legislation and impose a more stringent standard for GHG emission reductions, thereby replacing the goals established by the legislature.[98] The plaintiffs filed an appeal in July 2015, which is pending as of this writing.

This recent line of ATL cases at the state level reveals two important trends. First, several state courts have embraced the concept of ATL as a potential strategy to address climate change regulation in the courts, and it is rapidly gaining support. Second, even if the ATL theory does not succeed in its own right in the courts, it has already prompted valuable consideration or rethinking of how to most effectively goad state governmental entities to address climate change regulation initiatives to more effectively safeguard the rights of future generations to a safe and healthy environment. For example, following up on ATL litigation in the state of Washington that did not proceed to the merits, a petition for rulemaking was filed with the Washington Department of Ecology for climate change regulations. Although the Department denied the petition with a detailed response in 2014,[99] one year later a Washington trial court in *Foster v. Washington Department of Ecology* ordered the Department of Ecology to reconsider its denial of the plaintiffs'

---

95. *Id.* at 11.
96. *Id.* at 12.
97. *Id.* at 15–16.
98. *Id.* at 16.
99. Letter from State of Washington Department of Ecology, responding to Andrea Rogers Harris' Petition for Rule Making (Aug. 14, 2014), http://static1.squarespace.com/static/571d109b04426270152febe0/t/576081a01d07c05bf208e7c7/1465942439363/WA.EcologyDecision.pdf.

petition for rulemaking based on the Department's December 2014 report detailing imminent threats to the state from climate change impacts.[100] This case is an encouraging development that helps bring ATL closer to compelling climate change regulation as in *Massachusetts v. EPA*.

C.   Building on ATL and ATL-related Cases in the United States and Other Countries

Outside the United States, several lawsuits also have been filed in foreign domestic courts applying ATL litigation reasoning. For example, an ATL case was filed in 2011 in Ukraine seeking to compel the government to address its inactivity in implementing climate protection policies. The court ordered the Cabinet to prepare an assessment of the country's progress toward realizing the goals of the Kyoto Protocol, which secured an important victory for the plaintiffs.[101] Similarly, in Uganda, an environmental NGO filed an ATL case against the government invoking a public trust duty under the Uganda Constitution to protect the country's atmospheric resources from climate change.[102] Finally, in the Netherlands, 886 citizens served a summons to hold the government responsible for failing to take measures to prevent climate change. The summons requested the court to compel the government to fulfill its obligations under Dutch law, the United Nations Framework Convention on Climate Change, and the European Convention on Human Rights.[103] The citizens prevailed and the case is on appeal as of this writing.[104]

---

100. Foster v. Washington Dep't of Ecology, No. 14-2-25295-1 SEA (King County Sup. Ct., June 23, 2015), http://ourchildrenstrust.org/sites/default/files/Order_Fosterv.Ecology.pdf. *See also* Press Release, Our Children's Trust et al., Washington State Youth Win Unprecedented Decision in Their Climate Change Lawsuit (June 24, 2014), http://ourchildrenstrust.org/sites/default/files/15.06.24WADecisionPR.pdf.

101. *See* Our Children's Trust, *Global Legal Actions (Ukraine)*, http://www.ourchildrenstrust.org/ukraine.

102. *Id.* The case is in mediation as of this writing.

103. *See* RB-Den Haag [Hague District Court] 24 Juni 2015, ECLI:NL:RBDHA:2015:7196 (Stichting Urgenda/Nederlanden) [Urgenda Found. v. Netherlands], http://uitspraken.rechtspraak.nl/inziend ocument?id=ECLI:NL:RBDHA:2015:7145 (last visited Aug. 23, 2016), *translated at* http://www. urgenda.nl/documents/VerdictDistrictCourt-UrgendavStaat-24.06.2015.pdf.

104. For a full analysis of the *Urgenda* case, see Chapter 21 in this volume. Under a similar "protection of future generations" climate justice theory, a lawsuit is being prepared as of this writing against Norwegian authorities regarding recently opened blocks of oil and gas exploration acreage in Arctic waters. Atle Staalesen, *Lawyers Sue State Over Arctic Oil Drilling*, THE INDEP. BARENTS OBSERVER, Jan. 18, 2016, http://thebarentsobserver.com/ecology/2016/01/lawyers-sue-state-over-arctic-oil-drilling; Aleksander Melli et al., *Norway's Rush to Extract Arctic Oil Contradicts Its Constitution*, TRUTHOUT, Oct. 24, 2015, http://www.truth-out.org/news/item/33324-norway-s-rush-to-extract-arctic-oil-contradicts-its-constitution. If the government leases these blocks to oil and gas developers, a suit will be filed to prevent Arctic drilling under the Norwegian Constitution. Emily J. Gertz, *Shell May Be Leaving the Arctic, but Norway's High North Is Open for Business*, TAKEPART, Oct. 6, 2015. Article 112 of the Norwegian Constitution requires the government to impose policies that guarantee Norwegian citizens

The climate justice and intergenerational equity principles underlying ATL litigation also remain viable in ATL-related environmental human rights litigation in the United States and abroad. For example, the Supreme Court of Pennsylvania in *Robinson Township v. Commonwealth*[105] addressed key provisions of a Pennsylvania statute, Act 13, which authorized hydraulic fracturing ("fracking") operations to proceed with virtually no restrictions, even in residential areas. In striking down these provisions of Act 13, the court relied on the Environmental Rights Amendment in the Pennsylvania statute,[106] which mandates the conservation and maintenance of the environment in Pennsylvania.

The court focused on the environmental rights and public trust angle of the issue in resolving the case. The court reasoned that:

> [T]his dispute centers upon an asserted vindication of citizens' rights to quality of life on their properties and in their hometowns, insofar as Act 13 threatens degradation of air and water, and of natural, scenic, and esthetic values of the environment, with attendant effects on health, safety, and the owners' continued enjoyment of their private property. The citizens' interests, as a result, implicate primarily rights and obligations under the Environmental Rights Amendment—Article I, Section 27.[107]

In its analysis of the Environmental Rights Amendment, the court noted that §27 establishes two separate rights in the people of the commonwealth. The first is the declared "right of citizens to clean air and pure water, and to the preservation of natural, scenic, historic and aesthetic values of the environment."[108] Section 27 also separately requires the preservation of "natural, scenic, historic and esthetic values of the environment."[109] By calling for the "preservation" of these broad environmental values, the Constitution again protects the people from governmental action that unreasonably

---

and their descendants the right to a secure climate. Melli et al., *supra*. The lawyers preparing to bring suit assert that in drilling for oil in the Arctic, the government is violating the nation's constitutional requirement to avoid harming the planet for future generations. Hannah Hoag, *Executive Summary for January 19*, ARCTIC DEEPLY, Jan. 19, 2016, http://www.arcticdeeply.org/articles/2016/01/8334/arctic-deeply-executive-summary-january-19/.

105. Robinson Township v. Commonwealth, 623 Pa. 564 (Pa. 2013).
106. As stated in *Robinson Township v. Commonwealth*:

> The people have a right to clean air, pure water, and to the preservation of the natural, scenic, historic and esthetic values of the environment. Pennsylvania's public natural resources are the common property of all the people, including generations yet to come. As trustee of these resources, the Commonwealth shall conserve and maintain them for the benefit of all the people.

Id. at 584–85.
107. *Id.* at 631.
108. *Id.* at 646.
109. *Id.* at 642.

causes actual or likely deterioration of these features.[110] Therefore, any regulation is "subordinate to the enjoyment of the right . . . [and] must be regulation purely, not destruction"; laws of the commonwealth that unreasonably impair the right are unconstitutional.[111]

The court further observed that the second right that §27 protects is the common ownership of the people, including future generations, of Pennsylvania's public natural resources.[112] The court defined "natural resources" as including not only state-owned lands, waterways, and mineral reserves, but also resources that implicate the public interest, such as ambient air, surface and groundwater, wild flora, and fauna (including fish) that are outside the scope of purely private property.[113]

The court determined that the third clause of §27 establishes the commonwealth's duties with respect to Pennsylvania's commonly owned public natural resources.[114] It noted that "the Public Trust is an affirmation of the duty of the state to protect the people's common heritage of streams, lakes, marshlands and tidelands, surrendering that right of protection only in rare cases when the abandonment of that right is consistent with the purposes of the trust."[115] As trustee of the public trust, the commonwealth has two responsibilities: (1) to refrain from performing its trustee duties respecting the environment unreasonably, including via legislative enactments or executive action,[116] and (2) to act affirmatively to protect the environment, via legislative action.[117] Although not an ATL decision, the court's powerful reasoning in *Robinson Township* fully embraces the extension of the public trust doctrine to contexts beyond the traditional scope of the doctrine's coverage, including atmospheric resources.

Similarly, the intergenerational equity principles inherent in ATL are evident in a recent case in the Philippines. A petition was filed in the Supreme Court in Manila on behalf of youth and the 98% of the population without cars.[118] The petition is in the form of a legal instrument known as a Writ of Kalikasan, which provides a remedy for citizens whose environmental rights

---

110. *Id.*
111. *Id.* at 646.
112. *Id.* at 651.
113. *Id.* at 651–52.
114. *Id.* at 653.
115. *Id.* at 654.
116. *Id.* at 656.
117. *Id.* at 657.
118. Elyse Wynn Go, *Share the Road: Citizens' Group Seeks Writ of Kalikasan for Clean Air, Equitable Road Space*, INTERAKSYON, Feb. 14, 2014, http://www.interaksyon.com/article/80765/share-the-road--citizens-group-seeks-writ-of-kalikasan-for-clean-air-equitable-road-space.

have been violated.[119] The petition demands that one-half of the roads be set aside for citizens who do not drive.[120] Like the *Robinson Township* case, the theory in this case also offers support for the reasoning underlying ATL litigation in seeking to compel the government to manage resources beyond the traditional scope of the public trust doctrine for the benefit of future generations.

D.   Prospects for the Future of ATL Litigation

Within the past five years, ATL has been a primary focus of climate justice litigation and it has made significant progress in advancing its theory in U.S. and foreign domestic courts. This progress notwithstanding, ATL has faced significant resistance in state and federal courts in the United States, culminating in the D.C. Circuit's recent decision in *Alec L. v. McCarthy*.[121] This section of the analysis discusses reasons for hope and concern based on recent developments and the status of ATL as a tool to promote climate justice.

First, the cursory and rigid reasoning in the D.C. Circuit's opinion in *Alec L. v. McCarthy* is rooted in the tenuous foundation of the court's reliance on *PPL Montana v. Montana*.[122] The court relied on this case for the proposition that the public trust doctrine is a state law doctrine; however, *PPL Montana v. Montana* was not primarily a public trust doctrine analysis. The issue in this case was whether, under the equal footing doctrine, segments of rivers in Montana are non-navigable to determine if the state of Montana acquired title to the rivers.[123] The state alleged that it had acquired title to the disputed rivers under the equal footing doctrine on the basis that the rivers are navigable.[124] Consequently, the state sought rent from the plaintiff, a power company, for its use of the riverbeds for hydroelectric production of power.[125]

---

119. *Id.*

120. *Id.* In January 2016, the Congress of the Philippines allocated more than 85 million pesos to the Metropolitan Manila Development Authority "for transport and traffic management services particularly for road-sharing activities." *See* Joyce Ilias, *Road-sharing Scheme Along Major Roads in 2016*, CNN PHILIPPINES, Jan. 12, 2016, http://cnnphilippines.com/videos/2016/01/12/Road-sharing-scheme-along-major-roads-in-2016.html.

121. In addition, some recent scholarly writings have been critical of ATL. *See, e.g.,* Andrew Ballentine, *Full of Hot Air: Why the Atmospheric Trust Litigation Theory Is an Unworkable Attempt to Expand the Public Trust Doctrine Beyond Its Common Law Foundations*, 12 DARTMOUTH L.J. 98 (2014); Caroline Cress, *It's Time to Let Go: Why the Atmospheric Trust Won't Help the World Breathe Easier*, 92 N.C. L. REV. 236 (2013).

122. PPL Montana v. Montana, 132 S. Ct. 1215 (2012).

123. *Id.* at 1222.

124. *Id.*

125. *Id.*

The U.S. Supreme Court reversed the judgment in favor of the state for three reasons: (1) the trial court's failure to carefully consider the issue of navigability and required overland portage; (2) the reliance on recreational use to determine the navigability of the Madison River; and (3) the liberal interpretation of the navigability test.[126] The public trust doctrine only entered into the Court's analysis in a peripheral manner. The state alleged that denying title would undermine the public trust doctrine.[127] The Court simply made the distinction that the equal footing doctrine is based on federal constitutional foundations and the public trust doctrine is a matter of state law.[128] Thus, under the equal footing doctrine, federal law determines title to the riverbeds, but states retain the power to define the scope of the public trust of those waters.[129]

It is unfortunate that such an important legal question regarding whether ATL can be applied at the federal level was summarily dismissed through the D.C. Circuit's reliance on *PPL Montana v. Montana*. This case merely states a truism regarding the public trust doctrine, does not involve meaningful public trust doctrine analysis, and is not responsive to the legal question presented in the *Alec L.* case. It is certainly true, as a general principle, that the public trust doctrine has been considered a matter of state law. But the D.C. Circuit merely relied on that general principle without analysis of the question presented in *Alec L.*, which was whether this state law doctrine can be applied at the federal level under the appropriate circumstances. The D.C. Circuit's unresponsive evasion of the core question in the case is unlike previous public trust cases where state courts, presented with the question of whether the public trust doctrine can be extended to apply beyond its traditional water-based uses, did not respond merely by stating that the public trust doctrine had been tied to the traditional triad of uses and providing no further analysis. Unlike the D.C. Circuit's stunted analysis in *Alec L.*, state courts in the past fortunately were responsive to questions regarding the scope of the public trust doctrine's applicability and, for that reason, the doctrine now is understood to extend beyond the traditional triad of uses. Climate change is such a politicized issue in the United States that the D.C. Circuit simply may have been looking for a way to justify keeping climate change claims out of the court system. A related factual context that does not involve climate change could easily have yielded a different result in

---

126. *Id.* at 1226.
127. *Id.* at 1234.
128. *Id.* at 1235.
129. *Id.*

Alec L., or at least a result that would have generated more significant legal reasoning.[130]

The door to federal ATL relief appeared to be completely shut after the D.C. Circuit's decision in *Alec L.* and the subsequent denial of writ of certiorari in the case.[131] However, that door appears to have cracked open in a subsequent federal ATL case, which is pending before the U.S. District Court for the District of Oregon as of this writing. In *Juliana v. United States*, the plaintiffs asserted a claim based on ATL theory applicable to the federal government coupled with an alleged constitutional law duty regarding due process concerns of youth and future generations.[132] The court characterized the plaintiffs' creative claims as based on "a novel theory somewhere between a civil rights action and [National Environmental Policy Act]/Clean Air Act/Clean Water Act suit to force the government to take action to reduce harmful pollution."[133] In concluding that the plaintiffs' claims survived the federal government's motion to dismiss, the court offered compelling reasoning on standing, the political question doctrine, and the scope of the public trust doctrine that bodes well for the future of ATL litigation.

Regarding standing, the court concluded that the injury element was met. Although the personal harms alleged are a consequence of broader harms, the court determined "that does not discount the concrete harms already suffered by individual plaintiffs or likely to be suffered by these plaintiffs."[134] Furthermore, "[g]iven the allegations of direct or threatened direct harm, albeit shared by most of the population or future population, the court should be loath to decline standing to persons suffering an alleged concrete injury of

---

130. Two cases outside of the climate change context are relevant to support the plaintiffs' argument. The first case, *In re Steuart Transp. Co.*, 495 F. Supp. 38 (E.D. Va. 1980), involved claims filed by both the commonwealth of Virginia and the U.S. government against the defendant for damage to migratory waterfowl, statutory penalties, and cleanup costs arising from an oil spill in the Chesapeake Bay. Approximately 30,000 migratory birds allegedly were destroyed as a result of the oil spill. The sole issue before the court was whether the commonwealth and/or the federal government had a right to sue for the loss of migratory waterfowl. The court concluded that under the public trust doctrine, the state of Virginia, and the United States have the right and the duty to protect and preserve the public's interest in natural wildlife resources. *Id.* at 40. Similarly, the court in *United States v. Burlington N. R.R.*, 710 F. Supp. 1286 (D. Neb. 1989), noted that the public trust doctrine has been applied to the federal government. The court reasoned that although the public trust doctrine traditionally applied to tidal waters and the land submerged beneath them, the concept of the United States holding its land in trust for the general population is well established in U.S. jurisprudence. *Id.* at 1287.
131. Alec L. v. McCarthy, 135 S. Ct. 774 (2014).
132. Juliana v. United States, No. 6:15-cv-1517-TC, slip op. at 3 (D. Or. Apr. 8, 2016), http://www.lawandenvironment.com/wp-content/uploads/sites/5/2016/04/5456019-0-10918.pdf. On September 13, 2016, Judge Aiken heard arguments on the federal government's motion to overturn U.S. Magistrate Judge Coffin's April 8, 2016, order denying the federal government's motion to dismiss the case. A decision is expected in November 2016 to determine whether the *Juliana* case can proceed to trial.
133. *Id.*
134. *Id.* at 6.

a constitutional magnitude."[135] The court also concluded that there was sufficient causation between the defendants' actions and the plaintiffs' harms to allow the case to go forward[136] because "the failure to regulate the emissions has resulted in a danger of constitutional proportions to the public health."[137] Finally, the court determined that the plaintiffs' claim is redressable. The plaintiffs allege that a court order requiring the government to take action to reduce GHG emissions will have an impact on the constitutional harms they will suffer if the court does nothing.[138] The court held that there is a need for expert opinion and therefore the issue is better addressed at a later stage and will therefore not be a basis for dismissal.[139] The court relied on the *Urgenda* decision in the Netherlands to support its position on redressability.[140]

The *Juliana* court also provided powerful reasoning under the political question doctrine and the public trust doctrine to support ATL theory. On the political question doctrine, the court concluded that although "courts cannot intervene to assert 'better' policy . . . they can address constitutional violations by government agencies and provide equitable relief."[141] The plaintiffs allege that government action and inaction violates the Constitution, which is an issue that is within the courts' capacity to adjudicate.[142] While the court may not have the power to dictate regulations, it can "direct the EPA to adopt standards that prevent the alleged constitutional harms to youth and future generation plaintiffs."[143]

Regarding the scope of the public trust doctrine, the court determined that this case is distinguishable from *PPL Montana v. Montana*. The issue of whether the United States "has public trust obligations for waters over which it alone has sovereignty" was not presented or decided by the Court in *PPL Montana*.[144] This case, conversely, "does not at all implicate the equal footing doctrine or public trust obligations in the State of Oregon."[145] Here, the public trust doctrine is directed against the United States and its sovereign interests over the oceans and atmosphere of the nation.[146] The court stated that *PPL Montana* does not foreclose the "argument that the public

---

135. *Id.* at 7.
136. *Id.* at 9–10.
137. *Id.* at 10.
138. *Id.* at 12.
139. *Id.* at 12.
140. *Id.* at 11.
141. *Id.* at 13.
142. *Id.* at 14.
143. *Id.* at 14.
144. *Id.* at 18–20.
145. *Id.* at 20.
146. *Id.*

trust doctrine applies to the federal government" and that coastal seawaters could not "be privatized without implicating the principles that reflect core values of our Constitution and the very essence of the purpose of our nation's government."[147] EPA has a duty to protect the public health from pollutants in the atmosphere and the government's public trust duties are "deeply ingrained in this country's history" and therefore, the allegations in the complaint state a substantive due process claim.[148] The court concluded that it "cannot say that the public trust doctrine does not provide at least some substantive due process protections for some plaintiffs within the navigable water areas of Oregon."[149]

Additional support for the proposition that public trust doctrine principles apply to the federal government can be found in jurisprudence from other nations. For example, courts in the Philippines and India have concluded that the federal government has a trust responsibility to protect resources for the benefit of all of the people. In *Oposa v. Factoran*,[150] a group of Filipino minors represented by their parents sued the secretary of the Department of Environment and Natural Resources (DENR) for contracting to have large portions of the country's forested area logged. The court concluded that the right of the plaintiffs (and all those they represent) to a balanced and healthful ecology was as clear as the defendant's duty to protect and advance this right, and the denial or violation of that right gives rise to a cause of action.[151] Similarly, in *M.C. Mehta v. Kamal Nath*, the Supreme Court of India held that the public trust doctrine is embedded in the nation's jurisprudence.[152] The Court determined that "the State is a trustee of all natural resources, which are by nature meant for public use and enjoyment."[153] It further stated that the public at large is the beneficiary for these natural resources and the State owes a legal duty to the public to protect the natural resources.[154]

---

147. *Id.* at 23.

148. *Id.*

149. *Id.*

150. Oposa v. Factoran, G.R. No. 101083, 224 S.C.R.A. 792 (1993).

151. *See id.*

152. M.C. Mehta v. Kamal Nath & Ors, (1997) 1 S.C.C. 388, para. 39 (1996).

153. *Id.* para. 34.

154. *Id.* Another initiative to help protect future generations from the effects of climate change was adopted in Wales in 2015. The first law of its kind in the world, the Well-being of Future Generations Act requires public bodies in Wales to consider sustainable development in all of their decisions to ensure that the needs of present and future generations will be met. *See* Jessica Shankleman, *Government Passes "Groundbreaking" Law to Protect Future Generations From Climate Change*, BusinessGreen, Mar. 18, 2015, http://www.businessgreen.com/bg/news/2400206/wales-passes-groundbreaking-law-to-protect-future-generations-from-climate-change. The law requires Public Services Boards to prepare a local well-being plan setting out local objectives and steps it proposes to take to meet those objectives, including a report containing an assessment of the risks for the United Kingdom of the current and predicted impacts of climate change under the Climate Change Act 2008. *See* Act para.

The success of ATL should be gauged not by how many victories are achieved in state and federal courts under this theory. Rather, ATL's success ultimately should be judged on the basis of the role it played in facilitating state and federal government actors in the United States and abroad to establish and enforce rights and remedies for climate justice. One only needs to look back a few decades to observe similar successes secured through the environmental common law in the United States. Such efforts ultimately achieved effective federal legislative responses and significant damage awards in the contexts of tobacco, lead paint, and asbestos litigation.[155] Climate justice litigation in the United States is currently in the trenches of that struggle, but similar success in this context is on the horizon.

In addition, paralleling the evolution of ATL, scholars and leading NGOs have been active in international and foreign domestic arenas in seeking to promote climate justice from a variety of perspectives. Many of these approaches seek to advance the core goal of ATL and focus on how to leverage the rights of future generations in shaping a future climate justice regime. Some scholarly proposals offer solutions that would need to be crafted within the existing international climate change treaty system,[156] while others find more hope for climate justice outside of that system.[157] Regardless of the method ultimately employed to secure these goals, what is most important is that there is active dialogue and political will throughout the international community to promote climate justice as soon and as effectively as possible. These developments will help move ATL forward.[158]

---

24. The law also establishes the Future Generations Commissioner for Wales "to act as a guardian for the interests of future generations in Wales, and to support the public bodies listed in the Act to work towards achieving the well-being goals of the Act." DEPARTMENT FOR NATURAL RESOURCES OF THE WELSH GOVERNMENT, WELL-BEING OF FUTURE GENERATIONS (WALES) ACT OF 2015: THE ESSENTIALS 9 (2015), http://gov.wales/docs/dsjlg/publications/150623-guide-to-the-fg-act-en.pdf.

155. Similar to the ATL context, the use of the environmental common law to seek relief in these contexts also has been criticized by scholars. *See, e.g.*, Richard O. Faulk & S. John Gray, *Getting the Lead Out? The Misuse of Public Nuisance Litigation by Public Authorities and Private Counsel*, 21 TOXICS L. REP. 1172, 1176 (2006).

156. *See generally* PETER LAWRENCE, JUSTICE FOR FUTURE GENERATIONS: CLIMATE CHANGE AND INTERNATIONAL LAW (2014) (evaluating why and how climate justice principles should be incorporated into international climate change treaty law rules).

157. *See generally* TERESA M. THORP, CLIMATE JUSTICE: A VOICE FOR THE FUTURE (2014) (proposing to constitutionalize universally applicable principles and legal norms of international climate change law by drawing on a coalition of public, private, and civil society leadership).

158. A burgeoning body of ATL scholarship has emerged within the past few years, which has helped advance the theory as it progresses through the courts and legislatures in the United States and abroad. *See generally* KEN COGHILL & TIM SMITH EDS., FIDUCIARY DUTY AND THE ATMOSPHERIC TRUST (2013); Richard J. Lazarus, *Judicial Missteps, Legislative Dysfunction, and the Public Trust Doctrine: Can Two Wrongs Make It Right?*, 45 ENVTL. L. 1139 (2015); Tim Kline, *Alec L. and Federal Atmospheric Trust Litigation: Conceptual and Political Gains Amidst Legal Defeat?*, 42 ECOLOGY L.Q. 549 (2015); Kassandra Castillo, *Climate Change & The Public Trust Doctrine: An Analysis of Atmospheric Trust Litigation*, 6 SAN DIEGO J. CLIMATE & ENERGY L. 221 (2015); Kylie Wha Kyung Wager, *In Common*

The growth of ATL is due in part to the helpful synergy it enjoys with the climate change and human rights movement at the international level that began in the wake of the Inuit petition one decade ago and has gained significant momentum since that time. Within the past several years, numerous international conferences, studies, and reports have continued to address the interplay between climate change and human rights. The United Nations Human Rights Council also has weighed in on the issue.[159] A recent example of the international attention that climate change and human rights has received is a major report prepared by the International Bar Association Task Force on Climate Change Justice and Human Rights.[160] Released on September 22, 2014, the 240-page report proposes more than 50 recommendations to promote climate justice responses to protect environmental and human rights. Among the recommendations are proposed legal recognition for a new universal human right to a safe, clean, healthy, and sustainable environment and establishment of a new international dispute resolution framework for climate change issues, including a new International Court on the Environment.[161] Increasing international recognition of the need to engage dispute resolution frameworks to promote climate justice will help ATL achieve its objectives.

Within the U.S. court system, a promising development is unfolding at the state level in the wake of the federal displacement holdings in *AEP* and *Kivalina*. The Clean Air Act federal displacement rationale only applies to *federal* common law claims—the Court in *AEP* expressly left the door open for state common law claims seeking damages.[162] A 2014 decision by the Iowa Supreme Court[163] upheld plaintiffs' rights to seek damages from air pollution in a state common law tort action. Relying on savings clause analysis rooted in the U.S. Supreme Court's preemption analysis in *International Paper Co. v. Ouelette*,[164] the Iowa Supreme Court "rejected the defendants' arguments that the [Clean Air Act] displaced or otherwise preempted state common law nuisance, trespass, and other tort claims for property damage

---

Law We Trust: How Hawai'i's Public Trust Doctrine Can Support Atmospheric Trust Litigation to Address Climate Change, 20 Hastings W.-N.W. J. Envtl. L. & Pol'y 55 (2014); Jordan M. Ellis, *The Sky's the Limit: Applying the Public Trust Doctrine to the Atmosphere*, 86 Temp. L. Rev. 807 (2014).

159. *See, e.g., Human Rights and Climate Change*, U.N. Human Rights Council, Res. 7/23 (2008), http://ap.ohchr.org/documents/E/HRC/resolutions/A_HRC_RES_7_23.pdf.

160. International Bar Association, Achieving Justice and Human Rights in an Era of Climate Disruption, *supra* note 6.

161. *Id.*

162. *See* Hester, *supra* note 22, at 52 (citing American Elec. Power v. Connecticut, 131 S. Ct. 2527, 2540 (2011)).

163. Freeman v. Grain Processing Corp., No. 13-0723 (Iowa June 13, 2014).

164. International Paper Co. v. Ouelette, 479 U.S. 481 (1987).

and harms to human health" caused by air pollution.[165] Similarly encouraging, the Court relied on the Second Circuit's reasoning in *AEP* to underscore that "courts have successfully adjudicated complex common law public nuisance claims for more than a century"[166] and rejected the defendant's effort to dismiss as nonjusticiable under the political question doctrine a common law tort claim for air pollution damages. Therefore, this case (and ones that are likely to follow in the near future) that supports the capacity of state courts to adjudicate damage claims for air pollution will provide a helpful foundation for future ATL efforts. As state courts continue to depart from the principle that "damages from atmospheric sources are beyond the courts' capacity to address because the Clean Air Act addresses them," a door will remain open to enhance the opportunity for ATL claims to be successfully adjudicated at the state court level.

Conclusion

Although courts are not the best avenue to pursue effective and comprehensive regulation of climate change, the common law can be a powerful mechanism to goad proper regulatory responses to climate change impacts. The climate justice movement in the United States recently has shifted its jurisprudential reliance to another effective common law tool, atmospheric trust litigation. ATL involves a creative expansion of the public trust doctrine in suits primarily against state governments alleging that the state has a duty to manage its atmospheric resources to protect the interests of future generations.

Although extending the public trust doctrine to the federal government is supported by U.S. and foreign domestic jurisprudence, it is nonetheless possible that ATL plaintiffs may not be able to secure an opportunity to be heard before the U.S. Supreme Court and prevail on the merits of their claim to compel the federal government to regulate climate change. Notwithstanding this potential roadblock for ATL litigation, some recent ATL and non-ATL decisions in the United States and abroad offer hope that this common law theory will help promote climate justice within and outside the court system. Moreover, the growth of dialogue and responses in the international community and in foreign domestic arenas regarding climate change and human rights will enhance the receptivity of the judicial audience in evaluating ATL claims in the years ahead.

---

165. Howard A. Learner, *Emerging Clarity on Climate Change Law: EPA Empowered and State Common Law Remedies Enabled*, 44 ELR 10744, 10749 (2015).
166. *Freeman*, No. 13-0723, at 62.

The ultimate goal of ATL is to ensure that the federal government will regulate climate change, which, in turn, will help protect current and future victims of climate change impacts. The slow progression toward regulating climate change is already underway in the United States. Moreover, thanks to the power of the environmental common law as reflected in the climate justice litigation in the past decade, there will be significant progress toward this goal in the years ahead as ATL cases continue to achieve success in communicating the urgency of this need for federal regulation.

Chapter 21

Trends in Climate Justice Litigation: The Dutch Case and Global Repercussions

Jennifer Huang and Maria Antonia Tigre*

Introduction

It was the climate case heard around the world. *Urgenda Foundation v. The State of the Netherlands (Ministry of Infrastructure and the Environment)*[1] has been hailed as a historic decision, the first in Europe in which human rights and international law have been used to determine a government's duty of care to its citizens with respect to climate change regulation. The outcome has been lauded by environmentalists throughout the world. Later in 2015, the Paris Agreement[2] was universally adopted by Parties to the United

---

* *The authors would like to thank Teodora Siderova, Stetson University College of Law (J.D. 2016), for her research assistance.*

1.   RB-Den Haag [Hague District Court] 24 Juni 2015, ECLI:NL:RBDHA:2015:7196 (Stichting Urgenda/Nederlanden) [Urgenda Found. v. Netherlands], http://uitspraken.rechtspraak.nl/inziend ocument?id=ECLI:NL:RBDHA:2015:7145 (last visited Aug. 23, 2016), *translated at* http://www. urgenda.nl/documents/VerdictDistrictCourt-UrgendavStaat-24.06.2015.pdf [hereinafter Judgment].

2.   *Adoption of the Paris Agreement*, UNFCC Conference of the Parties, 21st Sess., U.N. Doc. FCCCC/ CP/2015/10/Add.1 (Dec. 12, 2015), http://unfccc.int/files/home/application/pdf/paris_agreement. pdf [hereinafter *Paris Agreement*].

Nations Framework Convention on Climate Change (UNFCCC), a signal that countries are willing to work together to do more to address climate change. In that context, the judgment can be seen as pushing for the most ambitious climate action in a world where greater action is urgently needed.

Despite these hopeful developments, the district court's judgment in *Urgenda* rests on legal assessments that raise questions regarding the obligations of a State, particularly a European Union (EU) Member State, to unilaterally act beyond the scope of existing legal obligations under domestic, regional, and international law. Clarity on the interplay between these levels of international environmental law, however, is critical. As countries prepare their nationally determined contributions (NDCs) to the Paris Agreement, they will want to anticipate whether they can be subject to similar climate litigation.

This chapter highlights some of the legal issues in the *Urgenda* case and the implications for similar climate justice litigation in other countries. Part I examines the court's decision in *Urgenda*. Part II assesses a number of views on three key legal questions raised by the *Urgenda* case. At the domestic level, legal experts remain divided over whether the court's decision overreaches its judicial authority or whether it presents a much-needed effort to correct a constitutional imbalance. At the European level, the district court may not have authority to issue a ruling that implies that the Netherlands' compliance with its EU obligations was unlawful. Finally, this section reviews various international and regional legal commitments and general principles that the Netherlands upholds under the general rules of treaty interpretation and international law.

Part III considers the implications of *Urgenda* for other climate cases, both in Europe and abroad. Many of the issues raised in Part III are limiting factors for other jurisdictions. The chapter concludes that both the *Urgenda* case and the Paris Agreement usher in a new era in climate action. Governments and civil society are engaging more than ever on climate change, with climate justice litigation providing some of the means by which to engage in a serious dialogue between governments and citizens on how to increase regulatory ambition. A new wave of climate pledges can provide the material from which to bring some of these cases, but overly zealous litigation can have the unintended effect of undermining aspirational policies and measures. Domestic courts, and perhaps even regional courts, will need to critically assess their role in reconciling these forces in seeking to promote climate justice.

I.   Background on the *Urgenda* Case

Urgenda Foundation, an Amsterdam-based environmental nongovernmental organization (NGO), laid the foundation for this lawsuit in November 2012 with a letter to the Dutch government. The letter highlighted the findings of the 2007 United Nations Intergovernmental Panel on Climate Change (IPCC) report to assert that the Netherlands was putting itself at risk by not committing to more ambitious greenhouse gas (GHG) emission reductions.[3] The group requested a written agreement that the Netherlands would take action to reduce GHG emissions by 40% relative to 1990 levels by 2020; otherwise, they would ask the courts to order the State to "take all measures necessary."[4] When the government replied that it was using both domestic and European climate policies to address climate change and cautioned against overly ambitious unilateral action,[5] Urgenda commenced its historic lawsuit.

A.   Theory of the Case

In November 2013, Urgenda, led by American climate change lawyer Roger Cox and representing nearly 900 Dutch citizens, initiated a judicial request to a Dutch district court asking for an order to the Dutch government to cut emissions by at least 25–40% below 1990 levels by 2020.[6] The organization's claims are based on Dutch civil law.

Article 305a of Book 3 of the Dutch Civil Code allows for NGOs to sue on behalf of the public or collective interest of other persons, without financial compensation.[7] Under this provision, Urgenda claimed the government of the Netherlands was in violation of Article 162, Book 6 of the Civil Code.[8] Article 162 addresses the violation of a personal right, a breach of statutory duty or of an unwritten standard duty of care, in which case a civil court may

---

3.   Letter from Urgenda to Mark Rutte, Prime Minister, Ministry of General Affairs, State of the Netherlands (Nov. 12, 2012), http://www.urgenda.nl/documents/121112BriefaanStaatderNL.pdf, *translated at* http://www.urgenda.nl/documents/Staat-der-NL-Engels1.pdf.

4.   *Id.* at 5–6.

5.   Letter from Wilma J. Mansveld, Ministry of Infrastructure and Environment, State of the Netherlands, to Marjan Minnesma, Director, Urgenda (Dec. 11, 2012), http://www.urgenda.nl/documents/BriefReactievandeStaatlp-i-m-0000002872.pdf.

6.   Urgenda, Volledige daagvarding [full summons] (Nov. 20, 2013), http://www.urgenda.nl/documents/DagvaardingUrgendaKlimaatzaak19-11-13.pdf, *translated at* http://www.urgenda.nl/documents/FINAL-DRAFT-Translation-Summons-in-case-Urgenda-v-Dutch-State-v.25.06.10.pdf (June 25, 2014) [hereinafter Summons].

7.   Art. 3:305a BW. *See also* Marjan Peeters, *Urgenda Foundation and 866 Individuals v. The State of the Netherlands: The Dilemma of More Ambitious Greenhouse Gas Reduction Action by EU Member States*, 25 Rev. Eur. Community & Int'l Envtl. L. 123, 124 (2016).

8.   Art. 6:162 BW; Summons, *supra* note 6, paras. 258–264. *See also* Peeters, *supra* note 7, at 124.

determine the applicable standard of duty.[9] Because the government is not immune from liability under Dutch law, government agencies can be liable as executive policymakers.[10]

Urgenda asserted that the Dutch government violated this statute by not adopting the aggressive emission reduction policies needed to protect Dutch citizens. In support of this benchmark, the organization relied on IPCC reports to supply the science behind global warming.[11] It also quoted findings from the World Bank and the International Energy Agency, which emphasized the need to keep global warming to 2°C above pre-industrial levels in order to safeguard human life, but warned that the current emissions trajectory indicates a possible warming of 4°C or more by 2100.[12] Finally, Urgenda cited the objective of the UNFCCC,[13] the long-term temperature goal of limiting global warming to 2°C established in the Cancun Agreements,[14] and the preamble of the Cancun decision under the Kyoto Protocol workstream that states that developed country Parties would have to reduce emissions in a range of 25–40% below 1990 levels by 2020 to avoid the worst impacts of climate change.[15] Because the Netherlands ranks fifth in per capita carbon dioxide (CO_2) emissions in the world,[16] and its current target of reducing emissions by 16% from 2005 levels by 2020 falls well below the reductions needed, Urgenda claimed the Netherlands can and must do more.[17]

---

9.   Art. 6:162 BW; Summons, *supra* note 6, paras. 258–264. *See also* Peeters, *supra* note 7, at 124.

10. Lucas Bergkamp & F. William Brownell, *Dutch Treat*, 33 ENVTL. F. 32, 33 (2016). For additional scholarly commentary on the *Urgenda* case, see generally Jesse Lambrecht & Claudia Ituarte-Lima, *Legal Innovation in National Courts for Planetary Challenges: Urgenda v State of the Netherlands*, 18 ENVTL. L. REV. 57 (2016); Suryapratim Roy & Edwin Woerdman, *Situating Urgenda Versus the Netherlands Within Comparative Climate Change Litigation*, 34 J. ENERGY & NAT. RESOURCES L. 165 (2016); Marc Loth, *Climate Change Liability After All: A Dutch Landmark Case*, 21 TILBURG L. REV. J. INT'L. & COMP. L. 5 (2016); J.H. Jans & K. de Graaf, *The Urgenda Decision: Netherlands Liable for Role in Causing Dangerous Global Climate Change*, 27 J. ENVTL. L. 517 (2015); Lucas Bergkamp & J.C. Hanekamp, *Climate Change Litigation Against States: The Perils of Court-made Climate Policies*, 24 EUR. ENERGY & ENVTL. L. REV. 102 (2015); Jolene Lin, *The First Successful Climate Negligence Case: A Comment on* Urgenda Foundation v. The State of the Netherlands (Ministry of Infrastructure and the Environment), 5 CLIMATE L. 65 (2015); Josephine van Zeben, *Establishing a Governmental Duty of Care for Climate Change Mitigation: Will* Urgenda *Turn the Tide?*, 4 TRANSNAT'L ENVTL. L. 339 (2015); Anne-Sophie Tabau & Christel Cournil, *New Perspectives for Climate Justice: District Court of The Hague, 24 June 2015, Urgenda Foundation Versus the Netherlands*, 12 J. EUR. ENVTL. & PLAN. L. 221 (2015).

11. IPCC reports are periodic, international reports that assess the scientific, technical, and socioeconomic information concerning climate change, its potential effects, and options for adaptation and mitigation. Summons, *supra* note 6, paras. 78–125.

12. *Id.* paras. 134–146.

13. *Id.* para. 185.

14. *Id.* para. 208.

15. *Id.* para. 201.

16. *Id.* paras. 347–354.

17. *Id.* para. 374 ("Based on the foregoing, it can be concluded that the EU reduction target of 20% and the linked Dutch target of 16% below 1990 [sic] levels are both insufficient.").

Urgenda contended that the applicable standard duty of care derives from the government's obligations under domestic, European human rights, and international environmental law. Citing Dutch case law on transboundary pollution, it argued that although other countries may contribute to GHG emissions, the Netherlands remains jointly liable for its share of emissions.[18]

Urgenda also relied on the European Convention on Human Rights (ECHR), an international treaty to protect human rights and fundamental freedoms in Europe.[19] The organization contended that three of the ECHR's articles could be interpreted to establish a duty of care: Article 1 (respecting rights), which it claimed infers strict liability on the State as a protector of rights and freedoms;[20] Article 2 (life), which it asserted compels the State to take "all the necessary measures" that can reasonably be expected to prevent any danger to life of which it is or ought to be aware;[21] and Article 8 (privacy), an article that can be interpreted broadly, which it emphasized comprises a positive obligation to *achieve* the protection of an Article 8 right, rather than merely *attempt* it.[22]

Finally, the organization stated that the "no harm" principle establishes an international legal duty with respect to transboundary pollution, obligating States to take effective and proportionate measures to prevent their emissions from damaging the environment of other States and their citizens.[23] Urgenda further requested that the court consider the Dutch government's obligations under the UNFCCC, the Kyoto Protocol, the Cancun Agreements, and through the EU's obligations under the same instruments.[24]

In April 2014, the Dutch government defended its climate policies. The State argued that its policies are consistent with the EU's Effort Sharing Decision,[25] which divided the EU's Kyoto Protocol target among its Member States and assigned the Netherlands a 16% reduction of CO_2 emissions below 1990 levels by 2020.[26] International or national law would not obligate the

---

18. *Id.* paras. 287–414.
19. Council of Europe, European Convention on Human Rights, as Amended by Protocols Nos. 11 and 14, Supplemented by Protocols Nos. 1, 4, 6, 7, 12, and 13 ETS 5 (1950), http://www.echr.coe.int/Documents/Convention_ENG.pdf [hereinafter ECHR].
20. *Id.* at art. 1; Summons, *supra* note 6, paras. 222–224.
21. ECHR, *supra* note 19, at art. 2; Summons, *supra* note 6, paras. 238–242.
22. ECHR, *supra* note 19, at art. 8; Summons, *supra* note 6, paras. 243–257 (emphasis added).
23. Summons, *supra* note 6, paras. 160–175, 291.
24. *Id.* paras. 176–217.
25. De Staat der Nederalanden, Reactie van de Staat [Reaction of the State], paras. 6:18–:24, Apr. 2, 2014, http://gallery.mailchimp.com/91ffff7bfd16e26db7bee63af/files/Conclusie_van_antwoord.pdf [hereinafter Government Reply].
26. Council Decision No. 406/2009/EC, 2009 O.J. (L 140) 136 (EC), Annex II (on the effort of Members States to reduce their GHG emissions to meet the Community's GHG emission reduction commit-

State to impose further reductions.[27] Although it did not challenge the science of global warming, the Netherlands emphasized that IPCC reports contain uncertainties and ambiguities that required using its discretion to design and implement its climate change policies.[28] A court order to revise those policies would violate the Dutch system's separation of powers,[29] undermine the Dutch negotiating position in the UNFCCC,[30] and be largely ineffective due to carbon leakage.[31] The State also contended that Urgenda lacked standing under the Dutch Civil Code and could not represent the future generations of the Netherlands, nor the present and future generations of other States.[32]

B.   The District Court's Decision

On June 24, 2015, the district court of The Hague issued its decision in favor of Urgenda, rejecting all of the State's defenses.[33] The court concluded that Article 305a of Book 3 of the Dutch Civil Code provided Urgenda standing to pursue its claim based on its mission of "a fast transition towards a sustainable society with a circular economy."[34] While it acknowledged that it ought to avoid intrusion into areas reserved for the executive and legislative branches of government, the court stated it was not prohibited from enforcing the government's duty of care in this case.[35]

Under Article 162, Book 6 of the Dutch Civil Code, Urgenda claimed that the government of the Netherlands was in breach of an unwritten standard duty of care. The court accepted Urgenda's assertions that international law informed the State's legal duty to protect its citizens from the impact of climate change and that such a duty could be enforced by the court.[36] It further ruled that the precautionary principle,[37] the government's commit-

ments up to 2020), http://eur-lex.europa.eu/LexUriServ/LexUriServ.do?uri=OJ:L:2009:140:0136:0148:EN:PDF.

27. Government Reply, *supra* note 25, paras. 12:13–:22.
28. *Id.* paras. 1.5, 2.5, 4.5.
29. *Id.* paras. 1.2, 12.14, 12.19, 12.28.
30. De Staat der Nederalanden, Tweede reactie van de Staat (dupliek) [Second reaction of the State (rejoinder)], para. 4.5, Jan. 21, 2014, http://www.urgenda.nl/documents/20150119-ConclvanDupliek-UrgendaKlimaatzaak.pdf.
31. *Id.* para. 6.17.
32. Government Reply, *supra* note 25, paras. 3.7, 3.9.
33. Judgment, *supra* note 1.
34. *Id.* paras. 4.4–10. *See* Urgenda, *Homepage*, http://www.urgenda.nl/en/ (last visited Aug. 24, 2016).
35. Judgment, *supra* note 1, paras. 4.94–102.
36. *Id.* paras. 4.46, 4.66, 4.74.
37. The precautionary principle, first established in the Rio Declaration, under Principle 15, provides that when there are threats of serious or irreversible damage, the lack of full scientific certainty shall not be used as a reason for postponing cost-effective measures to prevent environmental degradation.

ments under the UNFCCC, and its obligation to provide protection under the Treaty of the Functioning of the European Union informed this unwritten standard. Accordingly, the court determined that the Netherlands owed a legal duty to Urgenda to further reduce its GHG emissions.[38]

In crafting its order, the court considered the science and the future threat of global warming settled by the IPCC and other reports. Given that all GHG emissions contribute to climate change, the court concluded that the Netherlands had partial responsibility for its contributions.[39] The court relied on part of the preambular text of a 2010 Conference Meeting of the Parties to the Kyoto Protocol (CMP) decision that cites the IPCC's assessment that developed countries ought to reduce their emissions in the range of 25–40% below 1990 levels by 2020 to define the State's obligation,[40] and so ordered the Dutch government to take measures to reduce GHG emissions by 25% below 1990 levels by 2020.[41] The court determined that neither scientific uncertainty nor economic costs would justify delay;[42] both precautionary and prevention principles demanded that the government take immediate and effective action.[43]

In September 2015, the Dutch Cabinet announced that it would appeal the decision.[44] However, because an appeal does not suspend enforcement of the judgment, the Dutch government has begun taking action to more intensively reduce emissions.[45] In April 2016, the government formally filed its appeal.[46] Urgenda will reply before a hearing takes place before the Court of Appeal. A decision is not expected before the end of 2016. After the Court of Appeal's decision is issued, parties will have an opportunity to appeal to the Supreme Court of the Netherlands.[47]

---

38. Judgment, *supra* note 1, para. 4.93.
39. *Id*. para. 4.79.
40. *Id*. paras. 4.83–.86.
41. *Id*. para. 5.1.
42. *Id*. paras. 4.70, 4.73, 4.77.
43. *Id*. paras. 4.29, 4.76, 4.79.
44. De Staat der Nederalanden, Kabinetsreactie Vonnis Urgenda/State [Government response to Urgenda v. The State], Sept. 1, 2015, https://www.rijksoverheid.nl/documenten/kamerstukken/2015/09/01/kabinetsreactie-vonnis-urgenda-staat-d-d-24-juni-jl.
45. Press Release, Government of the Netherlands, Cabinet Begins Implementation of Urgenda Ruling but Will File Appeal (Sept. 1, 2015), https://www.government.nl/latest/news/2015/09/01/cabinet-begins-implementation-of-urgenda-ruling-but-will-file-appeal; Bergkamp & Brownell, *supra* note 10, at 34.
46. De Staat der Nederalanden, Memorie van grieven [Statement of appeal], Apr. 9, 2016, https://www.rijksoverheid.nl/onderwerpen/klimaatverandering/documenten/publicaties/2016/04/09/memorie-van-grieven-9-4-2016.
47. Press Release, Urgenda, Despite Pressure From Parliament, the Dutch Government Refuses to Pull Appeal in Landmark Climate Case (Sept. 29, 2015), http://us1.campaign-archive2.com/?u=91ffff7bfd16e26db7bee63af&id=c5967d141c&e=46588a629e.

II.   Legal Implications of the *Urgenda* Case

In a world where the window of opportunity to keep global warming below 2°C to avoid the worst impacts of climate change is rapidly closing, the *Urgenda* victory is moral and timely. However, in light of other climate justice cases and the pending entry into force of the Paris Agreement, which will surely inspire more litigation, the *Urgenda* case raises three important legal issues with significant implications. Subpart A explores whether the court's decision exceeds its judicial authority or whether it presents an otherwise welcome attempt to correct a constitutional imbalance, a question also raised by a Pakistani court regarding the government's failure to implement climate legislation. Subpart B considers whether the Dutch district court had the authority to issue a ruling that implied that the Netherlands' compliance with its EU obligations was unlawful. Section C examines the international and regional legal environmental commitments and general principles that the Netherlands upholds under the general rules of treaty interpretation and international law.

A.   *Judicial Overreach or Restoring Constitutional Balance?*

The Dutch constitutional system, like many others, consists of three branches of government (executive, legislative, and judicial), each with its own responsibilities and personnel to prevent the concentration of power in any one branch. When supported by a system of checks and balances, each branch can "check" the potential abuse of power by the others, though the authority afforded to each branch is interpreted differently across jurisdictions. In the *Urgenda* case, an important question is whether it was appropriate for the district court in The Hague to adjudicate the science-based policymaking decisions of the government.

The views of European legal experts vary. Lucas Bergkamp, an attorney in the Brussels office of Hunton & Williams, considers the court's decision "a threat to [the] rule of law and constitutional democracy."[48] In a worst-case scenario, an activist civil court receptive to making policy at the behest of interest groups could result in policies supported by a small minority and achievable only with high compliance costs.[49] Legal scholar T.J. Thurlings, though citing Bergkamp's concerns, considers the judicial foray into policymaking short-lived: the ruling will likely be overturned on appeal because

---

48.   Lucas Bergkamp, *The Urgenda Judgment: A "Victory" for the Climate That Is Likely to Backfire*, ENERGY POST, Sept. 9, 2015, http://www.energypost.eu/urgenda-judgment-victory-climate-likely-backfire/.
49.   *Id.*

the Dutch Supreme Court has previously ruled that the court cannot obligate the State to create new law.[50] Under EU and European Court of Human Rights law, a national court may hold a State liable for any omission, or failure to act where obligated, and assess damages.[51] It cannot, however, require the State to act.[52] On the other hand, Prof. Ceri Warnock believes that rather than heralding a new era of judicial activism, this case and others reflect a growing trend of courts "taking up the slack" when the other branches of government fail to protect fundamental rights.[53] The courts act with the intent of restoring the constitutional equilibrium.[54] Climate change, as a massive environmental threat to people, is revealing whether the legislative branches of government are willing and able to fulfill their responsibility to protect their citizens' rights in the face of such danger, and where they cannot, courts have a duty to enforce that obligation.[55]

The Dutch court justified its use of judicial authority by characterizing the Dutch system as "balancing" State powers, rather than "separating" them.[56] The court noted that it walks a fine line in the pursuit of ensuring the protection of rights by reducing the minimum standard to quantifiable terms and leaving it to the State to determine how to achieve the standard.[57] However, as Warnock points out, the decision is so detailed and precise that it leaves the State with a few means by which to achieve it.[58]

A case from Pakistan raises similar questions of potential judicial overreach. Ashgar Leghari, a farmer, sued the national government for failure to carry out the 2012 National Climate Policy and Framework (NCCPF).[59]

---

50. T.J. Thurlings, The Dutch Climate Case—Some Legal Considerations 7 (2015), http://papers. ssrn.com/sol3/Papers.cfm?abstract_id=2696343.

51. Id.

52. Id.

53. Ceri Warnock, *The Urgenda Decision: Balanced Constitutionalism in the Face of Climate Change?*, OUPblog, July 22, 2015, http://blog.oup.com/2015/07/urgenda-netherlands-climate-change/; Elbert R. de Jong, Case Note, *Dutch State Ordered to Cut Carbon Emissions*, 6 Eur. J. Risk Reg. 448, 449 (2015).

54. Id.

55. Warnock, *supra* note 53; de Jong, *supra* note 53 ("Governmental action is paralysed by *inter alia* scientific uncertainties about the nature, gravity and magnitude of risks, economic interests that may be negatively impacted by regulation, changing political views, influences of corporate lobbying, a lack of public support, externalization of the effects of climate risks and the global nature of climate risks, which makes it necessary to take action on an international level. Ultimately these circumstances may lead to a failure of the State to provide the level of protection that is socially and legally demanded.").

56. Judgment, *supra* note 1, para. 4.95.

57. Id. para. 4.101.

58. Warnock, *supra* note 53. *See also* van Zeben, *supra* note 10, at 354 (The district court's argument "is unconvincing as the order contains a comparatively high level of specificity, which severely reduces the government's discretion with respect to mitigation options.").

59. Government of Pakistan, Ministry of Climate Change, National Climate Policy (2012), http://www.nidm.gov.pk/Documents/Policies/National_Climate_Change_Policy_2012.pdf.

The NCCPF is the result of Pakistan's commitments as a UNFCCC Party. The country agreed to develop Nationally Appropriate Mitigation Actions (NAMAs) under the Bali Action Plan,[60] and National Adaptation Plans under the Cancun Agreements, which require domestic climate change policies and an implementation framework.[61] Leghari argued in his petition that climate change has led to water scarcity and temperature shifts, which in turn had severe impacts on food security. The government's failure to implement the NCCPF, including practical steps like promoting crop irrigation practices that waste less water and new crop varieties that require less water, has contributed to the worsening of this scenario. Instead of seeking compensation, Leghari requested that the government promote irrigation practices suited to the current water availability, as well as green energy practices.

The Lahore High Court ruled that climate change significantly impacts communities in Pakistan, requiring the protection of fundamental rights, particularly for the vulnerable and weak segments of society.[62] The Pakistani State's delay in implementing the NCCPF offended the right to life, which includes the right to a healthy and clean environment, and the right to human dignity, as established in Pakistan's constitution.[63] The court therefore directed government ministries to take specific actions to implement the NCCPF on human rights grounds.[64]

Like *Urgenda*, a national court has directed a national government to take specific climate action: the Lahore High Court ordered the executive government to properly exercise its executive powers and to effectively implement a law previously passed by the legislative branch.[65] The Pakistani court also had precise directions on how to do so: the judge summoned the country's main officials[66] before him; appointed climate change focal points for each government department; identified individual capacity needs of departments; and appointed a Climate Change Commission to ensure implementation of the

---

60. PAKISTAN, SUBMISSION BY PAKISTAN: NATIONALLY APPROPRIATE MITIGATION ACTIONS BY THE DEVELOPING COUNTRIES (BALI ACTION PLAN 1bii) (2011), https://unfccc.int/files/meetings/ad_hoc_working_groups/lca/application/pdf/submission_by_pakistan_on_namas_ghh.pdf.

61. Tracy Bach, *Human Rights in a Climate Changed World: The Impact of COP21, Nationally Determined Contributions, and National Courts*, 40 VT. L. REV. 1, 32 (2016).

62. *Id.*

63. *See* CONST. OF PAKISTAN arts. 9, 14.

64. Elaw Digest, *Ashgar Leghari v. Federation of Pakistan*, https://elaw.org/pk_Leghari (last visited Sept. 4, 2016).

65. Jessica Wentz, *Lahore High Court Orders Pakistan to Act on Climate Change*, COLUMBIA LAW SCHOOL CLIMATE LAW BLOG, Sept. 26, 2015, http://blogs.law.columbia.edu/climatechange/2015/09/26/lahore-high-court-orders-pakistan-to-act-on-climate-change/#sthash.KqDcQHo9.dpuf.

66. Including ministers in the federal government (e.g., finance, foreign affairs, and climate change) and members of departments at the provincial government.

NCCPF.[67] Like *Urgenda*, the Pakistani case relied on a blend of international climate change law and domestic constitutional norms, which are mutually supportive.[68] Rights and principles set forth in the national law supported the legal reasoning of climate change implementation, innovatively linking climate change to human rights.

B.   The Competence of the Civil Court Under EU Law

Dutch law professor Marjan Peeters raises the important question of whether any national court could rule that an EU's Member State's compliance with EU legislation is unlawful under domestic law.[69] Doing so, she asserts, likely exceeds judicial authority, while ordering a Member State to supersede obligations under EU legislation could undermine EU climate law in several ways.[70] First, the Dutch district court omits any assessment of the legality of the EU's climate policies, the key regulatory instruments of which are the EU Emissions Trading Scheme (EU ETS) and the EU Effort Sharing Decision.[71] The EU ETS is a regional cap on total emissions on all sectors, which, through a market mechanism, can reduce GHG emissions in a cost-effective way.[72] The EU Effort Sharing Decision complements the EU ETS, setting individual emission reduction targets for its Member States.[73] Trading of national emission reduction commitments between Member States or use of international credits to comply with national targets is permitted.[74] Distribution of the overall EU effort to reduce emissions among its Member States allows for the coordinated, cost-effective reduction of GHG emissions. A Member State may adopt more stringent policies beyond its assigned target, so long as they are compatible with EU treaties under Article 93 of the Treaty on Functioning of the European Union (TFEU) and scrutinized for environmental effectiveness.[75]

Only the Court of Justice of the European Union (CJEU) is competent to review the lawfulness of EU legislation[76] and to interpret the UNFCCC,

---

67. Leghari v. Federation of Pakistan, W.P. No. 25501, slip op. at 6–7 (Lahore High Court Sept. 4, 2015); Malini Mehra, *Pakistan Ordered to Enforce Climate Law by Lahore Court*, CLIMATE HOME, Sept. 20, 2015, http://www.climatechangenews.com/2015/09/20/pakistan-ordered-to-enforce-climate-law-by-lahore-court/.

68. Bach, *supra* note 61, at 32.

69. Peeters, *supra* note 7, at 124–26.

70. *Id.* at 124.

71. *Id.* at 124–26.

72. Directive 2003/87/EC, Oct. 13, 2003, Establishing a Scheme for Greenhouse Gas Emission Allowance Trading Within the Community and Amending Council Directive 96/61/EC, 2003 O.J. (L 275/32).

73. Council Decision No. 406/2009/EC, *supra* note 26.

74. *Id.* at arts. 3, 5.

75. Peeters, *supra* note 7, at 125.

76. Consolidated Version of the Treaty on the Functioning of the European Union, 2012 O.J. (C326/47), art. 263. A preliminary reference is mandatory if a national court has some doubts about the legality

Kyoto Protocol, and decisions taken under these treaties.[77] A national court can, however, consult the CJEU on the validity of an EU act of law, particularly through a preliminary reference procedure.[78] Despite its groundbreaking decision, the Dutch district court did not assess the legality of the EU GHG emissions reduction target of 20%, nor assess the legality of the Effort Sharing Decision, which set a 16% emissions reduction target compared to 2005 levels for the Netherlands.[79] "Remarkably," Peeters observes, "the civil court does not consider the question of its own competence to rule on the lawfulness of acts by the State of the Netherlands in light of international law to which the EU has adhered or that also may affect the EU legal order."[80] A threshold question should have been addressed to the CJEU to clarify whether a national court may adopt reasoning implying the insufficiency of EU legislation in ordering a Member State to adopt more ambitious measures and whether international decisions and EU statements made in the course of international negotiations would have implicit binding effect giving rise to legal commitments for EU Member States.[81]

Second, the court makes no mention of the principle of loyal or sincere cooperation in external relations, which pertains to the need for unity in the international representation of the EU.[82] In instances where the power of negotiation and conclusion of treaties is shared, each Member State is prohibited from "distanc[ing] itself from an agreed Union strategy by taking action within an international organization that could potentially bind the Union." Peeters acknowledges that it is not clear whether the principle has consequences for this case, but its relevance should not be overlooked.[83]

Third, by forcing the Dutch State to achieve greater emissions reductions than assigned under EU law, it "raises the question of the extent to which action by an EU Member State may influence the total amount of available emission allowances in the EU ETS."[84] In other words, one Member State acting unilaterally could drive up prices for other Member States, and

---

of a European Union measure; *see* Court of Justice of the European Communities, Case C-314/85, Foto-Frost v. Hauptzollamt Lubeck-Ost, 1987 E.C.R. 4199, explained by A. Albors-Llorens, *Judicial Protection Before the Court of Justice of the European Union*, *in* EUROPEAN UNION LAW 287 (Catherine Barnard & Steve Peers eds., 2014).

77.   Peeters, *supra* note 7, at 126.
78.   *Id.* at 125.
79.   *Id.* at 126.
80.   *Id.*
81.   *Id.* at 125.
82.   *Id.* at 126–27.
83.   *Id.* at 126 (citing Geert De Baere, *EU External Action*, *in* EUROPEAN UNION LAW 704 (Catherine Barnard & Steve Peers eds., 2014)).
84.   *Id.* at 127.

potentially subject them to legal action by affected EU industries, which had heretofore relied on the EU ETS and the Efforts Sharing Decision.[85]

C.   Defining Parties' Obligations Under the UNFCCC

Just as the district court of The Hague ordered the Dutch government, a Member State of the EU, to do more than legally required under its EU obligations, the court ordered the government, a UNFCCC Party, to do more than legally required by its obligations under the Convention. The court seems to accept at face value Urgenda's descriptions of Parties' rights and obligations under the Convention,[86] and by doing so, misses a critical opportunity to distinguish between the principles embedded in, and the legal obligations required by, the Convention and its attendant instruments.

The UNFCCC sets out the legal framework under which various instruments more clearly define the legal and political obligations of Parties.[87] These instruments can include legally binding commitments. Key decisions, such as to adopt such instruments, are made annually by the entire body of the Parties to the Convention, or the Conference of the Parties (COP). Ordinarily, COP decisions have the legal status of recommendations and are therefore not legally binding.[88] Rather, they rest on those powers ascribed to the COP by the Convention,[89] and generally serve to adopt and implement the various instruments.

---

85.   *Id.*

86.   As Josephine van Zeben points out, "The judicial process in the Netherlands does not allow for the judge to gather information in addition to that provided by the parties." van Zeben, *supra* note 10, at 353.

87.   United Nations Framework Convention on Climate Change, May 9, 1992, S. Treaty Doc. No. 102-38, 1771 U.N.T.S. 107 (entered into force Mar. 21, 1994) [hereinafter UNFCCC].

88.   Robin Churchill & Geir Ulfstein, *Autonomous Institutional Arrangements in Multilateral Agreements*, 94 Am. J. Int'l L. 623, 639–40 (2000); Jutta Brunnée, *COPing With Consent: Law-making Under Multilateral Environmental Agreements*, 15 Leiden J. Int'l L. 1, 21–33 (2002); Raj Bavishi, Ross Wolfarth & Brian Troxler, The Status of UNFCCC COP and Other Treaty Body Decisions Under US Law, Legal Response Initiative Briefing Paper 3 (2011), http://legalresponseinitiative. org/wp-content/uploads/2013/09/BP35E-Briefing-Paper-Status-of-COP-Decisions-under-US-Law-23-November-2011.pdf; Foundation for International Environmental Law and Development (FIELD) & Mary Robinson Foundation-Climate Justice, Briefing Note on the "Legal Form" of a New Climate Agreement 1–2 (2011), http://www.mrfcj.org/pdf/Briefing_Note_on_the_legal_form_of_a_new_climate_agreement.pdf.

89.   The Convention does not contain a provision explicitly granting binding authority to the COP. *Cf.* Montreal Protocol COP/CMP has an explicit grant of authority in this respect. Montreal Protocol on Substances that Deplete the Ozone Layer, Sept. 16, 1987, art 2.9, 1522 U.N.T.S. 3, 26 I.L.M. 1550 (granting the COP the authority to change the obligations of Parties to reduce consumption and production of controlled substances and providing binding effect to decisions once adopted). COP decisions can have legally binding effect if the UNFCCC expressly authorizes it to adopt rules on a particular subject, such as the preparation of national GHG inventories. UNFCCC, *supra* note 87, at arts. 4.1(a), 4.2(c), and 7.2(d). Other provisions, such as Article 9.3, authorize the COP to

The text of the Convention itself sets out the responsibilities of Parties in broad terms. The ultimate objective of the Convention and any related legal instruments is to achieve the

> stabilization of GHG concentrations in the atmosphere at a level that would prevent dangerous anthropogenic interference with the climate system. Such a level should be achieved within a time frame sufficient to allow ecosystems to adapt naturally to climate change, to ensure that food production is not threatened, and to enable economic development to proceed in a sustainable manner.[90] Although framed as thresholds for determining the level and time frame of mitigation, Article 2 of the Convention stresses the need for adaptation to occur.[91]

In order to achieve these aims, Parties have crafted agreements that swung between two approaches that enjoyed limited success until recently. The first of these efforts was the Kyoto Protocol, a legally binding treaty that entered into force in 2005 and set internationally legally binding emissions reduction commitments for developing countries only.[92] A second effort to forge an effective and universal climate agreement was the 2009 Copenhagen Accord, a political agreement born of an unsuccessful attempt to create a global, legally binding treaty to replace the Kyoto Protocol.[93] The Accord was widely considered a failure,[94] giving rise in the following year to the Cancun Agreements, a set of significant decisions by the international community to address climate change through an enhanced pledge and review process, to further institutionalize support to developing countries to meet adaptation needs, and to facilitate their plans to adopt sustainable development paths to low-emission economies.[95] Under this approach, countries

---

elaborate the functions and terms of reference of the Subsidiary Body for Scientific and Technological Advice.

90.   UNFCCC, *supra* note 87, at art. 2.

91.   Irene Suarez & Jennifer Huang, Addressing Adaptation in a 2015 Climate Agreement 1 (2015), http://www.c2es.org/docUploads/adaptation-cover.pdf.

92.   Kyoto Protocol to the United Nations Framework Convention on Climate Change, Dec. 10, 1997, U.N. Doc FCCC/CP/1997/7/Add.1, 37 I.L.M. 22 (1998) [hereinafter Kyoto Protocol].

93.   *Report of the Conference of the Parties on Its Fifteenth Session, Held in Copenhagen From 7 to 9 December 2009—Addendum, Part Two: Action Taken by the Conference of the Parties at Its Fifteenth Session, Decisions Adopted by the Conference of the Parties,* UNFCCC, 15th Sess., Decision 2/CP.15, U.N. Doc. FCCC/CP/2009/11/Add.1 (2010), http://unfccc.int/resource/docs/2009/cop15/eng/11a01.pdf.

94.   *See, e.g.,* Navroz K. Dubash, *Copenhagen: Climate of Mistrust,* 44 Econ. & Pol. Wkly. 8, 10 (2009) (referring to the Accord as a "paper-thin cover up of what was a near complete failure" and suggesting Copenhagen may "represent[] the worst possible outcome"); Kelly Inman, *The Symbolic Copenhagen Accord Falls Short of Goals,* 17 U. Balt. J. Envtl. L. 17, 219 (2010) (Copenhagen had "a few bright spots, but overall the conference was a failure.").

95.   *Report of the Conference of the Parties on Its Sixteenth Session, Held in Cancun From 29 November to 10 December 2010—Addendum, Part Two: Action Taken by the Conference of the Parties at Its Sixteenth*

undertook national pledges for 2020 that represented political rather than legal commitments.

The text of the Paris Agreement adopted in 2015 marks the latest step in the evolution of the UNFCCC, reflecting a "hybrid" approach that blends the bottom-up flexibility of the Copenhagen Accord and Cancun Agreements, and the top-down rules-based approach of the Kyoto Protocol.[96] The Agreement is a treaty under international law, but only certain provisions are legally binding; while Parties' "nationally determined contributions" to the Paris Agreement are not legally binding, obligations to report on their progress and to be reviewed are.[97]

Urgenda Foundation repeatedly and incorrectly asserted that adaptation is not the same caliber of commitment that mitigation is under the UNFCCC, and dismisses the Dutch government's attempts to remind Urgenda and the court of its efforts to adapt and make the Netherlands more resilient to the impacts of climate change.[98] While it is true that the Convention has historically placed a greater emphasis on mitigation than adaptation,[99] and some interpret Article 2 as an entirely mitigation-focused obligation, adaptation in the Convention has been increasingly emphasized. It has become more critical for human and ecosystem survival and has been seen for some time to be as important an obligation as mitigation under the Convention.[100] Although the Paris Agreement was not yet

---

Session, Decisions Adopted by the Conference of the Parties, UNFCCC, 16th Sess., Decision 1/CP.16, U.N. Doc. FCCC/CP/2010/7/Add.1 (2011), http://unfccc.int/resource/docs/2010/cop16/eng/07a01.pdf.

96.   CENTER FOR CLIMATE AND ENERGY SOLUTIONS, OUTCOMES OF THE U.N. CLIMATE CHANGE CONFERENCE IN PARIS 2 (2015), http://www.c2es.org/docUploads/cop-21-paris-summary-02-2016-final.pdf.

97.   *Paris Agreement, supra* note 2. *See id.* Annex, art. 3 ("As nationally determined contributions to the global response to climate change, all Parties are to undertake and communicate ambitious efforts . . ."); art. 4.8 ("In communicating their nationally determined contributions, all Parties shall provide the information necessary for clarity, transparency and understanding . . ."); art. 4.13 ("Parties shall account for their nationally determined contributions."); art. 13.7 ("Each Party shall regularly provide the following information . . ."); art. 13.11 ("Information submitted by each Party under paragraphs 7 and 9 of this Article shall undergo a technical expert review . . .").

98.   Urgenda, Repliek op de argumenten van de Staat [Reply to the arguments of the State], paras. 53–70, Sept. 10, 2014, http://www.urgenda.nl/documents/Conclusie-van-Repliek-10-09-2014.pdf, *translated at* http://www.urgenda.nl/documents/FINAL_Draft_Translation_-_Statement_of_Reply_case_Urgenda_v_Dutch_State_v.21.05.2015.pdf (May 21, 2015).

99.   SUAREZ & HUANG, *supra* note 91, at 1.

100.   *Report of the Conference of the Parties on Its Eighteenth Session, Held in Doha From 26 November to 8 December 2012—Addendum, Part Two: Action Taken by the Conference of the Parties at its Eighteenth Session, Decisions Adopted by the Conference of the Parties*, UNFCCC, Decision 1/CP.18, at 11, U.N. Doc. FCCC/CP/2012/8/Add.1 (2013) ("Also reaffirming that adaptation must be addressed with the same priority as mitigation and that appropriate institutional arrangements are required to enhance adaptation action and support"), http://unfccc.int/resource/docs/2012/cop18/eng/08a01.pdf; *Report of the Conference of the Parties on Its Nineteenth Session, Held in Warsaw From 11 to 26 November 2013—Addendum, Part Two: Action Taken by the Conference of the Parties at Its Nineteenth Session, Decisions Adopted by the Conference of the Parties*, UNFCCC, 19th Sess., Decision 4/CP.19, at 11,

adopted when The Hague district court was considering the *Urgenda* case, the negotiations on the Agreement had made the equality between the two obligations a high and clear priority.

The *Urgenda* court fails to acknowledge, and therefore fails to clarify, the hierarchy of legal and political obligations of the Netherlands under the Convention and international environmental law. Until the Paris Agreement enters into force, the Netherlands currently has one internationally binding target under the Kyoto Protocol (a reduction of GHG emissions by 6% relative to 1990 in the period 2008–2012).[101] In 2007, the EU made a unilateral commitment to reduce its GHG emissions by 20% below 1990 levels by 2020,[102] which was further embedded in the 2015 ratification of the second commitment period of the Kyoto Protocol (also known as the Doha Amendment) by the EU, its Member States, and Iceland.[103] Because the Doha Amendment has yet to enter into force, the Netherlands' targets of reducing GHG emissions by 21% by 2020 compared to 2005 levels for emissions covered by the EU ETS and reducing emissions by 16% by 2020 compared to 2005 levels for emissions not

---

U.N. Doc. FCCC/CP/2013/10/Add.1 (2014) (requesting the Green Climate Fund to "balance the allocation of resources between adaptation and mitigation"), http://unfccc.int/resource/docs/2013/cop19/eng/10a01.pdf; *Report of the Conference of the Parties on Its Twentieth Session, Held in Lima From 1 to 14 December 2014—Addendum, Part Two: Action Taken by the Conference of the Parties at Its Twentieth Session, Decisions Adopted by the Conference of the Parties*, UNFCCC, 20th Sess., Decision 1/CP.20, Annex, at 7, U.N. Doc. FCCC/CP/2014/10/Add.1 (2015) ("Option (a): Emphasizing that adaptation is a global challenge and a common responsibility that requires global solidarity that must be addressed with the same urgency as, and in political/legal parity with, mitigation, Option (b): Emphasizing that adaptation is a global challenge that must be addressed with the same urgency as, and in balance with, mitigation, and that enhanced action and international cooperation on adaptation is urgently required in order to enable and support the implementation of adaptation actions, Option (c): Emphasizing that enhanced action and international cooperation on adaptation is urgently required to enable and support the implementation of adaptation actions aimed at reducing vulnerability and building resilience in developing country Parties, taking into account the urgent and immediate needs of those developing countries that are particularly vulnerable, Option (d): Noting that adaptation is a global challenge that must be addressed with the same urgency as mitigation"), http://unfccc.int/resource/docs/2014/cop20/eng/10a01.pdf.

101. Council Decision No. 2002/358/CE, 2002 O.J. (L 130/1) (EC), Annex II, http://eur-lex.europa.eu/legal-content/EN/TXT/PDF/?uri=CELEX:32002D0358&from=EN; Kyoto Protocol, *supra* note 92, at Annex B, http://unfccc.int/resource/docs/convkp/kpeng.pdf.

102. Council Decision No. 406/2009/EC, *supra* note 26.

103. Council Decision No. 10400/5/14 REV 5, 2015 O.R. (EC) (council decision on the conclusion, on behalf of the European Union, of the Doha Amendment to the 406/2009/EC Protocol to the UNFCCC and the joint fulfillment of commitments thereunder), http://data.consilium.europa.eu/doc/document/ST-10400-2014-REV-5/en/pdf; Council Decision No. 10883/5/14 REV 5, 2015 O.R. (EC) (council decision on the conclusion, on behalf of the European Union, of the Agreement between the European Union and its Member States, of the one part, and Iceland, of the other part, concerning Iceland's participation in the joint fulfillment of commitments of the European Union, its Member States, and Iceland for the second commitment period of the Kyoto Protocol to the UNFCCC), http://data.consilium.europa.eu/doc/document/ST-10883-2014-REV-5/en/pdf.

covered by the EU ETS remain under the EU only.[104] In 2014, the EU committed as a group to a 40% reduction in GHG emissions compared to 1990 levels by 2030, a commitment that it repackaged as its intended nationally determined contribution (INDC) to the Paris Agreement in 2015.[105] Once the European Commission determines the respective obligations of its Member States, the Netherlands will have a new emissions reduction target for the 2020–2030 commitment period under the EU. If the EU submits its INDC as its NDC, unchanged, then this target will be under the UNFCCC as well.

To define the Dutch government's obligation towards its people, the court reiterates a portion of a preamble to a CMP decision on the "Outcome of the work of the Ad Hoc Working Group on Further Commitments for Annex I Parties under the Kyoto Protocol at its fifteenth session," which "recognize[es]" the IPCC report that indicates that achieving the lowest levels of emissions reductions to avert climate damage would require developed country Parties to reduce emissions in a range of 25–40% below 1990 levels by 2020.[106]

Under general rules of treaty interpretation and international law, the Netherlands' legally binding obligations are limited to its international emissions reduction targets that have been given domestic binding effect through its legal obligations under the EU. However, the court used the language from the preamble of a COP/CMP decision to set the standard against which the climate action of the Netherlands—its mitigation actions only—may be judged. A preamble of an international agreement, which usually sets out the context in which the agreement was negotiated, is not considered to be part of the legally binding or operative text of the agreement. But in this instance, much to the Dutch government's chagrin,[107] The Hague court afforded

---

104. *See, e.g.*, NETHERLANDS MINISTRY OF INFRASTRUCTURE AND THE ENVIRONMENT, SIXTH NETHERLANDS NATIONAL COMMUNICATION UNDER THE UNITED NATIONS FRAMEWORK CONVENTION ON CLIMATE CHANGE 57 (2013), https://unfccc.int/files/national_reports/annex_i_natcom/submitted_natcom/application/pdf/the_netherlands_nc6[1].pdf.

105. Council Conclusion No. EUCO 169/14, 2014 (EC), http://www.consilium.europa.eu/uedocs/cms_data/docs/pressdata/en/ec/145397.pdf; LATVIA AND THE EUROPEAN COMMISSION, INTENDED NATIONALLY DETERMINED CONTRIBUTION OF THE EU AND ITS MEMBER STATES (2015), http://www4.unfccc.int/submissions/INDC/Published%20Documents/Latvia/1/LV-03-06-EU%20INDC.pdf. The INDC will likely become the EU's NDC, unless the EU decides to increase the ambition of its EU-wide target.

106. *Report of the Conference of the Parties Serving as the Meeting of the Parties to the Kyoto Protocol on Its Sixth Session, Held in Cancun From 29 November to 10 December 2010, Decisions Adopted by the Conference of the Parties Serving as the Meeting of the Parties to the Kyoto Protocol*, UNFCCC, 6th Sess., Decision 1/CMP.6, at 3, U.N. Doc. FCCC/KP/CMP/2010/12/Add.1 (2011), http://unfccc.int/resource/docs/2010/cmp6/eng/12a01.pdf.

107. Government Reply, *supra* note 25, para. 9.14–.26.

unprecedented normative and prescriptive significance to a preamble paragraph of a non-binding COP decision.[108]

By claiming this standard of care, the court endorsed Urgenda's claims that, despite achieving and being on track to achieve its legally binding mitigation targets, the Netherlands is not, in principle, living up to the spirit of the environmental agreements to which it has committed. As such, it remains to be seen whether the Paris Agreement and its future implementation supports or undermines this assertion.

The successful adoption of the Paris Agreement, from its text to the way in which it was negotiated, has been attributed to the careful respect of countries' national capacities and domestic circumstances, most evident in the treatment of *nationally determined* contributions. To remedy the lack of ambition in past pledges, the Paris Agreement creates several means by which to "ratchet" up ambition over time: a transparency process that aims to make clear how and why Parties have assembled their contributions;[109] an obligation to submit new NDCs every five years,[110] guided by the principles of progression and highest possible ambition; the establishment of a mechanism for "implementation and compliance";[111] and a periodic global stocktake.[112] After many decades of negotiations, the Paris Agreement puts Parties behind the wheel; although it sets the final destination, Parties are both obligated and empowered to arrive at the destination on their own terms: setting their own targets, and determining their own pace, according to their domestic situation, limitations, and responsibilities under the Convention.

By implying the unlawfulness of the EU's emissions reductions target and deploring the deficiency of the Netherlands' mitigation actions, the *Urgenda* decision can be read as contrary to the spirit of the Paris negotiations and its agreement by curtailing the Dutch government's right to determine the means and extent of its mitigation law and policies. As a more practical matter, as others have noted, if governments are subject to the revision of their climate policies by domestic actors, this could undermine the negotiating positions of countries and erode trust between Parties under the UNFCCC.[113] However, it is possible to read the court's determination as

---

108. Judgment, *supra* note 1, at 1 ("the *norm* of 25% to 40% for developed countries deemed necessary in climate science and international climate policy") (emphasis added), para. 4.85. Additionally, neither Urgenda nor the court explains why the Netherlands ought to unilaterally undertake a reduction that can be read as applying *across* developed country Parties.

109. *Paris Agreement*, *supra* note 2, at Annex, art. 13.

110. *Id.* at art. 4.9.

111. *Id.* at art. 15.

112. *Id.* at art. 14.

113. *See also* Bergkamp & Brownell, *supra* note 10; Peeters, *supra* note 7, at 33, 127.

the ultimate fulfillment of the spirit of the Paris Agreement: by mainstreaming climate change action into the domestic law of Parties and empowering them to act on their own terms; national actors, including courts, can also be agents of change by influencing the decisions taken by their governments. By judging existing obligations against higher principles contained in international environmental agreements, courts may determine whether they are morally and environmentally sufficient.

For this reason, the implications of the Paris Agreement on current and future climate litigation are unclear but noteworthy. Gibson Dunn & Crutcher attorneys Peter Seley and Richard Dudley note that a recent wave of climate litigation was due to the lack of internationally binding emissions reduction targets.[114] It seems unlikely that the Paris Agreement, with its non-binding INDCs and NDCs and interlinked processes to increase ambition over time, will stem the flow of that wave of that litigation.

III.   Implications for Future Climate Justice Litigation

Given the prominence of the *Urgenda* case, its outcome can have significant implications for other climate justice cases. Other jurisdictions with more rigid interpretations of the separation of powers will likely forestall a similar kind of lawsuit, either for lack of standing, or because the judicial branch will be curtailed from impinging on the responsibilities of the legislative or executive branches, or both.[115] The case also relies, to a large extent, on EU law, making the case unique to Europe. Although this means that the case may have applicability to other EU Member States, it limits the applicability of the case to other countries.

A.   Foreign Domestic Courts

A similar case has already been initiated in Belgium.[116] A coalition of Belgian citizens,[117] represented by the association Klimaatzaak, filed a summons in the Court of First Instance in Brussels in April 2015.[118] The suit was brought against the federal and regional governments of Belgium for

---

114. Peter Seley & Richard Dudley, *Emerging Trends in Climate Change Litigation*, Law360, Mar. 7, 2016, http://www.gibsondunn.com/publications/Documents/Seley-Dudley-Emerging-Trends-In-Climate-Change-Litigation-Law360-3-7-16.pdf.

115. van Zeben, *supra* note 10, at 354.

116. VZW Klimaatzaak v. Kingdom of Belgium, et al. Court of First Instance, Brussels [2015].

117. Already composed of 11,000 co-plaintiffs. *See* Klimaatzaak, *Homepage*, http://klimaatzaak.eu/fr/ (last visited Aug. 24, 2016).

118. Klimaatzaak, Citation [full summons] (Apr. 2016), http://klimaatzaak.eu/wp-content/uploads/2015/12/Citation.pdf.

failing to reduce GHG emissions. According to the plaintiffs, the absence of emission reductions constitutes a violation of human rights laws, including international climate conventions, the ECHR, and the Constitution of Belgium. Klimaatzaak seeks to compel the government to reduce GHG emissions 40% below 1990 levels by 2020 and 87.5% below 1990 levels by 2050. The case is pending as of this writing.[119] Questions regarding the court's authority to interpret EU law will likely be impacted by the outcome of the *Urgenda* appeal.

In Pakistan, a case has been brought by a seven-year-old girl, which questions the validity of the country's INDC.[120] Rabab Ali filed a lawsuit against the federation of Pakistan and the province of Sindh in the Supreme Court based on the younger generation's fundamental constitutional rights to life, liberty, property, human dignity, information, and equal protection of the law.[121] The lawsuit asserts that the lack of mitigation measures in Pakistan's INDC is a violation of fundamental constitutional rights.[122] The plaintiff asks the court to, in cooperation with government institutions, rewrite the INDC to include a comprehensive national climate recovery plan with CO_2 reduction targets and mitigation actions, transition away from the use of fossil fuels, and engage in massive reforestation and other methods of carbon sequestration.[123] The case is still pending, but it represents one of the first legal cases questioning the sufficiency of an INDC. INDCs not only present an opportunity for developing countries to establish climate change policies and contribute to climate change mitigation, but also a chance for citizens to examine whether their governments are doing enough to safeguard the environment and present and future generations.

Similarly, a case in 2015 was filed in the High Court of Wellington,[124] New Zealand, by Sarah Thomson, a recent law graduate. The suit challenges

---

119. The parties are currently in the process of submitting written statements to the court. Afterwards, the court will hold a hearing, and a decision will be issued one to three months later. *See* Jennifer Klein, *Lawsuit Seeks to Force Belgian Government to Take Action Against Climate Change*, COLUMBIA LAW SCHOOL CLIMATE LAW BLOG, June 8, 2015, http://blogs.law.columbia.edu/climatechange/2015/06/08/lawsuit-seeks-to-force-belgian-government-to-take-action-against-climate-change/#sthash.Ly1zNVuI.dpuf; Columbia Law School, *Sabin Center for Climate Change Law*, http://web.law.columbia.edu/climate-change (last visited Aug. 24, 2016). *See also* Kilimaatzaak, *Le Proces [The Trial]*, http://klimaatzaak.eu/fr/le-proces/ (last visited Aug. 24, 2016).

120. Pakistan, Constitutional Petition [full summons] (Apr. 2016), http://ourchildrenstrust.org/sites/default/files/PakistanYouthClimatePetition.pdf.

121. Our Children's Trust, *Pakistan, Legal Updates*, http://ourchildrenstrust.org/legal/international/Pakistan (last visited Aug. 24, 2016).

122. Constitutional Petition, *supra* note 120, at 9 (items xxxii and xxxiii).

123. *Id.* at 38.

124. Thomson v. Minister for Climate Change Issues, High Court, Wellington, CIV-2015-__, filed Nov. 10, 2015 (N.Z.), http://web.law.columbia.edu/sites/default/files/microsites/climate-change/files/Resources/Non-US-Climate-Change-Litigation-Chart/nz_case_statement_of_claim.pdf.

the legality and reasonableness of the government's domestic GHG emission targets and its INDC[125] and requests a judicial review of the government's climate change policy. New Zealand's 2002 Climate Change Response Act[126] requires the environmental minister to review the government's emissions reduction target whenever the IPCC releases an updated assessment.[127] Since its last revision was done in 2011, New Zealand has proposed a reduction of 11% below 1990 levels by 2030, which the plaintiff claims is inadequate to prevent temperature rise below 2°C.

These cases are notable in that the government is being sued for pledges that, unless incorporated into national domestic processes, are not legally binding and serve as "intended" pledges for more formal and future NDCs, raising a number of other interesting questions. If an NDC has become part of a country's domestic law, such a party could be sued if it fails to implement or is not acting to achieve its target. However, once formalized and implemented, at what point could a Party be sued for failing to meet its NDC—when it seems less than likely it will meet its target, or after the commitment period has ended? What bearing does its subsequent NDC have to "make up for" its failed target? Can Parties be sued where an NDC is not part of its domestic law? And, once formalized, can Parties under the Convention be sued for failing to collectively meet the goals that they have set out for themselves?

B.   U.S. Courts

It would be difficult, if not impossible, to bring a case like *Urgenda* in the United States. First, the case largely relies on laws that are not applicable or have no equivalent in U.S. law. Though relying in part on Dutch private nuisance and tort law, which is similar to U.S. private nuisance and tort law, the ruling also rests on the ECHR, the EU constitution, and the EU decision establishing binding annual GHG emissions targets for Member States—to which the United States is neither a Party nor Member State.

Second, unlike in the Netherlands, U.S. citizens cannot directly sue the government in court. Sovereign immunity is a legal privilege by which the American federal, state, and tribal governments cannot be sued unless it has

---

125. Kennedy Warne, *Sarah vs the State: Government's Climate Targets "Illegal, Unreasonable, Irrational*,*" N.Z. Geographic, Nov. 12, 2015, https://www.nzgeo.com/stories/sarah-vs-the-state-governments-climate-targets-illegal-unreasonable-irrational/.
126. Climate Change Response Act 2002 (CCRA 2002).
127. Thomson v. Minister for Climate Change Issues, High Court, Wellington, CIV-2015-__, filed Nov. 10, 2015 (N.Z.).

waived its immunity or consented to suit.[128] The relevant exception is the Clean Air Act's (CAA's) citizen suit provision, which allows any person to initiate an action in one of three ways: (1) against any person in violation of an emissions standard or limitation; (2) against the U.S. Environmental Protection Agency (EPA) administrator for failure to perform a nondiscretionary act; or (3) against a person who builds a new or modified major emitting facility without a permit or in violation of the conditions of a permit.[129]

Federal common law actions initiated outside this provision have not succeeded. These cases have generally rested on either public nuisance theory, alleging that an action threatens the health, safety, or welfare of a community; or public trust doctrine, under which the government is required to safeguard certain resources for the public's reasonable use. Public trust cases against the government have generally been dismissed on the grounds that the public trust doctrine does not extend to the atmosphere, that the courts do not set emissions limitations, or that the plaintiffs have not been affected by climate change in a manner that is distinct from the public at large.[130]

In the 2011 U.S. Supreme Court case *American Electric Power v. Connecticut*, the Court held that a federal statute (the CAA's authority to regulate GHG emissions) displaced any federal common law right of state, city, and private parties to seek abatement of CO_2 emissions.[131] This holding leaves two courses of legal action available at the federal level. Where EPA does not enforce existing emissions limitations against regulated sources, citizens can bring civil enforcement action in federal court.[132] If EPA does not set emissions limits for certain pollutants or pollution sources, states and private parties can petition for rulemaking in federal court.[133] However, on discretionary matters such as whether EPA is doing enough to reduce emissions, the Court will give substantial deference to EPA's regulatory judgment and

---

128. U.S. Const. art. XI. A state may not be sued in federal court by its own citizen or a citizen of another state, unless the state consents to jurisdiction. Hans v. Louisiana, 134 U.S. 1 (1890). Consent to the jurisdiction of the federal court may be manifested by the state voluntarily appearing in the court to defend itself on the merits of the case. Gunter v. A. Coast Line R.R., 200 U.S. 273, 284 (1906). Eleventh Amendment immunity extends to suits filed against the state in state courts and before federal administrative agencies. Alden v. Maine, 527 U.S. 706 (1999); Federal Mar. Comm'n v. South Carolina Ports Auth., 535 U.S. 743 (2002). Unless the state or the federal government creates an exception to the state's sovereign immunity, the state is immune from being sued without consent by any citizen in federal courts, state courts, or before federal administrative agencies.

129. Clean Air Act Amendments of 1977 (Pub. L. No. 95-95, 91 Stat. 685); 40 C.F.R. §51.18(j)(1)(i)–(ii) (1983). Other major federal environmental statutes such as the Clean Water Act, the Resource Conservation and Recovery Act, and the Endangered Species Act have similar citizen suit provisions.

130. For an extensive discussion of these common law climate justice cases in the United States, see Chapter 20 in this volume.

131. American Elec. Power v. Connecticut, 131 S. Ct. 2527 (2011).

132. 42 U.S.C. §7604 a(2).

133. 42 U.S.C. §§7671a(c)(3), 7671e(b), 7671j(e).

such judgment is subject to judicial review only where EPA's actions are "arbitrary, capricious," or illegal.[134]

This case presents a high hurdle for any similar case brought against the federal government. However, it applies to federal common law only and does not govern state common law actions. Therefore, common law climate justice cases have been proceeding in the United States on a state-by-state basis.

The nonprofit organization, Our Children's Trust, has been responsible for several legal proceedings in the United States and abroad based on youth-driven claims for the protection of the atmosphere through enforceable science-based climate recovery plans.[135] The U.S. suits are part of a larger litigation strategy to have nonfederal courts declare that the public trust doctrine requires intergenerational protection against climate change harms.[136] Although several cases were dismissed on procedural grounds,[137] a recent decision in Washington shows the strategy can be successful. The case, *Foster v. Washington Department of Ecology*, was brought by eight teenagers who filed a petition to compel the Department of Ecology (WDOE) to exercise its statutory authority and regulate GHG emissions.[138] The petition called for reducing the concentration of CO_2 from the current level of more than 400 ppm to 350 ppm by the year 2100 based on a Washington statute that creates a "fundamental and inalienable right" to live in a "healthful and pleasant environment and to benefit from the proper development and use of its natural resources."[139] The petition is largely based on the Greenhouse Gas Emission Limits Statute,[140] which sets specific GHG emission limits enacted by the legislature, and requires periodic updates by the WDOE.[141]

In June 2015, the King County Superior Court ordered the WDOE to reconsider the rulemaking petition that asked the Department to use best available science, including the IPCC, when making emissions reduction recommendations to the state legislature.[142] In November 2015, the court

---

134. Chevron U.S.A., Inc. v. Natural Res. Def. Council, 467 U.S. 837 (1984).

135. Our Children's Trust, *Our Mission,* http://www.ourchildrenstrust.org/mission-statement/ (last visited Sept. 12, 2016).

136. Our Children's Trust, *State Legal Actions,* http://www.ourchildrenstrust.org/state-legal-actions (last visited Aug. 24, 2016).

137. *See, e.g.,* Kanuk v. Alaska, 335 P.3d 1088, 1100–01 (Alaska 2014); Butler v. Brewer, No. 1 CA-CV 12-0347, slip op. at 17–19, 21 (Ariz. Ct. App. Mar. 14, 2013).

138. Petition From Andrea Rodgers Harris on Behalf of Youth Petitioners to Washington Department of Ecology 3–7 (June 7, 2014), http://static1.squarespace.com/static/571d109b04426270152febe0/t/5785909d9de4bb340b8b75df/1468371110844/Petition.Final_.6.17.14.pdf.

139. *Id.*

140. WASH. REV. CODE §70.235.020(1)(a) (2014).

141. Wash. Exec. Order No. 13-04, at 1 (2014).

142. Foster v. Washington Dep't of Ecology, No. 14-2-25295-1 SEA, slip op. at 4 (Wash. Super. Ct. June 23, 2015).

determined that the state environmental authority has a mandatory duty to regulate climate change.[143] Nonetheless, the agency withdrew the proposed rule to reduce carbon emissions.[144] As a result, King County Superior Court Judge Hollis Hill ordered the agency to promulgate an emissions reduction rule by the end of 2016 and make recommendations to the state legislature on science-based GHG reductions in the 2017 legislative session.[145]

Foster therefore represents a landmark decision as the court ordered the executive branch of a subnational government to implement a rule by the legislative branch according to the best available science and latest policy-related guidance, including the IPCC. The WDOE relied on the Paris outcomes and the UNFCCC's framework, albeit a subnational government, showing another example of a network of intersecting sources of climate change law.[146] Like *Urgenda* and *Leghari*, *Foster* relies on climate science to prove the government is not doing enough to ensure environmental protection. The plaintiffs therefore sought judicial enforcement of a domestic law to take specific action on climate change.[147]

Another case was brought in Massachusetts attempting to ensure implementation of a previous law. Similar to the *Leghari v. Pakistan* case, environmentalists sued the government of Massachusetts for its failure to set goals to reduce carbon emissions required under the 2008 Global Warming Solutions Act.[148] The state Supreme Judicial Court ruled in favor of the plaintiffs due to the lack of concrete targets.[149] As such, it overturned a 2015 Suffolk Superior Court decision, which found that the state was in compliance with the Act because it adopted rules on vehicle emissions on the Regional Greenhouse Gas Initiative and on sulfur hexafluoride.

Conclusion

One of the defining features of the Paris Agreement is its "enhanced transparency framework for action and support," which is needed to "build mutual

---

143. Foster v. Washington Dep't of Ecology, 2015 WL 7721362 (Wash. Super. Ct. Nov. 19, 2015), http://ourchildrenstrust.org/sites/default/files/15.11.19.Order_FosterV.Ecology.pdf.
144. Press Release, Our Children's Trust et al., Youths Secure Second Win in Washington State Climate Lawsuit (Apr. 29, 2016), http://ourchildrenstrust.org/sites/default/files/2016.04.29WAFinalRulingPR.pdf.
145. Foster v. Washington Dep't of Ecology, No. 14-2-25295-1 SEA, slip op. at 4 (Wash. Super. Ct. June 23, 2015).
146. Bach, *supra* note 61, at 29.
147. *Id.* at 32.
148. Kain v. Massachusetts Dep't of Envtl. Prot., 2015 SJC11961 (Mass. Super. Ct. Mar. 23, 2015).
149. Conservation Law Foundation, Mass Energy Consumers Alliance, and four Massachusetts high school students.

trust and confidence and to promote effective implementation."[150] Such a system will compel countries to regularly provide information on their national circumstances, emissions reductions, adaptation measures, and the need for or provision of support. Such transparency, while useful for governments to know how others are doing, also makes it clear to their constituents what they are or are not doing as well. Such clarity can be a double-edged sword, however. Kurt Winter of ClientEarth acknowledges the enhanced transparency framework as an important development, but observes that it can also "help with coordinating evidence of whether governments are complying with targets and whether a case can be launched."[151]

Such cases, as Prof. Tracy Bach points out, provide "a potentially potent route for assuring national accountability for the NDCs pledged under international law . . . . In doing so, they act on the aspirational human rights language in the Paris Agreement's preamble."[152] *Urgenda* and other citizen suits have proceeded in parallel with a historic negotiation to develop a global climate agreement that ultimately acknowledged the importance of human rights in climate action, creating for the first time a high-level platform to showcase the initiatives and action of non-State actors, and may allow for some kind of civil society participation in its global stocktaking process. Together, these developments herald a new era of non-State climate action for civil society, one in which increased dialogue with governments can invite collaboration and cultivate mutual motivation to do more.

Climate litigation is a critical part of this dialogue. For now, in the eyes of Dennis van Berkel, legal counsel for Urgenda, the case stands for the idea that "states have an independent legal obligation towards their citizens."[153] Where that idea fails to inform States' NDCs, "they can expect pressure from courts in their own jurisdictions."[154] It is essential for citizens to hold governments accountable for their climate action, or inaction, while avoiding impinging on the prerogatives of regional entities and national governments to determine their climate policies and potentially killing the spirit of ambi-

---

150. *Paris Agreement, supra* note 2, at Annex, art. 13.1.
151. Sara Stefanini, *Next Stop for Paris Climate Deal: The Courts*, POLITICO, Jan. 11, 2016, http://www.politico.eu/article/paris-climate-urgenda-courts-lawsuits-cop21. *See also* Lucas Bergkamp, *The Hidden Trigger of Paris: Why the Climate Battle Will Now Be Taken to the Courts*, ENERGY POST, Jan. 6, 2016, http://www.energypost.eu/hidden-trigger-paris-climate-battle-will-now-taken-courts/ ("[T]he Paris Agreement will bolster climate activists' claims about the inadequacy of governments' climate policies.").
152. Bach, *supra* note 61, at 36.
153. Arthur Neslen, *Dutch Government Ordered to Cut Carbon Emissions in Landmark Ruling*, THE GUARDIAN, June 24, 2015, http://www.theguardian.com/environment/2015/jun/24/dutch-government-ordered-cut-carbon-emissions-landmark-ruling.
154. *Id.*

tion that has fortified the recent climate negotiations and Parties' NDCs.[155] The question of whether countries may be held accountable for achieving their NDCs under the Paris Agreement was a sensitive question already raised in the negotiations; the Paris Agreement represents a careful balance to achieve both broad participation and genuine ambition. Until the *Urgenda* litigation is resolved, however, its real takeaways have yet to be determined. But they will certainly inform the global conversation on how to close the ambition and action gap, how to transition to a low carbon world, and how to protect communities in an increasingly warming climate.

---

155. *Cf.* van Zeben, *supra* note 10, at 356 ("In the enthusiasm regarding the pro-environmental outcome of *Urgenda*, the perceived desirability of the outcome must not be seen as a cure for the democratic legitimacy concerns that this mandatory order raises.").

Chapter 22

Climate Justice for Future Generations: A Case Study in the Great Barrier Reef World Heritage Site of Australia

Keely Boom

Introduction

The 1972 World Heritage Convention[1] seeks to protect the world's cultural and natural heritage of outstanding universal value for present and future generations. In 2005, a group of nonprofit organizations and individuals alerted the World Heritage Committee to the threats posed by climate change to World Heritage sites around the world. These petitioners sought to have threatened sites added to the List of World Heritage in Danger, including the Great Barrier Reef of Australia.[2]

---

1.   Convention Concerning the Protection of the World Cultural and Natural Heritage, Nov. 16, 1972, 11 I.L.M. 1358 [hereinafter World Heritage Convention].
2.   SYDNEY CENTRE FOR INTERNATIONAL AND GLOBAL LAW, GLOBAL CLIMATE CHANGE AND THE GREAT BARRIER REEF: AUSTRALIA'S OBLIGATIONS UNDER THE WORLD HERITAGE CONVENTION 5 (2004), a report prepared for the Environmental Defender's Office (NSW), Climate Action Network Australia, and Greenpeace Australia Pacific [hereinafter SCIG REPORT].

Australian laws require these sites to be protected, particularly under the Environment Protection and Biodiversity Conservation Act 1999 (Cth) (EPBC Act),[3] which gives effect to the World Heritage Convention. A court case brought by the Australian Conservation Foundation (ACF) in November 2015 challenged the commonwealth government's approval of the Carmichael coal mine. ACF argued that the minister failed to properly consider the impacts to the Great Barrier Reef from the pollution and carbon emissions from the burning of the mine's coal, and thereby failed to comply with Australia's obligations under the World Heritage Convention. The Federal Court dismissed the case on August 29, 2016.[4] ACF has announced that it is appealing the decision.[5]

Part I of this chapter addresses the international climate change regulatory regime and the role of intergenerational equity. Part II examines the World Heritage Convention, and specifically considers the interpretation of the World Heritage Convention provided by the High Court of Australia. It also describes the Great Barrier Reef, including its value and vulnerability to climate change. Part III addresses the List of World Heritage in Danger from climate change, and the possible role of intergenerational climate justice. It highlights the petition to list the Great Barrier Reef in danger, and the responses by the World Heritage Committee and the World Heritage Centre to this and other similar petitions. Part III also considers Australian legislation, the proposed Carmichael coal mine, and the legal challenge brought by ACF. The legal challenge is examined to assess the potential role of World Heritage in promoting climate justice in Australia, particularly for future generations.

I. The International Climate Regime and Intergenerational Equity

The international climate regime is comprised of the United Nations Framework Convention on Climate Change (UNFCCC),[6] the Kyoto Protocol,[7] the Paris Agreement,[8] and other instruments. These treaties and other instru-

---

3. Environment Protection and Biodiversity Conservation Act 1999 (Cth) (Austrl.).
4. Australian Conservation Foundation v. Minister for the Environment (2016) FCA 1042 (No. QUD1017/2015). For a full discussion of this case, see *infra* Part III.
5. Joshua Robertson, *Adani Carmichael coalmine faces new legal challenge from conservation foundation*, THE GUARDIAN, Sept. 19, 2016, https://www.theguardian.com/business/2016/sep/19/adani-carmichael-coalmine-faces-new-legal-challenge-from-conservation-foundation.
6. United Nations Framework Convention on Climate Change, *opened for signature* May 9, 1992, 1771 U.N.T.S. 107, 165 (entered into force Mar. 21, 1994) [hereinafter UNFCCC].
7. Kyoto Protocol to the United Nations Convention on Climate Change, *opened for signature* Mar. 15, 1998, 37 I.L.M. 22 (entered into force Feb. 16, 2005).
8. *Adoption of the Paris Agreement*, UNFCCC Conference of the Parties, 21st Sess., U.N. Doc. FCCC/CP/2015/10/Add.1 (Dec. 12, 2015), http://unfccc.int/files/home/application/pdf/paris_agreement.pdf [hereinafter *Paris Agreement*].

ments provide the primary means through which the international community has sought to respond to the challenge of climate change. The UNFCCC provides a framework for the climate regime. It provides an objective, principles, obligations, and dispute resolution mechanisms, and it divides countries up according to responsibilities and rights. The ultimate objective of the UNFCCC is "to achieve . . . stabilization of greenhouse gas concentrations in the atmosphere at a level that would prevent dangerous anthropogenic interference with the climate system."[9]

The Kyoto Protocol established quantitative obligations for mitigating greenhouse gas (GHG) emissions by country in the period 2008–2012. The Paris Agreement was drafted in December 2015 and aims to hold the increase in the global average temperature to "well below 2°C above pre-industrial levels and pursuing efforts to limit the temperature increase to 1.5°C above pre-industrial levels, recognizing that this would significantly reduce the risks and impacts of climate change."[10] In accordance with Article 4, each Party shall prepare, communicate, and maintain successive nationally determined contributions that it intends to achieve.[11]

The preamble of the UNFCCC provides that change in the earth's climate, and its adverse effects, are part of the "common concern of humankind"[12] and refers to the principle of intergenerational equity.[13] The preamble of the Paris Agreement recognizes the "importance for some of the concept of 'climate justice.'"[14] This reference to "climate justice" in the Paris Agreement is the first time that it has been recognized in an international agreement.

Conceptualizations of "future generations" range from today's children[15] to the unborn persons of the remote future.[16] Generally, definitions of future generations are not restricted by a time factor. For example, the Earth Charter of 2002 affirms the need to "[s]ecure Earth's bounty and

9. UNFCCC, *supra* note 6, at art. 2.
10. *Paris Agreement*, *supra* note 8, at art. 2(1)(a).
11. *Paris Agreement*, *supra* note 8, at art. 4.
12. UNFCCC, *supra* note 6, at pmbl., para. 1.
13. *See, e.g.*, F. Biermann, *Common Concern of Humankind: The Emergence of a New Concept of International Environmental Law*, 34 ARCHIV DES VOLKERRECHTS 426 (1996); KEMAL BASAR, THE CONCEPT OF THE COMMON HERITAGE OF MANKIND IN INTERNATIONAL LAW (1998); Thomas Cottier & Sofya Matteoti-Berkutova, *International Environmental Law and the Evolving Concept of Common Concern of Mankind*, *in* INTERNATIONAL TRADE AND THE MITIGATION OF CLIMATE CHANGE (Thomas Cottier, Olga Nartova & Sadeq Z. Bigdeli eds., 2009); LUCA TACCONI & JEFF BENNETT, IMPLICATIONS OF INTERGENERATIONAL EQUITY FOR BIODIVERSITY CONSERVATION (1993); EDITH BROWN WEISS, IN FAIRNESS TO FUTURE GENERATIONS: INTERNATIONAL LAW, COMMON PATRIMONY, AND INTERGENERATIONAL EQUITY (1989).
14. *Paris Agreement*, *supra* note 8, at pmbl.
15. *See, e.g.*, LAURA WESTRA, ENVIRONMENTAL JUSTICE AND THE RIGHTS OF UNBORN AND FUTURE GENERATIONS: LAW, ENVIRONMENTAL HARM, AND THE RIGHT TO HEALTH xv–xviii (2006).
16. *See, e.g.*, EDWARD A. PAGE, CLIMATE CHANGE, JUSTICE, AND FUTURE GENERATIONS 53 (2006).

beauty for present and future generations," but does not specify a time factor for future generations.[17] Elise Boulding has proposed that policy-makers consider thinking in a time span that she calls the "two hundred year present."[18] This two hundred year present is marked by centenarians, who are celebrating their 100th birthday today, and extends to the 100th birthday of babies born today. This perspective encompasses our parents, grandparents, and great-grandparents, and then our children, grandchildren and great-grandchildren.[19]

Some have argued that since future generations do not exist at present that they cannot have any rights.[20] However, the decisions in all legal systems, and especially in common law countries, are "as much about the future as they are about the past."[21] There is significant support within international law for the view that future generations have interests and rights.[22]

Dr. Edith Brown Weiss argued that there are three basic principles of intergenerational ecological equity or justice: conservation of options, conservation of quality, and conservation of access.[23] Conservation of options requires that each living generation "does not unduly restrict the options available to future generations in solving their problems and satisfying their own values."[24] Conservation of quality means that each living generation "maintain[s] the quality of the earth so that it is passed on in no worse condition than [it] received it."[25] Finally, conservation of access requires each living

17. The Earth Charter http://earthcharter.org/discover/the-earth-charter/.

18. Elise Boulding, *The Dynamics of Imaging Futures*, 12 World Future Soc'y Bull. 7 (1978).

19. For some authors, "future generations" only refers to those who are unborn. For others, future generations include both children of today and the unborn generations. *See also* Oposa v. Factoran, G.R. No. 101083 (S.C. July 30, 1993), *reprinted in* 33 I.L.M. 173 (1994). This chapter uses the term "future generations" to refer to both children of today and the unborn generations.

20. *See, e.g.*, Richard T. DeGeorge, *The Environment, Rights, and Future Generations, in* Responsibilities to Future Generations: Environmental Ethics 157, 159 (Ernest Partridge ed., 1981) ("Future generations by definition do not now exist. They cannot now, therefore, be the present bearer or subject of anything, including rights."); Ruth Macklin, *Can Future Generations Correctly Be Said to Have Rights?, in* Responsibilities to Future Generations: Environmental Ethics 153 (Ernest Partridge ed., 1981) ("Sentience is not only a sufficient condition for ascribing rights to persons; it is also a necessary condition.").

21. *See* Weston Burns, *Climate Change and Intergenerational Justice: Foundational Reflections*, 9 Vt. J. Envtl. L. 375 (2007/2008).

22. *See, e.g.*, Convention for the Protection of the Mediterranean Sea Against Pollution, Feb. 16, 1976, 1102 U.N.T.S. 27, *reprinted in* 5 International Law and World Order, at W.F.18a; World Charter for Nature, G.A. Res. 37/7, U.N. GAOR, 37th Sess., Annex, Supp. No. 51, at 17, U.N. Doc. A/RES/37/51 (1983), *reprinted in* 5 International Law and World Order: Basic Documents V.B.3 (Burns H. Weston & Jonathon C. Carlson eds., 12th ed. 2006); Declaration on the Responsibilities of the Present Generations Towards Future Generations, G.C. Res. 31, UNESCO, 29th Sess., art. 4, UNESCO Doc. 29 C/Res. 31 (1997), http://www.unesco.org/cpp/uk/declarations/generations.pdf.

23. Brown Weiss, *supra* note 13, at 39.

24. *Id.*

25. *Id.*

generation to "provide its members with equitable rights of access to the legacy of past generations" and "conserve this access for future generations."[26]

International climate regulation is an effort by the international community to protect the climate for future generations. Recognition of intergenerational equity in the UNFCCC reflects the important role of this principle. Climate change threatens the rights of future generations in a myriad of ways, including their enjoyment of sites protected by the World Heritage Convention.

II. World Heritage Convention

The World Heritage Convention[27] is considered one of the centerpiece multilateral environmental agreements concerned with the conservation of wildlife and habitat.[28] The treaty is one of the world's most widely adopted multilateral agreements. The World Heritage Convention emerged in the 1950s and 1960s in recognition of serious threats posed by human activities to sites of cultural and natural significance.[29]

Much attention was given to a decision by the Egyptian government to build the Aswan Dam that would have flooded the valley containing the Abu Simbel Temples, which were constructed during the 13th century BC.[30] In response to a request from Egypt and Sudan, the United Nations Educational, Scientific, and Cultural Organization (UNESCO) assisted with the relocation of the Abu Simbel Temples. The General Assembly of UNESCO adopted the World Heritage Convention in 1972, and it entered into force in 1975.

The World Heritage Convention aims to establish an effective system of collective protection of the world's cultural and natural heritage of outstanding universal value. Protection of World Heritage sites is primarily a matter for the State in which the site is situated. However, the international community must also participate to protect the world's cultural and natural heritage. The World Heritage Convention provides that each State:

---

26. *Id.*
27. World Heritage Convention, *supra* note 1.
28. Patricia Birnie, Alan Boyle & Catherine Redgwell, International Law and the Environment 672 (3d ed. 2009). *See also* Mary Wood et al., *Securing Planetary Life Sources for Future Generations: Legal Actions Deriving from the Ancient Sovereign Trust Obligation, in* Threatened Island Nations: Legal Implications of Rising Seas and a Changing Climate (Michael B. Gerrard & Gregory E. Wannier eds., 2012).
29. United Nations Education, Scientific & Community Organization (UNESCO) World Heritage Centre, World Heritage Information Kit 7 (2008), whc.unesco.org/documents/publi_infokit_en.pdf.
30. *Id.*

Recognises that the duty of ensuring the identification, protection, conservation, presentation and transmission to future generations of the cultural and natural heritage [of outstanding universal value] situated on its territory, belongs primarily to that State. It will do all it can to this end, to the utmost of its own resources and, where appropriate, with any international assistance and co-operation, in particular, financial, artistic, scientific and technical, which it may be able to obtain.[31]

Thus, the focus of the World Heritage Convention is on the protection, conservation, presentation, and transmission of World Heritage sites to future generations. A number of other international environmental agreements also mention the interests of future generations.[32]

The World Heritage Convention provides definitions for natural and cultural heritage. "Natural heritage" is defined in Article 2 of the World Heritage Convention as:

Natural features consisting of physical and biological formations or groups of such formations, which are of outstanding universal value from a scientific point of view;

Geological and physiographical formations and precisely delineated areas which constitute the habitat of threatened species of animals or plants of outstanding universal value from the point of view of science or conservation;

Natural sites or precisely delineated natural areas of outstanding universal value from the point of view of science, conservation or natural beauty.[33]

"Cultural heritage" is defined as including monuments or groups of buildings of outstanding universal value "from the point of view of history, art or science" and "works of man or the combined works of nature and man, and areas including archaeological sites which are of outstanding universal value from the historical, aesthetic, ethnological or anthropological point of view."[34] The Operational Guidelines further define "outstanding universal value" as "cultural and/or natural significance which is so exceptional as to transcend national boundaries and to be of common importance for present and future

31. World Heritage Convention, *supra* note 1, at art. 4.
32. *See, e.g., Declaration of the United Nations Conference on the Human Environment,* U.N. Conference on the Human Environment, Stockholm, Sweden, June 5–16, 1972, at 3, U.N. Doc. A/CONF.48/14/ REV.1 (1972), *reprinted in* 5 INTERNATIONAL LAW AND WORLD ORDER: BASIC DOCUMENTS V.B.3 (Burns H. Weston & Jonathon C. Carlson eds., 12th ed. 2006).
33. World Heritage Convention, *supra* note 1, at art. 2.
34. *Id.* at art. 1.

generations of all humanity. As such, the permanent protection of this heritage is of the highest importance to the international community as a whole."[35]

Part II of the World Heritage Convention sets out the key obligations held by Australia and other States. Australia has a duty to ensure the identification, protection, conservation, presentation, and transmission to future generations of those properties. In accordance with Article 4 of the World Heritage Convention, Australia must "do all it can," "to the utmost of its own resources" to discharge the duty of "ensuring the identification, protection, conservation, presentation and transmission to future generations" of World Heritage sites.

Article 5(d) of the World Heritage Convention provides that States Parties must take the appropriate legal and administrative measures necessary for the protection, conservation, and rehabilitation of World Heritage sites. The obligation in Article 5(d) builds on the duty set out in Article 4 by stipulating that the measures taken by States Parties must be both legal and administrative.

Article 6(1) provides that the international community has a duty to cooperate to protect the cultural and natural heritage of World Heritage sites, which is of particular relevance to the global problem posed by climate change. Article 6(3) provides that each State Party "undertakes not to take any deliberate measures which might damage directly or indirectly" the World Heritage sites situated in the territory of other States Parties. Given the state of scientific knowledge around climate change and its impact on World Heritage sites, Article 6(3) requires all States Parties to the World Heritage Convention to ensure, both individually and in cooperation with other States Parties, that GHG emissions are reduced.[36] This language recognizes that impacts on World Heritage sites are no longer unintentional or unforeseeable.[37] Indeed, climate change impacts on future generations and thus intergenerational equity are foreseeable for States Parties to the World Heritage Convention.

Within this context, the World Heritage Convention contains 15 references to "international assistance." The frequency of this phrase reflects the critical importance of global cooperation and partnerships in protecting world heritage.[38] The preamble of the World Heritage Convention provides that:

---

35. Operational Guidelines for the Implementation of the World Heritage Convention, para. 49, http://whc.unesco.org/en/guidelines/.
36. World Heritage Convention, *supra* note 1, at art. (6)(3).
37. Anna Huggins, *Adverse Impacts of Climate Change: Obligations for States Parties to the World Heritage Convention*, 14 Australian Int'l L.J. 121, 135 (2007).
38. *See* Tom Baxter, *Legal Protection for the Great Barrier Reef World Heritage Area*, 3 Macquarie J. Int'l & Comp. Envtl. L. 67 (2006).

[I]t is incumbent on the international community as a whole to participate in the protection of the cultural and natural heritage of outstanding universal value, by the granting of collective assistance which, although not taking the place of action by the State concerned, will serve as an efficient complement thereto.[39]

The wording of the preamble emphasizes that although the primary responsibility rests with the State Party in which the World Heritage site is situated, States Parties are obliged to engage in internationally cooperative effort. The global nature of climate change requires an international response to protect, conserve, and transmit World Heritage sites to future generations. The World Heritage Convention provides authority for the position that the international community as a whole is obliged to engage in international cooperation to achieve this outcome.

The World Heritage Convention established the World Heritage Committee, which is comprised of 21 Parties, and elected by the Parties.[40] The responsibilities of the committee include establishing the List of World Heritage Sites; monitoring the state of conservation of World Heritage properties; establishing the terms for use of the World Heritage Trust, which is used to help protect World Heritage sites; and allocating financial assistance upon requests by Parties.[41] The World Heritage Committee maintains a List of World Heritage in Danger, which is reserved for sites "threatened by serious and specific dangers . . . for the conservation of which major operations are necessary and for which assistance has been requested under this Convention."[42]

If the World Heritage Committee finds that a site should be listed as "in danger," it then is empowered to define a program of corrective actions to be undertaken by the Party.[43] The committee reviews the List of World Heritage in Danger, and may decide that: (1) additional measures are required to protect a site; or (2) the property is to be deleted from the List of World Heritage in Danger if the threat has been removed; or (3) the property is to be deleted from both the List of World Heritage in Danger and the World Heritage List if the property has deteriorated to such an extent that it has lost the characteristics for which it was inscribed on the World Heritage List.

---

39. World Heritage Convention, *supra* note 1, at pmbl.
40. *Id.* at art. 8(1).
41. *Id.* at arts. 8–14.
42. *Id.* at art. 11(4).
43. *Id.* at art. 13.

A.   Interpretation by the High Court of Australia

A key interpretive question is whether the obligations contained in Articles 4, 5, and 6 are binding on States Parties as substantive obligations, or whether they amount to mere recommendations. Articles 4 and 5 are broadly worded and include qualifying language such as "as far as possible" and only require States Parties to "recognise" certain responsibilities.

The High Court of Australia has provided the first judicial interpretation of Articles 4 and 5. In *Commonwealth v. Tasmania*[44] (the "Tasmanian Dam Case"), the High Court of Australia held that, for the purposes of the commonwealth's constitutional power to legislate with respect to external affairs, Articles 4 and 5 of the World Heritage Convention constituted binding obligations for Australia.[45] The case involved a constitutional challenge to the validity of the World Heritage Properties Conservation Act 1983 (Cth). The High Court upheld the constitutional validity of this legislation. The World Heritage Properties Conservation Act 1983 (Cth) was later replaced by the EPBC Act.

In relation to Article 5 of the World Heritage Convention, Justice Mason stated that:

> [Article 5] cannot be read as a mere statement of intention. It is expressed in the form of a command requiring each party to endeavour to bring about the matters dealt with in the lettered paragraphs. Indeed, there would be little point in adding the qualifications "in so far as possible" and "as appropriate for each country" unless the article imposed an obligation . . . . There is a distinction between a discretion as to the manner of performance and a discretion as to performance or non-performance. The latter, but not the former, is inconsistent with a binding obligation to perform.[46]

Thus, the rationale of the High Court was that Articles 4 and 5 must impose substantive mandates on States Parties, because otherwise the qualifying language would be superfluous.[47] The decision recognized that States

---

44. Commonwealth v. Tasmania (1982–1983) 46 ALR 625.
45. *Id.* per Justice Mason at 697–99, Justice Murphy at 735, Justice Brennan at 777–79, and Justice Deane at 807–08. Contrary to the majority, Chief Justice Gibbs (at 660–63) and Justice Wilson (at 745–47) held that Articles 4 and 5 did not impose binding obligations on Australia.
46. *Id.* at 698. This view was later affirmed by the High Court in *Richardson v. Forestry Commission* (1988) 164 CLR 261 per Chief Justice Mason and Justice Brennan at 289, per Justice Deane at 313, per Justice Toohey at 332, and per Justice Gaudron at 334, and in *Queensland v. Commonwealth* (1989) 167 CLR 232 per Chief Justice Mason and Justices Brennan, Deane, Toohey, Gaudron, and McHugh at 235–36.
47. Erica Thorson, *On Thin Ice: The Failure of the United States and the World Heritage Committee to Take Climate Change Mitigation Pursuant to the World Heritage Convention Seriously*, 38 ENVTL. L. 139, 161 (2008).

Parties have discretion in determining what measures are appropriate, meaning that Articles 4 and 5 confer discretion to States Parties in fulfilling these substantive duties.[48]

The discretion exercised by States must be exercised in good faith.[49] The element of good faith is derived from the principle of *pacta sunt servanda*,[50] which provides that States must implement their international obligations in good faith.[51]

B.   The Great Barrier Reef

The Great Barrier Reef World Heritage Area was included on the World Heritage List in 1981 as a natural property possessing World Heritage values.[52] The Great Barrier Reef is the most extensive coral reef in the world, with more than 2,500 individual reefs over 2,000 km in length and 350,000 km² in area. The Great Barrier Reef has more than 400 species of coral, 1,500 species of fish, 4,000 species of mollusks, and 242 species of birds.[53] It provides habitat for the dugong and the green and loggerhead turtles, which are listed as threatened species.[54] The Great Barrier Reef is the largest World Heritage area in the world.[55]

The Great Barrier Reef has extensive environmental, cultural, and economic significance. It encompasses outer coral reefs, coastal reefs, islands and lagoons, coastal estuaries, seagrass beds, and mangroves.[56] The Great Barrier Reef is "sea country" of integral importance to local Aboriginal and Torres Strait Islander communities.[57] It also provides significant economic value for

---

48. *See also* Michael Jeffery, *An International Legal Regime for Protected Areas*, in INTERNATIONAL ENVIRON-MENTAL GOVERNANCE: AN INTERNATIONAL REGIME FOR PROTECTED AREAS—IUCN ENVIRONMENTAL POLICY AND LAW PAPER NO. 49, at 9, 15 (John Scanlon & Françoise Burhenne-Guilmin eds., 2004) ("Although terminology such as 'to the utmost of its own resources' and 'in so far as possible' might be seen as adding a subjective mechanism from which States can easily escape responsibility, it still places a legal obligation on each contracting party.").

49. Huggins, *supra* note 37, at 134.

50. *See* I.M. SINCLAIR, THE VIENNA CONVENTION ON THE LAW OF TREATIES 3 (1973); LORD MCNAIR, THE LAW OF TREATIES 493–505 (1961); Josef L. Kun, *The Meaning and the Range of the Norm of Pacta Sunt Servanda*, 39 AM. J. INT'L L. 180 (1945).

51. IAN BROWNLIE, PRINCIPLES OF PUBLIC INTERNATIONAL LAW 620 (5th ed. 1998). *See also* Vienna Convention on the Law of Treaties, May 23, 1969, art. 26, 1155 U.N.T.S. 331, 339.

52. Great Barrier Reef Marine Park Authority, *About the Reef—Heritage*, http://www.gbrmpa.gov.au/about-the-reef/heritage (last visited Aug. 23, 2016).

53. World Heritage Nomination, International Union for the Conservation of Nature Technical Review, July 1981.

54. *Id.*

55. *Id.*

56. *See, e.g.*, J.E. BOWEN & M.J. BOWEN, THE GREAT BARRIER REEF: HISTORY, SCIENCE, HERITAGE (2002).

57. *See, e.g.*, Paul Havemann et al., *Traditional Use of Marine Resource Agreements and Dugong Hunting in the Great Barrier Reef World Heritage Area*, 22 ENVTL. PLAN. L.J. 258 (2005); D. Smyth, *The Indigenous Sector: An Anthropological Perspective*, in VALUING FISHERIES: AN ECONOMIC FRAMEWORK (T.

the Australian economy, particularly for tourism. Approximately 1.8 million people visit the Great Barrier Reef each year and generate more than AU\$5.1 billion.[58]

The Great Barrier Reef Marine Park, which was declared in 1975, makes up about 99.3% of the Great Barrier Reef World Heritage Area. The Marine Park includes areas that have been declared under §31 of the Great Barrier Reef Marine Park Act 1975 (Cth). A number of other statutes apply to the Great Barrier Reef.[59] The Great Barrier Reef Marine Park Authority (GBRMPA) is responsible for the protection and management of the Great Barrier Reef.

The Great Barrier Reef was also the first site to be declared a Particularly Sensitive Sea Area by the International Maritime Organization. A Particularly Sensitive Sea Area is one that needs special protection through action by the International Maritime Organization due to its ecological, socioeconomic, or scientific importance, and which may be vulnerable to damage by international shipping.[60]

Beyond the World Heritage Convention, other international laws that impose obligations on Australia to protect the Great Barrier Reef are the International Convention for the Prevention of Pollution from Ships (MARPOL),[61] the United Nations Convention on the Law of the Sea (UNCLOS),[62] the UNFCCC,[63] and the Convention on Biological Diversity (CBD).[64]

Climate change is a major threat to the Great Barrier Reef and other coral reefs around the world. Additional threats include shipping,[65] fishing, tourism, and declining water quality. However, climate change poses the most

Hundloe ed., 2002); D. Smyth, *Management of Sea Country: Indigenous People's Use and Management of Marine Environments, in* WORKING ON COUNTRY: CONTEMPORARY INDIGENOUS MANAGEMENT OF AUSTRALIA'S LAND AND COASTAL REGIONS (R. Baker, J. Davies & E. Young eds., 2001).

58. AUGUSTIN COLETTE, CASE STUDIES ON CLIMATE CHANGE AND WORLD HERITAGE 35 (2007).

59. *See* Environment Protection (Sea Dumping) Act 1981 (Cth); Historic Shipwrecks Act 1976 (Cth); Native Title Act 1993 (Cth); Protection of the Sea (Prevention of Pollution from Ships) Act 1983 (Cth); Sea Installations Act 1987 (Cth).

60. International Maritime Organization, Guidelines for the Designation of Special Areas Under MARPOL 73/78 and Guidelines for the Identification and Designation of Particularly Sensitive Sea Areas, Assembly Res. A.927 (22) (2001).

61. International Convention for the Prevention of Pollution from Ships, Nov. 2, 1973, 1340 U.N.T.S. 184, 12 I.L.M. 1319 (entered into force Oct. 2, 1983).

62. United Nations Convention on the Law of the Sea, *opened for signature* Dec. 10, 1982, 1833 U.N.T.S. 3, 21 I.L.M. 1261 (entered into force Nov. 16, 1994).

63. UNFCCC, *supra* note 6.

64. Convention on Biological Diversity, *opened for signature* June 5, 1992, 1760 U.N.T.S. 79, 31 I.L.M. 818 (entered into force Dec. 29, 1993).

65. *See* Kathryn Berry et al., *Simulated Coal Spill Causes Mortality and Growth Inhibition in Tropical Marine Organisms*, 6 SCI. REP. 1 (2016).

significant long-term threat to the heritage values of the Great Barrier Reef. The sustainability of the Great Barrier Reef is threatened by a number of climate parameters, including sea-level rise, sea temperature increase, storm frequency and intensity, precipitation, drought, land runoff, changing oceanic circulation, and ocean acidification.[66]

The global average heat content of the oceans is increasing.[67] The oceans act as a sink for carbon dioxide (CO_2), with the increasing uptake of CO_2 causing acidification of the water, which causes corals to grow more slowly or with weaker skeletons.[68] The Intergovernmental Panel on Climate Change (IPCC) has stated that the increase of sea surface temperature and the uptake of CO_2 by oceans represent the most serious threats to coral reefs this century.[69]

The Great Barrier Reef is significantly threatened by coral bleaching, which occurs when there are abrupt changes to temperature, light, salinity, or turbidity. Scientific literature did not mention mass bleaching events until 1979.[70] These mass bleaching events occur when sea surface temperature exceeds seasonal highs by 1.5°C to 2°C. Scientific records show that during the past century the sea surface temperature of the Great Barrier Reef Lagoon had an upward trend of about 1°C.[71] As a result, the habitat of coral reefs in the Great Barrier Reef has significantly diminished.[72]

Climate change scientists predict that the Great Barrier Reef will experience warming of 2°C to 5°C by 2100.[73] It is expected that mass bleaching events, with widespread death of corals, will become increasingly frequent.[74] Coral bleaching is "not amenable to management in the short to medium term."[75]

---

66. UNESCO, CLIMATE CHANGE AND WORLD HERITAGE: REPORT ON PREDICTING AND MANAGING THE IMPACTS OF CLIMATE CHANGE ON WORLD HERITAGE AND STRATEGY TO ASSIST STATES PARTIES TO IMPLEMENT APPROPRIATE MANAGEMENT RESPONSES 22 (Augustin Colette ed., 2007) [hereinafter UNESCO Report].

67. Daniel L. Albritton et al, *Summary for Policymakers in* CLIMATE CHANGE 2001: THE SCIENTIFIC BASIS. CONTRIBUTION OF WORKING GROUP II TO THE THIRD ASSESSMENT REPORT OF THE INTERGOVERNMENTAL PANEL ON CLIMATE CHANGE (2001), http://www.grida.no/climate/ipcc_tar/wg1/pdf/WG1_TAR-FRONT.pdf

68. COLETTE, *supra* note 58, at 29.

69. Daniel Albritton et al, *supra* note 67, §6.4.5.

70. *See* O. Hoegh-Guldber, *Coral Reefs, Thermal Limits, and Climate Change, in* CLIMATE CHANGE IMPACTS ON BIODIVERSITY IN AUSTRALIA (M. Howden et al. eds., 2002).

71. J.M. LOUGH, RESEARCH PUBLICATION NO. 57: SEA SURFACE TEMPERATURES ON THE GREAT BARRIER REEF: A CONTRIBUTION TO THE STUDY OF CORAL BLEACHING (Great Barrier Reef Marine Park Authority 1999).

72. *See* J. Guinoette et al., *Future Coral Reef Habitat Marginality: Temporal and Spatial Effects of Climate Change in the Pacific Basin*, 22 CORAL REEFS 551 (2003).

73. COLETTE, *supra* note 58, at 32.

74. *Id.*

75. UNESCO Report, *supra* note 66, at 22.

In 1998 and 2002, the Great Barrier Reef was impacted by major bleaching events. In 1998, about 65% of inshore reefs suffered high levels of coral bleaching and 14% of offshore reefs were impacted by severe bleaching. While most of the corals recovered, there were some areas where more than 50% of the corals died.[76] In 2002, between 60% and 95% of the corals were impacted. Approximately 5% of those corals suffered high mortality, losing 50–90% of their corals. Even when corals survive bleaching events, they often show decreased growth and reproductive capacity.[77] In 2016, the Great Barrier Reef experienced the worst coral bleaching ever recorded. As much as 93% of the reef has suffered some level of bleaching in 2016, according to a report by the ARC Centre of Excellence for Coral Reef Studies.[78]

A climate change response program was developed with the goal of better preparation for and response to climate change impacts to the Great Barrier Reef.[79] As part of this program, the Coral Bleaching Response Plan detects and measures bleaching and other impacts through satellite imagery, aerial and underwater surveys, and community observations.[80] The Coral Bleaching Response Plan has since been adapted for other areas of the world, including the Florida Keys and Indonesia.[81] A further component of the program is the Climate Change Action Plan, which seeks to identify and implement relevant management actions, develop adaptation policy, and foster collaboration.[82] However, in 2016, the Australian Government successfully prevented mention of the Great Barrier Reef from an international scientific report on climate change impacts on World Heritage sites.[83] Despite these actions, the Australian government is bound by the World Heritage Convention to protect, conserve, and transmit the Great Barrier Reef to future generations, including from the threats posed by climate change.

---

76. COLETTE, *supra* note 58, at 32.
77. *See* A. Baird & P. Marshall, *Mortality, Growth, and Reproduction in Scleractinian Corals Following Bleaching on the Great Barrier Reef,* 237 MARINE ECOLOGY PROGRESS SERIES 133 (2002).
78. Press Release, ARC Centre of Excellence Coral Reef Studies, Only 7% of the Great Barrier Reef Has Avoided Coral Bleaching (Apr. 20, 2016), https://www.coralcoe.org.au/media-releases/only-7-of-the-great-barrier-reef-has-avoided-coral-bleaching.
79. *See* Great Barrier Reef Marine Park Authority, *Managing the Reef,* http://www.gbrmpa.gov.au/managing-the-reef/threats-to-the-reef/climate-change (last visited Aug. 23, 2016).
80. GREAT BARRIER REEF MARINE PARK AUTHORITY, CORAL BLEACHING RESPONSE PLAN 2010–2011, http://www.gbrmpa.gov.au/__data/assets/pdf_file/0019/4285/gbrmpa_CoralBleachingResPlan2011.pdf.
81. COLETTE, *supra* note 58, at 32.
82. GREAT BARRIER REEF MARINE PARK AUTHORITY, CORAL BLEACHING RESPONSE PLAN 2010–2011, *supra* note 80.
83. Tim Flannery, *The Great Barrier Reef Is Losing Its Adjective and It's Our Fault,* BRISBANE TIMES, June 3, 2016, http://www.brisbanetimes.com.au/comment/the-great-barrier-reef-is-losing-its-adjective-and-its-our-fault-20160602-gp9qsh.html.

III.   World Heritage in Danger Petitions

The Great Barrier Reef is seriously threatened by climate change, trigger-ing a role for the World Heritage Convention as a tool to promote climate justice for future generations. This part explains the history of an effort to list the site as in danger from climate change. Subpart A briefly highlights national legislation applicable to the site, particularly in relation to Australia's World Heritage commitments. Subpart B describes the specific threat posed to the Great Barrier Reef from the proposed Carmichael coal mine. Subpart C analyzes the national legislation and World Heritage commitments held by Australia and Subpart D assesses the recent decision in *Australian Conservation Foundation v. Minister for the Environment (2016) FCA 1042*. This part evaluates the interaction of these national and international laws on the government's decision to approve the mine, shedding light on the potential of the World Heritage Convention as a mechanism to protect the rights of future generations in relation to climate change.

Article 11(4) of the World Heritage Convention provides that the World Heritage Committee is required to establish, update, and publish a List of World Heritage in Danger. The World Heritage Committee exercises discretion as to whether to include a site on the List of World Heritage in Danger.[84]

In 2004, four petitions were filed with the World Heritage Committee for World Heritage sites to be added to the List of World Heritage in Danger. These sites were the Great Barrier Reef, Sagarmatha National Park in Nepal, Huascaran National Park in Peru, and the Barrier Reef Reserve System in Belize. In 2006, a petition was made for the Waterton-Glacier International Peace Park to be added to the List of World Heritage in Danger.[85] Although not cited by the petitioners, Article 13(7) provides that the World Heritage Committee will cooperate with international and national governmental and nongovernmental organizations that have objectives consistent with the World Heritage Convention.

The petition seeking the listing of the Great Barrier Reef argued that cli-mate change had already resulted in massive bleaching events and that the site might be without coral by 2100.[86] Similar arguments were made in the petition that related to the Barrier Reef Reserve System in Belize. The other three petitions cited the threat of climate change through glacial melting.

---

84. World Heritage Convention, *supra* note 1, at art. 11(4).
85. Lewis & Clark Law School, *International Environmental Law Project (IELP)*, http://law.lclark.edu/ live/news/4473-watertonglacier-international-peace-park-petition (last visited Aug. 23, 2016).
86. The petition was actually a report, but the World Heritage Committee addressed it as a petition.

The petition to list the Great Barrier Reef argued that Australia needed to make "deep cuts" in its GHG emissions.[87] The petition also called for Australia to include in its periodic reporting to the General Conference of UNESCO "information and documentation concerning the development of Australia's climate change policy and an assessment of the extent to which the integrity of the GBRWHA has been impaired by the effects of climate change."[88]

In response to the petitions made in 2004, including the one relating to Australia, the World Heritage Committee issued a decision in 2005. The World Heritage Committee acknowledged the "genuine concerns" of the petitioners and the impacts of climate change on World Heritage sites; however, it decided not to add the sites to the List of World Heritage in Danger.[89] The Committee established a working group of experts to work in conjunction with the petitioners, other Parties, and advisory bodies to assess the potential impacts of climate change on World Heritage sites, and to assist Parties with the development of appropriate management responses.[90] The Committee requested that the working group and other relevant bodies prepare a report on predicting and managing the impacts of climate change on World Heritage sites.[91]

The working group of experts drafted a "strategy to assist States Parties to implement appropriate management responses in 2006 (the Strategy)."[92] In relation to mitigation, the Strategy emphasized the role of the UNFCCC negotiations. It stated that the World Heritage community had "a role" to play in mitigation, but restricted this role to providing information to the UNFCCC and IPCC, and encouraging site-based reductions of GHG emissions.[93]

The working group also drafted a joint report, Predicting and Managing the Effects of Climate Change on World Heritage.[94] The report outlined the potential impacts of climate change on World Heritage sites. It presented a

---

87. SCIG REPORT, *supra* note 2, at 4.
88. *Id.* at 5.
89. *Decisions of the 29th Session of the World Heritage Committee (Durban 2005)*, UNESCO World Heritage Committee, 29th Sess., para. 7, UNESCO Doc. WHC-05/29.COM/22 (2005), http://whc.unesco.org/archive/2005/whc05-29com-22e.pdf.
90. *Id.*
91. *Id.*
92. *Issues Related to the State of Conservation of World Heritage Properties: The Impacts of Climate Change on World Heritage Properties*, UNESCO World Heritage Committee, 30th Sess., UNESCO Doc. WHC-06/30.COM/7.1 (2006), http://www.unesco.org/archive.org/archive/2006/whc06-30com-07.1e.pdf.
93. *Id.* at 4–5.
94. *Id.* at 21–59.

strategy for site-based mitigation and adaptation responses, and cooperation with other regimes.[95]

Ahead of the next World Heritage Committee meeting, the United States submitted a position paper regarding the "in danger" petitions. The paper stated that "There is no compelling argument for the Committee to address the issue of global climate change—especially at the risk of losing the unified spirit and camaraderie that has come to be synonymous with World Heritage."[96] The U.S. position was based in part on the view that "there is no unanimity regarding the impacts, causes, and how to or if man can affect the changes we are observing."[97] However, given the advances in scientific understanding of climate change, these arguments no longer apply. Moreover, the development of international climate law indicates that there is a unified spirit and camaraderie among States to address climate change, although there are variations in the preferred approach. The sheer magnitude of the threat posed by climate change to World Heritage sites means that it cannot be ignored.[98]

At the 30th Session in 2006, the World Heritage Committee endorsed the Strategy and took note of the Joint Report.[99] The World Heritage Committee requested[100] that the World Heritage Centre prepare a policy document on the impacts of climate change on World Heritage sites for discussion at the General Assembly of States Parties in 2007.[101] In 2007, the General Assembly of States Parties endorsed the Policy Document, which emphasized the role of the UNFCCC and the IPCC, and that the focus of the World Heritage Convention should be on the management of World Heritage sites. The Policy Document recognized that Article 6(3) required a "collaborative approach" among States Parties to the threats posed by climate change.[102]

95. *Id.* at 34–55.
96. Climate Justice Programme, *US Government to Oppose World Heritage Action on Climate Change*, Mar. 15, 2006, http://www.climatelaw.org/cases/by-country/international-tribunals/unesco-waterton-glacier-peace-park-petition/us-government-oppose-world-heritage-action-climate-change/.
97. *Id.*
98. *See* Thorson, *supra* note 47.
99. UNESCO, *World Heritage-Working Group Meeting to Develop the Draft Policy Paper on Impacts of Climate Change on World Heritage Properties, 5–6 Feb. 2007*, http://whc.unesco.org/en/activities/471/ (last visited Sept. 3, 2016).
100. *Decisions Adopted at the 30th Session of the World Heritage Committee*, UNESCO World Heritage Committee, 30th Sess., at 8, UNESCO Doc. WHC-06/30.COM/19 (2006).
101. *Policy Document on the Impact of Climate Change on World Heritage Properties*, UNESCO World Heritage Committee, UNESCO Doc. WHC-07/16.GA/10 (2007), http://whc.unesco.org/uploads/activities/documents/activity-397-2.pdf.
102. *Id.* at 7.

In 2007, the World Heritage Centre stated that World Heritage properties "will be used wherever appropriate and possible as a means to raise awareness about climate change impacts on World Heritage, act as a catalyst in the international debate and obtain support for policies to mitigate climate change."[103] It further stated that climate change will be "considered in all aspects of nominating, managing, monitoring and reporting on the status of these properties."[104]

The World Heritage Centre has updated the Operational Guidelines for the Implementation of the World Heritage Convention to reflect the threats of climate change to World Heritage sites. It now provides that where a site could be in danger due to environmental pressures, such as climate change, the nomination of the site as in danger should "[l]ist and summarise major sources of environmental deterioration affecting building fabric, flora and fauna."[105]

A.   Environmental Protection and Biodiversity Conservation Act

The EPBC Act is the key Australian legislation that governs World Heritage, Ramsar wetlands, nationally listed threatened species, commonwealth areas, and other "matters of national environmental significance." Its objectives include:

- promotion of "a co-operative approach to the protection and management of the environment involving governments, the community, landholders and indigenous peoples";[106]

- "co-operative implementation of Australia's international environmental responsibilities";[107] and

- "a partnership approach to environmental protection and biodiversity conservation."[108]

Australia's federal political system requires cooperation between the federal government and state governments on a range of matters, including the management of matters of national environmental significance.

---

103. *Id.* at 9.
104. *Id.*
105. World Heritage Centre, Operational Guidelines for the Implementation of the World Heritage Convention 92 (2015), http://whc.unesco.org/en/guidelines.
106. Environment Protection and Biodiversity Conservation Act 1999 (Cth), §3(1)(d).
107. *Id.* §3(1)(e).
108. *Id.* §3(1)(g).

The EPBC Act applies to any "action" that has, will have, or is "likely to have" a "significant impact" on a matter of national environmental significance, which includes the world heritage values of World Heritage sites such as the Great Barrier Reef.[109] Some of these actions may fall within the ambit of the GBRMPA, which provides a regulatory framework including offenses for certain activities and legislative instruments (e.g., zoning plans). Section 322(2) of the EPBC Act provides that:

> (2) The Commonwealth and each Commonwealth agency must take all reasonable steps to ensure it exercises its powers and performs its functions in relation to the property in a way that is not inconsistent with:
>
> (a) the World Heritage Convention; and
>
> (b) the Australian World Heritage management principles; and
>
> (c) if the property is on the World Heritage List and a plan for managing the property has been prepared as described in section 321—that plan.

Section 137 of the EPBC Act contains the minister's obligation to act not inconsistently with the World Heritage Convention. It provides:

> In deciding whether or not to approve, for the purposes of section 12 or 15A, the taking of an action and what conditions to attach to such an approval, the Minister must not act inconsistently with:
>
> (a) Australia's obligations under the World Heritage Convention; or
>
> (b) the Australian World Heritage management principles; or
>
> (c) a plan that has been prepared for the management of a declared World Heritage property under section 316 or as described in section 321.

Section 322(2) gives effect to the World Heritage Convention within Australia, and provides a basis for enforcement of the country's obligations. The next three subparts will consider the Carmichael coal mine, and the question of whether approval of this coal mine violates Australia's World Heritage commitments as recognized in the EPBC Act.

B.   Adani's Carmichael Coal Mine

Adani Mining, a subsidiary company of the Indian Adani Group, proposes to operate a thermal coal mine in the north of the Galilee Basin in Central

---

109. *Id.* §12-15A. *See also* Chris McGrath, *Avoid the Legal Pitfalls in the EPBC Act by Understanding Its Key Concepts*, 3 Nat'l Envtl. L. Rev. 32 (2005).

Queensland. Adani proposes to produce 60 million tons of coal per year[110] and 2.3 billion tons over the next 60 years from the Carmichael coal mine.[111] The project represents a $16.5 billion investment. If it proceeds, the coal mine will be the largest in Australia and one of the largest in the world. The extracted coal will be transported by a new 189 km rail line, and then by ship from port facilities at Hay Point and Abbot Point, to be exported primarily to India.

It is estimated that the Adani project would emit 4.6 billion tons of CO_2 during its lifetime. The CO_2 emissions would be "approximately 0.53–0.56% of the carbon budget that remains after 2015 to have a likely chance of not exceeding 2 degrees warming."[112] Adani has struggled to secure funding for the project. News reports have stated that Commonwealth Bank, National Australia Bank (NAB), and the Australia and New Zealand Banking Group Limited (ANZ) have refused to fund it, and that Westpac is also hesitant.[113]

In 2014, the coordinator-general released a report on the environmental impact of the Adani project. The report concluded that because the Great Barrier Reef World Heritage Area is 320 km upstream from the project, it was unlikely to have "any direct impacts" on the reef, but did note that polluted water could end up in the Great Barrier Reef.[114]

Environment Minister Greg Hunt granted initial approval to the mine in July 2014. The initial approval was successfully challenged on the basis that Hunt had failed to comply with the requirements of the EPBC Act by not considering the impact on threatened species, the yakka skink, and the ornamental snake.[115] Re-approval was granted by the federal minister in October 2015.[116]

---

110. Queensland Department of State Development, *Carmichael Coal Mine and Rail Project*, http://www.statedevelopment.qld.gov.au/assessments-and-approvals/carmichael-coal-mine-and-rail-project.html (last visited Aug. 23, 2016).

111. CHRIS TAYLOR & MALTE MEINSHAUSEN, JOINT REPORT TO THE LAND COURT OF QUEENSLAND ON "CLIMATE CHANGE—EMISSIONS" (2014), http://envlaw.com.au/wp-content/uploads/carmichael14.pdf.

112. *Id.*

113. Josh Taylor, *Adani Coal Mine Still Faces Two Big Legal Hurdles*, CRIKEY, Apr. 4, 2016, http://www.crikey.com.au/2016/04/04/adani-coal-mine-still-faces-two-big-legal-hurdles/.

114. QUEENSLAND GOVERNMENT AND ADVISIAN, ABBOT POINT GROWTH GATEWAY PROJECT: ENVIRONMENTAL IMPACT STATEMENT, VOLUME 1—EXECUTIVE SUMMARY (2015), http://www.coordinatorgeneral.qld.gov.au/resources/project/abbot-point-apx/abbot-pt-eis-vol-01-exec-summary.pdf.

115. Mackay Conservation Group v. Commonwealth of Australia & Adani Mining (FCA), https://www.comcourts.gov.au/file/Federal/P/NSD33/2015/3715277/event/28181487/document/607760.

116. The mine is also subject to a legal challenge by indigenous landholders. *See* Adani Mining Pty Ltd. & Another v. Adrian Burragubba, Patrick Malone, and Irene White on Behalf of the Wangan and Jagalingou People [2015] NNTTA 16.

The federal government has responded to legal challenges by developing draft legislation to stop so-called "green lawfare."[117] The bill seeks to amend §487 of the EPBC Act by removing the ability for public interest litigants such as conservation groups to challenge approvals in court. The bill has passed the lower house and is still before the Senate.[118] It is unclear whether the present government will approve the bill. The Australian and Queensland governments have previously demonstrated vigorous opposition to legal challenges to their approvals of coal mines likely to impact the Great Barrier Reef.[119]

C.   Legal Challenge Against the Carmichael Coal Mine to Promote Climate Justice

Environment Minister Greg Hunt re-approved the Adani coal mine project in 2015, but he did not consider the impact that the burning of coal exported from the mine would have on the Great Barrier Reef on the basis that these consequences were not sufficiently "direct." National contributions to GHG emissions under the UNFCCC process are calculated according to whether the country burns the fossil fuels, not on the basis of which country exports them.

However, ACF, represented by Environmental Defenders Office Qld, sought the federal court's review of the legality of Environment Minister Greg Hunt's re-approval of the Adani Carmichael coal mine project in Queensland.[120] The challenge was launched in November 2015. The ACF case is the first climate case to consider the relationship between federal approvals of fossil fuel projects and the World Heritage Convention. If the challenge had been successful, it would have required the federal government to consider the impact of fossil fuel exports on World Heritage listed sites.

The case concerned whether the minister correctly applied the law when considering the impacts of the Adani project on the Great Barrier Reef World Heritage Site. Australia is bound by the World Heritage Convention and, according to the EPBC Act, the minister must not act inconsistently with those responsibilities. The court hearing occurred in May 2016 and a decision was provided in August 2016 (see subpart D).

---

117. Josh Taylor, *Call in the Green Army! Threat of "Green Lawfare" Takes Down . . . Wait . . . Only Two Projects?*, Crikey, Aug. 19, 2015, http://www.crikey.com.au/2015/08/19/call-in-the-green-army-threat-of-green-lawfare-takes-down-wait-only-two-projects/.
118. *Id.*
119. *See* Chris McGrath, *Greenhouse Emissions Case Update*, 3 Nat'l Envtl. L. Rev. 19 (2005).
120. EDO Qld., *Case Summary: Adani Carmichael Federal Court Challenge*, http://www.edoqld.org.au/carmichael-coal-mine-federal-court-challenge/ (last visited Sept. 3, 2016).

The challenge also had other grounds. Two of these grounds related to the characterization of emissions from the coal mine, and the other ground is whether the minister failed to adequately consider the impact of the coal mine on the black-throated finch. The focus of this analysis is whether the minister took all reasonable steps to ensure that he exercised his powers and performed his functions regarding the Great Barrier Reef in relation to the coal mine approval that is not inconsistent with the World Heritage Convention.

In an originating application lodged with the federal court, Greg Hunt stated that it was "not possible to draw robust conclusions on the likely contribution of [the Adani mine] to a specific increase in global temperature." Hunt found that it is too "difficult to identify the necessary relationship between the taking of the action" and damage to the Great Barrier Reef. The minister has given some consideration to the impact of the emissions on the Great Barrier Reef, but ACF argued that he had not given appropriate weight to the impacts.[121]

As discussed above, Australia must act "to the utmost of its resources" to ensure the identification, protection, conservation, presentation, and transmission of the Great Barrier Reef to future generations under Article 4 of the World Heritage Convention. ACF claimed that the minister's decision to approve the mine was inconsistent with this obligation, relying on a literal construction of that obligation.[122] ACF also claimed that the decision was inconsistent with the World Heritage Management Principles, particularly that the identification, protection, conservation, presentation, and transmission to future generations must be the "primary purpose" of the management of the Great Barrier Reef World Heritage Area.[123]

Climate change has been identified as the greatest long-term threat to the Great Barrier Reef, particularly as mass coral bleaching events become increasingly common. In this context, the development of the Adani coal mine, which would result in emissions amounting to approximately 0.53–0.56% of the remaining carbon budget, is inconsistent with Article 4. The protection and conservation of the Great Barrier Reef's World Heritage values will be compromised if the Adani coal mine proceeds.

ACF did not rely on Article 5(d) of the World Heritage Convention, which requires Australia to take the appropriate legal and administrative measures necessary for the protection, conservation, and rehabilitation of the Great

---

121. Thom Mitchell, *Explainer: Adani Big Coal Case Could Make It Harder to Get Mines Approved*, NEW MATILDA, May 3, 2016, https://newmatilda.com/2016/05/03/adani-case-coal-mines-approved/.
122. Australian Conservation Foundation v. Minister for the Environment (2016) FCA 1042, para. 65.
123. *Id.*

Barrier Reef. ACF also did not cite Article 6(1), which provides that the international community has a duty to cooperate to protect the cultural and natural heritage of World Heritage sites. Australia holds this duty jointly with other States Parties to the World Heritage Convention. Although it could have been argued that Australia is obliged to engage in international cooperation to address climate change, it is possible that Australia cannot breach this obligation as an individual State because it is held jointly. However, the EPBC Act only requires that the decision not be "inconsistent" with Australia's obligations under the World Heritage Convention, which is distinct from the question whether Australia is in breach of Article 6(1).

Article 6(3) provides that Australia "undertakes not to take any deliberate measures which might damage directly or indirectly" the World Heritage sites situated in the territory of other States Parties, which would include other sites threatened by climate change. This article was not relied on in the case, but it is possible that the court could have found that the minister's decision directly and indirectly threatens the World Heritage sites situated in the territory of other States. If so, then this determination would be another ground to conclude that the decision is inconsistent with Australia's obligations under the World Heritage Convention.

D.   The Federal Court's Decision

On August 29, 2016, Judge Griffiths delivered his judgment in the matter, dismissing ACF's application for judicial review of the minister's decision. Judge Griffiths considered a number of issues, and in relation to arguments concerning World Heritage, he found that the issue of compliance with s 137 is justiciable.[124] However, he concluded that ACF had failed to establish any breach of the statutory obligation imposed by s 137. Judge Griffiths accepted that the World Heritage Convention imposes obligations on Australia.[125] In his interpretation of Article 4, Judge Griffiths stated that in accordance with Article 31 of the Vienna Convention on the Laws of Treaties 1969,[126] it is appropriate to have regard for the whole of the text of the treaty.

Judge Griffiths noted that the chapeau to Article 5 indicates that the obligations of a State Party to take appropriate measures to protect its cultural and natural heritage is qualified by the words: "each State Party to this Convention shall endeavor, in so far as possible, and as appropriate for each country . . ." to do the matters specified. He further noted that the reference in

---

124. *Id.* para. 205.
125. *Id.* para. 188.
126. Vienna Convention on the Law of Treaties, 23 May 1969, 1155 U.N.T.S. 331 [VCLT].

Article 5(d) to "appropriate" measures necessarily indicates the non-absolute nature of the obligation. On this basis, Judge Griffiths found that Articles 4 and 5 provide "considerable latitude to State Parties as to the precise action they may take to implement their 'obligations' under the relevant provisions" of the World Heritage Convention.[127]

However, there are inadequacies in the approach taken by Judge Griffiths. While Article 4 is qualified by the subjective language "to the utmost of its resources," Judge Griffiths did not offer any interpretation of the meaning of these specific words. Article 31(1) of the Vienna Convention on the Law of Treaties states that "A treaty shall be interpreted in good faith in accordance with the ordinary meaning to be given to the terms of the treaty in their context and in the light of its object and purpose." Judge Griffiths did not interpret the terms of Article 4 according to its ordinary meaning because he did not consider the specific words adopted in Article 4. Furthermore, Judge Griffiths gave no consideration to the object and purpose of the World Heritage Convention, despite this also being a critical component in treaty interpretation that is provided for in Article 31 of the Vienna Convention on the Law of Treaties. It is reasonable to conclude that if Judge Griffiths had considered the specific wording of Article 4 in light of the object and purpose of the World Heritage Convention, the discretionary element of the obligation would have been given much less weight.

Furthermore, Article 31(1) of the Vienna Convention requires treaties to be interpreted in good faith, and Australia must exercise its discretion under Article 4 of the World Heritage Convention in good faith. Judge Griffiths did not consider the role of good faith in his decision, neither in the context of treaty interpretation nor in Australia's fulfilment of the obligation held under Article 4.

In relation to emissions that would be created through the burning of the coal, ACF had argued that the minister had only considered Scope 1 and 2 emissions, rather than the separate issue of combustion emissions. There was no specific reference to combustion emissions in paragraphs 168 to 171 of the statement of reasons, which addresses the requirements of s 137. Judge Griffiths found that the fact that the minister did not refer to "combustion emissions" in the statement of reasons "does not mean that the minister did not turn his mind to combustion emissions in concluding that the approval would not be inconsistent" with the World Heritage Convention.[128] Judge Griffiths considered that it was plain that the minister had given consid-

---

127. *Australia Conservation Found.*, (2016) FCA 1042, para. 199.
128. *Id.* para. 204.

eration to greenhouse gas emissions resulting from combustion emissions and "made an express finding that the proposed action would not have an unacceptable impact on the world heritage values of the Reef."[129] Paragraph 48 of the statement of reasons stated that "after giving consideration to the greenhouse gas emissions from mining operations and from the burning of the mined coal, I found that the proposed action would not have an unacceptable impact on the world heritage values of the Great Barrier Reef World Heritage Area."[130]

The minister's statement of reasons provided that a determination of the combustion emissions of the project would be "speculative" on the basis that the GHG emissions of the project would be managed and mitigated through national and international emissions control frameworks in Australia and internationally. The minister's approach was accepted by Judge Griffiths, who stated that "I accept the Minister's submission that these matters reinforced his conclusion that the proposed action would have no relevant impact on the Reef."[131]

However, in making this finding, Judge Griffiths did not consider the decision in a different Australian climate case, *Gray v. Minister for Planning*,[132] under the Environmental Planning and Assessment Act 1979 (NSW). In this case, the applicant, Gray, argued that because the coal mining company did not include an assessment of the impacts of burning the coal (Scope 3 emissions) on the environment, the environmental assessment failed to comply with the requirement to include a "detailed greenhouse gas assessment." In response, the coal mining company argued that an environmental assessment of Scope 3 emissions was not required for activities of third parties, and that such a requirement is foreign to planning law.

Judge Pain found in favor of the applicant, concluding that the precautionary principle required that the cumulative impacts of the mine, including downstream emissions and the impact of those emissions, must be assessed.[133] This decision lends support to the view that the downstream emissions from the Carmichael coal mine must be considered, particularly given the potential impact on the Great Barrier Reef. It may be that on appeal the approach

---

129. *Id.* para. 204.
130. *Id.* para. 58.
131. *Id.* para. 165.
132. Gray v. The Minister for Planning, Director-General of the Department of Planning and Centennial Hunter Pty Ltd. (2006) NSWLEC 720. *See also* Anna Rose, *Gray v Minister for Planning: The Rising Tide of Climate Change Litigation in Australia*, 29 Syd. L. Rev. 725 (2007).
133. Gray v. The Minister for Planning, Director-General of the Department of Planning and Centennial Hunter Pty Ltd. (2006) NSWLEC 720, at 122, 131, 126.

taken by the minister will be found to be inadequate for the purposes of s 137.

ACF has appealed the decision.[134] Despite the lack of success for ACF in the federal court decision, the World Heritage Convention provides an important tool in Australia for efforts to promote climate justice for future generations. Section 137 provides a valid basis to challenge a decision made by the minister where World Heritage obligations are relevant. Similar cases might also be brought in other jurisdictions where the World Heritage Convention attracts enforceability within national courts.

Conclusion

The threats that climate change poses to World Heritage sites such as the Great Barrier Reef will undermine the ability of future generations to enjoy the values of these sites. States Parties in which these sites are situated have limited ability to take measures to adapt their sites to the impacts of climate change. Mitigation of GHG emissions is the most important action that States can take to protect and conserve these sites for future generations.

Australia's decision to approve a huge coal mine in Queensland has been challenged on the basis that it is inconsistent with the legal obligations that Australia holds under international law. Australia is bound by a number of obligations under the World Heritage Convention, which have previously been confirmed as substantive commitments by the High Court of Australia. While the application for judicial review was dismissed by Judge Griffiths, the matter may be overturned on appeal. The interpretation of Article 4 in the decision failed to consider the ordinary meaning of the article, the object and purpose of the World Heritage Convention, or the need for good faith. Furthermore, the analysis in the decision regarding the downstream or combustion emissions that will be caused by the burning of the coal may be overly restrictive.

Climate change promises to be the greatest threat to future generations. The international community has shown a spirit of cooperation in promoting the protection of World Heritage sites around the world for the benefit of future generations. Australia should be held to this spirit of cooperation and required to consider the total climate change impacts of the Adani coal mine. If properly considered by the minister, a project of such damaging magnitude on the rights of future generations should be rejected.

---

134. Joshua Robertson, *Adani Carmichael coalmine faces new legal challenge from conservation foundation*, THE GUARDIAN, Sept. 19, 2016, https://www.theguardian.com/business/2016/sep/19/adani-carmichael-coalmine-faces-new-legal-challenge-from-conservation-foundation.

Chapter 23

Climate Justice Litigation in the Inter-American Human Rights System to Protect Indigenous Peoples in Mexico

Verónica de la Rosa Jaimes*

Introduction

Government initiatives to address climate change have tended to regard climate change exclusively as an environmental or economic problem.[1] However,

* *The author would like to thank Justin Pon, law student at Dalhousie University, for his excellent research assistance; and Claribel Gonzalez, Esq. for her thorough analysis of Mexico's General Climate Change Law and the Climate Change Fund.*

1.   The impacts of global climate change are readily observed, ranging from rising global temperatures to extreme weather events such as floods, droughts, and storms, as well as food shortages, spread of diseases, loss of housing and shelter, and cultural extinction. Because of these effects, climate change has been acknowledged as one of the greatest threats to human development, making those with the least resources most vulnerable. *See* Kevin Watkins, Human development Report 2007/2008 (United Nations Development Programme 2007), http://hdr.undp.org/sites/default/files/reports/268/hdr_20072008_en_complete.pdf; Christopher B. Field et al., *Summary for Policymakers, in* Climate Change 2014: Impacts, Adaptation, and Vulnerability. Contribution of Working Group II to the Fifth Assessment Report of the Intergovernmental Panel on Climate Change

the link between climate change and human rights has been acknowledged recently, as climate change impacts are in some cases so severe that they violate the human rights of individuals and communities. In fact, the United Nations has recognized the connection between human rights and climate change. United Nations Human Rights Council (UNHRC) Resolutions 18/22[2] and 26/27[3] acknowledge that Parties need to respect human rights in climate change-related actions. At a general level, the United Nations Environment Programme (UNEP) in its publication "Climate Change and Human Rights" states that "[t]he core international human rights treaties do not recognize a freestanding right to a clean environment. However, it is generally understood that inadequate environmental conditions can undermine the effective enjoyment of other enumerated rights, such as the rights to life, health, water, and food."[4]

Indigenous communities, living mostly under conditions of inequality and disadvantage, are especially vulnerable to the impacts of current climate variability.[5] Climate change "poses a serious threat to indigenous peoples, who often live in marginal lands and fragile ecosystems that are particularly sensitive to alterations in the physical environment,"[6] and therefore can threaten indigenous rights to self-determination.[7]

In 2007, the Intergovernmental Panel on Climate Change (IPCC) noted that litigation was "likely to be used increasingly as countries and citizens become dissatisfied with the pace of decision making on climate change."[8] This tendency has increased with time. Generally, three types of lawsuits have been used by indigenous communities challenging entities responsible for impacts linked to climate change: "(1) law suits based on procedural rights; (2) law suits based on common law legal principles; and (3) law suits

---

(2014), http://ipcc-wg2.gov/AR5/images/uploads/IPCC_WG2AR5_SPM_Approved.pdf [hereinafter WG II FIFTH ASSESSMENT REPORT ON CLIMATE CHANGE 2014].

2.   United Nations Human Rights Council Res. 18/22, Human Rights and Climate Change, 18th Sess., U.N. Doc. A/HRC/RES/18/22 (2011).

3.   United Nations Human Rights Council Res. 26/27, Human Rights and Climate Change, 26th Sess., U.N. Doc. A/HRC/RES/26/27 (2014).

4.   UNEP & COLUMBIA LAW SCHOOL, CLIMATE CHANGE AND HUMAN RIGHTS 12 (2015), http://apps. unep.org/publications/index.php?option=com_pub&task=download&file=011917_en [hereinafter UNEP Report].

5.   See JAMES ANAYA, INDIGENOUS PEOPLES IN INTERNATIONAL LAW (2d ed. 2004); FEDERICO LENZERINI, REPARATIONS FOR INDIGENOUS PEOPLES (2008).

6.   UNEP Report, supra note 4, at 28.

7.   UNITED NATIONS OFFICE OF THE HIGH COMMISSIONER FOR HUMAN RIGHTS, UNDERSTANDING HUMAN RIGHTS AND CLIMATE CHANGE 14 (2015), http://www.ohchr.org/Documents/Issues/ClimateChange/COP21.pdf.

8.   IPCC, CLIMATE CHANGE 2007: SYNTHESIS REPORT 13.4.3 (2007), https://www.ipcc.ch/pdf/assessment-report/ar4/syr/ar4_syr.pdf.

based on public international law."[9] Although numerous petitions have been filed in the Inter-American system for violations of land titles and resources, litigation alleging human rights violations from climate change impacts has been used as a resource at a regional level only recently, and the success of this new strategy is not yet clear.[10]

This chapter addresses climate change impacts on the human rights of Mexican indigenous peoples and the use of Inter-American human rights instruments to support arguments to require governments to take action in response to climate change. It reviews jurisprudence of the Inter-American Court of Human Rights and the Inter-American Commission on Human Rights. Part I of this chapter considers the interrelation between climate change impacts on the human rights of Mexican indigenous peoples. Part II briefly examines Mexican climate change legislation. Part III reviews the evolution of the Inter-American human rights system focusing on its supervisory bodies: the Inter-American Commission on Human Rights (IACHR) and the Inter-American Court of Human Rights (IACtHR).

Part IV examines the extent to which the Inter-American supervisory bodies have found governmental duties to protect indigenous communities from environmental damage. The chapter focuses on those human rights that have been recently interpreted as protecting a right to life and a right to a healthy environment. These rights include the right to enjoy the benefits of culture, the right to preservation of health, and the right to use and enjoyment of property. Part V analyzes the Athabaskan Petition, which has been presented to the IACHR with an approach to climate change as an example of creative lawyering and comprehensive human rights protection. The chapter concludes with some reflections on the adequacy of the Inter-American system to address the interaction of climate change, indigenous peoples, and human rights violations.

I.   Climate Change Impacts on Mexican Indigenous Peoples

Mexico is the 12th largest greenhouse gas (GHG) emitter in the world[11] and it is already seeing substantial changes in its climate such as more droughts,

---

9.   Randall S. Abate & Elizabeth Ann Kronk Warner, *Commonality Among Unique Indigenous Communities: An Introduction to Climate Change and Its Impacts on Indigenous Peoples, in* Climate Change and Indigenous Peoples: The Search for Legal Remedies 15 (Randall S. Abate & Elizabeth Ann Kronk Warner eds., 2013) [hereinafter *Commonality Among Unique Indigenous Communities*].

10.   For a detailed discussion, see Verónica de la Rosa Jaimes, *The Arctic Athabaskan Petition: Where Accelerated Arctic Warming Meets Human Rights*, 45 Cal. W. Int'l L.J. 213 (2015).

11.   Working Group I of the IPCC Fifth Assessment Report notes that the most significant driver of climate change is the increase in the atmospheric concentration of carbon dioxide since 1750 and that human

heavier rain, and more extreme climate.[12] There is high agreement that climate change over the 21st century is projected to reduce renewable surface water and groundwater resources significantly in dry subtropical regions like Mexico.[13] In particular, the Office of the United Nations High Commissioner for Human Rights (OHCHR) has recognized that climate change "poses a serious threat to indigenous peoples, who often live in marginal lands and fragile ecosystems which are particularly sensitive to alterations in the physical environment."[14]

This is significant because 17% of Mexican people identify as indigenous,[15] and speak 62 different languages.[16] The percentage of identified Mexican indigenous peoples has even been criticized as being under representative of the total population.[17] These difficulties range from the necessity for people to self-identify in the government census,[18] to "migratory flows, shifting notions of indigenous identity, and deficiencies in government surveying methods [making] estimating the indigenous population of Central America and southern Mexico a complicated task."[19] The majority of the Mexican indigenous population is concentrated in the southern and south-central region of Mexico in eight of Mexico's 31 states—the three largest populations being Oaxaca, Chiapas, and Veracruz.[20] These coastal regions are prone to tropical hurricanes and uniformly high temperatures.[21] The indigenous

influence is evident in the warming of the atmosphere, global rising sea levels, and changes in some climate extremes; *see* Thomas F. Stocker et al., *Summary for Policymakers, in* CLIMATE CHANGE 2013: THE PHYSICAL SCIENCE BASIS. CONTRIBUTION OF WORKING GROUP I TO THE FIFTH ASSESSMENT REPORT OF THE INTERGOVERNMENTAL PANEL ON CLIMATE CHANGE (2013), http://www.ipcc.ch/pdf/assessment-report/ar5/wg1/WG1AR5_SPM_FINAL.pdf.

12. *See* World Bank, *Mexico Seeks to Adapt to Climate Change and Mitigate its Effects*, http://www.world-bank.org/en/results/2013/04/17/mexico-seeks-to-adapt-to-climate-change-and-mitigate-its-effects (last visited Aug. 2, 2016).

13. FOOD AND AGRICULTURE ORGANIZATION OF THE UNITED NATIONS, CLIMATE CHANGE AND FOOD SECURITY: RISKS AND RESPONSES 7 (2016), http://www.fao.org/3/a-i5188e.pdf.

14. UNEP Report, *supra* note 4, at 28.

15. PANORAMA SOCIODEMOGRÁFICO DE MÉXICO 2015, INEGI, http://fcps.uaq.mx/descargas/ineg_en-cuesta_intercensal_2015/Panorama%20Sociodemogr%C3%A1fico%202015.pdf (last visited Sept. 17, 2016).

16. MINORITY RIGHTS GROUP INTERNATIONAL, WORLD DIRECTORY OF MINORITIES AND INDIGENOUS PEOPLES—MEXICO: INDIGENOUS PEOPLES (2008), http://www.refworld.org/docid/49749ce423.html [hereinafter WORLD DIRECTORY OF MINORITIES].

17. *Id.*

18. *Id.*

19. CENTER FOR THE SUPPORT OF NATIVE LANDS AND NATIONAL GEOGRAPHIC, INDIGENOUS PEOPLES AND NATURAL ECOSYSTEMS IN CENTRAL AMERICA AND SOUTHERN MEXICO (2001), http://www.eli.org/research-report/indigenous-peoples-and-natural-ecosystems-central-america-and-southern-mexico.

20. *Id.*

21. World Meteorological Organization Programmes, *World Weather Information Service*, http://world-weather.wmo.int/en/home.html (last visited Aug. 23, 2016); U.S. Central Intelligence Agency, *The World Factbook*, https://www.cia.gov/library/publications/the-world-factbook/geos/mx.html (last visited Aug. 23, 2016).

communities in these areas have also retained local forms of self-governance to defend their culture and their livelihood.[22]

Working Group (WG) II Fifth Assessment Report on Climate Change 2014 defined vulnerability as "[t]he propensity or predisposition to be adversely affected . . . [which] encompasses a variety of concepts and elements including sensitivity or susceptibility to harm and lack of capacity to cope and adapt."[23] The report explains that "[p]eople who are socially, economically, culturally, politically, institutionally, or otherwise marginalized are especially vulnerable" to the impacts of climate change.[24] Globally, indigenous peoples "exist under conditions of severe disadvantage relative to others within the states constructed around them."[25] Therefore, their "cohesiveness as communities has been damaged or threatened, and the integrity of their cultures has been undermined."[26] In particular, because of contact with newly formed states constructed around them, "indigenous communities [have] suffered generations of abuse and subjugation."[27] As the vulnerability of a community increases, so do the potential consequences for something of value to be at risk such as life, health, property, or culture.[28]

WG II Fifth Assessment Report on Climate Change 2014 also notes that in Central and South America, there is a risk of decreased food production and food quality.[29] As Mexican indigenous peoples are dependent on agriculture for their livelihood,[30] they would have a greater exposure to extreme climate effects and general global climate change. In accordance with Article 2 of the Mexican Constitution, the government acknowledges that its society has its roots in indigenous identity, but they also form a discrete culture in the nation.[31] It recognizes that Mexican indigenous peoples have a right to self-determination in governing its social, economic, political, and cultural affairs,[32] but the state must also provide equal opportunities so that they may exercise their constitu-

---

22. See Rodolfo Stavenhagen, *Indigenous Movements and Politics in Mexico and Latin America, in* ABORIGINAL RIGHTS AND SELF-GOVERNMENT: THE CANADIAN AND MEXICAN EXPERIENCE IN NORTH AMERICAN PERSPECTIVE 72–98 (Curtis Cook & Juan D. Lindau eds., 2000).
23. WG II FIFTH ASSESSMENT REPORT ON CLIMATE CHANGE 2014, *supra* note 1, at 5.
24. *Id.* at 6.
25. ANAYA, *supra* note 5, at 4.
26. *Id.* at 3.
27. See *Commonality Among Unique Indigenous Communities, supra* note 9, at 15.
28. WG II FIFTH ASSESSMENT REPORT ON CLIMATE CHANGE 2014, *supra* note 1, at 6–7.
29. *Id.* at 24.
30. WORLD DIRECTORY OF MINORITIES, *supra* note 16.
31. Instituto de Investigaciones Juridicas, *Constitución Política de los Estados Unidos Mexicanos [Political Constitution of the United Mexican States]*, http://www.juridicas.unam.mx/legislacion/ordenamiento/constitucion-politica-de-los-estados-unidos-mexicanos (last visited Aug. 23, 2016).
32. *Id.*

tionally guaranteed rights.[33] Article 27 VII of the Mexican Constitution states that the law "protects the integrity of the lands of indigenous groups."[34]

In recognition of the unique relationship that governments have with indigenous communities, in 2007 the United Nations General Assembly adopted the United Nations Declaration on the Rights of Indigenous Peoples (UNDRIP) in a 143-4 vote, with Mexico voting in favor of adoption. UNDRIP addresses the rights of indigenous peoples and its purpose is to "[emphasize] the rights of indigenous peoples to maintain and strengthen their own institutions, cultures and traditions and to pursue their development in keeping with their own needs and aspirations."[35] It also explicitly acknowledges the disproportionate impact that climate change has on indigenous peoples and how the international community should strive to remedy this reality.[36] It imposes a positive obligation on the state to enable indigenous peoples to exercise their right to the environment and to refrain from taking actions that would interfere with that right.[37] Although this declaration is not legally binding, it reflects the normative principles that the international community is aspiring to achieve.

Indigenous communities have been said to "experience a double form of discrimination—both because of their low economic standing and poor levels of formal education, and also on grounds of language, dress and other cultural manifestations."[38] Moreover, "while other environmental justice communities typically come to gather as informal groups whose legal rights flow from environmental laws, indigenous nations' legal rights flow as an initial matter from their sovereignty."[39] UNDRIP also signals the gradual acceptance by the international community of the link between indigenous peoples' human rights and its connection to the environment. It acknowledges that "control by indigenous peoples over developments affecting them and their lands, territories and resources will enable them to maintain and strengthen their institutions, cultures and traditions."[40] That is to say that

---

33. *Id.*
34. *Id.*
35. United Nations Permanent Forum on Indigenous Issues, Frequently Asked Questions: Declaration on the Rights of Indigenous Peoples 1 (n.d.), http://www.un.org/esa/socdev/unpfii/documents/FAQsindigenousdeclaration.pdf.
36. *See* United Nations, United Nations Declaration on the Rights of Indigenous Peoples (2008), http://www.un.org/esa/socdev/unpfii/documents/DRIPS_en.pdf [hereinafter UNDRIP].
37. Article 29 of UNDRIP: "1. Indigenous peoples have the right to the conservation and protection of the environment and the productive capacity of their lands or territories and resources. States shall establish and implement assistance programmes for indigenous peoples for such conservation and protection, without discrimination."
38. World Directory of Minorities, *supra* note 16.
39. Elizabeth Ann Kronk Warner & Randall S. Abate, *International and Domestic Law Dimensions of Climate Justice for Arctic Indigenous Peoples*, 43 Ottawa L. Rev. 113, 124 (2013).
40. UNDRIP, *supra* note 36, at Annex.

their connection to the environment embodies their human rights to culture, health, and property.

While Mexican indigenous rights have been enshrined in the Mexican constitution, in practice, "much remains to be done."[41] This can partially be attributed to the fact that each individual Mexican state is able to establish its own constitution to further limit rights of local indigenous populations resulting in varied and limited indigenous rights between states.[42] For example, indigenous peoples are traditionally highly dependent on the agricultural sector but have seen an eroding of their rights to their communal lands at the hands of the State.[43]

The international community and the Mexican government have recognized that climate change impacts threaten Mexican indigenous peoples' ability to exercise their human rights.[44] Today more than ever, Mexican indigenous peoples have recourse in claiming that there has been a violation of their rights from climate change, as "the engagement of non-state actors in the development of the climate regime, and other multilateral environmental regimes, is growing although non-state actors have limited or no formal role in the negotiations."[45] The international community has recognized that more legal protections are needed to address climate change impacts on indigenous peoples, but some steps have been taken to address this concern through instruments such as the Paris Agreement and various United Nations resolutions. The Mexican government has created plans and legislation that attempt to address climate change and human rights, but the effectiveness of these efforts warrant further discussion.

II.   Mexican Climate Change Legislation and Policies

Mexico has had polarizing opinions regarding its attempts to address the effects of climate change. Some have lauded the government's efforts,[46] such

---

41. U.N. Human Rights Office of the High Commissioner, *Advancing Indigenous Peoples' Rights in Mexico*, http://www.ohchr.org/EN/NewsEvents/Pages/IndigenousPeoplesRightsInMexico.aspx (last visited Aug. 23, 2016).

42. *Id.*

43. World Directory of Minorities, *supra* note 16.

44. *Report of the Conference of the Parties on Its Twenty-first Session, Held in Paris From 30 November to 13 December 2015—Addendum, Part Two: Action Taken by the Conference of the Parties at Its Twenty-first Session, Decisions Adopted by the Conference of the Parties*, UNFCCC, 21st Sess., Decision 11/CP.21, at 25, U.N. Doc. FCCC/CP/2015/10/Add.1 (2016), http://unfccc.int/resource/docs/2015/cop21/eng/10a02.pdf.

45. Heike Schroeder, *Agency in International Climate Negotiations: The Case of Indigenous Peoples and Avoided Deforestation*, *in* 10 Int'l Envtl. Agreements: Pol., L. & Econ. 4, 324 (2010).

46. Anne-Marie O'Connor, *Mexico City Drastically Reduced Air Pollutants Since 1990s*, Wash. Post, Apr. 1, 2010, http://www.washingtonpost.com/wp-dyn/content/article/2010/03/31/AR2010033103614.

as being the first developing country to submit an intended nationally determined contribution (INDC).[47] Others have been considerably more critical claiming that "current initiatives fall short."[48] The most significant measure that the government has implemented was the passing of Mexico's General Law on Climate Change (GLCC).[49] This law, together with Mexico's National Climate Change Strategy (NCCS),[50] provides a framework for state-level governments to create policies, programs, and regulations.

The purpose of this law is to "guarantee the right to a healthy environment."[51] It defines the powers of the government at the federal, state, and municipal levels to address the effects of climate change through climate change mitigation, adaptation, research, and education.[52] In the same vein, the NCCS outlines the strategy to address the negative effects of climate change and to transition to a sustainable low carbon economy.[53]

Under Article 7 of the GLCC, the majority of the powers assigned to the federal government are setting national climate change strategy and policy; public consultation; establishment, regulation, and implementation of adaptation and mitigation actions; and the creation and funding of different entities such as the Climate Change Fund.[54] The Climate Change Fund provides resources for funding initiatives that address the effects of climate change under Article 80 of the GLCC. This fund was to mobilize $10 billion funded through both national and international donors[55] and prioritizes attention to the most vulnerable communities of Mexico.[56] While well intentioned, it has only allocated $78,000 for administrative operations and has yet to fund any projects that address climate change.[57]

html?sid=ST2010033103622.

47. Timmons Roberts & Guy Edwards, *Showing a New Way Forward? Implications of Mexico's Pledge for Global Climate Action*, Brookings, Mar. 30, 2015, http://www.brookings.edu/blogs/planetpolicy/posts/2015/03/30-mexico-pledge-global-climate-action-roberts-edwards.

48. Victoria Burnett, *As Mexico Addresses Climate Change, Critics Point to Shortcomings*, N.Y. Times, Nov. 29, 2014, http://www.nytimes.com/2014/11/30/world/americas/as-mexico-addresses-climate-change-critics-point-to-shortcomings-.html.

49. Ley General de Cambio Climático [LGCC] [General Law on Climate Change], Diario Oficial de la Federación [DO] el 6 de junio de 2012 (Mex.) [hereinafter GLCC].

50. Estrategia Nacional de Cambio Climático [National Climate Change Strategy], Diario Oficial de la Federación [DO] el 31 de mayo de 2013 (Mex.) [hereinafter NCCS].

51. GLCC, *supra* note 49, at art. 2.

52. *Id.*

53. NCCS, *supra* note 50, at pmbl.

54. GLCC, *supra* note 49.

55. Frank Biermann, Philipp Pattberg & Fariborz Zelli, Global Climate Governance Beyond 2012, at 121 (2010).

56. GLCC, *supra* note 49, at art. 82 I.

57. Emilio Godoy, *Mexico's Climate Change Law—More Than Just Empty Words?*, Inter Press Service News Agency, Apr. 21, 2014, http://www.ipsnews.net/2014/04/mexicos-climate-change-law-just-empty-words/.

Another significant entity that was created through the GLCC is the National Institute of Ecology and Climate Change (INECC).The INECC focuses on mitigation actions and developing effective systems designed to best manage the effects of climate change.[58] Its mandate is to provide technical support and evaluations on adaptation and mitigation objectives as well as participating in the design of economic, fiscal, and financial and market-based tools in connection with national environmental and climate change polices for the sustainable use and conservation of natural resources.[59]

A more recent development is the submission of the Mexican government's INDC to the United Nations on March 30, 2015. With the conclusion of the United Nations Framework Convention on Climate Change (UNFCCC), each Member Nation outlined what specific steps it would take to mitigate climate change post-2020. Mexico's INDC is a two-pronged approach—adaptation and mitigation.[60] The adaptation actions include protection of communities from adverse impacts, and increasing the resilience of infrastructure and ecosystems.[61] Of particular importance to the Mexican indigenous communities is the plan to "strengthen the adaptive capacity of at least by 50 per cent the number of municipalities in the category of 'most vulnerable.'"[62] The mitigation actions are further broken down into unconditional and conditional actions. Mexico has committed to unconditionally reduce its GHGs and short lived climate pollutants emissions by 25% by 2030.[63] Accompanying that is a conditional action by which the above-mentioned reduction can be increased to 40% "subject to global agreement addressing important topics including international carbon price, carbon border adjustments, technical cooperation, access to low cost financial resources and technology transfer."[64] While the targets may sound ambitious, when measured against the Paris Agreement, Mexico's targets have been criticized as "not yet consistent with limiting warming below 2°C unless other countries make much deeper reductions and comparably greater effort."[65]

---

58. GLCC, *supra* note 49, at art. 15.
59. *Id*. at art. 22.
60. Mexico Gobierno de la República, Intended Nationally Determined Contribution (2015), http://www4.unfccc.int/submissions/INDC/Published%20Documents/Mexico/1/MEXICO%20INDC%2003.30.2015.pdf.
61. *Id*. at 3.
62. *Id*.
63. *Id*. at 2.
64. *Id*.
65. Climate Action Tracker, *Mexico*, http://climateactiontracker.org/countries/mexico.html (last visited Aug. 23, 2016).

Pursuant to Article 8 of the GLCC, the Mexican states have the responsibility to establish state-level policy consistent with policy set by the federal government.[66] Similarly, each state should develop climate change programs by promoting public consultation, fostering scholarship on climate change, and developing strategies to mitigate contributors to climate change.[67] The delegation of authority by the federal government to the state government level allows more flexibility to adapt to local conditions, but it has been noted that "of Mexico's 32 states, only 14 have drawn up a state plan on climate change, just seven have passed their own laws, and only 11 have measured their CO_2 emissions."[68]

While Mexico's government has created several bodies and passed legislation that addresses the effects of climate change, there is a substantial lack of action on measures that directly assist Mexico's most vulnerable—in particular, the indigenous communities—and the measures that are in place are seemingly limited in their effectiveness. Consequently, the Mexican indigenous communities must refer to regional fora, such as the Inter-American human rights system, for opportunities to assert their rights. Both the IACHR and IACtHR have issued recommendations and judgments that affirm the connection between the environment and the rights of indigenous communities.

III.   The Inter-American Human Rights System

In 1948, the adoption of the Charter of the Organization of American States (OAS) formally created the Organization.[69] The bodies created to protect and promote human rights were the IACHR and the IACtHR.[70] These supervisory bodies, through the enforcement of the American Declaration of the Rights and Duties of the Man (American Declaration) and the American Convention on Human Rights (American Convention), promote and protect human rights.

The Inter-American system of human rights was developed more than 65 years ago.[71] It was formally created with the adoption of the American Declaration just months before the Universal Declaration of Human Rights

---

66.   GLCC, *supra* note 49, at 8.
67.   *Id.*
68.   Godoy, *supra* note 57.
69.   Charter of the Organization of American States, 1948, 119 U.N.T.S. 3 (entered into force Dec. 13, 1951) [hereinafter Charter of the OAS].
70.   OAS, *Our History*, http://www.oas.org/en/about/our_history.asp (last visited Aug. 23, 2016).
71.   *Id.*

was adopted by the General Assembly of the United Nations.[72] The American Declaration was the first international instrument that gave context and validation to the claim of the universality of human rights.[73]

Twenty years later, on November 22, 1969, the American Convention was adopted in San José, Costa Rica.[74] Currently, 25 of the 35 OAS Member States have ratified it.[75] The American Convention affords treaty-level protection to the human rights previously included in the American Declaration.[76] The Additional Protocol to the American Convention on Human Rights in the Area of Economic, Social, and Cultural Rights ("Protocol of San Salvador"), which was adopted in San Salvador, El Salvador, in 1988 and entered into force in 1999, added an array of economic, social, and cultural rights to the American Convention.[77] To date, 16 of the 35 OAS Member States have ratified the Protocol of San Salvador.[78]

A.   Inter-American Commission on Human Rights

In 1959, the IACHR was created by the OAS with the function of serving as a consultative organ of the OAS in human rights protection matters.[79] To achieve its mission, the IACHR was assigned authority under the Charter of the OAS to analyze and monitor human rights in the Americas[80] as well

---

72. *See* OAS Inter-American Court of Human Rights, Basic Documents Pertaining to Human Rights in the Inter-American System 1, 6 (2003) (OEA/Ser.L./V/II.82 doc.6 rev.1), http://www.corteidh.or.cr/docs/libros/Basingl01.pdf. [hereinafter Basic Documents].

73. *See id.* at 6 ("[T]he introduction to the American Declaration states 'the essential rights of man are not derived from the fact that he is a national of a certain state, but are based upon attributes of his human personality.' The American States thus acknowledge that when the State legislates in this area, it is neither creating nor granting rights. Instead, it is recognizing rights that existed before the State was ever created and that flow from the very nature of the human person.").

74. OAS, American Convention on Human Rights, Nov. 22, 1969, O.A.S.T.S. No. 36, 1144 U.N.T.S. 123 [hereinafter American Convention].

75. OAS, American Convention on Human Rights "Pact of San Jose, Costa Rica" (B-32), Nov. 22, 1969, O.A.S.T.S. No. 36, 1144 U.N.T.S. 123, http://www.oas.org/dil/treaties_B-32_American_Convention_on_Human_Rights_sign.htm.

76. American Declaration of the Rights and Duties of Man, OEA/Ser.L./V.II.23, doc. 21 rev. 6 (1948), *reprinted in* Basic Documents Pertaining to Human Rights in the Inter-American System, OEA/Ser.L./V/II.82, doc.6 rev.1, at 17 (1992) [hereinafter American Declaration].

77. *See* San Salvador Protocol to the American Convention on Human Rights in the Area of Economic, Social, and Cultural Rights, O.A.S.T.S. No. 69, 28 I.L.M. 156 (Nov. 17, 1988), *reprinted in* Basic Documents Pertaining to Human Rights in the Inter-American System, OEA/Ser.L./V/II.82, doc.6 rev.1 (1992) [hereinafter Protocol of San Salvador].

78. OAS, *A-52: Additional Protocol to the American Convention on Human Rights in the Area of Economic, Social, and Cultural Rights "Protocol of San Salvador"* (Nov. 17, 1988), http://www.oas.org/juridico/english/sigs/a-52.html.

79. Charter of the OAS, *supra* note 69, at art. 106.

80. *See* David J. Padilla, *The Inter-American Commission on Human Rights of the Organization of American States: A Case Study*, 9 Am. U. Int'l L. & Pol'y 95, 96 (1993).

as "promot[ing] and protect[ing] human rights in OAS member states."[81] In 1965, the IACHR functions were expanded to include the power to issue recommendations on complaints or petitions from citizens alleging human rights violations.[82]

The IACHR was entrusted with a twofold role: "it retained its status as an organ of the OAS, thereby maintaining its powers to promote and protect human rights in the territories of all OAS member states; in addition, [it also became] a monitoring body of the American Convention."[83] The core task of the Commission is "to promote respect for and defense of human rights."[84] In the exercise of its mandate, visits *in loco* and country reports remain an important part of the IACHR's work; nevertheless, the consideration of individual petitions plays an increasing role in its activities in recent years.[85]

According to Article 44 of the American Convention, "[a]ny person or group of persons, or any non-governmental entity legally recognized in one or more member states of the [OAS], may lodge petitions with the Commission containing denunciations or complaints of violation of [the American Convention] by a State Party."[86] Filing a petition is only the first step towards an IACHR recommendation being issued.[87] In order for a petition to be admitted and then considered by the IACHR, the petition must comply with numerous procedural and substantive requirements such as meeting jurisdictional requirements and alleging enough facts to amount to a violation.[88]

B. Inter-American Court of Human Rights

The IACtHR was not established and organized until the American Convention entered into force in 1979. The IACtHR consists of seven judges, who may be nationals of any Member State of the OAS regardless of whether they

---

81. *See* Eugenio Matibag, *Inter-American Commission on Human Rights*, 2 Encyclopedia U.S.-Lat. Am. Rel. 479–80 (2012).
82. *See id.*
83. Cecilia Cristina Naddeo, *The Inter-American System of Human Rights: A Research Guide*, Hauser Global L. Sch. Program, N.Y.U. Sch. L. §3.1 (2010), http://www.nyulawglobal.org/globalex/Inter_American_human_rights.htm#_edn51.
84. American Convention, *supra* note 74, at art. 41.
85. Patrick Thornberry, Indigenous Peoples and Human Rights 272 (2002); *see also* Thomas Buergenthal, *The Inter-American System for the Protection of Human Rights*, *in* 2 Human Rights in International Law: Legal and Policy Issues 479–81 (Theodor Meron ed., 1986).
86. American Convention, *supra* note 74, at art. 44.
87. *See* OAS, *Inter-American Commission on Human Rights, Individual Petition System Portal*, http://www.oas.org/en/iachr/portal/ (last visited Sept. 2, 2016).
88. *Id.*

are Parties to the American Convention.[89] The IACtHR is an autonomous judicial institution whose objective is to apply and interpret the American Convention. To attain this objective, the Court has two functions: a judicial function[90] and an advisory function.[91]

As to the judicial function, only the Commission and the States Parties to the American Convention that have recognized the jurisdiction of the Court are authorized to submit a case regarding the interpretation or application of the American Convention for its decision, on condition that the procedure before the Commission has been exhausted.[92] As to the advisory function of the Court, any Member State of the Organization may consult the Court regarding the interpretation of the American Convention or other treaties concerning the protection of human rights in the American States.[93] The Court may also, at the request of any Member State of the Organization, issue an opinion concerning any of their domestic laws and the treaties concerning the protection of human rights in the American States.[94] As of 2016, 25 Members of the OAS have ratified the American Convention and 22, including Mexico, have recognized the jurisdiction of the IACtHR.[95]

As Mexico is a signatory to the American Declaration and the American Convention, it is bound by precedent set by the IACtHR regarding climate change and human rights. Accompanying case precedents are the many formal recommendations issued by the IACHR regarding the effects of environmental degradation on human rights.[96] The decisions of these two bodies can be used to determine on what grounds Mexican indigenous peoples can pursue claims for climate change impacts on the exercise of their human rights.

IV. Climate Change and Human Rights in the Inter-American System

To understand the relevance of the role that the Inter-American human rights system could play in climate change litigation, two topics must be

---

89. American Convention, *supra* note 74, at art. 52.

90. *Id.* at arts. 61–63.

91. *Id.* at art. 64.

92. *Id.* at arts. 48–50.

93. *Id.* at art. 64.

94. *Id.*

95. Canada has not signed the American Convention. The United States signed the Convention in 1978; however, it has not been ratified. Cuba is technically a Member of the OAS, but its government has been excluded from participation since 1962. *See* Henry Steiner, International Human Rights in Context 1021 (3d ed. 2006).

96. *See* David R. Boyd, The Right to a Healthy Environment, Revitalizing Canada's Constitution 133–39 (2012).

considered: (1) the extent to which violations of human rights could be used to take cases before the supervisory bodies; and (2) the scope of the jurisprudence that could be used for future claims on this topic. This section first examines the right to enjoy the benefits of culture, the right to the protection of health, and the right to property as possible grounds for claims for climate change impacts. It then explores the potential use of regional human rights instruments to support arguments for requiring governments to take action in response to climate change. The act of filing climate change-based petitions or complaints in regional fora advances innovative arguments and pushes international law in a new direction.[97]

A.   Right to Enjoy the Benefits of Culture

The American Declaration enshrines the right to the benefits of culture, stating that "[e]very person has the right to take part in the cultural life of the community."[98] Article 14 of the Protocol of San Salvador also recognizes the right to benefits of culture, stating that it is the right of everyone "[t]o take part in the cultural and artistic life of the community."[99]

The IACHR has established that lands traditionally used and occupied by indigenous communities play a central role in their physical, cultural, and spiritual vitality.[100] The Inter-American system had emphasized the "special relationship between indigenous and tribal peoples and their territories."[101] Particularly, the Commission recognizes that "the use and enjoyment of the land and its resources are integral components of the physical and cultural survival of the indigenous communities and the effective realization of their human rights more broadly."[102] Their lands represent a cultural bond of collective memory, and this relationship must be internationally protected.[103] The IACHR has acknowledged that "the right to culture includes distinctive forms and modalities of using territo-

---

97.   For a detailed analysis of the European Court of Human Rights jurisprudence and United Nations committees reports, see Verónica de la Rosa Jaimes, *Climate Change and Human Rights Litigation in Europe and the Americas,* 5 SEATTLE J. ENVTL. L. 165 (2015).

98.   American Declaration, *supra* note 76, at art. XIII.

99.   Protocol of San Salvador, *supra* note 77, at art. 14.

100. Maya Indigenous Communities of the Toledo District v. Belize, Admissibility, Case 12.053, Inter-Am. C.H.R., Report No. 78/00, para. 155 (2000).

101. Indigenous and Tribal Peoples' Rights Over Their Ancestral Lands and Natural Resources, Norms and Jurisprudence of the Inter-American Human Rights System, Inter-Am. C.H.R, OEA/ser.L/V/II, doc. 56/09, paras. 55–57 (2009) [hereinafter Indigenous and Tribal Peoples' Rights].

102. *Maya Indigenous Communities of the Toledo District,* Case 12.053, Inter-Am. C.H.R., Report No. 78/00, para. 114.

103. Indigenous and Tribal Peoples' Rights, *supra* note 101, para. 78.

ries such as traditional fishing, hunting, and gathering as essential elements of indigenous culture."[104]

The IACtHR has recognized the close ties between the culture of indigenous peoples and their traditional or ancestral lands in numerous cases. In *Yakye Axa Indigenous Community v. Paraguay*, the IACtHR held that the culture of the members of the indigenous communities directly relates to a specific way of being, seeing, and acting in the world, developed on the basis of their close relationship with their traditional territories and the resources therein. Their traditional territories and resources therein constitute their main means of subsistence, and are part of their worldview, spirituality, and cultural identity. Therefore, activities that depend on natural resources, such as hunting, fishing, and gathering, are essential components of their culture.[105] States must take into account that indigenous land encompasses a broader and different concept that relates to the collective right to survival as an organized people, with control over their habitat as a condition to preserve their cultural heritage for their own development and to carry out their life aspirations.[106] In *Xákmok Kásek Indigenous Community v. Paraguay*, the IACtHR held that in the case of indigenous tribes or peoples, the traditional possession of their lands and the cultural patterns that arise from this close relationship form part of their identity. Such identity uniquely contributes to the collective perception they have as a group, their *cosmovision*, their collective imagination, and the relationship with the land where they live their lives.[107]

An interview of 70 Mexican indigenous people from varying *ejidos*[108] noted that "the majority said that they had never heard of climate change"[109] but "they don't know when to work the crops anymore; the heat is so strong they can only work outside half the time as in the past; and that

---

104. In *Dann v. United States*, the Commission states: "culture manifests itself in many forms, including a particular way of life associated with the use of land resources, especially in the case of indigenous people." Dann v. United States, Case 11.140, Inter-Am. C.H.R., Report No. 75/02, doc. 5 rev. 1, 860, para. 130, n.97 (2002) (*citing* United Nations Human Rights Council, general cmt. 23, International Covenant on Civil and Political Rights, art. 27, U.N. Doc. HRI/GEN/1/Rev.1 (1994)), http://www.cidh.oas.org/annualrep/2002eng/USA.11140.htm.

105. Yakye Axa Indigenous Community v. Paraguay, Merits, Reparations, and Costs, Judgment, Inter-Am. C.H.R. (ser. C) No. 125, paras. 135–140 (2005).

106. *Id.* para. 146.

107. Case of the Xákmok Kásek Indigenous Community v. Paraguay, Merits, Reparations, and Costs, Judgment, Inter-Am. C.H.R. (ser. C) No. 214, para. 234 (2010).

108. In Mexico, the *ejido* is a communal tenure of land and a community of farmers, who collectively possess the land rights. The Mexican Constitution recognizes the *ejido* and protects it for both human settlement and productive activities. *Constitución Política de los Estados Unidos Mexicanos, supra* note 31, at art. 27.

109. Alejandra Rabasa, *Climate and Resource Protection for Indigenous Communities in Mexico*, ENVTL. L. INST., Sept./Oct. 2014, https://www.eli.org/sites/default/files/docs/rabasa_forum_sept-oct_2014.pdf.

most of the streams running through their lands are gone."[110] Even their lands have been determined to be insufficient to sustain themselves.[111] All of these climate change effects represent a substantial concern for society's most vulnerable, particularly Mexican indigenous peoples who rely on the environment for their culture, traditions, and lifestyle. This vulnerability represents a large impact on the exercise of their right to enjoy the benefits of the culture.

A key concept of the Inter-American jurisprudence concerns the rights of future generations. Climate change adversely affects indigenous peoples' "ability to transmit cultural knowledge to future generations."[112] Knowledge developed over millennia about traditional lands, weather, ecology, and the use of natural resources is fundamental to indigenous peoples as it "provides a basis for the elders to educate the younger generation in traditional ways of life, kinship and bonding."[113] The ability to pass knowledge from one generation to the next is crucial for indigenous peoples' cultural survival.

B.   Right to Health and Well-being

The American Declaration enshrines in its Article XI the right to the preservation of health and well-being.[114] Article 10 of the Protocol of San Salvador states that "[e]veryone shall have the right to health, understood to mean the enjoyment of the highest level of physical, mental and social well-being."[115]

The OAS recognizes the close link between health and the environment through the Protocol of San Salvador, and extends the scope of the right to health by including the right to a healthy environment in Article 11. The Protocol stipulates this provision as the obligation of the States to "promote the protection, preservation, and improvement of the environment."[116]

---

110. *Id.*
111. World Directory of Minorities, *supra* note 16.
112. Arctic Athabaskan Council et al., Petition to the Inter-American Commission on Human Rights Seeking Relief From Violations of the Rights of Arctic Athabaskan Peoples Resulting From Rapid Arctic Warming and Melting Caused by Emissions of Black Carbon by Canada 61 (2013), http://earthjustice.org/sites/default/files/SummaryAACpetition13-04-23.pdf [hereinafter Athabaskan Petition].
113. *Id.* at 8.
114. "Every person has the right to the preservation of his health through sanitary and social measures relating to food, clothing, housing and medical care, to the extent permitted by public and community resources." American Declaration, *supra* note 76, at art. XI.
115. Protocol of San Salvador, *supra* note 77, at art. 10.
116. However, Article 11 has been weakened because Article 19 of the Protocol states that only progressive measures must be taken by State Parties to ensure due respect for the rights set in the Protocol, and, therefore, violations of these rights cannot give rise to an individual petition. As a result, none of the

Regarding the Inter-American system, the IACtHR considered in *Yakye Axa* the fact that Paraguay did not guarantee the communal property rights of the members of the Yakye Axa community, and the negative effect that this lack of guarantee had on the rights of members of the community to a decent life. It deprived them of the possibility of access to their traditional means of subsistence, as well as the right of use and enjoyment of the natural resources necessary to obtain clean water and to practice traditional medicine to prevent and cure illnesses.[117] The Court also emphasized that any infringement of the right to health has a major impact on the right to a decent existence and basic conditions to exercise other human rights, such as the right to education or the right to cultural identity.[118]

An example of climate change directly adversely affecting the health of Mexican indigenous peoples is that "temperature increase modifies several habitats and allows for dissemination of disease vectors such as those of dengue and malaria."[119] The World Health Organization has estimated that "climate change is responsible since 1970 for nearly 150,000 deaths per year as a result of the increase in diarrhea, malaria and malnutrition."[120] Disease is only one consequence of climate change among others affecting the production of agriculture and increased water scarcity that directly impairs the exercise of Mexican indigenous peoples' right to health and well-being.[121]

As to the right to preservation of health, two significant aspects should be highlighted. First, the IACHR and the IACtHR have recognized that there is a direct link between environment and health, and addressed the impacts when environmental degradation had harmed human health.[122] Second, the positive obligation of States to protect the right to the preservation of health has been recognized.[123] The WG II Fifth Assessment Report on Climate Change 2014 predicts with high confidence risks of injury, ill-health, and coastal and inland flooding caused by rising sea levels,[124] which could represent a direct violation to the right to the preservation of health. Thus, the creation and enforcement of policies and regulations to mitigate GHG emis-

---

IACtHR decisions has directly addressed the right to a healthy environment. DAVID R. BOYD, THE RIGHT TO A HEALTHY ENVIRONMENT: REVITALIZING CANADA'S CONSTITUTION 133–36 (2012).

117. Yakye Axa, *supra* note 105, para. 168.
118. *Id.* para. 1674.
119. UNITED NATIONS DEPARTMENT OF ECONOMIC AND SOCIAL AFFAIRS, COMMENTS OF MEXICO ON CLIMATE CHANGE AND SECURITY 2 (n.d.), http://www.un.org/esa/dsd/resources/res_pdfs/ga-64/cc-inputs/Mexico_CCIS.pdf.
120. *Id.*
121. *Id.*
122. ATHABASKAN PETITION, *supra* note 112, at 73.
123. Yakye Axa, *supra* note 105, para. 221.
124. WG II FIFTH ASSESSMENT REPORT ON CLIMATE CHANGE 2014, *supra* note 1.

sions and to adapt to climate change impacts is a path to protect the health of hundreds of indigenous peoples that will be subject to potential harm in the near future. For many indigenous communities, their spirituality is deeply connected to their land and as "the effects of climate change ravage their environment, indigenous peoples may experience both a physical and spiritual loss connected with the negative impact on the environment."[125]

C.   Right to Use and Enjoyment of Property

In the Inter-American system of human rights, the right to property is included in the American Declaration. Article XXIII states that "[e]very person has a right to own such private property as meets the essential needs of decent living and helps to maintain the dignity of the individual and of the home."[126] The American Convention recognized this right to the use and enjoyment of one's property, which may be subordinate to the interest of society. It also stresses that "[n]o one shall be deprived of his property except upon payment of just compensation, for reasons of public utility or social interest, and in the cases and according to the forms established by law."[127]

The Inter-American system has primarily dealt with cases involving the right to property and the protection of natural resources on indigenous and ancestral lands. The case of *Awas Tingni v. Nicaragua*[128] gave rise to the first decision that protected human rights of first nations and indigenous peoples with respect to the right to property. In that case, the IACtHR made the following conclusions regarding the right to property on indigenous lands:

> Among indigenous peoples there is a communitarian tradition regarding a communal form of collective property of the land, in the sense that ownership of the land is not centered on an individual but rather on the group and its community. Indigenous groups, by the fact of their very existence, have the right to live freely in their own territory; the close ties of indigenous people with the land must be recognized and understood as the fundamental basis of their cultures, their spiritual life, their integrity, and their economic survival. For indigenous communities, relations to the land are not merely a matter of possession and production but a material and spiritual element which

---

125. *Commonality Among Unique Indigenous Communities, supra* note 9, at 12.
126. American Declaration, *supra* note 76.
127. American Convention, *supra* note 74, at art. 21.
128. Mayagna (Sumo) Awas Tingni Community v. Nicaragua, Merits, Reparations, and Costs, Judgment, Inter-Am. C.H.R. (ser. C) No. 79 (2001).

they must fully enjoy, even to preserve their cultural legacy and transmit it to future generations.[129]

Similarly, in *Sawhoyamaxa Indigenous Community v. Paraguay*, the IACtHR once again confirmed the ties to culture and communal property, and stated that the close ties of indigenous peoples with their traditional lands and the native natural resources thereof associated with their culture must be secured under the right to property.[130]

The IACtHR has extended the scope of the right to property with regards to the use of the natural resources that are necessary for the survival of indigenous peoples. In *Saramaka People v. Suriname*[131] and *Kichwa Indigenous People of Sarayaku v. Ecuador*, the Court held that the right to use and enjoy their territory would be meaningless in the context of indigenous and tribal communities if this right were not connected to the natural resources that lie on and within the land.[132] Resources allow them to maintain their way of living and ensure their survival through their traditional activities.[133] The Court has established that in order to determine the existence of a relationship between indigenous peoples and communities, and their traditional lands, this relationship can be expressed in different ways depending on the indigenous group concerned and its specific circumstances, and the relationship with the land must be possible.[134]

In the same vein, the IACHR deemed in *Maya Indigenous Communities of the Toledo District v. Belize*,[135] the seminal case regarding the right to property, that this right has been recognized as one of the rights having a collective aspect

---

129. *Id.* para. 149.

130. Sawhoyamaxa Indigenous Community v Paraguay, Merits, Reparations, and Costs, Judgment, Inter-Am. C.H.R. (ser. C) No. 146, para. 189 (2006).

131. Saramaka People v. Suriname, Merits, Reparations, and Costs, Judgment, Inter-Am. C.H.R. (ser. C) No. 172, para. 141 (2007).

132. *Id.* paras. 141–142; Kichwa Indigenous People of Sarayaku v. Ecuador, Merits and Reparations, Judgment, Inter-Am. C.H.R. (ser. C) No. 245, para. 23 (2012).

133. Sarayaku, *supra* note 132, para. 147.

134. The ways in which this relationship is expressed may include traditional use or presence, through spiritual or ceremonial ties; sporadic settlements or cultivation; traditional forms of subsistence such as seasonal or nomadic hunting, fishing or gathering; or use of natural resources associated with their customs or other elements characteristic of their culture. The second element implies that community members are not prevented, for reasons beyond their control, from carrying out those activities that reveal the enduring nature of their relationship with their traditional lands. *Id.* paras. 147–148. *See also* Sawhoyamaxa, *supra* note 130, para. 132; Xákmok, *supra* note 107, para. 113.

135. The Mayan Toledo people claimed that the rights to the lands that they had traditionally used and occupied had been violated by Belize granting logging and oil concessions in and otherwise failing to adequately protect those lands, failing to recognize and secure the territorial rights of the Maya people in those lands. *See* Maya Indigenous Communities of the Toledo District v. Belize, Admissibility, Case 12.053, Inter-Am. C.H.R., Report No. 78/00, para. 5 (2000). They argued that these actions negatively impacted the natural environment upon which the Mayan people depended for subsistence and had jeopardized the Mayan people and their culture. *Id.* para. 28.

in the sense that it can only be properly ensured through its guarantee to an indigenous community as a whole.[136] The Commission also emphasized that the resources of the land are integral components of the physical and cultural survival of the indigenous communities, and that property rights of indigenous peoples "are not defined exclusively by entitlements within a State's formal legal regime, but also include that indigenous communal property that arises from and is grounded in indigenous custom and tradition."[137]

The impact of climate change on the right to property for Mexican indigenous peoples is demonstrated through the risk of "flooding and landslides in urban and rural areas due to extreme precipitation."[138] This poses a risk to both agriculture and housing for Mexican indigenous peoples given their aforementioned vulnerability. A trend of "environmentally induced migration"[139] is emerging where a "decrease in water and food security, as well as the increasingly inhospitable character of areas affected by climate change, will certainly hasten these migratory flows."[140] The impact of this reality can be seen in northern Mexico where the impacts of environmentally induced migration have been shown to disproportionally affect "impoverished rural populations, whose livelihoods depend on rain-fed agriculture."[141] Because of environmentally induced migration, Mexican indigenous peoples are forced out of their own land and unable to exercise their right to their property.

The Inter-American system emphasizes the linkage between land, culture, spiritual life, and economic survival, as well as the strong collective aspect inherent in these concepts. These notions are closely related to the WG II Fifth Assessment Report on Climate Change 2014 and its predictions of the risk of loss of rural livelihoods, particularly for people in the agricultural industry in semi-arid regions, in low-lying coastal zones, and developing small-island States.[142] The IACHR and the IACtHR can play a significant role in the enforcement of regulations regarding climate change mitigation.

---

136. *Id.* para. 113.
137. *Id.* para. 117. The Commission has previously observed that respect for and protection of the private property of indigenous peoples on their territories is equivalent in importance to non-indigenous property: "From the standpoint of human rights, a small corn field deserves the same respect as the private property of a person that a bank account or a modern factory receives." IACHR, Fourth Report on the Situation of Human Rights in Guatemala, OEA/Ser.L/V/II.83, doc. 16 rev. (1993).
138. WG II Fifth Assessment Report on Climate Change 2014, *supra* note 1, at 24.
139. Environmentally induced migration is defined as people being "forced to leave their traditional habitat, temporarily or permanently because of a marked environmental disruption (natural and/or triggered by people) that jeopardized their existence and/or seriously affected the quality of their life." Essam El-Hinnawi, Environmental Refugees 4 (1985).
140. Alexandra Deprez, *Climate Migration in Latin America: A Future "Flood of Refugees" to the North?*, Council on Hemispheric Aff., Feb. 22, 2010, http://www.coha.org/climate-migration-in-latin-america-part-1/.
141. *Id.*
142. *See* WG II Fifth Assessment Report on Climate Change 2014, *supra* note 1.

This chapter has emphasized the applicability of Inter-American human rights instruments for Mexican indigenous communities affected by climate change impacts. Government infringement of the rights of indigenous communities is not a problem unique to Mexico, but is evident in many vulnerable indigenous communities around the world. One such example is the Athabaskan Petition in Canada.[143] This unique case provides a valuable overview of an indigenous community filing a claim against the government alleging that climate change impacts are violating their human rights.

V.   Where Climate Change Meets Human Rights: The Athabaskan Petition

On April 23, 2013, the Arctic Athabaskan Council (AAC), represented by Earthjustice and Ecojustice Canada, on behalf of all the Athabaskan peoples of the Arctic regions of Canada and the United States, filed a petition with the IACHR seeking relief from violations of their rights resulting from rapid Arctic warming and melting caused by emissions of black carbon for which Canada has international responsibility.[144] The petition includes a thorough analysis of international human rights law and case law, as well as the evidence of some Athabaskan people claiming violations of their human rights.

The AAC's claim asserts that Canada's failure to regulate black carbon emissions is accelerating Arctic warming and that this failure violates the human rights of Arctic Athabaskan peoples.[145] The petition contends that, since Athabaskan peoples depend on natural resources for their livelihood, the effects of climate change (e.g., higher temperatures, melting snow, melting permafrost, shrinking glaciers, longer dry seasons, increase in forest fires, and severe climate extremes) are felt most acutely by their populations and therefore, human rights instruments should provide protection for them. The ACC states that when black carbon deposits on ice and snow, it not only reduces albedo,[146] but also absorbs sunlight and heats the atmosphere, thereby accelerating Arctic warming. Thus, due to the nature of black carbon[147] and the proximity of the emissions to the Arctic, Canada's emissions of black carbon affect Athabaskan lands the most.

---

143. *See* ATHABASKAN PETITION, *supra* note 112.
144. For detailed discussion on this petition, see de la Rosa Jaimes, *supra* note 10.
145. ATHABASKAN PETITION, *supra* note 112, at 16.
146. Albedo is the ability of snow to reflect the sunlight.
147. Black carbon is the sooty pollution emitted from diesel engines, residential heating stoves, agricultural and forest fires, and some industrial facilities. It is considered a "short lived" climate pollutant as it stays in the atmosphere for only about one week. ATHABASKAN PETITION, *supra* note 112, at 16.

The petitioners requested that the IACHR investigate and declare that Canada's failure to implement measures to reduce black carbon emissions violates the Athabaskan peoples' right to the benefits of their culture,[148] right to property,[149] and right to health[150] enshrined in the American Declaration. The ACC also requested that the IACHR recommend that Canada take steps to limit black carbon emissions and to protect the Athabaskan culture and resources from the effects of the accelerated Arctic warming. The ACC alleges that Canada does not provide effective domestic remedies to restore the rights for which they have alleged violations.[151] The Canadian government will have to respond to the Commission after which the Commission will determine the admissibility of the petition. If deemed admissible, the Commission will proceed to review the petition on its merits.[152]

The IACHR has issued recommendations on cases related to the right to property, where it recognizes that the right to property protects traditional forms of ownership and cultural survival, and rights to land, territories and resources.[153] Other cases have been taken by the IACHR to the IACtHR on behalf of the alleged victims of human rights violations, giving rise to decisions that protect human rights of First Nations and indigenous peoples, with specific reference to the right to property, due to the close link between indigenous communities and their traditional lands that they must fully enjoy, to preserve their cultural legacy and transmit it to future generations.[154] In the past decade, the Inter-American jurisprudence has transformed the international legal status of indigenous peoples' lands and has done this by "taking seriously the property rights of indigenous peoples."[155] The Athabaskan Petition is giving the IACHR a second chance[156] to advance human rights claims related to climate change impacts.

---

148. *Id.* at 61.
149. *Id.* at 71.
150. *Id.* at 76.
151. *Id.* at 82–84.
152. As of this writing, the petition is still waiting for admission by the IACHR.
153. Maya Indigenous Communities of the Toledo District v. Belize, Admissibility, Case 12.053, Inter-Am. C.H.R., Report No. 78/00, para. 115 (2000).
154. Xákmok, *supra* note 107; Awas Tingni, *supra* note 128; Saramaka, *supra* note 131; Sawhoyamaxa, *supra* note 130.
155. Nigel Bankes, *International Human Rights Law and Natural Resources Projects Within the Traditional Territories of Indigenous Peoples*, 47 Alta. L. Rev. 491 (2010).
156. In 2005, Sheila Watt-Cloutier, chair of the Inuit Circumpolar Conference (ICC), filed a petition to the IACHR on behalf of all Inuit of the Arctic regions of the United States and Canada, seeking relief from violations of human rights resulting from the impacts of global warming and climate change caused by U.S. GHG emissions. Inuit Circumpolar Conference, Petition to the Inter-American Commission on Human Rights seeking Relief From Violations Resulting From Global Warming Caused by Acts and Omissions of the United States, http://www.inuitcircumpolar. com/uploads/3/0/5/4/30542564/finalpetitionicc.pdf. In November 2006, the petition was dismissed

Climate justice litigation helps shape the tone and framing of the debate by the use of claims from those who suffer from climate change damages and who turn to diverse fora seeking to assign liability, obtain compensation, raise awareness, and achieve policy and legislative changes. If Mexican indigenous peoples were to present a claim regarding human rights violations within the Inter-American system due to climate change, they will face a critical challenge. As with any litigation related to responsibility for environmental damage, the petitioners would have to prove legally sufficient causation between the harm resulting from climate change and the acts or omissions of the Mexican government. The key element to success is to provide scientific evidence to demonstrate how environmental degradation due to anthropogenic climate change violates their human rights. Thus, the main challenge for a regional human rights claim to be successful would be the level of certainty and the nature of the evidence necessary to show a causal link between GHG emissions, climate change, and the threat to life, health, or enjoyment of property, among other rights.

Conclusion

Indigenous peoples have contributed the least to global climate change and yet they are among the first to face direct environmental, social, and human rights impacts of climate change. The integrity and cohesiveness of indigenous peoples' culture have been undermined; their access to life-sustaining resources has reduced dramatically in the past decades; and their life and health have been threatened because of environmental hazards caused by climate change. In the past two decades, indigenous peoples have appealed to the international arena and looked to international law as a vehicle to advance their cause, especially within institutions designed to examine complaints of human rights violations that can to lead to decisions or recommendations.

In Mexico, as in every country, climate change impacts significantly impair indigenous peoples' human rights. The Mexican government has attempted to address the effects of climate change and the resulting infringement of indigenous peoples' rights through legislation, strategies, and plans, but these efforts have made limited progress. Mexico has stan-

---

through a brief letter response to the ICC, in which the IACHR concluded that the petition failed to establish "whether the alleged facts would tend to characterize a violation of rights protected by the American Declaration." Letter from Ariel E. Dulitzky, Assistant Executive Secretary, IACHR, to Paul Crowley, Legal Representative, Re: Sheila Watt-Cloutier et al. (Nov. 16, 2006), http://graphics8.nytimes.com/packages/pdf/science/16commissionletter.pdf. *See* Kronk Warner & Abate, *supra* note 39; de la Rosa Jaimes, *supra* note 97.

dards that it must meet in order to fulfill its obligations to its indigenous communities.

As per the Inter-American human rights supervisory bodies, providing a judgment or recommendation will require bold and innovative thinking. However, earlier decisions of the IACHR and the IACtHR suggest that they are well equipped to interpret the American Declaration and American Convention in light of broader developments in international human rights law. In the meantime, human rights systems are evolving to cover the needs of the communities that will be affected by the key risks associated with climate change in all continents.

Chapter 24

Indigenous Peoples Bringing Climate Justice to Canada

Karine Peloffy*

* *The author would like to thank Lisa Koperqualuk, author of* Traditions Relating to Customary Law of Nunavimmiut, *for her extremely valuable input on indigenous law, Vanita Sachdeva for her outstanding research assistance as well as the numerous interns who conducted background research, and the many people who have contributed through insightful discussions toward this chapter.*

Introduction

This chapter explores a hypothetical case on how indigenous communities affected by climate change in Canada[1] could bring a legal action against the federal government using constitutional arguments to compel the government to abide by more ambitious greenhouse gas (GHG) emissions reduction targets and provide funding and resources to adapt to climate change. The case is structured similarly to the successful *Urgenda* case but in a Canadian context, focusing on the different legal tools available to Aboriginal peoples of Canada for two reasons. First, indigenous peoples in Canada are disproportionately affected by climate change. Second, the government has a unique fiduciary duty toward indigenous peoples, and Canadian indigenous peoples enjoy additional constitutional protections and avenues to bring a claim that the general Canadian public cannot access.

The chapter proposes that the inclusion of indigenous laws and concepts into climate court cases and policy development would have a beneficial impact on climate action in Canada. Canada simultaneously is one of the world's leading emitters of greenhouse gases (GHGs) and home to the most heavily impacted peoples on the planet. The chapter calls on Canada to be receptive to the teachings that have governed its territory for far longer than confederation, if indigenous peoples still have the patience and generosity to share their wisdom.

The difficulty remains that Aboriginal peoples of this land are the last people who should shoulder the burden of action on this matter, having contributed little to the problem and suffering most of the impacts.[2] However, as with other environmental issues, they are thankfully often already at the forefront of the fight against extractive industries affecting the environment.

Part I of the chapter reviews Canada's historical inaction on climate change and the climate change impacts that indigenous peoples have already endured. Part II charts a constitutional climate case brought by indigenous peoples by highlighting the recognized collective and individual rights they could rely on, the various rights limitation tests that would have to be met, and the possible remedies available. Part III explores principles of indigenous law that would be beneficial in developing climate policy and the challenges in attempting to reconcile settler and indigenous systems. The culturally spe-

---

1.   This chapter explores in greater detail the hypothetical test case put forward in Karine Peloffy, *Kivalina v. Exxonmobil: A Comparative Case Comment*, 9 McGill Int'l J. Sustainable Dev. L. 121 (2013).
2.   Although the chapter explores relatively novel arguments and unchartered territory, it is not meant to serve as an endorsement for indigenous peoples or communities to undertake the monumental task of the legal action contemplated or that it would be beneficial to any single community.

cific indigenous legal principles could, despite certain difficulties, be included in a court's analysis of the hypothetical case or form the basis of a new nation to nation constitutional dialogue.

Looking into other legal traditions occurs from an author's culturally defined lens and can therefore lead to some misconstruction in translating principles and norms across legal systems. Any possible misconception or oversimplification of the diversity of indigenous legal systems arising from this exploratory exercise is entirely unintended.

I. Factual Background

On June 24, 2015, the Dutch Urgenda Foundation and 886 individual Dutch citizens prevailed in their claim seeking to hold their State liable for its role in causing dangerous global climate change. The district court of The Hague delivered its judgment in favor of Urgenda making it the first instance in which a district court used principles from the United Nations Framework Convention on Climate Change (UNFCCC) to order a State to adopt emissions reduction targets in accordance with the Intergovernmental Panel on Climate Change (IPCC) recommendations.[3] The case relied on the IPCC report and public sources rather than adducing specific evidence of harm to individuals or future generations, which allowed the court's inquiry to focus on the wrongfulness of State action rather than impacts on specific victims. Indeed, since States participate in the IPCC process, the Dutch government did not dispute the reports' conclusions, only their legal implications, which constituted evidence of particularly probative value.[4] Ultimately, the court ruled that the Netherlands had acted negligently by failing to do its fair share in reducing GHG emissions to avoid dangerous levels of climate change.[5]

A. Canadian Historical Inaction on Climate Change

Like the Netherlands, Canada also has failed to adequately respond to the threat of climate change. Since the global community has started to take action on climate change, Canada has neither adopted reduction targets that

---

3. The Hague District Court (Chamber for Commercial Affairs), June 24, 2015, C/09/456689 / HA ZA 13-1396 (English translation), http://www.urgenda.nl/documents/VerdictDistrictCourt-UrgendavStaat-24.06.2015.pdf.
4. Urgenda Counsel Roger Cox, Climate Change and Rule of Law: Could Domestic Public Interest Litigation Contribute to Enforcing International Commitments? (Sept. 15, 2015).
5. For a detailed discussion of this case and its implications for climate justice, see Chapter 21 in this volume.

are sufficient in view of the international scientific and political consensus,[6] nor implemented them in binding legislation. National GHG emissions have actually risen, rather than diminished, since the international community took action in the 1990s.

The past 10 years (2006–2015) have been particularly dire for climate policy in Canada. Despite repeated efforts led by opposition parties, the Conservative government led by Prime Minister Stephen Harper undermined Canada's environmental legal regime and weakened Canada's role in climate change governance nationally and internationally.[7]

Canada became the first and only country to withdraw from the Kyoto Protocol,[8] which was the only internationally binding agreement mandating GHG reductions to date. The Conservative Party also dismantled Canada's environmental, scientific, and legal frameworks[9] through many amendments instituted by Bill C-38,[10] which overhauled more than 70 laws under the auspices of an omnibus "budget" bill, a move perceived by many as an affront to democracy.[11] The many attempts by opposition parties to introduce legislation "to ensure that Canada meets its global climate change obligations under the United Nations Framework Convention on Climate Change" have all failed.[12]

Canada's current GHG targets are to reduce emissions by 17% by 2020[13] and by 30% in 2030,[14] both compared to 2005 levels. Both targets represent

6.   The national targets that Canada set immediately after the adoption of the UNFCCC in 1992 and under the Kyoto Protocol could be considered potential exceptions to this otherwise consistent pattern of climate inaction. DAVID SUZUKI FOUNDATION, HISTORY OF CLIMATE NEGOTIATIONS (n.d.), http://www.davidsuzuki.org/issues/History%20of%20climate%20negotiations.pdf.

7.   See Peloffy, supra note 1, at 129. However, Canada's environmental policy was deemed a miserable failure even before Stephen Harper became prime minister. Lynda Collins, Tort, Democracy, and Environmental Governance: The Case of Non-enforcement, 15 TORT L. REV. 107, 108 (2007); see also DAVID BOYD, UNNATURAL LAW: RETHINKING CANADIAN ENVIRONMENTAL LAW AND POLICY (2003); ENVIRONMENTAL LAW ASSOCIATION, SHATTERING THE MYTH OF POLLUTION PROGRESS IN CANADA: A NATIONAL REPORT (2004).

8.   Bill C-38, An Act to implement certain provisions of the budget tabled in Parliament on March 29, 2012, and other measures, 41st Parliament, 1st Sess. ch. 19 §699 (June 29, 2012) [hereinafter Bill C-38].

9.   Elizabeth May, Bill C-38: The Environmental Destruction Act, THE TYEE, May 9, 2012, http://thetyee. ca/Opinion/2012/05/10/Bill-C38/; DAVID SUZUKI FOUNDATION, BILL C-38: WHAT YOU NEED TO KNOW (2012), http://www.davidsuzuki.org/publications/downloads/2012/C-38%20factsheet.pdf.

10.   Bill C-38, supra note 8.

11.   Id.; Andrew Coyne, Voting Endlessly Oddly Appropriate Way to Protest Abuse of Parliament, NAT'L POST, June 13, 2012, http://newcomment.nationalpost.com.

12.   See, e.g., Bill C-619, An act to ensure Canada assumes its responsibilities in preventing dangerous climate change, 41st Parliament, 2d Sess., 62–63 Elizabeth II (June 16, 2014), http://www.parl.gc.ca/ HousePublications/Publication.aspx?Language=E&Mode=1&DocId=6676830&File=4&Col=1.

13.   ENVIRONMENT CANADA, CANADA'S EMISSIONS TRENDS ii (2014), https://www.ec.gc.ca/ges-ghg/ E0533893-A985-4640-B3A2-008D8083D17D/ETR_E%202014.pdf.

14.   CANADA'S INDC SUBMISSION TO THE UNFCCC (2015), http://www4.unfccc.int/Submissions/ INDC/Published%20Documents/Canada/1/INDC%20-%20Canada%20-%20English.pdf.

absolute increases in yearly emissions compared to 1990 levels, when action on climate change started. International experts rate these targets as inadequate in the sense that Canada is not doing its fair share to avoid dangerous climate change.[15] Under existing regulations, Canada will likely fail to meet even these inadequate targets: if the status quo remains, Canada's GHG emissions are projected to be 768 metric tons of carbon dioxide equivalent (Mt CO_2-eq) in 2020 (emission reduction target is 622) and 815 Mt CO_2-eq in 2030 (emission reduction target is 524).[16]

As a result, Canada ranks 56 out of 61 countries on climate action[17] and yet is one of the leading nations in the world in per capita GHG emissions. Despite the country's small population, it is one of the 10 top emitters of GHGs in the world in absolute terms.[18]

The Liberal government elected in 2016 played a positive role during the 21st Conference of the Parties negotiations in Paris in 2015, in stark contrast to its predecessor. Canada supported a reference to striving for 1.5°C above pre-industrial levels as the ultimate temperature goal of the UNFCCC.[19]

B.   Indigenous Peoples in Canada and Climate Change

It is impossible to provide a comprehensive account of the situation of indigenous peoples in Canada in this chapter. Suffice it to say that climate change impacts are the latest injustice to befall indigenous peoples, who have suffered genocide and oppression since the settlement of Europeans. The road to reconciliation is not an easy one and will involve efforts that go well beyond the topics covered in this chapter. Climate change is already having a devastating impact on indigenous communities, especially in Canada's North,

---

15.   As of this writing, dangerous climate change is understood as global warming exceeding 2°C. *See* Climate Action Tracker, *Canada*, http://climateactiontracker.org/countries/canada.html (last visited Aug. 24, 2016).

16.   *See* Government of Canada, *Canada's Greenhouse Gas Emissions Projections in 2020 and 2030*, http://news.gc.ca/web/article-en.do?nid=1030489&_ga=1.159941502.238940361.1461000980 (last visited Aug. 24, 2016).

17.   *See* JAN BURCK, FRANZISKA MARTEN & CHRISTOPH BALS, THE CLIMATE CHANGE PERFORMANCE INDEX RESULTS 2016, at 9 (2015), https://germanwatch.org/en/download/13626.pdf. Brazil, the only other country assessed in this article that is part of the ranking, is outperforming Canada at 43 out of 61.

18.   *See* Mengpin Ge, Johannes Friedrich & Thomas Damassa, *6 Graphs Explain the World's Top 10 Emitters*, WORLD RESOURCES INST., Nov. 25, 2014, http://www.wri.org/blog/2014/11/6-graphs-explain-world%E2%80%99s-top-10-emitters.

19.   *See* Mychaylo Prystupa, *Trudeau Fights to Keep Indigenous Rights in Paris Climate Deal*, NAT'L OBSERVER, Dec. 7, 2015, http://www.nationalobserver.com/2015/12/07/news/trudeau-fights-keep-indigenous-rights-paris-climate-deal; *see also* Bruce Cheadle, *COP21: Catherine McKenna Endorses Goal of Limiting Warming to 1.5 Degrees C*, CBC NEWS, Dec. 8, 2015, http://www.cbc.ca/news/politics/mckenna-cop21-paris-goal-1.3355409.

and impacts will continue to worsen unless swift mitigation and adaptation actions are taken.

The close relationship between indigenous peoples and the environment make them especially sensitive to climate change impacts. Indigenous peoples generally live in rural areas rather than cities, and grow their food rather than purchase what they eat at a supermarket. In fact, the majority of their food is either wild or migratory. This noncommercial food supply has declined due to climate change impacts on wildlife habitat and migration routes.[20] Given that there is an intimate bond and interdependency between the traditional food sources of indigenous peoples and the state of the environment,[21] it is inevitable that any significant change to the climate ultimately causes a significant impact on the communities that directly depend on it. As an example, traditional wisdom passed from generation to generation on what time of year to plant crops and where to hunt for food is proving to no longer be valid with the changes and shifts in the climate. A similar trend is observed in Inuit communities, where the elders traditionally used their skills and knowledge to predict the weather, which is key to assessing the risks of venturing on ice or land. However, this climate-related weather predicting knowledge does not fit with the present-day weather patterns altered by climate change.[22] Some link these changes in environmental conditions with mental and social distress including suicide in northern communities.[23]

From 1948–2013, the average annual temperature in Canada increased by 1.6°C (relative to the 1961–1990 average), a higher rate of warming than in most other regions of the world. Warming trends are seen consistently across Canada, but the regions showing the strongest warming are found in the far North.[24] Indeed, the atmosphere is warming twice as fast in the Arctic.[25] A large portion of indigenous peoples inhabit the most northern regions of the globe where changes in climate are felt faster and to a greater extent. The thinning of the sea ice has led to diminished access to

20. FIONA J. WARREN & DONALD S. LEMMEN EDS., CANADA IN A CHANGING CLIMATE: SECTOR PERSPECTIVES ON IMPACTS AND ADAPTATION 125 (2014).
21. RACHEL BAIRD, THE IMPACT OF CLIMATE CHANGE ON MINORITIES AND INDIGENOUS PEOPLES, MINORITY RIGHTS GROUP INTERNATIONAL (2008), http://www.ohchr.org/Documents/Issues/ClimateChange/ Submissions/Minority_Rights_Group_International.pdf.
22. Nunavut Climate Change Centre, *Climate Change Impact*, http://climatechangenunavut.ca/en/ understanding-climate-change/climate-change-impact (last visited Aug. 24, 2016).
23. Chris Furgal & Terry D. Prowse, *Northern Canada*, *in* FROM IMPACTS TO ADAPTATION: CANADA IN A CHANGING CLIMATE 2007, at 57, 105 (2008).
24. Government of Canada, *Impacts of Climate Change*, http://www.climatechange.gc.ca/default. asp?lang=En&n=036D9756-1 (last visited Aug. 24, 2016).
25. BAIRD, *supra* note 21, at 4.

food and wildlife resulting in food-security problems. In addition, higher health and safety risks are involved in following their traditional herding routes.[26] To highlight the impact of climate change on food security, one study found that thinning-ice conditions in northern Manitoba caused by rising global temperatures resulted in a shortage of healthy groceries being delivered to the 25 northernmost communities.[27] Furthermore, where the cold temperatures of the North are used for food storage and to preserve meat catches, the increasing temperatures cause the meat to spoil, leading to food shortages.[28]

II.   Existing Constitutional Legal Framework

In addition to international law and tort-based arguments, indigenous claimants in Canada also benefit from constitutional protections specific to this country. This section will explore the different collective and individual rights afforded to indigenous peoples under the Canadian Constitution, analyze whether a court could find an infringement justified, and consider remedies that may be available if a violation is established.

A.   Rights Protected Under the Canadian Constitution

There are two major pathways to bring a constitutional action: (1) an Aboriginal rights claim under §35, or (2) a claim under the Charter §§2A, 7, and 15. The Constitution Act 1982 recognized individual rights of all Canadians and collective rights of indigenous peoples. Indeed, §35 is a rare recognition of collective Aboriginal rights that preexisted the arrival of Europeans in the Constitution of Canada (1982).

The remaining constitutional protections are more conservatively understood through the lens of individual rights specific in Western legal traditions. The Canadian Charter of Rights and Freedoms was also inserted into the Constitution to "guarantee the rights and freedoms set out in it subject only to such reasonable limits prescribed by law as can be demonstrably justified in a free and democratic society."[29]

---

26.   *Id.*; Nunavut Climate Change Centre, *supra* note 22.

27.   WARREN & LEMMEN, *supra* note 20, at 215.

28.   Nunavut Climate Change Centre, *supra* note 22. *See generally* Sheila Watt-Cloutier, Petition to the Inter American Commission on Human Rights Seeking Relief From Violations Resulting From Global Warming Caused by Acts and Omissions of the United States (Dec. 7, 2005), http://www.ciel.org/Publications/ICC_Petition_7Dec05.pdf.

29.   CANADIAN CHARTER OF RIGHTS AND FREEDOMS, §1, enacted as Schedule B to the Canada Act 1982, ch. 11 (U.K.), which became effective on Apr. 17, 1982.

Demonstrating an infringement of an individual charter right arguably necessitates a less burdensome evidentiary standard in not having to prove a collective right extending back to first contact. In addition to the financial resources necessary to satisfy such a claim, asserting collective rights involves lengthy court cases, which may only be worthwhile if the remedies sought include compensation. Since climate action is urgently needed, cases that ascertain only individual rights may proceed more quickly through the court system.

I.   Section 35: Collective Rights of Aboriginal Peoples

Canada's judiciary has produced favorable opinions in the past decades for Aboriginal communities in Canada. Since 1982, Canada's courts have developed a significant body of jurisprudence comprising more than 150 cases[30] concerning Aboriginal and treaty rights. Aboriginal rights have helped make indigenous peoples ideal environmental claimants. For the past few decades, they have been able to stop ecologically harmful developments in their traditional territories through court actions.[31]

One of §35's fundamental objectives is the reconciliation of Aboriginal peoples' distinctive societies, practices, traditions, and culture, and non-Aboriginal peoples in a way that respects their claims, interests, and ambitions.[32] Thus, §35 guarantees the protection through the recognition of Aboriginal title, rights, or in treaties between the Crown and Aboriginal peoples.[33] The exis-

---

30. BILL GALLAGHER, RESOURCE RULERS: FORTUNE AND FOLLY ON CANADA'S ROAD TO RESOURCES 1 (2012).

31. Mikisew Cree First Nation v. Canada (Minister of Canadian Heritage), [2001] F.C.J. No. 1877 (F.C.T.D.); Halfway River First Nation v. British Columbia (Ministry of Forests), 1999 B.C.C.A. 470; Tsawout Indian Band v. Saanichton Marina Ltd., [1989] 57 D.L.R. (4th) 161 (B.C.C.A.). *See also* JOHN BORROWS, CANADA'S INDIGENOUS CONSTITUTION (2010); John Borrows, *Living Law on a Living Earth, in* LAW AND RELIGIOUS PLURALISM IN CANADA (2008); JOHN BORROWS, LIVING LAW ON A LIVING EARTH (2006); Lynda M. Collins & Meghan Murtha, *Indigenous Environmental Rights in Canada: The Right to Conservation Implicit in Treaty and Aboriginal Rights to Hunt, Fish, and Trap*, 47 ALTA. L. REV. 959 (2010); Randy Kapashesit & Murray Klippenstein, *Aboriginal Group Rights and Environmental Protection*, 36 McGILL L.J. 925 (1991); Geoffrey W.G. Leane, *Indigenous Peoples Fishing for Justice: A Paradigmatic Failure in Environmental Law*, 7 J. ENVTL. L. & PRAC. 279 (1997); L. Little Bear, *Relationship of Aboriginal People to the Land and the Aboriginal Perspective on Aboriginal Title, in* FOR SEVEN GENERATIONS: AN INFORMATION LEGACY OF THE ROYAL COMMISSION ON ABORIGINAL PEOPLES (1996); Monique M. Ross & Cheryk Y. Sharvit, *Forest Management in Alberta and Rights to Hunt, Trap, and Fish Under Treaty 8*, 36 ALTA. L. REV. 645 (1998).

32. Mikisew Cree First Nation v. Canada (Minister of Canadian Heritage), [2005] 3 S.C.R. 388.

33. Many Aboriginal communities, especially in the North, have surrendered or have had their rights extinguished by signing treaties, but jurisprudence confirms that treaties cannot be unilaterally abrogated and must be interpreted in accordance with the understanding of the indigenous parties. *See* Andrew Stobo Sniderman & Adam Shedletzky, *Aboriginal Peoples and Legal Challenges to Canadian Climate Change Policy*, 4 W. J. LEGAL STUD. 1, 14 (2014); *see also* R. v. Sioui, [1990] 1 S.C.R. 1025; U.N. GENERAL ASSEMBLY, HUMAN RIGHTS COUNCIL, TWENTY-SEVENTH SESSION, REPORT OF THE SPECIAL

tence and content of these rights do not depend on their recognition by European colonizers.[34]

In cases such as *R. v. Sioui* and *R. v. Sparrow*, the Supreme Court advocated for a broad, liberal, and generous approach towards Aboriginal rights. The evidentiary requirements of claims to Aboriginal rights or title are modified to recognize the inherent difficulty of producing historical records.[35]

In 1997, the seminal case *Delgamuukw v. British Columbia* (and confirmed in *Tsilhqot'in*[36]) established Aboriginal title as a proprietary right to land, based on occupation at the start of British colonialism, which may only be infringed for public purposes with fair compensation and consultation. Other Aboriginal customs, practices, and traditions were affirmed in *R. v. Van der Peet*, including the rights to fish, to hunt, and to access lands for cultural and economic purposes.

The Supreme Court of Canada ruled that the Tsilhqot'in peoples have Aboriginal title to their lands in Northern British Columbia, which entailed

> ownership rights similar to those associated with fee simple, including the right to decide how the land will be used; the right of enjoyment and occupancy of the land; the right to possess the land; the right to the economic benefits of the land; and the right to pro-actively use and manage the land.[37]

The Court noted that "governments and individuals proposing to use or exploit land, whether before or after a declaration of Aboriginal title, can avoid a charge of infringement or failure to adequately consult by obtaining the consent of the interested Aboriginal group."[38]

Two positive obligations flow from §35: a fiduciary duty and the duty to consult. The Crown's fiduciary relationship towards Aboriginal people imposes on the government the duty to act in good faith, as opposed to an adversarial relationship. On that matter, the Supreme Court wrote:

> [F]irst, the Crown's fiduciary duty means that the government must act in a way that respects the fact that Aboriginal title is a group interest that inheres

---

RAPPORTEUR ON THE RIGHTS OF INDIGENOUS PEOPLES, JAMES ANAYA, THE SITUATION OF INDIGENOUS PEOPLES IN CANADA, para. 7, at 5 (2014) (A/HRC/27/52/Add.2), http://unsr.jamesanaya.org/docs/countries/2014-report-canada-a-hrc-27-52-add-2-en.pdf.
34. *See* Mitchell v. M.N.R., [2001] 1 S.C.R. 911, para. 9-10.
35. R. v. Van der Peet, [1996] 2 S.C.R. 507.
36. Tsilhqot'in Nation v. British Columbia, [2014] 2 S.C.R. 257.
37. *Id.* para. 73.
38. *Id.* para. 97.

in present and future generations. The beneficial interest in the land held by the Aboriginal group vests communally in the title-holding group.[39]

With respect to consultation, since the *Haida Nation v. British Columbia*[40] case in 2004, federal and provincial governments have been subject to a formal duty to consult indigenous peoples and accommodate their interests whenever their asserted or established Aboriginal or treaty rights may be affected by government conduct. Although the duty to consult does not grant veto power, it requires the government to consider Aboriginal interests, which tend to be aligned with environmental interests. Or "where climate change threatens treaty and Aboriginal rights, the government may be required to take steps to protect these rights."[41] The recent decision canceling the government approval of the Northern Gateway pipeline highlights the importance of engaging in a two-way dialogue meaningfully and in good faith showing an openness to change conditions of a project based on consultation as well as providing feedback on expressed concerns.[42]

There is now a greater opportunity to bring an environmental claim under §35 since Canada at last officially endorsed the United Nations Declaration on the Rights of Indigenous Peoples (UNDRIP).[43] From 2010–2016, the Conservative government had not treated UNDRIP as significant, claiming that it is not legally binding. However the current government announced at the United Nations Permanent Forum on Indigenous Issues in New York in 2016, that "we intend nothing less than to adopt and implement the declaration in accordance with the Canadian Constitution"[44] because "Canada is in a unique position to move forward."[45]

The implementation of UNDRIP could extend the recognition of fundamental principles for Aboriginal communities by defining more precisely the reach of §35 of the Constitution, as the minister of indigenous and northern affairs stated: "by adopting and implementing the Declaration, we are excited that we are breathing life into Section 35 and recognizing it now as a full box of rights for Indigenous peoples in Canada."[46] In UNDRIP, Parties

---

39.   *Id.* para. 86.
40.   Haida Nation v. British Columbia (Minister of Forests), [2004] 3 S.C.R. 511.
41.   Sniderman & Shedletzky, *supra* note 33, at 12.
42.   Gitxaala Nation v. Canada, [2016] F.C.A. 187, para. 279.
43.   United Nations Declaration on the Rights of Indigenous Peoples, G.A. Res. 61/295, U.N. GAOR, 61st Sess., U.N. Doc. A/RES/61/295 (2007), 46 I.L.M. 1013 (2007), http://www.un.org/esa/socdev/unpfii/documents/DRIPS_en.pdf [hereinafter UNDRIP].
44.   Carolyn Bennett, Speech Delivered at the United Nations Permanent Forum on Indigenous Issues, New York (May 10, 2016), http://news.gc.ca/web/article-en.do?mthd=advSrch&crtr.page=2&crtr.dpt1D=6680&nid=1064009.
45.   *Id.*
46.   *Id.*

like Canada "reaffirm that indigenous peoples, in the exercise of their rights, should be free from discrimination of any kind"[47] and "recogniz[e] that respect for indigenous knowledge, cultures and traditional practices contributes to sustainable and equitable development and proper management of the environment."[48] It will also reify the duty to consult as a meaningful tool through the notion of "free, prior, and informed consent" that is explicitly stated in Articles 11, 19, 28, and 29 of UNDRIP.

2. Rights Protected by the Charter of Rights and Freedoms

The Canadian Charter endows every person in Canada with human and civil rights with regards to State interaction. Social, political, and cultural rights are not directly protected by the Canadian Charter and, therefore, are generally understood as not justiciable. Some jurists have concluded that a certain degree of cultural rights of an indigenous person could be protected under a combination of individual rights such as §2 (freedom of religion), §7 (life, liberty, and security), and §15 (equality).[49]

For example, the purpose of §2(a) is to prevent interference with profoundly personal beliefs that govern one's perception of oneself, humankind, nature, and, in some cases, a higher or different order of being.[50] Given the spiritual relationship Aboriginal peoples have with nature, it could be argued that the destruction of the natural world by the government can constitute an infringement of their freedom of religion. However, such an individual framing of indigenous spiritual practice and culture, which is a collectively understood phenomenon, may not be palatable for indigenous peoples.[51]

---

47. UNDRIP, *supra* note 43, at pmbl.
48. *Id.*
49. The authors thank Maître Frederic Paquin and Maître Elisabeth Patterson for an enlightened dialogue on the complex and layered understanding of cultural rights in the context of indigenous peoples.
50. Religion itself is not defined, but at least requires: a particular and comprehensive system of faith and worship; a belief in a divine, superhuman or controlling power; and/or a personal conviction or belief that fosters a connection with the divine or with the subject or object of that spiritual faith. *See* Syndicat Northcrest v. Amselem [2004] 2 S.C.R. 551, at para. 39.
    The first stage of a religious freedom analysis, an individual advancing an issue premised upon a freedom of religion claim must show the court that (1) he or she has a practice or belief, having a nexus with religion, which calls for a particular line of conduct, either by being objectively or subjectively obligatory or customary, or by, in general, subjectively engendering a personal connection with the divine or with the subject or object of an individual's spiritual faith, irrespective of whether a particular practice or belief is required by official religious dogma or is in conformity with the position of religious officials; and (2) he or she is sincere in his or her belief. Only then will freedom of religion be triggered.
    Syndicat Northcrest v. Amselem, [2004] 2 S.C.R. 551, [2004] S.C.C. 47, at paras. 39 & 56.
51. For these reasons, cases considering individual indigenous people as plaintiffs should ideally be developed with the consent of the indigenous community.

An individual can satisfy the threshold for the tests laid out in many of these sections; however, the remedies are largely granted at an individual level. All of these sections recognize rights as something held by the individual and not the community. Community rights under the Charter are understood as derived from the collection of individual rights, but the community itself has no rights. In many Aboriginal communities, individual rights are not recognized as legitimate and invoking a §7 claim without the backing of the community can create rifts and fissures within the collective and could ultimately erode their cultural rights.[52]

Section 7 of the Charter states that "everyone has the right to life, liberty and security of the person and the right not to be deprived thereof except in accordance with the principles of fundamental justice." It requires a two-step analysis to determine whether a State action (which includes law and regulation, but also government policies, programs, practices, and activities executed pursuant to statutory authority, as well as action of agencies under government authority[53]) infringes one of the protected rights. First, one must determine if there is an infringement of the right to "life, liberty and security of the person." If so, the court must consider whether the infringement is contrary to the principles of fundamental justice. Furthermore, it is not necessary that the State directly caused the rights violation; rather, it is sufficient that its policies contributed to the prejudice or influence on the life, liberty, or security of a person in their most fundamental aspects or where "state compulsions or prohibitions affect important and fundamental life choices."[54]

Scholars such as Lynda Collins and David Boyd have argued that §7 safeguards environmental rights.[55] Section 7 could serve as a foundation to invalidate laws and regulations that allow pollution at levels significant enough to

---

52. Interestingly, the Charter protects aboriginal rights and freedoms from negative effects. Section 25 provides:

    The guarantee in this Charter of certain rights and freedoms shall not be construed so as to abrogate or derogate from any aboriginal, treaty or other rights or freedoms that pertain to the aboriginal peoples of Canada including (*a*) any rights or freedoms that have been recognized by the Royal Proclamation of October 7, 1763; and (*b*) any rights or freedoms that now exist by way of land claims agreements or may be so acquired.

53. Nathalie J. Chalifour, *Environmental Justice and the Charter: Are sections 7 and 15 Available to Protect Against Environmental Injustices in Canada?*, 28 J. ENVTL. L. & PRAC. 89 (2015).

54. Blencoe v. British Columbia (Human Rights Comm'n) [2000] 2 S.C.R. 307, at para. 49; *see also* Carter v. Canada (Attorney Gen.), [2015] S.C.C. 5, [2015] 1 S.C.R. 331, at para. 68.

55. *See* Collins & Murtha, *supra* note 31; BOYD, *supra* note 7; Sophie Thériault, *La justice environnementale au Québec et les droits fondamentaux : analyse des potentiels écologique et distributif des chartes en lien avec la pollution toxique diffuse, dans* UN REGARD QUÉBÉCOIS SUR LE DROIT CONSTITUTIONNEL. MÉLANGES EN L'HONNEUR D'HENRI BRUN ET DE GUY TREMBLAY (Cowansville, Éditions Yvon Blais, 2015).

interfere with human health and increase the risk of death, thus violating the right to life and security. The right of liberty also includes the right to make "decisions of fundamental importance free from state interference"[56] relative to "matters that can properly be characterized as fundamentally or inherently personal such that, by their very nature, they implicate basic choices going to the core of what it means to enjoy individual dignity and independence."[57] Thus, it could be used to protect the right to choose to live in an environment free from pollution and environmental harm created or allowed by the government. Furthermore, it can be argued that the introduction of harmful substances into one's body without one's consent is a violation of the right to liberty.

Whether the Charter creates positive obligations on the government's part to act remains controversial. Currently, §7 does not require the government to provide the means to enable the life, liberty, or security of the person—rather they cannot deprive someone of it. Justice Arbour stated in her dissenting opinion in *Gosselin* that she believed that §7 includes a dimension of positive obligations, noting "this Court has consistently chosen instead to leave open the possibility of finding certain positive rights to the basic means of subsistence within s. 7. In my view, far from resisting this conclusion, the language and structure of the *Charter*—and of s. 7 in particular—actually *compel* it."[58] Thus, different types of State actions may give rise to positive obligations under §7 of the Charter, such as cases where the State chose "to exercise its legislative choice in a non-inclusive manner that significantly affects a person's enjoyment of a Charter right."[59]

Furthermore, in *Dunmore*, the Supreme Court confirmed that, in certain contexts, the State is under a positive duty to extend legislative protections where it fails to do so inclusively.[60] As such, "state inaction—the failure of the state to exercise its legislative choice in connection with the protected interests of some societal group, while exercising it in connection with those of others—may at times constitute 'affirmative interference' with one's Charter rights."[61] Furthermore, Judge McLachlin in her obiter of the *Gosselin* case by an evolutive interpretation of the Constitution reinforces that §7 may have the effect of creating positive obligations:[62]

---

56. *Blencoe*, 2 S.C.R. 307, para. 49.
57. Godbout v. Longueuil (Ville), [1997] 3 S.C.R. 844, para. 66.
58. Gosselin v. Québec (Attorney Gen.), [2002] 4 S.C.R. 429, para. 309.
59. *Id*. para. 328.
60. Dunmore v. Ontario (Attorney Gen.), [2001] 3 S.C.R. 1016.
61. *Gosselin*, 4 SCR 429, at para. 327.
62. *Id*. at para. 82.

S[ection] 7 may be interpreted to include positive obligations. To evoke Lord Sankey's celebrated phrase in *Edwards v. Attorney-General for Canada*, [1930] A.C. 124 (P.C.), at p. 136, the Canadian Charter must be viewed as "a living tree capable of growth and expansion within its natural limits": see *Reference re Provincial Electoral Boundaries (Sask.)*, [1991] 2 S.C.R. 158, at p. 180, *per* McLachlin J. It would be a mistake to regard Section 7 as frozen, or its content as having been exhaustively defined in previous cases.

Since indigenous peoples are particularly reliant on the land for their livelihoods, the interference with natural cycles brought about by climate change and exacerbated by unbridled Canadian emissions have a detrimental impact on their life, liberty, and security. Aboriginal people living in northern communities, especially those who rely on fishing, hunting, or ice roads to survive, can argue that their security of the person is at risk by depriving these lifelines of survival.[63] One study links changes in environmental conditions with increased symptoms of psychosocial, mental and social distress, such as alcohol abuse, violence and suicide.[64] As a whole, these facts support an argument that climate change threatens a right to security of the person protected by section 7.[65]

Another Charter tool that can be used is §15, which prohibits discrimination on either grounds enumerated within the section (race, national or ethnic origin, color, religion, sex, age, or mental or physical disability) or analogous grounds. Analogous grounds are defined as characteristics that are immutable or "constructively immutable," defined as a characteristic whose modification would come as an unacceptable cost to personal identity. The list of bases of discrimination is not exhaustive, although the court does exercise control of the list of accepted analogous grounds. Aboriginal peoples can be protected on grounds of race, nationality, ethnicity, or also whether or not they live on a reserve;[66] however, the reductionist race-based characterization of §15 is problematic.[67] This section is open to a group bringing a claim, but it is often individuals bringing an action on behalf of their community, where the remedy will benefit the entire community.

The core of §15 is to attain substantive equality, and not just formal equality, a distinction affirmed in *Andrews*.[68] This means that the definition of

---

63. SHEILA WATT-CLOUTIER, THE RIGHT TO BE COLD 202 (2015).
64. *See* Furgal & Prowse, *supra* note 23, at 105.
65. *Id.* at 100-105.
66. Corbiere v. Canada (Minister of Indian and N. Affairs), [1999] 2 S.C.R. 203.
67. *See* Nathalie J. Chalifour, *Environmental Discrimination and the Charter's Equality Guarantee: The Case of Drinking Water for First Nations Living on Reserves*, 43 REVUE GENERALE DE DROIT 183 (2013).
68. Andrews v. Law Soc'y of British Columbia, [1989] 1 S.C.R. 143.

equality is not treating all people alike, rather, "the Court in the final analysis must ask whether, having regard to all relevant contextual factors, including the nature and purpose of the impugned legislation in relation to the claimant's situation, the impugned distinction discriminates by perpetuating the group's disadvantage or by stereotyping the group."[69] *R. v. Kapp* established a test to assess the validity of claims: (1) Does the law create a distinction based on an enumerated or analogous ground? and (2) Does the distinction create a disadvantage by perpetuating prejudice or stereotyping?[70]

Indigenous communities in the North suffer disproportionate impacts from climate change. Furthermore, they have more limited possibilities for adaptation due to historical and current racism.[71] Studies have shown the tendencies of industrialized societies to impose excessive environmental risks—a concept known as "disproportionate burden"—on minority and other marginalized communities, including and especially Aboriginal people.[72] As a result, the guarantee of equality of §15 is violated when a marginalized group receives less environmental protection than others, on the grounds of discrimination enumerated in §15(1) or on grounds analogous to them. Once the inequality in treatment and protection is proven, the burden shifts to the government to justify why, in a democratic society, a marginalized community should bear environmental pressures.[73]

B. Rights Infringement Justification Analysis

No constitutional right is absolute and in some circumstances it can still be lawfully infringed by government action. Hence, if a court were to find a constitutional rights infringement, whether Aboriginal or under the Charter, the government action would have to be justified under the applicable constitutional tests.

Constitutional justification analysis is a factually driven inquiry. Therefore, the likelihood that a rights violation will be justified will depend greatly on the specific circumstances of the case and the nature of the rights asserted.

---

69. Withler v. Canada (Attorney Gen.), [2011] 1 S.C.R. 396, at para. 54.
70. R. v. Kapp, [2008] 2 S.C.R. 483, at para. 17. *See also* Quebec (Attorney Gen.) v. A, [2013] 1 S.C.R. 61, at para. 142; Kahkewistahaw First Nation v. Taypotat, [2015] 2 S.C.R. 548, at paras. 10 & 18.
71. *See* Malcolm King, Alexandra Smith & Michael Gracey, *Indigenous Health Part 2: The Underlying Causes of the Health Gap*, 374 Lancet 76 (2009).
72. *See* Tara Ulezalka, *Race and Waste: The Quest for Environmental Justice*, 26 Temp. Envtl. L. & Tech. J. 51 (2007); Laura Westra & Bill E. Lawson eds., Faces of Environmental Racism: Confronting Issues of Global Justice (1995); *see also* Julian Agyeman et al., Speaking for Ourselves: Environmental Justice in Canada (2009).
73. *See* Chalifour, *supra* note 67 (describing a hypothetical case study in which Aboriginal peoples brought an action against the government for a lack of access to potable water on reserves).

This section highlights the different tests for constitutional rights and then analyzes how these tests could be satisfied in the context at issue.

I.   Jurisprudential Tests to Justify Constitutional Rights Infringements

All Charter rights infringement actions are subject to the §1 limitation clause. Furthermore, specific Charter rights, such as §7, have an additional internal justification test. Here, the Crown has the burden to demonstrate that its actions were prescribed by law and the Charter rights infringement was justified in a free and democratic society. The justification test was set out in the internationally renowned *Oakes* case:

> Two central criteria must be satisfied. First, the objective, which the measures responsible for a limit on a Charter right or freedom are designed to serve, must be "of sufficient importance to warrant overriding a constitutionally protected right or freedom": . . . It is necessary, at a minimum, that an objective relate to concerns which are pressing and substantial in a free and democratic society before it can be characterized as sufficiently important.
>
> . . .
>
> [T]hen the party invoking s. 1 must show that the means chosen are reasonable and demonstrably justified. This involves "a form of proportionality test" . . . Although the nature of the proportionality test will vary depending on the circumstances, in each case courts will be required to balance the interests of society with those of individuals and groups. There are, in my view, three important components of a proportionality test. First, the measures adopted must be carefully designed to achieve the objective in question. They must not be arbitrary, unfair or based on irrational considerations. In short, they must be rationally connected to the objective. Second, the means, even if rationally connected to the objective in this first sense, should impair "as little as possible" the right or freedom in question. Third, there must be a proportionality between the effects of the measures which are responsible for limiting the Charter right or freedom, and the objective which has been identified as of "sufficient importance."
>
> . . .
>
> Even if an objective is of sufficient importance, and the first two elements of the proportionality test are satisfied, it is still possible that, because of the severity of the deleterious effects of a measure on individuals or groups, the measure will not be justified by the purposes it is intended to serve. The more

severe the deleterious effects of a measure, the more important the objective must be if the measure is to be reasonable and demonstrably justified in a free and democratic society.[74]

This case has had a rich legacy in the past three decades,[75] a discussion of which is beyond the scope of this chapter.

Before even contemplating the *Oakes* test, an aggrieved party would need to allege a deprivation of the right to life, liberty, and security of the person "in accordance with the principles of fundamental justice."[76] Since §7 jurisprudence was historically developed in the criminal law context, the principles of fundamental justice developed thus far are mostly concerned with issues specific to that context. Still, courts refused to limit their understanding of §7 protections to a simple enumerative definition or to a restrictive content. Instead, the Supreme Court favored a broad interpretation and defined the principles of fundamental justice as "the basic tenets and principles not only of our judicial process but also of the other components of our legal system"[77] and added that "whether any given principle may be said to be a principle of fundamental justice within the meaning of s. 7 must rest on an analysis of the nature, sources, rationale and essential role of that principle within the judicial process and in our evolving legal system."[78] In addition, the establishment of a principle of fundamental justice, while possibly not gaining unanimity, can be created to the extent that there is consensus.[79] Thus, the principles of fundamental justice are yet to be fully defined and "will take on concrete meaning as the courts address alleged violations of s. 7."[80]

In *Bedford*, Chief Justice McLachlin wrote that the principles of fundamental justice set out "the minimum requirements that a law that negatively impacts on a person's life, liberty, or security of the person must meet"[81] and represent an attempt at capturing the basic values underpinning Canadian constitutional order. Among them are the basic values against: (1) arbitrariness (where there is an absence of a link between the objective of the law and its negative impact on security of the person);[82] (2) overbreadth (where the law imposes limits on security of the person that goes beyond what is

---

74. R. v. Oakes, [1986] 1 S.C.R. 103, at paras. 69–71 (internal citations omitted).
75. *See, e.g.*, Sujit Choudhry, *So What Is the Real Legacy of Oakes? Two Decades of Proportionality Analysis Under the Canadian's Section 1*, 34 N.Y.U. Sup. Ct. L. Rev. 501 (2006).
76. Canadian Charter of Rights and Freedoms §7.
77. Re B.C. Motor Vehicle Act, [1985] 2 S.C.R. 486, at para. 31.
78. *Id.* at para. 66.
79. Rodriguez v. British Columbia (Attorney Gen.), [1993] 3 S.C.R. 519.
80. *Id.* at para. 67.
81. Canada (Attorney Gen.) v. Bedford, [2013] 3 S.C.R. 1101, at para. 94.
82. *Rodriguez*, 3 S.C.R. 519, at 594–95.

required to achieve its objective); and (3) gross disproportionality (where the effects of the impugned law are so extreme that they cannot be justified by its object).[83]

Whether Aboriginal rights infringement could be justified would depend on the nature and strengths of the rights being asserted from ancestral rights to the lighter right to be consulted. Still, governments can infringe Aboriginal rights protected by §35 if it can be demonstrated that it is in the broader public interest to do so.[84] Indeed, the Supreme Court affirmed that:

> The range of legislative objectives that can justify the infringement of aboriginal title is fairly broad. Most of these objectives can be traced to the *reconciliation* of the prior occupation of North America by aboriginal peoples with the assertion of Crown sovereignty, which entails the recognition that "distinctive aboriginal societies exist within, and are a part of, a broader social, political and economic community". In my opinion, the development of agriculture, forestry, mining, and hydroelectric power, the general economic development of the interior of British Columbia, protection of the environment or endangered species, the building of infrastructure and the settlement of foreign populations to support those aims, are the kinds of objectives that are consistent with this purpose and, in principle, can justify the infringement of aboriginal title. Whether a particular measure or government act can be explained by reference to one of those objectives, however, is ultimately a question of fact that will have to be examined on a case-by-case basis.[85]

The government is "required to bear the burden of justifying any legislation that has some negative effect on any aboriginal right protected under section 35(1)."[86] Its action must be reasonable and not impose undue hardship, a valid objective on the part of the Crown must exist, and the means employed must be consistent with the government's fiduciary duty. For example, the government must first consult the Aboriginal people affected, minimize the infringement of their rights as much as possible, and give priority to their claims over other groups' interests; only then may its action be justified.[87]

---

83. *Bedford*, 3 SCR 1101, at para. 35.
84. TRUTH AND RECONCILIATION COMMISSION OF CANADA, HONOURING THE TRUTH, RECONCILING FOR THE FUTURE: SUMMARY OF THE FINAL REPORT OF THE TRUTH AND RECONCILIATION COMMISSION OF CANADA 302 (2015), http://www.trc.ca/websites/trcinstitution/File/2015/Honouring_the_Truth_Reconciling_for_the_Future_July_23_2015.pdf.
85. Delgamuukw v. British Columbia, [1997] 3 S.C.R. 1010, at para. 165 (emphasis in original) (citations omitted).
86. R. v. Sparrow, [1990] 1 S.C.R. 1075.
87. *Id.*

However, "incursions on Aboriginal title cannot be justified if they would substantially deprive future generations of the benefit of the land."[88]

2. Is Canadian Inaction on Climate Change Justified?

The Supreme Court has in recent years emphasized the importance of environmental protection and has increasingly developed its jurisprudence to protect the people against risks created by the State.[89] Moreover, Canadian courts have often recognized that environmental protection is a fundamental value of Canadian society worth protecting.[90] The courts have also established a progressive jurisprudence to protect indigenous peoples. In evaluating the parameters of a justification analysis, this section will focus on the Canadian government's GHG emissions targets and their contribution in bringing about dangerous climate change.

Faced with an acute prejudice (i.e., the disproportionate burden of climate change impacts on Canadian indigenous peoples), Canadian courts would likely undertake a rigorous justification analysis. Unbridled climate change is already deeply affecting indigenous peoples' practices, culture, and ability to hunt and fish on their traditional territories as they have done for thousands of years. Furthermore, the current trajectory towards dangerous climate change would mean future generations of indigenous peoples would be deprived of the benefit of their lands if their ice paths are melting, their permafrost subsiding, and their territories being ravaged by pests or massive species extinction.

Here, an argument could be made that Canadian climate inaction, an important contribution to global climate inaction, has a grossly disproportionate effect on indigenous peoples and their constitutionally protected rights. It is also arbitrary in the sense that there is no link between the creation of harm and suffering for indigenous peoples and the objective of muted climate action, which is to further short-term economic development at the expense of mid- to long-term development. Indeed, the current government, like its predecessors, has made public statements supporting GHG emission-intensive

---

88. Tsilhqot'in Nation v. British Columbia, [2014] 2 S.C.R. 257, at para. 86.
89. R. v. Hydro-Québec, [1997] 3 S.C.R. 213; Friends of the Oldman River Soc'y v. Canada (Minister of Transp.), [1992] 1 S.C.R. 3; R. v. Crown Zellerbach, [1988] 1 S.C.R. 401.
90. British Columbia v. Canadian Forest Prods. Ltd., [2004] 2 S.C.R. 74, [2004] S.C.C. 38; Ontario v. Canadian Pac. Ltd., [1995] 2 S.C.R. 1031, [1995] CanLII 112, at para. 55; see also Lynda M. Collins, Safeguarding the Longue Durée: Environmental Rights in the Canadian Constitution, 71 Sup. Ct. L. Rev. 2d 519 (2015).

industries.[91] Although a court could conclude that the infringements are justified because climate inaction promotes employment in extractive and carbon-
intensive industrial sectors, the fact remains that indigenous peoples benefit
disproportionately little from economic development in Canada. Very little
beyond scientific research has been done in the way of enhancing indigenous
peoples' resilience to the impacts of climate change.

Here, the court would likely consider the reasonableness of Canadian
action on climate change described in Part I.A in comparison to global
efforts, as well as those of industrialized countries. While it could be argued
that Canada has made fewer declarations of support for internationally set
targets as had the Netherlands, its actions on climate policy are much more
egregious and represent a greater contribution to global GHG emissions than
the smaller European country. Principles of equity in effort-sharing distribution as well as historical responsibility promoted in international law would
also support a court finding of "unreasonableness" of Canadian policy. However, a court could also focus on the absolute Canadian emissions and conclude they are minimal on a global scale.[92]

Historical and current Canadian climate policy likely cannot be reasonably justified infringements on Aboriginal titles and rights, but a court could
reach a different conclusion. Furthermore, the inclusion of indigenous principles into the justification inquiry could appropriately elevate the standard
of justification for reasons discussed below.

C.   Possible Court Remedies

The remedies to these Charter challenges fit into two categories: §52 and
§24. Section 52 renders a written law inoperative once it is deemed unconstitutional, whereas §24 provides compensation for an unconstitutional
government action. The two remedies are generally treated as mutually exclusive.[93] The courts tend to refrain from stating which action the government is
obliged to undertake, but Nathalie J. Chalifour suggests that there is nothing
constitutionally barring the courts from enforcing a specific action.[94]

---

91. Elizabeth McSheffrey, *Trudeau Says Pipelines Will Pay for Canada's Transition to a Green Economy*, NAT'L
      OBSERVER, Mar. 2, 2016, http://www.nationalobserver.com/2016/03/02/news/trudeau-says-pipelines-
      will-pay-canadas-transition-green-economy.
92. ENVIRONMENT AND CLIMATE CHANGE CANADA, CANADIAN ENVIRONMENTAL SUSTAINABILITY INDI-
      CATORS: GLOBAL GREENHOUSE GAS EMISSIONS (2016), https://www.ec.gc.ca/indicateurs-indicators/
      54C061B5-44F7-4A93-A3EC-5F8B253A7235/GlobalGHGEmissions_EN.pdf.
93. Kent Roach, *Enforcement of the Charter—Subsections 24(1) and 52(1)*, 62 SUP. CT. L. REV. 2D 473,
      490 (2013).
94. Chalifour, *supra* note 67, at 218.

I.   Injunctive Remedy: Dutch-type, Court-imposed National GHG Targets

Positive action from the government could be required in the form of an injunction similar to the one issued by the Dutch court. Similar to the Netherlands, it could be argued that it is a national legal duty to take actions to "stabiliz[e] greenhouse gas concentrations in the atmosphere at a level that would prevent dangerous anthropogenic interference with the climate system"[95] knowing that "such a level should be achieved within a time frame sufficient to allow ecosystems to adapt naturally to climate change, to ensure that food production is not threatened and to enable economic development to proceed in a sustainable manner."[96] Developed countries like Canada have agreed to common but differentiated responsibilities, understood as including notions of responsibility for historic emissions and per capita emissions.[97]

The issuance of a Fifth Assessment Report by the IPCC, the Paris Agreement, and the mere passage of time make it unlikely that a Canadian court would require exactly the same target as in the Netherlands. The *target* of 25–40% by 2020 represents suggested reductions for industrialized countries such as Canada and the Netherlands based on climate data to prevent "dangerous climate change," understood as limiting global temperature increase below 2°C.[98] The general average that needs to be collectively achieved to avoid dangerous climate change and satisfy the international obligations set out in the UNFCCC was translated as a national minimal reduction or policy floor deemed reasonable and necessary for the government to achieve. These numbers would need to be updated and discussed in the context of Canada by using a historical responsibility distribution model, for example, and citing their inaction and recently increased emissions as evidence for a more stringent emissions target.

A court could demand beyond the minimal policy floor and require Canada to adopt specific targets that would be compatible with the Canadian Constitution, or develop the legal framework and principles that must be

---

95. United Nations Framework Convention on Climate Change, May 9, 1992, art. 2, 1771 U.N.T.S. 107, 31 I.L.M. 849 (1992), https://unfccc.int/resource/docs/convkp/conveng.pdf; *see also* Urgenda, *Urgenda Foundation v. State of the Netherlands—Legal Documents*, http://www.urgenda.nl/en/climate-case/legal-documents.php (last visited Aug. 24, 2016).

96. *Id.*

97. Roger H.J. Cox, *The Liability of European States for Climate Change*, 30 Utrecht J. Int'l & Eur. L. 125, 133 (2014).

98. *Id.*; *see also* Sujata Gupta et al., *Policies, Instruments, and Co-operative Arrangements*, in Climate Change 2007: Mitigation, Contribution of Working Group III to the Fourth Assessment Report of the Intergovernmental Panel on Climate Change 745, 776, tbl. Box 13.7 (B. Metz et al. eds., 2008), http://www.ipcc.ch/pdf/assessment-report/ar4/wg3/ar4-wg3-chapter13.pdf.

applied by government in developing such targets. A debate would inevitably include the thorny issue of the long-time future of the fossil fuel industry in Canada, the industry responsible for and capable of reducing most emissions.

The latest IPCC report stresses that the issue of effort sharing among individual countries involves ethical considerations:

> Many areas of climate policy-making involve value judgements and ethical considerations. These areas range from the question of how much mitigation is needed to prevent dangerous interference with the climate system to choices among specific policies for mitigation or adaptation. Social, economic and ethical analyses may be used to inform value judgements and may take into account values of various sorts, including human wellbeing, cultural values and non-human values.[99]

This awareness of the ethical dimensions of climate change policymaking may be an opportunity for the government to include indigenous voices and principles into the dialogue, especially after Canada championed the inclusion of indigenous rights in the Paris climate agreement. Indeed, many indigenous principles could bring a new, much-needed perspective in climate debates. Adopting indigenous peoples' perspectives and teachings regarding collective legal duties would radically transform the current political debate on national action on climate by bringing in intergenerational, intragenerational, and interspecies equity-like principles to the discussion on required action.[100] Taking these principles seriously would seem to imply choosing a decarbonization pathway that is in line with the most preventative climate scenarios put forward by the IPCC, very few of which still allow the world a chance to avoid warming beyond 1.5° C through rapid action.

In the wake of the Paris Agreement, efforts are only starting to assess what should be Canada's share of global emission reductions efforts under different approaches involving the ultimate temperature target and effort-sharing principle used. The implications of these choices seem quite stark: one study indicated reductions ranging from 90–99% would be necessary by 2030 based on a conservative effort-sharing principle. Taking a fair-share approach based on equal cumulative per capita emissions towards limiting temperature rise to 2° C has a similar effect of requiring Canadian emissions to near zero in 2030. Attempting to do its fair share towards a 1.5° C goal would lead Canada to a carbon budget that would be exhausted in less than

---

99.   Brigitte Knopf & Oliver Geden, *A Warning From the IPCC: The EU 2030's Climate Target Cannot Be Based on Science Alone*, ENERGY POST, June 26, 2014 (citing Summary for Policymakers of IPCC WGIII), http://www.energypost.eu/warning-ipcc-eu-2030s-climate-target-based-science-alone.
100.   *See infra* Part III.B.2.

two years at current rates.[101] Considering these findings, current Canadian emissions reduction targets need to be significantly more ambitious if justice has any bearing on the matter.

2. Other Remedies: Compensation and Declaratory Judgments

Plaintiffs could also obtain damage awards for the infringement of their constitutional rights[102] and damage to land. They could also attempt to recover from costs or future costs of having to adapt to climate change in terms of infrastructure investments, displacements, or other costly but necessary measures.

Lastly, the remedy sought could also include declarations as to the nature of the duty to consult and seek prior informed consent from indigenous peoples in the establishment of climate policy. Ideally this requirement should be conducted in a manner that allows for indigenous law to emerge and offer guidance on projects and policies that will impact national emissions and adaptation to climate change.

III. Starting a New Constitutional Dialogue Between Settlers and Indigenous Legal Frameworks

A. Transforming Constitutions to Include Indigenous Peoples

Some scholars have advocated for the inclusion of indigenous principles through the drafting of constitutions. Proverbially stated, "present constitutions, it is said must be shaken out, to become more inclusive, less conflictual, [and] more accommodating of cultural diversity through deployment of a wider range of constitutional devices."[103] It has been proposed that constitutions should both capture the diversity among groups, as well as afford equal recognition to other nations by other nations. The goal of constitution writing should be as inclusive as possible to affirm, and not exclude, the already marginalized.

Canada is already a legally pluralistic country, recognizing civil law and common law as applicable legal systems in the country. A third legal tradition is partly recognized in §35, but could grow towards broader constitu-

---

101. Dr. Simon Donner & Dr. Kirsten Zickfeld, Canada's Contribution to Meeting the Temperature Limits in the Paris Climate Agreement (2016), http://blogs.ubc.ca/sdonner/files/2016/02/Donner-and-Zickfeld-Canada-and-the-Paris-Climate-Agreement.pdf.
102. See, e.g., Vancouver (City) v. Ward, [2010] S.C.C. 27, [2010] 2 S.C.R. 28.
103. H. Patrick Glenn, Legal Traditions of the World: Sustainable Diversity of Law 92 (4th ed. 2010).

tional application. The Supreme Court has acknowledged the long-standing history of Aboriginal people and rejected the theory of terra nullius, which European nations used to assert sovereignty to the land:

> Nomadic peoples and their modes of occupancy of land cannot be ignored when defining the concept of aboriginal title to land in Canada. The natural and inevitable consequence of rejecting enlarged terra nullius was not just recognition of indigenous occupants, but also acceptance of the validity of their prior possession and title. To ignore their particular relationship to the land is to adopt the view that prior to the assertion of Crown sovereignty Canada was not occupied. Such an approach is clearly unacceptable and incongruent with the Crown's recognition that aboriginal peoples were in possession of the land when the Crown asserted sovereignty. Aboriginal title reflects this fact of prior use and occupation of the land together with the relationship of aboriginal peoples to the land and the customary laws of ownership. This aboriginal interest in the land is a burden on the Crown's underlying title.[104]

The Supreme Court has confirmed the existence of written, and unwritten, rules and principles guiding the Constitution.[105] Since the Constitution cannot accommodate every situation or problem that arises, those unwritten rules and principles are necessary to maintain a complete legal framework that evolves with changing times. Sources of these unwritten principles are diverse: some are rooted in the history and Constitution of the United Kingdom, while others come from the Supreme Court's understanding and interpretation of constitutional texts. "Unwritten constitutional principles" (UCPs) is a concept that was formally defined in the Quebec Secession Reference:

> Behind the written word is an historical lineage stretching back through the ages, which aids in the consideration of the underlying constitutional principles. These principles inform and sustain the constitutional text: they are the vital unstated assumptions upon which the text is based . . . . These defining principles function in symbiosis.
>
> . . .
>
> Although these underlying principles are not explicitly made part of the Constitution by any written provision, other than in some respects by the oblique

---

104. R. v. Marshall; R. v. Bernard, [2005] 2 S.C.R. 220, at para. 134 (citing Samantha Hepburn, *Feudal Tenure and Native Title: Revising an Enduring Fiction*, 27 Syd. L. Rev. 46 (2005)).

105. New Brunswick Broad. Co. v. Nova Scotia (Speaker of the House of Assembly), [1993] 1 S.C.R. 319; Ref re Remuneration of Judges of the Prov. Court of P.E.I.; Ref re Independence and Impartiality of Judges of the Prov. Court of P.E.I., [1997] 3 S.C.R. 3; Reference re Secession of Quebec, [1998] 2 S.C.R. 217.

reference in the preamble to the *Constitution Act, 1867*, it would be impossible to conceive of our constitutional structure without them. The principles dictate major elements of the architecture of the Constitution itself and are as such its lifeblood.

. . .

The principles assist in the interpretation of the text and the delineation of spheres of jurisdiction, the scope of rights and obligations, and the role of our political institutions. Equally important, observance of and respect for these principles is essential to the ongoing process of constitutional development and evolution of our Constitution as a "living tree . . . ."[106]

There is a recurrence of biological language in this passage (e.g., "symbiosis," "lifeblood," "living tree"). Implicit in this use of language is an acknowledgment that all our human structures depend on our biological survival. In this sense, there is no principle more fundamental than that of a healthy environment.

The Supreme Court of Canada has acknowledged only a limited number of guiding principles to date: judicial independence, federalism, democracy, the rule of law, and the protection of minorities.[107] It is conceivable that a Canadian court could recognize unwritten principles of indigenous law as part of the constitutional order. Examples of these unwritten principles are explored in the next section.

B.   Aspects of Indigenous Law Important for a Pluralistic Legal Dialogue on Climate Change

Indigenous peoples are governed by resilient social structure including a form of law that has never been extinguished, at least not in its entirety, despite great efforts of many governments throughout Canada's history. Canada is comprised of diverse Aboriginal, First Nations, Métis, and Inuit communities with different languages, cultures, legal structures, and social mechanisms. Despite the diversity, there are commonalities shared across indigenous legal traditions, sometimes referred to as original instructions.

Indigenous principles that may be particularly relevant to climate change have to do with the sanctity of the natural world.[108] Indigenous principles

---

106. Reference re Secession of Quebec, [1998] 2 S.C.R. 217, at paras. 49–52.
107. Warren J. Newman, *"Grand Entrance Hall," Back Door or Foundation Stone? The Role of Constitutional Principles in Construing and Applying the Constitution of Canada*, 14 Sup. Ct. L. Rev. 2d 197, 198 (2001).
108. Glenn, *supra* note 103, at 77.

share the overall goal of preserving the critical order of the natural world, which can create a more ecological society.

These legal structures may not mirror Western legal structures, but still fulfill similar functional purposes. For example, there is no distinct judiciary, which creates a slower but more open and accessible system, without financial barriers to entry.[109] As explained by Lisa Oiluqqi Koperqualuk:

> A description of Inuit justice would involve three main elements: the Inuit definition of transgressions; conflict resolution procedures; and a set of individuals whose task was to re-establish order. In other words a justice system would be based on the existence of Inuit societal norms, their possible transgression and applicable sanctions for such transgressions.[110]

The sources of law tend to be a combination of sacred, natural, and deliberative law,[111] rather than codal or legislative. It is often oral in nature and passed through human speech and memory. The unstructured or fluid structure of indigenous law draws on the natural world as a source of law to guide and mediate human interactions. As a result, there is a greater tendency to embrace, preserve, and protect the environment rather than restrain or exploit it.[112] This also makes deliberation a source of law, which gives rise to a consensus-based character. Councils and communities go through a process of discussion and persuasion to come to a decision, either in a formal or informal process. Dispute resolution tends to be informal in conciliation of interests.

For example, valuing consensus would engage a broader scope of stakeholders in decisionmaking processes, inherently diversify opinions and priorities, and ultimately lead to an environmentally oriented outcome. Adopting dialogue-based conflict resolution allows for a more collaborative solution with a compromise, as opposed to going to court, which can be an antagonistic channel of communication with only one winner.

Indigenous legal traditions firmly embrace the principle of intergenerational equity—the notion that future generations should not have to be burdened with inequality generated in the present. The absence of a valid temporal distinction between the dead, the living, and the yet to be born creates obligations to nature for the future generations.[113] Hence, indigenous peoples going to court to assert their standing in the inter-

---

109. *Id.*
110. Lisa Oiluqqi Koperqualuk, Traditions Relating to Customary Law in Nunavik 444 (2015)
111. John Borrows, Canada's Indigenous Constitution (2010).
112. Glenn, *supra* note 103, at 77.
113. *Id.* at 80.

est of future generations has implications to preserve the environment for the future.[114] This indigenous principle of rights of future generations is starting to emerge and be recognized in Western legislatures as well.[115] For example, the Quebec Sustainable Development Act[116] and the Quebec Residual Materials Management Policy[117] explicitly recognize this premise.

Another attribute of indigenous law is to generally hold land communally, rather than individually.[118] The right to exploit certain swaths of land is apportioned to individuals for hunting, fishing, or cultivation; however, there is no right to alienation. This social organization of land supports a centralized, coordinated effort to prevent overexploitation and a tragedy of the commons-like degeneration, a problem plaguing many aspects of current global issues from fisheries collapse to climate change.

For example, whether natural habitats such as boreal forests are net sources or sinks of GHGs in Canada is highly variable and will require further study and development of governance structures to manage these vital ecosystems. Here again, indigenous peoples have been stewards of these ecosystems and can provide key guidance in understanding, managing, and preserving them for biodiversity conservation and GHG sequestration.

C.   Challenges to Pluralistic Constitutional Dialogue

Such a leap to constitutional recognition might not feel respectful toward indigenous peoples already in the grips of their respective fights to exercise self-determination and often simply struggling to survive the onslaught of extractive industries. There could be a justifiable reluctance on the part of Aboriginal leaders to engage with the Western law that has systematically erased, oppressed, and destroyed aboriginal communities. If the non-Aboriginal population of Canada becomes governed by Aboriginal law and has access to its democratic process, it could become employed as another tool to appropriate, criticize, and once again extinguish Aboriginal law.[119] There

---

114. The Labrador Metis Nation v. Her Majesty in Right of Newfoundland & Labrador, [2006] N.L.T.D. 119.

115. The courts have, however, acknowledged the concept in a financial context where artificially low water or gas prices accumulate cumbersome debts for the future. *See, e.g.*, Calgary (City) v. Alberta (Energy & Utils. Bd.), [2010] A.B.C.A. 132.

116. CanLII, *Sustainable Development Act, CQLR, c. D-8.1.1*, http://canlii.ca/t/5239p (last visited Aug. 28, 2016).

117. CanLII, *Québec Residual Materials Management Policy, CQLR c. Q-2*, http://canlii.ca/t/l23r (last visited Aug. 28, 2016).

118. GLENN, *supra* note 103, at 77.

119. JOHN BORROWS, CANADA'S INDIGENOUS CONSTITUTION 148 (2010).

might be an understandable resentment towards the government that fuels a desire to simply not engage with it.[120]

However, addressing the impacts of climate change on indigenous peoples' lands and rights seems to require such radical engagement. In order to exercise self-determination and their Aboriginal rights on their lands and terminate the violation of their individual and collective rights, they must be involved in decisionmaking processes that directly and indirectly affect their daily lives. Indigenous peoples should be able to engage at the level of policy determination where the impacts on their rights get negotiated, in a manner that is compatible with their culture.

Current constitutionalism has been denounced by Aboriginal legal scholars. Neither the prevailing school of modern Western constitutionalism nor postmodern constitutionalism provide a just way of adjudicating such diverse claims to recognition because they rest on untenable assumptions inherited from the age of European imperialism. However, by means of a historical and critical survey of 400 years of European and non-European constitutionalism, with special attention to the American Aboriginal peoples, James Tully develops a post-imperial philosophy and practice of constitutionalism. This consists of the conciliation of claims of recognition over time through constitutional dialogues in which citizens reached agreements on appropriate forms of accommodation of their cultural differences, guided by common constitutional convention.[121]

Other challenges associated with bringing indigenous law into the mainstream legal fold exist as well. Understanding any new legal system poses a challenge and requires training to become familiar with the broad, generic style of writing meant to capture the breadth of interactions. This challenge can be overcome by providing more institutional opportunities to learn and engage with Aboriginal law and with more accessibility. The oral nature of Aboriginal law does not lend itself to being easy accessible. "The easiest way to rectify this challenge is through systematic publishing, however, a central element of aboriginal law is its flexibility, which may be lost through transcription." Therefore, the process of recording must not hinder Aboriginal law's ability to evolve. The method of evolution is equally important: all those governed by indigenous law should have democratic access to change and alter the laws that rule them. If indigenous laws are to be incorporated as a source that brings sweeping change, such laws must also be applied to

---

120. *Id.*
121. James Tully, Strange Multiplicity: Constitutionalism in an Age of Diversity (1994).

non-Aboriginal people, so as not to segregate Aboriginal people by creating a separate legal order applicable only to them.[122]

Other countries have successfully achieved the integration of Aboriginal constitutions into State legal frameworks. Some Latin American constitutions were broadly discussed and build on citizen participation in communities and villages. They all reference the notion of nature's rights, which the people, through State institutions and through collective practices of care, have a duty to protect.[123] Important traits of "ecolaw" can be found in the constitutional rights granted to nature or to Pacha Mama from Ecuador to Bolivia to Venezuela.[124]

Conclusion

A constitutional challenge by indigenous peoples or individuals would contribute to the dialogue on the obligation to avoid dangerous climate change by showing that constitutional rights violations are already happening because of unabated climate change, adding a much-needed sense of urgency to climate change mitigation efforts. Beyond showing impacts and starting dialogues on compensation for irreparable harm, such a case also may highlight how indigenous law can contribute to ethical dialogues about what level of responsibility Canada is held to, bringing novel yet ancient perspectives on how to achieve harmony in a rapidly decarbonizing world.

Indigenous peoples are entitled to expedient, deep, and justice-based decarbonization and adaptation. They might also hold the key to legal principles that facilitate the transformation of the Canadian legal system to enable governance of new, more sustainable types of development.

Two scholars recently proposed ideas regarding what a future legal system in tune with nature and community could look like. Some distinguishing features seem to embody futuristic-sounding principles already shared by indigenous legal traditions:

---

122. BORROWS, *supra* note 119, at 150.
123. FRITJOF CAPRA & UGO MATTEI, THE ECOLOGY OF LAW: TOWARD A LEGAL SYSTEM IN TUNE WITH NATURE AND COMMUNITY 141–43 (2015).
124. *See generally* JAMES R. MAY & ERIN DALY, GLOBAL ENVIRONMENTAL CONSTITUTIONALISM (2014). *See also* BOLIVIA (PLURINATIONAL STATE OF)'S CONSTITUTION OF 2009 pmbl. (2016), https://www. constituteproject.org/constitution/Bolivia_2009.pdf. This new constitution was drafted pursuant to the International Labour Organization Convention No. 169 about indigenous foundations (entry into force in 1991) and UNDRIP (adopted in 2007). Indigenous peoples' rights that have a collective vocation are constitutionalized at the national level and separated into four categories: land and territories rights, cultural identity right, self-development right (in terms of health, education, and economic development), and autonomy rights (in terms of jurisdiction and policies).

This process requires that we now, as a consequence of our new ecological knowledge, displace the individual owner from the center of the legal system in favor of the commons. To do this we must rethink the most intimate structure of the law to reflect the basic principles of ecology and the new systemic thinking of contemporary science: no mechanistic separation between subject and object; no individual atom, but community and relationship as building blocks of the legal order. The reality follows what we collectively think and do.[125]

Achieving the effective protection of human health and the environment through the Charter is analogous to an attempt to stretch the leaves of our constitutional tree. Maybe all that is necessary to move forward fairly and swiftly is to recognize that the founding laws of Canada have roots stretching back in time through the continued existence of indigenous peoples. These laws seem to require us to safeguard this living planet.

---

125. CAPRA & MATTEI, *supra* note 123, at 12.

Notes